MERCATOR PROJECTION

SOCIETIES, NETWORKS, AND TRANSITIONS

A GLOBAL HISTORY

CRAIG A. LOCKARD

University of Wisconsin—Green Bay

HOUGHTON MIFFLIN COMPANY   Boston   New York

Senior sponsoring editor: Nancy Blaine
Senior development editor: Julie Swasey
Senior project editor: Carol Newman
Associate project editor: Deborah Berkman
Senior art and design coordinator: Jill Haber
Senior photo researcher: Jennifer Meyer Dare
Composition buyer: Chuck Dutton
Associate manufacturing buyer: Brian Pieragostini
Senior marketing manager for history: Katherine Bates

Cover image: Hagia Sophia, Istanbul. M.Taner/Zefa/Masterfile.

Printed in the U.S.A.

Library of Congress Catalog Card Number: 2006928173

ISBN 13: 978-0-618-38611-6
ISBN 10: 0-618-38611-4

1 2 3 4 5 6 7 8 9-DOW-10 09 08 07

BRIEF CONTENTS

CONTENTS

SOCIETIES · NETWORKS · TRANSITIONS

Classical Blossomings in World History, 600 B.C.E.–600 C.E.
253

MAPS

FEATURES

PREFACE

Awareness of the need for a universal view of history—for a history which transcends national and regional boundaries and comprehends the entire globe—is one of the marks of the present. Our past [is] the past of the world, our history is the first to be world history.[1]

British historian Geoffrey Barraclough wrote these words over two decades ago, yet historians are still grappling with what it means to write world history, and why it is crucial to do so. Twenty-first-century students, more than any generation before them, live in multicultural countries and an interconnected world. The world's interdependence calls for teaching a wider vision, which is the goal of this text. My intention is to create a meaningful, coherent, and stimulating presentation that conveys to students the incredible diversity of societies from earliest times to the present, as well as the ways they have been increasingly connected to other societies and shaped by these relationships. History may happen "as one darn thing after another," but the job of historians is to make it something more than facts, names, and dates. A text should provide a readable narrative, supplying a content base while also posing larger questions. The writing is as clear and thorough in its explanation of events and concepts as I can make it. No text can or should teach the course, but I hope that this text provides enough of a baseline of regional and global coverage to allow each instructor to bring her or his own talents, understandings, and particular interests to the process.

I became involved in teaching, debating, and writing world history as a result of my personal and academic experiences. My interest in other cultures was first awakened in the multicultural southern California city where I grew up. Many of my classmates or their parents had come from Asia, Latin America, or the Middle East. There was also a substantial African American community. A curious person did not have to search far to hear music, sample foods, or encounter ideas from many different cultures. I remember being enchanted by the Chinese landscape paintings at a local museum devoted to Asian art, and vowing to one day see some of those misty mountains for myself. Today many young people may be as interested as I was in learning about the world, since, thanks to immigration, many cities and towns all over North America have taken on a cosmopolitan flavor similar to my hometown.

While experiences growing up sparked my interest in other cultures, it was my schooling that pointed the way to a career in teaching world history. When I entered college, all undergraduate students were required to take a two-semester course in Western Civilization as part of the general education requirement. Many colleges and universities in North America had similar classes that introduced students to Egyptian pyramids, Greek philosophy, medieval pageantry, Renaissance art, and the French Revolution, enriching our lives. Fortunately, my university expanded student horizons further by adding course components (albeit brief) on China, Japan, India, and Islam while also developing a study abroad program. I participated in both the study abroad in Salzburg, Austria, and the student exchange with a university in Hong Kong, which meant living with, rather than just sampling, different customs, outlooks, and histories.

Some teachers and academic historians had begun to realize that the emphasis in U.S. education on the histories of the United States and western Europe, to the near exclusion of the rest of the world, was not sufficient for understanding the realities of the mid-twentieth century. Young Americans were being sent thousands of miles away to fight wars in countries, such as Vietnam, that few Americans had ever heard of. Newspapers and television reported developments in places such as Japan and Indonesia, Egypt and Congo, Cuba and Brazil, which had increasing relevance for Americans. Graduate programs and scholarship directed toward Asian, African, Middle Eastern, Latin American, and eastern European and Russian history also grew out of the awareness of a widening world, broadening conceptions of history. I attended one of the new programs in Asian Studies for my M.A. degree, and then the first Ph.D. program in world history. Thanks to that program, I encountered the stimulating work of pioneering world historians from

North America such as Philip Curtin, Marshall Hodgson, William McNeill, and Leften S. Stavrianos. My own approach owes much to the global vision they offered.

To bring some coherence to the emerging world history field as well as to promote a global approach at all levels of education, several dozen of us teaching at the university, college, community college, and high school level in the United States came together in the early 1980s to form the World History Association (WHA), for which I served as founding secretary. The organization grew rapidly, encouraging the teaching, studying, and writing of world history not only in the United States but all over the world. The approaches to world history found among active WHA members vary widely, and my engagement in the ongoing discussions at conferences and in essays, often about the merits of varied textbooks, provided an excellent background for writing this text.

The Aims and Approach of the Text

Societies, Networks, and Transitions: A Global History provides an accessible, thought-provoking guide to students in their exploration of the landscape of the past, helping them to think about it in all its social diversity and interconnectedness and to see their lives with fresh understanding. It does this by combining clear writing, special learning features, current scholarship, and a comprehensive, global approach that does not omit the role and richness of particular regions.

There is a method behind these aims. For nearly thirty-five years I have written about and taught Asian, African, and world history at universities in the United States and Malaysia. A cumulative seven years of study, research, or teaching in Southeast Asia, East Asia, East Africa, and Europe gave me insights into a wide variety of cultures and historical perspectives. Finally, the WHA, its publications and conferences, and the more recent electronic listserv, H-WORLD, have provided active forums for vigorously discussing how best to teach world history.

The most effective approach to presenting world history in a text for undergraduate and advanced high school students, I have concluded, is one that combines the themes of connections and cultures. World history is very much about connections that transcend countries, cultures, and regions, and a text should discuss, for example, major long-distance trade networks such as the Silk Road, the spread of religions, maritime exploration, world wars, and transregional empires such as the Persian, Mongol, and British Empires. These connections are part of the broader global picture. Students need to understand that cultures, however unique, did not emerge and operate in a vacuum but faced similar challenges, shared many common experiences, and influenced each other.

The broader picture is drawn by means of several features in the text. To strengthen the presentation of the global overview, the text uses an innovative essay feature entitled "Societies, Networks, and Transitions." Appearing at the end of each of the six chronological parts, this feature analyzes and synthesizes the wider trends of the era, such as the role of long-distance trade, the spread of technologies and religions, and global climate change. The objective is to amplify the wider transregional messages already developed in the part chapters and help students to think further about the global context in which societies are enmeshed. Each "Societies, Networks, and Transitions" essay also makes comparisons, for example, between the Han Chinese, Mauryan Indian, and Roman Empires, and between Chinese, Indian, and European emigration in the nineteenth century. These comparisons help to throw further light on diverse cultures and the differences and similarities between them during the era covered. Finally, each essay is meant to show how the transitions that characterize the era lead up to the era discussed in the following part. In addition, the prologues that introduce each of the six eras treated in the text also set out the broader context, including some of the major themes and patterns of wide influence as well as those for each region. Furthermore, several chapters concentrate on global developments since 1750 C.E.

However, while a broad global overview is a strongly developed feature of this text, most chapters, while acknowledging and explaining relevant linkages, focus on a particular region or several regions. Most students learn easiest by focusing on one region or culture at a time. Students also benefit from recognizing the cultural richness and intellectual creativity of specific societies. From this text students learn, for instance, about Chinese poetry, Indonesian music, Arab science, Greek philosophy, West African arts, Indian cinema, and Anglo-American political thought. As a component of this cultural richness, this text also devotes considerable attention to the enduring religious traditions, such as Buddhism, Christianity, and Islam, and to issues of gender. The cultural richness of a region and its distinctive social patterns can get lost in an approach that minimizes regional coverage. Today most people are still mostly concerned with events in their own countries, even as their lives are reshaped by transnational economies and global cultural movements.

Also a strong part of the presentation of world history in this text is its attempt to be comprehensive and inclusive. To enhance comprehensiveness, the text balances social, economic, political, and cultural and religious history, and it also devotes some attention to geographical and environmental contexts as well as to the history of ideas and technologies. At the same time, the text also highlights features within societies, such as economic production, technological innovations, and portable ideas that had widespread or enduring influence. To ensure inclusiveness, the text recognizes the contributions of many societies, including some often neglected in texts, such as sub-Saharan Africa, pre-Columbian America, and Oceania. In particular, this text offers strong coverage of the diverse Asian societies. Throughout history, as today, the great majority of the world's population have lived in Asia.

All textbook authors struggle with how to organize the material. To keep the number of chapters corresponding to the twenty-eight or thirty weeks of most academic calendars in North America, and roughly equal in length, I have often had to combine several regions into a single chapter in order to be comprehensive, sometimes making decisions for convenience sake. For example, unlike texts that may have only one chapter on sub-Saharan Africa covering the centuries from ancient times to 1500 C.E., this text discusses Africa in six chronological eras, devoting three chapters to the centuries prior to 1500 C.E. and three to the years since 1450 C.E. But this sometimes necessitated grouping Africa, depending on the era, with Europe, the Middle East, or the Americas. The material is divided into eras so that students can understand how all regions were part of world history from earliest times. I believe that a chronological structure aids students in grasping the changes over time while helping to organize the material.

Distinguishing Features

Several features of *Societies, Networks, Transitions: A Global History* will help students better understand, assimilate, and appreciate the material they are about to encounter. Those unique to this text include the following.

Introducing World History World history may be the first and possibly the only history course many undergraduates will take in college. The text opens with a short essay that introduces students to the nature of history, the special challenges posed by studying world history, and why we need to study it.

Balancing Themes Three broad themes—uniqueness, interdependence, and change—have shaped the text. They are discussed throughout in terms of three related concepts—societies, networks, and transitions. These concepts, discussed in more detail in "Introducing World History," can be summarized as follows:

- **Societies** Influenced by environmental and geographical factors, people have formed and maintained societies defined by distinctive but often changing cultures, beliefs, social forms, institutions, and material traits.
- **Networks** Over the centuries societies have generally been connected to other societies by growing networks forged by phenomena such as migration, long-distance trade, exploration, military expansion, colonization, the spread of ideas and technologies, and webs of communication. These growing networks modified individual societies, created regional systems, and eventually led to a global system.
- **Transitions** Each major historical era has been marked by one or more great transitions sparked by events or innovations, such as settled agriculture, Mongol imperialism, industrial revolution, or world war, that have had profound and enduring influ-

ences on many societies, gradually reshaping the world. At the same time, societies and regions have experienced transitions of regional rather than global scope that have generated new ways of thinking or doing things, such as the expansion of Islam into India or the European colonization of East Africa and Mexico.

Through exposure to these three ideas integrated throughout the text, students learn of the rich cultural mosaic of the world. They are also introduced to its patterns of connections and unity as well as of continuity and change.

"Societies, Networks, and Transitions" Minichapters A short feature at the end of each part assists the student in backing up from the stories of societies and regions to see the larger historical patterns of change and the wider links among distant peoples. This comparative analysis allows students to identify experiences and transitions common to several regions or the entire world and to reflect further on the text themes. These features can also help students review key developments from the preceding chapters.

Historical Controversies Since one of the common misconceptions about history is that it is about the "dead" past, included in each "Societies, Networks, and Transitions" feature is a brief account of a debate among historians over how an issue in the past should be interpreted and what it means to us today. For example, why are the major societies dominated by males, and has this always been true? Why and when did Europe begin its "great divergence" from China and other Asian societies? How do historians evaluate contemporary globalization? Reappraisal is at the heart of history, and many historical questions are never completely answered. Yet most textbooks ignore this dimension of historical study; this text is innovative in including it. The Historical Controversy essays will help show students that historical facts are anything but dead; they live and change their meaning as new questions are asked by each new generation.

Profiles It is impossible to recount the human story without using broad generalizations, but it is also difficult to understand that story without seeing historical events reflected in the lives of men and women, prominent but also ordinary people. Each chapter contains a profile that focuses on the experiences or accomplishments of a woman or man, to convey the flavor of life of the period, to embellish the chapter narrative with interesting personalities, and to integrate gender into the historical account. The profiles try to show how gender affected the individual, shaping her or his opportunities and involvement in society. Several focus questions ask the student to reflect on the profile. For instance, students will examine a historian in early China, look at the spread of Christianity as seen through the life of a pagan female philosopher in Egypt, relive the experience of a female slave in colonial Brazil, and envision modern Indian life through a sketch of a film star.

Special Coverage This text also treats often-neglected areas and subjects. For example:

- It focuses on several regions with considerable historical importance but often marginalized or even omitted in many texts, including sub-Saharan Africa, Southeast Asia, Korea, Central Asia, pre-Columbian North America, ancient South America, the Caribbean, Polynesia, Australia, Canada, and the United States.
- It includes discussions of significant groups that transcend regional boundaries, such as the caravan travelers of the Silk Road, Mongol empire builders, the Indian Ocean maritime traders, and contemporary humanitarian organizations such as Amnesty International and Doctors Without Borders.
- It features extensive coverage of the roots, rise, reshaping, and enduring influence of the great religious and philosophical traditions.
- It blends coverage of gender, particularly the experiences of women, and of social history generally, into the larger narrative.
- It devotes the first chapter of the text to the roots of human history. After a brief introduction to the shaping of our planet, human evolution, and the spread of people around the world, the chapter examines the birth of agriculture, cities, and states, which set the stage for everything to come.
- It includes strong coverage of the world since 1945, a focus of great interest to many students.

Witness to the Past Many texts incorporate excerpts from primary sources, but this text also keeps student needs in mind by using up-to-date translations and addressing a wide range of topics. Included are excerpts from important Buddhist, Hindu, Confucian, Zoroastrian, and Islamic works that helped shape great traditions. Readings such as a collection of Roman graffiti, a thirteenth-century tourist description of a Chinese city, a report on an Aztec market, and a manifesto for modern Egyptian women reveal something of people's lives and concerns. Also offered are materials that shed light on the politics of the time, such as an African king's plea to end the slave trade, Karl Marx's *Communist Manifesto*, and the recent *Arab Human Development Report*. The wide selection of document excerpts is also designed to illustrate how historians work with original documents. Unlike most texts, chapters are also enlivened by brief but numerous excerpts of statements, writings, or songs from people of the era that are effectively interspersed in the chapter narrative so that students can better see the vantage points and opinions of the people of that era.

Learning Aids

The carefully designed learning aids are meant to help faculty teach world history and students actively learn and appreciate it. A number of aids have been created, including some that distinguish this text from others in use.

Part Prologue and Map Each part opens with a prologue that previews the major themes and topics—global and regional—covered in the part chapters. An accompanying world map shows some of the key societies discussed in the part.

Chapter Outline, Primary Source Quotation, and Vignette A chapter outline shows the chapter contents at a glance. Chapter text then opens with a quotation from a primary source pertinent to chapter topics. An interest-grabbing vignette or sketch then funnels students' attention toward the chapter themes they are about to explore.

Focus Questions To prepare students for thinking about the main themes and topics of the chapter, a short list of thoughtfully prepared questions begins each chapter narrative. These questions are then repeated before each major section. The points they deal with are then revisited in the Chapter Summary.

Special Boxed Features Each chapter contains a Witness to the Past drawn from a primary source, and a Profile highlighting a man or woman from that era. The Historical Controversy boxes, which focus on issues of interpretation, are included in each "Societies, Networks, and Transitions" essay. Questions are also placed at the end of the primary source readings, historical controversies, and profiles to help students comprehend the material.

Maps and Other Visuals Maps, photos, chronologies, and tables are amply interspersed throughout the chapters, illustrating and unifying coverage and themes.

Section Summaries At the end of each major section within a chapter, a bulleted summary helps students to review the key topics.

Chapter Summary At the end of each chapter, a concise summary invites students to sum up the chapter content and review its major points.

Annotated Suggested Readings and Endnotes Short lists of annotated suggested readings, mostly recent, and websites providing additional information are also found at the end of each chapter. These lists acknowledge some of the more important works used in writing as well as sources of particular value for undergraduate students. Direct quotes in the text are attributed to their sources in endnotes, which are located at the end of the book.

Key Terms and Pronunciation Guides Important terms likely to be new to the student are boldfaced in the text and immediately defined. These key terms are also listed at the end of the chapter and then listed with their definitions at the end of the text. The pronunciation of foreign and other difficult terms is shown parenthetically where the terms are introduced to help students with the terminology.

Ancillaries

A wide array of supplements accompany this text to help students better master the material and to help instructors in teaching from the book:

- Online Study Center student website

  Online Study Center

- Online Teaching Center instructor website

  Online Teaching Center

- HM Testing CD-ROM (powered by Diploma)
- Online Instructor's Resource Manual
- PowerPoint maps, images, and lecture outlines
- PowerPoint questions for personal response systems
- Blackboard™ and WebCT™ course cartridges
- Eduspace™ (powered by Blackboard™)
- Interactive ebook

The *Online Study Center* is a companion website for students that features a wide array of resources to help students master the subject matter. The website, prepared by Robert Shannon Sumner of the University of West Georgia, is divided into three major sections:

- "Prepare for Class" includes material such as learning objectives, chapter outlines, and preclass quizzes for a student to consult before going to class.
- "Improve Your Grade" includes practice review material like interactive flashcards, chronological ordering exercises, audio mp3 files of chapter summaries, primary sources, and interactive map exercises.
- "ACE the Test" features our successful ACE brand of practice tests as well as other self-testing materials.

Students can also find additional text resources such as an online glossary, an audio pronunciation guide, and material on how to study more effectively in the General Resources section. Throughout the text, icons direct students to relevant exercises and self-testing material located on the *Online Study Center*. Access the *Online Study Center* for this text by visiting **college.hmco.com/pic/lockard1e.**

The *Online Teaching Center* is a companion website for instructors. It features all of the material on the student site plus additional password-protected resources that help instructors teach the course, such as an electronic version of the *Instructor's Resource Manual,* blank maps of world history, and PowerPoint slides. Access the *Online Teaching Center* for this text by visiting **college.hmco.com/pic/lockard1e.**

HM Testing (powered by *Diploma*) offers instructors a flexible and powerful tool for test generation and test management. Now supported by the Brownstone Research Group's market-leading *Diploma* software, this new version of *HM Testing* significantly improves functionality and ease of use by offering all the tools needed to create, author, deliver, and customize multiple types of tests. *Diploma* is currently in use at thousands of college and university campuses throughout the United States and Canada. The *HM Testing* content was developed by Candace Gregory-Abbott of California State University, Sacramento, and Timothy Furnish of Georgia Perimeter College and offers key term identification, multiple-choice questions (with page references to the correct responses), short-answer questions, and essay questions (with sample answers) as well as unit examination questions, for a total of approximately two thousand test items.

The *Instructor's Resource Manual,* prepared by Siamak Adhami of Saddleback Community College and Doug T. McGetchin of Florida Atlantic University, contains advice on teaching the World History course, suggestions on how to utilize the book's boxed feature program, instructional objectives, chapter outlines and summaries, lecture suggestions, suggested debate topics, writing assignments with sample answers, and cooperative learning activities.

We are pleased to offer a collection of world history PowerPoint lecture outlines, maps, and images for use in classroom presentations. Detailed lecture outlines correspond to the book's chapters and make it easier for instructors to cover the major topics in class. The art collection includes all of the photos and maps in the text, as well as numerous other images from our world history titles. PowerPoint questions and answers for use with personal response system software are also offered to adopters free of charge.

A variety of assignable homework and testing material has been developed to work with the *Blackboard™* and *WebCT™* course management systems, as well as with *Eduspace™*: Houghton Mifflin's online learning tool (powered by *Blackboard™*). *Eduspace™* is a web-based online learning environment that provides instructors with a gradebook and communication capabilities such as synchronous and asynchronous chats and announcement postings. It offers access to assignments, such as over 650 gradable homework exercises, writing assignments, interactive maps with questions, primary sources, discussion questions for online discussion boards, and tests, all ready to use. Instructors can choose to use the content as is, modify it, or even add their own. *Eduspace™* also contains an interactive ebook that contains in-text links to interactive maps, primary sources, audio pronunciation files, and review and self-testing material for students.

Formats

The text is available in a one-volume hard cover edition, a two-volume paperback edition, a three-volume paperback edition, and as an interactive ebook. *Volume 1: To 1500* includes Chapters 1–14; *Volume 2: Since 1450* includes Chapters 15–31; *Volume A: To 600* includes Chapters 1–9; *Volume B: From 600 to 1750* includes Chapters 10–18; and *Volume C: Since 1750* includes Chapters 19–31.

Acknowledgments

The author would like to thank the following community of instructors who, by sharing their teaching experiences and insightful feedback, helped shape the final textbook and ancillary program:

Siamak Adhami, Saddleback Community College

Sanjam Ahluwalia, Northern Arizona University

David G. Atwill, Pennsylvania State University

Ewa K. Bacon, Lewis University

Bradford C. Brown, Bradley University

Gayle K. Brunelle, California State University–Fullerton

Rainer Buschmann, California State University, Channel Islands

Jorge Canizares-Esguerra, State University of New York–Buffalo

Bruce A. Castleman, San Diego State University

Harold B. Cline, Jr., Middle Georgia College

Simon Cordery, Monmouth College

Dale Crandall-Bear, Solano Community College

Cole Dawson, Warner Pacific College

Hilde De Weerdt, University of Tennessee, Knoxville

Anna Dronzek, University of Minnesota, Morris

James R. Evans, Southeastern Community College

Robert Fish, Japan Society of New York

Robert J. Flynn, Portland Community College

Gladys Frantz-Murphy, Regis University

Timothy Furnish, Georgia Perimeter College

James E. Genova, Ohio State University

Deborah Gerish, Emporia State University

Kurt A. Gingrich, Radford University

Candace Gregory-Abbott, California State University, Sacramento

Paul L. Hanson, California Lutheran University

A. Katie Harris, Georgia State University

Gregory M. Havrilcsak, University of Michigan–Flint

Timothy Hawkins, Indiana State University

Don Holsinger, Seattle Pacific University

Mary N. Hovanec, Cuyahoga Community College

Jonathan Judaken, University of Memphis

Thomas E. Kaiser, University of Arkansas at Little Rock

Carol Keller, San Antonio College

Patricia A. Kennedy, Leeward Community College-University of Hawaii

Jonathan Lee, San Antonio College

Thomas Lide, San Diego State University

Derek S. Linton, Hobart and William Smith Colleges

David L. Longfellow, Baylor University

Erik C. Maiershofer, Point Loma Nazarene University

Afshin Marashi, California State University, Sacramento

Robert B. McCormick, University of South Carolina Upstate

Doug T. McGetchin, Florida Atlantic University

Kerry Muhlestein, Brigham Young University–Hawaii

Peter Ngwafu, Albany State University

Monique O'Connell, Wake Forest University

Annette Palmer, Morgan State University

Nicholas C. J. Pappas, Sam Houston State University

Patricia M. Pelley, Texas Tech University

John Pesda, Camden County College

Pamela Roseman, Georgia Perimeter College

Paul Salstrom, St. Mary-of-the-Woods

Sharlene Sayegh, California State University, Long Beach

Michael Seth, James Madison University

David Simonelli, Youngstown State University

Peter Von Sivers, University of Utah

Anthony J. Steinhoff, University of Tennessee–Chattanooga

Nancy L. Stockdale, University of Central Florida

Robert Shannon Sumner, University of West Georgia

Kate Transchel, California State University, Chico

Sally N. Vaughn, University of Houston

Thomas G. Velek, Mississippi University for Women

Kenneth Wilburn, East Carolina University

The author has incurred many intellectual debts in developing his expertise in world history, as well as in preparing this text. To begin with, I cannot find words to express my gratitude to the wonderful editors and staff at Houghton Mifflin—Nancy Blaine, Julie Swasey, Carol Newman, and Jean Woy—who had enough faith in this project to tolerate my missed deadlines and sometimes grumpy responses to editorial decisions or some other crisis. I also owe an incalculable debt to my development editor, Phil Herbst, who prodded and pampered, and helped me write for a student, rather than scholarly, audience. Carole Frohlich, Jessyca Broekman, Susan Zorn, and Jake Kawatski ably handled the photos, maps, copyediting, and indexes, respectively. Sandi McGuire and Katherine Bates provided great help with marketing. I also owe a great debt to Pam Gordon, whose interest and encouragement got this project started. Ken Wolf of Murray State University prepared the initial drafts of several of the early chapters and in other ways gave me useful criticism and advice. I would also like to acknowledge the inspiring mentors who helped me at various stages of my academic preparation: Bill Goldmann, who introduced me to world history at Pasadena High School in California; Charles Hobart and David Poston, University of Redlands professors who sparked my interest in Asia; George Wong, Bart Stoodley, and especially Andrew and Margaret Roy, my mentors at Chung Chi College in Hong Kong; Walter Vella and Danny Kwok, who taught me Asian studies at Hawaii; and John Smail and Phil Curtin, under whom I studied comparative world history in the immensely exciting Ph.D. program at Wisconsin. My various sojourns in East Asia,

Southeast Asia, and East Africa allowed me to meet and learn from many inspiring and knowledgeable scholars. I have also been greatly stimulated and influenced in my approach by the writings of many fine global historians, but I would single out Phil Curtin, Marshall Hodgson, L. S. Stavrianos, William McNeill, Fernand Braudel, Eric Hobsbawm, Immanuel Wallerstein, and Peter Stearns. Curtin, Hobsbawm, and McNeill also gave me personal encouragement concerning my writing in the field, for which I am very grateful.

Colleagues at the various universities where I taught have been supportive of my explorations in world and comparative history. Most especially I acknowledge the friendship, support, and intellectual collaboration over three decades of my colleagues in the Social Change and Development Department at the University of Wisconsin–Green Bay (UWGB), especially Harvey Kaye, Tony Galt, Lynn Walter, Larry Smith, Andy Kersten, Kim Nielsen, and Andrew Austin. I have also benefited immeasurably as a world historian from the visiting lecture series sponsored by UWGB's Center for History and Social Change, directed by Harvey Kaye, which over the years has brought in dozens of outstanding scholars. My students at UWGB and elsewhere have also taught me much.

I also thank my colleagues in the World History Association, who have generously shared their knowledge, encouraged my work, and otherwise provided an exceptional opportunity for learning and an exchange of ideas. I am proud to have helped establish this organization, which incorporates world history teachers at all levels of education and in many nations. Among many others, I want to express a special thank-you to several longtime friends, early officers and members of the WHA from whom I have learned so much and with whom I have shared many wonderful meals and conversations: Ross Dunn, Lynda Shaffer, Kevin Reilly, Jerry Bentley, Heidi Roupp, Mark Gilbert, Steve Gosch, Judy Zinsser, and Anand Yang.

Finally, I need to acknowledge the loving support of my wife Kathy and our two sons, Chris and Colin, who patiently, although not always without complaint, put up for the ten years of the project with my hectic work schedule and the ever-growing piles of research materials, books, and chapter drafts scattered around our cluttered den and sometimes colonizing other space around the house. Now perhaps we shall have a chance to once again smell the roses and marvel at the sunsets without my obsessing about a chapter revision to complete, after I clear away the clutter.

About the Author

Craig A. Lockard is Ben and Joyce Rosenberg Professor of History in the Social Change and Development Department at the University of Wisconsin–Green Bay, where since 1975 he has taught courses on Asian, African, comparative, and world history. He has also taught at SUNY-Buffalo, SUNY-Stony Brook, and the University of Bridgeport, and twice served as a Fulbright-Hays professor at the University of Malaya in Malaysia. After undergraduate studies in Austria, Hong Kong, and the University of Redlands, he earned an M.A. in Asian Studies at the University of Hawaii and a Ph.D. in Comparative World and Southeast Asian History at the University of Wisconsin–Madison. His published books, articles, essays, and reviews range over a wide spectrum of topics: world history; Southeast Asian history, politics, and society; Asian emigration; the Vietnam War; and folk, popular, and world music. Among his major books are *Lands of Green, Waters of Blue: Southeast Asia in World History* (forthcoming); *Dance of Life: Popular Music and Politics in Modern Southeast Asia* (1998); and *From Kampung to City: A Social History of Kuching, Malaysia, 1820–1970* (1987). He was also part of the task force that prepared revisions to the U.S. National Standards in World History (1996). Professor Lockard has served on various editorial advisory boards, including the *Journal of World History* and *The History Teacher,* and as book review editor for the *Journal of Asian Studies* and the *World History Bulletin.* He was one of the founders of the World History Association and served as the organization's first secretary. He has lived and traveled widely in Asia, Africa, and Europe.

NOTE ON SPELLING AND USAGE

Transforming foreign words and names, especially those from non-European languages, into spellings usable for English-speaking readers presents a challenge. Sometimes, as with Chinese, Thai, and Malay/Indonesian, several romanized spelling systems have developed. Generally I have chosen user-friendly spellings that are widely used in other Western writings (such as *Aksum* for the classical Ethiopian state and *Ashoka* for the classical Indian king). For Chinese, I generally use the *pinyin* system developed in the People's Republic over the past few decades (such as *Qin* and *Qing* rather than the older *Chin* and *Ching* for these dynasties, and *Beijing* instead of *Peking*), but for a few terms and names (such as the twentieth-century political leaders *Sun Yat-sen* and *Chiang Kai-shek*) I have retained an older spelling more familiar to Western readers and easier to pronounce. The same strategy is used for some other terms or names from Afro-Asian societies, such as *Cairo* instead of *al-Cahira* (the Arabic name) for the Egyptian city, *Bombay* instead of *Mumbai* (the current Indian usage) for India's largest city, and *Burma* instead of *Myanmar*. In some cases I have favored a newer spelling widely used in a region and modern scholarship but not perhaps well known in the West. For example, in discussing Southeast Asia I follow contemporary scholarship and use *Melaka* instead of *Malacca* for the Malayan city and *Maluku* rather than *Moluccas* for the Indonesian islands. Similarly, like Africa specialists I have opted to use some newer spellings, such as *Gikuyu* rather than *Kikuyu* for the Kenyan people. To simplify things for the reader I have tried to avoid using diacritical marks within words. Sometimes their use is unavoidable, such as for the premodern Chinese city of *Chang'an;* the two syllables here are pronounced separately. I also follow the East Asian custom of rendering Chinese, Japanese, and Korean names with the surname (family name) first (e.g., *Mao Zedong, Tokugawa Ieyasu*). The reader is also referred to the opening essay, "Introducing World History," for explanations of the dating system used (such as the Common Era and the Intermediate Era) and geographical concepts (such as Eurasia for Europe and Asia, and Oceania for Australia, New Zealand, and the Pacific islands).

A journey of a thousand miles begins with the first step.

CHINESE PROVERB

This introduction is designed to help you take the important "first step" toward understanding the scope and challenge of studying world history. By presenting the main concepts and themes of world history, it will serve as your guide in exploring the story of the world presented in the rest of the book. The introduction will also give you a foretaste of the lively ongoing debates in which historians engage as they try to make sense of the past, especially how societies change and how their contacts with one another have created the interconnected world we know today. By examining world history, you can better understand not only how this connection happened, but also why.

What Do Historians Do?

History is the study of the past that looks at all of human life, thought, and behavior and includes both a record and an interpretation of events, people, and the societies they developed. Therefore, the job of the historian is to both describe *and* interpret the past. Both tasks are important. Although beginning students generally see history as the story of "what happened," most professional historians regard the attempt to make sense of historical events as the more exciting part of their work. Two general concepts help historians in these efforts. When they look at humans in all their historical complexity, historians see both changes and continuity. The legal system in the United States, for example, is unlike any other in the world, and yet it has been shaped in part by both English and ancient Roman legal practices.

Historians face their greatest challenges in their role as interpreters of the past. Although historians agree on the need for extensive evidence to support their generalizations, they often disagree on how an event should be interpreted. Often the disagreements reflect differences in political points of view. In 1992 a widely publicized disagreement took place on the occasion of the 500-year anniversary of the first cross-Atlantic voyage of Christopher Columbus to the Western Hemisphere in 1492. Depending on their political biases, historians used the well-known records of this event in different ways. Some historians pictured Columbus as a farsighted pioneer who made possible communication between the hemispheres, while others saw him as an immoral villain who mistreated the local American peoples, beginning a pattern of exploitation by Europeans. Similar debates have raged about whether it was necessary for the United States to drop atomic bombs on Japan in 1945, a deadly decision that killed thousands of Japanese civilians but nevertheless ended World War II.

While the events of the past do not change, our understanding of them does, as historians both acquire new information and use the old information to answer new questions. Only within the past fifty years, for example, have historians studied the diaries and journals that reveal the important role of women on the home front during the American Civil War. Even more recently historians have used long neglected sources to conclude that, a millennium ago, China had the world's most dynamic economy and sophisticated technology. Similarly, historians have recently discovered, in the West African city of Timbuktu, thousands of old books written in African languages, forcing a rethinking of literacy and scholarship in West African societies hundreds of years ago.

What history "tells us" is constantly evolving. New evidence, changing interests, and the asking of new questions all add up to seeing things in a new light. As you read the text, remember that no text contains the whole or final truth. **Historical revision**, or changing understanding of the past, is at the heart of historical scholarship. This revision and the difficulties of interpretation also make history controversial. In recent years heated debates about what schools should teach about history have erupted in many countries, including Japan, India, and the United States.

Historians bridge the gap between the humanities and the social sciences. As humanists, historians study the philosophies, religions, literatures, and arts that people have generated over the ages. As social scientists, historians examine political, social, and economic patterns, though frequently asking questions different from those asked by anthropologists, economists, political scientists, and sociologists; the last three groups especially are generally more concerned with the present and often more interested in theoretical questions. Because they study people in their many roles and stations in life—the accomplishments of the rich and famous as well as the struggles and dreams of common women and men—historians must be familiar with the findings of other relevant academic disciplines.

Why Study World History?

World history is the broadest field of history. It studies the human record as a whole and the experiences of people in all the world's inhabited regions: Africa, the Americas, Asia, Europe, and the Pacific Basin. World history helps us better understand individual societies and their traditions by making it easier to look at them comparatively. Studying history on a global scale also brings out patterns of life, cultural traditions, and connections between societies that go beyond a particular region, such as the spread of long-distance trade and Buddhism, which followed the trade routes throughout southern and eastern Asia nearly two thousand years ago. World, or global, history takes us through the forest of history in which the individual societies represent the individual trees. World history helps us comprehend both the trees and the forest, allowing us to situate ourselves in a broader context.

The study of world history helps us understand our increasingly connected world. Decisions made in Washington, D.C., Paris, or Tokyo influence citizens in Argentina, Senegal, and Malaysia, just as events in Africa, the Middle East, or Latin America often affect the lives of people in Europe, North America, and Australia. World historians use the widest angle of vision possible to comprehend a world in which diverse local traditions and international trends intermingle. International trends spread from many directions. Western phenomena such as McDonald's, Hard Rock Cafes, French wines, Hollywood films, churches, the Internet, and cell phones have spread around the world. Non-Western products and ideas, however, have also gained global followings; among these are Mexican soap operas, Chinese food, Japanese cars, Indonesian arts, African rhythms, and the Islamic religion. While it is important to study the histories of individual nations, we must remember that, for all their idiosyncrasies, each nation develops in the context of a wider world.

Along with the growing interconnectedness of the world, a global perspective highlights the past achievements of all peoples. The history of science, for example, shows that key inventions—printing, sternpost rudders, the compass, the wheelbarrow, gunpowder—originated in China and that the modern system of numbering came from India, reaching Europe from the Middle East as "Arabic" numerals. Indeed, various peoples—Mesopotamians, Egyptians, Greeks, Chinese, Indians, Arabs—built the early foundation for modern science and technology, and their discoveries moved along the trade routes. The importers of technology and ideas often modified or improved on them. For example, Europeans made good use of Chinese, Indian, and Arab technologies, as well as their own inventions, in their quest to explore the world in the fifteenth and sixteenth centuries. The interdependence among and exchanges between peoples is a historical as well as a present reality.

The World History Challenge

When we study world history, we see other countries and peoples, past and present. We do not, however, always see them accurately. Nevertheless, by studying the unfamiliar, world history helps us to recognize how some of the attitudes we absorb from the particular society and era we live in shape, and may distort, our understanding of the world and of history. Coming to terms with this mental baggage means examining such things as maps and geographical concepts and acquiring intellectual tools for comprehending other cultures.

Broadening the Scope of Our Histories

During much of the twentieth century, high school and college students in English-speaking countries were often taught some version of a course, usually called Western Civilization, that emphasized the rise of western Europe and the European contributions to modern North American societies. The Western Civilization course recognized the undeniably influential role of Western nations, technologies, and ideas in the modern world, but it was also a reflection of historians' extensive acquisition of data on Europe and North America compared with the rest of the world. This approach exaggerated the role that Europe played in world history before the sixteenth century, pushing Asian, African, and Native American peoples and their accomplishments into the background while underplaying the contributions these peoples made to Europe. Students usually learned little about China, India, or Islam, and even less about Africa, Southeast Asia, or Latin America.

In the 1960s the teaching of history began to change, particularly in North America. The political independence of most African nations from Western nations and the civil rights movement in the United States, which demanded equality between blacks and whites, forced a reappraisal of African history that was less influenced by colonialism and racism. By the 1970s the academic study of not only African but also Asian, Latin American, Native American, and Pacific island history in North America and Europe had become far more sophisticated. The increased knowledge has made it easier to write a world history that takes into its scope the entire globe. As a result, world history courses, rare before the 1960s, became increasingly common in U.S. universities, colleges, and high schools by the late twentieth century and have been proliferating in several other countries, such as Australia, Canada, South Africa, China, and the Netherlands.

Revising Maps and Geography

Maps not only tell us where places are; they also create a mental image of the world, revealing how peoples perceive themselves and others. For example, Chinese maps once portrayed China as the "Middle Kingdom," the center of

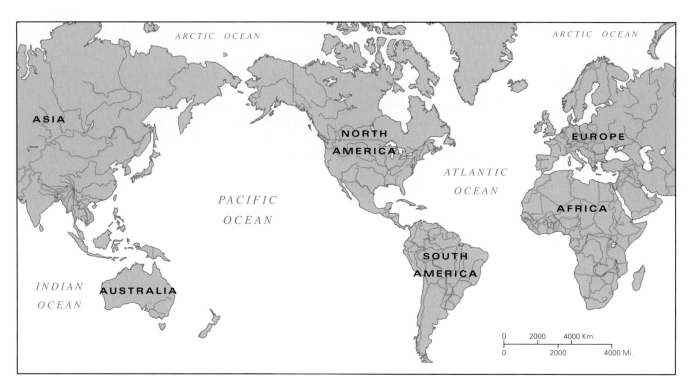

Mercator Projection

the world surrounded by "barbarians." This image reflected and deepened the Chinese sense of superiority over neighboring peoples. Similarly, 2,500 years ago, the Greeks developed a map that showed Greece at the center of the inhabited world known to them.

Even in modern times, maps can be misleading. For example, the Mercator projection (or spatial presentation), a map still used in many schools in North America and elsewhere and standard in most atlases, is based on a sixteenth-century European model that distorts the relative size of landmasses, greatly exaggerating Europe, North America, and Greenland while diminishing the lands around the equator and in the Southern Hemisphere. In this projection, Africa, India, Southeast Asia, China, and South America look much smaller than they actually are. In the United States, maps using a Mercator projection have often tellingly placed the Americas in the middle of the map, cutting Asia in half. The implicit message is that the United States, appearing larger than it actually is, plays the central role in the world.

Alternative maps have emerged that give a more accurate view of relative size. For example, the Eckert projection is an oval-shaped projection using an ellipse that shows a better balance of size and shape while minimizing distortion of continental areas. A comparison between the Mercator and Eckert world maps is shown on this page and the next.

The same shaping of mental images of geography found in maps is also seen in concepts of geographical features and divisions, such as continents, the large landmasses on which most people live. The classical Greeks were probably the first to use the terms *Europe*, *Africa*, and *Asia* in defining their world 2,500 years ago, and later Europeans transformed these terms into the names for continents. For centuries Western peoples have taken for granted that Europe is a continent. Actually, however, Europe is not a separate landmass, and the physical barriers between it and Asia are not that significant. If mountains and other geographical barriers define a continent, one can make a better case for India (blocked off by truly formidable mountains) or Southeast Asia than for Europe. At the same time, seeing Asia as a single continent is also a problem, given its spectacular size and geographical diversity. Today world geographers and historians usually consider Europe and Asia to constitute one huge continent, Eurasia, containing several subcontinental regions, such as Europe, South Asia, and East Asia.

Popular terms such as *Near East*, *Middle East*, or *Far East* are also misleading. They were originally formulated to describe regions as Westerners saw them in relationship to Europe. Much depends on the viewer's position; Australians, for example, often label nearby Southeast and East Asia as the "Near North." But, rejecting a Europe-centered approach, few Western scholars of China or Japan today refer to the "Far East," preferring the more neutral term *East Asia*. This text considers the term *Near East*, long used for western Asia, as outdated, but it refers to Southwest Asia and North Africa, closely linked historically (especially after the rise of Islam 1,400 years ago), as the Middle East, since that term is more convenient than the alternatives. The text also uses the term *Oceania* to refer to Australia, New Zealand, and the Pacific islands.

Eckert Projection

Rethinking the Dating System

A critical feature of historical study is the dating of events. World history challenges us by making us aware that all dating systems are based on the assumptions of a particular culture. Many Asian peoples saw history as moving in great cycles of birth, maturation, and decay (sometimes involving millions of years), while Westerners saw history as moving in a straight line from past to future (as can be seen in the chronologies within each chapter). Calendars were often tied to myths about the world's creation or about a people's or country's origins. Hence, the ancient Roman calendar was based on the founding of the city of Rome around 2,700 years ago, reflecting the Romans' claim to the territory in which they had recently settled.

The dating system used throughout the Western world today is based on the Gregorian Christian calendar, created by a sixteenth-century Roman Catholic pope, Gregory XIII. It uses the birth of Christianity's founder, Jesus of Nazareth, 2,000 years ago as the turning point. Dates for events prior to the Christian era were identified as B.C. (before Christ); years in the Christian era were labeled A.D. (for the Latin *anno domini*, "in the year of the Lord"). Many history books published in Europe and North America still employ this system, which has spread around the world in recent centuries.

The notion of Christian and pre-Christian eras has no longer been satisfactory for studies of world history because it is rooted in the viewpoint of only one religious tradition, whereas there are many in the world, usually with different calendars. The Christian calendar has little relevance for the non-Christian majority of the world's people. Muslims, for example, who consider the revelations of the prophet Muhammad to be the central event in history, begin their dating system with Muhammad's journey, within Arabia, from the city of Mecca to Medina in 622 A.D. Many Buddhists use a calendar beginning with the death of Buddha around 2,500 years ago. The Chinese chronological system divides history into cycles stretching over 24 million years. The Chinese are now in the fifth millennium of the current cycle, and their system corresponds more accurately than does the Gregorian calendar to the beginning of the world's oldest cities and states, between 5,000 and 6,000 years ago. Many other alternative dating systems exist. Selecting one over the others constitutes favoritism for a particular society or cultural tradition.

Therefore, in recent years most world historians and an increasing number of specialists in Asian, African, and European history have moved toward a more secular, or nonreligious, concept, the Common Era. This system still accepts as familiar, at least to Western and Latin American readers, the dates used in the Western calendar, but it calls the period after the transition, identified by Christians with the birth of Jesus, a "common" era, since many influential, dynamic societies existed two millennia ago in various parts of the world, not only in the Judeo-Christian Holy Land. Around two millennia ago, the beginning of the Common Era, the Roman Empire in the West was at its height while Chinese and Indian empires ruled large chunks of Asia. At the beginning of the Common Era many peoples in the Eastern Hemisphere were also linked by trade and religion to a greater extent than ever before. At the same time, several African societies flourished, and states and cities had long before developed in the Americas. Hence this period makes a useful and familiar benchmark.

In the new system, events are dated as B.C.E. (before the Common Era) and as C.E. (Common Era, which begins in year 1 of the Christian calendar). This change is an attempt at a method of dating that includes all the world's people and avoids favoring any particular religious tradition.

Rethinking the Division of History into Periods

To make world history more comprehensible, historians divide long periods of time into smaller segments, such as "the ancient world" or "modern history," each marked by certain key events or turning points. Historians call this process of dividing time **periodization**. For example, scholars of European, Islamic, Chinese, Indonesian, or United States history generally agree among themselves on the major eras and turning points for the region they study, but world historians need a system that can encompass all parts of the world. Finding such a system, however, presents difficulties, since most historic events did not affect all regions of the world. For instance, developments that were key to the eastern half of Eurasia, such as the spread of Buddhism, or to western Eurasia and North Africa, such as the spread of Christianity, did not always affect southern Africa, and both the Western Hemisphere, or the Americas, and some Pacific peoples remained isolated from the Eastern Hemisphere for centuries.

Given the need for a chronological pattern that is inclusive, this book divides history into periods, each of which is notable for significant changes around the world:

1. **Ancient (100,000–600 B.C.E.)** The Ancient Era, during which the foundations for world history were built, can be divided into two distinct periods. During the long centuries known as Prehistory (ca. 100,000–4000 B.C.E.), Stone Age peoples, living in small groups, survived by hunting and gathering food. Eventually some of them began simple farming and living in villages, launching the second period, the era of agrarian societies. Between 4000 and 600 B.C.E., agriculture became more productive, the first cities and states were established in both hemispheres, and some societies invented writing, allowing historians to study their experiences and ideas.
2. **Classical (600 B.C.E.–600 C.E.)** The Classical Era is marked by the creation of more states and complex agrarian societies, the birth of major religions and philosophies, the formation of the first large empires, often encompassing entire regions, and the expansion of long-distance trade, which linked distant peoples.
3. **Intermediate (600–1500 C.E.)** The Intermediate Era comprises a long middle period of expanding horizons that modified or displaced the classical societies.

It was marked by increasing trade connections between distant peoples within the same hemisphere, the growth and spread of several older religions, the rapid rise of a new religion, Islam, and oceanic exploration by Asians and Europeans.

4. **Early Modern (1450–1750 C.E.)** During the Early Modern Era, the whole globe became intertwined as European exploration and conquests in the Americas, Africa, and southern Asia fostered the rise of a global economy, capitalism, and a trans-Atlantic slave trade; undermined American and African societies; and enriched Europe.
5. **Modern (1750–1945 C.E.)** The Modern Era was characterized by industrialization and empire building on an unprecedented scale. These centuries featured rapid technological and economic change in Europe and North America, Western colonization of many Asian and African societies, the rise of nationalism and socialism, political revolutions, world wars, and a widening gap between rich and poor societies.
6. **Contemporary (1945–present)** The Contemporary Era has been marked by a more closely interlinked world, including the global spread of commercial markets, cultures, and communications, the collapse of Western colonial empires, international organizations, new technologies, struggles by poor nations to develop economically, environmental destruction, and conflict between powerful nations.

Understanding Cultural and Historical Differences

The study of world history challenges us to understand peoples and ideas very different from our own. The past is, as one writer has put it, "a foreign country; they do things differently there."[1] As human behavior changes with the times, sometimes dramatically, so do people's beliefs. Even moral and ethical standards have changed. For example, in Asia centuries ago, Assyrians and Mongols sometimes killed everyone in cities that resisted their conquest. Some European Christians seven hundred years ago burned suspected heretics and witches at the stake and enjoyed watching blind beggars fight. Across the Atlantic, American peoples such as the Aztecs and Incas engaged in human sacrifice. None of these behaviors would be morally acceptable today in most societies.

Differences in customs complicate efforts to understand people of earlier centuries. We need not approve of empire builders and plunderers, human sacrifice and witch burning, but we should be careful about applying our current standards of behavior and thought to people who lived in different times and places. There is always the danger of **ethnocentrism**, viewing others narrowly through the lens of one's own society and its values. Historians are careful in using value-loaded words such as *primitive*, *barbarian*, *civilized*, or *progress*. Such words carry negative meanings and are often matters of judgment rather than fact. For instance, soldiers facing each other on the battlefield may consider themselves civilized and their opponents barbarians. And progress, such as industrialization, often brings negative developments, such as pollution, along with the positive.

Today anthropologists use the term **cultural relativism** to remind us that, while all people have much in common, societies are diverse and unique, embodying different standards of correct behavior. For instance, cultures may have very different ideas about children's obligations to their parents, what happens to people's souls when they die, or what constitutes music pleasing to the ear. Cultural relativism still allows us to say that the Mongol empire builders in Eurasia some eight hundred years ago were brutal, or that the mid-twentieth-century Nazi German dictator, Adolph Hitler, was a murderous tyrant, or that laws in some societies today that blame and penalize women who are raped are wrong and should be protested. But cultural relativism discourages us from criticizing other cultures or ancient peoples just because they are or were different from us. Studying world history can make us more aware of our ethnocentric biases.

The Major Themes

Determining major themes is yet another challenge in presenting world history. This text uses certain themes to take maximum advantage of world history's power to illuminate both change and continuity as we move from the past to the present. Specifically, in preparing the text, the author asked himself: What do educated students today need to know about world history to understand the globalizing era in which they live?

Three broad themes help you comprehend how today's world emerged. These themes are shaped around three concepts: societies, networks, and transitions.

1. **Societies** are broad groups of people that have common traditions, institutions and organized patterns of relationships with each other. The societies that people have organized and maintained, influenced by environmental factors, were defined by distinctive but often changing cultures, beliefs, social forms, governments, economies, and ways of life.

2. **Networks** are arrangements or collections of links between different societies, such as the routes over which traders, goods, diplomats, armies, ideas, and information travel. Over the centuries societies were increasingly connected to other societies by growing networks forged by phenomena such as population movement, long-distance trade, exploration, military expansion, colonization, the diffusion of ideas and technologies, and communication links. These growing networks modified individual societies, connected societies within the same and nearby regions, and eventually led to a global system in which distant peoples came into frequent contact.

3. **Transitions** are passages, changes, events, or movements that reshape societies and regions. Each major historical era was marked by one or more great transitions that were sparked by events or innovations that had profound, enduring influences on many societies and that fostered a gradual reshaping of the world.

The first theme, based on societies, recognizes the importance in world history of the distinctiveness of societies. Cultural traditions and social patterns differed greatly. For example, societies in Eurasia fostered several influential philosophical and religious traditions, from Confucianism in eastern Asia to Christianity, born in the Middle East and nourished both there and in Europe. Historians often identify unique traditions in a society that go back hundreds or even thousands of years.

The second theme, based on networks, acknowledges the way societies have contacted and engaged with each other to create the interdependent world we know today. The spread of technologies and ideas, exploration and colonization, and the growth of global trade across Eurasia and Africa and then into the Western Hemisphere are largely responsible for setting this interlinking process in motion. Today networks such as the World Wide Web, airline routes, multinational corporations, and terrorist organizations operate on a global scale. As this list shows, many networks are welcome, but some are dangerous.

The third theme, transitions, helps to emphasize major developments that shaped world history. The most important include, roughly in chronological order, the beginning of agriculture, the rise of cities and states, the birth and spread of philosophical and religious traditions, the forming of great empires, the linking of Eurasia by the Mongols, the European seafaring explorations and conquests, the Industrial Revolution, the forging and dismantling of Western colonial empires, world wars, and the invention of electronic technologies that allow for instantaneous communication around the world.

With these themes in mind, the text constructs the rich story of world history. The intellectual experience of studying world history is exciting and will give you a clearer understanding of how the world as you know it came to be.

Online Study Center
Improve Your Grade Flashcards

Key Terms

history	cultural relativism
historical revision	societies
periodization	networks
ethnocentrism	transitions

Suggested Reading

After each chapter and essay, you will find a short list of valuable books and useful websites to help you explore history beyond the text. The general books and websites listed below will be of particular value to beginning students of world history.

Books and Journals

Bender, Thomas. *A Nation Among Nations: America's Place in World History*. New York: Hill and Wang, 2006. Looks at the history of the United States as part of modern world history.

Bentley, Jerry H. *Shapes of World History in 20th Century Scholarship*. Washington, D.C.: American Historical Association, 1996. A brief presentation of the scholarly study of world history.

Christian, David. *Maps of Time: An Introduction to Big History*. Berkeley: University of California Press, 2004. A detailed but path-breaking study mixing scientific understandings into the study of world history.

Dunn, Ross, ed. *The New World History: A Teacher's Companion*. Boston: Bedford/St. Martin's, 2000. A valuable collection of essays on various aspects of world history and how it can be studied. Useful for students as well as teachers.

Hodgson, Marshall G. S. *Rethinking World History: Essays on Europe, Islam, and World History*. Edited by Edmund Burke, III. New York: Cambridge University Press, 1993. Written by one of the most influential world historians for teachers and scholars but also offering many insights for students.

McNeill, J. R., and William H. McNeill. *The Human Web: A Bird's-Eye View of World History*. New York: W.W. Norton, 2003. A stimulating overview of world history using the concept of human webs to examine interactions between peoples.

McNeill, William H., et al., eds. *Berkshire Encyclopedia of World History*, 5 vols. Great Barrington, Mass.: Berkshire, 2005. One of the best of several fine encyclopedias, with many essays on varied aspects of world history.

Stavrianos, Leften S. *Lifelines from Our Past: A New World History*. Rev. ed. Armonk, N.Y.: M. E. Sharpe, 1997. A brief but stimulating reflection on world history by a leading scholar.

Stearns, Peter N. *Western Civilization in World History*. New York: Routledge, 2003. A brief examination of how Western civilization fits into the study of world history.

Wiesner-Hanks, Merry E. *Gender in World History*. Malden, Mass.: Blackwell, 2001. A pioneering thematic survey of a long-neglected subject.

Websites

The Encyclopedia of World History (http://www.bartleby.com/67/). A valuable collection of thousands of entries spanning the centuries from prehistory spanning the centuries to 2000.

Internet Global History Sourcebook (http://www.fordham.edu/halsall/global/globalsbook.html). An excellent set of links on world history from ancient to modern times.

Women in World History (http://chnm.gmu.edu/wwh/). Invaluable collection of links covering many societies and all eras.

World Civilizations (http://www.wsu.edu/~dee/MAIN/HTM). An internet anthology maintained at Washington State University.

World History for Us All (http://worldhistoryforusall.sdsu.edu). A growing site with useful essays and other materials, sponsored by San Diego State University.

World History Sources (http://worldhistorymatters.org). Valuable annotated links on different subjects, based at George Mason University.

PART I

Foundations: Ancient Societies, to 600 B.C.E.

Most of us carry pictures in our minds of the world's ancient peoples and their ways of life: prehistoric cave dwellers huddling around a fire, wandering desert tribes, towering pyramids, and spectacular ruins of cities and temples. In fact, the centuries between 100,000 and 600 B.C.E. saw the evolution of these and many other social and cultural phenomena, more complex and often more significant to us today than these mental pictures convey. These centuries also saw humans take the first steps in establishing regular contacts and exchanges, often those of trade, with one another, creating the networks that linked many societies over wide areas.

Human societies have emerged only recently in earth's long history. Simple life began on earth over 3 billion years ago. Several million years ago in Africa the earliest near ancestors of humans began to walk upright and use simple tools. Gradually they evolved into modern humans who commanded language, controlled fire, and eventually populated the entire world. For thousands of years, small bands of people, carrying their stone and wood tools as they moved from campsite to campsite, lived by hunting and gathering. With the first great transition in human history, the introduction of agriculture some 10,000 years ago, people began to deliberately cultivate plants and raise draft animals. Although some societies remained hunters and gatherers or herders, most people around the world shifted eventually to farming. Congregating in villages and towns and farming the neighboring fields with their simple hoes and plows, they experienced profound changes in their ways of life. For some societies, the production of an agricultural surplus—more food than was needed by the farmers—and growing commercial activity provided the economic and labor support that enabled the development of formal governments and religious institutions. Farming, town life, trade, and more advanced technology set the stage for the second great transition, the building of cities and the forming of states.

The world's first societies emerged in various parts of the world, and each society gradually created its own distinctive traditions. The first cities and states arose between 5,500 and 4,000 years ago in the lands stretching from southern Europe and northern Africa eastward through western and southern Asia to China. For most of history the vast majority of the

Cuneiform Tablet This letter, impressed on a clay tablet in Mesopotamia around 1900 B.C.E., records a merchant's complaint that a shipment of copper that he had paid for contained too little metal. Mesopotamian letters, written chiefly by merchants and officials, were enclosed in envelopes made of clay and marked with the sender's private seal. (Courtesy of the Trustees of the British Museum)

1

world's people lived in these regions of Africa and Eurasia. Between 5,000 and 3,000 years ago cities and states also developed in the Americas. The most densely populated ancient societies emerged where agriculture, aided by irrigation, flourished: in large river valleys, particularly the floodplains of the Nile in Egypt, the Tigris-Euphrates in Mesopotamia, the Indus in India, and the Yellow in China. The ancient world also benefited from great advances in metalworking, especially of copper, bronze, and iron, which spread widely. Growing networks of trade and transportation increasingly connected many societies to each other by land and sea. Although they exchanged ideas, products, and technologies with others, each ancient society created unique religions, cultural values, social structures, and systems for recording information. These traditions sometimes continued over several thousand years, even though modified with time. A few traditions, such as the ancient Hebrew and Indian religions, have survived into the present.

Contacts between peoples in different regions had already begun to increase greatly with the appearance of farming. Societies traded agricultural and hunting tools, as well as minerals, wood, clothing, and food. Between 2500 and 600 B.C.E. the Eastern Hemisphere experienced much more active trading networks. Improved transportation, including seaworthy sailing vessels, horse-drawn chariots, and camel caravans, fostered trade by shrinking distances. Long-distance trade served to spread ideas and expand horizons. Some peoples migrated far from their ancestral homes, with major movements into the Pacific islands (Oceana) and the southern half of Africa. Like trade, other encounters between societies, friendly or hostile, often became major forces for change.

Most ancient societies, such as Egypt and Mesopotamia, have long since disappeared, leaving only crumbling ruins or long-buried artifacts to remind us of their achievements. In their ancient forms, these societies never survived through the centuries, although their religions and values often influenced the societies that displaced them, and many of their descendants still live in the region. On the other hand, the Chinese and Indian societies persisted in some recognizable form and are familiar to us today. The Ancient Era built the framework for much that came later.

NORTH AND CENTRAL AMERICA
The ancestors of Native Americans migrated into North America from Asia thousands of years ago. They gradually occupied the Americas, working out ways of life compatible with the environments they lived in. While many remained hunters and gatherers, the first American farming began in Mexico and spread to various North American regions. The Olmecs of Mexico built cities atop huge artificial mounds and created an alphabet and religious traditions that influenced nearby peoples. Other North Americans also built settlements around large mounds.

SOUTH AMERICA
Some Native Americans reached South America thousands of years ago. Farming developed early along the Pacific coast and in the Andes Mountains region. The first cities, such as Caral in coastal Peru, arose around the same time as early cities in Egypt and India. Cities were later established in the Andes Mountains. The major Andean states influenced the art and religion of many other South American societies.

EUROPE

Ancient cities and states formed on the Mediterranean island of Crete and in Greece. Minoans, the residents of Crete, were successful maritime traders. After their collapse, the Mycenaeans of mainland Greece traded widely and exercised regional power until they declined. Migrants into Greece mixed with the Mycenaeans to form the foundation for later Greek society. These southern European societies worked bronze and participated in trade networks linking them to North Africa, eastern Europe, and western Asia.

WESTERN ASIA

The world's first farmers probably lived in western Asia, east of the Mediterranean Sea, where the oldest known cities and states also arose. The diverse societies that formed in the Tigris-Euphrates River Valley in Mesopotamia developed bronzeworking, writing, science, and mathematics, and they also traded with India and Egypt. Western Asians perfected iron technology, which eventually spread around Eurasia. The Phoenicians were the greatest traders of the Mediterranean region and also invented an alphabet later adopted by the Greeks. Another notable people, the Hebrews, introduced a monotheistic religion, Judaism.

EASTERN ASIA

Farming developed very early in the Yellow and Yangzi River Basins in China, fostering the region's first cities and states. Chinese culture then expanded into southern China. The Chinese invented a writing system and worked bronze and iron. Mixing Chinese influences with their own traditions, Koreans took up farming and metalworking. Some Koreans migrated into Japan, where they and the local peoples mixed their traditions to produce the Japanese culture.

Map labels: ARCTIC OCEAN · EUROPE · ASIA · Danube · GREECE · Carthage · CRETE · ISRAEL · MESOPOTAMIA · Harappa · HIMALAYAS · Ganges R. · CHINA · JAPAN · EGYPT · Nile · INDIA · NUBIA · SUDAN · Niger R. · AFRICA · Congo R. · Mekong R. · ATLANTIC OCEAN · INDIAN OCEAN · AUSTRALIA

AFRICA

Farming appeared very early in North, West, and East Africa. Africa's earliest cities and states formed along the Nile River Valley in Egypt. The Egyptians invented a writing system and flourished from productive agriculture and trade with other African societies and Eurasia. Cities and states also arose in Nubia, just south of Egypt. Africans south of the Sahara Desert developed ironworking technology very early, and iron tools and weapons helped the Bantu-speaking peoples gradually expand from West Africa into Central and East Africa.

SOUTHERN ASIA AND OCEANIA

Farming and metalworking developed early in South and Southeast Asia. The people of the Harappan cities in the Indus River Basin grew cotton, made textiles, and traded with western and Central Asia. After the Harappan society collapsed, Aryan peoples from western Asia moved into India, and the mixing of Aryan and local traditions formed the basis for the Hindu religion. Meanwhile, Austronesian peoples migrated from Taiwan into the Southeast Asian and Pacific islands. Southeast Asians pioneered in maritime trade and formed their first states. Hunters and gatherers flourished in Australia.

The Origins of Human Societies, to ca. 2000 B.C.E.

Online Study Center

This icon will direct you to interactive activities and study materials on the website: college.hmco.com/pic/lockard1e

Tassili Archers Thousands of ancient paintings on rock surfaces and cave walls record the activities of African hunters, gatherers, and pastoralists. This painting of archers on a hunt was made in a rock shelter on the Tassili plateau of what is today Algeria, probably long before the Sahara region had dried up and become a harsh desert. (Kazuyoshi Nomachi/Pacific Press Photo)

CHRONOLOGY

The Spread of Modern Humans

135,000–100,000 B.C.E.	Eastern and Southern Africa
100,000 B.C.E.	Palestine
50,000–45,000 B.C.E.	Australia
50,000–40,000 B.C.E.	India, Southeast Asia
50,000–35,000 B.C.E.	China
45,000–35,000 B.C.E.	Europe
40,000 B.C.E.	Japan, Americas (disputed)
35,000–30,000 B.C.E.	New Guinea
20,000 B.C.E.	Siberia
15,000–12,000 B.C.E.	Americas (traditional view)
2000 B.C.E.	Western Pacific Islands
1500 B.C.E.	Samoa
200 B.C.E.	Marquesas Islands
400–500 C.E.	Hawaii
1000 C.E.	New Zealand

China between 35,000 and 50,000 years ago, and in Europe between 35,000 and 45,000 years ago. Dates for settlement in frigid eastern Siberia range from 28,000 to 14,000 B.C.E. By 40,000 years ago they had migrated to Japan, which could then be reached by land bridges. To reach Australia from Southeast Asia across a very shallow sea required rafts or boats, but, according to controversial findings, modern humans had settled in Australia between 50,000 and 45,000 B.C.E. While New Guinea and the nearby Solomon Islands had human settlers between 35,000 and 30,000 years ago, the peopling of the Pacific Islands to the east began much later, around 2000 B.C.E.

Beginning around 200,000 years ago, a vibrant new tool culture developed in Europe that has been identified with the **Neanderthals** (nee-AN-der-thals), hominids who were probably descended from *Homo erectus* populations. By 100,000 B.C.E. this culture was well developed. The Neanderthals gradually spread to inhabit a wide region stretching from Spain and Germany to western and Central Asia; fossils have also been found in North Africa. Neanderthals were committed to social values, burying their dead, and caring for the sick and injured. In general, their cranial capacity equaled or even exceeded that

of *Homo sapiens,* and they had larger bodies. Although they probably lacked spoken language, they were capable of communication. They also used tools, made bone flutes, and wore jewelry. They were skillful hunters, and their dietary protein came mainly from meat.

The relationship of the Neanderthals to *Homo sapiens sapiens* is unclear. By 70,000 years ago both Neanderthals and modern humans lived in Palestine, and the two species apparently resided in the same areas for many centuries. When the modern, tool-using humans known as **Cro-Magnons** (krow-MAG-nuns) arrived in Europe, probably from western Asia, they also coexisted with Neanderthals for several millennia. DNA studies suggest that Neanderthals were a rather different species from Cro-Magnons. Although there is little convincing evidence of interbreeding, a few fossil discoveries hint that it may have occurred at least occasionally. The two species seem to have both traded and fought. Around 28,000 years ago, the last Neanderthals died out or disappeared as a recognizable group. Whether they were ultimately annihilated, outnumbered, outcompeted, or assimilated by the more resourceful and adaptable *Homo sapiens sapiens,* who had better technology and warmer clothing, remains unknown.

Archaeologists long thought that the peopling of the Americas came very late and that the earliest migration into North America occurred only 12,000 to 15,000 years ago. But recent discoveries have led a few scholars to speculate that the pioneer arrivals may have crossed from Northeast Asia as early as 20,000 or possibly even 30,000 or 40,000 years ago. The scientific community is deeply divided on the antiquity of the first Americans (see Chapter 4). At various times a wide Ice Age land bridge connected Alaska and Siberia across today's Bering Strait, and the evidence for a migration chiefly from Asia over thousands of years is strong. The first settlers moved by land, or by boat along the coast. Gradually people of Asian ancestry settled throughout the Western Hemisphere, becoming the ancestors of today's Native Americans.

SECTION SUMMARY

- Early hominids first evolved in Africa (most likely East Africa) 4 to 6 million years ago.
- Of the early hominids, our direct ancestor *Homo habilis* was most successful because it used simple stone tools.
- *Homo erectus* developed more refined tools and migrated to Eurasia and throughout Africa.
- *Homo sapiens* had larger brains and evolved into modern humans, who developed language and spread throughout the world.
- Though humans from different parts of the world may have different appearances, their genetic differences are insignificant.

Neanderthals   Hominids who were probably descended from *Homo erectus* populations in Europe and who later spread into western and Central Asia.

Cro-Magnons   The first modern, tool-using humans in Europe.

The Odyssey of Early Human Societies

How did hunting and gathering shape life during the long Stone Age?

For thousands of years humans lived at a very basic level during what is often called the Stone Age, although they also used other materials, such as wood and bone, to help them sustain life. The Stone Age included three distinct periods, each showing evidence of more efficient tools and stoneworking. The long **Paleolithic** (pay-lee-oh-LITH-ik) period (or Old Stone Age) began about 100,000 years ago. The **Mesolithic** (mez-oh-LITH-ik) period (Middle Stone Age) began around 15,000 years ago, when the glaciers from the final Ice Age receded. With this warming trend, the vast herds of large mammals that had flourished on the grasslands of Eurasia and North America began to thin rapidly. Major meat sources that were adapted to Ice Age climates, such as the woolly mammoth and mastodon, died out from warming climates, catastrophic disease, or zealous hunting by humans. The **Neolithic** (nee-oh-LITH-ik) period (New Stone Age) began between 9500 and 8000 B.C.E. in Eurasia, with the transition from hunting and gathering to simple farming. During the many centuries of the Paleolithic and Mesolithic eras the various peoples organized themselves into small, usually mobile, family-based societies.

Hunting and Gathering

Small groups of twenty to sixty members were the earliest and simplest forms of society. Their subsistence life depended on fishing, hunting live animals, scavenging for dead or dying animals, and gathering edible plants, a way of life that depended on naturally occurring resources. Members cooperated in gathering or hunting to obtain food, and usually they obtained just enough food to ensure the group's survival. Improved tools made possible both more food options and better weapons against predators or rivals. Whether early humans obtained their meat primarily through hunting or scavenging is unclear. Hunting became more important when the bow and arrow were invented in Africa, Europe, and southwestern Asia at least 15,000 years ago. Now hunters could kill large animals at a safer distance. Although men gained prestige from being the main hunters, meat was usually a small part of the diet.

The gathering by women of edible vegetation such as fruits and nuts was probably more essential for group survival than obtaining meat, and it gave women status and influence.

Paleolithic   The Old Stone Age, which began 100,000 years ago with the first modern humans and lasted for many millennia.

Mesolithic   The Middle Stone Age, which began around 15,000 years ago as the glaciers from the final Ice Age began to recede.

Neolithic   The New Stone Age, which began between 10,000 and 11,500 years ago with the transition to simple farming.

Ethnographic studies indicate that this is still true among many of the remaining hunting and gathering peoples today. Furthermore, women probably helped develop new technologies such as grinding stones, bone needles, nets (possibly used to catch small animals like rabbits and foxes), baskets, and primitive cloth. The oldest known woven cloth clothing was made in eastern Europe some 28,000 years ago.

The hunting and gathering way of life may not have been as impoverished and unfulfilling as we sometimes imagine it was, with people continually searching for food in harsh environments. Many societies were creative, inventing fishhooks, harpoons, fuel lamps, dugout boats and canoes, and perhaps even beer. Studies over the past fifty years of groups who still hunt and gather, such as the Mbuti (em-BOO-tee) of the Congo rain forest and the !Kung of the Kalahari Desert, have found that they enjoy varied, healthy diets, surprisingly long life expectancies, considerable economic security, and a rich communal life. Many spend only ten to twenty hours a week in collecting food and establishing camps. Work itself, often done cooperatively, is fully integrated into daily life. Generally these people have plenty of time for activities such as music, dance, and socializing. The Mbuti live in a symbiotic and mystical relationship with the forest and possess an intimate knowledge of the natural world, trying to work with rather than against their surroundings. Although we cannot know for sure, the hunting and gathering life millennia ago may have offered similar pleasures.

On the other hand, hunters and gatherers have always faced serious challenges. Early humans had to make their own weapons and clothing and construct temporary huts. For some groups, life remained precarious and many died young, since not all enjoyed access to adequate food resources. Some, like the Inuit Eskimos who live along the Arctic Rim of North America and Greenland, had to survive in harsh climates with few plants. The Inuit of today, like their Stone Age ancestors, are mostly hunters.

Communities of Kinship and Cooperation

Hunting and gathering generally encouraged cooperation, which led to more closely knit communities based on kinship. Community members were able to communicate with one another, and, as language developed, they also passed information from one generation to another, conveying a sense of the past and traditions. Gradually humans increased in numbers, and societies, still based on kinship, became more complex. In societies founded on family ties, personal relationships were paramount, while little value was given to obtaining material wealth. The mostly nomadic way of life made individual accumulation of material possessions impractical. These small groups shared food resources among the immediate family and friends, thus helping to ensure success and hence ultimate survival for both the individual and the group. Cooperative work and food sharing promoted the intense social life that is still common among hunting and gathering peoples today. But living close to others did not always result in harmony and mutual affection. Those who violated group customs could be killed or banished, temporarily or permanently, and sometimes groups split apart because of conflicts.

Most hunters and gatherers lived in small bands that had no system of government or leader. In these egalitarian social structures, all members in good standing often had equal access to resources. Everyone played a needed role, and social responsibilities linked people together. At the same time, groups often tended to reward the most resourceful members, and some societies had a headman who was chosen for his favored personal qualities. However, these headmen had limited authority over other group members, and early European explorers in the Americas and Australia were amazed at the degree to which many of the hunting and gathering peoples they encountered belittled or insulted their own leaders and could not comprehend the notion of high rank.

Women and men probably enjoyed a comparable status, as they do in many hunting and gathering societies today. As key providers of food, women may have participated alongside men in group decision making. They also likely held a special place in religious practice as bearers of life. Midwives were highly respected. **Matrilineal** (mat-ruh-LIN-ee-uhl) **kinship** patterns, which trace descent and inheritance through the female line, were probably common, as they are today in these societies. But these societies mostly maintain a clear sexual division of labor and give men some advantages over women. Sometimes men could have more than one wife.

Although childbearing influenced women's roles, women were not constantly pregnant. Since it was necessary to limit group size to avoid depleting resources from the environment, most hunting and gathering societies practiced birth control. The practice of breastfeeding an infant for several years suppressed ovulation and created longer intervals between pregnancies. Many groups also imposed ritual taboos against intercourse after childbirth or during specified periods. Plants and herbs were used as contraceptives or to induce abortions. If these schemes failed, unwanted babies might be killed. Paleolithic populations grew slowly, perhaps by only 10 percent a century.

Cultural Life and Violence

Some aspects of culture that we might recognize today were taking shape, such as religious belief. As people sought to understand dreams, death, and natural phenomena, they developed a perspective known as **animism** (ANN-uh-miz-um), the belief that all creatures, as well as inanimate objects and natural phenomena, have souls and can influence human well-being. For many hunting and gathering peoples today, for example, animals have souls and often play an important role in folktales. Many early peoples also practiced **polytheism**

(PAUL-e-thee-ism), the belief in many spirits or deities. Since spirits were thought capable of helping or harming a person, **shamans** (SHAW-mans), specialists in communicating with or manipulating the supernatural realm, became important members of the group. Many shamans were women. The widespread practice of burying the dead suggests that many people believed in an afterlife.

Like many hunters and gatherers today, these societies may have had ample time for leisure, engaging in such group-oriented activities as story-telling. Some scholars think some of them may have enjoyed an early form of wine, slurping the juice of naturally fermented wild grapes from crude wooden bowls or animal-skin pouches. Some activities with a social function that we might consider essential for enjoyment developed early, including music, dance, and painting on rocks and cave walls. Primitive flutes can be traced back 45,000 years. Dancing and singing may have promoted feelings of togetherness and lessened personal rivalries. They may also have led to nonviolent competition.

Egalitarian, self-sufficient societies enriched by spirituality and leisure activities may sound appealing to many modern people, but this was not the complete story. Violence between and within different societies has been a part of human culture throughout history, and the seeds were planted in the Paleolithic period. People were hunters, but they were also hunted by predators such as bears, wolves, and lions. This reality may have instilled in early societies not only a terror of dangerous animals, apparent in myths and folklore, but also a tendency to justify violence. Men were often expected to prove their bravery to attract females. And some prehistoric peoples may have practiced cannibalism.

Anthropologists disagree about whether humans are inherently aggressive and warlike or peaceful and cooperative. The experiences of societies still based on hunting and gathering or simple agriculture suggest that both patterns are common. Some peoples, such as the Hopi and Zuni Indians of the American Southwest, the Penan of Borneo, and many Australian Aborigines, have generally avoided armed conflict. But most societies have engaged in at least occasional violence, such as when their survival or food supply was threatened. Some societies admired military prowess and male bravado. For example, the Dani of New Guinea, who engaged in frequent conflict with their neighbors, lost a third of their men to war-related death.

Social and cultural patterns that promoted certain behaviors, such as violence against neighboring groups, arose in response to environmental conditions. Despite their carnivorous diets and primate origins, humans may not be genetically programmed for either violence or cooperation. They have a capacity but not a compulsion for aggressive behavior. Some primate species find ways to avoid conflict, and most engage in forms of reconciliation after fights. Humans may naturally seek self-preservation, but the influence of cultural patterns

---

matrilineal kinship A pattern of kinship that traces descent and inheritance through the female line.

animism The belief that all creatures as well as inanimate objects and natural phenomena have souls and can influence human well-being.

polytheism A belief in many spirits or deities.

---

shamans Specialists in communicating with or manipulating the supernatural realm.

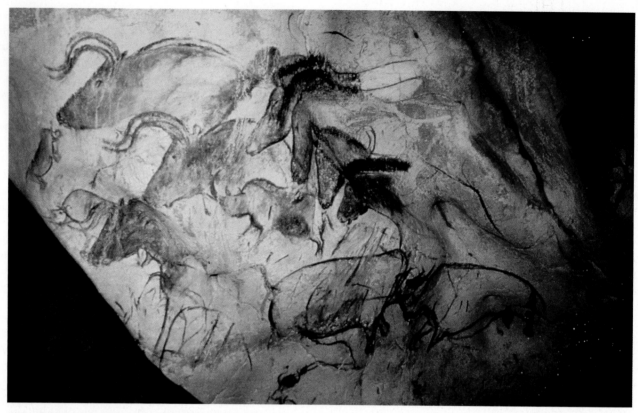

Cave Paintings in Europe   This Ice Age painting of bison is from a cave at Altamira, Spain. Many paintings on cave walls have been found in France and Iberia. Paleolithic peoples all over the world painted pictures of the animals they hunted or feared as well as of each other, suggesting an increasing self-awareness. (Jean Cottes)

can channel behavior in one direction or another. Changing contexts can alter behavior too. For example, the normally gentle and nonviolent Semai (Se-MY) of the Malayan mountains can be transformed into enthusiastic soldiers when drafted into the Malaysian military and removed from their home communities.

The Heritage of Hunting and Gathering

Hunting and gathering never completely disappeared. Throughout history some peoples have found this way of life the most realistic strategy for survival. Although not environmentalists in the modern sense, most recent hunting and gathering societies have made only a marginal impact on the surrounding environment because of their small numbers and limited technology. Since they have learned to live within environmental constraints, these peoples could be seen as highly successful adapters. Although it has generated little material wealth, hunting and gathering has remained viable for many societies, such as Australian Aborigines, until modern times. Indeed, Australia was the only inhabitable continent where agriculture never developed before modern times, largely because populations remained small, much of the continent was harsh desert, and the Aborigines were such skillful hunters and gatherers. But trade routes spanned the continent, and many Aborigines developed detailed notions of land management as

well as rich mythologies about their origins and their relationship to the fragile environment.

As already mentioned, some version of hunting and gathering is practiced even in modern times. Although we must be cautious in comparing modern hunters and gatherers to peoples who lived several millennia ago, today's few remaining hunting and gathering peoples, to the extent that they have not yet been significantly changed by the outside world, can probably reveal much about ancient societies (see Profile: The !Kung Hunters and Gatherers). Prehistoric peoples undoubtedly developed a wide range of behaviors and values, adapting to differing environments just as hunting and gathering societies do today.

But this way of life, which has survived for many millennia, may disappear during the twenty-first century. In recent decades many hunters and gatherers have seen their lives disrupted or destroyed by logging, commercial fishing, plantation development, dam building, tourism, and other activities that exploit their environments. For example, revenue-hungry governments lease the Borneo rain forests inhabited by the reclusive Penan to timber companies for logging. In the Amazon Basin, the burning of rain forests and opening of new land for farming or mining overwhelms many Native American groups. In the end these peoples, defenseless against modern technology, may have to make the same transition to new survival strategies as other peoples did millennia ago.

THE !KUNG HUNTERS AND GATHERERS

Although we need to remember that all societies change over time, often in response to environmental conditions, the remaining hunting and gathering peoples today may give us a glimpse of how some prehistoric peoples lived. The !Kung, a subgroup of the San people (once known as Bushmen), live in the inhospitable Kalahari Desert in southwestern Africa, chiefly in what is today Botswana and Namibia. Several thousand years ago they were widespread in the southern half of Africa, and some probably adapted to desert life a long time ago.

The !Kung became skilled hunters and gatherers. Women obtain between 60 and 80 percent of the food, collecting nuts, berries, bulbs, beans, leafy greens, roots, and bird eggs, as well as catching tortoises, small mammals, snakes, insects, termites, and caterpillars. While the women gather, the men hunt animals, snare birds, and extract honey from beehives. These hunters are skilled trackers who can follow animal tracks and other clues for many miles without rest. The !Kung utilize some fifty species of plants and animals for food, medicine, cosmetics, and poisons. Although Western peoples may disregard many of the food sources because of cultural biases, these sources are in fact highly nutritious. Termites, for example, are about half protein.

The !Kung have adapted well to a harsh environment. Even during periodic drought conditions that devastate the more vulnerable farmers, the diversity of !Kung food sources ensures a steady supply. Furthermore, their diet is low in salt, carbohydrates, and saturated fats, and high in vitamins and roughage. Their diet, combined with a relatively unstressful life, helps them avoid modern health problems like high blood pressure, ulcers, obesity, and heart disease. But because they live far from clinics, they die more easily from accidents and malaria, and some scholars doubt that their diet is nutritionally sound. Nonetheless, !Kung life expectancy is similar to that in many industrialized countries.

Since they spend only about fifteen to twenty hours a week in maintaining their livelihood, the !Kung have ample free time for resting, conversing, visiting friends, and playing games. Children have few responsibilities because their labor is not needed for the !Kungs' survival. The !Kung value interdependence between the genders and are willing to do the work normally associated with the opposite sex. For example, fathers take an active role in child rearing. The intense social life is symbolized by a large communal space in the midst of the camp surrounded by family sleeping huts; they prefer companionship to privacy. The !Kung strongly discourage aggressiveness. Their folk stories praise the animal tricksters who evade the use of force.

Throughout history farming peoples have affected hunters and collectors. The !Kung faced many challenges in recent decades that have altered the lives of many bands. Most are no longer completely self-sufficient. They trade desert products to nearby farming villages for tools and food. Others have been drafted into the military, have taken up wage labor, or have been displaced because their territory has been claimed by governments or business interests. Today, forced or induced to abandon their traditional ways of life, some disoriented !Kung have moved to dilapidated, impoverished villages on the edges of towns. The future for their ancestral lifestyle is unpromising.

THINKING ABOUT THE PROFILE

1. What role does the gathering by women play in the !Kung economy?
2. How does the traditional !Kung way of life promote leisure activity?
3. What problems do the !Kung face today?

!Kung Women Returning to Camp
These !Kung women in the Kalahari Desert of southwestern Africa are returning to camp after gathering wild berries and vegetables, sometimes by using digging sticks. Many Stone Age societies were sustained by such activity. (M. Shostak/Anthro-Photo)

SECTION SUMMARY

■ During the Paleolithic and Mesolithic eras, people lived in small groups of hunters and gatherers.

■ In general, women gathered fruits and nuts, which provided the majority of the food, while men hunted game.

■ Hunting and gathering groups were usually close-knit and egalitarian, though violence was not unknown.

■ Anthropologists are undecided as to whether humans have a natural tendency toward violence or peace.

■ Some hunting and gathering groups still exist, but they are threatened by modernity.

◆ The Agricultural Transformation, 10,000–4000 B.C.E.

What environmental factors explain the transition to agriculture?

Between 10,000 and 11,500 years ago, people who had survived largely by hunting and gathering during the Mesolithic period began to develop simple agriculture. This momentous change marked the beginning of the Neolithic period, a time when humans began to master the environment and change natural biological relationships in unprecedented ways. As agriculturalists, people now deliberately altered the ecological system by cultivating the soil, selecting seeds, and breeding animals that could help them survive. The often-used term *Agricultural Revolution* is misleading, because the development did not involve rapid, electrifying discoveries but occurred over hundreds of years. Nonetheless, the shift from hunting and gathering to farming was one of the greatest transitions in history, and it changed human life all over the world. The earth's surface was also transformed as trees and grass were cleared from one-tenth of the planet for plowing. The production of a food surplus set the stage for everything that came later, including cities, states, social classes, and long-distance trade.

Environmental Change and the Roots of Agriculture

Agriculture started with small preliminary steps. Even before farming began, some people were preparing themselves for permanent village life. Some, like the villagers at Abu Hureyra in Syria, were settling alongside lakes or in valleys rich in wild grains that were easy to collect. Around the world, archaeologists have discovered clay-walled houses from the Neolithic Period, as well as baskets, pottery, pits for storing grain, and

equipment for hunting, fishing, and grain preparation. Probably the first farmers did not even see themselves as pioneers forging a new way of life. As will be discussed shortly, they were probably reacting to environmental changes that were dooming the old ways.

However, documenting the steps taken in the transition to agriculture and settled life is not easy. For the earliest periods we have no written sources, since writing appeared only around 3500 B.C.E. Many material artifacts still lie buried, while others have long since turned to dust or were covered by rising sea levels. Historical reconstruction depends largely on archaeological evidence such as bones, artifacts, seeds, wild plants, tools, buildings, campsites, and the radiocarbon dating of the soils where these things are discovered.

Climate change was probably one key factor in triggering the shift to agriculture. After the last great Ice Age, the earth entered a long period of unusual warmth, which still persists. The melting glaciers caused rising sea levels, covering about a fifth of previously available land. Some scholars contend that the spread of the Persian Gulf, the Black Sea, and the Mediterranean onto once occupied lowlands may have led to legends in the Middle East of a great flood and human expulsion from a "garden of Eden." Rising sea levels also covered over many land links, including those connecting the British Isles to continental Europe and Japan to Asia.

Another factor was probably population growth. Around 10,000 B.C.E., the world population had grown to perhaps 5 or 10 million, and in some regions hunting and gathering could no longer meet the basic needs of everyone, especially as good land was submerged. Neighboring lands were already occupied by other bands of people. But the warmer climate encouraged the spread of grasses such as barley and wild wheat, which attracted grazing animals. Soon food gatherers gravitated to these areas, some of them abandoning their nomadic ways to live permanently near these rich food sources.

The Great Transition to Settled Agriculture

The environment continued to change, posing new challenges. The earth cooled again briefly about 9000 B.C.E., reducing food supplies, and a drought in the Middle East presented a crisis for some food-gathering societies because they had no real concept of saving or storing for the future. Eventually it was no longer enough to just exploit local resources more efficiently. Responding to the challenges, hunters and gatherers like those at Abu Hureyra began to store food and learn how to cultivate their own fields. Some people experimented with new foods, especially cereal grains collected in a wild state. These grains were generally most plentiful in mountain areas, where many settled. Others planted the grains after migrating to the plains in search of better prospects. Former hunters and gatherers began to pioneer **horticulture** (HORE-tee-kuhl-chur), the growing of crops with simple methods and tools,

---

horticulture   The growing of crops with simple methods and tools.

Ruins of Abu Hureyra The site of this ancient village overlooks the floodplain of the Euphrates River in northeastern Syria. The earliest settlement included intersecting pits that were turned into huts by roofs of reeds, branches, and poles. (Courtesy, Andrew M. T. Moore)

such as the hoe or digging stick. These efforts eventually resulted in a profound reorganization of human society.

Women may well have taken the lead in domesticating plants and some animals and in molding clay for storage and cooking pots. People in southwest Asia made pottery by 7500 B.C.E. to serve as waterproof containers. As the chief gatherers, women knew how plants grew in certain types of soil and sprouted from seeds, and they also knew the amount of water and sunshine needed to sustain plants. Women are generally the main food producers in horticultural societies today.

One major food-producing strategy was shifting cultivation, a method still practiced today by millions of people, especially in Southeast Asia, Africa, and Latin America. Shifting cultivation was especially adaptable in wooded areas, where people could clear trees and underbrush by chopping and burning (hence the common term *slash and burn*). Once the area was cleared, they loosened the soil with digging sticks and finally scattered seeds around the area. Natural moisture such as rain helped the crops mature. But since the soil became eroded after a few years, shifting cultivators moved periodically to fresh land, returning to the original area only after the soil had recovered its fertility. Most shifting cultivators still rely on men to supply protein by hunting and fishing.

The Consequences of Settled Agriculture

Farming promoted many radical changes in the way humans lived and connected with their environments. Whether agriculture made life more secure, predictable, and healthy than hunting and gathering remains subject to debate. But the domestication of plants and animals increased the production of food in a given amount of land. A farmer could not necessarily grow more food than might be collected from the wild in a favorable setting with ample land, but agriculture could produce a much higher yield per acre and thus could support much denser populations in the same area. Permanent settlements also made possible the storage of food for future use, since the pots and buildings did not have to be moved periodically. Most people apparently believed farming was necessary for survival.

But farmers faced new problems. Since they depended on fewer plant foods than food gatherers, they were in some ways more vulnerable to disaster from drought or other natural catastrophes. Food shortages may have become more rather than less common with farming. The earliest farmers could probably grow enough to feed themselves and their families with three or four hours of work a day. But as they required more food to feed growing populations, they were forced to exploit

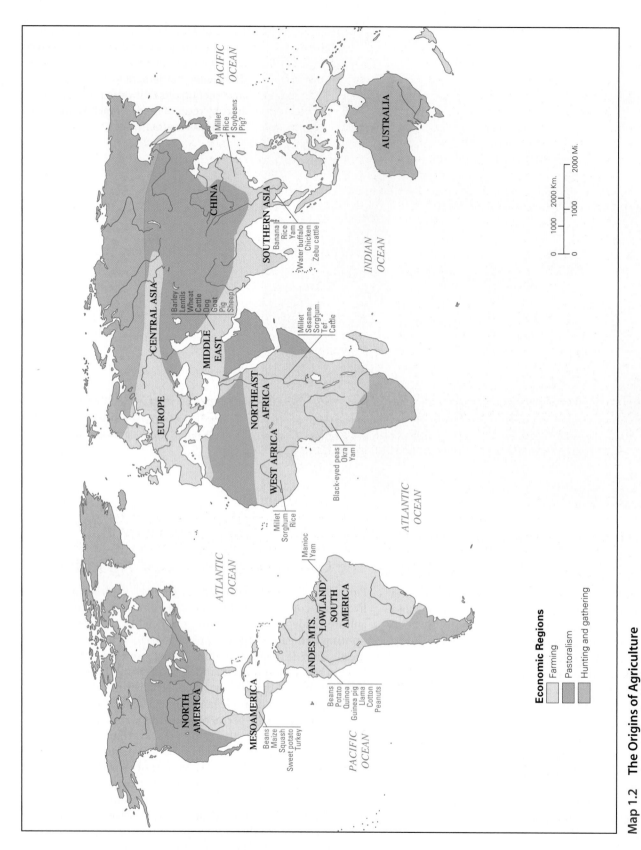

Map 1.2   The Origins of Agriculture

Between 11,500 and 7000 years ago, people in western Asia, North and sub-Saharan Africa, southern Asia, East Asia, New Guinea, Mesoamerica, and South America developed agriculture independently and domesticated available animals. Later most of these crops and some of the animals spread into other regions.

*Online Study Center   **Improve Your Grade** Interactive Map: River-Valley Civilizations, 3500–1500 B.C.E.

local resources more intensively and to work harder in their fields. And some domesticated foods, like corn and bread, caused more dental problems and gum diseases than their wild counterparts. Some people complained. The Hebrew writer who recorded the biblical garden of Eden story blamed women for the hard work of farming: "Cursed is the ground for your sake; in toil you shall eat of it all the days of your life. In the sweat of your face you shall eat bread til you return to the ground."[3] Agriculture eventually depended on peasants, mostly poor farmers who worked small plots of land that were often owned by others. Although most lived at little better than subsistence levels, they had to share some of their crop with their landlords. Hard-working peasants were the backbone of most societies before the Industrial Revolution.

Whether for spiritual reasons or because of a new understanding of natural forces, some early farming peoples all over the world constructed megaliths, huge stone monuments. For example, Stonehenge was built in southern England in stages between 3100 and 1800 B.C.E. Some of the stone, weighing several tons, was obtained up to 140 miles away. Many scholars think Stonehenge was a temple for shamanistic religious rites. It may also have been a secular ceremonial center, where the community gathered at special times. It clearly served as an astronomical observatory, because its axis aligns with the summer solstice sunrise, an important time for Neolithic farmers.

The Globalization and Diversity of Agriculture

The agricultural transformation eventually reached across the globe. Agriculture came first to Eurasia, where geography favored the movement of people to the east or west along the same general latitude, without abrupt climatic changes. By contrast, the Americas are constructed along a north-south axis, and northern and southern temperate regions are linked only through a huge tropical zone stretching from southern Mexico to northern and eastern South America. Some peoples, such as those in Australia and the Arctic, did not or could not make the transition from food gathering because of environmental and geographical constraints. Nonetheless, the different regions all contributed significantly to the discovery and production of the food resources we use today.

The Multiple Origins of Farming   Where did agriculture begin? Although some controversial evidence points to mainland Southeast Asia, most archaeologists believe the earliest transition to farming occurred in the area of southwestern Asia known as the "Fertile Crescent." This includes what is today Iraq, Syria, central and eastern Turkey, and the Jordan River Valley. This region had many fast-growing plants with high nutritional value, such as wheat, barley, chickpeas, and peas. The breakthrough came between 9500 and 8000 B.C.E.. There is good evidence for the growing of grain crops by 8000 B.C.E., and scattered evidence for even earlier farming at a few sites such as Abu Hureya.

Food growing also began independently in several other parts of the world, although we still do not know precisely when (see Map 1.2). Hot, humid climates such as those in Southeast Asia, tropical Africa, and Central America are poor for preserving plant, animal, and human remains, so archaeologists may never learn the full story. But clearly several Asian peoples were among the earliest farmers. A few scholars think farming began in northern Vietnam by 8000 B.C.E.. Crop cultivation began around 7000 B.C.E. in China and New Guinea, 7000 or 6000 B.C.E. in India, 5000 or 4000 B.C.E. in Thailand, and 3000 B.C.E. in Island Southeast Asia.

Elsewhere the dates varied considerably (see Chronology: The Transition to Agriculture, 10,000–500 B.C.E.). In the Mediterranean region, farming began in the Nile Valley by at least 6000 B.C.E., if not earlier, and in Greece by 6500 B.C.E. Agriculture reached northward to Britain and Scandinavia between 4000 and 3000 B.C.E. Farming may have spread into Europe with migrants from western Asia who intermarried with local people. While some historians suspect that farming in the southeast Sahara is very ancient, dating to between 8000 and 6000 B.C.E., others doubt it began that early. People in Ethiopia were farming by 4500 B.C.E. In the Americas cultivation apparently began in central Mexico between 7000 and 5500 B.C.E. and in the Andes (ANN-deez) highlands by 6000 B.C.E., if not earlier. Farming reached Panama by 4900 B.C.E., the Amazon Basin by 1500 B.C.E., Colorado by 1000 B.C.E., and the southeastern part of North America by 500 B.C.E.

CHRONOLOGY
The Transition to Agriculture, 10,000–500 B.C.E.

9500–8000	Southwestern Asia (Fertile Crescent)
8000	Vietnam (date disputed)
7000	Nubia (date disputed), China, Mexico, New Guinea
6500	Greece
6000	Northwestern India, Egypt, Andes, West Africa (disputed)
5000	Thailand (traditional)
4900	Panama
4500	Ethiopia
4000	Britain, Scandinavia
3000	Island Southeast Asia, Tropical West Africa
1500	Amazon Basin
1000	Colorado
500	Southeast North America

Food and Farming in Ancient Cultural Traditions

As agriculture became an essential foundation for survival, it became increasingly important in the traditions and mindsets of societies around the world. The following excerpts show three examples of how food and farming were reflected in the cultural traditions of ancient societies. The first, an Andean ritual chant many centuries old, is a prayer for successful harvests addressed to an ancient deity. The second is from a farmer's almanac from eighteenth-century B.C.E. Mesopotamia that offers guidance on cultivating a successful grain crop; this excerpt deals with preparing the field and seeding. The third reading, a song collected in China around 3,000 years ago, celebrates a successful harvest and explains how some of the bounty will be used.

Andean Chant
Oh Viracocha, ancient Viracocha, skilled creator,
who makes and establishes
"on the earth below may they eat, may they drink" you say;
for those you have established, those you have made
may food be plentiful.
"Potatoes, maize, all kinds of food may there be"

Excerpt from Farmer's Almanac
Keep a sharp eye on the openings of the dikes, ditches and mounds [so that] when you flood the field the water will not rise too high in it. . . . Let shod oxen trample it for you; after having its weeds ripped out [by them and] the field made level ground, dress it evenly with narrow axes weighing [no more

than] two thirds of a pound each. . . . Keep your eye on the man who puts in the barley seed. Let him drop the grain uniformly two fingers deep. . . . If the barley seed does not sink in properly, change your share. . . . Harvest it at the moment [of its fill strength].

Chinese Harvest Song
Abundant is the year, with much millet, much rice;
But we have tall granaries,
To hold . . . many myriads and millions of grain.
We make wine, make sweet liquor,
We offer it to ancestor, to ancestress,
We use it to fulfill all the [religious] rites,
To bring down blessings upon each and all.

THINKING ABOUT THE READING
1. Who did the Andeans believe determined the success of their harvest?
2. How did Mesopotamian farming depend on draft animals and cooperation?
3. How did ancient Chinese farmers use surplus grain and rice to fulfill obligations?

Sources: Brian M. Fagan, *Kingdoms of Gold, Kingdoms of Jade* (London: Thames and Hudson, 1991), p. 88; Samuel Noah Kramer, *Cradle of Civilization* (New York: Time-Life, 1967), p. 84; *The Book of Songs*, translated by Arthur Waley (London: George Allen and Unwin, 1954), p. 161. © 1954 by permission of the Arthur Waley Estate.

Varieties of Crops and Methods The earliest crops that were grown varied according to local environments and needs. Millet dominated in cold North China, rice in tropical Southeast Asia, wheat and barley in the dry Middle East, yams and sorghum in West Africa, corn in upland Mesoamerica, and potatoes in the high Andes. Food, however, was not the only concern. Some crops such as flax were grown for fiber to make clothing. Other plants had medicinal properties. Chinese were mixing herbs, acids, rice, and beeswax together to make a potent fermented alcoholic beverage by 7000 B.C.E. Southwest Asians began making wine from grapes and beer from barley between 6000 and 3000 B.C.E. The growing of fruits and nuts added variety to the diet. Over time farming became deeply ingrained in the psychology, social life, and traditions of many societies (see Witness to the Past: Food and Farming in Ancient Cultural Traditions).

Farming technology gradually improved. People living in highlands where slopes are steep, such as in Peru, Indonesia, China, or Greece, made their fields on terraces, which were laborious to construct and maintain. Then, as more people moved from highlands into valleys, they needed new techniques. Some people used water from nearby marshes or wells. On less well watered plains, they built large-scale water projects such as irrigation canals.

Animal Domestication

The domestication of animals for human use developed in close association with crop raising and brought many advantages. As they continued to be bred in captivity, animals were gradually modified from their wild ancestors. Men may have tamed and looked after the larger animals such as oxen and cattle, while women may have taken charge of smaller species such as sheep and pigs. Wild boars were domesticated into pigs in several different regions. Animals were raised to supply meat and leather, to aid in farming, to produce fertilizer, or to supply transportation. For example, horses and camels made long-distance travel and communication easier. Plows, probably developed from hoes, became more efficient tools when pulled by oxen or cattle. The oldest cart wheels so far discovered date back over 5,000 years. One disadvantage was that domesticated animals passed on diseases to humans, although this eventually led to immunities among peoples in Eurasia.

Much remains unclear about the chronology and location of animal domestication. For example, dogs may have been domesticated from gray wolves by 15,000 years ago in East Asia, but some scholars think this change came much earlier. Dogs were welcome for companionship, guarding, assistance in hunting, and sometimes food. Migrants took Asian dogs to the Americas. Sheep, goats, pigs, and cattle were all domesticated in the Middle East between 9000 and 7000 B.C.E., but it is possible that cattle and pigs were exploited during the same period in southern Asia, where chickens were domesticated. Some contested evidence also suggests cattle domestication in East Africa around 13,000 B.C.E. and in the Sahara region between 9000 and 8000 B.C.E. Indeed, cows were used in several parts of Africa by 7000 B.C.E. The first domesticated horses and donkeys, which date back to around 4000 B.C.E., enabled the improved transportation that stimulated long-distance trade networks. In some places animals may have been domesticated for herding even before the shift to farming occurred.

Zoological differences among the continents were crucial to the evolution of advanced agriculture. Eurasia contained many species of large, plant-eating, herding mammals whose habits and mild dispositions made their domestication into draft animals possible. But outside Eurasia, the lack of draft animals hindered the development of agriculture. Africa (except for cattle) and Australia lacked such animals, and most of the candidates in the Americas, such as the horse and camel, were extinct by 10,000 B.C.E. The only American possibilities were the gentle llamas and alpacas of the South American highlands. Though Andean people used them as pack animals by 3500 B.C.E., they were not well suited for farming.

Agriculture and Its Environmental Consequences

At the same time that the environment influenced farming, the resulting population growth also contributed to environmental changes, some with negative consequences. Human activities have had an impact on environments since the time of *Homo habilis*. Indeed, Stone Age hunters in both hemispheres may have contributed to the extinction of many animal species. But most hunters and gatherers, with limited technology and small numbers, left only a modest impact on their physical environment. Intensive agriculture more radically altered the ecology, especially as technology improved.

Technological innovation solved some problems for a while, but it did not always prove advantageous in the long run. For example, the invention of the plowshare made it easier to loosen dirt and eliminate weeds so that seeds could be planted deeper in nutrient-rich soil. But it also exposed topsoils to water and wind erosion. Similarly, vast irrigation networks provided the economic foundations for flourishing agriculture and denser settlement. But irrigation requires more labor than dry farming, and it also tends to foster centralized governments that can allocate the water resources among the people, with the result that more controls are placed on people's behavior. In addition, adding water to poor soils can produce waterlogged land and also change the mineral content of the soil, eventually producing a thick salt surface that ruins farming. In Mesopotamia and the Americas, where irrigation ultimately created deserts, it helped account for the rise and fall of entire societies.

Various activities contributed to environmental destruction. Farming and animal raising placed new demands on the land. Goats, for example, caused considerable damage as they browsed on shrubs, tree branches, and seedlings, thus preventing forest regeneration. Cattle required much pasture. People exploited nearby forests for lumber to build wagons, tools, houses, furniture, and boats. As early as 2700 B.C.E. Egyptians were ravaging the famed cedar forests of nearby Lebanon for wood to build their fleets, and the seafaring Phoenicians of Lebanon soon did the same. Contemporary observers were aware of the deforestation. For example, twenty-four centuries ago the philosopher Plato bemoaned the deforestation of the Greek mountains, which he called "a mere relic of the original country. What remains is like the skeleton of a body emaciated by disease. All the rich soil has melted away, leaving a country of skin and bone."[4] Overgrazing and deforestation in the mountains feeding the main rivers produced silt that contained harmful salt and gypsum, which moved downstream to the sea, clogging canals and dams. Water evaporated in the hot sun, leaving a salt residue. Later, much once fertile land in the Tigris-Euphrates and Indus River Basins of Mesopotamia and India became a salt desert.

The changing relationship of humans to their environment with farming generated new religious ideas. Early sacred and philosophical texts often justified human domination over nature. For example, the authors of the Hebrew book of Genesis believed God told humans to "be fruitful and multiply; fill

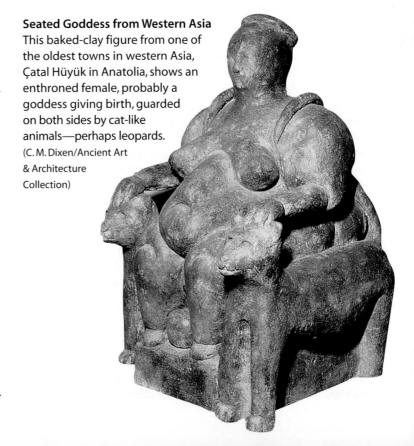

Seated Goddess from Western Asia
This baked-clay figure from one of the oldest towns in western Asia, Çatal Hüyük in Anatolia, shows an enthroned female, probably a goddess giving birth, guarded on both sides by cat-like animals—perhaps leopards.
(C. M. Dixen/Ancient Art & Architecture Collection)

the earth and subdue it; have dominion over the fish of the sea, over the birds of the air, and over every living thing that moves upon the earth."[5] Similarly, the Greek thinker Socrates argued that the gods were careful to provide everything in the natural world for human benefit. Many ancient thinkers saw an ordered world in which every part had a role and purpose in a divine plan, with humans the ultimate beneficiaries.

SECTION SUMMARY

- The shift from hunting and gathering to farming had tremendous consequences, but it occurred gradually, over hundreds of years.

- The end of the last great Ice Age and increased population density led people to shift from hunting and gathering to farming.

- Settled farming could support much denser populations and allowed for food storage, but it also led to some new health problems.

- Farming probably began in the area of southwestern Asia known as the "Fertile Crescent."

- Irrigation and other technological advances led to larger crops but also caused great environmental damage.

✦ The Emergence of Cities and States

How did farming and metallurgy establish the foundations for the rise of cities, states, and trade networks?

The cause-and-effect link between farming and more complex societies can be described in the following scenario. Given the prospects for ample food, some western Asian people moved to fertile areas to farm. They unloaded their stone tools, clay pots, and plant seeds and built flimsy huts of mud and reeds. Families formed small villages, and, with the food surpluses that were produced, they had more children to help in the fields. They built houses with a sleeping platform, bread oven, grain silo, and a corral for their domesticated animals. Older women served as religious specialists, acting as midwives, reciting myths, and composing verses and incantations. Over time hamlets grew into larger villages, and people began to see themselves as part of larger communities. To honor a special deity the villagers built a temple, not just brick and mortar but a holy place. Eventually these villages with their temples grew into the first cities. In turn, cities established a foundation for the rise of states, trade networks, and writing.

The Rise of New Technologies

While making possible such complex societies, agriculture also fostered new technology. Many times in history people came up against a serious resource problem, such as lack of food and water, and had to overcome the problem or perish. Often their solution was to develop some new technology, and many of these had long-lasting value. One innovation, metalworking, made possible a new level of human control over resources supplied by the environment.

The first metalworking was done with copper. Copper was being used in Europe for making weapons and tools as early as 7000 B.C.E. and in the Middle East by 4500 B.C.E. In fact, copper mining may have been the first real industry of the ancient world; for example, the Egyptians maintained substantial mining operations in the Sinai Peninsula. Traded over considerable distances, copper also became perhaps the first major commodity to enjoy a world market. Gold was also used and valued very early. These two soft metals could be fairly easily cut and shaped with stones.

Soon specialist craftsmen emerged to mine and work metals. By 3000 B.C.E. some of these specialists in western Asia had developed heating processes by which they could blend copper together with either tin or arsenic to create bronze. The bronze trade became a major spur to commerce in early Mesopotamia. By 1500 B.C.E. the technology for making usable iron had also been invented, although it took many centuries for people to perfect the new alloy for practical use. Bronze and iron made better, more helpful, and more durable tools (such as plows), but also more deadly weapons, and their use shaped many societies of the ancient and classical worlds (see "Societies, Networks, Transitions," page 101).

Urbanization and the First Cities

Agriculture also fostered population growth. By using cow's milk and grain meal for infant's food, women could now breast-feed for a shorter period and consequently bear children more frequently. In the Middle East the population is believed to have grown in the space of 4,000 years (some 160 generations) from less than 100,000 in 8000 B.C.E. to over 3 million by 4000 B.C.E.

In more densely populated areas, farming villages grew into substantial, often prosperous towns. In one of the oldest towns, Çatal Hüyük (cha-TAHL hoo-YOOK) in central Turkey, roughly 10,000 residents lived in cramped mud-brick buildings from 6700 to 5700 B.C.E. The residents decorated the white plaster walls of their houses with paintings. The town's wealth derived from volcanic obsidian, which people converted into polished mirrors and traded around the region. Çatal Hüyük and similar towns became centers of long-distance trade and the basis for the first cities. For example, by around 3700 B.C.E. Tell Hamoukar (Tell HAM-oo-kar) in northeastern Syria had grown from a village into a town enclosed by a defensive wall. It contained both a bakery and a brewery, evidence of some residents organizing people and resources, and seems to have had some occupational divisions and a growing bureaucracy, perhaps even a king. By 3500 B.C.E. Tell Hamoukar had grown into a city, which later traded with the cities of southern Mesopotamia. Road networks linked the various cities of the Tigris-Euphrates Basin.

Çatal Hüyük   A view of rooms and walls in one of the first known towns, Çatal Hüyük in eastern Turkey. The ruins contained many art objects, murals, wall sculpture, and woven cloth.   (Courtesy Arlene Mellaart)

As people grouped together, they pioneered new ways of living. Through the process of urbanization permanent settlements became larger and more complex, dominating nearby villages and farms. A city is a permanent settlement with a greater size, population, and importance than a town or village, and it usually contains many shops, public markets, government buildings, and religious centers. Cities emerged only where farmers produced more food than they needed for themselves and so could be taxed or coerced to share their excess crops. This surplus was critical to sustain people with no time or land for farming, and priests, scribes, carpenters, and merchants increasingly congregated in the larger settlements that eventually became cities.

What some call the urban revolution constituted a major achievement in different parts of the world, perhaps as significant as the agricultural transformation. In southwest Asia the first small cities were formed between 3500 and 3200 B.C.E.; they were administered by governments and dominated by new social hierarchies. Soon cities appeared elsewhere (see Chronology: The Rise of Cities). Many were surrounded by walls, which the Greek philosopher Aristotle later called a city's "greatest protector [and] best military measure."[6] City people enjoyed many new amenities. Many streets were lined by small shops and crowded with makeshift stalls selling foodstuffs, household items, or folk medicines. Hawkers peddled their wares from door to door, some announcing their presence with calls or songs. Craftsmen in workshops fashioned the items used in daily life, such as pottery, tools, and jewelry. Some of the goods made, mined, or grown locally were traded by land or sea to distant cities. Thus the rise of cities reshaped societies and fostered networks of communication and exchange.

CHRONOLOGY	
The Rise of Cities	
3500–3200 B.C.E.	Western Asia
3100–3000 B.C.E.	Egypt
3500–3000 B.C.E.	Northwestern India
3000–2500 B.C.E.	Peru
2000 B.C.E.	Northern China
1800 B.C.E.	Nubia
1600 B.C.E.	Crete
1200 B.C.E.	Mesoamerica (Mexico)
100 C.E.	West Africa

The Rise of States, Economies, and Recordkeeping

Food production and urbanization eventually led to the formation of states: formal political organizations or governments that controlled a recognized territory and exercised power over both people and things. The people within them, often from diverse ethnic and cultural backgrounds, did not necessarily share all the same values or allegiances. Furthermore, they exchanged influences with neighboring peoples. Complex urban societies organized into states developed at least 3,000 years ago on all the inhabited continents except Australia, and by 1,000 years ago they were widespread around the world.

These urban societies relied on diversified economies that generated enough wealth to permit a substantial division of labor and to support a social, cultural, and religious hierarchy. Farmers, laborers, craftsmen, merchants, priests, soldiers, bureaucrats, and scholars served specialized functions. The priests served the religious institutions that emerged as societies organized and standardized their beliefs. Some states constructed monumental architecture, such as large temples, palaces, and city walls. While men dominated most of the hierarchies and heavy labor, women also played key economic roles. In all of the ancient urban societies, women made the cloth. They prepared the raw materials; spun the yarn; wove the yarn into fabrics; and fashioned and sewed the clothing, blankets, and other useful items, passing along their knowledge from mother to daughter.

Most urban societies were connected to elaborate trade networks extending well beyond the immediate region. The earliest known long-distance trade, by dugout canoes in Europe, dates to around 9000 B.C.E. By 4000 B.C.E. a network of merchant contacts linked India and Mesopotamia, 1,250 miles apart. Very crude mathematical calculations were being etched in bones by people in western Asia by 15,000 or 10,000 B.C.E., and clay counting tokens used for trade had appeared by 3100 B.C.E., if not earlier. By 5000 B.C.E. the first seafaring vessels had been built around the Persian Gulf to serve increased long-distance trade, and by 3500 B.C.E. these and other developments had set the foundation for more extensive networks linking diverse societies.

The early urban societies also introduced cultural innovations such as recordkeeping and literature. A system of recordkeeping could involve a written language, such as those developed by the Egyptians, Greeks, Arabs, Chinese, and Mayans, among others. Or records could be kept by a class of memory experts, such as the professional "rememberers" that lived among some South American peoples and were common in Africa. In most literate societies writing was usually reserved for the privileged few until recent centuries, so knowledge of literature was not widespread unless it was passed on orally. Both nonliterate and literate societies created rich oral traditions of stories, legends, historical accounts, and poems, often nourished by specialists, that could be shared with all the people.

Some historians apply the term *civilization* to larger, more complex societies such as ancient Egypt and China, but this is a controversial concept with a long history of abuse. From ancient times up to today, some peoples have seen themselves as "civilized" and dismissed or criticized their neighbors, or any people unfamiliar to them, as "barbarians." Another problem is that modern historians may focus too much on societies, such as Egypt, that left more of an archaeological and written record, giving lesser attention to those societies that did not. The historian can cast a wide or narrow net in choosing which societies to consider "civilized." The term could refer to a large grouping of people with a common history and traditions, such as the Chinese, Mayans, Arabs, Bantu Africans, Brazilians,

or western Europeans. Or it could be restricted to those large, complex urban societies that developed or borrowed certain useful patterns such as bureaucratic governments, monumental architecture, and writing. Thus the term is too subjective to have much value in understanding world history, and many historians refuse to use it altogether. It is not used in this text.

The Rise of Pastoral Nomadism

Some societies adopted an alternative to agriculture and cities known as **pastoral nomadism**, an economy based on breeding, rearing, and harvesting livestock. The interaction between pastoral nomads and settled farmers was a major theme in history for many centuries. On the marginal land unsuitable for farming, some people began specializing in herding, moving their camps and animals seasonally in search of pasture. They traded meat, hides, or livestock to nearby farmers for grain. Both trade and conflict between the two contrasting groups, farmers and herders, became common. Pastoral nomadism was a highly specialized and developed way of life involving dispersed rather than concentrated populations. Yet some pastoral nomads exercised a strong influence on societies with much greater populations.

Pastoral Societies   Pastoral nomads mostly concentrated in grasslands and deserts, which could sustain only small populations. Grasslands covered much of central and western Asia from Mongolia to southern Russia, as well as large parts of eastern and southern Africa. An even more inhospitable area was the Sahara region of northern Africa, which was part of a great arid zone stretching from the western tip of Africa eastward through Arabia into western Asia and then to the frontiers of China. By 2500 B.C.E. a long drought had intensified the drying out of the Sahara region, and by 2000 B.C.E. it had become a huge, inhospitable desert habitable only by pastoralists.

Living along or beyond the frontiers of settled farming, the pastoralists lived very differently than farmers, but they were not culturally "unsophisticated." For example, they domesticated horses in Central Asia around 4300 B.C.E. (Horses reached western Asia by 2000 B.C.E. Although camels were domesticated around 3000 or 2500 B.C.E. in Arabia, they were not widely used in western Asia until sometime after 1500 B.C.E.) Pastoralists were also capable of undertaking ambitious projects. Around 5000 B.C.E. Sahara cattle herders built a remarkable megalithic ceremonial center of large stones to mark astronomical changes. Like other societies, pastoralists had humane values and a rich cultural life, and many were connected to other peoples by various networks.

The nomadic pastoral life had many similarities regardless of the region. Since a large area was needed to support each animal, herds had to be kept small and separated some distance from other herds to prevent overgrazing. As a result, the herders lived in small, dispersed groups, generally organized by extended families that were often part of **tribes**, associations of clans that traced descent from a common ancestor; sometimes they were

pastoral nomadism An economy based on breeding, rearing, and harvesting livestock.

part of federations of tribes. While most pastoralists had few material possessions, they did not necessarily envy the settled peoples. For example, the pastoral nomads who today herd yak, sheep, and goats across the windswept high plateaus of northern Tibet enjoy ample leisure time and believe, despite the harsh conditions, that they have an easier life than farmers.

There were also many differences among pastoralists. While some societies maintained egalitarian social structures, others were headed by chiefs. In some of the pastoral societies of Central Asia women seem to have held a high status and to even have served as warriors. Burial mounds in Turkestan contain the remains of what may be female warriors from 2,500 years ago. These women, unusually tall, were buried with daggers, swords, and bronze-tipped arrows. Some pastoralists became tough, martial peoples who were greatly feared by the farmers. As discussed in later chapters, Central Asian pastoralists like the Huns and Mongols played a central role in world history before modern times.

The Indo-Europeans   Among the pastoral nomads who had a great influence on world history were the various tribes known collectively as the **Indo-Europeans** (IN-dough-YUR-uh-PEE-uns). Historians derive this term from the original common tongue that spawned the many related languages spoken today by these peoples' descendants. All these languages have many similar geographic, climatic, botanical, and zoological terms. Scholars have long debated where the original Indo-European homeland was located. Many think these societies arose either in the Caucasus Mountains or in the adjacent plains to the north, in what is now southern Russia. Others place them in eastern Anatolia (modern Turkey). Eventually, because of the spread of these seminomadic and strongly patriarchal tribes and their languages, most people in Europe, Iran, and northern India came to speak Indo-European languages.

Indo-European expansion apparently occurred in several waves. According to recent studies, some Indo-Europeans may have moved into Europe and central Asia as early as 6500 or 7000 B.C.E., perhaps carrying with them not only their language but also farming technology, both of which they shared with, or imposed on, the local peoples. The culturally mixed people who resulted may have been the ancestors of, among others, the Celts and Greeks. Sometime between 3000 and 2000 B.C.E. many of the Indo-Europeans remaining in Anatolia and the Caucasus, most of them pastoralists, were driven from their homeland by some disaster, perhaps drought, prolonged frost, overpopulation, plague, or invasions by even more warlike peoples. The various tribes dispersed in every direction, splitting up into smaller, more cohesive units and driving their herds of cattle, sheep, goats, and horses with them. As they encountered farming peoples, they turned to conquest in order to occupy the land (see Map 1.3).

This dispersal of peoples from the Indo-European heartland set the stage for profound changes across Eurasia. The

Hittites gained dominance in Anatolia and then, around 2000 B.C.E., expanded their empire into Mesopotamia. Other tribes pushed on between 2500 and 1500 B.C.E., some to the west across Anatolia into Greece, some to the east as far as the western fringe of China, some south into Persia. From Persia some tribes moved southeast through the mountain passes into northwestern India. Everywhere they went the Indo-Europeans spread their languages and imposed their military power, eventually absorbing or subduing the peoples they encountered. Most eventually abandoned pastoral nomadism for farming, but their spread opened a new chapter in the history of Europe, the Middle East, and India.

SECTION SUMMARY

- Metals such as bronze and iron helped improve farming tools and weaponry.
- Highly productive farming allowed for the formation of the first cities, which became centers of trade.
- People in cities developed forms of recordkeeping and writing.
- Pastoral nomads, or herders, kept their animals in areas that were unsuitable for farming.
- Herders played an important role in spreading culture across Eurasia, though most eventually took up farming.

 Online Study Center   ACE the Test

 Chapter Summary

The story of humans and their societies constitutes only a tiny part of the broader 4.5-billion-year history of the Earth. Some 4 million years ago our hominid ancestors emerged in Africa, learning to walk upright, to make and use tools, and to control fire. Eventually, after several stages, evolution produced modern humans, who developed language and more complex social structures. For thousands of years, during the long Paleolithic age, all humans, using simple technologies and living in small groups, hunted wild animals and gathered wild plants. Hunters and gatherers survived and even flourished by maintaining a balance with their environment. While many such societies survived over the millennia, eventually environmental changes and other factors encouraged most peoples to adopt farming.

Beginning between 10,000 and 11,500 years ago, the climate began to warm and populations increased. In response some people gradually began to grow their own food. The great transition from hunting and gathering to a farming-based economy also involved the domestication of wild animals. Farming probably emerged first in southwestern Asia or possibly Southeast Asia. Over the next few thousand years various peoples in Eurasia, Africa, and the Americas began farming. By 2000 B.C.E. agriculture had been established widely

---

tribes   Associations of clans that traced descent from a common ancestor.

Indo-Europeans   Various tribes who all spoke related languages deriving from some original common tongue and who eventually settled Europe, Iran, and northern India.

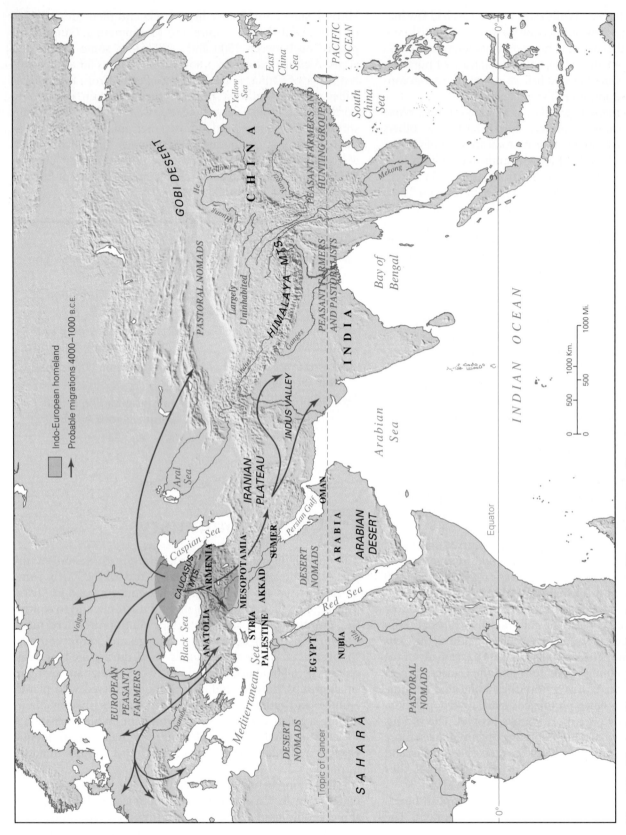

Map 1.3   The Indo-European Migrations and Eurasian Pastoralism
Some societies, especially in parts of Africa and Asia, adapted to environmental contexts by developing a pastoral, or animal herding, economy. One large pastoral group, the Indo-Europeans, eventually expanded from their home area into Europe, southwestern Asia, Central Asia, and India.

around the world. Agriculture led to larger populations and changed people's relationship to the environment. It also set the stage for another transition, the emergence of the first societies with cities, states, social classes, and recordkeeping. In the Afro-Eurasian zone, where many peoples were in contact with others, these societies first developed between 3000 and 3500 B.C.E. Early trade and transportation networks linked some of them together. The first cities and states formed in sub-Saharan Africa and the Americas between 3000 and 1000 B.C.E. At the same time, some people living in the grasslands and deserts became nomadic pastoralists and interacted with settled farmers. The formation of distinctive societies and increased contact between peoples inaugurated a new era of human history.

Online Study Center **Improve Your Grade** Flashcards

Key Terms

hominids	Paleolithic	polytheism
australopithecines	Mesolithic	shamans
Homo habilis	Neolithic	horticulture
Homo erectus	matrilineal	pastoral nomadism
Homo sapiens	kinship	tribes
Neanderthals	animism	Indo-Europeans
Cro-Magnons		

Suggested Reading

Books

Bellwood, Peter. *First Farmers: The Origins of Agricultural Societies.* Malden, M.A.: Blackwell, 2005. A detailed scholarly account summarizing recent knowledge.

Bogucki, Peter. *The Origins of Human Society.* Malden, Mass.: Blackwell, 1999. A detailed and up-to-date scholarly study of human prehistory.

Christian, David. *Maps of Time: An Introduction to "Big History."* Berkeley: University of California Press, 2004. The most extensive presentation of the "big history" approach.

Clark, Robert B. *The Global Imperative: An Interpretive History of the Spread of Humankind.* Boulder, Colo.: Westview, 1997. A well-written, brief overview of human expansion and the development of agriculture.

Diamond, Jared. *Guns, Germs and Steel: The Fates of Human Societies.* New York: W.W. Norton, 1997. A fascinating interpretation of early human societies, with emphasis on environmental influences.

Fagan, Brian. *People of the Earth: An Introduction to World Prehistory.* 11th ed. Upper Saddle River, N.J.: Prentice-Hall, 2003. A standard overview of human evolution and prehistory, from early hominids through the Neolithic.

Fagan, Brian. *The Long Summer: How Climate Changed Civilization.* New York: Basic Books, 2004. An up-to-date assessment of the connection between history and climate over the past 5,000 years.

Goudsblom, Johan. *Fire and Civilization.* London: Penguin, 1992. Examines the impact of fire use on prehistorical and early farming societies.

Lewin, Roger. *The Origin of Modern Humans.* New York: Scientific American Library, 1998. A well-illustrated survey of human evolution and early society.

Manning, Patrick. *Migration in World History.* New York: Routledge, 2005. Provocative study of human migrations, with much on prehistory and ancient history.

Megarry, Tim. *Society in Prehistory: The Origins of Human Culture.* New York: New York University Press, 1995. A sociological study of human evolution and Stone Age societies.

Mithen, Steven, *After the Ice: A Global Human History, 20,000-5000 BC.* Cambridge: Harvard University Press, 2004. an unorthodox but fascinating portrayal, based on the latest research, of 15,000 years of prehistory.

Smith, Bruce D. *The Emergence of Agriculture.* New York: Scientific American Library, 1994. An account for the general reader of the origins of food production.

Websites

About Archaeology
(http://archaeology.about.com/science/archaeology).
Contains much material on archaeology and ancient societies.

ArchNet Home Page
(http://archnet.asu.edu/). This Arizona State University site contains links to information on human origins, prehistory, and archaeology.

Evolution of Modern Humans
(http://anthro.palomar.edu/homo2/default.htm).
Valuable site maintained by Palomar College.

Internet Ancient History Sourcebook
(http://www.fordham.edu/halsall/ancient/asbook.htm).
Good collection of essays and links on prehistory.

The Internet Public Library: Archaeology
(http://www.ipl.org/div/subject/browse/soc06.00.00/).
Extensive collection of links on the ancient world and prehistory.

World Civilizations
(http://www.wsu.edu/~dee/TITLE.HTM).
A useful collection of materials on prehistory and ancient history, operated by Washington State University.

CHAPTER 2

Ancient Societies in Mesopotamia, India, and Central Asia, 5000–600 B.C.E.

Online Study Center

This icon will direct you to interactive activities and study materials on the website: college.hmco.com/pic/lockard1e

Bull's Head from Sumerian Lyre   This bull's head is part of the soundbox of a wooden harp. The harp, made in Sumeria around 2600 B.C.E., is covered with gold and lapis lazuli and reflects the popularity of music in Mesopotamian society.   (Michael Holford)

Inanna filled Agade [a Mesopotamian city], her home, with gold. She filled the storerooms with barley, bronze, and lumps of lapis lazuli [a stone used in jewelry]. The ships at the wharves were an awesome sight. All the lands around rested in security.

POEM PRAISING THE GODDESS OF LOVE AND GENEROSITY, WRITTEN IN 2250 B.C.E.[1]

Some 5,000 years ago in the Mesopotamian (MESS-uh-puh-TAIM-ee-an) city of Uruk (OO-rook), an unknown artist carved a beautiful narrative relief on a large stone-pedestaled vase, the first such sculpture known in history, and donated it to the city's temple for the goddess of love, Inanna (ih-NON-a), the first known goddess in recorded history. The scenes of domestic and religious life celebrate a festival honoring the goddess. The artist divided the vase into three bands, each illustrating different aspects of Uruk life and traditions. The lowest band presents an agricultural scene, with ewes and rams, barley and flax, and water, the staples of the area's economy. Inanna, the sculptor believed, had blessed Uruk's people with growing herds and good crops. The central band portrays a procession of naked men carrying jars and baskets overflowing with foodstuffs that they will present as gifts of gratitude to Inanna. Finally, the uppermost band features a female figure wearing a tall horned headdress, perhaps Inanna or her priestess. The Warka vase, as it is known today, reflects the artistic skill of a fine craftsman and also pictures for us the social order and rituals of one of the world's earliest cities.

Sometime after the people in southwest Asia and India had become comfortable with the farming technology necessary for successful living, they began to make the next great transition by founding the first cities, like Uruk and Agade (uh-GAH-duh), and the first states. Various urban societies eventually formed in the Indus Valley in northwestern India and all along the **Fertile Crescent**, a large semicircle of fertile land that included the valleys of the Tigris (TIE-gris) and Euphrates (you-FRAY-teez) Rivers stretching northwest from the Persian Gulf, the eastern shores of the Mediterranean Sea, and, to some historians, the banks of the Nile River in Egypt. The Mesopotamians in the Fertile Crescent divided their labor into specialized tasks assigned to full-time farmers, professional soldiers, government officials, artisans, and priests. To the east, the people in ancient India also divided their society into social classes and established the foundations for several religions of wide and enduring appeal.

Fertile Crescent A large semicircular fertile region that included the valleys of the Tigris and Euphrates Rivers stretching northwest from the Persian Gulf, the eastern shores of the Mediterranean Sea, and, to some scholars, the banks of the Nile River in North Africa.

Among the Mesopotamians and Indians, the first dramatic changes in human life arose from contact through trade and migration networks or warfare. Various Afro-Eurasian peoples built the foundations to sustain large populations. For at least three millennia a large majority of the world's population has lived in an arc stretching from Egypt and Mesopotamia eastward through India and China to Japan. The people of western Asia created many innovations: the first systematic use of writing for both business transactions and literature, the first working of bronze, the first large state structures and empires, and the first institutionalized religions to worship deities like Inanna. These societies also constructed networks to exchange products and information over long distances by land and sea. Agade, the hub for such a network, was visited by traders from near and far. Over time the Middle East, which includes North Africa and western Asia, became a crossroads or bridge between Europe, Africa, and southern Asia. And Mesopotamia was for centuries a great hub for trade and communication networks extending to distant lands.

FOCUS QUESTIONS

1. Why did farming, cities, and states develop first in the Fertile Crescent?
2. What were some of the main features of Mesopotamian societies?
3. What were some of the distinctive features of the Harappan cities?
4. How did the Aryan migrations reshape Indian society?
5. How did Indian society and the Hindu religion emerge from the mixing of Aryan and local cultures?

◆ Early Mesopotamian Urbanized Societies, to 2000 B.C.E.

Why did farming, cities, and states develop first in the Fertile Crescent?

The creation of small city-states around 5,000 years ago made Mesopotamia, and especially the southern part of the Tigris-Euphrates Valley, the home of some of the world's earliest urban societies. Geography played a key role in this region's transition to farming and then to urbanization and state building. Even in these early millennia, the connections between diverse peoples helped cultures change and grow. Over the centuries various peoples moved into the area, each adopting and building on the achievements of their predecessors. They built the first great cities and developed a written language. The cities were dominated by religious temples and had elaborate social class structures. As conquerors combined various city-states into a series of ever larger states, empires were formed, and Mesopotamian societies were soon linked by trade to the Mediterranean and North Africa.

Western Asian Environments

Life in these early societies owed much to the geographic features that brought people together. Most early urban societies began first in wide river valleys such as the Tigris-Euphrates, Indus, and Nile Valleys because such places provided life-giving irrigation for the crops that supported larger populations. In the case of Mesopotamia (the Greek word for the "land between the rivers"), the flooding of the Tigris and Euphrates Rivers made possible a flourishing society. The first known cities and states arose in the Tigris-Euphrates Basin, a region stretching from the western edge of the Persian Gulf through today's Iraq into Syria and southeastern Turkey. The long river valley promoted interaction between peoples, both friendly and hostile. For example, it invited frequent invasions through mountain passes by people living to the north and east. To the northwest the mountainous Anatolia (ANN-uh-TOE-lee-uh) Peninsula (modern Turkey) provided the key link between Asia and Europe. East of Mesopotamia lay Iran (known through most of history as Persia), a land of mountains and deserts and the pathway to India and Central Asia. To the south the Arabian peninsula, largely desert, was characterized by oasis agriculture and nomadic pastoralism.

Although the rivers provided water, other characteristics of this region and its climate were not so generous. Ancient

C H R O N O L O G Y

	Mesopotamia	India and Central Asia
3000 B.C.E.	**3000–2300** B.C.E. Sumerian city-states	
2500 B.C.E.	**2350–2160** B.C.E. Akkadian Empire	**2600–1750** B.C.E. Harappan city-states **2200–1800** B.C.E. Oxus cities
2000 B.C.E.	**1800–1595** B.C.E. Old Babylonian Empire	**1600–1400** B.C.E. Aryan migrations **1500–1000** B.C.E. Aryan Age
1000 B.C.E.	**1115–605** B.C.E. Assyrian Empire	

Mesopotamia had a climate similar to southern California today. Most rain fell in the winter, and summer temperatures in some places reached 120 degrees Fahrenheit. During the long and incredibly hot summer, the land, mostly composed of clay soils, baked stone-hard. Under a scorching sun searing winds blew up a choking dust. Vegetation withered. The winter was little more comfortable, as winds, clouds, and the occasional rains made for stormy and bleak days. In spring the green was welcome, but the rains and melting snows in the nearby mountains swelled the rivers to flood level, sometimes submerging the plains for miles around. Still, the annual but unpredictable floods created natural levees that could be drained and planted, and the nearby swamps contained abundant fish and wildlife.

Diverse peoples and languages contributed to the history and identity of western Asia. Many different peoples settled the region, some of them speaking Semitic languages, including Arabic and Hebrew, which are related to some African tongues. Speakers of Turkic and of Indo-European languages such as Persian, Armenian, and Kurdish arrived later. The various names given by outsiders to these lands hint at other influences and concepts. Two millennia ago the Romans called the lands from the eastern shores of the Mediterranean Sea to the Persian Gulf the "Orient" ("east"). Later Europeans referred to southwestern Asia as Asia Minor or the Near East (since it was part of the "East" nearest to them), and to the region along the eastern Mediterranean coast (today's Israel, Lebanon, and Syria) as the Levant (luh-VANT) ("rising of the sun"). Geographers today use the label "southwest Asia," and often lump the region together with Islamic North Africa under the broader concept of the "Middle East," since Europeans saw it as midway between East Asia (the "Far East") and themselves ("the West").

Mesopotamian Foundations

Despite its harsh geography and climate, Mesopotamia saw the first transitions to settled agriculture and then to urbanization. Long before Sumerians built the first cities at the head of the Persian Gulf, the transition to farming had taken place in various places of the Tigris-Euphrates Basin as well as in Palestine. For example, by 9000 B.C.E. Jericho (JER-ah-ko), located near the Jordan River, was an agricultural community that had some 2,000 people at its height. Excavated storage rooms, town walls, and a round storage tower indicate a complex town organization. Towns like Jericho in Palestine and Çatal Hüyük in south central Anatolia foreshadowed the beginnings of urban society in Mesopotamia.

The Tigris and Euphrates Rivers fostered several Mesopotamian societies. Both rivers begin in eastern Anatolia and flow southeast over a thousand miles to the Persian Gulf. The modern city of Baghdad is midway up the Tigris, and the ancient city of Babylon was only a few miles away on the Euphrates where the two rivers flow closest to each other. Sometime after 6500 B.C.E., the population of farmers and herders in the fertile hills on either side of these rivers increased. Because of their greater need for food, and possibly pushed by a cooler climate between 6200-5800 B.C.E, they left the hill country and created the first towns in the marshy but fertile areas near the head of the Persian Gulf. Although these people had been raising cattle and sheep and growing wheat and barley for several thousand years, after moving to the river valleys they worked together to build elaborate irrigation canals so they could grow food after the annual floods. Thus irrigation had significant historical consequences, for it necessitated the cooperation that laid the foundations for organized societies and then cities. Yet, irrigation also slowly degraded the soil, the salts it added eventually creating infertile desert.

The Pioneering Sumerians

People built the first Mesopotamian cities and states in Sumer (soo-MUHR), the lower part of the Tigris-Euphrates Valley in southern Iraq (see Map 2.1). Historians think the Sumerians originally came from the north or the east and that they settled in southern Mesopotamia about 5500 B.C.E. Over time villages grew into towns. By 3500 B.C.E. Uruk had grown into a city,

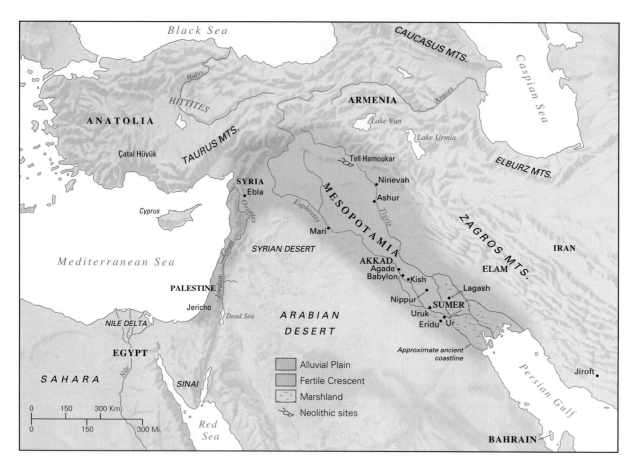

Map 2.1 Ancient Mesopotamia
The people of Mesopotamia and the adjacent regions of the Fertile Crescent pioneered farming. The Mesopotamians also built the first cities and formed the first states. The Sumerian cities dominated southern Mesopotamia for over a millennium, only to lose power to societies from northern Mesopotamia.

Online Study Center **Improve Your Grade** Interactive Map: Ancient Mesopotamia Through the Persian Empire

eventually reaching a population of 50,000. From the archaeological discoveries at Tell Hamoukar, on the northern fringe of the Tigris-Euphrates Valley in modern Syria, some scholars suspect that other peoples may have been as important as the Sumerians in forging the first states. But our knowledge of the Sumerians is much more extensive.

The various settlers created elaborate canal systems and, by 3000, a network of city-states, urban centers surrounded by agricultural land controlled by the city and used to support its citizens. These earliest territorial political units allowed Sumerian societies to grow, to perhaps several million people, by 2500 B.C.E. For example, Uruk was surrounded by 5 miles of fortified walls and had extended its influence through trade as far north as modern Turkey by 3500 B.C.E. An attack by Uruk on the city of Tell Hamoukar in northern Mesopotamia is the world's oldest known example of large-scale organized warfare. Uruk also exercised regional power. A document from the era reported that Uruk was obsessed with weapons and used them to conquer the nearby city of Ur (see Chronology: Mesopotamia, 5500–330 B.C.E.).

Sumerians had little sense of being citizens, as we understand that term, but they were clearly proud of their cities. A Sumerian myth begins with the lines "Behold the bond of Heaven and Earth, the city. Behold the kindly wall, the city, its pure river, its quay where the boats stand. Behold its well of good water. Behold its pure canal."[2] The Sumerians felt that city life made them superior to others and referred scornfully to the various desert peoples and tribes living to the west and south of the valley as "people who have never known a city." The city-dwellers lived in mud-baked brick houses constructed around courtyards. The largest building in any Sumerian city was the temple, or **ziggurat** (ZIG-uh-rat), a stepped, pyramidal-shaped building (almost an artificial mountain) that was seen as the home of that city's chief god. One of these temples may have inspired the later Hebrew story of the tower of Babel (BAY-buhl/BAH-buhl).

---

ziggurat A stepped, pyramidal-shaped temple building in Sumerian cities, seen as the home of the chief god of the city.

CHRONOLOGY

Mesopotamia, 5500–330 B.C.E.

5500	First Sumerian settlements
3200	First cuneiform writing
3000–2300	Sumerian city-states
2750	Model for legendary Gilgamesh rules Uruk
ca. 2500–2100	Jiroft
ca. 2350–2160	Akkadian Empire unified Mesopotamia
ca. 2100–2000	Neo-Sumerian Empire led by city of Ur
ca. 2000	*Epic of Gilgamesh* written in cuneiform
ca. 1800–1595	Old Babylonian Empire
ca. 1790–1780	Hammurabi's Law Code
ca. 1600–1200	Hittite Empire
ca. 1115–605	Assyrian Empire
745–626	Height of Assyrian Empire
ca. 626–539	Chaldean (Neo-Babylonian) Empire
ca. 539–330	Persian Empire

Sumerian Society and Economy

The social, political, and economic structures of Sumerian society became hierarchical, with some people having higher ranks than others. In the early years, decision-making assemblies of leading citizens governed the cities. Scholars have long debated whether these assemblies, which included elders and other free citizens, amounted to a kind of democratic government. The assemblies seem to have appointed a city leader, sometimes a woman, with both secular and religious authority. However, with the waging of wars, rulers, priests, and nobles came to dominate large numbers of lower-class people, workers, and slaves. Women lost the right to be elected leader and serve in the assemblies. War leaders became kings, or hereditary monarchs. By increasing their power and forming large armies, they weakened the power of the assemblies and priests. Either the nobility or the priests controlled most of the land in and around the city, which was tilled by tenant farmers or slaves, and many of these common people became dependent on the nobles or priests for their survival. A Sumerian proverb claimed that "the poor man is better dead than alive; if he has bread, he has no salt; if he has salt, he has no bread."[3] The many slaves, who included captives taken in battles and criminals, were treated as

personal property but allowed to marry. If a slave married a free woman, the children were free. Eventually royal officials, nobility, and priests controlled most of the economic life of the cities. In many places, for example, temple priests distributed seed for planting and planned crop distribution.

As the first of many male-governed societies, Sumeria introduced **patriarchy**, a system in which men largely control women and children and also shape ideas about appropriate gender behavior. Sumerian women were generally subservient to men and excluded from government, but they could inherit property, run their own businesses, and serve as witnesses in court. A queen enjoyed much respect as the wife of the king. Sumerian religion also allowed a woman to be the high priestess if the city divinity was female. Sumerians treasured the family; a proverb said: "Friendship lasts a day; kinship endures forever." Another proverb suggested the importance of women in the family but also the stereotypes they faced: "The wife is a man's future; the son is a man's refuge; the daughter is a man's salvation; the daughter-in-law is a man's devil."[4]

The trade networks involving Sumeria may have been some of the first in world history with significant consequences. Because of their location and lack of natural resources, the Sumerian cities engaged in extensive trade, which helped form networks with neighboring societies. Even today satellite images reveal the outlines of the 5,000-year-old road system that linked Mesopotamian cities. Sumerians imported copper from Armenia in the Caucasus Mountains and then discovered how to mix it with tin to make bronze. This alloy made for stronger weapons, which they often used against each other. Thus the Bronze Age originated in western Asia, and later the use of bronze helped shape other societies in Eurasia and North Africa. The Sumerians also imported gold, ivory, obsidian, and other necessities from Anatolia, the Nile Valley, Ethiopia, India, the Caspian Sea, and the eastern shore of the Mediterranean.

The Persian Gulf became a major waterway, with many trading ports. Bahrain (Bah-RAIN) Island served as a transshipment point for goods flowing in from all directions and as a hub where various traders and travelers met. Mesopotamian merchants traveled to this port of exchange carrying cargoes of textiles, leather objects, wool, and olive oil, and they returned with copper bars, copper objects, ivory, precious objects, and rare woods from various Western Asian societies and India. Some Mesopotamian traders lived in central Iran and others traveled widely. Already this early in history, trade helped people learn and profit from each other's skills and surplus goods.

The Sumerians also seem to have had some trade and other connections with another urban-based farming society known as Jiroft [JEER-oft], located in southeastern Iran. Scholars debate where the still sparsely documented Jiroft fits into the development of the most ancient urban societies. Jiroft seems to have emerged sometime between 3000 and 2500 B.C.E., with a rural economy based on cultivating date palms.

---

patriarchy A system in which men largely control women and children and shape ideas about appropriate gender behavior.

Overview of Early City of Uruk   This photo shows the ruins of one of the earliest Mesopotamian cities, a rich source of art objects and fine architecture. The best-known king of Uruk was the legendary Gilgamesh.   (Hirmer Verlag Munchen)

Some scholars think inscribed lines and images on seals constituted a form of writing. Mesopotamian texts describe a state they called Aratta, a possible reference to Jiroft. Aratta's gaily decorated capital city had lofty red brick towers, and the rulers supplied artisans and craftsmen to Uruk. The ruins of the main Jiroft city, a regional commercial center, include a two-story citadel and a Sumerian-like ziggurat. Archaeologists have found the world's oldest known board games and staggering numbers of decorated vases, goblets, cups, and boxes. The people adorned their products with precious stones from India and Afghanistan. Some decorations on Jiroft pottery resemble the gods, plants, and beasts of Sumeria.

Sumerian Writing and Technology

The Sumerians were innovators in many areas. Although a few scholars think the Egyptians, Indians, or Chinese might have developed a simple writing system at least as early as the Sumerians, most still credit the Sumerians with producing the first written records. Trade and the need to keep accurate records of agricultural production and public and private business dealings led around 3200 B.C.E. to one of the most significant Sumerian contributions. This was their **cuneiform** (kyoo-NEE-uh-form) (Latin for "wedge-shaped") writing system, in which temple recordkeepers, or scribes, began to keep records

of financial transactions by making rough pictures (say, of an animal or fish) on soft clay with a stylus that made wedges in the clay. They then baked the bricks on which these pictograms were scratched. Archaeologists have discovered hundreds of thousands of such bricks intact. Sumerian scribes soon let a stylized version of the pictogram stand for an idea, and later they converted an even more abstract version into a phonetic sign describing a speech sound.

Writing provided a way of communicating with people over long distances and allowed rulers to administer larger states. Those who controlled the written word, like those who master electronic communication in our day, had power, prestige, and a monopoly over a society's official history. Writing also gave temple scribes and other religious leaders the power to determine how written texts attributed to the gods or political authorities should be interpreted.

Since writing required mastery of at least three hundred symbols, few people learned to write, and those that did largely came from the upper class. In part to produce scribes, the Sumerians created the world's first schools, where strict instructors beat students for misbehavior or sloppy work. A clay tablet from the eighteenth century B.C.E. describes the life of a pupil who spent twenty-four days a month in school and was frequently beaten: "The fellow in charge of Sumerian said: 'Why didn't you speak Sumerian?' [He] caned me. My teacher said: 'Your hand [writing] is unsatisfactory.' [He] caned me. I [begin to hate] the scribal art."[5] However, because cuneiform eventually transformed pictures into phonetic sounds, it made

---

cuneiform ("wedge-shaped")   Latin term used to describe the writing system invented by the Sumerians.

the written word more accessible, even for people whose only goal was a good recipe for a meal of red broth and meat.

Writing became crucial in human history for a number of reasons. First, written language made it easier to express abstract ideas and create an intellectual life based on a body of literature. The oldest known signed poetry was composed by Enheduanna (en-who-DWAHN-ah), a Sumerian priestess and princess living around 2300 B.C.E. Since some of her poems dealt with religious issues, some consider her the first theologian. Royal women were often authors. Eventually writing also helped explain the physical world in rational instead of magical terms. In addition, a written language based on clearly understood symbols, whether phonetic or pictographic, allowed communication among people who spoke different languages but understood the same written symbols. For example, the number 5 is understood today the same way by Spanish speakers, who pronounce it "cinco," and German speakers, who say "funf." Finally, writing was one key to the interaction among societies. It not only gave a strong sense of identity to all who shared the language but also eventually encouraged the spread of trade and culture, including religion, to those outside a particular homeland. Through this process some people became, by choice or necessity, multilingual.

These first city builders were innovative in many areas. They pioneered the first use of the wheel, glass, and fertilizer, inventions that we still live with today. Sumerians also created some of the earliest calendars, which were based on their observations of the movements of various celestial bodies, and one of the first mathematical systems, based on the number 60. Remnants of this system can be seen today in our 60-minute hours and 60-second minutes. Later the Babylonians improved Sumerian mathematics by developing a simple calculator with tables of squares, cubes, reciprocals, square roots, and cube roots. Many other peoples eventually adopted all of these inventions. They were also used by the Sumerians who became the world's first known accountants. Humanity also owes to the Sumerians the decision to divide night and day into twelve hours each. In leisure-time endeavors, the Sumerians were innovative as well. Although they were not the first to convert barley into beer, they designated a special goddess to supervise its production, called Ninkasi or "the lady who fills the mouth." The many taverns fostered early drinking songs: "I will summon brewers and cupbearers to serve us floods of beer and keep it passing round! Our hearts enchanted and our souls radiant."[6]

The Akkadian Empire and Its Rivals

Eventually the political structure of the region changed. In the beginning the Sumerian cities were related by a common culture and not a common ruler. Each city had its own king who ruled the people in the name of the city's god. This independence ended about 2350 B.C.E. when Sargon (SAHR-gone), the ruler of Akkad (AH-kahd), a region just north of Sumer whose capital was Agade, conquered Uruk as a prelude to uniting the other Sumerian cities under the rule of his family. Sargon formed the world's first known empire, a large state controlling other societies through conquest or domination. He claimed a

humble origin, boasting that "in secret [my mother] bore me. She set me in a basket in the river which rose not over me." Later, he said, "I conquered the land, and the sea three times I circled."[7] The Akkadians enslaved many other people in addition to the Sumerians; in fact, slaves constituted perhaps a third of the empire's population in 2300 B.C.E. Under Sargon trade between Mesopotamia and India reached a peak. Indeed, Akkad became the major center for regional trade, and merchant ships from as far as Oman (O-mahn) in eastern Arabia docked at the wharves, carrying copper and various exotic products.

Struggles between rival cities became endemic, generating frequent warfare. Sargon's empire soon came into conflict with one created by another imperial city, Ebla (EBB-luh), in northern Mesopotamia. Ebla had a population of 30,000 and subject peoples totaling another 200,000 or more. It had created a large empire based on trade that stretched from eastern Turkey to the ancient city of Mari (MAH-ree), several hundred miles north of Akkad.

The Akkadian Empire was destroyed by the twenty-first century B.C.E., probably from a combination of internal conflicts, external attacks, and climate change. Less rainfall may have prompted many to migrate. Mesopotamian societies such as Sumer and Akkad were powerless against abrupt climate change which could reduce rainfall dramatically. Sumerian legends celebrated years of plenty: "Behold, now, everything on earth. The harvest was heaped up in granaries and hills." But they also expressed dread of the periodic droughts: "The famine was severe, nothing was produced. The fields are not watered. In all the lands there was no vegetation [and] only weeds grew."[8] A disastrous drought began in 2200 B.C.E., affecting much of Eurasia, and lasted for 300 years. Irrigation canals silted up and settlements became ghost towns.

As the Akkadian Empire collapsed, a new Sumerian dynasty led by Ur took over much of the lower valley between 2100 and 2000 B.C.E., forming what historians term the Neo-Sumerian Empire. Some Ur kings boasted of their commitment to art and intellectual life, one ordering that the places of learning should never be closed. But Ur was devastated by a coalition of enemies and sacked and burned along with other Sumerian cities. Its temples were destroyed, its populations killed or enslaved, and its treasures plundered. These horrific events may have left an enduring mark on the cultures of these cities. A surviving lamentation describes the destruction of Ur in graphic detail: "Ur is destroyed, bitter is its lament. The country's blood now fills its holes like hot bronze in a mould. Our temple is destroyed, the gods have abandoned us, like migrating birds. Smoke lies on our city like a shroud."[9]

The Akkadians, Eblaites, and the later Sumerians established the first empires in history, even though their creations were short-lived and were not the large bureaucratic organizations we see in later empires. They were largely collections of city-states that acknowledged one city as overlord, especially when the ruler's troops were present. However, once the pattern of one city dominating others was established, it soon became clear that whoever had the best army would dominate Mesopotamia.

The Royal Standard of Ur This mosaic from around 2500 B.C.E., made of inlaid shells and limestone, was found in a royal tomb. It depicts various aspects of life in the Mesopotamian city-state of Ur. The bottom panel shows a four-wheeled battle wagon drawn by a horselike animal. The middle panel features soldiers wearing armor and helmets. The top panel shows war prisoners being brought before the king. (British Museum/Michael Holford)

SECTION SUMMARY

- The first urban societies of Mesopotamia developed in the Tigris-Euphrates Basin.
- The ziggurat, or temple, was the largest building in Sumerian cities.
- Sumerian society was hierarchical and patriarchal.
- The earliest writing system was the cuneiform system.
- The world's first empire, the Akkadian Empire, was founded by Sargon.

 ## Later Mesopotamian Societies and Their Legacies, 2000–600 B.C.E.

What were some of the main features of Mesopotamian societies?

The Sumerians and Akkadians established a pattern of city living, state building, and imperial expansion. From 2000 B.C.E. and continuing for the next 1,500 years, a series of peoples, coming mainly from the north, successively dominated Mesopotamia and created new empires. The most important of these peoples were the Babylonians, Hittites, and Assyrians. Each made important contributions to the politics, laws, culture, and thought of the region. This pattern changed only when the entire area was incorporated into the Persian Empire in 539 B.C.E., an event that inaugurated a new era in the history of the region.

The Babylonians and Hittites

Several states dominated Mesopotamia during the second millennium B.C.E., beginning with the Amorite kingdom of Babylon (BAB-uh-lawn). In 1800 B.C.E. the Amorites (AM-uh-rites), a Semitic people, conquered Babylon, a city about 300 miles north of the Persian Gulf on the Euphrates, and gradually extended their control in the region. Babylon's most famous king, Hammurabi (HAM-uh-rah-bee), who ruled from 1792 to 1750 B.C.E., reunified Mesopotamia. Hammurabi had nearly three hundred laws collected and "published" on a black basalt pillar erected near the modern city of Baghdad. These laws were designed, he said, "to make justice appear in the land, to destroy the evil and the wicked [so] that the strong might not oppress the weak."[10] Hammurabi's law code was really a collection of earlier Sumerian concepts and practices. It remains famous today because some of its principles appeared later in the laws of the Hebrews and also because of its most noted principle, the law of retaliation: an eye for an eye and a tooth for a tooth. Hammurabi's successors were able to hold his empire together for little over a century.

By 1595 B.C.E., the Babylonian Empire had disintegrated in the face of attacks by the Hittites (HIT-ites), an Indo-European people who moved into Mesopotamia from their base in central Anatolia. The Hittites were most famous for their later use of iron weapons, which were superior to those made of bronze, but these had not yet been invented when the Hittites invaded Mesopotamia. Iron technology was introduced around 1500 B.C.E., although it took several centuries to perfect. Whether the Hittites invented ironworking or obtained the technology from nearby people in Anatolia, with iron weapons they expanded their power until they met the equally strong Egyptians in Syria and Palestine. The Hittites may also have used the first known biological weapons, since one of their tactics was to send plague victims into enemy lands. The Hittite Empire dominated various parts of western Asia from 1600 to 1200 B.C.E. The Hittites treated their subjects less harshly than the Babylonians. They followed a tolerant attitude toward other religions and adopted many Mesopotamian gods, establishing a tradition of tolerance in the region.

The Assyrian Empire and Regional Supremacy

For several centuries after Hittite power declined, no one group dominated Mesopotamia for long. In 1115 B.C.E., however, the Assyrians (uh-SEER-e-uhns), named for their major city, Ashur, created an empire in western Asia larger than any before, the first that was more than a collection of city-states. They did this in three ways: by creating a large, well-organized, and balanced military; by systematically using terror against enemies; and by devising methods of bureaucratic organization that later empires, especially the Persian, imitated. One of the greatest kings, Tiglath-pileser (TIG-lath-pih-LEE-zuhr) III (745–727 B.C.E.), conquered the entire eastern shore of the Mediterranean as far south as Gaza. Later Assyrian rulers added much of Egypt to the empire. One Assyrian king described himself with some accuracy as "obedient to his gods and receiving the tribute of the four corners of the world."[11]

Assyrian armies made war serious business. Using iron weapons while their enemies still relied on softer bronze ones, the Assyrians launched armies of over 50,000 men that were carefully divided into a core of infantrymen aided by cavalry and horse-drawn chariots. In addition to fighting traditional battles in the open, the Assyrians conducted sieges in which they used battering rams and tunnels against the city walls of their enemies. They also employed guerrilla, or irregular hit-and-run, tactics when fighting in the forests or mountains.

Assyrian kings created a systematic bureaucracy by increasing the number of administrative districts and making local officials responsible only to the kings. They ruled over several million people in the Tigris-Euphrates heartland alone. To improve their administrative control, the rulers used horsemen to create an early version of the "pony express," which allowed them to send messages hundreds of miles within a week. Some kings were both brutal, and learned. Ashurbanipal (ah-shur-BAH-nugh-pahl) (680–627 B.C.E.) founded a great library to collect tablets from all over the country, and boasted of his learning. He noted that, in school, he learned to solve complex mathematical problems and discovered the "hidden treasure" of writing, enabling him to read tablets in Sumerian and Akkadian.

Violence and the Fall of the Assyrians

The Assyrians were most remembered, and deplored, for their brutality, which ultimately contributed to their downfall. King Ashurbanipal bragged about mutilating and burning prisoners. After destroying the state of Elam, he boasted that "like the onset of a terrible hurricane I overwhelmed Elam [a state in southwestern Iran]. I cut off the head of Teumman, their braggart king. In countless numbers I killed his warriors." As to the capital city, "I destroyed it, I devastated it, I burned it with fire."[12] Soldiers routinely looted cities, destroyed crops, and both flailed and impaled their enemies. To prevent revolts, the Assyrians often simply moved people to another part of the vast empire. For example, according to legends, inhabitants of one of the two Hebrew kingdoms were sent to Mesopotamia, where they disappeared from history (see Chapter 3). The rulers sent thousands of people from Syria to the mountains east of the Tigris, and many Mesopotamians to the Mediterranean coast. And yet the Assyrians also tolerated other religions, a policy that allowed the Hebrew faith to survive the conquest of their state.

The terror tactics understandably undermined Assyrian popularity. In 612 B.C.E., a coalition including the Chaldeans (kal-DEE-uhns) (also known as neo-Babylonians) captured the Assyrian capital at Nineveh (NIN-uh-vuh). Soon the Assyrian Empire collapsed, but the Chaldeans, who formed the last Mesopotamian empire, adopted the Assyrian administrative system. The Chaldeans retained most of the Assyrian territories and flourished from 626 B.C.E. until they were conquered by the much larger Persian Empire in 539 B.C.E. Their most memorable ruler, Nebuchadnezzar (NAB-oo-kuhd-nez-uhr) II (r. 605–562 B.C.E.), a brutal strongman, rebuilt Babylon and adorned it with magnificent palaces and the elaborate terraced "hanging gardens," which were built to please one of his wives and which became famous throughout the ancient world. Nebuchadnezzar led the conquest of the remaining Hebrew kingdom in 586 B.C.E.

Not all of these ancient peoples disappeared from history. Although most scholars consider their direct ancestry doubtful, today several million people, mostly Christians in Syria and Iraq, identify themselves as Assyrians or Chaldeans, and they speak an ancient Semitic language. Many emigrated in recent decades to North America and Australia.

Mesopotamian Law

Several very different documents tell us much about Mesopotamian life and beliefs. The eighteenth-century B.C.E. law code of Hammurabi gives us a good look at the social structures of this early urban society (see Profile: Hammurabi the Lawgiver). Hammurabi's code makes clear both what people valued and the value of people, and it also reveals much about society. The code is also one of the earliest systematic records we have of how ancient peoples viewed laws, government, and social norms.

The code probably reflected a high crime rate in the cities, no doubt because of the tremendous gap between rich and

HAMMURABI
THE LAWGIVER

No person personifies Mesopotamian society better than Hammurabi, a Babylonian king (r. 1792–1750 B.C.E.) who was also at times a diplomat, warrior, builder of temples, digger of canals, and, most famously, lawgiver. Many surviving tablets, inscriptions, and letters, some from Hammurabi himself, made the king and his era the best documented in Mesopotamian history. He seems to have been a good administrator and able general who governed fairly and efficiently. Like other Mesopotamian kings, Hammurabi probably had a chief queen and various concubines, as well as several sons and daughters.

When Hammurabi became king, Babylon (which meant "gateway of the gods" in Akkadian) was an insignificant city-state. To expand its power, Hammurabi shrewdly allied with the powerful king of Ashur, probably by becoming a vassal, and allowed him to conquer some nearby cities. For some years Hammurabi's small domain remained one of many rival states, as noted by one of his officials: "There is no king who by himself is strongest. Ten or fifteen kings follow Hammurabi." Like other kings, Hammurabi had intelligence agents in other cities keeping him abreast of important developments such as pending alliances and troop movements. A spy for another king became close to him, writing that "whenever Hammurabi is perturbed by some matter, he always sends for me. He tells me whatever is troubling him, and all of the important information I continually report to my lord." After his army repulsed an invasion by a coalition of rivals, a confident Hammurabi engaged in a long series of wars that added all of southern Mesopotamia and then much of the north to his kingdom. Finally he conquered the strongest power, his former ally Ashur.

Kingship brought responsibilities. His letters reveal Hammurabi sitting in an office at his palace, dictating to a secretary who recorded his orders or thoughts with a reed stylus on a clay tablet. Most letters conveyed commands to governors. Messengers brought letters from officials, which the secretary read aloud. In his replies, Hammurabi tried to resolve problems, for example, suggesting ways to clear a flooded shipping channel, warning delinquent tax collectors of their obligations, punishing corrupt officials, improving agricultural productivity, or protecting frontiers. He also held daily audiences for petitioners seeking justice. Many decisions concerned temple property and administration, indicating the link between church and state.

Hammurabi realized the need to have uniform laws in his diverse country. He compiled older laws, recent legal decisions, and social customs, arranged them systematically, and placed them on an 8-foot block of basalt stone in the temple of Babylon's patron god, Marduk. At the top, an artist pictured Hammurabi receiving the symbols of kingship from Shamash, the sun-god and lawgiver. The code of 282 laws informed citizens of their rights and demonstrated to both gods and people that the king was doing his job to uphold justice in a moral universe.

For close to four millennia, the principles of this ancient Mesopotamian law code have intrigued us. The code reflected the harsh views of the era. It mandated two kinds of punishments, a

Hammurabi Receiving the Law Code The top of this stela, which is 7 feet high, shows the powerful sun-god, Shamash, on his throne bestowing the famous law code to King Hammurabi. (Hirmer Verlag Munchen)

monetary penalty and a retribution in kind, and the harshness of the punishment depended on the class of the people involved. The code recognized three social classes: nobles and landowners, commoners, and slaves. Many of Hammurabi's laws discouraged burglary by prescribing instant death for those caught. This emphasis may have reflected the fact that mud-brick homes were not very secure. On the other hand, prostitution was legal. Some laws protected women and children from abuse and arbitrary treatment. For example, a husband who divorced his wife because she bore no sons had to return the dowry she brought into the marriage and forfeited the money he had given her parents for a bridal price. Since the Hebrews borrowed some of these laws, often in modified form, and passed them into Christian and Islamic traditions, Hammurabi's legacy remains influential today.

THINKING ABOUT THE PROFILE

1. How did Hammurabi increase the power of Babylon?

2. What were the purposes of his great law code?

Note: Quotations from William H. Stiebing, Jr., *Ancient Near Eastern History and Culture* (New York: Longman, 2003), pp. 88–89.

also contain many toys made from clay or wood, indicating a prosperous society that valued leisure for children.

Harappan society had unusual gender relations for that era, different from the rigid patriarchies that characterized Mesopotamia or China as governments grew more powerful. Apparently Harappan husbands moved into their wives' households after marriage, a practice that suggests a matrilineal system. Yet, some practices harmed women. One set of double graves suggests that at least some Harappans practiced a form of *sati* (suh-TEE), the custom of a widow killing herself by jumping onto the funeral pyre as her dead husband is being cremated.

Scholars debate the identity of the Harappan people. Most believe that those who created the society spoke a **Dravidian** (druh-VID-ee-uhn) language, although speakers of Iranian and possibly Indo-European languages may also have lived there. The term *Dravidian* refers to a specific language family, as well as to the people who speak these languages. Most modern Dravidian speakers live in southern India, where they are the great majority of the population.

Culture and Religion Harappan city-dwellers developed an artistic appreciation, mixing art with religion and even commerce. Harappans made small, square, clay seals, possibly used by merchants for branding their wares. Some of the seals contain brilliant portraits of indigenous animals, including bulls and water buffaloes as well as the tigers, elephants, and rhinoceros that inhabited the forests in ancient times. Pottery shows animal and geometric motifs. Small bronze statues of dancers suggest the Harappans enjoyed dance.

Most scholars argue that the Harappans created a written language by at least 2600 B.C.E., although a few believe abstract symbols or graffiti on pots may indicate an even more ancient writing. There are also some historians who question whether the Harappans had a true writing system comparable to the Mesopotamians and ancient Chinese. By Harappan times the seals, pottery, and various clay tablets contained some four hundred different signs that were completely unrelated to the scripts of Mesopotamia and Egypt. Perhaps the writing represents a mix of images representing concepts and phonetic symbols. Unfortunately, modern scholars have not been able to decipher the Indus language. Most likely many of the signs represent the personal or business names of merchants, and perhaps the commodities being sold.

Some Harappan religious notions contributed to Hinduism (HIN-doo-ism), a religion that developed after Harappan times. For example, one of the seals features a human figure sitting in a yogalike position, surrounded by various animals. He wears a horned headdress, an apparent tiger skin on his torso, and bangles on his arms. The figure also appears to have multiple faces, a regular feature of later Hindu icons, and may depict what later became the great Hindu god **Shiva** (SHEEV-uh) in one of his major roles as "Lord of the Beasts."

Harappan Seal The seal from Mohenjo-Daro features a humped bull. The writing at the top has yet to be deciphered. (J. M. Kenoyer/Courtesy, Department of Archaeology and Museums, Government of Pakistan)

Harappans apparently already worshiped Shiva in his dual role as god of destruction and of fertility and the harvest. Possibly the later Hindu notions of reincarnation and the endless wheel of life derived from Harappan beliefs.

Mother-goddess worship seems also to have been prominent in Harappan religious life, as it was in the Fertile Crescent and ancient Europe. Many small clay figurines have a female theme, and some figurines with exaggerated breasts and hips may have represented the mother goddess. Such artistic representations of voluptuous female deities remain common today in India. The goddesses symbolized earth and the life-bearing nature of women. Whereas a female orientation largely disappeared or became a minor element in the religions of many other societies, it remained prominent in India as Hinduism evolved over the centuries.

The Harappan Economy and the Wider World

The Harappan cities were hubs tied to surrounding regions, especially southwestern and Central Asia, through trade and transportation networks that fostered extensive contact. This foreign trade grew out of a vibrant and diverse local economy based on the cultivation of the staples barley and wheat and the production of cotton and metal products. Harappans were also among the pioneers in using animals for economic support. These innovations helped Harappan society to remain stable and prosperous for hundreds of years.

A highly sophisticated irrigation system and animal husbandry aided farming. Harappans or their ancestors domesticated the camel, zebu (oxen), elephant, and, perhaps most importantly, the chicken and water buffalo. The raising of fowl enriched the diet, and water buffalo and zebu greatly aided farming as draft animals. Possibly the Harappans worshiped

---

Dravidian A language family whose speakers are the great majority of the population in southern India.

Shiva The Hindu god of destruction and of fertility and the harvest.

these two animals; if they did, this worship may have been the basis for the later respect accorded cows in Hinduism.

Harappans invented cotton cloth and learned to produce cotton textiles for clothing, one of ancient India's major gifts to the world. For many centuries, cotton spinning and weaving remained the most significant Indian industry, producing materials for eager markets both at home and abroad. Cotton was probably a chief item in the interregional trading system, and it was shipped in bulk to Mesopotamia. Since there were few metals in the Indus Basin, the Harappans had to develop external sources of supply. With the metals obtained in exchange for cotton and other products, metallurgists made tools and art works of copper, bronze, and stone.

The desirable Harappan agricultural and manufactured products led to extensive foreign trade that linked India with the wider world of western and Central Asia. A huge dock, massive granaries, and specialized factories at the coastal port of Lothal reflected a high-volume maritime trade. Some Harappan trade outposts have been found along the Indian Ocean coast as far west as today's Iran-Pakistan border. The Harappans traded with Jiroft in Iran. A continuous trade with Sumer was particularly brisk when the dynamic king Sargon of Akkad ruled that land. Many Harappan seals found at the Mesopotamian city of Ur suggest a steady trade for over 300 years, between 2300 and 2000 B.C.E. Bahrain Island in the Persian Gulf functioned as a major crossroads for the Harappan-Sumerian trade. Indeed, the Persian Gulf was a major contact zone where ancient communication networks linked with each other and where ideas, technologies, and products from a wide area were exchanged.

Many different products were traded through these networks. The Harappans exported surplus food, cotton, timber products, copper, and gold, as well as luxury items such as pearls, precious stone products, ivory combs, beads, spices, peacock feathers, and inlay goods made from shell or bone. Many of these items found their way as far west as Palestine. The Harappans imported precious stones from southern India and silver, turquoise, and tin from Persia and Afghanistan. The imports from Mesopotamia probably included various perishable commodities.

The Decline and Collapse of Harappan Society

Eventually, Harappan society declined, for reasons not altogether clear. Sometime between 1900 and 1750 B.C.E. a combination of factors disrupted the urban environment and diminished the quality of life of this once wealthy, highly efficient, and powerful society. By 1700 B.C.E. most of the Harappan cities had been destroyed or abandoned, although a considerable rural population remained. The decay is obvious in the archaeological excavations. Seals and writing began to disappear around 1900 B.C.E. The careful grid pattern for city streets was abandoned, the drainage systems deteriorated, and even home sizes were reduced. Some evidence points to plundering and banditry. Squatters from elsewhere may have occupied the declining cities.

Harappan decline may have resulted from several factors. Perhaps the Harappans overextended their economic networks, putting too much pressure on the land and exhausting their resources. Some evidence points to ecological catastrophes resulting from climate change, deforestation, increased flooding, excessive irrigation of marginal lands, and soil deterioration. Apparently rainfall decreased significantly between 2000 and 1500 B.C.E., and one major river seems to have dried up entirely. These catastrophes probably led to economic breakdown. The crop surpluses that had long sustained the cities disappeared, and people abandoned farms. Perhaps disease epidemics weakened the population.

The end of some of the Indus Valley cities may have been sudden, the result perhaps of a disastrous flood. Some scholars think that sometime between 1900 and 1700 B.C.E., volcanic or earthquake activity in the mountains to the north generated a mud slide that may have temporarily dammed the Indus River or one of its tributaries, changing its course and unleashing an awesome flood that quickly overwhelmed low-lying cities and their surrounding farms. The hoards of jewelry, skeletons buried in debris, and cooking pots found strewn across kitchens indicate hastily abandoned homes. Floods were not unusual, and many people may have been trapped by such a catastrophe. Some centuries later a Greek visitor reported seeing a land with more than a thousand cities and villages abandoned after the Indus shifted to a new riverbed. The rising floodwaters may have been accompanied by more earthquakes, a double blow. The chaos of the last days spread rapidly along the river. Harappa, located on higher ground, and some other cities survived a while longer, although with much reduced populations.

The fate of the Harappan people and their cultures is unclear. Many remained in the area, and some Harappan material technology and symbolism survive there today. Some cities well east of the Indus Valley remained populated for several more centuries, practicing modified but diverse forms of Harappan culture until around 1300 B.C.E. Many Harappans may have migrated into central and southern India, mixing with local Dravidian populations. They carried with them a culture, technology, and agriculture that contributed to the Indian society to come. Whatever the causes of their decline, the calamities left the remaining Indus peoples weak and unable to resist later migrations of peoples from outside.

Central Asian Environments and Oxus Cities

Central Asia is the vast area of plains (**steppes**), deserts, and mountains that stretches from the Ural Mountains and Caspian Sea eastward to Tibet, western China, and Mongolia. Before modern times Central Asians played a role in history far greater than their relatively small populations would suggest, not only as invaders and sometimes conquerors but also as middlemen in the long-distance trade that developed on the land routes between China, India, the Middle East, and Europe.

Much of Central Asia offered a harsh living environment suitable only for the nomadic way of life. It was inhabited largely by people speaking Ural-Altaic languages, including various Turkish and Mongol tongues. Many different peoples speaking

steppes The plains of Central Asia.

Hindu Values in the Bhagavad Gita

The *Bhagavad Gita*, a philosophical poem in the *Mahabharata*, helped shape the ethical traditions of India while providing Hindus with a practical guide to everyday life. The following excerpt is part of a dialogue between the god Krishna (Vishnu) and the poem's conflicted hero, the warrior Arjuna (are-JUNE-ah), on the eve of a great battle in which Arjuna will slaughter his uncles, cousins, teachers, and friends. The reading summarizes some of Krishna's advice in justifying the battle. Krishna suggests that Arjuna must follow his destiny, for while the physical body is impermanent, the soul is eternal. The slain will be reborn. Furthermore, humans are responsible for their own destiny through their behavior and mental discipline. They also, like Arjuna, need to fulfill their obligations to society.

The wise grieve neither for the living nor for the dead. There has never been a time when you and I and the kings gathered here have not existed, nor will there ever be a time when we will cease to exist. As the same person inhabits the body through childhood, youth, and old age, so too at the time of death he attains another body. The wise are not deluded by these changes.

When the senses contact sense objects, a person experiences cold or heat, pleasure or pain. These experiences are fleeting; they come and go. Bear them patiently. . . . Those who are not affected by these changes, who are the same in pleasure and pain, are truly wise and fit for immortality. Assert your strength and realize this!

The impermanent has no reality; reality lies in the eternal. Those who have seen the boundary between these two have attained the end of all knowledge. Realize that which pervades the universe and is indestructible; no power can affect this unchanging, imperishable reality. The body is mortal but he who dwells in the body is immortal and immeasurable. . . . As a man abandons worn-out clothes and acquires new ones, so when the body is worn out a new one is acquired by the Self, who lives within. . . . Death is inevitable for the living; birth is inevitable for the dead. Since these are unavoidable, you should not sorrow. . . .

Now listen to the principles of yoga [mental and physical discipline to free the soul]. By practicing these you can break through the bonds of karma. On this path effort never goes to waste, and there is no failure. . . . When you keep thinking about sense objects, attachment comes. Attachment breeds desire, the lust of possession that burns to anger. . . .

They are forever free who renounce all selfish desires and break free from the ego-cage of "I," "me," and "mine" to be united with the Lord. This is the supreme state. Attain to this, and pass from death to immortality. . . . Strive constantly to serve the welfare of the world; by devotion to selfless work one attains the supreme goal of life. Do your work with the welfare of others always in mind.

THINKING ABOUT THE READING

1. What key aspects of Hindu thought are revealed in the poem?
2. How do the attitudes toward life, death, and desire influence the behavior of individuals?
3. What are some of the viewpoints in this ancient poem that might be considered universal in their appeal?

Source: Lynn H. Nelson and Patrick Peebles, eds., *Classics of Eastern Thought* (San Diego: Harcourt Brace Jovanovich, 1991), pp. 43–47. From *The Bhagavad Gita*, trans. by Eknath Easwaran, founder of the Blue Mountain Center of Meditation, copyright 1855. Reprinted by permission of the Nilgiri Press: www.easwaran.org.

Indo-Aryan Social Life and Gender Relations

The Vedas reveal some of the expectations and attitudes of ancient Indian society. For example, contained within the *Mahabharata* is a philosophical poem called the **Bhagavad Gita** (BAA-guh-vad GEE-tuh) ("Lord's Song"), the most treasured piece of ancient Hindu literature (see Witness to the Past: Hindu Values in the *Bhagavad Gita*). It encourages people to do their duty to their superiors and kinsmen resolutely and unselfishly. It also explains that death is not a time of grief because the soul is indestructible. The other great ancient epic, the *Ramayana*, resembles the *Odyssey* of Homer in that it tells of a hero's wanderings while his wife remains chaste and loyal. The *Ramayana* conveys insights into the character of court life, which apparently involved endless intrigues.

We know something also of gender relations in Indo-Aryan society. The *Ramayana* illustrates the early Hindu notion of perfect manhood and womanhood through the main characters: Rama, the husband, and Sita (SEE-tuh), his wife. The couple demonstrate mutual loyalty, devotion, truthfulness, and self-sacrifice. But Sita is also patient, faithful, and pure in supporting her husband and family. The Sita ideal strongly influenced cultural expectations of womanhood, and Sita became a familiar figure of strength and affection, especially in north India.

Compared to the Aryan-dominated north, women seem to have enjoyed a higher status in mostly Dravidian south India. There both matriarchal and matrilineal traditions persisted for centuries, and goddesses remained especially central to religious life. Dravidian women also exercised some economic power and owned property. But even in the north during the Vedic Age, some women mastered the Vedas and mixed freely with men.

Bhagavad Gita ("Lord's Song") A poem in the *Mahabharata* that is the most treasured piece of ancient Hindu literature.

Indo-Aryan Technology and Economy

Indo-Aryan technology derived from both foreign and local developments. The Hittites might have passed iron technology along to fresh waves of Indo-Europeans migrating into India. Certainly the Aryans used iron, initially for weapons and horse harnesses, once they reached iron-rich districts in the Ganges region around 1000 B.C.E. But some metalworking derived from pre-Aryan cultures, which worked bronze and used gold in jewelry and ritual sacrifices.

Soon after they arrived in India the Aryans made the transition from a largely nomadic pastoral economy to a combination of pastoral and agricultural pursuits that emphasized grains like barley and wheat. One Veda prays: "Successfully let the good ploughshares' thrust part the earth, successfully let the ploughman follow the beasts of draft."[20] The use of plows and the expansion of irrigated agriculture greatly increased the available food supply and thus fostered population growth. India's population in 500 B.C.E. has been estimated at 25 million, including 15 million in the Ganges Valley.

Hinduism: A New Religion of Diverse Roots

Although Indian religion has changed much since the Harappans, it has remained unique. Nothing in the Middle East or Europe remotely resembles basic Indian beliefs such as reincarnation. These are part of the bedrock of Indian society, molding thought and daily lives. What modern Indians would clearly recognize as Hinduism had probably not fully formed until the second half of the first millennium B.C.E., and perhaps not until the early centuries of the Common Era. But the foundations were clearly established in ancient times. Hinduism can be seen historically as a synthesis of Aryan beliefs with Harappan and other Dravidian traditions that developed over many centuries. As the religion became more complex, it probed ever more deeply into cosmic mysteries. Eventually this spiritual quest resulted in a period of ferment and questioning.

Religious Synthesis The religious system became one of the richest and most complex in the world, with gods, devotions, and celebrations drawn from various regional and village cultures. The Aryans gradually turned from their old tribal gods to deities of probable Harappan origin such as Shiva. Hence the rise of the great gods of Hinduism: *Brahma* (BRA-ma) (the Creator of life); *Vishnu* (VISH-noo)(the Preserver of life); and *Shiva* (among other functions, the destroyer of life). In popular worship Vishnu and Shiva have had the most devotees. Vishnu is a benevolent deity who works continually for the welfare of the world. Shiva personifies the life force and embodies both constructive and destructive power.

Earlier Aryan nature worship was soon transformed by a relentless desire to understand and control the larger cosmic forces. Hinduism never developed a rigid core of beliefs uniting all followers; instead, it loosely linked together diverse practices and cults that shared a reverence for the Vedas. For over 3,000 years ago Indians posed questions and offered possible answers to cosmic mysteries that even today remain little understood. The Vedic thinkers were influenced by pre-Aryan meditation techniques and mystical practices of possible Harappan origin, such as those that were later known as *yoga*. In the eternal quest for divine favor, the Hindus came to believe that everyone must behave properly so that the universe can function in an orderly manner. They came to see human existence as temporary and fleeting and only the realm of the gods as eternal.

Religious Explorations The Vedas underwent three major stages of development to become accepted as revealed literature. The earliest stage included the poems and hymns in the *Rig Veda* and several other collections. A half millennium later, from around 1000 to 700 B.C.E., a series of prose commentaries on the earlier Vedas appeared. They elaborated on the meaning of the Vedic literature and also prescribed proper procedures for sacrificing to and worshiping the gods. These commentaries are called the **Brahmanas** (BRA-ma-nus), since they emphasize the central role of the priests, or brahmans ("those who chant the sacred words"). At this time, the prevailing religion can be termed Brahmanism. The authors of the *Ramayana* portrayed the powerful force of religious law in dictating proper behavior, even for the monarch.

Later still, between 800 and 600 B.C.E., a third group of more philosophical writings appeared, mostly in the form of 108 poetic dialogues known as the **Upanishads** (oo-PAHN-ih-shahds)("sitting around a teacher"). These writings, which speculated on the ultimate truth about the creation of life, offered a striking contrast to the emphasis on ritual, devotion, and ethics in the older works. One mystic pleaded, "From the unreal lead me to the real. From the darkness lead me to light. From death lead me to immortality."[21] These writings also gave women more importance; for example, the dialogues include the story of an exceptionally learned female. The *Upanishads* probably came out of the same atmosphere of questioning, ferment, and rebellion against priestly power that produced the great religious teacher Buddha in the sixth century B.C.E.

The religious atmosphere of ancient India seems to have been dynamic, with growing tensions between competing ideas about the nature of existence and appropriate human behavior. The *Ramayana* contrasts the luxury-filled decadence of the royal courts with the austere existence of hermit-sages dwelling in the forest and practicing forms of meditation and mysticism. By the middle of the first millennium B.C.E. the debate and disenchantment that produced the *Upanishads* resulted in much more far-reaching critiques of the brahman-led system. The movements that developed out of this ferment transformed the framework of Indian religion, fostering both Buddhism and the modified form of Brahmanism known today as Hinduism, as we shall see in Chapter 7.

Brahmanas Commentaries on the Vedas that emphasize the role of priests (brahmans).

Upanishads Ancient Indian philosophical writings that speculated on the ultimate truth about the creation of life.

SECTION SUMMARY
- Aryan and local cultures mixed together over the centuries and eventually produced a unique four-tiered caste system.
- The *Bhagavad Gita,* which emphasizes one's earthly duty and the soul's immortality, became the most treasured piece of Indian literature.
- Hinduism developed over many centuries but never became a rigid belief structure.
- The philosophical *Upanishads* represented a departure from the emphasis on priestly ritual.

Online Study Center ACE the Test

Chapter Summary

Mesopotamian society and early Indian society were two of humankind's first experiments with farming, cities, and states. While varying in size, complexity, and duration, both used technologies that were unheard of in Neolithic times. These ancient societies also developed different religious notions, social systems, and political structures. They were shaped, at least in part, by the challenges and opportunities of flood-prone river valleys: Mesopotamian society arose in the Fertile Crescent between the Tigris and Euphrates Rivers, and Harappan society arose in the Indus River Valley. Mesopotamians introduced the first cities and states, the cuneiform system of writing, bronze metalworking, mathematics, and science. Their many kingdoms were united under several different empires. Mesopotamia was also part of the early trade networks linking the Mediterranean Basin with India. Such connections among societies were a crucial and continuing part of history.

One of the oldest Eurasian urban societies emerged in northwest India, where the Harappan people built peaceful, bustling, and well-planned cities. They produced cotton products and developed sophisticated sanitation systems. The Harappans also participated in a trading network that reached into the Fertile Crescent and Central Asia, where the Oxus cities flourished for several centuries. After the Harappan collapse, Aryan migrants established political control. The mixing of Harappan and Aryan cultures shaped a new Indian society. This Indo-Aryan synthesis established the foundation for a caste system and for the religion of Hinduism, whose holy books interweaved many Harappan gods with Aryan stories and poems.

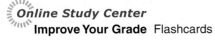

Online Study Center
Improve Your Grade Flashcards

Key Terms

Fertile Crescent	Harappan	Aryans
ziggurat	Dravidian	Vedas
patriarchy	Shiva	Sanskrit
cuneiform	steppes	*Mahabharata*
Indo-Aryan synthesis	vaisyas	*Bhagavad Gita*
brahmans	sudras	*Brahmanas*
kshatriyas	caste system	*Upanishads*
	pariahs	

Suggested Reading

Books

Allchin, F. R. *The Archaeology of Early Historic South Asia: The Emergence of Cities and States*. Cambridge: Cambridge University Press, 1995. A scholarly overview.

Basham, A. L. *The Wonder That Was India*. 3rd ed. London: Macmillan, 1968 (reprinted 1999 by Rupa and Company, New Delhi). An older study but still the best survey of premodern India.

Bottero, Jean. *Everyday Life in Ancient Mesopotamia*. Baltimore: Johns Hopkins University Press, 2001. Summarizes recent discoveries about Mesopotamian social and cultural life.

Crawfurd, Harriet. *Sumer and the Sumerians*. 2nd ed. Cambridge: Cambridge University Press, 2004. An up-to-date and interdisciplinary summary of the achievements of the Sumerians.

Dunstan, William E. *The Ancient Near East*. New York: Harcourt Brace, 1998. Designed for the general reader, this work makes sense of the confusing array of states and empires in western Asia.

Kenoyer, Jonathan Mark. *Ancient Cities of the Indus Valley Civilization*. New York: Oxford University Press, 1998. A valuable, well-illustrated summary of the most recent discoveries.

McIntosh, Jane. *A Peaceful Realm: The Rise and Fall of the Indus River Civilization*. Boulder, Colo.: Westview, 2001. A comprehensive, well-illustrated survey of the Harappans, based on recent archaeological research.

Sandars, N. K. (translator). *The Epic of Gilgamesh*. New York: Penguin Books, 1972. Easy introduction to the ancient Mesopotamian world view.

Stiebing, William H. *Ancient Near Eastern History and Culture*. New York: Longman, 2003. An up-to-date survey of ancient western Asia, Egypt, and the eastern Mediterranean.

Thapar, Romila. *Early India from the Origins to AD 1300*. Berkeley: University of California Press, 2002. A valuable revision of the standard history of early India, detailed and comprehensive.

Wolpert, Stanley. *A New History of India*. 7th ed. New York: Oxford University Press, 2003. One of the most readable survey texts.

Websites

Exploring Ancient World Cultures
(http://eawe.evansville.edu/index/htm). Excellent site run by Evansville University, with essays and links on the ancient Near East and Europe.

Indus Valley Civilization
(http://ancienthistory.about.com/cs/indusvalleyciv/). Gives access to many sites and links on ancient India, run by About.com.

Internet Ancient History Sourcebook
(http://www.fordham.edu/halsall/ancient/asbook.html). Exceptionally rich collection of links and primary source readings.

Internet Indian History Sourcebook
(http://www.fordham.edu/halsall/india/indiasbook.html). An invaluable collection of sources and links on ancient India.

CHAPTER 3

Ancient Societies in Africa and the Mediterranean, 5000–600 B.C.E.

Online Study Center

This icon will direct you to interactive activities and study materials on the website: college.hmco.com/pic/lockard1e

Abu Simbel The great temple with its colossal statues at Abu Simel overlooking the Nile River in Egypt was built as a monument to honor the powerful thirteenth century B.C.E. pharaoh Rameses the Great, who presided over empire building and economic prosperity. (George Holton/Photo Researcher, Inc.)

They adopted Egyptian customs and wrote their language in hieroglyphics. Finally, Egypt was conquered by the Assyrians in the seventh century and by the Persians in the late sixth century B.C.E.

Egyptian Society, Economy, and Culture

What were some unique features of Egyptian society?

Like other ancient societies, the Egyptians had many distinctive customs, technologies, and beliefs. Compared to most places, Egypt was a generally tolerable place to live. Perhaps because of the Nile inundation each fall, Egyptians of all social classes, blessed with many centuries of good crops, seemed to view themselves as favored. One writer celebrated the Nile Delta as "full of everything good—its ponds with fish and its lakes with birds. Its meadows are verdant, its melons abundant. Its granaries are so full of barley that they come near to the sky."[8] Although many peasants and workers worked very hard and had far fewer comforts than those in the upper classes, they at least had a life that was secure and a routine that was predictable. In addition, women enjoyed considerable freedom. Finally, although Egyptian cities had few close neighbors that could attack them, they could grow rich by trading with many distant suppliers and markets.

Social Life and Organization

Like other societies with cities and states, Egypt was divided into classes. During the Old Kingdom members of each social class had different responsibilities and roles. The head of this social hierarchy, the pharaoh, theoretically owned everything in the kingdom and had particular estates reserved for him in each of the provinces. The priests and nobles owned 80 to 90 percent of all the usable land (see Profile: Hekanakhte, an Egyptian Priest). However, the scribe, or "writing man," held the most honored upper-class occupation. "Be a scribe," a young man was advised in one

source. "Your limbs will be sleek. Your hands will grow soft. You will go forth in white clothes with courtiers saluting you."[9]

Not all enjoyed such amenities. Peasants maintained the irrigation works and paid taxes that could be as high as 20 percent of their crop. At the bottom of society were slaves, perhaps 10 or 15 percent of the population. They were mostly prisoners of war and foreigners, including Nubians and people from Palestine, among them some Hebrews. Most worked in the homes of the wealthy, in the palaces, or on temple estates. Some helped build pyramids and monuments.

Influenced by the Nile environment, Egyptians valued security and regularity more than social equality. Since it was relatively easy to plant in the soft soil left after the floods, they did not need heavy plows. After harvesting men hunted and fished in the marshes. Despite occasional grueling labor on construction projects, peasants showed little discontent except during the troubled intermediate periods. Although the rich ate meat and the poor had beer, bread, and beans ("beer and bread" was an ancient Egyptian greeting, much like "have a good day"), most people thought themselves lucky. Their massive tombs and mummies may seem gloomy to us today, but their temples were once bright with paint and gold, and people seemingly enjoyed life so much they wished to perpetuate it in tombs equipped with the trappings for everyday life.

Numerous temple paintings show people at work and play. Egyptians told bawdy stories (often about their gods), played musical instruments such as flutes, pipes, and harps, got drunk, and gave boring lectures to children. Both men and women used cosmetics to enhance their physical attractions, massaging themselves with scented oils and decorating their eyes with colorful eyeliners. In seeking beauty aids, Egyptians became the world's first chemists. Young people wrote sentimental poems to sweethearts. One love poem by a girl reported on a swim with her lover:

> Diving and swimming with you here,
> Gives me the chance I've been waiting for,
> To show my looks,
> Before an appreciative eye.
> My bathing suit of the best material.
> Nothing can keep me from my love,
> Standing on the other shore.[10]

Scholars debate whether stone carvings in a tomb that show two men embracing and kissing indicates a homosexual relationship or instead portrays identical or conjoined ("Siamese") twins.

Gender roles were flexible, and women had more independence and rights, especially in law, than women in any other ancient society. Hatshepsut was the most famous of at least four women pharaohs. By the New Kingdom the status of Egyptian women was higher than that of women in Mesopotamia or later in classical Greek and Roman society, and legal distinctions among persons seemed to be based more on class than on gender. A woman could inherit, bequeath, and administer property, conclude legal settlements, take cases to court, initiate divorce, and testify. She could bring a lawsuit against another woman or a man and have a real chance of winning. Some women could probably read and write. Many were

HEKANAKHTE,
AN EGYPTIAN PRIEST

Hekanakhte (Heh-KHAN-akt) who lived about 2000 B.C.E., was the *ka*-priest of a chief government minister who had died a generation earlier. As a *ka*-priest, it was his duty to tend the tomb of his patron, near the city of Thebes, in order to protect the deceased individual's guardian spirit or soul (*ka*). Wealthy individuals, like the great minister Ipi whom Hekanakhte served, left money or other resources to support a priest who would perform these duties. If the *ka* were not honored with these ceremonial offerings, Egyptians feared that it would die a "second death" or be annihilated.

In this case, the minister Ipi had left a large estate to support Hekanakhte and his family. Hekanakhte also supervised other properties left to his care, and he had to be gone visiting them much of the year. We know much about him because during his absences he wrote many letters to his eldest son, Mersu. Mersu read and eventually discarded them in a local tomb, where they were forgotten but where the dry desert climate preserved them until they were discovered by an archaeologist in 1922. These letters give us an interesting picture of family life in the Middle Kingdom. We discover that Hekanakhte had a large family that included five sons, two of them married, and all of them living at home. He also supported his mother, a poor female relative, and a widowed daughter.

Perhaps because he had such a large household, Hekanakhte's letters to Mersu give advice on cultivating and tending the grain crops. Some of the letters were written during a bad year, when harvests were slim because of inadequate Nile flooding. The priest tells his son that he is sending some food, but he carefully lists what each family member is to receive. He tells Mersu to remind family members not to complain, since "half life is better than dying together." Hekanakhte orders that only those who work should get food and urges Mersu to "make the most of my land, strive to the uttermost, dig the ground deep with your noses." He also tells his son exactly what seeds to plant and where to plant them. And he warns his son not to overpay the help, saying that if he does, his own personal funds will be reduced. Trust between father and son seems to have been in short supply.

Family disputes in Hekanakhte's household were a frequent topic in these letters. Apparently Hekanakhte had spoiled Mersu's younger brother, Snerfu, because he constantly reminds Mersu to give this youngest son things he wants. In addition, Hekanakhte apparently decided late in life, after his wife died, to take a young concubine, Iutenhab (YOU-ten-hob), who disrupted the household with her many requests. In one letter, the priest tells his son to fire a maid who had offended Iutenhab. Given the nagging tone of many of Hekanakhte's letters to his long-suffering son, it may not surprise us that one of the letters found in the debris of the tomb had been left unopened.

THINKING ABOUT THE PROFILE

1. What were the duties of a *ka*-priest?
2. What do these letters tell us about family relationships in this social class?

Note: Quotations from Barbara Mertz, *Red Land, Black Land: Daily Life in Ancient Egypt* (New York: Dodd, Mead, 1978), p. 127.

Measuring and Recording the Egyptian Harvest This wall painting from a tomb in the city of Thebes shows officials and peasants figuring the size of the annual harvest. (Michael Holford)

involved in well-paying economic activities, and they were paid the same as men for the same work. Women weavers produced some of the finest cloth in world history. Wives also enjoyed rough equality with husbands and assumed the public and family responsibilities of their deceased spouses. Women served as doctors and priestesses, and a few women even held administrative positions. Despite all these exceptions, however, most women were wives and mothers, and public duties were normally reserved for men. An Old Kingdom sage advised men to "love your wife at home, as is proper. Fill her belly and clothe her back. Make her heart glad as long as you live. You should not judge her, or let her gain control."[11]

Cities, Trade, and Regional Networks

Mesopotamian cities had been trading centers almost from their beginnings. Egyptian cities, by contrast, were largely administrative centers created by the pharaoh to house tax collectors, artisans in government workshops, shopkeepers, and the priests who cared for the local temple. Even the larger cities such as Memphis and Thebes did not begin as centers for long-distance trade and commerce, since most trade involved the import of luxury goods by the wealthy. Also, Egyptian city-dwellers, unlike their Mesopotamian counterparts, did not think of themselves as attached to the city. They were, like all Egyptians, subjects of the pharaoh. Since the Nile floods were more predictable than those along the unruly Euphrates, fewer people were needed to manage the irrigation system. Therefore, more Egyptians lived in villages, and market towns were scattered up and down the river.

Yet, although the cities were not commercial centers, the Egyptians' long-distance trade systems were more wide-ranging than those of the Mesopotamians. Either directly or through intermediaries, Egyptians traded with sub-Saharan Africans as far south as the Congo River Basin, with the Berber peoples of Libya and Algeria to the west, with the societies along the Red Sea to the east, with Palestine, Phoenicia, and Mesopotamia to the northeast, and with southeastern Europe. Gold, semiprecious stones, and such exotic things as frankincense, myrrh, ivory, ostrich feathers, and monkeys came from sub-Saharan Africa through Nubia or via the Red Sea and were exchanged for furniture, silver, tools, paper, and linen. Egyptians mined copper in the nearby Sinai (SIGH-nigh) Peninsula and along the Red Sea coast, and the Nile Delta provided papyrus as well as waterfowl.

Science and Technology

The geometrical precision of the pyramids tells us that the ancient Egyptians understood some mathematics and physics. They knew enough to make the pyramids level and to match the corners of each pyramid with the four points of the compass. The Egyptians also used a solar calendar that divided the year into 365 days, using twelve months of thirty days each and adding five days at the end. This was more accurate than the Sumerian lunar calendar. Egyptian arithmetic, however, was less sophisticated than their calendar might suggest. They understood fractions, but they had no concept of zero and dealt with numbers only by adding them. In medicine, Egyptians used both surgery and herbal remedies to treat illnesses. They recognized that the heart

was a pump, were able to cure some eye diseases, and did some dental work. In science and mathematics generally, however, they had much technical skill but little theoretical understanding.

Modern observers still admire Egyptian technical skill in treating the dead. If pyramids are the first things that come to mind when we think of ancient Egypt, mummies are probably the second. Using a form of salt found abundantly in Egypt, and taking advantage of the extremely dry climate (which probably created the first mummies in the Nile valley by accident), Egyptian morticians were able to preserve human tissue well enough that the distinct features of individuals could be seen 4,000 years later.

Religion

Egyptian religious and moral beliefs included some two thousand gods and goddesses, most of them benevolent, many myths, and unique views of death. Like their Mesopotamian counterparts, the Egyptian gods were created to explain nature, but were also made in the image of humans and shared human weaknesses. Eventually they were seen as responsive to human needs. For instance, the twelfth-century B.C.E. pharaoh Rameses IV asked the gods to give him good health, a long reign, and strength to all his limbs.

The emphasis on preserving bodies indicates another chief feature of Egyptian religion, the belief that a person's soul could be united with his or her body after death, but only if the body was properly preserved. In the Old Kingdom, only pharaohs could expect this afterlife, which mirrored life on earth. By the Middle Kingdom, however, all who could afford some form of mummification and whose souls passed a final moral judgment after death were candidates for immortality. As a result, people devoted vast resources to this quest.

The most dramatic and long-lived of the Egyptian myths is the story of Osiris (oh-SIGH-ris) and his wife Isis (EYE-sis). One version describes Osiris as the god-king who originally established peace and justice on earth. By this act he incurred the jealousy of his brother Set, who murdered him by sealing him in a box and throwing it into the sea. Isis, grief-stricken, found the body of her husband washed ashore. With the help of other gods, she revived Osiris long enough for him to impregnate her. Their son Horus later took revenge on Set, and Osiris descended to the underworld, where he established justice there as he had done on earth. A famous Egyptian drawing from the *Book of the Dead*, which depicts the afterlife, shows Osiris weighing the heart of a dead princess against the symbol

Online Study Center **Improve Your Grade**
Primary Source: Egyptian Book of the Dead

The *Book of the Dead* describes a confession that the dead person is to repeat as part of this judgment by Osiris. This confession includes statements by the deceased indicating that he or she has not murdered or cheated anyone. The following affirmations by the person facing judgment also show the practical side of Egyptian religion:

I have not stolen temple property.
I have not harmed the food of the gods [left in temples].

I have not held up water in its season.
I have not dammed running water.
I have not put out a fire that should have stayed alight.[12]

Because of the *Book of the Dead,* the durability of the pyramids, other Egyptian tombs, and mummified remains, some scholars have viewed the ancient Egyptians as people preoccupied with death and the afterlife. However, the tombs are the only artifacts that remain because they were made of stone. The less durable mud-brick houses of most Egyptians, in which a great deal of activity took place, were washed away or dissolved into mud long ago. Thus the Egyptians were probably not as preoccupied with death as the physical remains suggest. They no doubt enjoyed life as much or more than other people and, like the hero in one Egyptian tale, considered their homeland the only place where they could be happy. Many wall paintings suggest that even the lower classes accepted their lot as part of the natural order of things and found ways to cope. They show farmers and herders telling jokes, women bringing them their lunches, children squabbling, and shepherds asleep under a tree, a dog or flask of beer beside them. If conditions became too harsh, the peasants and workers might move elsewhere or go on strike. They could find solace in religion and awe of the pharaoh who sat, as the gods ordained, at the apex of the social pyramid.

SECTION SUMMARY

- Though Egyptian society was divided into classes, with the rich enjoying lavish lifestyles, even the poor were relatively comfortable.

- Women had greater independence and rights in Egypt than in any other ancient society, but their roles were still quite limited.

- Ancient Egyptians had great technical skill in architecture, medicine, and preserving the dead, but little theoretical understanding of science and mathematics.

- Ancient Egyptians believed they could obtain immortality if their bodies were mummified and if they passed a moral judgment after death.

- Ancient Egyptians traded widely with societies in sub-Saharan Africa and western Asia.

 # The Roots of Sub-Saharan African Societies

How did environmental factors help shape ancient sub-Saharan African history?

Africa is the original homeland for all of humanity, and Egypt was only the best-known of the early farming societies and states which emerged on the continent. Africans fostered varied societies, some of which also built cities,

formed states, and became linked to each other and the wider world by growing networks. Just as the annual Nile floods fostered Egypt's distinctive development, so the environment also influenced the varied traditions of sub-Saharan Africans and helped or hindered their early development of farming and technology.

African Environments

Both geography and climate have shaped African history. Africa, with one-fifth of the earth's landmass, is the second-largest continent after Eurasia and occupies more space than the United States, Europe (excluding Russia), China, and India combined. The equator almost exactly bisects Africa, giving most of the continent a tropical climate. Lush rain forests have flourished along West Africa's Guinea coast and in the vast Congo River Basin in the heart of the continent. These forests and other areas near the equator are home to many insects, parasites, and bacteria that cause debilitating diseases like malaria, yellow fever, and sleeping sickness. Since the last is deadly to cattle and horses, it was impractical to use a plow or wheel in much of ancient Africa. Despite the common image of Africa as a vast jungle, most of the continent has long been parched desert or savannah grasslands. African weather can be erratic, with fluctuating and often unpredictable rains. In addition, rain quickly diminishes north and south of the equator, producing a huge dry zone that receives less than 10 inches of rain a year. The deserts and some of the grasslands have largely been occupied by pastoral societies and herds of large wild animals. In some regions the poor-quality soil has been easily eroded by overuse, and erosion has fostered low agricultural productivity. Nonetheless, early farmers cultivated the grassland-covered region known as the **Sudan** (soo-DAN), which stretches along the southern fringe of the Sahara Desert from the western tip of Africa to the Nile Basin, where the modern nation of Sudan is located south of Egypt.

Geography has often hindered communication. The eastern third of Africa includes extensive plateau and mountain regions, which in Ethiopia rise to 15,000 feet. Deep valleys and gorges complicate travel. Even so, in some plateau districts great lakes and volcanic soils have permitted denser populations. The eastern highlands also produced great river systems, including the Nile, the Congo (which drains the vast central African rain forests), and, in the south, the Zambezi (zam-BEE-zee). but all these rivers have numerous rapids and waterfalls that have limited boat travel. Only the Niger (NIGH-jer) River, which flows mostly through the flat West African plains, is navigable over large distances. Nor was maritime transportation easy in the past. Prevailing winds made it difficult to sail along the West African coast, and much of the African coast has sandbars that create great swells, making it difficult to land a boat. Furthermore, much of Africa's coastline is unbroken by bays, gulfs, and inland seas. Hence, along

---

Sudan A grassland region stretching along the southern fringe of the Sahara Desert from the western tip of Africa to the Nile valley.

the entire Atlantic coast, historically there have been no great natural harbors to serve as maritime hubs. Only along the eastern, Red Sea, and Mediterranean coasts did a few protected bays and prevailing winds favor seagoing trade.

The Expanding Sahara Desert

The catastrophic climatic change that created and expanded the Sahara Desert strongly shaped early African societies. The Sahara region was once a rich grazing land with lakes and rivers, occupied by a large human population that flourished from hunting, gathering, fishing, and some farming. Ancient rock art portrays people dancing, worshiping, riding chariots, and tending horses and cattle. The paintings endow women with dignity as they raise children, gather plants, and make baskets, pottery, and jewelry. The history of rainfall explains why **desertification**, the process by which productive land is transformed into mostly useless desert, set in. For several millennia the region became relatively wet. This pattern reached a peak in 3500 B.C.E., making settlement more attractive. Then, as rain patterns shifted southward again, the gradual "drying out" of the continent began. By 2000 B.C.E. the Sahara region was harsh desert, and animals and plants had disappeared along with the water. People contributed to this process by overgrazing marginal lands and burning forests to create grasslands. The same desertification processes continue today on the Sahara's southern fringe.

Desertification influenced societies. The Sahara was left largely to nomadic herders of cattle and other animals, and most other inhabitants migrated to the north and south or into the lower Nile valley. This migration may have helped generate ancient Egyptian development. Eventually the Sahara marked a general boundary between the Berber and Semitic peoples along the southern Mediterranean coast and the darker-skinned peoples in the rest of Africa. But the desert barrier did not prevent considerable social, cultural, and genetic intermixing and exchange. For example, several West African spoken languages are closely related to Arabic.

The Origins of African Agriculture

Africa's geographical disadvantages did not prevent agriculture from developing early as the result of both local and imported discoveries. Recent discoveries suggest that, some 12,000 or 13,000 years ago, people in the eastern Sahara were perhaps the first in the world to make pottery, probably for storing food and water, two centuries earlier than Middle Eastern people. Between 8000 and 5000 B.C.E., people in the north-central Nile (Nubia) and the Sahara region had become among the world's first farmers (see Chronology: Ancient Sub-Saharan Africa, 8000 B.C.E.–350 C.E.). People in the Ethiopian highlands domesticated *teff* (tef) (a nutritious grain) and the banana-like *ensete* (en-SET-ay/en-SET-ee), probably between

desertification The process by which productive land is transformed into mostly useless desert.

CHRONOLOGY	
Ancient Sub-Saharan Africa, 8000 B.C.E.–350 C.E.	
8000–5000	Earliest agriculture in the Sahara and Nubia
5000–4000	Earliest agriculture in Ethiopia
3100–2800	First Nubian kingdom (disputed)
2500	Widespread agriculture in West, Central, and East Africa
2000	Beginning of Bantu migrations
1800–1500	Kerma kingdom in Nubia
1200	Early urbanization in western Sudan
1000–500	Bantu settlement of Great Lakes region
1000–500	Beginning of trans-Saharan trade
1000–500	Early ironworking technology
900–800	Mande towns
900–350 C.E.	Early Kush

5000 and 4000 B.C.E. By 2500 B.C.E. farming was widespread in West, Central, and East Africa. In West Africa and the Sahara almost all food crops developed from local wild African plants like sorghum, millet, yams, and African rice. Probably domesticated in the Niger River region, rice gradually spread south to become a major crop in the rain forest zone of the west coast. People in the eastern Sahara had also domesticated cotton and worked it into fabrics using spindles of baked clay, perhaps as early as 5000 B.C.E. Other crops came later from outside Africa, including wheat, barley, and chickpeas from the Middle East and bananas from Southeast Asia. But the movement went in both directions. Crops domesticated in West Africa such as sorghum and sesame reached India and China well before 2000 B.C.E.

Animal domestication presented a great challenge to sub-Saharan Africans. Cattle were probably domesticated from local sources in what is now the southern Sahara Desert and East Africa. Some scholars think this came as early as 9000 B.C.E., while others favor later dates. But no other African animals were suitable for domestication, and some were dangerous predators. Rock art and other evidence reveal possible attempts to domesticate giraffes, antelopes, and elephants. Failure to do so meant that most draft animals would have to come from North Africa and Eurasia. Goats and sheep were brought in from the Middle East by 6000 B.C.E. and were adopted in the Saharan region by both farmers and pastoralists.

African peoples overcame geographical challenges in many ways. The major response to difficult climate and soils was to create a subsistence economy, rather than the high-productivity agriculture possible in Egypt, China, India, Southeast Asia, or southern Europe. One such subsistence strategy, pastoral nomadism, became the specialty of some groups in dry regions. Others chose farming by shifting cultivation, a creative adaptation to prevailing conditions. As explained earlier, shifting cultivators moved their fields around every few years, letting recently used land lie fallow for a while to regain its nutrients. If not abused, this system worked well for centuries. Only in a few fertile areas was intensive sedentary agriculture possible, especially around the Great Lakes region of Central and East Africa and in the Ethiopian highlands.

Ancient African Metallurgy

Most sub-Saharan peoples learned to make metal tools and weapons, but unlike in Egypt and Eurasia, they probably used iron first. Copper may have been mined in the Sahara by 1500 B.C.E. and in the Niger valley between 600 and 400 B.C.E. But there was no pronounced bronze age, and generally the use of bronze, copper, and gold came around the same time or later than iron. Sub-Saharan Africans were among the world's earliest ironworkers, probably making iron by at least 1000 B.C.E. on the northern fringe of the Congo Basin rain forests. Iron smelters were built around 900 B.C.E. in the Great Lakes region of East Africa—modern Burundi, Rwanda, and Tanzania (TAN-zeh-NEE-uh). This date makes them slightly older than the earliest Egyptian works. Between 600 and 300 B.C.E., iron was being mined, smelted, and forged in West, East, and North Africa, and by around 500 B.C.E. true steel was being made in Tanzania. Iron and bronze metallurgy established on the North African coast after 700 B.C.E., especially at the Phoenician colony of Carthage (KAR-thage), may have influenced West Africans. Since most of the major iron ore deposits were located in far western Africa and Ethiopia, ore and iron artifacts had to be transported over long distances.

Mining and working iron were both difficult operations, and those who did them probably occupied a special position in the community. Sometimes blacksmiths were ranked with the priests and nobility. According to the oral traditions of the Haya (HI-uh) people in Tanzania, when a new king was installed on the throne, one important ritual was to visit the hut of the blacksmiths which symbolized the special relationship between the king and the iron workers.

The technology gradually improved and the number of products increased. Although some iron ore could be easily obtained from surface outcrops or riverbeds, in many places miners had to dig open pits and trenches or even put down vertical shafts to reach deposits deep underground. Furnaces for smelting ranged from simple open holes in the ground to elaborate clay structures 6 or 8 feet high with blower systems that used animal skin bellows. The craftsmen made spear blades and arrowheads for warriors and hunters; hoes, axes, machetes, and knives for farmers and traders; bangles and rings for jewelry; gongs to produce music; hammers, hinges, and nails for household use; and iron bells for ceremonies and rituals. The iron industry and its workers became a central feature of African life.

Recent discoveries show how some early farmers and metalusers lived. The ruins of a 2800-year-old village in Eritrea in the northeastern highlands revealed a people who lived in stone houses, drank beer, and ate cow and goat meat. They made gold earrings, bracelets, and rings as well as copper and bronze daggers and pottery jugs. Villagers also carved stone figurines, possibly for religious purposes.

Agriculture and metallurgy came to various African regions at different times, depending on circumstances, and they spread to the southern half of the continent last. Originally much of this region was inhabited by expert hunters and gatherers such as the !Kung (see Chapter 1), successful adapters to their environment who had little incentive to develop agriculture or ironworking. Gradually most of these groups were pushed farther south by iron-using farmers.

SECTION SUMMARY

■ African geography is extremely varied, ranging from jungles with abundant rainfall to deserts with practically no rainfall.

■ The area now covered by the Sahara Desert was once lush and fertile, but it gradually dried out as rain patterns shifted southward.

■ Small-scale agriculture flourished in Africa, though widespread disease made it difficult to domesticate animals.

■ Sub-Saharan Africans worked with iron at the same time or before they worked with bronze or gold.

■ Ironworkers held a special position in sub-Saharan society.

Early African States, Networks, and Migrations, 1800–600 B.C.E.

What were some achievements of the ancient Nubian, Sudanic, and Bantu peoples?

Historians tend to emphasize state building and the rise of political leaders, and some Africans formed states in this era, but the establishment of royal or centralized government did not always improve people's lives. Unlike the Egyptians and Nubians, many Africans rejected political centralization. Before the twentieth century, millions of people in sub-Saharan Africa, and many other parts of the world, remained by choice within loosely organized political structures, without kings, chiefs, or bureaucracies. In contrast to the citizens of most premodern kingdoms, these societies often enjoyed considerable democratic decision making and little tyranny.

However, some sub-Saharan peoples were linked, regularly or sporadically, to societies in North Africa and western Asia, and thus participated in the iron and commercial revolutions of

Afro-Eurasia. Most early sub-Saharan states probably developed around trading centers. As demonstrated by the expeditions to Punt, the Egyptians traded extensively with some of the peoples in northeastern Africa, and this trade probably helped foster the rise of states, especially of Nubia in the central Nile basin just south of Egypt. But the complex societies in the Sudan, some of which may have fostered kingship by 600 B.C.E., probably owed less to Egyptian connections. Meanwhile, migrating **Bantu** (BAN-too)—African people who developed traditions based on farming and iron metallurgy (the name is also used for the large family of African languages these people speak)—spread their languages, cultures, and technologies widely in the southern half of the continent. This migration brought farming and metallurgy to once remote regions.

Early Urban Societies in Nubia

The first known urban African state after Egypt emerged in the region known in ancient times as Nubia (see Map 3.1). The Nubians occupied the land that today is the northern half of the country of Sudan and far southern Egypt. Like Egyptians, Nubians turned to the Nile for survival. Today the region is mostly desert, and even several millennia ago it presented a difficult environment. But a thin area along the Nile was fertile, and copper and gold could be mined nearby. By 6000 B.C.E. villages in the region were among the world's earliest pottery makers. The first Nubian kingdom may have formed as early as 3100 B.C.E.

Egypt enjoyed a long connection with Nubia and dominated the region for many centuries, occasionally through military occupations. Many Nubians served willingly or unwillingly in the Egyptian army. Egypt and Nubia also established a two-way trade, with Egypt exporting materials such as pottery and copper items to Nubia and importing ivory, ebony, ostrich feathers, and slaves from the Nubians. This trade provided an economic incentive for local state building.

An independent Nubian kingdom, Kerma (CARE-ma), appeared between 1800 and 1600 B.C.E., as Egyptian power temporarily waned. Immigrants to this kingdom arrived from the Sahara and the south. Extensive ruins of massive cemeteries and large towers, as well as of a fortified city with stone and mud brick buildings, testify to a prosperous and well-organized society. Kerma was also distinguished for painted pottery and copper vessels and weapons. The Kerma religion mixed Egyptian and local African elements. Around 1500 B.C.E. Egyptian forces once again occupied Nubia and destroyed the Kerma state.

The Rise of Kush

When Egyptian power declined around 900 B.C.E., after the end of the New Kingdom, a larger Nubian state known as Kush (koosh) emerged, laying the foundations for a golden age of trade, culture, and metallurgy. The remains of many Kushite towns and cities have been found. The Kushites conquered Egypt in the eighth century B.C.E. but were pushed out by the Assyrians after nearly a century of occupation. Kush became a major regional trading hub, connected to growing networks of communication. Overland caravan routes linked Kush with the Niger Basin, the Congo Basin, and the Ethiopian highlands. This enterprising society provided goods from central and southern Africa to the Mediterranean and Red Sea regions, as well as to markets as distant as India and China. From these places Kush imported Roman goblets and Chinese copper vessels.

Kush clearly benefited from its contacts with other societies, adding imported ideas to Nubian traditions. For example, mechanical irrigation technology imported from Egypt and western Asia made farming possible in this barren area. Kushite culture mixed Egyptian and local ideas, along with touches from Hellenistic Greece and India. In religion, Kushites worshiped both Egyptian and local gods and buried their kings in Egyptian-style pyramids. A sixth-century B.C.E. inscription tells us that King Aspelta (as-PELL-ta), as the son of the Egyptian sun-god, Ra, built for his son a pyramid of white stone and made many offerings of gold and silver. Although the Kushites welcomed these foreign influences, they also reshaped them. For example, Kushite art reflected considerable Egyptian and even sometimes Greek influence, but the overall effect remained distinctively Nubian. The unique Kushite society may have also been matrilineal, and some women held key political positions, including that of queen. Kings sometimes traced their descent back through female ancestors.

Coronation Stela of Kushite King Aspelta (ca. 600 B.C.E.). The stela and inscription celebrate the coronation of King Aspelta. Related to the royal line through his mother, he was chosen from among many candidates by high priests acting in the name of the gods. (From Derek A. Welsby, *The Kingdom of Kush* (Princeton, NJ: Markus Weiner Publishers). Reproduced with permission of the the British Museum.)

Bantu Sub-Saharan peoples who developed a cultural tradition based on farming and iron metallurgy, which they spread widely through great migrations.

Eventually Kush linked the peoples of Africa and the Mediterranean. By 600 B.C.E. Kush had become the major African producer of iron, a position that gave it an even more crucial economic influence on the ancient world. The ancient Greek poet Homer described Kushites as "the most just of men; the favorites of the gods. The lofty inhabitants of Olympus (oh-LIM-pus) (home of Greek gods) journey to them, and take part in their feasts."[13] Kush played an even more prominent historical role during the Classical Age (see Chapter 9).

The Sudanic Societies and Trade Networks

In ancient times peoples in the Sudan grasslands also began developing towns and long-distance trade routes, and perhaps a few small kingdoms. Although trade extended to Nubia and Egypt, the Nubian and Egyptian influences in this region remain unclear. Urban societies existed in the Sudan three millennia ago, and perhaps earlier. By 1200 B.C.E. farmers in Mauritania (MORE-ee-TAIN-ee-uh) had built over two hundred stone villages and towns in what is now mostly uninhabited desert. They may have been the ancestors of the Mande (MAN-da) peoples, who now occupy a large area of the western Sudan, and they probably domesticated African rice. By 900 or 800 B.C.E. the population increase had changed walled villages into large, well-constructed towns. Then, between 500 and 300 B.C.E., this flourishing society was swallowed by the expanding Sahara and the people probably moved south.

Long-distance trade, especially the caravan routes crossing the Sahara Desert, greatly aided the growth of Sudanic societies by forging enduring networks of communication. The earliest caravan activity dates back to 1000 or 500 B.C.E. Gradually trade networks formed, and some groups took up commerce as their primary activity. The trans-Saharan trade depended on pack animals introduced by Berbers from North Africa, initially mules and horses and later camels. First domesticated in parched Arabia and used in the Nile valley by 700 B.C.E., camels stimulated trans-Saharan trade because they could endure many days of caravan travel without water, and they also provided meat and milk. Eventually a large trade system spanned the Sahara, linking the Sudanic towns with the peoples of the desert and the southern Mediterranean coast as well as the forest zone to the south.

On the southern fringe of the Sudan, in what is now central Nigeria, the Nok people, mostly farmers and herders, were working iron by 500 B.C.E., and they created enduring artistic traditions. Nok artists fashioned exquisite terra cotta pottery and sculpture, including life-size and realistic human heads. The later art of several Nigerian societies shows Nok influence. The worldviews of other peoples in the region, such as the ancestors of the Igbo (EE-boh) people in what is today southeastern Nigeria, may derive in part from Nok traditions.

During the Ancient Era African societies, such as the people who later coalesced into the Mande and Igbo groups, were shaping their longstanding beliefs into complex religious traditions (see Witness to the Past: The Worldview of an African Society). While each society developed some distinctive notions of

Nok Terra Cotta Sculpture of Head   Elaborate, life-size, technically complex sculptures reveal something of Nok material life in ancient Nigeria. Some figures sit on stools, carry an axe, or wear beads.   (Werner Forman/Art Resource, NY)

the cosmic order and their place within in, there were common patterns. Many peoples, like the Mande and the Igbo, believed in one divine force or supreme being, either male or female, who created the cosmos, earth, and life, and then either completely ignored the human sphere entirely or at least remained remote from human affairs. Africans needing immediate spiritual help appealed to secondary gods and spirits. By 6,000 or 7,000 years ago some West Africans were perhaps the world's first monotheists, and a few historians wonder if their ideas influenced later Middle Eastern peoples such as the Hebrews. Sub-Saharan African religion became a mix of monotheism, polytheism, and animism.

The Bantu-Speaking Peoples and Their Migrations

The Bantu-speaking peoples, who developed a cultural tradition based on farming and iron metallurgy, spread these techniques widely by their great migrations. Today people who speak closely related Bantu languages occupy most of the continent south of a line stretching from Kenya in the northeast to Cameroon in west-central Africa. All of these societies can trace their distant ancestry back to the same location in west-

Few primary sources survive for the ancient period in sub-Saharan Africa. Although it is difficult to extrapolate the distant past from contemporary oral traditions, we can get some insight into ancient understandings of the natural and spiritual realms from such accounts. This excerpt on the worldview of the Igbo people in southeastern Nigeria was compiled by an Igbo anthropologist, who summarized Igbo thought. Many Igbo perspectives may well derive from the Nok and Bantu cultures, whose ancestral homelands are near the region where the Igbo live today.

There is the world of man peopled by all created beings and things, both animate and inanimate. The spirit world is the abode of the creator, the deities, the disembodied and malignant spirits, and the ancestral spirits. It is the future abode of the living after their death. . . . Existence for the Igbo is a dual but interrelated phenomenon involving the interaction between the material and the spiritual, the visible and the invisible, the good and the bad, the living and the dead. . . . The world of the "dead" is a world full of activities. . . . The principle of seniority makes the ancestors [in the world of the "dead"] the head of the [extended kinship system in the world of man]. . . .

The world as a natural order which inexorably goes on its ordained way according to a "master plan" is foreign to Igbo conceptions. Rather, their world is a dynamic one—a world of moving equilibrium. It is an equilibrium that is constantly threatened, and sometimes actually disturbed by natural and social calamities. . . . But the Igbo believe that these social calamities and cosmic forces which disturb their world are controllable and should be "manipulated" by them for their own purpose. The maintenance of social and cosmological balance in the world becomes . . . a dominant and pervasive theme in Igbo life. They achieve this balance . . . through divination, sacrifice, and appeal to the countervailing forces of their ancestors . . . against the powers of the malignant spirits. . . . The Igbo world is not only a world in which people strive for equality; it is one in which change is constantly expected. . . . Life on earth is a link in the chain of status hierarchy which culminates in the achievement of ancestral honor in the world of the dead. . . .

The idea of a creator of all things is focal to Igbo theology. They believe in a supreme god, a high god, who is all good. . . . The Igbo high god is a withdrawn god. He is a god who has finished all active works of creation and keeps watch over his creatures from a distance. . . . Although the Igbo feel psychologically separated from their high god, he is not too far away, he can be reached, but not as quickly as can other deities who must render their services to man to justify their demand for sacrifices. . . . Minor gods [can] be controlled, manipulated, and used to further human interests. . . . Given effective protection, the Igbo are very faithful to their gods.

THINKING ABOUT THE READING

1. How do the Igbo understand the relationship between the human and spiritual worlds?
2. What is the role of the supreme god in their polytheistic theology?
3. How might their beliefs about the relationship of the human and spiritual realms shape Igbo society?

Source: Victor C. Uchendu, *The Igbo of Southeast Nigeria* (New York: Holt, Rinehart and Winston, 1965), pp. 11–13, 15–16, 94–95. Copyright © 1965. Reprinted with permission of Wadsworth, a division of Thomson Learning: www.thomsonrights.com.

---

central Africa. The Bantus incorporated many of the peoples they encountered and modified their own cultures to suit local conditions.

The Bantu occupation of central, eastern, and southern Africa is the result of one of the great population movements in premodern world history, a saga similar to that of the sea voyages that resulted in the settlement of the Pacific islands, the Indo-European migration into western and southern Eurasia, and the Native American settlement of the Western Hemisphere. During this process, the Bantu population multiplied many times and formed networks that fostered trade and the diffusion of technology. As the Bantus spread out over a wider area, they became less cohesive and gradually divided into the over four hundred different ethnic groups that today dominate this vast region.

Archaeological and linguistic evidence allows us to reconstruct the Bantu migrations (see Map 3.2). The Bantus originated along the Benue (BAIN-way) River in what is now eastern Nigeria and western Cameroon (KAM-uh-roon). By 3000 B.C.E. they were already combining farming (especially of yams) with hunting, gathering, and fishing. But agricultural progress fostered overcrowding by 2000 B.C.E., or perhaps earlier, spurring some to migrate eastward into the lands just north of the Congo River Basin. Bantus settled the Great Lakes region of East Africa between 1000 B.C.E. and 500 B.C.E., and by 1000 B.C.E. some land-short Bantus from the Benue began moving to the south and southeast. Some moved up the Congo River, setting up small farms. Often whole family groups moved together. As they settled in new areas, Bantus mixed with the local peoples, exchanging technologies and cultural patterns.

The Bantus benefited from metallurgy and agricultural technologies. Well before the Common Era the Bantus in the Benue region had learned to smelt iron, perhaps from the

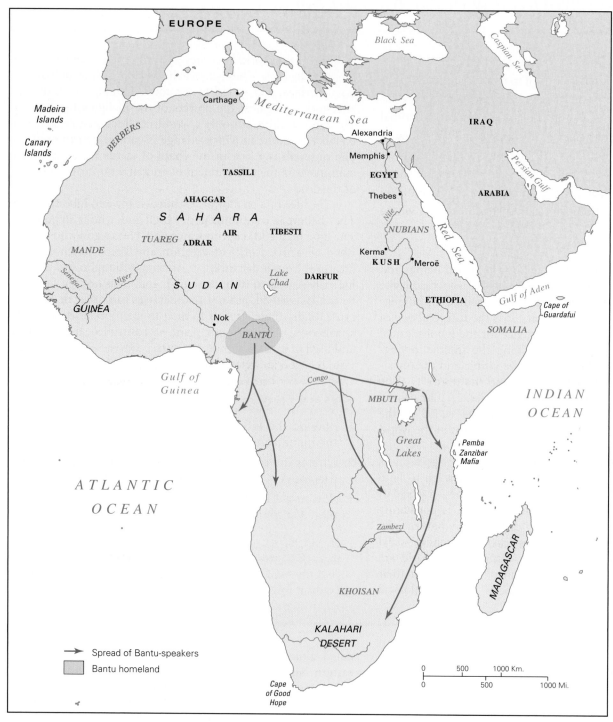

Map 3.2 Bantu Migrations and Early Africa

The Bantu-speaking peoples spread over several millennia throughout the southern half of Africa. Various societies, cities, and states emerged in West and North Africa.

nearby Nok culture. Iron spread along the Bantu communication network. But Bantus migrating eastward may also have adopted the ironworking technology developed by peoples living there. Metallurgy allowed the Bantus to use iron tools and weapons to open new land and subdue the small existing populations. They were also skilled farmers. Some adopted cattle and goat raising as a sideline, while others made these a major economic activity. By 2,000 years ago some Bantus living in northeast Africa had also learned to grow domesticated bananas and plantains (large bananas) imported from Southeast Asia, as well as sorghum (SOAR-gum) from the Nile valley. These high-yielding crops replaced yams as their primary staple food and provided a spur to population growth, encouraging new migration into southern Africa.

SECTION SUMMARY

- Early sub-Saharan societies were linked by trade and loosely organized, without centralized rule.
- Nubia had a close relationship with Egypt, which eventually destroyed the Nubian kingdom of Kerma.
- The Nubian kingdom of Kush increased in power as Egypt declined and became a major trading hub linking the peoples of Africa to the Mediterranean.
- Caravan routes through the Sahara allowed for trade and for links among widely separated African peoples.
- The Bantus spread widely throughout Africa, mixing their culture and traditions with those of local peoples.

◈ Early Societies and Networks of the Eastern Mediterranean

What were the contributions of the Hebrews, Minoans, Mycenaeans, Phoenicians, and Dorian Greeks to later societies in the region?

During the second millennium B.C.E., when the Egyptians and various Mesopotamian empires were growing in strength and competing with one another, smaller bronze- and then iron-using societies in the eastern half of the Mediterranean Basin were developing influential ideas or establishing cities and states. Among these, the Hebrews created the base for three major religions. The Minoans became a flourishing society and an economic bridge between western Asia and southeastern Europe, and the trade-oriented but warlike Mycenaeans built the first cities in Greece. The Phoenicians created an important new alphabet, established colonies in the western Mediterranean, and forged trade links with people as far away as England. Phoenician migration and trade fostered networks connecting many ancient societies. Greek migrants also began building an important society that eventually nourished other societies in Europe, western Asia, and North Africa.

Eastern Mediterranean Environments

The history and diet of peoples living around the eastern Mediterranean, such as the Phoenicians, Minoans, and Greeks, were influenced by the regional climate, with its cool, rainy winters and hot, dry summers, and by the Mediterranean Sea and its coastal areas. On the narrow coastal or interior plains of the northern shores, grain was planted in the late fall and harvested in the spring before the heat of summer killed it, and bread became a basic product. The many hills also encouraged the planting of olive trees and grape vines, and both olive oil and wine became export crops for Greece and Anatolia. Since the mountains and hills of Greece and Anatolia, as well as the drier lands of Lebanon and Palestine, made the development of large herds of cattle impractical, people raised pigs, sheep, and goats. Indeed pastoralism was common inland from the Levant coast. Finally, the eastern Mediterranean Sea, a large and mostly placid body of water, fostered boat building, maritime trade, and other contacts over long distances and between diverse societies (see Map 3.3).

One of the densest populations emerged in Greece, an appendage of southern Europe located less than 100 miles from Anatolia across the Aegean (ah-JEE-uhn) Sea. The Greeks were destined to live in relatively small, independent city-states and to be a seafaring, trading people. Unlike western Asia and Egypt, where long and wide river valleys invited the creation of large political units, Greece consists of small valleys separated by numerous mountains, some 8,000 to 10,000 feet high. This physical separation encouraged political fragmentation, which meant that people with unpopular or new ideas could move from one small state to another. This mobility encouraged intellectual diversity. Greece also has an extensive coastline with many good harbors, and most Greek cities were built on or near the coast. Greeks could travel by sea east to Ionia (today western Turkey), south to Crete, or west to southern Italy more easily than they could establish connections with nearby inland towns. Thus the Mediterranean linked the societies of the Greek peninsula to other peoples such as the Minoans, Egyptians, and Phoenicians.

The Hebrews and Religious Innovation

For over a thousand years the Hebrews, a Semitic people, were one of many groups of pastoral nomads, led by powerful men known as patriarchs (from the Greek word for "rule by the father"). Their population was smaller, and their economic and technological developments less impressive, than those of many of their neighbors, and when they did organize themselves into a state, their political achievements were short-lived. The united Hebrew monarchy lasted less than a century. Yet the Hebrew contribution to religious history, especially to Christian and Islamic traditions, exceeds that of either the Mesopotamians or Egyptians.

Early Hebrew Society and Politics The various books of the Hebrew Bible contain the basic laws of the Hebrews and are the main source for their early history. The Hebrews trace their ancestry as a people back to Abraham, a patriarch who supposedly lived in Mesopotamia sometime between 2000 and 1500 B.C.E. (see Chronology: The Eastern Mediterranean, 2000–539 B.C.E. on page 73). The question of whether Abraham was a real person or, as most scholars suspect, mythical may never be resolved by archaeological research. Nevertheless, the patriarch and his two sons, Isaac and Ishmael, are considered the spiritual ancestors of three monotheistic religions—Judaism, Christianity, and Islam—which are often called the Abrahamic faiths and collectively have some 3 billion followers today.

Historians and archaeologists, among them modern Israelis, have heatedly debated the historical reliability and antiquity of the Hebrew Bible, which was probably based in part on older oral

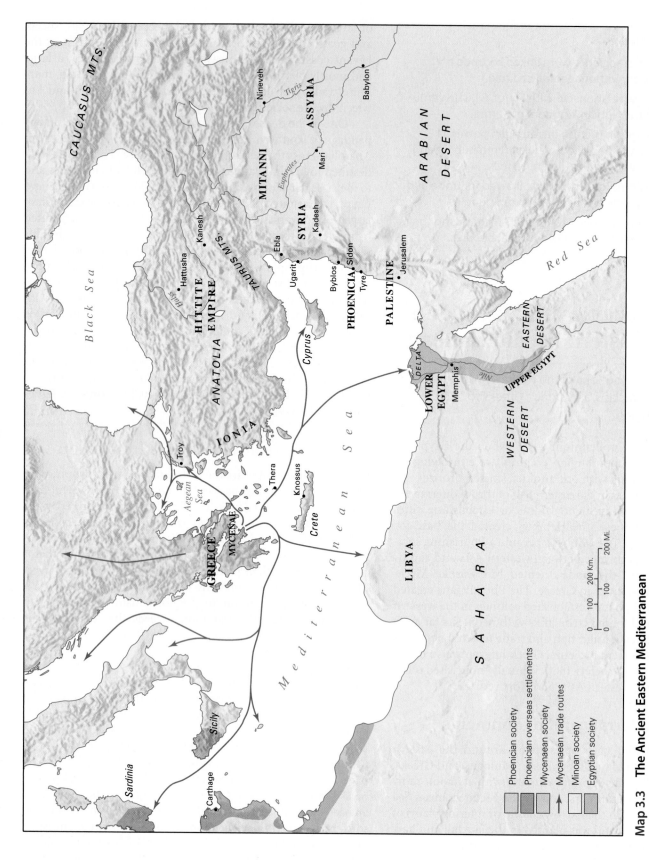

Map 3.3 The Ancient Eastern Mediterranean
The Hebrew, Minoan, Mycenaean, Phoenician, and Greek societies developed along the eastern shores of the Mediterranean Sea. They exchanged goods and ideas with each other and with other western Asians and the Egyptians.

The Eastern Mediterranean, 2000–539 B.C.E.

2000–1500	Possible time frame for Abraham (biblical account)
2000–1400	Minoan society
1630	Volcanic eruption destroys Thera (Santorini)
1600–1200	Mycenaean society
1500–650	Phoenician society
1300–1200	Hebrew Exodus from Egypt led by Moses (biblical account)
1200–800	Greek "Dark Age"
1250	Destruction of Troy, possibly by Mycenaeans
1000	First Hebrew kingdom (biblical account)
922–722	Hebrew kingdoms of Israel and Judah
750	Carthage colony established by Phoenicians
722	Assyrian conquest of Israel
586	Neo-Babylonian (Chaldean) conquest of Judah
539	End of Babylonian captivity

polytheistic world, Abraham recognized one supreme god. Peoples from Palestine, probably including some Hebrews, had migrated, either voluntarily or as slaves, to Egypt since at least 2000 B.C.E. A group of Hebrews who had gone to Egypt to escape drought and been enslaved were freed and left Egypt, probably in the thirteenth century. This "Exodus" from Egypt and eventual return to Palestine was led by Moses, whom the later Hebrews believed to be the founder of their religion. Moses gave his name to a code of laws, including the Ten Commandments, by which the Hebrews governed themselves. Egyptian and Mesopotamian ideas influenced some of the laws and religious views. The biblical account indicates that not all Hebrews were monotheists who followed the Mosaic laws, but that around 1000 B.C.E. the Hebrews had enough unity to establish a monarchy centered in the small city of Jerusalem.

Hebrew unity proved short-lived. After the death of King Solomon in 922 B.C.E., the monarchy split into a northern kingdom of Israel and a southern kingdom of Judah. In 722 the Assyrians conquered Israel and resettled its inhabitants elsewhere in their empire. When Assyria fell, the Hebrew prophet Nahum (NAY-hum) expressed the joy of many: "Nineveh [the Assyrian capital] is laid waste; who will bemoan her? All who hear the news of you will clap their hands over you."[14] In 586 the Chaldeans conquered the kingdom of Judah and moved its leaders to the Euphrates near Babylon. The bitterness of the "Babylonian Captivity" was reflected in a Hebrew psalm: "By the rivers of Babylon, there we sat down, yea, we wept when we remembered Zion."[15] This exile ended in 539 when the Persians conquered the Chaldeans and allowed the Hebrews to return to Palestine. Later Palestine became part of the Roman Empire. The Jews (from the word *Yehudin*, a term Hebrews used to describe themselves by about 500 B.C.E.) were again dispersed after a revolt against Roman rule in 70 C.E. From that time until the establishment of modern Israel in 1948 C.E., there was no Hebrew or Jewish state.

traditions. Little of it can be confirmed by nonbiblical sources such as archaeology. Some scholars think the biblical books are quite old while others argue that most or all of the books, even those offering accounts of very ancient events, were composed after 700 B.C.E. to support the claims of Hebrew political and religious factions. The earliest known material evidence for biblical passages are inscriptions found on silver scrolls dating from the late 500s B.C.E. Some bible stories seem based on Mesopotamian and Egyptian traditions, such as the great flood in the *Epic of Gilgamesh,* suggesting the spread of ideas. For example, some of the advice in the Hebrew Book of Proverbs, such as helping neighbors rather than acquiring wealth, and treating the disabled with dignity, closely echoes advice in more ancient Egyptian writings. These ongoing controversies in biblical scholarship underline the importance of Hebrew religion to later history.

In the biblical account, during the second millennium Abraham led a small group of people on a migration from southern Mesopotamia to Palestine, an area on the Mediterranean coast between Egypt and Syria. Although born into a

Hebrew Religion and World History

The religious history of the Hebrews, especially their ethical code, makes them memorable in world history. Over their long history both as nomads and as settled state builders, the Hebrews developed or refined four religious concepts that made them stand out among ancient peoples and that later influenced the Western and Islamic traditions. These concepts are found in their sacred writings; they include monotheism, morality, messianism, and meaning in history.

The first concept, monotheism, developed in two stages. At first, while polytheism remained influential for some centuries among other peoples, many Hebrews worshiped a single god, *Yahweh* (YA-way). They believed Yahweh had made an agreement, or covenant, with their earliest patriarchs and reinforced it when Moses received the Ten Commandments. If they would obey him, he would protect them. This form of monotheism, similar to that proposed by the Egyptian pharaoh Akhenaton to replace the two thousand Egyptian gods, did not deny that other peoples had gods but asserted that the Hebrews had only one. Some neighboring peoples may also have adopted

The Captivity of Israeli Women at Ninevah This relief comes from the palace of the Chaldean king Sennacherib in Ninevah. It was probably carved at the beginning of the seventh century B.C.E.
(Erich Lessing/Art Resource, NY)

monotheistic views around the same time. Gradually, however, the Hebrews reshaped monotheism, asserting that there is only one God, Yahweh, for all peoples, as the prophet Isaiah proclaimed: "There is no other God besides Me, a just God. Look to Me, and be saved, all you ends of the earth!"[16]

Hebrew holy men known as prophets refined a second Hebrew religious concept, morality. Working in the troubled times between the end of the united monarchy and the fall of Israel to the Assyrians, these men emphasized that it was not enough to obey the Bible's social and ritual commandments. Following Yahweh also meant leading a moral life, that is, refraining from lying, stealing, adultery, and persecution of the poor and oppressed. For example, the prophet Amos advised his people to hate evil and love good. One of the differences between the code of Hammurabi and the law of Moses was that the latter, while accepting the belief in retaliation, also emphasized compassion for the poor, for example, by ordering that all debts be canceled every seven years. Also, unlike the Mesopotamian law, Hebrew law required that only the wrongdoer be punished, and not members of his or her family. Hebrew ethics emphasized mercy as well as justice.

The third Hebrew contribution to religious thought was **messianism**, the belief that God had given the Hebrew people

a special mission in the world. As the Hebrews faced their time of troubles after the division of Solomon's kingdom, and especially after the fall of Judah to the Chaldeans, messianism acquired a broad spiritual meaning of bringing proper ethical behavior to all peoples. This idea is found in the book of Isaiah, where the prophet refers to Israelites as models from whom other people can learn moral truth: "I will give you as a covenant to the people, as a light to the [nations]. To open blind eyes, to bring out prisoners from the prison, those who sit in darkness."[17] This idea later inspired Christian missionary work.

The final important Hebrew religious contribution is the idea that history itself has meaning and that it moves forward in a progressive, linear fashion and not in great repetitive cosmic cycles of thousands or millions of years. The Hebrews believed that Yahweh acted in history by making specific agreements with particular individuals, such as Abraham and Moses. Sanctifying a linear view of time meant that the material, time-bound world was where human beings worked out their salvation by choosing good over evil. This belief helped shape the attitudes toward the material world found in all Western religions, and it also helped give birth later to the idea of progress, the notion that the future will be better than the past. It stood in contrast to ideas enshrined in the Indian religions of Hinduism and Buddhism that the material world is illusory and that time is cyclical.

---

messianism The Hebrew belief that their God, Yahweh, had given them a special mission in the world.

Minoan Crete and Regional Trade

An important urban society and network hub, now called Minoan (mi-NO-an), thrived on the island of Crete (kreet) between about 2000 and 1400 B.C.E. Crete lies just south of the Aegean Sea and the Greek peninsula, a strategic location that made it a logical center for sea trade between Egypt, western Asia, and southeastern Europe. Archaeologists who discovered the remains of an elaborate royal palace at Knossos (NAW-sus), on the northern shore of the island, named it Minos (MY-nus), after a Greek legend about a king who had once ruled in Crete. In the story, Minos "made himself master of the Greek waters, and for the safer conveyance of his revenues, he did all he could to suppress piracy."[18]

Historians have remained intrigued by the achievements of Minoan society. Some of the buildings had plumbing, and some towns had streets with drains and sewers, like the cities in ancient India. Paintings and sculptures show some Mesopotamian and Egyptian influences, but they are also different in style. Particularly interesting was the apparent worship of a large number of female deities, including an im-

portant mother goddess, and many paintings of flowers, animals, and bare-breasted females. The Minoans built no fortresses, and the towns lacked defensive walls. They apparently relied on their fleet alone to protect them. Around 1630 B.C.E. many cities on the island were destroyed, perhaps from earthquakes that followed a massive volcanic explosion that blew apart the nearby island of Thera (THER-uh) (today's Santorini). The sinking of most of Thera and the dispersal of the survivors may have given rise to the legend of the lost continent of Atlantis.

The first great Mediterranean sea power, the Minoans were innovators and played a very important role in regional trade. They pioneered a mixed agriculture that was well suited to the region's sunny, dry climate, growing both olives and grapes as well as grain. Already by 3000 B.C.E. they were using copper and trading intermittently with Egypt, and this trade became regular after 2000. Minoans traded extensively with Sicily, Greece, and the Aegean islands and sent wine, olives, and wool to Egypt and southwest Asia. Though their writing has not been deciphered, tablets found in the palace at Knossos appear to be written in two scripts, one of which may be related

Wall Painting from Thera, Crete   The paintings in palaces and homes show slices of Minoan life. This portrays female boxers, hinting that women played many roles in Minoan society.   (Julie M. Fair)

to a Mesopotamian language and the other to early forms of Greek. This suggests that ancient Crete served as a hub or meeting place connecting, through trade, western Asians and North Africans with various European societies. The Cretan ports were counterparts to the Persian Gulf ports that linked western and southern Asia.

The Mycenaeans and Regional Power

The Mycenaeans, Indo-Europeans named after the city of Mycenae (my-SEE-nee) in southern Greece, also became an important power between 1600 and 1200 B.C.E. after migrating into the Greek peninsula. Like the Hyksos then moving into Egypt, they were a warrior society. Their graves, which contain swords and armor, show that they valued fighting and had a command of bronze technology. They had a state-controlled economy that was tightly organized from the top down by the king and his scribes. By the middle of the second millennium, the Mycenaeans controlled Crete, whose Minoan society had already collapsed. The Mycenaeans also conquered all of southern Greece and the Aegean islands, forming an empire from which they collected taxes and tribute. They continued the Minoan trading networks, dispatching ships to Sicily, Italy, and Spain and into the Black Sea. This trade spread bronze technology. Mycenaeans also engaged in war with rivals, operating, unlike the Minoans, out of strong fortresses.

According to legends, around 1250 the Mycenaeans conquered Troy, a trading port along the northwestern coast of Anatolia. This event inspired Homer's epic story, the *Iliad*, some 500 years later. Scholars differ as to whether an actual Trojan War ever took place, and some suspect that the Homeric stories combine oral accounts of various conflicts. Whatever their accuracy, they strongly influenced the later Greeks and Romans.

By 1200 B.C.E., however, the Mycenaeans themselves faced collapse, although the reasons remain unclear. A prolonged drought resulting from climate change or a possible series of earthquakes, which may also have destroyed Troy, may have been factors. Many historians blame civil wars and attacks by warlike Indo-Europeans known as the Dorian Greeks, who were migrating into the peninsula. In the several centuries after 1200 various groups known as "Sea Peoples" pillaged and disrupted trade throughout the Aegean and eastern Mediterranean. In Homer's *Odyssey*, a king boasts that he "wandered and suffered much to collect these treasures and bring them home in my ships,"[19] a statement probably referring to regional piracy networks. But eventually a creative society emerged in Greece that incorporated many influences from the Dorian Greeks, Mycenaeans, Phoenicians, and Egyptians, as will be discussed below.

The Phoenicians and Their Networks

The Phoenicians, one of the greatest ancient trading societies, linked Mediterranean and southwest Asian peoples by trade networks and by their invention of a phonetic alphabet.

Between 1500 and 1000 B.C.E. this Semitic people, known to the Hebrews as the Canaanites (Kay-nan-ites), established themselves along the narrow coastal strip west of the Lebanon mountains, where they built the great trading cities of Tyre (tire), Sidon (SIDE-en), and Byblos (BIB-los). Described by Hebrew sources as the crowning city whose merchants were also princes, Tyre was a major hub, the place where luxury goods from many societies were collected and the finest artists and craftsmen worked. The Hebrew prophet Ezekial denounced the rich, vibrant city and listed the extraordinary network of mercantile connections: "Tyre, You who are situated at the entrance of the sea, merchants of the peoples on many coastlands. Your borders are in the midst of the seas. All the ships of the sea were in you to market your merchandise."[20]

Although sometimes dominated by Egypt, these cities were fiercely competitive and independent states headed by kings. Although the Phoenicians spoke a common language and worshiped the same gods, they never united to form one country. The Greek word for book, *byblos,* was taken from the name of the Phoenician city that was famous for its high-quality papyrus, which was used to make written scrolls, the ancient equivalent of our bound books. The Phoenicians' relatively rich, well-situated land was the home of the now long-gone "cedars of Lebanon" prized by the tree-starved Sumerians, Egyptians, and Hebrews. The most famous cultural achievement of the Phoenicians, their simplification of Mesopotamian cuneiform writing into an alphabet of twenty-two characters, became the basis of later European alphabets.

Only a few tablets containing information on government and religion survive, while the papyrus documents which might record their views on trade and daily life, or provide a glimpse of their stories, songs, and jokes, have mostly disappeared. As a result, most of what we know comes from Egyptian, Greek, and Hebrew sources; these peoples generally admired the Phoenicians' skills as scribes, seafarers, engineers, and artisans but also denounced them as immoral profiteers and cheaters. For example, an Egyptian report from around 1100 B.C.E. describes the difficult mission of a pharaoh's envoy, Wen-Amon, who was sent to Byblos to purchase some cedarwood for a new temple. Such trade had gone on for centuries, often with Egypt dictating the terms, but by now Byblos was strong and Egyptian power had waned. On his sea journey the hapless Wen-Amon was robbed. In Byblos he waited days for an audience with the Byblos king, Zakar-Baal, who wanted to sell timber but realized Wen-Amon now had little money left to purchase anything. After a chilly meeting, Zakar-Baal sold the demoralized Egyptian a small amount of wood. The king made clear he would deal with Egypt and any other power on his own terms. The Phoenician image as schemers, deserved or not, survives into modern times. Our term for a shameless woman, Jezebel, is derived from a princess of Tyre.

The Phoenician creation of this alphabet helped spread Phoenician influence in the Mediterranean and the networks they created. Between 1000 and 800 B.C.E., the seafaring Phoenicians began to replace the declining Mycenaeans as the leaders in Mediterranean trade with western Asia. They also may have helped spread knowledge of ironworking to Europe. In addition, the Phoenicians became experts in new methods of dyeing cloth, and they may have traveled as far as England to get supplies of tin. In the process, they established colonies or trading posts beyond the Strait of Gibraltar on the southern coast of Spain, as well as in Morocco, Sicily, and southern Italy. They fished for tuna in the Atlantic and some historians think the Phoenicians may have reached the Canary Islands and Madeira, off the coast of Morocco, and conceivably the more distant Azores, nearly a third of the way to North America. Thus the Phoenicians became the greatest mariners of the ancient Mediterranean. They also traded overland with Arabia and Syria.

Between 1000 and 500 B.C.E., the Mediterranean Sea became a major source of goods and wealth, partly because of Phoenician efforts. Although coins were probably not used widely until the seventh century B.C.E., centuries earlier solid bars of precious metals served as currency. By 1200 B.C.E., if not earlier, ships capable of carrying two hundred copper bars were sailing the Mediterranean. Using their colonies as ports for resupply and repair, the Phoenicians traveled long distances to secure iron, silver, timber, copper, gold, and tin, all valuable commodities in western Asia and Egypt during the second and first millennia B.C.E. Legends suggest that around 600 B.C.E., under the sponsorship of the Egyptian king, a Phoenician fleet may even have sailed around Africa in an expedition lasting three years, but these journeys cannot be substantiated. In 650 B.C.E. the Assyrians conquered the Phoenician home cities and brought an end to their dynamic power, but some Phoenician colonies lived on. The most famous colony was Carthage in North Africa, established around 750 B.C.E. near what is today Tunis. A legend tells of Elissa, the sister of a king in Tyre who was caught in a political feud and left with some followers in search of a new home. They eventually established the city of Carthage, which became the capital of a major trading empire and the chief competitor to the Romans in the western Mediterranean by the third century B.C.E. As great sailors the Carthaginians later explored far down the coast of West Africa.

The Eclectic Roots of Greek Society

The fall of the Phoenicians and the Mycenaeans set the stage for another seafaring people, the Greeks, to found an influential urban society. Historians have referred to the centuries from the destruction of Mycenae around 1200 B.C.E. down to around 800 B.C.E. as the Greek "Dark Age," because during this time organized states and writing disappeared and social and political conditions were chaotic on the peninsula. During these centuries the economic and social environment changed considerably, and there was great population movement. This was the period of the "Sea Peoples" mentioned earlier. Dorian Greeks, whose migrations had contributed to the fall of Mycenae, settled much of the Greek peninsula, and many Mycenaeans dispersed, some settling the offshore islands and others crossing the Aegean Sea to Ionia, where they established cities.

The Greek world, scattered, as the philosopher Plato later put it, like frogs around a pond, became a mix of Mycenaean and Dorian peoples and traditions. In the absence of strong governments, various tribes struggled for power. The Homeric epics, which were written during this period, became an integral part of the Greek tradition in an era of much political and economic change.

Although the Greeks were famous as maritime traders, they were also warriors. Their respect for military strength is reflected in the works of Homer, oral epics written down between the eleventh and the eighth centuries B.C.E. Historians disagree as to whether Homer was an actual person or the collective name for several authors who compiled these epic poems into a narrative. As mentioned earlier, they also debate whether the epics reflect actual events from the Mycenaean era or represent a composite of various stories from the past. Some scholars argue that many themes and plots in the epics reflect influences from Mesopotamian literature such as *The Epic of Gilgamesh*, indicating the spread of ideas around the eastern Mediterranean world.

The first Homeric epic, the *Iliad*, is set during an attack by some Greek cities, led by their king Agamemnon (ag-uh-MEM-non), on Troy across the Aegean in Anatolia. The poem emphasizes the aristocratic value of valor in war but also warns its readers against excessive pride. Arrogance leads the Greeks to make some nearly fatal mistakes. For example, the Greek hero Achilles (uh-KIL-eez) refuses to fight after a quarrel with Agamemnon. When the Trojans, led by Hector, try to burn the enemy ships, Achilles' friend Patroclus (puh-TROW-klus) takes Achilles' place in the battle and is killed by Hector. An angry and remorseful Achilles then kills Hector, warning that friendship between them is impossible, and there could be no truce until one of them has fallen. The poem ends when Hector's father, Priam, comes to ask Achilles for his son's body. Achilles is moved by Priam's courage, and both men share their grief. The Greek victory also costs many lives on both sides.

This poem and Homer's second epic, the *Odyssey* (ODD-eh-see), a story of the adventures of Odysseus (oh-DIS-ee-us), or Ulysses (YOU-lis-eez) returning home after the Trojan War, portrayed the Greek gods as superheroes who intervened frequently to help their human friends and hinder their enemies. The Homeric world measured virtue by success in combat. Both gods and men took more joy in competition and battle than they did in justice or mercy. Yet these great epics continue to be read, not only because of their dramatic and often brutal war scenes, but also because they tell us something about the tragedy and pathos of human life. This emphasis on both human power and suffering remained a part of Greek literature throughout the following centuries. The Homeric epics and belief in the gods that they introduced greatly influenced the emerging Greek society.

As mentioned above, Greek society eventually became a synthesis of Mycenaean and Dorian traditions. The Greeks also borrowed ideas from neighboring peoples, including the Egyptians and western Asians, although the degree of outside influence on early Greek culture is debated (see the Historical

Controversy feature in "Societies, Networks, Transitions," page 101). Certainly the Mediterranean was a zone of interaction for peoples living around its rim. Phoenician ships, which had avoided a turbulent Greece for several hundred years, began to show up again, restoring Greek contact with the eastern Mediterranean and its regional trade networks. Soon the Greeks adopted and modified the Phoenician alphabet and began trading with western Asia again as they had during the Mycenaean period. These centuries built a foundation for a dynamic Greek society in the Classical Era.

> ## SECTION SUMMARY
>
> ■ Mountainous Greece favored the development of many small, independent communities, rather than one homogenous community.
>
> ■ The Hebrews were politically fragmented, but their religious writings, with their emphasis on monotheism, morality, messianism, and meaning in history, have had a tremendous impact on religious history.
>
> ■ Minoan Crete was the first great Mediterranean sea power and had a well-developed urban infrastructure.
>
> ■ Around 1250 B.C.E., the Mycenaeans possibly conquered Troy; this event later inspired Homer's epic, the *Iliad*.
>
> ■ The Phoenicians, the region's greatest maritime traders, simplified the Mesopotamian cuneiform writing into an alphabet, which served as the basis for later European alphabets.
>
> ■ The Homeric epics, the *Iliad* and the *Odyessy*, greatly influenced the emerging Greek society, which was a synthesis of Mycenaean and Dorian Greek peoples.

Online Study Center   **ACE the Test**

✦ Chapter Summary

Egypt is often called "the gift of the Nile" because it arose in the flood-prone Nile River valley. The Egyptian system was extraordinarily durable, lasting for several thousand years in its basic form. Like the Mesopotamians, the Egyptians developed a state led by kings and invented the hieroglyphics writing system. In their stable and predictable environment, the Egyptians developed a more optimistic worldview and culture than the Mesopotamians, who were buffeted by chronic power struggles. Egyptians also participated in trade networks linking western Asia and the Mediterranean Basin with sub-Saharan Africa and India.

Many of the peoples of sub-Saharan Africa also made the great transition to farming by inventing or adopting agriculture and metallurgy, both of which built the framework for cities and states. These societies were often modified by contacts with other peoples around them. An environment of grasslands, forests, and the expanding Sahara Desert helped to

shape their history, and the gradual drying out of the Sahara region forced many people to migrate. Cities arose early in Nubia (along the central Nile), probably stimulated by long-distance trade and contacts with Egypt. The Sudan fostered distinctive cultures. The Bantu peoples, in one of the greatest migrations in history, spread their farming and iron-based culture and languages widely in the southern half of Africa and established networks over vast distances.

The Mediterranean societies also benefited from regional connections. The trade routes of the Minoans, Mycenaeans, and especially the seafaring Phoenicians enriched the peoples of western Asia and the Mediterranean Basin by bringing them material goods, markets, cultural contacts, and a practical new alphabet. The Hebrews' evolving understanding of their mission, and of Yahweh, was influenced by their contact with Egyptians and Mesopotamians. Some of these contributions, such as the Phoenician alphabet and Hebrew religious and ethical concepts, have influenced many peoples down to the present day. Greece arose from interaction among several Mediterranean societies in a turbulent period during which Homer wrote his great epics.

 *Online Study Center*   **Improve Your Grade** Flashcards

Key Terms

pharaohs	Sudan
hieroglyphics	desertification
ma'at	Bantu
monotheism	messianism

Suggested Reading

Books

Castledon, Rodney. *Minoans: Life in Bronze Age Crete.* New York: Routledge, 1993. Valuable recent survey.

Connah, Graham. *African Civilization: An Archaeological Perspective.* 2nd ed. Cambridge: Cambridge University Press, 2004. A good overview of early African societies; emphasizes the rise of cities and states.

Dunstan, William E. *The Ancient Near East.* New York: Harcourt Brace, 1998. Designed for the general reader, this work makes sense of the confusing array of states and empires in western Asia and Egypt.

Ehret, Christopher. *The Civilizations of Africa: A History to 1800.* Charlottesville: University of Virginia Press, 2002. A pathbreaking introduction to African history, with nearly half devoted to the ancient period.

Grimal, Nicholas. *A History of Ancient Egypt.* Oxford: Blackwell, 1992. A clear account of this society for beginning students.

Harris, Nathaniel. *History of Ancient Egypt: The Culture and Lifestyle of the Ancient Egyptians.* New York: Barnes and Noble, 1997. A richly illustrated overview of Egyptian life.

Markoe, Glenn E. *The Phoenicians.* Berkeley: University of California Press, 2000. A fine account of the history, cities, economy, and literature of this maritime society.

McNutt, Paula M. *Restructuring the Society of Ancient Israel.* Louisville: Westminster John Knox Press, 1998. Recent survey of knowledge and scholarly debates.

Mertz, Barbara. *Red Land, Black Land: Daily Life in Ancient Egypt.* Rev. ed. New York: Peter Bedrick, 1990. A lively and readable re-creation of the lives and values of ancient Egyptians.

Newman, James L. *The Peopling of Africa: A Geographic Interpretation.* New Haven: Yale University Press, 1995. An excellent summary of what we know about the early history and migrations of Africa's people.

Niditch, Susan. *Ancient Israelite Religion.* New York: Oxford University Press, 1997. An account of the Hebrew religion that shows its debt to the Canaanites as well as those features that made it unique.

Stiebing, William H. *Ancient Near Eastern History and Culture.* New York: Longman, 2003. An up-to-date survey of ancient western Asia, Egypt, and the eastern Mediterranean.

Tyldesley, Joyce. *Hatshepsut: The Female Pharaoh.* New York: Viking, 1996. Readable biography of this remarkable leader.

Welsby, Derek A. *The Kingdom of Kush: Napatan and Meroitic Empires.* Princeton: Markus Wiener, 1996. A well-illustrated and up-to-date survey of kushite society.

Websites

African Timelines
(http://web.edu/cagatucci/classes/hum211/timelines/htimelinetoc.htm). Offers many links to essays and other sources on Africa; maintained by Central Oregon Community College.

Ancient Jewish History
(http://www.us-israel.org/jsources/Judaism/jewhist.html). Offers much useful information.

Exploring Ancient World Cultures
(http://eawe.evansville.edu). Excellent site run by Evansville University, with essays and links on the ancient Near East and Europe.

Internet African History Sourcebook
(http://www.fordham.edu/halsall/africa/africasbook.html). This site contains much useful information and documentary material on ancient Africa.

Internet Ancient History Sourcebook
(http://www.fordham.edu/halsall/ancient/asbook.html). Exceptionally rich collection of links and primary source readings.

CHAPTER 4

Around the Pacific Rim: Eastern Eurasia and the Americas, 5000–600 B.C.E.

Online Study Center

This icon will direct you to interactive activities and study materials on the website: college.hmco.com/pic/lockard1e

Shang Axe Head The Shang Chinese made some of the ancient world's finest bronze tools. This axe head, decorated with a human face, may have been used to behead rivals of the Shang rulers. (Bildarchiv Preussischer Kulturbesitz/Art Resource, NY)

He encouraged the people and settled them. He called his superintendent of works [and] minister of instruction, and charged them with the building of the houses. Crowds brought the earth in baskets. The roll of the great drum did not overpower [the noise of the builders].

CHINESE POEM FROM THE SECOND MILLENNIUM B.C.E.[1]

According to Chinese tradition, around 1400 B.C.E. a ruler named Pan Keng supervised the building of a new capital city, Anyang (ahn-yahng), on a flat plain alongside the Huan River. The king and his officials supervised the citizens in the hard construction labor, which was done to the beat of a drum. Because Anyang's location had many advantages, the king had high expectations for his new capital. Thanks to the rich soil, productive farms would stretch out into the distance. The river could supply water and aid in defense. People could find timber, hunt animals, or—the king himself probably thought of this—seek relief from the summer heat in mountains a short chariot ride away. Anyang was likely China's first planned city. Surrounded by four walls facing the points of the compass, it reflected the ancient adage that without harmony nothing lasts. This basic system governed city planning for the next 3,000 years.

Three and a half millennia later archaeologists digging at Anyang found exquisite ritual bronzes and "dragon bones," animal bones carved with some of the earliest Chinese writing. For hundreds of years, local chemists, not knowing their priceless historical value, had been grinding up these bones to make folk medicine. To the archaeologists, however, they showed that ancient China, like Mesopotamia and Egypt, had both cities and a writing system. The Chinese concern for posterity is reflected in their writing. An Anyang artisan, Ts'ai Shu, had inscribed on a bronze vessel: "I myself made this. May my sons and grandsons for a myriad years treasure it and use it without limit."[2] Although Anyang's buildings crumbled with time and ruling families came and went, the legacy of early China did live on for centuries.

Cities, states, agriculture, and trade networks developed in various societies on both sides of the Pacific Ocean. On the Asian side, ancient cities like Anyang confirm that, as in India, Mesopotamia, and Egypt, distinctive urban societies appeared very early in China, developing largely from local roots. People in China, Southeast Asia, and Korea were among the first people in the world to develop farming, metalworking, and maritime technology and to establish enduring traditions. The ancient Chinese established a foundation for a society that has retained many of its original ideas and customs down to the present day. Despite formidable geographical barriers, China and Southeast Asia also became connected very early to other parts of Eurasia by trade networks. On the

American side of the Pacific, too, many peoples underwent the great transitions to farming, cities, and complex social structures, while others, less involved with urbanization or state formation, nevertheless flourished by using various strategies for survival. Although environmental factors such as mountains, deserts, and forest barriers tended to isolate North, Central, and South American societies from each other, regional networks of exchange still formed even here during the ancient period.

FOCUS QUESTIONS

1. How did an expanding Chinese society arise from diverse local traditions?
2. What were some key differences between the Shang and Zhou periods in China?
3. How did the traditions developing in Southeast and Northeast Asia differ from those in India and China?
4. How do scholars explain the settlement of the Americas and the rise of agriculture in these continents?
5. What were some of the main features of the first American societies?

◆ The Formation of Chinese Society, 6000–1750 B.C.E.

How did an expanding Chinese society arise from diverse local traditions?

China was one of the first societies with cities and states, joining Harappa, Mesopotamia, Egypt, and Minoan Crete in pioneering new ways of life. Societies change in part through contact with each other, but this was less true for ancient China than for India, southwestern Asia, or the Mediterranean Basin. Forbidding desert and mountain barriers, including the high Tibetan (tuh-BET-en) Plateau, on China's western borders complicated travel, although they did not prevent some influences from crossing borders. This relative remoteness resulted in limited contact with the other ancient urban societies. But productive farming, creative cultures, and the rise of states laid the framework for a distinctive society, now at least 4,000 years old, that dominated a sphere of interaction in eastern Eurasia.

China and Its Regional Environments

The Chinese faced many challenges in communicating both with each other and with distant peoples. China's vast size, combined with a difficult topography, made transportation difficult and also encouraged regional cultural and political loyalties. The Chinese were often divided into competing states, especially in early times, and governments struggled to enforce centralizing policies. The Himalayas (him-uh-LAY-uhs), the Tibetan Plateau, and great deserts inhibited contact with South and West Asia. However, the ancient Chinese did have regular exchanges, including both trade and conflict, with the various peoples in Central Asia, North Asia, Southeast Asia, and Tibet, whose cultures, languages, and ways of life were very different from the Chinese. Over the centuries the Chinese sometimes extended political control over these peoples and sometimes were invaded and even conquered by them.

China's large land area was one major factor that fostered regionalism (division into different regions). Modern China covers as much land as western and eastern Europe combined. The eastern third of the modern country, where most of the people live, is about half the size of the continental United States. Before modern times, most Chinese lived in inland river valleys rather than along the coast. As a result, maritime, or ocean, commerce was not very significant until 1000 C.E. In the interior, extensive mountains, deserts, and wetlands hindered transportation, and therefore communication, between one region and another.

China's three major river systems helped shape Chinese regionalism. The Yellow, or Huang He (hwang ho), River; the Yangzi (yahng-zeh), or Yangtze, River; and the West, or Xijiang (SHEE JYAHNG), River all flow from west to east and hence do not link the northern, central, and southern parts of China. The Yellow River, sometimes termed "China's sorrow" because of its many destructive floods, flows some 3,000 miles through north China to the Yellow Sea, but it is easily navigable only in some sections. The more navigable but also flood-prone Yangzi, the world's fourth-longest river, flows through central China, a region of moderate climate that has had the densest population for the past thousand years. The shorter West River system helps define mountainous and subtropical south China.

China's neighboring regions had diverse environments and distinctive cultures. The deserts and grasslands of Central Asia, with their blazing hot summers and long, bitterly cold winters, were unpromising for intensive agriculture except in the Oxus River Valley (see Chapter 2). The rugged, pastoralist

CHRONOLOGY

	China	Japan and Southeast Asia	The Americas
10,000 B.C.E.		**10,000–300 B.C.E.** Jomon culture	
5000 B.C.E.	**5000–3000 B.C.E.** Yangshao culture	**4000–2000 B.C.E.** Austronesian migrations	
3000 B.C.E.	**3000–2200 B.C.E.** Longshan culture		**3000–1600 B.C.E.** Peruvian cities
2000 B.C.E.	**1752–1122 B.C.E.** Shang dynasty **1122–221 B.C.E.** Zhou dynasty		**1200–300 B.C.E.** Olmecs **1200–200 B.C.E.** Chavín
1000 B.C.E.		**1000–800 B.C.E.** First Southeast Asian states	

Central Asian societies that lived there traded with, warred against, and sometimes conquered the settled farmers of China, Korea, and India. The Central Asians who most affected Chinese history included diverse Turkish-speaking peoples, some of whom still live in the dry Xinjiang (SHIN-jee-yahng) region of far western China. South of the deserts, the Tibetans of the high plateau were subsistence farmers and herders. The ancient Chinese also forged occasional relations with people in mainland Southeast Asia, Manchuria, and Korea.

Early Chinese Agriculture

Agriculture in China began around 7000 B.C.E., perhaps 1,000 years later than in Mesopotamia, and fine food became a Chinese preoccupation (see Chronology: Ancient China, 7000–600 B.C.E.). The remains of Neolithic settlements have been discovered all over China, and they have revealed various regional traditions, suggesting the diverse roots of Chinese society. The Yellow and Wei River Valleys in north China were major centers of early farming. The modest annual rainfall and tendency toward flooding made the region somewhat similar to the Nile, Tigris-Euphrates, and Indus Basins. In addition, winds blowing in from the Gobi Desert of Mongolia to the northwest deposited massive amounts of dust, known as **loess** (LESS), which enriched the soils of north China. The people planted the wheatlike, highly drought-resistant prairie grass called millet. Later, wheat, likely imported from India or Mesopotamia, became northern China's main cereal grain.

loess The dust blown in from the Mongolian deserts that enriched the soils of northern China.

Ancient songs tell us something about the farming routine:

They clear away the grass, the trees; Their ploughs open up the ground. In a thousand pairs they tug at weeds and roots, Along the low grounds, along the ridges. They sow the many sorts of grain, The seeds that hold moist life. How that blade shoots up, How sleek, the grown plant.[3]

Further south, the Chinese in the Yangzi River Basin began cultivating rice by 5000 B.C.E. Whether they were the first to grow rice or learned it from people in southern China or

CHRONOLOGY

Ancient China, 7000–600 B.C.E.

7000	Agriculture begins in Yellow River Basin
5000	Agriculture begins in Yangzi River Basin
5000–3000	Yangshao culture in northern China
3000–2200	Longshan culture in northern China
2600	Copper mining
2183–1752	Xia dynasty in northern China (disputed)
1752–1122	Shang dynasty in northern China
1400	Beginning of bronze-casting industry
1122–221	Zhou dynasty

Southeast Asia remains unclear. Thus very early two distinct agricultural traditions emerged. In the north, where the climate was cold and dry, drought-tolerant crops like wheat, millet, pears, and apricots were mainstays. In the wetter, warmer southern half of China, irrigated rice and more temperate crops came to predominate. But rice became so important that for several thousand years Chinese have greeted each other by asking, Have you eaten rice yet?, and have described losing a job as breaking one's rice bowl.

Highly productive agriculture was always a key to China's success. Making wise use of the land, the Chinese sustained reasonably adequate diets over many millennia. In part because of climate changes, famine was fairly common, as it was elsewhere, yet the Chinese people were basically well fed, well clothed, and well housed throughout much of history, beginning in ancient times. Productive farming also promoted population growth: northern and central China contained between 2 and 4 million people by 3000 B.C.E.

The Chinese ate well enough and grew enough food that they came to perceive food as more than simple fuel. Cooking became an art form, an arena for aesthetic involvement and sensory delight, and an essential component of social life. A God of the Kitchen became an important deity of folk religion. Many distinctive regional variations in cooking developed, as any traveler will see if he or she explores the Cantonese, Hunanese (hoo-nahn-eez), Mandarin, and Sichuanese (SUH-chwahn-eez) restaurants in large cities around the world. Boiling and steaming were the most common cooking methods during ancient times, but gradually stir-frying replaced roasting in preparing meat. The use of chopsticks for eating meals probably goes back 4,000 years.

The First Farming Societies

Neolithic China included several societies with distinctive regional traditions that established a foundation for Chinese cultural development. The best known of these societies is the Yangshao (YANG-shao) ("painted pottery") culture, which began in the middle Yellow River region around 5000 B.C.E. and covered an area of north China larger than Mesopotamia or Egypt. Several excavated villages from around 4000 B.C.E. tell us that people made fine painted pottery, used kilns, fashioned stone and bone tools, bred pigs and dogs, weaved thread, lived in houses constructed partly with timber, and buried their dead in cemeteries, suggesting belief in an afterlife. They also raised silkworms and fashioned the silk into clothes. In the centuries to follow silk making become a unique Chinese activity, and Chinese silk was exported all over Eurasia.

Farming life in this early society was hard, and probably much communal effort was needed to produce a small agricultural surplus. Village layouts suggest that people already were organizing themselves into larger kinship groups such as clans, a feature of Chinese life thereafter. However, there is little evidence for a ruling elite or warfare.

Neolithic Chinese developed some long-lasting cultural patterns. Music was popular; a 7,000-year-old seven-holed flute is the oldest still playable musical instrument ever found anywhere in the world. The Chinese also created the first known numerical system. Evidence for jade carving, for which the Chinese later became famous, has been found in several regions. Since floods and earthquakes were common, the early Chinese sought various ways to avert disaster. This search led to religious speculation and experimentation with techniques to predict the future.

The Growth and Spread of Chinese Culture

About 3000 B.C.E., when the Sumerians were building their cities, the exchange of ideas and technologies over the developing trade networks began to produce an expansive Chinese culture out of various regional traditions, although apparently there were not yet any true states. The Chinese in the Yellow River Basin developed a society more complex than the Yang-

Peasant Life in Zhou China   The decorations on bronze vessels from Zhou China offer information on peasant life. This decoration, from the Warring States Period, shows people in varied activities: fighting, hunting, making music, performing rituals, and preparing food.   (E. Consten, Das alte China)

shao society, with permanent settlements and irrigated farming, and there were also major achievements elsewhere. As late as 2000 B.C.E. many societies with different cultures and languages remained in China, but gradually the societies in northern and central China merged their traditions into a common social and cultural zone.

Various societies arose in river basins. The Yellow River Basin was always a major core of creativity. The Longshan (LUNG-shahn) ("black pottery") culture dominated the eastern Yellow River area between around 3000 and 2200 B.C.E. Because occupations were more specialized in this society than in the Yangshao society, a division of labor was created and social classes began to emerge. The Longshan people built strong houses, lived in walled villages and towns, had weapons for warfare, and developed farming. They also made pottery almost as hard as metal, carved high-quality jade, and created a simple pictographic writing system. Millennia before any other society, the Chinese of this era also used industrial diamonds to polish ceremonial ruby and sapphire axes, giving them a fine sheen. Societies to the south, east, and north of the Yellow River also made contributions to the emerging Chinese society. For example, the people in the Yangzi Basin produced distinctive traditions of agriculture, animal domestication, town building, and bronze metallurgy that were at least as old, if not older, than those of north China.

Later, during the first millennium B.C.E., Chinese identity and customs gradually expanded from the Yellow and Yangzi Basins into south China. The Chinese displaced or absorbed most of the indigenous (in-DIJ-uh-nuhs) peoples (the original inhabitants) in the south, although many ethnic minorities still live there. An old folk song celebrated the expansion: "We shall extend to the limits of the east, Even to the states along the sea. Tribes to the south will all proffer their allegiance."[4] This mixing of different peoples produced a Chinese culture that encompassed many regional traditions and, at times, different states, all held together by many common customs and values as well as a standardized written language. Political unity helped but was not essential to this sense of a shared cultural identity. Indeed, the political states that arose in the first two millennia never encompassed all the Chinese people.

Population growth and shared culture made possible the first states, which may have appeared during the third millennium B.C.E. The Chinese trace their political ancestry to several culture heroes who supposedly lived in north China during Longshan times. The honorable deeds of these men, real or mythical, led later Chinese philosophers to make them models of behavior for all Chinese. Chinese historians labeled this era the Xia (shya) (Hsia) dynasty (2183–1752 B.C.E.), but its existence is still debated. A possible Xia capital city, one square mile in size, was built around 2000 B.C.E. near the Yellow River. The Xia may have presided over an occupationally diverse society including scribes, metallurgists, artisans, and bureaucrats. If the Xia were the first real Chinese state, the extent of their rule remains unclear.

Ancient China built on its foundations in such an original fashion as to almost create a world apart. Some influences filtered in from Central Asia, including the horse and chariot, ironworking, and certain philosophies, but in general, the Chinese themselves developed the ideas and institutions that gave their society the ability to expand, grow, adapt, and coordinate large populations. Many of the ancient traditions remain influential even today.

SECTION SUMMARY

■ Early Chinese society was concentrated inland from the sea and was frequently fragmented into various states.

■ In the cold, dry Chinese north, crops such as wheat and millet were grown, while in the wetter, warmer south, rice was dominant.

■ Members of the Yangshao ("painted pottery") society were skilled craftspeople who excelled at carving, weaving, and village design.

■ As time passed, the widely diverse Chinese peoples began to knit themselves together in one broad society with traditions that persist to this day.

 # The Reshaping of Ancient Chinese Society, 1750–600 B.C.E.

What were some key differences between the Shang and Zhou periods in China?

China had clearly made the great transition to cities and states when the Shang (shahng) dynasty established a powerful state and an expanding culture based on bronze technology. The Shang were followed by a more decentralized, iron-using system under the Zhou (joe) dynasty, during which time the Chinese improved writing and developed a literature. Some religious notions of enduring influence in China also appeared in these centuries. In addition, isolation from other Eurasian states convinced the Chinese that they needed little help from others, and a feeling of cultural superiority gradually developed. They perceived themselves surrounded by less developed neighbors who either adopted Chinese customs or invaded China to enjoy its riches. There was much truth to these assumptions, since strong governments, technological developments, and writing helped make China the most influential East Asian society.

The Shang Dynasty Reshapes Northern China

The Shang (1752–1122 B.C.E.), the first Chinese dynasty that can be fully documented, began around the same time that Hammurabi ruled in Babylon and the Harappan society was

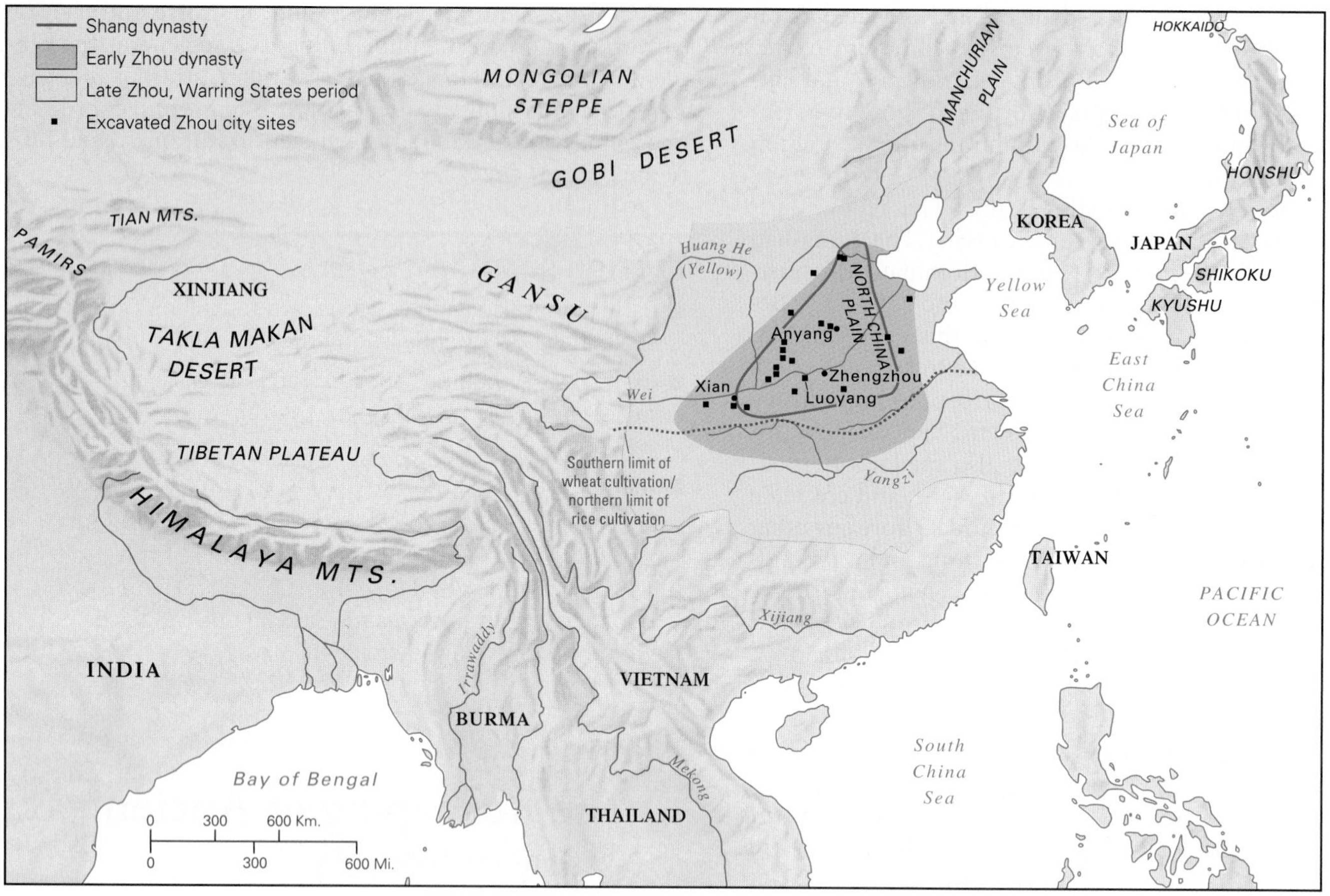

Map 4.1 Shang and Zhou China
The earliest Chinese states arose in north China along the Yellow River and its tributaries. The bronze-using Shang dynasty presided over the first documented state and were succeeded by the iron-using Zhou, who governed much of north and central China.

collapsing in India. A people from the western fringe of China, the Shang, like the Aryan migrants into India, had adopted horse-drawn chariots for warfare and owed their success partly to networks linking them with Central Asian pastoralists. They conquered the eastern Yellow River Basin and imposed a hierarchy dominated by landowning aristocrats (see Map 4.1). Shang kings presided over a growing economy and the building of more cities, and the influence of Shang culture reached far beyond their state. However, many Chinese maintained their own states and unique customs. For example, large cities with complex technology and highly developed art also flourished in places such as the western Yangzi Basin.

The Shang established an authoritarian state, perhaps in part to coordinate irrigation and dam building. Shang kingship was hereditary and was passed on to a monarch's male relative, usually a brother or son. Kings presented themselves as patriarchal and undisputed father figures who headed the country as a father did a family. The Shang made little distinction between the secular and the sacred, and their kings claimed both political and spiritual leadership. Like the Aryans who were then moving into India, they devoted much of their energy to military matters, using a lethal combination of

archers, spearmen, and charioteers. One of their concerns was defending their northern borders, a recurring theme in Chinese history. The relative prosperity of China in comparison to the marginal existence possible in the grasslands and deserts beyond the frontiers often prompted pastoral nomads to invade the Yellow River Valley.

Economically the Shang was a flourishing period. Commerce developed, and many cities were built as administrative and economic centers. The largest of the successive Shang capital cities, Anyang, was the ruler Pan Keng's new capital city discussed in the opening to this chapter. It was surrounded by a wall 30 feet high and 60 feet wide that enclosed 4 square miles; altogether, the city and its suburbs spread out over some 10 square miles. It apparently took some 10,000 workers 18 years to build Anyang, and the project reflected the considerable political and social organization of the time.

Technology improved, especially with the introduction of bronze and the earliest porcelain. The Chinese used copper by 2600 and bronze by 1400 B.C.E. This was the great age of bronze in the Afro-Eurasian Zone. The Shang and other Chinese are often considered the most skilled bronze casters the world has ever known. They used complex methods to produce flawless

Shang Bronze Pots These bronze ritual vessels, some featuring animal designs, were made during the Shang or early Zhou period. They were used for ceremonies. (Courtesy of the Trustees of the British Museum)

bronze arrows, spears, sculpture, pots, and especially ritual vessels for drinking wine. The Shang also produced glazed pottery that was the forerunner of the porcelain ("china") for which the Chinese would later become so famous.

Shang Society and Culture

The Shang fostered a new social organization. As already mentioned, their social hierarchy was dominated by landowning aristocrats, many of whom also served as government officials. These elite individuals enjoyed luxurious and extravagant surroundings and engaged in regular royal-sponsored hunts for tigers, bears, boars, and deer. Their residences were built on cement-like foundations in a style that closely resembled the houses of the wealthy many centuries later. Aristocratic women also enjoyed a high status. For example, Fuhao (foo-HOW), a wife of a Shang king, led military campaigns and owned large estates. These leaders and their families were buried in elaborate royal tombs surrounded by great quantities of valuable objects.

Most people were commoners or slaves. The Shang middle class consisted of skilled artisans, scribes, and merchants. The most valued artisans were the bronze casters. The scribes, most of them employed in government service, may have formulated the world's earliest simple decimal system, around 1500 B.C.E. Farmers and laborers occupied the bottom of the social hierarchy, and they were often mobilized by the powerful state for major building projects. Many of these laborers were war captives who had become slaves. The Shang were harsh masters. They practiced human and animal sacrifice as part of their religious observances, often using slaves as victims.

The Shang's momentous contribution was an elaborate writing system. Some scholars believe that 4,800-year-old inscriptions on pottery can be considered writing, but most conclude that oracle bones from Shang times provide the earliest examples of Chinese writing. In an attempt to predict the future, influential people wrote questions addressed to the gods on bones of animals and tortoise shells. The variety of subjects included the abundance of the next harvest, the outcome of a battle, the weather, or the birth of an heir. For example, one inquired "whether today there would be prolonged rain," and another asked whether "if the king hunted, whether the chase would be without mishap."[5] Some officials, probably those with great prestige, seem to have been experts in interpreting the future with these bones. The writing found on oracle bones was clearly the forerunner of today's Chinese writing. In the later Shang period, people also wrote inscriptions on bronze vases.

The Early Zhou and Their Government

As Shang power faded, the Zhou, a state on the western fringe of China, invaded and overthrew the Shang. The new rulers formed a new dynasty, the Zhou (1122–221 B.C.E.), and established a new type of government. The triumph of the Zhou occurred about the time that the Assyrian Empire was rising in western Asia and the Mycenaean society in Greece disintegrated. The Duke of Zhou, credited by early Chinese historians for completing Zhou expansion, supposedly urged that "we must go on, abjuring all idleness, until our reign is universal and from the corners of the sea and the sun rising there shall not be one who is disobedient to our rule."[6] But the decentralized Zhou system differed considerably from the Shang system. A relatively weak central government ruled over small states that had considerable autonomy but owed service obligations to the king, somewhat like the earlier Akkadian Empire in Sumeria.

The decentralized system reflected the Zhou realization that, despite their impressive military technology, Chinese culture had spread too far for them to administer the entire society effectively. The royal family directly ruled the area around their capital, the present-day city of Xian (SEE-an), but parceled out the rest to followers, relatives, and Shang collaborators. The regional leaders became local lords with much local power. This system allowed the Zhou kings to preside, however symbolically, over a much larger land area than that of the Shang, from southern Manchuria to the Yangzi Basin (see Map 4.1).

To solidify their position, the Zhou justified their triumph over the Shang with a new concept: the **Mandate of Heaven**. According to this belief, rulers had the support of the supernatural realm ("heaven") so long as conditions were good. However, when there was war, famine, or other hardships, heaven withdrew its sanction and rebellion was permissible. The decadent and cruel Shang, the Duke of Zhou argued, lost their right to rule because their last kings mocked the gods by their behavior and "did not make themselves manifest to Heaven."[7] But over time this radical new concept was used against the Zhou and all later dynasties, since it added the criterion of morality to kingship. Monarchs lost their legitimacy if their misrule led to a crisis. Ever since the Zhou, the Chinese have invoked the Mandate of Heaven to justify and explain the demise of a discredited dynasty or government.

The Mandate of Heaven was not the only enduring political idea fostered by the Zhou. In about the sixth century B.C.E., Chinese scholars began to view their political history in terms of the **dynastic cycle**. Instead of seeing a straight line of progress in history, as the Hebrews did, the Chinese focused on dynasties of ruling families, all of which more or less followed the same pattern as their predecessors. The cycle always began with a new dynasty, which brought peace and prosperity for a few decades. Then overexpansion and corruption led to increasingly costly government, bankruptcy, social decay, and rebellions. This disorder eventually resulted in a new dynasty, beginning the cycle anew. Modern scholars consider this narrative too simple because it ignored many factors, such as the continuity of government institutions from one dynasty to the next, but it shaped Chinese thinking for the next 2500 years.

The Zhou system was unstable, plagued by chronic warfare between the various substates and outsiders. Over the centuries, larger substates conquered smaller ones. The worst warfare occurred during the Era of the Warring States, beginning around 500 B.C.E. (see Chapter 5). As a result, the 1,700 substates of the early Zhou years were reduced to 7 by 400 B.C.E. These larger substates now had considerable power in counteracting the weakening Zhou kings. External pressures also threatened political order. The Central Asians were obtaining faster ponies, forcing the Chinese to erect better defenses against the relentless pressure.

Mandate of Heaven A Chinese belief that rulers had the support of the supernatural realm as long as conditions were good, but rebellion was justified when they were not.

dynastic cycle The Chinese view of their political history, which focuses on dynasties of ruling families.

Early Zhou Society and Economy

Zhou government not only brought political fragmentation and a figurehead monarchy, but it also fostered a rigid social structure. Zhou society clearly divided aristocrats, commoners, and slaves. The nobility owed allegiance to the king as vassals but governed their own realms as they liked. Most aristocratic families owned large estates that were worked by slaves, and they hired private armies to defend their property. As influential commoners, the merchants and artisans were more insulated from the aristocracy. Indeed, merchants had much freedom of action and often became rich. The majority of slaves were soldiers from rival ministates who were captured in the frequent wars. Criminals and sometimes their relatives were enslaved for their misdeeds.

Peasants, the largest group of commoners, were mostly bound to the soil on aristocracy-owned land (see the Witness to the Past: The Poetry of Peasant Life in Zhou China). Their superiors assigned them work and punished them if it was not done. Peasants were assigned houses, wore prescribed clothes to indicate their status, and had specified tax obligations. Their songs reflected resignation: "We rise at sunrise, We rest at sunset. Dig wells and drink, Till our field and eat—What is the strength of the emperor to us?"[8] Yet, there were some checks on landowner power. A major rebellion or massive desertion could ruin a landlord, so he had an incentive to develop reasonably humane policies toward the common people on his lands. The more repressive and exploitive lords did indeed lose many of their workers and slaves, who migrated or absconded, depopulating the land.

Gender roles were rigid in this patriarchal society. Both men and women were expected to marry, but all marriages were arranged by parents. A song from the times states: "How does one take a wife? Without a matchmaker she cannot be got." Whatever their class status, before or after marriage most women worked hard, and their assigned place was in the home. They prepared food, did housekeeping, and made clothes. Women at all levels were expected to be meek and submissive, and they enjoyed no official role in public affairs, although some women exercised considerable informal influence. While many elite women were literate, few peasant women or men enjoyed opportunities to learn to read and write. But some women could travel beyond their villages. Both genders valued friendship and kinship, as another song illustrates: "Of men that are now, None equals a brother. When death and mourning affright us, Brothers are very dear."[9]

Zhou social life often revolved around food: the Zhou-era Chinese clearly appreciated the culinary arts. The Chief Cook of the ruler was a high state official. Written sources describe many lavish feasts, often used to cement social ties. Indeed, the banquet was a chief tool of diplomacy at all levels of society, often lubricated by wine: "When we have got wine, we strain it; When we have got none, we buy it!"[10] The costly and complicated ceremonies enjoyed by the rich did not extend down to peasants, who had little money for anything more than basic hospitality.

We can learn something of the lives of ancient Chinese common folk, especially the peasants who worked the land, from *The Book of Songs*, a collection of 305 poems, hymns, and folk songs compiled between 1000 and 600 B.C.E.

Some songs address ordinary people at their labor. Men weed the fields, plant, plow, and harvest. Women and girls gather mulberry leaves for silkworms, carry hampers of food to the men in the fields for lunch, and make thread:

The girls take their deep baskets, And follow the path under the wall, to gather the soft mulberry-leaves.

Some of the songs deal with courtship and love, sometimes revealing strong emotion, as in this song by a girl about a prospective sweetheart:

That the mere glimpse of a plain cap, Could harry me with such longing, Cause me pain so dire. . . . Enough! Take me with you to your house. . . . Let us two be one.

Within the family, the father had nearly absolute authority over his wife and children. When the family patriarch died, his wife became the family head. Children were expected to obey their parents, but some songs reveal that mutual affection and gratitude were common:

My father begot me. My mother fed me, Led me, bred me, Brought me up, reared me, Kept her eye on me, tended me, At every turn aided me. Their good deeds I would requite.

Peasant lives were filled with toil and hardship, but they could find some relief from drudgery in friendship and kinship. Entertaining relatives and friends was a major leisure activity:

And shall a man not seek to have his friends? He shall have harmony and peace. I have strained off my liquor in abundance, the dishes stand in rows, and none of my brethren are absent. Whenever we have leisure, let us drink the sparkling liquor.

Peasants faced many demands on their time and labor. Songs complain and even protest about an uncaring government and its rapacious tax collectors:

Big rat, big rat, Do not gobble our millet! Three years we have slaved for you. Yet you took no notice of us. At last we are going to leave you, And go to the happy land . . . where no sad songs are sung.

Some songs record abject poverty and misery.

Deep is my grief. I am utterly poverty-stricken and destitute. Yet no one heeds my misfortunes. Well, all is over now. No doubt it was Heaven's [the supernatural realm's] doing. So what's the good of talking about it!

Zhou peasants needed all the help they could get and some songs seem to be prayers to Heaven to bless their lives:

Good people, gentle folk—Their ways are righteous. . . . Their thoughts constrained. . . . Good people, gentle folk— Shape the people of this land. . . . And may they do so for ten thousand years!

THINKING ABOUT THE READING

1. What do the songs tell us about the importance of families and friends to the Zhou Chinese?

2. What did peasants think about those who ruled them? Can you say why?

Source: The Book of Songs, translated by Arthur Waley (London: George Allen and Unwin, 1954), pp. 26, 316–317, 309, 305, 174. George Allen & Unwin LTD. © copyright 1954 by permission of the Arthur Waley Estate.

Online Study Center **Improve Your Grade**
Primary Source: The Book of Documents

Zhou China nurtured many significant technological and economic developments. Ironworking reached China over trade networks from Central Asia by around 700 B.C.E. From the Zhou states iron reached southern Chinese, who improved the technology by 500 B.C.E. Iron made much better plows and tools than bronze but also improved weaponry for the increasing warfare. Newly introduced soybeans provided a rich protein source and also enriched the soil. Chinese agriculture became so productive, and surpluses so common, that the population by 600 B.C.E. was around 20 million. Trade grew, and merchants became more prominent. Copper coins were issued as China developed a cash economy.

The Evolution of Chinese Writing

During the Shang and Zhou periods, a distinctive Chinese writing system arose to solve the special problems posed by the many spoken languages. Some six hundred dialects of Chinese are still spoken today, a heritage of many local cultures. Most of the Chinese north of the Yangzi River speak closely related Northern Mandarin dialects, but other Chinese, especially in the southern half of China, have different dialects that are often mutually unintelligible. Chinese from Guangzhou (GWAHN-Cho), Shanghai (shahng-hie), and Beijing (bay-JING) would not understand each other if they only spoke their local dialects. Another diffi-

Large *(frontal view of "large" man)*		
Sun		
To speak *(mouth with protruding tongue?)*		
Mouth		
Speech *(vapor or tongue leaving mouth)*		
Door, house *(left leaf of double door)*		
Heart, mind *(picture of physical heart)*		
Evening, dusk *(crescent moon)*		
Tree, wood *(tree with roots and branches)*		
Fish		
Grass *(growing plants)*		
Drum *(drum on stand; hand with stick)*		

Figure 4.1 Evolution of Chinese Writing
This chart shows early and modern forms of Chinese characters, revealing how pictographs, often recognizable, matured into increasingly abstract ideographs.

culty is that the monosyllabic Chinese languages are tonal: that is, the stress or tone placed on a sound changes its meaning. For example, depending on the tone employed by the speaker, in Mandarin the sound *ma* can mean "mother," "hemp," "horse," or the verb "to curse." It can also indicate a question.

To overcome these problems, the Shang and Zhou Chinese gradually developed one written language based not on sound but on characters. The pictographs of early Shang times resemble crude pictures of an object, such as a man or bird. Over some centuries they evolved into complex ideographs, in which characters stand for ideas and concepts. Some 50,000 new characters have been created since the Shang (see Figure 4.1). The practicality of this system became apparent in modern times when Chinese linguists faced great difficulty converting tonal words into a Western-type alphabet.

As in Mesopotamia and Egypt, writing had vast social and cultural implications. The writing system promoted political and cultural unity, making possible communication between people whose dialects were often very different from each other. Without such a system, the Chinese might have split into many small countries, as occurred in India and Europe for much of history. Thus writing helped to create the largest society on earth, unifying rather than dividing peoples of diverse ancestries, regions, and languages. Chinese writing also reinforced a strong feeling of historical continuity and a deep reverence for the past and one's ancestors. The written language gained a certain mystique, giving prestige to those who mastered it. As the writing brush became the main writing instrument, writing became an art form, and every literate Chinese became something of an artist. Perhaps this written language has endured for over 3,500 years in part because it possesses so many artistic qualities.

To be sure, the demands of memorizing and mastering thousands of characters, as well as of acquiring acceptable brushwork skills, mostly limited literacy to those in the upper classes with the time and money to study writing. Those who could master the system gained special status, and education, scholarship, and literature became valued commodities. Rulers and administrators also gained legitimacy through their literacy.

Ancient Philosophy and Religion

Chinese ideas on the deeper mysteries of life and the cosmic order also developed in ancient times. The diverse Shang religion emphasized ancestor worship, magic, and mythology as well as agricultural deities and local spirits. Gradually these ideas evolved by later Zhou times into distinctive ideas, including the notion of a generalized supernatural or moral force the Chinese called *tian* (tee-an), which was believed to govern the universe. Western Christian visitors later translated this term, somewhat inaccurately, as "heaven."

The first books probably appeared during the Shang period, including the **Yijing** (Yee-CHING) (Book of Changes), an ancient collection of sixty-four mystic hexagrams and commentaries upon them that were used to predict future events. It was used regularly during the Zhou period and later became influential throughout East Asia. The *Yijing*'s main theme was that heaven and earth are in a state of continual transition. This book helped the Chinese to understand the process of change.

The *Yijing* was closely related to Chinese cosmological thinking as expressed in the theory of *yin* and *yang*, which had appeared in simple form as early as the Shang period and was elaborated in later centuries. To the Chinese, yin and yang are the two primary cosmic forces that make the universe run through their interaction. Neither one permanently triumphs;

Yijing (Book of Changes) An ancient Chinese collection of sixty-four mystic hexagrams and commentaries upon them that was used to predict future events.

rather they are balanced, in conflict and yet complementary in a kind of cosmic symphony. Many things were correlated with these principles:

> Yang: bright, hot, dry, hard, active, masculine, heaven, sun
> Yin: dark, cold, wet, soft, quiescent, feminine, earth, moon

Given the Chinese preference for hierarchy, yang was superior to yin, and male superior to female. Thus the philosophy justified inequalities in society.

The yin-yang dualism remains important throughout East Asia. For example, the symbol is found on the modern South Korean flag. Because China was the cultural heartland of East Asia, the Chinese strongly influenced their neighbors in Korea, Vietnam, and Japan, beginning in Shang times, and over the centuries many Chinese ideas and institutions diffused to the peoples on their fringe.

SECTION SUMMARY

- The western Shang established an authoritarian state, with the king playing the role of father to the entire country.
- Under the Shang, society became increasingly stratified, divided up into a dominant aristocracy, a middle class, farmers and laborers, and slaves.
- After a slave rebellion overthrew the Shang, the Zhou established a more widespread, less centralized empire.
- The Zhou introduced the concepts of rule by the "Mandate of Heaven," and of the dynastic cycle, which have endured to this day.
- A common written language provided a unifying link for the Chinese, who spoke hundreds of different dialects (many of which are still spoken today).
- One of the first Chinese books was the *Yijing*, which was related to the idea of the universal opposing forces, *yin* and *yang*.

 ## Ancient Southeast and Northeast Asians

How did the traditions developing in Southeast and Northeast Asia differ from those in India and China?

While the Chinese and Indians created some of the first urban societies, the neighboring societies of Southeast and Northeast Asia also made important early contributions in farming and technology in an environment somewhat different from their large neighbors. The resulting cultures, although influenced by China or India or both, demonstrated many unique characteristics. These societies and the networks of trade and migration that formed provided the foundations for enduring traditions.

Southeast Asian Environments and Early Agriculture

While historically linked to both China and India, Southeast Asian peoples developed in distinctive ways that were shaped in part by geography and climate. Southeast Asia, which stretches from modern Burma (or Myanmar) eastward to Vietnam and the Philippines and southward through the Indonesian archipelago, is separated from the Eurasian landmass by significant mountain and water barriers. The region has a tropical climate, with long rainy seasons. Before modern times rain forests covered much of the land. But the great rivers that flow through mainland Southeast Asia, such as the Mekong (MAY-kawng), Red, and Irrawaddy (ir-uh-WAHD-ee) Rivers, also carved out broad, fertile plains and deltas that could support dense human settlement.

The topography both helped and hindered communication. Southeast Asians say that the sea unites and the land divides. The shallow oceans fostered maritime trade, encouraging seafaring and fishing. Mastery of the seas linked the peoples of large islands such as Sumatra (soo-MAH-truh), Java (JA-veh), and Borneo (also known as Kalimantan) to their neighbors. But the heavily forested interior highlands of the mainland and the islands inhibited travel and encouraged cultural diversity, including a wide variety of religions, worldviews, languages, states, and economic patterns. An old Indonesian proverb well describes the complex mosaic of cultures that resulted: different fields, different grasshoppers; different pools, different fish.

Agriculture arose early, but archaeologists still debate how early. Some think the transition to food growing began in what is today Thailand and northern Vietnam by 8000 or perhaps even 9000 B.C.E., roughly the same time as in southwest Asia, but most doubt that it began much earlier than 6000 B.C.E. Certainly farming was widespread by 5000 B.C.E. In New Guinea, the large island just east of Southeast Asia, horticulture also developed very early, sometime between 7000 and 4000 B.C.E. Rice was apparently first domesticated in northern Southeast Asia or southern-central China 6,000 or 7,000 years ago; the two areas were closely linked in Neolithic times. Between 4000 and 3000 B.C.E. rice growing became common. Southeast Asians may have been the first to cultivate bananas, yams, and taro and domesticated chickens, pigs, and perhaps even cattle (see Chronology: Northeast and Southeast Asia, 10,000–600 B.C.E.).

Southeast Asians also developed or improved technologies, some of which may have come originally from India, Mesopotamia, and China. Bronze-working appeared very early, sometime before 2000 B.C.E. By 1500 B.C.E. fine bronze was being produced in what is today northeast Thailand in villages like Ban Chiang (chang), founded around 3600 B.C.E., whose people lived in houses perched on poles above the ground, still a common pattern in Southeast Asia. Ban Chiang women made beautiful hand-painted and durable pottery. Village artists fashioned necklaces and bracelets as well as many household items of bronze and ivory.

Elsewhere in Eurasia the Bronze Age was synonymous with states, cities, kings, armies, huge temples, and defensive

CHRONOLOGY	
Northeast and Southeast Asia, 10,000–600 B.C.E.	
10,000–300	Jomon culture in Japan
8000–6000	Agriculture begins in Southeast Asia
7000–4000	Agriculture begins in New Guinea
5000–2000	Agriculture begins in Korea
4500–2000	Bronze Age begins in Southeast Asia
4000–2000	Austronesian migrations into Southeast Asia islands
1600–1000	Melanesian and Austronesian migrations into South Pacific
1000–800	First Southeast Asian states
1000	Austronesian settlement of Fiji and Samoa

walls, but in Southeast Asia bronze metallurgy derived from peaceful villages with few hints of warfare. Evidence for trade networks can be found in Dong Son village, Vietnam, where people made huge bronze drums that have been found all over Southeast Asia. Tin mined in Southeast Asia may have been traded to the Indus cities and Mesopotamia to be used in making bronze there; if so, this trade would suggest involvement in even larger networks. Southeast Asians worked iron by 500 B.C.E., several centuries later than northern China.

Dong Son Bronze Drum   These huge Dong Son bronze drums, named for a village site in Vietnam, were produced widely in ancient Southeast Asia and confirm the extensive long-distance trade networks.
(Erich Lessing/Art Resource, NY)

Migration and New Societies in Southeast Asia and the Pacific

Gradually new societies formed from local and migrant roots. The early Southeast Asians probably included the Vietnamese, Papuans (PAH-poo-enz), Melanesians (mel-uh-NEE-zhuhns), and Negritos (Ne-GREE-tos). Several waves of migrants came into mainland Southeast Asia from China sometime before the Common Era, assimilating local peoples or prompting them to migrate eastward through the islands. Today Papuans and Melanesians are found mostly in New Guinea and the western Pacific islands, while the few thousand remaining small-statured, dark-skinned Negritos mostly live in the mountains of the Malay Peninsula and the remote Andaman and Nicobar Islands west of the peninsula. Migration fostered some of the oldest networks linking peoples over a wide area. The newcomers probably mixed their cultures and languages with those of the remaining indigenous inhabitants, shaping the region's societies. The ethnic merging produced new peoples such as the Khmers (kuh-MARE) (Cambodians), who later established states in the Mekong River Basin.

Over the course of several millennia peoples speaking Austronesian (AW-stroh-NEE-zhuhn) languages and possessing advanced agriculture entered island Southeast Asia from the large island of Taiwan, just east of China. Beginning around 4000 B.C.E., Austronesians began moving south from Taiwan into the Philippine Islands, and some later moved southward into the Indonesian archipelago (see Map 4.2). Sometime before 2000 B.C.E. they had settled Java, Borneo, and Sumatra, and by 1000 B.C.E. Austronesian languages were dominant from the northern Philippines through what is today Indonesia to the Malay Peninsula and the central Vietnam coast. Indonesian islanders were the major seafaring traders and explorers of eastern Eurasia before the Common Era.

The Austronesian migrations brought new settlers and cultures to Southeast Asia and had a profound effect on other regions as well. Melanesians migrated eastward by boat into the western Pacific islands beginning around 1500 or 1600 B.C.E., carrying Southeast Asian domesticated crops, animals, house styles, and farming technology as far east as Fiji. Traveling in outrigger canoes and, later, in large double-hulled canoes, some Austronesians also sailed east into the open Pacific, mixing their cultures, languages, and genes with those of the Melanesians. By around 1000 B.C.E. Austronesian settlers had reached Samoa and Tonga.

These voyages were intentional efforts at discovery and colonization by fearless mariners who developed remarkable navigation skills, reading the stars with their eyes and the swells with their backs as they lay down their canoes. The an-

Map 4.2   The Austronesian Diaspora
Austronesians migrated from Taiwan into Southeast Asia, settling the islands. Later some of these skilled mariners moved east into the Western Pacific, settling Melanesia. Eventually some of their ancestors settled Polynesia and Micronesia.

cient western Pacific culture known as **Lapita**, stretching some 2,500 miles from just northeast of New Guinea to Samoa, was marked by a distinctive pottery style and a widespread trading network over vast distances. In Samoa and Tonga, Polynesian culture emerged from Austronesian roots. Some Polynesians eventually reached as far east as Tahiti and Hawaii, both 2,500 miles from Tonga.

The Austronesians, Vietnamese, and others established a foundation for societies based on intensive agriculture, fishing, and interregional commerce. By 1000 B.C.E. dynamic Austronesian trade networks stretched over 5,000 miles, from western Indonesia to the central Pacific, forming a commercial system unparalleled in the ancient world. Austronesians built advanced boats and carried out maritime trade with India by 500 B.C.E. Indonesian cinnamon even reached Egypt. The Vietnamese created the first known Southeast Asian states between 1000 and 800 B.C.E. and believed in a god that, according to their myths, "creates the elephants [and] the grass, is omnipresent, and has [all-seeing] eyes."[11]

Lapita The ancient western Pacific culture that stretched some 2,500 miles from just northeast of New Guinea to Samoa.

Northeast Asian Environments

The Chinese strongly influenced their neighbors in Northeast Asia, the Koreans and the Japanese, beginning in the Shang period and continuing for many centuries afterward. But the Koreans and Japanese had already established the foundations for complex societies. Over the following centuries they integrated Chinese influences with their own ideas and customs, producing unique cultures and separate ethnic identities.

Korea and Japan are neighbors, but they were shaped by different environments (see Map 4.1). The 110 miles of stormy seas that separate them at their closest point did not prevent contact between the two societies but did make it sporadic. Korea occupies a mountainous peninsula some 600 miles long and 150 miles in width. Japan, on the other hand, is a group of 3,400 islands stretching across several climatic zones. Over 90 percent of the land is on three islands: densely populated Honshu (hahn-shoo), frigid Hokkaido (haw-KAI-dow) in the north, and subtropical Kyushu (KYOO-shoo) in the south. Because mountains occupy much of Japan, only a sixth of the land is suitable for intensive agriculture. The archipelago is also weak in all metals except silver.

The Roots of Korean Society

Despite centuries of contact, the Koreans were never assimilated by the neighboring Chinese, in part because the Korean and Chinese spoken languages were very different. Korean belongs to the Ural-Altaic language family and is therefore related (although not closely) to Mongol, Turkish, and the Eastern Siberian tongues. Ural-Altaic languages are polysyllabic and nontonal, unlike Chinese.

Korean lives gradually changed as they began farming between 5000 and 2000 B.C.E., perhaps borrowing the technology from China. Later they creatively adapted rice growing, which originated in warm southern lands, to their cool climate. As Korean agriculture became more productive, the population grew rapidly, generating a persistent migration of Koreans across the straits to Japan. Growing occupational specialization led to small states based on clans. In a pattern still common today, female shamans led the animistic religion.

The ancient Koreans imported some useful ideas and also made several technological innovations. Sometime between the fifteenth and eighth century B.C.E. they adopted bronze, probably from China, and mining and metallurgy became significant activities. Ironworking reached Korea from China or Central Asia between 700 and 300 B.C.E. Shang refugees fleeing in the wake of dynastic collapse brought more Chinese culture and technology, but Koreans also created their own useful products and technology. For example, they produced some of the era's finest pottery. To contend with the frigid winters, the early Koreans invented an ingenious method of radiant floor heating, still widely used today, that circulates heat through chambers in a stone floor. Much later both the Chinese and Romans devised similar schemes.

The Roots of Japanese Society

The ancient Japanese were more isolated than the Koreans from China and no less creative. Human settlement began perhaps 40,000 years ago, before rising sea levels isolated Japan from the mainland. Pottery, for example, was produced on Kyushu by 10,700 B.C.E., earlier than in China, and this date makes Japanese pottery among the oldest in the world. The identity of these early settlers and pottery-makers is unknown, but they were probably the ancestors of the Ainu (I-noo), who are genetically close to other East Asians despite their light skin and extensive body hair, which are unusual in the region. The ancestral Ainu seem to have built seaworthy boats, for they settled the Kurile (KOO-reel) Islands north of Japan and traded with the people of eastern Siberia. Ainu relics have also been found in the Aleutian (ah-LOO-shan) Islands off Alaska, suggesting some connection there in prehistoric times. Several scholars think that ancestors of the Ainu were among the northeast Asians who settled the Americas. Today the remaining few thousand Ainu, who mostly live in their own villages on Hokkaido and Sakhalin Island, face cultural extinction.

Migration influenced Japan no less than Southeast Asia, but little is known about when the non-Ainu ancestors of most of today's Japanese arrived in the islands. Some may have come from northeastern Asia by way of Korea beginning 3,000 or

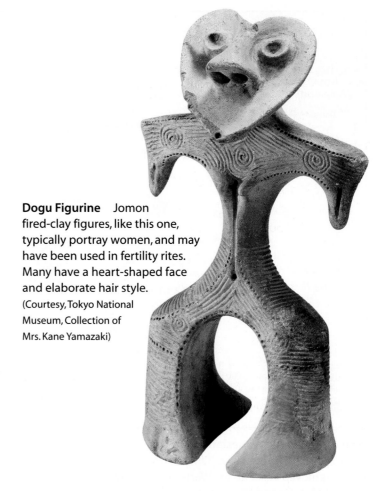

Dogu Figurine Jomon fired-clay figures, like this one, typically portray women, and may have been used in fertility rites. Many have a heart-shaped face and elaborate hair style. (Courtesy, Tokyo National Museum, Collection of Mrs. Kane Yamazaki)

4,000 years ago. Ainus and newcomers mixed over the millennia. Genetic studies link modern Japanese to the Ainu, Siberians, and especially Koreans.

Jomon Society

The best documented Japanese early society is called **Jomon** (JOE-mon) ("rope pattern"), because of the ropelike designs on their pottery. The Jomon period began around 10,000 B.C.E. and endured until 300 B.C.E. The Jomon evidently had little contact with China but did some trade with Korea and Siberia. Most scholars suspect it was a primarily Ainu culture that was divided by various languages and regional customs. The diversity may reflect the arrival of migrants from Korea, especially in southern Japan. The Jomon and other ancient islanders were only partially the ancestors of the modern Japanese. The major migrations that brought waves of iron-using settlers from Korea came later, between 500 B.C.E. and 700 C.E.

The Jomon lived primarily from hunting, gathering, and fishing, but by 5000 B.C.E. they lived in permanent wooden houses containing elaborate hearths, probably the centers for family gatherings. Scholars are impressed with the wide range of foods that made up their well-balanced, highly nutritious

---

Jomon The earliest documented culture in Japan, known for the ropelike design on its pottery.

diet, which included shellfish, fish, seals, deer, wild boar, and yams. The Jomon may have been better fed than the Chinese and Korean farmers. They may also have grown millet by 1000 B.C.E., but there is no evidence for more complex agriculture until around 500 B.C.E.

As in Korea, a very different spoken language helped preserve cultural distinctiveness despite much Chinese cultural influence over the centuries. Whether the Japanese language was spoken by some of the Jomon or brought by later immigrants remains uncertain. Japanese is related, but not closely, to modern Korean, and not at all to the surviving Ainu languages. At some point, probably between 500 B.C.E. and 500 C.E., most of the Ainu languages were overwhelmed by a Japanese language with diverse roots that was possibly based on a now lost Korean dialect. The environment helped shape the language. Perhaps in response to increasingly crowded conditions as Japan's population grew, the language structure and vocabulary came to promote tact and vagueness, and the Japanese became adept at nonverbal understanding and at feeling out other people's moods. It is much harder to directly insult or provoke someone in Japanese than in most languages. These tendencies, which are useful in discouraging social conflict, remain part of Japan's unique heritage.

SECTION SUMMARY

- The peoples of Southeast Asia established early maritime trading networks, while inland geographical boundaries led to the development of extremely diverse cultures.

- Extensive migration occurred among China, Southeast Asia, and the Pacific islands.

- Korea and Japan, while being strongly influenced by the Chinese, were shaped by different environments and created unique cultures and societies.

- Partly because of its distinct language, Korea was never assimilated into China and developed special technologies, such as radiant floor heating, to meet its needs.

- The ancestors of modern Japanese probably included, among others, the Ainu, the Jomon, and later the Koreans.

- Japan's language promoted tact and vagueness, probably to prevent social conflict in an increasingly populated area.

 # Migration and Settlement in the Americas

How do scholars explain the settlement of the Americas and the rise of agriculture in these continents?

After the migrations of humans from Eurasia to the Americas thousands of years ago, American societies developed in isolation from those in the Eastern Hemisphere. Early Americans created diverse cultures that often flourished from hunting and gathering, and later Americans, in some regions, created urban societies, states, writing, and trade networks. Population movement and adaptations to differing environments shaped these varied people's most ancient history.

Diverse American Environments

Most of the land area of the Western Hemisphere is found on two continents, North and South America, which are linked by the long, thin strand of Central America. A string of fertile islands, both large and small, also rings the Caribbean Sea from Florida to Venezuela. Unlike the east-west axis of Eurasia, the Americas lie on a north-south axis, with a large forest-covered tropical zone separating more temperate regions. This meant that migrating peoples or long-distance travelers encountered very different environmental and climatic zones.

Although the total land area is smaller, the Western Hemisphere contains as much diversity of landforms and climate as the Eastern. Extensive tropical rain forests originally covered much of Central America and parts of the Caribbean islands as well as the vast Amazon and Oronoco (or-uh-NO-ko) River Basins of South America. In these tropical regions intensive farming was difficult, although some people developed simple farming. Rain-drenched forests also once covered much of the northern Pacific coast and southern Chile, while the eastern part of what is now the United States had more temperate woodlands. The long, harsh winters in much of North America made hunting and gathering the most practical subsistence option.

Great mountain ranges shaped human life by discouraging communication, while river systems encouraged it. Like the Himalayas in Asia, the high Andes (AN-deez), which stretch nearly 5,000 miles from the Caribbean coast down the western side of South America, limited human interaction. Similarly, in North America, the Rocky Mountains provided an east-west barrier from New Mexico to northwestern Canada. Mountains also run along the Pacific coast from Alaska to southern Mexico. By trapping rain clouds, these formidable coastal and Andes mountain complexes helped create huge deserts in western North America and along the Pacific coast of South America, as well as extensive grasslands in the interior of the continents. On the other hand, some of the great river systems, such as the Mississippi, drained fertile regions and fostered long-distance trade.

The Antiquity and Migration of Native Americans

The ancestry of Native Americans, and the antiquity of settlement, generate exciting debate among scholars. Most anthropologists agree that modern Native Americans are descended chiefly from stone tool–using Asians who crossed the Bering Strait from Siberia to Alaska. Most likely entered North America when Ice Age conditions lowered ocean levels and created a wide land bridge. This natural bridge is also probably how mammoths crossed from Eurasia to North America. Even today people sometimes walk the few miles across the winter ice of the Bering Sea. Some may have crossed by boat even when no land bridge existed. Seeking game like bison, caribou, and mammoths, migrants could have moved south through ice-free corridors or by boat along the Pacific coast, and gradually dispersed throughout the hemisphere. Waves of migrants from different cultural backgrounds in East and North Asia might account for the over two thousand languages among Native Americans. The last wave some 5,000 years ago brought the Inuit (IN-oo-it) and Aleuts (AH-loots).

The traditions of many Native American peoples place their origins in the Americas, usually in the areas where they lived 500 years ago, but some may have lived in these places for many centuries before that. In many North American origin stories, the first man and woman emerged from the earth and relied on the help of various animals to survive. While the stories, rich in spiritual meaning, deserve respect, much evidence supports the notion of ancient migration from Asia. The fact that no remains of any hominids earlier than modern humans have been found in the Americas suggests that all human evolution took place in the Eastern Hemisphere. Furthermore, the common ancestry of modern Native Americans is clear from the remarkable uniformity of DNA, blood, virus, and teeth types, which all connect them clearly to ancient peoples in East Asia and Siberia. For example, DNA studies link some Native Americans to the Chukchi (CHOOK-chee) people, pastoral nomads who live in the northeastern corner of Siberia. Some early American flake tools and housing styles resemble those from northern Asia, and some American languages can also be linked distantly with northeast Asian languages. As already mentioned, some evidence hints that the ancestors of the Ainu might have been early migrants. Skilled boat builders, especially of canoes, their settlements once stretched from southern Japan northward through the islands and peninsulas of eastern Siberia, and their artifacts have been discovered in the Aleutian Islands.

Recent tool and skeletal finds raise the possibility that some early immigrants may have come from someplace other than Northeast Asia. A few physical remains found in Brazil and the Pacific Northwest bear some resemblance to ancient Southeast Asians or Australian aborigines (ab-uh-RIJ-uh-neez). Several scholars have also suggested that some ancient tool cultures in eastern North America are similar to those of Stone Age peoples who lived in Spain and France several millennia earlier. Perhaps, they believe, such migrants from Europe may have used boats to skirt the edge of the ice then covering a large section of the northern Atlantic Ocean. But the evidence for possible European, Southeast Asian, or Australian migrations is sparse and controversial. If such migrants did once settle in the Americas, they likely died out or were absorbed by the peoples of Northeast Asian ancestry.

The question of when the first migrants arrived in the Americas perplexes archaeologists. For many years, most traced the migration back to the **Clovis** (KLO-vis) culture some 11,500 to 13,500 years ago, named after spear points discovered at Clovis, New Mexico (see Chronology: The Ancient

Americas, 40,000–600 B.C.E.). Clovis-type sites are widespread in North and Central America. However, human skeletons and artifacts have lately been discovered in North and South America that have much older radiocarbon dates. Monte Verde (MAWN-tee VAIR-dee), a campsite in southern Chile, which is over 10,000 miles from the Bering Strait, may be at least 12,500 years old. Monte Verde people lived in two parallel rows of rectangular houses with wooden frameworks and log foundations, and they exploited a wide variety of vegetable and animal foods. A few archaeologists think some material from Monte Verde might be as much as 33,000 years old, but many scholars doubt these are human-made artifacts.

A variety of other sites challenge the Clovis theory, but none offers conclusive evidence that convinces skeptics. Bones and diverse projectiles as old as Clovis have been found at various North American, Mexican, and Brazilian sites. A rock shelter near Pittsburgh, with possible blade knives and bone needles for sewing warm clothes, and another site in Virginia may place people in eastern North America between 17,000 and 19,000 years ago. These scattered discoveries hint at but do not prove an ancient migration somewhere between 20,000 and 40,000 years ago. The debate will rage for years to come as more sites are excavated.

CHRONOLOGY	
The Ancient Americas, 40,000–600 B.C.E.	
40,000–20,000	Possible earliest migrations to Americas (disputed)
11,500–9,500	Beginning of Clovis culture
8000	Beginning of agriculture in Mesoamerica and Andes
6000	Potato farming in Andes
4000	Early trade routes in North America
2500	Earliest mound-building cultures
3000–2500	Farming along Peruvian coast
3000–1600	Peruvian city of Caral
2500	Agriculture in lower Mississippi Valley
2000	Earliest agriculture in southwestern North America
1500	Agriculture in Amazon Basin
1200–300	Olmecs
1200–200	Chavín
1000–500	Poverty Point culture
650	Olmec writing

Clovis A Native American culture dating back some 11,500 to 13,500 years.

Hunting, Gathering, and Ancient American Life

The earliest Americans, known to scholars as Paleo-Indians, survived by hunting, fishing, and gathering while adapting to varied environments. Being skilled hunters, they may have helped bring about the extinction of large herbivore animals such as horses, mammoths, and camels, which disappeared from the Western Hemisphere between 9000 and 7000 B.C.E. But the extent to which these peoples depended on big game hunting is unclear, since they were armed only with spears and spear-throwers. A similar die-off of animals also occurred in Eurasia at the end of the Ice Age, suggesting that climate change was a factor. Most likely, the extinctions of the animals in both hemispheres was caused by some combination of over-hunting, environmental change, and perhaps an apocalyptic disease that originated with humans but then jumped to the large mammals.

In most places these trends forced a shift to hunting smaller game. But on the North American Great Plains, many peoples existed for some 10,000 years hunting bison, without benefit of horses. By 500 B.C.E. some people constructed corrals to hold captured bison. Only in the nineteenth century C.E. did this hunting way of life become impossible, as newly arrived white Americans slaughtered the bison herds on which these Native Americans depended. Abundant deer fed hunters in many other parts of North America.

Some people in favored locations flourished from hunting, fishing, and gathering for many millennia, even into modern times. This was the case in the Pacific Northwest, where coastal peoples built oceangoing boats and sturdy wood houses. Along the Peruvian coast deep-sea fishermen were exploiting the rich marine environment by 7600 B.C.E. The Monte Verde villagers, who had extensive knowledge of the available resources, used more than fifty food plants and twenty medicinal plants. In the Santa Barbara channel region of southern California beginning between 6000 and 5000 B.C.E., the Chumash (CHOO-mash) society, like the Jomon culture of Japan, lived well from a varied vegetation and meat diet that included large marine mammals such as seals. The Chumash built large, permanent villages headed by powerful chiefs, and they also used shell beads as a kind of money to distribute resources. Yet, Pacific coast peoples such as the Chumash were also subject to climate change, which periodically brought drought and hunger by altering plant and animal environments.

The eastern third of what is now the United States also provided an abundant environment for hunting and gathering, and this way of life was augmented by trade. By 4000 B.C.E. extensive long-distance trade networks linked people over several thousand miles from the Atlantic coast to the Great Plains. Dugout canoes moved copper and red ocher from Lake Superior, jasper (quartz) from Pennsylvania, obsidian from the Rocky Mountains, and seashells from both the Gulf and East Coasts. Great Lakes copper was traded as far away as New England and Florida. Indeed, copper objects made in Wisconsin around 3000 B.C.E. reached Mexico.

Early Societies and Their Cultures

Over many millennia Americans organized larger societies and developed some distinctive social and cultural patterns that emphasized cooperation within family units, animistic religion, and, for some, building huge mounds. Most people lived in egalitarian bands linked by kinship and marriage. Hunting was often a communal activity. For example, bison hunting might involve the entire village.

Americans shared with people in the Eastern Hemisphere a belief in supernatural forces, spirits, or gods. For example, perhaps like their descendants in many societies from the Amazon to the North American Great Plains, men sought a personal guardian spirit through a visionary experience induced by fasting, enduring physical pain, or taking hallucinogenic drugs. Shamans claiming command over spirits or animal souls played an important role as vehicles to connect the human and spirit worlds, often through ceremonies fueled by their showmanship. The ceremonies for such events as initiations into adult life and courtship probably included ritual dancing. Since the land furnished food, most Americans revered the earth as sacred. Some of them also adopted creation stories that were widely shared with other peoples. For example, the following Mandu creation myth from central California has much in common with the legends of some peoples a continent away on the East Coast:

> Long ago there were no stars, no moon, no sun. There was only darkness and water. A raft floated on the water, and on the raft sat a turtle. Then from the sky, a spirit came and sat on the raft. Then the spirit said that something else was needed, and he made people.[12]

Some ancient Americans organized communities around **mound building**, the construction of huge earthen mounds, often with temples on top. The oldest mound so far discovered, in Louisiana, dates to 2500 B.C.E.. Beginning around 1600 B.C.E., some peoples in the eastern woodlands and Gulf Coast of North America developed a distinctive mound-building culture. One major site, Poverty Point in northeastern Louisiana, was occupied between 1000 and 500 B.C.E., which makes it contemporary to the urban Olmec society in southern Mexico, discussed below (see Profile: The Poverty Point Mound Builders).

Occupying about three square miles, and home to perhaps five thousand people at its height, Poverty Point had the most elaborate and massive complex of earthworks in all the Americas at that time. The largest mound, an effigy of a bird that can only be seen from the air, was 70 feet high, comparable to an eight-story apartment building. It stretches nearly 700 feet from north to south and east to west. Poverty Point served as the hub of a lower Mississippi River trading system. Trade goods found there came from as far away as the Ohio and upper Mississippi River Valleys, and their exports of stone and clay products such as pendants and bowls reached what are today the states of Florida, Missouri, Oklahoma, and Tennessee.

mound building The construction of huge earthen mounds, often with temples on top, by some ancient peoples in the Americas.

THE POVERTY POINT MOUND BUILDERS

While the spectacular mounds at Poverty Point are the site's most striking legacy, the archaeological research has also revealed a remarkable community. The inhabitants did not need farming because their location, in a fertile valley nourished by annual Mississippi River floods, offered a benign hunting and gathering environment and a gentle climate. The people enjoyed a rich and varied diet that many modern people might envy. Men used simple weapons—for example, spears, spear throwers, darts, and knives—to hunt. The woods provided turkey, duck, deer, and rabbit, while the rivers offered bass, catfish, alligator, and clams. Women collected acorns, hickory nuts, walnuts, wild grapes, persimmons, sunflower seeds, squash, and gourds.

Life seems to have been agreeable. The people lived in wood houses around a central plaza and six mounds, probably governed by chiefs. In their houses men and women crafted many tools and art objects, some of which they traded hundreds of miles away. Small decorated baked-clay balls, found by the thousands in the ruins, were heated for use in cooking or boiling water. Since cooking was women's work, women probably made these clay balls, perhaps helped by their children. Each woman had her own preference for design and shape. Stoneworkers also ground and polished hard stones into ornaments and useful artifacts, and they chipped various stones into points, blades, and cutting tools. Those with an artistic bent made solid-clay female figurines, sometimes pregnant, possibly as fertility symbols. Using red jasper, they fashioned beautiful bead necklaces, bird-head pendants, and human effigies.

Located at the intersection of important waterways, Poverty Point was the central hub for a large region and was linked to trade networks that supplied the townsmen with Appalachian metal for bowls and platters, stone from the Ozarks and Oklahoma, and flint from as far away as Illinois and Ohio. The finely crafted red jasper items, often shaped like animals such as owls, have been found in distant settlements. Some of the Poverty Point men may have ventured out on trading expeditions or to bring home valuable stones from as far away as Missouri. Men and perhaps women undoubtedly arrived regularly in canoes full of trade goods to exchange.

At times the people were mobilized to build new mounds or rebuild old ones that were eroding with time. The complete earthworks contain an immense 1 million cubic yards of soil; to make them, the people probably had to transport 35 to 40 million 50-pound basket loads to the site. Several thousand people may have participated in the construction, and the project had to be carefully planned and directed so that it followed a geometric design. The mounds perhaps aided astronomical observations as a solar calendar, or perhaps served as a regional ceremonial center for social, political, or religious purposes. Some priestly or ruling class may have lived atop the mounds, as was common in some mound-building societies around the hemisphere. At least 150 smaller satellite sites, scattered along the Mississippi for several hundred miles, all contain similar artifacts, suggesting that Poverty Point was the center of both an economic and a political network.

The culture disappeared by 500 B.C.E., the people having dispersed to smaller settlements. There are no signs of war or major environmental change. Perhaps some political or religious crisis disrupted society. Whatever the case, the Poverty Point people and their culture were lost to history, leaving only the badly eroded but still impressive ruins of today.

THINKING ABOUT THE PROFILE

1. What sort of life did the Poverty Point people experience?
2. What role did Poverty Point play in the region?

Poverty Point Jasper Bead
Trade goods, such as this red jasper bead shaped like a locust, were produced at Poverty Point in Louisiana and traded over many hundreds of miles in eastern and central North America.
(Gilcrease Museum, Tulsa, Oklahoma)

SECTION SUMMARY

- The lands of the Western Hemisphere are smaller in area than those of the Eastern and are constructed on a north-south axis rather than an east-west one, but they are just as varied in terms of landforms and climate.

- Scientific evidence suggests that Native American peoples migrated from Eurasia to North America from Siberia to Alaska at least 12,000 years ago, and possibly between 20,000 and 40,000 years ago.

- Early American peoples survived by hunting, gathering, and fishing, as well as trading over large distances, but some societies clustered around huge mounds that served religious purposes.

- Mutual cooperation, earth worship, personal connections with guardian spirits, and shamanism were prominent features in early American cultural and spiritual life.

◈ The Roots of American Urban Societies

What were some of the main features of the first American societies?

In ancient times Americans, like people in the Eastern Hemisphere, developed agriculture, trade systems, institutionalized religions, monumental architecture, and creative technologies to support them. These set the stage for more complex and highly diverse cultures, and eventually the first cities, states, and written languages. The traditions of peoples in different regions shared some common ideas, but distinctive societies also arose in various places, such as the Andes and Mexico

The Rise of American Agriculture

Americans were some of the earliest farmers, but they developed very different crops than the peoples of Afro-Eurasia. Population growth and long-distance trade were key influences sparking this great transition. The ebb and flow of weather conditions may also have contributed to the shift. Some hunting and gathering peoples were vulnerable to devastating droughts in years when the periodic weather change known today as *El Niño* (EL NEE-nyo) warmed the Pacific Ocean, shifting both rainfall patterns and the marine environment. This may have prompted them to experiment with growing food sources, and eventually several quite different agricultural traditions emerged. Some of the chief crops, such as maize (corn), were much more difficult to master than the big-seeded grains of the Fertile Crescent. Furthermore, since there were no potential draft animals, farmers needed to be creative in growing and transporting food.

Some Native Americans made the transition not long after southwest Asians had. By 8500 or 8000 B.C.E. bottle gourds and pumpkins may have been raised in **Mesoamerica**, the region stretching from central Mexico southeast into northern Central America. Avocados and chili peppers have been traced to 7000 B.C.E., and by 3500 B.C.E. some Mesoamerican farmers also grew maize, sweet potatoes, and beans. Andes people cultivated chili peppers and kidney beans by about 8000 B.C.E. Later potatoes and maize flourished there. By 3400 B.C.E. some Andeans, like early farmers in Eurasia, built elaborate irrigation canals that created artificial garden plots. By 3000 or 2500 B.C.E. societies along the Peruvian coast had also made the shift to farming, often using irrigation. They raised cotton, squash, and maize as a supplement to their still lucrative exploitation of marine resources. By 2800 B.C.E. Mound Builders in what is today Uruguay, thousands of miles from Peru, were growing corn, squash, and beans. By 1500 B.C.E. farming had spread to the Amazon Basin.

Farming later spread over trade networks to North American societies, probably influenced by environmental change with a wetter climate. Maize and squash were grown in the Southwest by 2000 or 1500 B.C.E., and beans and cotton by 500 B.C.E. The southwestern peoples were particularly ingenious in adapting farming to their poor soils and desert conditions. By 2500 B.C.E. people in the lower Mississippi Valley had discovered farming and were growing sunflowers and gourds. Eventually maize, beans, and squash became mainstays from the Southwest to the northeastern woodlands, providing a nutritionally balanced diet.

Diverse Farming Patterns and Their Consequences

Three basic farming patterns eventually shaped American societies. People in the highland and valley regions of Mesoamerica relied heavily on maize, beans, and squash. Difficult to grow, maize requires considerable labor. Another farming pattern was developed by people dwelling at the high altitudes of the Andes, who cultivated potatoes and other frost-resistant tubers. Tropical forest societies in South America evolved the third pattern, growing manioc, sweet potatoes, and root crops. The differing farming patterns proved significant for later world history because the great diversity of crops later enriched modern food supplies. Americans domesticated more different plants than had all the Eastern Hemisphere peoples combined, including three thousand varieties of potatoes, as well as chocolate, quinine, and tobacco. The shifting cultivation used in most places also limited population densities and hence fostered smaller societies.

The Americans practiced less intensive agriculture than those in the Eastern Hemisphere for one simple reason: the lack of draft animals. This fact had significant consequences. The only large herd animals available for domestication, the

---

Mesoamerica The region stretching from central Mexico southeast into northern Central America.

cameloids of the Andes like the llama and alpaca, were tamed by 3500 B.C.E., mostly for use as pack animals and wool sources. Americans domesticated dogs, and turkeys and guinea pigs were bred for eating in North America and the Andes, respectively. But there were no surviving counterparts to horses, cattle, and oxen. With no animals to aid in pulling, people could not use a plow or wheel. In any case, wheeled vehicles were useless in the steep Andes and the tropical rain forests. However, people made other innovations, including various ingenious irrigation schemes. For example, terracing allowed many hillsides to be farmed, and the floating gardens later developed in Central Mexico, which turned swamps into highly productive fields, provided large surpluses. To build floating gardens, farmers dug ditches to drain away water and then built long artificial islands to form planting surfaces, piling up mud and muck from the swamp bottom and organic matter to fertilize the fields. But the sort of intensive farming, aided by draft animals, that supported huge populations in China or India was not possible in the Americas.

The lack of draft animals also meant that Americans were exposed to fewer infectious diseases and epidemics. In the Eastern Hemisphere, domesticated animals passed diseases such as measles and smallpox to humans through infectious organisms such as germs and parasites, precipitating outbreaks that could kill many people and spread to adjacent regions. Historians disagree over whether, lacking these diseases, Americans may have been healthier than people across the oceans. Skeletons reveal that many of them enjoyed long lives but many people also suffered from many ailments. Furthermore, isolation from the Eastern Hemisphere left Native Americans vulnerable to the diseases brought by Europeans and Africans beginning in 1492 C.E., for which they had no immunity. These diseases eventually killed the great majority of Native Americans.

Early Farming Societies

Archaeologists are learning more about the social and cultural patterns, such as village life and religion, of early farming peoples. Permanent lakeside villages may have appeared in Mexico's fertile central valley as early as 5500 B.C.E. Communal activity was essential in these early settlements as people cooperated for survival. In the northern Andes, people fashioned the oldest known ceramics in the hemisphere between 3000 and 2500 B.C.E. By 1600 B.C.E. societies in Baja (ba-ha) California made mural paintings on rocks and in caves.

Institutionalized religions began to take shape, led by a priestly caste. Some Mesoamericans may have practiced human sacrifice by 7000 B.C.E. Later human sacrifice became common in both Mesoamerica and the Andes to honor the gods and keep the cosmos in balance. Some South American and several North American societies developed processes for mummifying the bodies of the deceased through drying. This began with the Chonchorros people in what are today southern Peru and northern Chile by 5500 B.C.E., far earlier than the more famous Egyptian mummies. Probably people noticed how bodies became naturally mummified in a dry climate and

then devised techniques for deliberate preservation, perhaps because of religious beliefs about death and the afterlife.

Like the Mound Builders in North America, some societies in the Andes region and Mesoamerica began building permanent structures for religious, governmental, or recreational purposes. Pacific coast cultures in South America constructed some of the oldest monumental architecture, including stepped pyramids. Similar public buildings appeared in the Andes by the third millennium B.C.E., about the same time as monumental construction was taking place in Egypt, India, and China. Some buildings were made for recreational activities. A site in southern Mexico from 5000 B.C.E. contained a dance ground or ball court. Ceremonial ballgames involving small teams of players attempting to knock a rubber ball through a high stone hoop became a fixture of Mesoamerican life for millennia.

The Foundations of Cities and States

Agriculture, monumental construction, and long-distance trade provided a foundation for several societies to build the first cities and form the first states in the Americas (see Map 4.3). Between 3000 and 1000 B.C.E. farming people in Mesoamerica and the Andes made the technological breakthroughs and experienced the population growth that eventually led to urbanization. They worked metals like copper, gold, and silver to create tools, weapons, and jewelry, and they devised more productive farming systems, often including irrigation. Growing towns with public buildings became centers of political, economic, and religious activities. Massive ceremonial centers hundreds of feet long were constructed along the Peruvian coast, and huge mounds were erected in several places, laying the framework for the great pyramids that followed. Long-distance trade also become more common. By 1300 B.C.E. various trade routes wound around and through the Andes. Among the most valuable commodities traded over vast areas were obsidian, mirrors, seashells, and ceramics.

Growing populations and trade networks fostered the first cities. Between 4000 and 1 B.C.E. the population of the Americas grew from 1 or 2 million to around 15 million; over two-thirds of this number were concentrated in Mesoamerica and western South America. The first settlements built around massive stone structures emerged around 3100 B.C.E. in the Norte Chico region stretching from the western foothills of the Andes to the Pacific in central Peru. The largest of these settlements with some 3000 residents, and America's first known city, Caral in north-central Peru, was built perhaps as early as 2500 or 3000 B.C.E., about the same time as the Harappan cities and the Egyptian pyramids. Caral was a 150-acre complex of plazas, pyramids, and residential buildings that probably required many thousands of laborers to build. The major pyramid is 60 feet tall and covers the equivalent of four football fields. It contained a sunken amphitheater capable of seating hundreds of spectators for civic or religious events. These findings show that the local economy was able to support an elite group of priests, planners, builders, and designers. The elite seem to have lived in large, well-kept rooms atop the pyramids, the craftsmen at ground-

Map 4.3   Olmec and Chavín Societies
The earliest known American states arose in Mesoamerica and the Andes. The Olmecs and Chavín both endured for a millennium.

Online Study Center **Improve Your Grade**
Interactive Map: Olmec and Chavîn Civilizations

level apartments, and the workers in outlying neighborhoods. Eventually some twenty pyramid complexes occupied land for many miles around.

We know only a little of Norte Chico life. The economy was based on obtaining marine resources such as fish and growing squash, sweet potatoes, fruits, and beans as well as cotton, which they traded to coastal fishermen for making nets. The Norte Chico people do not seem to have made ceramics, unusual for a farming society, nor did they produce many arts and crafts. Caral was a major hub for trade routes extending from the Pacific coast through the Andes to the Amazonian rain forest. There is evidence for human sacrifice. The people evidently enjoyed music, and many animal bone flutes have been found in the ruins. But Caral collapsed for unknown reasons around 1600 B.C.E., several hundred years before the rise of the better-known American societies of the Olmecs and Chavín.

Mesoamerican Societies: The Olmecs

The **Olmecs** (OHL-mecks), a people who lived along the Gulf coast of Mexico, formed the earliest known urban society in Mesoamerica by 1200 or 1000 B.C.E., and they flourished until 300 B.C.E. (see Map 4.3). Each Olmec city was probably ruled by a powerful chieftain, who made alliances with chiefs in other districts. Olmec cities reflected engineering genius. The earliest city, known today as San Lorenzo, was built on an artificial dirt platform three-quarters of a mile long, half a mile wide, and 150 feet high. Home to some 2,500 people, San Lorenzo was situated above fertile but frequently flooded plains. The most famous Olmec city, La Venta, included huge earth mounds that required massive labor to build. Indeed, the mobilization of many workers was central to the construction

---

Olmecs The earliest urban society in Mesoamerica.

Olmec Head This massive head from San Lorenzo is nearly 10 feet high. The significance of such heads (and the helmets they wear) remains unclear, but they might represent chiefs, warriors, or gods. (Nathaniel Tarn/Photo Researchers, Inc.)

west coast and as far south as modern Costa Rica, importing basalt, obsidian, and iron ore. One of the major trade goods was jade, probably obtained in Guatemala, which the Olmec fashioned into ceremonial objects, masks, rings, and necklaces. The Olmecs may also have exploited cocoa trees for chocolate, later an important Mayan crop.

Extensive communication between the Olmecs and neighboring peoples contributed to some cultural homogeneity in Mesoamerica, especially in religion. Olmec religious symbols and myths emphasized a pantheon of fearsome half-human, half-animal supernatural beings, the prototypes of later Mesoamerican deities. Olmec leaders conducted great public ceremonies and honored gods feared or respected by many Mesoamerican peoples. The developing religion required precise measurement of calendar years and time cycles, which fostered the development of mathematics and writing. Although Olmec society eventually disappeared, the Olmecs established enduring patterns of life, thought, and kingship in Mesoamerica that influenced later peoples like the Maya (see Chapter 9).

South American Societies: Chavín

The earliest known Andean urban society, the **Chavín** (cha-VEEN), emerged 10,000 feet above sea level in northwestern Peru the same time as the Olmecs, around 1200 or 1000 B.C.E., and collapsed by 200 B.C.E. The Chavín created flamboyant sculpture and monumental architecture, including the large pyramid that still sits in the ruins of their major city. They also developed a highly original art focusing on real animals and anthropomorphic creatures, and they knew how to work gold and silver. As in Mesoamerica, jaguar motifs were common, but the Chavín people also seem to have venerated eagles and snakes, among other animals.

Chavín lasted for a millennium and exercised considerable influence in surrounding regions. At its height, between 860 and 200 B.C.E., the main city probably had some three thousand inhabitants. Elaborate burial sites clearly reveal a pronounced class division. The Chavín people became a major regional power, trading widely with the coast and spreading their religious cult to distant peoples. They worshiped two main deities, one of which was the "smiling god," depicted as a human body with a feline head and clawed hands and feet. Their ceremonial center became a site of pilgrimage for the faithful from a wide area. Chavín helped to establish or perpetuate some of the architectural and religious patterns that became common in the Andes.

of these cities. The stones for their sculptures and temples had to be brought from 60 miles away, and some of the blocks weigh more than 40 tons. The Olmecs studied astronomy in order to correctly orient their cities and monuments with the stars.

The Olmecs created remarkable architecture and art, as well as a writing system. The purpose of the huge sculptured stone heads they erected is unknown, but they might represent rulers. Olmec builders also constructed temples and pyramids in ceremonial centers and in palace complexes. The artists created a distinctive style, carving human and animal figures (especially jaguars) as well as supernatural beings in sculpture and relief. Knowing that the monuments or buildings would be a center of religious veneration and ceremonies for generations, astronomers and priests probably watched the artists work. By around 650 B.C.E. the Olmecs had also developed perhaps the first simple hieroglyphic writing in the Americas, which influenced other Mesoamerican peoples, especially the Mayan. Unlike in Mesopotamia, where writing developed from commercial needs, Mesoamerican writing kept records of kings, rituals, and the calendar, much as writing did in Egypt.

Commerce and the networks it created were a key to Olmec success and influence. The Olmecs traded with Mexico's

Chavín The earliest-known Andean urban society.

Xunzi also contributed to the authoritarian tendencies of Confucianism by claiming that Confucian writings were the source of all wisdom. But not all of his proposals were harsh. For example, Confucius had praised music, and Xunzi also argued that music was joy and produced an emotion that stirred people to find an outlet through movement and voice. Approved by sages for fostering harmony, music played a central role in court life and in village ceremonies.

Daoism and Chinese Mysticism

The second major philosophy to develop during the Hundred Flowers Period was **Daoism** (DOW-iz-um), which taught that people should adapt to nature. The main ideas of Daoism are attributed to Laozi (lou-zoe) (Lao Tzu or "Old Master"). However, we have no direct evidence such a man ever lived. According to the legends about his life, Laozi was an older contemporary of Confucius and a disillusioned bureaucrat who became a wandering teacher. If such a man existed, he probably did not write the two main Daoist texts, which were most likely composed during the third century B.C.E.

Daoism was a philosophy of withdrawal for people appalled by the warfare of the age. Daoist thinkers held that the goal of life for each individual was to follow the "way of the universe," or *dao*. Daoist teachers described the dao as "unfathomable, the ancestral progenitor of all things, everlasting. All-pervading, dao lies hidden and cannot be named. It produces all things. He who acts in accordance with dao becomes one with dao."[7] Convinced that people could never dominate their environment, Daoist philosophy urged them to ally themselves with it. This meant being simple, formless, without desire and without striving, and content with what is. An early Daoist text expressed disgust with everyday life: "To labor away one's whole lifetime but never see the result, and to be utterly worn out with toil but have no idea where it is leading, is this not lamentable?"[8] Daoists advised Chinese to conform to the great pattern of the natural world rather than, as was the emphasis of Confucians, to social expectations and governments. One of the main texts argued that the wise person prefers fishing on a remote stream to serving as emperor. To the Daoists societies were an obstacle and all governments corrupt and oppressive. Politicians were urged to rule a big country as you would fry small fish, that is, don't overdo it.

Daoism was mystical and romantic, fostering an awareness of nature and its beauties. This attitude became pronounced in Chinese poetry and landscape painting, which often recorded towering mountains, roaring waterfalls, and placid lakes. Daoists viewed nature as good; indeed, people and nature were one. This was different from the Western view growing out of the Greco-Roman and Christian traditions, where the wilderness was to be subdued. Thanks to Daoist influences, one of the main functions of a Chinese ruler was to maintain the balance between human society and nature, to govern well and follow correct rituals.

Daoism later fragmented into several traditions. Popular Daoism became a religion of countless deities and magic. Some followers sought to find the elixir of immortality, often by experimenting with a wide variety of foods. By contrast, philosophical Daoism, which appealed to the better educated, stressed mysticism, suggesting that the individual could live in harmony with nature by turning inward and experiencing oneness with the universe. Like all mystics seeking the heart of spirituality, Daoists found it difficult to express their basic ideas in words. Daoist writers claimed that "those who know do not speak; those who speak do not know."[9]

Some of the early Daoist writings contained stories such as this one, which is filled with mysticism, a sense of unity with nature, and a humbling relativism:

> One time, Chuang-tzu dreamed he was a butterfly, flitting around, enjoying what butterflies enjoy. The butterfly did not know that it was Chuang-tzu. Then Chuang-tzu started, and woke up, and he was Chuang-tzu again. And he began to wonder whether he was Chuang-tzu who had dreamed he was a butterfly or was a butterfly dreaming that he was Chuang-tzu.[10]

Balancing Confucianism, Daoism tapped a different strand of Chinese experience. It added enjoyment, reflection, and a sense of freedom. Daoists advised Confucianists to flow with the spirit and the heart rather than struggle with the intellect. The man in power was a Confucianist, but out of power became a Daoist. The active bureaucrat of the morning became the dreamy poet or nature lover of the evening. Daoism complemented Confucianism by enabling Chinese to balance the conflicting needs for social order and personal autonomy.

Legalism and the Chinese State

Among the dozens of other competing philosophies of the Warring States Period, **Legalism**, which advocated that the state maintain harsh control of people, also had an enduring influence. Borrowing ideas from the Confucian Xunzi, who believed people were inherently selfish and power hungry, the Legalists emphasized the need for an authoritarian government to secure prosperity, order, and stability. To ensure the survival of the whole, they believed, the state must control all economic resources, and people should be well disciplined, subject to military duty and harsh laws.

Taken to extremes, Legalism led to unrestrained state power. The ruler needed to be strong and to have no regard for the rights or will of the people, since the larger goal was to maintain unity and stability. One of the leading Legalists wrote that people can be controlled by means of punishments and rewards, commands and prohibitions, with force keeping them in subjection. Legalists ridiculed Confucian humanism. One Legalist, in a pointed attack on the Confucians, argued that "the intelligent ruler does not speak about deeds of humanity and righteousness, and he does not listen to the words of learned men."[11]

Daoism A Chinese philosophy that emphasized adaptation to nature.

Legalism A Chinese philosophy that advocated harsh control of people by the state.

Although Legalism exercised a long-term influence on Chinese politics, the Chinese always balanced it with the more humane ideas of Confucius and Mengzi, who stressed moral persuasion rather than coercion. Hence, the Chinese during the Classical Era did not follow one philosophy to the exclusion of others. In the resulting mix, leaders were to be obeyed but also ethical and benevolent. Laws were sometimes severe, but local officials had flexibility in implementing them and took into account the social context.

SECTION SUMMARY

■ Despite being marred by chronic civil warfare, China became the most populous society on earth and its economy evolved rapidly.

■ The belated development of iron technologies, as well as many other breakthroughs, finally made China competitive with western Asia.

■ Instability resulting from military conflict led intellectuals to question basic tenets of society and government, thus creating the era of the "hundred schools of thought."

■ Three enduring Chinese philosophies from this period—Confucianism, Daoism, and Legalism—have influenced Chinese state and culture through two millennia.

■ Chinese philosophies emphasized humanism rather than the supernatural or gods.

◆ Chinese Imperial Systems and Eurasian Trade

What developments during the Han dynasty linked China to the rest of Eurasia?

Chinese society, more than Indian, Middle Eastern, or European societies, was characterized by cohesion and continuity, as well as by balancing and blending of diverse influences. For example, although China was often attacked and even occasionally conquered by Central Asians, the invaders maintained continuity with China's past by adopting Chinese culture, a process known as **Sinicization**. But before modern times, there was one major transition that quickly changed the face of China: the replacement of the multistate Zhou system by a centralized empire. This made China since 221 B.C.E. different from the China before it and set the pattern for the centuries to follow. The new imperial China was forged by the harsh rulers of Qin (chin). Their despotic rule was followed by the Han dynasty, which conquered a large empire, fostered foreign trade, and restored Confucianism as a guiding philosophy, establishing enduring political patterns.

Sinicization   The process by which Central Asian invaders maintained continuity with China's past by adopting Chinese culture.

The Qin Dynasty

The political turmoil of late Zhou times ended when the Qin dynasty (221–206 B.C.E.) conquered the other states and implemented repressive Legalist ideas, a political change that transformed the China of many states into an empire with a powerful and highly authoritarian central government. Located on the northwest borders, the state of Qin had gradually become the strongest state within the Zhou system. Some of the Legalist scholars had moved there and been appointed to high office. Under their policies, the state controlled the economy, establishing government monopolies over many trade goods. Like Sparta in Greece around the same time, the population was regimented and militarized, the men serving as citizen-warriors. Slowly Qin began conquering other Zhou states. The prime minister, Li Si (lee SHE) (Li Ssu), a Legalist thinker, was a brutal man; he argued that those who used the past to oppose the present, the Confucians, had to be exterminated. Li Si was the chief deputy to the man who would eventually become the ruler, and first emperor, of all of China.

In 221 B.C.E. the Qin, finally defeating and absorbing all the remaining Zhou states, established a new government that ruled most of the Chinese people. The first Qin ruler assumed the new and imposing title of Shi Huangdi (SHE hwang-dee) (first emperor) and prophesied that his dynasty would last 10,000 generations. The son of a Qin prince and his concubine, he was not yet forty when he became ruler of China. This extraordinary autocrat surrounded himself with mystery and pomp to enhance his prestige, but in so doing he also concealed himself from the consequences of his decrees. Shi Huangdi lived in carefully guarded privacy, moving secretly from one apartment to another in his vast palaces. To reveal his movements was a crime that was instantly punished with death. The first emperor was also superstitious and devoted considerable resources to the search for an elixir of immortality.

The new dynasty implemented dramatic policies, including military expansion. Not content with conquering the Chinese heartland, the Qin also sent armies to incorporate much of southern China and, for a while, Vietnam, into the empire. In the following centuries many in the south were assimilated into Chinese society. The first emperor also mandated a total reordering of China along Legalist lines. In doing so, he constructed a monolithic state that sought to control all aspects of Chinese life. The growing bureaucracy that was needed to supervise these operations strengthened the centralized state system. The Qin goal of creating a unified state was accomplished once they embraced nearly all regions where Chinese society was dominant. Given this unification, the name *Qin* is quite fittingly the origin of the Western name for China.

Later Chinese historians viewed the Qin Empire as one of the most terrible periods in the country's long history. The common people hated the forced labor and strict laws. Spies, general surveillance, and thought control were paramount in the Qin police state, which closely monitored the citizenry. Intellectuals despised the Qin because the state launched attacks on all aspects of culture, including Confucianism. In the campaign to stamp out what they perceived to be subversive doctrines, the

Qin burned thousands of books, sparing only practical and scientific manuals, and executed many scholars, often by burying them alive. In so doing the Qin ended the intellectual creativity of the hundred schools. No other era could match the late Zhou for the wide range of creative thought.

The Qin Legacy

Despite the repression, Shi Huangdi's policies led to many achievements. A dazzling series of public works projects and state policies promoted communication, economic growth, and social change. The Qin standardized weights and measures, unified economic and agricultural practices, and codified laws. For example, to aid communication, roads, bridges, dams, and canals were built. They also ordered that all wheel axles be the same length so that wagons could use the ruts made by other wagons in the dusty roads. In addition, the Qin standardized the written language so that all literate Chinese anywhere in the empire could communicate easily; they also developed an "express" postal service, which conveyed documents written on slips of bamboo around the country. To foster economic growth, the Qin established state monopolies over essential commodities like salt, and ever since the Chinese have accepted a strong government role in economic matters. Taxes were high and often included devoting significant time to forced labor on government projects. The harsh Qin laws also ended crime, as a later Chinese scholar conceded: "Nothing lost on the road was picked up and pocketed, the hills were free of bandits, men avoided quarrels at home."[12] Finally, Qin land reform undermined the power of the old aristocracy, a mighty blow to the Zhou social structure.

The most famous public works project was the construction of an early and limited version of a Great Wall along China's northern borders. This wall had two purposes. First, it marked the boundary between the grasslands of the Central Asian pastoralists and the Chinese farmlands. Second, it served as a barrier to the encroachment of Central Asian warriors into China. Chinese traded with their Central Asian neighbors but also fought with and feared them, and conflict between them became more frequent during the Qin. A few partial earthen walls had already been built in Zhou times, but the Qin consolidated these into a more formidable structure, later known as the Great Wall. As part of their tax obligation, vast numbers of laborers were drafted for building the wall.

The Great Wall   This panorama from the region just north of Beijing shows a portion of the wall reconstructed in the fifteenth century C.E. The wall was an attempt to mark the northern boundary of China and keep out nomadic invaders.   (Georg Gerster/Photo Researchers, Inc.)

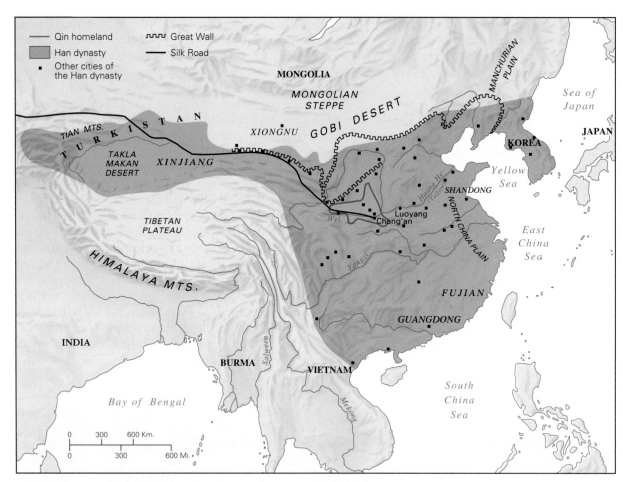

Map 5.2 The Han Empire
The Han Empire fluctuated in size but at its height controlled most of today's China, Korea, northern Vietnam, and a long corridor through Central Asia to Turkestan.

Online Study Center **Improve Your Grade** Interactive Map: Han China

The Great Wall was one of the greatest architectural feats of the ancient world. Later dynasties periodically rebuilt and added to the wall. The present brick and stone wall that so astounds tourists derives mostly from reconstruction and expansion work around 600 years ago, after which the wall stretched over 1,400 miles across north China, with watchtowers every few miles. Properly manned, it could be an effective defense, but that was an expense only the most affluent emperors could afford. The wall was seldom as successful as the Chinese had hoped in curbing invaders. Still, it was a symbolic affirmation of empire and a statement of territorial limits.

But the Qin dynasty itself was short-lived. Shi Huangdi was a tyrant who fostered much general hatred, and his expansionist policies provoked conflict with neighboring peoples. The first emperor's death in 210 B.C.E. was kept secret by his inner circle for fear of general revolt. He was buried in a huge underground mausoleum together with seven thousand astonishingly realistic life-size terra cotta horses and warriors brandishing real bronze weapons. It took 700,000 laborers to construct the final resting place and its contents. When news finally spread of Shi Huangdi's death, peasant revolts broke out. In 206 B.C.E. the Qin forces were defeated by an alliance of various rebel armies. In the

chaos that followed, as the various rebel groups vied for power, a former peasant led his forces to victory, establishing a new dynasty, the Han (HAHN).

The Han Empire

The Han is the most respected dynasty in Chinese history because during these four centuries (206 B.C.E.–220 C.E.). China became a major force in the affairs of Eurasia, participating in networks of trade, diplomacy, and imperialism. The Han built a huge empire stretching far into Central Asia (see Map 5.2), and trade across this area allowed greater contact with people to the west. Like the Qin, the Han built a strong state, but they also greatly modified the Qin's harsh Legalist structure. The brilliance of the Han and the expansion of Chinese society southward led the Chinese who followed to call themselves the Sons of Han, since this classical period set the pattern for later dynasties.

Large empires like the Han were common in this era. The middle Classical Era was the age of empires, when large segments of the Eurasian landmass and North Africa were under the domination of large imperial structures. In organizing their societies, all the empires built on the ideas of the Axial Age sages, resolving the crises that had sparked their rise. But the classical empires eventually declined as their structures and finances weakened, the conquered populations revolted, and nomadic peoples invaded the imperial heartlands.

The Han and Roman Empires reached their zenith around the same time and resembled each other in population, although Rome's empire was larger in territorial size. In 2 C.E. the Han Empire contained at least 60 million people and the Roman Empire ruled some 55 million. However, unlike the situation in the Roman Empire, most of the Han subjects lived in China itself, around two-thirds of them in the Yellow and Wei River Valleys of north China. In contrast, the people in Italy were greatly outnumbered by the colonized populations.

The pinnacle of Han imperial power came under the emperor mentioned in the opening of this chapter: Wu Di, who ruled for over half a century (141–87 B.C.E.). Wu Di's imperialism came after several decades of national revival and dynastic consolidation. After he established firm control at home, Wu Di, a firm believer, like many Chinese emperors, that the best defense is a good offense, counteracted the encroaching pastoral nomads of the northern and western grasslands. In a series of bloody campaigns, Chinese forces pushed some nomads toward Europe, where they then disrupted the Roman Empire. Among the groups deflected toward the west were the Huns, who had menaced China for centuries. The branch of Huns the Chinese called Xiongnu had forged a large confederation of tribes in the third century B.C.E. that constantly threatened China. Indeed, the Qin built the Great Wall in part to deflect the Huns.

Empire building and diplomacy soon linked China to western Eurasia as well as to neighboring societies in East and Southeast Asia. In search of allies against threatening nomads, the Han used both diplomatic and military strategies. To foster diplomacy, they sent ambassadors such as Zhang Qian to distant Central Asians seeking support against common enemies. But to neutralize nearby threats, Wu Di also dispatched a series of great armies, some numbering as many as 150,000 men, into the fringe areas of China and then beyond. Within a few years they had conquered southwestern China, the Xinjiang (shin-jee-yahng) region on China's western borders, Mongolia, and parts of Turkestan. Wu Di wrote a poem about a successful military campaign in 101 B.C.E. that brought many horses as tribute: "The heavenly horses are coming from the Far West. They crossed the Flowing Sands, for the barbarians are conquered."[13] His armies also established colonial control over northern Korea and Vietnam. The Chinese ruled the former for four centuries and the latter for 1,000 years. Soon Chinese power extended even further, as states in today's Afghanistan acknowledged themselves vassals of China, sending tribute to Han emperors. By controlling the local peoples, Han military forces brought security to a narrow corridor that could be used for increased trade. But not all soldiers celebrated these achievements. One Han soldier wrote a protest song: "We fought south of the city wall. We died north of the ramparts. In the wilderness we dead lie unburied, fodder for crows. Tell the crows for us, 'We've always been brave men.'"[14]

During this time the Chinese even made contact with the Roman Empire. In later Han times a Chinese army of 90,000 men reached as far as the Caspian Sea in southeastern Russia, and a small force led by General Gan Ying apparently traveled through Parthia to the Persian Gulf in 97 C.E., the first Chinese known to reach there. On his return General Gan reported on the customs and topography of these western states and discussed the Roman Empire, noting it was a massive state ruling many smaller ones, with many large cities.

The Silk Road and Eurasian Trade

The Han presence in Central Asia allowed for the establishment of overland trade routes between China and western Asia. A lively caravan route, known as the **Silk Road** for its most valuable cargo, linked China with India, the Middle East, and southern Europe. Central Asian cities such as Kashgar (kahsh-gar), Bactra (BAK-tru), and Samarkand (SAM-mar-kahnd) grew up along the overland route to service the trade and the merchants, becoming network hubs. Indeed, the string of cities was an important contact zone between East and West. Chinese silk, porcelain, and bamboo were carried west across the deserts and mountains to Baghdad and the ports of the eastern Mediterranean. Eventually some of these Chinese goods reached Rome. Silk was the most desired product. Since it was lightweight and easily packed, large quantities were carried west by each caravan. Caravans then returned with horses and luxury goods such as Egyptian glass beads, Red Sea pearls, and Baltic amber.

The Silk Road and the trade networks that it shaped greatly influenced the peoples who participated in the trade. To pay for Chinese luxuries, the Romans dispatched considerable quantities of silver to China. A serious trade imbalance ensued that contributed to the decline of the Western Roman Empire. In such ways, the Han Empire ultimately had a political and economic impact on distant Europe. Relations with Central and West Asians during the Han and later periods also brought new products to China, such as stringed musical instruments and new foods. Imperial power and foreign trade generated an economic boom and the rapid growth of commerce in China. The Silk Road network also affected populations, even those that were not directly involved in the trade. For example, trade activities fostered a Central Asian melting pot as peoples moved, met, and mixed.

Han Government

The Han period also saw the emergence of a government structure that survived in its basic form until the early twentieth century. Whereas the Qin had sought to transform China in one brutal stroke, the Han were more pragmatic and cautious. The Han combined many elements of Qin authoritarianism but used less repression and coercion, and they retained a strong central government but also had some respect for local political power. The Han softened Legalism with Confucian

Silk Road A lively caravan route through Central Asia that linked China with India, the Middle East, and southern Europe.

humanism, demonstrating that Confucian philosophy could maintain stability in the wake of momentous change. They adopted the advice of the Confucian Mengzi, who argued that "when the personal life is cultivated, the family will be regulated; when the family is regulated, the state will be in order; and when the state is in order, there will be peace throughout the land."[15] This Han pattern of mixing Legalism with Confucianism, power with ethics, characterized the Chinese political system for the next 2,000 years.

During Han times the civil service developed. In the early Han era the bureaucracy comprised some 130,000 officials, or 1 for every 400 to 500 people. This small number in relationship to the total population was the norm throughout Chinese history and can be explained by the relatively restricted role of the imperial administration. The central government mainly existed to ensure law, order, and border defense, and its bureaucrats collected taxes, administered the legal system, and officered military forces. Han officials boasted that they did not interfere in the daily lives of the people and kept public works to a minimum. And yet, the many rebellions during Han times suggest that the reality of government often included high taxes and onerous demands on the peasants to provide the regime with military or labor service, such as rebuilding river dikes or repairing washed out roads. These demands generated occasional unrest.

The bureaucracy was staffed by educated men later called **mandarins** (MAN-duh-rinz). Chinese proverbs claimed that the country might be won by the sword but could be ruled only by the writing brush—in other words, by an educated elite. The Han Chinese invented the civil service examination system to select officials based on merit. Wu Di even established a national university, which by the late Han period trained up to 30,000 students who were studying for the exams. These exams tested knowledge of the Confucian writings, an indication that Confucianism was becoming the official ideology of the state. With its emphasis on deference, Confucianism legitimized the regime and promoted faithful service. The prestige of the scholars staffing the bureaucracy also moderated the tendency toward despotism. In their role as officials, Confucian scholars served as intermediaries between the emperor and the people.

The development of the Han bureaucracy marked the rise of the **scholar-gentry**, a social class based on learning and officeholding but also on landowning, since many of the mandarins came from wealthy landowning families. Still, the social system was somewhat fluid. Scholars could not guarantee that their sons would be competent, and some poor men did rise by passing the civil service exams. Most of the scholar-gentry lived in towns, where they had some influence on local government officials. Gentry men frequently met together in teahouses to discuss local affairs and forge common positions on government policies.

---

mandarins Educated men who staffed the Chinese bureaucracy.
scholar-gentry A Chinese social class of learned officeholders and landowners that arose in the Han dynasty.

Heavenly Mandates and Dynastic Cycles

During the Han the Chinese came to view rulership in terms of the Mandate of Heaven, or sanction by the supernatural realm, and history in terms of the dynastic cycle, the rise and fall of dynasties (see Chapter 4). These concepts became ingrained in Chinese thinking. Most premodern Chinese scholars believed that emperors ruled as deputies of the cosmic forces, but only so long as they possessed the virtues of justice, benevolence, and sincerity. In each dynasty, able early rulers with these virtues were succeeded by debauched weaklings, who left government more and more to the bureaucracy while they indulged their pleasures. Emperors had vast harems of wives, concubines, and sometimes boys, and usually enjoyed fine wine and foods. When an emperor misruled, he lost the Mandate of Heaven and rebellion was justified.

The rise and fall of dynasties also correlated with economic trends. A strong new dynasty initially generated security and prosperity, which led to population increase and additional tax revenues. However, these prospects lured ambitious emperors into overextending imperial power and squandering human and financial resources, not only on wars of expansion but also on palaces and court luxury. Extraordinary art was produced for the Han elite; for example, the tomb of one princess contained a 2,000-piece jade suit that was sown with gold wire.

Overspending led to decline. Wasteful expenditures created financial difficulties and military stagnation. Governments such as the Han could no longer fund the large military commitment to protect the country, and it became vulnerable. After a century or so, decay set in, and some bureaucrats became corrupt. To meet the growing deficits the government raised taxes, forcing many poorer peasants to sell their land to large landlords, who could then evade taxes through their wealth and influence. Hence revenues further declined.

This pattern was illustrated by Han emperor Wu Di. His glorious empire came at a huge cost, straining the imperial treasury. The resulting inflation led to the world's first price stabilization board and generated a heated debate in China about the economic benefits of empire. Some Han scholars opposed military expansion as a senseless waste of lives and tax revenues. In 81 B.C.E. Wu Di's successor as emperor invited some of them to make their case before him. They did so, arguing that,

> *at present, morality is discarded and reliance is placed on military force. Troops are raised for campaigns and garrisons are stationed for defense. It is the long-drawn-out campaigns and the ceaseless transportation of provisions that burden our people at home and cause our frontier soldiers to suffer from hunger and cold.*[16]

But higher government officials responded that the spending was necessary to protect the country from the Xiongnu.

The Han dynasty finally collapsed in 220 C.E., not unlike the fall of Rome several centuries later. Critical factors for both empires included inadequate revenues, peasant revolts, powerful landed families contending for power, and raids by pastoralists from the borderlands. Across Eurasia the unusually warm conditions between 200 B.C.E. and 200 C.E. came to an end, and the colder weather affected agriculture. Both empires were also ravaged by epidemics in the second century C.E., which killed millions and thus reduced tax revenues.

SECTION SUMMARY

- Through military conquest, the Qin dynasty unified the warring states into a new centralized, imperial China.

- Legalism, with its strict authoritarianism and negative view of human nature, was the dominant philosophy of the Qin rulers.

- Both the Han dynasty and the Roman Empire reached their peaks at about the same time, with roughly similar population sizes.

- The diplomatic and military expansion under the Han rulers set the stage for expanded trade, including the development of the Silk Road linking China to western Asia and Europe.

- The structure of government established during the Han, characterized by a blending of central and local authority and a softening of Legalism with Confucian humanism, endured until the early twentieth century.

◆ Society, Economy, and Science in Han China

How was Chinese society organized during the Han?

The Han era was formative for many aspects of Chinese life. During the Han the Chinese family matured into its basic form and the economy grew dramatically, affecting peasant life. Chinese examined their own history, looking for lessons from the past. The Han were also highly creative in technology and science, making advances, for example, in mathematics and health.

Social Life and Gender Relations

Han social life revolved around the family system, which endured for over 2,000 years because it offered many strengths. In part because of Confucian ideas, the family became an elaborate institution, the central focus of allegiance for most Chinese. Each Chinese saw himself as belonging to a large, continuing family that went backward and forward in time. They were expected to honor their ancestors while also keeping in mind the welfare of future generations. The family provided great psychological and economic security, despite the inevitable tensions that disrupted family harmony. The Chinese ideal was the joint family, that is, three or four generations living together under one roof. But only wealthy families could support the large houses and private courtyards that made the joint family way of life possible. Most peasant families could not afford to follow this pattern.

The family was an autocratic institution that exercised considerable influence over its members. It was led by a patriarch, or senior male, who commanded respect. Chinese traced descent exclusively through the male line. Children were expected to respect not only the senior male, but also both parents, and to venerate their elders. Reflecting these obligations, Han law stated that a child who concealed a parent suspected of wrongdoing, or a wife a husband, or a grandchild a grandparent, should not to be brought to trial. Family interests always took precedence over individual ones. Because laws held the family accountable for the actions of its members, they discouraged disgraceful behavior by individuals.

The family system increasingly put most women at a disadvantage compared to men. Women were expected to be devoted first to their parents, then later to their husband, and finally to their sons; care of the family and children was their central preoccupation. A young wife joined her husband's family and was subject to the authority of his parents. Parents arranged marriages with the goal of linking families. Betrothed couples often eventually developed affection for each other, and many marriages seem to have been happy. Nonetheless, the sorrows of unhappy women became a common literary theme. Many Chinese novels and plays concerned unrequited love or lovers forced to marry others. In one small part of central China some women developed among themselves a special and secret form of writing, known as **nuxu** (nushu), to share their life experiences. It was passed down from mother to daughter. Although its origins remain obscure, some historians think it developed as early as the Han. Others believe it emerged much later.

We know much about gender roles in Chinese society and about the experiences of Han women. For example, Ban Zhao (ban chao), the most famous woman scholar in Han China and an accomplished historian, astronomer, and mathematician, wrote an influential book on women's place in society. Her advice to women stressed the Confucian obligations of selfless behavior, devotion, and obedience. Under the influence of patriarchal Confucianism reflected in Ban Zhao's advice, women's virtues became family virtues, and gender roles became more rigid than they had been a few centuries earlier. Still, many women engaged in some small-scale trade; as a Han proverb said, "To prick embroidery does not pay as much as leaning upon a market door." Most women worked long hours in the fields or the marketplace in addition to doing housework and caring for children. But they also formed groups to spin or weave together, "to economize on the expense of light and heat,"[17] as a Han source put it.

In spite of the preeminence of Confucian patterns, women's experiences were never standardized. The amount of independence and influence they enjoyed depended on their age, social class, and local practices. There were always women like Ban Zhao who achieved wide acclaim. The Han scholar

---

nuxu A secret form of writing developed by some Chinese women to share their experiences, possibly beginning in the Han period.

Liu Xiang (loo shang) wrote biographies of 125 women in antiquity who were noted for their unselfish behavior and gallant deeds, such as maintaining loyalty to the ruler or offering wise advice to husbands or fathers. Some elite women received an education, and some were celebrated for their poetry writing. The mother of the Confucian thinker Mengzi was widely esteemed as a model of astuteness and assertiveness, though these traits had not allowed her to completely overcome Confucian expectations of womanhood. She was reported by a male Han era biographer to have said that a "woman's duties are to cook the five grains, heat the wine, look after her parents-in-law, make clothes, and that is all! Therefore, she had no ambitions to manage affairs outside the house."[18] In contrast, some peasant women, who worked in the fields alongside their men, were strong-willed and exercised influence in their families and villages. Indeed, male power was strongest at the elite level and often weaker among the lower classes.

The Rural Economy

Beginning in the early Han and continuing for the next 2,000 years, China's economy was dominated by intensive farming, especially the growing of cereal crops. Peasants constituted the vast majority of the population. Although trade gradually became more significant, farming remained the basis of Chinese society, and landowning became the major goal of economic endeavor and investment. Peasants had to produce a food surplus for the 20 percent of the people living in towns and cities. The fertile Chinese land and peasant labor made this possible: Chinese peasants were able to achieve high yields, becoming some of the world's most efficient farmers. But Chinese agriculture also depended on hard physical labor, especially in growing rice. Fields had to be flooded with irrigation water and drained, and the rice had to be sown, transplanted, and harvested, all by hand.

Peasants did not lead easy lives. Most rarely went farther than the local market town to which they brought their produce. Family land and movable property were divided equally among sons, a form of inheritance that fragmented landholdings and stood in contrast to landholding patterns in pre-Han China, Japan, and Europe. In addition, a lack of capital kept many peasant families at the mercy of middlemen for advances until the crop came in. A Han scholar complained that poor peasants were left with too little land to live on and thus reduced to eating the food of pigs and dogs. As a result, many peasants were forced into tenancy to landlords. However, few were slaves. Slavery, an important feature of Shang and Zhou society, became less common during the Han.

Population pressure and land shortage posed problems to peasants and also created political stability. No great land problem existed before the Han, since virgin land was still available. By the second century B.C.E., however, practically all the good agricultural land in north and north-central China was being used. The dynastic cycle was partly a result of land shortage and population pressure, which fermented rebellion. At times of endemic unrest, caused by bad harvests, high rents, or official corruption, peasants would revolt.

Han Farmer   Stone relief of Han farmer using an ox-drawn plow. These plows fostered the expansion of cultivated land during the Han.   (From Patricia Buckley Ebrey, *The Cambridge Illustrated History of China,* 1996)

The labor-intensive nature of the economy was also apparent outside agriculture. Transportation meant porters with carrying poles, men pushing wheelbarrows, and men bearing the sedan chairs of the elite. Men also walked along narrow paths pulling boats upriver through the narrow gorges of the Yangzi River. Even the famous silk industry required endless labor. **Sericulture** (silk making) produced silks and brocades of the finest weave by Han times. But producing 150 pounds of silk required feeding and keeping clean the trays of 700,000 worms.

Chinese Historiography

The Chinese developed one of the greatest traditions of studying and writing about history, known as historiography, among premodern societies. The recording of history was probably inevitable among a people who looked to the past for guidance in the present. History writing in China goes back at least as far as the Zhou dynasty. One of the classics of Confucian learning, *The Spring and Autumn Annals,* attributed traditionally but probably inaccurately to Confucius, provided a largely factual and chronological recounting of political events

sericulture   Silk making.

in the eastern state of Lu (loo) from 722 to 481 B.C.E. But Confucians also read into the prose a moral assessment of history.

In Han times history writing made perhaps the greatest contribution to literature. Beginning with the Han, most dynasties employed a group of professional historians, such as the Han era's Sima Qian (SI-mu tshen) (see Profile: Sima Qian, Chinese Historian). Later Chinese historians were influenced by Sima Qian's belief that past events, if not forgotten, also taught about the future. To insulate them from retribution by outraged emperors, often their work was not published until after the emperors had passed on. The Chinese historians tended to ignore social and economic history in favor of political history, concentrating on personalities, stories, wars, and the doings of emperors while neglecting long-term trends.

The greatest Chinese historians wrote monumental works and had much in common with each other. They aimed for objectivity, carefully separating their editorial comments from the narrative text, all in elegant prose. Although quoting generously from original documents, like all historians they still had to decide what to include and omit. They paid little attention to events of alleged supernatural intervention and focused more on information about human beings and their foibles. Historical literature also served as a manual for government, since it discussed the success and failure of past policies with the goal of achieving wisdom and promoting morality. The Chinese evaluated their culture by what they had done in the past.

Science and Technology

China developed one of the world's oldest and most influential scientific and technological traditions, establishing along with the Indians, Mesopotamians, Egyptians, and Greeks the foundation for modern science. The Zhou and Han are credited with many important breakthroughs. Among the inventions originating in these centuries were porcelain ("china"), rag paper, the water-powered mill, the shoulder harness for horses, the foot stirrup (possibly adapted from crude Central Asian models), the magnetic compass, the seismograph, the wheelbarrow, the stern-post rudder for boats, the spinning wheel, and certain kinds of textiles, including linen. Most of these inventions did not reach western Eurasia over the trade routes until a few centuries—in some cases a millennium—later.

Paper may have been the most significant innovation. Before paper Chinese scribes wrote with a pointed stylus on strips of wood or bamboo, but these were difficult to use and store. Then they tried woven cloth as a writing surface. Eventually an ingenious artisan tried beating the cloth into fiber and forming thin sheets. Traditionally Chinese historians attribute the invention of paper to the scholar-bureaucrat Chai Lun (tshai lun), who reported the discovery to the emperor in 105 C.E. But the first experiments had probably been done over the course of decades until paper was perfected.

The Han also made great strides in mathematics. Among the major achievements was the most accurate calculation of pi at the time. In addition, the Chinese were many centuries ahead of the rest of the world in the use of fractions, a simple decimal system, the concept of negative numbers, and in certain aspects of algebra and geometry. Han Chinese used bamboo rods, much like mini-chopsticks, to do arithmetic calculations. This system was widely used until the invention around 190 C.E. of the *abacus,* a primitive computer still used widely in Asia today, that proved an unparalleled tool for calculations. The abacus was constructed by fastening balls on wires attached to a board carved with divisions.

In the study of astronomy, the Han compiled catalogues of stars and speculated on sunspots. Around 100 C.E. the astronomer Zhang Heng (jang hoeng) explained the causes of lunar eclipses, writing that the moon reflects the sunshine and will be eclipsed when it travels into earth's shadow. Astronomy was also essential for an agricultural society, which needed accurate calendars to regulate planting and harvesting.

Chinese science, especially medicine, also owed much to the cosmological thinking exemplified in yin-yang dualism and also to Daoism, which inspired an interest in nature. To the Daoists the body was a microcosm of the universe. An influential early Han book on medicine advised readers that when yin and yang are in proper harmony, a person is filled with strength and vigor. An enduring medical discovery, *acupuncture,* also developed from the belief that good health was the result of proper yin-yang balance in the body. In this procedure, thin needles are inserted at predetermined points to alleviate pain or correct some condition. While pursuing acupuncture, Chinese experts learned the parts of the body and discovered how to read a pulse. Acupuncture is still practiced today and has spread around the world.

The Chinese made other contributions in medicine. They stressed good hygiene and preventive medicine, including proper dress, a well-balanced diet, and regular exercise. In their quest for the elixir of immortality, Daoist alchemists discovered many edible foods, herbs, and potions that improved health. They developed the greatest list of pharmaceuticals in the premodern world, which in turn promoted the study of botany and zoology. By the Han period doctors could diagnose gout and cirrhosis of the liver. The Chinese pioneered many medical innovations, and many ancient Chinese folk remedies remain popular to this day in China.

SECTION SUMMARY

■ The family structure became the central social institution; its patriarchal hierarchy, codified in law, put the needs of the group above the needs of the individual.

■ Despite subservience to all males in the family, some women of this period made many artistic and intellectual contributions.

■ Peasant labor, as well as backbreaking labor in general, continued to be the foundation of the economy and characterized most people's existence.

■ Developments in science and medicine were influenced by Daoism, which promoted the idea of a yin-yang balance in the natural world.

SIMA QIAN,
CHINESE HISTORIAN

Perhaps the greatest Han dynasty historian was Sima Qian (ca. 145–90 B.C.E.). His father, a high court official who also wrote about Chinese history, begged his son on his deathbed to continue compiling a history of China and its neighbors from earliest times. "I have failed to set forth a record of all the enlightened rulers and wise lords, the faithful ministers and gentlemen who were ready to die for duty," he conceded. His dutiful son replied, "I shall not dare to be remiss," and made the project his life's work. At the age of twenty, Sima Qian, who had grown up in the ancestral home in northwest China, began a grand tour of the empire. During the tour, he devoted time to examining historical sites, such as the tomb and family home of Confucius.

After receiving an official appointment, the Han government sent the young scholar on a mission to newly conquered territories in the southwest. Later he visited far northwestern outposts, including Mongolia, and also traveled extensively with the emperor Wu Di. Like his father, Sima Qian was appointed Grand Astrologer, a post dealing with time and the heavens, and helped to reform the calendar. But, being an honest man who spoke his mind, he alienated the emperor by defending a respected general whose brave attack against the Huns had failed for lack of support. As punishment Sima Qian was castrated.

Using his immense learning, combined with access to the vast imperial library containing the public records, Sima Qian produced his major book, *Records of the Grand Historian.* An invaluable source, *Records* covered some 2,000 years of history in 130 chapters, roughly 10,000 pages of text. Attempting to be universal, this monumental history ranges across a variety of topics, including astronomy, astrology, science, music, religious sacrifices, and economic patterns. It offers sketches of famous men from many walks of life, including political and military leaders, merchants, philosophers, scholars, comedians, assassins, rebels, bandits, and poets. *Records* also describes all foreign peoples and lands well known to the Chinese, from Korea to Afghanistan. Because it also covers rivers and canals, we know much of Wu Di's ambitious conservation and irrigation schemes. In addition, Sima Qian was the first historian to offer a comparative appraisal of China's various philosophical traditions, in which he showed particular sympathy to Daoism.

The book is strongest on the history of his times. Because Sima Qian's castration had embittered him toward Wu Di, some chapters are filled with covert satires on the emperor and warnings about his increasing power. His most original writing came in the chapters on people and contemporary affairs. Consider this criticism of those abusing their power:

We see that men whose deeds are immoral and who constantly violate the laws end their lives in luxury and wealth and their blessings pass down to their heirs with-

Sima Qian   Painting of Sima Qian. This modern painting, by an unknown artist, imagines what Han China's great historian, Sima Qian, might have looked like.   (British Library)

out end. And there are others who expend anger on what is not upright and just, and yet, in numbers too great to be reckoned, they meet with misfortune and disaster. I find myself in much perplexity.

Its vital narrative made this book popular reading among Chinese scholars for many centuries. Sima Qian's lively prose style made him an excellent storyteller. Above all, the historian was concerned with both his literary and his moral legacy. As Sima Qian concluded, in words that still stir historians everywhere: "I have assembled and arranged the ancient traditions, and if they may be handed down and communicated surely I would have no regrets," and, "those who do not forget the past are masters of the future." Sima Qian set the standard to be followed by later historians in China.

THINKING ABOUT THE PROFILE

1. How did Sima Qian become a historian?

2. What does his life tell us about the pleasures and hazards of being a high official in Han China?

3. What made his historical writing so valuable to later readers?

Note: Quotations from Ben-Ami Scharfstein, *The Mind of China: The Culture, Customs, and Beliefs of Traditional China* (New York: Dell, 1974), pp. 89–91; and Sima Qian, *Historical Records,* translated by Raymond Dawson (Oxford: Oxford University Press, 1994), p. 177.

Chinese influence soon overwhelmed these states. Chinese refugees from the Zhou wars and from Qin repression migrated across the frontier, bringing with them culture and technology. Then in 108 B.C.E. Wu Di's armies, reportedly 60,000 troops strong, conquered northern Korea against fierce resistance. China ruled the territory as a colony for the next four centuries, providing models to the Koreans in government structure, architecture, and city planning (see Chronology: Classical Japan and Korea).

The end of Chinese colonization in 313 C.E. allowed Korean society to flower, and three native kingdoms emerged. These powerful states dominated Korea between the fourth and seventh centuries, occasionally warring against each other for control of fertile agricultural land. At the same time, however, Chinese cultural influences, including the writing system, spread more widely. Mahayana Buddhism, introduced from China into northern Korea in 372 C.E., had a strong influence on Korean painting, sculpture, and architecture. Confucian doctrines also became popular. But the Koreans never became carbon copies of the Chinese. For example, unlike in China, where family status rose or fell with dynastic change and civil service examination success or failure, an aristocracy of inherited position, living in considerable luxury, thrived for most of Korean history. Korean music remained distinctive even if the instruments were adapted from Chinese models. And although most Koreans eventually adopted Buddhism, the animism that had long flourished never disappeared.

Eventually one Korean kingdom, Koguryo (go-GUR-yo), became the most influential (see Map 5.3). In the fifth century, with China divided, Koguryo expanded far to the north, annexing much of Manchuria and southeastern Siberia in addition to the northern half of the Korean peninsula. In its expansion, Koguryo became one of the largest states in Eurasia at that time. The empire, which lasted from 350 to 668 C.E., also boasted a substantial population of several million people by

Map 5.3　Korea and Japan in the Fifth Century C.E.
During the Classical Era Korea was often divided into several states. Koguryo in the north was the largest state, ruling part of Siberia. By the sixth century the Yamato state governed much of the main Japanese island, Honshu.

the seventh century. At the same time, several much smaller Korean states controlled the southern part of the peninsula.

Koguryo proved a strong regional force. Its army repulsed seven major Chinese invasions by the Sui and Tang dynasties between 598 and 655 C.E., when a resurgent China was the most powerful state in the world. The great Koguryo generals commanded skilled and mobile legions. In 612 C.E. they routed an invading Sui army that, according to legend, numbered at least 1 million soldiers but was probably closer to a still formidable 300,000. The huge cost of the Chinese campaigns in Korea contributed to the collapse of the Sui dynasty. Finally, in 668 C.E., Chinese armies, allied with the southern Korean state of Silla (SILL-ah or SHILL-ah), overran Koguryo and destroyed the kingdom, carrying 200,000 prisoners back to China. This event allowed for the reunification of Korea under Silla, which then flourished for several centuries.

Yayoi Japan

Like Korea across the straits, Japan experienced dramatic change between 600 B.C.E. and 600 C.E. The prehistoric, pottery-making Jomon culture (see Chapter 4) persisted until around 300 B.C.E., when a new pattern emerged that archaeologists term Yayoi (ya-YOI). This emergence correlated with the rise of an exceptionally productive wet rice-farming society

CHRONOLOGY	
Classical Japan and Korea	
300 B.C.E.–552 C.E.	Yayoi culture in Japan
18 B.C.E.	Rise of Koguryo in northern Korea
108 B.C.E.–313 C.E.	Han Chinese colonization of Korea
250 C.E.	Beginning of Yayoi tomb culture
350–668 C.E.	Koguryo Empire
514–935 C.E.	Silla state in southern Korea
538 C.E.	Introduction of Buddhism to Japan
552–710 C.E.	Yamato state in Japan
604 C.E.	First Japanese constitution

that established close links with Korea, a relationship that fostered migration from Korea. Hence, Japan owes its flowering in part to networks of trade and migration in Yayoi times.

During the long Yayoi era (300 B.C.E.–552 C.E.), Korea remained a source of learning and population for Japan. A relationship between people in southwestern Japan and southeastern Korea promoted a continuous flow of Korean immigrants as well as both Korean and Chinese ideas and technology from the mainland into the islands. Some Korean migrants brought horses, and the armored warrior on horseback later became a vivid feature of Japanese life. In addition, Koreans worked in Japan as skilled craftsmen, scribes, and artists. Immigration from Korea continued until the ninth century. By 600 C.E. the Japanese people as we know them today had come together from the genetic and cultural mixing over many centuries of Korean immigrants with earlier settlers and the indigenous Ainu people.

The Yayoi also traded sporadically with China. A Chinese visitor in 297 C.E. left us much information about Yayoi society. He reported that the Yayoi were much concerned with taboos, class distinctions, and especially ritual cleanliness, writing that "when [a] funeral is over, all members of the family go into the water to cleanse themselves in a bath of purification."[22] The Chinese visitor also reported that the Yayoi were fond of dancing, singing, drinking rice wine, and eating raw vegetables; experienced no theft and little other crime; revered nature; and clapped their hands in worship. All these behaviors characterize modern Japanese, suggesting that these early customs never eroded. The Chinese also noted that the Yayoi used the potter's wheel, were expert weavers, and had mastered both bronze and iron technology. Later they would fashion iron into highly effective swords and armor.

The Yayoi formed no centralized governments but did have a class structure. They were organized into a large number of clans, each ruled by a hereditary priest-chieftain. According to a Chinese source, during the second century C.E., when Japan was engulfed in war and conflict, a woman, Pimiko (pih-MEE-ko), became a powerful queen-priestess and brought peace by imposing strict laws. She lived in a palace surrounded by a tower and employed a thousand female attendants. But aside from a few women leaders such as Pimiko, the clan elites were men who governed large numbers of farmers, artisans, and a few slaves and who mobilized people to build hundreds of large earthen tombs, often surrounded by moats, all over south-central Honshu Island. The tombs housed the remains of prominent leaders, who were buried with prized possessions such as jewels, swords, and clay figurines.

Yamato: The First Japanese National State

Japan entered the light of written history in the sixth century C.E., with the beginning of the Yamato (YA-ma-toe) period (552–710 C.E.), named for the first state ruling a majority of the Japanese people. The Yamato was centered in south-central Honshu, where the cities of Kyoto (kee-YO-toe) and Osaka

(oh-SAH-kah) now stand. The Japanese population had by then probably reached 3 million. Yamato leaders exercised some control from what is today Tokyo in the north to the southern tip of Korea. Yamato was not a centralized state like Han China or Koguryo but rather a national government ruling over smaller groups based on clans and territorial control, each headed by a hereditary chief. Eventually Yamato extended its influence into southern Japan while expanding the northern frontier deep into Ainu territory.

Yamato was headed by emperors and occasionally empresses—all ancestors of the same imperial family that rules Japan today, fifteen centuries later. Political continuity under the same royal family gave the Japanese a strong sense of identity and a corresponding sense of cultural unity. The imperial family owes its longevity in part to an identification with Japanese origins. The Japanese saw their history before the sixth century C.E. in mythological terms: they believed the imperial family descended from the Sun Goddess. This beautiful spirit, *Amaterasu* (AH-mah-teh-RAH-soo), and her male consort experienced violent mood swings and periodic conflict that may have been modeled on the frequent storms, volcanic eruptions, and earthquakes that rock the islands. Despite her tantrums, a female creator deity may also have reflected a high status for women in early Japan. The Chinese reported that the Yayoi made no distinction in status between men and women, and before the eighth century C.E. around half of the imperial sovereigns were women, some of whom had charismatic personalities. But female power eventually eroded, and patriarchy became the common pattern by 1000 C.E.

Japanese Isolation and Cultural Unity

The Japanese forged a particularly distinctive society in late classical times through a mixing of the local and the foreign. Many of Japan's unique features resulted from the fact that the islands were over a hundred miles from the Eurasian mainland, which meant that communication with other societies was sporadic, mainly restricted to Korea and China, and the Japanese had to become very creative. At the same time, physical isolation severely restricted the space and resources available to the steadily growing population on the mountainous islands. The result was a tightly woven society with intense social pressures. Since personal privacy became rare in this crowded land, and since the Japanese lived in houses with thin walls, people learned how to erect psychological walls that allowed them to "tune out" the surrounding noise and activity.

Isolation made the Japanese expert at borrowing selectively from the outside during periods of intensive contact. Much of Japanese history can be understood as an interplay between the indigenous (native) and the foreign; ultimately a native element survived despite a flood of borrowing from Korea, China, and, much later, the West. The Japanese have been very conscious of borrowing, but they have always selected and adapted foreign ideas that suit their own needs. Seldom have

Prince Shotoku This painting from the eighth century C.E. shows Prince Shotoku, one of the major Yamato leaders, and his sons in the Japanese clothing style of the times. Prince Shotoku launched a period of intensive borrowing from China. (Imperial Household Collection)

they left a borrowed idea in its original form. For example, the Japanese adopted the Chinese idea of an exalted emperor but not the concept of the Mandate of Heaven, which allowed for incompetent or tyrannical dynasties to be overthrown. The Japanese imperial family had, according to their myths, been granted a permanent mandate by the Sun Goddess, which could not be withdrawn.

The Japanese also created a large proportion of their own culture. Japan has been a leading technological innovator for millennia; for instance, it developed the best tempered steel of the classical world. This creative ability is particularly striking in the traditional arts, where the Japanese created forms and styles of universal appeal, such as carefully planned gardens and *bonsai* (bon-sigh) (miniature) trees, and in social organization, where they have evolved ingenious solutions to chronic problems such as urban crowding and limited resources. Thus, the Japanese house itself, containing thick straw floor mats,

sliding paper panels rather than interior walls, a hot tub for communal bathing, and charcoal-burning braziers, conserved building materials and minimized fuel needs for heating and cooking.

Japanese Encounters with China

Japan was greatly influenced by the Chinese several times in history. The importation of Chinese ideas began on a large scale in the middle of the sixth century C.E. In this period Mahayana Buddhism was introduced around 538 and became a major medium for cultural change, bringing, for example, new forms of art and ideas about the cosmos and afterlife. Chinese teachers, artisans, and Buddhist monks crossed over to Japan, and Japanese journeyed to Korea and China, coming back as converts to Buddhism. Just as the Chinese maintained three distinct traditions of thought, in Japan Buddhism coexisted with the ancient animistic cult later known as **Shinto** (SHIN-toe) ("way of the gods"), which emphasized closeness to nature and enjoyed a rich mythology that included many deities.

During the sixth century, a growing realization among Japanese leaders that China and Korea were much stronger than Japan in the political, economic, and cultural spheres led the Japanese to embrace new ideas. The adaptation of Buddhism as well as the Chinese written language launched an era of deliberate borrowing from China to reshape Japanese society. The Yamato state was strong enough to support radical change without losing its independence. It expanded relations with Sui China and began to reorganize government structures, integrating Confucian notions of social organization and morality.

The adoption of Chinese ideas accelerated at the beginning of the seventh century under the auspices of Prince Shotoku (show-TOW-koo) (573–621 C.E.), an ardent Buddhist who sponsored the building of temples, used Buddhism to unify the politically fragmented society, and also promoted Confucian values. "Punish that which is evil and encourage that which is good," he wrote into the first Japanese constitution, issued in 604. His ideas also foreshadowed later Japanese values emphasizing group interests: "Harmony is to be cherished, and opposition for opposition's sake must be avoided as a matter of principle."[23] Shotoku became one of the most revered figures in Japanese history. His support for Buddhism has led some historians to compare Shotoku to the Indian king Asoka, who also embraced Buddhism, and the Roman emperor Constantine, who promoted Christianity. Over the next two and a half centuries many official embassies were exchanged between China and Japan, further promoting the exchange of ideas.

SECTION SUMMARY

■ Like most of China, Korea and Japan were agricultural societies, a similarity that facilitated the easy transmission of Chinese culture.

■ Korea's proximity to China, along with the alternating military dominance of one culture over the other, led to the adoption of Chinese writing and other technologies in Korea.

■ Both Buddhism and Confucianism permeated Korean culture from China and were blended with the native belief system of animism, keeping Korean culture distinctive.

■ The flow of ideas and people from Korea and China to Japan introduced Buddhism, writing, and other influences into Japan, but the Japanese culture, arts, and religion remained distinctive.

■ From the beginning, Japan's small land area prompted the Japanese to deal creatively with lack of space and the social problems of overcrowding.

Shinto ("way of the gods")   The ancient animistic Japanese cult that emphasized closeness to nature and enjoyed a rich mythology that included many deities.

Online Study Center **ACE the Test**

 # Chapter Summary

The classical societies that flowered in eastern Asia were distinctive in many ways. China was large, densely populated, and an innovator in government, culture, religion, science, and technology. During the late Zhou period, a time of warfare and political instability, Chinese philosophers such as Confucius as well as the Daoists and Legalists promoted ideas to restore order and promote personal happiness. Confucius promoted ethical values and suggested how people could live in harmony with each other through a well-defined and hierarchical social structure. In contrast, the Daoists advocated a life in accordance with the rhythms of the natural world. Third among these three dominant Chinese philosophies, the Legalists argued that a powerful government must harshly regulate society to preserve order. These classical ideas persisted in Chinese thought into modern times. The Legalist leaders of the Qin dynasty used brutal policies to transform China into a centralized imperial state.

Following the short-lived Qin, the great Han dynasty established a large Asian empire and traded with western Asia and Europe across the Silk Road. By constructing a centralized government and expansive empire, Han China became a major force in eastern Eurasia and traded with societies as far away as Europe. Directly or indirectly, the networks linking China with other Eurasian societies influenced all the societies involved. During the Han the social structure became more patriarchal and women were expected to be dutiful to their men. Peasant labor provided the economic foundation for the society.

After the Han collapsed, Central Asians frequently invaded and divided China politically. In this turbulent period, Mahayana Buddhism, which originated in India, became popular in China, where it mixed with Confucianism, Daoism, and animism to create various blends. At the end of this period China became reunified in an imperial state under the Sui dynasty, an achievement that contrasted with the Roman Empire in the West, which disintegrated into various fragments.

China became a model for neighboring societies. First the Koreans and then the Japanese adopted many Chinese ideas, including some technologies, writing, Confucianism, and Buddhism. But they also creatively blended them with their own unique traditions. The societies that resulted were thus a distinctive mix of the imported with the local. The East Asian societies continued to blend local creativity with foreign influences in the centuries to follow.

Online Study Center **Improve Your Grade** Flashcards

Key Terms

Confucianism	Sinicization	sericulture
The Analects	Silk Road	geomancy
filial piety	mandarins	Shinto
Daoism	scholar-gentry	
Legalism	nuxu	

Suggested Reading

Books

Adshead, S. A. M. *China in World History*. 3rd ed. New York: St. Martin's, 2000. A good introduction to Han China's interaction with Central Asia, western Asia, and Europe.

Clements, Jonathan. *Confucius: A Biography*. New York: Sutton, 2005. Brief study written for a popular audience.

Cotterell, Arthur. *The First Emperor of China*. New York: Penguin, 1981. A readable and fascinating study of the first emperor and his times.

Di Cosmo, Nicole. *Ancient China and Its Enemies: The Rise of Nomadic Power in East Asian History*. Cambridge: Cambridge University Press, 2002. An important study of China and the northern peoples from the Zhou through the Han dynasties.

Ebrey, Patricia Buckley, et al. *Pre-Modern East Asia: to 1800: A Cultural, Social, and Political History*. Boston: Houghton Mifflin, 2006. An excellent survey of China, Japan, and Korea.

Ebrey, Patricia Buckley. *The Cambridge Illustrated History of China*. New York: Cambridge University Press, 1996. A very readable survey with much on the classical period.

Hane, Mikiso. *Premodern Japan*. 2nd ed. Boulder, Colo.: Westview, 1991. A readable survey.

Hinsch, Bret. *Women in Early Imperial China*. Lanham, Md.: Rowman and Littlefield, 2002. A stimulating study of the factors shaping women's experiences in Qin and Han China.

Holcombe, Charles. *The Genesis of East Asia, 221 B.C.–A.D. 907*. Honolulu: University of Hawai'i Press, 2001. Provocative examination of this era.

Imamura, Kenji. *Prehistoric Japan: New Perspectives on Insular Japan*. Honolulu: University of Hawaii Press, 1996. A scholarly study of the Yayoi and Yamato periods.

Loewe, Michael. *Everyday Life in Early Imperial China: During the Han Period 202 B.C.–A.D. 220*. Indianapolis: Hackett, 2005. Reprint of classic work on Han life and society.

Mote, Frederick W. *Intellectual Foundations of China*. 2nd ed. New York: Knopf, 1989. A brief, readable introduction to classical Chinese philosophy.

Shaughnessy, Edward L. ed. *China: Empire and Civilization*. New York: Oxford University Press, 2005. Contains many short essays on premodern Chinese society and culture.

Sima Qian. *Historical Records* (translated by Raymond Dawson). New York: Oxford University Press, 1994. A brief introduction to the writings of the Han era historian.

Wright, Arthur. *The Sui Dynasty: The Unification of China, A.D. 581–617*. New York: Alfred A. Knopf, 1978. A valuable study of government and society.

Websites

History of China
(http://www.chaos.umd.edu/history). Collection of essays and timelines on Chinese history maintained by the University of Maryland.

Internet East Asian History Sourcebook
(http://www.fordham.edu/halsall/eastasia/eastasiasbook.html). An invaluable collection of sources and links on China, Japan, and Korea from ancient to modern times.

Internet Guide for China Studies
(http://www.sino.uni-heidelberg.de/igcs/). Good collection of links on premodern and modern China, maintained at Heidelberg University.

Monks and Merchants
(http://www.asiasociety.org/arts/monksandmerchants/index/html). Interesting essays, timelines, maps, and images for an Asia Society exhibition on the Silk Road as a zone of communication.

A Visual Sourcebook of Chinese Civilization
(http://depts.washington.edu/chinaciv/). A wonderful collection of essays, illustrations, and other useful material on Chinese history.

CHAPTER 6

Western Asia, the Eastern Mediterranean, and Regional Systems, 600–200 B.C.E.

CHAPTER OUTLINE
- The Persians and Their Empire
- The Emergence of the Greeks
- Greek Thought, Culture, and Society
- Greeks, Persians, and the Regional System
  The Hellenistic Age and Its Afro-Eurasian Legacies

▉ **PROFILE**
Archimedes, a Hellenistic Mathematician and Engineer

▉ **WITNESS TO THE PAST**
Good, Evil, and Monotheism in Zoroastrian Thought

Persepolis   During the height of their empire, Persian kings built a lavish capital at Persepolis, in today's Iran. This photo shows the audience hall, the part of the grand palace where the kings greeted their ministers and foreign diplomats.   (Ancient Art & Architecture Collection)

Wonders are many on earth, and the greatest of these, is man, who rides the ocean. He is master of the ageless earth. The use of language, the wind-swift motion of brain he learned; found out the laws of living together in cities. There is nothing beyond his power.

CHORUS IN *ANTIGONE*, BY THE FIFTH-CENTURY GREEK PLAYWRIGHT SOPHOCLES (SAHF-UH-KLEEZ)[1]

The Greeks Thales (THAY-leez) and Anaximander (uh-NAK-suh-MAN-der), pioneering philosophers and scientists, had the great fortune to grow up in the prosperous city of Miletus (my-LEET-uhs), a great commercial center on the southwestern coast of Anatolia (modern Turkey). For hundreds of years Miletus had served as a crossroads for the entire region, mingling Greek and foreign cultures. Young men like Thales and Anaximander haunted the bustling docks and seaside bars, listening to the reports of sailors returning from distant shores and of travelers from foreign lands, as well as the ideas of Persian and other non-Greek residents. Milesian merchants sent ships to the far corners of the Mediterranean carrying the treasured wool developed by Miletus sheep breeders and the fine furniture produced by its cabinetmakers. Along the shores of the Black Sea Milesians established settlements that supplied fish and wheat that enriched the city's traders.

Milesians benefited from cultural cross-fertilization fostered by trade. Some sailors brought scraps of learning from older societies such as Egypt and Mesopotamia. This intermingling led to pioneering thinking about geography and cartography. Inspired by the maritime trade, Thales, around 600 C.E., worked out a geometrical system to calculate the position of a ship at sea. Fifty years later Thales' student, Anaximander, made the first map of the Mediterranean world and the first Greek chart of the heavens, and five decades after that Hecataeus (HEK-a-TAU-us) of Miletus published a map of the world known to the Greeks, from India to Spain. Miletus matured into a great intellectual center and a meeting place for the Greek and Persian worlds.

The Greeks such as those at Miletus developed not only a penchant for maritime trade and an understanding of regional geography but also a unique society on the rocky shores of the Aegean Sea. In cities such as Miletus and Athens, they introduced many ideas and institutions that endured through the centuries. The view of humanity's greatness offered by Sophocles in the opening quotation reflects an obsession with individuality and freedom that made the Greeks role models for modern democracies, where people today engage in some of the same debates as did the Greeks about the interplay between individual freedom and the community. Sophocles also shared the bias, common in classical times, that men, not women, were responsible for human progress and should dominate society. But the Greek achievements that we know today are only part of the story. Connected to a wider world through cities like Miletus, the Greeks flourished by participating in regional trade, colonizing other territories, and borrowing ideas from neighboring societies. This world included another creative society and even greater regional power, the Persian Empire, which dominated the eastern Mediterranean and western Asia and also introduced many innovations that affected the lives of many peoples. Ultimately the rival Greek and Persian societies were brought together in a political union that extended Greek culture into Asia and Africa but also added Persian culture to the mix. The resulting Hellenistic Age was an era of unprecedented cross-cultural sharing.

FOCUS QUESTIONS

1. How did the Persians acquire and maintain their empire?
2. How did democracy develop in Greece, and what were its advantages and inadequacies?
3. What were some features of Greek philosophy and science?
4. In what ways did Persians and Greeks encounter and influence each other?
5. What impact did Alexander the Great and his conquests have on world history?

 # The Persians and Their Empire

How did the Persians acquire and maintain their empire?

Although its period of greatest political influence lasted only two centuries, the Persian Empire played an important role in world history. The Persians established a larger empire than any people before them. Theirs was also the first large multicultural empire in Eurasia, encompassing Anatolian Greeks, Phoenicians, Hebrews, Egyptians, Mesopotamians, and Indians. Domination of the east-west trade routes made the empire the meeting ground of the early classical world. The Persians also tried unsuccessfully to conquer Greece. Their wars with Greece and their empire building in western Asia paved the way for the later rule of the Greek Alexander the Great and his successors. Finally, the Persians fostered an influential new religion.

Geography and the Early Persians

The Persian homeland was located on a plateau just north of the Persian Gulf (see Map 6.1 on page 148). Overland networks for traders and migrants connecting Mesopotamia and Anatolia to India and Central Asia passed through Persia, and cities emerged along the trade routes. Travelers between Mesopotamia and India encountered many mountains and deserts. For example, the area between the Black and Caspian Seas contained the Caucasus Mountains, an area of much linguistic diversity but also closely linked to Persia historically.

Various pastoral societies on the Persian plateau competed for power. Two of these, the Indo-European Medes (MEEDZ)

and the Persians, had sent tribute payments to the powerful Assyrian Empire. By 600 B.C.E. the Persians were living in southeastern Iran under their own ruling family but were subjects of the Medes, who became the dominant regional power after they joined with the Babylonians in 612 B.C.E. to overthrow the Assyrians (see Chronology: Persia, 1000–334 B.C.E.). The Median Empire extended from Anatolia in the west to Afghanistan in the east. But the Medes were soon overshadowed by the Persians.

Building a Regional Empire

The Persian Empire, usually known as **Achaemenid** (a-KEY-muh-nid) Persia after the ruling family, was an extraordinary achievement. At its peak, it extended from the Indus Valley in the east to Libya in the west and from the Black, Caspian (KASS-pee-uhn), and Aral (AR-uhl) Seas in the north to the Nile valley in the south. This empire was created by a series of four kings. Cyrus (SY-ruhs) II (r. 550–530 B.C.E.), better known as Cyrus the Great, began the expansion. Cyrus and his successors, Cambyses (kam-BY-seez) II (r. 530–522 B.C.E.), Darius (duh-RY-uhs) I (r. 521–486 B.C.E.), and Xerxes (ZUHRK-seez) I (r. 486–465 B.C.E.), conquered vast territories and created an autocratic but effective and tolerant government. They established a model for later Middle Eastern empires and challenged the Greeks in the west. But they also suffered some setbacks in this empire building.

Achaemenid   The ruling family of the classical Persian Empire.

CHRONOLOGY

	Greece	Persia	Hellenistic World
600 **B.C.E.**	**ca. 594 B.C.E.** Solon's reforms in Athens	**550–530 B.C.E.** Kingship of Cyrus the Great **525–523 B.C.E.** Conquest of Egypt **521–486 B.C.E.** Kingship of Darius I	
500 **B.C.E.**	**499–479 B.C.E.** Greco-Persian Wars **460–429 B.C.E.** Periclean era in Athens **431–404 B.C.E.** Peloponnesian War		
400 **B.C.E.**			**338 B.C.E.** Macedonian conquest of Greece **336–323 B.C.E.** Reign of Alexander the Great **330 B.C.E.** Occupation of Persia

The Foundations of Empire

Cyrus the Great was the real founder of the Persian Empire. In 550 B.C.E. he overthrew the Median king to become the "king of the Medes and Persians." By 539 he had conquered Mesopotamia, Syria, Palestine, Lydia (LID-ee-uh) (a kingdom in the western part of Anatolia), and all the Greek cities in Anatolia that had prospered under the loose and pro-trade rule of the Lydians. In one decade Cyrus had built an empire stretching from the Aegean to Central Asia. As much diplomat as soldier, Cyrus followed moderate policies in the conquered territories, making only modest demands for tribute. After conquering Babylonia, Cyrus issued a proclamation on a cylinder, which some historians interpret as the world's first charter of human rights: "Protect this land from rancor, from foes, from falsehood, and from drought." Cyrus claimed that the main Babylonian god, Marduk (MAHR-dook), ordered him to help the Babylonians by becoming their ruler and bringing them "justice and righteousness," boasting that he and Marduk hence "saved Babylon from oppression."[2] Under Cyrus's authority, the Jews taken to Babylon by the Assyrians were allowed to return to Palestine and rebuild their temple.

Cyrus was killed in 530 B.C.E. while campaigning against nomads east of the Aral Sea. He was replaced by his son Cambyses II, who had learned to accept cultural differences while being governor of Babylonia. Cambyses II subjugated Egypt in 525 B.C.E. and wisely presented himself to the ruling class of priests as a new Egyptian ruler instead of a foreign conqueror. He carved in a granite slab that he would bring stability, good fortune, health, and gladness while ruling Egypt forever.

Cambyses' successor and distant cousin, Darius I, faced new challenges. For one thing, he was a usurper who had seized power at the age of twenty-eight. Not a modest man, he boasted that "over and above my thinking power and understanding, I am a good warrior, horseman, bowman, spear-

man."[3] Darius began his reign by crushing a revolt in Egypt. He spread Persian power east and west, even annexing the Sind region in northwestern India, and he claimed that within his territories he cherished good people, rooted out the bad, and prevented people from killing each other (see Map 6.1). To

CHRONOLOGY

Persia, 1000–334 B.C.E.

ca. 1000	Life of Zoroaster
640	Persians become vassals of Medes
550–530	Kingship of Cyrus the Great
547–546	Conquest of Lydia
530–522	Kingship of Cambyses II
525–523	Conquest of Egypt
521–486	Kingship of Darius I
518	Persian conquest of Indus Valley
499	Rebellion by Ionian Greeks against Persian rule
499–479	Greco-Persian Wars
486–465	Kingship of Xerxes
404	Egyptian independence from Persia
334	Conquest of Persian Empire by Alexander the Great

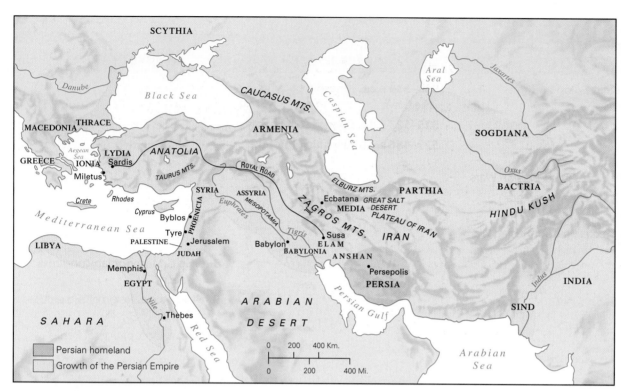

Map 6.1 The Persian Empire, ca. 500 B.C.E.
At its height around 500 B.C.E., the Persians controlled a huge empire that included northern Greece, Egypt, and most of Western Asia from the Mediterranean coast to the Indus River in India.

promote justice and ensure his posterity as a great lawgiver, Darius also supervised the organization and codification of Egyptian law. In 519 he fashioned a law code for Babylonia that basically reaffirmed Hammurabi's laws made almost 1,500 years earlier.

The Persians were among the classical world's greatest engineers and builders. For example, to forge closer links with Egypt, Darius completed the first Suez Canal, an amazing engineering achievement that briefly connected the Mediterranean and the Red Seas. The channel was 125 miles long and 150 feet wide. In 539 Darius began the building of a new capital at Persepolis (puhr-SEP-uh-luhs). This spectacular city was centered on a massive stone terrace, on which stood monumental royal buildings. The city's architecture and decoration were drawn from many traditions, including Egyptian, Mesopotamian, and Greek, and its craftsmen and workers included Egyptians, Greeks, Hittites, and Mesopotamians.

Challenges to Persian Power

Darius and his successors eventually encountered some major problems. In 520 and 513 Darius campaigned unsuccessfully against the Scythians (SITH-ee-uhnz), warlike Indo-European pastoral nomads whose territory stretched from southern Ukraine and Russia eastward to Mongolia. Skilled horsemen and master workers of gold and bronze, the Scythians were among the Central Asians whose interactions with settled farmers helped shape Eurasian history. They had both fought and traded with the Greek trading cities. Later, the

Scythians were one of the few peoples to defeat the formidable armies of Alexander the Great.

A more serious defeat came with the first Greco-Persian War, in which the tiny disunited Greek states turned back the world's most powerful empire. Persians and peninsular Greeks were rivals for regional power, but many Greeks lived in Persian territories, including merchants and political exiles as far east as Mesopotamia. Inspired by Scythian resistance to Darius and concerned about losing trade to rivals, at the beginning of the fifth century B.C.E. some Greek cities on the Ionian (eye-OH-nee-uhn) coast of Anatolia rebelled against Persian control (see Map 6.1). In response Darius decided to go further west and attack the cities on the Greek peninsula that supported the Ionian Greek rebels. The Greek historian Herodotus (heh-ROD-uh-tuhs) reported that a Persian general favored expansion because Europe was blessed with trees of all sorts and a very fertile soil, which only the Persian king was worthy of possessing. While the Persians failed to occupy most of peninsular Greece, they reclaimed the Ionian Greek cities, brutally punishing the most rebellious such as Miletus. Darius then turned to favoring democratic forces in Ionian cities, a tactical move he hoped would inspire democrats in the peninsula to replace anti-Persian conservatives and cooperate with Persian aims.

His hopes proved unrealistic. Xerxes, the son of Darius, tried again to conquer the Greeks in 480 B.C.E. He attacked with a huge army and naval force, and a fierce two-year struggle resulted. Perhaps Xerxes' most effective ally was Queen Artemisia (AHRT-uh-MIZH-ee-uh) of the Ionian Greek city

Bas relief of Darius and Xerxes Holding Court   This relief was carved in one of the palaces at the Persian capital of Persepolis.   (Oriental Institute, University of Chicago, Photo #P57121)

of Halicarnassus (hal-uh-kar-NASS-uhs), who was praised for her bravery, daring, and the wise counsel she gave the Persian king. But the Persian thrust failed, and Xerxes returned home. Xerxes still held a large chunk of the Greek world, including the Ionian states, and he regained control of Egypt, so he could rightly boast that he was still "the king of kings." However, defeat in this second Greco-Persian war was a turning point in Persian history.

Imperial Policies and Networks

Unlike their Assyrian and Babylonian predecessors, the Persian empire builders used laws, economic policies, and tolerance toward the conquered to rule successfully, and many people benefited from the peace that Persian rule provided for two centuries. Leading citizens came from many backgrounds. Generals might be Medes, Armenians, Greeks, Egyptians, or Kurds (curds), a people living in the mountains just north of Persia and Mesopotamia. Some of the Persian techniques were imitated by their successors, including the Greeks and Romans, when they created even larger imperial structures several centuries later.

The Persians followed and improved upon the systematic bureaucracy first used by the Assyrians. Although their power was in theory absolute, Persian kings were expected to consult with important nobles and judges. Each of the twenty-three Persian provinces was governed by a **satrap** (SAY-trap) ("protector of the kingdom"), an official who ruled according to established laws and procedures and paid a fixed amount of taxes to the king each year. The Persians had several grand capitals, including Babylon and Susa (SOO-zuh) in Mesopotamia, before Persepolis was completed. Darius also set up courts with permanent judges.

Communication between imperial officials was aided by the "royal road" stretching 1,700 miles from east to west. A messenger of the king could travel the road by horse in nineteen days by exchanging horses at a series of stations along the way. The Persians became famous for building roads and then protecting those who traveled them. Herodotus marveled at the communication network, writing that "neither snow, nor rain, nor heat, nor darkness of night prevents these couriers from completing their designated stages with utmost speed."[4] Today that is the motto of the United States Postal Service.

The highways promoted economic growth and exchange, a second Achaemenid practice that strengthened their empire. For instance, Darius minted coins, a practice derived from the Lydians. The use of standard weights and measures, along with a currency of recognized value, made trade easier throughout the empire. In addition, the Persian rulers did not steal the wealth of the lands they conquered, but allowed them to continue to engage in and benefit from the same economic activities as before. Phoenicia, for example, continued its Mediterranean trade. The Persians gained their revenue from land taxes, road tolls, and taxes on the production and consumption of goods. To open new networks for exchanging goods and technologies, Darius sent an expedition to visit India. It returned by sailing around Arabia to Suez (SOO-ez). This expedition laid the foundation for the conquest of the southern Indus River Valley and also more maritime trade.

satrap ("protector of the kingdom")   A Persian official who ruled according to established laws and procedures and paid a fixed amount of taxes to the emperor each year.

Perhaps most crucial to their imperial success, the Persians generally treated the people they conquered with respect, allowing them to maintain their own social and religious institutions. In Egypt, for instance, Cambyses was a pharaoh, not a Persian ruler. Similarly, Cyrus sought the approval of the local god Marduk in Babylon in claiming ancient titles, announcing that he was king of the universe and of Babylon, Sumer, and Akkad. The Persians prided themselves on their ability to unify the vastly different peoples of western Asia under the "king of kings," a title that recognized the existence of other rulers whose limited rights in their own territories were respected. For this reason, many Greeks fought for Persia in the Persian-Greek Wars.

The Persians also utilized various official languages. Eventually, Aramaic (ar-uh-MAY-ik), spoken by many peoples of western Asia, became the official language. Most official documents were written in Aramaic using the Phoenician alphabet. Greek also became widely used as a written language in the western empire. Herodotus reported of the Persians that "there is no nation which so readily adopts foreign customs. They have taken the dress of the Medes and in war they wear the Egyptian breastplate. As soon as they hear of any luxury, they instantly make it their own."[5]

Zoroaster and Persian Religion

The Persians made another distinct contribution to later world history in their promotion of **Zoroastrianism** (zo-ro-ASS-tree-uh-niz-uhm), a religion founded by Zoroaster (whose name means "With Golden Camels") that later became the state religion of Persia. Some of the key ideas in Judaism, Christianity, and Islam are foreshadowed by, and perhaps even derived from, this early Persian religion. The prophet Zoroaster was one of the first non-Hebrew religious leaders to challenge the prevailing polytheism of his day. Although he is usually thought to have lived between 630 and 550 B.C.E., at the beginning of the Eurasian Axial Age, many scholars believe he lived much earlier, between 1400 and 900 B.C.E. Zoroaster may have been a priest in the early Persian religion, which was closely related to the religion of the Aryans who migrated to India, and the language of his writings and the *Rig Veda* have much in common.

In contrast to the polytheism of other Persians, Zoroaster had a monotheistic vision. He believed in one supreme god, **Ahura Mazda** (ah-HOOR-uh-MAZZ-duh) (the "Wise Lord"), who was opposed by an evil spirit, a Satan-like figure who was the source of lies, cowardice, misery, and other forms of evil (see Witness to the Past: Good, Evil, and Monotheism in Zoroastrian Thought). Zoroaster speculated that Ahura Mazda allowed humans to freely choose between himself and evil,

between heaven and hell. By serving Ahura Mazda, men and women were serving the spirit of ultimate goodness and truth while simultaneously improving the world. At the end of time, Zoroaster believed, there would be a final judgment at which Ahura Mazda would win a final victory over the spirit of evil. At that time, even hell would come to an end.

Many core Zoroastrian ideas, especially the notion of a contest between a good God and an evil spirit or devil and the corresponding belief in heaven and hell, were developed in later Jewish scriptures, and then in the sacred writings of both Christians and Muslims. The Jews may have adopted some of their ideas about good and evil, the afterlife, and a last judgment from Zoroastrians while the Jews were held captive in Babylon (586–539 B.C.E.). The Zoroastrian watchwords of "good thoughts, good words, good deeds" became key ideas of other religions, including Christianity and Buddhism. Darius I did much to spread Zoroastrianism. He publicly attributed his victories to Ahura Mazda, whose name figured prominently in carved stone memorials honoring him for creating earth, sky, and humankind. While Zoroastrianism was displaced in western Asia by Christianity and, later, Islam, the faith lives on today among small groups in Iran as well as in the wealthy Parsee (PAR-see) minority in western India, descendants of Persian Zoroastrians.

Social Life and Gender Relations

The Persians did not develop as politically diversified a society as did the Greeks. No class of active citizens helped make political decisions at the imperial level. At the top of the system were the nobles, many of them warriors who had been granted large estates by the king, followed by priests, merchants, and bankers. In Babylonian cities ruled by Persia these citizens met in formal assemblies to make important judicial decisions, and routine administration was done by councils of twenty-five leading men. Zoroastrian priests schooled the princes of the noble families to prepare for government careers. The middle class included brewers, butchers, bakers, carpenters, potters, and coppersmiths. Affluent Persians enjoyed feasting and wine drinking.

Peasants and slaves constituted the bottom of the social structure. Over the centuries, as wealthy landowners acquired their land, more and more peasant farmers were impoverished and became poor renters or sharecroppers, bound to the land. There were also some slaves, mainly debtors, criminals, and prisoners of war. The slave population filled a variety of functions. Some were apprenticed in trades, and others were allowed to take up business.

Persian society was patriarchal. Herodotus reported that Persian men believed that the greatest proof of masculinity was to father many sons. Persian society was also polygynous: many men, especially at upper levels, had several wives. Persian women were usually kept secluded in harems and many probably veiled themselves, an ancient practice in western Asia. But some queens and other noble women exercised strong influences on their husbands, and many even controlled large estates. Herodotus commented that some queens were more outgoing and aggressive than their husbands. A few women

---

Zoroastrianism A monotheistic religion founded by the Persian Zoroaster, and later the state religion of Persia. Its notion of one god opposed by the devil may have influenced Judaism and later Christianity.

Ahura Mazda (the "Wise Lord") The one god of Zoroastrianism.

Good, Evil, and Monotheism in Zoroastrian Thought

The Persian thinker Zarathustra, better know today by the name given him by the Greeks, Zoroaster, offered an ethical vision that, he believed, came from God. The early Persians apparently believed in three great gods and many lesser ones, but Zoroaster preached that only one of these, *Ahura Mazda* (The Wise Lord), was the supreme deity in the universe, responsible for creation and the source of all goodness. But a rival entity, *Angra Mainyu* (Hostile Spirit), embodied evil and was the source of all misery and sin. Zoroaster asked people to join the cosmic battle for good and worship Ahura Mazda while opposing evil and Angra Mainyu, referred to as the Liar. This excerpt outlining Zoroaster's beliefs comes from one of the devotional hymns, the *Gathas*, contained within the Zoroastrian holy scriptures. It was written down in final form centuries after Zoroaster's life but was probably based on earlier writings by the prophet or his disciples.

Then shall I recognize you as strong and holy, Mazda, when by the hand in which you yourself hold the destinies that you will assign to the Liar [Angra Mainyu] and the Righteous [Ahura Mazda] . . . the might of Good Thought shall come to me.

As the holy one I recognized you, Mazda Ahura, when I saw you in the beginning at the birth of Life, when you made actions and words to have their reward—evil for the evil, a good Destiny for the good—through your wisdom when creation shall reach its goal. At which goal you will come with your holy Spirit, O Mazda, with Dominion, at the same with Good Thought, by whose action the settlements [human societies] will prosper through Right. . . .

"I am Zarathustra, a true foe to the Liar, to the utmost of my power, but a powerful support would I be to the Righteous, that I may attain the future things of the infinite Dominion, so I praise and proclaim you, Mazda. . . ."

As the holy one I recognized you, Mazda Ahura, when Good Thought [a good spirit created by Ahura Mazda] came to me, when the still mind taught me to declare what is best: "Let not a man seek again and again to please the Liars, for they make all the righteous enemies."

And thus Zarathustra himself . . . chooses the spirit of thine that is holiest, Mazda. May Right be embodied, full of life and strength! May Piety abide in the Dominion where the sun shines! May Good Thought give destiny to men according to their works [good actions]!

This I ask you, tell me truly, Ahura. . . . Who determined the path of sun and stars? Who is it by whom the moon waxes and wanes again? . . . Who upheld the Earth beneath and the firmament from falling? Who the water and the plants? Who yoked swiftness to winds and clouds? . . .

This I ask you, tell me truly, Ahura—whether we shall drive the Lie away from us to those who being full of disobedience will not strive after fellowship with Right, nor trouble themselves with counsel of Good Thought. . . .

I will speak of that which Mazda Ahura, the all-knowing, revealed to me first in this earthly life. Those of you that put not into practice this word as I think and utter it, to them shall be woe at the end of life. I will speak of that which the Holiest declared to me as the word that is best for mortals to obey: he, Mazda Ahura said, "They who at my bidding render [Zarathustra] obedience, shall all attain Welfare and Immortality by the actions of the Good Spirit." In immortality shall the soul of the righteous be joyful, in perpetuity shall be the torments of the Liars [the followers of evil]. All this does Mazda Ahura appoint by his Dominion.

THINKING ABOUT THE READING

1. What supreme powers did Zoroaster attribute to Ahura Mazda?

2. How did Zoroaster expect individuals to work for good and combat evil?

3. What fate awaited those who chose the path of evil?

Source: Yasnas 43–45, in James Hope Moulton, *Early Zoroastrianism* (London: Williams and Norgate, 1913), 364–370.

---

became independently wealthy. For instance, one entrepreneur of commoner origins, Irdabama, was a major landowner who not only controlled a large labor force of several hundred but also operated her own grain and wine business. Egyptian women kept many of the rights they enjoyed before Persian rule, and most marriages there were monogamous.

The Decline of Achaemenid Persia

Although the Persian empire was not finally conquered until the army of Alexander the Great defeated Persian forces in 330 B.C.E., the seeds of decline were planted more than a century earlier when the policies of Xerxes I, especially a policy of heavy taxation of the satrapies, began to weaken support for Persian rule. Vast amounts of pure silver paid as taxes were sent to the Persian capital. By 424 B.C.E. the Persian Empire was suffering from civil unrest caused by fights within the Achaemenid family, currency inflation, and difficulty collecting taxes.

Under Xerxes and his successors, the wise policies of Cyrus and Darius, which promoted trade and treated non-Persians with respect, were gradually reversed. Many merchants and landlords were ruined by having to borrow money at very high interest rates. At the same time, fewer attempts were made to include other ethnic groups in the governing of the empire.

Some regions rebelled. For example, Egypt ended Persian control in 404 B.C.E. and restored pharaonic rule. Thus support for the increasingly remote kings weakened long before the superior armies of the Macedonian conqueror Alexander brought an end to Achaemenid Persia and its once great empire.

SECTION SUMMARY

- The Persian Empire, centered on a trade crossroads, lasted for only two centuries, but it was larger than any empire that preceded it.
- The Persian Empire suffered several setbacks, including an unsuccessful campaign against the Scythians and repeated failure to completely conquer Greece.
- The Persians often won the support of peoples they had conquered through their respect for native cultures and their institution of the rule of law.
- The monotheistic Persian religion, Zoroastrianism, may have contributed some key ideas to Judaism, Christianity, and Islam.
- Though the Persian Empire was conquered by Alexander the Great in 330 B.C.E., it had begun to decline over a century earlier.

CHRONOLOGY	
The Greeks, 750–338 B.C.E.	
ca. 750–550	Greek colonization in Mediterranean, Black Sea
ca. 594	Solon's reforms in Athens
561–527	Peisistratus tyrant in Athens
507	Athenian democracy under Cleisthenes
499–479	Greco-Persian Wars
477	Founding of Delian League
469–399	Life of Socrates
ca. 460–429	Era of Pericles in Athens
431–404	Peloponnesian War
428–347	Life of Plato
384–322	Life of Aristotle
338	Philip of Macedonia's conquest of Greece

◆ The Emergence of the Greeks

How did democracy develop in Greece, and what were its advantages and inadequacies?

Historians of Persia's greatest rival, Greece, have tended to emphasize Greek achievements, especially the birth of democratic thought, but these were only part of a complex, often conflicted society. The Greeks had to struggle to forge democracy. How much of their culture the Greeks created and how much they adopted from others remains subject to debate. Whatever the truth, the Mediterranean was a zone of interaction for peoples living around its rim, and by 700 B.C.E. the Greeks had become active participants in maritime trade. Soon this activity led to prosperity for many Greek cities and new forms of government.

Cities and Citizenship

The Greek world was shaped by varied influences. On the Greek peninsula, a geographical context of mountains, coastal plains, and islands encouraged the development of a dozen or so major city-states rather than one centralized state. This same context also stimulated maritime trade, which was the main reason for the growth and prosperity of most Greek cities between 800 and 500 B.C.E. A growing population, a shortage of good farmland at home, and commercial interests led many Greeks to leave their home cities (see Chronology: The Greeks, 750–338 B.C.E.). In what is called the Greek diaspora

(dye-ASS-puh-ruh), meaning dispersion or spreading out, they established some 250 new settlements along the Ionian coast, around the Black Sea, in Italy, and even as far west as the Mediterranean coasts of what is today France and Spain (see Map 6.2). Trade and migration opened the Greeks to new ideas. By the sixth century B.C.E. Greeks were even visiting and living in Egypt, where they worshiped Egyptian gods under Greek names.

Prosperity led to a new conception of the city and the citizen's role in it. The result was a unique Greek political unit, the **polis** (POE-lis), a city-state that embraced nearby rural areas whose agricultural surplus helped support the urban population. The polis, whether in the peninsula or the Greek diaspora, became the major institution of classical Greek life, a living community that gave citizens a sense of personal identity and meaning. All business, from building a new temple to making war, was decided by the free male citizens meeting in an open assembly. Even loyalty to one's family or clan was less important than loyalty to the polis. The worst punishment a Greek could suffer was being asked to leave the polis. Some Greeks committed suicide rather than face ostracism.

City-states competed fiercely with each other, including in sports events. The Olympic Games, begun in the eighth century B.C.E., were associated with a religious festival to honor the god Zeus (ZOOSS). Each polis sent athletes, both men and

---

polis A Greek city-state that embraced nearby rural areas, whose agricultural surplus then helped support the urban population.

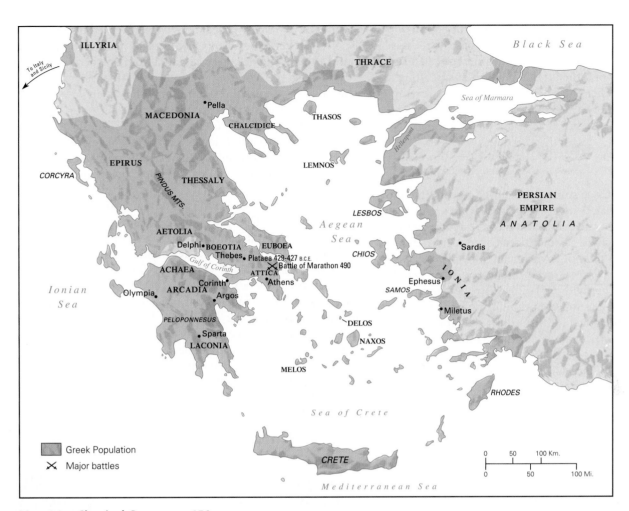

Map 6.2 Classical Greece, ca. 450 B.C.E.
Greek settlements, divided into rival city-states, occupied not only the Greek peninsula but also Crete and western Anatolia. Two alliances headed by Athens and Sparta respectively fought each other in the Peloponnesian War (431-404 B.C.E.).

Online Study Center **Improve Your Grade** Interactive Map: Ancient Greece

unmarried women, who competed naked in track and field events or personal contests of strength, such as wrestling. The idea was to win, even if it meant cheating. The Greek athlete might have viewed our modern concept of a "good loser" as somewhat bizarre.

Not all inhabitants of the polis were equal. Many cities developed **oligarchy** (AHL-uh-gar-kee), rule by a small group of wealthy leaders. As much as 80 percent of the population in most Greek cities, including women, slaves, children, and resident foreigners, were not citizens and thus had no right to participate in political life by voting or holding office. Even among the citizens, members of old, aristocratic families were treated with greater respect than others. Most Greek cities, despite their elected assemblies, were long dominated by a monarch or other executives who were supervised by a council of aristocrats.

Trade, Warfare, and Politics

By the seventh century two factors had weakened aristocratic power. One was the growth of trade. Aristocrats generally scorned trade in favor of the wealth to be gained from the land. Moreover, trade helped create wealth for other citizens, allowing them to compete with the upper class. The second factor was the development of a new battle formation that relied on infantry more than the aristocracy-dominated cavalry. By this time, the city of Sparta had perfected an infantry formation, the phalanx (FAY-langks), that was quickly adopted by other cities. The phalanx consisted of a square of soldiers eight wide and eight deep that moved in unison. Each man was protected with heavy armor and carried either a short sword or a nine-foot spear. Each soldier bought his own armor and weapons. With this development Greek armies became citizen-armies, not paid professional forces. As men other than aristocrats paid to risk their lives for their polis, they wanted a greater role in governing it.

---

oligarchy Rule by a small group of wealthy leaders.

In sum, a new military system combined with population expansion and increased wealth from trade with the Greek cities in Ionia contributed to the rise of democracy, most notably in the city-state of Athens. But the Greeks also fought many wars with each other and other enemies, and these struggles undermined some of the Greek political ideals.

Reform, Tyranny, and Democracy in Athens

Between 600 and 350 B.C.E. some Greeks tried to combine the contradictory ideas that people are politically free and that they owe their loyalty to the community. The resulting tension was not as great as it would be for citizens of modern democracies, since the Greeks did not envision anything like "perfect" liberty. Nevertheless, some Greeks discovered how people could live with each other without being controlled by gods or kings, and many cities developed notions of political freedom and equality that were radical for that era, or even for ours. Although reserved for adult male citizens only, these ideas had never been seen before.

The most dramatic political changes occurred in Athens, a polis on the eastern Greek peninsula of Attica. Athens became progressively more democratic, partly a result of a crisis. The soil on which Athenians grew wheat was wearing out, and as farmers produced less, they borrowed money and went deeply into debt. As the bad harvests continued, farmers were reduced to selling themselves and their families into slavery. The poor demanded reform.

Around 594 B.C.E. the Athenians elected Solon (SOH-luhn), a general, poet, and merchant, to lead the city and rewrite the old constitution. He canceled the debts of the poor, forbid enslavement for default of debts, and made wealth rather than birth the criterion for membership on the council of hereditary aristocrats who controlled the city. Solon also established a new Council of 400 to review issues before they came before an Assembly of Citizens, which now served as a court of appeals where people, rich or poor, could bring a case to court. Solon boasted of his attempts to gather back the common people and set straight laws alike for lowly and lords, in order to prevent mob violence and avoid civil war. While many of Solon's reforms were progressive, he also reduced the freedom of women. For example, laws now gave fathers the right to sell into slavery daughters who lost their virginity before marriage.

The Athenian path to a more democratic system came in several stages, from reform to tyranny to democracy. Solon's reforms failed to please either side in this social and economic struggle. The poor wanted him to take land from the rich and redistribute it to them, while the aristocrats resented their loss of power. After his death tensions returned, allowing Peisistratus (pie-SIS-truht-uhs) (r. 561–527 B.C.E.) to seize power as a **tyrant**, not necessarily a brutal ruler but someone who ruled outside the law. Many Greek cities were governed by tyrants in this period. Peisistratus appealed directly to the poor, giving some of them land he had confiscated from aristocratic estates. He also aided the economy and culture of Athens by launching a building program, one result of which was an aqueduct to bring water directly to the city center.

Another aristocrat, Cleisthenes (KLICE-thuh-neez), finally established genuine democracy in Athens in 507 B.C.E. Instead of emphasizing noble birth or wealth as a criterion of citizenship, Cleisthenes organized people geographically. He created geographical units that chose people by lot to serve in a new Council of 500, which submitted legislation to the Assembly for approval. The Assembly consisted of 40,000 citizens; about 6,000 generally showed up for meetings, and these selected by lot the city officials. Cleisthenes' version of Athenian democracy was extended in the mid-fifth century when the power of the aristocrats was further reduced and lower-income citizens were allowed to serve as officials. Euripides (you-RIP-uh-deez) described the system in his play, *The Suppliant Woman*: "The city is free, and ruled by no one man. The people reign, in annual succession. They do not yield power to the rich; the poor man has an equal share in it."[6]

Although the majority of people were excluded from political life, for those who were citizens, the system was more radically democratic than most modern governments. The

Narrative Drawing on Pottery   The Francois vase, made around 570 B.C.E., is considered a masterpiece of narrative drawing on pottery, with fine detail and vivid coloring. It shows scenes of battle.   (Scala/Art Resource, NY)

---

tyrant   Someone who ruled a Greek polis outside the law, not necessarily a brutal ruler.

Martin, Thomas R. *Ancient Greece from Prehistoric to Hellenistic Times.* New Haven, Conn.: Yale University Press, 1996. A clear survey of Greek history, written for the general reader.

Pomeroy, Sarah B. *Goddesses, Whores, Wives and Slaves: Women in Classical Antiquity.* New York: Schocken, 1975. An excellent study of women's lives in classical Greece and Rome.

Samons, Loren J., ed. *Athenian Democracy and Imperialism.* Boston: Houghton Mifflin, 1988. Valuable collection of writings on an important theme.

Vernant, Jean-Pierre, ed. *The Greeks,* translated by Charles Lambert and Teresa Lavender Fagan. Chicago: University of Chicago Press, 1995. A collection of essays interpreting Greek political, economic, social, and religious life.

Wood, Michael. *In the Footprints of Alexander the Great: A Journey from Greece to Asia.* Berkeley: University of California Press, 1997. A fascinating recreation of Alexander the Great's route to, and experiences reaching, India.

Websites

Ancient/Classical History
(**http://ancienthistory.about.com/library**).   Essays and timelines for many ancient civilizations and societies.

Diotima: Women and Gender in the Ancient World
(**http://www.stoa.org/diotima/**).   Contains excellent materials on gender and women in the early Mediterranean world.

Exploring Ancient World Cultures
(**http://eawc.evansville.edu/**).   Excellent site run by Evansville University, with essays and links on the ancient Near East and Europe.

Internet Ancient History Sourcebook
(**http://www.fordham.edu/halsall/ancient/asbook.html**).
Exceptionally rich collection of links and primary source readings.

Livius: Articles on Ancient History
(**http://www.livius.org**).   Very useful site with many short essays on the Greeks, Persians, Parthians, Romans, and other ancient and classical societies.

CHAPTER 7

Classical Societies in Southern and Central Asia, 600 B.C.E.–600 C.E.

Online Study Center

This icon will direct you to interactive activities and study materials on the website: college.hmco. com/pic/lockard1e

Gold Coin This gold coin, showing a horseman, was made in India during the reign of King Chandragupta II, who presided over a great and prosperous Indian empire, with a dynamic economy, between 380 and 415 C.E. (C. M. Dixon/Ancient Art & Architecture Collection)

Ashoka spent his remaining years in power promoting the pacifist teachings of the Buddha. He wrote that his duty was the good of the whole world. He pledged to bear wrong without violent retribution, to look kindly on all his subjects, and to ensure the safety, happiness, and peace of mind of all living beings. To fulfill his pledge, he designed laws to encourage Buddhist virtues such as simplicity, compassion, mutual tolerance, vegetarianism, and respect for all forms of life. He also sponsored many public works, including hospitals and medical care paid for by the state. Trees were planted, parks developed, wells dug, and rest houses built along highways. Ashoka dispatched Buddhist missions to various foreign countries, spreading the religion into Sri Lanka, Southeast Asia, and Afghanistan. According to one legend, a Buddhist monk sent by Ashoka reached Greece, where he debated with Greek thinkers about the nature of being. Such contacts indicate that Eurasian networks of religious and philosophical exchange were forming.

Despite his own devotion and strong beliefs, Ashoka neither made Buddhism the state religion nor persecuted other faiths. Indeed, while Ashoka financed the building of Buddhist temples and *stupas* (STOOP-uhz) (domed shrines), government aid was distributed to all religious groups. The king argued that "all sects deserve reverence for one reason or another. By thus acting a man exalts his own sect and at the same time does service to the sects of other people."[12]

Although reflecting Buddhist attitudes, Ashoka was also a practical statesman. He sought to spread humane ideas peacefully both within and without the borders of the state while also maintaining the system of courts and a military force. Public respect for his pacifist ideals and behavior discouraged rebellion. Ashoka styled himself "Beloved of the Gods," which in practice meant he was considered at least a semi-deity. For both Hindus and Buddhists, the Mauryas created a political legacy of the universal emperor, a divinely sanctioned leader with a special role in the cosmic scheme of things.

The Decline of the Mauryas

Ashoka ruled with popular acclaim, but his successors were less able. Within a half century after his death, regions were seceding, the Mauryas were overthrown, and the empire destroyed. Perhaps Ashoka's policies had made India too peace-loving and had weakened Mauryan military forces. But difficult communications in a large empire also fostered local autonomy, and the mounting costs of a centralized bureaucracy drained the treasury. Perhaps caste divisions and ethnic and religious diversity also undermined political unity.

The end of the Mauryan Empire set a political pattern different from that of China. In China, long periods of unity were interspersed with short intervals of political fragmentation. In India, on the other hand, periods of unity were relatively brief, followed by prolonged fragmentation. But while India did not always possess political unity, it did possess a strong sense of cultural unity. This culture and mindset emphasized loyalty to the social order, including the family and caste, rather than to the state.

SECTION SUMMARY

■ Through the conquests by Darius and Alexander the Great, northwest India experienced significant influence from the West.

■ After Alexander's retreat, Chandragupta established the first imperial Indian state, the centralized, autocratic Mauryan Empire, which included the Indus and Ganges Basins.

■ The Mauryan capital city, Patna, was among the largest in the world, and the empire excelled in crafts and trade.

■ King Ashoka, Chandragupta's grandson, became a pacifist convert to Buddhism, which he helped to spread to Sri Lanka, Southeast Asia, and Afghanistan.

■ Unlike those of China, India's periods of unity were relatively brief; and, several decades after Ashoka died, the Mauryan Empire broke down.

South and Central Asia After the Mauryas

What were some of the ways in which classical India connected with and influenced the world beyond South Asia?

Although the end of the Mauryas in the early second century B.C.E. was followed by 500 years of political fragmentation before the rise of the next empire, that of the Guptas, these centuries saw increasing contact between India and the outside world. This contact had strong repercussions for both sides. India's contact with peoples in Central Asia increased, and Indian cultural influence, especially Buddhism, spread into that region. Various Central and West Asian peoples swept into northwestern India from time to time, conquering the Indus Valley and mixing with local peoples, who eventually absorbed the invaders and their ways. Substantial foreign trade and Buddhist missions to neighboring societies also occurred. In world history, change has often come from contact with other peoples, and this was certainly true of India.

India, Central Asia, and the Silk Road

India's relations with Central Asia, the area stretching from Russia eastward to the borders of China, were constant and included several dimensions. Central Asia, especially the Turkestan region north of India, so known since many people spoke Turkish languages, was a key contact zone and hub for networks stretching east to China, south to India, and west to Persia and Russia. As trade between China and western Asia developed, cities developed in Central Asia along the overland route (known as the "Silk Road") through Turkestan. A Persian-speaking society, the Sogdians (SAHG-dee-uhns), mostly

Zoroastrians or Buddhists, dominated the commerce of many cities along the trade network, and they also linked the trade to India. The Sogdians, who had a written language and literature, developed a flourishing mercantile society based on their interaction with Persians, Turks, Indians, Chinese, and others. A Chinese traveler described the country around the major Sogdian city, Samarkand (SAM-uhr-kand), as "a great commercial entrepot, very fertile, abounding in trees and flowers, its inhabitants skillful craftsmen, smart and energetic."[13]

Over the centuries various pastoral groups living on China's borders, unable to penetrate China's defenses or under pressure from Chinese expansion, moved westward. Among the best known were the Huns, who developed the most effective weapon of the day, a reflex bow. Pressure from the horseback-riding Hun soldiers had long pushed various Indo-Europeans, including the Germanic peoples, into Europe. Some Huns migrated into the fertile plains of southern Russia and Hungary. In the fourth and fifth centuries C.E. Huns invaded and inflicted much damage on the weakened Roman Empire (see Chapter 8). Various other Central Asians settled in eastern Europe, southern Russia, and the Caucasus. Others moved south through Turkestan into Persia, Afghanistan, and India, helping shape developments there.

Migrations into Northwest India

Throughout the Classical Era new peoples migrated through the mountain ranges into northwest India from Central Asia and western Asia. These invasions introduced new cultural influences, adding to India's hybrid character. The newcomers were diverse. Invaders from the Hellenistic kingdom of Bactria in Afghanistan, for instance, occupied parts of the Indus Basin, reintroducing Greek influence. Bactria was a crossroads between east and west where Greek, Persian, and Indian cultures met and mixed. There Greeks and Indians exchanged knowledge of medicine and astronomy. Bactrian Greeks adopted Hinduism or Buddhism and inspired a Greek- and Roman-influenced form of Buddhist painting and sculpture, known as Gandhara after the region where it emerged west of the Indus. Gandharan art became preeminent in parts of the northwest, reaching its height in the fourth and fifth centuries C.E. Eventually the Bactrian Greeks became absorbed into the broad fold of Indian society. Various Central Asians migrated into northwest India beginning around 50 B.C.E. Like their predecessors, the new rulers adopted Hinduism and fit themselves into the caste system, mostly as warriors.

In the first century C.E. the **Kushans** (KOO-shans), an Indo-European people from Central Asia, conquered much of northwest India and western parts of the Ganges Basin, and they constructed an empire that also encompassed Afghanistan and parts of Central Asia, including many Silk Road cities. This expansion brought occasional conflicts with first the Parthians

and then the Sassanians, two groups who successively dominated Persia (see Chapters 6 and 8). This empire building promoted communication and extensive trade between India and China, the Middle East, and the eastern Mediterranean.

Some Kushan leaders embraced Buddhism and sought to become world leaders of the faith. Indeed, the Kushans were instrumental in spreading the religion into Central Asia, from which it then diffused to China. The Kushans also encouraged the Gandhara and other schools of Buddhist art. Hence, they promoted and spread a mix of Indian and Greco-Roman culture over a wide area. Some Kushan kings, especially the much respected Kanishka (ka-NISH-ka) (r. 78–144 C.E.), patronized artists, writers, poets, and musicians and tolerated all religions. Like invaders before them, the Kushans intermarried with local people, enhancing the hybrid character of the culture in northwestern India.

South India and Sri Lanka

The Kushan Empire lasted from 50 to 250 C.E. When it eventually faded, northern Indians replaced it with a patchwork of competing states. The political instability in northwestern India was duplicated elsewhere in the subcontinent, where there was frequent warfare between competing states. But the post-Maurya period also saw considerable political and cultural development in both south India and the large island of Sri Lanka. The culture of north India, partly rooted in Aryan traditions, spread southward. At the same time, south Indians and Sri Lankans developed distinctive cultures of their own.

South India   North Indian influence spread south in part because some Dravidian peoples extended their political power northward into the Ganges Basin. Aryan myths, values, rituals, and ideas such as divine kingship from north India appealed to south Indian rulers. South Indians also adopted the caste system, although in a less rigid form than that practiced in north India. These adaptations strengthened southern states, some of which had already flourished for centuries from maritime trade networks stretching from China to the Persian Gulf. South India was renowned as far west as Greece and Rome for its prosperity and for products such as gold.

However, Aryan influence did not destroy regional traditions in south India. For example, the Dravidians, who speak a Dravidian language and inhabit India's southeastern corner, developed a vigorous cultural tradition distinct from that of the Ganges Basin. Poetry became the Tamils' most esteemed art. The mountain city of Madurai (made-uh-RYE), the temple-filled cultural center for the Tamils, had several important colleges and developed into a major center of Hinduism, literature, and education. A Tamil poem from the second century C.E. describes Madurai's function as a religious center filled with devout people:

The great and famous city of Madurai, Is like the lotus flower of God Vishnu. Its streets are the petals of the flower. God Shiva's temple is the center. The citizens are the plentiful pollen; The poor, the crowding beetles. And

---

Kushans   An Indo-European people from Central Asia who conquered much of northwest India and western parts of the Ganges Basin, constructing an empire that also encompassed Afghanistan and parts of Central Asia.

Kulke, Hermann, and Dietmar Rothermund. *History of India*. 3rd ed. London and New York: Routledge, 1998. A concise but stimulating general history that incorporates recent scholarship on the Classical Era.

Mabbett, Ian, and David Chandler. *The Khmers*. London: Blackwell, 1995. An authoritative study of early Cambodian history.

Oxtoby, Willard G. *World Religions: Eastern Traditions*. New York: Oxford University Press, 1996. Contains valuable essays on the Budhist, Hindu, and Jain traditions.

Ray, Himanshu Prabha. *The Archaeology of Seafaring in Ancient South Asia*. New York: Cambridg University Press, 2003. Scholarly study of India's maritime trade and contacts in this era.

Shaffer, Lynda Norene. *Maritime Southeast Asia to 1500*. Armonk, N.Y.: M.E. Sharpe, 1996. A very readable brief introduction to premodern Southeast Asia, including Funan and the Austronesian maritime trade.

Stein, Burton. *A History of India*. Malden, M.A.: Blackwell, 1998. A survey text especially strong on social and religious history.

Taylor, Keith Weller. *The Birth of Vietnam*. Berkeley: University of California Press, 1983. The major study on Vietnam before and during Chinese colonization.

Thapar, Romila. *A'soka and the Decline of the Mauryas*. Delhi: Oxford University Press, 1997. An update of an earlier study, with much information on the Mauryas.

Thapar, Romila. *Early India from the Origins to AD 1300*. Berkeley: University of California Press, 2002. A valuable revision of the standard history of early India, detailed and comprehensive.

Websites

Austronesian and Other Indo-Pacific Topics (http://w3.rz-berlin.mpg.de/~wm/wm3.html). A useful collection to sources on Austronesian languages and cultures, operated by Germany-based scholars.

Internet Indian History Sourcebook (http://www.fordham.edu/halsall/india/indiasbook.html). An invaluable collection of sources and links on India from ancient to modern times.

Silk Road Narratives (http://depts.washington.edu/uwch/silkroad/texts/texts.html). Explores cultural interaction in Eurasia through excerpts from Silk Road travelers.

Virtual Religion Index (http://virtualreligion.net/vri/). An outstanding site with many links on the history of Buddhism and Hinduism.

Empires, Networks, and the Remaking of Europe, North Africa, and Western Asia, 500 B.C.E.–600 C.E.

Online Study Center

This icon will direct you to interactive activities and study materials on the website: college.hmco. com/pic/lockard1e

Santa Sophia The magnificent Santa Sophia Church in Constantinople, rebuilt during the reign of the emperor Justinian in the sixth century C.E., had interior walls covered in gold mosaics that glowed from reflected sunlight. This mosaic from the Zoe panel shows Jesus holding a Bible. (Erich Lessing/Art Resource, NY)

Remember, Roman, that it is for you to rule the nations. This shall be your task: to impose the ways of peace, to spare the vanquished and to tame the proud by war.

ROMAN POET VIRGIL[1]

Around 320 B.C.E. Pytheas (PITH-ee-us), a scientist from the Greek colony of Massalia (ma-SAL-ya), today's city of Marseilles (mahr-SAY) on the Mediterranean coast of France, wrote a book about his remarkable travels in Europe. A brave, curious man, some ten years earlier, according to his account, Pytheas had reached the western coast of France by sea or over land. From there he arranged to sail on a boat owned by local Celtic (KELL-tik) people to southwest England. He continued north through the Irish Sea and may have reached Iceland. He then ventured down the east coast of Britain before turning north, exploring the North Sea coast as far as Denmark before retracing his journey back to Massalia. Some of his contemporaries were awed by his daring adventure. Others called him a liar. Today some scholars consider Pytheas one of the world's great explorers because he gave Mediterranean societies their first eyewitness account of the remote northern coast and its mysterious peoples.

Pytheas's story tells us much about the western Eurasia of those times. The people of the Mediterranean knew little of the lands north of the Alps and Balkans, whose peoples they considered dangerous barbarians. Many goods were exchanged between Mediterranean and northern societies, but mostly by being passed from community to community. However, the western Mediterranean where Pytheas lived was crisscrossed by trade networks: Greeks, Etruscans (ee-TRUHS-kuhns), Carthaginians (kar-thuh-JIN-ee-uhns), and the upstart Romans competed intensely for economic resources and political power. These societies were all part of an interdependent world incorporating southern Europe, North Africa, and western Asia, where commodities flowed and ideas were exchanged. Three hundred years after Pytheas's voyage, Europe was much more closely linked, thanks largely to a people who in Pytheas's time were an ambitious but still minor power, the Romans.

By the time Pytheas wrote his book, the Romans had begun their rise to power in the region. The Roman success in creating a large empire and rich society, celebrated in the opening quote by the Roman poet Virgil, had a considerable impact on world history. As Rome flowered, many societies became its subjects. Under Rome, diverse societies were changed in many ways, and networks were expanded. Roman expansion helped reshape much of Europe, marginalizing or incorporating the northern peoples while also transforming North African and western Asian politics. In addition, when the Roman Empire finally ended after half a millennium, it left several legacies for later European, western Asian, and even African societies. The Romans passed on to later Europeans useful ideas on law and government, some of which derived from the Greeks. In addition, during Roman times Christianity emerged to form the cultural underpinning of a new, post-Roman European society while also spreading in Asia and Africa.

A version of the Roman Empire, Greek-speaking Byzantium (buh-ZANT-ee-uhm), continued to exist in the eastern Mediterranean for a thousand years, a Christian society serving as an important center of transcontinental trade and a buffer between western Europe and the states of western Asia. The Romans and their successors also had conflicts with societies in western Asia and North Africa, including a revived Persian Empire; these conflicts continued long after the Classical Age. Finally, these various struggles set the stage for the rise of another society, the Arabs.

FOCUS QUESTIONS

1. What were the main political and social features of the Roman Republic?
2. How did the Romans maintain their large empire?
3. What were the relations between Romans and other societies, including Celts and Germans?
4. How did Christianity develop and expand?
5. How did the Byzantine and Sassanian Empires reinvigorate the eastern Mediterranean world?

 # Etruscans, Carthage, Egypt, and the Romans

What were the main political and social features of the Roman Republic?

By 300 B.C.E. the Mediterranean world was politically and culturally diverse, divided between Etruscans, Carthage, small Greek city-states, various Hellenistic kingdoms including Egypt, and the rising Romans, who eventually dominated the entire region. Roman society was built on several foundations. The Romans learned much from the older Etruscan society that they eventually absorbed, and they were influenced by Greek ideas in building their republic. The regional environment also played a part, as Roman political expansion was made possible by good access to the Mediterranean Sea. Eventually Rome conquered peoples in southern Europe and then beyond, establishing the framework of a huge empire.

Western European Geography

Geography and climate were influential in shaping Roman society. The geological spine of Italy is the Apennine mountain range running down the eastern side of the narrow peninsula. The rich agricultural Po Valley lies north of the Apennines, and smaller plains spread west from the Apennines to the Mediterranean. This topography directed the at-

tention of the early settlers to the sea, where they took up maritime trade. But the Roman newcomers had to adapt to seagoing. One Roman poet wrote in 30 B.C.E.: "Whoever first dared to float a ship on the grim sea must have had a heart of oak coated with a triple layer of bronze."[2] In addition, Italy's geography, unlike the rocky hills of Greece, offered considerable fertile land suitable for intensive agriculture, especially along the west coast. The Mediterranean climate was perfect for growing grapes and olives, and as the Roman state grew, the Romans were able to increase their export of wine and olive oil while importing grain from the nearby islands of Sicily and Sardinia (sahr-DIN-ee-uh) and from northern Africa, which is only 100 miles from Sicily. Agricultural success, and the ease of north-south contact in the peninsula, also made it easier than in Greece to develop large states. The mild climate of Italy also encouraged attacks by the Indo-European Celtic and Germanic peoples living in the forested hills and plains of western and northern Europe. Attracted to the warmer lands in the south, these northern peoples made frequent invasions using passes through the Alps, a formidable complex of mountains. By forcing the early inhabitants of the peninsula to emphasize military defense, these attacks had a significant effect on the history of Roman society and the entire region.

As the Romans themselves expanded beyond Italy, they drew upon the natural resources of the larger Mediterranean world (see Map 8.1 on page 202) and beyond. In Spain, they found a rich supply of silver, copper, and tin. Egypt provided

CHRONOLOGY

	Roman Republic	Roman Empire	Byzantium and Western Asia
500 B.C.E.	**509 B.C.E.** Roman Republic		
300 B.C.E.	**264–146 B.C.E.** Punic Wars		
100 B.C.E.		**31 B.C.E.–180 C.E.** *Pax Romana* **7–6 B.C.E.–30 C.E.** Life of Jesus	
1 C.E.			**240–272 C.E.** Founding of Sassanian Empire
300 C.E.		**395 C.E.** Division of eastern and western empires **476 C.E.** Official end of western Roman Empire	**330 C.E.** Founding of Constantinople
500 C.E.			**527–565 C.E.** Reign of Justinian

wheat. Beginning about 200 B.C.E., overland trade routes connected the Mediterranean with China along the famous Silk Road, named after the most important product acquired from East Asia, which was bartered in return for gold, silver, precious stones, and some textile products from the west.

The Etruscans and Early Rome

The Romans were greatly influenced by the Etruscans, who established the first urban society in the peninsula. A non-Indo-European people who may have come originally from western Asia, the Etruscans had founded a dozen or so city-states in central and northern Italy by the eighth century B.C.E. They were aggressive chariot warriors but also sailors who traded with the western Mediterranean islands and Spain. Eventually Etruscans expanded their territory to include more of Italy as well as the nearby island of Corsica (KOR-si-kuh). They also had considerable contact with Greeks and Phoenicians. They adopted a form of the Greek alphabet, as well as Greek craft styles and myths, and Greek craftsmen worked in some Etruscan cities. As more Greeks settled in Italy after 550 B.C.E., they had increased conflict with the Etruscans.

We do not know very much about the Etruscans. Their language is only partially understood, and none of their major literature survives. Later Roman writers portrayed them as barbarians, a view that distorted the picture of Etruscan culture. The Etruscans' huge cemeteries with impressive, well-decorated tombs show that they were skilled artists and artisans. Some of their cities, which could include as many as 35,000 people, were well planned and were linked together by a good road system. Each city apparently had its own king. The Etruscans were known for mining and working iron ore, and their excellent iron axes, sickles, and tools were carried by merchants to every region. Their rigid social system included slavery, although Etruscan women apparently had a higher social status than women in most classical societies. Etruscan women conversed openly with men in public, drove their own chariots, owned real estate, and sometimes ran businesses like pottery workshops.

Initially the relationship between the Romans and the Etruscans was peaceful. Rome began as a small city-state just south of Etruscan territory in central Italy. It was established in the eighth century B.C.E. by a group of Indo-European pastoralists known as the Latins (see Chronology: The Roman Republic, 753–58 B.C.E. on page 203). The major Latin city, Rome, built on seven hills along the Tiber (TIE-buhr) River, was originally founded as a base from which the early Romans could trade with the Etruscans.

Map 8.1   Italy and the Western Mediterranean, 600–200 B.C.E.
During the early Classical Era the Etruscan cities in the north and the Greek city-states in the south held political power in Italy. Carthage held a similar status in northeast Africa. Eventually the Latins, from their base in Rome, became the dominant political force in the entire region.

CHRONOLOGY

The Roman Republic, 753–58 B.C.E.

753	Founding of Rome (traditional date)
ca. 616–509	Etruscan kings rule over Rome
509	Beginning of Roman Republic
265	Roman control of central and southern Italy
264–241	First Punic (Roman-Carthaginian) War
218–201	Second Punic War
149–146	Third Punic War
113–105	First German-Roman conflicts
60–58	Julius Caesar completes conquest from Rhine to Atlantic

During the sixth century B.C.E. the Etruscans came to dominate Rome, and their influence was significant. The Romans adopted the twenty-six-character alphabet that the Etruscans had themselves borrowed from the Greek colonies in southern Italy and Sicily, as well as the Etruscan phalanx infantry formation originally devised by the Greeks. Skilled Etruscan engineers taught the Romans to make the weight-bearing semicircular arch, which Romans used to construct city walls, aqueducts to carry water, and doorways. Although Etruscan kings won support in Rome by building new public buildings, at the end of the sixth century B.C.E. the last Etruscan king was driven out for his brutality, and Rome became independent. Later the Romans conquered and assimilated the Etruscans.

The Roman Republic

The Romans also borrowed many political ideas from the Greeks. As the Greeks did in Athens, the Romans built a system of self-government for their city-state. While doing so, however, they also began their territorial expansion. Again like Athens, Rome then faced the challenge of how to maintain its democratic aspirations while expanding an empire. And, like the Greeks, the Romans ultimately failed to keep their fragile system of self-government alive.

A New Government System After deposing the last Etruscan monarch, in 509 B.C.E. Romans established a republic, a state in which supreme power is held by the people or their elected representatives. Over the next three centuries, the Romans developed a system of representative government that introduced many enduring political ideas. Many modern English words taken from Latin—such as *senate, citizenship, suffrage* (the right to vote),

dictator (a man given full power for a limited time, usually during a war), *plebiscite* (PLEB-i-site), and even *republic*—remind us of the influence of the Romans on modern political life.

The system changed over time. Initially, power rested entirely in the hands of the aristocratic upper class, or **patricians** (puh-TRISH-uhnz). Patricians controlled the Senate, a small body that had previously advised the kings and later dominated foreign affairs, the army, and the legislative body made up of soldiers, known as the **Centuriate Assembly**. The Senate, composed of three hundred older men, all former government officials, claimed the right to ratify resolutions of the Centuriate Assembly before they became law. As the Republic developed, the Centuriate Assembly elected two men each year to serve as **consuls,** who had executive power. Consuls were assisted by other patrician officials, such as judges and budget directors.

The Patrician-Plebeian Conflicts The patricians were heavily outnumbered by the commoners, or **plebeians** (pli-BEE-uhnz), who were plagued by debts owed to the patricians. Wealth flowed into Rome as a result of military expansion in the peninsula and then beyond. As the soldiers who fought to make this expansion possible, the plebeians wanted to share in this wealth. The long, hard-fought wars left many plebeians in debt because long years of service in the army had taken them away from their farms, which were now in ruin. The plebeians therefore demanded a greater political voice, hoping that by gaining access to political power they could secure economic equality. A Roman historian reported the bitterness of a plebeian leader toward those who opposed reform: "[You] realize vividly the depth of the contempt in which you are held by the aristocracy. They would rob you of the very light you see by; they grudge you the air you breathe, the words you speak."[3] Political power, the plebeians believed, would allow them to pass laws that distributed the wealth of the state more fairly.

Gradually social and political rights expanded. In 494 B.C.E. the plebeians selected two of their number, called **tribunes**, to represent their interests in the Centuriate Assembly, much as the consuls represented patrician interests. By 471 a separate Plebeian Assembly was established to elect tribunes and to conduct votes of the plebeian class, called plebiscites. In 451 the plebeians also demanded that the law code be published so that all could know the laws. The laws were carved on tablets and placed in the Forum, the public gathering place in Rome. Plebeians later gained the right to share with the patricians lands that the Roman state had won in war. In 367 B.C.E.

patricians The aristocratic upper class who controlled the Roman Senate.

Centuriate Assembly A Roman legislative body made up of soldiers.

consuls Two patrician men, elected by the Centuriate Assembly each year, who had executive power in the Roman Republic.

plebeians The commoner class in Rome.

tribunes Roman men elected to represent plebeian interests in the Centuriate Assembly.

The Roman Forum   The Forum, located amidst various religious and governmental buildings, was the center of Roman political life.   (Bruce Coleman, Inc.)

plebeians also became eligible to serve as consuls, a major step that eventually led to their full acceptance into the political system. Full equality for plebeians was won by 267 B.C.E., when their assembly became the principal lawmaking body of the state.

Expanding Roman Power in Italy

In the fourth century, the Roman Republic turned to imperialism, the control or domination by one state over another, as a way of resolving some of its problems. Roman political expansion began with a major defeat at the hands of the Gauls (gawlz), a Celtic people who plundered Rome in 390 B.C.E. Shocked by this defeat, Roman leaders decided to expand their territory to keep their frontiers safely distant from the city of Rome. Their military successes were due in part to their wise decision to enlist defeated enemies as allies in future conquests.

During the rest of the fourth century, Romans successfully fought a series of wars with other Italian city-states. At the end of each successful war, they granted either full or limited Roman citizenship to the inhabitants of many of the defeated cities. Being a Roman citizen became a great honor entitling a person to special legal treatment, an honor that fathers were proud to pass on to their sons. By treating former enemies

fairly, the Romans spread their power without encouraging revolts and ensured that more men would enlist in their army. They first conquered the Etruscan cities, which had been weakened by conflicts with the Gauls. After securing their power in north and central Italy, the Romans were then able to conquer the remaining Greek cities in southern Italy and Sicily. Across the sea from Sicily, however, the Romans encountered their greatest enemy, the Carthaginians.

Carthage, Egypt, and Regional Trade

Both Carthage and Egypt played key roles in Mediterranean trade. The city-state of Carthage (KAHR-thij) was originally a Phoenician colony founded in 814 B.C.E. on the North African coast near where the city of Tunis (TOO-nis) is today. The other great power on the southern shores of the Mediterranean was Egypt, ruled by the Hellenistic Greek Ptolemaic (tawl-uh-MAY-ik) dynasty, which had fostered great prosperity for over a century.

With a fine harbor and a strategic position, Carthage rapidly grew into the wealthiest and strongest Phoenician outpost. A Greek from Sicily reported that Carthage in the third century B.C.E. had "gardens and orchards of all kinds, no end of country houses built luxuriously, land cultivated partly as vineyards and partly as olive groves, fruit trees, herds of cattle and flocks of sheep."[4] However, the autocratic city government experienced much political instability as rival leaders vied for power, and differences between the Phoenician settlers, who owned most of the wealth, and the native Berbers also created tensions. The Carthaginians also fought frequent wars with their main commercial rivals, the Greeks.

The Carthaginians were great sailors and used their maritime skills to develop trade networks. Around 425 B.C.E. an admiral, Hanno (HAN-oh), led a naval expedition through the Strait of Gibraltar and down the coast of West Africa, seeking markets and perhaps a sea route to Asia. He founded trading posts along the Morocco (muh-RAHK-oh) coast and sailed at least as far as the Senegal River. Some historians think Hanno may have sailed much further along the West African coast. Other Carthaginian expeditions apparently reached the British Isles and perhaps several of the Atlantic islands off the northwest African coast, such as Madeira and the Canary Islands.

Gradually the Carthaginians created an empire along the southern and western shores of the Mediterranean Sea. By the third century B.C.E. they controlled a large part of Spain, much of the North African coast, and the islands of Corsica and Sardinia. In 264 B.C.E. they moved troops to Sicily to aid several Greek cities allied with them against Rome.

To the east there was Egypt. Although it had long flourished, the Ptolemaic hold on that country was becoming more tenuous by the second century B.C.E. The Ptolemies were hard-headed businessmen and worked to increase agricultural and crafts production, in part by demanding more work from Egyptians. As it had been under the ancient pharaohs, Egypt remained a major producer of wheat. The Hellenistic Greeks introduced a new variety of hard wheat, popular with non-Egyptians, which made Egypt a major supplier of wheat to other Mediterranean societies. Egypt also exported papyrus, the preferred medium for scientific, philosophical, and literary texts throughout the region; textiles, including linen and woolen fabrics; and pottery and metal objects. Greeks and Phoenicians owned some of the ships which carried these goods to foreign ports. Despite the economic growth, many Egyptians tired of foreign occupation, hardship, and high taxes, and several rebellions threatened the government, including an attack on Alexandria. At the same time, the ruling Greeks gradually became somewhat Egyptianized, and the more privileged sectors of Egyptian society became relatively Hellenized.

Women had long exercised power behind the Egyptian throne, but in 180 B.C.E. Cleopatra (KLEE-oh-PA-truh) I became sole ruler, the first in a long chain of assertive queens who competed with men for the dominant position. During this time Egyptian rulers sought alliances with rising Rome in order to maintain their own independence. In 47 B.C.E., with Roman assistance, an ambitious eighteen-year-old became ruler as Queen Cleopatra VII, just as years of poor harvests and official corruption fostered more unrest. Her skills enabled the unstable state to maintain domestic peace and deflect Rome for nearly two decades.

The Punic Wars and Afro-Eurasian Empire

The result of Roman expansion southward was the Punic (PYOO-nik) Wars, which pitted the two major powers and bitter rivals of the western Mediterranean, Rome and Carthage, against each other. In 264 B.C.E. the Romans began the first of three wars against the Carthaginians. The first Punic War (264–241 B.C.E.) resulted in several Roman naval expeditions against Carthage and finally ended with Roman occupation of Sicily, Corsica, and Sardinia. In the second of the wars (218–201), the brilliant Carthaginian general Hannibal (HAN-uh-buhl) (247–182 B.C.E.) led his troops through Spain and France to invade Italy across the Alps, defeating every Roman army sent against them. Hannibal's father had instilled in him an intense hatred of the Romans, and he used every tactic at his disposal to achieve victory, including drafting Celts from Spain and southern France into his army. Modern people may have images in their mind, probably accurate, of war elephants used by Hannibal's army lumbering through the rugged mountains. The Carthaginians had carefully trained these elephants to charge and possibly terrify the enemy on the battlefield. But the elephants and Hannibal's troops were not used to the snow and ice of the mountains, and perished by the thousands.

The arrival and early military success of Hannibal's still formidable force alarmed the Romans. In a Roman play of the time, a character implored Romans to "conquer by inborn valor, as you have done before; increase resources; destroy your foes; laud and laurels gather."[5] With his supply lines overstretched, however, Hannibal could not conquer the Italian cities. Eventually the Romans drove him out and defeated Carthage, which had to surrender all its overseas possessions, including Spain. In the final Punic War (149–146), Rome laid siege to the city of Carthage and destroyed it, spreading salt on the fields around the city to make it difficult to plant crops there in the future. Northwest Africa became a Roman province, a source of copper, grain, and West African gold.

Roman victory in the wars not only destroyed Carthage but also encouraged additional Roman imperial expansion in the Mediterranean region, aimed either at punishing Carthage's allies or at restoring stability. Rome went to war with Macedonia and ended Macedonian control of the Greek cities in 197 B.C.E. When the Hellenistic Seleucid rulers in Anatolia attempted to conquer Greece, the Romans intervened in 146 B.C.E. and made Greece and Macedonia into a Roman province. Few could resist the Roman infantrymen, who were armed with swords and rectangular shields, or the armor-clad Roman archers, who rode in carts carrying large crossbows, among the era's most feared weapons.

Through these struggles, a Roman Empire was being built that eventually commanded the entire Mediterranean and its vast resources, binding together Europe, western Asia, and North Africa. By the middle of the first century B.C.E., Roman power extended throughout the entire Mediterranean basin and beyond. The empire included most of Anatolia, Syria, and Palestine, as well as much territory in northern and western Europe. The Ptolemies still controlled Egypt, but the rulers were careful to do nothing to offend the Romans. The Romans absorbed much of the Hellenistic east, with its rich web of international commerce centered on several hubs, including Alexandria in Egypt, which distributed goods from as far away as India and East Africa. But imperial success also led to major changes in Roman society.

SECTION SUMMARY

- The agricultural plenty of Italy allowed for the development of larger states than had been possible in Greece, and the Mediterranean Sea allowed for Roman expansion.

- The Etruscans, a non-Indo-European people most likely from western Asia, formed the first urban society in Italy; they influenced and were eventually conquered by the Romans.

- Rome formed a republic, in which citizens rule the state; initially upper-class patricians dominated, but over time the plebeians attained increasing amounts of power.

- After a major defeat by the Gauls, the Romans decided that the key to safety was to expand their territory so their frontiers would be safely distant from Rome.

- Rome defeated Carthage, its primary rival, in the Punic Wars and then conquered an empire.

◈ Roman Society During the Imperial Era

How did the Romans maintain their large empire?

Athenians had pondered whether empire and democracy were compatible, and eventually they proved incompatible. Likewise, in Rome the rise of empire, with its clash of personal ambitions and greed created by the wealth gained through conquest, had important consequences. In particular, the expanding empire led to the decline and replacement of the Republic with a more autocratic and arrogant imperial system. The Roman historian Tacitus (TASS-uh-tuhs) observed how the growth of empire increased the love of power: "It was easy to maintain equality when Rome was weak. World-wide conquest and the destruction of all rival[s] opened the way to the secure enjoyment of wealth and an overriding appetite for it."[6] This period of imperial rule saw the full development of Roman culture and of those elements of the Roman heritage, such as law, that formed a significant legacy to European society.

The Decline of the Republic

Imperial expansion provoked various crises that reshaped Roman politics and undermined the Republic, turning the representative institutions into window-dressing. Warfare gave excessive power to military leaders, weakening the influence of the Senate. In addition, growing Roman wealth increased the gap between rich and poor. As the empire expanded, upper-class families bought farmland from peasants who had become impoverished by long service in the army and the cheaper grain being imported from Sicily and North Africa. Many farmers moved to the city of Rome, where the government supported hundreds of thousands of displaced people to maintain their loyalty. Thus Roman society became polarized between the very rich and the desperately poor.

Some leaders attempted to deal with this impoverishment. With fewer farmers willing to serve in the army, the tribune Tiberius Graccus (tie-BIR-ee-uhs GRAK-uhs) proposed turning over public land to farmers who agreed to serve in the Roman legions when needed. When the poor gathered in Rome to support this measure, some wealthy Romans panicked and spurred a mob to club Tiberius and many of his followers to death. This event demonstrated both the determination of the wealthy not to give up power and the fact that many poor people could be mobilized to support one leader or another. In addition, the Senate was unable to control the military leaders.

The changing nature of military power also undermined democracy. In 107 B.C.E., Gaius Marius (GAY-uhs MER-ee-uhs), who defeated Roman enemies in North Africa and southern France, was elected consul for five straight years, despite a law that prohibited a person from holding the office more than one year. Marius set an undemocratic precedent for the future when he brought his military veterans to pressure the senators to vote for a law that gave the veterans public land. As a result, skillful military leaders thereafter used their armies to enhance their political power and outmaneuver civilian leaders and the Senate. The result was a series of civil and foreign wars. Between 78 and 31 B.C.E., several ambitious military leaders used their power to expand Roman territory in Asia and Europe while finally destroying republican institutions within Rome itself. Crassus (KRASS-uhs) gained power by putting down a great slave revolt in 71 B.C.E., and Pompey (pahm-PAY) conquered more wealthy lands in the east, including Syria and Palestine. At one point, both joined with the young Julius Caesar (SEE-zer) in an alliance to share power.

Caesar proved the most ambitious. During his years as Roman governor in Gaul (France), he completed the conquest of Europe from the Rhine River west to the Atlantic and sent the first Roman forces into Britain. These victories enhanced his influence. His power was further increased when he won a civil war against his former allies. In addition, Caesar weakened the Senate by enlarging it to nine hundred men, making it too large to be an effective governing body. Finally, in 44 B.C.E. he took charge of the state by having himself declared Perpetual Dictator (see Chronology: The Roman Empire and Its Successors, 60 B.C.E.–526 C.E.). This act led to his assassination, made famous centuries later in the play *Julius Caesar* by the English author William Shakespeare.

Caesar's death led to another civil war, the end of any pretence of democracy, and conquest of Egypt. Caesar's adopted son, Octavian (ok-TAY-vee-uhn), fought Mark Anthony, a general who had fallen in love with the Egyptian ruler Cleopatra. A

CHRONOLOGY

The Roman Empire and Its Successors, 60 B.C.E.–526 C.E.

60–44 B.C.E.	Julius Caesar rises to dominance in Roman politics
31 B.C.E.–14 C.E.	Reign of Octavian (Caesar Augustus)
31 B.C.E.–180 C.E.	Pax Romana
6–7 B.C.E.–30 C.E.	Jesus's life and preaching in Palestine
64 C.E.	Death of Peter (first bishop of Rome) and of Paul of Tarsus
66–73 C.E.	Jewish revolt against Rome
251 C.E.	Germans defeat Roman armies and sack Balkans
306–337 C.E.	Reign of Constantine
313 C.E.	Legalization of Christianity
325 C.E.	Council of Nicaea
354–430 C.E.	St. Augustine of Hippo
391 C.E.	Paganism banned by Emperor Theodosius I
395 C.E.	Final division of eastern and western empires
410 C.E.	Alaric and Ostrogoths sack Rome
451–452 C.E.	Huns invade western Europe
455 C.E.	Vandals sack Rome
476 C.E.	Official end of western Roman Empire
481–511 C.E.	Clovis and Franks conquer Gaul
493–526 C.E.	Ostrogoths rule Italy

remarkable personality who had borne a son by Julius Caesar, Cleopatra was described by the Greek historian Plutarch (PLOO-tark), who wrote that "her presence was irresistible; the attraction of her person, the charm of her conversation, was something bewitching. She could pass from one language to another."[7] The turmoil and the Republic itself ended when Octavian defeated Anthony and Cleopatra at the naval Battle of Actium (AK-tee-uhm), in Greece, in 31 B.C.E. Anthony and Cleopatra escaped to Egypt and eventually committed suicide. Soon their armies surrendered to Octavian, giving Rome control of Egypt. The Romans placed Egypt under a tighter grip than most of their colonies, passing laws to discourage Greek-Egyptian intermarriage, imposing heavy taxes, and encouraging more wheat production to feed the city of Rome.

Augustus and the *Pax Romana*

Rome and its empire were now ruled by emperors who controlled the military and much of the government bureaucracy. This trend was begun by Julius Caesar's nephew, Octavian (63 B.C.E.–14 C.E.), who called himself Augustus (aw-GUHS-tihs), a Latin term meaning "majestic, inspiring awe." Augustus became the empire's effective ruler in 31 B.C.E., and the Senate affirmed his exalted position in 27 B.C.E. His long reign (r. 27 B.C.E.–14 C.E.) gave Augustus time to establish and consolidate a system in which he allowed the Senate to appoint governors to the peaceful provinces while he took charge of provinces where troops were stationed. Augustus gained the power to legally enact or veto legislation and to call the Senate into session. The writer Juvenal (JOO-vuhn-uhl) deplored the consequences of the lost popular voice and its replacement by entertainments to divert public attention: "The people that once bestowed commands now meddles no more and longs eagerly for just two things: bread and circuses."[8]

The period in Roman history from the beginning of the reign of Augustus through that of Emperor Marcus Aurelius (aw-REE-lee-uhs) in 180 C.E. is known as the **Pax Romana** ("Roman Peace"). For the first and last time, the entire Mediterranean world was controlled by one power and remained at peace for two centuries (see Map 8.2). During this time Rome experienced few challenges from the Germanic peoples, who for the most part remained east of the Rhine and north of the Danube Rivers. In the east the Romans faced only a weak Parthian kingdom in Persia and Mesopotamia. Whether in London or Paris, Vienna or Barcelona—all cities founded by the Romans—people lived under the same laws.

Peace and prosperity encouraged trade and population growth. Great fleets of ships moved mountains of goods across the Mediterranean Sea. Trade also flourished along the Silk Road between China and Rome through Central and western Asia. Rome governed a huge population, which has been estimated at 54 million in the first century C.E., including 6 million in Italy, 17 million in the rest of Europe, 20 million in western Asia, and 11 million in North Africa. Rome may have been the world's largest city, with a half million to 1 million inhabitants.

In this diverse empire the Roman ideal, like that of the Hellenistic Greeks, was cosmopolitan. Hence, Emperor Marcus Aurelius (r. 161–180 C.E.) wrote: "Rome is my city and country, but as a man, I am a citizen of the world."[9] Non-Romans were incorporated into the ruling class. By the second century C.E., half of the members of the Roman Senate were non-Italians from the provinces. Men of wealth and military skill, whatever their ethnic background, could rise to the highest levels in the army and civil administration. Many people from outside Italy migrated to Rome, bringing with them cultural forms such as new musical instruments and dances. As the cosmopolitan

Pax Romana ("Roman Peace") The period of peace and prosperity in Roman history from the reign of Augustus through that of Emperor Marcus Aurelius in 180 C.E.

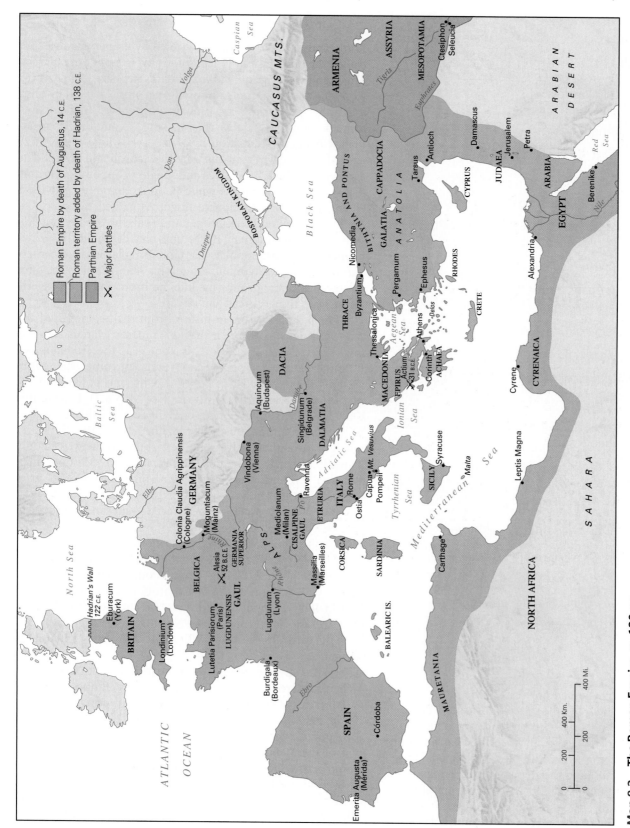

Map 8.2 The Roman Empire, ca. 120 C.E.
The Romans gradually expanded until, by 120 C.E., they controlled a huge empire stretching from Britain and Spain in the west through southern and central Europe and North Africa to Egypt, Anatolia, and the lands along the eastern Mediterranean coast.

Online Study Center **Improve Your Grade** Interactive Map: The Roman World in the Republic and Early Empire

When the day dawns the trader betakes himself to his trade; the spinner takes her spindle; the warrior takes his shield; the farmer awakes, he and his hoe handle; the hunter awakes with his quiver and bow.

ANCIENT YORUBA PROVERB ABOUT DAYBREAK IN A WEST AFRICAN TOWN[1]

In the classical world, few settlements were as specialized as those serving the caravans that crossed the trackless sands of the vast Sahara Desert of Africa, a barren landscape where scorching sun and arid soil made it nearly impossible to plant crops or trees. A later traveler with these caravans commented that "the desert is haunted by demons, nothing but sand blown hither and thither by the wind."[2] The journeys were interrupted by rest stops at caravan way stations, isolated oasis towns with gardens, date palms, and flocks of sheep where weary travelers could find fresh water and restock before resuming their journeys.

The round trip of many weeks between the cities of the North African coastal zone and those on the southern fringe of the desert held many dangers besides thirst and discomfort, including fierce raiders on horseback. Camels, the major beast of burden in the caravan trade, were not always cooperative animals and often waged battles of wills with their handlers, but they could travel many days without water. On an average day camels could carry their riders and cargo some 30 miles. In the Sahara, wealth was measured more in camels than in gold. Thanks to these caravans and the brave men who led them, sub-Saharan African products reached a wider world, and goods and ideas from North Africa and Eurasia found their way along the trade networks to peoples living south of the Sahara.

The diverse societies that arose in sub-Saharan Africa, the Americas, and Oceania (the Pacific Basin) were all shaped by their environment, whether that was a desert like the Sahara, a highland, a flood-prone river valley, or a rain forest, savannah, seacoast, or small island. Societies were also influenced by their contacts—friendly, hostile, or both—with other societies, whether near and familiar or distant and alien. In Africa, for example, Egyptians, Nubians, and Ethiopians, although sometimes bitter rivals, exchanged products, ideas, and technologies with each other, with other Africans, and with Eurasian societies. Various Africans established connections with the wider world through long-distance trade, such as that carried on by the camel caravans across the bleak Sahara or by boat around the Indian Ocean. These connections ensured that few societies, regardless of where they were located, were completely isolated and unique. During the Classical Era diverse and distinctive societies developed in sub-Saharan Africa, the Americas, and Australia, and intrepid mariners settled most of the Pacific islands. These various communities worshiped their own deities, created their own artistic styles, valued some products more than others, and evolved their own political and social structures. At the same time, they had much in common. In parts of Africa and the Americas cities and states emerged that resembled each other, and in some societies there were many parallels to classical societies in Eurasia. This was truly a classical era, as societies and networks flourished and cultural influences spread over a wide area.

FOCUS QUESTIONS

1. What were some of the similarities and differences between Kush and Aksum?
2. How did the spread of the Bantus reshape sub-Saharan Africa?
3. What were the similarities and differences between the Maya and Teotihuacan?
4. How did the Mesoamerican, Andean, and North American societies compare and contrast with each other?
5. How were some of the notable features of Australian and Pacific societies shaped by their environments?

Classical States and Connections in Northeast Africa

What were some of the similarities and differences between Kush and Aksum?

In classical times tropical Africa and Eurasia were connected largely through intermediaries, including the North Africans linked to the trans-Saharan caravan trade and the maritime traders of the Indian Ocean who visited the East African coast. Two African societies, Kush (koosh) in Nubia and Aksum (AHK-soom) in Ethiopia, also served as intermediaries, becoming trading hubs and forming powerful states. Both enjoyed particularly close ties with Egypt and western Asia. Their relationship to networks of exchange strongly shaped some African societies.

Iron, Cities, and Prosperity in Kush

The kingdom of Kush, along the Nile south of Egypt, existed from about 800 B.C.E. to 350 C.E. (see Chronology: Classical Africa). From 600 to 100 B.C.E. Kush was the major African producer of iron and an important crossroads for the middle Nile region (see Map 9.1 on page 230). Its capital city, Meroë (MER-uh-wee), became an industrial powerhouse of the classical world. The Kushites acquired iron technology either from

Egypt or from the Africans who worked iron in Central and West Africa (see Chapter 3). Whatever the case, Kush had many sources of iron ore, and heaps of iron slag litter the ruins of Meroë today. Through trade networks Kush linked various peoples of sub-Saharan Africa and the Mediterranean, and hence played a central economic role in the Afro-Eurasian

CHRONOLOGY	
Classical Africa	
2000 B.C.E.–1000 C.E.	Bantu migrations into Central, East, and South Africa
800 B.C.E.–350 C.E.	Meroë kingdom in Kush
500 B.C.E.–600 C.E.	Garamante confederation dominates trans-Saharan trade
400 B.C.E.–800 C.E.	Aksum kingdom in Ethiopia
300 B.C.E.	Beginning of maritime trade to East African coast
200 B.C.E.	Founding of Jenne-Jenno
300 C.E.	Introduction of Christianity to Kush and Aksum
ca. 500 C.E.	Founding of kingdom of Ghana

CHRONOLOGY

	Africa	The Americas	Oceania
800 B.C.E.	**800 B.C.E.–350 C.E.** Kush		
400 B.C.E.	**400 B.C.E.–800 C.E.** Aksum		**300 B.C.E.–1200 C.E.** Polynesian settlement of Pacific
200 B.C.E.	**200 B.C.E.** Founding of Jenne-Jenno	**200 B.C.E.–600 C.E.** Hopewell Mound Builders	
		200 B.C.E.–700 C.E. Moche	
		200 B.C.E.–750 C.E. Teotihuacan	
		150 B.C.E.–800 C.E. Flourishing of Maya society	
500 C.E.	**ca. 500 C.E.** Founding of Ghana		

zone. Kush imported pottery, fine ceramics, wine, olive oil, and honey from Egypt and western Asia, and it exported both iron and cotton cloth. Roman sources reported that Egyptian priests preferred Kushite cloth for their garments. Both the Greeks and Romans admired the Nubians. Some Nubians seem to have visited Greece and others were members of the Persian armies that attacked Greece. Roman sources report that Africans, possibly Nubians, came to Rome to trade or work, noting numerous African musicians, actors, gladiators, athletes, and day laborers in the city.

At its height Meroë was a grand city of perhaps 25,000 inhabitants. Built around a walled palace along the Nile, it contained massive temples, large brick-lined pools that may have been used for public baths, and rows of pyramids, similar to those in Egypt, where kings and queens were buried in splendor. In fact, Kush built more royal pyramids than did Egypt. The highly skilled builders used masonry, stonework, fired brick, and mud brick. As in the Indus cities, washing and sanitation facilities, with many latrines, serviced Meroë's population.

Kush Social Patterns and Culture

Although influenced by Egypt, Kushite society and the culture it produced were distinctive. At the top of the social hierarchy were absolute monarchs, including some queens, who both governed the state and served as guardians of the state religion, responsible for supporting and building the temples. In addition to worshiping some Egyptian gods, Kushites considered their monarchs, like those in Egypt, to be divine. Inscriptions testify to the piety of rulers, and Roman sources report that kings were guided by laws and traditions:

It is their custom that none of the subjects shall be executed, even if the person condemned to death appears to deserve punishment. Instead the king sends one of his servants bearing a symbol of death to the criminal. He upon seeing [it], immediately goes to his own house and kills himself.[3]

Queen mothers seem to have played an influential role in politics; some historians believe that the occasional succession of women to power indicates matrilineal succession.

Below the ruler were the military and bureaucratic elite. Kush's military officers led an army feared for both its weapons and the appearance of its soldiers. The Greek historian Herodotus described the soldiers of Kush:

[They] were clothed in panthers' and lions' skins, and carried long bows made from branches of palm trees, and on them they laced short arrows made of cane tipped with stone. Besides this they had javelins, and at the tip was an antelope horn, made sharp like a lance; they also had knotted clubs. When they were going into battle they smeared one half of their body with chalk, and the other half with red ocher.[4]

Some government officials dealt with trade, since the state dominated this activity, but the role of private merchants remains unclear. Below the bureaucratic and military elite were free peasants and slaves. Women played a variety of economic roles, working in gold mines and engaging in farming and craft production. They also served as priestesses, perhaps specializing in the honoring of female deities.

Kushites enjoyed a rich culture, as well as some activities that seem universal to all cultures. Some Greek-speaking teachers apparently lived at Meroë, perhaps immigrants or the descendants of immigrants, and at least one Kushite king studied Greek

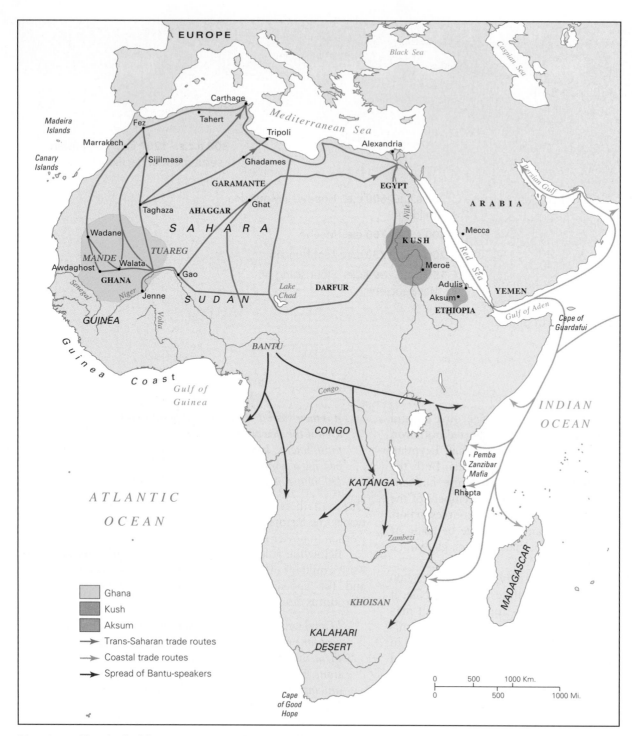

Map 9.1 Classical Africa, 1500 B.C.E.–600 C.E.
During this era, Kush, Aksum, and Jenne were major African centers of trade and government.
Trade routes crossed the vast Sahara Desert and the Bantu-speaking peoples expanded into
central, southern, and eastern Africa.

philosophy. Meroë also had artists who produced highly polished, finely carved granite statues of their monarchs, and music
played on trumpets, drums, harps, and flutes was a part of ceremonial and religious life. Some of the instruments may have been
imported from Egypt and Greece. People of all classes and both

genders wore jewelry made from gold, beads, iron, and copper alloy, and the ruins of at least one tavern have been found littered
with thousands of goblet fragments, suggesting that wine was a
popular drink. Finally, the presence of writing on numerous
tombstones as well as graffiti suggests that literacy was wide-

spread among all classes. Along with other distinctive achievements, Kushites developed their own alphabet, **Meroitic** (mer-uh-WIT-ik), a cursive script that can be only partly read today. Meroitic gradually replaced Egyptian hieroglyphics in monumental inscriptions. Indeed, over time Egyptian influence apparently faded while indigenous culture flourished.

The Legacy of Kush

After a millennium of power and prosperity, by 200 C.E. Kush was in decline, in part from environmental deterioration. Centuries of deforestation and overgrazing had helped produce a drier climate. In fact, climate change was widespread in the world at that time, and it may have also hastened the decline of the Han Chinese and Roman Empires. Chronic warfare with the Ethiopian state of Aksum also contributed to Meroë's problems. In 350 C.E. an invasion by the Aksum army destroyed what remained of the Kush kingdom.

However, the culture of Kush was kept alive in some neighboring societies. Some of its people, including the rulers, may have migrated elsewhere in Africa, spreading their iron technology and culture. Some West African societies developed political traditions not unlike those in Kush and have a folklore that identifies their origins to the northeast, though many historians doubt the connection. Nonetheless, some peoples now living a few hundred miles to the southwest of Meroë still show many signs of Kushite influence, including recreational activities (such as wrestling), fashion, body art, and material life. Indeed, like the Romans in Europe or the Han in China, the people of Kush may well have established classical patterns that still survive today.

Several new kingdoms arose from the ashes of Kush, and contacts with the outside world eventually brought a new religion, Christianity, which became dominant in Nubia between the fourth and sixth centuries C.E. Many churches were built, and ecclesiastical authorities had close ties to the monarchies. Nubian Christianity was a branch of the **Coptic** (KAHP-tik) **Church,** which followed Monophysite thought (see Chapter 8) and had become influential in Egypt. Many Copts still live in Egypt. With its patriarchal tendencies, Christianity seems to have replaced Nubian matrilineal traditions with patrilineal ones, monarchies now passing exclusively from fathers to sons. But the Christian kingdoms of Nubia, isolated from other Christians to the north by the Islamic conquest of Egypt in the seventh century C.E., gradually faded. Around 1400 C.E. Muslims conquered the last Christian Nubian state and converted most people to Islam. This religious change proved the most long-lasting transition for the societies of the middle Nile basin. Today only the ruins of Christian churches and monasteries of Nubia remain, along with the Meroite pyramids, the material legacy of Kush.

Meroitic   A cursive script developed in the Classical Era by the Kushites in Nubia that can be read only partly today.

Coptic Church   A branch of Christianity, based on Monophysite ideas, that had become influential in Egypt and became dominant in Nubia between the fourth and sixth centuries C.E.

Queen Amanitere   Queen Amanitere ruled Meroë along with her husband, King Natakamani, around 2,000 years ago. In this relief on the Lion Temple at Naqa, Kush, she holds vanquished foes by the hair while brandishing swords, thus demonstrating the power of the royal couple and the Kushite state.   (From Graham Connah, *African Civilizations,* p. 44. Reproduced by permission of Cambridge University Press.)

The Aksum Empire and Trade

Another literate urban African state, **Aksum,** emerged in the rocky but fertile Ethiopian highlands beginning around 400 B.C.E. Despite the difficult geographical terrain and the unpredictable climate of the this area, its peoples traded with Egypt from ancient times. They also benefited from proximity to the Red Sea, the major maritime route between the Mediterranean Sea and the Indian Ocean. This proximity linked northern Ethiopia to a widespread network of exchange and contact. In addition, at the Red Sea's narrowest point only 20 miles of water separates the southern tip of Arabia from northeast Africa. Many Semitic people from Arabia crossed into Ethiopia and settled among the original inhabitants. Although many deep

Aksum   A literate, urban state that appeared in northern Ethiopia before the Common Era and grew into an empire and a crossroads for trade.

gorges inhibited communication across the plateau, the northern Ethiopians benefited greatly from accessibility to Arabia.

This accessibility may have allowed them to establish links to the Hebrews, as suggested at least in Ethiopian legends. In these legends, the Queen of Sheba who, according to biblical accounts, met the Hebrew King Solomon was in fact an early Ethiopian monarch, Queen Makeda (Ma-KAY-da), who went to Israel in search of knowledge. In the tale as reported in an old Ethiopian book, Makeda supposedly told her people:

> Let my voice be heard by all of you, my people. I am going in quest of Wisdom and Learning. My spirit impels me to go and find them out where they are to be had, for I am smitten with the love of Wisdom and I feel myself drawn as tho by a leash toward Learning. Learning is better than treasures of gold, better than all that has been created upon earth.[5]

Semitic immigrants from Yemen (YEM-uhn), the probable location of the ancient Sheba (Saba) kingdom, may have brought the story with them to Ethiopia and adapted it for local needs. The son of Solomon and Makeda, Menelik (MEN-uh-lik), supposedly founded a new kingdom, called Aksum.

The Aksum region, located on the northern edge of the Ethiopian plateau near the Red Sea, was already a center of agriculture and both bronze- and ironworking when Queen Makeda supposedly made her visit. It was inhabited by the ancestors of the Amharic (am-HAR-ik) people who today dominate central Ethiopia. Between 400 B.C.E. and 100 C.E. Aksumites built their first temples and palaces of masonry, as well as a city, dams, and reservoirs. Irrigation and terracing supported a productive farming. The Aksumites also developed an alphabet.

For centuries Aksum enjoyed close economic and cultural exchange with the peoples of both southwestern Asia and eastern Africa, becoming something of a network hub between these regions. In about 50 C.E. the Aksumites built an empire that dominated a large section of Northeast Africa and flourished chiefly from trade. One Aksumite king boasted that he compelled the nations bordering on his kingdom to live in peace and then restored their territories to them if they paid tribute to him. Soon Aksum had eclipsed Meroë and gained control of the trade between the Red Sea and the central Nile. Aksum became so well known that a Persian observer, the prophet Mani, included it with Persia, Rome, and China among the world's four great kingdoms.

The Aksumites traded all over the Middle East, eastern Mediterranean, and East Africa. A Mesopotamian poet celebrated the ships from the main Aksumite port, Adulis (A-doo-lis) on the Red Sea, whose prows cut "through the foam of the water as a gambler divides the dust with his hand."[6] The trade network also reached to Sri Lanka and India, and many Indian coins have been found at Aksum (see Witness to the Past: A Shopper's Guide to Aksum). The Aksumites exported ivory, gold, obsidian, emeralds, perfumes, and animals and imported metals, glass, fabrics, wine, and spices. A visiting Greek merchant reported that every second year the king sent agents to an African society south of Aksum to bargain for gold. Several hundred merchants accompanied the agents, taking along iron, oxen, and lumps of salt for trade. Aksumites used the Greek language in foreign commerce and were the first sub-Saharan Africans to mint their own coins.

The Aksum empire flourished from cultural interchange with many societies. Byzantium sent envoys to the court, seeking alliances against common enemies in Arabia. In addition, the Aksumites' extensive ties with the Semitic peoples of Yemen across the Red Sea led to considerable genetic and cultural intermixing between these two peoples. The classical Amharic language, **Geez** (gee-EZ), is a mixture of African and Semitic influences. There was also much Hebrew influence on Ethiopian literature and religion. Indeed, the modern Amharic royal family, descendants of Aksumite kings, claimed ancestry from King Solomon and Queen Makeda. The Jewish communities known as *Falasha* (fuh-LAHSH-uh) have lived in northern Ethiopia for many centuries.

Aksum Society and Culture

Aksum's highly stratified social structure was dominated by kings. However, these kings had a paternalistic attitude toward their people. A fourth-century C.E. king left an inscription in which he claimed: "I will rule the people with righteousness and justice, and will not oppress them."[7] Judging from their spectacular palaces, kings also enjoyed great wealth and power. A sixth-century Byzantine ambassador reported on the royal family's pomp and ceremony, writing that the king wore

> a golden collar. He stood on a four-wheeled chariot drawn by four elephants; the body of the chariot was high and covered with gold plates. The king stood on top carrying a small gilded shield and holding in his hands two small gilded spears.[8]

Below the royal family was an aristocracy that supplied the top government officials. A substantial middle class included many merchants, and at the bottom of the social order were peasants and slaves, who could be conscripted for massive building projects.

The capital city of Aksum was a wealthy and cosmopolitan trading center, widely known for its monumental architecture. Its magnificent pillars, thin stylized representations of multistoried buildings, were erected chiefly at burial grounds. The largest stands over 100 feet high. The city also contained many stone platforms and huge palaces. The making and transporting of the huge monoliths and stone slabs required remarkable engineering skills.

Christianity became influential just as Aksum reached its height of economic and military power in the fourth century C.E. Christian missionaries traveled the trade routes from western Asia, especially from the societies along the eastern

---

Geez The classical Amharic language of Ethiopia, a mixture of African and Semitic influences.

The following account of the trade of Aksum comes from the *Periplus of the Erythrean Sea*, written by an unknown Greek sometime in the second half of the first century C.E. The *Periplus* was a guide prepared for merchants and sailors that outlines the commercial prospects to be found in Arabia, the Indian Ocean, and the Persian Gulf. It also describes many of the bustling ports of this region. Hence, the *Periplus* is an excellent source for understanding Classical Era networks of exchange. In this excerpt, we learn about the port city of Adulis on the Red Sea. Adulis, now called Massawa (muh-SAH-wuh), was the chief Aksumite trade distribution center, where goods from the Ethiopian interior and from faraway places such as India, Egypt, and the Mediterranean were brought for sale or transshipment.

Adulis [is] a port . . . lying at the inner end of a bay. . . . Before the harbor lies the so-called Mountain Island, . . . with the shores of the mainland close to it on both sides. Ships bound for this port now anchor here because of attacks from the land [by bandits]. . . . Opposite Mountain Island, on the mainland, . . . lies Adulis, a fair-sized village, from which there is a three day's journey to Coloe, an inland town and the first market for ivory. From that place to the [capital] city of the people called Aksumites there is a five day's journey more; to that place all the ivory is brought from the country beyond the Nile. . . .

There are imported into these places [Adulis], undressed cloth made in Egypt for the Berbers; robes from . . . [modern Suez]; cloaks of poor quality dyed in colors; double-fringed linen mantles; many articles of flint glass, and others of . . . [agate] made in . . . [Thebes, Egypt]; and brass, which is used for ornament and in cut pieces instead of coin; sheets of soft copper, used for cooking utensils and cut up for bracelets and anklets for the women; iron, which is made into spears used against the elephants and other wild beasts, and in their wars. Besides these, small axes are imported, and adzes and swords; copper drinking cups, round and large; a little coin for those coming to the market; wine of Laodicea [on the Syrian coast] and Italy . . . ; olive oil . . . ; for the King, gold and silver plate made after the fashion of the country, and for clothing, military cloaks, and thin coats of skin. . . . Likewise from the district of Ariaca [on the northwest coast of India] across this sea, there are imported Indian cloth [fine-quality cotton]. . . . There are exported from these places ivory, and tortoise-shell and rhinoceros-horn. The most [cargo] from Egypt is brought to this market [Adulis] from the month of January to September.

THINKING ABOUT THE READING

1. What were some of the societies that were linked to the trade at Adulis?

2. What does this reading tell us about the networks of exchange that connected Aksum to a wider world?

Source: W. H. Schoff (trans. and ed.), *The Periplus of the Erythraen Sea: Travel and Trade in the Indian Ocean by a Merchant of the First Century* (London, Bombay & Calcutta, 1912).

Mediterranean coast with whom the Aksumites had long exchanged goods and ideas. The king adopted the new faith, making Christianity the official religion of the kingdom. According to a Roman source, the king "began to search out Roman merchants [at Aksum] who were Christian and to give them great influence and to urge them to establish [churches], supplying sites for buildings, and in every way promoting the growth of Christianity."[9] The king had political reasons for conversion, since he wanted to establish closer relations with Rome, Byzantium, and Egypt. But the Amharic population only slowly adopted the new faith. Ethiopian Christianity resembled the Coptic churches of Egypt and Nubia but also incorporated some of the long-entrenched spirit worship and various Hebrew practices, including the Jewish sabbath and kosher food.

The Aksum Legacy and Ethiopian History

Aksum eventually collapsed as a result of several forces. New challenges isolated Aksum and destroyed its dynamism. It had flourished during an era of adequate rainfall, but by 400 C.E., reduced rainfall and the resulting pressure on the land had produced an ecological crisis. Political problems added to imperial decline. The conquest of southern Arabia by Aksum's enemy, Sassanian Persia, in 575 diverted the Indian Ocean commerce from the port of Adulis. Then the rapid Islamic conquests of western Asia and North Africa beginning in the middle of the seventh century cut Aksum off from the Christian world. Aksum's trade withered, and it fell into economic stagnation, cultural decline, and political instability. By 800 C.E. the capital city was abandoned and the remnants of the kingdom had moved several hundred miles south.

Unlike Kush, however, Ethiopian society persisted in recognizable form. Indeed, the culture demonstrated a continuity for nearly 2,000 years, confirming that the Aksumite period was the Classical Age in northeast Africa. In particular, over the centuries Christianity became a deeply ingrained local religion among the Amharic and some of the neighboring peoples, producing the unique Ethiopian Christianity of today. The Ethiopian church, which became closely connected to the monarchy, benefited from owning many landed estates. Ethiopia remained relatively isolated in its mountain fastness for the next ten centuries.

SECTION SUMMARY

■ The kingdom of Kush in Nubia, with its capital city of Meroë, was a major African iron producer and crossroads of trade between sub-Saharan Africa and the Mediterranean.

■ Kush was influenced by Egypt but was also remarkable for its rich culture, its fearsome warriors and absolute monarchs, and its strong laws and traditions.

■ Aksum, in the Ethiopian highlands, had contact with Egypt and Arabia, may have forged links with the Hebrews, and after a time eclipsed Meroë as the region's primary trade center.

■ Aksum's king converted to Christianity as a means of establishing closer relationships with Rome, Byzantium, and Egypt.

■ Like Kush, Aksum may have declined in part because of climate change, but it was also hurt by the Islamic conquest of its neighbors; unlike Kush, however, the society endured for another 2,000 years.

✦ The Blossoming of Sudanic and Bantu Africa

How did the spread of the Bantus reshape sub-Saharan Africa?

While Kush and Aksum maintained the closest connections to Eurasia, complex urban societies also arose in the Sudanic region, on the Sahara's southern fringe, among peoples like the Mande (MAHN-day). These societies were linked to North Africa and beyond by trade networks. Meanwhile, Bantu-speaking Africans, first discussed in Chapter 3, continued to spread their languages, cultures, and technologies widely, occupying the southern half of the continent. Some became connected to trade networks linked to east coast port cities.

Sudanic Societies, Farming, and Cities

In the vast but dry grassland region known as the Sudan (soo-DAN), lying between the Sahara and tropical Africa, societies composed of farmers and city-dwellers, and sharing some common features, germinated during classical times. The Sudanic peoples had long before adapted their economic life to the prevailing ecology. Most Sudanese became farmers living in small, largely self-sufficient farming villages. Cereal crops, especially millet and sorghum, mixed with vegetables, were the most basic food sources. Reliance on grains suited the dry Sudanic soils;

millet and sorghum both require little water. West Africans also grew cotton and developed richly colored cotton clothing. The fertility of a large delta region along one stretch of the Niger (NYE-juhr) River made intensive farming possible there. The food grown in the delta as well as the fish caught in the river helped to feed the people of the trading cities.

Some Sudanese congregated in large towns and cities reaching 30,000 or 40,000 in population, of which Jenne-Jenno was perhaps the major hub of a network of commercial centers along the Niger River. Located in what is now the nation of Mali (MAHL-ee), Jenne-Jenno developed as early as 200 B.C.E., with the residents building circular houses made of straw and coated with mud. By the Common Era the city's people worked copper, gold, and iron, which they obtained from mines several hundred miles away. Gold and copper had probably been brought to the city by boat for several centuries, and gold dust and small copper ingots (ING-guhts) apparently served as currency throughout the Sudan in the later Classical Era. By 400 C.E. Jenne-Jenno had

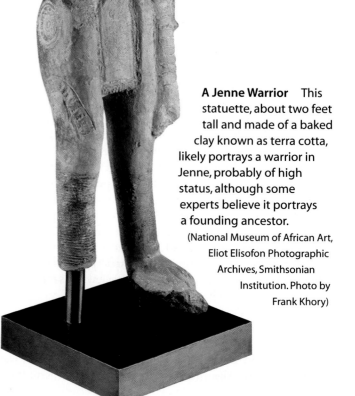

A Jenne Warrior This statuette, about two feet tall and made of a baked clay known as terra cotta, likely portrays a warrior in Jenne, probably of high status, although some experts believe it portrays a founding ancestor. (National Museum of African Art, Eliot Elisofon Photographic Archives, Smithsonian Institution. Photo by Frank Khory)

become a crucial transshipment point where goods arriving by camel or donkey caravan were exchanged for goods moved by boat along the Niger River. This position made Jenne-Jenno the major early trading city of the Sudan.

Jenne-Jenno continued to flourish as a commercial hub for many centuries, closely tied, like other Sudanic cities, to hemispheric trade by the caravans across the Sahara. Eventually a wall over a mile in circumference surrounded the city for protection of the residents, most of whom lived in houses made from dried mud. Jenne-Jenno was built upon a productive agriculture, and it exported grain, fish, and animal products in exchange for metals. States of some sort may have existed around urban centers like Jenne-Jenno, but the ruins have yielded few clues to political organization. Historians suspect that Jenne-Jenno and other Classical Age commercial centers in the Niger Valley were probably independent city-states for most of the first millennium C.E.

Large cities and states were less common in sub-Saharan Africa than in Eurasia and North Africa, in part because of the smaller population densities in Africa. The African agricultural system, mostly based on shifting cultivation, suited the soils but could not generally support the kinds of large settled populations that developed in parts of Eurasia and the northern Nile valley. At the beginning of the Common Era the African continent may have contained between 15 and 25 million people, much less than half that of China alone. About half lived in Egypt, Kush, and along the Mediterranean coast. Elsewhere in Africa, including the Sudan, small population densities meant that societies were held together by social and economic ties and did not require a powerful state to maintain order.

Trans-Saharan Trade Networks

The establishment of caravan routes crossing the Sahara, which greatly aided the growth of Sudanic societies by fostering interregional trade, began well before the Common Era. Eventually a large trade system spanned the Sahara that linked the Sudanic towns with the peoples of the desert and southern Mediterranean coastal societies such as Carthage. From ancient times Carthage sporadically carried on some trade with the Sudanic peoples, although the volume remains disputed. By the third century C.E. the gold used in coins minted in Carthage may have come from western Africa.

Salt moving south to the Sudan and gold moving north to the Mediterranean drove the complex Saharan trade. The several trade routes that crossed the barren sands eventually became one of the major trade networks of the Classical Era. However, many other goods were traded as well. Sudanic cities shipped north cotton cloth, leather goods, pepper, slaves, and most important, gold, which the merchants in North Africa then sold to Europe. The Sudanic peoples also traded meat animals to the forest societies along the West African coast, and they imported copper from the region east of the Niger. Sudanic societies were largely self-sufficient, but they needed salt mined in the central Sahara and along the West African coast.

The salt trade was mostly controlled by the *Garamante* tribal confederation, which inhabited the desert region in what is now southwestern Libya, southeastern Algeria, and northern Niger. These Berber (BUHR-buhr) people dominated the caravan trade routes as intermediaries from around 500 B.C.E. to 600 C.E., managing a vast commercial network that included trading of enslaved Africans. The Garamantes used camels as pack animals and horses to pull light chariots. The Greeks and Romans considered the Garamantes to be warlike barbarians, an ethnocentric viewpoint. As an example of this prejudice, the Roman writer Pliny complained that the Romans could not open a road to Garamante country because bandits filled up the wells with sand. Pliny underestimated the Garamantes. In fact, these Saharans made the parched desert livable by combining pastoral stock raising with irrigated farming; they constructed several thousand miles of underground canals to cultivate their farms; and they lived in walled cities and villages, built stone citadels as military outposts, and were apparently governed by royal families. Products from around West Africa, Egypt, and the Mediterranean Basin have been found in the ruins of the Garamantian capital. Their state collapsed around the same time as the Roman Empire, and the remnants were later overrun by Muslims.

Sudanic States and Peoples

As in Kush and Aksum, commerce stimulated the growth of states in the Sudan. Kingdoms apparently grew out of markets and flourished from taxing the trade in gold and other commodities. The Soninke (soh-NIN-kay) people of the middle Niger Valley formed the first known major Sudanic state, **Ghana** (GAH-nuh). Ghana existed by at least 700 C.E., but it probably formed by 500 C.E. and perhaps a century or two earlier. Excavations of the probable capital city, not far from Jenne-Jenno, show a stone town that was built sometime between 500 and 600 C.E. Ghana reached its height as a trade-based empire in the ninth century and flourished until the thirteenth.

Diverse **Mande** (MON-day) peoples may have been typical of many classical Sudanic societies. The Mande spoke closely related languages, shared many customs, and dominated the western Niger River Basin and adjacent areas. Mande speakers included such ethnic groups as the Soninke (who established Ghana), Mandinka (man-DING-goh), Malinke (muh-LING-kee), and Bambara (bam-BAHR-uh) peoples. These Mande peoples combined farming with fishing along the Niger River. The ancestors of the Mande were the likely domesticators of African rice. By 900 or 800 B.C.E. Mande farmers lived in large walled villages, and they may have built Jenne-Jenno. Later, Mande speakers dominated much of the western Sudan.

Although divided into different groups, the Mande shared many common social, political, and religious traditions. They

Ghana The first known major Sudanic state, formed by the Soninke people of the middle Niger valley.

Mande Diverse Sudanic peoples who spoke closely related languages, shared many customs, and dominated the western Niger River Basin and adjacent areas of West Africa.

had highly stratified societies, with aristocratic, warrior, and commoner classes, and a special group of ritual and religious specialists. Across the early Sudan political structures varied, but the Mande eventually developed a theocracy in which chiefs and village heads combined religious and secular duties. A respected class of oral historians and musicians known widely as **griots** (GREE-oh) memorized and recited the history of the community, emphasizing the deeds of leaders. The common folk had to content themselves with living in the reflected glory of their exalted leaders. Still, many Mande of all classes enjoyed considerable prosperity, often from growing cotton or making their elaborate and beautiful cotton clothing, which was traded widely. The Mande and other Sudanic peoples also developed some common ideas about religion, including animism. People believed in a distant creator god, but spirits of nature and ancestral spirits loomed large in daily life. Like many African peoples, the Mande drew no neat line between the living and the dead. They also wanted to keep the favor of good spirits and avoid the hostility of bad ones.

The Guinea Coast

Over time various peoples, including some from the Sudan, migrated into the Guinea (GIN-ee) coast just south of the Sudan, a migration made possible by new tools and agricultural techniques. The Guinea coast, which stretches some 2,000 miles from modern Senegal (sen-i-GAWL) to southeastern Nigeria (nie-JEER-ee-uh), was mainly covered by forest and swamp and had few edible plants or game animals. The mixing of Sudanic and other traditions in this area produced unique new societies.

The challenging life on the Guinea coast led to some pragmatic solutions. To survive, the people lived mostly in small, self-sufficient villages with rich social networks. They practiced subsistence agriculture, with yams and bananas as the staple crops. Although some land was privately owned, most Guinea peoples developed a tradition of cooperative labor. Furthermore, the Guinea peoples traded with the Sudanic societies, over land or by boat up the rivers such as the Niger and Volta (VAHL-tuh), and thus became linked to wider networks of economic and cultural exchange. Over time, many of the coastal societies came to practice some common customs, including Sudanese traditions such as theocratic political systems and pronounced social class divisions.

The Bantu-Speaking Peoples and Their Migrations

Over several thousand years, many iron-using speakers of Bantu languages had migrated from their original homeland in eastern Nigeria into Central and East Africa (see Chapter 3). During the Classical Era, Bantu peoples accelerated their expansion to the south and east. They carried with them many traditions of art, music, farming, and religion that had originated in the Sudan, thus spreading Sudanese influence into other areas of Africa.

Expansion of the Bantu World Some Bantu-speaking peoples moved into the southern Congo region now known as Katanga (kuh-TAHNG-guh), which they reached by 400 B.C.E. Katanga is an area of savannah grasslands like the region they had left, but it is less fertile and more prone to drought and disease. Much of the region south of the Congo Basin rain forest is relatively arid because of irregular rainfall. Fortunately, sorghum and millet from the Sudanic region and Ethiopia spread among the Bantus, who successfully adapted these cereal crops to the dry southern climate.

From Katanga many Bantus began moving to the west, south, and east. In the east they met Bantus migrating from the Great Lakes in the East African highlands. By 200 B.C.E. Bantu culture had reached the Zambezi (zam-BEE-zee) River Basin, and by the third century C.E. the first Bantu settlers entered what is now the nation of South Africa. Networks of trade and migration spanning vast distances eventually connected the southern third of Africa to the Sudan and the East African coast.

As Bantu-speaking migrants settled in a new location, they encountered local peoples and incorporated new influences. Because they worked iron, the Bantus possessed military and agricultural technologies more effective than those of many non-Bantus, which allowed them to push some of the local peoples into marginal economic areas suitable only for hunting and gathering. For example, the Mbuti Pygmies of the Congo region moved into thick rain forests, while many of the Khoisan (KOY-sahn) peoples in southern Africa, such as the Kung! hunters and gatherers discussed in Chapter 1, became desert dwellers. But many Bantus intermingled with, and probably culturally assimilated, those they met. Sudanese cultural forms carried by the Bantus, such as drums and percussive music, woodcarving, and ancestor-focused religions, became widespread.

Cultural Mixing in Southern and Eastern Africa The contacts also influenced the Bantu cultures, especially in southern and eastern Africa. For example, the Xhosa (KOH-sah) and Zulu (ZOO-loo) peoples, who lived along the southeastern coast of today's South Africa by the fourth century C.E., mixed their languages and cultures with the local Khoisan cattle herders. Cattle herding was incorporated into Xhosa and Zulu economic life alongside farming and trade.

The migrating Bantus also encountered and gradually absorbed various societies in East Africa, some of them pastoralists and some farmers. Various ironworking pastoralists from the eastern Sudan, known as **Nilotes** (nie-LAHT-eez) because they speak Nilotic (nie-LAHT-ik) languages very different from

---

griots A respected class of oral historians and musicians in West Africa who memorized and recited the history of the group, emphasizing the deeds of leaders.

Nilotes Ironworking pastoralists from the eastern Sudan who settled in East Africa and there had frequent interactions with the Bantus.

the Bantu tongues, were also settling in East Africa. Although their relationships to each other were not always peaceful, Bantus and Nilotes mutually modified their cultures as a result of contact. Some Bantus adopted pastoralism (cattle and goats) while others mastered new agricultural techniques and diets, including Southeast Asian foods like bananas, coconuts, sugar cane, and Asian yams available on the East African coast.

These foods, as well as domesticated chickens and possibly pigs, were brought to East Africa by Indonesian mariners and migrants in outrigger canoes early in the Common Era (see Chapter 7). Eventually these crops and domesticated animals spread throughout Africa. Some of the Indonesian mariners settled along the coast and married local people, intensifying cultural exchange. These Indonesians and later arrivals also introduced Austronesian housing styles and musical instruments, which were incorporated into local cultures. They established trading posts to barter pottery, beads, and utensils for ivory and animal products. Indonesian influences reached as far west as the Congo River Basin. Between 100 and 700 C.E. Indonesians settled the large island of Madagascar. Eventually most of the descendants of the Indonesian settlers on the East African coast relocated to that large and previously uninhabited island, implanting there a mixed Indonesian-Bantu culture and language that still survives.

Maritime Trade and the East African Coast

The East African coast, where many Bantu speakers settled, developed a cosmopolitan society based on maritime trade. The winds and currents along the coast reverse direction every six months, allowing boats from southwestern Asia to sail to East Africa and back each year. The same wind reversal is true for the Indian Ocean, making possible two-way communication between East Africa and India or Southeast Asia. A seagoing trade between Arabia and the East African coast developed even before the Common Era. The trading ports to which merchants from southern Arabia sailed were located along the coast from Somalia to present-day Tanzania. The main port city in this era, Rhapta (RAHP-ta) in Tanzania, had a large merchant community from southern Arabia.

The east coast trade grew slowly during the Classical Era and was not yet an integral component of the great trading network forming around the Indian Ocean Basin. A first-century C.E. survey of maritime trade by an Alexandria-based Greek traveler reported that ships left Egypt's Red Sea ports and then visited Adulis and various Somalian ports before sailing to East African ports such as Rhapta. The author reported that local people made sown boats, used dugout canoes (of probable Bantu origin), and behaved "each in his own place like chiefs,"[10] indicating that there were independent local communities rather than a centralized state. He and his party then headed to India rather than venturing further down the coast, avoiding what they considered the mysterious ocean stretching southward.

Growing numbers of traders came to the coastal towns. Various Roman accounts reported that East Africa exported ivory, rhinoceros horn, and tortoise shell to Egypt, India, and western Asia and imported iron goods, pottery, and glass beads. Egyptian, Roman, and West Asian coins found in the region date from 300 B.C.E. to 200 C.E., indicating trade with the Mediterranean area, and Persian pottery produced between 400 and 600 C.E. was distributed widely along the coast and inland. Eventually, the coast developed many large and flourishing port cities and a culture that mixed Bantu ideas with those of southwestern Asia. But it was many centuries before any ships ventured out into the "western seas" and established contact with the Western Hemisphere, to which we now turn.

SECTION SUMMARY

- The Sudan region included trading hubs such as Jenne-Jenno, but the population in the Classical Era was not dense enough to require a powerful state; Ghana was the first state to arise, probably around 500 C.E.

- The Garamante peoples controlled the extensive caravan routes through the Sahara Desert to bring salt from the African Mediterranean coast to Sudan, which exported gold in return.

- The Bantu peoples, equipped with iron tools, continued to migrate south and east, mixing with and sometimes pushing out other peoples, and they made their way to South Africa by the third century C.E.

- Indonesian mariners settled on the East African coast and, to a greater extent, in Madagascar, where a mixed Indonesian-Bantu culture survives to this day.

- Winds that switched direction every six months made it easy to travel back and forth between East Africa and southwestern Asia, India, and Southeast Asia.

 # Classical Mesoamerican Societies and Networks

What were the similarities and differences between the Maya and Teotihuacan?

As in Eurasia and Africa, the first cities and states in the Americas had developed during ancient times, including the Olmecs in Mesoamerica and the Chavín in the Andes (see Chapter 4). And in common with Eurasia and Africa, population increase helped to stimulate the growth of more American urban societies during the Classical Era. By the beginning of the Common Era there may have been around 15 million people in the Americas. Over two-thirds of them were concentrated in Mesoamerica and western South America, where the most significant developments were taking place. The most long-lasting and widespread of these societies were the **Maya**

Maya The most long-lasting and widespread of the classical Mesoamerican societies, who occupied the Yucatan Peninsula and northern Central America for almost 2,000 years.

(MIE-uh) of Mesoamerica, who forged a literate culture that excelled in some sciences and mathematics. Mesoamerica also provided a fertile environment for the rise of several cities that became the centers of prosperous states.

The Emergence of the Early Maya

To the east of the pioneering Olmecs, in the lowland rain forests of Central America and the Yucatan (YOO-kuh-TAN) Peninsula in southeast Mexico facing the Caribbean Sea, a society coalesced that became the Maya (see Map 9.2). Farming by shifting cultivation and ceramic making dates back to at least 1100 B.C.E. The Maya introduced intensive cultivation of maize (corn) and other foods into the tropical forests. Maize was the key crop. According to Maya legends, the gods had fashioned people out of corn. Maya farmers built artificial platforms and terraces on which they could grow enough crops to generate surpluses that would support a ruling elite, as well as large underground reservoirs to store groundwater where rainfall was scarce. As more productive agriculture led to more population, the Maya spread southward into the mountains and coastal zones of what is today Chiapas (chee-AHP-uhs) (Mexico), Guatemala (GWAHT-uh-MAHL-uh), Honduras (hahn-DUR-uhs), El Salvador (el SAL-vuh-DOR), and Belize (buh-LEEZ).

As their power increased, the Maya elite organized ambitious building projects. The first Maya pyramids and elaborate stone buildings were constructed by 600 B.C.E. Unlike Egyptian pyramids, which served as burial tombs for top leaders, Maya pyramids had temples on top and were built for religious worship and ceremonies. According to ancient Maya folklore, these temples housed the gods:

> There had been five generations of people since the origin of light, of continuity, of life and of humankind. And they built many houses there. And they also built houses for the gods, putting these in the center of the highest part of the citadel. They came and they stayed. After that their domains grew larger; they were more numerous and more crowded.[11]

By 100 B.C.E. notions of divine kingship became widespread, and the Maya began making stone statues and carvings of their rulers. By this time they also painted sophisticated murals on walls, illustrating Mayan myths such as their creation story.

Maya society was based on urbanization and cultural innovations such as writing. At the height of their culture, 150 B.C.E.–800 C.E., the Maya built many cities, each boasting masonry buildings, large temples, spacious plazas and pyramid complexes, and elaborate carvings (see Chronology: Classical Americas). The major early city was El Mirador, built between 150 B.C.E. and 50 C.E. In its ruins archaeologists have discovered the first examples of Maya writing, inscribed on pot fragments and sculpture. The Maya developed the most comprehensive writing system in the Americas. Their hieroglyphic script, which had phonetic as well as pictographic elements, was used for calendars, religious regulations, and many sacred books, as well as to record dynastic histories, genealogies, and

Map 9.2 Classical Societies in the Americas
The major American centers of complex agriculture, cities and states emerged in Mesoamerica, where the Mayans were the largest and longest-lasting society during the era, and the Andes regions, where Chavin, Moche, and Tiahuanaco were important societies.

Online Study Center **Improve Your Grade**
Interactive Map: Mesoamerican Civilizations

military successes. A later Spanish observer later admired "those who carried with them the black and red ink, the manuscripts and painted book, the wisdom, the annals, the books of song."[12] The heritage of the early Maya cities such as El Mirador also included a distinctive architecture, royal dynasties, and a highly stratified social system. In some cities, suburbs containing residences, markets, and workshops stretched for several miles out from the city centers. Even the Spanish who conquered the Maya lands in the 1500s marveled at the city buildings. One wrote that "the buildings and the multitude of them is remarkable. So well built are they of cut stone that it fills one with astonishment."[13]

Tikal (ti-KAHL), in what is today eastern Guatemala near the border with Belize, was one of the major Maya cities between 200 and 900 C.E. and had a population of 50,000 at its height. Tikal contained three hundred large ceremonial buildings dominated by temple pyramids 200 feet high. The pyramids were topped by temples decorated with carvings made of stucco plaster. The first ruler used the jaguar as the symbol of kingship, military bravery, and religious authority. His descendants, King Great Jaguar Paw and General Smoking Frog, led Tikal to a great victory over the rival city Uaxactun in 378 C.E., ensuring Tikal's regional supremacy for the next two hundred years.

Maya identity was more cultural than political. There was much cultural uniformity among the competing cities, proba-

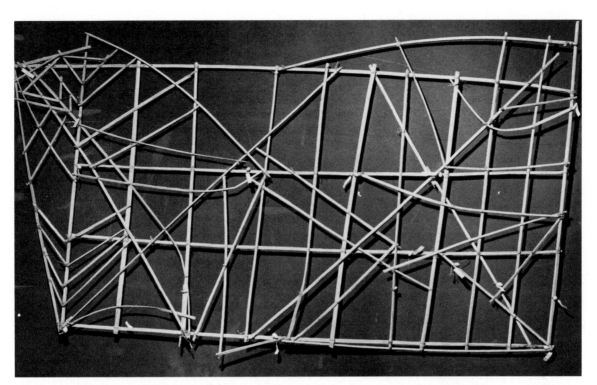

Polynesian Palm-Frond Navigational Map   This nautical map, made in the Marshall Islands from palm fronds, shows distances between islands as measured by time traveled. The map may have originally had bits of shell or coral to mark islands. Polynesians and Micronesians often made such maps for their ocean voyages.   (Bishop Museum)

Polynesian Migrations and Societies

Polynesian culture seems to have flowered first in the neighboring Fiji (FEE-jee), Tonga (TAHN-guh), and Samoa (suh-MO-uh) island groups around 500 B.C.E. Ancestors to the Polynesians had reached these islands between 1100 and 800 B.C.E. (see Map 9.3), and within a few centuries some were on the move again. The voyages must have involved incredible hardships, as men, women, children, animals, and precious seed plants were crammed into open canoes. By around 300 or 200 B.C.E. Polynesian mariners from Tonga may have reached the Marquesas (mar-KAY-suhs) Islands and soon thereafter Tahiti (tuh-HEE-tee), 1,500 miles east of Tonga. Sometime in the early Common Era Polynesians sailed from Samoa 1,500 miles north to the Kiribati (kear-uh-BAH-tee) Islands, and then on to the Marshall Islands. Later, between 400 and 600 C.E., mariners from the Marquesas settled Hawaii after crossing over 2,000 miles of ocean, followed around 1100 or 1200 C.E. by a migration from Tahiti. Then Tahitians journeyed some 2,500 miles east to Easter Island. Finally, between 800 and 1000 C.E., some Tahitians moved west another 2,500 miles to Aotearoa (which a Dutch explorer much later named New Zealand), the largest landmass settled by Polynesians. These settlers, the ancestors of the Maori (MAO-ree) people faced a very different climate and topography from that of the tropical Pacific islands, as well as a new mix of plants and animals. Polynesian sailors may even have visited the Peruvian coast. Such contact might explain the presence of sweet potatoes, a South American crop, in eastern Polynesia and New Zealand for at least 1000 years.

Polynesian settlement required adapting to varied island environments. Their agriculture was based on Southeast Asian crops such as yams, taro, bananas, coconuts, and breadfruit, and animals included pigs, chickens, and dogs. But survival required some modifications. Sometimes farmers needed elaborate terracing, artificial ponds, and irrigation. Polynesians also exploited local food sources such as coconuts as well as the abundant marine life of the lagoons, coral reefs, and deep sea. Cloth made out of bark furnished clothing. But fragile island ecologies were easily unbalanced. Imported animals like pigs, dogs, and (unintentionally) rats consumed local birds. Overhunting also eliminated some species, and deforestation was also a problem. As an extreme example, Easter Island, which was heavily forested when Polynesians arrived, was completely denuded over the centuries, and the people were reduced to poverty and chronic conflict over ever scarcer resources.

Early Polynesians lived in clans that were generally dominated by hereditary chiefs who controlled the lands. Conflict between rival clans and chiefdoms over status and land led to tensions and sometimes war. Those who felt aggrieved might seek a better life by sailing to new lands. Eventually the most elaborate social hierarchies emerged in Tonga, Tahiti, and Hawaii, where paramount chiefs ruled many thousands of followers and controlled much of the economy. In these island

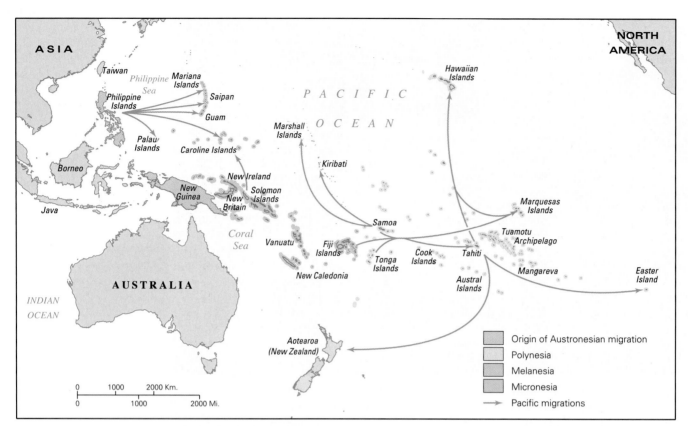

Map 9.3 Pacific Migrations in the Classical Era
During this era, Austronesian peoples scattered across the vast Pacific Basin, using ingenious canoes and navigation techniques to settle nearly all the inhabitable islands. From bases in Tonga and Samoa in the west, the Polynesians settled a large expanse of the basin ranging from Hawaii in the north to Easter Island in the east and New Zealand in the south.

groups a deep divide developed between the families of the chiefs and the commoners. While men held most political power, women often enjoyed a high status. Most Micronesian and some Polynesian societies were matrilineal. In addition, Polynesian women often ranked higher than their brothers in spiritual and ritual authority and, by marrying into other clans or ruling families, could help political relations.

The Austronesian Dispersal in the Pacific and Beyond

Today some 1,200 different Austronesian languages are spoken across the huge span of space from Madagascar eastward through Indonesia, Malaysia, and the Philippines to Easter Island, a few hundred miles off the west coast of South America. All the Pacific islanders except those on and around New Guinea speak Austronesian languages. This book has elsewhere discussed the migrations of Indo-Europeans from southern Russia into Europe, western Asia, and India, as well as the long movement of Bantu-speaking peoples into the southern half of Africa. But no premodern peoples migrated over as wide an area in so short a time as did the Austronesians. The huge tri-

angle of Polynesia, anchored at the ends by Hawaii, New Zealand, and Easter Island, is one of the largest expanses of territory in the world. One of the first outsiders to explore the area, British captain James Cook, wrote in 1774 C.E.: "It is extraordinary that the same [people] should have spread themselves over all the isles in this vast Ocean, almost a fourth part of the circumference of the Globe."[20]

Migration over such vast distances did not necessarily mean isolation. The Austronesian languages may have been spread through the large maritime trading network that developed. As an example of this network, obsidian was mined on the island of New Britain, northeast of New Guinea. From there it was traded as far west as Borneo and as far east as Fiji, some 4,000 miles apart. On a smaller scale nearby island groups traded with each other and maintained social links. For example, the Tongan and Fijian chiefly families frequently intermarried. But even after sea routes were established, the sailing required remarkable observation and could be dangerous, as Captain Cook reported from Tonga in 1777: "In these Navigations the Sun is their guide by day and the Stars by night; when these are obscured they have recourse to the points from whence the Wind and waves come upon the vessel. If [these] shift, they are bewildered."[21] Even today Polynesian traditions honor great navigators of the past such as Moikeha and Pa'ao, who sailed back and forth between the Marquesas and Hawaii over a millennium ago.

Regular trade and communication ensured that the far-flung Polynesian societies shared many linguistic and cultural traits, including elaborate facial and body tattooing (the word *tattoo* is of Polynesian origin), myths, reverence for ancestors, and art forms such as woodcarving. Many of these customs were also common in Melanesia and Micronesia. And all these Pacific peoples derived not only their languages but also some of their culture, maritime prowess, and subsistence strategies from the Austronesians who ventured into Southeast Asia and then into the western Pacific in ancient times.

SECTION SUMMARY

■ Aboriginal Australians developed great understanding of natural phenomena and were very successful hunters and gatherers for thousands of years.

■ Aborigines across Australia believed in the dreamtime of the mythic past and felt that spirits and ghosts inhabited much of the physical world.

■ Austronesian peoples from Southeast Asia took to the sea and settled on various Pacific islands.

■ Polynesian culture probably began in Fiji, Tonga, and Samoa, but it spread out over a remarkable expanse of the Pacific Ocean.

■ An extensive trading network developed among the Pacific islands and, despite their isolation from each other, the islands' cultures remained quite homogenous.

Online Study Center ACE the Test

◆ Chapter Summary

During the Classical Era some sub-Saharan Africans became more closely linked by trade with North Africa and the western half of Eurasia, and two societies, Kush and Aksum, also served as trade intermediaries. Kush, along the central Nile, became a center for iron production, and Aksum, in the Ethiopian highlands, flourished as a trading hub linked with many other societies of Africa and Eurasia. Cities and small states that emerged in the Sudanic region of West Africa participated in the growing trans-Saharan caravan trade network linking them with the Mediterranean world. Trading cities also appeared along the East African coast, which became tied by trade networks to the Mediterranean, western Asia, and India. Bantu-speaking peoples settled the southern half of Africa, carrying with them iron technology and many Sudanic influences. Many also settled on the East African coast.

Various urban societies dominated Mesoamerica and the Andes in classical times, including the Maya, Moche, Tiwanaku, Teotihuacan, and Monte Alban. The Maya forged a particularly enduring society based on competing city-states, developed a writing system, and understood much about astronomy and mathematics. The Moche on the Peruvian coast and Tiwanaku in the highlands formed empires. In Mesoamerica, Teotihuacan became the greatest city in the Americas and a major trading hub. In North America many peoples adopted farming. Southwestern peoples built permanent towns, and some societies in eastern North America took up mound building. In the Pacific, Australian Aborigines adapted well to their harsh environment, flourishing for millennia from hunting and gathering. And various Austronesian peoples, particularly the Polynesians, made spectacular migrations into the vast Pacific Ocean by using remarkable seagoing technologies and adapting to diverse island environments.

Online Study Center **Improve Your Grade** Flashcards

Key Terms

Meroitic	griots
Coptic Church	Nilotes
Aksum	Maya
Geez	Teotihuacan
Ghana	Moche
Mande	dreamtime

Suggested Reading

Books

Adams, Richard E. W. *Ancient Civilizations of the New World.* Boulder: Westview, 1997. Brief survey of Mesoamerican and South American societies before 1500 C.E.

Coe, Michael. *The Maya.* 7th ed. London and New York: Thames and Hudson, 2005. The standard overview of Maya history.

Connah, Graham. *African Civilization: An Archaeological Perspective,* 2nd ed. Cambridge: Cambridge University Press, 2001. An overview of early African societies, emphasizing the rise of cities and states.

Ehret, Christopher. *An African Classical Age: Eastern and Southern Africa in World History, 1000 B.C. to A.D. 400.* Charlottesville: University Press of Virginia, 1998. A pathbreaking study rethinking the role of classical Africa in world history.

Fagan, Brian M. *Kingdoms of Gold, Kingdoms of Jade: The Americas Before Columbus.* London and New York: Thames and Hudson, 1991. A nicely illustrated and readable introduction to the premodern American societies.

Fischer, Steven Roger. *A History of the Pacific Islands.* New York: Palgrave, 2002. Readable introduction to Pacific societies and history.

Kehoe, Alice Beck. *America Before the European Invasions.* New York: Longman, 2002. A recent overview of the North American peoples and history before 1600 C.E.

Kirch, Patrick. *On the Road of the Winds: An Archaeological History of the Pacific Islands.* Berkeley: University of California Press, 2000. The most recent and comprehensive study of the Austronesians in the Pacific.

Knight, Alan. *Mexico: From the Beginning to the Spanish Conquest*. New York: Cambridge University Press, 2002. An introduction to Mesoamerican societies.

Mann, Charles C. *1491: New Revelations of the Americas Before Columbus*. New York: Alfred A. Knopf, 2005. A readable summary of recent scholarship on the American societies.

Newman, James L. *The Peopling of Africa: A Geographic Interpretation*. New Haven, Conn.: Yale University Press, 1995. An excellent summary of what we know about the early history and migrations of Africa's people.

Nile, Richard, and Christian Clark. *Cultural Atlas of Australia, New Zealand and the South Pacific*. New York: Facts on File, 1996. A well-written overview with much on early histories and cultures.

Phillipson, David W. *African Archaeology*. 3rd ed. Cambridge: Cambridge University Press, 2005. A general study of the archaeology of premodern Africa, from prehistory into the second millennium of the Common Era.

Shillington, Kevin. *History of Africa*, revised 2nd ed. New York: Palgrave Macmillan, 2005. A recent survey text.

Welsby, Derek A. *The Kingdom of Kush: The Napatan and Meroitic Empires*. Princeton: Markus Wiener, 1996. A well-illustrated and up-to-date survey of Kushite society.

Whitlock, Ralph. *Everyday Life of the Maya*. Reprint of 1976 edition. New York: Dorset Press, 1987. Although somewhat dated, this remains an excellent introduction to Maya life.

Websites

About Archaeology
(http://archaeology.about.com/library).   About.com offers many essays and links relevant to early Africa and the Americas.

Africa South of the Sahara
(http://www-sul.stanford.edu/depts/ssrg/africa/guide.html). Useful collection of links from Stanford University.

African Timelines
(http://www.cocc.edu/cagatucci/classes/hum211/timelines/htimeline.htm).   Has many links to specific periods and cultures as well as essays on controversial topics.

Ancient Mesoamerican Civilizations
(www.angelfire.com/ca/humanorigins).   Links and information about the premodern societies.

Austronesian and Other Indo-Pacific Topics
(http://w3.rz-berlin.mpg.de/~wm/wm3.html).   A useful collection of sources on Austronesian languages and cultures, operated by Germany-based scholars.

History and Cultures of Africa
(http://www.columbia.edu/cu/lweb/indiv/africa/cuvl/cult.html). Extensive links provided by Columbia University.

Internet African History Sourcebook
(http://www.fordham.edu/halsall/africa/africasbook.html). This site, maintained at Fordham University, contains much useful information and documentary material on African societies.

Mystery of the Maya
(http://www.civilization.ca/civil/maya/nminteng.html). Canadian site offering useful essays on various aspects of Mayan history and society.

Classical Blossomings in World History, 600 B.C.E.–600 C.E.

In the second century B.C.E. a Greek historian, Polybius, recognized the expanding horizons of his time and concluded that "the world's history has been a series of unrelated episodes, but from now on history becomes an organic whole. The affairs of Europe and Africa are connected with those of Asia and all events bear a relationship and contribute to a single end."[1] In his perception of increasing connections across cultures, Polybius identified a crucial transition. During the Classical Era a vast exchange of ideas, cultures, and products grew in the Afro-Eurasian zone. For example, the Chinese sent missions into western Asia, where they met Persians and Greeks. Alexander the Great, born on the northern fringes of Greece, conquered Egypt, and later looked out on the Indus River in India, dreaming of moving on to the Ganges and even further.

The commercial exchanges that were carried out along the trade routes represented the first glimmerings of a world economy centered on Asia. Greek merchants traveled as far as south India, and one, based in the Egyptian city of Alexandria, wrote a manual describing the ports and listing the products traded in East Africa and South Asia. Warehouses in the south Indian port of Pondicherry were filled with caskets of Roman wine. Goods from Persia and Rome reached Funan in Southeast Asia, while the statue of an Indian goddess was carried to the Italian city of Pompeii. Romans craved Chinese silk, Arabian incense, and Indian spices. Merchants near Kabul, in today's Afghanistan, dealt in Greek glass, Egyptian pots, Chinese lacquer ware, and Hindu carvings.

Thanks in part to greater interregional communication over widening networks of exchange, the Classical Era was a period of flowerings of many kinds. Creative philosophies established new value systems or reinforced existing ones in the Mediterranean world and Asia. Between 350 B.C.E. and 200 C.E. the Afro-Eurasian world was also transformed by large regional empires. In the wake of these empires, universal religions such as Buddhism and Christianity crossed cultural boundaries, becoming permanent fixtures of world history. Classical peoples also refined their economic and social patterns. In this process, each society, while having its own dynamics, was also altered by contact with others.

THE AXIAL AGE OF PHILOSOPHICAL SPECULATION

Between around 600 and 400 B.C.E., several societies of Eurasia faced a remarkably similar set of crises. People in China, India, Persia, Israel, and Greece were all beset by chronic warfare, population movement, political disruption, and the breakdown of traditional values. Improved ironworking technology produced better tools but also more effective weapons. Political instability was common, as rival states competed with each other for power in China, India, the Middle East, and Greece.

These troubled conditions led to a climate of spiritual and intellectual restlessness, provoking a questioning of the old order. Because of the many influential and creative thinkers of this age, some scholars have called this an "axial period" or turning point, a crucial transition in history. This idea understates some crucial religious developments that occurred after 350 B.C.E., such as the reshaping of Hinduism, the division of Buddhism, and the rise of Christianity and Islam. Yet, the Axial Age produced enduring philosophical, religious, and scientific ideas that became the intellectual underpinning of many cultural traditions and fostered new ways of thinking.

Axial Age Thinkers

Many of the greatest thinkers in history were near-contemporaries; that is, they lived at roughly the same time, between 600 and 350 B.C.E. Laozi (credited by tradition as the inspiration for Daoism) and Confucius in China lived and taught in the sixth century around the same time as Buddha and Mahavira (the founder of the Jain faith) in India and the Greek thinkers Thales and Heraclitus. Other major Axial Age thinkers included the Hebrew prophets Jeremiah, Ezekiel, and the second Isaiah, as well as Socrates, Plato, and Aristotle in Greece. Although he may have lived much earlier, the teachings of the Persian Zoroaster also became prominent in this era. Many people today are still influenced by these thinkers: Laozi's advice to live in accordance with nature, the Confucian dream of an ordered society based on proper ethical conduct, the Buddha's rules for ending human suffering, Mahavira's belief in absolute nonviolence, the prophetic Hebrew vision of universal justice, the Greek emphasis on rational analysis, and the Zoroastrian notion of opposing forces of darkness and light still have meaning.

Some of these men were not only thinkers but also teachers. To pass along their ideas, leading intellectuals such as Confucius and Plato took on students. Confucius reflected the passion for education: "I am not someone who was born wise. I am someone who tries to learn [from the ancients]."[2] It was a time of exciting exchanges, as mystics and teachers traveled through India, dozens of philosophers spread their ideas in China, and students of Socrates competed with followers of the Stoics in the schools of Athens.

Causes and Characteristics of Axial Age Thought

In trying to identify the causes of the Axial Age, historians point to social and political instability, the effects of commercial exchanges along far-flung trade networks, economies productive enough to support a class of thinkers, and the first glimmerings of the belief that individuals have intrinsic worth apart from their role in society. Other possible causes include the increase in cultural exchanges among Afro-Asian peoples with the spread of writing, iron tools and vehicles, and

Confucius and Laozi in Conversation   This picture engraved on a stone tablet in an old Confucian temple shows Confucius visiting Laozi in the city of Loyang and amiably discussing with him views on ritual and music.   From Carl Crow, Master Kung: The Story of Confucius (New York and London: Harper and U Brothers Publishers, 1938)

improved boats. These inventions helped widen intellectual horizons and stimulated human intellect and imagination. Exactly where many of the great Axial Age ideas began, however, has led to controversy (see Historical Controversy: The Afrocentric Challenge to Historians of Antiquity).

Whatever the causes, several themes became common to Axial Age thinkers. First, especially in China and Greece, thinkers questioned the accepted myths and gods and promoted a humanistic view of life, one more concerned with the social and natural order than the supernatural order. Second, most thinkers stressed moral conduct and values, a vision that often rejected the violent, selfish pursuit of material power they saw around them. Some, like the Buddha, Mahavira, and Laozi, were pacifists who denounced all violence, the Jains going to the extreme of preventing harm even to insects. Third, Confucius, the Hebrew prophets, and several Greeks were also among the first people to think about history and its lessons for societies. Fourth, while few of these thinkers favored social equality, many argued that rulers should govern with a sense of obligation to the powerless and less fortunate. Finally, all the Axial Age thinkers believed that the world could be improved, either by the actions of ethical individuals or by the creation of an ideal social order, or both. For example, Plato devised a model government led not by kings but by a special class of wise men.

But the Axial Age thinkers disagreed as to whether truth was absolute. Socrates and Plato, for example, argued for universal concepts, Plato writing that "those who see the absolute and eternal have real knowledge and not mere opinions." Yet, some Greeks and Chinese also explored the notion that truth was relative and dependent on circumstances. As one Chinese thinker wrote: "Monkeys prefer trees: so what habitat can be said to be absolutely right? Fish flee at the sight of women whom men deem lovely. Whose is the right taste absolutely?"[3] Philosophers still struggle with the question of universal or relative truth.

The Axial Age had not only philosophical and religious but also scientific and political consequences. Across Eurasia people raised fundamental questions about many phenomena and answered them by systematic investigation. Greek thinkers such as Aristotle, who pondered and classified everything from political systems to animals, influenced European and Middle Eastern science, and their ideas inspired new discoveries by Hellenistic, Roman and, later, Islamic scientists. At the other end of Eurasia, Chinese influenced by Confucianism and Daoism also created another rich scientific tradition. Indians became some of the classical world's greatest mathematicians and astronomers. Together, the classical Greeks, Chinese, Indians, and the ancient Mesopotamians and Egyptians built the foundations for modern science. Axial Age ideas also became the basis for new political ideologies. For example, in China, Confucianism mixed with Legalism provided the ideas for building stronger states, while Romans rose to power using modified Greek ideas of democracy. As a result of strengthening state institutions and leaders, in China, India, Persia, and Greece the Axial Age ended in mighty empires that reflected a new order of technological and organizational planning.

THE AGE OF REGIONAL EMPIRES

The empires that arose in much of Eurasia during or at the end of the Axial Age were greater in size and impact than those that had flourished in ancient times. The Persian Empire set the

Expanding Horizons: Encounters and Transformations in the Intermediate Era, ca. 600–1500

By 600 C.E. most of the great classical Eastern Hemisphere empires and states, such as Rome, Han China, Gupta India, and Kush, were only memories. The classical American societies, such as the Maya, were to flourish a few centuries longer, only to collapse. Yet vigorous new societies were emerging. Even while some classical patterns hung on or were modified to suit new needs, the Afro-Eurasian zone was in transition. During this era many societies developed a more cosmopolitan outlook. New trade networks emerged and old ones were revitalized. Though characterized by long periods of conflict, this era also saw worldwide innovations.

Historians disagree as to what this era should be called. Borrowing from European history, scholars often refer to the medieval period, a "middle ages" stretching from around 600 to 1500. The term *medieval* suggests societies with relatively weak governments, rigid social orders, and one dominating religion, a description that best fits Europe in this era and perhaps Japan and parts of India. However, the term has little relevance for China, the Islamic states, and most of Africa, Southeast Asia, and the Americas. *Intermediate Era* is a more neutral term to describe this creative transitional period, which linked the Classical Era, when contacts between distant societies were still limited, with the rise of global connections that marked the centuries after 1500.

The Intermediate Era experienced dramatic transformations of societies. The explosive rise of Islam from a local faith in Arabia in the early 600s to a hemispheric-wide religion by 1400 was one of the main transitions. The resurgence of China as a political, economic, and cultural force was another. Also during this time, Buddhism became a major influence in the eastern half of Eurasia, while Christianity became Europe's dominant faith. Mighty empires arose in Africa, Southeast Asia, and the Americas.

These nine centuries also differed from the preceding Classical Era by virtue of the increasing contacts between peoples. Contacts became more frequent and substantial beginning around 600. New interregional communications took place across Afro-Eurasia, including trade, cultural exchange, and religious links. As a result, a maritime trading network connected China and Southeast Asia

Sape Ivory Saltholder Africans had traded and carved ivory since ancient times. This magnificent ivory carving, made, probably in the fifteenth century, by an artist of the Sape people, who lived in what is today Sierra Leone in West Africa, was used to store salt. The carving reflected artistic influence brought to the region by the earliest Portuguese explorers and traders. (Courtesy, Museo Prehistorico et Etnografico, Rome) through India and the Persian Gulf to East Africa and the Mediterranean. A growing caravan trade across the Sahara Desert brought West Africa and the Mediterranean closer together. The spread of religions also reshaped societies. For example, Arab culture expanded with Islam. The cosmopolitan Islamic world, stretching from Morocco to Indonesia, enjoyed much cultural diversity but also shared many beliefs and practices. In the Western Hemisphere, Mesoamerican cultural and agricultural influences spread deep into North and Central America.

The era was also marked by conflicts that changed societies. Spurring the rise of interregional encounters was the expansion of several Central Asian peoples. Turkish migrations and conquests in western Asia occurred throughout the period. In the thirteenth century the Mongols conquered the largest land empire in world history, stretching from Korea and China westward to Russia and eastern Europe, a momentous achievement with major consequences. For example, as a result, East Asian technology flowed along the trade routes to Europe. However, the Mongol period also witnessed the spread along these same trade routes of a catastrophic plague, known as the Black Death, that devastated societies all across Eurasia and North Africa, killing countless millions of Chinese, Persians, Arabs, and Europeans.

The Intermediate years also saw major innovations such as economic growth, technological change, the rise of new states, and maritime exploration. China became the world's most commercialized and industrialized society, often exercising influence far from its borders. In the 1400s Chinese maritime expeditions reached East Africa and the Persian Gulf. Islamic states were also dynamic, and Muslim scholars and artisans made numerous contributions to the world. West African kingdoms, East African coastal cities, and Southeast Asian states were closely tied to world trade. In the Americas, the Aztec and Inca Empires had arisen on the foundations of earlier societies. Europeans made key intellectual and technological discoveries, and they also benefited when the expansion of Islam and the Mongols introduced to Europe Asian-derived ideas, plants, and tools. In the 1400s, making good use of naval technology and weaponry from all over Eurasia and energized by economic growth and religious fervor, Europeans began voyages of discovery that set the stage for connecting the entire world after 1500.

NORTH AND CENTRAL AMERICA
The Maya city-states flourished for centuries until the cities were abandoned. The Toltecs dominated central Mexico for two hundred years. In the 1400s the Aztecs conquered a large empire in Mexico and built a huge capital city. North of Mexico, societies such as the Anasazi lived in towns and farmed in the desert for centuries. To the east the Mississippian peoples built mounds and a grand city while trading over a vast area. Farming villages also dotted the east coast.

SOUTH AMERICA
For most of the era Tiwanaku, in the Andes, and the Chimu Empire, based on the Peruvian coast, were the dominant powers in western South America. In the 1400s the Incas conquered most of the region, creating the largest empire in the history of the Americas. Skilled farmers, the Incas used a powerful but paternalistic state to rule millions of people.

EUROPE

In western Europe a rigid society, dominated by a powerful Christian church, slowly emerged, reaching its zenith around 1000 C.E. Dozens of small rival states fought each other. Urban and commercial growth, technological innovation, and the Black Death eventually undermined feudalism and church power, and political, intellectual, artistic, and religious change began reshaping western Europe in the 1400s. At the same time, imported Chinese and Arab naval and military technology helped spur maritime explorations. Meanwhile, Byzantium struggled to hold its eastern Mediterranean empire but also spread its culture to the Russians.

WESTERN ASIA

The rise of Islam in Arabia in the 600s transformed the region. Arab Muslim armies conquered much of western Asia, and most of the region's peoples eventually embraced Islam. Islam also spread west through North Africa and into Spain, as well as east to India, Central Asia, and Indonesia, linking western Asians with a vast Islamic community. Islam divided into rival Sunni and Shi'a schools. Muslim scholars fostered science and literature, and major Islamic states, especially the Abbasid Empire, dominated the region. Eventually the Ottoman Turks formed the most powerful western Asian state, conquering Byzantium.

EASTERN ASIA

China stood out for its influence and creativity. During the Tang and Song dynasties, China's economy grew rapidly and science flourished, attracting merchants and scholars from many countries. At the same time, Chinese cultural influences spread to neighboring Korea, Japan, and Vietnam. Under Mongol rule, China remained open to the world, but it later turned inward. Meanwhile, Japanese and Koreans combined Chinese influences, such as Buddhism, with their own traditions.

ARCTIC OCEAN

RUSSIA

ENGLAND

EUROPE

FRANCE

Danube

SPAIN

BYZANTIUM

OTTOMAN EMPIRE

ABBASIDS (IRAQ)

MOROCCO

EGYPT

Nile

ARABIA

MALI

Niger R.

AFRICA

MONGOLS (MONGOLIA)

ASIA

JAPAN

HIMALAYAS

CHINA

Ganges R.

INDIA

PAGAN

Mekong R.

VIETNAM

ANGKOR

BENIN

Congo R.

KONGO

SWAHILI

INDIAN OCEAN

ATLANTIC OCEAN

ZIMBABWE

INDONESIA

AUSTRALIA

AFRICA

Islam swept across North Africa, becoming the dominant religion north of the Sahara. It also reshaped societies as it spread into West Africa and East Africa. Sub-Saharan African peoples formed large empires, such as Mali, and flourishing states, such as Benin, Kongo, and Zimbabwe. West African kingdoms and East African coastal cities were closely tied to world trade. In the 1400s the Portuguese explored the West African coast and disrupted African states.

SOUTHERN ASIA AND OCEANIA

Although politically fragmented into diverse rival states, India remained a major commercial and manufacturing center. Muslims from West and Central Asia conquered parts of north India, spreading Islam there. In response, Hinduism became reinvigorated. Southeast Asians flourished from farming and maritime trade, and major kingdoms, notably Angkor and Pagan, emerged. Southeast Asians imported ideas from India, China, and the Middle East, and many people adopted Theravada Buddhism or Islam. Maritime trade, especially the export of spices, and the spread of Islam and Buddhism linked Southeast Asia to the wider Afro-Eurasian world. Meanwhile, Polynesians settled the last uninhabited Pacific islands, including Hawaii and New Zealand.

CHAPTER 10

The Rise, Power, and Connections of the Islamic World, 600–1500

Online Study Center

This icon will direct you to interactive activities and study materials on the website: college.hmco.com/pic/lockard1e

Pilgrimage Caravan Every year caravans of Muslim pilgrims converged on Islam's holiest city, Mecca, in Arabia. This painting shows such a caravan led by a band. Pilgrims came from as far away as Morocco and Spain in the west and Indonesia and China in the east. (Bibliotheque nationale de France)

Then came Islam. All institutions underwent change. It distinguished [believers] from other nations and ennobled them. Islam became firmly established and securely rooted. Far-off nations accepted Islam.

IBN KHALDUN, FOURTEENTH-CENTURY ARAB HISTORIAN[1]

In 1382 the author of these words on history, the fifty-year-old Arab scholar Abd al-Rahman Ibn Khaldun (AHB-d al-ruh-MAHN ib-uhn kal-DOON), left his longtime home in Tunis in North Africa and moved east to Egypt. He was already a well-traveled man and renowned as a thinker, and his work, like his life, reflected the expansive cosmopolitan nature of Islamic society, which crossed many geographical and cultural borders. After seven years of research and writing he had recently completed his greatest work, a monumental history of the world known to educated Muslims. While writing this work, he said, ideas and words poured into his head like cream into a churn. The book was the first attempt by a historian anywhere to discover and explain the changes in societies over time, especially those shaped by Islam. Rational, analytical, and encyclopedic in coverage, it also offered a philosophy of history rooted in the scientific method.

Ibn Khaldun came from an Islamic family with ancient roots in Arabia that had later settled in Spain. Several generations later they relocated across the Mediterranean to Tunis. After growing up there, Ibn Khaldun visited and worked in various cities of North Africa and Spain. He served diverse rulers as a jurist, adviser, or diplomat. Now he was settling finally in Cairo (KYE-roh), Egypt, a city he praised as the "metropolis of the world, garden of the universe, meeting-place of nations, ant hill of peoples, high place of Islam, seat of power."[2] Cairo remained his home for the rest of his life as he served as a judge and a teacher, reading, writing voluminously, and traveling with high Egyptian officials to Palestine, Syria, and Arabia. Six centuries after his family left Arabia for the western Mediterranean, he could visit their ancestral homeland and feel at home. The Islamic world he chronicled enjoyed an extraordinary unity of time and space.

The rise of Islam that produced Ibn Khaldun and his world was a major historical turning point that led to widespread social, cultural, and political changes over the centuries. The Islamic religion originated in seventh-century Arabia and eventually spread across several continents. Today Islam is, after Christianity, the largest religion in the world, embraced by about one-fifth of the world's population. The impact of Islam on a multitude of societies and networks was complex and varied. A dynamic faith, Islam adapted to new cultures while remaining close to its founding ideals. It also had extensive dialogue with, and often tolerance toward, other traditions, establishing contacts that enriched both sides. For nearly a thousand years Islamic peoples greatly influenced or dominated much of the Eastern Hemisphere. Muslim thinkers salvaged or developed major portions of the science and mathematics that formed the basis for later industrial society, and Muslim sailors and merchants opened or extended networks that spread goods, technologies, and ideas throughout Afro-Eurasia.

FOCUS QUESTIONS

1. How did Islam arise?
2. How did Islam shape a distinctive new society from diverse sources?
3. What were the major achievements of the Islamic states and empires?
4. What were the major concerns of Muslim thinkers and writers?
5. Why do historians speak of Islam as a hemispheric culture?

Early Islam: The Origins of a Continuous Tradition

How did Islam arise?

The Islamic religion was founded in the seventh century in the Arabian peninsula, a land inhabited mainly by nomads who lived on the fringes of more powerful societies. A fervently monotheistic faith influenced by Jewish and Christian thought, Islam was inspired by the visions of a single influential man, Muhammad (moo-HAM-mad). His followers considered him to be the last of God's prophets. Islam quickly developed explosive energies that propelled it from a small Arab sect into the dominant faith of many millions of people from one end of the Eastern Hemisphere to the other.

The Middle Eastern Sources of Islam

Islam developed in a part of the Middle East known as Arabia, which occupies a peninsula in southwestern Asia. Much of the Middle East, including Arabia, is a harsh, parched land that provides a challenging environment for human settlement. Living by farming or herding, the region's peoples tamed camels, horses, donkeys, and cattle to lighten the agricultural labors or help merchants cross the deserts.

In Muhammad's day the Middle East was a region of great cultural diversity, a major factor in the rise of Islam. The peoples of Egypt, Mesopotamia, and Achaemenid Persia had produced flourishing societies in ancient times. Later the Hellenistic Greeks had conquered much of western Asia and Egypt, and later still the Byzantine Empire filled the vacuum left by the collapse of Roman control in western Asia and North Africa. Between 611 and 619 Sassanian Persia conquered Syria, Palestine, and Egypt, and during the sixth century the

Persians, Byzantines, and Ethiopians all interfered in Arabian politics. By the end of the Classical Era many Middle Eastern people were Christians, including sects such as the Monophysites (among them the Copts of Egypt) and Nestorians, which were considered heretical by orthodox Christians. These diverse traditions eventually influenced Islam.

Islam was also the product of a distinctive Arab culture and society. The Arabs, a Semitic people, occupied the desolate Arabian peninsula, where life was sustained by scattered oases and a few areas of fertile highlands. Survival in a sparsely populated environment depended on cooperation within small groups of related peoples divided into clans and tribes. Each tribe was usually governed by a council of senior males, who selected a supreme elder respected for his generosity and bravery. Some Arabs, like the Nabataeans, became traders who ranged widely in the Middle East, and Arab trading cities and farmers flourished in Yemen in the south. But many Arab tribes were tent-dwelling nomadic pastoralists, known as **Bedouins** (BED-uh-wuhnz), who wandered in search of oases and grazing lands. Some resorted at times to raiding trade caravans.

Arab culture and literature reflected the nomadic existence of many Arabs. A pre-Muslim Arab poet wrote: "Ah, but when grief assails me, straightway I ride it off mounted on my swift, lean-flanked camel, night and day racing."[3] Poetry was so popular that, one month a year, raids and battles were halted so that poets could gather and compete. The Arab romantic poetry tradition may have been taken to Europe centuries later by Christian crusaders, and there it may have influenced the chivalric love songs of medieval European performers known as troubadours.

Arabia was saturated with ideas from diverse religious traditions, including Judaism, Christianity, and Zoroastrianism. Like their Hebrew neighbors, the Arabs believed that they were

---

Bedouins Tent-dwelling nomadic Arab pastoralists who wandered in search of oases, grazing lands, or trade caravans to raid.

CHRONOLOGY

	Middle East	Europe	Central Asia
600	**622** Hijra of Muhammad to Medina **634–651** Arab conquests in Middle East **632–661** Rashidun Caliphate **661–750** Umayyad Caliphate		
700	**750–1258** Abbasid Caliphate	**711–1492** Muslim states in Spain	**705–715** Islamic Conquests
1000		**1096–1272** Christian Crusades in Middle East	
1200			**1218–1360** Mongol conquests in Central and western Asia
1300		**1300–1923** Ottoman Empire	**1369–1405** Reign of Tamerlane

descended from Abraham, but through his son Ishmael, not Issac, as the Hebrews claimed to be. While some Arabs had adopted Judaism or Christianity, and some practiced a monotheism similar to that of the ancient Hebrews, most were polytheistic, believing in many gods, goddesses, and spirits. Some tribes believed that the chief god was housed in a huge sacred cube-shaped stone, known as the **Ka'ba** (KAH-buh), in Mecca (MEK-uh), a bustling trading city in central Arabia near the Red Sea to which people made annual pilgrimages. Meccan merchants obtained hides, leather goods, spices, and perfumes in Yemen and exchanged them in Syria for textiles, olive oil, and weapons.

The Prophet Muhammad and His Revelations

The founder of Islam was Muhammad Ibn Abdullah (ca. 570–632). Historians debate the origins of all the major religions, and Islam is no exception. Just as historians disagree with each other about the accuracy of the historical accounts contained in the Hebrew Bible and the Christian gospels, and lack adequate sources to trace fully the lives of the Buddha and Confucius, there is controversy, especially among non-Muslim scholars, concerning Muhammad's life, how much Islamic thought arose out of older ideas, and the factors that shaped the expansion of the Arabs and Islam. The sources available for understanding early Judaism, Christianity, and Islam were compiled decades, sometimes centuries, after the events described,

and can be interpreted by historians in different ways, fostering disagreement.

According to the traditional accounts by both Muslim and Western historians, Muhammad was a member of the Hashimite (HASH-uh-mite) clan of the prosperous mercantile Quraysh (KUR-aysh) tribe of Mecca (see Chronology: The Islamic World, 570–1220). His father died before his birth and his mother died when he was six, so he was raised by an uncle. After becoming a merchant, Muhammad began shipping goods for a wealthy and prominent twice-widowed older woman, Khadija (kah-DEE-juh), who had capitalized on the opportunities that city life sometimes gave ambitious women. They soon married. Although Muhammad's business operating trade caravans flourished, he came to believe that Meccan merchants had become greedy and materialistic, contrary to Arab traditions of generosity.

In seeking answers to his concerns, Muhammad often retreated to meditate in the barren mountains around Mecca. His prophetic career began in 610 when he had a series of visions in the mountains in which he believed God revealed the secrets of existence. He reported that he was visited by an angel, who brought the command from God to "recite in the name of your lord who created the human."[4] Alarmed, he consulted one of his wife's cousins, a monotheist who encouraged him to accept the visions he received as revelations, or messages, from God. Fearing that he was possessed by demons, Muhammad often agonized about the visions, once even reaching a state of suicidal despair. The spiritual experiences continued over the next twenty-three years.

However, Muhammad eventually came to accept the authenticity of the messages, largely because of the support given

Ka'ba A huge sacred cube-shaped stone in the city of Mecca to which people made annual pilgrimages.

by his wife Khadija, his closest spiritual adviser: "She believed in me when no one else did. She considered me to be truthful when the people called me a liar. She helped me with her fortune when the people had left me nothing."[5] Once convinced of the messages' truth, Muhammad began preaching the new

faith of *Islam* ("submission to God's will") to a few followers. The early believers, or *Muslims* (MUZ-limz) ("those who had submitted to God's will"), were mostly drawn from among his middle-class friends and relatives and a few other Meccans, some from lower-class backgrounds. Gradually some rich members of the Quraysh tribe also joined.

In the 650s, several decades after Muhammad's death, his followers compiled his revelations into an official version, the **Quran** (kuh-RAHN), meaning "Recitation." The Quran, beloved by Muslims for its beautiful poetic verses, became Islam's holiest book, to believers the inspired word of God. A second book revered by many Muslims as a source of belief, the **Hadith** (hah-DEETH), meaning "narrative," compiled by Muslim scholars into an official version during the ninth and tenth centuries, collected the remembered words and deeds of Muhammad himself. A source of religious guidance and law, the Hadith helped explain the principles of the Quran.

Muhammad insisted that he was human, not divine, and his followers accepted him as a prophet rather than as a manifestation of God. To believers, Muhammad's visions were the last of several occasions in history during which God spoke to prophets, communicating through them from the divine to the human realm. The earlier prophets were Adam, Abraham, Moses, and Jesus, and Muhammad was considered the final voice superseding the others (see Witness to the Past: The Holy Book, God, and the Prophet in the Quran).

Muhammad's faith mixed older traditions with new understandings. Both Jews and Christians lived in Mecca, and many of the principal ideas of Islam clearly resemble some Judeo-Christian traditions. Like these traditions, Muhammad's views were strictly monotheistic. All other gods were put aside, and believers were assured of an afterlife. In contrast to the social customs dominant in Arabia at the time of Muhammad, Islam guaranteed women certain rights formerly denied them and promoted the equality of all believers. Muhammad also advocated sharing all wealth, living simply, and creating a spirit of unity. In Islam, Muhammad established principles of equality and justice.

Emigration and Triumph

Muhammad soon faced challenges that led him to leave Mecca. His ideas earned him some enemies among the Quraysh and divided the tribe, and the Mecca leaders rejected Muhammad's views and saw him and his followers as a threat to their position. He and his allies were harassed, and some enemies even plotted his murder. In 619 Khadija died, followed by the uncle who raised him, an influential tribal chief. The loss of his two most powerful supporters left Muhammad in despair. Meanwhile, the nearby city of Medina became engulfed in strife. To

CHRONOLOGY	
The Islamic World, 570–1220	
ca. 570	Birth of Muhammad in Mecca
622	Hijra of Muhammad and followers to Medina
632	Death of Muhammad; Abu Bakr becomes first caliph
634	Muslim conquests begin
632–661	Rashidun Caliphate
636–637	Arab military victories over Byzantine and Sassanian forces
642	Arab conquest of Egypt
651	Completion of Arab conquest of Persia
661	Murder of Ali and establishment of Umayyad dynasty in Damascus
705–715	Arab conquests of Afghanistan and Central Asia
711–720	Arab conquest of Spain
732	European defeat of Arabs at Battle of Tours
750	Abbasid defeat of Umayyads and new caliphate
756–1030	Umayyad dynasty in Spain
825–900	Arab conquest of Sicily
969–1171	Fatimid dynasty in Egypt and neighboring areas
1061–1091	Norman conquest of Sicily from Arabs
1071	Beginning of Seljuk Turk conquest of Anatolia
1085	Spanish Christian seizure of Umayyad capital
1095–1272	Christian Crusades in western Asia and North Africa
1171–1193	Reign of Saladin in Egypt
1220	Beginning of Mongol conquests in Muslim Central Asia

Quran ("Recitation") Islam's holiest book; contains the official version of Muhammad's revelations, and to believers is the inspired word of God.

Hadith ("narrative") The remembered words and deeds of Muhammad, revered by many Muslims as a source of belief.

Social Life and Gender Relations

Most Muslims were settled farmers, craftsmen, and traders. As Islamic culture expanded and matured, the social structure became more complex and marked by clear ethnic, tribal, class-occupational, religious, and gender divisions, especially in the Middle East. Arabs generally had a higher social status than Turkish, Berber, African, and other converts. The descendants of the Prophet and members of the Hashimite clan to which he belonged held an especially honored status. Even in modern times people who can trace, or claim to trace, their ancestry to Muhammad and his family enjoy special influence in many Islamic societies around the world. Many Arabs were also members of tribes, such as Muhammad's Quraysh tribe. In addition, because the first Muslims were merchants, the religion had a special appeal for people in the commercial sector, providing spiritual sanction of their quest for wealth. This wealth could finance their pilgrimage to Mecca and also help the poor through almsgiving. Merchants and artisans established guilds that were sometimes affiliated with a particular sect or Sufi order.

Slavery was common in Islamic societies. Slaves were bureaucrats and soldiers, workers in businesses and factories, household servants and concubines, musicians, and plantation laborers. One Abbasid caliph kept 11,000 slaves in his palace. Islamic law encouraged owners to treat slaves with consideration, and many slaves were eventually freed. Many slaves were war captives and children purchased from poor families, but Christian European states like Byzantium and Venice also sold slaves to Muslims. For over a dozen centuries, but especially after 1200, perhaps 10 to 15 million African slaves were brought to the Middle East across the Sahara or up the East African coast by an Arab-dominated slave trade. African slave soldiers were common in Egypt, Persia, Iraq, Oman (oh-MAHN) in eastern Arabia, and Yemen.

The Islamic religion imposed some divisions in society. For example, Christian and Jewish communities did not always have the same rights as Muslims. They also paid higher taxes and were prohibited from owning weapons, and so were exempt from military duty. However, these non-Muslim communities did enjoy some protection under the law. Although the level of that protection varied in different societies and under different rulers, on the whole these communities were allowed to follow their own laws, customs, and beliefs and to maintain their own religious institutions.

Families were at the heart of the social system. Marriages were arranged, with the goal of cementing social or perhaps business ties between two families. As elsewhere in the world at the time, people assumed that love followed matrimony rather than the reverse. Although law allowed men to have up to four wives at a time, this situation remained fairly rare and largely restricted to the rich and powerful. Many poor men never married at all because they could not afford the large bridal gifts expected. While divorce was theoretically easy for men, marriage contracts sometimes discouraged divorce by specifying that men pay a large gift to the wife upon divorce. Parents

Persian Women at a Picnic This miniature from sixteenth-century Persia shows women preparing a picnic. The ability of women to venture away from home varied widely depending on social class and regional traditions. (Bodleian Library, Oxford University, MS Elliot 189)

expected children to obey and respect them, even after they became adults. Both women and men in a family entertained their friends at home. These gatherings, which were usually segregated by gender, often involved poetry recitations, musical performances, or Quran readings. Picnics were also popular family activities. Islamic law harshly punished homosexuality; yet, homosexual relationships were not uncommon, and same-sex love was often reflected in poetry and literature, most notably in Muslim Spain. European visitors were often shocked at the tolerant attitudes of Arabs, Persians, and Turks toward homosexual romantic relationships.

The status of women in Islamic society has been subject to debate by both Western and Islamic observers in modern times, and by Muslim thinkers for centuries. For example, the philosopher Ibn Rushd (IB-uhn RUSHED) (1126–1198), known in the West as Averroes (uh-VER-uh-WEEZ), attacked restrictions on women as an economic burden, arguing that "the ability of women is not known, because they are merely used for procreation [and] child-rearing."[14] Although the Quran recognized certain rights of women, prohibited female infanticide, and limited the number of wives men could have, it also accorded women only half the inheritance of men and gave women less standing in courts of law. Both Muslim and non-Muslim observers have criticized the many restrictions on women as institutionalizing their social inferiority. Many Muslim men and women have contended that these restrictions liberate women from insecurity and male harassment. Scholars have also disagreed over whether restrictions such as veiling and seclusion were based on Quranic mandates or on patriarchal pre-Islamic Arab, Middle Eastern, and Byzantine customs. Some Muslim communities in the Middle East, and many outside the region, never adopted these practices.

Women played diverse roles in Muslim societies. Muhammad's wives enjoyed great political influence. Some of the wives of Abbasid caliphs also played political roles, albeit mostly behind the scenes. For instance, Khayzuran, noted for her compassion and generosity, rose from a simple Yemenite slave girl to become the great love and wife of the Caliph Mahdi, dominating his harem, investing in land reclamation and charitable works, and giving strong support to her husband. On his death, she helped smooth the transition to the rulership of her son, Harun al-Rashid. During Abbasid times some elite women, while excluded from public life, enjoyed considerable power behind the scenes, and some exceptional women circumvented restrictions. For example, Umm Hani (also known as Mariam) in fifteenth-century Cairo studied law and religion with many famous teachers, wrote poetry, owned a large textile workshop, and became a renowned teacher and scholar of the Hadith. She also had seven children by two husbands and made thirteen pilgrimages to Mecca. While formal education for girls in the Middle East was generally limited, women monopolized certain occupations such as spinning and weaving, and they also worked in the fields or in some domestic industries beside men. And in some Muslim societies, particularly in sub-Saharan Africa and Southeast Asia, women often maintained their relative independence and were free to dress as they liked, socialize outside the home, and earn money. Turks and Mongols also seem to have been more liberal on gender issues than Arabs and Persians. In short, patterns of gender relations varied considerably.

Pen and Brush: Writing and the Visual Arts

Although Islamic societies became identified with literacy and literature, writing derived from pre-Islamic roots. The Arabic alphabet originated in South Arabia long before Muhammad's time. In Mecca the script had been used chiefly by merchants to keep their books. But Islam enhanced the script further by emphasizing literacy. The Quran stated: "Read, and thy Lord is most generous, Who taught with the pen, Taught man what he knew not."[15] Muslims adopted the Arab poetic tradition but modified romantic ideas into praise not for a lover but for the Prophet and Allah. Islamic culture also developed a written and oral prose literature, including tales of Alexander the Great.

One of the greatest writers of Abbasid times, also an astronomer and mathematician, was the Persian Omar Khayyam (OH-MAHR key-YAHM). In his famous poem *Rubaiyat* (ROO-bee-AHT), he noted the fleeting nature of life: "O, come with old Khayyam, and leave the Wise, to talk; one thing is certain, that Life flies; one thing is certain, and the rest is Lies; the flower that once has blown forever dies." This led him to regret never knowing the purpose of existence:

> *Ah, make the most of what ye yet may spend, Before we too into the Dust descend; Dust unto Dust, and under Dust to lie, [without] Wine, Song, Singer, and End! Into this Universe, and Why not knowing, Nor Whence, like Water willy-nilly flowing; And out of it, as Wind along the Waste, I know not Whither, wily-nilly blowing.*[16]

The most famous Sufi poet was the thirteenth-century Persian Jalal al-Din Rumi (ja-LAL al-DIN ROO-mee). Born in what is today Afghanistan, as a youth he lived in Central Asia and Anatolia, which reflected Islam's wide reach. Al-Din Rumi blended liberal spirituality with humor in writings about love, desire, and the human condition. His vision was optimistic, joyful, and ecumenical: "I am neither Christian, nor Jew, nor Zoroastrian, nor Muslim."[17] He often danced while reciting his poems to his disciples. At the beginning of the twenty-first century, over seven hundred years after his death, Rumi became the best-selling poet in the United States after his poems were translated into English.

Some Muslims emphasized the visual arts. For example, since Arabic is written in a flowing style, the artful writing of words, or **calligraphy** (kuh-LIG-ruh-fee), became a much admired art form. An elegant script offered not just a message but also decoration. Calligraphy appeared in manuscripts and also on the walls of public buildings. Islamic Persia, India, and Central Asia also fostered a tradition of painting, especially landscapes. In addition, Muslims produced world-class architecture, some of it monumental, that included lavishly decorated buildings such as the Taj Mahal in India. Some architecture, such as mosques with domes and towers, reflected Byzantine church influence. Muslims also produced ceramics, and then as now they were famed for weaving carpets and fabrics that were valued in many non-Muslim societies.

Science and Learning

During the Islamic golden age many creative thinkers emerged. Muslims borrowed, assimilated, and diffused Greek and Indian knowledge and were familiar with some Chinese technologies. By the seventh century certain classical and Hellenistic Greek

---

calligraphy The artful writing of words.

traditions of philosophy and science had been nearly forgotten in Europe, but they survived in the Middle East. Thanks to the mixing of ideas as cultures encountered each other, science and medicine flourished, and Muslims also made many contributions to mathematics and astronomy.

Science and Medicine   Many advances in science and medicine were made in the Islamic world as experts synthesized the learning of other societies with their own insights. Some knowledge was carried into the Middle East by Nestorian Christians, who taught Greek sciences under Abbasid sponsorship and helped make Baghdad a center of world learning. The Abbasid caliphs opened the House of Wisdom in Baghdad, a research institute staffed by scholars charged with translating Greek, Syrian, Sanskrit, and Persian works into Arabic. The works included books on philosophy, medicine, astronomy, and mathematics. Aristotle's writings were particularly influential. The institute also included schools, observatories, and a huge library. Other scientific centers arose in many Muslim lands, from Spain and Morocco to Samarkand in Central Asia. For example, in the tenth and eleventh centuries the Shi'ite Fatimids built the House of Knowledge in Cairo with a massive library holding 2 million books, many on scientific subjects.

After the ninth century, Arab and Persian scholars were not just translating but also actively assimilating the imported knowledge. As the influential eleventh-century Persian philosopher Al-Biruni (al-bih-ROO-nee) wrote: "The sciences were transmitted into the Arabic language from different parts of the world; by it [the sciences] were embellished and penetrated the hearts of men, while the beauties of [Arabic] flowed in their veins and arteries."[18] For example, many Muslim intellectuals adopted the Greek idea that an underlying order underpinned the apparent chaos of reality and that this order, or laws, could be understood by human reason.

The dialogue resulting from a diversity of ideas produced an open-minded search for truth that is apparent in the work of Ibn Khaldun, Ibn Sina, al-Kindi, and Ibn Rushd. For instance, the philosopher al-Kindi wrote that Muslims should acknowledge truth from whatever source it came because nothing was more important than truth itself. Ibn Rushd (Averroes), who lived in twelfth-century Cordoba (Spain), influenced Christian thinkers with his assertion of the role of reason. In the eleventh century, Christian Europe became aware of the Muslim synthesis of Greek, Indian, and Persian knowledge from libraries in Spain.

Muslims also turned their attention to medicine, where they enjoyed considerable success. Although much influenced by Greek ideas, Muslim medical specialists did not accept ancient wisdom uncritically. Instead, they developed an empirical tradition. Baghdad hospitals were the world's most advanced. Muslim surgeons learned how to use opium for anesthesia, extract teeth and replace them with false teeth made from animal bones, remove kidney stones, and do a colostomy by creating an artificial anus. These achievements attracted attention. For example, after many Islamic medical books were translated into Latin in the twelfth century, they became the major medical texts in Europe for the next five centuries.

Two medical scientists stand out. Abu Bakr al-Razi (aboo BAH-car al-RAH-zee) (ca. 865–ca. 932) and Ibn Sina (Avicenna) compared Greek ideas with their own research. Al-Razi, a Persian, directed several hospitals and wrote more than fifty clinical studies as well as general medical works. The latter included the *Comprehensive Book,* the longest medical encyclopedia in Arabic (eighteen volumes), which was used in Europe into the 1400s. In distinguishing smallpox from measles, he added much to the clinical knowledge of infectious diseases. Al-Razi also studied what we would today call sociological and psychological aspects of medicine. A century later Ibn Sina, who was born in Central Asia, placed considerable stress on psychosomatic medicine and treated depression. He also pioneered the study of vision and eye disease and performed complicated operations on the eye. His medical encyclopedia provided about half of the medical curriculum in medieval European universities. Ibn Sina served princes as both a physician and a political adviser.

Mathematics and Astronomy   As with science, Islamic mathematics moved well beyond the imitative, and it also helped spur astronomy. The scientific revolution that later occurred in Europe would have been impossible without Arab and Indian mathematics. In Baghdad the Persian Zoroastrian al-Khuwarizmi (al-KWAHR-uhz-mee) (ca. 780–ca. 850) developed the mathematical procedures he called algebra, building on Greek and Indian foundations. Omar Khayyam, the beloved Persian poet who worked at Baghdad's House of Wisdom, helped formulate trigonometry. Meanwhile, Arab thinkers also made advances in geometry. From Indian math books Muslims adopted a revolutionary system of numbers, including the concept of the zero. Today we know them as Arabic numerals because Europe acquired them from Muslim Spain. The most revolutionary innovation of Arabic numerals was not just their greater convenience but also the use of a dot to indicate an empty column. This dot eventually became the zero. Muslims also used decimal fractions. All these innovations had practical uses. Thus, advances in mathematics and physics made possible improvements in water clocks, water wheels, and other irrigation apparatus that spread well beyond the Islamic world.

The Muslim world also improved astronomical observations. Muslim astronomers combined Greek, Persian, and Indian knowledge of the stars and planets with their own observations. Applying their knowledge of mathematics to optics, Muslim scholars constructed a primitive version of the telescope, and one astronomer reportedly built an elaborate planetarium that reproduced the movement of the stars. A remarkable observatory built at Samarkand in Central Asia in 1420 produced charts for hundreds of stars. Some astronomers noted the eccentric behavior of the planet Venus, which challenged the widespread notion of an earth-centered universe. Indeed, many Muslim astronomers accepted that the world was round.

IBN BATTUTA,
A MUSLIM TRAVELER

Among the Islamic travelers who journeyed to, and often sojourned in, distant lands, the most famous was Abdallah Muhammad Ibn Battuta, a gregarious and pious fourteenth-century Moroccan who spent thirty years touring the length and breadth of the Islamic world, as far east as Southeast Asia and, he claimed, the coastal ports of China. His travels demonstrated the reach of the Islamic community. He was a pilgrim, judge, scholar, Sufi, ambassador, and connoisseur of fine foods and elegant architecture. Ibn Battuta's writings about his remarkable journeys, the autobiographical *Rihla* (Book of Travels), provide detailed, often unique eyewitness accounts of many societies. A collaborator compiled the *Rihla* in a literary form near the end of the adventurer's life.

Born in Tangier, Morocco, in North Africa, to a Berber family of scholars and trained in Islamic law, Ibn Battuta left home in 1325 at the age of twenty-one to seek adventure and learning. His apparent wanderlust proved difficult to quench. Such extensive travel would have been impossible for any woman, Muslim or otherwise, in that era, since women were expected to stay close to home and family. Traveling by camel, horse, wagon, or ship, Ibn Battuta covered between 60,000 and 75,000 miles and visited dozens of countries. He never had a conventional family life and married several times for short periods, leaving children all over the hemisphere. The politically ambitious jurist often sojourned in a society for months or years; his largest career stint was seven years' service in the Delhi Sultanate of northern India. But wherever he went, Ibn Battuta made observations on a wide variety of subjects, from cuisine and botany to political practice and Sufi mystics. For example, he marveled at the "continuous series of bazaars [along the Nile] from Alexandria to Cairo. Cities and villages succeed one another without interruption." And, coming from a more patriarchal North African society, he marvelled at the "respect shown to women by the [Central Asian] Turks, for they hold a more dignified position than the men. Turkish women do not veil themselves."

Although a repeated visitor to Mecca and the Islamic heartland, his experiences in the frontier regions of Islam, such as India and the Maldive Islands, Southeast Asia, the East African coast, the western Sudan, Turkish Central Asia, Anatolia, and Mongol-ruled southern Russia, provide the most useful information for the historian. They reveal a vivid picture of an expanding, vigorous Islamic realm encountering diverse structures, peoples, and practices. For example, from him we learn about the sexual customs of the Maldive Islands, where he married the widow of a sultan, and the Arab religious scholars, Persian merchants, and Chinese painters who gathered at Delhi "like moths around a candle."

Whereas the Christian Marco Polo a century earlier was always a stranger in his travels in Asia, in most places Ibn Battuta went he encountered people who shared his worldview and social values. From Morocco to Central Asia and around the In-

The Journey to Mali   No known paintings of Ibn Battuta exist. However, this map of Africa and the Mediterranean world, made by a Jewish cartographer in Spain in 1375, features a drawing of a camel-riding Muslim traveler that some historians think represents the journey of the Moroccan to Mali.
(Bibliotheque nationale de France)

dian Ocean Rim, people worshiped in mosques and recognized the Shari'a as a legal framework. Far and wide, Ibn Battuta enjoyed the company of merchants, scholars, Sufis, and princes, with most of whom he could converse in Arabic on many topics, including developments in faraway lands. His knowledge of Islamic law and Arabic allowed him to work as a judge and legal scholar from Morocco to India. But, while cosmopolitan and open-minded by the standards of the day, he was clearly uncomfortable in non-Islamic societies such as China and in those frontier Islamic cultures where Islamic orthodoxy was greatly modified by local custom, such as Mali in West Africa. The traveler finally returned home to Tangier, where he died around 1368.

THINKING ABOUT THE PROFILE

1. Why was Ibn Battuta one of the great travelers of the Intermediate Era?

2. What do his travels tell us about the values and reach of Islamic religion and culture?

Notes: Quotations from Ross Dunn, *The Adventures of Ibn Battuta: A Muslim Traveller of the 14th Century* (Berkeley: University of California Press, 1986), pp. 45, 183; Nikki R. Keddie, "Women in the Middle East Since the Rise of Islam," in Bonnie G. Smith, ed., *Women's History in Global Perspective*, Vol. 3 (Urbana: University of Illinois Press, 2005), p. 81.

Social Science and Historiography

The modern study of social sciences and history owes much to Muslim research and writing. For example, Muslims made a major contribution to geography. With the expansion of Islam and Arab trading communities to the far corners of the Eastern Hemisphere, some pious Muslims were able to travel to distant lands, and many became long-distance traders. Educated Muslims enjoyed reading these travelers' accounts of other countries and peoples. Modern historians are indebted to Muslim travelers such as the Moroccan jurist Ibn Battuta (IB-uhn ba-TOO-tuh) for much of what we know today about the geography and societies of sub-Saharan Africa and Southeast Asia from the ninth to the fifteenth centuries (see Profile: Ibn Battuta, a Muslim Traveler). Aided by travel accounts, geographers and cartographers such as Al-Idrisi (al-AH-dree-see) from Muslim Spain produced atlases, globes, and maps.

Ibn Khaldun (1332–1406), the well-traveled North African introduced at the beginning of the chapter, was apparently the first scholar anywhere to look for patterns and structure in history. For example, his monumental work connected the rise of states among tribal communities with a growing feeling of solidarity between leaders and their followers, often enhanced by a coherent religion. His recognition of the role in history of "group feeling" (what today we call ethnic identity) and the powerful role of religion was pathbreaking. In studying other cultures, he advocated "critical examination":

> Know the rules of statecraft, the nature of existing things, and the difference between nations, regions and tribes in regard to way of life, qualities of character, customs, sects, schools of thought, and so on. [The historian] must distinguish the similarities and differences between the present and the past.[19]

Ibn Khaldun put the Arab expansion into the broader flow of regional history, in the process focusing on various regional cultures.

SECTION SUMMARY

- Sufism, a mystical approach to Islam that emphasized flexibility and a personal connection with God, drew both Sunni and Shi'ite followers.

- Although the Quran and most Muslim societies restricted women, some Muslim societies did not, and both Muslims and non-Muslims have debated the origins and benefits of such practices as wearing a veil.

- Literature, especially poetry, was very important in Islamic culture, as was calligraphy, the artful writing of words.

- Islamic science and medicine were very advanced and pioneered such practices as anesthesia and the replacement of false teeth.

- The Scientific Revolution would not have occurred without the help of Islamic mathematicians who passed on to Europe Indian mathematics.

✦ Globalized Islam and Middle Eastern Political Change

Why do historians speak of Islam as a hemispheric culture?

The major theme of early Islam was the transformation of a parochial Arab culture into the first truly hemisphere-wide culture that was connected by many religious and commercial networks. Between the eighth and seventeenth centuries Islam expanded out of its Arabian heartland to become the dominant religion across a broad expanse of Africa and Eurasia, and Muslim minorities emerged in places as far afield as China and the Balkans. From this expansion was created **Dar al-Islam** (the "Abode of Islam"), the Islamic world stretching from Morocco to Indonesia and joined by both a common faith and trade. Networks fostered by Islam reached from the Atlantic eastward to the Pacific, spreading Arab words, names, social attitudes, cultural values, and the Arabic script to diverse peoples. Eventually several powerful military states rose to power and ruled over large populations of Muslims and non-Muslims. The Islamic world also faced severe challenges—expanding Turks, Christian crusaders, Mongol conquerors, and horrific pandemics—that set the stage for the rise of new political forces in the fifteenth and sixteenth centuries. Yet, the Islamic tradition was resistant and overcame factionalism and political decay to remain creative well past the 1400s.

The Global Shape of Dar al-Islam

To identify the Muslim world with the Arab world is misleading. More than half of the world's 1.3 billion Muslims today live outside the Middle East, and Arabs are significantly outnumbered by non-Arab believers. The majority of all Muslims live in South and Southeast Asia. This chapter largely focuses on the Middle East, since the spread of Islam in Africa and southern Asia is discussed in Chapters 12 and 13. But this is only a part of a larger global whole of Islam, a zone stretching from West Africa and Spain east to Indonesia and the southern Philippines.

After the destruction of the cosmopolitan Abbasid Caliphate in 1258, Arab political power diminished, but Islam grew rapidly in both Africa and South Asia. Dozens of prosperous Muslim trading cities, from Tangier in northwest Africa to Samarkand in Central Asia to Melaka in Malaya, offered goods from distant countries. Beginning in the thirteenth century, Muslims constructed a hemisphere-spanning system based not just on economic exchange but also on faith. This system, built on a shared understanding of the world and the cosmos, was linked by informal networks of Islamic scholars and saints. The Quran and its message of a righteous social order provided a framework for Dar al-Islam.

Dar al-Islam ("Abode of Islam") The Islamic world stretching from Morocco to Indonesia and joined by both a common faith and trade.

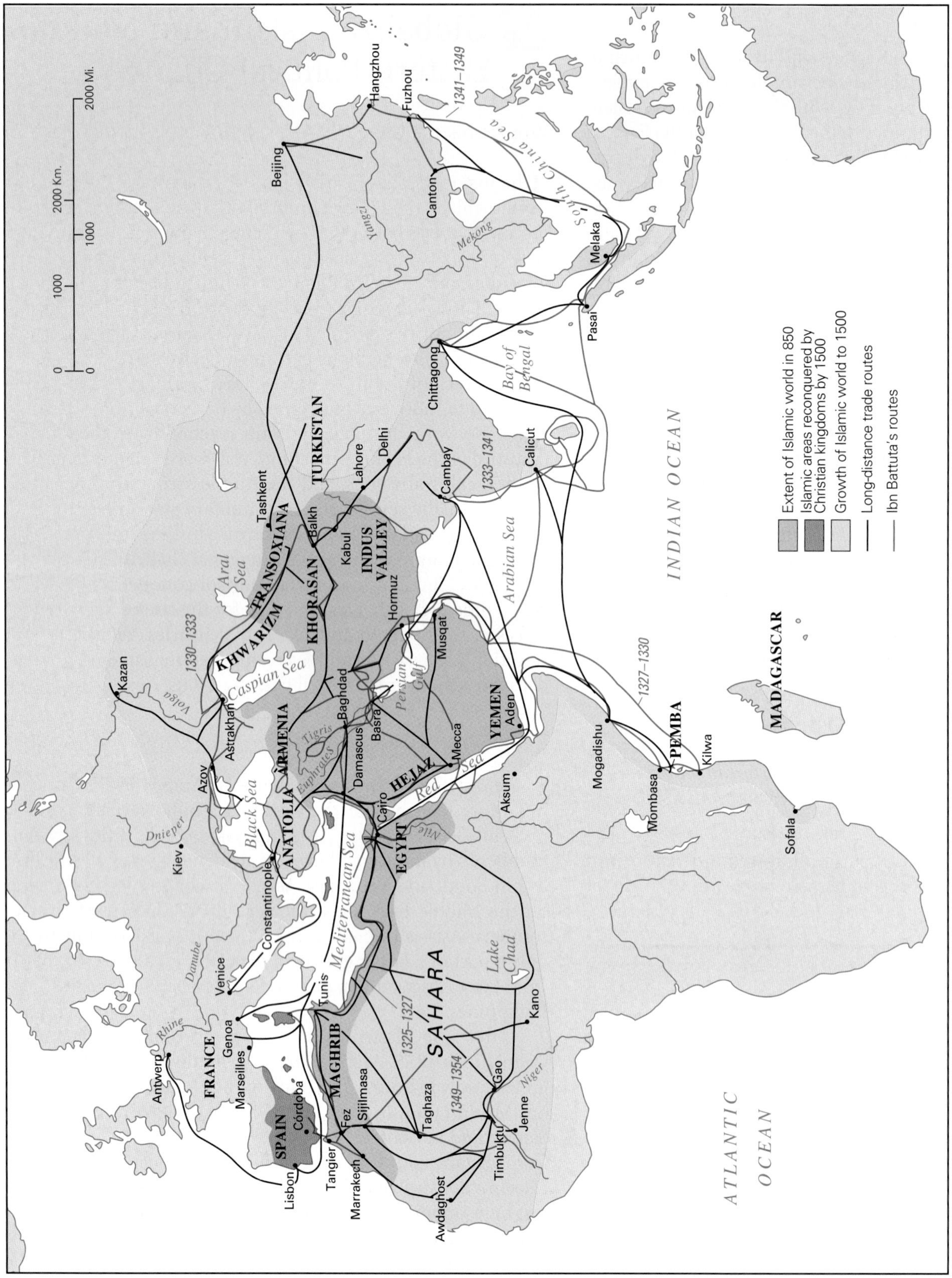

Map 10.3 Dar al-Islam and Trade Routes, ca. 1500 C.E.
By 1500 the Islamic world stretched into West Africa, East Africa, and Southeast Asia. Trade routes connected the Islamic lands and allowed Muslim traders to extend their networks to China, Russia, and Europe.

China is a sea that salts all rivers that flow into it.

ITALIAN TRAVELER MARCO POLO (1275 C.E.)[1]

Early in the twelfth century the Chinese artist Zhang Zeduan, noted for his realistic drawings, painted a massive scroll of people at work and leisure throughout the city of Kaifeng (KIE-FENG), then China's capital and home to perhaps 1 million people. The scroll, the surviving portions of which are 17 feet long, portrays a bustling city and its peoples' daily lives during one of premodern China's most creative and prosperous eras. The viewer can experience the grandeur of the city, from its riverside suburbs to the high protective walls and the towering city gates to the downtown business district. In Zhang's scroll, set during the annual spring festival, Kaifeng's streets are crowded with people (mostly men) going about their daily activities. Foreign merchants and other visitors can be seen, as well as streetside hawkers touting their goods, fortunetellers, scholars, and monks. The scroll also shows industrial activities, with people working in warehouses, iron smelters, arsenals, and shipyards. Zhang's record of Kaifeng's commercial life is particularly vivid: building material suppliers, textile firms, and drug and chemical shops, as well as hotels, food stalls, teahouses and restaurants, amenities for local people and visitors alike. Cargo barges cruise the river, while camels heavily laden with goods enter the city, some arriving from distant countries.

Much of the prosperous city life Zhang portrayed was familiar to Chinese of earlier and later generations, for Chinese society showed considerable continuity over time. The Han's eventual succession by the Sui and then by the Tang (tahng) and Song (soong) dynasties ensured that Chinese society continued along traditional lines, in contrast to the dramatic changes that took place in Japan, the Middle East, India, Southeast Asia, and Europe during the Intermediate Era. Once the Tang adopted a modified version of the Han system, the ensuing millennium, from the seventh through the eighteenth centuries, proved to be a golden age, broken only occasionally by invasion or disorder. Some scholars call the Intermediate Era in world history the "Chinese Centuries." China became and remained perhaps the world's richest and most populous society, enjoying a well-organized government and economy, a flourishing artistic and literary culture, and creativity in technology and science. Many commercial and cultural networks connected China to the rest of Eurasia. Furthermore, China's neighbors in Korea and Japan adopted many aspects of Chinese culture, though they also forged their own highly distinctive societies during this period. China did indeed, as Marco Polo recognized, influence or awe all those with whom it came into contact.

FOCUS QUESTIONS

1. What role did Tang China play in the Eurasian world?
2. Why might historians consider the Song dynasty the high point of China's golden age?
3. How did China change during the Yuan and Ming dynasties?
4. How did the Koreans and Japanese make use of Chinese culture in developing their own distinctive societies?
5. How did Korean and Japanese society change in the late Intermediate Era?

Tang China: The Hub of the East

What role did Tang China play in the Eurasian world?

The harsh Sui dynasty that united China after the disintegration of the Han ruled for only a short time (581–618 C.E.) before rebellions brought it to an end. The victor in the struggles between rival rebel forces established the Tang dynasty (618–907), regarded by many historians as the most splendid of all the Chinese dynasties. Many peoples admired Tang China. The three centuries of Tang rule set a high watermark in many facets of Chinese life and provided a cultural and political model for neighboring Asian societies. The only comparable power in Eurasia at that time was the expanding Muslim empire of the Abbasids; India and Europe were then divided into many small states and often threatened by invaders. The Tang made important advances in political organization, economic production, science, technology, art, literature, and philosophy, and many of these advances dominated China until the early twentieth century.

The Tang Empire and Eurasian Exchange

In the seventh and eighth centuries Tang China—an empire of some 50 or 60 million people—was the largest and most populous society on earth, and it had an immense influence in the eastern third of Eurasia (see Map 11.1 on page 302). Like the Han before them, the Tang launched a series of ambitious campaigns that brought Central Asia (as far west as the Caspian Sea), Tibet, Mongolia, Manchuria, and parts of Siberia under Chinese rule. Vietnam had already long been a colony. The Koreans became a vassal state, and the Japanese established close ties. Kingdoms as far away as Afghanistan acknowledged Chinese leadership, and Chinese garrisons protected the Silk Road, fostering the flow of goods and people across Eurasia. In western Asia, the powerful Abbasid caliph Harun al-Rashid testified to China's diplomatic clout by signing a treaty with the Tang.

The Tang were the most outward-looking of all Chinese dynasties, and during these years China became an open forum, a world market of ideas, people, and things arriving over the networks of exchange. The Silk Road, established during the Han era, remained a sort of transcontinental highway. Along this network traders, adventurers, diplomats, missionaries, and pilgrims traveled east or west, carrying goods and ideas, and many made their way to China. Nestorian Christian, Manichean, Buddhist, and Muslim missionaries arrived. Merchants from around Asia formed communities in several Chinese cities, and many arrived by sea. For example, perhaps two-thirds of the 200,000 inhabitants of the southern port of Guangzhou (gwahng-jo), also known as Canton, a great trading hub, were immigrants, including Arabs, Persians, Indians, Cambodians, and Malays. For the many Muslim residents, the city boasted both Sunni and Shi'ite mosques. Indian astronomers and mathematicians joined the Tang government as scientific officials, bringing with them Indian traditions of knowledge. Meanwhile, several hundred Chinese scholars visited or sojourned in India, most of them seeking Buddhist literature.

Tang wealth and power stimulated commerce throughout Eurasia. A lively sea trade linked China with Southeast Asia, India, Persia, and the Arabs. By land or sea, many Chinese inventions reached into western Eurasia. In 753 C.E. a Chinese craftsman reported that, in Baghdad: "As for the weavers who make light silks, the goldsmiths who work gold and silver there, and the painters; the arts which they practice were started by Chinese technicians."[2] Chinese products such as silk and porcelain were much prized in Europe and the Middle East. Because of the Tang's fame, Chinese culture also spread in this period to Korea and Japan.

This multicultural exchange also benefited China. New products appeared, most notably tea from Southeast Asia. Chinese began drinking tea, originally a medicinal substance, as a beverage, and it became the national drink. Teahouses selling boiled tea opened in every marketplace. Another new arrival was the chair, probably from the Middle East. Over the next centuries it replaced seating pads, and the Chinese became the only chair users in East Asia. Diverse societies in places such as Burma, Java, and Nepal regularly sent embassies to the Tang court bearing gifts. Renewed contacts with India and the Middle East as well as many other peoples helped foster China's creativity. But some Chinese scholars criticized the cosmopolitan attitude and complained about too much foreign culture.

The Eurasian exchange during the Tang fostered dynamic and culturally rich cities. Tang China boasted many cities larger than any contemporary cities in Europe or India, and the capital, Chang'an (CHAHNG-ahn), present-day Xi'an (SHEE-AHN), the Mandate of Heaven. Soon rebellions broke out all over China. The turmoil was ended by a Chinese commoner who established a new Chinese dynasty, the Ming. Mongol military forces left China and returned to Central Asia.

Ming Government and Culture

The new Ming dynasty (1368–1644) became a great period of orderly government and social stability, with a rich culture. The founder, Zhu Yuanzhang (JOO yuwen-JAHNG) (1328–1398), was a former Buddhist monk and the son of an itinerant farm worker who, like the founder of the Han, rose from abject poverty through sheer ability and ruthless behavior in a time of opportunity. Under the Ming, China's people lived for nearly three centuries in comparative peace and considerable prosperity, with living standards among the highest and mortality rates among the lowest of anywhere in the world. China more than doubled in population, from around 80 million to between 160 and 180 million.

The Ming installed a government similar to that of the Han and Tang but were somewhat more despotic. Perhaps because of the bitter experience of Mongol rule, the Ming emperors exercised more power than Song or Tang emperors and placed the bureaucracy under closer imperial scrutiny. Yet, the bureaucracy was still small, some twenty-thousand officials, of whom some 25 percent were from nonelite backgrounds. The Ming also eliminated the office of prime minister, which had been traditional since the Han. The man who filled this post had been the highest-ranking mandarin and had kept his hand on the pulse of the country. The Censorate also became more timid, reducing the checks on royal abuses. As a result of these changes, the Ming emperors became more isolated from the real world. As in previous dynasties, some Ming emperors had male lovers as well as many wives and concubines. This reflected a tolerance of same-sex relationships among many Chinese court officials and commoners.

A sense of order infused the arts, which saw several genres mature during the Ming. Theater flourished, reaching its highest level in this period. The most popular form of theater at the peasant level, Chinese opera (musical drama), included extended arias and spoken dialogue. Most operas were witty and unrealistic, often with lowbrow humor. Each performance of a play aimed at harmonizing all the elements: song, speech, costume, makeup, movement, and musical accompaniment. The stage settings were minimal, since the audience focused intently on the actors, who triggered their imagination by telling a story by word and gesture. Much Chinese music was composed for operas or for ritual and ceremonial purposes. String, wind, and percussion instruments were popular, especially the flute, lute, and zither.

Although most Ming scholars considered fiction worthless, it had a large audience. Most novels had a Confucian moral emphasizing correct behavior, but some offered social criticisms or satires. Perhaps the greatest Ming novel, *The Water Margin* (also known as *All Men Are Brothers*), presented heroes who were also bandits, Robin Hoods driven into crime by corrupt officials. Another great work, *The Golden Lotus*, re-

A Ming Imperial Workshop   Printer's shops, such as the one shown here, used movable type to publish encyclopedias with information on engineering, medicine, agriculture, and other practical topics.   [Courtesy of South China University of Technology Library, Canton (Guangzhou)]

vealed the hedonistic lives of the rich. Both these novels offered psychological depth. Ming authors also wrote some of the world's first detective stories.

Ming rulers encouraged intellectual pursuits, expanding the *Hanlin* ("Forest of Culture") Academy, which was established in the Tang. The brightest scholars were assigned there as research fellows and were paid to read and write whatever they liked. Ming scholars also compiled a 11,000-volume encyclopedia (with 20,000 chapters) and a 52-volume study of Chinese pharmacology.

Ming China and the Afro-Eurasian World

Rather than building a new empire, the Ming turned to overseas exploration, which resulted in closer political and economic relations with Southeast Asia. The early Ming rulers pursued territorial expansion, including a failed attempt to

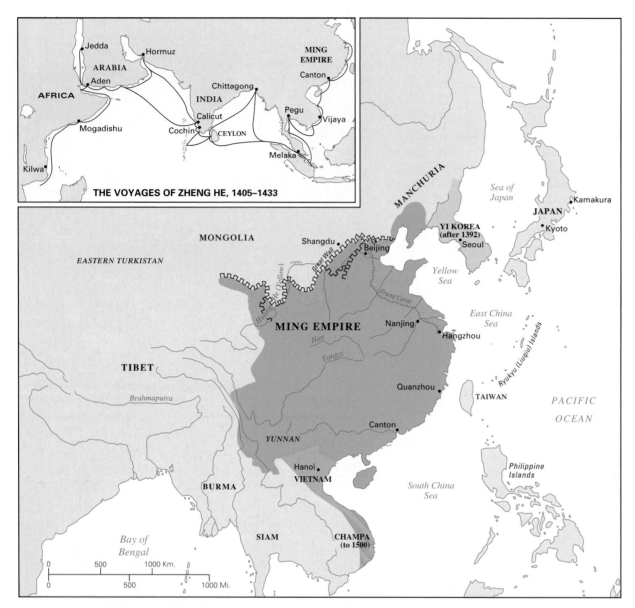

THE VOYAGES OF ZHENG HE, 1405–1433

Map 11.3 The Voyages of Zheng He
After replacing the Mongols, the Ming reestablished a strong Chinese state, attempted to recolonize Vietnam, and rebuilt the Great Wall. Ming emperors dispatched a series of grand maritime expeditions in the early 1400s that reached the Middle East and East Africa.

recolonize Vietnam. But China was now oriented more to the sea. Rather than send armies far into Central Asia, the emperor dispatched a series of grand maritime expeditions to southern Asia and beyond to reaffirm China's preeminence in the eastern half of Asia by, as official sources put it, "showing off the wealth and power of the Central Kingdom."[15] Admiral Zheng He (jung huh) (Cheng Ho) (ca. 1371–1435), a huge man and a trusted court eunuch of Muslim faith, commanded seven voyages between 1405 and 1433. The world had never before seen such a large-scale feat of seamanship: the largest fleet comprised sixty-two vessels carrying 28,000 men, and the largest "treasure ships," as they were known, weighed 1,500 tons, were

450 feet long, boasted nine masts nearly 500 feet high, and carried a crew of five hundred. Observers must have been astounded as these ships approached their harbors. A few decades later Christopher Columbus sailed from Spain in three tiny vessels carrying only about a hundred men total.

Zheng He's extraordinary voyages carried the Chinese flag through Southeast Asia to India, the Persian Gulf, and the East African coast (see Map 11.3). Had they continued, the Chinese ships had the capability of sailing around Africa to Europe or the Americas but had no incentive to do so. The expeditions expressed the exuberance of an era of great vitality. Even though the Chinese came mostly in peace and undertook only a few military actions, some thirty-six countries in southern and western Asia officially acknowledged Chinese preeminence. Even the ruler of the East African city of Malindi sent ambassadors bearing tribute, including a giraffe.

Historians still debate the reasons for Zheng He's great voyages. Some point to ideology, the desire to have so many foreign countries reaffirm the emperor's position as the Son of Heaven. Zheng He may also have sought to locate a deposed boy emperor who had disappeared, possibly fleeing into exile. Others suspect the ambitious emperor wanted to demonstrate China's military capabilities. Some historians, however, see commercial motives as primary, since these voyages occurred at a time of increased activity by Chinese merchants in Southeast Asia. During the early Ming many thousands of Chinese had settled or were sojourning in what is today the Philippines, Indonesia, Siam, and Vietnam, creating a closer commercial link to China. Chinese merchants also visited trading ports in India and forged extensive trade links across the Indian Ocean, transporting Yuan and Ming porcelain as far west as the interior of south-central Africa.

The voyages of Zheng He may also have helped revitalize the traditional tribute system. During Han and Tang times this tribute system helped shape China's relations with its neighbors. Under this system China considered the various East, Southeast, and Central Asian states as vassals or tributaries and granted them trade relations and protection. The protection was mostly symbolic, however, since the Chinese rarely intervened to support their allies, except in nearby Korea. In return the tributary states sent periodic envoys bearing gifts to the emperor, confirming his superiority in ritual form. The vassal states played along, whatever their true feelings, because they desired China's goodwill and trade goods. In Ming times tribute came regularly from states in Korea, Vietnam, Cambodia, Borneo, Indonesia, South Asia, and Central Asia. The tribute system also enabled the Chinese to benefit from trade with various countries.

Inevitably the Chinese saw themselves as the Middle Kingdom surrounded by vassal states in various degrees of barbarism. Beginning in the Han, the Chinese never recognized any other society as an equal, at least not symbolically. They developed the notion that they were superior not just materially but also culturally and that barbarians could not resist their appeal. This view was reinforced by the fact that other East Asian societies borrowed from China. For the Chinese, to be civilized was to embrace Chinese culture, and a virtuous ruler, they believed, irresistibly attracted barbarians. When a tribute mission arrived in the capital, part of the rite was the **kotow**, the tribute-bearers' act of prostrating themselves before the emperor, a practice from which we get the modern English word *kowtow*, to pander to authority. This practice, above all others, left little doubt as to who was superior and who was inferior, reflecting a Confucian sense of hierarchy.

---

kotow The tribute-bearers' act of prostrating themselves before the Chinese emperor.

Ming China Turns Inward

In the early Ming, China remained at the cutting edge, perhaps the world's wealthiest and most developed country. Hindu India faced Muslim conquests, the Middle Eastern societies were struggling to recover from various setbacks, and the western Europeans were just beginning to enjoy political and economic dynamism. Commercially vibrant and outward-thrusting, Ming China had the capability to open maritime communication between the continents and become the dominant world power. But world dominance never came and China turned inward. The grand voyages to the west and the commercial thrust in distant lands came to a sudden halt when the Ming emperor ordered them ended and recalled the overseas Chinese merchants from Southeast Asia. Soon the state outlawed Chinese emigration altogether. But the withdrawal was by no means total. Some Chinese continued to illegally travel abroad for trade, and foreign merchant ships still came to China. The tribute system provided cover for extensive trade and smuggling.

The causes of the stunning reversal of official Chinese engagement with the world that, in the perspective of later history, seemed so counterproductive remain subject to debate. Some causes were economic. Perhaps Zheng He's voyages were too costly even for the wealthy Ming government. The voyages were not cost-effective, since the ships mostly returned with exotic goods (such as African giraffes for the imperial zoo) rather than mineral resources and other valuable items. Other causes were cultural and ideological. Unlike Christian and Muslim societies, the Chinese lacked any missionary zeal, having little interest in spreading Chinese religion and culture except to near neighbors such as Vietnam. Furthermore, despite their flourishing guilds and frequent wealth, the merchants held a low status in the Confucian social and ideological system. Indeed, Ming leaders were even more convinced than their predecessors that profit was evil, and mercantile interests inevitably conflicted with social and political ones. Confucian officials often despised the merchants, and a later Ming scholar wrote that "one in a hundred [Chinese] is rich, while nine out of ten are impoverished. The poor cannot stand up to the rich. The lord of silver rules heaven and the god of copper cash reigns over the earth."[16] In keeping with these feelings, many mandarins opposed foreign trade.

Military and economic factors also influenced the turn inward. With the Mongols regrouping in Central Asia, the Ming court shifted its resources to defense of the northern borders and the pirate-infested Pacific coast, spending millions rebuilding and extending the Great Wall. What tourists see today of the Great Wall near Beijing is mostly work that the Ming did. But military operations along the northern border and an ill-fated invasion of Vietnam generated a fiscal crisis that weakened the government. In dealing with this crisis, the Ming began concentrating on home affairs.

Finally, the turn inward can be seen as a reaction to the Mongols. After the bitterness of the Mongol era, the Chinese became more ethnocentric and antiforeign. The early Ming maritime expeditions were an aberration, because China had always been land-based and self-centered. Ming Chinese believed that they needed nothing from outside, since the Middle Kingdom considered itself to be self-sufficient. China remained powerful, productive, and mostly prosperous, enjoying generally high living standards, well into the eighteenth century, when profits from overseas colonies and the Industrial Revolution tipped the balance in favor of northwest Europe. By the later Ming, China had entered a period of relative isolation that was ended only by the forceful intrusion of a newly developed Europe in the early 1800s.

SECTION SUMMARY

- The ancient Chinese fear of Central Asian nomads was realized when the Mongols, under Genghis and Khubilai Khan, conquered China and established the Yuan dynasty.

- Khubilai Khan made a number of improvements in China's transportation system and moved the capital to Beijing.

- Because of lack of cooperation from Chinese scholars and bureaucrats, the Mongols established an international civil service, in which Marco Polo served.

- After the decline of the Mongols, the Chinese enjoyed three centuries of prosperity under the Ming dynasty, and their sense of well-being was displayed in Zheng He's grand sailing expeditions, which enhanced China's position among its neighbors.

- The Ming dynasty received tribute from many peoples throughout Asia.

- For reasons that are still debated, the Ming emperor suddenly ordered all overseas activity halted and China. turned inward, beginning an isolation that ended only in the 1800s.

✦ Cultural Adaptation in Korea and Japan

How did the Koreans and Japanese make use of Chinese culture in developing their own distinctive societies?

As the cultural heartland of East Asia, China strongly influenced its three large neighbors of Vietnam (see Chapter 13), Korea, and Japan. Both Vietnam and Korea derived considerable culture from China, including writing systems, philosophies, and political institutions. At the same time, all these societies adapted these Chinese influences to their indigenous customs. Both Vietnamese and Koreans retained their sense of cultural identity. Although sharing many common traits with Korea, Japan produced a variant of East Asian culture even more distinctive, especially in its political and social structures.

Silla Korea and Tang China

As Korean society developed, several strong states emerged on the peninsula. In the mid-seventh century the southern Korean state of Silla (SILL-ah) defeated its main rival, Koguryo, and united all Koreans, but at the price of becoming a vassal of China. Political unity, which Koreans enjoyed into the 1900s, allowed Korean culture to became homogenized. But like earlier states, Silla also borrowed Chinese culture and institutions. Buddhism triumphed, and the Tang system became the model in government, with Confucianism used as a political ideology. Many Korean monks traveled to China, and some even visited India. But Koreans were selective in their borrowing. The Korean social structure continued to place more emphasis than the Chinese did on inherited status instead of merit, and Korean peasants faced many legal restrictions on their movements. In addition, the gap between rich and poor was much wider than in China. Yet, among Silla's rulers were three queens, two of them among the state's most effective rulers, suggesting less gender bias than in China. For instance, Queen Sondok (r. 632–647) fostered science and promoted a tolerant mixing of Buddhism and shamanism. Silla women generally shared in the social status of their menfolk, enjoyed many legal rights, and could even head families.

During the Silla era (688–918), Koreans mixed influences from Tang China with their own traditions to produce a distinctive culture. For example, they adapted Chinese writing to their own very different spoken language, though it never fit very well. Using this writing system, during the Silla era Koreans began creating a distinctive literary tradition, composing works of history, religion, and poetry. To mass-produce these works, Silla craftsmen also developed woodblock printing as early as China. The oldest still extant example of woodblock printing in the world, a Korean Buddhist writing, dates from 751. Perhaps influenced by the Chinese, Koreans also studied astronomy. A great observatory built in this era is the oldest still standing in East Asia.

While remaining culturally tied to East Asia, Korea also formed connections with the rest of the world. Buddhist pilgrims came from as far away as India, and many Arabs traded at Silla, some settling down there. One Arab wrote that "seldom has a stranger who has come there from Iraq or another country left it afterwards. So healthy is the air there, so pure the water, so fertile the soil and so plentiful of all good things."[17]

Korea During the Koryo Era

Gradually Silla declined, damaged by elite rivalries, corruption, and peasant uprisings, and it was replaced by a new state, Koryo (KAW-ree-oh), which lasted for over four centuries (918–1392). Chinese influence continued in politics and philosophy: Koreans set up an examination system like that of China and Confucian schools, and neo-Confucianism became popular. But Koreans retained a distinctive political and social system. For example, Korean kings, never as strong as Chinese emperors, were greatly influenced by the court, military, and aristocratic landowning families. In contrast to Silla, Koryo court women mainly exercised influence behind the scenes. For example, Lady Yu successfully urged her reluctant husband, Wang Kon, the founder of the Koryo dynasty, to seize power from a despotic ruler, arguing that "It is an ancient tradition to raise a banner of revolt against a tyrant. How can you, a great military leader, hesitate?"[18] While Koryo women played a lesser role in public affairs and faced more restrictions than Silla women, they took full responsibility for family affairs and farmed. Unlike in China, Korean farming relied on large estates. These patterns persisted long after the Koryo dynasty ended.

Thanks to the continued mixing of Chinese and Korean influences, substantial religious, cultural, and technological change characterized the Koryo years. Buddhism gradually became a more powerful economic and political force but also assimilated many elements from animism. The involvement of monks in political life fostered religious corruption and a more worldly orientation that alienated some believers. For the past 1,500 years Korea has been a nominally Buddhist society, but the religion gradually lost influence beginning in Koryo times. More secular artistic trends emerged, including landscape painting and some of the world's finest porcelain. Wide interest in religious and secular literature fostered a publishing industry. The first movable-type printing made of clay came from China in the eleventh century, and Koreans invented the world's first metal movable-type printing by 1234.

Like China, Korea had to occasionally fend off northern pastoralists. The Mongols conquered the peninsula in the early 1200s, making Koryo a colony in their vast empire. When Koreans resisted, the Mongols devastated the land, carrying off hundreds of thousands of captives and imposing heavy taxes on peasants. Yet, thanks to closer links to trade networks, more Chinese and western Asian learning and technology reached Korea during the Mongol era.

Nara Government and Its Challenges

Although using many Chinese and Korean influences, Japan, like Korea, produced a highly distinctive society. In the mid-sixth century the Japanese embarked on three centuries of deliberate cultural borrowing from China, and the ideas and methods they imported helped to create a robust, expansive, and sophisticated society. The changes began with the *Taika* (TIE-kah) ("Great Change") reform of 646 C.E., which the rulers hoped would transform Japan into a centralized empire on the Tang model. The country was divided into provinces that were ruled by governors who derived their power from the emperor. Japanese leaders also established a governmental system made to resemble, on the surface at least, the Chinese centralized bureaucracy. Moreover, the Japanese were now able to record their history and conduct their daily activities using the Chinese writing system. Finally, the adoption of Buddhism from China brought with it a rich constellation of art and architecture.

The height of the period of conscious borrowing from China (710–784) takes its name from Nara (NAH-rah), Japan's

CHRONOLOGY	
Korea and Japan During the Intermediate Era	
645	Taika reforms in Japan
688	Destruction of Koguryo
688–918	Domination of Korea by Silla
710–784	Nara period in Japan
794–1184	Heian period in Japan
918–1392	Unification of Korea by Koryo
1180–1333	Kamakura Shogunate in Japan
1274, 1281	Mongol invasions of Japan
1338–1568	Ashikaga Shogunate in Japan
1392–1910	Yi dynasty in Korea

first capital city, which was built on the model of the Tang capital, Chang'an (see Chronology: Korea and Japan During the Intermediate Era). Nara had a population of some twenty thousand, half of them government officials and their families. At that time the total Japanese population was probably 5 or 6 million. Many Buddhist temples reflected Tang influence. In addition, during the Nara period land was nationalized in the name of the emperor and, using Tang models, reallocated on an equal basis to the peasants. In return, the peasants paid a land and labor tax. This system was abandoned as unworkable after a few decades, but it illustrated that in agrarian societies land control is the key to political power, a fact demonstrated vividly throughout Japanese history.

Although these changes were designed to strengthen imperial authority, the Japanese emperor never became an unchallenged and activist Chinese-style ruler. Powerful aristocrats maintained control of the bureaucracy and also retained large tax-exempt landholdings. In practice Japan became a **dyarchy**, a form of dual government whereby one powerful family dominated the emperors, whose power was mostly symbolic. The powerful family filled the highest government posts but never aspired to the throne. The emperors passed their lives in luxurious seclusion, with the main goal of guaranteeing an unbroken succession through having sons. This dyarchical system, so different from China's, remained the pattern in Japan into the nineteenth century.

Economic unrest characterized the late Nara period. Peasants resented corvée (forced labor) and military conscription, which often resulted in economic ruin. Many abandoned their

dyarchy A form of dual government that began in Japan during the Nara period (710–784) whereby one powerful family ruled the country while the emperor held mostly symbolic power.

fields, becoming wandering, rootless *ronin* (ROH-neen) ("wave people"), some of whom were hired by large landowners as workers. To stop people from becoming ronin, the government abolished compulsory service and gave the responsibility for police and defense to local officials. Eventually the ronin these officials hired as troops were transformed into the provincial warrior class, whose activities reshaped Japanese life.

Nara Culture and Thought

Nara leaders promoted aspects of Chinese culture but blended them with Japanese traditions. For example, they encouraged their people to wear Chinese clothing and to construct Chinese-style buildings. The rituals and ceremonies of the imperial court, largely based on Tang Chinese models, included stately dances and orchestral music using Japanese versions of Chinese musical instruments such as the flute, lute, and zither. These ceremonial forms, which are still maintained at the Japanese court, constitute the oldest fully authenticated music and dance tradition in the world. More significantly, the Chinese written language gained great prestige, and Chinese ideographs were adapted to Japan's very different nontonal spoken language, in what must have been a difficult conversion process. Chinese literary forms, including poetry and calligraphy, became popular. One Nara collection contains 4,500 poems.

The Japanese also adopted and reshaped Chinese philosophical and religious doctrines that they found appealing. They borrowed Confucianism and modified its ethical and political doctrines to suit their own social structure. They also borrowed Mahayana Buddhism, whose worldview that all things are impermanent greatly influenced their art and literature. For example, many artists and poets focused their work on the passage of time and the changing of the seasons. They were also attracted to Buddhist ethics.

But the Japanese also retained their original animist religion known today as Shinto, a kind of nature worship. Shinto and Buddhism addressed different needs and easily blended into a synthesis. The deities of Shinto were not gods but beautiful natural phenomena such as Mt. Fuji (FOO-jee), waterfalls, thunder, or stately trees. This worship reflected the intensity with which the Japanese have loved beauty in all forms. No line separated humanity from nature. Shinto also stressed ritual purity, encouraging bathing and personal cleanliness, and the Japanese became the world's best-scrubbed people. Shinto worshiped the land and ancestors but had no coherent theology or moral doctrine, no concept of death or an afterlife. The faithful flocked to shrines, such as the famous Ise (EE-say), for festivals or to seek help from spirits.

Heian Cultural Renaissance

The period of imitation and direct cultural borrowing from China came to an end during the Heian (HAY-en) period (794–1184). After the capital moved from Nara to Heian, or Kyoto (kee-YO-toe), 28 miles north, Japan gradually returned, over some decades, to a period of relative isolation. The leaders discontinued foreign contacts in the ninth century and set about consciously absorbing and adapting the Chinese cultural patterns imported during the Nara era under the slogan "Chinese learning, Japanese spirit." The centralized government gave way to a resurgence of aristocratic rule, and Buddhism gradually harmonized with Shinto beliefs and practices while generating new sects, art, and temple building.

A rich and uniquely Japanese court society arose, and in turn supported the development of purely Japanese art and literary styles. Heian culture fostered a distinctly Japanese writing system and worldview. The modification of Chinese influence was exemplified in the development of **kana** (KAH-nah), a phonetic script consisting of some forty-seven syllabic signs derived from Chinese characters. Now Japanese could write their language phonetically. This allowed more freedom of expression, especially when the kana letters were combined with Chinese characters. The Japanese written language of today combines the two.

Heian elite culture, a world enormously remote from us today in time, attitudes, and behavior, reached its high point around 1000 C.E. It flourished among a very small, highly inbred group of privileged families in Kyoto, which then had a population, including both the elite and commoners, of around 100,000. Many elite residents derived their incomes from bureaucratic jobs and land ownership. The Kyoto aristocracy became extraordinarily withdrawn from the realities of the outside world, creating a culture that was governed by standards of form and beauty and in which the distinction between art and life, and fact and fiction, was not clearly made. Passionately concerned with their rank and status in society, they created some of Japan's greatest literature and art. The Heian elite admired nothing so much as the ability to write in an artistic hand, compose a graceful poem, and create an elegant costume.

Guided by these priorities, the finest energies of the period went into creating beauty in a variety of forms, such as putting together harmonious syllables and lines of ink on the page or perfumes on the body. The Heian period was probably unique in world history for the careful attention spent in choosing an undergarment, or the time writing a love note, always exquisite down to the last detail, with perhaps a tastefully faded chrysanthemum to emphasize the melancholy nature of the contents. The homely, color-blind, or unromantic person would have felt terribly out of place in this culture. The Heian aristocrats were not interested in pure intellect or social morality; their value system was superficial. They were obsessed by mood, especially the sense of the transience of beauty. But they left a wonderful cultural legacy.

Women from affluent families had their highest position in Japanese history during the Heian, at least in the capital city. They were free to have romantic affairs, and sexual promiscu-

---

kana A Japanese phonetic script developed in the Heian period (794–1184) that consisted of some forty-seven syllabic signs derived from Chinese characters.

LADY MURASAKI,
HEIAN NOVELIST

Women produced much of the best Heian literature. The greatest of the books was *The Tale of Genji*, the world's first psychological novel, written by a lady-in-waiting, Lady Murasaki (Murasaki Shibiku), beginning around 1008. Murasaki worked as the maid to Empress Akiko, who was a consort of the emperor and the daughter of a political leader. We know only a little of Murasaki's life, much of it from a diary she kept. She was born around 978 into a leading aristocratic family steeped in literature. Her grandfather was a famed poet and her father a provincial governor. Her father apparently lamented that she had not been a boy and allowed her to study. Murasaki's writing showed that she was familiar with Chinese history, literature, and poetry and had a considerable education. Indeed, she criticized young people who expected good jobs without undergoing the appropriate training.

Perhaps because she avidly pursued learning, she was married late, at age twenty, but her much older husband died only a few years later from illness. She had at least two children, including a daughter who later became a well-known writer. Murasaki is believed to have died sometime between 1025 and 1031, perhaps after several years as a Buddhist nun. Her self-description in her diary suggests an introverted woman:

> Pretty yet shy, unsociable, fond of old tales, conceited, so wrapped up in poetry that other people hardly exist, spitefully looking down on the whole world—such is the unpleasant opinion that people have of me. Yet when they come to know me they say that I am strangely gentle, quite unlike what they had been led to believe.

Murasaki's novel, *The Tale of Genji*, is much more sophisticated in language and thoughtful in sensibility than the literature that came before in Japan. In *Genji* she made contemporary language rather than the formal Chinese writing style a medium for art. Even today words and phrases from *Genji* are common in Japanese language. She also had other goals, claiming that the novel should always have "a definite and serious purpose." In focusing on the emotional and psychological interplay of her characters, her writing betrays a strongly feminine perspective. *Genji* also constitutes a treasure trove on social history, revealing much about the times.

The engaging *Genji* story chronicles the life and amorous adventures of Prince Genji, the son of an emperor and a model for all the qualities of taste and refinement admired by the Kyoto aristocracy. Genji is an accomplished poet, painter, dancer, musician, and athlete. But his supreme gift is the art most prized: "pillowing" (lovemaking). Genji and his friends devote little time to their government jobs. They spend their days largely in the search for pleasure, attend countless ceremonial functions, recite poetry endlessly, and move from one romantic affair to another. The mood of the novel is subdued melancholy and nostalgia for the passing of lovely things. Both men and women freely express their emotions. Hence, Genji shows a keen sensitivity to nature: "I hope that I shall have a little time left for things which I really enjoy—flowers, autumn leaves, the sky, all those day-to-day changes and wonders that a single year brings forth; that is what I look forward to." The novel ends with Genji making plans to give up his posts and retire to a mountain village, perhaps to continue with his poetry, music, and painting while focusing more on religious knowledge.

Lady Murasaki This eighteenth-century painting of Lady Murasaki writing while observing the moon reflected the styles of the artist's times but also suggests the continuing significance of the beloved Heian era writer. (Kyusei Atami Art Museum, Japan)

THINKING ABOUT THE PROFILE

1. What sort of background did Murasaki come from?

2. Why is *Genji* such an important work of literature?

Notes: Quotations from Ivan Morris, *The World of the Shining Prince* (New York: Kodansha, 1994), p. 251; Ryusaku Tsunoda et al., eds., *Sources of Japanese Tradition*, vol. 2 (New York: Columbia University Press, 1958), pp. 178–179; and Mikiso Hane, *Japan: A Historical Survey* (New York: Charles Scribner's, 1972), p. 56.

ity was acceptable for both men and women. Aristocratic women spent their days playing games, writing diaries, listening to romantic stories, or practicing art. Some women, such as the novelist Lady Murasaki (MUR-uh-SAH-kee), gained a formal education and learned to write (see Profile: Lady Murasaki, Heian Novelist). Many elite women wrote because, without demanding jobs, they had abundant free time and could focus on their feelings. In poetry, a writer might deftly turn a scene of nature into one of emotion: "The flowers withered, their color faded away, while meaninglessly, I spent my days in the world, and the long rains were falling."[19]

The Heian aristocracy saw love as an art to be cultivated and given maximum artistic expression. People wrote poems before meeting their lover and then the next morning following their meeting. Here are two morning-after poems from the diary of a prominent woman writer, Izumi Shikibu:

> Woman: "painful though it were, to see you leave before dawn [to avoid discovery], better by far than when the dawn's grey light, so cruelly tears you from my side." Prince: "to leave you while the leaves are moist with dew, is bitterer by far, than if I were to say farewell at night, without a single chance to show my love."[20]

Heian standards of feminine beauty were distinctive: women wore their hair long to the ground, applied white skin powder and lipstick, plucked their eyebrows, and blackened their teeth with dye. In one novel, a lady refuses to do these things, and her attendants are disgusted: "Those eyebrows of hers, like hairy caterpillars, aren't they; and her teeth—like peeled caterpillars."[21] Men also used cosmetics and were equally concerned with their personal dress and appearance.

The Decline of Heian Japan

Heian culture was perhaps too removed from real life to survive. Only a tiny fraction of Japan's population could afford to enjoy this hedonistic way of life. The common people outside Kyoto lived vastly different lives, usually working at bare subsistence levels as farmers and craftsmen. They were mostly illiterate and saddled by unremitting work, their rural lives brightened only by the occasional festival or family activities. Most peasants knew nothing of Heian court life or Chinese literature. Likewise, aristocrats feared leaving Kyoto; they called peasants "doubtful, questionable creatures" and the provinces "uncivilized, barbarous, wretched" places.[22]

The literature written during the late Heian period shows a growing sense of pessimism. The Kyoto elite became aware that their world of aesthetic perfection was a fleeting phenomenon that might soon vanish. Such indeed was the case. While aristocrats pursued hedonism in Kyoto, social and economic changes were clearing the path for a more decentralized system. Emperors became figureheads while powerful regional families gained considerable wealth and began building up their own warrior bands to keep the peace. These bands were transformed into hierarchical military organizations based on kinship and vassal ties to lords. By the twelfth century the

Heian era had ended and Japan had moved into a new phase of its history with a much different social system.

SECTION SUMMARY

■ The Korean state of Silla was subordinate to China and borrowed a great deal from China's culture, adapting it to Korean traditions.

■ The Koryo state was dominated by the aristocracy and saw the decline of Buddhist influence.

■ In the Nara period, Japan borrowed heavily from Chinese culture, but its government was a dyarchy in which one powerful family dominated the emperor, and imports such as Buddhism were melded with native cultural features such as Shinto.

■ In the Heian period, borrowing from China ended, foreign contacts were stopped, and a small elite group, concerned almost exclusively with the pursuit of aesthetic beauty, created some of Japan's best art and literature.

■ Affluent women in the Heian period had great sexual freedom and the time to learn to write.

◆ Changing Korea and Japan

How did Korean and Japanese society change in the late Intermediate Era?

During the second half of the Intermediate Era the Koreans came under the sway of a new dynasty while the Japanese changed substantially, producing a very different way of life and outlook than they had enjoyed a few centuries earlier. For all its cultural brilliance, the Heian aristocracy was not the prototype of later Japanese society. It had grown too inward-looking to continue its dominance. Instead, it served as a transmitter of the now fully assimilated residue of Chinese culture to another vigorous group, the provincial warrior class, in whose hands the future of Japan was to lie. As a result, the post-Heian centuries constituted another important transition in East Asia.

Korea During the Early Yi Dynasty

In 1392 a new Korean dynasty took over from the Mongols, the Yi (yee), whose state was known as Choson (cho-suhn) (see Map 11.4). They lasted until 1910, an incredible longevity of 518 years. Yi rulers sought good relations with China and maintained a tribute relationship with their large neighbor. During this time Koreans learned to better use Chinese social and political models; for example, mastery of Confucian scholarship became the road to careers in government. To Koreans Confucianism provided a philosophical justification for government by a benevolent bureaucracy under a virtuous ruler. Education expanded to prepare students for the civil service exams, which tested for both Confucian and scientific knowledge, and gradually this knowledge came to define the intellectual elite. As in China, government became the main way to wealth. Confucian influence also remade Korean social institutions such as the family. The Yi believed that Korean women had too much freedom and hence behaved immorally. They introduced policies to encourage women's seclusion at home and imposed arranged marriages, veiling of the face when out in public, female chastity, and strict obedience to husbands and fathers. However, commoner women, needing to work in the fields, usually had more freedom of movement and faced less segregation from men. Today Confucianism is arguably a stronger force than Buddhism, especially in rural areas.

Aided by extensive use of movable-type printing, Yi Korea continued to develop literature, technology, and science, including mathematics and astronomy. King Sejong (say-jong) (r. 1418–1450) was a particularly strong supporter of scientific progress. Respected by his people for improving the Korean economy and military, helping poor peasants, and prohibiting cruel punishments, Sejong wrote books on agriculture and formed a scholarly think tank, the Hall of Worthies. Aided by Sejong, fifteenth-century Yi scholars invented a phonetic system for indicating Korean pronunciation of Chinese characters and for writing the Korean language. Some experts consider it the most scientific system of writing in the world. But Chinese was still used for serious scholarship. These years also saw a renaissance of intellectual activity, including a 365-volume encyclopedia of medical knowledge. In technology, Koreans created the world's first rain gauges, which were installed throughout the country to keep accurate rainfall records. In these ways, Choson was able to remain among the more creative and sophisticated of the late Intermediate Afro-Eurasian societies.

Map 11.4 Korea and Japan, ca. 1300
Japanese society developed in an archipelago, the major early cities rising in central Honshu. In 1274 and 1281 the Japanese repulsed Mongol invasions by sea. Throwing off the Mongols, Korea was unified under the Yi dynasty in 1392.

Online Study Center **Improve Your Grade**
Interactive Map: Korea and Japan Before 1500

King Sejong This modern painting portrays the Yi dynasty King Sejong, revered by Koreans for his political, economic, and scientific achievements, observing stars, supervising book printing, and contemplating a musical instrument he commissioned. Sejong patronized learning, supported agricultural innovations that increased crop yields, introduced humane laws, and fostered economic growth.
(Courtesy, Yushin Yoo)

The Warrior Class and a New Japanese Society

When the Heian period ended, a new warrior class gradually became the dominant force in Japanese politics and society, helping to produce a very different Japanese government and culture. The warrior class triumphed for several reasons. First, Heian provincial governors, who were too fond of the refinements of Kyoto, had a growing tendency to delegate their powers and responsibilities to local subordinates. Second, rural society was changing. Powerful local families and Buddhist communities were always hungry for land and often able to seize it by force. By gaining tax exemptions, they increased the tax load on peasants, some of whom in turn fled to the north to open new land or joined roving bands of unattached ronin. Other peasants signed over themselves and their lands to lords of manors, which released the peasants from paying taxes and provided them with protection, but at the cost of becoming bound to the land and supplying food in exchange for protection. Thus the Heian era estates were replaced by a system of scattered landholdings in which a lord ruled over the villages on his parcel of land. This system led to more direct ties between peasants as vassals and the warrior class as lords.

The net result was that, by the end of the twelfth century, tax-paying land amounted to 10 percent or less of the total cultivated area, and local power had been taken over by the new aristocracy in the rural provinces. As this aristocracy expanded their landholdings, they needed military assistance. Soldiers and ronin signed on as military retainers to aristocratic families, the leaders of whom themselves became mounted warriors. Since conscription had ended earlier because it was too burdensome for the peasants, imperial forces were weak. In this way political and military power dispersed to rural areas.

As this warrior class moved to the center of the historical stage, it led Japan into a type of social and political organization more like that of Zhou China or medieval Europe than the centralized Tang state. Historians disagree as to when between the twelfth and fourteenth centuries the transition to a new, warrior-based system—Japanese called it the Age of Warriors—was completed, but it continued in some form to the nineteenth. During this time, military power absorbed into itself political and economic authority, and all three became defined in terms of rights to land and relations between lords and vassals. Although some historians have stressed the many similarities between post-Heian Japan and medieval Europe, the Japanese rulers were at times stronger than most European kings.

The warrior class, or **samurai** (SAH-moo-rie) ("one who serves"), moved gradually into a position of military supremacy over the emperor and the court. The samurai resulted from a relationship formed between the rural lords and their military retainers, based on an idealized feudal ethic later known as **Bushido** (boo-SHEE-doh) ("way of the warrior"), which was not completely developed until the seventeenth century. The samurai had two great ideals derived from Bushido: loyalty to leaders, and absolute indifference to all physical hardship. They enjoyed special legal and ceremonial rights and in return were expected to give unquestioning service to their lords. Although only a few women of the samurai class, most famously Tomoe Gozen in the twelfth century, engaged in combat, most received some martial arts training. Their main job was to run and defend the family estates.

The samurai occupied the highest level of the social system, but they were a small percentage of the population. In return for loyalty, they received material rewards and secure employment. If they failed to do their duty or achieve their purpose, suicide was a purposeful and honorable act. This act served as conclusive evidence that, although he had failed his purpose, here was a man who could be respected by friend and enemy alike for his physical courage, determination, and sincerity. Homosexuality was also common among the samurai, as among several other warrior castes in history, such as the Spartans in classical Greece, perhaps because of male bonding and an ethic extolling male values. Japanese society generally tolerated same-sex relations. Such unique cultural patterns as Zen Buddhism and the tea ceremony also rose to prominence among the samurai class.

The Shogunates

The periodic fighting of the warrior society resulted in part from overpopulation: too many people competing for control of too little good land. By the twelfth century Japan was controlled by competing bands of feudal lords, and a civil war broke out between two powerful families and their respective allies. One lord, Minamoto-no-Yoritomo (MIN-a-MO-to-no-YOR-ee-TO-mo), emerged victorious and set up a military government in Kamakura (kah-mah-KOO-rah), near Tokyo (TOE-kee-oh), which lasted from 1180 to 1333. The emperor commissioned him **shogun** (SHOW-guhn) ("barbarian-subduing generalissimo"), in effect a military dictator controlling the country in the name of the emperor, who remained in seclusion in Kyoto. The shogun was responsible for internal and external defense of the realm, and he also had the right to nominate his own successor.

Although the imperial house, which traced its origins back to the Sun Goddess in an unbroken line, had become politically impotent, no shogun seriously attempted to abolish it. To many Japanese, the emperors symbolized the people and the land. The Kamakura shoguns were nominally subordinate to the emperors but had real power in many parts of the country. However, before 1600 the system was not very centralized. In many regions, local leaders paid only nominal respect to the shoguns and governed their own districts as they liked.

---

samurai ("one who serves")   A member of the Japanese warrior class, which gained power between the twelfth and fourteenth centuries and continued until the nineteenth.

Bushido ("Way of the Warrior")   An idealized ethic for the Japanese samurai.

shogun ("Barbarian-subduing generalissimo")   In effect a military dictator controlling the country in the name of the emperor.

During the Kamakura Shogunate the Mongols failed twice, in 1274 and 1281, to invade Japan. The 1281 Mongol attempt involved the largest force, in some accounts up to 150,000 men transported by over 4,000 conscripted Chinese ships. These ships were armed with ceramic projectile bombs, the world's first known seagoing exploding projectiles. On both occasions, the Mongol armies landed, met fierce resistance, and were destroyed when great storms scattered and shipwrecked their fleets. These divine winds, or *kamikaze* (KAHM-i-KAHZ-ee), convinced the Japanese of special protection by the gods. Japan was never successfully invaded and defeated until 1945. Any inferiority complex toward China had ended.

Japanese Society, Religion, and Culture

The new Japanese society and culture, shaped by the warrior class, differed substantially from that during the Heian era. Japanese society had always been hierarchical, but now the special status of the samurai reflected a more rigid structure than before. Inequality started in the family: children owed obedience to their parents, and the young honored the old. Each family was headed by a patriarchal male. Women now commonly moved into their husband's household, where they were considered his property and served his parents. Women were expected to be dutiful, obedient, and loyal to their menfolk. Marriages were arranged for the interest of the family, not from romantic love. Women were socialized to stay home and raise children. Yet, while women lost some freedom, marriage became more durable and divorce more difficult, giving married women more security. Furthermore, women from aristocratic families also dominated the staff of the imperial court and ran the emperor's household, giving them some political influence. As in China, the interest of the group always took precedence over that of the individual.

The Japanese developed new forms of religion and the arts between 1200 and 1500. Many Buddhist sects emerged, but three became the most significant and enduring. The largest, the *Pure Land*, emphasized prayer and faith for salvation and was very popular among the lower classes. Arising during civil war, the Pure Land school stressed the equality of all believers and minimized distinctions between monks and laypeople. It also rejected the notion of reincarnation, maintaining that believers went straight to nirvana. Another Buddhist sect, *Nicheren* (NEE-chee-ren), has sometimes been compared to Christianity and Islam because of its militant proselytizing and concern for the afterlife. Most Japanese Buddhist sects were peaceful and tolerant, but Nicheren was angry and outspoken, seeing rival views as heresy.

The third major Buddhist sect originated in China under Daoist influence. **Zen** is called the meditation sect because it emphasized individual practice and discipline, self-control, self-understanding, and intuition. Knowledge came from seeking within, deep into the mind, rather than from outside assistance. One Zen pioneer wrote, "Great is mind. Heaven's height is immeasurable but Mind goes beyond heaven; the earth's depth is unfathomable, but Mind reaches below the earth. Mind travels outside the macrocosm."[23] Zen practitioners expected enlightenment to come in a flash of understanding. The Zen culture was devised over the centuries to bring people in touch with their nonverbal, nonrational side. It stressed simplicity and restraint, contending that "great mastery is as if unskillful."[24] We might say today that "less is more."

Religious perspectives, especially Zen, affected the arts. Zen values can be seen in Japanese rock gardens, landscape gardening, and flower arrangements. Whereas the Chinese preferred their nature unspoiled, the Japanese liked it ordered. Japanese gardens, ponds, and buildings, such as the beautiful Golden Pavilion of Kyoto, built in the thirteenth century, were all constructed in harmony with their natural surroundings. The tea ceremony, which also resulted from Zen, emphasized patience, restraint, serenity, and the beauty of simple action involving the commonplace, that is, preparing and drinking tea. The highly formalized ceremony could last two hours, suggesting withdrawal from the real world. It also reflected a Japanese beverage preference. For example, a Zen monk wrote that tea was the most wonderful medicine for nourishing health and fostering a long life.

Other arts also flourished in this era. Japanese ceramics and pottery later became famous throughout the world for their subtlety and understated beauty, and they are considered by some to have been the world's greatest. Potters specialized in making cups, bowls, and vases using rough textures and irregular lines to suggest weathering and the effects of time, a Japanese preoccupation. By the fourteenth century they were mass-producing pottery. Japanese painting was also an old art and, as in other visual arts, emphasized not creativity or self-expression but skill and technique through self-discipline. Poetry too continued to be popular. The **Noh** drama, plays that presented stylized gestures and spectacular masks, also appeared in this era.

Japanese Political and Economic Change

Although a samurai-dominated hierarchical society became well established, these centuries also saw considerable political and economic change. In 1333 the Kamakura Shogunate was ended through intrigues and civil wars and replaced by a government headed by the Kyoto-based Ashikaga (ah-shee-KAH-gah) family (1338–1568). But the Ashikaga shoguns never had much power beyond the capital, although they were theoretically lords over the provincial governors. Furthermore, a growing population, which reached 5 million by the 1300s, became harder to control. Political power became increasingly decentralized, as local lords struggled to obtain more land. This

---

Zen A form of Japanese Buddhism called the meditation sect because it emphasizes individual practice and discipline, self-control, self-understanding, and intuition.

Noh Japanese plays that use stylized gestures and spectacular masks that began in the fourteenth century.

competition led to the rise of great landowning territorial magnates called **daimyo** (DIE-MYO) ("great name"), who monopolized local power. Each of the several hundred daimyo had his supporting samurai and derived income from the peasants working on their land.

By the 1400s Japan had experienced rapid change in both economic and political spheres. Agriculture became more productive, and an increasingly active merchant class lived in the fast-growing towns. The Japanese developed a new interest in foreign trade, and Japanese sailors and merchants traveled to China and Southeast Asia. The rigid political and social system strained to accommodate these new energies. In the next century civil war and the arrival of European merchants and Christian missionaries aggravated these problems and resulted in a dramatic modification of the political system.

SECTION SUMMARY

■ The Yi, who ruled Korea after the Mongols, sought good relations with China and instituted the Chinese educational and civil service exam system.

■ In Japan, the warrior class, or samurai, gradually attained supremacy over the emperor and the court, and an organization like that of medieval Europe, based on lords and vassals, became dominant.

■ The Kamakura Shogunate began after the winner of a Japanese civil war was given the title of shogun, or military dictator, who ruled while the emperor retreated behind the scenes.

■ Three enduring Buddhist sects developed in Japan: Pure Land, which stressed equality; Nicheren, which was militant; and Zen, which stressed meditation, discipline, and simplicity, qualities that are shown in the tea ceremony and such Japanese arts as gardening and flower arranging.

■ The Ashikaga Shogunate, which followed the Kamakura, had little power over the provinces, which became ruled by landowning lords called daimyo.

Online Study Center **ACE the Test**

✦ Chapter Summary

The Intermediate Era was in many respects a golden age for much of East Asia. With their increasingly sophisticated ways of living, the Tang and Song dynasties represented perhaps the high point of Chinese history and culture. While the Tang enjoyed great external power, the Song featured dramatic commercial growth. The Chinese continued to develop distinctive forms of literature, visual arts, philosophy, and government, as

well as new technologies and scientific understandings. Major aspects of Chinese culture, such as writing, Confucianism, and Buddhism, spread to Korea, Japan, and Vietnam. The Mongol conquest and brief period of rule weakened China's dynamism but extended overland trade routes that linked China even more closely to the outside world and promoted the spread of Chinese science and technology to western Eurasia. China became the richest segment of a vast empire spanning half of Eurasia. During the Ming, China briefly reasserted its transregional power and maintained an advanced technology. But, in part because of the experience of Mongol rule, Ming China also increasingly turned inward, becoming less involved in world affairs.

The Koreans and Japanese synthesized Chinese learning with their own native traditions to produce highly distinctive societies. Significant change occurred in Japan as it moved from the aristocratic court culture of Heian to a warrior-dominated culture based on large landowning families and their military retainers, or samurai. By the end of the 1400s the East Asian societies remained strong but faced new challenges when Europeans began to expand their power in the world.

Online Study Center **Improve Your Grade** Flashcards

Key Terms

neo-Confucianism	Bushido
qi	shogun
kotow	Zen
dyarchy	Noh
kana	daimyo
samurai	

Suggested Reading

Books

Adshead, S. A. M. *China in World History*. 3rd ed. New York: St. Martin's, 2000. A study of China's relations with the world during this era.

Adshead, S. A. M. *T'ang China: The Rise of the East in World History*. New York: Palgrave Macmillan, 2004. Provocative examination of the rise and decline of China.

Benn, Charles. *China's Golden Age: Everyday Life in the Tang Dynasty*. New York: Oxford University Press, 2002. A comprehensive look at the society, economy, and culture of Tang China.

Cohen, Warren. *East Asia at the Center: Four Thousand Years of Engagement with the World*. New York: Columbia University Press, 2000. A good summary of China, Koria, and Japan in Eurasian history.

Ebrey, Patricia Buckley, Anne Walthall, and James B. Palais. *East Asia: A Cultural, Social, and Political History*. Boston: Houghton Mifflin Company, 2006. A readable, comprehensive survey, especially strong on the Intermediate Era.

Ebrey, Patricia Buckley. *The Inner Quarters: Marriage and the Lives of Chinese Women in the Sung Period*. Berkeley: University of California Press, 1993. A fascinating study of this neglected topic.

---

daimyo ("Great name") Large land-owning territorial magnates who monopolized local power in Japan beginning during the Ashikaga period (1338–1568).

Gernet, Jacques. *Daily Life in China on the Eve of the Mongol Invasion 1250–1276.* Stanford: Stanford University Press, 1962. Dated but still a fascinating study of Song life.

Lee, Ki-Baik. *A New History of Korea.* Cambridge: Harvard University Press, 1984. One of the most comprehensive and readable surveys.

Levathes, Louise. *When China Ruled the Seas: The Treasure Fleet of the Dragon Throne, 1405–33.* New York: Simon and Schuster, 1994. A recent study of the Ming voyages for the general reader.

Merson, John. *The Genius That Was China: East and West in the Making of the Modern World.* Woodstock, N.Y.: Overlook Press, 1990. Lavishly illustrated with good coverage of Song and Ming China.

Morris, Ivan. *The World of the Shining Prince: Court Life in Ancient Japan.* New York: Kodansha International, 1994. A reprint of the classic 1964 study of Heian society and culture.

Rossabi, Morris. *Kublai Khan: His Life and Times.* Berkeley: University of California Press, 1987. A study of China under Mongol rule.

Shaughnessy, Edward, ed. *China: Empire and Civilization.* New York: Oxford University Press, 2005. Contains essays on many aspects of Chinese society in this era.

Souyri, Pierre F. *The World Turned Upside Down: Medieval Japanese Society,* translated by Kathe Roth. New York: Columbia University Press, 2001. A major study of later Intermediate Japan and warrior society.

Storry, Richard, and Werner Forman. *The Way of the Samurai.* London: Orbis, 1978. A nicely illustrated examination of the samurai and their culture.

Varley, Paul. *Japanese Culture,* 2nd ed. updated and expanded. Honolulu: University of Hawai'i Press, 2000. A good overview.

Websites

Ancient Japan
(http://www.wsu.edu:8080/~dee/ANCJAPAN/CONTENTS/HTM). A useful site from Washington State University offering many essays and links on premodern Japan.

A Visual Sourcebook of Chinese Civilization
(http://depts.washington.edu/chinaciv/). A wonderful collection of essays, illustrations, and other useful material on Chinese history.

East and Southeast Asia: An Annotated Directory of Internet Resources
(http://newton.uor.edu/Departments&Programs/ AsianStudiesDept/index.html). Varied collection of links, maintained at University of Redlands.

Internet East Asian History Sourcebook
(http://www.fordham.edu/halsall/eastasia/eastasiasbook.html). An invaluable collection of sources and links on China, Japan, and Korea from ancient to modern times.

Internet Guide for China Studies
(http://www.sino.uni-heidelberg.de/igcs/). A good collection of links on premodern and modern China, maintained at Germany's Heidelberg University.

Silk Road Narratives
(http://depts.washington.edu/uwch/silkroad/texts/texts.html). Explores cultural interaction in Eurasia through excerpts from Silk Road travelers.

CHAPTER 12

Expanding Horizons in Africa and the Americas, 600–1500

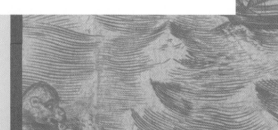

Online Study Center

This icon will direct you to interactive activities and study materials on the website: college.hmco.com/pic/lockard1e

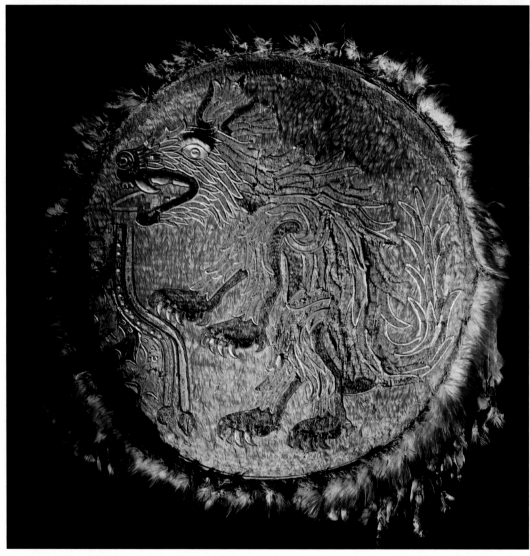

Feathered Shield This brightly colored feathered mosaic shield, used for ceremonial purposes by an Aztec warrior in the fifteenth century, has an image of the Aztec water god, a monster that resembled a coyote, outlined in gold. (Erich Lessing/Art Resource, NY)

A long time ago, when the Arabs arrived in Lamu [a port in today's Kenya, East Africa], they found local people there. The Arabs were received with friendliness and they wanted to stay on. The local people offered to trade land for cloths. Before the trading was finished, the Arabs had the land, and the [local people] had the cloth.

A LAMU ORAL TRADITION[1]

round 912 the Baghdad-born Arab geographer Abdul Hassan Ibn Ali al-Mas'udi sailed to East Africa with mariners from Oman (OH-mahn), in eastern Arabia, on their regular trading expedition to what Arabs described as *Zanj* ("the land of black people"). Al-Mas'udi discovered that the journey up and down the East African coast could be perilous, with reefs and strong winds that generated high waves that "grow into great mountains and open deep gulfs between them." Altogether al-Mas'udi spent three years traveling from port to port, venturing as far south as Sofala (so-FALL-a), a city in what is today Mozambique (moe-zam-BEEK). After further travels to Persia, India, and China, al-Mas'udi finally returned to Africa to settle in Cairo, where he wrote several scholarly books before his death around 956. His most influential book, provocatively titled *Meadows of Gold and Mines of Gems*, reported on his discoveries. He intended the book "to excite a desire and curiosity about its contents, and to make the mind eager to become acquainted with history."[2]

Al-Mas'udi's informative account pictured East African society in a key period of state formation while also recording the many links between these coastal towns and the Arabs, and through the Arabs to other Eurasian societies. He praised the energetic traders and skilled workers of the coast, reported that the Sofala region produced abundant gold for export, and provided details about the international ivory trade. Arabs carried ivory from Zanj to Oman, from where they shipped it to India and China. He wrote that "in China the Kings and military and civil officers use ivory [to decorate furniture]. In India ivory is much sought after. It is used for the handles of daggers. But the chief use of ivory is making chessmen and backgammon pieces."[3]

During the Intermediate Era many societies in East Asia, Southeast Asia, South Asia, West Asia, North Africa, and Europe benefited from extensive links across long distances over which they exchanged technologies, products, religions, and ideas. Some sub-Saharan Africans also became connected to this vast network through trade and the spread of world religions. As al-Mas'udi's description of the Zanj ports confirms, transregional trade was significant. As trade networks expanded, some African peoples, such as the gold producers near Sofala, became integral parts of hemispheric commerce while remaining part of networks within Africa. But many sub-Saharan Africans had only indirect links, and the American societies across the Atlantic Ocean had no known links at all, to these busy Afro-Eurasian networks of exchange.

Americans and many Africans had to independently address the challenges they faced. Yet, despite lack of contact with each other, Africans and Americans also shared some patterns of social and political development. Using their own creativity, some of these peoples thrived in forbidding desert, forest, or highland environments. Between 600 and 1500 African and American states rose and fell, among them a few regional empires. However, in contrast to the more densely populated areas of Eurasia, for many African and American societies politics was mainly a matter of self-governing villages rather than large, centralized governments. In the Western Hemisphere, trade routes existed over wide areas, but geography inhibited the growth of long-distance networks such as those linking, for example, East Africa to China. Only after 1492 did maritime exploration permanently connect African, American, and Eurasian peoples.

FOCUS QUESTIONS

1. How did contact with Islamic peoples help shape the societies of West Africa?
2. What networks linked East Africa and the Bantu societies to the wider world?
3. What were some distinctive patterns of government, society, thought, and economy in Intermediate Africa?
4. What factors explain the collapse of the Early Intermediate Era American societies?
5. How were the Aztec and Inca Empires different, and how were they similar?

 # The Power of West African States

How did contact with Islamic peoples help shape the societies of West Africa?

After 600, major changes took place in West Africa that resulted in the rise of several important kingdoms in the Sudanic region (the area stretching from west to east just below the Sahara Desert) and along the Guinea (GINN-ee) coast. As in Eurasia, empires sprouted, flourished, and decayed. Scholars studied and disputed in centers of learning, and what Chinese artists accomplished with ink and Europeans with paint, African artists achieved with bronze and wood. Networks of exchange and travel helped shape societies. The rise of great kingdoms in the Sudan coincided with the expansion of both a global religion, Islam, and a global commerce that linked West Africa with North Africa, the Mediterranean Basin, and western Asia.

Trade and the Expansion of Islam in the Sudan

For hundreds of years camel caravans had plied the trackless Sahara sands, a barren landscape where dry conditions, towering sand dunes, and searing sun conspired against crops, grasses, and trees. The caravans transported valuable products such as gold, salt, ivory, slaves, and ceramics between West and North Africa. The people benefiting the most from these networks lived in the Sudan (soo-DAN), the largely grasslands region just south of the Sahara. Because its generally flat geography and the long but sluggish Niger River allowed for easy communication, the Sudan became a meeting place of people and ideas.

Beginning in the 800s Islam filtered down the Saharan trade routes, carried peacefully by merchants, teachers, and mystics in much the same way it arrived in the islands of Southeast Asia (see Chapter 13). As Muslim merchants settled in towns involved with the trans-Saharan trade, they helped form stable governments to protect the trade and the caravans, and their religion was absorbed into the Sudanic societies.

CHRONOLOGY

	Africa	The Americas
700	ca. **500–1203** Ghana	**700–1400** Anasazi
		800–1475 Chimu Empire
		900–1168 Toltec Empire
1000	ca. **1000–1450** Zimbabwe	
1200	**1220–1897** Benin	
	1234–1550 Mali Empire	
1400	**1464–1591** Songhai Empire	**1428–1521** Aztec Empire
		1440–1532 Inca Empire

Islam introduced a complex, literate tradition to the Sudan. Many political and economic leaders of the Sudanese cities converted to the religion, and eventually most Sudanic peoples embraced Islam. Islamic influence produced changes in customs, names, dress, diet, architecture, and festivals, and Islamic schools spread literacy in the Arabic language. The Sudanic religious atmosphere promoted tolerance, by Muslims toward animists and vice versa. Still, Islamic practice was often superficial, and it took several centuries for the religion to permeate into the villages.

The First Sudanic Kingdom: Ghana

A few kingdoms with similar features already existed by the time that Islam reached the Sudan. Reflecting their peoples' animist beliefs, the kings in these societies were considered divine and enjoyed direct access to the spirits. They remained aloof from the common people and ruled through bureaucracies. But the kings' power was often limited. Many kings had to consult a council of elders, who frequently had to approve a decision to go to war, and some kings were elected by elders or chiefs. The women of the royal families also had great power, and, in a few societies, they could rule as queens. Some kingdoms became empires by either conquering neighboring peoples or linking states together through ties of kinship. States had no fixed territorial boundaries, only fluctuating spheres of influence, and they often included diverse ethnic groups. Their lack of political, ethnic, and cultural cohesion made them inherently unstable.

The earliest known Sudanic kingdom was Ghana (GON-uh), centered on the northwestern part of the Niger River (see Map 12.1). Founded by Mande speakers of the Soninke (soh-NIN-kay) ethnic group, Ghana was probably established around 500 C.E. but reached its golden age in the ninth and tenth centuries (see Chronology: Africa in the Intermediate Era). Ghana prospered from its control of the trans-Saharan gold trade between West and North Africa. Of Ghana and its

profitable commerce, the Spanish Muslim traveler Abu Hamid al-Andalusi wrote: "In the sands of that country is gold, treasure immeasurable. Merchants trade salt for it, taking the salt on camels from the salt mines. They travel on the desert as if it were a sea, having guides to pilot them by the stars or rocks."[4] For generations, gold and various tropical crops had been traded northward for salt, dates, textiles, and horses. The Ghana capital, Koumbi, was a major trade center located near gold deposits. Many of the city's 20,000 inhabitants were immigrants, including Arab and Berber merchants.

Ghana flourished for centuries before collapsing in 1203. By the tenth century Ghana's rulers, at their pinnacle of power,

CHRONOLOGY

Africa in the Intermediate Era

ca. 500–1203	Kingdom of Ghana
1000–1200	Rise of Hausa city-states
ca. 1000–1450	Zimbabwe kingdom
1200–1500	Golden age of East African coastal cities
1220–1897	Kingdom of Benin
1234–1550	Mali Empire
ca. 1275	Rise of Yoruba kingdom of Oyo
1324–1325	Mansa Musa's pilgrimage to Mecca
ca. 1375	Rise of Kongo kingdom
1464–1591	Songhai Empire
1487	Bartolomeu Dias rounds Cape of Good Hope

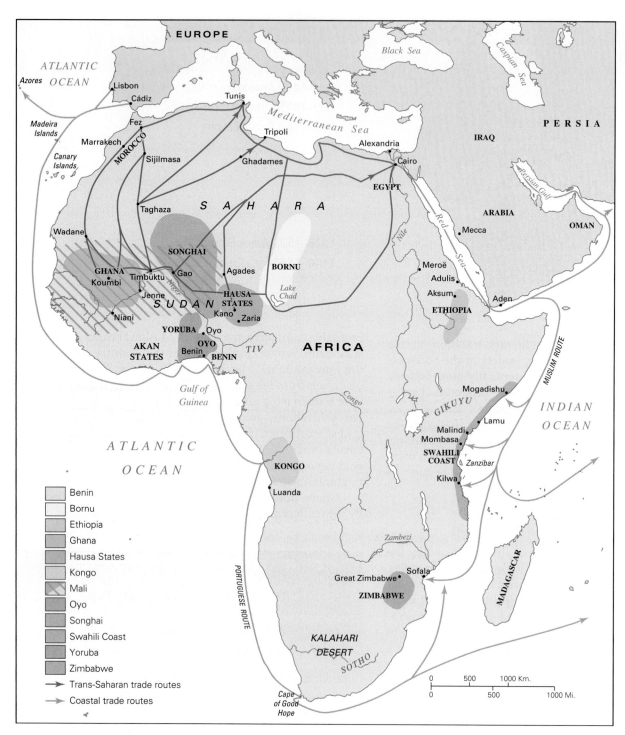

Map 12.1 Major Sub-Saharan African Kingdoms and States, 1200–1600 C.E.
Many large kingdoms and states emerged in Intermediate Africa. Large empires dominated the
Sudan in West Africa. Prosperous trading cities sharing a Swahili culture dotted the east coast.

Online Study Center **Improve Your Grade** Interactive Map: Africa Before 1500

had converted to Islam, a move that apparently increased the wealth and splendor of the royal court. An Arab visitor in 1067 said that the king's attendants had gold-plaited hair and carried gold-mounted swords, and that even the guard dogs wore collars of gold and silver. But early in the eleventh century a civil war erupted and Berbers from North Africa took advantage of the turmoil to attack the kingdom. Perhaps the empire had incorporated so many different peoples that it lost its cohesion. The court was destroyed and the merchants moved away.

Mali: Islam and Regional Power

The next great Sudanic empire, Mali (MAHL-ee), was formed in 1234 by another Mande-speaking group, the Malinke (muh-LING-kay), led by the Keita (KAY-ee-tah) clan. The Keita leader, Sundiata (soon-JAH-tuh), became the **mansa** (MAHN-suh), or king, of Mali (see Profile: Sundiata, Imperial Founder). Famed farmers and traders, the Malinke conquered much of the western Sudan, including the territory once controlled by Ghana. The empire's total area stretched some 1,500 miles from east to west and incorporated dozens of ethnic groups. The Malinke *mansa* was both a secular and religious leader who surrounded himself with displays of wealth and ceremonial regalia and expected his subjects to approach him on their knees. This emphasis on his dignity and power helped instill respect and obedience in his people. At some point Sundiata apparently converted to Islam, perhaps to secure better relations with North Africa, but he never seriously practiced that religion. Indeed, he also made use of Malinke animism, developing a reputation as a magician.

Islamic influence, however, gradually grew stronger, expanding the networks of communication and travel. Some of the later Mali emperors made glittering pilgrimages to Mecca. When Sundiata's descendant, Mansa Musa (MAN-sa MOO-sa) (r. 1312–1337), went to Mecca in 1324 riding a white Arab horse, he took fifty slaves bearing golden staffs, one thousand followers, and one hundred camels, each loaded with 300 pounds of gold. His fabulous journey exhibited the wealth and power of his state. According to an Arab official writing of Mansa Musa's visit to Egypt en route to Arabia, he "spread upon Cairo the flood of his generosity; there was no person, officer of the court, or holder of any office who did not receive a sum of gold from him. The people of Cairo earned incalculable sums from him, whether by buying and selling or by gifts."[5] Mansa Musa reportedly spent so much money in Cairo that the Egyptian currency was devalued. An Arab observer credited Mansa Musa with being a student of religious sciences who built grand mosques in Mali and imported Islamic jurists. But whatever the attention Mansa Musa lavished on Islam, the majority of the Mali people continued to follow animism, and even the elite were lax in their Islamic practice. Mali remained an essentially secular state.

Mali's economic base included farming, commerce, and control of the gold and salt trade across the desert. The kingdom supplied most of Europe's gold reserves and about two-thirds of the world's gold supply in this era. Local Africans mined the gold in open pits or in underground passages through loose dirt along streambeds, the miners digging while crouching in waist-deep water. At the surface, women extracted the gold dust from the dirt dug out by the men. Acquiring the gold, traders then met salt merchants from the north and silently matched piles of gold and salt until a fair exchange was agreed upon. Other imports came to Mali from as far away as China and India. In the thirteenth century the Mali trading

city of Timbuktu (tim-buk-TOO) emerged as the major southern terminus of the trans-Saharan caravan trade. Cities and towns like Timbuktu were filled with craftspeople, but most Malians lived in small villages and cultivated rice, sorghum, or millet, supplemented by herding or fishing. The wealth of rulers like Mansa Musa may have dazzled the world, but most Malians lived simply.

Mali benefited from network connections. The international links provided by Islam and the trans-Saharan commerce enticed many visitors and sojourners to the Sudan, including poets, architects, teachers, and traders from places such as Spain and Egypt. Even a few bold European Christians braved the desert to visit the area, and at least one Italian merchant reached Timbuktu. The fourteenth-century Moroccan traveler Ibn Battuta spent months in Mali and had mixed feelings about the empire. He admired the Malians' many "admirable qualities," commenting that "they are seldom unjust, and have a greater abhorrence of injustice than any other people." He also found "complete security in the country. Neither traveler nor inhabitant in it has anything to fear from robbers or men of violence."[6] But the pious Muslim frowned on what he considered the immodest dress and independent behavior of women and the custom of eating dogs.

Mali rapidly declined in the 1400s because of internal factionalism and raids by other peoples. Soon the fringes broke away, and by 1550 the Mali of former days was gone. A much smaller Mali kingdom limped into the 1600s, one of numerous small states in the western Sudan.

The Songhai Empire

The third great Sudanic empire was Songhai (song-GAH-ee), a kingdom formed by several ethnic groups that seceded from Mali in 1340. Over the next decades, Songhai increased its power, and by 1464 it was a major empire roughly as large as the former Mali Empire. Some of the Songhai rulers were nominal Muslims, and others were devout. The most revered leader was Aksia (ACK-see-a) the Great (1483–1528), a humane, pious, and tolerant man who was devoted to learning. The imperial capital at Gao (ghow) on the Niger River was a substantial city containing perhaps 100,000 people. A Moroccan visitor around 1500 wrote that Gao's rich merchants traveled continuously around the region to sell their wares, while many people came to Gao bringing gold to purchase goods from North Africa and Europe. As demand for gold and slaves increased in both North Africa and Europe, Songhai flourished from the trans-Saharan caravan trade, even more than Ghana and Mali had done before. Slaves were obtained from nearby peoples and sold in the Gao slave market, and many were taken on the arduous journey across the Sahara to the Mediterranean societies. In exchange for gold and slaves, Songhai received glass, copperware, cloth, perfumes, and horses.

Under Songhai rule, Timbuktu flourished. The city on the Niger became a major Islamic intellectual center with a famous Islamic university that specialized in teaching astronomy, astrology, medicine, history, geography, Arabic, and Quranic studies. The thousands of scholars and students in the city

---

mansa ("king")   Mande term used by the Malinke people to refer to the ruler of the Mali Empire.

SUNDIATA,
IMPERIAL FOUNDER

According to tradition, the founder of the great Mali Empire was Sundiata Keita, the "Lion Prince" of the Malinke people. It is difficult to separate myth from fact about his life, but most historians believe there was a real Sundiata. Arab historians such as Ibn Khaldun mention him in their accounts. Nonetheless, any account must use oral epics, which tend to glorify his heroism and reflect a Malinke view of a glorious past.

At the time Sundiata was born in the early thirteenth century, Ghana was collapsing and various other groups were contending to fill the power vacuum. Sundiata was one of twelve sons of a Malinke king, Nare Fa Maghan, and Sogolon Conde, a hunchback. As a child Sundiata was sickly and had stiff legs that made walking difficult. Hence he was spared when a rival state, Kaniaga, under their brutal king, Sumaguru, conquered Sundiata's town, Niane, and executed all his brothers as potential threats. According to the oral epic:

He had a slow and difficult childhood. At the age of three he still crawled along on all-fours. He had nothing of the great beauty of his father. He had a head so big that he seemed unable to support it. He was taciturn and used to spend the whole day just sitting in the middle of the house. Malicious tongues began to blab. All Niane talked of nothing but the stiff-legged son.

However, soothsayers predicted greatness for him, and eventually he overcame his physical problems so that "at the age of eighteen he had the stateliness of the lion and the strength of the buffalo."

As a young man he went into exile, and then he returned to rally his people against the tyrannical Sumaguru: "The sun will arise, the sun of Sundiata." Determined and diplomatic, he skillfully used traditional clan and kinship groups as well as a reputation for possessing knowledge of magic to build and solidify his power. Persuading other Malinke chiefs to surrender their titles to him, he became his peoples' sole king, enhancing his position in preparation for war. Sundiata put together a military force and triumphed over Sumaguru in the battle of Kirina about 1235, and then he conquered much of the old Ghana territories.

As king, Sundiata acquired the power to reshape Malinke government and society. According to the epics, "He left his mark on Mali for all time and his [rules] still guide men in their conduct [today]." As ruler for over two decades, Sundiata transformed his small state into the core of an imperial system based in his hometown of Niane, alongside the Niger River and near valuable goldfields. His rule brought peace, happiness, prosperity, and justice: "He protected the weak against the strong. The upright man was rewarded and the wicked one punished." The epic account is undoubtedly an idealized version of truth, but it also recorded that Sundiata punished his enemies. Malinke custom allowed high-status men to have

Sundiata This modern depiction of Sundiata Keita memorializes the legendary founder of the Mali Empire. Even today, nearly a millennium after his death, Sundiata remains a hero to Africans for his political and military skills. [From Ada Konare Ba, *Sunjiata: Le Fondateur L'Empire du Mali* (Dakar: Nouvelles Editions Africaines, 1983.)]

many wives, and Sundiata, like his father, followed this practice, leaving many descendants.

Sundiata died about 1260, but his legend lived on. As the epics retold even today put it:

Sundiata was unique. In his time no one equaled him and after him no one had the ambition to surpass him. Men of today, how small you are beside your ancestors. Sundiata rests but his spirit lives on and today the Keitas still come and bow before the stone under which lies the father of Mali.

THINKING ABOUT THE PROFILE

1. What does Sundiata's career tell us about the personal qualities admired by the Malinke people and helpful in forging a Sudanic empire?

2. How do the epic stories told over the centuries remember Sundiata and his deeds?

Note: Quotations from D. T. Niane, *Sundiata: An Epic of Old Mali* (London: Longman, 1965), pp. 15, 40, 47, 81, 83–85.

Nurse, Derek, and Thomas Spear. *The Swahili: Reconstructing the History and Language of an African Society, 800–1500.* Philadelphia: University of Pennsylvania Press, 1985. An excellent summary of what we know about the Swahili and their early history.

Pearson, Michael. *The Indian Ocean.* New York: Routledge, 2003. Integrates east Africa into the hemispheric trading system.

Shaffer, Lynda Norene. *Native Americans Before 1492: The Mound-building Centers of the Eastern Woodlands.* Armonk, N.Y.: M. E. Sharpe, 1992. A brief overview, for the general reader, of some early North American societies.

Smith, Michael E. *The Aztecs,* 2nd ed. Malden, M.A.: Blackwell, 2003. A recent scholarly study.

Thobhani, Akbarali. *Mansa Musa: The Golden King of Ancient Mali.* Dubuque, Iowa: Kendall-Hunt, 1998. A readable introduction to Mali and its rulers.

Townsend, Richard F. *The Aztecs.* Rev. ed. New York: Thames and Hudson, 2000. A readable, well-illustrated survey of Aztec history and society.

Websites

Africa South of the Sahara
(**http://www-sul.stanford.edu/depts/ssrg/africa/guide.html**).
Useful collection of links from Stanford University.

Ancient Mexico.com
(**http://www.ancientmexico.com/**).   Contains useful features on art, culture, and history.

Ancient Mesoamerican Civilizations
(**http://www.angelfire.com/ca/humanorigins/**).   Links and information about the premodern American societies.

Civilizations in Africa
(**http://www.wsu.edu:8080/~dee/CIVAFRCA/CIVAFRCA.htm**).
Contains useful essays on premodern Africa.

History and Cultures of Africa
(**http://www.columbia.edu/cu/lweb/indiv/africa/cuvl/cult/html**).
Provides valuable links to relevant websites on African history.

Internet African History Sourcebook
(**http://www.fordham.edu/halsall/africa/africasbook.html**).
This site contains much useful information and documentary material on ancient Africa.

The Aztecs/Mexicas
(**http://www.indians.org/welker/aztec.htm**).   Essays and information on the Aztecs.

South Asia, Central Asia, Southeast Asia, and Afro-Eurasian Connections, 600–1500

Online Study Center

This icon will direct you to interactive activities and study materials on the website: college.hmco. com/pic/lockard1e

Xuan Zang Arriving in China A seventh-century C.E. Buddhist Chinese pilgrim, Xuan Zang, spent many years traveling in India, collecting Buddhist wisdom and observing Indian life. This Chinese painting shows him and his caravan returning to China with pack loads of Buddhist manuscripts. (Fujita Art Museum)

India's shape is like the half-moon. The administration of the government is founded on benign principles. The taxes on the people are light. Each one keeps his own worldly goods in peace. The merchants come and go in carrying out their transactions. Those whose duty it is sow and reap, plough and [weed], and plant; and after their labor they rest awhile.

XUAN ZANG, SEVENTH-CENTURY CHINESE VISITOR TO INDIA[1]

In 630 C.E. a brave and determined Chinese Buddhist monk, Xuan Zang (swan tsang) (ca. 600–664), traveled the Silk Road, mostly alone, to India on an extended pilgrimage to collect holy books and ended up spending fifteen years there, visiting every corner of the subcontinent. He was very observant and politically astute, but he also chafed at the perception of many Indian Buddhists that China was too remote and backward to truly claim Buddhism. In a debate at the great Nalanda (nuh-LAN-duh) Monastery, Xuan Zang told the monks that

> *Buddha established his doctrine so that it might be diffused to all lands. Who would wish to enjoy it alone? Besides, in my country the laws are everywhere respected. The emperor is virtuous and the subjects loyal, parents are loving and sons obedient, humanity and justice are highly esteemed. How then can you say that the Buddha did not go to my country because of its insignificance?[2]*

Despite Xuan Zang's Chinese pride, he found much to admire in India, including the Indian tolerance for diverse viewpoints. Even though Hinduism had become dominant, Buddhism enjoyed protection and royal patronage. Xuan Zang's writings described an Indian society that had a rigid social structure but also one that was creative and diverse and open to foreign influences, including regular contact over networks of exchange with China, Europe, the Middle East, and Indonesia. Xuan Zang was much impressed with India's high standard of living, efficient governments, and generally peaceful conditions. But some customs troubled him. Despite the bias in Indian religions against eating animals, many Indians consumed fish, venison, and mutton. He also criticized the caste restrictions, such as the practice of confining untouchables to their own neighborhoods.

After covering some 40,000 total miles in his many years of travel, Xuan Zang returned to China in 643, taking with him hundreds of Buddhist books to be translated into Chinese. He also became a confidant of the Tang emperor and fostered closer relations between India and China.

The cultural diversity and openness to foreign influence that Xuan Zang admired in India was due in part to the repeated invasions of Central Asian peoples, who brought with them diverse beliefs and customs. Over the centuries Hindu religion and society absorbed these newcomers and their ideas. Groups with differing customs generally lived peacefully side by side, and Indian ideals were spread through trade with neighboring peoples. But Hindu political domination and the assimilation of newcomers into Hinduism or Buddhism faced a particularly severe challenge with the arrival of Muslims, who gained control over large parts of the subcontinent. Having their own strong religious ideas, Muslims were not easily absorbed into the complex world of Hindu culture. The coming of Islam constituted a great turning point in the region's development, a transition comparable to that initiated by the Aryan migrations into India several millennia earlier.

Like Indians, Southeast Asians also adopted new political systems and religions. Powerful kingdoms emerged, some of them strongly influenced by Hindu and Buddhist culture from India. By the fifteenth century new faiths from outside, Theravada Buddhism and Islam, had reshaped the political map and created many diverse cultural and religious patterns. This diversity, as well as trade, remained a hallmark of Southeast Asian societies.

FOCUS QUESTIONS

1. What were some of the main features of Hindu society at its height?
2. How did Hinduism and Buddhism change in this era?
3. How did Islam alter the ancient Indian pattern of diversity in unity?
4. What political and religious forms shaped Southeast Asian societies in the Early Intermediate Era?
5. What was the influence of Theravada Buddhism and Islam on Southeast Asia?

◆ Hindu Politics and Indian Society

What were some of the main features of Hindu society at its height?

Political disunity and regional diversity marked the Early Intermediate Era in India. No Hindu leaders were able to recreate an empire like the earlier Maurya or Gupta, and India became a region of many states, cultures, and languages. In spite of a broad Hindu tradition and the extensive common heritage and historical continuity it created, most South Asians were split into many microcultures. Rather than a melting pot, India became a collage in which many images coexisted on the same canvas, shaping each other while retaining their own distinctive character. These pronounced regional distinctions within a widely shared Hindu culture demonstrated one of the great themes in Indian history: diversity in unity.

Unity and Disunity in Hindu Politics

The political disunity following the fall of the Gupta state in the fifth century proved to be a long-term pattern, with political fragmentation becoming the norm. King Harsha Vardhana (600–647) briefly united parts of north India, but this consolidation proved short-lived (see Chronology: South Asia, 600–1500 on page 360). Harsha came to power at the age of sixteen and ruled for forty-one years. A man of enormous energy, he put together an army that, at its strongest point,

C H R O N O L O G Y

	South Asia	Southeast Asia
600	**600–647** Empire of Harsha	**600–1290** Srivijaya Empire
800	**846–1216** Chola dynasty	**802–1432** Angkor Empire
1000	**1192–1526** Delhi Sultanate	**1044–1287** Pagan Kingdom
1200	**1336–1565** Vijayanagara state	**1238–1419** Sukhotai state **1403–1511** Melaka state
1400		

included 100,000 cavalry and 60,000 elephants, together with many thousands of infantrymen, a formidable force. He skillfully held together his small empire while cultivating close relations with Tang China. But his empire collapsed on his death.

We know about Harsha and his society from a biography written by a close adviser and an account by Xuan Zang, whose pilgrimage to India opened the chapter and who spent years in Harsha's domain. Much more than a warrior-king, Harsha had a fondness for philosophy and was renowned as a poet. While enjoying the pomp of kingship, he also listened patiently to the complaints of his humbler subjects. Harsha also fostered religions. A strong Buddhist like Ashoka centuries earlier, he tolerated all faiths. But Harsha opposed some practices. For example, he prevented his beloved sister, a Hindu, from committing sati at her husband's cremation.

Despite Harsha's brilliant reign, in the post-Gupta centuries dozens, and sometimes hundreds, of small states proliferated in the subcontinent. The Hindu states had varied types of government, including many absolute monarchies. Rulers owned many economic resources, such as irrigation works, forests, mines, and spinning and weaving operations. Kings tried to control outlying regions through appointed governors or patronage over local leaders. Since they occupied a precarious position of power, they attempted to buttress their rule by claiming a divine mission. The Brahmans (Hindu priests) who served as court advisers gave them legitimacy.

North and south India developed somewhat different political patterns. **Rajputs** ("King's sons"), members of a warrior caste formed by earlier Central Asian invaders who adopted Hinduism, controlled some of the north Indian states. This military aristocracy was raised in traditions of chivalry, honor,

and courage not unlike those of Japanese samurai or medieval European knights. The Rajput code emphasized respect for women, mercy toward enemies, and precise rules of conduct in warfare. However, the Rajput-led kingdoms never united and often fought wars against each other for regional power. In contrast to the north, many south Indian states were oriented to the sea and hence specialized in piracy, plunder, and foreign trade. South Indian merchants had more political influence than merchants did in north India, and various south Indians continued their lucrative maritime trade with Southeast Asia, China, and the Middle East. Indeed, many visited or settled in Southeast Asia, bringing with them lasting south Indian ideas on art, politics, and religion.

Villages and Cities

The continuity of Indian culture was reflected in village life. In an economy based mainly on agriculture, the village remained the basic unit of Indian life; even today, about 80 percent of Indians still live in villages. Farmers had to feed an Indian population that reached around 100 million by 1500. Rulers also depended on villages for income. Since ancient times land was regarded as the property of the sovereign, who was entitled to either a tax or a share of the produce. The land tax remained the main source of state revenue and the main burden on the peasant. This was a collective responsibility, since the village paid as a unit. As long as they regularly met their tax obligations, villages ran themselves and peasants had the hereditary right to use the land they farmed. A well-entrenched pattern of village government included a council, elected annually from among village elders and caste leaders, which dispensed local justice and collected taxes.

The typical Hindu village remained largely self-sufficient economically and organized itself through the caste system,

---

Rajputs ("King's sons")   An Indian warrior caste formed by earlier Central Asian invaders who adopted Hinduism.

C H R O N O L O G Y
South Asia, 600–1500

606–647	Empire of Harsha in north India
620–649	First Tibetan kingdom and introduction of Buddhism
711	First Muslim invasion of northwest India
846–1216	Chola kingdom in south India
1192–1526	Delhi Sultanate
1336–1565	Kingdom of Vijayanagara in south India
1398–1399	Devastation of Delhi by Tamerlane

which promoted stability. Within the village the individual served his or her caste. Members of different castes lived separately in their own neighborhoods, but all contributed to the livelihood of the larger community. Each village had a potter, carpenter, blacksmith, clerk, herdsman, teacher, astrologer, and priest as well as many farmers. These villagers with different specializations and caste levels served each other on a barter basis in what was essentially a symbiotic community. The village structure probably did not change substantially during the Intermediate Era.

Some modern Indian writers have romanticized traditional village life, portraying a society living peacefully from generation to generation. This picture contains some truth. Village life offered great psychological and economic security. Each individual had a recognized status as well as certain rights and duties, not to mention a built-in sense of community and many personal relationships. During those periods when the rulers kept the region at peace, repressed banditry, and kept the tax burden reasonable, most people were probably contented with their lot.

A large number of Indians also lived in towns and cities, many of which were commercial hubs. Urban merchants helped administer the towns, but, as in China, they were heavily taxed and not allowed to become too independent of government. Some merchant groups were immigrants. For example, during the eighth century some Zoroastrians fled to western India to escape the Islamic conquest of Persia and formed the distinctive *Parsee* (PAHR-see) (Persian) community, known for its commercial prowess in several cities of western India. Over the centuries the Parsees had adopted local languages and some Indian traditions.

Manufacturers as well as merchants lived in the cities. Indeed, India was one of the world's leading manufacturing centers. Workshops located mainly in or near cities and towns produced cloth, textiles, pottery, leather goods, and jewelry for local use or export, and some artisans spun and wove cotton to

be eventually sold as far away as China, Africa, or eastern Europe. India and China provided most of the world's industrial goods until the eighteenth century, and during this era the average per capita income for both urban and rural dwellers remained high by world standards.

Hindu Social Life and Gender Relations

The Hindu social system demonstrated great continuity over the centuries and, as in China, subordinated the individual to the group. The Indian owed an even more basic social obligation to the extended family than to the caste. An old saying described this extended family as "joint in food, worship, and property." The family, which included people of several generations, lived together in the same compound (residential area), enforced caste regulations among their members, and also collectively owned their economic assets, such as farmland. Because families helped their weaker members and shared their wealth, they constituted an effective source of social security. Most families, especially in north India, were patriarchal, headed by a senior male with strong authority, although older women held considerable influence. In a family compound children lived in close contact with many cousins, aunts, uncles, and grandparents. Child rearing became a group obligation, and children enjoyed warm support and great security.

Marriage customs reflected regional differences. In north India, parents arranged marriages for their children and hoped that love would follow marriage. Girls were married off young, sometimes by the age of seven or eight, usually to a boy in a neighboring village. Because the bride's family paid for the wedding and was expected to give lavish presents, families preferred sons. South Indians enjoyed more variation in marriage practices. Girls were more likely than in north India to marry boys whom they already knew, often a cousin. In Kerala (CARE-a-la) in southwestern India, one large group practiced **polyandry**, marriage of a woman to several husbands. However, since some male characters in the *Mahabharata* have the same wife, polyandry may have been a more common pattern in north India 3,000 years ago. Most Indian families discouraged divorce, viewing it as a humiliation.

The Indian social system of the Intermediate Era clearly favored men, who enjoyed many privileges. In ancient India, especially in merchant families, women seem to have had considerable freedom, often choosing their own husbands and circulating freely in local society. But by 600 C.E. customs had become more conservative as male leaders became obsessed with preserving social stability and controlling female sexuality. For example, from puberty females of all castes were now taught to keep a distance from all men except their closest relatives. High-caste women were expected to spend their time at home, only occasionally visiting friends or family. Low-caste and untouchable women enjoyed more mobility because they had to

polyandry Marriage of a woman to several husbands.

enter public society to earn the incomes needed for family survival.

Women by and large led lives marked by obedience, sacrifice, and service. From an early age they were taught to sacrifice themselves for parents, husband, and children. The stereotypical role model was the loyal and submissive wife who always followed her husband's lead. The young bride, usually much younger than her husband, moved into her husband's household and was expected to be submissive to her new mother-in-law. Yet, husbands often treated their brides indulgently and tenderly. Indians also revered motherhood and equated childbearing with success. After she bore children (especially sons), the wife's status improved considerably, and she enjoyed more freedom and respect inside and outside the household. As a woman grew older and became a mother-in-law herself, she gained even more influence, especially in domestic matters.

Women faced a complex situation. They enjoyed some legal rights, and ill-treatment of women, including physical brutality, was condemned, although it was undoubtedly common. In practice not all wives were silent and subservient. But widowhood could prove catastrophic, particularly if a woman had no son to care for her. Since Hindu custom frowned on remarriage, to be a young and childless widow was to face an especially difficult situation. This helps to explain the practice of *sati*, whether voluntary or coerced. To avoid surviving their deceased husband, some women, especially in north India, died on their husband's funeral pyre. An ancient Indian expression captures the challenge for women: "As a girl she is under the tutelage of her parents; as an adult her husband; as a widow her sons." Some women, such as actresses, singers, and prostitutes, flouted social custom and mainstream values. However, although sometimes wealthy, these women suffered from having a low status in the community.

Indians held diverse views about sex. Many books commended celibacy and advised married men to exercise their sexual prerogatives sparingly if they wanted health and virtue. Indeed, devout Hindu Brahman men frequently adopted celibacy after fathering several children. Yet, the worldly views of many, especially among the elite, are reflected in many Indian texts such as the *Kama Sutra*, a manual of lovemaking and related matters written around the third century C.E. Even the Hindu gods and goddesses were portrayed in art and writings as highly sexual beings, a view very unlike that of the virginal Madonna and celibate Jesus of Christian tradition, the image of a spiritually and morally pure Buddha, and the puritanical restrictions of Islam.

Science and Mathematics

During this era Indians made many contributions in mathematics and science. One of the greatest Indian mathematicians, Bhaskara (bas-CAR-a), lived in the twelfth century. In addition to proving that zero was infinity, he also designed a perpetual-motion machine by filling a wheel rim with quicksilver, in the process demonstrating the Hindu belief in perpetual change in

Sculpture of Two Lovers from Konarak Temple   This sculpture of two embracing lovers comes from the Konarak temple in the north Indian state of Orissa. The Hindu temple, dedicated to the sun-god, was built in the thirteenth century and featured many erotic sculptures.   (Benoy K. Behl)

the universe. Bhaskara's book on the subject was later translated into Arabic and reached Europe by 1200 C.E. Soon after, drawings of quicksilver wheels appeared there, generating ideas of perpetual motion that influenced modern scientific thought in the West. The first weight-driven clocks, built in Europe after 1300, may have been based in part on Bhaskara's ideas. A seventh-century Syrian astronomer said that "no words can praise strongly enough" the Hindus' discoveries in astronomy and their rational system of mathematics.[3] Some Indian astronomers and mathematicians found employment in Tang China, fostering a fruitful exchange of knowledge between the two societies.

Underlying many Indian creative investigations could be found the basis for scientific reasoning. But growing intercaste jealousy and the indifference of the higher castes to applied or practical inquiry hindered the development of science after Gupta times. The Brahmans became more powerful and controlled education, while those who pursued technical activities or physical labor sank lower in the status system. By the tenth century some visitors reported a growing ethnocentrism and disdain among Hindu thinkers for foreign ideas, including scientific ones. An astute Muslim observer wrote that "the Hindus believe that there is no country, king, religion, [or] science like theirs."[4]

SECTION SUMMARY

- In the Intermediate Era, India was fragmented into many small states; the north was influenced by earlier Central Asian invaders and the south by maritime trade with Southeast Asia.

- The village, which was based on cooperation and caste, remained the basic unit of Indian life and provided people with a sense of security.

- Indian merchants in the cities were heavily taxed, but India and China produced most of the world's manufactured goods in this era.

- In the Hindu social system, the individual was subordinate to the group and people tended to live in extended families that supported their members.

- Indian men had much more power than women, who were forced to marry early and earned respect through bearing children, particularly boys.

- The mathematician Bhaskara discovered perpetual motion, which influenced science in the West.

◈ Hinduism and Buddhism in South and Central Asia

How did Hinduism and Buddhism change in this era?

Hinduism experienced a renaissance in the Early Intermediate centuries. Although it increasingly divided into competing schools of thought and practice, it also grew in popularity, developing into a faith that emphasized offerings and devotion. While Hinduism increasingly shaped Indian life, Buddhism faded in India but found new influence in neighboring societies. Hindu culture flourished in India for half a millennium before facing the concerted challenge from Islamic peoples and ideas.

Hindu Diversity and a Common Culture

Hinduism provided the spiritual framework for the great majority of South Asians until the coming of Islam. Its strength lay in its diversity, which could accommodate all classes, personalities, and intellects. For example, it gave the scholar and mystic an opportunity for abstract and speculative thought, while also giving the more worldly individual a wealth of ritual, art, and gods for every occasion. Because they satisfied so many needs, the values of Hinduism came to permeate the diverse Indian society.

Recognizing that individuals varied in their spiritual and intellectual capacities, Hindus tolerated many different practices and beliefs and relied on no fixed and exclusive theology or set of beliefs. As the earliest Hindu holy book, the *Rig Veda*, put it: "Reality is one; sages speak of it in different ways."[5] Concepts of spiritual power ranged from an indescribable but all-pervading, omnipotent God, to personal gods with human attributes, to demons and spirits. An Indian proverb welcomed all to sample the essence of Hindu ideas: "Life is a river; virtue is its bathing place; truth is its water; moral convictions are its banks; mercy is its wave. In such a pure river, bathe."[6] Because it had these characteristics, Hinduism remained undogmatic, a philosophy and way of life with no central institution or church to monitor the faith. Since no single leader codified their beliefs, Hindus did not even agree on which sacred writings were most important. During the Intermediate Era, Muslims introduced the collective term *Hindu*, from the Persian term for "Indians," to describe the varied Indian sects, and in the nineteenth century C.E. Europeans began referring to the diverse collection of Indian beliefs as "Hinduism."

The tradition of tolerance suggested that all approaches to God were equally valid, although mystics and intellectuals tended to consider their approaches more worthy than those of the peasantry. For example, mother goddess worship was particularly common among the lower castes living in thousands of villages, especially in south India, but was less popular among the higher castes. The many gods and goddesses were worshiped in various ways. Although India was a patriarchal society, men and women often believed that the wives and consorts (companions) of the main male gods were more responsive to their needs than the male gods themselves. For example, many cults worshiped Shiva's wife, Shakti (SHAHK-tee), who was a composite of opposites: kind and beautiful but also cruel and fearsome.

For all their diversity of beliefs, most Hindus perceived the universe as a collection of temporary living quarters inhabited by individual souls going through a succession of lives. The most devout had the ultimate goal of liberation from finite human consciousness, which freed one from the endless cycle of birth and rebirth. Yet most Hindus accepted the natural world in which people must work out their own salvation, and only a small minority seriously sought to escape from the earthly world with all its pain and pleasures. Wandering holy men were respected for their withdrawal from worldly activities but not role models for most people. Rather, Hindus were obligated to meet their social obligations to family, caste, and village. Stressing moderation and temperance, Hindu thinkers typically advised all to combine spiritual and worldly spheres.

Hinduism helped establish a common culture throughout India. Brahmans served as advisers to kings, ensuring a certain standardization of political ideas and rituals in Hindu states. While Brahmans had a monopoly on reading the Sanskrit scriptures, the Hindu classics were available to all through storytellers. Legends and traditions were also handed down through the generations by word of mouth. By around

1000 C.E. the collections of ancient prayers and hymns, the Vedas, were also being translated from Sanskrit into various regional languages. These trends in Hinduism contributed to the broader pattern of cultural unity in diversity.

The Hindu Renaissance

Many thinkers who embellished or revitalized Hindu traditions lived during the Intermediate centuries, creating what has been called the Hindu Renaissance. Perhaps the greatest was Shankara (shan-kar-uh) (788–820), a south Indian Brahman who helped refine Hindu thinking. Shankara's religious ideas harked back 1,500 years to the *Upanishads*, but he systematically organized the diffuse strands for the first time. Through his itinerant preaching, debates with rivals, and written commentaries on the *Upanishads*, Shankara revitalized the mystical *Vedanta* tradition, with its belief in the underlying unity of all reality. To Shankara, all the Hindu gods were manifestations of the impersonal, timeless, changeless, and unitary Absolute Reality, *Brahman*, and the individual soul only a tiny part of the whole unity of the universe.

Shankara tried to balance reason and intuition. While accepting the Hindu scriptures as divine revelation, he wanted to prove them through logical reasoning and debate. Yet, contradictorily, he also argued that all knowledge was inconclusive and relative, impaired because humankind's grasp of reality is warped by ignorance and illusion. The truth of existence, he believed, could only be understood through ascetic meditation. Shankara's views remain very popular among modern Indian intellectuals.

Other philosophers offered different visions of Hinduism. In the eleventh century Ramanuja (RAH-muh-NOO-ja) rejected both reliance on Brahman priests and Vedanta meditation and instead emphasized **bhakti**, devotional worship of a personal god, arguing that the gods should be accessible without priestly help. As a Hindu poet-saint put it: "The lord comes within everyone's reach."[7] A few centuries later some Christian reformers in Europe would develop a similar notion of establishing a personal relationship with God without priestly aid. Whereas Shankara had seen the human soul as identical to god, Ramanuja believed them to be quite distinct entities. To him, the goal of life was to bring communion between the two. Salvation could be achieved by pure, childlike devotion to a personal god. The bhakti tradition emphasized pilgrimage to holy places such as the city of Benares (buh-NAHR-uhs) (Varanasi), alongside the Ganges. Hindus who died in Benares, it was believed, had their sins washed away. Ramanuja and other early bhakti thinkers, most of them non-Brahmans, also opposed or downplayed the caste system. The bhakti tradition appealed particularly to women, marginalized in brahmanic worship. An early female poet, Antal, in the ninth century, urged women devotees to revere Lord Krishna (an incarnation of Vishnu). Later the bhakti movement became part of mainstream Hinduism.

The Hindu Renaissance included the building of increasingly flamboyant temples, whose sculptural art was designed to illustrate the intricate mythology of the faith. One of the best examples of such a temple was constructed in the tenth century by a prince in his home city of Khajuraho (kah-ju-RA-ho). Dedicated to Vishnu, sculptures carved into the temple walls suggested the delights enjoyed by the gods, including lovemaking. The countless erotic, sexually explicit paintings or carvings in many Hindu temples, some of them clearly presentations of sexual intercourse, reflected a rather open view about portraying sexuality.

Decline and Change in Indian Buddhism

During the first half of the Intermediate Era, while Hinduism was enjoying its resurgence, the influence of Buddhism gradually declined in much of India. However, it retained considerable support in northeast India, where many Buddhist holy sites were located. The governments there continued to patronize the religion and its institutions, such as the college at the Nalanda Monastery, which attracted religious students from around Asia, as well as the Chinese pilgrim Xuan Zang. Pilgrims from distant lands, such as Xuan Zang, showed how much Buddhism was becoming a major influence in the eastern half of Eurasia, a trend that continued throughout the Intermediate Era as the faith spread in Central Asia, Tibet, China, Korea, Japan, and Southeast Asia, adapting to different cultures.

The intellectual and cultural environment of northeast India also promoted a dialogue between Hinduism and Mahayana Buddhism that fostered new schools of Buddhist and Hindu thought. One new Buddhist school, the **Vajrayana** ("Thunderbolt"), featured female saviors and the human attainment of magical powers. It spread during the eighth century into Nepal and Tibet, where it became the predominant form of faith.

In Bengal the continued contact between Mahayana Buddhists and Hindu followers of Shiva, many of whom revered his consort, the goddess Shakti, led to a new approach called **Tantrism** (TAN-triz-uhm), which worshiped the female essence of the universe. Both the Tantric and Vajrayana schools exalted female power, as earth mother and as the highest form of divine strength. Tantric sects developed within both Hinduism and Buddhism. Some were mystical and presented male-female sexual union as an action form of worship, a symbolic unity between the earthly and cosmic worlds. Other sects promised release from life's pain in a single lifetime to those who cultivated hedonism (including drinking of alcoholic beverages), pleasure, and ecstasy. Tantric Hindus were often hostile to the caste system. Most Hindus and Buddhists denounced Tantrism as an excuse for debauchery and sexual desire, and Tantrism gradually became a minor strand in the two religions.

---

bhakti Devotional worship of a personal Hindu god.

Vajrayana ("Thunderbolt") A form of Buddhism that featured female saviors and the human attainment of magical powers.

Tantrism An approach within both Buddhism and Hinduism that worshiped the female essence of the universe.

State Building and Buddhism in Tibet

While Buddhism declined in India, the remote high plateau of Tibet became a refuge for the religion. The first known pre-Buddhist Tibetan state emerged when Songsten-gampo (SONG-sten-GOM-po) (r. 620–649 C.E.) unified several tribes. Like other Tibetan leaders during this time, he was interested in connecting to an Asian world where Buddhism was expanding. He established close relations with Tang China and married a Chinese princess, and although not a Buddhist, he allowed the religion to spread in his kingdom and tolerated Buddhist practice. Several trade routes linked Tibet to the Silk Road and China, and some young Tibetans went to China for study. Tibetans also borrowed the Sanskrit script from India and made it their written language. A Tibetan epic poem about the revered first king, one of the longest in history, eventually became a beloved part of the folk tradition in India, China, and Mongolia.

By the eighth century Buddhism had become the dominant Tibetan faith, and its monasteries enjoyed many legal protections and financial support from the government. But many Tibetans also continued to follow the ancient folk religion, *bon*. The two faiths competed for popular support and political influence for the next several centuries, and late in the ninth century violent religious conflicts destroyed the unified state.

However, both Buddhism and state building were reinvigorated in later centuries. Several factors can account for this change. In the thirteenth century many Buddhist monks fled to Tibet to escape Islamic persecution in India. Political relations with the predominantly Buddhist Mongols, who had conquered China and established loose control over parts of Tibet, also boosted Tibetan Buddhism. A unified Tibetan government was established in 1247 under the leadership of one Buddhist sect allied to the Mongols. But the end of Mongol rule in China brought a return to aristocratic lay leadership in Tibet, which persisted into the seventeenth century.

Tibetans developed a distinctive religious system in their harsh highlands environment, and many of their customs differed from those of East and Southeast Asian Buddhists. Tibetan Buddhism, which is divided into four sects, is often termed **Lamaism** (LAH-muh-iz-uhm) because of the centrality of monks, or *lamas* (LAH-muhz), and huge monasteries. Perhaps a quarter to a third of male Tibetans became career monks, and Buddhism came to permeate every aspect of Tibetan life. Believers practiced magic, chanted mantras, made pilgrimages to shrines, and provided generous support to monasteries and Buddhist teachers. Tibetans also blended Buddhism with strong beliefs in the supernatural, including evil spirits. For example, people spun hand-held or roadside prayer wheels and carved prayers into stones, seeking the help of the Buddha. Tibetan Buddhism also featured elaborate death rites to propel the soul to the next rebirth.

Lamaism   The Tibetan form of Buddhism, characterized by the centrality of monks (*lamas*) and huge monasteries.

SECTION SUMMARY

- Hinduism adapted itself to the needs of a wide variety of people, from the worldly to the scholarly, and helped to establish a common culture throughout India.
- Shankara, a major thinker of the Hindu Renaissance, emphasized the importance of reason and of ascetic meditation, while Ramanuja emphasized the worship of a personal god.
- Indian Buddhism declined generally, but it remained important in the northeast, where Vajrayana and Tantrism grew out of the interplay between it and Hinduism.
- Buddhism became the dominant religion in Tibet, where it became Lamaism, and many Indian Buddhist monks took refuge there to escape Islamic persecution.

◆ The Coming of Islam to India and Central Asia

How did Islam alter the ancient Indian pattern of diversity in unity?

The spread of Islamic religion and government in India was a major transition in Indian history, as important as the coming of the Aryans several millennia earlier. Since Muslims and Hindus were almost exact opposites in their beliefs, Islam created a great divide in South Asian society. As Al-Biruni, an eleventh-century Muslim scholar, put it: "Hindus entirely differ from us in every respect. They differ from us in every thing which other nations have in common. In all manners and usages they differ from us to such a degree as to frighten their children with us."[8] For centuries Hinduism had absorbed invaders and their faiths, but Islam, a coherent and self-confident religion, could not be assimilated. The tension between the two faiths sometimes resulted in conflict. However, Islam enriched Indian culture, establishing new connections with western Asia while also promoting the spread of Indian ideas, especially in mathematics and science, to the Middle East and Europe. Many Indians embraced the new faith, and Muslims also gained political dominance over large parts of India, though Hindu power remained strong in south India.

Early Islamic Encounters

Islamic forces reached Central Asia and India within a few decades of the religion's founding. Western Asians had long been linked to Central Asia through Silk Road trade, and they were well aware of India's riches. Arab sailors had been active in South Asia for centuries before the rise of Islam, linking India by trade to western Asia and East Africa. Initially Indian and Central Asian encounters with Islam were sporadic and often peaceful. But Islamic rulers hoped to dominate these valuable regions, and military conflict increased.

Coming from a Hindu family that had recently converted to Islam, Kabir was well acquainted with both religious traditions. His mystical poems of passionate love for a monotheistic god rejected religious prejudice, rigid dogmatism, and the caste system. Modern Indian intellectuals seeking to bridge the gap between the two faiths particularly admired his attempt to see beyond the limitations of the two religions and his absolute opposition to violence. The following poem argues that individuals must experience God for themselves.

O servant, where dost thou seek Me? Lo! I am beside thee.

I am neither in temple nor in mosque; I am neither in Kaaba [Muslim shrine] nor in Kailash [abode of Shiva].

Neither am I in rites and ceremonies, nor in Yoga and renunciation.

If thou art a true seeker, thou shalt at once see Me: . . .

It is needless to ask of a saint the caste to which he belongs;

For the priest, the warrior, the tradesman, and all the thirty-six castes, alike are seeking for God.

It is but folly to ask what the caste of a saint may be; The barber has sought God, the washerwoman, and the carpenter . . .

Hindus and Muslims alike have achieved the End, where remains no mark of distinction. . . .

O brother! when I was forgetful, my true Guru [teacher] showed me the Way.

Then I left off all rites and ceremonies, I bathed no more in the holy water: . . .

From that time forth I knew no more how to roll in the dust in obeisance:

I do not ring the temple bell; I do not set the idol on its throne; I do not worship the image with flowers.

It is not the austerities that mortify the flesh which are pleasing to the Lord,

When you leave off your clothes and kill your senses, you do not please the Lord,

The man who is kind and who practices righteousness, who remains passive amidst the affairs of the world, who considers all creatures on earth as his own self,

He attains the Immortal Being, the true God is ever with him.

Kabir says: "He attains the true Name whose words are pure, and who is free from pride and conceit."

If God be within the mosque, then to whom does this world belong?

If Ram [God] be within the image which you find upon your pilgrimage, then who is there to know what happens without?

Hari [Lord Vishnu] is in the East; Allah is in the West. Look within your heart, . . .

All the men and women of the world are His Living Forms.

Kabir is the child of Allah and of Ram [God]: He is my *Guru* [Hindu teacher], He is my *Pir* [Sufi saint].

THINKING ABOUT THE READING

1. Why would someone of mixed religious background be open to questioning rigid doctrines?

2. What does Kabir think about the traditions of organized religions?

3. Where does Kabir believe that God is to be found?

Source: William Theodore De Bary, ed., *Sources of Indian Tradition*, Vol. 1 (New York: Columbia University Press, 1958), pp. 355–357. Copyright © 1958 Columbia University Press. Reprinted with permission of the publisher.

Muslims and Hindus also engaged each other culturally. For example, Muslim influences, including Persian words and Persian food, were incorporated into Hindu social life. In addition, many Hindu males adopted Muslim clothing styles, and in north India some Hindus began practicing the local Muslim custom of **purdah**, seclusion of women. Under the challenge of the new missionary faith, which was often supported by the local rulers, Hinduism became more conservative, emphasizing tradition and priestly leadership. Some intermarriage also occurred, and, at the village level, Muslims fit themselves into the caste system to some extent. Thus the Muslim society that developed in India, like the Hindu society, was not egalitarian but rather was led by an upper class who descended from immigrants. Many Muslims also adopted some Hindu religious customs, including music and dance.

However, despite some mixing, from the thirteenth century onward, the life of India became two distinct currents flowing side by side. Most Muslims refused to be assimilated into the social and religious fold of Hinduism and remained separate, disdainful of Hindus and of the caste system. But Hinduism was not destroyed either. Unlike Buddhism, which was centered in vulnerable monasteries, Hinduism's decentralized structure proved stable. Thus Hindus and Muslims mingled to some extent along the lines of contact but never united to form a single stream. This persistent division greatly affected twentieth-century India, when the British colony of India (most of the subcontinent) was eventually divided into separate nations, the Hindu-dominated India and the Muslim-dominated Pakistan. A third religion also maintained

purdah The Indian Muslim custom of secluding women.

a South Asian base, since the island of Sri Lanka remained a bastion of Theravada Buddhism.

SECTION SUMMARY

- Hindu warriors fended off Muslim invaders for a time, but they were outmatched and eventually defeated by their aggressive opponents.
- The destruction inflicted by Muslim invaders caused long-term Hindu resentment and also contributed to the decline of Buddhism in India.
- The Islamic Delhi Sultanate brought unity to north India for the first time in centuries, but its rulers ranged from the enlightened to the tyrannical.
- Various Hindu monarchies, including the Cholas, maintained power in southern and eastern India, while Hindu traditions died out in the north.
- The Delhi Sultanate declined because of climate change and civil war, and north Indian unity was shattered by the invasion of Tamerlane.
- Muslim and Hindu beliefs were radically opposed, but over time Muslim rulers came to tolerate Hindu subjects, many of whom eventually converted to Islam.
- While there was some cultural interchange between Hindus and Muslims in India, for the most part, the traditions remained separate.

✦ Cultural Adaptation and New Southeast Asian Societies

What political and religious forms shaped Southeast Asian societies in the Early Intermediate Era?

Owing partly to the stimulus from India and, to a lesser extent, China, several great Southeast Asian kingdoms developed near the end of the first millennium C.E., establishing their main centers in what is today Cambodia, Burma, the Indonesian islands of Java and Sumatra, and Vietnam, which managed to throw off the Chinese yoke in the tenth century (see Map 13.2). These Southeast Asian states mixed outside influences with their own traditions to produce new societies. As they experienced many changes, they also preserved considerable continuity, much as Funan and Champa had done early in the Common Era (see Chronology: Southeast Asia, 600–1500).

Indianized Kingdoms

From early in the Common Era until around the fourteenth century C.E., many Southeast Asian societies made selective use of Indian models in shaping their political patterns, a process known as Indianization. For example, the rulers declared

CHRONOLOGY	
Southeast Asia, 600–1500	
192–1471	Kingdom of Champa
600–1290	Srivijaya Empire
802–1432	Angkor Empire
939	End of Chinese colonization in Vietnam
1044–1287	Pagan kingdom in Burma
1292–1527	Madjapahit kingdom on Java
1238–1419	Sukhotai kingdom in Siam
1350–1767	Ayuthia kingdom in Siam
1403–1511	Melaka kingdom and Sultanate
1428–1788	Le dynasty in Vietnam (founded by Le Loi)

themselves god-kings, or **devaraja**, not just China-style intermediaries between the human realm and the cosmos but rather a reincarnated Buddha or Shiva worthy of cult worship. By maintaining order in the world, they ensured cosmic harmony. In theory absolute rulers, in reality their power faded with distance from the capital cities. Kings enjoyed enormous prestige but also faced continuous threats from rivals, who often succeeded in acquiring the throne. Warfare was no less frequent in Southeast Asia than in other areas of the world as rulers sought more land and labor to supply revenues.

The Indianized kingdoms of Southeast Asia were not all alike, and the economic foundations of their prosperity differed. Some were based largely on agriculture and generally located inland. Others, including the states alongside the Straits of Melaka, depended heavily on maritime trade and international networks of exchange. In many respects these contrasting patterns represented skillful adaptations to the environment. In the agriculture-based economies, rice-growing technology improved considerably beginning in the ninth century, becoming productive enough to sustain large centralized states. But in places with large areas of swampland, such as Malaya and Sumatra, people compensated for their lack of good farmland by maximizing their access to the open frontier of the sea and becoming seafaring traders.

Indianized Social and Cultural Patterns

The migration and mixing of peoples and their cultures were significant themes in Southeast Asia, as they had been in India,

---

devaraja ("God-king") The title used by Indianized Southeast Asian rulers, who wished to be seen as a reincarnated Buddha or Shiva worthy of cult worship.

Map 13.2 Major Southeast Asian Kingdoms, ca. 1200 C.E.
By 1200 the Khmer Empire (Angkor), which once covered much of mainland Southeast Asia, had declined. Sukhothai, Pagan, Srivijaya, Champa, and Vietnam were other major states.

Online Study Center **Improve Your Grade**
Interactive Map: South and Southeast Asia in the Thirteenth Century

Europe, and Africa. Many influences came from immigrants. Following in the footsteps of earlier arrivals, peoples such as the Burmans (BUHR-muhnz) in the ninth century and the Tai (tie) peoples in the seventh to thirteenth centuries immigrated from Tibet and China into mainland Southeast Asia and reshaped the region. For example, the Burmans established the dynamic state of Pagan (puh-GONE) in central Burma after assimilating Buddhism and Hinduism from local people.

Religion played a central role in these states. Though the peasantry remained chiefly animist, Southeast Asian elites adopted Mahayana Buddhism and Hinduism from India. At its height in the twelfth century, the city of Pagan, the capital of a great kingdom, was one of the architectural wonders of the world, a city filled with temples and shrines for the glory of Buddhism and Hinduism. Spurred by piety, Pagan's kings and commoners alike spent as much wealth as they could spare on magnificent religious buildings, using Hindu and Buddhist sculpture and architecture from India as models. At Pagan and elsewhere religion infused government and the arts, and Hindu priests became advisers on ritual in the courts. Hindu Indian epics such as the *Ramayana* and *Mahabharata* became deeply imbedded in both the folk and elite culture, and the Hindu kings, gods, and demons animated the arts.

Southeast Asian societies shared many common features. Extensive trade networks, both land and maritime, had linked the region from earliest times, and many people specialized in local or foreign commerce. Most of the larger states were multiethnic in their population, including many foreign merchants in temporary or permanent residence. This social and ethnic diversity fostered a cosmopolitan attitude in many cities. Still, like Indians, most Southeast Asians were farmers and fishermen and lived in villages characterized by a spirit of cooperation for mutual survival. Unlike in India, however, Southeast Asian family patterns were diverse, ranging from flexible structures to a few patriarchies and matriarchies. In contrast to India and China, women held a relatively high status in most Southeast Asian societies, and some, like the Burmese queen Pwa Saw, exercised political influence behind the scenes (see Profile: Pwa Saw, a Burmese Queen).

An enduring gap separated the social and cultural traditions of the courts, including the royal families, administrations, and capital cities, and the villages. The two traditions differed significantly in religious orientations, worldviews, and ways of life. For example, Indian scripts (especially Sanskrit) became the basis for many Southeast Asian written languages, such as Khmer, Burman, and Thai, and fostered literature of various types, especially poetry, philosophical or religious speculations, and historical chronicles. These literatures became an important component of Southeast Asia's elite culture but were less known among the peasantry.

The Angkor Empire

The Khmer people created the greatest Indianized state, the kingdom of Angkor (ANG-kor), in what is today Cambodia. It was established by a visionary king, Jayavarman (JAI-a-VAR-man) I (r. 802–834), in 802 C.E. The name *Angkor* derives from the Sanskrit term meaning "holy city," and Jayavarman identified himself with the Hindu god Shiva. His successors extended and consolidated the kingdom, which persisted until 1432. Angkor was notable for its substantial empire,

PWA SAW,
A BURMESE QUEEN

Women in royal families played important political roles in many Southeast Asian states, mostly behind the scenes, but few had the influence of thirteenth-century Queen Pwa Saw (pwah saw) of Pagan. Much of what we know about her life comes from a chronicle of the country's history compiled by Burmese scholars in the nineteenth century, and modern historians are divided on whether it represents more myth than fact. Whatever the accuracy, in their traditions the Burman people remember Queen Pwa Saw as witty, wise, and beautiful and as exercising political influence for forty years during one of their most difficult periods.

The girl who would become queen was born to a prosperous peasant family in a remote village around 1237. According to the legends, a deadly king cobra approached her when she was asleep but failed to attack, considered a favorable omen for a bright future, and a jasmine bush she tended astonished her neighbors by blooming in three colors. This unusual event drew the attention of the young King Uzana (r. 1249–1256), a playboy fond of hunting and drinking who was visiting the district with a large entourage of attendants. The unexpected visit of a king and his party riding on elephants spurred the villagers into frenzied preparations for a proper reception to demonstrate their respect. Infatuated with the bright, pretty, graceful, and talkative sixteen-year-old girl, Uzana took her back to Pagan as one of his many wives and appointed her a deputy queen. A short time later, Uzana died in an accident while hunting wild elephants.

With her husband's death, Pwa Saw was thrown into the schemes and rivalries of the royal court as various factions maneuvered for power. Placed in a precarious position as a young bride resented by rival queens, she quickly forged an alliance with the able and wily Chief Minister Yazathingyan (YAH-za-THING-yan), who feared the accession of the king's oldest son, the unpopular Prince Thitathu (thee-TAH-thoo), with whom he had long quarreled. Together they convinced officials to support another son, Narathihapade (NAR-a-THITH-a-PAH-dee) (r. 1256–1287), as king and make Pwa Saw chief queen. But the young king proved arrogant, quick-tempered, and ruthless, alienating many at court and earning the nickname "King Dog's Dung." While the economy declined, the king boasted that he was "the commander of 36 million soldiers, the swallower of 300 dishes of curry daily," and had 3,000 concubines. His zeal to build an expensive Buddhist pagoda fostered the proverb that "the pagoda is finished and the great country ruined." Pwa Saw remained loyal but lost respect for the king.

After her ally Yazathingyan died leading royal forces to suppress a rebellion in the south, Pwa Saw skillfully survived the king's paranoid suspicions and the constant intrigues of the court nobles, attendants, and other queens. Because the king trusted the widely revered queen, she could often overrule his destructive tendencies and talk him into making wiser state decisions. She also convinced the erratic king to appoint capable officials. But she had to maintain her wits. Increasingly paranoid, Narathihapade executed any perceived enemies and burned another queen to death. In the 1270s, anxious to prove himself a great leader, he rejected Pwa Saw's advice to meet Mongol demands for tribute and avoid conflict and instead escalated tensions, thus bringing on war, disaster, and the temporary Mongol occupation of Pagan.

Even as the Pagan state declined, Pwa Saw asserted a benevolent influence. For instance, in 1271 she donated some

advanced architecture, and unique social system. The magnificent temples still standing today testify to the prosperity and organization of Angkor society. By the twelfth century the bustling capital city, Angkor Thom (ANG-kor tom), and its immediate environs contained perhaps a million people. It was much larger than any medieval European city and comparable to all but the largest Chinese and Arab cities. Trade with China and other countries flourished, and many Chinese merchants lived in the kingdom.

The Angkor kings presided over a vigorous imperial system. At its height in the twelfth and thirteenth centuries, Angkor had an empire controlling much of what is now Cambodia, Laos, Thailand, and southern Vietnam. The Khmers acquired and maintained their empire by a skillful combination of warfare, diplomacy, and pragmatism. The system was loosely integrated, and regional governors usually had considerable autonomy. Only the most ruthless kings wielded unchallenged power, and many were art patrons and builders. For example, Jayavarman VII (r. 1181–1219) was a devout Buddhist who boasted of his compassion for his people. He expanded the empire, commissioned important artworks, built roads, and sponsored the construction of many monuments and temples. Zhou Daguan (joe ta-kwan), a Chinese ambassador in Angkor in 1296, left vivid descriptions of Angkor, including the system of justice presided over by the king: "Disputes of the people, however insignificant, always go to the king. Each day the king holds two audiences for affairs of state. Those of the functionaries or the people who wish to see the king, sit on the ground to wait for him."[15]

The state held much power over the population and often used that power to enrich the society. For example, the well-financed government supported substantial public services, including hospitals, schools, and libraries. It also used conscripted workers to construct an extensive canal network for efficient water distribution, exhibiting some of the most advanced civil engineering in the premodern world. Although historians debate how much farming depended on irrigation from these canals, they agree on the fact that the Khmers may

Court Life of Pwa Saw
No known paintings of Pwa Saw exist. This fresco, from the Ananda Buddhist temple at Pagan, shows rich court ladies, much like Pwa Saw herself, relaxing in an upstairs room of a magnificent Buddhist temple while, downstairs, stallholders hawk their wares to visitors. (Robert Harding World Imagery)

of her lands and properties to a Buddhist temple, expressing hope that in future existences she would "have long life, be free from illness, have a good appearance, melodic of voice, be loved and respected by all men and gods, [and] be fully equipped with faith, wisdom, nobility." In 1287 the mad king was murdered by one of his sons. In 1289 Queen Saw and surviving ministers selected a new king, Kyawswar (kee-YAH-swar) (1287–1298). With that last effort to help her country, she retired in style to her home village.

THINKING ABOUT THE PROFILE

1. What skills did Pwa Saw use to influence the court?
2. What does this profile tell us about the relations between queens and kings at Pagan?

Notes: Quotations from D. G. E. Hall, *A History of South-East Asia,* 4th ed. (New York: St. Martin's Press, 1981), p. 169; and Michael Aung-Thwin, *Pagan: The Origins of Modern Burma* (Honolulu: University of Hawaii Press, 1985), p. 41.

have had the most productive agriculture in world history, producing three to four crops a year in a marginally fertile rice-growing region.

Angkor Religion and Society

Religion played an important political and cultural role in Angkor, and Indian influence was considerable. The Angkor government structure resembled a theocratic state: it presided over a well-developed cult for the popular worship of the god-kings, and priestly families held a privileged position. Perhaps as many 300,000 Hindu priests lived in the heart of the empire at its height, and the numerous temples controlled massive wealth. Hindu values were also reflected in many aspects of culture, including theater, art, and dance.

Many magnificent stone temples, some of them as huge as small mountains, were built during the Angkor period. They were designed to represent the Hindu conception of the cosmos centered on the abode of the gods. Built as sanctuaries and

mausoleums, these temples also provided vivid and concrete symbols of a monarch's earthly power, since the construction involved amazing engineering skills and massive amounts of conscripted labor. The most famous temple was part of the largest religious complex in the premodern world, Angkor Wat (ANG-kor waht). The complex, containing buildings, towers, and walls was built by some 70,000 workers in the twelfth century. Angkor Wat dwarfed other Intermediate Era monumental religious buildings, including the magnificent cathedrals of Europe and the grand mosques of Baghdad and Cairo. The reliefs carved into stone at Angkor Wat and other temples provide glimpses of daily life, showing fishing boats, midwives attending a childbirth, merchant stalls, festival jugglers and dancers, peasants bringing goods to market, the crowd at a cockfight, and men playing chess.

In exchange for considerable material security and the protection of a patron to whom they owed allegiance, Khmer commoners tolerated a highly inequitable distribution of wealth and power as well as substantial labor demands, such as

Angkor Wat Temple Complex   This photograph shows the inner buildings of the Angkor Wat temple complex in northern Cambodia. The towers represented the Hindu view of the cosmos. Mount Meru, the home of the gods, rises 726 feet in the middle.   (Robert Harding World Imagery)

the draft of workers to build Angkor Wat. Like many hierarchical societies of the era, Angkor had numerous slaves and people in some form of temporary or permanent involuntary servitude. Although no India-style caste system existed despite the strong Hindu influence, the social structure was rigid. Each class had its appointed role: below the king were the priests, and below them were the trade guilds. The vast majority of the population were of the farmer-builder-soldier class, which had some labor obligations to the sovereign. Peasants were tied to the soil they plowed, to the temples they served, and to the king's army.

Khmer women played a much more important role in society and politics than women did in most other places in the world. According to Zhou Daguan, women operated most of the retail stalls: "In this country it is the women who are concerned with commerce."[16] Some royal women were noted for intellectual or service activities. Jayarajadevi (JAI-ya-RAJ-a-deh-vee), the first wife of King Jayavarman VII, took in hundreds of abandoned girls and trained and settled them. After her death the king married Indradevi (IN-dra-deh-vee), a renowned scholar who lectured at a Buddhist monastery and was acclaimed as the chief teacher of the king. Women domi-

nated the palace staff, and some were even gladiators and warriors. Chinese visitors were shocked at the liberated behavior of Khmer women, who went out in public as they liked. Women were also active in the arts, especially as poets. Khmer society in this era was matrilineal, giving women status in the family.

Indianized Urban Societies in Java and Sumatra

Of the other important Indianized states in Southeast Asia, several developed in the Indonesian archipelago, on the large islands of Java and Sumatra. The encounters between Indian influence and local traditions produced in Java a distinctive religious and political blend known as Hindu-Javanese, which was based on an agricultural economy and which included many unique beliefs. Among the core beliefs were the notions that the earthly order mirrored and embodied the cosmic order and that, to preserve the cosmic order, people must avoid disharmony and change at all cost. The duty of the god-king was to prevent social deterioration in a turbulent human world by maintaining order. As in Angkor, the capitals and palaces of

Javanese kingdoms were built to imitate the cosmic order. Hindu-Buddhist ideas can be seen most vividly in the temple complexes of that time, such as the famous temple mountain of Borobodur (BOR-uh-buh-door) in central Java. They were also reflected in the stories and content of arts such as the shadow puppet play, or **wayang kulit** (WHY-ang KOO-leet), which was based on the Hindu epics like the *Ramayana* but had much local content as well.

The greatest Javanese kingdom of this era was Madjapahit (MAH-ja-PA-hit) (1292–1527). Madjapahit reached its peak in the fourteenth century under the fabled Prime Minister Gajah Mada, when it loosely controlled a large empire embracing much of present-day Indonesia. A court poet in 1365 described the reigning monarch, King Hayam Wuruk, as follows: "He is praised like the moon in autumn, since he fills all the world with joy. His retinue, treasures, chariots, elephants, horses are (immeasurable) like the sea. The land of Java is becoming more and more famous for its blessed state throughout the world."[17]

Social inequality permeated Hindu-Javanese society. A complex etiquette regulated the relations between those of varied status, and hence confirmed the social hierarchy. The aristocracy, who administered the realm, expected deference from commoners, most of whom lived in villages whose cultures and ways of life differed substantially from those of the royal capital. Much of village work was planned and carried out on a communal basis, following a tradition of indigenous democracy and mutual self-help. The villagers' main link with the government was through tax and labor obligations. Peasants identified more with their village community than with distant kings in their palaces.

Coastal states on Sumatra were shaped much more heavily by international trade than were the inland agricultural kingdoms of Java and Cambodia. The Straits of Melaka separating Sumatra from the Malay Peninsula was a major contact zone throughout history and a passageway for trade and religious networks. Throughout the first millennium of the Common Era a complex maritime trading system gradually emerged that linked the eastern Mediterranean, Middle East, East African coast, Persia, and India with the societies of East and Southeast Asia. A vigorously mercantile variation of Indianized culture formed to capitalize on this growing trend.

Between 600 and 1290 many of the small trading states in the Straits region came under the loose control of Srivijaya (SREE-vih-JAI-ya), a great empire based in southeastern Sumatra and a fierce rival of the Cholas in South India. Srivijaya exercised considerable power over the international commerce of the region and maintained a close trade relationship with powerful China. It was not a centralized system but rather a federation of linked trading ports held together by a naval force that both fought and engaged in piracy. Besides being a trading hub, Srivijaya was also a major international center of Buddhist study, attracting thousands of Buddhist monks and students from many countries.

International Influences and the Decline of the Indianized States

The great Indianized states of Southeast Asia came to an end between the thirteenth and fifteenth centuries, for a variety of complex reasons, but the changes were mostly gradual. Some causes of decline were internal. For example, Angkor experienced a combination of military expansion that overstretched resources; increased temple-building resulting in higher tax levies and forced labor that antagonized much of the population into rebellion; and growing breakdown of the irrigation system. But international influences also played a major role in the disintegration of Angkor and neighboring states. These included the migrations of the Tai peoples, the intervention of the Mongols, and the arrival of Theravada Buddhism and Islam.

Over several centuries various groups from mountainous southwestern China speaking Tai languages migrated into Southeast Asia. By the thirteenth century the Tai began setting up their own states in the middle Mekong valley and northern Thailand. These were the ancestors of the closely related Siamese (SYE-uh-meez), today known as the Thai, and the Lao (laow) peoples. As they moved south, the Tai conquered or absorbed the local peoples while also adopting some of their cultural traditions. Eventually they came into conflict with Angkor. By the mid-1400s they had repeatedly sacked Angkor and seized much of the empire's territory. The Khmer Empire soon disintegrated, and the Angkor capital was abandoned. The Khmers became pawns perched uneasily between the expanding Vietnamese and Siamese states.

Meanwhile, the Mongols encountered Angkor's neighbors, but their impact was smaller than that of the Tai. After conquering China, in 1288 they attacked Pagan because the Burmans refused to recognize Mongol overlordship. Although the Mongols soon withdrew, in their wake they left instability in Burma as rival groups competed for power. Elsewhere in Southeast Asia the Mongols found mostly frustration. Although an ill-fated land-and-sea invasion of Vietnam and Champa at first inflicted terrible damage, it was ultimately repelled by a temporary Vietnamese-Cham military alliance. A Mongol naval expedition to Java also proved a costly failure. Southeast Asians were among the few peoples to successfully resist Mongol conquest and power.

The third force for change was religion. By early in the second millennium of the Common Era, two new universal religions began filtering peacefully into the region from outside: Theravada Buddhism and Islam. Theravada Buddhism had been present in the region for several centuries and had been a strong influence among the Burmans at Pagan, but a revitalized form came from Sri Lanka and provided a challenge to the hierarchical order of the Indianized regimes. The Buddhist message of egalitarianism, pacifism, and individual worth proved attractive to peasants weary of war, public labor projects, and tyrannical kings. Furthermore, Theravada Buddhism was a tolerant religion able to exist alongside the rich animism of the peasants, who could honor the Buddha while worshiping local spirits. By the fourteenth century most of the Burman, Khmer, Siamese,

---

wayang kulit Javanese shadow puppet play, developed during the Intermediate Era, based on Hindu epics like the *Ramayana* and local Javanese content.

and Lao peasants had adopted Theravada Buddhism, while the elite mixed the new faith with the older Hindu–Mahayana Buddhist traditions.

About the same time, from the thirteenth through sixteenth centuries, Sunni Islam filtered in from the Middle East via India and spread widely. Like Buddhism, Islam also offered an egalitarian message that challenged the power of traditional elites, as well as a complex theology that appealed to peasants and merchants in the coastal regions of the Malay Peninsula, Sumatra, Java, and some of the other islands. Some Southeast Asians adopted Sunni Islam in a largely orthodox form, while others mixed it with animism or Hinduism-Buddhism. The adaptable mystical Sufi ideas embedded in missionary Islam also blended well with the existing mysticism. This blending fostered conversion by promoting an emotional spirituality rather than dry, dogmatic theology.

As Theravada Buddhism and Islam spread across Southeast Asia, only a few scattered peoples maintained Indianized societies, among them the Balinese (BAH-luh-NEEZ). On the Indonesian island of Bali, Hinduism and other classical patterns remained vigorous, emphasizing arts like dancing, music, shadow plays, and woodcarving. Thus the many visitors to Bali today get a glimpse of patterns that were once widespread in the region.

SECTION SUMMARY

- Southeast Asian kingdoms were heavily influenced by India, and, as in India, their rulers considered themselves god-kings, although their power was limited in the provinces.

- Most Southeast Asian states were multiethnic and were influenced by immigrants and the migration of Mahayana Buddhism and Hinduism from India.

- The Indianized kingdom of Angkor controlled a large swath of Southeast Asia and completed advanced civil engineering projects, such as an extensive canal system and the huge temple complex of Angkor Wat.

- Hindu priests played a very important role in Angkor and the social structure was extremely rigid, though an Indian-style caste system did not take hold and women were more important in society and politics than in most places in the world.

- On Java, a highly stratified Indianized society that championed harmony developed, while on Sumatra, Srivajaya became a powerful commercial empire.

- Southeast Asians fended off the Mongols, but new peoples such as the Tai invaded and destroyed Angkor, and the gradual introduction of Theravada Buddhism and Sunni Islam challenged the hierarchical order and displaced Indian influence in many states.

 # Changing Southeast Asian Societies

What was the influence of Theravada Buddhism and Islam on Southeast Asia?

By the fifteenth century Southeast Asia had experienced a major transition. The Indianized kingdoms such as Angkor, Pagan, and Srivijaya had gradually been replaced by new states with less despotic governments and more dynamic economies Networks of trade and religion linked the region even more closely to wider areas of Afro-Eurasia. In these centuries the major Southeast Asian societies began to diverge in many directions from the earlier Indian and Chinese-influenced patterns, and Theravada Buddhism and Islam permeated further into the countryside. By the fifteenth century three broad but very distinctive social and cultural patterns had developed: the Theravada Buddhist, the Vietnamese, and the Malayo-Muslim or Indonesian.

Theravada Buddhist Society in Siam

The Siamese formed one of the most influential Theravada Buddhist societies, establishing several states in northern and central Thailand. The first major Siamese state, Sukhotai (SOO-ko-TAI), was founded in 1238 by former Angkor vassals and controlled much of the central plains of what is today Thailand. While some modern historians are skeptical, according to Siamese tradition, Sukhotai's glory was established by Rama Kamkheng (RA-ma KHAM-keng) ("Rama the Brave"), a shrewd diplomat who established a close tributary relationship with the dominant regional power, China. Under Rama's leadership, Siam adopted the Khmer script and experienced other Khmer influences in literature, art, and government. Siamese chronicles portray Rama as a wise and popular ruler. A temple inscription of the time tells us that

> the Lord of the country levies no tolls on his subjects. If he sees someone else's wealth he does not interfere. If he captures some enemy soldiers he neither kills them nor beats them. In the [palace] doorway a bell is suspended; if an inhabitant of the kingdom has any complaint or any matter irritates his stomach and torments his mind, and he desires to expose it to the king ring the bell.[18]

This may have exaggerated his merits, but Rama did make Theravada Buddhism the state religion and adopted laws that were humane by world standards.

By 1350 Sukhotai was eclipsed by another Siamese state that emerged in the southern Thai plains, with its capital at Ayuthia (ah-YUT-uh-yuh). While Sukhotai declined and finally collapsed in 1419, Ayuthia developed a regional empire whose influence extended into Cambodia and the small Lao states along the Mekong River. Its rivalry with the Burmans and Vietnamese for regional dominance occasionally led to war.

Buddhist states like Sukhothai and Ayuthia were monarchies. People viewed Siamese kings as semidivine reincarnated Buddhas. Kings lived in splendor and majesty and were advised by Brahman priests in ceremonial and magical practices. They had many wives and therefore many sons, all of whom could be rivals for the throne. This problem, as well as unclear or unenforceable political succession rules, meant that the top levels of government were plagued with instability. But these rivalries generally had little impact in the villages, which had substantial autonomy. Despite a bureaucratic government, royal power lessened as distance to the capital increased.

The Siamese society and culture had many similarities to those of other Theravada Buddhist peoples such as the Khmer, Burmans, and especially the Lao. Like them, the Siamese social order was divided into a small aristocracy, many commoners, and some slaves (many of them prisoners of war). Male slaves did a variety of jobs, from farming and mining to serving as trusted government officials. Slave women were often concubines, domestic servants, or entertainers. Deference to higher authority and recognition of status differences were expected among the Siamese people. In contrast to the extended families of China or India, small nuclear families were the norm. While Theravada peoples encouraged cooperation and mutual obligations within the family and village, they also valued individualism.

Although women did not enjoy absolute equality with men and were expected to show their respect for men, free women enjoyed many rights. They inherited equally with men and could initiate marriage or divorce. They also operated most of the stalls in village or town markets. Visitors from China, India, Europe, and the Middle East were often shocked at the relative freedom of Siamese women. A Muslim Persian diplomat in Ayuthia wrote that "it is common for women to engage in buying and selling in the markets and even to undertake physical labor, and they do not cover themselves with modesty. Thus you can see the women paddling to the surrounding villages where they successfully earn their daily bread with no assistance from the men."[19]

Siamese society reflected Theravada Buddhist values, such as gentleness, meditation, and reincarnation, as well as the concept of *karma*, the idea that one's actions, either in this life or a past life, determined one's destiny. To escape from the endless round of life, death, and rebirth, believers were expected to devote themselves to attaining merit by practicing merciful and generous deeds, with the ultimate goal of reaching *nirvana*, or release from pain. Many men became Buddhist monks, and monks played key roles in local affairs, operating many village schools. Hence Theravada societies had some of the highest literacy rates (especially for males) in the premodern world. Women could not gain merit as monks, although some became nuns. Despite this piety, most Siamese were tolerant of those who were less devout, believing that individuals' spiritual state was their own responsibility. Peasants moved easily between supporting their local Buddhist temple and placating the animist spirits of the fields.

Vietnamese Society

A Chinese colony for over a thousand years, Vietnam also constituted a major Southeast Asian society. In 939 C.E., with the Tang dynasty collapsing, a rebellion finally succeeded in pushing the Chinese out and establishing independence, but China remained a permanent threat. Vietnamese leaders wisely continued to borrow ideas and institutions from China and, to placate the Chinese, even became a vassal state, sending regular tribute missions to the Chinese emperor. By the fourteenth century Vietnam, still strongly influenced by Chinese political and philosophical ideas, offered a striking contrast to Theravada Buddhist societies.

Despite Vietnam's formal subservience, Chinese forces occasionally attempted a reconquest, inspiring the Vietnamese to become masters at resisting foreign invasions. In 1407 the new Ming dynasty invaded and conquered Vietnam in an attempt to restore China's control. In response to the harsh Chinese repression, Le Loi (lay lo-ee) (1385–1433), a mandarin from a landlord family, organized a Vietnamese resistance movement that struggled tenaciously for the next two decades. After it finally expelled the Chinese in 1428, Le Loi became founding emperor of a new Vietnamese dynasty, the Le (1428–1788). His efforts to launch social and economic reforms to reduce the power of the traditional elite, as well as his struggle against Chinese domination, made him one of the heroes of Vietnam's long struggle for independence and self-determination. As Le Loi told his people in his proclamation of victory: "Over the centuries, we have been sometimes strong, sometimes weak; but never yet have we been lacking in heroes. In that let our history be the proof."[20]

Some historians believe the Vietnamese also possessed a sense of national feeling centuries before such ideas developed elsewhere in the world. Over the centuries, this sense of common identity greatly aided Vietnamese survival in a sometimes dangerous regional environment. Vietnam successfully survived on the fringes of powerful China, and when the country was at peace, a cultural renaissance, including literature, poetry, and theater, flourished.

Vietnam had an imperial system modeled on China's. For example, the Vietnamese considered the emperor a "son of heaven," not a god-king but an intermediary between the terrestrial and supernatural realms, ruling through the Mandate of Heaven. As in China, emperors governed through a bureaucracy staffed by scholar-administrators (*mandarins*) chosen by civil service examinations designed to recruit men of talent. The emperor and his officials followed the official ideology of Confucianism, which stressed ethical conduct, social harmony, and social hierarchy. Vietnam also adopted the Chinese model of tributary states and sought to influence or control the peoples of the highlands as well as the neighboring Cham, Khmer, and Lao states.

Peasant society differed considerably from the Chinese-influenced culture of the imperial court and political elite. In the villages religious life mixed Mahayana Buddhism, Confucianism, and Daoism, all adopted from China, with the preexisting

Le Dynasty Ruler This Vietnamese drawing shows the Le emperor being carried in state, accompanied by his mandarins, parasol-and fan-bearers, and a royal elephant. The drawing was printed in an eighteenth-century British book, with an English description of the procession. (From Churchill, *A Collection of Voyages and Travels,* 1732)

Vietnamese spirit and ancestor worship. Villages were self-governing and closely knit communities, and their autonomy was summarized in the peasant expression that "the authority of the emperor ends at the village gate." While individual families owned most of the land, villages also developed a built-in social security system by setting aside communal land that could be farmed by landless peasants. The Vietnamese social system was patriarchal and patrilineal, giving family and village power to senior males. But women dominated the town and village markets, doing most of the buying and selling of food and crafts, and they saw their influence increase with age.

Beginning in the tenth century some Vietnamese left the overcrowded Red River Valley and Tonkin Gulf to migrate southward along the coast in a long process known as the **Nam Tien**, or "Drive to the South." Over the centuries these Vietnamese settlers, supported by imperial forces, overran the Cham people and their states, in what is today central Vietnam. By the sixteenth century they were pushing toward the Khmer-dominated Mekong River Delta in southern Vietnam. As a result of this migration, the Vietnamese became more involved with Southeast Asia and the central and southern dialects and cultures gradually came to differ from those in the northern part of Vietnam.

Islam, Maritime Networks, and the Malay World

Southeast Asian people had excelled as seafaring traders since the beginning of their history, trading as far away as East Africa. Some Indonesians had probably even been visiting the north coast of Australia for centuries to obtain items like orna-

mental shells. During the Intermediate Era world trade more closely connected diverse Eurasian and African peoples, and Southeast Asian port cities became essential intermediaries in the Indian Ocean trade between China, India, and the Middle East. Peoples like the Malays and Javanese played active roles in this maritime trade.

Trade also brought Southeast Asians into contact with the Muslim traders who dominated interregional commerce. As Islamic merchants from Arabia, Persia, and India spread Islam along the Indian Ocean trading routes, Islam became a major influence in the Malay Peninsula and Indonesian archipelago. Commercial people were attracted to a religion that sanctioned the accumulation of wealth and preached cooperation among believers. By the fourteenth century Islam was well established in northern Sumatra, and some Hindu-Buddhist rulers of coastal states in the Malay Peninsula and Indonesian islands grew eager to attract Muslim traders. Impressed by the cosmopolitan universality of Islam, they adopted the new faith, converting themselves into sultans.

The increased trade fostered by the spread of Islam spurred other changes, among them the growth of cities and the increasing influence of merchants in local politics. In addition, a new type of maritime trading state emerged to handle the increased amounts of products being procured and transported. Revenue from trade became more important than agricultural tribute in many states. This transformation in the international maritime economy created an unprecedented commercial prosperity and cosmopolitan culture in Southeast Asia. At the same time, more intensive agricultural growth, including new crops and varieties of rice, spurred population increase, migration, and more bureaucratic states, some large and many small ones.

The spread of Islam in the region coincided with, and was spurred by, the rise of the great port of Melaka (muh-LACK-uh) on the southwest coast of Malaya facing the Straits of Melaka. In 1403 the Hindu ruler of the city, Parameswara,

---

Nam Tien ("Drive to the South") A long process beginning in the tenth century in which some Vietnamese left the overcrowded north to migrate southward along the coast of Vietnam.

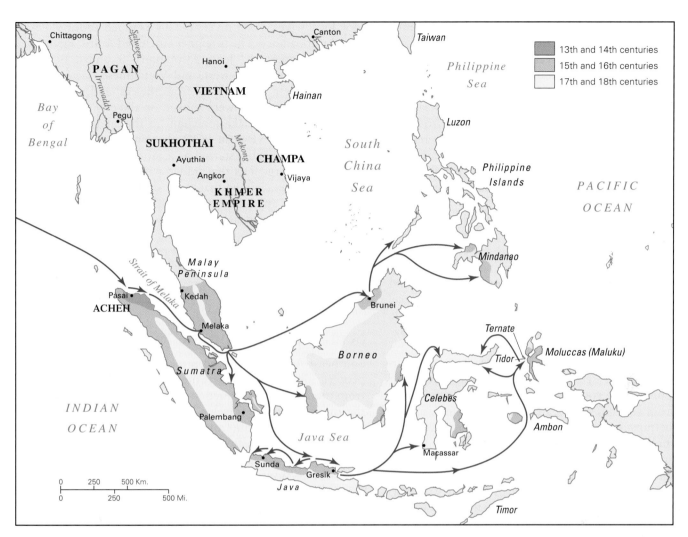

Map 13.3 The Spread of Islam in Island Southeast Asia
Carried by merchants and missionaries, Islam spread from Arabia and India to island Southeast Asia,
eventually becoming the major faith on many islands and in the Malay Peninsula.

adopted Islam and transformed himself into a sultan. His motivation was probably as much political and commercial as spiritual. In Southeast Asian fashion, the Melakans blended Islamic faith and culture with the older Hindu-Buddhist (and, for peasants, animist) beliefs, creating a cultural pattern that remained eclectic for generations. Because Islam in the region was closely identified at first with the Malay people of the Melaka region, historians often refer to the Muslim Southeast Asian societies as Malayo-Muslim. Malay identity spread to many societies in Malaya, Sumatra, and Borneo who practiced Islam and spoke the Malay language.

Melaka became the main center for the spread of Islam in the peninsula and western archipelago (see Map 13.3), spurring political change and economic growth. Sultanates appeared in many districts and islands as rulers embraced the new faith for religious, political, and commercial reasons. Some Islamic states, such as Acheh (AH-chay) in northern Sumatra, became regional powers. The sultanates of Ternate

(tuhr-NAH-tay) and Tidor (TEE-door) in the Maluku (muh-LUKE-uh) (Moluccan) Islands of northeastern Indonesia prospered from the spices they produced (especially cloves and nutmeg) that were prized in Europe and the Middle East. Gradually many of the people in the region followed the example of their rulers and adopted Islam. As a result, the Malay Peninsula and Indonesian archipelago were joined to the great Islamic world. But there also remained many village-based societies, some of them still practicing animism, in more isolated or fringe areas such as the Philippine Islands, with no political authority higher than local chiefs.

As Islam was grafted onto different cultures, various patterns of Islamic belief and practice, more diverse than elsewhere in the Islamic world, emerged in the scattered island societies. In most cases Islam did not completely displace older customs. For example, on Java several religious patterns developed. While Indianized kings and courts combined Islamic beliefs with older Hindu-Buddhist ceremonies and mystical traditions, many peasants maintained their mystical animist beliefs and practices under an Islamic veneer, tolerating diverse religious views, while others (especially merchants) adopted a more orthodox Islamic faith, following prescribed Islamic practices and looking toward the Middle East for models. The complex Javanese religion mirrored a hierarchical social system. The sultans in their palaces remained aloof from the people, and the aristocracy, obsessed with practicing refined behavior rooted in mystical Hinduism, disdained the common folk. Like their pre-Muslim ancestors, Javanese of all classes placed a great value on maintaining a tranquil heart by avoiding interpersonal conflict.

Melaka: Crossroads of Trade

Melaka played a growing role in transregional trade, replacing Srivijaya as the region's political and economic power and becoming the crossroads of Asian maritime commerce. Melaka's rulers sent tributary missions to China and made their port a key way station for the series of grand Chinese voyages to the western Indian Ocean led by Admiral Zheng He (see Chapter 11), who called at the port in 1409 and 1414. In exchange for Melaka's service as a naval base, the Ming emperor supported the young state in regional disputes. Soon merchants from around Asia began coming to the new emporium, rapidly transforming the port into the archipelago's major trading hub, as well as the southeastern terminus for the Indian Ocean maritime trading network.

One of the major commercial centers in the world, Melaka rivaled other great trading ports such as Calicut, Cambay, Guangzhou (Canton), Hormuz, Alexandria, Genoa, and Venice. In 1468 Melaka sultan Mansur wrote to the king of the Ryukyu Islands, "We have learned that to master the blue oceans people must engage in commerce. All the lands within the seas are united in one body. Life has never been so affluent in preceding generations as it is today."[21] Melaka's rulers were actively involved in commerce, a pattern that became common among Muslim trading states in Southeast Asia. Gradually, Melaka became the center of a highly decentralized empire that dominated much of coastal Malaya and eastern Sumatra.

Melaka flourished until 1511 as a vital link in world trade. An early-sixteenth-century Portuguese visitor wrote that it had "no equal in the world" and extolled the importance of Melaka to peoples and trade patterns as far away as western Europe: "Melaka is a city that was made for merchandise, fitter than any other in the world. Commerce between different nations for a thousand leagues on every hand must come to Melaka."[22] Melaka had a special connection to the Indian port of Cambay, nearly 3,000 miles away. Every year trading ships from around the Middle East and South Asia gathered at Cambay and Calicut to make the long voyage to Melaka. They carried with them grain, woolens, arms, copperware, textiles, and opium for exchange. Goods from as far north as Korea also reached Melaka.

The flourishing trading port attracted merchants from many lands. By the late 1400s Melaka's 100,000 to 200,000 people included 15,000 foreign merchants, some of whom took local wives. Their diversity tells us much about Melaka's global importance. The foreigners included Arabs, Egyptians, Persians, Armenians, Jews, Ethiopians, Swahilis, Burmese, and Indians from the west, and Vietnamese, Javanese, Filipinos, Japanese, and Chinese from the east and north. Some eighty-four languages were spoken on the city's streets. Perhaps the richest Melaka merchant in the later 1400s, Naina Suradewana (NINE-a su-ROD-eh-won-a), a portly Hindu from southeast India, started as a moneylender but eventually owned a large fleet that traded with Java and the Maluku Islands. Visitors claimed that more ships crowded the Melaka harbor than in any other port in the world, attracted by a stable government and a free trade policy. City shops offered textiles from India, books from the Middle East, cloves and nutmeg from Maluku, batiks and carpets from Java, silk and porcelain from China, and sugar from the Philippines. Gold brought from various places was so plentiful that children played with it.

Southeast Asia and the Wider World

Southeast Asia had long been a cosmopolitan region where peoples, ideas, and products met, and visitors and sojourners from many lands continued to reach the region. For example, the intrepid Italian traveler Marco Polo passed through in 1292 on his way home from a long China sojourn. His writings praised the wealth and sophistication of Champa, Java, and Sumatra, arousing European interest in seeking direct trade connections with these seemingly fabulous lands. Polo wrote that "Java is of unsurpassing wealth, producing all kinds of spices, frequented by a vast amount of shipping. Indeed, the treasure of this island is so great as to be past telling."[23]

The Southeast Asia Marco Polo and other travelers such as the Moroccan Ibn Battuta encountered was one of the world's more prosperous and urbanized regions. Major cities like Ayuthia, Melaka, and Hanoi (huh-NOY) (Vietnam) each probably contained around 100,000 residents and thus were as large as the major European urban centers like Naples and Paris. But this was small by Chinese or Middle Eastern standards. By the 1400s, though having perhaps 15 to 20 million people, a fifth of them in Vietnam, Southeast Asia was dwarfed by the dense populations of nearby China and India. Still, blessed with fertile land and extensive trade, Southeast Asians often enjoyed better health, more varied diets, and adequate material resources than most peoples.

Southeast Asia's connections to the wider world, as well as its famed wealth, eventually attracted arrivals who were not welcome. By the beginning of the sixteenth century a few Portuguese explorers and adventurers, with deadly weapons, state-of-the-art ships, Christian missionary zeal, and desire for wealth, reached first India and then Southeast Asia seeking "Christians and spices." The Portuguese standard of living was probably inferior to that of Siam, Vietnam, Melaka, or Java. Yet, the Portuguese were the forerunners of what became a powerful, destabilizing European presence that gradually altered the region after 1500.

SECTION SUMMARY

- Siamese states such as Sukhotai and Ayuthia were Theravada Buddhist monarchies that valued individualism and peacefulness, offered women a fair amount of freedom, and were permeated by Buddhist values.
- Despite gaining freedom from Chinese rule, Vietnam retained a great deal of Chinese cultural influence.
- Inhabitants of the Malay and Indonesian archipelagoes embraced Islam, which arrived via increasing maritime trade, and grafted it onto Hinduism and Buddhism to create many different patterns of Islamic belief, while native animist traditions survived to some extent in the villages.
- Melaka displaced Srivajaya as the center of Southeast Asian trading power and became an international crossroads.
- Southeast Asia would eventually attract less friendly visitors, such as the Portuguese.

Online Study Center **ACE the Test**

 # Chapter Summary

Although many earlier patterns of life and thought persisted in India and Southeast Asia during the Intermediate Era, these regions also experienced tremendous changes. Islam was brought to India through violent conquest and to Southeast Asia through peaceful trade. In all cases societies adapted new ideas in different ways to their own distinctive cultures.

A constant stream of West Asian and central Asian peoples into India brought more diversity to Indian social patterns and beliefs. Although India remained politically fragmented, Hinduism enjoyed a kind of renaissance. Most people owed allegiance to their family, caste, and village. Hinduism spawned diverse ideas and cults, and gradually fostered many common cultural patterns, bringing some cultural unity. Buddhism gradually lost influence in much of India. Hindu society faced its greatest challenge from Muslim conquerors, who became politically dominant in north India. Unlike earlier ideas and peoples, Muslims would not be assimilated, although there was some mixing of Hindu and Muslim traditions. Islam added a major new strand to India's heritage, influencing the political, religious, and cultural realms but increasing diversity at the expense of unity.

Hindu and Buddhist ideas along with various other Indian traditions diffused to Southeast Asia, where they helped foster the rise of great kingdoms. The Angkor Empire dominated much of mainland Southeast Asia by mixing Indian and local patterns. New peoples, especially the Tais, and religions eventually reshaped Southeast Asia. Theravada Buddhism became a major influence of several societies, including Siam, while Islam became strong in peninsula and island societies such as Melaka and Java. International trade fostered economic dynamism, and Melaka served as a major international port in which many cultural traditions flourished.

Online Study Center **Improve Your Grade** Flashcards

Key Terms

Rajputs	Tantrism	devaraja
polyandry	Lamaism	wayang kulit
bhakti	purdah	Nam Tien
Vajrayana		

Suggested Reading

Books

Andaya, Barbara Watson, and Leonard Andaya. *A History of Malaysia*. 2nd ed. Honolulu: University of Hawaii Press, 2000. Contains an overview of Melaka and the spread of Islam in Southeast Asia.

Aung-Thwin, Michael. *Pagan: The Origins of Modern Burma*. Honolulu: University of Hawaii Press, 1985. The most comprehensive study of the Pagan society in Burma.

Basham, A. L. *The Wonder That Was India*. 3rd rev. ed. New Delhi: Rupa and Company, 1967 (reprinted 1999). Although dated, this is still the best general study of pre-Islamic India.

Chaudhuri, K. N. *Trade and Civilization in the Indian Ocean: An Economic History from the Rise of Islam to 1750*. Cambridge: Cambridge University Press, 1985. A scholarly study of trade and Islam, with much on India and Southeast Asia.

Hall, Kenneth R. *Maritime Trade and State Development in Early Southeast Asia*. Honolulu: University of Hawaii Press, 1985. One of the few studies of trade and politics in Southeast Asia before 1500 C.E.

Higham, Charles. *The Civilization of Angkor*. Berkeley: University of California Press, 2001. A scholarly but readable summary of Cambodia's early history.

Kulke, Hermann, and Dietmar Rothermund. *History of India*. 4th ed. London and New York: Routledge, 2004. A concise but stimulating general history, incorporating recent scholarship on India in this era.

Mabbett, Ian, and David Chandler. *The Khmers*. London: Blackwell, 1995. An authoritative study of Cambodian history, with much on Angkor.

Rizvi, S. A. A. *The Wonder That Was India*, Part 2. New Delhi: Rupa and Company, 1987 (reprinted 2000). A comprehensive discussion of India under the impact of Islam from 1200 to 1700.

Thapar, Romila. *Early India: From the Origins to A.D. 1300*. Berkeley: University of California Press, 2003. A recent revision of the standard work by an Indian historian.

Websites

Internet Indian History Sourcebook
(http://www.fordham.edu/halsall/india/indiasbook.html).
An invaluable collection of sources and links on India.

WWW Southeast Asia Guide
(http://www.library.wisc.edu/guides/SEAsia/). An impressive, easy-to-use site from the University of Wisconsin-Madison.

WWW Virtual Library: South Asia
(http://www.columbia.edu/cu/libraries/indiv/area/sarai/).
This Columbia University site offers many useful resources.

WWW Virtual Library: Southeast Asia
(http://iias.leidenuniv.nl/wwwvl/southeast.html). A Dutch site offering portals to all the countries of the region.

CHAPTER 14

Christian Societies in Medieval Europe, Byzantium, and Russia, 600–1500

Online Study Center

This icon will direct you to interactive activities and study materials on the website: college.hmco.com/pic/lockard1e

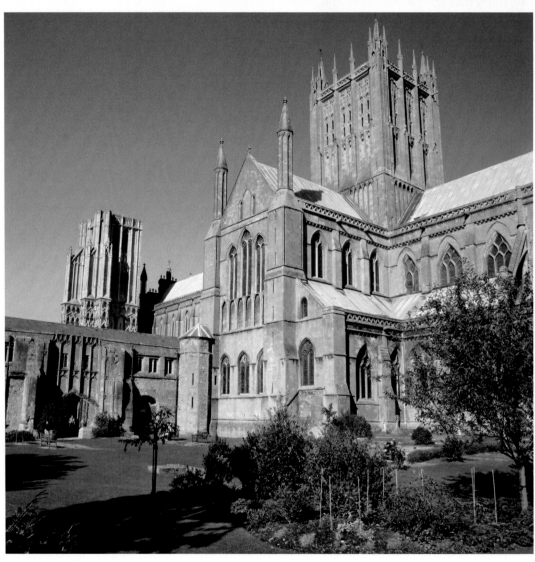

Wells Cathedral The importance of Christianity in European life was symbolized by magnificent cathedrals. This cathedral, built in the town of Wells in England in the thirteenth century C.E., was designed to reflect the glory of God.   (Robert Harding World Imagery)

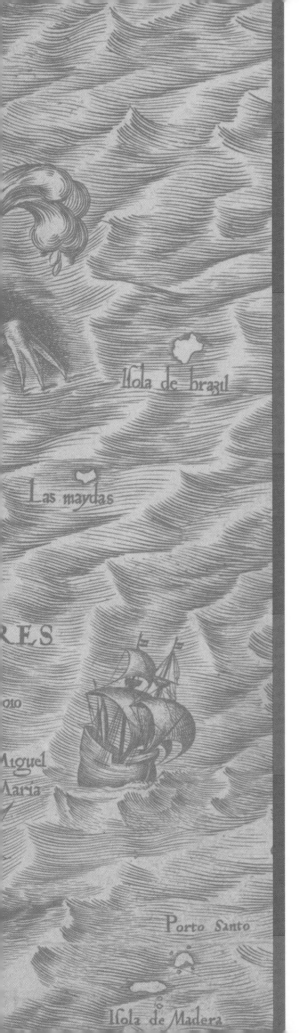

The most Christian man beloved by God, the glorious king of the Franks, while he was building this [Christian] monastery, wished that [its] consecration and the battles which he [waged] should not be consigned completely to oblivion.

 t was Christmas, 800 C.E., and the city of Rome, filled with magnificent buildings and monuments, still possessed majesty. Containing some three hundred Christian churches, Rome was the center of Roman Christendom. Along one of the many roads that connected the fabled metropolis to a wider Europe had come the most powerful ruler in Europe, Charlemagne (SHAHR-leh-mane), the Christian king of the Germanic people called the Franks, arriving from his capital of Aachen (AH-kuhn) some 700 miles away in what is now northwest Germany. He came to celebrate Christmas mass with Pope Leo III, the head of Christendom.

A towering man, 6 feet 4 inches tall, and wearing the Roman toga and colorful Greek cloak supplied by the pope, Charlemagne entered the spectacular St. Peter's cathedral. When the Christmas service ended, the pope placed upon Charlemagne's head a golden crown encrusted with sparkling jewels. Led by the pope, the crowd chanted, "Crowned by god, great and peace-loving Emperor of the Romans, life and victory."[2] Historians disagree as to whether Charlemagne expected to be crowned emperor of a new, church-blessed Roman Empire. But for the first time a pope had crowned an emperor and sought to shape monarchies. Indeed, for the next few centuries popes tried to influence secular affairs, while at the same time kings worked to control the church and, like Charlemagne, used religion—even the building of monasteries—for their own purposes. The complex relations between the Roman church and diverse European states helped shape the tapestry of European life in this era.

In the 1400s Italian historians first coined the term ***medieval*** to describe the centuries between the classical Romans and their own time. In their view, it was a superstitious and ignorant "Dark Age." But the reality of what later scholars often called the "Middle Ages" in Europe was more complex, and always in flux. Linked by networks of faith and culture, medieval western Europeans combined Christianity with practices inherited from both the Romans and Germanic groups like the Franks. The mix of religion and politics that saw Charlemagne anointed ruler by a church official and then build a monastery went back to an-

---

medieval   A term first used in the 1400s by Italian historians to describe the centuries between the classical Romans and their own time.

cient times. But in both western Europe and Byzantium to the east, the strong influence of the Christian churches in all aspects of society, including politics, was an innovation. Furthermore, Christian culture also spread into northeastern Europe and Russia. Medieval people tended to think of themselves as part of Christendom rather than Europe.

The role and spread of Christianity were only one aspect of a Europe that changed considerably over the millennium between 500 and 1500. Europeans made their own history, but they also borrowed much from other cultures, especially from Muslims. In addition, the many tensions of European life, including conflicts between Christian leaders and kings for power, struggles between kings and nobles, debates over how to reconcile faith and reason, and the differing priorities of the rural-based aristocracy and urban merchants, fostered a competitive spirit that helped spur overseas exploration in the fifteenth century.

FOCUS QUESTIONS

1. How did Europeans create new societies between 500 and 1000?
2. What institutions shaped medieval European life?
3. How did the Christian church influence medieval religious, political, and intellectual life?
4. How did Byzantine society differ from that of western Europe?
5. What developments between 1300 and 1500 gave Europeans the incentive and means to begin reshaping the world after 1500?

❖ Forming Christian Societies in Western Europe

How did Europeans create new societies between 500 and 1000?

The disintegration of the western Roman Empire in the fifth century C.E. led to political and social instability, which cleared the ground for the rise of new societies between 500 and 1000. Although classical education, building, and commerce faded in the first half of the medieval period, these were centuries of considerable creativity, spurred partly by the mixing of Roman and Germanic traditions as well as by relations with non-European peoples. While the societies of western Europe varied, they also developed many common cultural features, including a dominant Rome-based Christian church and similar social, political, and economic systems. The church helped create a unique European community of societies in this era. Economic change and technological development also set a foundation for a new Europe.

Environment and Geography

Climate change and disease were two of the factors that shaped post-Roman Europe. In contrast to the warmer weather of the middle Classical Era, a cooling climate brought shorter growing seasons between 500 and 900, after which warmer trends returned. The terrible plague that devastated Europe during Justinian's time reappeared occasionally through the eighth century. Given these challenges, it was not surprising that people turned to religion for support.

Between 200 and 800 western Europe also suffered repeated and prolonged incursions by migrating peoples. Various Germanic groups occupied much of the region, destroying forever the western Roman Empire and much of its culture. These developments prevented any imperial restoration like that in China, where classical society reemerged in stronger form during the Tang dynasty. Today few people study the Latin that was once the dominant language of the Mediterranean world.

Although classical unity was lost, Europe's favorable geography enabled many areas to develop similar religious, social, economic, and political patterns. Much of western and central Europe was blessed by fertile, well-watered plains rich in minerals, while a long coastline offered many fine harbors along the Mediterranean and Baltic Seas as well as along the Atlantic Ocean. Long navigable rivers such as the Danube (DAN-yoob) and Rhine (rine) and accessible mountain passes through the Alps made communication within the region much easier than for Asia, Africa, and South America. Hence, land and sea networks linked diverse societies, fostering the movement of ideas, products, peoples, technologies, and diseases.

Early Medieval Trade, the Muslim World, and Spain

Economic factors, especially trade, also shaped the new Europe. While most Europeans were peasants, growing food or raising livestock for sale at local markets, some were merchants who traded products such as wool hides, salt, fish, wine, and grain over long distances, often by sea or riverboat. As it had for centuries, trade continued briskly in the eastern Mediterranean, where it was tightly controlled by the Byzantine rulers. Trade between the Franks and Constantinople flourished at various times.

As time passed the east-west trade grew dynamic. The northeastern Italian city of Venice, built on its lagoons in the fifth century, was an active trading center throughout the Middle Ages. Venice and Genoa, on Italy's northwest coast, competed to dominate trade with the Middle East and Byzantium, negotiating agreements with Muslim rulers who distrusted most other Christian states. Other Italian cities, such as Milan and Naples, remained connected to the Byzantine economy. Even the most remote northern towns received occasional visits from merchants, and aristocrats purchased luxury goods such as silk produced in the East. By 800, multiple networks of exchange were reconnecting western Europeans to each other and to eastern Europe and the increasingly Islamic Middle East.

As trade increased, Europeans benefited from the growing connections with, and borrowings from, the Muslim world. Islamic expansion stimulated a wider movement of people, goods, and information, such as Asian science and classical Greek thought, that gradually influenced many Afro-Eurasian societies. The exchange of products and ideas between Islamic Spain and Sicily, where various cultures met, and Christian Europe proved especially fruitful for European intellectual life.

In the eighth and ninth centuries, Arab Muslims conquered Sicily and much of Spain, where they created cosmopolitan societies and several strong states (see Chapter 10). Scholars and merchants from all over the Mediterranean world gravitated to great Spanish cities such as Cordoba. For example, Jewish merchants from the Carolingian realm regularly visited Cordoba. The meeting of Christian, Jewish, and Muslim traditions in Muslim-ruled Spain and Sicily allowed the philosophical, scientific, and technological writings of many Classical Greek and Indian as well as Persian and Arab thinkers to spread among educated Europeans. In the 1140s, an Italian translator of Arabic texts wrote that "it befits us to imitate the Arabs especially, for they are our teachers and the pioneers."[6]

Technology, Agricultural Growth, and Industry

The development of new technology helped establish the economic foundations of medieval Europe, especially in farming and power generation. This technology was often borrowed from other societies, even across long distances, but it was adapted to suit local needs. Various technological improvements, some originating in Asia, came into common use in western Europe during these early centuries, laying the basis for European expansion after 1000.

Some of the major technological innovations improved agriculture. Three devices or practices spurred the higher grain yields that sparked population growth in Europe. The first was the rugged *moldboard plow,* which included a blade that dug the earth and an attached moldboard that turned over the furrow. This new plow enabled farmers to turn and drain the heavy, wet soil of northern Europe, where such difficult farming conditions had kept the populations sparse. Germans probably invented the moldboard plow after finding that the simpler Roman scratch plow used in the sandier Mediterranean soils was inadequate. The second improvement was the horseshoe, which Europeans adopted from Central Asians in the ninth century. Horseshoes allowed farmers to make greater use of horses to plow fields, especially when they were combined with the third device, the horse

"Tilling the Fields" Most medieval Europeans were peasants growing food. This French painting from the 1400s shows peasants working land on a manor. (The Bridgeman Art Library International)

collar. Invented in China and adopted by Germanic peoples, the horse collar distributed the weight of the burden across the animal's shoulders so that the horse could pull more weight and work longer hours.

The most crucial agricultural improvement was the three-field system, introduced in the eighth century to replace the Roman two-field system. Europeans divided their fields into three parts and let only one-third lie fallow each year; they then increased their yield by planting winter and summer wheat in the other two fields. Peasants were also learning to plant more beans and other nitrogen-fixing crops, which returned nutrition to the soil. Increased grain consumption produced a better-balanced diet. All of these measures multiplied the food supply.

Other innovations fostered the growth of industry. First invented in Roman times, watermills were built along rivers and streams to generate power. This technology spread widely in early medieval times, freeing up human and animal labor for other tasks. By 1056 there were over 5,600 watermills in England, providing power for such activities as sawing logs and grinding wheat into flour. Waterpower allowed some industries to be mechanized. For example, by the late tenth century a French mill was making beer. By the 1100s Europeans also used windmills, invented in Persia around 650, to generate power for such industries as grinding grain. By then the wheelbarrow had also reached Europe from China.

SECTION SUMMARY

- With the decline of the Roman Empire, the Christian church became a power in its own right with influence over kings, and monasteries created a new culture that respected manual labor.

- Under Germanic influence, Christians more aggressively spread their faith, assimilating pagan practices and transforming them into Christian ones and sometimes persecuting non-Christians, as well as beginning to value warfare and fighting.

- During this time the Papal States were created, Charlemagne's Carolingian empire temporarily united much of Europe, and Otto the Great began the tradition of calling Germany the "Holy Roman Empire."

- The Vikings of Scandinavia, who raided European lands for over four centuries, were also good traders and eventually settled in Iceland, Greenland, and various European territories; they also made forays to eastern Canada and experimented with democracy.

- As merchants engaged in growing networks of exchange, trade with the expanding Muslim world and contact with Muslim Spain introduced Europeans to Classical Greek, Indian, Arab, and Persian ideas.

- Technological advances such as the moldboard plow, the horseshoe, and the horse collar improved agriculture, as did the three-field system, and the watermill helped to improve European industry.

Medieval Societies

What institutions shaped medieval European life?

Medieval Europe was dominated by several institutions, three of which were paramount between 800 and 1300. The papacy, of course, was significant in religion and church-state relations. The other two institutions were feudalism in the realm of politics and social structure, and manorialism in the realm of economics. Both developed from roots that lay in the later centuries of the Roman Empire. Neither was uniform in western Europe, varying greatly across the region. Brisk economic activity also marked medieval Europe, including increasing trade encouraged in part by the growth of towns. The pluralism of religious, social, political, and economic institutions forged in early medieval Europe, combined with an unusually warm climate, spurred changes in many areas of life between 1000 and 1300, centuries historians term the "High Middle Ages."

The Emergence of Feudalism

A concept that is controversial among historians, **feudalism** was a term introduced in sixteenth-century England to describe the complex and decentralized social, political, and economic system of previous centuries. Eventually modern scholars defined feudalism as a political arrangement characterized by a weak central monarchy ruling over smaller states or influential families that were largely autonomous but owed service obligations to the monarch. In turn, these influential families, or "nobles," ruled over the warriors or farmers on their estates who owed them service. In both cases the ruler was a "lord" and his subordinates were **vassals.** Monarchs were lords to nobles, and nobles were lords to most of the common people. In medieval Europe noble families often held large estates in exchange for paying homage and offering military service or labor to the royal governments. Likewise, warriors in a landowner's service and farmers living and working on the land also owed obligations to the landowner. Church leaders supported this arrangement, arguing that "it is the will of the Creator that the higher shall always rule over the lower. Each individual and each class should stay in its place [and] perform its tasks."[7] This basic political and social formation, with its complex network of ties, was strongest in France, England, and parts of Italy.

Some historians consider the concept of feudalism to be simplistic and misleading, an overgeneralization of the complex lord-vassal relationship and land ownership patterns. But while it may be a flawed concept, feudalism can help illuminate

---

feudalism A political arrangement characterized by a weak central monarchy ruling over smaller state or influential families that were largely autonomous but owed service obligations to the monarch.

vassal In medieval Europe, a subordinate person owing service to a lord.

medieval life. For example, it helps explain why many monarchs of states where feudal relations prevailed had little power beyond the immediate area around their capital. Some small states were part of a larger unit, such as the Holy Roman Empire, their princes owing allegiance to the king but also exercising power in the states they ruled.

Despite the unifying role of the Christian church in creating a common culture and the accomplishments of strong rulers such as Charlemagne and Otto the Great, certain forces worked toward the decentralization and fragmentation that characterized feudalism during the early medieval period. The old Roman roads had fallen into disrepair, disrupting transportation and long-distance trade, and Europe remained sparsely populated and largely rural. Cities were few north of the Alps. The most densely populated region, France, boasted a population of only 8 or 9 million people, and, as late as 1000, England had only a million and a half. Europe as a whole was home to around 40 million by 950. By contrast, early Song China had around 100 million.

These conditions made it difficult for even a strong ruler to maintain a powerful central government. Since both money and talent were scarce and land was the source of wealth, Charlemagne often rewarded his best soldiers and administrators by giving them control over large areas of land. Vassals who held such grants of land from a lord, called **benefices**, took an oath of personal loyalty to the king and promised him military service. In return they had a virtually free hand to govern the territory, collect taxes from the people who lived on that land, and administer justice. This delegation of authority led to political fragmentation.

Historians of medieval Europe often use the concept of feudalism in a narrow sense of legal relations between lords and vassals. The term *fief* described the thing granted in a feudal contract. Although this was usually land, it could also be something such as the right to collect tolls on a bridge. The vassal might also be obliged to provide hospitality to the ruler when he traveled around his kingdom. If a fief of land were large enough, as many were, the vassal could subdivide it and have vassals of his own. Thus feudalism allowed a king to rule a large country without personally administering it through his own paid officials. This rule through subordinates, and subordinates of subordinates, was most common in England, especially after William, Duke of Normandy, conquered that island in 1066 and set up a feudal monarchy (see Chronology: The High Middle Ages, 1000–1300).

Feudal society included **knights**, armored military retainers who swore allegiance to their lord and who fought mostly on horseback. Since warhorses and elaborate armor were expensive, lords imposed this expense on their vassals. A large peasant class that was, for the most part, denied military and therefore political power, supported the warriors at the top.

CHRONOLOGY	
The High Middle Ages, 1000–1300	
987–1328	Capetian kings in France
1066	Norman conquest of England
1095–1272	Christian Crusades to reclaim Holy Land
1198–1216	High point of medieval papacy under Innocent III
1215	Signing of Magna Carta
1231	Beginning of Inquisition
1265	First English Parliament

Knights had a rigid code of behavior, including a sense of duty and honor known as **chivalry.** A thirteenth-century French writer explained the chivalric ideal: "A knight must be hardy, courteous, generous, loyal and of fair speech; ferocious to his foe, frank and debonair to his friend. [He] has proved himself in arms and thereby won the praise of men."[8] Most of us have romantic images of medieval knights wielding lances in jousts or defending maidens from fire-breathing dragons, but the reality was usually more mundane. Knights wore 60 pounds of chain-mail armor. As a result, they were often felled by heat exhaustion. The steel suits of armor seen in museums did not come into general use until the 1400s. Since states and rival lords fought each other regularly, knights were kept busy. But despite the dangers, the rewards could be great. For instance, one of the most renowned English knights, William Marshall (1145–1219), became very wealthy, an adviser to kings, and married a woman from an aristocratic family.

The mounted cavalry was medieval Europe's chief fighting force, and the innovation that made it possible was the stirrup. Central Asians probably borrowed stirrup technology from the Chinese and spread it to western Europe, where it was used by Frankish warriors when they defeated the Arabs in 732. The stirrup, which enabled the knight to stand when delivering a blow, made him much more powerful than if he delivered a blow while seated. Thus it contributed greatly to the knight's fighting power.

Manorialism and the Slave Trade

The rural economy was based on **manorialism**, a system of autonomous, nearly self-sufficient agricultural estates. The roots were laid in late Roman imperial practices. As the Roman cities

---

benefices   In medieval Europe, grants of land from lord to vassal.

fief   In medieval Europe, the thing granted in a feudal contract, usually land.

knights   In medieval Europe, armored military retainers on horseback who swore allegiance to their lord.

chivalry   The rigid code of behavior, including a sense of duty and honor, of medieval European knights.

manorialism   The medieval European system of autonomous, nearly self-sufficient agricultural estates.

became expensive places to live, wealthy Romans retreated to their large country estates and hired low-wage agricultural workers, who were also looking for security during dangerous times. Eventually these Roman states became the manors, the combination of farms and villages into which each territorial fief was divided. With money and trade goods in short supply, each manor was responsible for its own needs, from mills to grind the grain and press grapes for the wine to blacksmiths to shoe the horses.

The manors, often organized around a castle, were owned by nobles who had the right to the produce grown by the large class of hereditary **serfs,** peasants who were legally bound to their lord and tied to the land through the generations. Serfs tilled the lord's fields as well as their own and were given, instead of money, the use of the manor's resources, such as farming tools or crafts, and protection in the manor house or castle in case the settlement was attacked. Although serfs were not allowed to change their status or leave without permission, they were not the personal property of their lords. If they were tied to the land, the land was also tied to them. They could not be dispossessed unless they failed to live up to their obligations. Serfs were warned by lords and priests to work hard to receive their eventual reward in Heaven. Their security and stability were paid for with compliance and a lifetime of drudgery. Occasional peasant revolts, sometimes targeting the lords and ladies of the manor, indicated some dissatisfaction. But the rural life also had some pleasures. An Irish verse from the ninth century praised the "three sounds of increase: the lowing of a cow in milk; the din of the smithy; the swish of a plough."[9]

Although serfdom gradually became far more pervasive, slavery did not disappear altogether in Europe. Slaves were mostly used for farming in England, where they constituted perhaps 10 percent of the population until the eleventh century. They were also common in Italy and Spain, where many were domestic servants. Slaves worked the estates owned by the popes, and some French monasteries owned thousands of slaves to work their farms. Slavery was familiar enough that the Roman church developed rules for the humane treatment of slaves. Leading Christian thinkers like St. Thomas Aquinas argued that slavery was morally justified and an economic necessity.

Slave trading was a key part of the medieval economy. Complex networks of trade transported slaves all over Europe and the Middle East. An active Mediterranean slave trade based in Byzantium bought or seized slaves, mostly Slavs, Greeks, Turks, and Caucasus peoples, from the Black Sea region and shipped them to southern Europe and North Africa. The Carolingians and Venetians sold slaves from various European societies to the Arabs. Vikings enslaved captives and also sold English and French slaves to Byzantium and Islamic Spain. By the 1400s Arabs and Portuguese were selling some enslaved West Africans in southern Europe.

Medieval Cities and Towns

European societies experienced considerable change during the High Middle Ages, including the growth of population, towns, and cities. Compared to Byzantium, Tang China, and the Islamic world, early medieval western Europe was economically underdeveloped, a reality reflected in the size of cities: by 1000 Rome had only 35,000 people, Paris around 20,000, and London an insignificant 10,000. By contrast, Constantinople had 300,000, Kaifeng in China had 400,000, Cordoba in Muslim Spain nearly 500,000, and the world's largest city, Baghdad, a million people. However, between 1000 and 1300 the increased food resulting from the new methods of growing crops spurred Europe's population to double to about 75 million. As people from the neighboring countryside went to buy and sell agricultural produce and other goods necessary for daily life, western European cities increased in both population and importance, becoming centers of trade and industry. Milan and Paris grew to almost 100,000 during these three centuries. London had at least 30,000 people by 1300 and a problem with air pollution due to the burning of coal.

As in our own day, some medieval people thought cities were degenerate places. An eleventh-century English monk detested London:

> I do not like that city. All sorts of men crowd together there from every country under the heavens. Each race brings its own vices. No one lives in it without falling into some sort of crime. Actors, jesters, smooth-skinned lads, flatterers, effeminates, pederasts, singing and dancing girls, quacks, belly-dancers, sorceresses, extortioners, magicians, mimes, beggars, buffoons: all this tribe fill all the houses. Therefore, if you do not want to dwell with evildoers, do not live in London.[10]

Indeed, a variety of characters inhabited the medieval city. City life and the money to be made attracted many people to places such as London and Paris, then as now. A traditional German expression, "city air makes one free," referred to the fact that a serf who left the manor and was able to spend "a year and a day" in a city without being caught was considered legally free.

Cities increasingly operated outside the feudal social and political structure. City craftsmen and merchants organized themselves into **guilds,** collective fraternal organizations designed to protect the economic interests of members and to win exemptions from feudal obligations. Eventually city charters, secured from the local lord or the king, allowed the cities to have their own courts, run by local people, and other privileges of self-government. Rulers granted such privileges because of the great wealth that city commerce and payments brought them.

---

serfs In medieval Europe, peasants legally bound to their lord and tied to the land through generations.

guilds In medieval Europe, collective fraternal organizations of craftsmen and merchants designed to protect the economic interests of their members.

eastern and central Mediterranean, and the East African coast as far south as Mozambique. Over these routes the spices of Indonesia, the gold and tin of Malaya, the textiles, sugar, and cotton of India, the cinnamon of Sri Lanka, the gold and ivory of East Africa, the coffee of Arabia, the carpets of Persia, and the silks, porcelain, and tea of China moved to distant markets. Many of these products reached Europe, sparking interest there in reaching the sources of the riches of the East.

The spices, aromatic and pungent derivatives of vegetables grown in tropical lands, were among the main products moving from east to west. Black pepper was cultivated chiefly in India, Siam, and Indonesia, while cloves, nutmeg, and mace came from the Maluku (Moluccan) Islands of eastern Indonesia and cinnamon were grown in Indonesia and Sri Lanka. All of them found a market in the Middle East and Europe. Asia was not the only source for spices, since red or cayenne pepper from West Africa was traded to the Middle East and reached Europe in the 1300s. While they became ingredients in cosmetics and perfumes, spices were more commonly used as medicine or as condiments to flavor food. Intermediate Era people treated a range of illnesses and aided digestion with spices, and many cultures used copious quantities of spices in cooking. Asian spices such as almonds, ginger, saffron, cinnamon, sugar, nutmeg, and cloves improved late medieval European diets. An English book from the early 1400s reported the popularity of pepper, which helped disguise the bad taste of heavily salted preserved meat during the long European winter: "Pepper is black and has a good smack, And every man doth it buy."[5]

Various states around the Persian Gulf, Indian Ocean, and South China Sea were closely linked to maritime trade. However, no particular political power dominated the Indian Ocean trading routes. The trade dynamism depended on cosmopolitan port cities, especially hubs such as Hormuz in Persia, Kilwa in Tanzania, Cambay in northwest India, Calicut on India's southwest coast, Melaka in Malaya, and Quanzhou (chwan-cho) in southern China. These trading ports became vibrant centers of international commerce and culture, drawing populations from various societies. The thirteenth-century traveler Marco Polo was fascinated by the coming and going of ships at Quanzhou: "Here is a harbor whither all ships of India come, with much costly merchandise. It is also the port whither go the [Chinese] merchants [heading overseas]. There is such traffic of merchandise that it is a truly wonderful sight."[6]

A hemispheric trade system developed in which some people came to produce for a world market. This system was fueled by China and India, the great centers of world manufacturing in this era (see Historical Controversy: Eastern Predominance in the Intermediate World). Together China and India probably produced over three-quarters of all world industrial products before 1500. China exported iron, steel, silk, refined sugar, and ceramics, while India was the great producer of textiles. Their industrial products might be transported thousands of miles. Hence, the work of a cotton weaver in India might be sold in China or East Africa, and Chinese ceramics might reach Zimbabwe and Mali. The Muslim soldiers who resisted the Christian crusaders used steel swords smelted in India from East African iron. Merchants from all over Afro-Eurasia—Arabs,

Armenians, Chinese, Indians, Indonesians, Jews, Venetians, Genoese—traveled great distances in search of profits, often forming permanent trade diasporas. For instance, it was said of the Genoese, whose merchant networks stretched from Portugal to the Middle East and Russia, that they were so spread "throughout the world that wherever one goes and stays he makes another Genoa there."[7] One Cairo-based Jewish family firm had branches in India, Iran, and Tunisia. Most of the goods traded over vast distances were luxury items meant for the upper classes, but some goods, such as pepper and sugar, also reached consumers of more modest means.

UNIVERSAL RELIGIONS AND SOCIAL CHANGE

The power and reach of universal, or world, religions such as Buddhism, Christianity, and Islam increased during the Intermediate Era. Religion and its mandates dominated the lives of millions around the world. These religions were early agents of globalization, propagating ideas and fostering trade across regional boundaries. By 1500 the religious map of the Eastern Hemisphere looked very different than it had in 600. Millions of people had embraced ideas, beliefs, and ways of life vastly different from those of their ancestors. The religions promoted moral and ethical values that helped preserve harmony in societies that were increasingly cosmopolitan. The Christian injunction to "love thy neighbor as thyself," the Buddhist emphasis on good thoughts and actions, and the Muslim ideals of social justice and the equality of believers fostered goodwill and cooperation. Religious beliefs also spurred the emergence of new values and social forms.

The Triumph of Universal Religions

During the Intermediate Era, most people in Eurasia and many in Africa eventually embraced one or another universal religion. Islam became the most widespread, rapidly expanding through the Middle East and eventually claiming Central Asia and parts of Europe while gaining a large following in West Africa, the East African coast, South Asia, China, and Southeast Asia. Islam fostered religious, social, and economic networks that linked peoples from Morocco and Spain to Indonesia and the Philippines with a common faith, values, and trade connections. Some Muslim scholars and jurists, such as the Moroccan Ibn Battuta, traveled, sojourned, and even settled thousands of miles from their homelands.

Older faiths also spread in this era, changing societies in varied ways. Theravada Buddhism was established in Sri Lanka and then expanded into mainland Southeast Asia, where it gradually displaced earlier faiths and reshaped cultures by teaching moderation, pacifism, unselfish acts, and individualism. To the north, Mahayana Buddhism first reached Central Asia and then China early in the Common Era, and during the Intermediate Era it became entrenched in Japan, Korea, Vietnam, Mongolia, and Tibet. In most places Buddhism existed alongside rather than replacing earlier religious traditions, such as animism in Siam and Tibet, Shinto in Japan, and Confucianism in China. By 1000 a Buddhist world incorporating diverse societies and several sects stretched from India eastward to

Eastern Predominance in the Intermediate World

For over a century now the prosperous and powerful nations of North America and western Europe—often known today as the West—have dominated the world economically and politically. But before 1500 the world looked very different, and various societies in Asia and North Africa were much stronger and more influential than they are today. Some Eastern societies enjoyed power and status far beyond their borders, helping to shape much of the Eastern Hemisphere in these centuries. However, historians debate to what degree we can consider this to have been an era of Eastern predominance in Afro-Eurasia.

THE PROBLEM

Some historians believe that the rise to influence and prosperity of the East, especially China, India, and various Islamic societies, was a major theme of the Intermediate Era. In their view, for most of these centuries, these Eastern peoples developed and sustained more dynamic governments, productive economies, and creative technologies than any other societies. Others disagree, contending that after 1000 the advantage shifted to western Europeans, who laid the foundations for rapid growth and eventual world dominance. These arguments are part of a vigorous scholarly debate.

THE DEBATE

Many historians identify Eastern predominance in this era, but they disagree on which society made the greatest contributions to the world. The largest number point to China as the Eurasian leader in the Intermediate Era, and they offer a variety of factors to explain China's status. S. A. M. Adshead, for example, sees Tang China as taking center-stage in the world economy and becoming the world's best-ordered state between 600 and 900. William McNeill refers to an era of Chinese predominance especially from 1000 to 1500, with China as the engine of the Eurasian economy. Various historians of Asia, among them Rhoads Murphey, describe an especially dynamic and creative Song China that had many of the conditions that would, in the later eighteenth century, foster industrialization in northwest Europe: urbanization, commercialization, widening local and overseas markets, rising demand, and mechanical invention. A few scholars such as Mary Matossian label the entire Intermediate Era the "Chinese Millennium," when China was more populous, productive, and wealthy than any other society, enjoying an orderly society and advanced technology.

There is a growing consensus among world historians that Chinese innovations and commercial expansion energized Eurasian trade and that Chinese inventions contributed much to the Intermediate world. The British scholar Robert

Temple goes even further, crediting the Chinese with inventing modern agriculture, shipping, astronomical observatories, oil industries, paper money, decimal mathematics, wheelbarrows, fishing reels, multistage rockets, guns, umbrellas, hot-air balloons, chess, whiskey, and even the essential design of the steam engine. Without Chinese naval technology, he and others argue, Columbus would never have sailed to America. China and India were the two great centers of world manufacturing before 1500, and their exports fueled Afro-Eurasian trade.

But China was not the only Asian powerhouse and great source of knowledge. Indians fostered two universal religions, Buddhism and Hinduism, while inventing and exporting scientific, technological, and agricultural techniques to China, the Islamic world, and later Europe in a process the historian Lynda Shaffer terms "southernization." Such innovations as Indian granulated sugar crystals, the decimal system, "Arabic" numerals, and cotton plants had revolutionary implications for Eurasia. Then there are historians of the Middle East, such as Marshall Hodgson and Richard Eaton, who argue for the centrality of the Islamic societies. They contend that, before 1600, the Islamic culture and economy were the world's most expansive, influential, and integrating force. Islam provided a widespread, sophisticated culture as many peoples joined the Muslim-dominated hemispheric economy. Islam was cosmopolitan, egalitarian, and flexible, allowing Muslims to rebound from the Mongol conquests and Black Death and reestablish powerful states such as Ottoman Turkey.

Still other historians think China, India, and Islam all played key roles as powerhouses in an Eastern-dominated Intermediate world. For instance, Robert Marks argues that the Eastern Hemisphere in the 1300s and 1400s had three centers, with dynamic but linked regional systems based on China, India, and Islam. In the 1400s, from Ottoman Turkey eastward to Japan, agricultural efficiency, consumer goods, social welfare, and civilian and military technology were generally the equal of, and often superior to, European counterparts. British scholar John Hobson makes a strong case that the rise of the East made possible the later rise of the West. He argues that the globalization of the era allowed the advanced Eastern inventions, the products of more dynamic societies, to flow westward, where they were gradually assimilated by Europe. Many historians contend that Europe in this era was economically weak, with small, insignificant states, and did not show renewed vigor until 1400. Nor did Europe have, as some historians suggest, any unique cultural advantages. Jack Goody concludes that there were few decisive cultural differences between East and West in rationality, economic tools, family patterns, and political pluralism.

Other scholars doubt that any Eastern societies had a great advantage in this era, and they contend that medieval Europe was not backward compared to China, India, or Islam. David Landes, for example, while conceding that Europe was well behind China and Islam in many areas of life in 1000, suggests that things had changed considerably 500 years later. With what he considers many cultural and geographical advantages, Europeans, argues Landes, caught up to the East with the growth of manufacturing and trade. Landes and others describe an inventive Europe with impressive technological progress using increased nonhuman power, especially in agriculture. Toby Huff has favorably contrasted European science with its Chinese counterpart, especially after 1200. Restless human energy, influential merchants, and competing states made late medieval Europe dynamic. Rodney Stark credits the medieval Catholic Church's emphasis on reason and belief in progress for fostering economic growth, asserting that these ideas were lacking in other religions, a view many scholars have challenged. Landes and Huff also challenge the notion of Eastern leadership. They see China by 1450 as overpopulated, intellectually dormant, indifferent to technology, negating commercial success, and resistant to change. Some historians of China, such as Adshead, concur that the balance of power was shifting toward Europe in the later Intermediate Era.

If several Eastern societies, and especially China, did have some advantages and great power during much of the Intermediate Era, they lost their predominance between 1450 and 1800, raising the question of when and how the East declined. As for when, some historians believe the decline of the East preceded and made possible the rise of the West. Janet Abu-Lughod describes a well-integrated hemispheric system linking Afro-Eurasia by trade for several centuries, with no single country dominant. This network declined after 1350, reducing Europe's commercial competition. Other historians blame Eastern decline on the Mongols and their heirs, who devastated western Asia and North India and ended the creative Song dynasty.

Others credit what the historian L. S. Stavrianos termed the "Law of the Retarding Lead"—that nothing fails like success—for undermining China and helping underdeveloped Europe. This concept holds that the best-adapted, most successful societies have the most difficulty in changing and retaining their lead in a period of transition. They lose their dynamic thrust. Conversely, the less successful societies are more likely to eventually adapt and forge ahead. In the 1400s China still had an edge over other societies, with an advanced technology, efficient government, great regional power, and the world's largest commercial economy. As a result, the Chinese had a stake in preserving rather than dramatically altering their system, which seemed to work so well. Indeed, some argue that the leading Eastern societies, especially China, remained successful until overtaken by a rising West between 1600 and 1800.

EVALUATING THE DEBATE

A plausible case can be made for Eastern predominance, and most global historians now agree that, while other societies played key roles, China and the Islamic world were the two major poles of global trade and technological innovation for much of this era, at least before the 1400s. But the Eastern advantage was eventually lost. We are left with tantalizing questions. What if the Mongols or Ottomans had conquered some

Chinese Foundries By the second century B.C.E. Chinese iron masters had developed highly sophisticated techniques for producing iron and steel, including a basic blast furnace similar to those invented in Europe in the nineteenth century. (Courtesy of South China University of Technology Library, Canton [Guangzhon])

of western Europe, or Ming admiral Zheng He had continued his voyages and headed all the way to West Africa, Europe, or the Americas? Had they occurred, these Mongol, Ottoman, or Chinese achievements might have created a world unrecognizable to us today. Perhaps China, with many prerequisites already in place and enriched by greater trade with West Africa and Europe, might have sparked an industrial revolution. It did not happen, however. Humanity stood at a crossroads in the middle of the millennium, posed between several very different futures. During the next several centuries Europe gradually forged ahead—what some historians call "the rise of the West"—partly by assimilating Eastern technologies and science, while the Islamic societies, India, and finally China struggled, making the world after 1500 very different than the world before it.

THINKING ABOUT THE CONTROVERSY

1. Why do some historians emphasize China as the predominant power in this era?

2. What role did India and the Islamic societies play in the Intermediate world?

3. What points support the argument that Europe began its rise to world power in this era?

EXPLORING THE CONTROVERSY

Among books making the case for Eastern predominance and leadership are John M. Hobson, *The Eastern Origins of Western Civilisation* (New York: Cambridge University Press, 2004); Robert B. Marks, *The Origins of the Modern World: A Global and Ecological Narrative* (Lanham, Md.: Rowman and Littlefield, 2002); and Jack Goody, *The East in the West* (Cambridge: Cambridge University Press, 1996). On China as the major power, see S. A. M. Adshead, *Tang China: The Rise of the East in World History* (New York: Palgrave, 2004); William H. McNeill, *The Pursuit of Power: Technology, Armed Force, and Society Since A.D. 1000* (Chicago: University of Chicago Press, 1982); Rhoads Murphey, *East Asia: A New History*, 3rd ed. (New York: Longman, 2004); Mary Kilbourne Matossian, *Shaping World History: Breakthroughs in Ecology, Technology, Science, and Politics* (Armonk, N.Y.: M.E. Sharpe, 1997); and Robert Temple, *The Genius of China: 3,000 Years of Science, Discovery and Invention* (London: Prion Books, 1986). For Indian and Islamic influence, see Lynda Shaffer, "Southernization," *Journal of World History*, 5/1 (Spring 1994), pp. 1–22; Marshall Hodgson, *Rethinking World History* (Cambridge: Cambridge University Press, 1993); Richard Eaton, *Islamic History as Global History* (Washington, D.C.: American Historical Association, 1993). Among books that argue for European superiority are Toby E. Huff, *The Rise of Early Modern Science: Islam, China, and the West* (Cambridge: Cambridge University Press, 1993); David S. Landes, *The Wealth and Power of Nations: Why Some Are So Rich and Some Are So Poor* (New York: Norton, 1998); and Rodney Stark, *The Victory of Reason: How Christianity Led to Freedom, Capitalism, and Western Success* (New York: Random House, 2005). For a broader study of the rise and demise of the East, see Janet L. Abu-Lughod, *Before European Hegemony: The World System A.D. 1250–1350* (New York: Oxford University Press, 1989).

> *"O, wonder! How many goodly creatures are there here! How beauteous mankind is! O brave new world That hath such people in't!"*
>
> MIRANDA, IN *THE TEMPEST* BY WILLIAM SHAKESPEARE, 1611[1]

The European and world economy changed rapidly in the sixteenth century, and few places exemplified change more than the port city of Antwerp (AN-twuhrp), on the River Scheldt (skelt) in what is now Belgium. In 1567 an Italian diplomat and historian, Ludovico Guicciardini (loo-do-VEE-ko GWEE-char-DEE-nee), published a description of the mostly Flemish-speaking city and its fabulous Bourse (boors), a huge, multistory building in the city center that served as a combination of marketplace, not unlike a modern department store, and stock exchange. The Bourse posted a motto above its entrance: "For the service of merchants of all nations and all languages." An economic boom centered on the Bourse brought prosperity to Antwerp's merchants and bankers, as well as to the businesspeople from many lands who came to the Bourse to buy and sell. Guicciardini wrote that "all of these persons being people who are earning money, invest it not only in commerce but also in building, in buying lands and properties, and thus the city flourishes and increases marvelously."[2]

From the late 1400s until the late 1500s Antwerp was the European hub for ever-widening world networks of commerce. Every week fabulous merchandise arrived from all over the world, some delivered by wagons, some by ships. As many as 2,500 ships from different lands anchored at one time in the harbor, many laden with gold and silver from the Americas, and the Bourse became the clearinghouse for their cargo. Every day goods were put on sale, and bustling crowds of merchants, foreign visitors such as Guicciardini, and affluent local consumers thronged the rooms. They came to buy spices from Southeast Asia and India, sugar from the Americas, tin from England, Venetian glass, Spanish lace, German copper, paintings by great Flemish artists, and even the service of assassins or professional soldiers. Thus one great city linked the economies not only of Europe but also of the wider world. The Antwerp Bourse represented a postmedieval Europe shaped by the fruits of overseas exploration, conquest, and expanding commerce. The new economic thrust was one component of the changes in many areas of life and thought that Shakespeare referred to as a "brave new world."

In 1500, as the Early Modern Era began, western Europeans were still medieval in many respects: they were dominated by the multinational Roman church, their countries had little sense of national identity, they were skeptical of science, and they were minor participants in hemispheric commerce and barely aware of distant lands. By the mid-1700s, however, Europe and parts of the wider world had undergone a profound economic, intellectual, and political transition. Europeans were conquering and settling the Americas, and various European countries had established colonies or trading networks in Asia and Africa. As a result, wealth flowed into Europe, enriching some and fostering investment in science and technology. New knowledge of, and influences from, non-European cultures reshaped European thinking and cultures. The Catholic Church faced severe challenges. In cultural and religious life, some European thinkers were influenced as much or more by secular ideas, including science, as by Christian doctrines. Although such changes were not always beneficial, often resulting in strains that produced long and bloody wars, they nevertheless remade Europe's political and social systems. By 1750 Europeans had left many of their medieval institutions and beliefs behind and were on the verge of introducing even more profound changes to the world.

FOCUS QUESTIONS

1. How did exploration, colonization, and capitalism increase Western power and wealth?

2. How did the Renaissance and Reformation mark a crucial cultural and intellectual transition?

3. What types of governments emerged in Europe in this era?

4. How did major intellectual, scientific, and social changes help to reshape the West?

Transitions: Overseas Expansion and Capitalism

How did exploration, colonization, and capitalism increase Western power and wealth?

The foundations for the dramatic changes that reshaped many Early Modern European societies were established in late medieval times and embellished by developments after 1500. The European encounter with America and its riches, which began in the 1490s, the growth of a trans-Atlantic slave trade, and the opening of direct trade with Asia all increased European wealth and stimulated the development of **capitalism**, an economic system in which property, exchange, and the means of production, such as factories, are privately owned. By the 1600s huge quantities of valuable Asian spices and precious American metals and plantation crops were pouring into Europe. Inherently dynamic, capitalism gradually expanded its scale of operation to a global level. The economic revolution fostered stronger European states and reshaped the daily lives of nearly all Europeans.

capitalism An economic system in which property, exchange, and the means of production are privately owned.

Economic and Urban Roots

Some of the economic changes of the Early Modern Era simply continued trends already apparent in western Europe before 1500. During the 1400s commerce and merchants flourished, cities grew larger and more numerous, and the feudal social systems and the values that supported them broke down. Commerce, with its widening trade networks, became a part of everyday life. The ability of the middle classes to buy more luxury goods, especially fine clothes, spurred the growth of industries like textile manufacturing. However, most Europeans were still neither urban nor middle class; 80 percent were peasants who worked the soil. Their life was organized around the male-dominated household: men tilled the fields while women had responsibility for the house, barn, and gardens. Many peasants were now free or tenant farmers rather than serfs, but most farmers were still heavily burdened with taxes and service obligations to lords. They also tithed crops and livestock to the church. Only a few farm people, mostly boys, received any formal education.

Yet, despite being rooted in farming, the economy was changing, partly as a result of population growth and climate change. The European population (excluding Russia) increased from 70 to 100 million between 1500 and 1600, and then to 125 million by 1750, making for larger commercial markets. The global cooling that began around 1300 intensified, reached its height in the late 1600s, and then began to

CHRONOLOGY

	Cultural and Intellectual Changes	Political Changes
1300	**1350–1615** Renaissance	
1400		
1500	**1517–1615** Protestant Reformation	**1588** Defeat of Spanish armada
1600	**1600–1750** Scientific Revolution	**1618–1648** Thirty Years War
	1675–1800 Enlightenment	**1641–1645** English Civil War
		1688–1689 English Glorious Revolution

thaw around 1715, finally ending in the mid-1800s. This "Little Ice Age" brought winter freezing to canals and rivers, caused poor harvests, and helped motivate overseas explorers to seek better conditions and food sources elsewhere. Importing foods from the Americas, such as corn and potatoes, helped avert mass famine.

Political and economic changes were felt more strongly by urban populations. By 1500 cities such as Paris and London had grown to over 200,000. Although this was still small by Asian standards, such cities were unique in the world for their growing political power and autonomy. Unlike Chinese or Ottoman cities, European cities existed in a politically fragmented region rather than a centralized empire. Not having to answer to centralized authorities, city leaders could bargain with kings for advantages and autonomy.

Merchants also benefited from changing conditions. More favorable attitudes toward commerce gave some European merchants a status and power that were unusual in the world. In addition, many western European societies offered an opportunity for making profit and also had institutions, such as banks, that favored economic growth. Blessed with these advantages, late medieval Europeans laid the foundation for an economic transition that, in the fifteenth and sixteenth centuries, began to fundamentally alter western European life and later spread its influences around the world.

Some western European societies developed capitalism, a dynamic system that was highly oriented to economic growth. In the 1400s cities such as Venice and Genoa in Italy, and Bruges (broozh) and Antwerp in what is today Belgium, became centers of capitalistic enterprise. Venetians and Genoese,

Antwerp Marketplace The marketplace at the center of Antwerp, in what is today Belgium, was the main hub for European trade in the 1500s, the place where goods from all over Europe and from Africa, the Americas, and Asia were bought and sold. (Musées Royaux Beaux-Arts de Belgique)

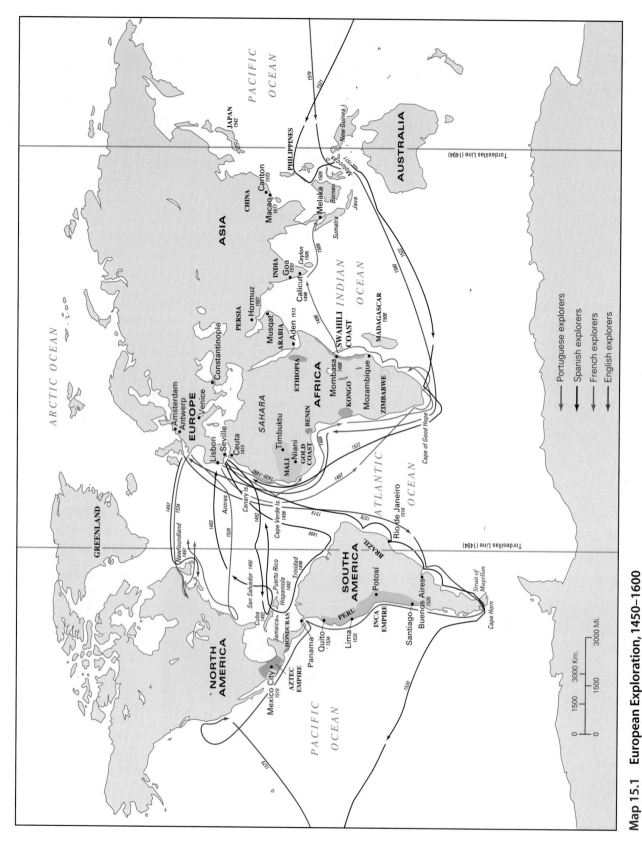

Map 15.1   European Exploration, 1450–1600

Between the early 1400s and mid-1600s explorers sponsored by Portugal, Spain, France, Holland, and England discovered the sea route around Africa to South and Southeast Asia, and crossed the Atlantic to the Americas, permanently connecting the two hemispheres. They also sailed across the Pacific Ocean from the Americas to Asia.

fierce competitors, traded all over Europe, western Asia, and North Africa. But early capitalism was limited by the Catholic Church's condemnation of usury and by cumbersome business methods. Not until after 1500 did the scope and nature of capitalism, fostered by overseas exploration and conquest, change dramatically, allowing the Antwerp merchants to build a Bourse that became a marketplace for world products.

Political, Intellectual, and Technological Roots

The political shape of western Europe also began to shift in the 1500s. After the ending of the Roman Empire in the Late Classical Era, western Europe had remained politically fragmented, and in 1500 it contained some five hundred states or ministates. Unlike in China, Ottoman Turkey, or Mughal India, which had powerful bureaucracies, no single imperial state could dominate the economy and enforce intellectual conformity. But in the 1500s some of the small states were gradually transformed into integrated monarchies, which became enriched by resources obtained by their merchants and adventurers in Africa, the Americas, and Asia. Both merchants and monarchs resented the power and independence of the landed aristocracy and cooperated to destroy their influence in a series of bloody wars. For the first time since the Roman Empire and the Carolingians, large centralized states developed in Europe, particularly in England and France. The growth of these strong but competitive states made the political system dynamic and unstable.

New intellectual currents also emerged that fostered broader horizons, especially improvements in mapmaking. In 1375 Abraham Cresques (kres-kay), a Jewish cartographer on the Spanish island of Majorca (muh-JOR-kuh), used Christian, Muslim, and Jewish traditions and the accounts of many travelers to produce a map that placed Jerusalem rather than Europe at the center of the world. Cresques also offered a much more realistic picture of northern Africa than was found in earlier maps. In the 1400s Portuguese mapmakers drew innovative maps that influenced Flemish mapmakers of the 1500s such as Gerardus Mercator (muhr-KAY-tuhr). But these maps were also misleading and, unlike Cresques' effort, did not decenter Europe. For example, Mercator's 1569 world map vastly exaggerated the size of Europe and North America while diminishing the size of Africa, India, China, and South America. In spite of these distortions, Mercator's approach, which pictures the earth as an uncurved rectangle intersected by straight lines for latitude and longitude, is still widely used.

The foundation for the reshaping of European societies also came from developments in technology and mathematics, some of them inspired by earlier Arab, Chinese, and Indian innovations. Between 1450 and 1550 Europe's technology surpassed that of the Arabs and was catching up to that of China. The major improvements came in shipbuilding, navigation, weaponry, and printing. European ships took advantage of lateen sails developed by Arabs and sternpost rudders from China, and they could also use the Chinese magnetic compass to navigate. Facing much rougher, stormier waters than the placid Mediterranean and Indian Ocean, the people along Europe's Atlantic coast also had to build sturdier ships, giving them a naval advantage over other maritime societies. Europeans also greatly improved gunpowder weapons and printing processes, both invented in China. The introduction of the European printing press in the mid-1400s made possible the dissemination of both Christian and secular knowledge to an increasingly literate audience. Some 13,000 books were published in Europe by 1500. Europeans also blended imported mathematical concepts, such as the Indian numerical system and Arab algebra, with their own insights to improve quantification. Countries that developed and marketed these new technologies and techniques increased their power, while those holding on to existing technologies fell behind.

"Gold, God, and Glory": Explorations and Conquests

During these centuries, the rise of Europe as a world power took place within a context of European overseas expansion and conquest (see Chapters 16–18). Historians use a standard shorthand, "Gold, God, and Glory," to describe European motives in going out into the world in this era. "Gold" was the search for material gain by acquiring and selling Asian spices, African slaves, American metals, and other resources. A desire to establish a direct connection to Asian trade led to the first European voyages of discovery in the 1400s. "God" refers to the militant crusading tradition of Christianity, including the rivalry with Islam and the hatred of non-Christian religions. Many Christians wanted to convert the world to what they believed to be the true faith. Reflecting this view, a missionary Catholic priest in Spanish America argued that "it is a great thing that so many souls should have been saved and that so many evils, idolatries, homicides, and great offenses against God [by Native Americans] should have been halted."[3] "Glory" describes the goals of the competing monarchies, who sought to establish their claims to newly contacted territories so as to strengthen their position in European politics. Motivated by these three aims, various western European peoples expanded overseas during the Early Modern Era, gaining control over widening segments of the globe. By the late nineteenth century Europeans dominated much of the world politically and economically.

During the 1400s the seafaring peoples of the Iberian peninsula, the Spanish and Portuguese, ventured out into the Atlantic and discovered the Azores (A-zorz), Madeira (muh-DEER-uh), and Canary island chains off northwest Africa (see Map 15.1). Several factors pushed Iberians to pioneer in overseas expeditions: a favorable geographic location facing the Atlantic Ocean and North Africa, a maritime tradition of deep-sea fishing, an aggressive Christian crusading tradition, and possession of the best ships and navigation techniques in Europe by the 1400s. The Iberians also had economic motives. For centuries gold from West Africa had passed through North Africa to southern Europe, where it was used for coins, treasuries, and jewelry and as tender (money) to buy valued Asian goods. But trade with Islamic North Africa and western Asia had stalled in the 1400s. Furthermore, the earliest Iberian exploration sought a way to circumnavigate the Venetian monopoly over the valuable trade from southern Asia through Persia and Egypt. The Iberians were also interested in finding new food sources, since Iberia did not produce enough meat and wheat to feed its growing population.

This maritime exploration and conquest required new technologies, such as a new type of ship to sail the rough Atlantic. The Portuguese invented the caravel, an easily maneuverable type of ship designed to travel long distances. However, since caravels used Chinese sternpost rudders and Arab lateen sails, they were not entirely a Portuguese invention. Some historians even argue that the caravel was modeled on the earlier Arab ship known as a carrack (KAR-uhk). Later the Iberians built larger ships such as galleons, which provided much more cargo space and room for larger crews than caravels. To chart the position of the sun and stars, Iberian sailors used the astrolabe (AS-truh-labe), invented by tenth-century Arabs. Some Europeans also learned how to mount weapons on ships, which increased their advantage at sea and enabled them to overwhelm coastal defenses and defeat lightly armed ships. The Spanish in the Americas and the Portuguese in Africa and Asia, using artillery, naval cannon, and muskets, could conquer or control large territories if the inhabitants lacked guns. By the late 1500s, the English were building the most maneuverable ships and the best iron cannon, and by the 1700s European land and sea weapons greatly outclassed those of once militarily powerful China, India, Persia, and Ottoman Turkey. Europeans now posed a threat to the great Asian states.

The intense competition between major European powers led to increased exploration, the building of trade networks, and a scramble for colonies, subject territories where Europeans could directly control primary production. In the 1400s the Portuguese began direct encounters with the peoples of coastal Africa, and by 1500 Portuguese explorers had reached East Africa and then sailed across the Indian Ocean to India. Soon, they seized key Asian ports such as Hormuz on the Persian Gulf, Goa in India, and Melaka in Malaya. Meanwhile, the Spanish discovered that a huge landmass to the west, soon to be named America, lay between Europe and East Asia. By the later 1500s the Spanish had explored large regions of the Americas and conquered many of its peoples, including the great Inca and Aztec Empires making them the most powerful European state for some decades. Portugal, England, France, and Holland also colonized other parts of the Americas and sent emigrants to what they called "the New World." At the same time, various European states established colonies in several African locations and carried increasing numbers of enslaved Africans to the Western Hemisphere to work on plantations growing cash crops, such as sugar, cotton, and coffee, for European consumption. In the sixteenth and seventeenth centuries, the Portuguese, Dutch, and Spanish colonized several Asian port cities and various Southeast Asian islands, including the Philippines, Java, and the Spice Islands of Indonesia. American minerals, especially silver, supported a great expansion of the European economy and allowed Europeans to buy into the rich Asian trade, especially from China. These conquests and economic activities enabled the transfer of vast quantities of resources to Europe, especially silver, gold, sugar, coffee, and spices, and the fortunes of leading European trading ports such as Venice, Genoa, Lisbon, Seville, Antwerp, and Amsterdam rose or fell depending on their importance in overseas trade.

During the Early Modern Era Europeans gradually brought various peoples into their economic and political sphere, laying the foundations for a system of Western dominance in the world after 1750. Several European societies benefited the most. The Portuguese and Spanish prospered in the 1500s from their overseas activities, while in the 1600s the overseas trade of the Dutch, English, and French enabled them to become the most powerful European countries. But European influence was still limited in many regions. During this era Asian and African societies such as China, Siam, Japan, and Morocco remained powerful and dynamic and were able to successfully resist or ignore European demands. Nonetheless, overseas trade and exploitation provided some European societies with valuable human labor and natural resources and contributed to the growth of capitalism.

Early Capitalism

Arising first in western Europe, capitalism has taken many forms and fostered new values around the world. Under capitalism, the drive for profit from privately owned and privately invested capital has largely determined what goods are produced and how they are distributed. Capitalism was unique when it first arose because, on a much greater scale than ever before, money in the form of investment capital was used to make profits. The various forms of capitalism that emerged as the economic system spread had certain common features: the need for constant accumulation of additional capital, economic self-interest, the profit motive, a market economy of some sort, and competition. These features shaped both economic and social relations between people. For example, individual carpenters who once shared their services with the community on a barter basis, or who belonged to a guild that operated for the benefit of all local carpenters, began to charge fees instead, competing for customers with other carpenters. By the 1800s capitalism also included private ownership of the means of production, such as factories, businesses, and farms.

Capitalism was not necessarily inevitable. The profit motive, wealth accumulation, and competition were incompatible with certain cultural values. For example, many traditional cultures had a bias against people accumulating more wealth than their neighbors or working hard for the sole purpose of maximizing income. Even today, some Asian, African, American Indian, and Latin American cultures value cooperation, religious piety, or generosity more than acquiring great wealth. For instance, many Malays in Southeast Asia respect Muslim pilgrims to Mecca more than successful businessmen and mistrust shopkeepers. In precapitalist societies governments siphoned off surplus wealth, and the elite spent their resources on conspicuous consumption of luxuries, such as the building of magnificent cathedrals, palaces, and pyramids that now impress tourists. In medieval Europe merchant and craft guilds emphasized ethics, accepting a strict regulation of economic activity for the greater good. By contrast, capitalists invested some profits in further exchange or production, always with the goal to make more money. This reinvestment fostered an economic expansion that differentiated capitalism from earlier economic systems, transforming small-scale trade into global capitalism.

While western Europe became increasingly capitalist, parts of eastern Europe discouraged capitalism. In the 1500s, as the demand for agricultural products increased while cooler climates hindered farming, eastern European nobles faced a labor shortage on their estates. Allied with the landowning aristocracy, kings in Poland, Lithuania, Prussia, and Russia mandated serfdom on the peasantries and imposed new laws forbidding people to leave the land. At the same time, by providing little support to the local merchant classes, these governments thwarted capitalist expansion and diminished the political influence of cities. As local merchants declined, foreign merchants, including Dutch, Germans, Jews, and Armenians, moved into eastern Europe, becoming the major middlemen and gradually dominating the region's commerce. As the economies became chiefly agrarian and serf-based, however, many once vibrant cities declined into sleepy provincial towns, inhabited by many foreign-born merchants or their descendants. For example, many Polish and Lithuanian cities had large populations of Jewish merchants and artisans.

The Rise of Capitalism

During the 1500s capitalism took hold in some cities and states of north and northwest Europe. Indeed, the English and the people of the Low Countries (today's Belgium and the Netherlands), especially the Flemish and Dutch, developed the most dynamic forms of capitalism, and soon they eclipsed Italy, shifting the economic balance of power in Europe from the Mediterranean to the English Channel and North Sea. Enriched by distributing American silver and controlling the Baltic grain trade, Antwerp became Europe's main financial capital until 1568, when Genoa temporarily regained dominance as a banking center. By the 1620s Amsterdam in Holland had emerged as Europe's capitalist powerhouse, dominating much European and Asian trade. This clean, orderly, and prosperous Dutch city boasted amenities rare elsewhere, such as street lamps and watch patrols to prevent crime. In 1728 the English writer Daniel Defoe concluded that "the Dutch must be understood as they really are, the Middle Persons of Trade, the Factors and Brokers of Europe. They buy to sell again, take in to send out, and the greatest part of their vast commerce consists in being supply'd from all parts of the world that they may supply the world again."[4]

Expanding capitalism fostered new economic ideas, social groups, and consumption patterns. For example, spurred by increasing trade, old concepts of investing wealth in land ownership gradually gave way to the view that capital should instead be invested in business and industry to help increase production of ships, armor, arms, and textiles. This increased production would then create more capital. Indeed, people needed more money because the import of American metals caused a rapid rise in prices. The increase in available capital began to change business methods, especially the use of credit on a large scale, which fostered banking. Society also changed. Capitalism produced a new social group known as the **bourgeoisie**, an urban-based, mostly commercial, middle class. Members of this group ranged from small-scale merchants to financiers. In addition to the bourgeoisie, many western Europeans were affected by the new materialism, which also encouraged lotteries and gambling. More people of all backgrounds purchased consumer goods, from tea, coffee, and sugar to clocks, china, and glassware.

As a new capitalist order emerged, many Europeans changed their attitudes toward charging interest for loans and seeking profit. The medieval church had denounced charging interest as usury, a mortal sin, and had also opposed commercial profit. A good Christian could not become a merchant or banker, leaving much commerce and banking to the Jewish minority. By the late 1500s, however, many rejected these church teachings and instead heeded the cynical saying that "he who takes usury goes to hell; he who doesn't goes to the poorhouse." Acceptance of interest by Christians reflected a gradual shift to an entirely different type of society in western Europe.

Jacob Fugger (FOOG-uhr) (1459–1525) of Augsburg (AUGZ-burg), a southern German city, was living proof that an ambitious commoner could prosper from the capitalist trends. The grandson of a weaver and son of a successful merchant, Fugger built a financial empire of banks, factories, silver mines, and farmlands. Earning an annual profit of 54 percent for sixteen years, Fugger became Europe's richest man, in the process loaning money to royal houses and acquiring a castle and the title of count. He wrote the epitaph for his own tomb, praising himself as "behind no one in attainment of extraordinary wealth, in generosity, purity of morals and greatness of soul."[5] His sons also published the first newsletter for merchants and bankers, which tracked political and economic developments in Europe.

Commercial Capitalism and Mercantilism

As a dynamic, flexible economic system, capitalism continually changed in character and expanded in scope. Under the form of capitalism dominant in western Europe between 1500 and 1770, **commercial capitalism**, most capital was invested in commercial enterprises such as trading companies, including the world's first joint-stock companies (see Chronology: Political, Economic, and Intellectual Developments, 1500–1750).

---

bourgeoisie The urban-based, mostly commercial, middle class that arose with capitalism in the Early Modern Era.

commercial capitalism The economic system in which most capital was invested in commercial enterprises such as trading companies, including the world's first joint-stock companies.

CHRONOLOGY

Political, Economic, and Intellectual Developments, 1500–1750

1500–1770	Era of commercial capitalism
1533–1586	Reign of Ivan the Terrible in Muscovy
ca. 1600–1750	Scientific Revolution
ca. 1600–1750	Baroque era
1609	Dutch independence
1618–1648	Thirty Years War
1641–1645	English Civil War
1648	Congress of Westphalia
1661–1715	Reign of Louis XIV in France
1675–1800	Enlightenment
1682–1725	Reign of Peter the Great in Russia
1688	Bill of Rights
1688–1689	Glorious Revolution and Declaration of Rights in England
1700–1709	Great Northern War
1701–1714	War of the Spanish Succession
1707	United Kingdom of England, Scotland, and Wales

To increase their efficiency and profits, these precursors of today's giant multinational corporations pooled their resources by selling shares, or stocks, to merchants and bankers. Joint-stock companies encouraged investment and mobilized great capital, and their directors were chosen for their experience. A typical company employed many cashiers, bookkeepers, couriers, and middlemen skilled in various languages, and it invested in diversified economic activities such as real estate, mining, and industry. Few Asian or African merchants could compete with this collective power.

Commercial capitalism was strongly shaped by the cooperation of the state and big business enterprises, which worked together for their mutual benefit. States practiced **mercantilism**, an economic approach based on a government policy of building a nation's wealth by expanding its reserves of precious metals. The Atlantic states of England, Holland, France, and Spain particularly pursued mercantilism. The purpose was to strengthen monarchies by amassing gold and silver bullion. Trading was controlled by semimilitary, government-backed

---

mercantilism An economic approach that emerged in Early Modern Europe based on a government policy of building a nation's wealth by expanding its reserves of precious metals.

companies protected from competition. To attract bullion held by other nations, these governments tried to limit imports and increase exports. In the 1600s the French finance minister Jean Baptiste Colbert (kohl-BEAR), the son of a merchant, used this approach brilliantly to support French industries and industrial exports. Some of the largest joint-stock companies obtained royal charters, which granted them monopolies and the right to colonize other lands in the name of the government. In England such companies, founded by business and government leaders, financed overseas exploration and supported piracy against Spanish and French shipping. Spurred by mercantilism, during the 1500s commercial capitalism expanded out of western Europe and into Africa, Asia, and the Americas.

SECTION SUMMARY

- Europe's political decentralization allowed for the growth of cities and the development of capitalism.

- Europeans made great strides in mapmaking and improved technologies such as shipbuilding, navigation, weaponry, and printing by borrowing and building on the work of Arabs, Chinese, and Indians.

- Motivated by "Gold, God, and Glory," Europeans, led by the Spanish and the Portuguese, set up colonies in the Americas, Africa, and Asia.

- Despite entrenched value systems that opposed its single-minded emphasis on accumulating wealth, capitalism took hold in western Europe, while eastern European leaders resisted it and instead mandated serfdom.

- By the early seventeenth century, Amsterdam had established itself as the center of capitalist Europe and the medieval Christian prohibition on usury was softening.

- Commercial capitalists, assisted by the mercantilist policies of their countries, increased their market power by pooling resources in such organizations as joint-stock companies.

✦ The Renaissance and Reformation

How did the Renaissance and Reformation mark a crucial cultural and intellectual transition?

Two major movements, the Renaissance and the Reformation, reshaped European thought and culture in the 1500s. During the Renaissance, a dramatic flowering in arts and learning that began in Italy around 1350 (see Chapter 14), new philosophical, scientific, artistic, and literary currents paved the way for more creative, secular societies. The movement reached its peak in the 1500s, when it spread throughout Europe as the large quantities of gold and silver imported from the Americas spurred economic expansion and provided more

the sides and then supported the nobles, who crushed the uprisings. The result was over 100,000 deaths. The Lutheran Church became closely linked to governments, and many German princes became Lutheran, while their overlord, the Holy Roman Emperor, remained staunchly Catholic.

Non-Germans were also inspired by Luther's example, founding Protestant movements. In Switzerland the theologian, priest, and humanist Ulrich Zwingli (ZWING-lee) (1484–1531) preached similar ideas. But Luther and Zwingli soon disagreed. Whereas Luther interpreted the Bible literally, Zwingli was more open-minded and applied reason to religious doctrine. Zwingli's activities sparked a civil war among Swiss Catholics and Protestants that resulted in Zwingli's death. Another Protestant movement, Calvinism, was more radical than Lutheranism in rejecting Catholic doctrine. Its founder, John Calvin (1509–1564), was forced to leave France for supporting Luther's ideas and settled in Geneva (juh-NEE-vuh), Switzerland. Like Luther, Calvin emphasized reading the Bible, practicing charity, and never questioning God. However, unlike Luther, Calvin believed not in human free will but in predestination, the doctrine that an individual's salvation or damnation was already determined at birth by God. Since good behavior and faith could not guarantee reaching Heaven, the authorities must enforce morality to maintain order. Under Calvin, Geneva became a theocratic society, ruled by church leaders with growing intolerance of other views. Some dissenters were even burned at the stake. Calvin demanded strict morality and attacked worldly pleasures. For example, inns had to forbid behavior such as swearing, dancing, dice, playing cards, indecent songs, or staying up after nine at night. Calvinism spread rapidly in Switzerland, England, and Holland and also developed centers of strength elsewhere. In 1561, for instance, the Calvinist John Knox founded the Presbyterian Church in Scotland, where it became the dominant church.

In England, unlike Germany and Switzerland, the initiative for religious change came from the king, Henry VIII (r. 1509–1547), who was then a Catholic. Henry had no male heir with his wife, Catherine of Aragon, a Spanish princess. To preserve his dynasty, he asked the pope to annul his marriage so that he could marry Anne Boleyn (1501–1536), the much-courted daughter of English aristocrats who had rebuffed Henry's invitations to become his mistress. When Rome refused the annulment, Henry chose to break with the church in 1532, rejecting papal supremacy. He announced his divorce, married Anne Boleyn, and arranged to be made head of the Church of England, later known as the Anglican Church, newly formed by his allies. Henry quickly moved to suppress both Calvinism and the Catholic Church. He closed the English monasteries and distributed their lands to his allies among nobles and businessmen. However, the Anglicans largely retained Catholic dogma. Ironically, Henry grew disenchanted with Anne Boleyn, who also bore him no sons, and had her beheaded in 1536 for alleged treason and adultery. Henry married four more times.

Henry's moves generated religious strife in England. His only male heir, the sickly Edward VI (r. 1547–1553), came to the throne at age ten but died at sixteen of tuberculosis. The Catholic reaction was led by Edward's successor, Henry's daughter by Catherine of Aragon, Queen Mary Tudor (TOO-duhr) (r. 1553–1558), who suppressed the Anglican Church. But she was succeeded by Elizabeth I (1533–1603), the daughter of Henry VIII and Anne Boleyn, who restored the Anglican Church. Calvinist influences then began reshaping Anglican dogma. English Calvinists (known as Puritans) were at first tolerated by Anglicans but later persecuted by Elizabeth's successors for opposing moves toward Catholic-Anglican reconciliation. Some Puritans emigrated to Holland. From there one small Puritan group, the Pilgrims, moved to North America in 1620 to seek more religious freedom, helping plant Puritan influence in the New England colonies.

Protestantism and Capitalism

Modern historians avidly debate the relationship between the rise around the same time of both capitalism and Protestantism. While many doubt any direct connection, other scholars believe that Protestant doctrines contributed to, and supplied religious underpinnings for, capitalist values. Some forms of Protestantism were certainly congenial to the thriving new economic attitudes. In particular, Calvinists believed that citizens demonstrated their fitness for salvation by being law-abiding, industrious, thrifty, and sober, all values that supported the capitalist order. Like Calvinists and other Protestants, capitalists also favored productive labor, frugality, and accumulation of wealth as good in themselves. Many Protestant hymns warned against wasting money on frivolous pleasures. Both Protestantism and capitalism also encouraged individualism, thus undermining the medieval values that the Catholic Church defended.

The relationship between capitalism and Protestantism certainly seems to have been congenial. Although capitalism also emerged in some Catholic societies, as with the Fuggers, the wealthy entrepreneurs in southern Germany mentioned earlier, it flourished in several Protestant societies, especially Holland, England, and northern Germany. The strongest capitalist societies were also the most Protestant; they were also the most intellectually diverse and gave rise to some secularized free thinkers. Although Luther and Calvin may have been intolerant of other religious views, they opened the doors to democracy: once people had freely voiced their opinions on religion, they moved on to seeking a voice in government. Similarly, when women were encouraged to become literate so that they could read the scriptures, they also gained some new options.

The Counter Reformation and Catholic Reform

The Protestant challenge generated a reaction, the **Counter Reformation**, a movement to confront Protestantism and crush dissidents within the Catholic Church. The church used varied strategies to fight Protestantism. Pope Paul IV praised

---

Counter Reformation A movement to confront Protestantism and crush dissidents within the Catholic Church.

Queen Elizabeth I Rallies Her People

Few women have ever enjoyed the power and respect of England's Renaissance queen, Elizabeth I. Her forty-five years of rule (1558–1603) marked a brilliant period for English culture, especially in literature and theater. On her death, the admiring playwright Ben Jonson wrote her epitaph: "For wit, features, and true passion, Earth, thou hast not such another." The queen may have been, as her detractors claimed, deceptive, devious, and autocratic, but her intelligence and formidable political skills helped her maneuver successfully through the snake pit of both English and European politics. But English-Spanish relations deteriorated, prompting war. In 1588, as the powerful Spanish armada sailed toward the English coast, Elizabeth launched the English ships with a speech to her subjects that ironically played off her gender to reinforce her link with the English people. With the help of foul weather, the English defeated the Spanish, changing the fortunes of both countries.

My loving people. We have been persuaded by some that are careful for our safety, to take heed how we commit ourselves to armed multitudes, for fear of treachery, but I assure you, I do not desire to live to distrust my faithful and loving people. Let tyrants fear; I have always so behaved myself, that, under God, I have placed my chiefest strength and safeguard in the loyal hearts and good will of my subjects, and therefore I am come amongst you, as you see, at this time, not for my recreation and disport, but being resolved in the midst and heat of the battle, to live or die amongst you all, to lay down for my God, and for my kingdoms, and for my people, my honor and my blood, even in the dust.

I know I have the body of a weak and feeble woman; but I have the heart and stomach of a king, and of a king of England too; and I think foul scorn that . . . Spain, or any prince of Europe should dare to invade the borders of my realm; to which rather than any dishonor shall grow by me, I myself will take up arms, I myself will be your general, judge, and rewarder of every one of your virtues in the field.

I know already for your forwardness you have deserved rewards and crowns; and we do assure you in the word of a prince, they shall be duly paid you. In the meantime my lieutenant general shall be in my stead, than whom never prince commanded a more noble or worthy subject; no doubting but by your obedience to my general, by your concord in the camp, and your valor in the field, we shall shortly have a famous victory over those enemies of my God, of my kingdoms, and of my people.

THINKING ABOUT THE READING

1. How did Elizabeth justify the forthcoming battle with Spain?

2. What personal qualities did this Renaissance monarch suggest she could offer to her people in their time of peril?

Source: Charles W. Colby, ed., *Selections from the Sources of English History* (Harlow: Longmans, Green, 1899), pp. 158–159. Quotation in introduction from A. L. Rowse, *The Elizabethan Renaissance: The Life of the Society* (New York: Charles Scribner's, 1971), p. 59.

the Holy Inquisition, the church court formed in medieval times to combat heretical ideas (see Chapter 14), as the apple of his eye. Persecution of dissidents by the Inquisition became especially ferocious in Spain, where several thousand people believed to hold dissident ideas were burned at the stake. In addition, the pope formed a new church office, the Congregation of the Index, to censor books and decide which ones, among them Protestant writings, were to be forbidden altogether. Missionary activity also entered into the Counter Reformation. The Spanish Basque former soldier, Ignatius of Loyola (loi-OH-luh) (1491–1556), founded a new missionary order, the Society of Jesus, in 1534. The Jesuits, as they were known, boasted strict discipline. One prominent Jesuit, the Spanish Basque St. Francis Xavier (ZAY-vee-uhr) (1506–1552), became a pioneering missionary in India, Southeast Asia, and Japan.

For all their harsh punitive measures, the Inquisition and Index did not manage to suppress dissidence within the church, prompting the pope to sponsor a series of conferences, the Council of Trent (a city in northern Italy), to reconsider church doctrines in free-wheeling discussions. However, the council (1545–1563) reaffirmed most Catholic dogma, including those ideas and practices rejected by Protestants. It supported the value of both tradition and scripture, condemned Calvin's doctrine of predestination and Luther's sole reliance on faith, endorsed the church hierarchy and papal authority, and maintained priestly celibacy. But the council did bring about some reform: it imposed more papal supervision of priests and bishops, and it mandated that all clergy be trained in seminaries. The Trent reforms were continued by three reforming popes, enabling Catholicism to check its loss of believers to Protestantism and recover some lost ground. The reforms within the church and the competition with Protestants allowed the Catholic Church to survive and flourish in a modified form. The church gradually turned from confronting Protestants to converting the peoples outside of Europe.

But religious passions continued to foster intolerance. Indeed, in Europe, religious minorities, such as Jews, French Protestants, and English Catholics, faced discrimination and sometimes violence. Several popes pursued anti-Jewish policies, as did some Protestants: Luther advocated burning synagogues, arresting rabbis, and confiscating Jewish property. Throughout the Early Modern Era many Jews faced expulsion from the countries where they lived or segregation in city ghettoes. Many Jews and minority Catholics and Protestants emigrated to other European countries or to the Americas to escape religious persecution.

Religious Wars and Conflicts

Religious divisions contributed to a series of European wars and other conflicts from the late sixteenth through early eighteenth centuries, which reshaped several societies. The Spanish Empire, ruled by a branch of the Habsburg family, was particularly troubled by religious tensions. During the 1500s Spain emerged as a major European power, which, thanks to exploration and conquest, controlled a vast empire in the Americas and Southeast Asia. The Spanish Habsburgs also ruled other Europeans, including Portugal, the Low Countries, and parts of Italy. King Philip II of Spain (r. 1556–1598), known as "the most Catholic of kings," put the resources of the Spanish crown toward defending the Catholic cause in Europe while spreading the faith abroad.

Philip faced one of his biggest challenges in the Low Countries, where his suppression of Calvinism antagonized businessmen and the nobility, who demanded autonomy and freedom of worship. Inflamed Protestants attacked Catholic churches, and Spain's execution of dissident leaders spurred a general revolt in 1566, in which both Catholics and Protestants rallied behind the Calvinist leader, the Dutchman William of Nassau (NAS-au), Prince of Orange. Philip dispatched an occupation army that executed over 1,100 Protestants and, in 1576, sacked Antwerp, Europe's wealthiest city. In 1579, hoping to divide his opponents, Philip promised political liberty to the ten largely Catholic Flemish- and French-speaking southern provinces of the Low Countries, thereby forging the foundations of modern Belgium and Luxembourg.

Because of English assistance to the Low Country rebels and English attacks on Spanish shipping in the Americas, Philip II tried to invade England by sea in 1588 but faced a determined foe in Queen Elizabeth I (see Witness to the Past: Queen Elizabeth I Rallies Her People). The English ships outmaneuvered Spain's armada of 130 ships and then triumphed when a fierce storm in the English Channel devastated the Spanish fleet. This disastrous defeat of Spain's once invincible navy weakened Philip. The mostly Protestant, Dutch-speaking northern provinces of the Low Countries broke away from Spain in 1588 and became fully independent in 1609, forming the country later officially called the Netherlands, but popularly known as Holland.

Between 1562 and 1589 religious conflicts also raged across France. The French Calvinists, known as Huguenots (HYOO-guh-nauts), were led by the powerful Bourbon (BOOR-buhn) family. In 1572, after the assassination of Calvinist leaders on royal orders sparked Huguenot rioting in Paris, Catholic forces massacred 30,000 Huguenots. Religious

rivalries also became enmeshed in succession disputes for the French crown. In 1593 Henry of Bourbon (1553–1610), remarking that "Paris is well worth a mass," renounced Calvinism for Catholicism in order to become King Henry IV. Remaining a Protestant sympathizer, in 1598 he signed the Edict of Nantes (nahnt), which ended the religious conflicts by recognizing Roman Catholicism as the state church of France but giving Huguenots the right to freely practice their religion.

While Protestant-Catholic tensions in Europe were intense, Christian-Muslim conflicts also simmered, as they had for centuries, and often translated into political and military conflict. Many Europeans worried in particular about the growing power of the Muslim Ottoman Turks (see Chapter 16). The Ottomans sought to expand their empire, which already included Greece, much of the Balkans, and Bulgaria. When some people in the Balkans abandoned Christianity for Islam, Christian leaders became alarmed, and the Holy Roman Emperor Charles V marshaled allies to defeat the Turks at Vienna in 1529. Then in 1571 the so-called Holy League of Spain, Rome, and Venice used advanced naval gunnery to destroy the Turkish fleet at the Battle of Lepanto (li-PAN-toh), off Greece, ending Turkish ambitions for a while. In 1683 the Turks besieged Vienna, and Austria was saved only by Polish intervention. Finally the Austrians pushed the Turks out of Hungary. Ottoman expansion in Europe had ended, and with it the Christian fear of more conversion to Islam.

SECTION SUMMARY

- Renaissance humanists questioned the authority of the Catholic Church, while thinkers such as Machiavelli, Leonardo da Vinci, and Copernicus challenged accepted truths of morality, science, and astronomy.

- Renaissance artists such as Michelangelo aimed to represent humanity more realistically, and writers such as Shakespeare and Cervantes examined the concerns of individuals and the broad sweep of society.

- Martin Luther, who criticized the corruption of the Catholic Church, set the Reformation in motion; it was propelled by figures such as John Calvin, whose ideas were taken up by the Puritans, and King Henry VIII of England, who made England Protestant.

- While not all capitalists were Protestant, many historians see a link between the individualism and thrift of Protestants and their success in business.

- In the Counter Reformation, the Catholic Church attempted to reassert its dominance, but ultimately it focused its energy on converting non-Europeans rather than combating Protestants.

- Religion sparked several wars: Spain's attempts to keep the Low Countries Catholic led to costly conflict with England and the eventual fragmentation of the area; Catholics massacred Huguenots in France; and several battles finally ended Ottoman expansion in Europe.

Changing States and Politics

What types of governments emerged in Europe in this era?

The encounters with the wider world, capitalism, Renaissance humanism, and the Protestant Reformation reshaped Europe, creating new institutions and beliefs to challenge old ones. European politics also changed. The transition from the medieval to the Early Modern order unleashed forces that threatened to consume Europe. Bloody wars drew much of Europe into conflict and produced political changes: kingdoms were torn asunder and reconfigured, old states declined, and new states gained influence. These states were probably not nations in the modern sense, since most were multiethnic entities ruled by royal families who married across national lines. Moreover, patriotic feelings of belonging to a nation, common today, were mostly restricted to the elites. Many of these states used mercantilist policies to provide them with monetary resources, and in some states, some form of royal absolutism flourished. A few other states developed representative governments with elements of democracy.

Regional Wars and National Conflicts

Various wars raged during much of this era; some were prompted by religious divisions, but others were spawned by tensions between rival states and within large multinational empires such as the Habsburg-ruled realms of Spain and the Holy Roman Empire. Even after religious tensions subsided, warfare remained a constant reality, involving most European societies at one time or another.

The major conflict was the Thirty Years War (1618–1648), a long series of bloody hostilities that claimed millions of lives and involved many countries. The Thirty Years War was a continuation of the religious wars and national rivalries of the 1500s. This complex struggle for regional power started in the Holy Roman Empire, as Czech (check) Protestants revolted against Habsburg Catholic rulers trying to limit religious freedom. Eventually the fighting also drew in German princes and two mostly Lutheran countries, Denmark and Sweden. Finally France, although a mostly Catholic country, went to war against its Habsburg rivals who ruled Austria and Spain. In 1648 the conflict ended after a four-year-long European congress in Westphalia (west-FALE-yuh), a German province. The Treaty of Westphalia reaffirmed freedom of religion but did not permanently end Protestant-Catholic conflict. The new balance of power in Europe favored France and curbed the Habsburgs, and France enjoyed unrivaled prestige after 1659 while two of its major rivals, Spain and the Holy Roman Empire, were militarily exhausted. The Holy Roman Emperor lost influence to German princes, Sweden gained territory, and the conference recognized Swiss independence from Habsburg rule. Perhaps the Dutch benefited the most, because the long struggle had weakened their longtime enemy and former ruler, Spain.

After Westphalia European warfare changed. The wars of the later 1600s and early 1700s were fought between states with well-drilled professional soldiers, large warships, and more deadly gunpowder weapons, including cannon and rifles. The most widespread conflict, the War of the Spanish Succession (1701–1714), brought together England, Holland, Austria, Denmark, Portugal, and some German states to battle France and Spain over who would inherit the Spanish throne from the

Soldiers' Return In the early 1600s the French artist Jacques Callot made a series of moving etchings about the Thirty Years War called "Miseries of War." This etching shows a group of discharged soldiers, so impoverished and brutalized by war that they either beg for food or die alongside the road.
(Courtesy of the Trustees of the British Museum)

last Habsburg king, and how the Spanish Empire might be partitioned as a result. With deadlier weapons, the human costs of war increased. For example, in the 1709 Battle of Malpaquet 40,000 French soldiers were killed or wounded.

The War of the Spanish Succession had major political and economic consequences for Europe. The Treaty of Utrecht (YOO-trekt), which ended the war, forced Spain to transfer its territory in Belgium and Italy to Austria. The once prosperous Dutch had overextended themselves in the war, damaging their economy, and Venice became a peripheral, declining state. Now a major maritime power, England received most of the spoils of war, including the strategic Gibraltar peninsula at Spain's southern tip, which commanded the entrance to the Mediterranean Sea, as well as some French territory in eastern Canada. Utrecht resulted in a new system of European states that was governed by the idea of maintaining a balance of power between rival states. Most of Europe entered a period of calm as the threat of war finally receded.

Absolutist and Despotic Monarchies

States changed during the Early Modern Era, with many governments moving far from medieval forms. New ways of thinking as well as political, social, and religious strife set the stage for diverse patterns of government by the seventeenth century. One trend among states was the rise of **absolutism**, a system of strong monarchial authority in which all power was placed under one supreme authority, a king or queen. Supporters saw absolutism as the best way to avoid chaos. Spain, ruled by the Habsburgs and, after 1715, the Bourbon dynasty, and Habsburg-ruled Austria exercised despotic power, as did the Papal States of central Italy, governed by the Vatican, and the Turk-dominated Ottoman Empire. But the French kings and the Russian czars best represented this increasing concentration of political power.

Absolutism in France For a time absolute monarchies dazzled Europe, with the France of King Louis XIV (r. 1661–1715) serving as the model. Other rulers admired and envied the French monarchy. French became the language of European diplomacy, while French art and architecture were imitated as far away as imperial Russia. By the mid-1600s France, with 18 million people, was western Europe's largest country, was self-sufficient in agriculture, and had some thriving industries. All groups were subordinate to the French crown. Some historians, however, question whether French absolutism was as dictatorial as is often thought, since French kings had to work within a context of legality, bureaucracies, and tradition, which limited their exercise of power.

Louis XIV believed that he was the state and that his power derived from God; thus he was a monarch by divine right. He wrote that "princes act as Ministers of God and are his lieutenants on Earth."[10] Known as "the Sun King" for the brilliant extravagance of his court, Louis enjoyed great power, demanding obedience from all at the expense of the nobility. The monarch admitted that his dominant passion was love of glory. Few French kings valued marital fidelity, and Louis had many mistresses and children, legitimate and illegitimate.

The king tried to control everything. He imposed mercantilism, fostering industries and companies subject to royal domination, and he revoked the Edict of Nantes, forbade Protestant pastors to preach, and closed Protestant schools and churches. His repression of Protestantism led 200,000 Huguenots to emigrate to England, Holland, and North America. Louis also ordered a spectacular palace built at Versailles (vuhr-SIGH), a Paris suburb. Some 5,000 servants and courtiers lived on the grounds, with 14,000 more nearby. Versailles became the center of French cultural life and was regularly visited by French nobles and foreign leaders, all of whom were spied upon by the king. Louis' finance minister, Colbert, complained that "every day is one long round of dances, comedies, music of all kinds, promenades, hunts and other entertainments."[11] The king patronized the arts and literature by giving annual allowances to a court composer and financing playwrights and ballet dancers. In gratitude, artists celebrated the king, comparing him to classical Greek and Roman leaders.

Louis XIV's search for power elsewhere in Europe caused four major wars aimed at preventing Habsburg dominance. Marrying his dreams of personal glory to his goal of state prestige, he built up an effective military force. French power reached its height around 1680, but the wars proved financially ruinous and fell short of their objectives. The War of the Spanish Succession sapped the French treasury and military and enabled Austria, England, and Holland to counterbalance French power. Although France remained a major state after 1715, it had lost some of its glory. The absolutist French monarchy collapsed in revolution in the late 1700s.

Russian Despotism and Expansion Just as France represented a concentration of power, Russia also developed a strong and often tyrannical government led by czars, some of whom pursued bold policies. The Russians had freed themselves from Mongol domination by the late fifteenth century. Ivan (ee-VON) IV (r. 1533–1584), known as Ivan the Terrible because of his paranoia and brutality, built a centralized Russian state while fighting wars with neighboring Poland and Sweden and conquering the Tartar (or Tartar) states, founded by Mongols and Turks three centuries earlier, along the lower Volga River. With the name of God on his lips, Ivan also ordered the death or torture of many thousands of Russians whom he considered enemies. Muscovite czars after Ivan imposed a rural economy based on serfdom to gain support from the landed nobility. Just as they sold land or horses, lords could sell their serfs, making them little better than slaves. The czars imposed tight control over the Russian Orthodox Church after it broke officially from the Greek Orthodox Church in the late 1500s. They also began extending their sovereignty toward the Black and Baltic Seas. In the early 1600s Muscovite expansion reached the southeastern Baltic region, where the Russians came into conflict with the Poles and Lithuanians.

absolutism A system of strong monarchial authority in which all power is placed in a supreme authority, a king or queen.

St. Petersburg   This painting, made around 1760, shows the Winter Palace, inhabited by the Russian royal family, occupying the left side of the Neva River in St. Petersburg, a major port that attracted many trading ships. Other government buildings occupy the right bank.   (Michael Holford)

Russia gradually developed an even more powerful state, especially during the reign of Peter I the Great (r. 1682–1725), an enlightened but despotic czar who encouraged Russia's integration with the West. Nearly 7 feet tall and possessed with tremendous energy, Peter dedicated himself to transforming his backward realm into a modern state. Peter saw Russia's only hope as copying Western technology and administrative techniques. To find out about the West, he secretly toured Europe under an assumed name for eighteen months, spending time in Austria, England, and Holland. He visited factories, museums, government offices, hospitals, and universities, and even worked as a carpenter in a Dutch shipyard to view firsthand the most advanced industrial and military technology. Returning to Russia in 1698, the czar launched ambitious political, economic, military, and educational reforms and hired foreign specialists to advise him.

Peter's policies had mixed though often significant consequences. Some policies to promote western European practices were superficial and unpopular, such as banning beards, no longer fashionable in western Europe, and the traditional long coats worn by men. He increased royal power at the expense of the church and nobility and often in a harsh manner, such as by mandating compulsory military service for some nobles. With such great power, Peter expanded Russia's frontiers, established industries, strengthened autocracy and serfdom, put together a navy to protect his Baltic flank, and developed a more efficient government. Since he hated gloomy Moscow, with its medieval flavor, in 1713 he began building a new capital on the Baltic, modeled on Amsterdam and Venice, and

named it St. Petersburg. For his summer place near St. Petersburg, Peter enlisted Italian architects and French garden designers.

Peter had many foreign achievements. Wanting a stronger presence on the Baltic Sea, which was mostly dominated by Sweden, in 1699 he forged a secret alliance with Sweden's rivals, Denmark and Poland. During the Great Northern War that began in 1700, Russia and its allies battled the Swedes. But Swedish power was formidable, and only in 1709 did an exhausted Sweden abandon the eastern rim of the Baltic to Russia. Russia's growing power unsettled European rivals. As one of Peter's diplomats admitted in 1721: "We know very well that the greater part of our neighbors view [us] very unfavorably. If they seek our alliance it is rather through fear and hate than through friendship."[12] Peter and other Russian czars also pursued expansion to the south and east. Anxious to forge permanent access to the warm Mediterranean Sea because it was open to shipping twelve months a year, Russian forces pushed south toward the Black Sea and the Straits of Bosporus (see Map 15.3). They also began acquiring territory in Siberia and Muslim Central Asia (see Chapter 16).

By eventually creating a huge colossus of an empire and exploiting the resources of the newly colonized areas, Russia developed a largely self-sufficient economy. It had limited trade with western Europe and attracted few merchants from that region. Despite Peter the Great's Westernization policies, most czars were wary of foreign influence. Today Russia remains the last great land empire, ruling over various non-Russian peoples.

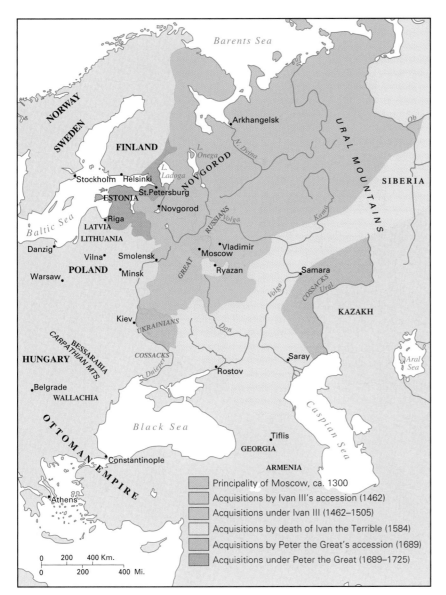

Map 15.3   Russian Expansion, 1300–1750
Beginning in the 1300s the Russians expanded from a small remote northern state, based in Moscow, into an empire. By the mid-1700s the Russians had spread over a wide area and gained political domination over western Siberia, the northern Caucasus, and part of what is today the eastern Baltic region and the Ukraine.

Online Study Center **Improve Your Grade**
Interactive Map: Expansion of Russia to 1725

The Rise of Representative Governments

Some European countries moved toward greater political freedom. In this era Iceland and Switzerland had the most democratic societies. Iceland enjoyed self-rule, including an elected assembly, for several centuries, while Switzerland was a multilingual, decentralized, and constitutional confederation of self-governing Catholic and Protestant districts. The Italian city-state of Venice was also a self-governing republic, although noble and merchant families dominated political life. Among the more powerful states, the Netherlands and England developed the most open and accountable governments. Both of these commercial powers were enriched by sea trade, which allowed the commercial class and many nobles to amass huge fortunes and hence play political roles. Eventually they demanded more influence. As a result, the Netherlands became a republic and England a constitutional monarchy.

The Dutch Republic   The Netherlands enjoyed a golden age during much of the 1600s. It built a colonial empire, including holdings in the Americas, South Africa, Sri Lanka, and Southeast Asia, and also dominated the Atlantic, Baltic, and Indian Ocean trade. Large Dutch joint-stock companies controlled the overseas market. The most powerful, the Dutch East India Company formed in 1602, monopolized the spice trade from Southeast Asia, making huge profits from the import of cinnamon and pepper. The company also imported other valuable Asian products, including Chinese silks and porcelain, Japanese art, Indian cotton textiles, and precious metals. These commercial activities amassed capital, some of which was invested in Dutch industry. The Netherlands became Europe's most prosperous society, with Amsterdam serving as a major hub of world trade. As an added benefit, economic prosperity fostered a market for Dutch artists.

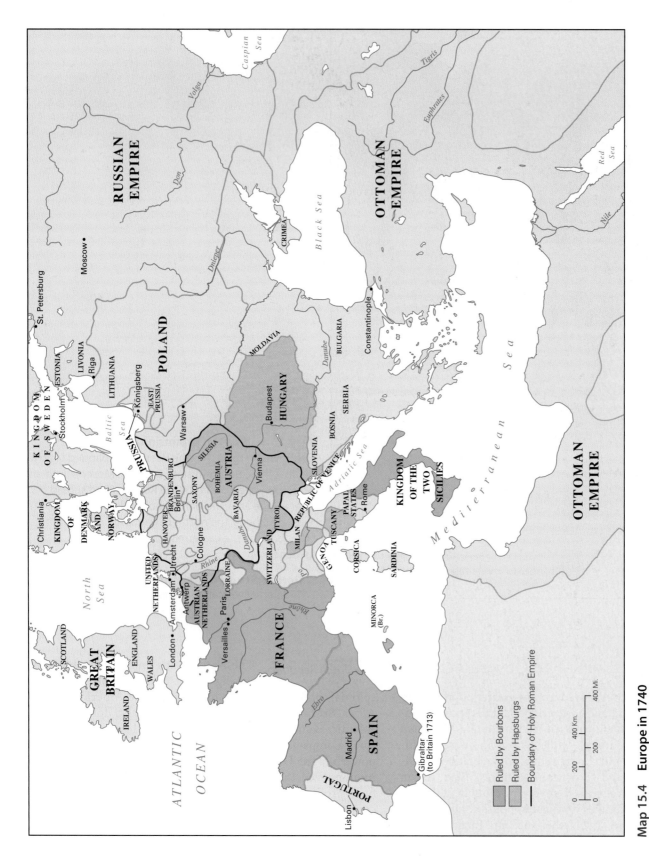

Map 15.4 Europe in 1740

By the mid-1700s France and Great Britain were the most powerful western European states. While once powerful Spain and Portugal had lost influence and the Germans and Italians remained divided, Prussia, Sweden, Russia, and Habsburg-ruled Austria were gaining strength.

Warriors will fight scribes for the control of your institutions; wild bush will conquer your roads; your soil will crack from the drought; your sons will wander in the wilds. Yes, things will fall apart.

IGBO ANCESTRAL CURSE[1]

Confirming the Igbo curse, things fell apart for many Africans in the Early Modern Era, while for others things were put together. Among the many Africans caught up in unprecedented new challenges was Ayuba Suleiman Diallo (ah-YOO-bah SOO-lay-mahn JAH-loh). In 1731 the thirty-year-old educated son of a leading family in the West African kingdom of Bondu visited the western Senegambia region, at the western tip of Africa, on a trading mission. There he was captured by enemies and sold to the British as a slave. Eventually he was shipped to Maryland, where he was put to work on a plantation growing tobacco. After an attempted escape, he was taken in by Thomas Bluett, an English entrepreneur who recognized both his talents and his connections to West African commercial life. Diallo's Islamic faith and ability to read and write Arabic reflected the influence of Islam and Arab traditions in parts of West Africa. Bluett emancipated Diallo and then took him to London and presented him at the English court. The British hoped he might help them to increase their commercial and slaving activity in the Senegambia, and he agreed to act as middleman in obtaining more slaves. Finally, after pledging friendship with the British, Diallo was able to return to Bondu and resume his life. Until his death in 1773, Diallo profited from his connection to British merchants as a trading partner. He had been both victim and beneficiary of the new economic forces of his times.

Some aspects of Ayuba Suleiman Diallo's story represent the changing Atlantic world of the Early Modern Era, when Europe, Africa, and the Americas became increasingly linked in unprecedented ways. African life changed during these years, in part because of contact with Europeans, whose presence in Africa gradually increased. The West African trading world that produced Diallo now included English, Portuguese, Dutch, and French companies seeking gold, gum, hides, ivory, and especially slaves. Goree (go-ray) Island, just off Senegambia near the present day-city of Dakar (duh-KAHR), became a major slave collection center, and several French garrisons had been established up the Senegal River near Bondu. Diallo's story is unique, partly because he gained freedom quickly and eventually returned home, and partly because he came from the mostly Muslim Fulani (foo-LAH-nee) ethnic group, a widely distributed inland people who rarely went as slaves to the Americas. But the ancient Igbo curse proved prophetic for the many other Africans who were shipped off as slaves, for they faced significant new challenges and often disaster.

Not all of Africa was affected by European activities. Like the Fulani, many Africans remained untouched by the various slave trades and other disruptive European activities and continued to pursue their ways of life as they always had, expanding and flourishing or declining and decaying from local conditions unrelated to what Europeans might be doing, often only with African agreement, along the coasts. Still, Diallo's experience illustrates the expanding influence of Europe in Africa and the Americas during the early modern centuries. Encounters with Europe reshaped parts of Africa and drew them into an emerging Atlantic world, as first the Portuguese and then other Europeans established trading posts along the West African coast. Soon these trading posts, such as Goree Island, became centers for acquiring and shipping slaves. The Portuguese and Dutch also began to conquer and settle several African regions.

The growing European power was also gradually felt in some of the Islamic lands of the Middle East (western Asia and North Africa) and Central Asia, though not to the extent that it was in certain parts of Africa. By the 1500s Islam, the monotheistic religion that had arisen in Arabia a millennium earlier, dominated a huge chunk of Afro-Eurasia, from the westernmost fringe of Africa to central Indonesia and the southern Philippines. Islamic political ideas, trade networks, and literary traditions linked many millions of people, and several large and dynamic Islamic states dominated much of the Middle East and South Asia, the successors to the great Islamic empires of earlier centuries. The powerful Ottoman Empire, which included much of western Asia, North Africa, and southeastern Europe, and a new Persian state, the Safavid Empire, had increasing connections of trade and conflict with non-Islamic societies. But while these Islamic societies experienced some changes, they also maintained long-standing traditions and remained largely in control of their own destinies.

FOCUS QUESTIONS

1. How did the larger sub-Saharan African societies and states differ from each other in the sixteenth century?
2. What were the consequences of African-European encounters in this era?
3. How did the trans-Atlantic slave trade develop and impact Africa?
4. What factors made the Ottoman Empire such a powerful force in the region?
5. How did the Persian and Central Asian experience differ from that of the Ottomans?

 # Sub-Saharan African Societies

How did the larger Early Modern Era sub-Saharan African societies and states differ from each other in the sixteenth century?

At the beginning of the Early Modern Era African societies reflected considerable political, economic, and cultural diversity, and many flourished. Some, especially in West and East Africa, had much in common with societies in western Asia, Europe, and China and formed great empires and states, engaging in extensive long-distance trade, fostering intellectual debate, and connecting with the wider Eastern Hemisphere. Many people in the Sudanic region of West Africa and along the East African coast had adopted Islam. But many other Africans had decentralized political systems based on villages and religions mixing monotheism, polytheism, and animism. Whatever their ways of life and thought, many African societies possessed valuable human and natural resources that attracted Europeans as the era progressed, posing new challenges and changing Africa's relationship to the world.

The Last Sudanic Empire: Songhai

The last of the great Sudanic empires, Songhai (song-GAH-ee), became the major power in interior West Africa during the 1400s and flourished through much of the 1500s (see Map 16.1 on page 462). From its capital of Gao (ghow) on the Niger River, Songhai built an empire stretching some 1,500 miles

C H R O N O L O G Y

	Sub-Saharan Africa	Middle East
1300		**1300–1923** Ottoman Empire
1400	**1497** Portuguese encounters with East Africa	
1500	**1526–1870** Trans-Atlantic slave trade	**1501–1736** Safavid Persia
		1520–1566 Suleiman the Magnificent
1600	**1591** Destruction of Songhai	**1554–1659** Sa'dian Morocco
	1652 Dutch settlement of Cape Town	

from east to west. The people of Songhai blended Islam with local customs. For example, in contrast to the gender segregation and female seclusion common in Arab society, the women of Songhai and some other Islamic states in the Sudan held a high social position and enjoyed considerable personal liberty, much to the shock of Arab visitors. Many women engaged in small-scale commerce, and in some Sudanic cities women were free to have lovers as they desired. Some Sudanic societies were matrilineal; the heir to the throne was not the king's son but the son of his sister.

The Songhai city of Timbuktu became a major terminus for the trans-Saharan trade that shipped to North Africa large supplies of gold and ivory as well as slaves for Arab and European markets. For nearly two centuries Timbuktu remained the greatest Islamic city in sub-Saharan Africa. It was not only a center of commerce but also a major center of Islamic scholarship, boasting schools, libraries, and several universities teaching theology, law, and literature. Its well-stocked bookstores sold books from many lands. An early sixteenth-century Arab visitor, Leo Africanus, reported that Timbuktu had "numerous judges, doctors of letters, and learned Muslims. The king greatly honors scholarship. Here too, they sell many hand-written books. More profit is had from their sale than from any other merchandise."[2] The Islamic University of Sankore at Timbuktu was modeled after the respected University of Cairo. Its faculty, which included several well-known Arab scholars, and the student body were drawn from throughout the Islamic realm. In recent years thousands of crumbling books from that era, written in Arabic and several African languages, have been found in forgotten Timbuktu storage rooms.

But Songhai did not remain a dominant state in West Africa. After several strong kings ruled the empire, Songhai's leadership deteriorated and succession struggles emerged. In 1591, when an army from Morocco seized much of the Niger River territory from Songhai, the kingdom collapsed (see Chronology: Africa and the Atlantic World, 1482–1750). One Timbuktu historian of the time wrote that everything changed, as danger, poverty, and violence replaced security, wealth, and peace. The end of Songhai marked the end of the era of huge imperial states in the western Sudan.

C H R O N O L O G Y

Africa and the Atlantic World, 1482–1750

1482	First Portuguese-Kongo encounter
1487	Portuguese discovery of Cape of Good Hope
1497	Vasco da Gama's first voyage to East African coast
1505	Portuguese pillage of Kilwa
1514	First African slaves to Americas
1507–1543	Rule of Alfonso I in Kongo
1526–1870	Trans-Atlantic slave trade
1562	Dutch settlement of Cape Town
1575	End of Portuguese technical assistance to Kongo
1591	Destruction of Songhai

Other West African States

Besides Songhai, several other Sudanic and Guinea Coast societies exercised regional influence and flourished from trade. The small Sudanic kingdoms formed by the Mandinka, Bambara (bahm-BAH-rah), and Mossi peoples in the upper Niger Basin after the fall of Songhai had effective, cavalry-based armies and were closely linked to the commercial networks of the Sudanic region. The Dyula (JOO-lah), a large Mandinka-speaking Muslim mercantile clan, became the most important trading group, with operations throughout West Africa. Dyula merchants moved goods such as gold and salt through the forest with caravans of porters, down the rivers in canoe fleets, and across the grasslands in donkey trains. Yet, women usually dominated the village markets. Many Sudanic and

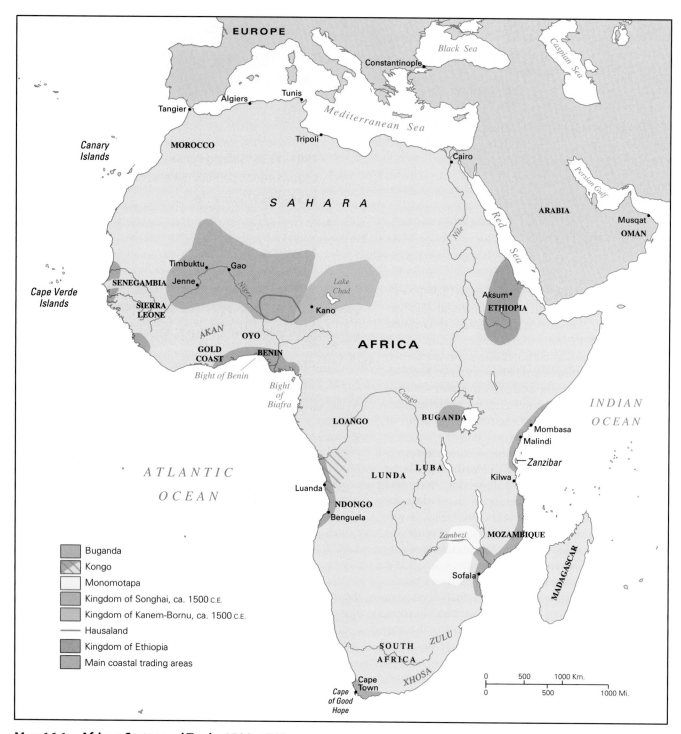

Map 16.1 African States and Trade, 1500–1700
Some African states, such as Songhai, Kanem-Bornu, Benin, Lunda, Buganda, and Ethiopia, remained powerful in this era. West African coastal societies were increasingly drawn into world trade while the East African coastal cities remained significant in Indian Ocean trade.

Online Study Center Improve Your Grade Interactive Map: The African Slave Trade, 1500–1800

Guinea societies were matrilineal, and some of these, as well as a few patrilineal societies, sometimes had women chiefs or queens. Queen mothers of kings enjoyed great power. The Igbo people of southeastern Nigeria worshiped female deities and some of them preferred female leaders. Africans often vener-

ated women elders for their wisdom and closeness to the ancestors.

Several strong Islamic kingdoms and states arose to the east of the Niger River. For example, the Islamic kingdom of Kanem-Bornu (KAH-nuhm-BOR-noo), centered on Lake

The Ottomans and Islamic Imperial Revival

What factors made the Ottoman Empire such a powerful force in the region?

The Islamic societies of the Middle East, the large region including North Africa and western Asia, did not experience the jarring transitions felt by many Africans during the Early Modern Era. While European nations established supremacy of the seas, Islamic states remained, as they were during the Intermediate Era, major land powers. The greatest of these, the Turkish Ottoman Empire, began in 1300 and survived until 1923, eventually ruling much of southeastern Europe, the western fringe of Asia, and much of North Africa, including Egypt. The Ottomans also nearly succeeded in conquering much of eastern and central Europe before being repulsed. Ottoman government remained powerful through most of the Early Modern Era. By the 1700s, however, the Ottomans and other Middle Eastern states were suffering from chronic warfare, poor leadership, a growing rigidity, and a superiority complex in relationship to the upstart Europeans. Their decline came when Europeans were on the rise, meaning that these Islamic societies soon became targets of European imperialism.

The Ottoman Empire

From their base in central Anatolia, the Ottoman Turks gained power over much of the once great Byzantine Empire in the 1300s. The Ottoman conquest of the Byzantine capital, Constantinople, in 1453 demonstrated conclusively the power of Islamic society, as the capital of Orthodox Christianity was transformed into Muslim-ruled Istanbul. By 1512 the Ottomans controlled all of Anatolia and what is today Bulgaria, Greece, Albania, Serbia, and much of Romania. They had also invaded southern Italy in 1480, but the death of the sultan led them to withdraw before marching on Rome. Had they conquered Italy, the history of Europe might have been very different. Between 1514 and 1517, the Ottomans defeated Persian forces and added Syria, Lebanon, Palestine, and Egypt to their domains. During the sixteenth century they controlled the Mediterranean, even raiding coastal Spain and Italy.

The Ottoman golden age came under the leadership of Sultan Suleiman (SOO-lay-man) the Magnificent (r. 1520–1566), a just man famed as a lawgiver but also a merciless conqueror to his enemies who presided over military expansion and the pushing back of Christian power (see Chronology: The Middle East, 1500–1750). Under Suleiman, the Ottomans pushed north of the Danube River and into the eastern Balkans, defeated the Hungarians, and besieged Vienna. They also gained control of Egypt—according to an Ottoman historian, in the twinkling of an eye—and then the North African coast. Suleiman's forces also pushed the Portuguese from their Red Sea bases and defeated the Persians, incorporating Iraq. Suleiman's empire now stretched from Algeria to the Persian Gulf and from Hungary to Armenia (see Map 16.3). But the Ottomans never controlled much of the Arabian peninsula, enabling independent sultanates such as Oman to extend their own power to the East African cities. Omani Arabs and other coastal Arabs remained active in the Indian Ocean trade network, enjoying a strong presence as far east as Indonesia.

Suleiman's reign revived the Islamic glory that had faded with the downfall of the Iraq-based Abbasid Empire in the 1200s. Suleiman and other Ottoman sultans claimed to have restored the caliphate, the governing system of early Islamic times that was thought to be ordained by God and that blended political and religious power. In 1538 the Ottoman ruler could boast proudly of his wide-ranging power:

> I am God's slave and sultan of this world. I am head of Muhammad's community. In Baghdad I am the shah, in Byzantine realms the Caesar, and in Egypt the sultan; who sends his fleets to the seas of Europe, the Maghrib [northwest Africa] and India. I am the sultan who took the crown and throne of Hungary and granted them to a humble slave.[15]

Suleiman's position at the center of an extensive international political system often involved him in conflicts. At various times, for example, the Ottomans allied with France or with northern European Protestants against the Habsburgs, the Catholic royal family that ruled Austria and a large area of eastern Europe bordering on Ottoman territories. But Suleiman's broad empire also gave him large commercial benefits; he controlled the overland trade routes between Europe and the Indian Ocean. Spices and other products from India, Southeast Asia, and China were shipped to the Ottoman-ruled port of Basra (BAHS-ruh), at the head of the Persian Gulf, and then transported to the Ottoman-controlled markets of Damascus, Cairo, Aleppo, and Istanbul for sale to Venetian and

CHRONOLOGY	
The Middle East, 1500–1750	
1501–1736	Safavid dynasty in Persia
1514–1517	Ottoman conquest of Syria, Egypt, and Arabia
1520–1566	Reign of Ottoman sultan Suleiman the Magnificent
1529	First Ottoman siege of Vienna
1554–1659	Sa'dian dynasty in Morocco
1682–1699	Ottoman wars with Habsburg Austria
1715	Beginning of Russian conquest of Turkestan
1722	Afghan invasion of Safavid Persia
1736–1747	Rule of Nadir Shah in Persia

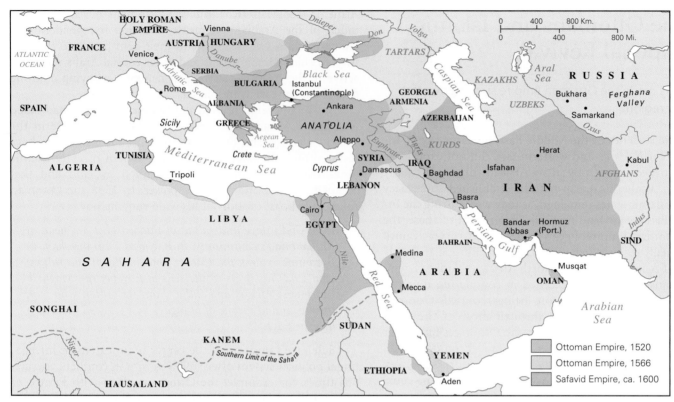

Map 16.3　The Ottoman and Safavid Empires, 1500–1750
By the later 1500s the Ottoman Empire included large parts of western Asia, southeastern Europe, southern Russia, and North Africa. Their major rivals, the Safavids, controlled Persia and parts of Iraq, the Caucasus, Afghanistan, and Central Asia.

other European merchants. Ottoman ships also controlled the Black Sea trade.

Ottoman political success owed much to military power and immigration. The Ottomans adopted gunpowder weapons, especially cannon, which were often built and operated by mercenary Hungarian Christians in Ottoman service. These weapons equaled the best of European gunnery until the late 1600s. The Ottomans also developed an effective navy, often led by Muslim refugees from Spain. These Muslims, among thousands of other emigrants, including Jews, who were expelled from or fleeing persecution in Spain in the 1400s and 1500s, settled in Ottoman territory, bringing with them valuable expertise and international connections.

Ottoman Government and Economy

Ottoman imperialism supported an effective state. For decades the Ottoman government was led by very able men. The Ottomans also chose officials based on merit, allowing Arabs and other non-Turks to serve in the government and military, often in high positions. Many European thinkers and diplomats admired the Ottoman leaders and system. For instance, a Habsburg envoy wrote in the sixteenth century: "No distinction is attached to birth among the Turks. Honors, high posts,

and judgeships are the rewards of great ability and good services."[16] The sultans governed through an imperial council headed by a prime minister. The ruling elite lived in luxury, residing in beautiful palaces with large harems of wives and concubines, children, and many servants. Sometimes favored wives or concubines had great influence over their husbands.

Christian princes remained the major landowners in Ottoman Europe, and the Ottomans especially recruited administrators and soldiers from Christian peoples. At regular intervals the sultan's agents swept through the provinces selecting Christian youth for training. Essentially becoming slaves, they were required to embrace Islam. The most talented, perhaps 10 percent of the total, were sent to the palace school to be trained for administration. There they learned to read and write Arabic, Persian, and Turkish. Many acquired power and influence; for example, prime ministers usually came from this group. The other conscripts joined the well-armed, highly disciplined, and generally effective elite military corps of infantrymen known as **janissaries** ("new troops"), who lived in barracks

---

janissaries ("new troops")　Well-armed, highly disciplined, and generally effective elite military corps of infantrymen in the Ottoman Empire.

and were not allowed to marry but were well paid for their loyalty. In referring to the janissary soldiers and their fortresses, an Austrian opponent in the 1700s wrote that "it is beyond all human powers of comprehension to grasp how strongly these places are built and how obstinately the Turks defend them."[17]

Under this dynamic state, the Ottoman commercial economy flourished. Istanbul and other major cities served as centers for transregional trade, where merchants from different lands bought or sold European woolens, Persian silk, Chinese porcelain, Indian spices, Arab sugar, and Anatolian iron. The Ottomans became major consumers of Indian textiles. Artisan and merchant guilds with elected leaders became central to urban life, controlling many economic activities. But the dynamic international trade mostly involved luxuries, and the empire was largely self-sufficient in necessities such as food.

Ottoman Society

The diverse Ottoman society thrived in this era. The empire's multiethnic population, about evenly divided between Christians and Muslims, was large, containing some 50 million people at its peak. This was small compared to China or India but dwarfed the largest European country of the time, France, which had less than a third of the Ottoman total. The size and diversity of the Ottoman population, including the number of religious minorities, posed administrative challenges, however. Following the pattern in most multicultural Muslim states, the sultans governed the Jewish, Greek Orthodox, and Armenian Christian communities through their own religious leaders. Each religious group had its own laws and courts. Although they faced some legal disabilities, religious minorities enjoyed a toleration rare in the world at that time.

Ottoman cities, where varied peoples mixed, were vibrant. City social life revolved around coffeehouses, public baths, and taverns. Coffeehouses became informal cultural centers where storytellers enjoyed a mass following. An Ottoman observer of one of these establishments wrote: "Some read books and fine writings, some were busy with backgammon and chess, some brought new poems and talked of literature. Pious hypocrites said: 'People have become addicts of the coffee-house; nobody comes to the mosques.'"[18]

Women had a higher status in Turkish society than in Arab tradition, and this pattern continued under the Ottomans. Women in the royal family, especially queen mothers, exercised considerable political clout. Princes were brought up in royal harems, whose women influenced their thinking while financing buildings and social service activities. Upper-class women often owned land, managed businesses, and controlled wealth. Throughout the empire women took their grievances to Islamic courts and were often treated sympathetically, the courts protecting their rights to inheritance and property. Turkish society was patriarchal but older women had control of both the young males and females in their families. Having sons provided even more security. Since men tended to die younger, women often became heads of households. Yet, women could also be abused by men and more easily divorced, and sometimes families punished or killed women suspected of illicit sexual activity.

The Ottomans attracted many immigrants, among them European merchants and technicians, from outside the empire by exempting them from taxes and laws. Later these privileges gave the European immigrants a big commercial advantage over their local-born competitors. Many Christian peasants from southern and eastern Europe migrated into Ottoman territory or welcomed Ottoman conquest, which generally brought them a better life. Indeed, there was a saying among Balkan peasants that the turban of the Turk was better than the tiara of the pope.

Ottoman Culture and Thought

The Ottomans also stimulated literary and artistic creativity, often with royal patronage. Istanbul attracted artists and artisans from all over Europe and the Middle East. For example, the Sultan Mehmed II (1432–1481) arranged with the Venetians to have their most famous artist, Giovanni Bellini, spend two years (1479–1480) decorating his palace with paintings. Suleiman the Magnificent welcomed humanist thinkers from Italy to the capital. Ottoman poets wrote ornate verse in Persian or Turkish, and architects, such as the highly innovative Pasha Sinan, designed beautiful domed mosques and other public buildings that combined form with function (see Profile: Pasha Sinan, Ottoman Architect). Artists also produced beautiful painted tiles and pottery. In this creative environment, Ottoman and European architects and artists influenced each other. One sultan who admired Italian art even tried to woo two of the greatest talents, Michelangelo and Leonardo da Vinci, to work in Istanbul.

Although the Ottomans pursued science, by the 1700s they were falling behind some rival states. Ottoman medicine remained vibrant, and scholars published many volumes on astronomy, mathematics, and geography. Muslim geographers also produced world maps more sophisticated than those of Europe. But Ottoman intellectuals remained largely disinterested in and uninformed about scientific and technological developments in western Europe and East Asia. The emphasis on law and theology rather than science in Ottoman higher education inhibited technological innovation.

In Ottoman religious life, various mystical Sufi sects, seeking a personal experience of God, had large followings. Seyh Bedreddin (SAY beh-DREAD-en), a famous mystic who founded an order of practitioners known as dervishes, wrote about his discoveries: "Ecstasy came to me, and I remained in wonderment at God's presence. The mystic who has perceived God spreads to the whole universe; he is one with the mountains and streams. There is no here or hereafter; everything is a single moment."[19] To achieve a trancelike state, dervishes feverishly danced, whirling around faster and faster while their long skirts billowed out, creating a hypnotic effect. Although some Sufi sects operated with official approval and financial support, others, including the order founded by Seyh

PASHA SINAN, OTTOMAN ARCHITECT

One of the most innovative architects in world history, Pasha Sinan (1491–1588), served as the royal architect to Ottoman sultans for fifty years and perfected the Ottoman style. Sinan's work reflected the meeting and mixing of Christian and Muslim cultures in Istanbul, the former Byzantine city of Constantinople that became the Ottoman capital. Spectacular architecture symbolized the grandiose Ottoman spirit, thanks in part to Sinan, who eventually occupied a key state office. In his long career Sinan designed over three hundred works, ranging from grand government buildings and mosques taking years to build to fountains, tombs, bridges, and baths.

Sinan was born into a Christian Greek family in central Anatolia. Selected for the Ottoman military in 1512, he was converted to Islam and then trained as a janissary warrior and fought in various military campaigns. During his military service Sinan developed a reputation for his engineering skills. For example, he figured ways to float artillery across lakes and engineered the quick building of a bridge across the Danube River. In 1538 he was appointed royal architect, based in Istanbul, by the great sultan Suleiman the Magnificent, a patron of art and architecture. In this highly visible post, Sinan developed, procured funding for, and supervised the construction of projects that would be seen by millions. To succeed, he needed the skills of a visionary, planner, administrator, and manager.

Istanbul was filled with inspiring architecture from Byzantine times, including the beautiful cathedral of Hagia Sophia, with its huge dome. Sinan was fascinated by these domed structures and concentrated on incorporating them into his own architecture. The Hagia Sophia church design, with its ascending hierarchy of sanctity ending at the altar, had reflected the Byzantine worldview and the values of the Greek Orthodox Church. Sinan sought to outdo the architects who built Hagia Sophia for the Byzantine emperor Justinian a thousand years earlier. He also wanted to adapt the dome structure to the needs of an Islamic house of worship, providing open spaces where all could face Mecca from an equal position. Sinan experimented constantly in pursuit of his vision.

During his career Sinan designed several great mosques in Istanbul in which he tried to incorporate the best features of Hagia Sophia into an Islamic setting. The Suleimaniye (SOO-lay-man-iya) mosque, for instance, finished in 1557, sits atop a high hill, dominating the city and proclaiming the triumph of Islam. A sixteenth-century English traveler, John Sanderson, exclaimed that the mosque passed "in greatness, workmanship, marble pillars, and riches all the churches of [Christian] emperors [and merited] to be matched with the 7 Wonders of the [ancient] World." The main dome is surrounded by over four hundred lesser domes. Within this huge complex were several of Istanbul's most elite schools.

Sinan's last great mosque, the Edirne (eh-DURN-a), completed in 1575, had a dome that surpassed that of Hagia Sophia. Sinan considered it his masterpiece and boasted that "architects among Christians say that no Muslim architect would be able to build such a large dome. With the help of God I erected a dome higher and wider than Hagia Sophia." In designing this mosque, Sinan tried to assert what he considered the superiority of Islam over Christianity and brought Ottoman architecture to its highest point. The mosque expressed the imperial Ottoman achievement and the splendor of Islam.

Various rich Ottomans, to show their piety and provide themselves with a burial place, endowed mosques. The women of the imperial family and the wives of wealthy Ottoman officials also financed mosques, among other good works. Sinan

Bedreddin, were suspected of political disloyalty and of modifying too many Islamic principles.

The Ottomans drew the religious establishment close to the state, which was headed by a leader who saw himself anointed by God. Some historians argue that, in the Ottoman realms and in other parts of the Middle East, Islam became more rigid during these centuries because it was too closely linked to the state. Religious leaders emphasized rote learning and memorization rather than analysis of the sacred texts, and some punished deviation from orthodoxy. Furthermore, Islamic leaders were increasingly conservative and hostile to technological innovation. Meanwhile, Christian minorities in the empire flocked to schools set up by Christian missionaries from Europe and North America, some of which taught commercial and technical subjects. Thus Christians but not Muslims were often exposed to knowledge from the wider world.

Ottoman Decline

Eventually the Ottomans faced new challenges that undermined the state and reduced the size of the empire. Well into the 1600s, however, Ottoman armies continued to effectively wage battles against European and Persian rivals. In the 1670s Ottoman forces annexed part of the Ukraine. Only in 1683, when Austria and its allies repulsed the last Ottoman attack of Vienna, did European observers begin to perceive the Ottoman decline. In the next few years the Ottomans were pushed out of much of the area north of the Danube River in eastern Europe and the Ukraine and southern Greece. By 1699 the Ottomans were forced to cede Hungary to the rival Habsburgs. Although in the early 1700s the Ottomans did reclaim some of these territories, Ottoman power was no longer feared. By 1800 European diplomats began calling the empire "the sick man of Europe."

lamps reflecting in a pool of water filled with floating lotus blossoms.

Persian Shi'ism underwent some changes. The Safavids encouraged passion plays and religious processions commemorating the tragic death of the prophet Muhammad's grandson, Husayn, in the Battle of Karbala in 680, the event that split the Islamic community. In the annual processions, hundreds of men fulfilled vows of faith by beating their bodies with chains while chanting religious dirges. Sufi influence gradually declined while religious teachers increasingly emphasized their own authority over that of the Quran and other early sacred texts. The result was increasing belief in the infallibility of Islamic leaders, who enjoyed greater power than was common elsewhere in the Islamic world. Even the shahs claimed to represent divine power, giving the state a theocratic cast. But tensions over religious power between the shahs and Shi'ite leaders, many of whom came to own vast tracts of land, continued to simmer.

Safavid Decline

By the eighteenth century the Safavid sultans had become weaker, the Shi'ite religious officials had become stronger, and the empire's economy had declined. Unable to control the clergy or trust their sons plotting for the throne, later Safavid rulers often turned to alcohol for comfort, and most were increasingly controlled by ministers and concubines. In any case, corruption grew rampant. In 1722 Afghans seized Isfahan and then repulsed Ottoman forces invading from the west. Isfahan, once one of the world's most beautiful cities and filled with splendid architecture, was nearly destroyed.

Soon a new government appeared. In 1736 a new Persian leader, Nadir Shah (1688–1747), led a force that drove out the Afghan invaders. Casting aside the remaining Safavids, he launched a vigorous new state. His armies went on the offensive, marching into Ottoman lands and north India, where his forces plundered the major city, Delhi. But Nadir Shah proved ruthless against suspected foes, antagonizing many, and economic collapse exposed millions to famine. After ill-advised efforts to reconvert the Persians from Shi'a to Sunni Islam, Nadir Shah was assassinated in 1747. His empire soon collapsed. In the decades to follow Persia was again divided into smaller states, and the early Safavid cultural dynamism became a distant memory. In this power vacuum Western pressure intensified.

Moroccan Resurgence and Expansion

While the Ottomans and Safavids dominated much of the Islamic world, the Moroccans on the far northwestern fringe of Africa forged one of the stronger Islamic states, conquered an empire, and linked themselves to various networks of exchange. Moroccan society comprised Berbers, Arabs, and an influential Jewish community. The gradual displacement of Islamic rule in Iberia resulted in many Muslims and Jews migrating across the Strait of Gibraltar to Morocco. Some Spanish Muslims joined Moroccan military forces, while Jews invigorated commercial life. Morocco traded widely with its North African neighbors, West Africa, and Europe, and during the 1400s and 1500s ships from Venice, Genoa, and other European trading ports regularly visited Moroccan ports, exchanging metals, textiles, spices, hardware, and wine for leather, carpets, wool, grain, sugar, and African slaves.

During the later 1400s and early 1500s Moroccan encounters with the Portuguese eventually brought the Sa'dians to power. Portugal's cultivation of sugar on the Atlantic islands began undermining the Moroccan economy, which was based partly on growing sugar, and the establishment of Portuguese forts along the coast threatened the Moroccan government. In response, growing mystical Sufi movements organized tribal coalitions to resist the Portuguese. In 1554 the Sa'dians, a Moroccan family who claimed descent from the prophet Muhammad and had fought against the Portuguese forts, conquered much of Morocco with the support of Sufi and tribal leaders, launching a new era.

The Sa'dians ruled Morocco until 1659, forging a powerful military and a regime quite different from those of the Ottoman territories. The greatest Sa'dian leader, Sultan al-Mansur (man-SOOR) (r. 1578–1603), recruited mercenary soldiers from elsewhere who knew how to use firearms. By 1603 the army of 40,000 included 4,000 Europeans, 4,000 Spanish Muslims, and 1,500 Turks, armed with modern artillery. The Netherlands and England, both rivals of the Portuguese, sold Morocco ships, cannon, and gunpowder. The resulting military power allowed the Moroccans to capture the Portuguese ports along the Atlantic coast, proving the value of possessing gunpowder weapons. In 1591 Moroccan forces seized the trading city of Timbuktu in Songhai, undermining that Sudanic state, and gained control of the trans-Saharan trade linking West and North Africa.

In the later 1600s the Sa'dian system broke down, and a new Moroccan dynasty, the Alawis (uh-LAH-wees), who also claimed descent from the prophet Muhammad, came to power in 1672. This dynasty still rules Morocco today. Sufi influence continued to expand, but powerful Sufi movements sometimes clashed with the royal governments. Morocco traded even more heavily with Europe, North Africa, and the Sudan.

Central Asia and Russian Expansion

The most direct and long-lasting confrontations between Muslims and Europeans resulted from Russian imperial expansion into Central Asia and Ottoman territories. The Russians had long coveted the dry lands of Central Asia, where long-distance trade flourished and a few regions supported productive farming. Islam had a strong foothold in Central Asia, and many places had large Sufi communities where Sufi masters often gained political power. In many of the cities, including Silk Road hubs such as Bukhara (boo-CAR-ruh) and Samarkand (SAM-ar-kand), social, political, and religious patterns closely resembled those of Persians and Arabs.

As the remnants of the Mongol Empire broke up into various rival societies by the 1400s, Russia capitalized on the political vacuum to extend its own power first into Siberia and then into the Black Sea region and Central Asia. While western European nations built maritime empires, Russia, seeking resources and land for possible settlement by Russians, transformed itself into a great land-based territorial empire. The Russian eastward and southward expansion over huge distances was a saga comparable to the later westward expansion of the United States and Canada across North America. A key role in this Russian expansion was played by the **Cossacks** (KOS-aks), tough, hard-drinking adventurers and soldiers from southern Russia who were descendants of Russians, Poles, and Lithuanians fleeing serfdom, slavery, or jail. Cossacks (the Turkish word for "free men") were fierce warriors and usually defeated rival forces.

The expansion east across sparsely populated Siberia began in the 1500s and accelerated during the seventeenth and eighteenth centuries. By 1637 Russian explorers had reached the Pacific Ocean. In 1689 conflict with China forced the Russians to temporarily abandon settlements in the Amur (AH-moor) River Basin north of China (see Chapter 18), but they continued to add other Siberian territory, often after overcoming fierce resistance from local peoples. Siberia yielded the Russians furs, metals, and forest products.

Seeking direct access to maritime trade routes, the Russians also began acquiring territories on their southern fringe. Looking south, Russian leaders coveted the Black Sea and the Straits of Bosporus bisecting Istanbul, through which Russian ships could reach the warm Mediterranean. The southward thrust meant confronting the Tartars (TAHR-tuhrz), Muslim descendants of Mongols and long a threat to the Russians. In the 1400s and 1500s Tartars, Russians, Ottoman Turks, Poles, and Lithuanians fought for control of today's southern Russia. Between 1552 and 1556 the Russians seized the Tartar state of Kazan (kuh-ZAN), slaughtering many residents in the capital, and then gradually gained more land. Russian commerce benefited from Russia's new domination of the northern Caspian Sea, which made possible direct trade between the Baltic lands and Persia through Russia.

Soon the Russians turned toward Muslim Central Asia, settled largely by Turkish peoples and often known as Turkestan. By the early 1700s the Russians had gained territory occupied by the Kazakhs (kah-ZAHKS), a pastoral people who had once ruled a large area, and by 1864 they controlled all the Kazakh lands to the eastern border with China. They then targeted the Silk Road cities, those centers of Islamic learning that attracted merchants from many societies, among them Jews and Hindu Indians.

In pursuing this goal the Russians faced formidable opponents in the Uzbeks (OOZ-beks), a people of mixed Turkish, Persian, and Mongol ancestry who controlled several rival states in southern Turkestan. But the Uzbeks eventually were weakened. Uzbek sultans promoted Sunni Islam, which made them enemies of the Shi'ite Safavids. When Safavid hostility

closed Persia to Uzbek trade, the prosperity of the Silk Road cities declined, and the roads that had once brought diverse religions, cultural influences, and trade goods into Turkestan saw fewer travelers. Eventually the Uzbeks and their neighbors earned smaller revenues and their merchants lost profits. In addition, the sultans lost power to tribal chiefs. In the early 1700s the Persians gained control of some Uzbek territory and much of Afghanistan, and by the later 1800s an expanding Russia was able to conquer all of southern Turkestan.

> ## SECTION SUMMARY
>
> ■ Under the leadership of a charismatic boy named Isma'il, the Safavids, originally from Azerbaijan, conquered Persia and made the Persians convert from Sunni to Shi'a Islam.
>
> ■ Under the Safavids, Persia was a major exporter of silk and remained a major conduit of trade, and its beautiful capital, built by Shah Abbas I, attracted merchants from many countries.
>
> ■ The Safavid Empire patronized art and literature, and Safavid artists became famous for their miniature painting and their carpet weaving.
>
> ■ Safavid religious leaders, increasingly relying on their own authority rather than that of the Quran, eventually became more influential as the power of Safavid rulers declined and then collapsed.
>
> ■ Morocco, the far western outpost of Islam, absorbed many fleeing Iberian Muslims and grew into a powerful state that, under the Sa'dians, eventually defeated the Portuguese.
>
> ■ With the aid of the Cossacks, Russia engaged in a large territorial expansion to create a land-based empire, an expansion that brought it into conflict with Siberian and Islamic Central Asian peoples, including the Uzbeks in Turkestan.

 *Online Study Center*   **ACE the Test**

 # Chapter Summary

The overseas expansion of Europe during the Early Modern Era affected different regions in different ways but was only one of the forces at work in most societies. Various African societies, among them Songhai, Kanem-Bornu, the Hausa states, Benin, and Buganda, remained strong in the 1500s. Eventually, however, the arrival of Europeans set in motion forces that began to reshape parts of Africa, especially societies along the western and eastern coasts, and many Africans became linked more closely to Europe and the Americas. The Portuguese undermined Kongo, Angola, and the city-states of East Africa and ultimately established the first European colonies in sub-Saharan Africa, Angola and Mozambique. The most prominent factor in changing the course of African history was the trans-

---

Cossacks Tough adventurers and soldiers from southern Russia who were descendants of Russians, Poles, and Lithuanians fleeing serfdom, slavery, or jail.

Atlantic slave trade, which arose in the sixteenth century. Soon various Europeans began procuring slaves in West Africa and shipping them across the Atlantic to meet the limitless demands of the American plantations. This trade benefited a few African societies, such as Dahomey and Ashante, but devastated others and created chronic conflict along the West African coast.

Several Islamic societies remained powerful during the 1500s and 1600s. These included the great Islamic empires of the Ottomans and Safavids and Morocco. The Ottomans, who were Sunni Turks, built an empire over much of western Asia, North Africa, and southeastern Europe, reuniting a large part of the Islamic world for the first time in some centuries. At their zenith they had a powerful military, flourishing economy, and vibrant cultural life. The Safavids dominated part of western Asia and fostered a lively culture and economy in Persia. They also converted the Persians from Sunni to Shi'a Islam, increasing the rivalry with the Ottomans. Sa'dian Morocco repulsed the Portuguese and built a regional empire. But by the early 1700s these great Islamic states as well as Muslim societies in Central Asia experienced new challenges, some posed by Russian expansion into Muslim lands.

 **Online Study Center** Improve Your Grade Flashcards

Key Terms

Darkest Africa	Middle Passage	colonialism
Boers	Atlantic System	janissaries
trekking	imperialism	Cossacks
racism		

Suggested Reading

Books

Balandier, Georges. *Daily Life in the Kingdom of the Kongo: From the Sixteenth to the Eighteenth Century.* New York: Meridian Books, 1968. A classic study of an important African kingdom.

Barendse, R. J. *The Arabian Seas: The Indian Ocean World of the Seventeenth Century.* Armonk, N.Y.: M. E. Sharpe, 2002. A lengthy but wide-ranging scholarly study of the political economy connecting Europe, Africa, India, and the Middle East.

Findley, Carter Vaughn. *The Turks in World History.* New York: Oxford University Press, 2005. A survey over many centuries.

Goldschmidt, Arthur, Jr. and Lawrence Davidson. *A Concise History of the Middle East.* 8th ed. revised and updated. Boulder, Colo.:

Westview Press, 2005. A good introduction, especially to the Ottoman and Safavid Empires.

Khodarkovsky, Michael, *Russia's Steppe Frontier: The Making of a Colonial Empire, 1500–1800.* Bloomington: Indiana University Press, 2002. A scholarly study.

Klein, Herbert S. *The Atlantic Slave Trade.* New York: Cambridge University Press, 1999. An overview that incorporates social, economic, political, and cultural history.

Northrup, David. *Africa's Discovery of Europe, 1450–1850.* New York: Oxford University Press, 2002. A sweeping survey of Africa's engagement with Europe and the varied responses.

Pearson, Michael N. *Port Cities and Intruders: The Swahili Coast, India, and Portugal in the Early Modern Era.* Baltimore: Johns Hopkins University Press, 1998. A scholarly study of the coast.

Robinson, Francis. *The Cultural Atlas of the Islamic World Since 1500.* Oxford: Stonehenge, 1992. A useful compilation of materials.

Savory, Roger. *Iran Under the Safavids.* Cambridge: Cambridge University Press, 1980. The standard survey.

Shillington, Kevin. *History of Africa,* revised 2nd ed. New York: Palgrave Macmillan, 2005. Readable survey with much on this era.

Thornton, John. *Africa and Africans in the Formation of the Atlantic World, 1400–1800.* 2nd ed. Cambridge: Cambridge University Press, 1998. An excellent examination of Africa and the diaspora.

Wheatcroft, Andrew. *The Ottomans.* New York: Viking, 1993. A readable, lively discussion with particular attention to the elites.

Websites

History and Cultures of Africa
(**http://www.columbia.edu/cu/lweb/indiv/africa/cuvl/cult/html**). Provides valuable links to relevant websites on African history.

Internet African History Sourcebook
(**http://www.fordham.edu/halsall/africa/africasbook.html**). This site contains useful information and documentary material.

Internet Islamic History Sourcebook
(**http://www.fordham.edu/halsall/islam/islamsbook.html**). Useful links and source materials.

Middle East Studies Internet Resources
(**http://www.columbia.edu/cu/lweb/indiv/mideast/cuvlm/ancient/html**). A useful collection of links.

The Trans-Atlantic Slave Trade
(**www.whc.neu.edu/afrintro.htm**). A demographic simulation created at Northeastern University.

CHAPTER 17

Americans, Europeans, Africans, and New Societies in the Americas, 1450–1750

Online Study Center

This icon will direct you to interactive activities and study materials on the website: college.hmco.com/pic/lockard1e

Español   3. Mestizo   2. Yndia

A Mestizo Family The intermarriage of Europeans and Indians was common in Latin America, especially in Mexico. This Mexican painting, by the eighteenth-century artist Las Castas, shows a Spanish man, his Indian wife, and their mixed-descent, or *mestizo*, son.   (Courtesy, Banco de Mexico)

Truly do we live on earth? Not forever on earth; only a little while here. Although it be jade, it will be broken. Although it is gold, it is crushed.

AZTEC POEM ON THE MEANING OF LIFE, CA. 1500[1]

In the sixteenth century Spanish colonists in Mexico trained an Aztec historian, Chimalpahin Cuahtlehuanitzin (chee-MAL-pin QUAT-al-WANT-zen), how to read and write in the Western alphabet. Using this alphabet but writing in his native Nahuatl (NAH-waht-l) language of central Mexico, the Aztec historian gave us one of the best records of the Mexican world at the threshold of the changes instigated by the coming of Europeans. He wrote, for example, of Aztec military triumphs over neighboring people and of how Aztec kings used their wealth to improve their great capital, Tenochtitlan (teh-noch-TIT-lan), constructing an aqueduct to convey fresh water and rebuilding temples to the gods. But Cuahtlehuanitzin also told of ominous developments. In particular, he recorded the reports that began to reach Tenochtitlan in 1519 of pale-skinned men in huge boats arriving on the eastern coast from the sea, where gods might come from. In fact, Aztec legends claimed that, centuries earlier, a Toltec king driven into exile by rivals had become a god, Quetzalcoatl (kate-zahl-CO-ah-tal) ("the plumed serpent"), who promised to return some day and seek revenge. These strange men on the coast seemed suspiciously godlike: they dressed in metal, had unfamiliar but lethal metal weapons, and rode on large animals as tall as the roof of a house—perhaps, Aztecs thought, some kind of deer. And they arrived around the year some believed that Quetzalcoatl would return. This was disturbing, Cuahtlehuanitzin remembered, because the god's reappearance threatened the Aztec social order.

To be sure, for all their military and cultural triumphs, the Aztecs had known challenges. Cuahtlehuanitzin wrote that, nearly three decades earlier, 13-Flint in the Aztec calendar (1492 in the Gregorian calendar) had been an unusually bad year, bringing an eclipse of the sun, volcanic eruptions, and widespread famine. The Aztec philosophy of life understood such occasional setbacks, as the poem opening the chapter suggests. But the Aztecs were not prepared for the arrival of the Europeans and the troubles they would provoke. The leader of the pale men who had arrived on the shore was the Spanish explorer Hernán Cortés. The invaders arrived in the Aztec lands, Cuahtlehuanitzin remembered, when a terrible and unknown disease, known to Europeans as smallpox, began killing off the people. And within two years, these men from afar, with horses, metal armor, and gunpowder weapons, had conquered the heart of the Aztec Empire, giving new meaning to the broken jade and crushed gold in the Aztec poem.

The first Europeans to arrive in the Americas claimed to have discovered a "new world," but it was actually an old one, long populated by a mosaic of peoples such as the Aztecs. The exploratory voyages of Christopher Columbus and the conquests of such adventurers as Cortés in Mexico often destroyed many long-existing American societies and reshaped them into new kinds of societies, in reality *creating* a "new world." In fact, the whole Western Hemisphere changed. During the 1500s the Spanish and Portuguese conquered and colonized large areas of what we now call Latin America, containing millions of people. A century later, in North America and the Caribbean, the English, French, and Dutch followed, gradually extending their power. As a result of these incursions during the Early Modern Era, with its forging of many new networks of travel and commerce around the world, few regions experienced more changes than the Americas, and the two hemispheres became closely linked. European exploration in the Americas and Southeast Asia also led to the first encounters between Europe and the diverse island societies of the Pacific Ocean.

The transitions that resulted from European encounters with Native American cultures affected both sides of the Atlantic. Among the most important consequences of European activities in the Americas was a complex global exchange of crops and animals, peoples and cultures. By the 1600s, European ships regularly crisscrossed the Atlantic, moving people, plants, animals, natural resources, and manufactured goods, while diseases carried from the Eastern Hemisphere set off a demographic disaster for Native American peoples. The societies that emerged from the European colonization of the Americas reflected diverse influences from all over the Atlantic world. Europeans, Africans, and Native Americans in Latin America and the Caribbean formed mixed cultures that differed in many respects from the societies formed in English- and French-ruled North America. Finally, in some regions of the Americas a plantation economy developed that engaged enslaved Africans and their descendants as a work force. For millions of Africans, transported across the Atlantic against their will, this consequence of Europeans' arrival meant that they now lived in conditions that were often unendurable, requiring them to develop strategies for survival.

FOCUS QUESTIONS

1. How did encounters between Europe and the Americas increase in the 1500s?

2. How did Europeans conquer and begin settling the American societies?

3. What were the major consequences of European colonization of the Americas?

4. How did the development of the American economies lead to the trans-Atlantic slave trade?

5. What impact did the emerging Atlantic System have on Europe and the American societies?

CHRONOLOGY

	Exploration	Latin America	North America
1400	**1492** First Columbian voyage		
1500	**1519–1521** Magellan's circumnavigation of the globe	**1521** Spanish conquest of Aztecs **1535** Spanish conquest of Incas	
1600			**1604** French settlement in Canada **1607** English settlement in Virginia **1627** Colony of New France
1700			**1759** English defeat of French in Quebec

✦ Early American-European-Pacific Encounters

How did encounters between Europe and the Americas increase in the 1500s?

American peoples developed their ways of life long before the European voyages of exploration permanently connected the two hemispheres, and a wide variety of societies, economies, and styles of governing existed in the Americas by the fifteenth century. But the Americans faced a great challenge from the coming of the Europeans. Christopher Columbus began the historic change in 1492. In the wake of the Columbian voyages, various European nations first explored and then gradually conquered, colonized, and settled the entire Western Hemisphere, drawing the Americas into commercial, travel, and religious networks centered on Europe. The exploration of the Americas also spilled over into the Pacific Ocean, though few Pacific islanders encountered the West in this era.

American Societies in 1500

In 1500 the Western Hemisphere contained many societies with distinctive institutions, customs, and survival strategies. Their differences resulted from adaptation to different environments. Those who lived by hunting, gathering, and fishing could be found particularly in the North American Great Plains, the Pacific Northwest coast, Alaska, northern Canada, and some of the tropical forest regions of Central and South America. Other peoples lived from small-scale farming, especially in eastern North America, parts of the North American desert and Amazon Basin, and southeastern Brazil.

For millennia the most complex Native American societies flourished from intensive farming in Mesoamerica (Mexico and northern Central America) and the Andes region of western South America. By 1500 the Aztecs, based in central Mexico, were the most powerful Mesoamerican society and the Incas (IN-kuhz), centered in central Peru, controlled most of the Andes region. Both the Aztecs and the Incas built states on the foundations of much older urban and farming-based societies. Like their predecessors, they worked metals and fibers for tools, decoration, and weapons.

The Aztec state, through military conquest by a strong army and a well-organized government, completed its empire building in 1428 (see Chronology: American Societies and European Discoveries, 1400–1524). Aztec warfare relied on disciplined battle formations, shrewd tactics, and deadly weapons such as bows and arrows, stone-bladed broadswords,

CHRONOLOGY

American Societies and European Discoveries, 1400–1524

1428–1521	Aztec Empire
1440–1532	Inca Empire
1492	Landing in Bahamas by Columbus
1494	Treaty of Tordesillas
1497	John Cabot's landing in North America
1500	Portuguese claim of Brazil
1513	Balboa's sighting of Pacific Ocean
1519–1521	Ferdinand Magellan's circumnavigation of globe
1524	French claim of Canada

spears, and spear-throwers. But the Aztecs only loosely controlled the various peoples in their empire, and by the early 1500s they faced mounting military confrontations with rival confederations of city-states, especially the Tlaxcalans (tlax-CALL-uns) on their eastern fringe. Cruel Aztec imperialism, including the widespread use of human sacrifice, had created enemies, some of whom were later willing to cooperate with the first European arrivals, the Spanish, to overthrow Aztec power. But Aztec society was still vigorous and expanding its influence in the early 1500s.

The Incas completed the conquest of their empire in 1440. Even more impressive than the Aztecs in material accomplishments, they formed an empire larger than the Roman or Han Chinese Empires of the Classical Era, stretching nearly 2,500 miles north to south, much of it above 8,000 feet in altitude. The Inca state was the most dynamic and integrated in all of the American states, and it was geared for conquest and paternalistic regimentation. Some Spanish colonizers admired it. For example, in the later 1500s Garcilaso de la Vega (GAHR-suh-LAH-so duh luh VAY-guh), the son of a Spanish captain and an Inca princess, wrote the most detailed study of Inca culture. While acknowledging the misery of people colonized by the Incas, he also praised the highly productive farming system, generosity, and other values of Inca society. The Incas, he concluded, "had attained to a high status of perfection. No thoughtful man can fail to admire so noble and provident a government."[2]

Probably in part due to climate change, some Native American societies had long passed their peak by 1500. By 1440 the last Maya cities and states of southern Mexico and northern Central America had collapsed. But some 5 to 6 million Mayan-speaking people, living mostly in villages, remained as examples of a once vibrant society, over 2,000 years old, whose city-states had once stretched from the northern Yucatan Peninsula southward into what is today Guatemala and Belize. In North America the mound-building and trade-oriented Mississippian culture had reached its peak in the 1100s, and the major Mississippian town, Cahokia (kuh-HOE-key-uh), had been deserted by 1250. The once vast Mississippian trading system was in steep decline by the 1400s, by which time the Anasazi (ah-nah-SAH-zee) and other societies of the southwestern desert had already abandoned their major settlements.

Flourishing Native American societies besides the Aztecs and Incas remained, however, such as the Taino (TIE-no) in the Caribbean islands and the diverse farming peoples along the Atlantic coasts of North America and Brazil. Indeed, while the first European settlers wrongly considered the Americas to be largely empty land, some regions were densely populated. By 1492 the population of the Western Hemisphere probably numbered between 60 and 75 million people, although some demographers place it at over 100 million. The majority of Americans lived in central and southern Mexico and the Andes region. The most complex agricultural and political systems

Arawak Women This woodcut, made in the sixteenth century, shows Arawak women on a Caribbean island preparing a meal of cornmeal tortillas and stew. (Courtesy of John Carter Brown Library at Brown University)

corresponded to the largest populations. Regardless of their success in mastering environments, however, because of many millennia of isolation from the Eastern Hemisphere, American peoples had no immunity to the diseases brought by Europeans and later African slaves. Hence, the coming of the West brought a terrible mortality. Native Americans also had no metal swords or firearms to resist Europeans. The vulnerability of the Western Hemisphere peoples made this the main region to suffer incursions by Europe in the Early Modern Era.

Bridging the Atlantic Barrier

The Atlantic Ocean was the major barrier between the hemispheres, but a few Europeans steadily overcame the challenge. The first known contact between Americans and Europeans did not have a long-lasting impact. In the later tenth century C.E. some Norse Vikings, whose ancestors had settled Iceland several generations earlier, sailed west and established small farming settlements in several glacier-free coastal valleys in southern Greenland. By around 1000 a few of these hardy Norse, perhaps blown off course, sighted what is now eastern Canada and explored the coast. They built a small village in Newfoundland, a large island off the coast of the Canadian region known today as Labrador, where they harvested fish and cut timber.

Largely as a result of conflicts between local Native Americans and the Norse, the Newfoundland settlement was abandoned after only a few years. The Greenland Norse, however, apparently sent occasional trading and lumbering expeditions to eastern Canada for several hundred years. A few Norse artifacts, possibly used as trade goods, have been found scattered across eastern Canada and the Arctic islands. The Greenland settlements also collapsed by 1450. There may have been factional disputes or conflicts with the native Inuit (IN-yoo-it) people of Greenland, while deforestation and colder climates made the already difficult farming impossible. But the Greenland Norse were not lost to history. Portuguese ships occasionally visited Iceland, where people knew of the Greenland and Labrador settlements, and this knowledge probably circulated in Europe.

The Norse may not have been the only people from the Western Hemisphere to spot the North American coast before 1492. The winters of the Little Ice Age in Europe brought poor harvests and reduced fish catches along Europe's Atlantic coast, pushing some desperate fishermen to venture farther from home. For many years Portuguese, Basque, Danish, English, Breton, and Moroccan fishermen had worked the waters of the North Atlantic in search of cod, whales, and sardines. Some of them probably found the fish-rich Grand Banks off Newfoundland. Perhaps a few of the fishermen also saw North America. A few scattered non-Norse European artifacts reported by early explorers in eastern North America have led some historians to suspect that some coastal people may have encountered Europeans in the later 1400s. If there were any landings they apparently went unreported in Europe. Fishermen may have kept any discoveries secret to keep rivals away from their rich fishing grounds.

Different motives, including the quest for riches, national glory, and Christian converts, encouraged other Europeans to venture out into the Atlantic on exploring expeditions (see Chapter 15). While early Portuguese expeditions concentrated on the African route to the East (see Chapters 16 and 18), others, led by Christopher Columbus, hoped to sail westward from Europe to Asia. Contrary to myth, many educated people in Europe accepted that the earth was round and hence could be circumnavigated.

Columbus's First Voyages to the Americas

The first explorers to brave the Atlantic directly from Europe with the purpose of reaching Asia came under the Spanish flag, beginning with Christopher Columbus (see Chapter 15). Columbus (1451–1506), born in the key Italian port of Genoa, had lived for many years in the Portuguese capital, Lisbon, which had a large Genoese merchant and sailing community. His connections to wealthy Genoese in Lisbon helped him court and marry Donha Felipa Moniz, the aristocratic daughter of a governor on the Portuguese-settled Atlantic island of Madeira (muh-DEER-uh). Thanks to this connection, Columbus worked in Madeira and visited the Canary and Azores (A-zorz) Islands farther out in the Atlantic. Donha Felipa died soon after giving birth to their son, Diego, but she had given Columbus social status and access to her family's navigational charts and records. Columbus had also likely sailed to Iceland and down the West African coast on Portuguese ships, and he was probably familiar with both the Norse discoveries and the tales of Portuguese fishermen.

Soon Columbus, described by a contemporary as a man of great spirit and lofty thoughts, formed grander plans of exploration. The mariner was inspired by the writings of the thirteenth-century Italian adventurer Marco Polo and owned a well-worn copy of Polo's book relating his travels in Asia and long sojourn in China. A devout Christian, Columbus claimed that he wanted to sail to China to introduce Christianity there. He also hoped to find the sea route to the silk- and spice-rich lands of China and Southeast Asia. But the inaccurate maps he acquired vastly underestimated the size of the earth and the distance to Asia.

Columbus eventually convinced the Spanish monarchs, King Ferdinand and Queen Isabella, fresh from their final triumph over the last Muslim state in southern Spain, to finance his voyages of exploration in hopes of establishing direct ties to Asia. Commanding ships far smaller than the great junks of the Chinese explorer Zheng He in the early 1400s, Columbus surveyed much of the Caribbean and some of the South American coast in four voyages over the next decade and believed that he had discovered outlying regions of Asia. When Ferdinand and Isabella realized he was wrong, they were at first disappointed. America was a heartbreaking obstacle on the route to eastern Asia.

On his first voyage in 1492, Columbus had encountered the Taino, an Arawak (AR-uh-wahk)-speaking people who lived on Caribbean islands (see Map 17.1). When Columbus and his crew sailed into the Bahamas, they were greeted by

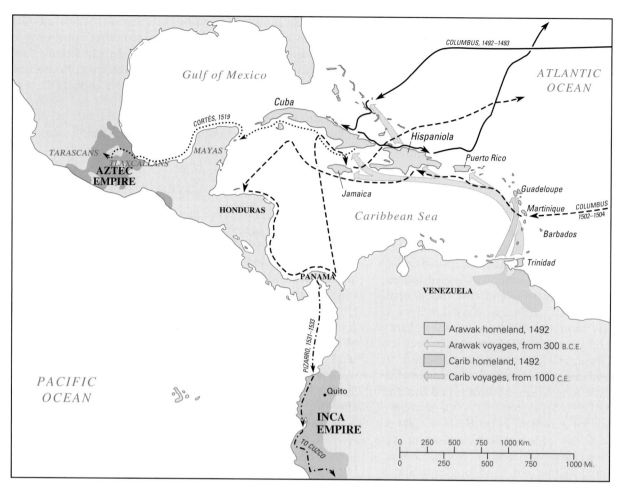

Map 17.1   The Americas and Early European Exploration
The several voyages across the Atlantic led by Columbus explored the Caribbean Basin and set the
stage for Spanish conquest of many American societies, most notably of the Aztec and Inca Empires.

curious Taino islanders. The Taino proved friendly, but the fact that they wore few clothes, a practical response to the tropical heat, shocked the straight-laced Spanish, who considered nakedness a sign of barbarism. The Taino themselves may have desired to cultivate a potential ally. Even before the arrival of the Spanish, they had often had to resist incursions by the Caribs (KAR-ibs), a more warlike Native American group that had originated in South America. By the fourteenth century Caribs were pushing Taino and other Arawaks toward more northern islands and also raiding the Yucatan coast of Mexico.

The Taino had a flourishing society; they smoked cigars, slept in hammocks, possessed a little gold, and some of them lived in sizeable towns built around Mesoamerican-style plazas and ball courts. They combined fishing with highly productive cultivation of corn (maize) and manioc, and they carried on extensive interisland trade in large canoes that were not much smaller than Columbus's ships and capable of holding up to 150 people. The women did the farming and often served as community leaders, exhibiting egalitarian gender relations that confounded the Spanish. After meeting with several communities, Columbus developed favorable views of the hospitable,

patient, and peaceable Taino, seeing them, according to the Western stereotype of certain non-Western peoples, as "noble savages," innocent children of nature: "They are a loving and uncovetous people. They love their neighbors as themselves."[3] Later, however, when Columbus encountered Taino noncooperation or armed resistance to Spanish demands, he modified his views, replacing the image of the "noble savage" with that of the "ignoble savage."

Columbus then moved on, first to the island he called Hispaniola (HIS-puhn-YO-luh), today the home of Haiti and the Dominican Republic but then dominated by six Taino chiefdoms. Leaving a small colony of Spaniards there, Columbus began his return voyage to Europe by way of Cuba, which Columbus believed might be China. There he dispatched a small party, led by a Jew who spoke Hebrew, Chaldean, and Arabic, to search the interior for, and possibly communicate with, the Chinese ruler. They returned only with some mysterious dried leaves called *tobacos*, which local people smoked. Some decades later other Europeans would take tobacco, widely consumed in the Americas, back to Europe and start a smoking fad. Columbus and his crew sailed back to Spain with six Taino Indians from the Bahamas to present at court as

messages, nursing infants, or taking care of the older Tolosa children. In exchange for better food and medical care than was given the field hands, they were expected to be obedient and loyal.

Caetana lived in a close-knit relationship to kin, including her mother, Pulicena, and her sister, married to the free-born mulatto, Joao Ribeira da Silva, who was probably a supervisor of field hands. Caetana was also close to her aunt, the freed slave Luisa Jacinta, whose husband, Alexandre, served as Caetana's godfather and male authority figure. Caetana grew up speaking Portuguese with no direct knowledge of African ways or the terrible Middle Passage across the Atlantic. From a young age she served in the Tolosa house as a personal maid to the Tolosa women, including two daughters, and was trusted and allowed into their private quarters.

In 1835 Tolosa, without consulting her, ordered Caetana, then around seventeen, to marry Custodio, a slave in his mid-twenties, in a wedding blessed by the Catholic Church. Custodio was a master tailor who may have cut and sewn the rough cotton clothes worn by slaves and probably also made clothes for the Tolosa family. Like many slave owners, Tolosa may have believed that slave marriages fostered social stability and diminished the threat of rebellion. Perhaps he also feared that an unmarried house slave, representing unyoked female sexuality, might be a bad influence on his two daughters, twelve and two years old, and temptation for his three adolescent sons. Most adult slave women at Rio Clara were married. Caetana, however, refused Tolosa's order, saying, according to court records, that she felt "a great repugnance for the state of matrimony" and found Custodio especially distasteful. In the end she obeyed, succumbing to the pleas of her family and fearing Tolosa's threats to punish her by assigning her to field work or selling her to another plantation. But after priests performed the ceremony and the couple moved into her aunt and uncle's house, she refused to sleep with Custodio, humiliating and enraging him.

After her uncle and godfather, Alexandre, threatened to beat her if she did not submit to her husband, and with few options, Caetana fled to Tolosa's mansion and pleaded to have the marriage ended. Her rebellion was apparently not against plantation slavery as such but against male authority over her. Caetana's action against the entire system of male power—slave owner, uncle, husband, church—threw Rio Clara into turmoil. After his threats to sell Caetana or reassign her to onerous field work failed, Tolosa relented, giving her protection from her husband and asking a church court to issue an annulment. In court, Caetana complained that she was "reduced to the hard necessity of obeying solely from fear of grave punishment and lasting harm." The legal case took five years, including appeals, with the church ultimately refusing the annulment request.

We do not know why, against such long odds, she rebelled, why she despised marriage, or what ultimately happened to Caetana. Perhaps she envied unmarried free women, who were often respected, or the chaste nuns in the convents. The records do not indicate whether she continued to evade the marriage, but it seems unlikely she complied. She might have been sold to another plantation, before or after Tolosa died in 1853. What we know is that Caetana bravely refused a demand to do something against her will.

THINKING ABOUT THE PROFILE

1. What does Caetana's experience tell us about life on a Brazilian plantation?

2. What does her rebellion tell us about the Brazilian system of patriarchy?

Note: Quotations from Sandra Lauderdale Graham, *Caetana Says No: Women's Stories from a Brazilian Slave Society* (New York: Cambridge University Press, 2002), pp. 2, 57.

and those consequences were often severe. Enslaved Africans experienced a high mortality rate, dying from mistreatment, disease, infant mortality, and disrupted family life. Slave women faced rape or sexual harassment by male owners and slaves.

Slaves owners organized slave labor to squeeze out profits. In Brazil, for example, while enslaved Africans and their unfree descendants labored in a wide variety of economic activities, including gold mining and cattle ranching, the great majority worked in agriculture, especially on sugar, coffee, and tobacco estates. The average Brazilian sugar plantation in the seventeenth and eighteenth centuries owned between eighty and one hundred enslaved workers. Some of them worked as mule drivers, sugar makers, household servants, or even low-level managers, but most were field hands who were each expected to produce three-quarters of a ton of sugar a year. The slave owner recovered the cost of purchasing and maintaining

slaves after about three years of such production. Brazilian slave owners earned profits from any additional years of hard work but had little incentive to maintain the health of slaves no longer able to work hard. With two men for every woman, the Brazilian population with African ancestry did not grow very rapidly and required constant replenishment from Africa. Encouraged by the Catholic Church to marry, many Brazilian slaves formed families, even though they could be broken up by sale.

Africans and their descendants often resisted the slave system. Some, like the Brazilian woman Caetana, risked severe punishment by defending their interests in a complex social system (see Profile: Caetana, Slave Rebel Against Patriarchy). Some slaves, known as **maroons** (muh-ROONS) in the English

maroons Slaves who escaped from plantations and set up African-type societies in the interior of several American colonies.

Caribbean, escaped from plantations and set up African-type societies in the interior of several American colonies, including Brazil, Colombia, Jamaica, Haiti, Dutch Guiana, and some of the southern colonies in North America. Maroons often recreated African cultures by mixing influences, such as religious concepts, from the various African ethnic groups involved. African women led at least two of the ten major maroon societies in Brazil. Since the colonial governments sent in military forces to recapture or control maroons, some of the maroon communities were only temporarily independent. The largest maroon community was formed in northeast Brazil, where rebellious slaves established a state around 1605, Palmares (paul-MARYS), with a government led by an African-style king and chiefs. With a population of perhaps 30,000, mostly of African ancestry, Palmares flourished, and resisted nearly annual Portuguese assaults, for nearly a century before being crushed by the Portuguese in 1694. According to legends, the last Palmares king, Zumbi, hurled himself from a cliff to avoid capture and reenslavement. Slave revolts also erupted in Haiti, Mexico, the North American colonies, and elsewhere, but they were brutally crushed and the leaders executed. For example, the 1739 Stono Rebellion in South Carolina, the deadliest of the North American uprisings, largely involved recently imported, frequently Catholic, Kongolese. The captured rebels were beheaded.

Africans and their descendants, free or unfree, became a part of local societies. Some slaves were eventually freed, a process known as *manumission.* Manumission was rare in the English colonies and more common in Latin America, especially Brazil, where women, mulattos, and local-born children were most likely to be freed. In both English and Latin America, a few slaves earned enough to buy their own freedom, and some slave owners gave favored slaves an inheritance. As a result, a slowly growing class of free blacks filled niches in Latin American life. Together the enslaved and freed people of color constituted some two-thirds of the population in parts of Brazil and Cuba. While racism—judging people based on observable physical traits such as skin color—remained influential throughout the Americas, Latin Americans tended to rank people according to their occupation and status as well as skin color, making for a flexible social order. In contrast, the English colonies rigidly divided people largely by skin color and whether they had any African ancestry.

African American Cultures

The harsh conditions of slave life notwithstanding, unique, new African American cultures emerged. Africans in the Americas and their descendants frequently mixed Western and African customs, and some created hybrid religions based on both African and Christian beliefs. For example, the ceremonies of such religions as Haitian voodoo, Cuban *santaria* (san-tuh-REE-uh), and Brazilian *candomblé* (can-dum-BLAY) involved practices derived from West Africa such as animal sacrifice and worship of African spirits and gods. Yet, many fol-

lowers of these faiths also believed in the Christian God and saints. Combining African rhythms with local European and sometimes Native American musical traditions, African Americans also invented musical forms of wide appeal, including North American jazz and blues; Caribbean salsa, reggae, and calypso; and Brazilian samba. A few African Americans even developed new languages, such as the Gullah (GULL-uh) dialect of the Georgia Sea Islands, which mixes English and African words.

African American cultures also influenced other ethnic groups in the Americas. For example, African words enriched the English, French, Spanish, and Portuguese spoken locally. Brazilian Portuguese, for instance, contains many words of Kongolese and Yoruba origin. In addition, many non-Africans enjoyed various folktales and traditions of African origin, such as the Brer Rabbit stories of the southern United States, and the Angolan-based *capoiera* martial arts of Brazil, which involved music as well as physical movements. Africans also introduced several crops from their homelands, including watermelons, black-eyed peas, okra, and rice, and contributed their invaluable knowledge of blacksmithing and ironworking to colonial life.

The survival of African cultural forms and values varied from place to place depending on circumstances. Survival was probably strongest in Brazil, Haiti, and a few Caribbean islands such as Cuba, Jamaica, and Trinidad. In Brazil, the Portuguese eventually learned to accept and sometimes appreciate African influences, which were brought by the thousands of Africans that arrived every year for over three centuries. Thus Brazilian culture developed as a complex mix of African and European influences. In contrast, Spanish American and North American authorities tried to repress African music and religion, with some success. Today cultural leaders in the Americas often disdain Africa-influenced cultural forms and hold up European and North American culture as the model.

The Americas and the Atlantic System

As already mentioned (see Chapter 16), trans-Atlantic migration, voluntary and forced, and increasingly close economic ties between Europe, Africa, and the Americas created an Atlantic System by which cargoes of plantation crops were shipped east across the Atlantic to Europe while cargoes of slaves moved west to the Americas. The Atlantic System comprised a large network that spanned western and Central Africa, the east coast and southern region of English North America, the Caribbean Basin, and the northern and eastern coastal zones of South America. Plantations, slavery, and the numerical prominence of Africans and their descendants in the Americas defined this system. Ultimately, this system of economic activities helped spur major developments in modern world history, including the rise of European capitalism and wealth.

As key economic activities in the Atlantic System, the slave trade and plantation economies provided enormous capital to

Europeans and North Americans. Slave trading became a hugely profitable enterprise that was operated on a sophisticated business basis and attracted large amounts of capital, which allowed for rapid expansion of the trade. The prosperity of eighteenth-century European cities such as Bristol and Liverpool in England, and of North American cities such as Boston, Providence, Charleston, Savannah, and New Orleans, depended heavily on the slave trade. Since the slavers, the cooperating African chiefs and merchants, the plantation owners, the shipbuilders, and the other groups linked directly or indirectly to the trade were all reluctant to abandon a lucrative activity, the trade endured for four hundred years, finally coming to an end only in the 1870s.

The Atlantic System also contributed to European industrialization and colonialism. Some of the profits from the slave trade and American plantations were invested in enterprises and technology in England, the Netherlands, France, and North America, helping to bring economic development to these societies and later spurring rapid industrialization in England. Some of the investment capital for inventing industrial technologies came from individuals and companies linked to the slave trade and plantations. For example, Glasgow merchants known as the "tobacco lords" because of their ties to North American tobacco plantations set up industries in Britain, such as printing companies, tanneries, and ironworks, and also invested in cotton textile plants and coal mines.

Colonial Wealth and Europe

Some Europeans made wiser use of American profits than others. However vast the profits earned from overseas commerce—the slave trade, plantation agriculture, and mining—these profits did not always result in substantial economic development in European countries. Mercantilist economic strategies could not necessarily convert the incoming wealth into a growing domestic economy. While Spain and Portugal largely squandered opportunities, by 1750 becoming poor countries within Europe, the Dutch and English pursued wiser investment policies.

Spain, the most powerful European country for most of the 1500s, had reaped vast riches from the silver mines of the Americas and the galleons that brought from the Philippines Chinese goods and tropical products. But they did not ultimately use this wealth in ways that promoted their own economic improvement. In fact, much of the exploitation of the Americas hurt Spain. For example, the flood of American bullion into Spain caused severe inflation, resulting in the need to import lower-priced products from other European countries. In addition, the thousands of Spaniards who went to the Americas and Asia created a labor shortage at home. Furthermore, the large investments in the colonies were obtained in part by heavily taxing peasants and merchants in Spain. Spanish investment also did not spur capitalism. Since most Spanish merchants were or hoped to be large landowners in Spain, they used their prof-

its to buy land rather than investing in trade or industry. By 1600 Spain was bankrupt, and a Spanish official charged that the country had wasted its wealth on frivolous spending rather than manufacturing, arguing that "the cause of [our] ruin is that riches ride on the wind, instead of [producing] goods that bear fruit. Spain is poor because she is rich [in gold and silver]."[23] Much of the silver ended up elsewhere in Europe or in China. The wealth also tempted the monarchy to pursue expensive and ultimately futile wars of expansion in Europe.

The Portuguese were second only to the English in the volume of slave trading. Their colony in Brazil was also the world's largest exporter of gold, diamonds, and sugar and a major producer of coffee and cotton. But the Portuguese squandered their colonial wealth through nonproductive investments, such as building magnificent churches and monasteries rather than financing local industry. As a small country with a small population and a weak local resource base, Portugal had a tiny domestic market and hence little incentive to build its local industries. Investment in Brazil was more profitable.

The Dutch did much better investing their profits than the Spanish and Portuguese. Enriched by its strong trade position in northern Europe, the Netherlands became a major banking center and also boasted the world's largest commercial fleet. During the 1600s, the Dutch earned vast profits from selling Indonesian coffee and spices to other Europeans, and they invested much of these profits in their domestic economy. In addition, a large share of Portuguese and Spanish wealth ended up in the Netherlands. The Dutch were the strongest European power for most of the seventeenth century until they were finally eclipsed by England.

The English enjoyed the most long-term success. Profits from the Americas and India greatly benefited England, which had replaced the Netherlands as the dominant European power by the end of the 1600s. In the 1700s England held the most powerful position in the Atlantic System, with large amounts of wealth flowing into cities such as Liverpool, Glasgow, and Bristol from the slave, tobacco, and sugar trades. The colonial wealth enriched businessmen and bankers, who could now easily mobilize capital for investment in trade, technology, and manufacturing. These factors gave England unique advantages that it fully exploited in the 1700s and 1800s.

During the Early Modern Era, the Americas were transformed and linked to the rest of the globe, and these two outcomes reshaped world history. The conquest and exploitation of Native Americans and the acquisition of American resources gave some Europeans a decided economic advantage over other Eurasian powers, such as China, India, and the Ottoman Empire. The profits from American metals, often mined by Native Americans, and American crops, chiefly grown by African slaves, enriched Europe and shifted economic power in the world. Ultimately, this economic power also added to European political and military strength. By the late 1700s or early 1800s several European countries, especially Britain, had surpassed a declining China in wealth, living standards, and power.

SECTION SUMMARY

■ African slaves in the Americas were treated as commodities, and resistance to slavery was rarely successful, though freed slaves had somewhat more success in Latin America than they did in North America.

■ Elements of African religion, music, language, and agriculture all found their way into American culture, though they were accepted more readily by the Portuguese than by other European colonists.

■ The slave trade and plantation economies helped spur European capitalism and were extremely profitable to Europeans and North American colonists.

■ Spain and Portugal wasted the wealth they derived from their colonies, but the Dutch and the English invested it wisely and, as a result, gained an advantage over other world powers.

 Online Study Center ACE the Test

✦ Chapter Summary

After Columbus first landed in the Americas in 1492, powerful forces were unleashed around the Atlantic Ocean that generated a great historical transition. During the Early Modern Era, European explorers seeking a route to Asia, beginning with Columbus, and then conquerors seeking wealth brought the Americas and their peoples into a permanent relationship with the Eastern Hemisphere. The Spanish, Portuguese, English, and French built vast colonial empires in the Americas, using their superior military power to subjugate American peoples. The majority of Native American people perished from disease and other causes; American societies, including the great Aztec and Inca Empires, were destroyed and placed under European colonial control; and the survivors saw their lives changed enormously. The encounters created new worlds for the surviving Native Americans as well as for the African slaves and Europeans who moved to the Americas. The Native American and mixed-descent peoples had to adjust to colonial rule, Africans to the trauma of servitude, and the European colonizers and settlers to cultural resistance.

Some of the main changes derived from economic activities. The economic evolution of the Americas, especially mining and plantation agriculture, created a tremendous market for labor. Mine owners conscripted Native American workers, and planters exploited enslaved Africans and their descendants. The slave trade linked the Americas closely to the larger world, and the emerging Atlantic System closely connected Europe, West Africa, and the Americas, mostly to the benefit of Europe and European colonists. Gradually American colonies became connected to the emerging world economy as producers of raw materials, usually metals or cash crops, and as consumers of European goods. Some colonists in English North America built more diversified economies, in contrast to the monocultures of the Caribbean and Latin America. The Spanish and Portuguese initially prospered from their conquests but later squandered the resources they obtained, while the English and Dutch capitalized on their activities to achieve greater wealth and power. American history was thus not only a dynamic saga of indigenous development but also, beginning in the late fifteenth century, the story of increasing integration into larger global processes.

 *Online Study Center* Improve Your Grade Flashcards

Key Terms

conquistadors	mestizos	monoculture
Paulistas	mulattos	development
voyageurs	Black Legend	plantation zone
Columbian Exchange	Metis	maroons
audiencias	haciendas	
creoles	encomienda	

Suggested Reading

Books

Altman, Ida, et al. *The Early History of Greater Mexico*. Upper Saddle River, N.J.: Prentice-Hall, 2003. An excellent survey of Mexico in this era.

Brown, Jonathan C. *Latin America: A Social History of the Colonial Period*. 2nd ed. Belmont, Calif.: Wadsworth, 2004. A detailed survey on Europeans, Indians, and Africans.

Captive Passage: The Transatlantic Slave Trade and the Making of the Americas. Washington, D.C.: Smithsonian Institution Press, 2002. Excellent collection of essays for the general reader.

Conniff, Michael L., and Thomas J. Davis. *Africans in the Americas: A History of the Black Diaspora*. New York: The Blackburn Press, 2002. An introduction to the slave trade and the African heritage in the Americas.

Cook, Noble David. *Born to Die: Disease and New World Conquest, 1492–1650*. New York: Cambridge University Press, 1998. One of the best scholarly introductions to the topic.

Crosby, Alfred W. *The Columbian Exchange: Biological and Cultural Consequences of 1492*. 30th anniversary ed. New York: Praeger, 2002. A pioneering study of the exchange of plants, animals, diseases, and foods.

Curtin, Philip D. *The Rise and Fall of the Plantation Complex: Essays in Atlantic History*. Cambridge: Cambridge University Press, 1990. One of the best studies of the plantation zone in the Americas.

Fischer, Steven R. *A History of the Pacific Islands*. New York: Palgrave, 2002. Provides coverage of these centuries.

Fuentes, Carlos. *The Buried Mirror: Reflections on Spain and the New World*. Boston: Mariner Books, 1999. A readable overview by a Mexican scholar of the interaction of peoples and cultures.

Hoffer, Peter C. *The Brave New World: A History of Early America*. Boston: Houghton Mifflin, 2000. A lively, comprehensive portrait of North America in this era.

Kicza, John E. *Resilient Cultures: America's Native Peoples Confront European Colonization, 1500–1800*. Upper Saddle River, N.J.: Prentice-Hall, 2003. A brief survey of the encounters throughout the Americas.

Martin, Cheryl E. and Mark Wasserman. *Latin America and its People.* New York: Longman, 2005. A readable survey text.

Mattoso, Katia M. de Queiros. *To Be a Slave in Brazil, 1550–1888.* Translated by Arthur Goldhammer. New Brunswick: Rutgers University Press, 1986. An in-depth look at the context of Brazilian slavery and the slave experience.

Mintz, Sidney W. *Sweetness and Power: The Place of Sugar in Modern History.* Reprint ed. New York: Penguin, 1995. The best introduction to the role of sugar and sugar planting in this era.

Thornton, John. *Africa and Africans in the Formation of the Atlantic World, 1400–1800.* 2nd ed. Cambridge: Cambridge University Press, 1998. A provocative examination of Africa and the African diaspora in the Atlantic world.

Viola, Herman J. and Carolyn Margolis, eds. *Seeds of Change: Five Hundred Years Since Columbus.* Washington, D.C.: Smithsonian Institution Press, 1991. Excellent collection of readable essays on the changes fostered by European exploration and conquest.

Websites

Africans in America: America's Journey Through Slavery (http://www.pbs.org/wgbh/aia/home.html). A useful website offering materials relevant to a documentary series broadcast on Public Television.

The Columbian Exchange (http://www.nhc.rtp.nc.us:8080/tserve/nattrans/ntecoindian/essays/columbian.htm). A useful set of essays compiled by Alfred Crosby.

Early America (http://earlyamerica.com/earlyamerica/index.html). Offers primary sources on the thirteen North American colonies in the eighteenth century.

Internet Resources for Latin America (http://lib.nmsu.edu/subject/bord/laguia/). An outstanding site with links to many resources.

1492: An Ongoing Voyage (http://metalab.unc.edu/expo/1492.exhibit/Intro.html). An electronic exhibit from the Library of Congress on pre- and post-Columbian Europe, Africa, and the Americas.

Pictorial Images of the Transatlantic Slave Trade: A Media Database (http://hitchcock.itc.virginia.edu/SlaveTrade/). A searchable collection of three hundred images on the experiences of enslaved Africans.

CHAPTER 18

South Asia, Southeast Asia, and East Asia: Triumphs and Challenges, 1450–1750

Online Study Center

This icon will direct you to interactive activities and study materials on the website: college.hmco. com/pic/lockard1e

"Southern Barbarians" This painting on a sixteenth-century Japanese screen, decorated with gold leaf, depicts a Portuguese sea captain, shaded by a parasol carried by his black servant, being greeted by black-robed Jesuit missionaries in the port of Nagasaki. His porters carry gifts for the Japanese merchants. (Michael Holford)

A Goa Market A Dutch traveler, Jan Huygen Van Linschoten, made this plate while living in the Portuguese-ruled port city of Goa in the 1580s. It shows a street scene, including market stalls and, on the far right, a Portuguese woman walking with two Indian maids. Some Indians, wearing crosses, have become Christians. (Cadbury Collection, Birmingham Central Library and City Archives)

South Asia's New Challenges

Before the mid-1700s European influence on India remained relatively modest. The European component of India's trade was small. For example, only some 10 percent of the silk and other cloth produced in Bengal in 1750 ended up in Europe. The internal dynamics of Indian politics, economic affairs, and religion still had more effect on the lives of most Indians than did the Europeans. But the Portuguese activity foreshadowed an increasingly active European presence. The Dutch, French, and English followed the Portuguese to Asia, and all attempted to impose their influence on parts of South Asia. The overextended Portuguese were hard-pressed to sustain their power against these European rivals, who had larger populations and were developing better ships and gunpowder weapons.

The Dutch challenged the Portuguese for domination of the Indian Ocean trade in the early 1600s, eventually destroying their power in South and Southeast Asia and gaining partial control over the Indian Ocean commerce. In 1602 Dutch merchants in Amsterdam, with the goal of tapping into the Asian trade, formed the well-financed Dutch East India Company, a private company with government backing that had its own armed fleet and operated in conjunction with other Dutch activities. In South Asia the Dutch concentrated their attention on Sri Lanka, gaining control of some of the coastal regions from the Portuguese in the 1640s. They remained in Sri Lanka, often intermarrying with local people, until they were ousted by the British in the early 1800s. Neither the Dutch nor the Portuguese before them were able to defeat and occupy the main kingdom of Kandy (KAN-dee) in central Sri Lanka. Only in 1815 did Kandy fall to the British.

Soon the French joined the competition, forming their own East India Company in 1664. In the later 1600s and early 1700s the French established a trading presence at Surat and Calcutta, and they built a military and commercial base at the southeast coast town of Pondicherry (pondir-CHEH-ree). The vigorous French competition for Indian merchandise generated tensions with the English. The two countries were also bitter rivals in Europe, and the resulting antagonisms sometimes spilled over into conflict in India. For example, in 1746 the English and French fought fierce battles for dominance in southeast India that also involved local Indian states and destabilized the region's politics.

The English, with a rapidly growing commercial economy, became the main threat to the Mughals, Dutch, and French in Asia. In 1600 British investors formed the British East India Company in London, and English traders working for the company visited various ports. But they also built a fort at Madras (muh-DRAS) (today known as Chennai) on the southeast Indian coast and established a stable commercial base at Surat in northwest India, with Mughal permission. At Surat the English forged a commercial alliance with the Parsis (PAHR-seez), the Zoroastrian descendants of Persian refugees who were leading traders in India.

By the late 1600s the English were increasing their presence in India and, in 1717, they established bases at Bombay (today called Mumbai) and Calcutta, both then sparsely populated backwaters, for collecting and exporting textiles, indigo, and saltpeter (an ingredient for gunpowder). Soon they controlled these towns. When Surat rapidly declined after a Mughal governor imprisoned the port's leading merchant, to whom he was deeply in debt, many Parsis left Surat for better prospects in Bombay, again working closely with the English for their mutual benefit. But outside of Bombay, Calcutta, and Madras, English officials still had to negotiate with the Mughals or local princes for trading privileges. When piracy and banditry grew rapidly as Mughal authority collapsed, the law and order in the three English-run towns, secured by an increasing English military presence, attracted Indian settlers. English and Indian merchants in the three English bases prospered. The growing English presence in India also had consequences in England, where competition from Indian textile imports spurred local textile manufacturers to cut costs, helping stimulate English industrialization.

By the mid-eighteenth century the English were strong enough to treat local rulers with less deference and expand their control from their three bases into the surrounding regions. When local Indian governments resisted this encroachment, the English resorted to military force. By the 1750s this had resulted in a war in Bengal, where, from their Calcutta base, the English now began their long period of military conquest in South Asia. Eventually they controlled nearly all of South Asia except for a few small enclaves, such as Portuguese Goa and French Pondicherry. The English conquest and its momentous impact recalled age-old patterns in South Asia, which had often been conquered by outsiders, including people, such as the Mughals, of different cultural and religious backgrounds. But now, with the English, India faced a major new challenge.

SECTION SUMMARY

- The Muslim Mughal Empire attained great riches and, especially under Akbar, maintained an enlightened rule over religiously diverse India, but it began to decline after the fall of Akbar.

- The Indian economy, already strong, expanded greatly as extensive foreign trade brought an influx of silver and enriched entrepreneurs.

- Tensions existed between Indian Muslims and Hindus, though some were able to bridge the gap through mysticism and others joined sects such as the Sikhs that blended or transcended the dominant religions.

- The Mughal decline hastened under Aurangzeb, a harsh and corrupt ruler who was particularly resented by non-Muslims, whom he persecuted and taxed at high rates.

- As a result of their military prowess, Portuguese traders gained a significant share of trade with India, though they never completely controlled it.

- The Dutch, French, and English all competed with each other and with the Portuguese for dominance of trade with India, with the English growing increasingly strong by the mid-eighteenth century.

Southeast Asia and Global Connections

How did Southeast Asia become more fully integrated into the world economy?

Southeast Asia, the region south of China and east of India, had long been a cosmopolitan center where peoples, religions, ideas, and products met. Southeast Asians participated in the wider hemispheric trade and most adopted Theravada Buddhism, Confucianism, or Islam. The Portuguese arrival at Melaka inaugurated a new era of transregional contacts during which European adventurers, traders, missionaries, and soldiers were active in the region. Several areas were influenced by the West before 1750, particularly Malaya, the Philippine Islands, and parts of Indonesia. However, in most parts of Southeast Asia, including strong kingdoms such as Siam, Burma, and Vietnam, Western influence remained weak until the nineteenth century.

Southeast Asian Transitions

European activity was only one aspect of the Early Modern Era in Southeast Asia. The region was undergoing a transition that included commercial growth, political change, increasingly productive agriculture, and expansion of Islam and Buddhism. Partly because of increasing connections with European, Chinese, Arab, and Indian merchants, commerce increased between the 1400s and 1700s, and Southeast Asia remained an essential hub in the maritime trade network linking East Asia with India and the Middle East. Sailing ships still stopped in the region's ports to exchange goods or wait for the monsoon winds to shift. The growing regional trade attracted merchants from afar. For example, in 1650 the capital city of Arakan (AIR-ah-kan), a coastal kingdom in today's western Burma, attracted many traders from the Middle East, Central Asia, Africa, and India. Among the region's maritime traders were the Indonesians, who for centuries had even visited the north coast of Australia to obtain items such as ornamental shells and pearls.

Increased trade encouraged political centralization, the growth of cities, and the spread of world religions. Larger, more centralized states absorbed neighboring smaller states: on the mainland some twenty states in the fourteenth century had been reduced to less than a dozen by the early eighteenth century, with Siam, Vietnam, and Burma being the most influential. Economic dynamism enhanced the value of regional ports such as Melaka, Ayuthia (ah-YUT-uh-yuh) in Siam, Pegu (Peh-GOO) in Burma's Irrawaddy Delta, and Banten (BAN-ten) in West Java. Thanks to the increased amounts of products being obtained and transported, and the wealth this created, urban merchants became a powerful group in local politics. Revenue from trade became more crucial than agricultural taxes in many states. However, agriculture remained a major activity, and new crops and varieties of rice spurred population growth. At the same

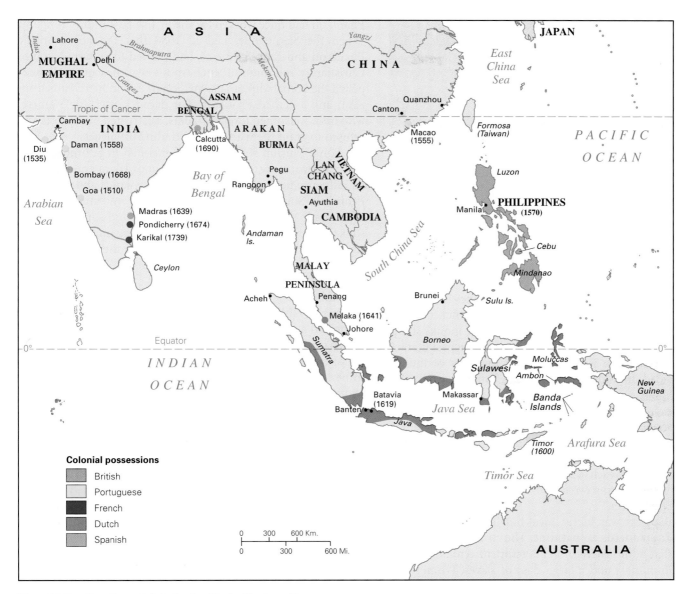

Map 18.2   Southeast Asia in the Early Modern Era
Much of Southeast Asia remained independent, able to deflect European ambitions, but the Portuguese
had captured the port of Melaka, Timor, and the Moluccas (Maluku), and the Spanish had colonized the
Philippines. In the 1600s the Dutch displaced the Portuguese from Melaka and the Moluccas, and ruled
part of Java from Batavia.

time, Theravada Buddhism dug deeper roots on the Southeast
Asian mainland, and Islam continued to spread throughout the
Malay Peninsula and the islands of Indonesia and the southern
Philippines. As a result of increased trade and exposure to new
religions, cultures were opened to the outside world.

Buddhist and Islamic Societies

Various Southeast Asian societies remained vigorous in this
era, in both the Buddhist and Islamic realms (see Map 18.2).
Among the strongest states with a mostly Theravada Buddhist
population was Siam, governed from 1350 to 1767 by kings
based at Ayuthia (see Chronology: Southeast Asia, 1450–1750).
Siam was involved in maritime trade and developed a regional

empire, extending its influence into Cambodia and some of
the small Lao (laow) states along the Mekong River. Its competition with the Burmese, Vietnamese, and the largest Lao state,
Lan Xang (lan chang), for regional dominance occasionally led
to war. Indeed, in the 1560s a Burmese army ravaged Siam and
sacked Ayuthia, carrying back to Burma thousands of Siamese
prisoners and their families. In Burma, the sophistication of
Siam's society was reflected in the occupational skills of these
Siamese captives: actor, actress, architect, artist, blacksmith,
carpenter, coiffeur, cook, coppersmith, goldsmith, lacquer-
ware maker, painter, perfume maker, silversmith, stone carver,
wood carver, and veterinarian.

Siam eventually recovered from Burma's conquest and
flourished. For example, during the reign of King Narai (na-RY)

(r. 1656–1688), the king used some of his revenues to promote literature and art, often with a Buddhist emphasis, thus fostering a cultural renaissance. Since Theravada Buddhist monks sponsored many village schools, Siam had one of the highest literacy rates in the premodern world. The high numbers of literate readers provided an audience for writers, some of whom focused on religious themes while others addressed more earthly affairs. For example, a long poem by Sri Mahosot (shree ma-HO-sut) describes the courtship rituals of young people along the Ayuthia riverside during the evening hours: "O beautiful night! Excited voices on the riverbank. Couples closely embraced they stare at each other. There is smiling, touching, singing in chorus, looking eye to eye. There is excitement, craving and longing forever."[8]

Siamese society was hierarchical but liberal and tolerant by the world's standards at that time. The royal family and the aristocracy that administered the government remained aloof from the commoners and a large class of slaves. Women enjoyed rights, including that of operating village and town markets. Most of the ruling elite, including the king, were ardent Buddhists, and Theravada Buddhism encouraged tolerance toward other faiths. In 1636 a Dutch trader contrasted the tolerance of Siamese Buddhists with the zealous proselytizing of Christians and Muslims in that era. He observed that the Siamese did not condemn any "opinions, but believe that all, though of differing tenets, living virtuously, may be saved, all services which are performed with zeal being acceptable to the great God. And the Christians [and Muslims] are both permitted the free exercise of their religions."[9] Ayuthia's openness to merchants and creative people from all over Eurasia made it a vibrant crossroads of exchange and influence.

However, while open to the outside world, Siam had to contend with increasing European activity. English, French, and Dutch traders all established operations in Ayuthia. King Narai, who had regularly sent missions to Persia, India, and China, sent three diplomatic missions to the French court of Louis XIV to obtain Western maps and scientific knowledge. Narai employed several foreigners as officials, including a Persian Muslim as prime minister and a Greek merchant, Constantine Phaulkon (FALL-kin), as superintendent of foreign trade.

Phaulkon had once worked for the British East India Company. When the Siamese learned in 1688 that the opportunistic Phaulkon and French officials had plotted to convert Narai to Christianity and station French troops near the capital, they expelled the French diplomats, missionaries, and merchants from Siam and executed Phaulkon. For decades after, the Siamese, who once welcomed foreign traders, mistrusted Europeans and refused to grant them any special trading privileges.

Some Muslim societies also flourished in Southeast Asia. Trade networks fostered the expansion of Islam and increased its influence throughout the Indonesian islands and the Malay Peninsula. Southeast Asian Muslims who could afford to do so often made the long pilgrimage to Mecca and some sent their sons to the Middle East for study, reinforcing links between the regions. Various societies adapted Islam to their own cultural traditions. The Javanese often superimposed Islam, often with a Sufi flavor, on the existing foundation of Hinduism and mystical animism (spirit worship), producing an eclectic and tolerant mix of faiths. Some other peoples, including most Malays, embraced a more orthodox version of Islam. As more Muslim merchants called at ports with Muslim rulers, the strengthening of trade ties enriched states. The mixing of Islam and maritime trade encouraged mobility and thus connections to the wider world. For example, Hamzah Fansuri (HOM-sah fan-SIR-ee), a Sufi poet from west Sumatra famed for his mystical and romantic writings, lived for a time in Ayuthia and for a time in Baghdad. Fansuri was a follower of an earlier Spain-born mystic, Ibn al-Arabi (1165–1240), who taught, like Vedanta Hinduism, that all reality is one and everything that exists is part of the divine. By implication, al-Arabi and Fansuri's approach downplayed ritual and law and emphasized dreams, visions, and achieving ecstasy to know God.

Islam also changed gender relations. As in most of Southeast Asia, women in Indonesia had often enjoyed independence. However, Islam, rooted in patriarchal Arab traditions, diminished women's rights in some Indonesian societies. For instance, in Acheh (AH-cheh) in northern Sumatra, where four successive women had ruled in the later 1600s, women were eventually prohibited from holding royal power. But elsewhere women often continued to play key roles. Muslim courts on Java and other islands were often filled with hundreds, sometimes thousands, of women. Some were wives and concubines, but most were attendants, guards, or textile workers. By the 1600s, if not earlier, *batik*, the beautiful cloth produced in Java by a wax and dying process, had appeared. The time-consuming work of making fine batik was mostly done by women in the courts and villages. Batik arts later spread throughout the world.

Southeast Asian Trade and the European Challenge

Southeast Asia's wealth and resources, especially spices such as cloves, nutmeg, and pepper, attracted European merchants and conquerors to the region. The Portuguese who occupied Melaka were the forerunners of a powerful and destabilizing European presence that transformed Southeast Asia between

1500 and 1900. By controlling Melaka, the Portuguese now had an advantage against their European and Malay rivals and had reshaped world trade, as the victorious admiral Albuquerque boasted: "Melaka is the source of all the spices and drugs which the [Muslims] carry every year to [the Middle East]. Cairo and Mecca will be entirely ruined, and Venice will receive no spices unless her merchants go and buy them in Portugal."[10] A few years later the Portuguese brutally conquered the Spice Islands, known as Maluku (muh-LOO-ku) (Moluccas), in northeast Indonesia, thus gaining nearly total control of the valuable spice trade to Europe.

But, as in India, Portuguese power in Southeast Asia proved short-lived. Like the East African ports they occupied earlier, Melaka languished under Portuguese control, since fewer Muslim merchants chose to endure the higher taxes and Portuguese intolerance of Islam. The Portuguese effort to convert subject peoples to Christianity made them unwelcome, and they also faced constant challenge from various neighboring states. In dealing with these challenges, Portuguese policies often involved brutal force. The Jesuit missionary St. Francis Xavier, a Spaniard, described Portuguese behavior in the Spice Islands as little more than discovering new ways of conjugating the verb *to steal*. Although the Dutch replaced the Portuguese in Melaka in 1641, a small Catholic, Portuguese-speaking community still lives in the city of Melaka. Furthermore, for several centuries Portuguese became a language of trade and commerce in some coastal regions of Asia, from Basra in Iraq to ports in Vietnam.

Portuguese activities spurred the Spanish, Dutch, English, and French to compete for markets, resources, Christian converts, and power in Southeast Asia. The Spanish conquered the Philippines, and the Dutch gained some control of the Indian Ocean maritime trade by force and conquered Java and the Spice Islands. Preoccupied with India and the Americas, the English mainly sought only trade relations in this era. The French became involved in Vietnam beginning in 1615. The French sought trade but also dispatched Catholic missionaries, who recruited a small following of Vietnamese. The Vietnamese used the Chinese writing system, and to undercut Confucian influence on Vietnamese culture, French missionaries created a romanized Vietnamese alphabet, which in the twentieth century became the official Vietnamese writing system. But European power had its limits. Southeast Asian states such as Siam, Vietnam, Burma, and Acheh were strong enough to resist over three hundred years of persistent effort by Westerners to gain complete political, social, and economic domination, which they achieved only by 1900.

The Philippines Under Spanish Colonization

The greatest Western impact in Southeast Asia before 1800 came in the Philippine Islands, which were conquered by Spain. For over nearly three centuries of its colonial rule, beginning in 1565, Spain imposed the Catholic religion and many aspects of Spanish culture on the people with a policy known as **Hispanization**. However, the Filipinos managed to develop a diversity of cultures by mixing their indigenous customs with the Spanish influences. Under Spanish rule, the Philippines became a key participant in the new world economy.

Spanish Colonization   Spanish interest in the Philippines was a result of their activities in the Americas and their quest for a sea route to Asia. The first Spanish ships to reach the islands in 1521, commanded by Ferdinand Magellan, were part of the first successful effort to circumnavigate the world, though Magellan himself did not complete the voyage. Magellan pressured the Filipinos he encountered to adopt Christianity. He ordered a local chief to burn all his peoples' religious figures and replace them with a cross, which every villager should worship every day on their knees. Magellan's arrogant demands inspired opposition, and he was killed in a skirmish with hostile Filipinos. Today, on the beach on Cebu Island where Magellan died, a memorial honors Lapulapu (LAH-pu-LAH-pu), the chief who led the attack, as the first Filipino to repel European aggression. When, after visiting the Spice Islands, Magellan's ships returned to Spain, they had proved that Columbus was correct that Asia could be reached by sailing west from Europe (see Chapter 17).

Magellan had chanced upon an island group inhabited by some 1 to 2 million people divided into many distinct ethnic groups and speaking over a hundred Malay languages. The population was scattered across 7,000 islands, although the majority lived on the two largest islands, Luzon (loo-ZON) and Mindanao (min-duh-NOW). Muslims occupied the southernmost islands, and Islam was slowly spreading northward, but most Filipinos mixed belief in one supreme being with animism, for which the Spanish labeled them immoral devil worshipers. Remote from the mainland and western Indonesia, the islands had historically received relatively little cultural influence from India or China. Nonetheless, they were not completely isolated. A few hundred Chinese traders lived in the major towns, and some Filipinos traveled as far as Melaka and Burma as maritime traders. Many Filipinos used a simple writing system. Unlike the kingdoms of Java or Siam, the largest Filipino political units were villages led by chiefs.

When, four decades after Magellan's death, the Spaniards returned to conquer and evangelize, they renamed the islands the Philippines after their monarch, Philip II, known as "the most Catholic of kings." Given the ethnic divisions and lack of a dominant Philippine state, the militarily superior Spanish had little trouble conquering the islands and co-opting local chiefs. But the Muslims in the south, called **Moros** by the Spanish, were never completely pacified, and Spanish authority there remained mostly nominal. Today some southern Muslims seek independence from the Christian-dominated country. The Spanish set up their colonial government in

---

Hispanization   The process by which, over nearly three centuries of Spanish colonial rule beginning in 1565, the Catholic religion and Spanish culture were imposed on the Philippine people.

Moros   The Spanish term for the Muslim peoples of the southern Philippines.

Manila (muh-NIL-uh), located on a fine natural harbor, which they also hoped to use as a base for trade with China.

The Catholic Church took a major role in the colonial Philippine enterprise. The church governed various regions outside of Manila and acquired great wealth. In many districts priests collected taxes and sold the crops, such as sugar, grown by Filipino parishioners. Catholic friars, accompanying the soldiers, began the process of conversion, and several religious orders competed to gain the most converts. Indeed, the Spanish colonial regime gave the missionaries special authority, and the Spanish crown financed the conversion efforts. Missionaries concentrated on the children of village leaders but, to better control and evangelize the Filipinos, they also required people to move into towns. Few schools were opened outside Manila, and what education existed was in church hands and emphasized religious doctrine. To control competing ideas, the Spanish destroyed nearly all of the pre-Spanish writings, which they considered pagan. The effort to spread Christianity took at least eighty years. Eventually around 85 percent of the Filipinos adopted Roman Catholicism.

However, Filipinos accepted Christianity on their own terms and incorporated their own animist traditions into the religion, to the disgust of the Spanish. Friendly spirits became Christian saints, and miracles attributed to Jesus or the Virgin Mary became the new form of magic. Some Filipinos even used religious festivals to subtly express opposition to Spanish rule. For example, the Spanish introduced passion plays on the life and death of Jesus as a way to spread Christian devotion and morality. But Filipinos wrote their own plays that expressed their anticolonial sentiments, such as by presenting Jesus as a social activist of humble background who was tormented by a corrupt ruling class. Since the Spanish conquerors had contempt for the common people, few Filipinos were able to rise in the church hierarchy or in government. Reflecting these biases, one Spanish observer mocked the Filipino priest as "a caricature of everybody. He is a patchwork of many things and is nothing. He is an enemy of Spain."[11]

Colonial Economy and Society

Inequality was not limited to government and the church; it also showed up in economic and social patterns. The colonial economy forged a rural society based on plantation agriculture and tenant farming, implanting a permanent gap between the extraordinarily rich landowners and the impoverished peasants. Traditionally the Filipinos had grown rice for themselves and some sugar to sell to foreign merchants. The Spanish encouraged a much stronger emphasis on lucrative cash crops, such as sugar and hemp, for sale on the world market. The religious orders, Spanish corporations, the Spanish crown, and the families of pro-Spanish chiefs owned most of the farmland. Peasants expressed their dissatisfaction by revolting against local landlords or the corrupt Spanish system. The Filipinos, once masters of the land, mostly became tenants working for a few powerful landowning families or the church. Priests and landowners told them their religious duty was to labor hard for others—they would get their just rewards later in heaven.

Although the Spanish created a country and expanded the economy, they did not construct a cohesive society. Regional and ethnic loyalties remained dominant. In fact, by their decentralized government, the Spanish encouraged regionalism. The Spaniards occupied the top spots, controlling the government and church. The great majority of Spanish lived in Manila, often in luxury, and few outside the church ever learned to speak local languages. Below them were mixed-descent people, known as mestizos, who resulted from intermarriage and cohabitation of Spanish men with Filipinas, and a few Filipino families who descended from chiefs. Below them were Chinese immigrants, who worked as merchants and craftsmen. Some Chinese became rich, but most remained middle class, especially those who opened small shops in rural towns. The Chinese often became Catholic, and Chinese men often married Filipinas, forming the basis for a Chinese mestizo community. Leaders of the Philippines today are frequently of Chinese or Spanish mestizo ancestry. But while the Spanish needed the Chinese as middlemen, they also despised, persecuted, and sometimes expelled them. On occasion, when

Chinese Mestizo Couple   This painting by a French artist shows two wealthy, well-dressed Chinese mestizos riding in Manila. Chinese mestizos, products of marriages between Chinese immigrants and Filipino or Spanish women, played a key role in colonial life.   [From Edgar Wickberg, *The Chinese in Philippine Life 1850-1898* (New Haven and London: Yale University Press, 1965)]

their resentment of Chinese wealth or concern with growing Chinese numbers became intense, Spanish forces slaughtered the residents of Manila's large Chinatown.

The lowest social status was held by the vast majority of Filipinos, whom the Spanish called **Indios** (Indies people). They faced many legal restrictions; for example, they were prohibited from dressing like Spaniards. The Filipinos retained their traditionally strong communal orientation, including powerful kinship networks and their close family ties. However, since the Spanish culture and church devalued women, Filipinas lost the high position they had enjoyed in pre-Spanish society and now faced restrictions on their activities. For instance, the female priestesses integral to Filipino animism were pushed to the margins of society by male Catholic priests, one of whom described the priestesses as "loathsome creatures, foul, obscene, truly damnable. My task [is] to reduce them to order."[12] Despite male prejudice and a narrowing of gender roles, Filipinas continued to control family finances and engage in small-scale trade.

Indonesia and the Dutch

In the seventeenth century the Dutch arrived, displacing the Portuguese from most of their bases and becoming the dominant European power in Southeast Asia. The Dutch gradually expanded their influence from the Spice Islands to other islands, notably Java. Since they built their empire in the Indies over a period of three hundred years, their impact varied widely over time. The Dutch sought wealth but, unlike the Portuguese and Spanish, cared little about spreading their culture and religion. Nonetheless, they fostered a unique colonial society.

The Rise of Dutch Power The Dutch became Europe's most prosperous society during the 1600s, in large part because of their trade and conquests in Asia, especially Indonesia. Dutch ships had long carried spices from Portugal to northern Europe. In 1595 a Dutch fleet visited the Spice Islands of Maluku and brought back spices to Holland. Over the next several decades the Dutch, after bloody battles, dislodged the Portuguese from most of their scattered outposts, including Maluku. Finally, they captured the Portuguese-controlled port of Melaka in 1641. But although they tried to revive Melaka as a trade entrepôt, the city never recovered its earlier glory.

Over the next several centuries the Dutch gradually gained control of the islands of Indonesia, except for the Portuguese-ruled eastern half of the island of Timor. They eliminated all competition, often by military force, and quickly became hated for their ruthlessness. For example, in 1623 the Dutch massacred the English residents of a base on Ambon (am-BOHN) Island. As Dutch forces attacked and occupied the prosperous trading city of Makassar (muh-KAS-uhr), in southeast Sulawesi (SOO-la-WAY-see), in 1659, the city's sultan asked: "Do you believe that God has preserved for your trade alone islands

which lie so distant from your homeland?" The sultan's secretary, Amin, wrote a long poetic account about the disaster: "Listen, sir, to my advice; never make friends with the Dutch. No country can call itself safe when they are around."[13] Both sides sparked conflict, but with their superior military power, the Dutch often slaughtered their Indonesian opponents by the thousands.

The Dutch were also well-organized, resourceful, and shrewd diplomats, allying themselves with one state against a rival state. While exploiting local conflicts, however, they sometimes were drawn into civil wars or were faced with stiff resistance. For example, Shaikh Yusuf (ca. 1624–1699) from Sulawesi had studied Islamic knowledge in Acheh and Arabia and had become a spiritual adviser to the sultan of Banten, a small trading state in western Java. Becoming enraged by Dutch practices that threatened Islamic morality, such as the toleration of gambling, opium smoking, and cock fighting, in 1683 he led 2,000 followers into a holy war against the Dutch. It failed, however, and Yusuf was exiled to Dutch-ruled South Africa, where he died.

With trade as their major goal, for several centuries the Dutch left administration of their Indonesian bases to the Dutch East India Company, which had great capital and large resources for pursuing profit. Since Holland was ten months away by boat, there was little guidance and few restraints on the company's power, and it used its goal of gaining a monopoly of trade in Southeast Asia to justify ruthless policies. If the people of a Spice Island grew restless, Dutch forces might exterminate them or carry them off as slaves to Java, Ceylon, or South Africa. For example, in 1621 the entire population of the spice-producing Banda (BAN-duh) Islands—some 15,000 people—were killed, taken away as slaves, or left to starve. To increase demand and reduce supply, the Dutch sometimes chopped down spice-growing trees and bushes en masse, leaving the population with no source of income.

The Dutch-Javan Encounter Eventually the Dutch concentrated on the rich island of Java, which had a flourishing mercantile economy tied to maritime trade and several competing sultanates. In the 1600s Java boasted at least two cities with over 100,000 people, and their population was a cosmopolitan mix drawn from throughout Asia. Javan artisans were noted for fine craftsmanship. For example, the island's smiths made perhaps the finest steel swords in the world. The commercial prowess of the Javanese, the main ethnic group on the island, was renowned in the region. Javanese women were prominent in business alongside the men, as an English observer noted: "It is usual for a husband to entrust his pecuniary affairs entirely to his wife. The women alone attend the markets, and conduct all the buying and selling."[14] Thus the Dutch did not come into an underdeveloped society, but one with living standards comparable to those in western Europe.

Capitalizing on Java's political instability and divisions, the Dutch slowly extended their power across the island after establishing a military and commercial base at a village they renamed Batavia, on the northwestern coast, in 1619. Batavia

---

Indios ("Indies peoples")   The Filipinos at the bottom of the Spanish colonial social structure, who faced many legal restrictions.

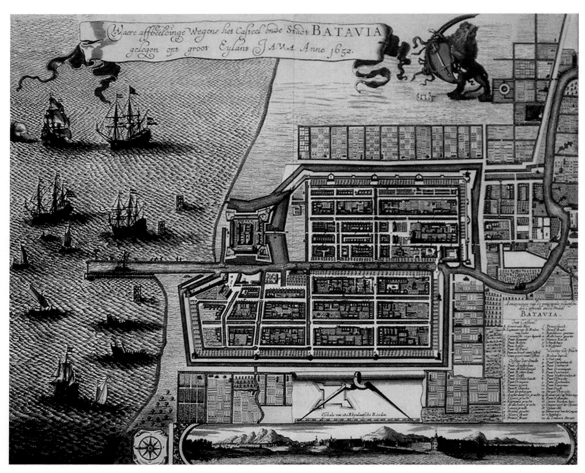

Batavia The Dutch built a port they called Batavia on the northwest coast of Java. Batavia, shown on this map from 1652, grew rapidly as the political and commercial center of the Dutch empire in Southeast Asia. (Royal Institute of Linguistics and Anthropology, Leiden)

later grew into a city, today known as Jakarta. Most of Java came under direct or indirect Dutch control by the end of the eighteenth century. The Dutch became preoccupied with consolidating their position in Java and the Spice Islands, especially after Batavia became a flourishing trading city. They co-opted the local elites and governed some districts through local rulers. Admiring the Chinese traders, who had operated in Java for centuries, the Dutch invited more Chinese to come in as middlemen. Dutch and Chinese entrepreneurs slowly displaced the Javanese merchant class, once major players in the world economy.

Soon the Dutch concentrated on making Java a source of wealth. The burden of economic change fell on the peasantry, most of whom grew rice. In the highlands of west Java, and later in Sumatra, peasants were forced to grow coffee for export through a system of annual quotas. Coffee, domesticated centuries earlier in Ethiopia and then grown in southern Arabia, had become a popular beverage in both the Middle East and Europe. The Dutch earned huge sums from this process, enough to finance much of Holland's industrialization in the nineteenth century. Coffee soon came to be called "java" in the West. Between 1726 and 1878 Holland controlled 50 to 75 percent of the world's coffee trade.

Through their political and economic activities, the Dutch gradually transformed Javan society and life. As in other colonies and pre-Dutch Java, inequality characterized the society. Europeans occupied the top rung, followed by those of mixed-descent, known as Eurasians, and the co-opted local aristocracy. Javanese now became even more preoccupied with social status, and the peasants were encouraged to treat the aristocratic officials with great awe and respect. The middle class was mostly Chinese. Like the Spanish in the Philippines, the Dutch came to fear the growing Chinese community, a fear that sometimes led to a massacre of Chinese in Batavia. The lower class included not only the peasants but also Javanese merchants. Denied real power, the Javanese royal courts turned inward to refine the traditional culture. As a result, the royal dances became fantastically fluid, graceful, and stylized; the batik fabrics produced by women at the courts more splendid and intricate.

Gradually the Dutch colonists, most of them men, became part of Javan society. Many Dutch found Javanese culture seductive and took local wives, owned slaves, dressed in Javanese clothes, and indulged in the delicious spicy curries, now enriched by American chilies. Other Dutch, however, criticized this behavior. Whatever their attitude toward local customs, most

Dutch lived in Batavia, which was built to resemble a city in the Netherlands. Its close-packed, stuffy houses and stagnant canals were poorly suited to the tropics, and the puritanical Dutch wore heavy woolen clothes in the tropical heat but bathed only once a week. The children of Dutch men and Javan women often grew up speaking Malay, the most common language in Batavia. Like many Southeast Asian cities, Batavia had a highly mixed, multiethnic society. The Dutch, who recognized religious freedom at home, spent little money on Christian missions.

Southeast Asians and the World Economy

The major changes experienced by Southeast Asians during the Early Modern Era reshaped global commerce. With the Portuguese, Dutch, and Spanish exporting luxury items such as Indonesian spices but also bulk products such as tin, sugar, and rice from their newly colonized possessions, the region became an even more crucial part of the developing world economy. Some historians trace the birth of a truly world economy to the founding of the Philippine city of Manila in 1571, which became the first hub linking Asia and the Americas across the Pacific. Each year Philippine crops and other Asian products, including Chinese silk and porcelain, were brought to Manila for export to Mexico. From there some products were shipped on to Europe. These Spanish galleons symbolized the new global reality. The galleons returned to Manila with European goods, mail, personnel, and vast amounts of silver to pay for Asian goods, draining Spanish imperial coffers and enriching Asian treasuries. Over half the silver mined in the Americas ended up in China. The American silver gave the Asian economy a great push, encouraging increased production of Philippine sugar, Chinese tea, and Indian textiles.

The Manila galleon trade was highly speculative, since Spanish businessmen bet their fortunes that the galleons would arrive in Mexico safely. Pirates, storms, and other obstacles made the voyages dangerous. For example, on a crossing in 1604, the *Espiritu Santo* became grounded on a shoal leaving Manila Bay, encountered a storm off California that destroyed much of its rigging, and was struck by lightning, which killed three crewman, before limping into the port of Acapulco two months late. Sometimes the galleons never completed their voyages. Thus, while investors could reap huge profits, they sometimes incurred huge losses. The unpredictable galleon trade fostered a "get rich quick" mentality rather than a long-term strategy to bring prosperity to the Philippines.

In spite of all the economic changes, Southeast Asians retained considerable continuity with the past. The West was not yet dominant in either political or economic spheres, except in a few widely scattered outposts such as Melaka, the Spice Islands, and the Philippines. The European interlopers had to compete with Chinese, Arab, Indian, and Southeast Asian merchants. Nor were Europeans the only growing political power. The Vietnamese, continuing their long expansion down the Vietnamese coast, had annexed the Mekong Delta by the late 1600s, and the Siamese forced the French to leave. In brief, the European powers had entered a wealthy, open, and dynamic region. Only by

the eighteenth century did the Southeast Asian commercial society begin to collapse under the weight of accelerating Western military and economic activity, combined with internal strife and increasingly expensive government structures.

SECTION SUMMARY

■ Increased trade in Southeast Asia led to greater political centralization and increased the influence of major world religions such as Islam and Buddhism.

■ Theravada Buddhism thrived in Siam, which was highly literate and cultured, while Islam flourished on the Malay Peninsula, where an orthodox form took hold, and in the Indonesian archipelago, where it blended with local traditions.

■ Europeans, beginning with the violent Portuguese and later including the Spanish, Dutch, English, and French, were attracted by Southeast Asia's riches and resources.

■ The Spanish conquered the Philippine Islands and eventually succeeded in converting local people to Christianity, though the Filipinos shaped Christianity to their own ends.

■ The militaristic Dutch came to dominate Southeast Asia, particularly Java, which they turned into a highly profitable coffee exporter, but whose culture they did not attempt to transform.

■ As a result of European colonization, Southeast Asia entered the world economy, though European speculators often focused on making quick money rather than strengthening the region's economy for the long term.

◆ Early Modern China and New Challenges

What factors enabled China to remain one of the world's strongest and most dynamic societies?

Two dynasties, the Ming followed by the Qing (ching), ruled China for more than half a millennium, between the overthrow of the Mongols and the advent of a republic in 1912 (see Map 18.3). These centuries make up one of the great eras of orderly government and social stability in history. Like western Europeans at this time, the Chinese enjoyed widening market networks and more cultivation of cash crops. China still remained one of the strongest, most industrialized societies through the eighteenth century, boasting a vibrant culture and economy. Because of its continuing strength and its location on the eastern fringe of Asia, European influence and pressure were relatively slight in the Early Modern Era. Although encounters with Europeans indicated the challenges ahead just as China began to experience political and technological decay, no other country could match the size, wealth, and power of Early Modern China.

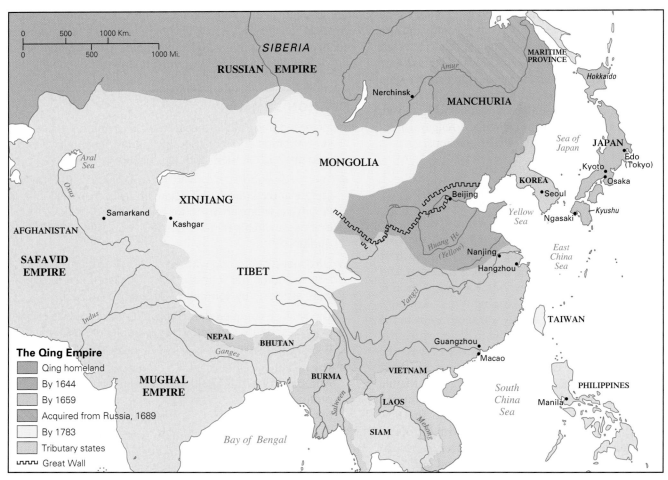

Map 18.3 Qing China and East Asia in the Early Modern Era
Qing China remained the colossus of eastern Eurasia, controlling a huge empire that included Tibet, Xinjiang, and Mongolia. Korea and Vietnam remained tributary states of China, but the Russians expanded into eastern Siberia. The Japanese partly secluded themselves from the outside world.

Online Study Center **Improve Your Grade** Interactive Map: The Qing Empire, 1644–1753

The Later Ming Dynasty

China under the Ming (1368–1644) remained strong and dynamic (see Chronology: China, 1450–1750). The imperial political system administered by the mandarins was supported by a highly productive agriculture and the world's largest, most diversified commercial economy. Although heavily regulated, commercial activity provided the people with numerous products and services, and the Mings' rebuilding of the transportation network centered on the Grand Canal made it easier to ship goods and hence stimulated manufacturing. Cotton fields in North China supplied a growing textile industry. Along with silk and tea, these textiles were exported to Japan and Southeast Asia for silver and spices.

For centuries China had been among the world leaders in scientific thought and technological invention. This inventiveness continued: late Ming and early Qing Chinese developed color woodblock printing and introduced new equipment into the textile industry. Better cotton gins, spinning wheels, and

other technologies for textile and silk production fostered growth and the employment of many more workers. Chinese also continued to publish scientific books.

At the same time, however, Ming China turned somewhat inward, concentrating on home affairs and the defense of the northern borders. Always self-sufficient and self-centered, China became increasingly ethnocentric, even antiforeign; the great maritime voyages of the early fifteenth century had ended, and the Ming court increasingly viewed foreign states as merely tribute providers. Although some foreign merchants continued to come to China, and Chinese merchants still went to Southeast Asia, the Ming launched a period of increased isolation, in contrast to the cosmopolitanism of the earlier Tang, Song, and Yuan periods. The Chinese, having turned inward, were not patrolling the Indian Ocean in their great junks when the first Portuguese ships arrived.

Misrule and other mounting problems helped undercut the Ming and led to dynastic change. During the later 1500s, crop failures, which caused famine, and a terrible plague killed millions in north China. In the 1590s the Ming had to dispatch soldiers and a large naval force to defend their Korean vassal from the Japanese, at a huge cost to the treasury. Adding to the pressure, Japanese pirates ravaged the southern coast and peasant revolts broke out. These problems opened the doors to the Manchus (MAN-chooz), a seminomadic pastoral people from Manchuria just northeast of China, who were angry at the migration of Chinese settlers into their homeland. United under a strong chief, the Manchus found collaborators among Chinese tired of the Ming failures. While peasant rebellions rocked the country, Manchu forces swept into China on horseback, routing the Ming. However, it took several decades to occupy and pacify the country, and Ming loyalists held out in the south and on the large offshore island of Taiwan for several decades.

Qing Empire and Society

The new Manchu rulers installed the Qing dynasty, which ruled from 1644 to 1912. The first Qing rulers were exceptionally competent overseers, governing from Beijing through the Chinese bureaucracy and patronizing Confucianism much like their Chinese predecessors. Although they retained their ethnic identity, forbidding Manchu intermarriage with Chinese, the Manchus knew that to be successful they would have to adopt Chinese institutions and culture to win the support of the Chinese people. Hence, like most earlier foreign rulers, the Manchus underwent voluntary assimilation to Chinese ways. Chinese served in high offices, and many villagers scarcely knew China had foreign rulers. Like earlier dynasties, the Qing relied on the mandarins, scholars educated in the Confucian classics, for administration.

Some Qing emperors were outstanding managers and hard workers, aware of their awesome responsibility and willing to temper arbitrary power. The most admired Qing ruler, the reflective Kangzi (kang-shee) (r. 1661–1722), wrote that "giving life to the people and killing people—these are the powers that an emperor has. He knows that administrative errors in government bureaus can be rectified, but that a criminal who is executed cannot be brought back to life any more than a chopped string can be joined together again."[15] Kangzi loved to tour the provinces inspecting public works and joining hunting expeditions. Like other emperors, he was also a

noted writer and painter, exemplifying the Confucian ideal of the virtuous ruler. His son and successor, Yongzheng (youngcheng) (r. 1723–1735), tried to improve social conditions. For example, he ordered that anyone held in hereditary servile status anywhere in the empire be freed. The law was aimed at groups in remote regions who still practiced forms of slavery.

The Manchus created the greatest Eurasian land empire since the Mongols, making China one of the world's major political powers. Qing armies reasserted Chinese control of the western and northern frontier, annexing Xinjiang (shinchang) ("New Dominions"), a desert region largely inhabited by Turkish-speaking Muslims, and Mongolia. For the first time in Chinese history, peace prevailed along the northern and western borderlands. Tibet, long a tributary state to China, was brought into the Manchu fold. While Tibetans shared with Manchus and Mongols the same mystical and magical version of Buddhism known as Lamaism (LAH-muh-iz-uhm), the Tibetans were ethnically and culturally different from Chinese. The Qing also incorporated Taiwan, off the east coast. This large, fertile island's original inhabitants were Malay peoples, but Chinese began immigrating there in large numbers in the 1600s.

Ming and Qing China owed their political and social stability in part to the Chinese gentry, whose power was based on their combined possession of land and office in an agrarian-based bureaucratic empire. As landlords and moneylenders, the gentry had dominated economic life in villages since the Tang dynasty. Natural disasters brought them even more land from bankruptcies. Because they owned land and could afford tutors, the gentry men also received a formal education and held scholarly degrees. The mid-Qing novel, *The Story of the Stone*, revealed the expectations for sons in gentry families: "A boy's proper business is to read books in order to gain an understanding of things, so that when he grows up he can play his part in governing the country."[16]

Under the Ming, a close relationship had developed between the local gentry and the imperial bureaucracy, a relationship that continued under the Qing. Most of the gentry made their peace with the Manchus and served the Qing, and together the Chinese gentry and the Manchu rulers sought to preserve the status quo. However, some of the gentry could not successfully negotiate the dynastic change. For example, the celebrated essayist, poet, and historian Zhang Dai (chang die) (1597–1680) lived a comfortable life during the late Ming, in part because the three generations of Zhang men before him had been high-ranking mandarins and he himself passed the rigorous civil service exams. His privileged status and wealth allowed him to support a wife and several consorts, by whom he had eight or ten children. As a rich man Zhang had ample leisure time, which he chiefly spent at a lakeside villa in Hangzhou (hahng choh), visiting tourist sites, collecting handcrafted lanterns, playing the lute, and getting together with a crab-eating club. However, in the 1640s the Zhangs ran afoul of changing political winds during the dangerous transition between the Ming and Qing dynasties, and they were reduced to poverty. Zhang Dai spent the remainder of his life writing about his family history, trying to recreate and memorialize the

Emperor Kangxi The Qing emperor Kangxi had one of the longest reigns in Chinese history, and his birthdays were given lavish public celebrations. In this print of Beijing, a crowd gathers around the royal dais while women observe the festivities from courtyards (foreground) and shopkeepers look on from their businesses. (Laurie Platt Winfrey, Inc)

Ming world in which the Zhangs had prospered.

Women had a complex status in the patriarchal society of Qing China. The education of women was frequently debated among the elite and was encouraged by some intellectuals. Some women from gentry and merchant families were educated informally, reading and even writing literature. Zhang Dai credited the Zhang women with keeping his extended family organized and with influencing major family decisions. However, elite women also had limited physical mobility because of footbinding, a custom introduced half a millennium earlier but which only became widespread during the Ming. Peasant women were usually illiterate but nonetheless played a key economic role. For example, women improved and promoted spinning and weaving tools. In the cloth industry, the men planted the cotton but the women picked the crop, processed it into yarn, and wove the finished product for sale. An eighteenth-century government report observed that "whole peasant families assemble, young and old; the mother-in-law leads her son's wives, the mother supervises her daughters; when the wicker lantern is lit and the starlight and moonlight come slanting down, still the click-clack of the spindle-wheels comes from the house."[17] But in many districts peasant women were gradually marginalized as their menfolk or large commercial farmers took over their livelihood in search of greater profits.

Chinese attitudes toward homosexuality fluctuated. The European traders and missionaries who visited in China in the sixteenth and seventeenth centuries were shocked at the Chinese tolerance toward homosexuality, fiercely punished in much of Europe. One Catholic missionary lamented that homosexual relations were neither forbidden in Chinese law nor considered shameful. However, some Chinese scholars blamed the downfall of the Ming on lax morality and convinced the Qing to penalize unconventional behavior, including homosexuality. Yet, by Europeans' standards, the Qing punishments were mild and the repression gradually ebbed. At least half of the Qing emperors are thought to have had same-sex bed-

mates. These relationships did not preclude marriage and family, and one Qing emperor with a male lover also fathered 27 children with his wives and concubines.

Thought and Culture

Along with social conditions and steady leadership, philosophy also contributed to the stability of the Ming and Qing period. Most Chinese remained comfortable with the eclectic philosophical and religious mix of Confucianism, Buddhism, and Daoism that had evolved in the Classical Era. Nonetheless, a renaissance of Confucian thought flourished during the Ming and early Qing, when changing times seemed to call for something more than mere memorization of Confucian classics written in the Classical Era. In response to these changes, some scholars developed an interpretation of Confucianism, known as neo-Confucianism, that incorporated elements of Buddhism and Daoism, stressed rational thinking, and reemphasized the natural goodness of people.

Like their contemporaries, the thinkers of the European Renaissance and Enlightenment, Ming and Qing philosophers sought knowledge for knowledge sake whether or not it conformed to religious doctrine. Some offered ideas similar to those of such European philosophers as Sir Francis Bacon, René Descartes, and John Locke. Like Bacon, the neo-Confucian Wang Yang-Ming (1472–1529) pondered the unity of knowledge and conduct, concluding that the first necessarily required the second. Like Descartes, Wang wondered how people know the external world and concluded that "whatever we see, feel, hear, or in any wise conceive or understand is as real as ever."[18] Like Bacon and Locke, many scholars espoused the idea that the mind is reason. Others turned to the critical study of the past, emphasizing historical linguistics and archaeology. Like Enlightenment thinkers, a few Chinese scholars studied knowledge from other societies. For example, the philosopher and poet Tai Chen, a merchant's son, made comparative studies of Chinese and Western mathematics.

However, as neo-Confucianism became more influential, it turned into a new orthodoxy, limiting Chinese interest in alternative ideas. Some Qing scholars wrote that no more writing was needed because the truth had been made clear by ancient thinkers: all that was left was to practice their teachings. By the 1700s, fewer Chinese intellectuals showed much interest in practical inquiry or technological development. Neo-Confucianism reinforced a growing social rigidity, including increasing male dominance over women. Thus, although it contributed to the unparalleled continuity of Chinese society, it did so at considerable cost: intellectual conformity was hostile to originality or ideas from outside.

While intellectual inquiry began to stagnate, China's art and literature, in contrast, remained creative. As they had for centuries, artists painted landscapes featuring misty distances, soaring mountains, and angular pine trees. However, many innovative painters drew on Daoist mysticism to create fanciful scenes at odds with tradition. For example, Zhu Da (ca. 1626–1705), famous for his eccentric personality, painted bizarre conceptions of nature: huge lotuses in ponds, birds with wise-looking eyes, and surging landscapes. Qing authors wrote some of China's greatest fiction. Some scholars who had failed the civil service examinations became writers, and their experience fostered a critical detachment from traditional society. For example, in the early 1700s the novel *The Scholars,* by Wu Jingzi (woo ching-see), satirized the examination system and revealed the foibles of the pompous and the ignorant.

Likewise, *The Story of the Stone,* by Cao Xueqin (tsao swee-chin), used a large and declining gentry family to discuss, and sometimes satirize, Qing life. Often considered China's greatest novel, *The Story* contains 120 chapters and runs to some 1,300 pages. An even longer work was the world's greatest encyclopedia, 5,000 volumes long, which Qing scholars compiled under imperial patronage.

China and the World Economy

China in the later Ming and early Qing had commercial vitality, flourishing industrial production, and extensive foreign trade. Indeed, the Chinese, whose goods often sold hundreds of miles from where they were produced, enjoyed the world's largest and best-integrated commercial economy (see Witness to the Past: A Mandarin's Critique of Chinese Merchants). Government taxation policies encouraged both agriculture and industry. A Chinese official wrote in 1637 that there was at least one cotton loom in every ten houses. Gradually the fertile lower Yangzi (yahng-zeh) Basin, linked by the Yangzi River and Grand Canal to west and north China, became China's industrial heartland, commercial hub, and most prosperous region. Throughout the 1700s the people of the Yangzi Basin enjoyed living standards comparable to those of the world's other wealthiest regions, England and the Netherlands, both enriched by overseas colonization. A French visitor in the early 1700s, amazed that China's internal trade vastly exceeded the commerce of all Europe, identified some of the factors promoting economic success, writing that the Chinese put "merit ceaselessly in competition with merit, diligence with diligence, and work with work. The whole country is like a perpetual fair."[19]

Ming and early Qing China remained a major force in an international economy. China exported such products and resources as porcelain, cotton textiles, silk, tea, quicksilver, and zinc, and was a market for and source of valuable products, it

Chinese Porcelain Like other peoples around Eurasia, people in southwestern Asia prized Chinese porcelain. This Turkish miniature painting shows several valued pieces of Chinese porcelain, probably part of a bride's dowry, being carried in a decorated cart for display during a wedding procession. (Topkapi Palace Museum)

A Mandarin's Critique of Chinese Merchants

In the late sixteenth century, a Ming official, Zhang Han (Chang Han) (1511–1593), wrote an essay criticizing merchants. Himself from a wealthy merchant family, Zhang had the ambivalent attitude toward merchants that was typical of the Confucian elite of the day. He asserted that merchants were greedy, self-serving, arrogant, and pampered. However, he also admired the products provided by commerce and the efficiency with which they were distributed throughout the empire. And he suggested that China could benefit from lower taxes on mercantile activity.

Money and profit are of great importance to men. They seek profit, then suffer by it, yet they cannot forget it. They exhaust their bodies and spirits, run day and night, yet they still regard what they have gained as insufficient. Those who become merchants eat fine food and wear elegant clothes. . . . Opportunistic persons attracted by their wealth offer to serve them. Pretty girls in beautiful long-sleeved dresses and delicate slippers play stringed and wind instruments for them and compete to please them. Merchants boast that their wisdom and ability are such as to give them a free hand in affairs. They believe that they know all the possible transformations in the universe and therefore can calculate all the changes in the human world, and that the rise and fall of prices are under their command. They are confident that they will not make one mistake in a hundred in their calculations. These merchants do not know how insignificant their wisdom and ability really are. As [the *Chuang Tzu,* an ancient Daoist text] says: "Great understanding is broad and unhurried; little understanding is cramped and busy."

Because I have traveled to many places during my career as an official, I am familiar with commercial activities and business conditions in various places. . . . Those who engage in commerce, including the foot peddler, the cart peddler, and the shopkeeper, display not only clothing and fresh foods from the fields but also numerous luxury items such as priceless jade from [K'un-lun], pearls from the [southern] island of Hainan, gold from Yunnan (in southwest China), and corals from Vietnam. These precious items, coming from the mountains or the sea, are not found in central China. But people in remote areas and in other countries, unafraid of the dangers and difficulties of travel, transport these items step by step to the capital, making it the most prosperous place in the empire. . . . The profits from the tea and salt trades are especially great, but only large-scale merchants can undertake these businesses. Furthermore, there are government regulations on their distribution. . . .

Turning to the taxes levied on Chinese merchants, though these taxes are needed to fill the national treasury, excessive exploitation should be prohibited. . . . But today's merchants are often stopped on the road [at checkpoints] for additional payments and also suffer extortions from the [marketplace] clerks. Such exploitation is hard and bitter enough but, in addition, the merchants are taxed twice. How can they avoid becoming more and more impoverished? . . . Levying taxes on merchants is a bad policy. We should tax people according to their degree of wealth or poverty.

THINKING ABOUT THE READING

1. What criticisms does Zhang make of merchants?
2. In Zhang's view, what benefits does China gain from merchant activity?
3. How does Zhang believe merchant activity could be stimulated?

Source: Patricia Buckley Ebrey, ed., *Chinese Civilization and Society: A Sourcebook,* 2nd ed. rev. (New York: The Free Press, 1993), pp. 216–218. Reprinted with permission of the Free Press, a division of Simon and Schuster Adult Publishing Group. Copyright © 1993 by Patricia Buckley Ebrey.

influenced economic decisions made in Southeast Asia, the Middle East, Europe, and the Americas. As Europeans shipped silver to China to pay for Chinese products, Chinese production increased in response. Chinese population growth was also due to China's link to the international economy, a result of the introduction by Spanish merchants of new crops from the Americas such as corn, sweet potatoes, and peanuts, as well as Chinese development of a new fast-growing rice. The thriving economy served a population that numbered some 100 million in 1500 and reached 250 or 300 million by 1750, a quarter of the world total. Several major cities had over a million residents, including Nanjing (nahn-JING), Beijing, and Guangzhou (gwong-joe) (known in the West as Canton).

However, despite Ming and Qing China's economic dynamism, full-scale capitalism and industrialization did not develop, a result that has puzzled historians. The commercial revolution and technological advances of the Tang, Song, and Ming failed to bring about in China the revolutionary changes that transformed western European feudalism into capitalism. One reason was that, unlike the English and Dutch, the Chinese lacked an overseas empire that could be exploited to acquire capital for investment. Another basic difference from Europe was the continuity of Chinese traditions. The Han pattern was continued in essentials by the Sui, the Sui by the Tang, and so on in unbroken succession until 1912. The traditional bureaucracy-gentry, often contemptuous of merchants and their values, could absorb the effects of economic growth, keeping merchants politically weak, whereas in Europe economic growth undermined the old system. In addition, with a fast-growing population, China had no labor shortage and hence no great spur for technological innovation. Its economy met its basic needs well.

The relations between the imperial government and the merchants may also have been a factor in preventing full-scale capitalism. The imperial system heavily restricted and taxed the merchant class, a major difference from early modern Europe, where big business enterprises and the commercial middle class had a growing influence in politics. In China a large and wealthy merchant class existed and the laws encouraged markets. But the government feared that if merchants became too rich and powerful they might pose a threat to the regime, and hence their activities had to be kept in check. For example, Chinese industrialists and merchants customarily organized themselves into guilds, but the guilds were certified by the government and responsible for the behavior of their members. This made the guilds subject to government interference. During the Song commercial revolution, many mandarins came from merchant backgrounds and tended to protect their family's enterprises as well as business generally. By the Qing this was no longer true. The government also deprived the merchants of valuable goods, and ultimately inhibited capitalism, by maintaining monopolies over the production and distribution of essential commodities, including arms, textiles, pottery, salt, iron, and wine.

Indeed, few opportunities for unrestricted entrepreneurship existed in Ming and Qing China. Government policies reflected China's priorities as a centralized, agriculture-based empire. Hence, in the fifteenth century, the Ming emperor, with little opposition, stopped Zheng He's overseas voyages and ordered Chinese merchants to return home. Of course, that edict did not stop Chinese merchants from going abroad. Those from Fujian (fu-JEN) province, on the southeast coast, remained prominent in Asian trade throughout the Early Modern Era, especially in Southeast Asia. Many had no other options, since their home province offered poor conditions for farming. A Chinese official commented that Fujian men, of necessity, made fields from the sea. But, unlike their European rivals, they received no official support and often had to pay bribes to local officials when they returned home. These fundamental differences from European patterns deflected Chinese energies inward at a fateful turning point in world history, leaving the world's oceans open to Western enterprise.

China's Encounter with Portugal and Christianity

Although it turned inward, China did not cut itself off completely from the outside world. In the 1500s and 1600s European ships seeking to acquire silk, tea, porcelain, lacquer ware, and other products reached Chinese shores. The Portuguese landed on the China coast in 1514 and began a troubled relationship with China by failing to request permission from imperial officials to trade. They soon wore out their welcome, earning reputations as pirates and religious fanatics. With their naval forces spread thinly around Asia and Africa, the Portuguese were no match for Chinese armed junks. In 1557, to stop the piracy, the emperor allowed the Portuguese to establish a trading base at a small unpopulated peninsula, Macao (muh-cow), near Guangzhou on the southeast coast. By the 1580s Macao had a population of 10,000, including some 500 Portuguese (many with Chinese wives), several hundred African slaves, and Chinese and Japanese merchants. When the Qing declined in the 1800s, the Portuguese transformed Macao from a trading base into the first Western colony on Chinese soil.

Christian missionaries from Europe, especially Jesuits, also became active in the late Ming and early Qing. The most influential Jesuit missionary, the Italian Matteo Ricci (ma-TAY-o REE-chee) (1552–1610), was a brilliant scholar and linguist who was trained in law, mathematics, and geography. In 1583 he entered China from Macao to study the Confucian classics and foster an interest in Christianity among Confucian scholars. Ricci impressed Chinese officials with his forceful personality and great learning, and he began training young scholars for the civil service exams. Eventually the emperor allowed Ricci and his Jesuit colleagues to settle in Beijing. Armed with his knowledge of European Renaissance science, Ricci became a scientific adviser to the imperial court, helping improve clocks, calendars, and astronomical observations. On Ricci's death the Chinese buried him with honors in Beijing. Despite earning Chinese respect, Ricci attracted only a few converts to his faith.

Online Study Center Improve Your Grade
Primary Source: Journals of Matteo Ricci

The encounter between the Jesuits and the Chinese expanded the horizons of both parties. Some Chinese leaders, in particular the emperor Kangzi, became interested in Western scientific knowledge. Kangzi wrote:

> In the 1690s I often worked several hours a day with [the Jesuits]. I had examined each stage of the forging of a cannon. I worked on clocks and mechanics. [Father] Pereira taught me to play a tune on the harpsichord and the structure of the eight-note scale. I also learned to calculate the weight and volume of spheres, cubes, and cones, and to measure distance and the angles of riverbanks.[20]

A few Chinese even visited Europe. One of them, the Christian convert Michael Alphonsus Shen, demonstrated chopstick techniques for French king Louis XIV and catalogued Chinese books in the Oxford University library.

For their part, the Jesuits, chiefly well-educated Italians, were much impressed with a China that seemed to have more wealth and a more impressive technology than did Europe. Jesuit letters home described Chinese ideas and advanced technology, knowledge that circulated widely in Europe. Enjoying their status, the Jesuits lived like mandarins and wore Chinese clothing. Their admiration of Chinese traditions led them to attempt to harmonize Christianity with Chinese philosophy and ethics as a way of attracting support from Chinese scholars. But they avoided discussing those aspects of Christian theology incompatible with Confucianism.

The efforts of Ricci and his colleagues laid some groundwork for introducing Roman Christianity to China, and by the end of the seventeenth century, some 100,000 Chinese had become Catholics. But this was a tiny percentage of the vast population, and the less tolerant Catholic missionaries who followed the early Jesuits made even less progress. After the pope prohibited any attempt at mixing Christianity and Confucianism, the faith had less appeal. Furthermore, the rival Catholic orders squabbled. Many neo-Confucian thinkers already considered Christianity intellectually false and resented the missionary enterprise for its arrogance. The emperor Yongzheng (young cheng) asked the missionaries: "What would you say if I sent a troop of Buddhist monks into your country to preach their doctrines? You want all Chinese to become Christians. Shall we become subjects of your king? You will listen to no other voices but yours."[21] In the early 1700s the Qing banned Christianity for undermining such Chinese traditions as ancestor worship, persecuted converts, and expelled missionaries.

China Confronts the Western Challenge

New challenges from the Western countries faced China in the 1600s. Before 1800 Europeans could be rebuffed because China was militarily and economically strong. But relations with the Dutch and Russians suggested changes to come. The Dutch had established a base on Taiwan in 1624 but were expelled in 1662 by the militarily stronger Ming resistance forces that had moved to the island. In 1683 the Qing took control of Taiwan, but the Dutch remained active in the China trade. In the late 1600s Russian expeditions crossed Siberia, seeking trade with China as well as sable fur. Over time they consolidated control of the sparsely populated regions north of Xinjiang and Mongolia. They coveted the Amur River valley, in eastern Siberia north of the Manchu homeland and under loose Qing suzerainty, as a gateway to the Pacific and China. In the late 1600s Russian and Chinese forces fought several battles in Siberia. The Chinese won these conflicts but granted Russians commercial privileges in the Treaty of Nerchinsk of 1689, the first treaty between China and a European power and a symbol of things to come. From this relationship the Russians obtained tea, which became popular in Russia. Furthermore, Russia maintained its ambitions in eastern Siberia, occasionally testing Qing resolve and power.

Needing little from outside, China still had considerable control of the relations with European powers before the 1800s. The Qing minimized contacts by restricting foreign trade to a few border outposts and southern ports, especially Guangzhou (Canton), and politely but firmly refused diplomatic relations on an equal basis with the Western nations. The Chinese were willing to absorb useful technologies to improve mapmaking and astronomy, as reflected in the fruitful relationship between Emperor Kangzi and the early Jesuits, but they were less interested in foreign ideas like Christianity. By the mid-Qing, China was also increasingly self-centered and complacent, underestimating the Western challenge.

China's internal problems, such as overpopulation, mounted just as Western economic, industrial, and military power increased and foreign pressures on China intensified in the later 1700s. The sequel was that China, despite full confidence in the superiority of its culture, was eclipsed within a few decades by the West. Having lived under foreign rulers such as the Mongols and Manchus, the Chinese understood political subjugation but could not comprehend that foreign forces might force them to rethink their cultural traditions, which they wanted to preserve at all costs. In late imperial China, culture and nation were one, but during the later 1800s the 2,000-year-old imperial system declined rapidly.

SECTION SUMMARY

- During the Ming dynasty, China maintained its economic power, but it turned increasingly inward and antiforeign and was ultimately undermined by plague, famine, and pressures from Japan.

- The Qing dynasty was established by foreign Manchus, who assimilated to many Chinese ways, amassed the greatest Eurasian land empire since the Mongols, and added Taiwan to China's holdings.

- Chinese neo-Confucians incorporated elements of Buddhism and Daoism in their thinking and, like their European contemporaries, emphasized reason, but over time neo-Confucianism hardened into a new orthodoxy and discouraged the growth of new ideas.

- China's economy remained extremely strong but never developed full-scale capitalism or industrialization, perhaps because it lacked an exploitable overseas empire, and perhaps because the government failed to encourage entrepreneurship.

- China had fitful encounters with Europeans, including Portuguese traders who irked Chinese authorities and established a colony at Macao, and missionaries who had little success and were ultimately banned for undermining Chinese traditions.

- Over time, China faced increasing pressure from the Russians, who fought for commercial privileges in the area north of China.

 # Continuity and Change in Korea and Japan

How did Korea and Japan change during this era?

For much of the Early Modern Era Korea and Japan remained more isolated than China from the wider world, although both maintained trade relations with China. Korea faced little Western pressure, local issues and conflicts with Japan being far more important. Japanese history also largely revolved around the country's changing economic and social patterns. For a brief period Japan encountered a significant European presence, but when the experience proved destabilizing, the Japanese became aloof from the West.

Choson Korea

The Koreans had learned over the centuries how to mix Chinese influences with local traditions, adapting and modifying Chinese political models, Confucian social patterns, and Mahayana Buddhism. The Yi (YEE) dynasty, which called its state Choson, came to power in 1392 and survived until 1910, a longevity of over five centuries (see Chronology: Korea and Japan, 1450–1750). Strongly Confucian in orientation, the Yi borrowed Chinese models and maintained close relations with their powerful neighbor. The early Yi era was creative, enjoying progress in science and technology as well as in writing and literature. However, Choson began to decline in the 1500s, damaged by factional disputes and a Japanese invasion.

The Japanese invasion proved most disastrous for Korea. In 1592 a Japanese army of 160,000 attempted to conquer some of the peninsula. With superior military power, the Japanese soon captured the capital, Seoul (soul). However, the Koreans, aided by China, fought back and eventually prevailed. They owed their successful defense to their invention, in 1519, of the first ironclad naval vessels, four centuries before such vessels were developed anywhere else. The Koreans used these boats to cut Japanese supply lines and hence undermine the Japanese occupation. Forced to the peace table, the Japanese agreed to withdraw. But the Japanese invasion destroyed countless buildings, weakened the central government, and generated severe economic problems.

After these invasions, while the Yi maintained their power, Koreans abandoned or modified some customs borrowed from China. In theory the Yi government remained Confucian, but practice varied considerably. The rigid old class system was modified, with class lines becoming more open. The society also enjoyed economic development and change: agriculture became more productive, and population grew, reaching 7 million by 1750. Commerce and the merchant class also expanded. Growing dissension fostered movements for change that became stronger after the mid-1700s, laying the foundations for a new era.

C H R O N O L O G Y	
Korea and Japan, 1450–1750	
1338–1568	Ashikaga Shogunate
1392–1910	Yi (Choson) dynasty in Korea
1549	Beginning of Christian missions in Japan
1592–1598	Japanese invasions of Korea
1603	Founding of Tokugawa Shogunate
1637	Christian rebellion against Tokugawa
1639–1841	Japanese seclusion policy

Ashikaga Japan and the West

Japanese society, with its samurai (SAH-moo-rie) warrior class, distinctive mix of Buddhism, Confucianism, and Shinto, and long history of adapting foreign influences, differed dramatically from those of neighboring Korea and China. But by 1500, Japan under the Ashikaga (ah-shee-KAH-gah) Shogunate (1338–1568), like Yi Korea, was experiencing rapid change that strained the samurai-dominated political and social system that had emerged during the Intermediate Era. The Kyoto-based Ashikaga shoguns, military leaders who dominated the imperial family in Kyoto and the central government, never had much power beyond the capital. A long civil war, during which Western powers intruded into Japan, unsettled conditions even more.

Growth and Conflict in Ashikaga Japan During the Ashikaga years, rapid economic and population growth had major consequences for Japanese society. As technological advances improved agriculture, production per acre tripled, and Japan's population doubled from 16 million in 1500 to perhaps 30 million in 1750. The increased productivity in turn stimulated trade and the gradual development of cities and towns. By 1600 the largest city, Kyoto, may have grown to some 800,000 people. In the cities and towns merchants and craftsmen organized themselves into guilds. Guilds obtained monopoly rights to sell or make a product by paying fees to local governments, thus getting higher status and more freedom than most Japanese enjoyed.

As merchants became more active and assertive, they spurred foreign and domestic trade. Before this time few Japanese other than a few diplomats, fishermen, and Buddhist monks had ventured beyond Korea and China. Now Japanese traders and pirates began visiting Korea, China, and Southeast Asia. Japanese settlers and soldiers of fortune were especially prominent in Vietnam, Cambodia, Siam, and the Philippines. Several thousand Japanese lived in Manila, and one Japanese even became a governor in Siam. Indeed, there was a sizeable Japanese community in King Narai's Siam. Japan became a major supplier of silver, copper, swords, lacquer ware, rice wine, rice, and other goods to Asia. Japanese were showing a highly developed mercantile spirit.

If the Ashikaga economic and military expansion had continued, the Japanese might have been in a position to challenge the Portuguese and other Europeans for influence in Southeast Asia. Perhaps Japan was on the verge of developing into an expansionist and capitalistic country with a flexible social structure, as England, the Netherlands, and France did around the same time, with the gradual replacement of feudalism by market economies and overseas colonization. But growing instability turned Japan in a different direction.

Political turmoil and civil war in Japan were a factor in this shift. Political power became increasingly decentralized, as great territorial landowning magnates, called daimyo, increasingly dominated the regions outside Kyoto. At the beginning of the 1500s there were several hundred of these daimyo, each with a supporting samurai force. The most powerful hoped to one day rule Japan. However, the rise of the daimyo precipitated a civil war that raged for over a century, from the mid-1400s into the late 1500s. The military engagements during the centuries of warrior dominance were mainly matters of hand-to-hand conflict between samurai wielding long, slightly curved, two-handed swords with great efficiency, supported by commoner spearmen. In the late 1600s a famous poet visited a historic battleground and offered a retrospective on the fighters and the fleeting nature of their causes: "The summer grasses! All that is left of the warrior's dream!"[22]

During the late sixteenth and early seventeenth century, three men who successively became shogun gradually restored order. All were brutal warlords but also devotees of the refined tea ceremony and pragmatists willing to challenge powerful institutions. The first, Oda Nobunaga (OH-da no-boo-NAG-ga) (1534–1582), was so wild as a youth that a family servant committed suicide hoping this desperate act might settle the young man down. With the slogan "rule the empire by force," Oda, from a minor daimyo family, became a brilliant military strategist who once defeated an army of 25,000 with his own small force of 2,000 men. He usually performed a folk dance and then sang a delicate verse about life's transience before leading his samurai into bloody battles, where they sometimes slaughtered thousands of rival fighters. Nobunaga deposed the last Ashikaga shogun. Hideyoshi Toyotomi (1536–1598), the second warlord and of peasant origins, had ambitions abroad. He demanded unsuccessfully that the Spanish governor of the Philippines send him tribute. In hopes of gaining land for his supporters, he also dreamed of conquering China. When the Koreans refused his request to use Korea as a staging base for the China invasion, he instead sent a large army into Korea in 1592. The fierce Korean resistance forced the Japanese to abandon the effort on Hideyoshi's death. The last of the three, Tokugawa Ieyasu (ee-yeh-YAH-soo) (1542–1616), one of Hideyoshi's chief generals, ended the warfare and became shogun in 1603.

The Japanese-European Encounter

During the civil war European traders and missionaries arrived in Japan, and their encounter with the Japanese sparked cultural exchange but also conflict. Thanks to the warfare and the absence of strong rule, Japan was now more open to borrowing from outside than it had been since the early Heian (HAY-an) era. The main imports during these decades were technological, especially Western guns, and religious, mainly Christianity. Nonetheless, Japanese leaders became alarmed by the superiority of Western military and naval technology, as well as the surprising effectiveness of Western Christian missionaries in Japan.

In 1542 the Portuguese reached Japan, starting an encounter that troubled both sides. The European arrivals caused a sensation, as we learn from a Japanese observer:

There came on a [merchant ship] a creature one couldn't put a name to, that [appeared to have] human form at first [glance], but might as well be a long-nosed goblin.

Careful inquiry [revealed] that the creature was called a "Padre." The first thing one noticed was how long the nose was! It was like a wartless conch-shell.[23]

The Europeans were equally astonished at what they found. An Italian Jesuit in the 1500s struggled with the cultural differences:

Japan is a world the reverse of Europe. Hardly in anything do their ways conform to ours. They eat and dress differently. Their methods of doing business, their manner of sitting down, their buildings, their domestic arrangements are so unlike ours as to be beyond description or understanding.[24]

But for all the mutual astonishment, the Europeans had an economic, religious, and military impact. The Portuguese traded Chinese silk for Japanese gold, and soon Spanish and Dutch merchants arrived to compete in the Japanese market. Francis Xavier (1506–1552), a Spanish Jesuit missionary, began to preach Christianity in 1549. As a result of energetic Spanish and Portuguese missionary efforts, by 1600 perhaps 300,000 Japanese were Christians, out of a total population of some 18 million. The converts included some of the daimyo on the southern island of Kyushu (KYOO-shoo), who converted to gain a closer relationship to European traders and acquire advanced military technology from the West. But many Japanese grew increasingly suspicious of the missionaries, resented their intolerance of Japanese faiths and local customs, and could not comprehend the fierce competition between Portuguese and Spanish priests, and between rival Catholic orders. Japanese leaders viewed the Christian communities, often armed by the missionaries, as posing a threat to their power.

But the Japanese adopted what was useful to them: Western technologies. Major consequences often followed. They acquired, then quickly improved, muskets from the Portuguese and Spanish. They also developed new tactics to use the firepower they now possessed. Indeed, European guns sharpened warfare and, since even nonsamurai could obtain them, contributed to the breakdown of social class lines. The increasingly common and deadly violence resulting from guns often prompted peasants to seek solace in religion, and some adopted Christianity.

The Tokugawa Shogunate: Stability and Seclusion

The civil war brought on by the rise of the daimyo, and intensified by gunpowder weapons, ended with the Tokugawa Shogunate, which ruled Japan from 1603 to 1868. Tokugawa Ieyasu was a great warrior and able administrator, but also cruel and treacherous. He subdued his rivals and established a shogunate at Tokyo, then known as Edo (ED-doe), presiding over the most centralized state in premodern Japanese history, in striking contrast to the weak Ashikaga shoguns a century earlier.

The Tokugawa leaders imposed a government mixing authoritarian centralization with the rigidly hierarchical social system that emerged in the later Intermediate Era, which resembled medieval European feudalism in some respects. Japan now had a more powerful shogunate than ever before, while the imperial family in Kyoto remained powerless. To discourage rebellion, some members of each daimyo family were required to live in Edo as hostages. The Tokugawa restored the pre–civil war social structure, with the samurais at the top. A samurai scholar instrumental in developing the code of chivalry (*bushido*) defended the special role of his class by saying that the farmers, merchants, and artisans were too busy to master the warrior ways. The samurai, he wrote, "is one who does not cultivate, manufacture, engage in trade. The business of the samurai consists in reflecting on his own station in life, in discharging loyal service to his master, in devoting himself to duty above all."[25]

To stop the conflict between the various Europeans and Catholic orders, Tokugawa eventually ordered a seclusion policy, closing off Japan from Western pressure and ordering home Japanese traders in Southeast Asia. In the process he ejected the feuding Catholic missionaries and merchants, and broke the power of the Christian communities. This led to a rebellion by Japanese Christians in 1637, to which Tokugawa responded by massacring 37,000 Japanese Christians. The shogun warned the Portuguese and Spanish that they were worthy of death and should justly be killed, but he generously spared their lives and instead ordered that they leave Japan and never return. But while Japan was closing itself to the West, trade with China, Korea, and Southeast Asia continued, with Japan paying for silk with its main mineral resource, silver.

While the Portuguese and Spanish were expelled, after 1639 a few Dutch traders were allowed to remain and set up a base on a small island, Deshima (DEH-shi-ma), in Nagasaki (nah-gah-SAH-kee) Bay. The Dutch were not interested in converting the Japanese to Christianity, only in commerce, and for the next two centuries the Dutch base served as Japan's only link to the European world. The Deshima station chief for the Dutch East Indies Company reported in 1650 that the restrictions and humiliations they endured were worth the gains, since Japan was the most profitable of all the company's operations.

Tokugawa Society and Culture

Tokugawa leaders believed that society could be frozen in a hierarchical pattern. But under the surface of the rigid Tokugawa rule new social forces simmered. For example, even though the rulers restricted travel between cities or regions, merchants found ways to evade the rules and move their wares. The Japanese population grew rapidly, straining the country's resources. Thousands of local peasant protests, riots, and uprisings reflected more dramatic discontent. Also a force for change, Tokugawa Japan boasted several large cities, with Tokyo and Osaka each over a million in population by 1800. The cities became centers of complex commercial networks, and their demands fostered agricultural productivity and economic prosperity, especially in the Edo region. Merchants and their values became more influential. By the mid-1700s Japan was a well-organized country, with rising living standards but growing tensions.

The Tokugawa tried to restrict Japanese women. European visitors in the 1500s were surprised that elite women seemed to have more independence than their European contemporaries. A Jesuit noted that, in contrast to Europe, women went where they wished during the day without informing their husbands. These European perceptions were partly accurate. In contrast to some Asian societies, Japanese women were never secluded and participated in community life. Some women were literate, and a few became noted writers. Nonetheless, like women in most societies, Japanese women had few legal or property rights, faced arranged marriages, and were encouraged to be dependent on men, all patriarchal customs reinforced during the early Tokugawa period. As a result, severe laws against adultery only punished women. Women in samurai families were raised to be courteous, conciliatory, and humble toward their husbands. The Tokugawa advised peasants that "however good looking a wife may be, if she neglects her household duties by drinking tea or sight-seeing or rambling along the hillside, she must be divorced."[26] However, gender expectations and relations among urban merchant and artisan families were less rigid.

In Tokugawa culture, distinctive new forms also emerged in the 1600s. In the major cities entertainment districts known as the "floating world" were filled with restaurants, theaters, geisha houses, and brothels. A playwright described a lively district in Osaka: "Through the thronged streets young rakes were strolling, singing folk-songs as they went, reciting fragments of puppet dramas, or imitating famous actors at their dialogues. From the upper rooms of many a teahouse floated the gay plucking of a *samisen* [lute]."[27] The writer Ihara Saikaku (ee-HAR-oo sigh-KOCK-oo), himself from a merchant family, chronicled the floating world and satirized urban merchant life in often erotic novels. The master artist Moronobu (more-oh-NOH-boo) introduced the colorful woodblock prints known as **ukiyo-e** (oo-kee-YO-ee), which celebrated the life of the floating world. Although many considered them vulgar, these prints achieved wide distribution, making famous the actors, geishas, and courtesans who were portrayed. Later, landscapes, such as views of Mt. Fuji, became popular themes for woodcuts. By the 1800s many European artists collected and were influenced by these prints.

New theater forms also appeared, such as the **bunraku** puppet theater and the racy **kabuki** drama, the favored entertainment of the urban population. Aimed particularly at the merchant class, kabuki featured gorgeous costumes, beautiful scenery, and scripts filled with violent passion. Men played all the roles. Professional female impersonators were highly honored and spent years mastering the voice, gestures, and other aspects of femininity.

---

ukiyo-e Colorful Japanese woodblock prints that celebrated the life of the "floating world," the urban entertainment districts.

bunraku The puppet theater of Tokugawa Japan.

kabuki The all-male and racy drama that became the favored entertainment of the urban population in Tokugawa Japan.

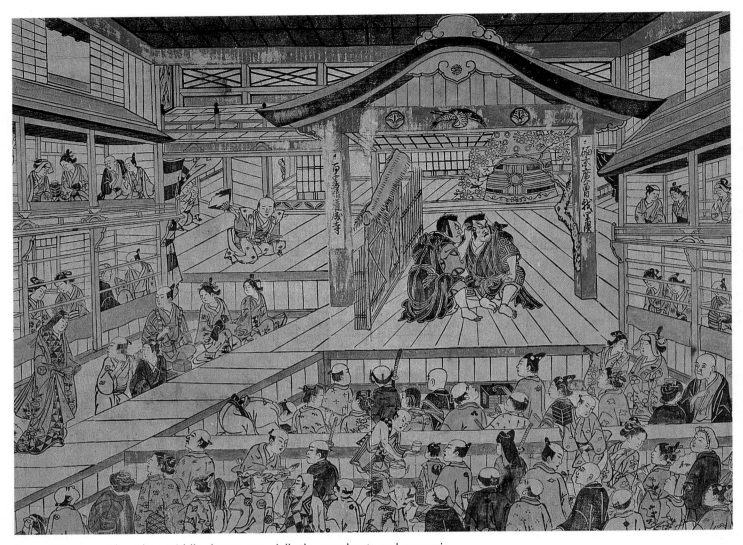

Kabuki Theater The urban middle classes, especially the merchants and samurais, enjoyed kabuki drama. This eighteenth-century print by one of the most acclaimed artists, Moronobu, shows the audience enjoying a play about a vendetta involving two brothers. (Tokyo National Museum/DNP Archives)

A new literary device, the seventeen-syllable **haiku** poem, also became popular. Haiku proved an excellent vehicle for discussing the passage of time or briefly summarizing some action or scene through a series of images, such as the famous presentation by the samurai turned wanderer and greatest haiku poet, Matsuo Basho (BAH-show) (1644–1694), of a sudden event on a quiet pond: "An old pond. Frog jumps in. Sound of water." Another Basho poem commented on the change of seasons and human emotions: "No blossoms and no moon, and he is drinking *sake* [rice wine], all alone."[28] Japanese did not need to be lonely on a dark winter's night, as portrayed in the poem, to appreciate Basho's delicate word art.

---

haiku The seventeen-syllable poem that proved an excellent vehicle for discussing the passage of time and the change of seasons in Early Modern Japan.

Tokugawa Stability and Its Costs

Tokugawa Japan largely enjoyed security, stability, and peace for 250 years, a pattern many other societies would envy. But it came at a price. Although commerce thrived, Japan, like China, experienced no political transformation or social rejuvenation, since Tokugawa policies preserved rigid class and gender divisions and shielded the people from outside influence. The lack of political and social dynamism left the Tokugawa vulnerable to a later return of Western power, as several Western nations rapidly acquired wealth and resources and improved their technology between 1500 and 1850. The Tokugawa had merely papered over the cracks, pushing social tensions, such as between samurai and merchants and between daimyo and shoguns, below the surface.

When the West intruded in the mid-nineteenth century, the latent tensions boiled over and the Tokugawa lost their grip on power, but Japan, unlike China, was able to respond creatively. Whereas Chinese feared cultural change more than political conquest, the Japanese were more afraid of conquest and more accepting of change. Japan's history of borrowing from abroad made it uniquely prepared to make the necessary adjustments, and the Japanese could assimilate Western techniques and customs to Japanese traditions, as they had done with Chinese and Western imports in earlier eras. These differences meant that China and Japan eventually met the challenge from the West in very different ways.

SECTION SUMMARY

- The Chinese helped Korea to rebuff a 1592 Japanese invasion, but as a result Korean culture began to liberalize and shed some customs borrowed from China.

- Ashikaga Japan saw tremendous economic and population growth, but it was undermined by a lengthy civil war, during which European merchants made incursions and introduced guns and Christianity, upsetting Japan's social order.

- The Tokugawa Shogunate ended Japan's civil war, restored strict order, and expelled European missionaries and traders, with the exception of a small group of Dutch traders who were uninterested in missionary work.

- Despite the Tokugawa leaders' attempt to halt change, the Japanese economy grew rapidly, tensions in Japanese society increased, and Japan's culture flourished in the urban "floating world" and in new theatrical and literary forms.

- Tokugawa Japan was quite stable, but its rigidity hampered its growth and made it vulnerable to overthrow when Western powers returned in the mid-nineteenth century.

 *Online Study Center* **ACE the Test**

 Chapter Summary

In the Early Modern Period communication between distant peoples intensified. European expansion at that time had much less impact in most of southern and eastern Asia than it had in the Americas and Africa. Many Asian societies remained strong and militarily powerful, able to manipulate or deflect the Europeans who came in search of valuable trade resources and products. Muslim-ruled Mughal India, especially under the tolerant Akbar, developed creative art and architecture and a prosperous export economy. By the 1700s, however, the Mughals weakened from overspending and religious intolerance as new challenges mounted. While various Southeast Asian states, among them Siam, remained strong, the Portuguese and then the Dutch successively captured Melaka and the Spice Islands, and the Dutch gradually conquered Java. The Spanish

carved out a colony in the Philippines and began exporting Asian goods from Manila to the Americas, helping build a world economy. Increasing commerce, fostered partly by European activity, more closely tied Southeast Asia to the growing world economy.

China during the late Ming and early Qing remained among the world's most powerful and prosperous countries, with several outstanding leaders, extensive industry, and the world's largest commercial economy. China traded with other countries on Chinese terms. However, while it remained creative in arts and philosophy, overpopulation and declining support for merchants eventually hindered China just as European pressures increased. Both Japan and Korea imposed policies of partial seclusion. After welcoming Western traders and missionaries, Japan restricted their access. The Tokugawa Shogunate maintained a rigid social and political system but also fostered a creative culture. Hence, European activity was only one of many factors influencing Asian societies.

Online Study Center **Improve Your Grade** Flashcards

Key Terms

Urdu	Moros	bunraku
Sikhs	Indios	kabuki
Hispanization	ukiyo-e	haiku

Suggested Reading

Books

Brook, Timothy. *The Confusions of Pleasure: Commerce and Culture in Ming China.* Berkeley: University of California Press, 1998. A readable exploration of Ming China, including the lives of China's people.

Chaudhuri, K. N. *Trade and Civilization in the Indian Ocean: An Economic History from the Rise of Islam to 1750.* Cambridge: Cambridge University Press, 1985. A scholarly study of trade and Islam, focusing on India and Southeast Asia.

Cohen, Warren. *East Asia at the Center: Four Thousand Years of Engagement with the World.* New York: Columbia University Press, 2000. A good summary of China, Korea, Japan, and Southeast Asia in Eurasian history.

Crossley, Pamela Kyle. *The Manchus.* Cambridge, Mass.: Blackwell, 1997. An excellent study of Manchu history and culture.

Ebrey, Patricia Buckley, Anne Walthall, and James D. Palais. *East Asia: A Cultural, Social, and Political History.* Boston: Houghton Mifflin, 2006. A readable, comprehensive survey.

Matsunosuke, Nishiyama. *Edo Culture: Daily Life and Diversions in Urban Japan, 1600–1868.* Honolulu: University of Hawaii Press, 1997. A detailed look at popular culture and ways of life during the Tokugawa era.

Mungello, D. E. *The Great Encounter of China and the West, 1500–1800.* 2nd ed. Lanham, Md.: Rowman and Littlefield, 2005. A readable account of the meeting of Chinese and European societies in the Early Modern Era.

Phelan, John L. *The Hispanization of the Philippines: Spanish Aims and Filipino Responses, 1565–1700.* Madison: University of Wisconsin Press, 1959. Dated but still the best general study of the topic.

Prakash, Om. *European Commercial Enterprise in Pre-Colonial India.* New York: Cambridge University Press, 1998. A valuable scholarly study.

Reid, Anthony. *Southeast Asia in the Age of Commerce, 1450–1680.* 2 vols. New Haven: Yale University Press, 1988 and 1993. A major scholarly source on the Southeast Asian societies and their interaction with the wider world.

Richards, John F. *The Mughal Empire.* Cambridge: Cambridge University Press, 1993. The major scholarly study of Mughal India.

Schimmel, Annemarie. *The Empire of the Great Mighals: History, Art and Culture.* New York: Oxford University Press, 2005. Well-illustrated survey emphasizing social and cultural history.

Spence, Jonathan D. *Emperor of China: Self-Portrait of Kang-Hsi.* New York: Vintage, 1974. A fascinating study of an important Qing emperor.

Statler, Oliver. *Japanese Inn.* Honolulu: University of Hawaii Press, 1981. A reprint of one of the best portrayals of life in Early Modern Japan.

Subrahmanyan, Sanjay. *The Portuguese Empire in Asia, 1500–1700: A Political and Economic History.* New York: Longman, 1993. An overview of the Portuguese and their impacts.

Taylor, Jean Gelman. *Indonesia: Peoples and Histories.* New Haven: Yale University Press, 2003. Highly readable survey with much on this era.

Websites

Internet East Asian History Sourcebook (http://www.fordham.edu/halsall/eastasia/eastasiasbook.html). An invaluable collection of sources and links on China, Japan, and Korea from ancient to modern times.

Internet Guide for China Studies (http://www.sino.uni-heidelberg.de/igcs/). A good collection of links maintained at Germany's Heidelberg University.

Internet Indian History Sourcebook (http://www.fordham.edu/halsall/india/indiasbook.html). An invaluable collection of sources and links on India from ancient to modern times.

East and Southeast Asia: An Annotated Directory of Internet Resources (http://newton.uor.edu/Departments&Programs/AsianStudiesDept/general.html). This site, prepared at the University of Redlands, offers many links on history, culture, and politics, with much on this era.

Nakasendo Highway: A Journey to the Heart of Japan (http://hkuhist2.hku.hk/nakasendo/). This website, hosted at Hong Kong University, uses a famous highway to introduce Tokugawa Japan.

A Visual Sourcebook of Chinese Civilization (http://depts.washington.edu/chinaciv/). A wonderful collection of essays, illustrations, and other useful material on Chinese history.

WWW Southeast Asia Guide (http://www.library.wisc.edu/guides/SEAsia/). An impressive, easy-to-use site from the University of Wisconsin-Madison.

WWW Virtual Library: South Asia (http://www.columbia.edu/cu/libraries/indiv/area/sarai/). This Columbia University site offers many useful resources.

Connecting the Early Modern World, 1450–1750

In 1552 a Spanish historian called the landing in the Americas by a naval expedition led by Christopher Columbus "the greatest event since the creation of the world."[1] It was a claim that ignored many previous achievements, yet the permanent connecting of the hemispheres that followed Columbus in fact reshaped the world, helping to make the Early Modern Era vastly different from the Intermediate Era that preceded it. History was now painted on a larger canvas and peoples' horizons around the world rapidly expanded. In this new global age, greatly increased communication and mobility resulted in encounters, some friendly others hostile, between societies once remote from each other. Travel and exploration revealed the resources of the inhabited world. As a result of this discovery, the exchange among societies of people, diseases, ideas, technologies, capital, resources, and products occurred on a greater scale than ever before. Europeans forged a new world economy, while disrupting, changing, and sometimes destroying the societies they encountered, especially in the Americas and parts of Africa and Southeast Asia. Because of the growing contacts spanning the two hemispheres, for the first time in history an interconnected world became a reality.

But the encounters between Europeans and peoples they could reach only after long sea voyages were only part of the story. The world had many political and economic centers between 1450 and 1750. In the Afro-Eurasian zone, Morocco, the Ottoman Empire, several western European societies, Safavid Persia, Mughal India, China, and a few Southeast Asian societies such as Siam were wealthy, populous, and linked to each other by trade networks and diplomatic ties. They all enjoyed military prowess, had effective states, and fostered creative thinkers. Some African kingdoms, such as Ashante and Buganda, also enjoyed influence and connections to hemispheric trade. No single country or region dominated world politics or the world economy. Yet, the links forged during the Early Modern Era laid a foundation for the building, often by force, of an even more integrated global system, encompassing even the most remote peoples, in the Modern Era.

NEW EMPIRES AND MILITARY POWER

From the dawn of recorded history some peoples have used military power to impose their will on others and create empires. As a result, people often think of history in terms of great empires such as Assyria, Rome, Tang China, the Inca, and, the largest of all, the Mongol. Increasing wealth and power, as well as more deadly weapons, led some Early Modern Era societies to build large empires. Some, such as Safavid Persia, Mughal India, Qing China, and Russia, ruled land empires. In contrast to these empires, which annexed nearby and often sparsely populated territories, the Ottoman Turks controlled large areas of southeastern Europe, western Asia, and North Africa, and the Omani Arabs established footholds in East Africa. The Portuguese, Spanish, Dutch, English, and French empires were even more ambitious, incorporating distant peoples in Africa, Asia, and the Americas. These conquests created empires on a geographical scale never imagined before, even by the Mongols. But empire also had limits, and many peoples were able to resist the imperial designs of the major powers.

Gunpowder Empires

Historians characterize most Early Modern empires as "gunpowder empires" because they depended on bigger and better gunpowder weapons, including cannon mounted on ships, field artillery, and guns used by individual soldiers. Gunpowder empires dominated Eurasia and the Americas. Various Asian and European societies sought to acquire resources and markets in neighboring societies by building empires rather than relying chiefly on trade. Only a few European countries, however, had the means, including sea power, to envision dominating very distant societies, and those countries sought resources and then territory in Africa, the Americas, Asia, and the Pacific. Only those few European countries also had the incentive: the quest for "gold, god, and glory." The worldwide exploration, trade, missionary activity, and conquest that took place during this era resulted from the transformation of various European societies by various forces—the rise of capitalism, powerful merchants, and competitive, centralizing states, as well as by rivalry between Christian churches actively seeking converts—while improved military and maritime technology provided the means for all this activity.

Europeans took advantage of their economic growth and military expansion to improve their position in the world and to compete more effectively for resources in the East, where Islamic societies, India, and China had long enjoyed the most political, economic, and cultural power. Advanced naval and military technology, including gunpowder weapons unknown in the Americas and in much of Africa and Southeast Asia, allowed the Portuguese to seize various African and Asian trading ports, and the Spanish to construct a huge empire in the Americas. The Dutch, English, and French soon followed, establishing footholds in North America, the Caribbean, coastal Africa, and southern Asia. The European powers used some of their weapons against each other. For example, the Dutch and Portuguese were bitter rivals for influence and territory in Southeast Asia, Sri Lanka, and Brazil. Europeans controlled Atlantic shipping and also gained considerable power over Indian Ocean trade, which brought them great wealth. As the English adventurer Sir Walter Raleigh recognized in 1608, "Who so commands the sea commands the trade of the world; who so commands the trade of the world commands the riches of the world."[2]

Dutch Diplomats In this print, a Dutch delegation, eager to make an alliance with the Kongolese against the Portuguese, prostrate themselves before the Kongolese king, sitting on his throne under an imported chandelier, in 1642. (From Olfert Dapper, *Beschreibung von Africa*, Amsterdam, 1670)

A Polycentric World

Despite the growth of empires, the Early Modern world had varied centers of political and economic power, a situation known as polycentrism. No one country could dominate all other rivals. Despite their weaponry, Europeans did not become dominant all over the world during this era. European power was limited in Asia, the Middle East, and parts of Africa and South America, and much of North America and the Pacific remained untouched by European exploration. For much of the era, the Ottomans, Mughals, and Chinese were more politically, economically, and culturally influential in Eurasia than European societies. For example, many Muslims admired Mughal India, which became a destination for merchants, writers, and religious scholars. A Persian poet proclaimed: "Great is India, the Mecca of all in need. A journey to India is of essence to any man made worthy by knowledge and skill."[3] The major Asian states also collected far larger tax revenues than did any European government. Societies in Eurasia, from China to England, and in Africa, from Buganda to Songhai (song-GAH-ee), extended their power into nearby territories, centralized their governments, fostered commerce, and worked to integrate ethnic minorities into the broader society.

The era was dynamic for many peoples. Across Eurasia varied societies experienced economic innovation, free markets, industrialization, and rising living standards. For example, cities such as Amsterdam in Holland, Isfahan (is-fah-HAHN) in Persia, and Ayuthia (uh-YUT-uh-yuh) in Siam were bustling trade crossroads, attracting merchants from all over Eurasia. A Jesuit who visited Surat (SOO-rat) in northwest India in 1663 found countless foreign ships and thousands of foreign merchants, among them traders from over a dozen European societies, including Swedes and Hungarians, as well as many Asians, from Turks to Chinese. Foreign merchants, such as the Dutch and Persians at Ayuthia or at Surat, had to adapt to local customs to succeed. Sometimes, as in Siam, Tokugawa Japan, and Morocco, Europeans who disregarded local customs or threatened local governments were expelled.

The encounters between peoples fostered compromises and information exchange. Many Asians and Africans adapted ideas from other cultures to meet their own needs. Among other leaders, the Chinese emperor Kangzi (KANG-see), the Siamese king Narai (na-RY), the Mughal sultan Akbar (AK-bahr), and the Kongo king Alfonso I showed a keen interest in Western ideas and technologies. Kangzi, for instance, studied Western science with Italian Jesuits, and Alfonso asked the Portuguese for technical assistance. But Europe was not the only source of knowledge. For example, Narai also borrowed architectural styles and medical knowledge from the Persians and Chinese.

The main European advantage had been in acquiring the resources of the Americas for exploitation, often using enslaved African labor. But the large-scale trans-Atlantic slave trade became possible because the kings or chiefs of some

African states, such as Ashante (ah-SHAN-tee) and Dahomey (da-ho-MAY), profited by collaborating with it. Similarly, Spanish rule in the Americas survived only because the conquerors ultimately made compromises with Indian societies. For example, in Peru, well-placed Spaniards intermarried with the Inca elite and Spanish officials adopted some Inca administrative traditions. In the Spanish empire, as well as in other empires of the era such as the Ottoman and Mughal, laws recognized local customs, and different groups often maintained their own legal codes.

Innovative thought reflected the vigor of many societies. Science and technology remained creative all over Eurasia. The Chinese and British, for example, published important scientific books and invented new technologies, especially for the textile industry. New astronomical observatories were built in China, India, and the Middle East, although Europeans had by now developed a much keener interest than Asians in clocks and mathematics. Japan's fostering of schools gave it the world's highest literacy rate and an audience for a publishing industry. Siam and Burma also enjoyed high rates of literacy, though it was chiefly restricted to males. Leaders of the European Renaissance, Reformation, and Enlightenment, Sufi mystics in the Ottoman and Mughal Empires, the Hindu bhakti (BUK-tee) movement in India, and some Chinese thinkers challenged accepted wisdom. Various European and Chinese philosophers emphasized reason, as did some Latin Americans such as the Mexican nun and scientist Sor Juana Ines de la Cruz. Indeed, some participants in the European Enlightenment were inspired by their growing knowledge of secular China, which was ruled by emperors who dabbled in philosophy. A French ambassador in 1688 praised Qing China for promoting "virtue, wisdom, prudence, good faith, sincerity, charity, gentleness, honesty [and] civility."[4]

European achievement of global power was not inevitable. In this era China as well as several western European societies had sizeable empires and the potential for great economic and political success (see Historical Controversy: The Great Divergence Between Europe and Asia). Early Modern China, boasting the world's largest commercialized economy, remained the engine of the Eurasian economy. Not only Europe but also China experienced commercial growth, increases in cash cropping, growing industrial production, and widening marketing networks.

The maritime expansion of Europe, however, contrasted sharply with that of the Chinese. Just as western Europeans turned outward and developed a naval technology to match that of the Chinese, the Chinese pulled back from their grand maritime expeditions of the early 1400s and turned inward, although some Chinese merchants continued to venture out to trade. China enjoyed huge budget surpluses until the late 1700s and did not need colonies or foreign trade to prosper. Unlike western European states, the Chinese government did not depend on rich merchants for economic and political support. Chinese rulers feared that if merchants gained more wealth and influence, they could threaten the state and undermine Confucian values. In contrast, western European merchants had the support of their mercantilist governments, especially in England, the Netherlands, Spain, and France. The resulting political competition between European states fostered exploration and colonization.

Gunpowder and Warfare

Gunpowder weapons were not new. The Chinese invented gunpowder and then made the first true guns in the tenth century C.E., primarily for defensive purposes. The Mongols improved these Chinese weapons into a more effective offensive force, to blow open city gates. By 1241 these weapons had reached Europe. Early Modern Europeans, Turks, Mughals, and Chinese owed their strength in part to improvements in gunpowder weaponry. Combined with better military organization and seagoing capability, advanced weaponry inevitably affected political and social systems.

As they spread around Eurasia and North Africa, gunpowder weapons changed warfare. Europeans learned how to make particularly deadly weapons, improving the technology in part because they had easier access to metals. In Europe—full of competitive, often hostile states—no ruler had a monopoly on weapons, such as siege cannon. Hence rulers had an incentive to constantly improve their armaments, such as handheld muskets, to maintain the balance of power. As a result, the wars in Europe became far more deadly. Indeed, even in Asia and the Americas, Europeans often used the weapons more against each other than against the local people. The French writer Voltaire wrote that after 1500 all the pepper from Calicut came dyed red with blood, and a Portuguese poet lamented that the spices of the Indies were bought with Portuguese blood. The Portuguese, Dutch, and English slaughtered each other in Southeast Asia, and the English and French fought long wars in North America. A similar increase in battlefield casualties came in Japan in the civil war era of the 1500s, when Japanese swordsmiths learned how to replicate Portuguese and Spanish guns and cannon. Japanese small arms soon proved superior to European rifles. In contrast, the Ottomans did not create a class of Turkish and Arab craftsmen and instead relied heavily on hiring European craftsmen to manufacture their military and naval technology. Ashante and Dahomey achieved military success in West Africa because they had large armies equipped with muskets acquired from European slave traders.

But Asians took the development of their gunpowder arsenals only so far. With gunpowder weapons, the Qing greatly expanded China's land frontier deep into Central Asia and Tibet, thereby stabilizing their border regions. After that, secure in their power, the Manchu emperors had little need to increase their offensive capability, while the land-oriented Mughals saw little gain in developing naval armaments. The Chinese, Japanese, and Koreans all had some naval power but no interest in challenging the Europeans in the Indian Ocean. When Chinese came into contact with foreign firearms in 1500s, they found them superior to their own. A Chinese military manual published in 1644 concluded that "nothing has more range than the Ottoman musket. The next best is the European one."[5] Nonetheless, Chinese firearms were adequate for ejecting the

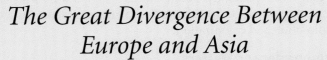

The Great Divergence Between Europe and Asia

In recent years historians have debated the roots of Europe's rise to world leadership, power, and wealth while other societies, especially in Asia, lost the political and economic leadership they once enjoyed—what some call "the great divergence." To many historians the surprising rise of Europe during the Early Modern Era needs explaining. It was not inevitable; history could have turned out very differently.

THE PROBLEM

How, why, and when Europe rather than a major Asian society like China came to dominate the world remain some of the principal questions of modern world history. If several Asian societies had an edge in power and wealth over other societies during most of the Intermediate Era, then why was the world so very different by 1800? Some western European societies, especially Britain, moved toward an unprecedented level of industrialization while once influential Asian societies, including China, increasingly faced challenges from the West. And when did western Europe begin to diverge from other dynamic, commercialized economies, especially China's? The debate divides into several schools of thought.

THE DEBATE

Many historians argue that the great divergence began in the Intermediate Era, when western Europe developed unique advantages that intensified after 1500. They contend that social, cultural, and political factors gave Europeans an advantage. David Landes believes Europe enjoyed a superior social heritage because its values and institutions promoted economic growth. In his view, European countries prospered because they were vital and open, valuing both hard work and knowledge, and these values led to increased economic productivity and positive attitudes toward change. Rodney Stark emphasizes what he considers a tradition unique to Christianity of stressing reason and progress. Offering another explanation, scholars such as E. L. Jones and Nathan Rosenberg stress the political pluralism represented by fiercely competing states. The chronic warfare between states stimulated a quest for increased revenues and more effective weapons. Furthermore, the flexibility of Western institutions, including the shift toward more representative government in England and Holland, made it easier to take advantage of overseas discoveries. In contrast to dynamic Europe, Landes and Jones argue, the rest of the world was static. China, in their view, had by 1700 reached an economic, political, and intellectual dead end, possessing wealth and power but introducing few inventions leading to any breakthroughs.

Other historians reject the notion of European social and cultural superiority. James Blaut and Andre Gunder Frank contend that the key to Europe's rise was not a unique culture but European countries' acquisition of wealth, especially in precious metals, from their conquests in the Americas. Between 1500 and 1800 the colonized Americas supplied 85 percent of the world's silver and 70 percent of the gold, a huge windfall to European merchants and governments, who were selling much of it to China in exchange for tea, silk, porcelain, and other valuable Chinese exports. The rise of the slavery-based plantation economy in the Americas in the 1600s produced additional profits for the Western colonizers. The sale of profitable American minerals and cash crops such as sugar not only stimulated European capitalism but also gave Europeans new advantages as they tapped into the lucrative Asian market. Blaut also believes that Europe benefited from being much closer than was Asia to the Americas.

Many who dispute the claim that Western social and cultural traditions or the pluralistic state system were an advantage agree that Europeans capitalized on events, such as the American conquests and the acquisition of Asian and Middle Eastern technology, to foster economic growth. Scholars such as John Hobson, Alan Smith, L. S. Stavrianos, and Eric Wolf have shown that western European economies were rapidly commercializing from late medieval times and produced a full-blown commercial capitalism between 1450 and 1800 that helped generate a more widespread and powerful world economy. Nonetheless, while Europeans developed better weaponry and business organization, some historians conclude that Europe had no real advantage over China until the late eighteenth or early nineteenth centuries, when industrialization gave the British and later some other western Europeans a vastly superior technology.

Many historians disagree that China was at a dead end and in economic decline. They argue that China's commercial economy dwarfed all others, making China a major player in world trade. In 1800 China still produced a third of all the world's manufactured goods. China also imported over half of all the silver mined in the Americas. Chinese in the commercialized core regions may have enjoyed as high, if not higher, standards of living, per capita incomes, and long life spans as northwest Europeans before 1800. Chinese merchants and craftsmen were intensely competitive, hardly constrained by the Ming and Qing state. Indeed, China's commercial economy grew rapidly from the early Ming to the mid-1700s, producing abundant export products which were eagerly sought by merchants from all over Afro-Eurasia.

Scholars also question whether other Asian societies, including India, were in decline, even though their states were clearly weakening. By 1800 India could not match China's economy but still produced around a quarter of the world's industry, about the same as Europe. With their many exports and imports, China and India remained the engines for the Eastern Hemisphere trading system well into the 1700s. In the early Mughal era India enjoyed a far larger, more productive economy than England. Although the Mughal state was collapsing by the early 1700s, Indian manufactured goods still attracted a vigorous international trade. R. Bin Wong, Kenneth Pomeranz, and Andre Gunder Frank suggest that eighteenth-century China, India, western Europe, and perhaps Japan had comparable levels of economic development. The Indian scholar Amiya Kumar Bagchi agrees, stressing that western Europeans enjoyed no decisive advantage over China and India in economic production, consumption, and growth before Britain's Industrial Revolution, and that China only fell behind in the 1850s. Furthermore, he argues, most Europeans saw little improvement in their lives until the late nineteenth century.

In asking why sustained economic growth began first in northwestern Europe rather than in eastern Asia, Pomeranz argues that the densely populated Yangzi River Delta of China, Japan's Tokyo region, and possibly even India's Gujerat region were similar in many respects to the northwest European core regions, England and the Netherlands, in the seventeenth and eighteenth centuries, and that all these regions were facing similar ecological and demographic stress, such as overpopulation. The great divergence came in the 1800s, he suggests, when one country, England, developed fossil fuels, especially its coal industry, for power while increasingly reaping the benefits of cheap, often slavery-produced resources from the Americas. China had used coal many centuries before Europe, but its remaining coal reserves were remote from the major population centers. The availability of slave-produced American wealth

and easily tapped coal reserves, Pomeranz suggests, put first England and then northwestern Europe on a completely new development path unavailable to China, Japan, and India, changing world history.

EVALUATING THE DEBATE

This debate will likely thrive for years, making thoughtful arguments on all sides. Some scholars see the rise of the West as inevitable, a result of certain advantageous trends building for centuries, while others argue that things could have turned out differently had Western nations not been able to exploit American resources and China had sustained its dynamism. The Industrial Revolution in Europe, beginning in the late 1700s, which gave Europeans the technology and wealth to achieve global dominance, may have been the product of long-standing and unique European attitudes, or it may have resulted from a late shift in global economic power, fueled by American resources, that favored Europe and undermined China and India. Whether or not Europe was exceptionally enterprising or simply lucky in finding useful resources, the new, expanded world economy that emerged between 1500 and 1800 benefited primarily western Europe and later North America, but it eventually touched everyone, bringing about changes in many aspects of life around the world.

Tea-Packing Factory in China This painting from the 1700s shows a tea-packing factory in China's major trading port, Guangzhou (Canton) in southern China. A European merchant negotiates with a Chinese manager while Chinese workers prepare tea for export. (Courtesy of the Trustees of the Victoria & Albert Museum)

THINKING ABOUT THE CONTROVERSY

1. Why do some historians believe the great divergence between Asia and the West did not come until after 1750?

2. How did Western expansion into the Americas give some European countries an advantage over Asian countries in the global economy?

EXPLORING THE CONTROVERSY

Historians emphasizing Europe's social, cultural, and political advantages include David S. Landes, *The Wealth and Power of Nations: Why Some Are So Rich and Some Are So Poor* (New York: Norton, 1998), Rodney Stark, *The Victory of Reason: How Christianity Led to Freedom, Capitalism, and Western Success* (New York: Random House, 2005); E. L. Jones, *The European Miracle: Environments, Economies and Geopolitics in the History of Europe and Asia*, 3rd ed. (Cambridge: Cambridge University Press, 2003); and Nathan Rosenberg and L. E. Birdzell, Jr., *How the West Grew Rich* (New York: Basic Books, 1986). On the rise of the European-dominated world economy, see Alan K. Smith, *Creating a World Economy: Merchant Capital, Colonialism, and World Trade, 1400–1825* (Boulder, Colo.: Westview Press, 1991); L. S. Stavrianos, *Global Rift: The Third World Comes of Age* (New York: William Morrow, 1981); and Eric Wolf, *Europe and the Peoples Without History* (Berkeley: University of California Press, 1983). Scholars dubious of innate European advantages include Andre Gunder Frank, *ReORIENT: Global Economy in the Asian Age* (Berkeley: University of California Press, 1998); James Blaut, *The Colonizer's Model of the World: Geographical Diffusionism and Eurocentric History* (New York: Guilford Press, 1993); Amiya Kumar Bagchi, *Perilous Passage: Mankind and the Global Ascendancy of Capital* (Lanham, M.D.: Rowman and Littlefield, 2005); and John M. Hobson, *The Eastern Origins of Western Civilization* (New York: Cambridge University Press, 2004). On China's continuing strength, see Kenneth Pomeranz, *The Great Divergence: China, Europe, and the Making of the Modern World Economy* (Princeton: Princeton University Press, 2000); and R. Bin Wong, *China Transformed: Historical Change and the Limits of European Experience* (Ithaca, N.Y.: Cornell University Press, 1997). For an excellent discussion of the great divergence debate and related issues, see David D. Buck, "Was It Pluck or Luck That Made the West Grow Rich?" *Journal of World History*, 10/2 (Fall, 1999), pp. 413–430.

Dutch from Taiwan and the Russians from the Amur Valley in the 1600s. But two centuries later, European military technology far surpassed that of Asian powers, dramatically changing the hemispheric balance of power.

THE EMERGING WORLD ECONOMY

With the opening of the Atlantic and Pacific Oceans to regular sea travel, connections spanning not just hemispheres but the entire world were forged during the Early Modern Era. Western Europeans gradually created a global network of economic and political relationships that increasingly shaped the destinies of people around the world. Rather than the luxuries of earlier times, such as silks and spices, long-distance trade increasingly moved bulk items: essential natural resources, such as sugar and silver from the Americas, and manufactured goods, such as textiles from Europe and Asia. Traders moved commodities and capital faster and more cheaply over greater distances than ever before. These trends wove together different societies in a world economy. European merchants were actually only a small part of global commerce; some Asian and African merchant groups also flourished, and some Asian states, particularly China and Siam, benefited from the increasing trade. Nonetheless, western Europeans usually benefited more, and it was Europeans who laid the foundations for a new global system to emerge after 1750.

The New Trading System

Europeans became the main beneficiaries of the increased communication and travel that shaped a gradual globalization of trade. The capitalist market economy that gradually developed was increasingly centered on northwestern Europe, especially England and the Netherlands, but a half dozen other European countries were also enriched by trade (see map). For example, the Portuguese as well as the Dutch established regular maritime trade routes between Europe and Asia around Africa that allowed Europeans to avoid the overland routes through the Middle East while harming their Muslim rivals by diminishing Persian and Ottoman commerce. The Spanish conquest of the Americas provided huge quantities of silver from Peru, Bolivia, and Mexico, which financed expansion of the European economy and, since Asian governments valued silver, enabled Europeans to gain access to Asian markets. The Spanish establishment of a base at Manila in 1571 provided an essential economic link between eastern Eurasia and the Americas, forging a major foundation for a truly world economy. European exploration and settlement in the Americas brought access to resources such as timber, marine mammals, fish, and wildlife (particularly furbearing beavers) only lightly exploited before by local peoples.

Growing commercial activity stimulated production for the market, in mining and manufacturing but especially in tropical agriculture. The highly profitable plantations that sprung up around the Caribbean Basin, along the Atlantic coast of North and South America, and on the Atlantic and Indian Ocean islands and the Philippines reflected the expansion of production. A growing trans-Atlantic slave trade provided cheap labor to the American plantations, enabling them to produce inexpensive calories for Europe in the form of sugar and, after 1700, abundant cotton for English mills. Thousands of slaves obtained in eastern Europe, East Africa, Sri Lanka, and Indonesia also labored for European and Muslim enterprises in the Middle East, South Africa, and Southeast Asia.

As a result of the growing commercial activity, including the slave trades, by 1750 millions of people worked thousands of miles from their place of birth or otherwise experienced lives very different from those of their ancestors. For example, Chinese merchants lived on Java, Persians served in the Siamese government, Turkish soldiers fought for the sultans of Acheh (AH-cheh) in Sumatra, Portuguese settled in Mozambique, Kongolese labored in Brazil, and French traders explored the Mississippi Basin. Some merchants flourished by having operations in many lands. One of the most successful was the German commercial agent Ferdinand Cron in the late sixteenth and early seventeenth century. Born in Augsburg and then based in Portuguese-ruled Goa on India's west coast, Cron supervised a network of couriers who collected information on markets and prices from Europe in the West to Melaka and Macao in the East and then used that information to make lucrative investments.

Asia and Europe in the New World Economy

The transition to a European-dominated trading system took place over several centuries in Asia. Before the 1800s, when the transition was completed, Asia boasted the bulk of world economic activity. Asians produced some 80 percent of goods as late as 1775, and this production had probably increased since 1500. The industries of China and India remained the twin pillars of Asian commerce well into the 1700s. Indian textiles such as cashmere and cotton cloth were so popular in Asia, Africa, and Europe that they almost constituted a form of currency. Handicraft industries also flourished in the Ottoman Empire, Persia, Sri Lanka, Burma, Siam, and Java during the sixteenth and seventeenth centuries. These societies imported raw materials from India (including raw cotton), China (especially silk), and Japan (copper) for production into exportable consumer goods. For example, Javanese women used beeswax and dying to transform Indian cloth into beautiful batik clothing. The economies of India and China dwarfed those of any other country. The most economically developed regions within China, Japan, India, and northwestern Europe may have enjoyed roughly comparable standards of living, including health and income levels.

Asian merchants, enjoying lower overhead and shrewd business skills, could often outcompete those from Europe. After 1670 Indian merchants even took the Indonesian textile market away from the Dutch. Like Europeans, Asians also traded over long distances. In the 1600s, for example, Arab and Persian traders remained influential at the main Mughal port, Surat, while north Indian merchants were found all over the Persian Gulf. Many wealthy Asian trading magnates had huge capital resources. The trader Virji Vohra (VEER-gee VOOR-ah) in Surat was as rich as Europe's wealthiest merchant family, the

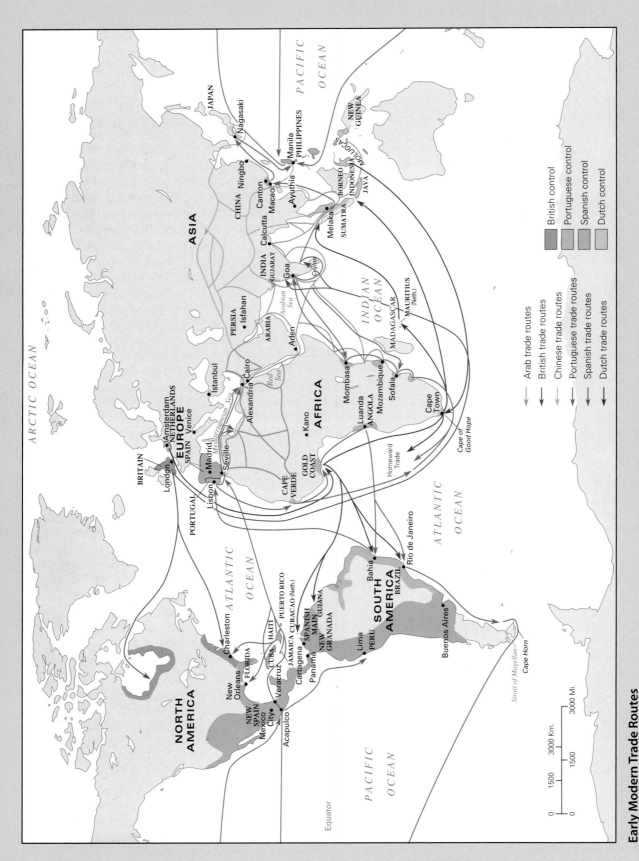

Early Modern Trade Routes

Between 1500 and 1700 the world economy developed and new trade routes proliferated. Major maritime routes linked Asia and the Americas across the Pacific; Europe, Asia, and the Americas across the Atlantic; and eastern and southern Asia with Africa and Europe across the Indian Ocean.

Fuggers in Germany. A European visitor to Goa in 1510 was amazed at the competition provided by fabulously rich Arab and Indian merchants: "We [Europeans] believe ourselves to be the most astute men that one can encounter, and the people here surpass us in everything. And they can do better calculations by memory than we can do with the pen."[6] European merchants competed best when they were, like the Dutch East Indies Company traders, supported by military force.

European-Asian trade relations often favored Asians. Since Asians had little interest in European manufactured goods such as clothing, which they considered inferior in quality to their own goods, Europeans bought Asian goods and resources with American silver and gold. For example, since Europeans traded with China for products such as tea, vast amounts of American silver ended up in China, where it served as the basis of the monetary system and promoted economic growth. The Ottoman, Safavid, and Mughal Empires also needed an expanding money supply to meet the investment needs of their expanding economies and were, like the Chinese, ready to trade goods for silver.

Asian goods found a ready market around the world. Europeans shipped bullion to Persia for silk, and Persia shipped bullion to India for cotton textiles. Chinese goods transported from the Philippines were so much cheaper than Spanish ones in Peru that the Spanish viceroy complained it was "impossible to choke off the trade since a man can clothe his wife in Chinese silks for 25 pesos, whereas he could not provide her with clothing of Spanish silks with 200 pesos."[7] While European ships carried a growing amount of seaborne trade, European merchants accounted for only a small proportion of trade from India and China. Mughal India traded far more with Central Asians and Ottomans than with the Dutch or English. Asian exports to Europe grew slowly; intra-Asian trade was far larger.

Expanding Trade Networks

The growth of long-distance trade corresponded to the expansion of trade networks operated by different commercial communities. The rise of European power allowed Dutch, English, and French merchants to establish themselves in India, Southeast Asia, West Africa, eastern Europe, Russia, and the Caribbean Basin. At the same time, Sephardic Jews, originally from Iberia, spread their trading networks throughout western Europe, flourishing particularly in Antwerp, Amsterdam, Seville, and Geneva. Eventually, Jews also became active as merchants in parts of South America, the Caribbean, and the Indian Ocean. Some entered the Asian spice trade, developing ties as far east as Melaka. The Mendes family, for instance, expelled from Spain in 1492 and eventually based in Istanbul, had business connections in several European cities and, with their banks, helped finance the gem and spice trades across Asia, Europe, and Africa.

Groups specializing in trade were prominent in many lands. Chinese remained active all over Southeast Asia, establishing permanent settlements in many cities and towns. For example, the Spanish in the Philippines depended on the Chinese merchant class to supply many consumer goods. A Spanish friar observed in the mid-1600s that although Manila "is small, and the Spaniards are few, nevertheless, they require the services of thousands of Chinese."[8] Traders of French or mixed French and Indian descent traveled deep into the North American continent contacting local peoples. In East Africa, it was the Omani Arabs who had a leading role. In West Africa, Hausa (HOUSE-uh) merchants increasingly dominated the trade networks of the Sudan by the 1600s. This trade domination brought prosperity to walled cities like Kano (KAH-no), famous for its cloth manufacturers, and Katsina. Hausa merchants became influential in the Niger Basin as far west as the Ashante kingdom and supplied resources such as kola nuts to the far-reaching trans-Saharan trade, which still flourished despite growing European trade along the west coast. In far western Africa the Dyula (JOO-lah), Mandinka Muslims, held the leading commercial position.

Similarly, some Asian merchants, especially Indians and Armenians, maintained and even expanded commercial networks over vast distances. The Indian maritime trade network stretched from Arabia, Persia, northeast Africa, and the Red Sea to Melaka, Sumatra, Siam, and China. Although the Portuguese cut into the Indians' power in the Indian Ocean, Indians remained active in the 1700s. Meanwhile, Indian overland trade networks extended across Central Asia, Afghanistan, Tibet, Persia, the Caucasus states, and much of Russia. Armenian merchants based in Safavid Persia flourished in the overland trade from India to Central Asia and the Middle East, and from Persia to Russia, England, and the Baltic. Some Armenians traveled widely. Hovannes Ter-Davtian (tur-DAHV-ti-an) left Isfahan in 1692, traded on the western and eastern coasts of India, and then spent seven years in Tibet before arriving in Calcutta in 1693 with a cargo of Chinese porcelain, gold, and musk that earned him a handsome profit. Growing Eurasian trade clearly involved, and often benefited, varied groups.

ENVIRONMENTAL CHANGES

Human activity reshaped the natural world and was influenced by it in turn. As they had for millennia, people tapped the Earth for underground resources, such as coal and iron ore, but large-scale manufacturing, which often pollutes the environment, was found in only a few widely scattered countries, mostly in Eurasia. For farming and light industries, Early Modern economies relied chiefly on traditional power sources, such as people, animals, water, and wind. For example, windmills were common in the Middle East and Europe, and spinning wheels, often operated by women, were widespread in Eurasia and North Africa. Nonetheless, natural systems came under more stress as the global population nearly doubled, putting severe pressure on land and resources. Expanding settlements and farming in frontier regions displaced woodlands, grasslands, and wetlands and reduced the variety of plant and animal life. More spectacularly, the exchange of diseases, plants, and animals across the Atlantic altered entire environments and resulted in huge population losses in the Americas.

Climate Change and Population Growth

Between 1300 and 1850 much of the world experienced a fluctuating "Little Ice Age," probably caused by a dimming sun and increased volcanic activity, that had significant consequences for many societies. In North America and Eurasia, this period brought cool temperatures, shorter growing seasons, and famine. The coldest years came between 1570 and 1730, and then through the early 1800s. For example, in the 1600s China often received either too much rain, which caused widespread flooding, or too little rain and late springs, which produced drought and reduced the growing season to allow for only one crop of rice rather than two. The lands bordering the North Atlantic saw much colder and wetter conditions, which diminished agricultural production and resulting in widespread starvation in much of Europe. Indeed, harsh weather conditions, combined with occasional outbreaks of bubonic plague, may have been one of the factors that spurred Europeans to seek new lands abroad. Climate change also affected topical regions. For example, West Africa had abundant rain until 1700, when rainfall began diminishing, allowing desert to claim much of the Sahel and pushing savannah farming southward by several hundred miles.

Nonetheless, despite the poor weather, the distribution of new food sources and other resources was widening. For instance, western European societies obtained more food, particularly grain, from eastern Europe, and thus became more linked to that region. Seaborne trade, especially from the Americas, also provided valuable resources, especially to coastal maritime states such as the Netherlands and Britain. The increased diffusion of resources fostered population growth. Indeed, American crops such as the potato helped Europe stave off even worse climate-related famines. To the east, the Mughals cleared the forests and wetlands of Bengal to create a large area for rice growing, which allowed them to feed more people. Around the world the expansion of farming to sustain more people came at the expense of shifting cultivators, pastoralists, and food collectors. Some peoples, such as the pastoral Khoikhoi (KOI-KOI) in South Africa, died off or were enslaved or killed.

Partly because of the spread of food crops, especially from the Americas to Afro-Eurasia, world population increased significantly. In 1500 the earth contained between 400 and 500 million people. Perhaps 60 percent lived in Asia, with China and India each accounting for nearly a quarter of the world total. By 1750 the world population had grown to between 700 and 750 million, probably 80 percent of them peasants living on the land. China and India together, totaling perhaps 400 million, still accounted for over half, while Europe held perhaps 20 percent and Africa 10 percent of the world total.

The Exchange of Diseases, Animals, and Crops

In this era people, chiefly Europeans and Africans, moved voluntarily or involuntarily to distant lands, deliberately or accidentally carrying with them species of animals, insects, bacteria, and plants that reshaped local ecosystems. These biological invasions, what historians have termed the Columbian Exchange, particularly accompanied the encounter between Eurasia and the Americas. The European settlers in the Americas brought with them horses and food animals: pigs, chickens, sheep, and cattle. To raise beef cattle, Europeans introduced ranching. Ships returning to Europe carried with them American turkeys, which enriched Eurasian diets.

The exchange of diseases between the Eastern and Western Hemispheres was not one-way, but it had a greater impact on the Americas than on Eurasia and Africa. Native Americans had never experienced, and hence had developed no immunities to, Afro-Eurasian diseases such as smallpox, diphtheria, measles, chicken pox, whooping cough, malaria, bubonic plague, yellow fever, cholera, typhoid fever, and influenza. These diseases devastated the Americas. Smallpox brought the greatest known demographic catastrophe in world history, killing off around 90 percent of the peoples of the Americas. This was a much greater percentage of population than that destroyed by the terrible Black Death, which ravaged much of Eurasia and North Africa in the 1300s. The demographic disaster for the Americas emptied productive land and hence paved the way for Europeans to settle the Americas and to import captive Africans to labor in mining and agriculture. Only in the highlands, such as the Andes Mountains in South America, where European diseases had a smaller impact, did substantial concentrations of Native Americans survive. In contrast, only a few American diseases, especially syphilis, brought suffering to people in Europe and Africa.

Crop exchanges also proved momentous. Eurasian and African crops transformed some American regions, and required the introduction of new agricultural practices. Most Native Americans had grown crops such as corn (maize) and potatoes on small plots, but settlers found that Afro-Eurasian crops such as wheat, rice, coffee, barley, and sugar were most successfully grown on large farms or estates. Among these imported crops, sugar had the most impact on the Americas, and vast acreage was devoted to its growth, mostly on plantations worked by African slaves and their descendants. Much of the sugar was exported to Europe for use to sweeten foods such as jam and breads, and beverages such as tea and coffee.

American crops spread widely in the Eastern Hemisphere, where people adopted them to enhance their lives or resolve some of their own food problems. Tobacco, for instance, gained popularity in China and Europe, generating both avid devotees (some of whom considered it medicinal) and opponents who considered it unhealthy or immoral. Many imports, such as tomatoes, made the once bland European meals more varied. Potatoes became a mainstay of the European diet and the major crop grown in several societies, including Ireland and Scotland. Maize (corn) could be grown on marginal land and proved a boon in Africa, southwest Asia, and China, where it was planted on unused hillsides. Corn also fed livestock, and the stalks could be used to make huts and sheds. American chilies, hotter than Asian black peppers, proved hugely popular in South and Southeast Asian cooking, adding a sharp bite to curries and other foods. Peanuts became a key crop in West

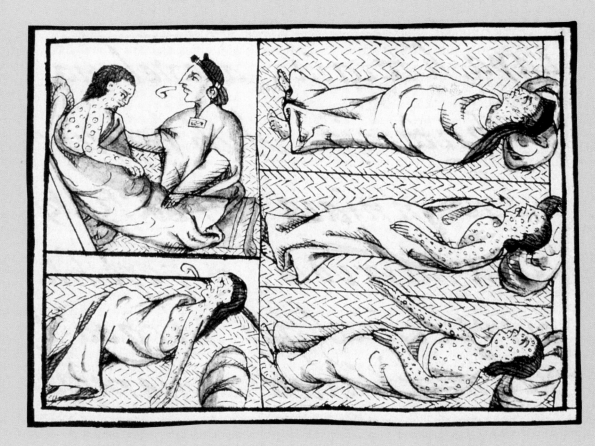

Smallpox Victims in the Americas Eurasian diseases accompanied the Europeans to the Americas, causing a catastrophic loss of life for the Native Americans, who had no immunity. As shown in this print from the 1500s, millions of people sickened and died from smallpox. (Biblioteca Medicea Laurenziana)

Africa. The new foods offered not only a more varied diet but also a healthier one. By 1750 a diner in many cities in the world could enjoy a fruit salad mixing pieces of Southeast Asian bananas and mangos, Chinese peaches, Southwest Asian pears, African watermelons, Mesoamerican papayas, South American pineapples, and Mediterranean grapes.

European expansion and colonization owed much to the spread of the Eurasian biota, a distinct package of plants, animals, and germs that overwhelmed the rest of the world, especially the Americas and, later, Oceania. Eurasian plants, such as wheat and apple trees, and animals, such as cattle, often replaced indigenous ones in the temperate zones of the Americas and, after 1800, Australia and New Zealand. These changes occurred in part because Europeans viewed animals, plants, and land largely as commodities, to be exploited for their own benefit. The English scientist Sir Francis Bacon expressed these attitudes well: "The world is made for man, not man for the world."[9]

SOCIAL AND CULTURAL CHANGE

During the Early Modern Era, the growing networks of trade, information, and technology fostered changes in societies all over the world. Some changes resulted from the increasing migration of peoples, voluntarily or by force. Intermarriage or sexual contact between people from different ethnic groups produced new peoples with mixed cultural backgrounds. Other contributing factors were changing economic systems, the growth of international trade, and the exchange of ideas.

Encounters with other ways of living and thinking stimulated curiosity and fostered rethinking. Several religions expanded their boundaries and sought converts, challenging the ancient faiths of the Americas and parts of Asia.

Migration and Hybrid Groups

Improved maritime technology made it possible for people to cross vast oceans and to do so in larger numbers than ever before. The resulting contacts between peoples reshaped societies. A new system of global migration brought people with very different customs and values together, not always happily. The largest population movement involved Europeans settling in the Americas and bringing with them enslaved Africans but few European women. Women comprised perhaps only a fifth of the Spanish and Portuguese who went to the Americas; men thus frequently sought partners among Native American and African women.

Intermarriage and sexual relations across social boundaries led to the creation of American societies that contained many mixed-descent people. By 1750 in Latin America and in French colonies such as Haiti and Louisiana a large part of the population blended European and Native American backgrounds, creating mestizos, or European and African ancestries, fostering mulattos. For example, many people in Mexico City were mestizo, while in New Orleans blacks and mulattos predominated. In turn, these groups' cultures often mixed the varying social influences, as in northeast Brazil, where people blended African religions and Catholic traditions. Unlike

English North America, where any African ancestry usually meant classification as black, in much of Latin America a complex hierarchy of social categories developed based on gradations of skin color.

Migration and intermarriage also occurred in the Eastern Hemisphere. Dutch and Portuguese adventurers and merchants, most of them men, settled in southern Africa and the port cities of South and Southeast Asia, often taking wives from the local population. Some of the Russians who moved into Siberia and the Black Sea region mixed with local peoples. As had been true for centuries, Arab and Indian traders relocated to distant lands in Africa and Eurasia, often settling permanently and sometimes taking local wives. Many Chinese also migrated, usually with their families, and moved into nearby territories such as Taiwan, and male merchants settled in Southeast Asia, where they often intermarried. For example, several thousand Chinese lived in the major Siamese city, Ayuthia; one of them wrote in the early 1600s that "Siam is really friendly to the Chinese."[10] Many of the Chinese married Ayuthia women and stayed permanently, their descendants mixing Chinese and Siamese culture. More Chinese also arrived, and by 1735 some 20,000 lived in the kingdom.

Groups of mixed European and Asian ancestry appeared in European colonies in Asia. For instance, the Portuguese men who settled in Goa, Colombo, and Melaka married local women and raised their children as Portuguese-speaking Catholics. But their descendants adopted many local customs. Hence, in Melaka today, while Catholic churches, schools, and festivals remain at the heart of Portuguese community life, the local Portuguese language contains many Malay words, the cuisine has borrowed extensively from Malay and Chinese cooking, and, unlike their merchant, sailor, and soldier ancestors, most men work as fishermen. Throughout the era Portuguese was the lingua franca of maritime Asia, spoken in many ports, and some of its words were incorporated into local languages such as Malay.

In Africa too—South Africa, Mozambique, Angola, and along the West African coast—the mixing of Europeans and Africans led to hybrid social groups. The offspring of relations between Dutch men and African or Asian women were so common in South Africa that they became a distinct racial group, known as the Coloreds. Prominent slave-trading and merchant families of West Africa often descended from Portuguese men who married women from local chiefly or royal families. Like Brazilian mulattos and many Asian mestizos, African mulattos often spoke a version of Portuguese, the first language with a global reach.

Changing Gender Relations

Although men, voluntarily or involuntarily, were much more likely than women to join overseas ventures or cross oceans, women were also affected by the changes of the era. In the Americas many European men sought Indian women, often by force. One-third of enslaved Africans taken to the Americas were women, some of whom were brought into close contact with slave-owning men, mostly white, who exercised control over their lives. The result was forced sexual activity and mixed-descent children. Since slave couples were often separated by sale, women held together many slave households, a social pattern that continued among many African Americans after the abolition of slavery. Christian missionaries working among North American Indians often pursued policies that marginalized women in once egalitarian cultures such as the Algonquians of eastern Canada and the Iroquois of New York.

Gender patterns were modified around the world, including in Africa. For instance, in the parts of Africa most affected by slave trading, the absence of men in their productive years encouraged the remaining men to take multiple wives, a practice that may or may not have made life easier for women. The traditional role of West African women in local commerce, however, also meant that, along the coast, some became active as slave traders. A few of these, such as Senhora Philippa, who in the 1630s controlled the trading center of Rufisque (ROO-feesk) in today's Senegal, became immensely wealthy and owned trading ships and magnificent houses. Women also played powerful roles in some of the newer kingdoms fostered by the trans-Atlantic slave trade, where they controlled access to the kings. For example, in Dahomey queen mothers wielded extraordinary power in a palace occupied by a few men and thousands of women, many of them wives and concubines of the king. Dahomey women also served as soldiers and bodyguards. A Portuguese missionary to one Senegambia kingdom described a powerful woman, the king's aunt, who was "so respected and obeyed that nothing of importance took place in the kingdom without her knowledge."[11] Of course, most African women, whether slave or free, enjoyed much less wealth and power in their communities than these merchants and royal women.

In much of Eurasia women experienced increasing subordination by men. Hence, women generally became more restricted in Mughal India, China, and Japan as patriarchal attitudes strengthened, largely as a result of internal factors. For example, Qing leaders turned more socially conservative, imposing harsher laws against behavior considered deviant, such as homosexuality, and stressing the purity of women, which meant less freedom for women to leave home. Adopting the idea of the "chaste widow," more Chinese widows than ever before, forever faithful to their late husbands, frequently refused to remarry. In addition, Western missionaries and officials often sought to impose their own patriarchal prejudices on Asians. Hence, in Southeast Asia, the Spanish and Portuguese were often appalled at the relative freedom of women. Spanish officials criticized Filipinos for tolerating adultery and premarital sex, and they punished those who engaged in these activities.

But there were exceptions to the growing restrictions on women. The Mughal emperor Akbar ordered that no woman could be forced by family or community pressures to immolate herself on her husband's funeral pyre, arguing that "it is a strange commentary on the magnanimity of men that they seek their own salvation by means of the self-sacrifice of their wives."[12] Many Qing women from elite families published essays and poetry that were widely read and admired. One Chinese poet recalled how her father nurtured her talent: "Understanding that I was quite intelligent, He taught his daughters as he taught his sons, [advising us to] Develop together, support, and do not impede each other."[13]

Missionaries and Religious Change

The encounters between widely differing cultures around the world also had a religious dimension, forcing people to confront different belief systems while widening or sparking divisions in established faiths. Some of the major conflicts came in Europe. Tensions simmering for several centuries finally fragmented Western Christianity into Catholic and diverse Protestant churches in the 1500s, spurring religious wars, militancy, and hostility toward non-Christians. Dissenters were punished by those in the majority. Scientists such as the Italian astronomer Galileo Galilei and the Flemish biologist Andreas Vesalius, (an-DRAY-us ve-SAL-yus) who produced the first reference manual on human anatomy, were tried by the Holy Inquisition, a Catholic Church institution organized to root out heresy.

Meanwhile, other religious traditions also dealt with tensions and divisions. Mystical Sufi orders became more influential in Islamic societies from Indonesia to West Africa. For example, the early Mughal emperors Babur (BAH-bur) and Akbar were fervent Sufis. Babur wrote in a poem that "I am their follower in heart and soul. I am a king, but yet a slave [follower] of the Dervishes [mystics]."[14] But the Sufis' popularity distressed dogmatists, fostering debate on Sufism's role and value among Ottoman, Mughal, and Central Asian Muslims. Islamic division hardened in Persia, too. Ordered by their Safavid rulers, Persians shifted from the Sunni to the Shi'a branch of Islam, causing many Sunnis to emigrate. But tensions sometimes led to secular approaches rather than to religious zeal. One such movement, neo-Confucianism, became a strong influence in China, helping secular values to triumph there while Buddhism lost influence among the elites. To comprehend a world charged with diverse and changing ideas, Chinese thinkers, European Enlightenment philosophers, and several Mughal emperors questioned religious dogmas and sought to broaden intellectual horizons.

In contrast to those who explored new ideas, many were religious militants and engaged in missionary activity. Christians actively sought converts in the Americas, Africa, and Asia. Christian missionaries were often intolerant of local traditions and scornful toward the people they were trying to reach. One prominent Spanish clergyman strongly supported conquest and evangelization as a way of "civilizing" Native Americans, whom he described as "these pitiful men, in whom you will scarcely find any vestiges of humanness. They were born for servitude. How are we to doubt that these people, so uncultivated, so barbarous, and so contaminated with such impiety and lewdness, have not been so justly conquered."[15] Catholicism eventually triumphed in Latin America, Kongo, and the Philippines, and it found a few thousand converts in East Asia. Protestant missionaries mostly concentrated on Catholic Europe, Southeast Asia, and North America, where they particularly targeted Native Americans and slaves.

At the same time, the Christian missionary enterprise faced challenges, including stiff resistance. To gain acceptance, missionaries often had to blend Christianity with local traditions, often against the opposition of church leaders. The intolerance of many Christian missionaries toward other faiths led to their expulsion from Japan and China. East Asians assimilated some useful Western technical and scientific knowledge from the missionaries, such as clock-making and mapmaking, but most rejected Christianity. Christian missionary efforts had little success among Muslims, Theravada Buddhists, and Hindus. Indeed, missionary activity sometimes prompted non-Christians to solidify support for traditional ways, as was the case in China and Japan.

Christianity was not the only missionary religion: millions of Europeans, Africans, and Asians embraced Islam. Islam spread into the Balkan societies under Ottoman control, and many Serbs, Albanians, and Bulgarians adopted the faith, forging a permanent divide between Christians and Muslims in the region. Islam continued to gain strength in sub-Saharan Africa, Mughal India, and Island Southeast Asia. Unlike Christianity, Islam was not identified with unpopular Western conquest, and it continued to link distant societies. For instance, in the 1600s Nuruddin al-Raniri, (new-ROOD-in al-RAN-eer-ee) from Gujerat in India, studied in Mecca and then traveled widely, finally settling in Acheh, Sumatra, and becoming an adviser to the king. Under Nuruddin's influence, the sultan promoted the more vigorous practice of Islamic customs, such as fasting, strict dietary laws, and alms-giving.

Some trends promoted accommodation between divergent faiths. For example, in India the Mughal emperor Akbar preached tolerance and cultural diversity. Indeed, in some respects Akbar and his ancient Indian predecessor, the Mauryan emperor Asoka, were global pioneers in promoting respect for different traditions. Akbar's more zealously Islamic successors, however, repressed Hinduism, reviving a long conflict between the two faiths. Theravada Buddhists generally respected all religions. Hence, when the French king, Louis XIV, sent a mission to King Narai of Ayuthia requesting that he and his people adopt Roman Catholicism, the Siamese monarch sent a letter back, arguing that God rejoiced not in religious uniformity but in theological diversities, preferring to be honored by different worships and ceremonies. Meanwhile, Muslims and animists lived side by side without conflict in parts of Africa. Similarly, in some European societies, notably the Netherlands and Poland, Protestants and Catholics learned to live in peace. And growing European knowledge of Chinese society, including Confucianism, led some leaders of the European Enlightenment, such as Voltaire, to view China as an admirable, secular alternative model to the religious divisions and orthodoxies of Europe. In this way Asian ideas influenced some Europeans just as European ideas spread to some non-European peoples, a testament to an increasingly connected world.

SUGGESTED READING

BOOKS

Adas, Michael, ed. *Islamic and European Expansion: The Forging of a Global Order*. Philadelphia: Temple University Press, 1993. Contains excellent essays by William McNeill, Alfred Crosby, and Philip Curtin on major developments in this era.

Black, Jeremy. *War in the World: Military Power and the Fate of Continents, 1450–2000*. New Haven: Yale University Press, 1998. A global history of land and sea warfare and its contexts.

Brandon, William. *New Worlds for Old: Reports from the New World and Their Effect on the Development of Social Thought in Europe, 1500–1800*. Athens: Ohio University Press, 1986. Examines the impact on Europe of the American discoveries and cultures.

Crosby, Alfred W. *Ecological Imperialism: The Biological Expansion of Europe, 900–1900*. Cambridge: Cambridge University Press, 1993. A pioneering exploration of the environmental changes in the past millennium.

Curtin, Philip D. *The World and the West: The European Challenge and the Overseas Response in the Age of Empire*. Cambridge: Cambridge University Press, 2000. Explores relevant themes in world history since 1500.

Eltis, David. *The Rise of African Slavery in the Americas*. New York: Cambridge University Press, 2000. Overview of slavery and the Atlantic system.

Gunn, Geoffrey C. *First Globalization: The Eurasian Exchange*. Lanham, Md.: Rowman and Littlefield, 2003. An idiosyncratic but absorbing study of East-West encounters.

Hobhouse, Henry. *Seeds of Change: Five Plants That Transformed Mankind*. New York: Harper and Row, 1985. A fascinating study of how quinine, sugar, tea, cotton, and the potato changed the world.

Marks, Robert B. *The Origins of the Modern World: A Global and Ecological Narrative*. Lanham, Md.: Rowman and Littlefield, 2002. A stimulating, readable, and concise account of how the modern world emerged.

Pacey, Arnold. *Technology in World Civilization*. Cambridge: MIT Press, 1990. Provides a global overview of technological change in this era.

Pilcher, Jeffrey M. *Food in World History*. New York: Routledge, 2006. Examines changing food cultures around the world.

Pomeranz, Kenneth and Steven Topic. *The World That Trade Created: Society, Culture, and the World Economy, 1400 to the Present*, 2nd ed., Armonk, N.Y.: M. E. Sharpe, 2006. Contains dozens of brief esasys written for the general public.

Richards, John F. *The Unending Frontier: An Environmental History of the Early Modern World*. Berkeley: University of California Press, 2003. A detailed but stimulating study of environmental change, with many case studies.

Smith, Alan K. *Creating a World Economy: Merchant Capital, Colonialism, and World Trade, 1400–1825*. Boulder, Colo.: Westview Press, 1991. A valuable survey of the world economy in this era.

Wiesner-Hanks, Merry E. *Christianity and Sexuality in the Early Modern World: Regulating Desire, Reforming Practice*. New York: Routledge, 2000. A wide-ranging study of the impact of spreading Christianity on sexual practices.

Wills, John E. *1688: A Global History*. New York: W.W. Norton, 2001. A very readable and informative exploration of various peoples and societies around the world in the late seventeenth century.

WEBSITES

The Columbian Exchange (http://www.nhc.rtp.nc.us:8080/tserve/nattrans/ntecoindian/ essays/columbian/htm).   Contains varied materials on the Columbian Exchange.

Columbus and the Age of Discovery (http://muweb.millersville.edu/_columbus/main/html). This site, maintained by Millersville University, offers many sources related to the linking of the hemispheres during this era.

Early Modern Resources (http://www.earlymodernwrb.org.uk/emr/).   A useful British site offering many links to essays and sources.

Internet Global History Sourcebook (http://www.fordham.edu/halsall/global/globalsbook.html). An excellent set of links on world history from ancient to modern times.

Internet Modern History Sourcebook (http://www.fordham.edu/halsall/).   An extensive online collection of historical documents and secondary materials.

PART V

Global Imbalances: Industry, Empire, and the Making of the Modern World, 1750–1945

The Early Modern Era from the mid-1400s to the mid-1700s, discussed in Part IV, constituted a key stage in the building of today's world. During that era European overseas expansion established permanent communication between the Eastern and Western Hemispheres, building ever closer political and economic ties between Europe, the Americas, the West and East African coasts, and some Asian societies. These ties in turn fostered a global economy while dramatically altering the lives, for better or worse, of many people.

The next key stage in creating the world we live in today came during the Modern Era, between around 1750 and 1945, which was marked by revolutions in political, intellectual, economic, and social life around the world. In countries such as France, Britain, the United States, and Japan, political revolutions or major reforms replaced old governments with more democratic or progressive governments, inspiring other peoples to seek similar changes. Latin Americans became independent from Spanish and Portuguese colonialism. In many countries political change went hand in hand with new ideas about the relationship between citizens and governments, new visions of a better life, and more skeptical attitudes toward organized religions. At the same time, Western nations transformed world politics by asserting their power in Asia, Africa, and Latin America, a few of them establishing huge colonial empires. The peoples they colonized, however, often resisted Western rule. Meanwhile, in the economic realm, the Industrial Revolution, which produced unprecedented goods and fostered technological advances, reshaped Western economic life. In some societies assertive workers', peasants', and women's movements challenged old aristocratic social orders. Overall, great progress was made toward improving social and economic conditions, especially in providing material goods. But the progress was purchased at a high cost in the dislocation of human lives, the suppression of colonized peoples, the ravaging of the natural environment, growing antagonism toward the powerful Western nations, and the deadliest wars in history.

The increasing military, political, and economic domination of the rest of the world by several

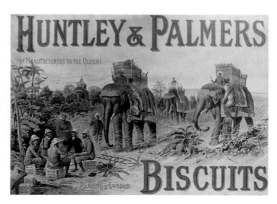

Colonial Advertisement As imperialism became a part of European life, advertisers capitalized on the interest in the colonial realm. This nineteenth-century advertisement for a British biscuit company shows a scene of the British in India. (The Robert Opie Collection)

561

European nations, soon joined by the United States, was a major trend in the nineteenth and early twentieth centuries. While Western peoples controlled some 35 percent of the world's land surface in 1800, they controlled over 84 percent by 1914. This domination encouraged European emigration and helped to spread capitalism, Western languages, and Western ideas such as Christianity and Marxism. It also contributed to huge changes in the world economy. Strongly shaped by Western activity, the world economy reshuffled natural resources, so that rubber, for example, a plant native to Brazil, became a major cash crop in Southeast Asia, often grown by Indian or Chinese immigrants. Around the world men and women now often worked for wages to produce goods primarily for sale in distant markets rather than the local community.

But Western expansion and domination also created imbalances. The major imbalance was a growing gap by the early 1900s between rich nations and poor societies. Rich nations enjoyed industrialization and, in some cases, imperial expansion. The poor societies, by contrast, were usually colonies of Western nations, economically subordinate to the West, or, like China and Latin America, subject to informal Western power. Most Asian societies powerful in the Early Modern Era, including China and India, declined. The West, including North America, increasingly exported industrial and consumer goods while people elsewhere largely exported raw materials. Six hundred years ago many Chinese and Southeast Asians and some Native Americans lived longer and healthier lives than did most Europeans. By the early twentieth century, however, the balance had changed and most societies in western Europe and North America were far richer and healthier, and had far more influence on the world, than other peoples.

By the first decade of the twentieth century Western imperialism had generated global integration, the increasing connections between societies. Sparked partly by these connections, major changes came to the world during the first half of the twentieth century, some of them creating widespread misery. The hopes for a more democratic, equitable world were undermined by two ruinous world wars, the decade-long collapse of the world economy, and some of history's most brutal, despotic governments. Meanwhile, people in Asia, Africa, and Latin America increasingly challenged Western power and unpopular local governments. These developments set the stage for a new world order to emerge after 1945.

NORTH AND CENTRAL AMERICA
In the later 1700s, the thirteen British colonies along the Atlantic coast revolted and established a new democratic nation, the United States, that gradually expanded across the continent. After a civil war ended slavery, the United States rapidly industrialized; as it became the world's major political and economic power in the later 1800s, it attracted immigrants. U.S. military power proved decisive in World Wars I and II. Meanwhile, Canada spread west to the Pacific and achieved self-government. After overthrowing Spanish rule, Mexico was reshaped by liberalism, dictatorship, and revolution.

SOUTH AMERICA
During the early 1800s the Latin American societies overthrew colonialism by force and became independent nations, but they also retained close economic links to Europe, reinforcing their natural resources-based economies and limiting industrialization. The struggles between liberal reformers and conservatives often led to military dictatorship. As European and Asian immigrants reshaped Latin American societies, Latin Americans created distinctive cultures by combining imported and local traditions.

EUROPE

The Industrial Revolution, which began in Britain in the later 1700s, sparked dramatic economic, social, and political change. The French Revolution and the rise of parliamentary democracy in nations such as Britain benefited the middle classes and fostered new national loyalties. Russia conquered Siberia and Central Asia. Britain, France, and Germany renewed imperialism in the later 1800s, forging large empires in Asia and Africa. After 1914 Europe was reshaped by World War I, Communist revolution in Russia, economic collapse, the rise of fascism, and World War II.

WESTERN ASIA

Although gradually losing its grip on southeastern Europe and North Africa, the Ottoman Empire maintained control of much of western Asia until after World War I, when Britain and France acquired the Arab territories and the Ottomans collapsed, replaced by a modernizing Turkish state. Persia attempted reforms but still fell under Western domination. Arab nationalism challenged Western power, while secular reformers and pro- and antimodern Muslims struggled for influence throughout the region.

EASTERN ASIA

China remained strong until the early 1800s, when, unable to reform and thwart Western ambitions, it lost several wars to the West and experienced rebellions. After a revolution ended the imperial system in the early 1900s, China lapsed into warlordism and then civil war, opening the door for Japanese invasion. Fearing Western power, the Japanese had rapidly industrialized and modernized their society in the later 1800s but, ravaged by economic depression, came under military rule in the 1930s, which eventually led to their defeat in World War II.

ARCTIC OCEAN

RUSSIA

BRITAIN
GERMANY
EUROPE
FRANCE
ITALY
Danube
TURKEY
PERSIA
EGYPT
Nile

ASIA

JAPAN

CHINA

HIMALAYAS
Ganges R.

INDIA

VIETNAM
THAILAND
Mekong R.

AFRICA
Niger R.

NIGERIA

ASHANTE
Congo R.
BUGANDA
CONGO

ATLANTIC
OCEAN

INDIAN OCEAN

INDONESIA

SOUTH
AFRICA

AUSTRALIA

AFRICA

Although some African states, such as Ashante, Buganda, and Egypt, remained strong into the 1800s and instituted reforms, they could not halt increasing Western power. The ending of the trans-Atlantic slave trade by the mid-1800s opened the door to Western colonization of the entire continent. The British and French built large empires in both sub-Saharan Africa and North Africa. Western imperialism created artificial countries, undermined traditional societies, and drained Africa of resources. After World War I African and Arab nationalist movements struggled against Western domination.

SOUTHERN ASIA AND OCEANIA

Overcoming local resistance, the British gradually conquered India, and their rule exploited India's resources, reshaped Indian life, and generated opposition from Indian nationalists seeking independence. Dynamic Southeast Asian states repulsed the West until the mid-1800s, when the British, French, and Dutch colonized all of these resource-rich societies, except Thailand, often against fierce resistance, and the United States replaced Spanish rule in the Philippines, crushing a local independence movement. To the east, Western powers colonized the Pacific islands and Europeans settled in Australia and New Zealand.

CHAPTER 19

Modern Transitions: Revolutions, Industries, Ideologies, Empires, 1750–1914

Online Study Center

This icon will direct you to interactive activities and study materials on the website: college.hmco.com/pic/lockard1e

Crystal Palace Exposition of 1851   Attracting more than six million visitors, the Great Exhibition, held at the Crystal Palace in London in 1851, showcased industrial products and the companies that produced them from all over the world but especially from Europe.
(British Museum/Laurie Platt Winfrey, Inc.)

From this foul drain the greatest stream of human industry flows out to fertilize the whole world. From this filthy sewer pure gold flows. Here humanity attains its most complete development and its most brutish.

FRENCH WRITER ALEXIS DE TOCQUEVILLE ON MANCHESTER, ENGLAND, 1835[1]

On a spring day in 1851 the people of London prepared to celebrate the technological achievements of their era. People of all social classes, from bankers and nobles to sailors, day laborers, and barmaids, crowded the city streets, heading for the spectacular new Crystal Palace in Hyde Park to see the official opening, led by Queen Victoria herself, of the Great Exhibition. The less affluent walked while the wealthy rode in horse-drawn carriages or steam-powered buses. Some people had come by railroad from other British cities or by steamships from France and Belgium. All shared in the excitement of an exhibition designed to celebrate "The Works of Industry of All Nations," with Progress as the organizing theme.

The first "world's fair," the Great Exhibition was dazzling. Some 14,000 firms participated in the displays, showcasing British industrial leadership in particular. Some exhibits featured the mineral basis for British industry: coal, iron ore, gypsum, granite, and agates. The hall of machinery contained power textile looms, hydraulic presses, printing presses, marine engines, and locomotives: inventions that had revolutionized British life. Some locomotives, for example, had attained the before unimaginable speed of 60 miles per hour. Another hall lavishly presented industrial products that British merchants sold all over the world, including fine textiles made from wool, cotton, linen, and silk. Many of these products were made in Manchester, the city condemned as a "foul drain" in the opening quote but praised for fostering development. Nearly half of the exhibitors represented other countries of Europe and North America, illustrating the spread of industrialization.

The Great Exhibition of 1851 celebrated the industrialization that had begun three-quarters of a century earlier and was already dramatically transforming the social and physical landscapes in Britain and in parts of Europe. The age of the machine had arrived. The British, enamored with the idea of progress, saw in modern industry, a growing economy, and creative science humanity's triumph over the natural world. Industrialization gave Britain and other European and North American countries the economic and military power to increase their influence around the world.

Along with industrialization, political revolutions and new ideologies were also defining developments in Europe and the Americas between 1750 and 1914. Historians refer to an age of revolutions, violent conflicts that spurred the rise of modern European, North American, and Latin American nations. In

565

turn, the economic and political changes resulting from industrialization and revolutions fostered new ideas about politics and government and about the relationship of citizens to the state. Great Britain, France, Germany, and Russia emerged as the main powers in Europe while the United States became the strongest American country. But the industrial and political trends yielded mixed blessings. The British writer Charles Dickens, commenting on the French Revolution, summed up the era: "It was the best of times, it was the worst of times. It was the age of wisdom, it was the age of foolishness, it was the season of light, it was the season of darkness, it was the spring of hope, it was the winter of despair."[2] By the later 1800s these trends had also sparked a renewal of the imperialism, begun in the 1500s, that resulted in various European nations acquiring or expanding empires in Asia and Africa.

FOCUS QUESTIONS

1. What were the major consequences of the American and French Revolutions?
2. How did the Caribbean and Latin American revolutions compare with those in North America and Europe?
3. How did industrialization reshape economic and social life?
4. How did nationalism, liberalism, and socialism differ from each other?
5. What factors spurred the Western imperialism of the later 1800s?

✦ The Age of Revolution: North America and Europe

What were the major consequences of the American and French Revolutions?

Some historians use the phrase "the **Age of Revolution**" to refer to the period from the 1770s through the 1840s, when revolutions rocked North America, Europe, the Caribbean, and Latin America (see Chronology: The North American and European Revolutions, 1770–1815). During these years revolutionaries employed armed violence to seize power and forge fundamental changes. Two types of revolutions emerged in modern times. Political revolutions changed the personnel and structure of government, while social revolutions transformed both the political and social order. The American Revolution was the most influential political revolution in this era because it ended British colonial rule, led to a new democratic form of government, and ushered in the Age of Revolution in Europe and the rest of the Americas. The French Revolution was the major social revolution, overthrowing a discredited old order of royalty and aristocratic privilege. The revolutionary tradition and values spawned in France remained a major influence

on modern Europe and also inspired other peoples to seek radical change. For the next two centuries revolutions transformed states, ideologies, and class structures, especially in Europe, Latin America, and Asia.

Modern Revolutions

Revolutions such as those in British North America and France have been momentous events in modern world history, erupting on every inhabited continent except Australia. While most revolutions have been local in impact, some have influenced other societies. In the late 1700s Europeans and Latin Americans watched fascinated as the disaffected citizens in the thirteen British colonies in North America struggled to overthrow British rule and then established an independent federation that soon became the United States. The American revolutionary leaders proclaimed Enlightenment political theories formulated in Europe, such as democracy and personal freedom, and then sought to apply these theories to their new representative government. The French Revolution electrified Europe by violently replacing the monarchy with a republic and spreading new values that stressed liberty and social equality. But the French Revolution also generated terrible violence, the rise of despotic leaders, and long years of war. The new political dialogue created by the French Revolution and the shock waves it generated strongly shaped nineteenth-century Europe.

Whether in North America, France, Latin America, or elsewhere, revolutions usually had much in common. Revolution-

Age of Revolution The period from the 1770s through the 1840s when revolutions rocked North America, Europe, the Caribbean, and Latin America.

French citizens, mostly rebellious peasants and provincial leaders, were executed, and tens of thousands more were arrested, often on flimsy evidence, to restore internal order. Some Jacobin leaders themselves were executed in factional disputes. The terror abated when the Jacobins lost power in 1795, but several constructive Jacobin policies endured down to today, including innovative laws guaranteeing the right to public education for all children and to public welfare for the poor.

The Legacy of the French Revolution

Although not all its accomplishments proved long-lasting, the French Revolution showed that an old regime could be destroyed and a new order created by its own people, providing both a model and an inspiration for generations of revolutionaries to come. The Revolution not only installed the middle class in power in France but also ultimately constructed a state much more powerful than that of the Bourbon kings. During these years much of the vocabulary of modern politics emerged, including terms such as *conservative* and *right-wing*, referring to those who favored retaining the status quo or restoring the past, and *liberal* and *left-wing*, meaning progressives wanting faster change. Revolutionary France also transformed warfare by introducing conscription and promotion through the ranks and by expanding the country's borders. The countries occupied or conquered by France, such as Belgium and some western German states, were turned into "sister republics," where new revolutionary governments promoted human rights.

But the terrible violence of the French Revolution dampened its appeal as the Jacobins' terror undermined personal liberty. The British-born American thinker Tom Paine, who had fervently admired the French Revolution and its assertion of the "Rights of Man," wrote that he despaired of seeing European liberty accomplished. Indeed, the French trauma and terror turned North Americans against revolutions, which they now feared too often degenerated into anarchy and then despotism, destabilizing societies and threatening property rights.

Observers also debated whether the French "Rights of Man" were intended to include women. Some women who today would be called feminists promoted women's rights. For example, Olympe de Gouges (1748–1793), a French butcher's daughter, published a manifesto complaining that women were excluded from decision making and tried to organize a female militia to fight for France, arguing that needles and spindles were not the only weapons women knew how to handle. For her efforts she was executed. A British campaigner for women's rights, Mary Wollstonecraft (1759–1797), whose outrage was spurred by watching her merchant father abuse her mother, moved to Paris and wrote the *Vindication of the Rights of Women* in 1792, calling for equal opportunities for women in education and society. The unconventional Wollstonecraft shocked polite society by having two children out of wedlock. But despite the efforts of reformers such as de Gouges and Wollstonecraft, women remained excluded from citizenship in France and nearly everywhere else.

The Napoleonic Era and Its Aftermath

Although the republican system had inspired many within and outside of France, the end result in France was a military dictatorship. The terror and the shifting fortunes of war led to a resurgence of pro-monarchy feelings in France and prompted antiroyalists to turn to the ambitious General Napoleon Bonaparte (BOW-nuh-pahrt) (1769–1821), a lawyer's son and a brilliant military strategist from the French-ruled island of Corsica. Bonaparte's ambitions and deeds would shake up the politics of France and Europe.

The Rise of Bonaparte Bonaparte's rise to power was astounding. In 1795 he was a lowly artillery officer just released from prison for alleged Jacobin ties. Through political connections and his forceful personality, he rapidly rose through the ranks to command major military victories in France, Italy, Austria, and Egypt, becoming the most influential French leader of his day. In 1799 Napoleon gained the most powerful political office in revolutionary France, that of First Consul. His military victories led to a treaty with rival nations in 1801, temporarily ending conflict.

In 1804, responding to a widespread belief that only a dictator could provide stability, Bonaparte crowned himself emperor in a regal coronation, attended by the pope, that harked back a millennium to the crowning of Charlemagne. Bonaparte then quickly began to promote reconciliation within France and to restore French economic prosperity. He also standardized revolutionary laws, including the equality of all citizens before the law, thus making permanent the Revolution's core values. However, the Corsican's general dictatorial tendencies betrayed French liberty, and he also developed a taste for the trappings of royal power. Wanting an heir, he divorced his childless wife, the popular Empress Josephine, and married an eighteen-year-old Austrian princess, Marie-Louise.

Rival nations still feared Bonaparte and the wars soon began again, upsetting the entire European state system. In 1805 Britain, the world's dominant sea power and longtime rival of France, forged a coalition with Austria, Prussia, and Russia to defeat France. In the following years France won most of the land battles, enabling it to occupy much of western Europe. By 1810, Bonaparte's family ruled Spain, Naples, and some German states. But Napoleonic power eventually waned. Armed resistance in Spain and the German states, a costly French invasion of Russia resulting in humiliating retreat, and an invasion of France by rival powers all sapped Bonaparte's military strength. In 1814 allied armies entered Paris, and Bonaparte abdicated and was imprisoned on an Italian island. He escaped and regrouped his forces, but he was finally overcome by British and Prussian armies at Waterloo, a Belgian village, in 1815. While the Bourbon family reclaimed the French throne, Napoleon, for a decade the most powerful man in Europe, spent his remaining years in exile on St. Helena, a remote, British-ruled South Atlantic island.

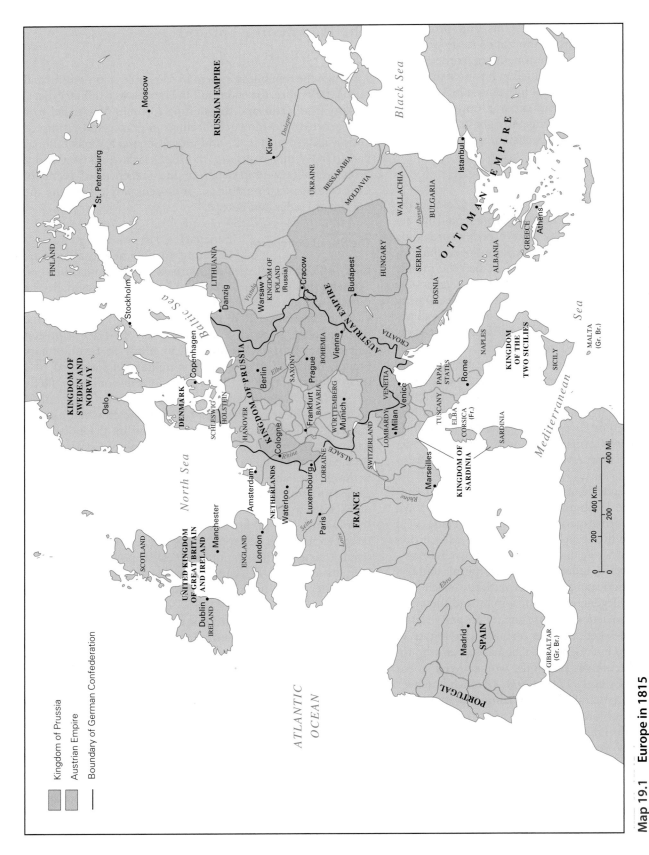

Map 19.1   Europe in 1815

With the Napoleonic wars ended, the Congress of Vienna redrew the map of Europe. France, Austria, Spain, Britain, and a growing Prussia were the dominant states, but the Ottoman Turks still ruled a large area of southeastern Europe.

A new European Politics The demise of revolutionary France and the dismantling of Napoleon's empire allowed for a partial return to the political status quo in Europe. The victorious allies met in 1815 at the Congress of Vienna to remold the European state system (see Map 19.1). Europeans who preferred monarchy and church-state alliance rejoiced at French defeat. The men who overthrew French control in Naples sang, "Naples won't stay a republic. Here's an end to equality. Here's an end to liberty. Long live God and his Majesty."[6] Dominated by Austria, Britain, Russia, and the revived royalist government of France, the Congress reaffirmed pre-Napoleonic borders and restored most of the former rulers displaced by revolutionaries and reformers. It also fostered some changes. For example, thirty-nine German states began moving toward national unity by forming the German Confederation. But some societies faced disappointment. Russia invaded Poland-Lithuania, destroying the constitutional government and partitioning the nation between Russia and Prussia. Wars and violent outbreaks also remained frequent in Europe between 1815 and 1914, many of them involving France.

Once the revolutionary genie generated by the French and American Revolutions was out of the bottle, however, all the best efforts of the established order could not put it back again. Revolutionary ideas combined with popular discontent continued to unsettle Europe, and various revolutions broke out in 1830–1831 because of discontent with despotic political systems. The French overthrew the increasingly despotic Bourbon king, Charles X, and installed his more progressive cousin and former Jacobin, Louis-Philippe (1773–1850), as a constitutional monarch who recognized democratic liberties. Uprisings in several German and Italian states and in Poland sought voting rights, and a peasant rebellion caused by poverty and unemployment rocked Britain.

Even more turbulent European revolts erupted in 1848, a result of poor harvests, rampant disease, trade slumps, rising unemployment, massive poverty, and a desire for representative government. These upheavals began in France, forcing the increasingly unpopular King Louis-Philippe to abdicate, and soon spread to Austria, Hungary, and many German and Italian states. For example, in German cities students inspired by the events in Paris met in city marketplaces to organize movements demanding elected parliaments and civil liberties such as free speech and a free press. But around Europe conservative regimes crushed the dissident movements, which had no central coordination, within a few months, often causing great bloodshed. A French observer said that "nothing was lacking" in the repression in Paris, "not grapeshot, nor bullets, nor demolished houses, nor martial law, nor the ferocity of the soldiery, nor the insults to the dead."[7] Still, the uprisings helped further spread democratic ideas, and monarchies lost ground as parliamentary power increased in countries such as Denmark and the Netherlands. To prevent revolutionary outbursts, many European governments also began to consider social and economic reforms, such as higher wages, to improve people's lives.

SECTION SUMMARY

- Many people in the North American colonies chafed against British rule and, inspired by Enlightenment thinkers, pushed for independence, while others, including many Indians and black slaves, sided with the British.

- After a first failed attempt at confederation, the thirteen American colonies agreed upon a system that balanced federal and state powers, but the American Revolution did little to change the social order and did not extend equal rights to blacks, women, and Indians.

- The French Revolution, which aimed to wrest control from the nobility and the clergy, achieved some of its progressive goals and was an inspiration to some societies, but it led to a period of war and widespread terror, and its excesses turned others away from revolution.

- In the tumultuous aftermath of the French Revolution, Napoleon Bonaparte seized power, implemented some of the Revolution's egalitarian ideals in law, and waged a series of overly ambitious wars that eventually led to his defeat and the Congress of Vienna, at which many pre-Revolution boundaries were restored. Throughout the first half of the nineteenth century, other revolutions against despotic regimes rose up and were usually crushed, but nevertheless democratic ideals made gradual progress.

The Age of Revolution: The Caribbean and Latin America

How did the Caribbean and Latin American revolutions compare with those in Europe and North America?

The Age of Revolution was not confined to North America and Europe. Just as in British North America, dissatisfaction with colonialism was common in the Caribbean and Spanish America, and it led to revolutions and wars of independence in these regions in the early 1800s. The first successful movement to overthrow colonialism came in Haiti, where slaves of African ancestry fought their way to power. Most of the American colonies of Spain eventually fought for and won their independence by the 1820s. During the same period Mexico and Brazil became independent without warfare.

Spanish and Portuguese America's Colonial Heritage

The Spanish and Portuguese ruled much larger American empires than did the British. By 1810 some 18 million people, many times the population of British North America, lived under Spanish rule from California in the north to the southern tip of South America. This population included 4 million people of European ancestry, 8 million Indians, 1 million blacks, and 5 million people of mixed descent. The empire was divided into four administrative units based in Mexico, Colombia, Peru, and Argentina, each supervised by Spanish governors. Corruption ran deep in the colonial system, but the planters, ranchers, mine owners, bureaucrats, and church officials who benefited from Spanish rule or profited from exploiting the economic resources opposed any major change. They preferred a system that sent raw materials, such as silver and beef, to Spain rather than one that developed domestic institutions or markets.

The Spanish fostered American societies with many problems and conflicts. They ruled their colonies differently than did the British in North America, allowing little self-government, maintaining economic monocultures that relied on the export of a single agricultural or mineral resource, and imposing one dominant religion: Roman Catholicism. Only a small minority of people, mostly those of European ancestry, shared in the wealth produced by the mines, plantations, and ranches. Latin American social conditions did not promote unity or equality. The creoles, whites born in the Americas, resented the influential newcomers from Spain, but they were also more cautious than the North American Patriots, fearing that resistance against Spain might get out of control and threaten their position. The great majority of the population, a dispossessed underclass of Indians, enslaved Africans, and mixed-descent people, faced growing unemployment and perhaps the world's most inequitable distribution of wealth.

In contrast to British America, Latin America, dominated by a rigid Catholic Church wary of dissent, enjoyed little intellectual diversity. The Inquisition denounced as seditious any literature espousing equality and liberty for all people and punished people it considered to be heretics. Local critics accused the government and church of "placing the strongest fetters on Enlightenment and [keeping] thought in chains."[8] Yet some thinkers sidestepped the repression. For example, the Mexican creole Jose Antonio Alzate y Ramirez (1738–1799) published a magazine that promoted science and Enlightenment rationalism.

Given the political and social inequalities, various revolts punctuated Spanish colonial rule. For example, Mexico experienced some 142 village revolts between 1700 and 1820, including a major upheaval in 1761 when the Mayas revolted against high taxes and church repression of Maya customs, leading to Spanish reprisals. The largest revolt in Spanish America, a mass uprising led by Tupac Amaru II (1740–1781), the wealthy, well-educated mestizo who claimed to be a descendant of an Inca king, spread over large areas of Peru in the 1780s. Tupac had been stirred by historical accounts of his Inca ancestors and memories of the many earlier anti-Spanish revolts in the Andes regions. Tupac and Michaela Bastidas, his wife and a brilliant strategist, organized a broad-based coalition of groups that quickly overran much of central and southern Peru, where they hoped to establish an independent state, with Tupac as king, and where Indians, mestizos, and creoles would live in harmony. But many of Tupac's peasant followers went further, reviving the Inca religion and attacking Catholic churches and clergy. The better-armed Spanish defeated the rebel bands and

executed Tupac and his family. The Tupac Amaru revolt paved the way for larger upheavals across South America several decades later.

Portuguese Brazil also experienced dissension. By the late 1700s Brazil was the wealthiest part of the Portuguese colonial realm, but only a small minority, especially white plantation and gold mine owners, benefited from the prosperity derived from exporting the raw materials chiefly produced by slaves of African ancestry. Since Brazil was the major importer of slaves, accounting for a quarter to a third of all Africans arriving in the Americas, blacks vastly outnumbered Native Americans in Brazil, in contrast to Spanish-ruled Mexico and South America. Disgruntled Afro-Brazilians demanded a better life, but they faced many setbacks. For example, in 1799 a revolt seeking social equality and political freedom was crushed in the northeastern state of Bahia (buh-HEE-uh).

Caribbean Societies and the Haitian Revolution

Most of the small Caribbean islands and the Guianas in northeast South America were colonies of Britain, France, or the Netherlands and were inhabited chiefly by African slaves and their descendants, most of whom worked on sugar plantations. The Afro-Caribbean peoples appropriated European cultural forms and languages, welding them with retained African forms. In British-colonized islands such as Jamaica, Barbados, and Antigua, for example, most slaves adopted Christianity and Anglo-Saxon names. The African influences that shaped slave life included African musical influences, such as drumming, improvisation, and varied rhythms.

Slave revolts were common throughout the colonial era, but only one, the Haitian Revolution, overthrew a regime. In 1791 some 100,000 Afro-Haitian slaves, inspired by the French Revolution and its slogans of liberty and equality, rose up against the oppressive society presided over by French planters, thus beginning years of war and bloodshed (see Chronology: The Caribbean and Latin American Revolutions, 1750–1840). Toussaint L'Ouverture (too-SAN loo-ver-CHORE) (1746–1803), a freed slave with a vision of a republic composed of free people, became the insurgent leader. Toussaint had status on the plantation because his father came from a chiefly family in Africa. Raised a Catholic, Toussaint learned French and Latin from an older slave.

The Haitian revolution went from triumph to tragedy. For a decade the Afro-Haitians, led by Toussaint, fought the French military and, at times, anti-French British and Spanish forces hoping to capitalize on the turmoil. By 1801 Toussaint's forces had gained control over Haiti and freed the slaves. But Napoleon Bonaparte sent in a larger French force to restore order, and in 1803 French soldiers captured Toussaint, who soon died in a French prison. In 1804 Afro-Haitians defeated Napoleon's army and established the second independent nation in the Western Hemisphere after the United States. Elsewhere in the Americas the Haitian Revolution cheered slaves and those favoring abolition of slavery but alarmed planters, who became more determined to preserve slavery. Reflecting

CHRONOLOGY

The Caribbean and Latin American Revolutions, 1750–1840

1791–1804	Haitian Revolution
1808	Move of Portuguese royal family to Brazil
1810–1826	Wars of independence in Spanish America
1810–1811	First Mexican revolution
1816	Argentine independence
1819	Founding of Colombian republic by Bolivar
1822	Mexican independence; Dom Pedro emperor of Brazil
1830	Independence of Colombia, Venezuela, and Ecuador
1839	Division of Central American states

South American Independence Wars

As in North America and Haiti, dissatisfaction in Spanish-ruled South America exploded into wars of national independence. In 1800 the Spanish colonial hold on its empire seemed secure, but, as in British North America, resentments simmered, especially among creoles, fostering anticolonial movements. Creole merchants and ranchers criticized Spain for its commercial monopoly, its increasing taxes, and the colonial government's favoritism toward those born in Spain. They also wanted a role in government. Creoles also often felt more loyalty to their American region than to distant Spain, and some were influenced by the Enlightenment and the American and French Revolutions. The British, who were pressuring the Spanish and Portuguese to open Latin American markets to British goods, also secretly aided anticolonial groups. At the same time, Spain was experiencing political problems at home, including French occupation during the Napoleonic wars, which weakened the country's ability to suppress unrest in Latin America.

Since Spain refused to make serious political concessions, creole revolutionaries of middle-class backgrounds waged wars of independence between 1810 and 1826, forming new countries. Two separate independence movements began in 1810–1811 in Venezuela and Argentina, and they soon came under the leadership of Simon Bolivar (bow-LEE-vahr) in the north and Jose de San Martin (san mahr-TEEN) in the south. Bolivar became the symbol of the liberation struggle. Born into a wealthy Caracas family that owned slaves, land, and mines, Bolivar (1783–1830) had studied law in Spain, was a free thinker who admired rationalist Enlightenment thought, and had a magnetic personality that inspired loyalty. He offered an inclusive view of his Latin American people: "We are a microcosm of the human race, a world apart, neither Indian nor Europeans, but a part of each."[9] Bolivar also spent time in Haiti and Jamaica, where he gained sympathy for blacks. In

white fears of slave revolt, the United States, still a slave-owning nation, withheld diplomatic recognition of the black Haitian republic. In Haiti, French planters were either killed or fled, and the ex-slaves took over sugar production. The promise of a better life for Haiti's people proved short-lived, however. Toussaint's successor as revolutionary leader, the Africa-born Jean Jacques Dessalines (de-sah-LEEN) (1758–1806), became emperor and ruled despotically, beginning two centuries of tyranny.

Simon Bolivar The main leader of the anti-Spanish war of independence in northern South America, Bolivar came to be known as "the Liberator," a symbol of Latin American nationalism and the struggle for political freedom.
(Courtesy, Archivo CENIDIAP-INBA, Mexico City. Collection, Fernando Leal Audirac)

Map 19.2   Latin American Independence, 1840

By 1840 all of Latin America except for Cuba and Puerto Rico, still Spanish colonies, had become independent, with Brazil and Mexico the largest countries. Later the Central American provinces and Gran Colombia would fragment into smaller nations, and Argentina would annex Patagonia.

Online Study Center **Improve Your Grade** Interactive Map: Latin America in 1830

1812 he formed an army to liberate northern South America, offering freedom to slaves who aided his cause. After many setbacks, Bolivar's forces liberated the north in 1824. San Martin (1778–1850), a former colonel in the Spanish army, led the southern forces against Spain and its royalist allies, helping Argentina gain independence in 1816 and Chile in 1818. In 1824 San Martin and Bolivar cooperated to liberate Peru, where royalist sympathies were strongest.

Online Study Center **Improve Your Grade**
Primary Source: The Jamaican Letter

But these victories over the colonial regimes did not always meet the expectations of the liberated or the liberators. The wars damaged economies and caused people to flee the fighting. In addition, the creoles who now governed these countries often forgot the promises made to the Indians, mestizos, mulattos, and blacks who had often provided the bulk of the revolutionary armies. And although some slaves were freed, slavery was not abolished. Women also experienced disappointment. Some enthusiastically served the revolution as soldiers and nurses. For example, Policarpa Salavarrieta helped Bolivar as a spy until she was captured by the Spanish. Before she was executed in Bogota's main plaza, she exclaimed: "Although I am a woman and young, I have more than enough courage to suffer this death and a thousand more."[10] But women soon found that they still lived in patriarchal societies that offered them few new legal or political rights. Finally, unlike the founders of the United States, Latin America's new leaders were largely unable to form representative and democratic governments. Simon Bolivar could not hold his own country together, and in 1830 it broke into Colombia, Ecuador, and Venezuela. Meanwhile, Uruguay and Paraguay split off from Argentina, and Bolivia separated from Peru. Disillusioned, Bolivar concluded that Latin America was ungovernable.

Independence Movements in Mexico and Brazil

Political change also came to Mexico and Brazil (see Map 19.2). In 1810 two progressive Mexican Catholic priests, the creole Manuel Hidalgo (ee-DAHL-go) and the mestizo Jose Maria Morelos (hoe-SAY mah-REE-ah moh-RAY-los), mobilized peasants and miners and launched a revolt promoting independence, the abolition of slavery, and social reform to uplift the mestizos and Indians. Creole conservatives and royalists suppressed that revolt and executed Hidalgo and Morelos. But a compromise between various factions brought Mexico independence in 1822 under a creole general, Agustin de Iturbide (ah-goos-TEEN deh ee-tur-BEE-deh) (1783–1824), who proclaimed himself emperor. However, although initially the anti-Spanish struggle had united creoles, mestizos, and Indians against a common enemy, the alliance unraveled and a republican revolt soon ousted Iturbide. The Central American peoples split off from Mexico and, after several attempts at unity, by 1839 had splintered into five states.

Brazil escaped many of the conflicts bedeviling Spanish America, enjoying a nearly bloodless transition to independence. In 1808 the Portuguese royal family and government sought refuge in Brazil to escape the Napoleonic wars, and in the following years Brazilians increasingly viewed themselves as separate from Portugal. When the Portuguese government tried to reclaim the territory, a member of the royal family still in Brazil, Dom Pedro (1798–1834), severed ties with Portugal in 1822 and became emperor of Brazil as Pedro I, Latin America's only constitutional monarch. However, although a parliament was set up and elections were held, most Brazilians had no vote and Pedro I governed autocratically. Politics involved a small group of merchants, landowners, and the royal family.

SECTION SUMMARY

■ Spain controlled its American colonies extremely tightly, leaving little room for intellectual freedom or economic mobility, and put down many revolts through the end of the eighteenth century.

■ After over a decade of revolutionary struggle, the Afro-Haitian slaves won their freedom from the French, but they soon fell under the control of an African-born despot.

■ Rising dissatisfaction among South Americans, particularly creoles, led to successful independence movements throughout the continent, though the newly free nations had trouble forming representative and democratic governments.

■ After Mexico obtained its independence, the coalition that had opposed the Spanish fell apart, while members of the Portuguese royal family who fled to Brazil helped it to obtain its independence peacefully.

The Industrial Revolution and Economic Growth

How did industrialization reshape economic and social life?

Along with political and social revolutions, the **Industrial Revolution**, a dramatic transformation in the production and transportation of goods, was a major force reshaping the economic, political, and social patterns of Europe and later of North America and Japan. For the first time in history, the shackles were taken off the productive power of societies and people could now manipulate nature for their own purposes. Henceforth, they became capable of the rapid, constant, and seemingly limitless increase of goods and services. This revolution was perhaps the greatest transformation in society since

Industrial Revolution A dramatic transformation in the production and transportation of goods.

settled farming, urbanization, and the first states arose thousands of years ago. Although the intellectual and economic roots of industrialization were laid in the Early Modern Era, it was in the late 1700s that breakthroughs in productivity were made. The transition began in Britain and then spread across the English Channel to western Europe, then across the Atlantic to North America, eventually helping transform the limited European power of 1750 into Western domination over much of the world by 1914.

The Roots of the Industrial Revolution

The Industrial Revolution and the changes it generated had deep roots in Early Modern Europe. The Renaissance, Reformation, and Enlightenment had generated new ways of thought, including the expanded quest to understand the natural and physical world reflected in the Scientific Revolution. The discovery of new lands, plants, peoples, cultural traditions, and animals stimulated curiosity about the world. In addition, the commercial capitalism that arose in the 1500s and 1600s generated trade and conquest overseas, forming political and economic links between the Americas, the African coast, some Asian societies, and western Europe by 1750. These connections allowed Europeans to acquire natural resources and great wealth overseas, which provided capital for investment in new technologies and incentives for producing more commodities for the world market.

Great Britain benefited more than other countries from these changes, becoming the world's leading trading nation by the 1700s. British inventors experimented with steam power, and by the 1730s spinning machines were making the English textile industry more efficient. The demands of the world market for textiles spurred Britain to replace India as the main supplier of cotton textiles. Britain had many advantages over rival countries, including an open intellectual atmosphere with diverse views and a reasonably democratic political system that included the middle classes in government. Britain also had the most productive economy, favorable terrain on which to build transportation networks, abundant raw materials like coal and iron, and many water sources to run machines. By contrast, the lack of minerals and water sources in the Netherlands explains why that prosperous and tolerant country did not initiate an industrial revolution. Between the 1780s and 1830s Britain dominated European industrialization.

Because of its earlier overseas activities in the Americas and Asia, Britain acquired one of the prerequisites for industrialization: adequate capital. Profits from the British-controlled Caribbean islands and from several colonies in North America, which produced huge amounts of sugar and tobacco, and from British trading posts in India were particularly crucial in funding the Industrial Revolution. Some British companies made

vast fortunes from the trans-Atlantic slave trade and the slavery plantations in the Americas. Although historians debate the exact connection between profits from slavery and the establishment of British industries, they tend to agree that companies owning sugar, cotton, and tobacco plantations in the Americas often invested their excess capital in new British industries. Most factories were built in the hinterland of great slave trade ports such as Liverpool. In this way the English region east of Liverpool and northern Wales known as the Midlands, near rich coal and iron ore fields, became the center of British industry (see Map 19.3). Concentrating production in large factories in or near cities such as Birmingham and Manchester in the Midlands lowered transport costs and tapped a ready labor supply.

The Age of Machines

The Industrial Revolution introduced an era in which machines produced the goods used by people and increasingly performed more human tasks, reshaping peoples' lives. Instead of making things by hand with the aid of simple tools, workers now used increasingly complicated machines and chemical processes. These machines were moved by energy derived from steam and other inanimate sources rather than human or animal sources. People were also increasingly able to tap the resources of the earth's crust and turn them into commodities. As a result, the Industrial Revolution created great material richness. Between the 1770s and 1914 a Europe of peasant

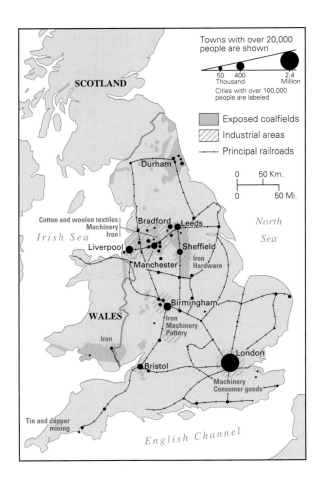

Map 19.3 Industrial Transformation in England
British industrialization mostly occurred near coalfields and iron ore deposits, spurring the rise of cities such as Birmingham, Leeds, Liverpool, and Manchester.

holdings, country estates, and domestic workshops became a Europe of sprawling and polluted industrial cities such as Manchester, with a wide gap between the few rich and the many poor (see Chronology: European Politics and Economy, 1750–1914).

In the past 250 years the material culture of the world, and particularly of Europe and North America, changed more than it did in the previous 750 years. Europeans in 1750 lived much more like Europeans in 1000 than like Western peoples in 1900. Today citizens of industrialized nations use transportation, wear fabrics, and employ building materials inconceivable in 1750. As one measure of how the world changed, one need only consider some of the words that first appeared in the English language between 1780 and 1850: *industry, factory, middle class, working class, engineer, crisis, statistics, strike,* and *pauper.*

The Industrial Revolution triggered continual technological innovations and a corresponding increase in economic activity. Inventions in one industry stimulated inventions in others. The cotton industry mechanized first. New cotton machines created a demand for more plentiful and reliable power than could be provided by traditional water wheels and horses. The steam pump invented by the Englishman Thomas Newcomen in 1712, possibly based on an earlier Chinese model and used mostly for pumping water out of mines, was innovative but inefficient. Seeking a more efficient power source, James Watt (1736–1819), a Scottish inventor who gained financial support from a wealthy merchant, Matthew Boulton, produced the first successful rotary steam engine in 1774. Watt transformed Newcomen's machine from a simple pump into a more versatile mover of energy that was useful in many types of industrial activities. Steam engines provided power not only for the textile mills but also for the iron furnaces, flour mills, and mines. When used in railroads and steamships, steam power conquered time and space, bringing the world much closer together. Watt's backer, Boulton, understood that profit required large sales, arguing that he had to sell steam engines to all the world to make money.

Technological innovations continued. The new cotton machines and steam engines required increased supplies of iron, steel, and coal. Mining and metalworking improved in response, creating a need for improved transportation facilities to move the coal and ore. After a while technological and economic growth came to be accepted as normal, provoking admiration and wonder. The British novelist William Thackeray celebrated the changes in 1860: "It is only yesterday, but what a gulf between now and then! *Then* was the old world. Stagecoaches, riding horses, pack-horses, knights in armor, Norman invaders, Roman legions—all these belong to the old period. But your railroad starts a new era."[11] In others, however, mechanization provoked fear, causing them to turn against industrialization. Between 1815 and 1830 anti-industrialization activists in Britain known as **Luddites,** mostly skilled textile

---

Luddites   Anti-industrialization activists in Britain who destroyed machines in a mass protest against the effects of mechanization.

CHRONOLOGY	
European Politics and Economy, 1750–1914	
1770s	Beginning of Industrial Revolution in England
1774	James Watt's first rotary steam engine
1776	Adam Smith's *The Wealth of Nations*
1800	British Act of Union
1821–1830	Greek war of independence
1830–1831	Wave of revolutions across Europe
1831	Formation of Young Italy movement by Mazzini
1845–1846	Irish potato famine
1848	Wave of revolts across Europe; *The Communist Manifesto* by Marx and Engels
1851	Great Exhibition in London
1859–1870	Unification of Italy
1862–1871	Unification of Germany
1870s–1914	Second Industrial Revolution

workers, invaded factories and, with guns, hatchets, and pikes, destroyed machines in a mass protest against the effects of mechanization. Ultimately the Luddite cause proved futile. The British government sent in 12,000 troops to stop the destruction and made the wrecking of machines a crime punishable by death.

The Spread of Industrialization

For decades Britain was the world's richest, most competitive nation, with a reputation as the workshop of the world. The new factories and machines mass-produced goods of better quality and lower price than traditional handicrafts, helping the British to overcome the old problem of finding commodities to trade to the world. They now had marketable goods and a powerful need to sell them to recoup their heavy investments in machinery and materials. By the mid-1800s Britain produced two-thirds of the world's coal, half the iron, and half the cotton cloth and other manufactured goods. A British poet boasted that "England's a perfect World, hath Indies, too, Correct your Maps, Newcastle [a center of the coal industry] is [silver rich] Peru."[12] The British enjoyed political, military, and economic supremacy in Europe and significant power in other regions of the world. No other state could substantially threaten Britain's economic and political position.

Industrial Sheffield This painting of one of the key British industrial cities, Sheffield, in 1858 shows the factories, many specializing in producing steel and metal goods, that dominated the landscape. (Courtesy, Sheffield Archives and Local Studies Library.)

However, the British invested some of their huge profits in western Europe, spreading the Industrial Revolution across the English Channel between the 1830s and 1870s. As iron-smelting technology improved, industrial operations became concentrated in regions rich in coal and iron ore. Capitalizing on its reserves of these resources, prosperous trading cities, and a strategic location between France, Holland, and Germany, Belgium industrialized in the early 1800s. By 1850 the Belgians had tripled their coal production and increased the number of steam engines from 354 to 2,300. Belgium also capitalized on the transportation revolution, building an ambitious railroad system to transport coal, iron, and manufactured goods and connecting it to neighboring countries. By the 1830s France had also begun constructing a national railroad network. In contrast to Britain and Belgium, France had to import coal, and, since it had fewer rich merchants than Britain, the government helped fund industrial activity. In the German states, political fragmentation before 1870 discouraged industrialization, except in several coal-rich regions such as the Ruhr Valley in western Germany and Silesia in Prussia. Some countries, including Portugal, Spain, and Austria-Hungary, remained largely agricultural. By 1914, however, industrialization was widespread around Europe and had also taken root in North America and Japan, and large numbers of people lived in cities and worked in factories.

Industrial Capitalism and Its Advocates

Beginning around 1770, industrialization and the vast increase in manufactured goods transformed commercial capitalism, dominated by large trading companies, into industrial capitalism, a system centered around manufacturing. During this era European industrial firms made and exported manufactured goods to other countries and in return imported raw materials, such as iron ore, to make more goods. The Industrial Revolution gave businesses marketable products and a powerful compulsion to market them in ever-increasing quantities. Because of the heavy investments in machines, success depended on a large and steady turnover of goods. Advertising developed to create demand, and banking and financial institutions expanded their operations to better serve business and industry. The industrialists, bankers, and financiers were also supported by political leaders who pursued policies of maximizing private wealth.

As economic and government efforts were made to support industrial capitalism, some thinkers felt the need to justify it. Economic philosophers emerged to praise British-style capitalism. The most influential, the Scottish professor Adam Smith (1723–1790), was a friend and supporter of Enlightenment thinkers. In his book *The Wealth of Nations* (1776), Smith helped formulate modern economics theory, known as neoclassical economics. In examining the consequences of economic freedom, Smith concluded that the market should be left alone. He advocated **laissez faire**, the restriction of government interference in the marketplace, such as laws regulating business and profits. Smith believed in self-interest, arguing that the "invisible hand" of the marketplace would turn the individual greed of the entrepreneur into a rising standard of living for all. Smith also introduced the new idea of a permanently growing economy, reinforcing the long-standing Western view of progress and of ever-increasing wealth as time went on. History was going somewhere. The popularity of Smith's writing shows how much things had changed since medieval times, when Christian leaders condemned mercantile activity. Smith's free trade ideas helped end the mercantilism of the Early Modern Era, when several European states worked closely with large commercial enterprises to accumulate wealth. The free traders like Smith believed that Britain should serve as the world's industrial center, into which flowed raw materials and out of which flowed manufactured goods.

But Smith saw the potential for both good and evil in industrial capitalism. He championed free trade but also found areas where government regulation might be useful and even essential. Smith acknowledged that free enterprise did not necessarily generate prosperity for all, since the interests of the manufacturers were not necessarily those of society or even of the broader economy. To ensure these larger interests, he encouraged businesses to pay their employees high wages, writing that "no society can surely be flourishing and happy of which the far greater part of its members are poor and miserable. [They should be] well fed, clothed and lodged."[13]

The Second Industrial Revolution

Beginning about 1870, what some historians call the Second Industrial Revolution, characterized by technological change, mass production, and specialization, got under way, continuing to 1914. The increasing application of science to industry spurred expansion and improvement in the electrical, chemical, optical, and automotive industries and brought new inventions such as electricity grids, radio, the internal combustion engine, gasoline, and the flush toilet. The United States and Germany led in implementing these changes, and by 1900 Germany was Europe's main producer of electrical goods and chemicals. By the early 1900s factory production was often done on the assembly line. Work was increasingly broken down into separate specialized tasks; for example, a worker in an automobile assembly line might only install wheels, leaving other tasks in building the automobile to others.

The Second Industrial Revolution promoted a shift to a form of capitalism in which giant monopolies, led by tycoons with unprecedented wealth, replaced the more competitive economy of industrial capitalism. The concentration of capital in what became known as "big business" gave a few businessmen and bankers, such as the Krupp family in Germany and the Rockefellers in the United States, vast economic power and control over many industries. For instance, Alfred Krupp (1812–1887) became Europe's leading manufacturer of arms and also owned steel mills and mines. His son Freidrich Krupp (1854–1902), who expanded the family empire to incorporate shipbuilding, was so influential that Germany's emperor and most top government officials attended his daughter's lavish wedding in 1906. The monopolies emerged because the huge capital investment needed for new factories eliminated many of the small businesses. Moreover, new industries producing such useful innovations as aluminum and electrical power required a heavy capital investment to start. A long depression in the late 1800s undermined competition, encouraging businesses to merge or cooperate and to moderate slumps, which hurt their profits, by fixing prices. The result was economic change that reshaped government policies and generated a drive to colonize more of the world to ensure access to resources and markets.

Industry and Social Change

The Industrial Revolution reshaped patterns of life in the industrializing countries, affecting both men and women and all social and economic classes (see Chapter 20). In 1800 Europe remained mainly agricultural. A century later many changes had occurred: a greater division of labor, growing social problems, most people living in cities, and the replacement of human workers by machines. The factory system compelled the migration of millions of people from the countryside into cities, where life was often difficult.

The cities of western Europe and North America in the 1800s were overcrowded and unhealthy, with high rates of alcoholism, prostitution, and crime. In the early industrial years city people crowded into festering slums, worked long hours for low wages, and learned new lifestyles. French writer Alexis de Tocqueville (TOKE-vill) described the atmosphere of Manchester in 1835:

> The footsteps of a busy crowd, the crunching wheels of machinery, the shriek of steam from boilers, the regular beat of the looms, the heavy rumble of carts, these are the noises from which you can never escape in the somber half-light of these streets. Crowds are ever hurrying this way and that, but their footsteps are brisk, their looks preoccupied, and their appearance somber and harsh.[14]

Factories, mines, and cities reshaped European life. Factory workers included highly skilled and experienced artisans but also millions of less skilled people who worked fourteen- and sometimes eighteen-hour days in a system of rigid discipline and punishments, including flogging, with no insurance provided in case of accidents, ill health, or old age. Many children worked seven days a week in mines or factories. In one reported case from 1887, a Scottish manufacturer on his trotting horse forced a sixteen-year-old, who had left work without permission, to run back to the factory alongside him while whipping the boy the entire way. In the English cotton mills during the 1830s and 1840s, about one-quarter of workers were adult men, over half were women and girls, and the rest

---

laissez faire   Restriction of government interference in the marketplace, such as laws regulating business and profits.

TOMMY ARMSTRONG, BARD OF THE ENGLISH COAL MINES

Tommy Armstrong (1849–1919) was one of the most famous song-makers who came out of the new industrial working class of Britain. From a poor family and with little formal schooling, Armstrong began working in the mine pits around Durham in the Northumbrian region of north England at age nine. Since the youngster was born with crooked legs, his older brother William carried him to work on his back. Tommy worked first as a trapper-boy, opening the ventilation doors for coal and miners to pass through. Later he went on to more demanding jobs in the pits.

In the later nineteenth century many miners in Durham and elsewhere composed rhymes and songs. Armstrong was already writing song lyrics at age twelve. Eventually he married, but miners' wages barely covered expenses for his large family—his overworked wife and fourteen children—prompting Armstrong to seek additional money by writing songs and having them printed. Single sheets, known as broadsides, containing lyrics were then sold in pubs to raise money for his family but also to buy beer for himself. The balladeer of Tyneside, as he was

known, referring to the nearby Tyne River, developed a legendary thirst. His son claimed, "Me dad's Muse was a mug of beer." Armstrong engaged in song duels with rival songwriters and even made up verses about the people in the houses he passed on his way home from work or pub. His songs usually had a strong sense of social class and social criticism. One of them encouraged educating the young, in part to avoid trouble with the law: "Send your bairns [children] to school, Learn them all you can. Make scholarship your faithful friend, and you'll never see the school-board man [truant officer]." He set his songs to folk and music-hall tunes as well as to Irish melodies brought by the thousands of Irish immigrants to the mines.

Armstrong became renowned for writing songs reflecting the miner's increasingly radical views and ballads to memorialize mining disasters, usually to raise money for union funds or the relief of orphans and widows. For example, in 1882, after an explosion killed seventy-four miners, Armstrong produced a song commemorating the lost men: "Oh, let's not think of tomorrow lest we disappointed be. Our joys may turn to sorrow as we all may daily see. God protect the lonely widow and raise each dropping head; Be a father to the orphans, never let them cry for bread." Conscious of his responsibility, he claimed that "when you're the Pitman's [coal miner's] Poet and looked up for it, if a disaster or a strike goes by without a song from you, they say: What's with Tommy Armstrong? Has someone let out all the inspiration?"

Armstrong was especially productive in the last two decades of the 1800s when strikes were common and the Miners' Union grew rapidly from 36,000 to over 200,000 members. As the struggles between miners and mine owners became more bitter, the union grew more assertive and organized. Armstrong wrote strike songs to give information and courage to miners, but also to collect money for hungry families of strikers. Some of the worst conflicts erupted in 1892, when the Durham miners were asked to take a large pay cut. When the union refused, the workers were locked out of their workplaces, prompting one of Armstrong's most famous songs: "In our Durham County I am sorry for to say, That hunger and starvation is increasing every day. For want of food and coals, we know not what to do, But with your kind assistance, we will stand the battle through. Our work is taken from us now, they care not if we die, For they [the mine owners] can eat the best of food, and drink the best when dry." After months of labor strife, the union pragmatically agreed to a lower pay reduction. The songs of Tommy Armstrong and other industrial balladeers provide a chronicle of the Industrial Revolution and the ways it shaped the lives of millions of people.

THINKING ABOUT THE PROFILE

1. How did Armstrong's life reflect the working conditions and often hardships imposed on workers by the Industrial Revolution?

2. What did the songs of industrial balladeers like Armstrong tell us about how working-class people confronted the realities of industrial society?

Tommy Armstrong Known as the "Pitman's (coalminer's) Poet," Armstrong worked in the coalfields around Durham, in England, and wrote many songs celebrating the miners' struggles for a better life. (Courtesy, Northern Recording Company, UK)

Note: Quotations from A. L. Lloyd, *Folk Song in England* (New York: International Publishers, 1967), pp. 359–361, 378, 380–381. Copyright © 1967 by International Publishers. Reprinted with permission.

were boys younger than eighteen. In these difficult conditions, workers such as the English coal miner Tommy Armstrong sometimes used cultural expression, such as songs, to express their solidarity with each other and resentment of those they worked for (see Profile: Tommy Armstrong, Bard of the English Coal Mines).

Gradually many people, especially in the cities, began to think of themselves as members in a social and economic class that had interests of its own in opposition to other classes. The working classes, such as the coal miners and factory workers, were the largest group. The middle classes included business-people, professionals, and prosperous farmers. A salaried labor force, today known as "white-collar" workers, emerged to handle sales and paperwork. For example, some 90,000 women worked as secretaries in Britain by 1901. The middle class prided itself on a keen work ethic and attributed poverty to poor work habits and lack of initiative. The rise of the middle class posed a challenge to the legal and social status of the beleaguered aristocrats, who struggled to maintain their dominance over the governments and churches in many countries. Crime increased as the gap between the haves and the have-nots became more apparent. In 1845 the British writer and politician Benjamin Disraeli described these two groups as inhabitants of different planets, between which there is no sympathy and no discourse.

SECTION SUMMARY

- The Industrial Revolution began in England, which had great stores of capital derived from overseas trade, an openness to new ideas, and abundant natural resources, and the revolution gradually spread throughout western Europe and North America.

- As technology played an increasingly important role in the economy and in people's lives, with machines constantly evolving and being put to new uses, some people marveled at the technological change while others, such as the Luddites, resisted it.

- Commercial capitalism was changed into industrial capitalism centered on manufacturing, and economic philosophers such as Adam Smith advocated laissez faire, the idea that the market, if left alone, would improve everyone's standard of living and create ever-increasing wealth and progress.

- The Second Industrial Revolution ushered in an age of specialization and mass production, and it favored monopolistic corporations that could afford enormous investments in new technology.

- The Industrial Revolution brought many people from the countryside to cities, where they encountered crowding, noise, new social problems, and hard labor conditions.

- As a result of the revolution, new classes arose—the working class; the middle classes, including a new secretarial force; and the aristocrats—and the gap between the haves and the have-nots widened.

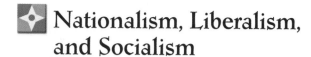

Nationalism, Liberalism, and Socialism

How did nationalism, liberalism, and socialism differ from each other?

Besides the political and economic revolutions, the Modern Era also produced three new ideologies—nationalism, liberalism, and socialism—that influenced the European and American political order and that continue to shape our world. An **ideology** is a secular faith or philosophy: a coherent, widely shared system of ideas about the nature of the social, political, and economic realm. In the Modern Era, nationalism fostered unified countries, liberalism encouraged democratic parliamentary governments in various nations, and socialism sparked movements to counteract the power of industrial capitalism and the social dislocations generated by industrialization.

Nations and Nationalism

Between 1750 and 1914 many societies in Europe and North America formed, or aspired to form, nations, communities of people united by a common language and culture and organized into independent states. The ideology that sparked this transition was **nationalism**, a primary loyalty to, and identity with, a nation bound by a common culture, government, and shared territory. Nationalists insisted that support for country transcended loyalty to family, village, church, region, social class, monarch, or ethnic group. Many peoples had a growing sense of belonging to a nation, such as France or Italy, that must be independent, have its own government, and share a common identity separate from that of other nations. For example, a Swiss newspaper proclaimed in 1848 that the "nation [Switzerland] stands before us as an undeniable reality with her own voice and equipped with extensive powers. The Swiss of different cantons [small self-governing states] will henceforth be perceived and act as members of a single nation."[15] Some historians conceive of the nation as an "imagined community" that grew in the minds of people living in the same society. Nationalism provided a cement that bonded all citizens to the state. But it also fostered wars with rival nations.

The ideology of nationalism converted older ethnic identities and traditions into political beliefs and solidarity. With its vision of uniting people who shared many traditions and a sense of common destiny, nationalism became a popular, explosive force in modern Europe and the Americas, and then in Asia and Africa. It particularly appealed to the rising middle classes and intellectuals struggling to gain more political power. They claimed that the nation included not just the monarchs and aristocrats but all the people, regardless of social

---

ideology A coherent, widely shared system of ideas about the nature of the social, political, and economic realm.

nationalism A primary loyalty to, and identity with, a nation bound by a common culture, government, and shared territory.

status, and that the nation's people were better than those in other nations. This perception of collective identity and the special nature of the nation was captured by the India-born English poet Rudyard Kipling: "If England was what England seems, An' not the England of our dreams, But only putty, brass an' paint, 'Ow quick we'd drop 'er! But she ain't!"[16]

Most historians credit the birth of modern nationalism to France and Great Britain in the late eighteenth and early nineteenth centuries. The French revolutionaries, in "The Declaration of the Rights of Man," proclaimed that all sovereignty emanated from the nation, rather than from individuals or groups, and the Jacobins identified themselves as custodians of French nationhood. The British also began to conceive of themselves as one nation composed of several peoples. England and Wales had united in 1536 under English monarchs, but by 1700 there was no Britain, and the peoples who shared the island identified themselves as English, Scottish, or Welsh. Even after England and Scotland were combined under one monarchy in 1707, the Scottish resented English domination. But the spread of English power led to the deliberate suffocation of the Scottish and Welsh cultures and languages in the 1800s. Although some people in Wales and Scotland remained wary of England, eventually most of the English, Scots, and Welsh accepted the reality of being part of Great Britain.

Nationalism transformed Europe's political landscape. In 1750 large parts of Europe were dominated by multinational states that had ethnically diverse populations. For instance, one royal family, the Vienna-based Habsburgs, ruled Austria, Hungary, the Czech lands, Belgium, and parts of Italy. Sweden ruled Finland, and Denmark ruled Norway. But during the 1800s nationalism fostered the emergence of **nation-states**, politically centralized countries with defined territorial boundaries, such as Italy, Belgium, and Norway. By 1914 only the Russian and Habsburg-ruled Austro-Hungarian empires remained major multinational states in Europe.

Unified Nations, Frustrated Nations

In the 1800s some of the most dramatic efforts to create unified nations were made in Greece, Italy, and Germany. The Greeks, long a part of the Turkish-dominated Ottoman Empire, were one of the first modern European peoples to claim nationhood through violence. Many Greeks served in the Ottoman government, and Greek merchants dominated commerce in Ottoman-ruled western Asia. Nonetheless, some Greek merchants sent their sons to western Europe to study, where they picked up nationalist ideas. Returning home, they organized a secret society that began an uprising for independence in 1821, killing many Turks. The Ottomans responded by massacring Greek villages, pillaging churches, and hanging the leader of the Greek Orthodox Church in Istanbul, acts that inflamed western European opinion. In 1827 the intervention of Britain, France, and Russia on the Greek side led to the de-

struction of the Turkish fleet. In 1830 Greece became independent, and in 1843 a rebellion against Greek royal absolutism resulted in a parliamentary government. Greek nationalism inspired other restless Ottoman subjects, and in 1862 Romania also became independent.

While the Greeks wanted independence, Italians wanted to realize a long-held dream of unity. The Italian speakers were divided into many small states, some of them part of the Habsburg and Holy Roman Empires, some ruled by the pope. In 1831 Giuseppi Mazzini (jew-SEP-pay mots-EE-nee) (1805–1872), a fiery Genoese exiled to France for membership in a nationalist secret society, founded the Young Italy movement as a brotherhood of Italians who believed that Italy was destined to become one nation. A political philosopher as well as an activist, Mazzini envisioned free nation-states eventually joining together to form a united Europe. He also promoted a republican form of government and women's rights, radical ideas in Italy. Mazzini's example inspired nationalists and democrats elsewhere in Europe, who formed imitative organizations such as Young Germany and Young Poland. In 1859 various nationalists, including Mazzini and Giuseppi Garibaldi (gar-uh-BOWL-dee) (1807–1882), who had nurtured his passion for Italy during years of exile in South America, began an armed struggle for Italian unity and drove the Habsburg forces out of the north. By 1861 Mazzini had lost influence, but Garibaldi helped create the kingdom of Italy, which included all the states except papal-dominated Rome. In 1870 Italian troops entered Rome, reuniting Italy for the first time since the Roman Empire. Thus the nation-state of Italy had been forged, but, as one leader told parliament, the job of creating Italians, people who shared a common national vision, would take longer.

German reunification also came in stages. In 1862 Otto von Bismarck (BIZ-mahrk) (1815–1898), the prime minister of Prussia, brought together many northern German states under Prussian domination. Bismarck came from the landed nobility and had spent his youth gambling and womanizing. But after marrying a devout Lutheran he changed his ways and began a rapid political ascent to Prussian leadership. Bismarck shared with the Prussian king William I a dislike of business and professional leaders, who favored expanding democratic political rights. Instead Bismarck looked to uniting the Germans through warfare, a policy he characterized as "blood and iron." War with Denmark in 1864 added Schleswig (SHLES-wig) and Holstein (HOLE-stine) to Prussian territory. Prussia quickly followed up with the defeat of Austria in 1866, driving the Habsburgs out of their last German holdings. A war with France in 1870 then brought southern Germany and the Alsace-Lorraine border region between France and Germany into the Prussian orbit. In 1871 King William I of Prussia was declared *kaiser* (emperor) of a united Germany, by now one of Europe's major powers.

Unlike the Greeks, Italians, and Germans, some peoples were unable to satisfy their nationalist aspirations. For example, the Poles frequently but unsuccessfully rebelled against the Russians and Germans who controlled Poland. The Jewish

---

nation-states Politically centralized countries with defined territorial boundaries.

Battle of Langhada The Greek war for independence from the Ottoman Turks gained strong support from liberals and nationalists all over Europe. This painting, by the Greek artist Panagiotis Zographos, uses Byzantine art traditions to show Greek soldiers riding to fight the Turks in the Battle of Langhada. (Gennadeion Library, Athens/Visual Connection Archive)

minorities faced even more difficult barriers, scattered as they were around Europe and often having little in common. Many Jews, especially in Russia, Poland, and Lithuania, had been restricted to all-Jewish villages and urban neighborhoods known as ghettoes, and they often maintained conservative cultural and religious traditions and avoided political activity. Other Jews, especially in Germany, France, and Britain, often adopted a more secular approach and moved toward assimilation with the dominant culture. Although often facing discrimination, they identified with the nations in which they lived. Reacting against widespread anti-Semitism, other Jews gravitated to revolutionary groups or to **Zionism** (ZYE-uh-niz-uhm), a movement founded by Hungarian-born journalist Theodor Herzl (HERT-suhl) (1860–1904) that sought a Jewish homeland. No Jewish state was possible in Europe, but in 1948 the Zionists formed the state of Israel in Palestine.

Zionism A movement that sought a Jewish homeland.

The Irish were particularly frustrated in their desire for their own nation. Ireland had been a colony of England for centuries, and Irish opposition to harsh English rule simmered, sometimes erupting in violence. The English attempted to destroy the language, religion, poetry, literature, dress, and music of the Irish people. As an Irish folk song from 1798 protested, "She's the most distressful country that ever yet was seen. [The English] are hanging men and women for the wearing of the green [Ireland's unofficial national color]."[17] Much of the best farming land in Ireland came under the control of rich English landlords. Conditions worsened after 1800, when English domination intensified. The English mounted even more severe laws to restrict Irish rights, deporting thousands who resisted to Australia. Many Irish men, with few job prospects, were recruited into the British army, to fight in England's colonial wars abroad. As a result, Irish ballads are filled with men going out to fight, of mothers or wives greeting their wounded men when they returned, or of grieving for those who would never return. Then during the 1840s the potato crop failed for several successive years because of a fungus blight. One and a half million Irish died from starvation while English landlords ejected Irish peasants from the land so that they could replace subsistence food growing with more profitable sheep raising. Millions of Irish people sought escape from poverty and repression by emigrating to the Americas and Australia.

But the Irish, not to be defeated, rebelled against British rule every few years. In the mid-1800s resistance became more organized, led by the Fenians (FEE-nians), a secret society dedicated to Irish independence. After experiencing many failures, by 1905 the Fenians were transformed into Sinn Fein (shin FANE) (Gaelic for "Ourselves Alone"), which first favored peaceful protest and then turned to violence against English targets. Sinn Fein extremists formed the Irish Republican Army, which organized a rebellion on Easter Monday, 1916, in which some 1,500 volunteers seized key buildings in Dublin, including the General Post Office, and proclaimed a republic in Ireland. The English quickly crushed the rising, shot the ringleaders, and jailed 2,000 of the participants, but Sinn Fein, the IRA, and acts of terrorism continued to bedevil the English colonizers.

Liberalism and Parliamentary Democracy

While nationalism reshaped states, another ideology emerged to offer a vision of democracy and individual freedom, including representative and inclusive government institutions. Influenced by Enlightenment thinkers such as John Locke and Baron de Montesquieu, **liberalism** favored emancipating the individual from all restraints, whether governmental, economic, or religious. Liberals, mainly from middle-class backgrounds, favored the sovereignty of the people, representative government, the right to vote, and basic civil liberties such as freedom of speech, religion, assembly, and the press. The liberal Scottish philosopher John Stuart Mill (1806–1873) offered the most eloquent defense of individual liberty and free expression, writing that no one should restrict what arguments a legislature or executive should be allowed to hear. Liberal politicians fought against slavery, advocated religious toleration, and worked for more popular participation in government.

Liberal ideas found their political and institutional expression in modern democracy, which involves choice and competition, usually between contending political parties and policies, within a constitutional framework that allows free choice for the electorate. Liberalism proved particularly popular in Britain and the United States, and it provided the bedrock for the United States Constitution and Bill of Rights. To protect against tyranny, the nation's founders mandated a separation of executive, legislative, and judicial powers.

Democratic decision making is an old and widespread idea. Village democracies that allowed many residents to voice their opinions and shape decisions had long existed in various tribal and other stateless societies of Asia, Africa, and the Americas. For example, the Tiv, Gikuyu, and Tswana (SWAN-a) peoples in Africa had village councils composed of elders from each family. The classical Greeks and Romans had also introduced democratic institutions, such as the mass public assemblies in Athens that selected leaders, but political rights were restricted to a small minority of male citizens. Representative institutions later appeared in England, the Netherlands, Switzerland, Iceland, and Poland. But in the nineteenth century more fully democratic and participatory systems, inspired in part by liberalism, emerged in parts of Europe. For some nations this meant evolution toward **parliamentary democracy**, government by representatives elected by the people.

Britain became the most successful parliamentary democracy in Europe. Democracy had gradually grown in Britain as royal power declined over several centuries and then flowered in the 1800s. The popular Queen Victoria (r. 1837–1901) reigned over Britain for sixty-four years after becoming queen at eighteen, and Victoria and her German-born husband, Prince Albert, provided a model of morality and stability. But by the 1800s the British monarch, even one as respected and shrewd as Queen Victoria, was no longer very powerful, exercising influence mostly behind the scenes. Instead prime ministers, elected by the majority of Parliament members, had become the major power holders. The base of democracy gradually widened as the elected House of Commons exercised more power than the appointed and hereditary House of Lords. Both houses offered extensive possibilities for dialogue and debate between political parties.

But democracy remained somewhat limited in Britain, whose leaders struggled with issues of democratic access. Throughout the 1800s British reformers wanted average people to have more voice in the electoral system. The Reform Act of 1832 increased the number of voters to about 650,000, all upper- and middle-class males, but this left out many men and all women. The major protest movement, Chartism, was based in the working class and called for universal adult male suffrage, a secret ballot, and paying members of Parliament so that people without wealth could run for office. Although the Chartists did not call for women's suffrage, many women supported the movement, founding political clubs and organizing boycotts of unsympathetic merchants. Some Chartists, led by Elizabeth Neesom, advocated the rights of women to participate in government. Chartists used demonstrations, strikes, and riots to support their demands, without much success. Fearing that radical ideas such as wealth redistribution might be proposed, Englishmen with property refused to allow the working class to have a say in government.

---

liberalism An ideology that favored emancipating the individual from all restraints, whether governmental, economic, or religious.

parliamentary democracy Government by representatives elected by the people.

Socialism and Marxist Thought

While liberals tended to favor preservation of wealth and property rights and therefore feared radical popular movements, a third ideology did encourage protest. In contrast to liberalism's promotion of individual liberty, **socialism** offered a vision of social equality and the common, or public, ownership of economic institutions such as factories. Socialism grew out of the painful social disruption that accompanied the Industrial Revolution.

The Rise of Socialism In the eighteenth and nineteenth centuries utopian socialists in Britain, France, and North America, many influenced by Christian ideals of a community based on faith and cooperation, offered visions of perfect societies shaped by the common good. A few even founded communal villages based on ideas such as service to the community and renunciation of personal wealth. For example, the British industrialist Robert Owen (1771–1858) set up a model factory town around his cotton mill, where workers put in ten hours a day on the job rather than the seventeen hours common elsewhere, and children attended school instead of working in the mill. Owen later moved to the United States and founded a model socialist community, New Harmony, in Indiana. Some proponents of women's rights, such as Emma Martin (1812–1851) in Britain and Flora Tristan (1801–1844) in France, promoted socialism as the solution to end female oppression. These views stirred controversy. For example, clergymen opposed to feminism and socialism urged their congregations to disrupt Martin's speeches, and sometimes outraged mobs chased and stoned her.

Karl Marx (1818–1883) had the most long-lasting influence on socialist thought, and his ideas, known as Marxism, became one of the major intellectual and political influences around the world. Marx, a German Jew with a passion for justice, came from a wealthy family, studied philosophy at the University of Berlin, and then worked as a journalist in several European cities before settling in London. Marx wrote his classic works in the middle and late 1800s. In England he worked closely with his German friend, Friedrich Engels (1820–1895), who had moved to England to manage his father's cotton factory. Engels, who collaborated in writing and editing some of Marx's books, introduced Marx to the degraded condition of English industrial workers. Marx called himself a communist to differentiate himself from earlier socialists such as Robert Owen, whom he dismissed as naive utopians divorced from working-class life.

In *The Communist Manifesto* (1848), Marx developed a vision of social change in which the downtrodden could redress the wrongs inflicted upon them by rising up in a violent socialist revolution, seizing power from the capitalists, and creating a new society (see Witness to the Past: The Communist View of Past, Present, and Future). Marx wrote that violence was the midwife of every old society, which is pregnant with the new. He argued that, through revolution, peoples can change their conditions and alter the inequitable political, social, and economic patterns inherited from the past. He also opposed nationalism, writing that working people had no country, only common interests, and needed to cooperate across borders. In 1864 Marx helped form the International Workingmen's Association to work toward those goals.

Marx was a product of his scientific age and considered his socialist ideas as laws of history. In his most influential work, the three-volume *Capital*, Marx argued that historical change resulted from class struggle, in which the confrontation between antagonistic social classes produced change. All social and economic systems, he suggested, contain contradictions that doom them to conflict, which generates a higher stage of development. For example, feudalism was undermined by the confrontation between nobles, merchants, and serfs, leading to capitalism. Eventually, Marx predicted, this process would replace capitalism with socialism, where all would share in owning the means of production and the state would serve the interests of the masses rather than the privileged classes. Finally would come communism, where the state would wither away and all would share the wealth, free to realize their human potential without exploitation by capitalists or governments. A revolutionary new society, Marx claimed, could create an equitable distribution of wealth and power. Such a vision of change proved attractive to many disgruntled people in Europe and later around the world.

The Marxist Legacy Marx offered some astute ideas that economists and historians have debated ever since. He believed that history was shaped by material conditions, that the nature of the economic system and technology determined all aspects of society, including religious values, social relations, government, and laws. Hence, in each type of system, such as feudalism or capitalism, the ways in which land and labor were allocated to production, work was organized (such as on medieval manors or in capitalist factories), and products were distributed, as well as the tools used, determined such patterns as family relationships, the gods people worshiped, and the ideas that emerged. Marx also argued that religion was the "opiate of the people," encouraging people to fatalistically accept their lot in this life in hopes of earning a better afterlife rather than protesting or rebelling. He criticized capitalism for creating extremes of wealth and poverty and for separating workers from ownership and management of the means of production—the farms, mines, factories, and businesses where they labored—to furnish wealth to the owners and managers as well as to the urban-based, mostly commercial, middle class that Marx called the bourgeoisie. Under capitalism, workers had become tenants and employees rather than self-employed farmers and craftsmen. Marx observed that the industrial working

---

socialism An ideology offering a vision of social equality and the common, or public, ownership of economic institutions such as factories.

The Communist View of Past, Present, and Future

In 1848 Karl Marx and Friedrich Engels published *The Communist Manifesto* as a statement of beliefs and goals for the Communist League, an organization they had founded. In this excerpt Marx and Engels outlined their view of history as founded on class struggle, stressed the formation of the new world economy, and offered communism as the alternative to an oppressive capitalist system. They ended their summary of the problems of contemporary society by inviting the working class to take its future into its own hands through unity and revolution.

A specter is haunting Europe—the specter of communism. All the powers of old Europe have entered into a holy alliance to excise this specter. . . . Where is the party in opposition that has not been decried as communistic by its opponents in power? . . . The history of all hitherto existing society is the history of class struggles. . . . Oppressor and oppressed stood in constant opposition to one another, carried on in an uninterrupted, now hidden, now open fight, a fight that each time ended, either in a revolutionary reconstitution of society at large, or in the common ruin of the contending classes.

In the earlier epochs of history, we find almost everywhere a complicated arrangement of society into various orders, a manifold gradation of social rank. In ancient Rome we have patricians, knights, plebeians, slaves; in the Middle Ages, feudal lords, vassals, guild-masters, journeymen, apprentices, serfs; in almost all these classes, again, subordinate gradations. The modern bourgeois [middle class] society that has sprouted from the ruins of feudal society has not done away with class antagonisms. It has but established new classes, new conditions of oppression, new forms of struggle in place of the old ones.

Our epoch, the epoch of the bourgeoisie, possesses, however, this distinctive feature: it has simplified the class antagonisms. Society as a whole is more and more splitting up into two great hostile camps, into two great classes directly facing each other: bourgeoisie and proletariat (working class). . . . The discovery of America, the rounding of the Cape [of Good Hope], opened up fresh ground for the rising bourgeoisie. The East Indian and Chinese markets, the colonization of America, trade with the colonies, the increase in the means of exchange and in commodities generally, gave to commerce, to navigation, to industry, an impulse never before known, and, thereby, a rapid development to the revolutionary element in the tottering feudal society. . . . Meantime the markets kept ever growing, the demand ever rising. Even manufacture no longer sufficed. Thereupon, steam and machinery revolutionized industrial production. The place of manufacture was taken by the giant, modern industry, the place of the industrial middle class, by industrial millionaires. . . .

Modern industry has established the world market, for which the discovery of America paved the way. . . . The bourgeoisie, by the rapid improvement of all instruments of production, by the immensely facilitated means of communication, draws all, even the most barbarian, nations into civilization. The cheap prices of its commodities are the heavy artillery with which it batters down all Chinese walls. . . . It compels all nations, on pain of extinction, to adopt the bourgeois mode of production. . . . It creates a world after its own image. . . .

[The Communists] have no interests separate from those of the proletariat as a whole. . . . The immediate aim of the Communists is . . . the formation of the proletariat into a class; the overthrow of the bourgeois supremacy; and the conquest of political power by the proletariat. . . . The Communists disdain to conceal their views and aims. They openly declare that their ends can be attained only by the forcible overthrow of all existing social conditions. Let the ruling classes tremble at a Communistic revolution. The proletarians have nothing to lose but their chains. They have a world to win. WORKING MEN OF ALL COUNTRIES, UNITE!

THINKING ABOUT THE READING

1. What did Marx and Engels identify as the opposing classes in European history?

2. What developments aided the rise of the bourgeoisie to power?

3. What is the goal of the Communists?

Source: From *The Communist Manifesto*, trans. 1880. http://www.anv.edu.au/polisci/marx/classics/manifesto.html.

---

class, the **proletariat**, grew more miserable as wealth became concentrated in giant monopolies in the later 1800s.

Marxist ideas attracted a wide following, first in Europe and later in various American, Asian, and African countries. In Europe they stimulated unrest. For example, in 1871, in the aftermath of a disastrous French war with Germany and the election of a conservative French government, a people's government comprising Marxists, other socialists, republicans, and other groups briefly gained control of the Paris city government, with the moderate goal of ensuring that all sectors of the population were represented in politics. The Paris Commune, as this government was called, experimented with some socialist programs such as better wages and working conditions, and thus led Karl Marx to believe that the end of capitalism was at hand. To suppress the Commune, the French government attacked Paris with ruthless force, and in response

proletariat   The industrial working class.

the Commune supporters, known as Communards, burned public buildings and killed the Catholic archbishop of Paris. The brutality of the French government troops prompted a horrified British reporter to conclude that "Paris the beautiful is Paris the ghastly, the battered, the burning, the blood-splattered."[18] When the dust had cleared, 38,000 Communards had been arrested, 20,000 executed, and 7,500 deported to the South Pacific. Not discouraged, later rebels across Europe would hoist the Marxist banner for radical redistribution of power and privilege.

With its promise of a more equitable society, Marxism became a major world force. Socialist parties were formed all over Europe in the late 1800s and early 1900s, and, in some cases, more radical socialists soon split off to establish parties that called themselves Communist. Marxism also influenced the founding of labor unions in the late nineteenth and early twentieth centuries in Europe and North America. But not all poor people or industrial workers in Europe gravitated to Marxism. While many envied the rich and thought life unfair, they were also inhibited by family, religion, and social connections from joining radical movements or risking their lives in a rebellion that might fail. An English pub toast from the 1800s reflected the desires of people for more immediate pleasures: "If life was a thing that money could buy, the rich would live and the poor might die. Here's oceans of wine, rivers of beer, a nice little wife and ten thousand a year."[19] North Americans had a weaker sense of social class, and Marxism never became as influential in the United States as in parts of Europe. Furthermore, Marx mistakenly believed that socialist revolution would first occur in leading capitalist nations such as Britain and Germany. Instead the first successful socialist revolution came, over three decades after Marx had died, in Russia.

Social Democracy and Social Reform

Eventually a more evolutionary version of socialist thought gained influence in many European societies. In contrast to the call by radical Marxists for revolution, some Marxists and other socialists favored a more gradual, evolutionary approach of working within constitutional governments. These socialists established the foundation for social democracy, a system mixing capitalism and socialism within a parliamentary framework. The first Social Democratic Party was formed in Germany in 1875. Soon other Social Democratic parties emerged in other western and eastern European countries. Criticizing Marxist revolutionaries, a German Social Democratic leader, Eduard Bernstein (1850–1932), argued that socialists should work less for the better future and more for the better present. Social Democrats and other socialists often felt a kinship with people of shared views and class backgrounds in other countries. This feeling of solidarity and the memory of the earlier International Workingmen's Association led in 1889 to the founding of the Second International Workingmen's Association by nonrevolutionary socialist parties, with the goal of working for world peace, justice, and social reform.

Social Democrats, Marxists, and other socialists actively supported labor unions and strikes to promote worker demands. Skilled workers were the first to organize unions. Although most employers were opposed, unions gradually gained recognition as representatives of the work force. Between 1870 and 1900 unions gained legal status in many nations, and in Britain, France, Germany, the Netherlands, and Sweden, trade unions and labor parties acquired enough political influence to force governments to legislate better working conditions.

In the later 1800s governments implemented social reforms to address the ills of the Industrial Revolution, laying the foundation for welfare states. This era saw the rise of the interventionist, bureaucratic state with state-run welfare systems. Many European nations passed laws regulating the length of the working day, laws regarding working conditions, and safety rules. Reformers pushed for nationalizing landed property, state inspections of housing, town planning, and slum clearance. To tackle the problem of poverty, Germany and Britain passed social legislation introducing health and unemployment insurance and creating old age pensions. Contrary to Marx's expectations, life for many European workers improved considerably by the early 1900s. But many people still worked in dangerous and unhealthy conditions or faced a ten-hour working day, and child labor continued.

SECTION SUMMARY

■ With the rise of nationalism, the inhabitants of a given country came to identify with each other as distinct from, and often better than, the inhabitants of other countries.

■ Greece attained nationhood through revolution, Italy through a unification movement, and Germany through collective war against others, while the Poles, the Irish, and the Jews struggled unsuccessfully to form nations.

■ Liberalism, which favored maximizing individual liberty, was particularly influential in Britain and the United States of America.

■ Socialism aimed to achieve economic equality through common ownership of industry, and its major proponent, Karl Marx, argued that history is driven by class struggle and that capitalism would inevitably give way to a communist society.

■ Marx's ideas exerted a strong influence on the Paris Communards and the founders of labor unions, but the first successful Marxist revolution took place not in an industrialized country as Marx had predicted, but in Russia.

■ Social Democrats, who rejected Marx's revolutionary ideas and instead favored working to better the lot of workers within a capitalist democracy, managed to greatly improve working conditions by the early 1900s.

The Resurgence of Western Imperialism

What factors spurred the Western imperialism of the later 1800s?

The Industrial Revolution provided economic incentives, and nationalism provided political incentives, for European merchants and states to exploit the natural and human resources of other lands in order to enrich their own nations and thwart the ambitions of rival nations. Initially the British were most successful in dominating the growing world economy. But economic, political, and ideological factors in the West eventually fostered a resurgence of imperialism, leading European nations to colonize and dominate much of Asia and Africa. The explosion of imperialism reshaped the global system. By virtue of imperialism, industrial capitalism became a genuine world economy. With the entire world connected by economic and political networks, history from now on transcended regions and became truly world history.

British Trade and Empire

The quest for colonies diminished somewhat in the first phase of the Industrial Revolution, even for the strongest European power, Great Britain. From the later 1700s through the mid-1800s, the British feared no competitor in world trade because they had none. The free traders who influenced the British government, wanting neither economic nor political barriers to their operations, viewed the acquisition of more colonies as too expensive. Adam Smith argued that colonialism actually impoverished the homeland. In any case, Britain already controlled or had gained access to valuable territories in the Americas, Africa, Asia, and the Pacific. While Britain lost its thirteen North American colonies, it took control of French Canada and Australia. Furthermore, Britain's Spanish and Portuguese rivals suffered even graver losses. The collapse of Spain and Portugal during the Napoleonic wars led to most of their Latin American colonies becoming independent in the 1820s, opening doors for British commercial activity.

British merchants also benefited from new technologies that enabled them to compete all over the world. Steam power meant that sailors were no longer dependent on trade winds. This revolution in transportation improved maritime shipping, allowing British ships to reach distant shores faster. The first exclusively steam-powered ships appeared in 1813 and took 113 days to travel from England around Africa to India, in contrast to eight or nine months by sailing ships. Then in 1869 the completion of the Suez Canal linking the Mediterranean Sea and the Red Sea dramatically cut the travel time between the Indian Ocean and Europe to several weeks. Britain, the canal's major shareholder, now found it easier to extend its influence to East Africa and Southeast Asia. By 1900 the England-India trip took less than twenty-five days, making for more efficient transport of resources and goods.

Despite a pragmatic preference for peaceful commerce, Britain did obtain some colonies between 1750 and 1870. The British took over territories or fought wars when local governments refused to trade or could not protect British commerce by establishing law and order. For example, as states in India grew weaker and banditry increased, the British began expanding the territory under their control in the subcontinent. Hence, during the later eighteenth and early nineteenth centuries the British gradually gained direct control or indirect power over most of India and also established footholds in Malaya, Burma, China, and South Africa. But the British preferred to undercut the power of their rivals. For example, British merchants were successful in gaining economic influence in some South American countries such as Argentina, Brazil, and Chile. Because of their economic power, the British could flood a society with cheap manufactured goods. In this way, by the late 1800s they had greatly diminished the crafts and industries of India for their own benefit. To protect their own position, British industrialists and merchants opposed any attempts to foster rival enterprises, such as textile mills, in Asian and African states, among them China, Burma, and Egypt.

However, the British economic advantage in world markets gradually diminished as economic leadership in the world changed during the later 1800s. The British invested many of the profits that they earned from India and their Caribbean colonies in other nations, much of it in the United States, Canada, and Australia, all countries settled by European, particularly British, immigrants. This investment helped develop these countries' economies, and the United States soon became a serious competitor. British investment also benefited some European nations, including Germany, and increasingly the United States and Germany were able to gain on Britain. Because British investors found it more profitable to invest abroad rather than at home, British industrial plants became increasingly obsolete. In 1860 Britain had been the leading economic power, with France a distant second followed by the United States and Germany. By 1900, however, the hierarchy had changed: the United States was now at the top, followed by Germany and then a fading Britain and France. Some British officials predicted accurately that the United States would soon dwarf Britain and other European countries economically.

Industrialization and Imperialism

As they industrialized, Germany, France, and the United States became more competitive with Britain, and the growing economic and political competition between the leading powers renewed the quest for colonies abroad. The shift to domestic economies dominated by large monopolies was a major factor in the new push for colonies in Africa and Asia. The monopolies stimulated empire building by piling up huge profits and hence excess capital that needed investment outlets abroad to keep growing. Furthermore, by the 1880s some of the wealth generated by the industrial economy began to filter down to the European working classes, stimulating new consumer interests in tropical products such as chocolate, tea, soap, and rubber for bicycle tires. To satisfy the need for resources and markets, businessmen in Britain, Germany, Italy, France, Belgium, and the United States looked for new opportunities to exploit in Africa, Asia, and the Pacific and then pressured their governments to pursue colonization to assist their efforts.

National rivalries also motivated imperialism. Nations often seized colonies to prevent competing nations from gaining opportunities. For example, the British sometimes occupied an African territory to block the French from doing so, and vice versa. While expanding British control in southern Africa, the British imperialist Cecil Rhodes (1853–1902) was moved by the words of his Oxford University professor, the philosopher and art critic John Ruskin: "This is what England must either do, or perish: found colonies as fast and as far as [it] is able, seizing every piece of waste ground [it] can get [its] foot on."[20] The national rivalries and the intense competition for colonies also planted the roots of conflict in Europe. By the early 1900s Germany and Austria-Hungary had forged an alliance, and this prompted Britain, France, and Russia to do likewise, setting the stage for future wars.

The conflicts between European powers led to a resurgence of Western imperialism between 1870 and 1914. Often this resulted in colonialism, or direct political control of another society, though Western imperialism also sometimes led to neocolonialism, or strong influence over another country's government and economy. Seizure of colonies not only brought profits for business interests but also strengthened a nation's power in competition with rival nations. The result was the greatest land grab in world history: a handful of European powers dividing up the globe between themselves.

The Scramble for Empire

With the resurgent Western imperialism, millions of people in Africa, Asia, and the Pacific Islands were conquered or impacted by Western nations and thus brought into the Western-dominated world economic system. These operations were bloody and costly for both sides. Many peoples fiercely resisted conquest. The Vietnamese, Burmese, and various Indonesian and African societies held off militarily superior European armies for decades, and even after conquest guerrilla forces often continued to attack European colonizers. For instance, in Vietnam, for fifteen years after the French annexed the country, anticolonial fighters refused to surrender, preferring to fight to the death. Countless revolts punctuated colonial rule, from West Africa to the Philippines, and Western ambitions were sometimes frustrated. In Africa, Ethiopians defeated an Italian invasion force bent on conquest. A few Asians maintained their independence by using creative strategies. The Japanese prevented Western political domination by modernizing their own government and economy, and the Siamese (Thai) used skillful diplomacy and selective modernization to deflect Western power.

Lipton Tea European imperial expansion brought many new products to European consumers. Tea, grown in British-ruled India, Sri Lanka (Ceylon), and Malaya, became a popular drink, advertised here in a London weekly magazine. (The Illustrated London News Library)

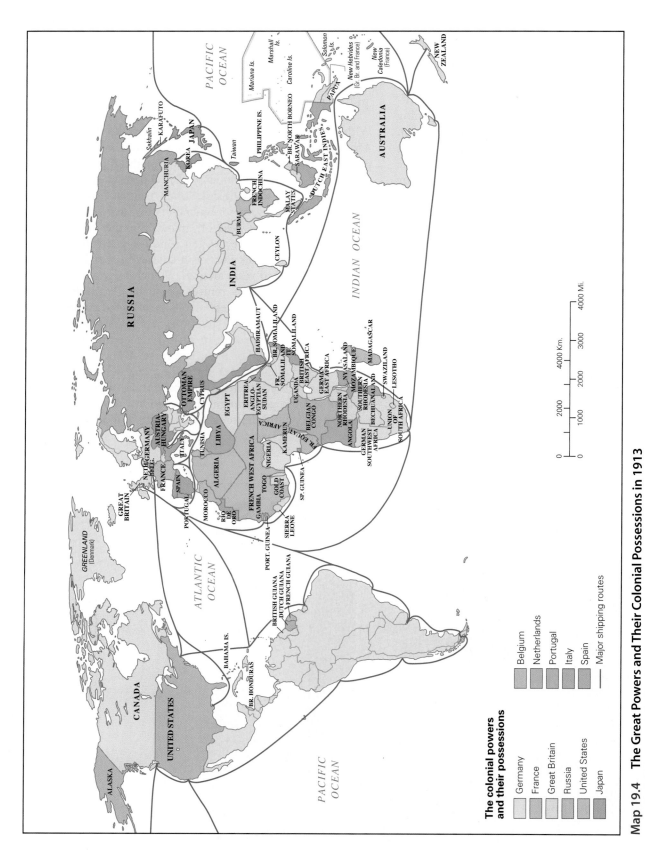

Map 19.4   The Great Powers and Their Colonial Possessions in 1913

By 1913 the British and French controlled huge empires, with colonies in Africa, southern Asia, the Caribbean zone, and the Pacific Basin. Russia ruled much of northern Eurasia while the United States, Japan, and a half dozen European nations controlled smaller empires.

New technologies permitted and stimulated imperial expansion. The Industrial Revolution gave Europeans better weapons, including the repeating rifle and the machine gun, such as the lightweight, quick-firing Maxim Gun invented in 1884, to enforce their will. A British writer boasted: "Whatever happens we have got the Maxim Gun, and they have not."[21] These weapons gave Europeans a huge advantage against Asians and Africans, and the discovery of quinine to treat malaria enabled European colonists and officials to survive in tropical Africa and Southeast Asia. Later, better communication and transportation networks, such as steamship lines, colonial railroads, and undersea telegraph cables, also helped consolidate Western control. They also more closely connected the world. In 1866 a speaker at a banquet honoring Cyrus Field, the American most responsible for building the transatlantic cable linking Europe and North America, one of the greatest engineering feats of the 1800s, noted that on the statue of Christopher Columbus in Genoa, Italy, was the inscription: "There was one world; let there be two." Now, with the cable, the speaker boasted, "There were two worlds and [now] they [are] one."[22]

As the scramble continued, old European empires grew and new ones were founded (see Map 19.4). By 1900 Western colonial powers controlled 90 percent of Africa, 99 percent of Polynesia, and 57 percent of Asia. By 1914 the British Empire, the world's largest, included fifty-five colonies containing 400 million people, ten times Britain's population, inspiring the boast that "the sun never sets on the British Empire." British leaders were proud of their empire, and some even compared it favorably to the Roman Empire. France acquired the next largest empire of twenty-nine colonies. Germany, Spain, Belgium, and Italy joined in the grab for African colonies. Between 1898 and 1902 the United States took over Hawaii, Samoa, Puerto Rico, and the Philippines. Russia also continued its expansion in Eurasia, which began in the Early Modern Era (see Chapter 23).

Western imperialism forged networks of interlinked social, economic, and political relationships spanning the globe. Hence, decisions made by a government or business in London or Paris soon affected people in faraway Malaya or Madagascar, and silk spun in China was turned into dresses worn by fashionable women in Chicago and Munich. Westerners had the strongest position in this network, ruling many subject peoples and enjoying advantageous trade relations with or strong influence over neocolonies such as China, Siam, Persia, and Argentina. Yet various Asian, African, and Caribbean peoples also mounted nationalist movements to challenge the colonial regimes and cultural movements to assert their own traditions (see Chapters 21, 22, and 25). For example, South African blacks, risking prison, demanded equality with whites, and South Asians reaffirmed the value of their Hindu, Muslim, and Buddhist beliefs.

The scope of Western imperialism changed world power arrangements. In 1750 China and the Ottoman Empire remained among the world's strongest countries, but by 1914 they could not match Western military and economic power.

In 1500 the wealth gap between the more economically developed and the less developed Eurasian and African societies was small, and China and India dominated world trade and manufacturing. By 1914 the gap in total wealth and personal income between industrialized societies, whether in Europe or North America, and most other societies, including China and India, had grown very wide.

Social Darwinism and Imperial Ideology

By the late 1800s, a new ideology, known as Social Darwinism, supported the revival of imperialism and colonialism. Supporters of imperialism used the ideas about the natural world developed by the British scientist Charles Darwin, who described a struggle for existence among species (see Chapter 20). This idea led other thinkers to conclude that this struggle led to the survival of the fittest, a notion that they then applied to the human world of social classes and nations. The industrialized peoples considered themselves the most fit and saw the poor or exploited as less fit. A German naval officer wrote in 1898 that "the struggle for life exists among individuals, provinces, parties and states. The latter wage it either by the use of arms or in the economic field. Those who don't want to, will perish."[23] Social Darwinists stereotyped the Asian and African societies as "backward" and held their own nations up as "superior" peoples who had the right to rule. Accepting Social Darwinism, most Westerners took the innate inequality of peoples for granted, and this ideology in fact created a relationship of inequality.

As a result of this ideology, Western racism and arrogance toward other peoples increased. For example, in the 1600s and 1700s many Western observers had admired the Chinese, and Enlightenment thinkers saw China as a model of secular and efficient government. But by the 1800s Europeans and North Americans had developed scorn for "John Chinaman" and the "heathen Chinee," as Europeans stereotyped them. Most Western peoples accepted these stereotypes, which were even popularized by intellectual and political leaders. The British imperialist Cecil Rhodes boasted, "I contend that we British are the finest race in the world, and that the more of the world we inhabit the better it is for the human race."[24]

This self-proclaimed superiority legitimized the effort to "improve" other people by bringing them Western culture and religion. The French proclaimed their "civilizing mission" in Africa and Indochina, the British in India claimed that they were "taking up the white man's burden," and the Americans colonized the Philippines claiming condescendingly to "uplift" their "little brown brothers." Western defenders argued that colonialism, despite much that was shameful, gave so-called stagnating non-Western societies better government and drew them out of isolation into the world market. A British newspaper in 1896 claimed that "the advance of the Union Jack means protection for weaker races, justice for the oppressed, liberty for the down-trodden."[25] This rationale also preserved the status quo favoring the European colonizers. However, most people in Asia, Africa, and the Pacific opposed colonialism, seeing it only for the terrible toll it took on their lives. The Indian nationalist leader Mohandas Gandhi, educated in Britain, reflected the resentment. When asked what he thought about "Western civilization," he replied that civilizing the West would be a good idea.

SECTION SUMMARY

■ Even after losing thirteen of its North American colonies, Britain continued to dominate the world economy through its other holdings and its technological advantages, but it gradually lost ground, especially to the United States.

■ As Germany, France, and the United States became more competitive with Britain, the powers competed for colonies that could provide natural resources for their industries and power over their rivals.

■ In the renewed scramble for colonial domination, many African, Asian, and Pacific peoples struggled for their independence, but the technological advantage of Western nations often proved insurmountable.

■ Westerners rationalized imperialism and colonization as good for the colonized, who were offered the fruits of Western culture in exchange for their independence.

Online Study Center **ACE the Test**

✦ Chapter Summary

The years between 1750 and 1914 were an age of revolutions that reshaped economies, governments, and social systems in Europe and the Americas. Political and social revolutions generated major changes. Colonists in North America overthrew British rule and established a republic that included democratic institutions such as an elected president and congress. The French Revolution ended the French monarchy and brought France's middle classes to power. Although the Revolution was consumed in violence and then modified by Napoleon Bonaparte's dictatorship, the shock waves of the upheaval in France reverberated around Europe, carrying with them new ideas about liberty and equality. The American and French Revolutions also inspired peoples in the Caribbean and Latin America. Haitians ended slavery and forced out the French colonial regime and planters, and in South America creoles waged successful wars of independence against Spanish rule.

People in North America and Europe also experienced other dramatic changes. The Industrial Revolution, which began in Britain in the late 1700s, transformed societies as profoundly as agriculture had transformed ancient societies millennia earlier, reorienting life to cities and factories and producing goods in unparalleled abundance. Until the 1850s Britain enjoyed unchallenged economic power. With the

spread of industrialization, however, positions of world economic leadership began to change. In the meantime, however, new ideologies contributed to the creation of new states and government structures. Appealing to hearts and minds, nationalism introduced new ideas of the nation and provided a glue to bind people within the same nation. Another ideology, liberalism, promoted increasing freedom and democracy. A third, socialism, addressed the dislocations industrialization created and sought to improve life for the new working classes by forging a system of collective ownership of economic property. Capitalism, industrialization, and interstate rivalries also generated in the West a worldwide scramble for colonies and neocolonies in the later 1800s, allowing Western businesses to seek resources and markets abroad. This imperialism brought many more societies into a global system largely dominated by the West.

Online Study Center **Improve Your Grade** Flashcards

Key Terms

Age of Revolution	laissez faire	liberalism
Jacobins	ideology	parliamentary
Industrial	nationalism	democracy
Revolution	nation-states	socialism
Luddites	Zionism	proletariat

Suggested Reading

Books

Anderson, Benedict. *Imagined Communities: Reflections on the Origin and Spread of Nationalism*. Rev. ed. London: Verso, 1991. An influential scholarly examination of the rise of nationalism.

Anderson, M. S. *The Ascendancy of Europe, 1815–1914*. 3rd ed. Harlow, U.K.: Pearson, 2003. A good overview of the era by a British historian.

Baumgart, Winfried. *Imperialism: The Idea and Reality of British and French Colonial Expansion, 1880–1914*. New York: Oxford University Press, 1986. A readable analysis of the imperial quest.

Connelly, Owen, and Fred Hembree. *The French Revolution*. Wheeling, Ill.: Harland Davidson, 1993. A thoughtful, brief survey emphasizing the Revolution's long-term consequences.

Countryman, Edward. *The American Revolution*. Rev. ed. New York: Hill and Wang, 2003. An excellent treatment of the conflict and its context.

Grosby, Steven. *Nationalism: A Very Short Introduction*. New York: Oxford University Press, 2005. Highlights social, historical, and philosophical perspectives.

Headrick, Daniel R. *The Tools of Empire: Technology and European Imperialism in the Nineteenth Century*. New York: Oxford University Press, 1981. A pathbreaking study of the role of technology in European expansion.

Heilbroner, Robert L. *The Worldly Philosophers: The Lives, Times and Ideas of the Great Economic Thinkers*. 7th ed. New York: Simon and Schuster, 1999. A classic and readable introduction to these thinkers.

SECTION SUMMARY

■ In Europe, better crops and health care produced higher populations, which led to increasing urbanization, impoverishment, and emigration.

■ As Europe became more industrialized and interconnected, the nuclear family and love marriages became increasingly common, and some began to question the institution of marriage itself.

■ Industrialization made men more powerful and relegated women to the home, but in the late nineteenth century women began to gain legal rights and economic opportunities.

■ While some Protestants attempted to stamp out behavior they considered sinful, Europeans as a whole became more secular and the Catholic Church's influence declined.

■ Artists, writers, and composers became dependent on the public marketplace rather than wealthy patrons, and artistic trends such as romanticism, realism, modernism, and impressionism became dominant.

■ Advances in science and technology led to improved medical care, the theory of evolution, greater understanding of the physical world, new sources of energy, and new concerns about pollution and its effects.

✦ The Rise of the United States

What impact did westward expansion have on American society?

After the American Revolution, in which the thirteen colonies successfully overthrew British control, the former colonists turned to building their new nation. The United States became an ongoing experiment as Americans learned how to balance regionalism and national unity, freedom and control, individualism and social obligation, popular representation and special interests, and national uniqueness and world leadership. During the early republic Americans established new forms of government, reshaped economic patterns, fostered a new culture, and began the movement westward, conquering Native Americans, acquiring Mexican territory, and becoming involved in the wider world.

Government and Economy

The new American republic, weak and small and surrounded by hostile neighbors in British Canada and the Spanish American Empire, found nation-building a challenge. Unity was fragile. In erecting a distinctive new system of representative government, Americans faced the daunting task of establishing principles to unite the diverse states and erecting a legal system. Ultimately they forged a new form of democracy and constructed an economic framework to preserve independence and encourage free enterprise capitalism.

American leaders were divided over many issues, including the power of a national government and the relative autonomy of the separate states. The Constitution and Bill of Rights, approved in 1787, established a relatively powerful central government, elected by voters in each state, within a system, known as federalism, that ensured the sovereignty and recognized the lawmaking powers of each member state (see Chronology: The United States and the World, 1750–1914). White Americans gained many civil liberties, and white adult males were granted the right to vote, but the government maintained slavery and excluded Native Americans and women from political activity. Professing a love for freedom, Americans ever since independence have had to constantly redefine—in political debates, legislative bodies, the workplace, schools, and the bedroom—the balance between the rights of the state and the individual, and of the majority and the minority.

The U.S. political system reflected a mix of liberalism, which underpinned the Bill of Rights, and fear of disorder. Inspired by a liberal hatred of despotic government in Europe, the founders made tyranny difficult through the separation of powers into executive and legislative branches and an independent judiciary, with each institution having defined roles. But wary of potential radicalism and shocked by the excesses of the French Revolution, the nation's leaders also discouraged attacks on the interests of the upper classes by limiting voting rights. For example, states imposed property and literacy qualifications for voting. The indirect election for the presidency through the Electoral College, in which each state chose electors to cast their votes, also reduced popular sovereignty and produced results that did not always reflect the choice of the majority of citizens.

American leaders also had to establish a sound economic foundation for the new nation. The southern plantation interests favored free trade to market their crops abroad without obstacles, especially cotton, tobacco, and sugar. But many founders insisted that economic independence was necessary to safeguard political independence and thus favored self-reliance and **protectionism**, the use of trade barriers to shield local industries from foreign competition. This strategy, they hoped, would be the first step toward fostering an Industrial Revolution like Britain's. The first treasury secretary, the West Indian–born Alexander Hamilton (1757–1804), laid the basis by establishing a national bank, favoring tariffs to exclude competitive foreign goods, and providing government support for manufacturing. A controversial figure, brilliant but arrogant, Hamilton later died in a duel with a political rival.

Hamilton's policies and protectionism encouraged manufacturing. Continued conflicts with Britain brought about a U.S. decision in 1807 to temporarily embargo all foreign trade, which stimulated domestic manufacturing to offset the lost imports. Conflicts between Britain and the U.S. over trade, U.S.-Canada border tensions, and other issues led to

---

protectionism   Use of trade barriers to shield local industries from foreign competition.

CHRONOLOGY

The United States and the World, 1750–1914

1787	U.S. Constitution
1803	Louisiana Purchase
1812–1814	U.S.-British War of 1812
1823	Monroe Doctrine
1825	Completion of Erie Canal
1846–1848	U.S.-Mexican War
1848	U.S. acquisition of Texas, California, and New Mexico
1849	California gold rush
1861–1865	Civil War
1862	Lincoln's Emancipation Proclamation
1867	U.S. purchase of Alaska from Russia
1869	Completion of transcontinental railroad
1898	U.S. incorporation of Hawaii
1898–1902	Spanish-American War
1902	U.S. colonization of Philippines
1903	First powered flight by Wright Brothers

the War of 1812 (1812–1814). The British captured Washington, burning down the White House, and repulsed a U.S. invasion of Canada but, after some U.S. victories, the two sides negotiated peace. Industrialization proceeded in the U.S. northeast and, in 1813 the first large textile mills to convert raw cotton into finished cloth opened in New England. The northern industrialists who favored protectionist policies soon prevailed over the southern planters who wanted free trade. Meanwhile, to move resources and products, Americans also built over 3,300 miles of canals by 1840. The Erie Canal, completed across New York State in 1825, connected the Hudson River at Albany to Lake Erie, linking the markets and resources of the Midwest and Mississippi Basin to the port of New York City.

Society and Culture

Gradually Americans forged a society distinct from Britain's. The French writer Alexis de Tocqueville (TOKE-vill) (1805–1859), who visited the United States in the early 1830s, noted the American commitment to democracy and individualism, the "blending of social ranks," and Americans' "unbounded desire for riches."[7] But he also considered slavery and racial prejudice a dark blot on American claims to equality, and he feared that too much individualism and greed for riches undermined

community. De Tocqueville was fascinated by America's gender relations, which differed from those in Europe. For instance, he admired the independence of single American women, the tendency to view marriage as a voluntary contract between loving equals, and the resulting influence of married women in the family, which gave them more responsibility for child rearing than in Europe, where fathers made most of the decisions about children's upbringing. Nonetheless, he noted, unmarried women and many wives were still under the strong control of fathers and other men, who believed that women's place was centered on the home.

Slavery shaped the society of the southern states. Enslaved African Americans, mostly plantation workers, were the majority in many southern districts, constantly replenished by new arrivals from Africa. They created music, including spirituals, which were based in part on African rhythms and song styles and used Christian images to indirectly protest slavery and to express a longing for freedom. In "Go Down Moses," for example, the refrain emphasized "let my people go," a clear call for emancipation, just as, in the biblical account, the Hebrews in Egypt were led to freedom by Moses. Many white Americans also wanted to eliminate slavery and other social ills. One abolitionist musical group, the Hutchinson Family, toured the country with songs that attacked slavery and the mistreatment of Native Americans, favored women's suffrage, and opposed smoking. The abolitionist Sojourner Truth (c. 1797–1883), a former slave, also eloquently advocated gender equality. Sarah Grimke (1792–1873), a Quaker from a South Carolina slaveholding family, became an active abolitionist and one of the first American feminists. She rejected the notion of different male and female natures and roles (see Witness to the Past: Protesting Sexism and Slavery). Discovering that their deceased brother had fathered two sons with one of his slaves, Sarah and her sister Angelina flouted custom and state laws by raising and educating their nephews, who both became active in the equal rights cause.

This period also saw the development of distinctively American religious and cultural beliefs. For example, Americans often ignored rigid doctrines and dogmatic church leaders. Like some of the nation's founding leaders, many Americans embraced secular values, such as tolerance for diverse ideas and indifference to organized religion. Others actively sought a personal and intense religious experience. Religious dissenters, such as Quakers and Methodists, had long flocked to North America, and Protestant denominations there multiplied, a pattern reinforced by the religious revivals that periodically swept the country, sometimes inspired by evangelical movements in Britain. At the same time, Puritan and Calvinist values remained influential, promoting a dedication to hard work at the expense of leisure and leading some Americans to criticize activities such as music, dancing, and reading for pleasure.

Manifest Destiny and Westward Expansion

The nation's boundaries gradually expanded westward, providing a counterpart to European imperialism in Asia and Africa (see Chapter 19) and allowing the acquisition of

Protesting Sexism and Slavery

Sarah Grimke and her younger sister, Angelina, were the daughters of a wealthy slaveholding family in Charleston, South Carolina. Adopting the Quaker faith, which emphasized human dignity, and rejecting their positions as members of the state's elite, they dedicated their lives to advocating women's rights and the abolition of slavery. In 1837 they moved north and began giving lectures before large audiences. Because they spoke out so publicly, they were often criticized by churches for violating gender expectations. Sarah Grimke responded in 1838 by writing letters to her critics that often used Christian arguments to defend women's right and obligation to voice their views. When the letters were published together in one volume, they became the first American feminist treatise on women's rights. The following excerpts convey some of Grimke's arguments.

Here then I plant myself. God created us equal; he created us free agents; he is our Lawgiver, our King and our Judge, and to him alone is woman bound to be in subjection, and to him alone is she accountable for the use of those talents with which her Heavenly Father has entrusted her. . . . As I am unable to learn from sacred writ when woman was deprived by God of her equality with man, I shall touch upon a few points in the Scriptures, which demonstrate that no supremacy was granted to man. . . . [In the Bible] we find the commands of God invariably the same to man and woman; and not the slightest intimation is given in a single passage, that God designed woman to point to man as her instructor. . . .

I hope that the principles I have asserted will claim the attention of some of my sex, who may be able to bring into view, more thoroughly than I have done, the situation and degradation of women. . . . During the early part of my life, my lot was cast among the butterflies of the *fashionable* world; and of this class of women, I am constrained to say, both from experience and observation, that their education is miserably deficient; that they are taught to regard marriage as the one thing needful, the only notice of distinction; hence to attract the notice and win the attentions of men, by their external charms, is the chief business of fashionable girls. They seldom think that men will be allured by intellectual acquirements, because they find, that where any mental superiority exists, a woman is generally shunned and regarded as stepping out of her "appropriate sphere," which, in their view, is to dress, to dance, to set out to the best possible advantage her person. . . . To be married is too often held up to the view of girls as [necessary for] human happiness and human existence. For this purpose . . . the majority of girls are trained. . . . [In education] the improvement of their intellectual capacities is only a secondary consideration. . . . Our education consists almost exclusively of culinary and other manual operations. . . .

There is another class of women in this country, to whom I cannot refer, without feelings of the deepest shame and sorrow. I allude to our female slaves. . . . The virtue of female slaves is wholly at the mercy of irresponsible tyrants, and women are bought and sold in our slave markets, to gratify the brutal lust of those who bear the name of Christians. . . . If she dares resist her seducer, her life by the laws of some of the slave States may be . . . sacrificed to the fury of disappointed passion. . . . The female slaves suffer every species of degradation and cruelty, which the most wanton barbarity can inflict; they are indecently divested of their clothing, sometimes tied up and severely whipped. . . . Can any American woman look at these scenes of shocking . . . cruelty, and fold her hands in apathy, and say, "I have nothing to do with slavery"? *She cannot and be guiltless.*

THINKING ABOUT THE READING

1. What do the letters tell us about the social expectations and education for white women from affluent families?

2. In what way do Grimke's letters address the issue of slavery?

Source: Sarah M. Grimke, *Letters on the Equality of the Sexes, and the Condition of Woman* (Boston: Issac Knapp, 1838).

---

abundant fertile land and rich mineral deposits. In the later 1700s American pioneers began moving across the Appalachian Mountains in search of new economic opportunities. As they expanded westward, Americans developed the potent notion of their **Manifest Destiny**, the conviction that their country's institutions and culture, which they regarded as unmatched, gave them a God-given right to take over the land, by force if necessary. Manifest Destiny offered a religious sanction for U.S. nationalism and the thrust outward, and American leaders promoted this view. In 1823 Secretary of State John Quincy Adams set a goal of transforming the United States into "a nation, coextensive with the North American continent, destined by God and nature to be the most populous and powerful people ever combined under one social compact."[8]

Expansion to the Pacific coast was achieved during the 1800s. After acquiring the Ohio territory, in 1787 the new nation extended from the Atlantic to the Mississippi River, and it was further enlarged in three expansionist waves. In the first, President Thomas Jefferson (g. 1800–1809) astutely bought from France, in the Louisiana Purchase (1803), a huge section

---

Manifest Destiny   Americans' conviction that their country's institutions and culture, regarded as unmatched, gave them a God-given right to take over the land.

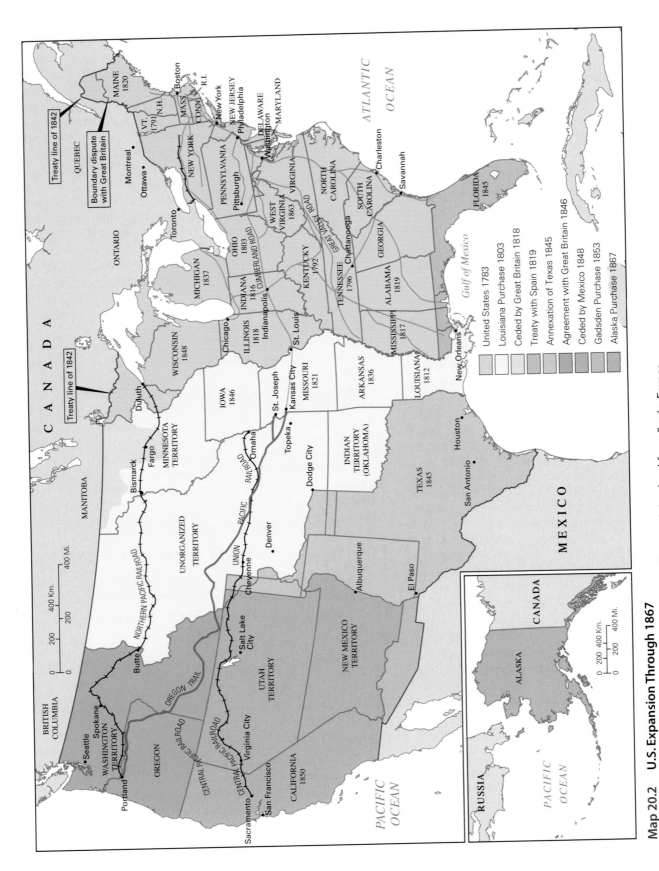

Map 20.2 U.S. Expansion Through 1867
The United States expanded in stages after independence, gaining land from Spain, France, Britain, and Mexico until the nation stretched from the Atlantic to the Gulf and Pacific coasts by 1867. During the same period Canadians expanded westward from Quebec to British Columbia.

Online Study Center **Improve Your Grade** Interactive Map: Territorial Growth of the United States

American Progress This 1893 painting by the American artist John Gast extols progress and shows Americans, guided by divine providence, expanding across, and bringing civilization to, the forests and prairies of the Midwest and West. The painting reflects views held by many Americans of their destiny and special role in the world. (Library of Congress)

of the Midwest and South that doubled the size of the country. In the second wave, the United States acquired Florida and the Pacific Northwest from Spain. Many Americans moved into the Midwest, and others continued on to Oregon by wagon train, crossing vast prairies, deserts, and mountains. In the third wave, the United States obtained from Mexico in 1848 Texas, California, and New Mexico as a result of the U.S.-Mexican War. The discovery of gold near what is today Sacramento in 1849 prompted over 100,000 Americans, known as "49ers," to board sailing ships or covered wagons and head for California from the distant east, hoping to strike it rich. In California the "49ers" sometimes clashed with the long-settled Mexicans and newcomers, such as immigrant Chinese, who were also seeking a better life. The 1867 purchase of Alaska from Russia eliminated all European rivals from North America (see Map 20.2). By 1913 the United States had grown to forty-eight states.

The gradual migration west shaped a pioneer society different from that on the eastern seaboard. The vast North American frontier offered conditions where settlers could develop new ways of life and ideas. For example, the rise of ranching, especially of cattle, on the Great Plains fostered the growth of a new occupation, that of the cowboy. Cowboys on horseback were needed to guide herds of several thousand cattle on long, lonely drives, sometimes hundreds of miles, to railroad towns

for shipment east. These cowboys—whites, Mexicans, African Americans, and men of mixed descent—often learned survival skills and knowledge of horses from Native Americans. Some historians argue that the frontier helped democratize the United States as individualists sought adventure, social equality, and a better life. But life on the frontier was often hard, especially on women. An Illinois farm wife, Sara Price, lamented her hardship in poetry, writing that "life is a toil and love is a trouble. Beauty will fade and riches will flee. Pleasures will dwindle and prices they double, And nothing is as I would wish it to be."[9]

Westward expansion came at the expense of the people already there, including Mexicans, Spaniards, and especially Native Americans. Indians saw whites as invaders in their territory and often resisted violently. To whites, Indians represented an alien way of living and thinking and needed to be controlled, that is, restricted to reservations. The U.S. Supreme Court ruled in 1831 that the Indians' "relation to the United States resembles that of a ward to his guardian."[10] Over time many Indians were removed from their native lands. Even tribes who lived in peace with whites and had adopted aspects of European culture were not spared. For example, the Cherokee, farmers who had developed their own written language, published a newspaper, and had a written constitution, had long cultivated good relations with their white neighbors. Yet, after gold was discovered on their land, 15,000 Cherokee from Georgia were forced into concentration camps and then in 1838 sent on a forced march of 1,200 miles, the "Trail of Tears," to Oklahoma. Four thousand Cherokee died from starvation or exposure on the journey. Other tribes were broken up in coerced relocations. For instance, the Delaware, who once controlled a vast mid-Atlantic territory, were scattered from Canada to Texas. Some tribes also resisted removal. The Seminole (SEM-uh-nole) in Florida, led by Chief Osceola (os-ee-OH-luh) (ca. 1804–1838), fought two wars with the U.S. army, attacking with guerrilla tactics and then retreating into the Everglades swamps. Fifteen hundred American soldiers died in the long conflict. Finally Osceola was captured, after which the Seminole resistance faded and many of the tribe were exiled to Oklahoma.

The United States, Latin America, and Asia

Although Americans avoided interference in European affairs until World War I, the belief that they had God's favor, along with the quest for resources and markets, led ultimately to territorial expansion into Latin America and the formation of a new kind of empire. In 1823 James Monroe (1758–1831), the fifth president of the United States, delivered a message to Congress that became one of the major principles of U.S. foreign policy. The Monroe Doctrine was a unilateral statement warning European nations against interfering in the Western Hemisphere and affirming U.S. commitment to shape the Latin American political future after the overthrow of Spanish colonialism. The doctrine claimed that the United States enjoyed a special political and economic status in the Americas, and it effectively marked off Latin America as an American **sphere of interest**, an area in which one great power assumes exclusive responsibility for maintaining peace and attempts to monopolize the resources of that area. Nearly a century after the Monroe Doctrine, Secretary of State Robert Lansing reaffirmed this pattern, claiming that the United States "considers its own interests. The integrity of other American nations is an incident, not an end."[11] As a result, the Monroe Doctrine forged complex links between the United States and the rest of the Americas, often provoking hostility in Latin America, and it set the stage for the rise of the United States as a world power.

As a result of the U.S.-Mexican War of 1846–1848, the United States more than doubled its national domain by seizing territory at the expense of a Latin American nation. Some 35,000 Americans and their slaves had settled in the Mexican province of Texas. Chafing at Mexican rule and its antislavery policies, the Americans rebelled and, despite a defeat at the Alamo, a fort in San Antonio, pushed the Mexican forces out and declared themselves an independent republic in 1836. Soon the Texans sought annexation to the United States, a move favored by the proslavery southern states and opposed

by the antislavery northern states. As antislavery forces stalled the annexation in the United States Congress, Texans talked of alliance with Britain, alarming U.S. leaders. In 1844 the U.S. president and Congress moved to admit Texas to statehood, provoking the pride of Mexicans, who had never recognized Texan independence and now reasserted their claims.

The war that followed stirred politically divisive and passionate debate among politicians and the media in the United States, where many people opposed the conflict. After President James Polk (1795–1849) ordered military action, the United States Congress went along, but some members were troubled that Polk evaded the constitutional mandate that only the Congress could declare war. The war badly divided Americans. A Massachusetts legislative resolution proclaimed "that such a war of conquest, so hateful, unjust and unconstitutional in its origin and character, must be regarded as a war against freedom, against humanity, against justice, against the Union."[12] The war ended when 14,000 U.S. troops invaded Mexico and captured Mexico City. This victory allowed the United States to annex Mexican territories from Texas to California. However, the conflict had killed 13,000 Americans and 50,000 Mexicans, and it had also fostered an enduring Mexican distrust of the United States.

Many Americans supported the extension of Manifest Destiny to Latin America and Asia, some citing economic factors. Polk wanted to seize California and its harbors from Mexico as a way of increasing the profitable commerce with China. In 1853 Senator William Seward placed expansion in global perspective, advising Americans: "You are already the great continental power. But does that content you? I trust that it does not. You want the commerce of the world. The nation that draws the most from the earth and fabricates most, and sells the most to foreign nations, must be and will be the great power of the earth."[13] Americans soon eyed trade opportunities across the Pacific. By the early 1800s traders were participating in the lucrative China trade, including opium smuggling. Meanwhile, the U.S. navy led the way in opening up reclusive Japan. American traders, missionaries, adventurers, diplomats, and soldiers flocked to Asia (see Chapters 22–23).

Many historians argue that during the nineteenth century the United States began to build a new kind of empire, not a territorial one like the British, French, Spanish, and Russian Empires, but chiefly an "informal" one based on using financial controls and military operations to extend U.S. power rather than gain formal political control. Hence, American naval forces intervened in Southeast Asia almost annually from the 1830s through the 1860s, often arrogantly. For example, in 1832 a U.S. naval expedition bombarded a port on the Indonesian island of Sumatra, whose officials had seized a private U.S. ship for illegal activities, and U.S. officials boasted that the demolition of the port had "struck terror" into the Sumatrans, forcing them to release the ship. Some American leaders advocated military action to gain trade agreements, an aggressive attitude that increasingly influenced U.S. policies during the century. Various presidents also sought to obtain nearby Cuba from Spain or helped to finance Cuban revolts to overthrow Spanish rule.

---

sphere of interest An area in which one great power assumes exclusive responsibility for maintaining peace and attempts to monopolize the area's resources.

SECTION SUMMARY

- Politically, the United States balanced individual liberty with systems designed to check disorder; economically, it balanced protectionist and free-market interests.

- Americans were more individualistic and offered more independence to women than Europeans, and a struggle raged between supporters and opponents of slavery.

- Americans gradually pushed toward the West Coast, taking advantage of abundant natural resources and inflicting great suffering on Native Americans.

- The Monroe Doctrine announced that the United States saw Latin America as its own sphere of interest, off limits to European powers.

- The bloody and divisive U.S.-Mexican War brought a large chunk of Mexican territory under American control.

 # An Industrial United States and Global Power

How did immigration and industrialization reshape U.S. society?

Between 1860 and 1914 the United States changed dramatically. The Civil War, which began in 1861 and lasted four years, maintained the territorial unity of the nation, ended slavery, and led to the increased centralization of the federal government at the expense of state and regional interests. This centralization, combined with economic protectionism, allowed the United States to duplicate the economic and political growth that was spurred by mercantilism in Early Modern western Europe. Industrialization created more wealth, supported U.S. power, and reshaped American social patterns. By 1900 the United States was rapidly changing as immigrants poured into the country. The country had a larger population than all but one European nation, boasted the world's most productive economy, owned half a continent, and enjoyed a powerful, stable, democratic government, all sustained by an abundance of natural resources. The nation also increasingly exercised its power abroad to extend its political and economic influence.

The Civil War, Slavery Abolition, and Social Change

The Civil War (1861–1865), a major transition for the United States, reshaped U.S. society by ending slavery. Like Sarah Grimke, many Americans had believed that slavery mocked liberal democracy. Slavery had largely disappeared from northern states by the early 1800s, and the U.S. government outlawed the slave trade in 1810, although it continued elsewhere. Thousands of free blacks occupied a precarious position in the southern states. The Civil War was a last gasp for the slavery-based southern society, which desperately tried to break free from the forces of urbanization, industrialization, and social change percolating in the northern states. Economic disparities exacerbated the North-South conflict. By 1860, the North was the home of industry, banks, and great ports such as New York, Boston, and Philadelphia. By contrast, the South was largely a monocultural plantation economy supported by 350,000 white families and 3 million black slaves. The northern leaders mostly favored high customs tariffs to protect their industries but this policy threatened the South, which depended on exports to survive.

In 1860–1861 eleven southern states seceded from the union, forming the proslavery Confederate States of America. President Abraham Lincoln (1809–1865), a lawyer from Illinois who wanted to end slavery and preserve the union, mobilized the military forces of the remaining states to resist the secession. In 1862 he issued the Emancipation Proclamation, freeing all slaves. After four years of war the North defeated the South, mainly because the North's dynamic economy better mobilized resources for war and the North also had a population advantage of nearly 4 to 1.

The Civil War was in many respects a social and political revolution. Not only did it end slavery, but it also ultimately displaced the southern planters and their plantation system: it crushed the southern struggle for self-determination, destroyed the South's economic link to Britain, firmly established protectionism as economic policy, and fostered a much stronger federal government. The war resulted in more deaths than all other wars combined that were fought by Americans before or since, killing 360,000 Union and 258,000 Confederate troops, and it devastated the southern countryside. The South began to enjoy balanced economic development only with the growth of industry in the mid-twentieth century, largely paid for by northern investors.

The Civil War emancipated African Americans from slavery but did not eliminate the disadvantages faced by them and other ethnic minorities. Determined to overcome barriers, many former slaves taught themselves to read—usually forbidden under slavery—and some opened schools to expand opportunities for young blacks. Many African Americans left the plantations to find work elsewhere, but their prospects were chiefly limited to sharecropping such as growing cotton, or physical labor, such as mining or longshoreman work. Long after slavery ended, African Americans faced discrimination reflected in laws restricting their rights and were often prevented from voting. The southern states and some northern states had rigid laws against intermarriage and, unlike Latin America, little separate recognition for people of mixed ancestry, who were lumped with African Americans and treated as such. Yet, many African Americans had some European ancestry. Classifications based on skin color and presumed ancestry were often codified in state laws. Any trace of African ancestry meant automatic relegation to inferior status. Skin color became the major determinant of social class, and segregation based on this physical feature remained the norm in the South until the 1960s. African Americans attended separate schools, were largely confined to their own neighborhoods, and could not use public facilities, such as parks, restaurants, and drinking fountains, reserved for whites. Those who violated these laws and customs faced jail, beatings, or even executions (some 235 in 1892 alone) by white vigilantes. The journalist Ida B. Wells (1862–1931), born into slavery, sparked a long movement to end mob violence, including hangings (known as "lynchings").

Native Americans also continued to suffer. In the aftermath of the Civil War, as peace brought a resumption of westward American expansion into central and western North America, more Native Americans lost control of their destinies. After 1865 whites subdued the Great Plains and its people with new technology, including the six-shooter, the steel plough, and the barbed-wire fence. Settlers, railroad builders, and fur traders massacred 15 million bison, the chief source of subsistence for Indian tribes on the Great Plains, while farmers and ranchers reshaped the environment of the prairies and northern woodlands, rendering the territory unfit for Indian survival. Indians resisted but eventually faced defeat. In 1886 the Apache of Arizona, under their chief, Geronimo (juh-RON-uh-moe) (1829–1909), finally surrendered after years of fighting. In 1890, the United States Army's massacre of three hundred Lakota Sioux followers of the Ghost Dance, an Indian spiritual revival movement, at Wounded Knee in South Dakota marked the triumph of U.S. colonization of the west. Defeated by the army, decimated by epidemics, and reduced to poverty, Indians were put on reservations controlled by the federal government. Their children, prohibited from speaking their native languages or practicing tribal traditions in boarding and public schools, were thereby stripped of their cultural heritage. Indians experienced the American dream in reverse, as democracy became tyranny and liberty became confinement.

Industrialization

The northern victory in the Civil War and economic policies of protectionism spurred the great industrial growth in the later 1800s, which fostered a better material life but also generated changes in American class structure and ways of living. These decades saw the rise of the food, textile, iron, and steel industries and the growth in coal, mineral, and oil production. The industrial economy in the United States resembled those in Europe but became more productive. In 1860 the United States ranked fourth among industrial nations, but by 1894 it ranked first; in addition, American exports had tripled, and the nation was second only to Britain as a world trader.

A surge in technological innovation changed economic life. Electricity as a power source, combined with improved factory production methods, turned out goods faster, more cheaply, and in greater quantities than ever before, increasing U.S. competitiveness in the world. New inventions by Americans such as the typewriter, cash register, adding machine, telegraph, and telephone increased business productivity, while American and European inventions such as water-tube boilers, steam-powered forging hammers, portable steam engines, and the internal combustion engine revolutionized industry. U.S. factories tripled their output between 1877 and 1892. Thomas Edison (1847–1931) benefited the public as well as industry by perfecting the light bulb.

American life and population patterns were also shaped by an improved transportation and communication network. The transcontinental railroad, completed in 1869, opened western lands for settlement, and by 1890 the U.S. railroad network was larger than all European railroad systems combined. Railroad construction owed much to ethnic minorities and

Women Textile Workers
In both Europe and North America women became the largest part of the workforce in the textile industry. These women, working in a New England spinning mill around 1850, endured harsh work conditions and the boring, often dangerous, job of tending machines.
(George Eastman House)

immigrants, since many of the workers who drove the spikes and blasted the passages through rocks and mountains were African Americans, Chinese, or Irish. The transportation revolution continued when Henry Ford (1863–1947) started a motor company in 1903 and began turning out the first affordable cars and refining the mass-production assembly line. In another transportation breakthrough, Orville and Wilber Wright became the first men to achieve powered flight in 1903, launching the age of aviation.

But industrialization also led to monopoly capitalism, a concentration of industrial and financial resources similar to Europe's that worsened the inequitable distribution of wealth. A few fabulously wealthy tycoons such as John D. Rockefeller and J. P. Morgan, known to their critics as the Robber Barons, had great influence over politicians, controlled much of the economy, and expected workers to labor at subsistence wages. Using Social Darwinist thinking (see Chapter 19), Rockefeller claimed that "the growth of large business is merely survival of the fittest and a law of God."[14] The wealthy flaunted their success and financed political allies, and many less affluent Americans also valued and hoped to acquire wealth, believing that the United States was a land of opportunity where anyone could succeed with hard work regardless of social background.

Industrialization reshaped the American social structure by creating new classes of workers. Although many Americans prospered, industrial workers often experienced a hard life. For example, in the coal mines of the southern Appalachians and Ohio River Valley, the work was dangerous, the hours long, and the wages low. Children worked alongside their parents, and miners often died young from breathing coal dust. Textile workers also faced hardship. Before the Civil War the textile industry, centered in New England, was based on exploitation of women and children. Companies recruited teenage girls from poor rural families to work in dark, hot mill rooms filled with cotton dust. They labored six days a week from 5 A.M. to 7 P.M. and were housed in company dormitories, six to eight girls per room. By the 1880s the textile industry had abandoned New England and moved south, to Virginia and the Carolinas, where wages were lower and people even more desperate for jobs. The mill town became a feature of southern life, with poor rural females the major labor force.

Immigration, Urbanization, and Social Movements

This era was also marked by social change, including the influx of millions of immigrants. Some 25 million Europeans immigrated to the United States between 1870 and 1916, and by 1900 over a million Europeans entered the nation each year in search of a better life. At first they came largely from northwestern Europe, especially English, Irish, Germans, and Scandinavians. Later many arrived from southern and eastern Europe, including Italians, Greeks, Serbs, and Poles. The population of European ancestry in the United States increased from 2.5 million in 1770 to 32 million in 1860 and 92 million by 1910. For example, many Jews fleeing persecution in Europe saw the United States as the Promised Land. In 1870 the number of Jews, mostly from Germany, that were living in the United States was 250,000, and by 1927 immigrants from Russia and eastern Europe had swelled this total to 4 million. Meanwhile, thousands of Chinese and Japanese immigrants landed on the Pacific Coast in the later 1800s, followed by Filipinos after 1900. Most of these newcomers, both European and Asian, typically faced discrimination. For instance, some businesses posted signs saying, "No Irish need apply." Chinese and Japanese immigrants, mostly living in the western states, faced even harsher restrictions and sometimes violence.

In less than a century the United States went from a mostly rural nation along the Atlantic coast to a transcontinental powerhouse. The federal government encouraged migration westward by passing liberal land laws such as the 1862 Homestead Act, which allotted 160 acres in parts of the Midwest to every pioneer family free of charge. Farming became dominant in the Midwest, pushing cattle ranching westward. Frontier territories became states within the Union. During this time the United States also became urbanized, with half of the people living in cities, including metropolises such as New York and Chicago.

The decades between 1865 and 1914 were also marked by movements seeking economic and social change. Since factories poured out more goods than Americans could consume, by the 1890s the nation was in turmoil. Economic depression, panics, and bloody labor conflicts fostered working-class radicalism, which threatened the wealthy and the middle class. Farmers and workers resented the wealth of the Robber Barons and the power of large corporations and railroads. Even while increased agricultural output made the United States the world's leading agricultural producer, many farmers went bankrupt, losing their land to banks. Political leaders worried that an inflamed public mood would spark a revolution.

Popular movements, some led by women and others by men, fought those with power and privilege. Labor unions had first appeared in the 1820s. Two decades later mill girls, led by Sarah Bagley, campaigned for better conditions and a shorter workday in the textile mills of Lowell, Massachusetts. In 1860 female strikers in the textile mills of nearby Lynn chanted, "American ladies will not be slaves." Eugene Debs (1855–1926), the socialist leader of the railway union, explained in 1893 that "the capitalists refer to you as mill hands, farm hands, factory hands. The trouble is he owns your head and your hands."[15] By the early 1900s the radical, Marxist-influenced International Workers of the World (better known as the Wobblies) were gaining influence among industrial workers, miners, and longshoremen. Employers and their political allies disparaged union members as communists and fought their demands, eventually destroying the Wobblies as a mass movement.

Women also struggled for their civil rights. The republic excluded more than half of the population from democracy for the first 150 years. During the 1800s, although large numbers of women worked in factories, shops, and offices, they also managed their homes. Despite their increasing economic roles, women were also urged by religious leaders to be more pious, self-sacrificing, and obedient to men. They wore stiff, uncomfortable whalebone corsets that constrained movement and accentuated their figure, a symbol of their submission to male taste and expectations. Many women wanted more options; the banners carried by striking factory workers in 1912 read, "We want bread and roses too."

Women gained basic privileges more on a par with men only after a long, nonviolent effort. The suffrage movement for the vote was born in 1848, when women meeting in Seneca Falls, New York, declared, in a reference to the U.S. Declaration of Independence, that "all men and women are created equal." They opposed a system in which women had no rights to property or even to their own children in case of divorce. After seven decades of marching, publicizing their cause, and lobbying male politicians, suffragettes convinced Congress to give women the right to vote in 1920.

Thought, Religion, and Culture

While some Americans, especially on the East Coast, still looked to Europe for cultural inspiration, the nation increasingly created its own distinctive literary and intellectual traditions. Later-nineteenth-century writers such as Walt Whitman and Mark Twain helped forge a uniquely American literature that examined society and its problems. Whitman (1819–1892), a journalist influenced by European romanticism, celebrated democracy, the working class, and both heterosexual and homosexual affection while addressing the transformations of the Industrial Revolution. In 1855 Whitman described his ethnically diverse and dynamic nation as "a newer garden of creation, dense, joyous, modern, populous millions, cities and farms. By all the world contributed."[16] Twain (1835–1910), a former printer and riverboat pilot from Missouri turned journalist, was inspired by European realism and sought material for his essays, short stories, and novels all over the country and the world. Unlike the optimistic Whitman, Twain emphasized the underside of American life and character, was skeptical about technology's value, and opposed the increasing U.S. imperial thrust in the world.

American philosophy and religion also went in new directions. In a constantly changing world, some thinkers concluded, eternal ideas were harder to justify. The leading American philosophers, such as William James and John Dewey, broke with the European tradition by claiming that ideas had little value unless they enlarged people's concrete knowledge of reality, an approach known as pragmatism. While many Americans embraced secular and humanist views, many others took a different view, seeking truth in religion. The Protestant missionary impulse, inherited from the first settlers and augmented by the growth of evangelical churches, fostered religious and moral fervor. As a result, Americans became active as Christian missionaries around the world. At the same time, the nation itself became more religiously diverse. In 1776 most Americans were Protestant, often Calvinist. By 1914 the United States contained followers of many faiths, including some Buddhist and Muslim immigrants from Asia.

Americans also produced unique music, largely the result of the mixing of black and white traditions. In the South, especially the states along the Mississippi River, new forms of music developed in the early 1900s out of African American culture. One of these, the blues, grew out of the plantation economy. Sung mainly by blacks on street corners or in saloons, the blues detailed personal woes in a world of harsh reality and racism. Bluesmen sang of lost love, the brutality of police, jail, joblessness, and oppression. The blending of black blues with white folk music and popular music provided a foundation for several forms of American popular music in the twentieth century, including jazz, rock, rhythm and blues, and soul, which spread around the world.

American Capitalism and Empire

As in Europe, industrial capitalism fostered imperialism and warfare. A series of economic depressions from the 1870s through the 1890s spurred public demand for foreign markets and for extending Manifest Destiny to other parts of the world. As a result, by the later 1800s many American businessmen, farmers, and workers favored acquiring territories overseas to improve national economic prospects. Others hoped to spread American conceptions of freedom, which they increasingly equated with individualism, private property, and a capitalist marketplace economy. Since domestic problems, such as the wide gap between the very rich and very poor, were not easily resolved, many argued, only the imposition of direct or indirect control over other societies, in order to acquire resources and markets, could generate enough wealth to avoid domestic turmoil.

These pressures led to military interventions. The United States sent military forces to at least twenty-seven countries and territories between 1833 and 1898 to protect the economic interests of American businesses during insurrections or civil strife or to suppress the piracy that threatened U.S. shipping. Troops were dispatched at various times to nearly a dozen Latin American nations, China, Indonesia, Korea, North Africa, and Hawaii. For example, for decades U.S. gunships patrolled several of China's rivers to protect American businessmen and missionaries from Chinese who resented Western imperialism.

U.S. forces also brought the Hawaiian Islands, a Polynesian kingdom where Americans had long settled as traders, whalers, planters, and missionaries, into the U.S. empire. The growing American population in Hawaii, led by sugar planters, resented the Hawaiian monarchy. In 1891 Liliuokalani (luh-lee-uh-oh-kuh-LAH-nee) (1838–1917), a Hawaiian nationalist who wanted to restrict settler political influence, became queen. She was strong and resolute, spoke excellent English, and was beloved by her people as a songwriter, but she faced economic disaster when the United States Congress abandoned preferential treatment for Hawaiian sugar imports.

Hoping to reestablish close ties to the United States, in 1893 American settlers, aided by 150 U.S. troops, overthrew the monarchy, formed a provisional government, and announced that they would seek affiliation with the U.S. Americans already dominating the island economy, effectively making Hawaii a neocolony. A heated debate in the United States on the advantages and disadvantages of direct colonization as opposed to informal control delayed annexation of the islands as a territory until 1898. The end of the monarchy transformed the islands not only politically but also socially, as thousands of Japanese, Chinese, Korean, and Filipino immigrants become the main labor force, mostly working on plantations owned by American settlers and companies. By the 1930s, Asians constituted the large majority of Hawaii's population.

The major conflict involving the United States was the Spanish-American War (1898–1902), which pitted American against Spanish forces in several Spanish colonies. The war was a watershed in U.S. foreign affairs that helped make the United States a major world power and empire. On the eve of the war, President William McKinley (1843–1901) argued for the necessity for obtaining foreign markets for America's surplus production, linking expanding markets with the maintenance of prosperity. In what Secretary of State John Hay called "that splendid little war," the United States fought with Spain over that country's remaining, restless colonies: Cuba, Puerto Rico, Guam, and the Philippines. The war unleashed American nationalist fervor. One observer described patriotism as oozing out of every boy old enough to feed the pigs.

The United States quickly triumphed against the hopelessly outmatched Spanish. However, 5,500 Americans died in Cuba, largely because of malaria and yellow fever rather than enemy gunfire. A surgeon who labored among the disease-ridden survivors wrote of pale faces, sunken eyes, staggering gaits, and emaciated forms, which marked these veterans as wrecks for life. The war also changed Americans' outlook on the world. A future president, Woodrow Wilson, boasted about America's emergence as a major power in the global system: "No war ever transformed us quite as the war with Spain. No previous years ever ran with so swift a change as the years since 1898. We have witnessed a new revolution, the transformation of America completed."[17] However, to colonize the Philippines, the United States had to brutally suppress a fierce nationalist resistance by Filipinos opposed to U.S. occupation (see Chapter 22). The U.S. struggle against Filipinos seeking independence and democracy after three and a half centuries of unpopular Spanish rule, while ultimately successful, resulted in the deaths of thousands of Filipinos and Americans and indicated the challenges and costs of exercising power in the world. The colonization of the Philippines, Puerto Rico, and Guam, and economic and political domination over nominally independent Cuba, also transformed the United States from an informal into a territorial empire much like the Netherlands and Portugal.

SECTION SUMMARY

■ The Civil War killed hundreds of thousands, did tremendous damage to the South's economy, and freed the slaves, though discrimination and segregation continued for at least another century.

■ American industry advanced rapidly, producing immense wealth for a small number of tycoons, helping others to prosper, and creating difficult, hazardous work for many.

■ Millions of immigrants poured into the United States, seeking opportunity and often finding discrimination, while social movements seeking better treatment for workers and greater rights for women came into being.

■ A distinctive American culture developed that celebrated democracy and practicality and that reflected the diverse origins of the American people.

■ In the interests of promoting and protecting American business interests, the U.S. military intervened in the affairs of many foreign countries and territories, most notably in the Spanish-American War, which brought the United States its first formal colonies.

✦ Latin America and the Caribbean in the Global System

What political, economic, and social patterns shaped Latin America after independence?

Brazil and most of Spain's Latin American colonies won their independence in the early 1800s, although the Caribbean islands mostly remained colonies (see Chapter 19). But the new Latin American states did not forge the enduring democracy of their northern neighbors or foster significant social and economic change. Most Latin Americans experienced considerable turmoil, including political instability, economic decline, and regional conflicts. However, by the 1870s conditions stabilized somewhat. Expanding European markets by then had created a greater demand for Latin American exports and stimulated economic growth, though free-trade policies also deepened the Latin American and Caribbean monocultures. Black slaves gained their freedom, and waves of European immigrants poured into some nations, changing the social landscape. Latin American and Caribbean societies also forged new cultural forms, and the United States increasingly exercised power in the region.

Latin American Nations

After winning their independence from Spain and Portugal, Latin Americans faced new challenges. Some countries, such as Argentina, Brazil, and Mexico, were large and unwieldy, while others, such as El Salvador and the Dominican Republic, were small and had limited resources. Except for Brazil, which was governed by an emperor, the new countries were republics. Creating stable political systems proved to be a struggle. Despite efforts to forge national identities and unity, the new governments did not always win the allegiance of all the people within the country. Civil wars for dominance continued some places into the 1860s, often pitting those favoring federalism and regionalism against partisans of a strong centralized government. In addition, various frontier disputes fostered occasional wars. For example, Chile fought Peru and Bolivia in 1837 and again in 1879–1884, acquiring territory from those two countries as a result (see Chronology: Latin America and the Caribbean, 1750–1914).

Political instability dominated Latin American politics in the decades to follow, often leading to military dictatorships and wars. Unlike England, Spain and Portugal had never fostered democratic conditions at home or in their colonies. Most of the Latin American countries adopted U.S.-style constitutions, but their provisions were often ignored in the authoritarian political systems. Many nations had regular elections but enjoyed little democracy. Furthermore, tensions between central governments and remote regions became chronic. For example, the Argentine government did not impose its authority on remote provinces until the 1870s.

Although the Latin Americans achieved political independence, most leaders did not favor dramatic social and economic change. The wealthy upper class largely consisted of creoles who owned large businesses, plantations, and haciendas or had seized them from the departing Spaniards. The small middle class of shopkeepers, teachers, and skilled artisans was mainly composed of mestizos and mulattos. Over half of the population, including most Indians and blacks, remained at the bottom of the social structure. Whether in North America, the Caribbean, or Latin America, economies based chiefly on plantation agriculture or mining had similar, highly unequal social structures. These societies offered limited education for the workers because little alternative employment was available.

In Latin American countries politics usually remained chiefly an affair among planters, ranchers, mine owners, merchants, and military officers, and political and economic leaders often restricted the political participation of the poor nonwhite majority. To contain or prevent unrest resulting from the severe gap between rich and poor, military strongmen, known as **caudillos**, who acquired and maintained power through force, gained control of many Latin American countries. Some of these, such as the dictator Juan Manuel de Rosas (huan man-WELL deh ROH-sas) (1793–1877) in Argentina, were tyrants. To defend the interests of the big ranchers and merchants, Rosas's police and thugs beat up, tortured, or murdered opponents, often poor peasants. For their armies, caudillos and regional leaders sometimes recruited local cowboys, known as **gauchos** in Argentina and Uruguay, who worked on large ranches and were skilled horsemen and fighters. Like North American cowboys, the gauchos were European, Indian, black, or of mixed descent.

Most Latin American nations established some stability by the 1850s, although politics remained highly contentious. Many countries sought both "progress and order," which often led to caudillo rule. But a few fostered multiparty systems in which competing parties sought access to national power in order to

CHRONOLOGY	
Latin America and the Caribbean, 1750–1914	
1861–1872	Benito Juarez president of Mexico
1876–1911	Diaz dictatorship in Mexico
1842	End of trans-Atlantic slave trade by most nations
1862–1867	French occupation of Mexico
1886	Abolition of slavery in Cuba
1889	Abolition of slavery in Brazil
1889	Brazilian republic
1879–1884	War between Chile and Peru-Bolivia
1885–1898	Cuban revolt against Spain
1898–1902	Spanish-American War
1901	Platt Amendment to Cuban constitution
1910–1920	Mexican Revolution
1912	U.S. intervention in Nicaragua
1914	Completion of Panama Canal

reward supporters. The political elite often disagreed on policies. Liberals generally favored federalism, free trade, and the separation of church and state. Often irreligious or anticlerical, they viewed the institutional power of the Catholic Church as being opposed to individual liberty. Conservatives sought centralization, trade protectionism, and maintenance of church power. Conflicts between these groups were sometimes violent.

Brazil was the only Latin American nation to maintain a monarchy rather than a republic. By the 1880s Brazilians had begun debating the legitimacy of the monarchy, which seemed unwilling to consider popular aspirations. Many Brazilians favored abolishing slavery, the source of growing social conflict, and forming a republic. As tensions simmered, the army seized power in 1889, exiled Emperor Dom Pedro II, and replaced the monarchy with a republic. However, although a federal system on the U.S. model emerged, suffrage was highly restricted, the majority of Brazilians gained neither property nor civil rights, and many remained desperately poor. In the end Brazil maintained an authoritarian tradition, but rebellions and regionalism constantly challenged the government.

Revolution in Mexico and Cuba

Social and economic inequalities in Latin American countries often led to reforms and sometimes to revolutions. Revolution was most notable in Mexico; however, the birth of the Mexican republic in 1824 did not bring stability to the vast country,

---

caudillos Latin American military strongmen who acquired and maintained power through force.

gauchos Cowboys in Argentina and Uruguay who worked on large ranches and were skilled horsemen and fighters.

which stretched from northern deserts to southern rain forests and was difficult to administer effectively. Between 1833 and 1855 a caudillo, General Antonio Lopez de Santa Anna (SAN-tuh AN-uh) (1797–1876), led a series of dictatorships punctuated by civil war. By leading his country into the disastrous U.S.-Mexican War (1846–1848), Santa Anna also lost half of Mexico's territory, including Texas and California, to the United States, a humiliation that is still felt by Mexicans today.

Santa Anna's misadventures and growing social problems sparked upheaval. In 1861 Mexican liberals led by Benito Juarez (WAHR-ez) (1806–1872), a pragmatic lawyer and Zapotec Indian, defeated the conservatives and suspended repayment of the foreign debt. In 1862 this provoked a short-lived occupation by France, whose ruler, Napoleon III, dreamed of renewed American empire. The French made a member of the Habsburg family, Maximilian of Austria (1832–1867), emperor of Mexico. However, under pressure from Mexican liberals and the United States, France withdrew its troops, and Maximilian's regime collapsed in 1867. Juarez again served as president from 1867 until his death in 1872, seeking social justice, fighting corruption and the privileged classes, and subordinating the church to the secular state. Juarez sold church lands and dissolved Indian communes, assigning individual properties to their tenants in order to create free peasants. His reformist policies and his Indian ancestry—his admirers called him the "man of bronze" because of his dark skin—made Juarez Mexico's most honored leader and a symbol of the nation.

In 1876 Mexico came under the dictatorship of Porfirio Diaz (DEE-ahs) (1830–1915), a caudillo of mestizo ancestry who ruled until 1911. Diaz brought stability and economic progress, allowing the country's population to grow from 9 million in 1874 to 15 million in 1910. But Diaz also allowed foreign business interests and investors to take over much of Mexico's economy, and he did little to help the growing mass of impoverished people. Under Diaz and his free enterprise policies many Indians sold their land to pay off debts, and much of it became owned by large haciendas and land companies. Women such as Dolores Jimenez (hee-MEH-nes), who led a working-class organization advocating women's empowerment, were among those opposed to Diaz.

Although Diaz brought some development to Mexico, he did so at the expense of most Mexicans, and his rule ended in civil war and revolution. In 1910 various forces coalesced to fight the unpopular Diaz regime in the Mexican Revolution (1910–1920). One faction was led by political liberals such as the creole Francisco Madero (muh-DER-oh) (1873–1913), a landowner's son who was also a spiritualist and vegetarian and who was educated in France and the United States. Another rebel leader, Pancho Villa (VEE-uh) (1877–1923), a field laborer's son and former cowboy, attracted support chiefly from ranchers in northern Mexico. In the south, the mestizo Emiliano Zapata (zeh-PAH-teh) (1879–1919), a charismatic former peasant, organized a peasant army that seized haciendas and fought the federal army. With the defeat of Diaz, largely by Zapata's forces, the idealistic Madero was elected president but proved a weak leader, unable to hold the revolutionary movement together, and was murdered by a rival. Madero's death

Women Revolutionaries in Mexico Women joined men in fighting, and sometimes dying, for one or another faction during the Mexican Revolution. Many women hoped that the revolution would bring social change and a greater emphasis on improving women's political and economic rights. (Archivo General de la Nación, Mexico, courtesy of Martha Davidson)

generated a free-for-all for power between the armies of Madero, Villa, Zapata, and other leaders. For years Mexico was engulfed in sporadic violence, all factions used ruthless tactics, and alliances formed and collapsed, often confusing Mexicans. A novel of the period concluded that "thinkers prepare the Revolution; bandits carry it out. At the moment no one can say with any assurance: 'So-and-so is a revolutionary and What's-his-name is a bandit.' Tomorrow, perhaps, it will be clearer."[18] Zapata was assassinated by a rival in 1919, but his reputation lived on in death, making him the most celebrated revolutionary hero.

The fighting had raised expectations for social change and fostered a yearning for peace. For example, hoping to gain more rights and influence, women played a critical revolutionary role. They cooked and commanded troops, served as spies and couriers, shot carbines and pistols, and fought disguised as men. Some of their hopes seem realized in a constitution introduced in 1917, which set forth progressive goals such as an eight-hour work day and paid maternity leave. But the constitution ignored other goals set out by liberal women, such as women's suffrage. In 1920 the revolutionary conflict wound down after claiming 1 million lives. While most Mexicans remained impoverished, a new party led by former revolutionaries formed a government and brought political stability while also opening some space for women to enter the business world and state governments.

In the Caribbean, Cuba also experienced revolt. The Spanish retained a tight control of Cuba and its valuable sugar plantations, but by the later 1800s an independence movement had developed. Its major spokesman, the journalist Jose Marti (mahr-TEE) (1853–1895), was a true citizen of the world who had travelled and lived in Europe, the United States, and various Latin American nations. Marti wrote innovative poetry and essays promoting freedom, social justice, and equitable distribution of wealth, and his writings helped inspire a Cuban revolt in 1895. Marti welcomed Afro-Cubans and women, who became the backbone of the struggle. However, Marti was killed in the fighting, and eventually the revolution was sidetracked by U.S. intervention during the Spanish-American War, which turned Cuba into a U.S. neocolony, Americans dominating the economy and having strong influence over the Cuban government.

Latin American Economic Patterns

Like North Americans, Latin Americans debated the benefits of free trade as opposed to protectionism, of heavy involvement in the world economy as opposed to self-sufficiency. After the destructive wars of independence, Latin American exports and investments declined. However, in contrast to the protectionist United States, this decline did not prompt Latin American leaders to move toward economic independence. Instead, they largely pursued free trade and maintained the monoculture based on plantations, mines, and ranches, concentrating on the export, mainly to the United States and Europe, of raw materials such as Ecuadorian cocoa, Brazilian coffee, Argentine beef, Cuban sugar, and Bolivian and Chilean ores.

The decision to concentrate on exporting natural resources left Latin American societies economically vulnerable. Around the region, earnings from minerals and cash crops ebbed and flowed with the fall or rise of world commodity prices. For instance, the "boom-and-bust" pattern for Brazil's coffee and rubber made sustained growth difficult and created regional pockets of alternating prosperity and decline. By the twentieth century the fate of Brazil and other Latin American countries became closely tied to fluctuating world prices for those countries' exports. Reflecting this fact, the politically unstable Central American countries, whose economies depended on tropical agriculture, were derisively called "banana republics." Unbalanced development had its hazards. For example, when silver deposits were exhausted at Potosi in Bolivia, the once famed mining city that had supplied so much wealth to Spain rapidly declined to a sleepy Andean town offering few jobs. In addition, because Latin American economic policies fostered growth but not development, the majority of people saw few benefits and the gap between the rich and the poor widened.

Some countries may have had few viable alternatives to free trade. The impoverished state of most Indians and blacks, in contrast to prosperous white North Americans, gave them little purchasing power to support any local industries that might be developed. And attempts to foster economic change often failed. Efforts to industrialize in Brazil, Colombia, and Mexico in the 1830s and 1840s failed because of competition from European imports. Only Argentina had some success fostering modest manufacturing in the later 1800s.

Investment by North Americans and Europeans in mines and plantations drew Latin America more firmly into the global market, exposing the region's peoples to continued exploitation by outsiders. Independence opened Latin America to North American, French, and especially British merchants and financiers, who used their economic power to dominate banking and the import trade for industrial goods such as cotton textiles and who also invested in mines and plantations. Brazil became heavily dependent on Europe and North America for loans, investment, technology, and markets. By the mid-1800s British businessmen and bankers controlled the imports and exports of both Brazil and Argentina. Argentina was sometimes called an informal member of the British Empire, and in 1895 an Argentine nationalist complained that "English capital has done what English armies could not do. Today our country is tributary to England."[19] After 1890 the United States also became a powerful economic influence in Latin America.

Foreign investment and domination had several consequences for Latin Americans. First, foreign corporations increasingly owned the plantations and mines. For example, the U.S.-based United Fruit Company dominated Central American banana growing. Such companies sent their profits to the United States or Europe rather than investing further in Latin America. Second, Latin America became a major contributor to world commodity markets, producing some 62 percent of the world's coffee, 38 percent of the sugar, and 25 percent of the rubber by World War I. Third, by the later 1800s, increased communication and transportation, as well as growing U.S. demand for markets and raw materials, fostered economic expansion in many countries. Despite this growth, however, inequalities grew. In some rural areas of Brazil, for example, powerful landed families maintained the peasantry in what was essentially bondage through private armies and gunmen. Throughout Latin America powerful families or foreign corporations increasingly owned the usable land, creating social and economic imbalances that produced political unrest in the twentieth century.

Slavery, Abolition, and Social Change

The abolition of slavery opened the door to social change in Latin America. Some of the leaders who overthrew Spanish rule, such as Simon Bolivar and Jose de San Martin, had favored emancipation and freed slaves who fought in the wars of independence. The emancipation movement continued. Between

1823 and 1854 slavery was legally abolished in most of Latin America and the Caribbean. Most European and American countries outlawed the trans-Atlantic slave trade by 1842 although the smuggling of African slaves to the Americas continued on a gradually diminishing scale through the 1870s. By the 1880s only Cuba and Brazil still maintained legal slavery. The Spanish rulers finally granted Cuban slaves their freedom in 1886, and abolitionists became more outspoken in Brazil, where slavery remained common in the sugar and coffee industries. Their most fiery spokesman, Joaquim Aurelio Nabuco de Araujo (wah-KEEM na-BOO-ko day ah-RAO) (1849–1910), a diplomat and the son of a rich landowner, denounced slavery for corrupting everything and robbing workers of their virtues. Increasing resistance by slaves, growing opposition by educated Brazilians, and the desire to promote European immigration led finally to abolition in 1889.

However, as in the United States, emancipation brought Latin American and Caribbean blacks freedom but did not dramatically improve their economic conditions. Many blacks shifted from being slaves to sharecroppers, tenant farmers, and laborers, experiencing little change in their low social status. As a popular Brazilian verse lamented: "Everything in this world changes; Only the life of the Negro [black] remains the same. He works to die of hunger."[20]

While life for most blacks changed little, the immigration of millions of Europeans and Asians reshaped many Latin American societies. European immigrants, especially Italians, Spaniards, Germans, Russians, and Irish, sought better economic prospects in new lands, particularly in Argentina, Brazil, Chile, Uruguay, and Venezuela. European arrivals most strongly shaped Argentina and Uruguay. The majority of people in Buenos Aires today trace their roots to Italy. The continued immigration encouraged Latin Americans to emulate European fashions, which generated a long-term market for European products. Owing in part to immigration, Latin America's population doubled between 1850 and 1900 to over 60 million.

Seeking, like Europeans, a better life, people from overcrowded lands in Asia and the Middle East also immigrated to the Americas in the later 1800s and early 1900s. In Trinidad, British Guiana, and Dutch Guiana, the abolition of slavery prompted labor-short planters to import workers in large numbers from India, and Indians eventually accounted for around half of the population in these colonies. Japanese settled in Brazil, Peru, and Paraguay as farmers and traders. Arab immigrants from Lebanon and Syria developed trade diasporas throughout Latin America, and Indonesians moved to Dutch Guiana as plantation workers. Chinese flocked to Peru and Cuba and, in smaller numbers, to Jamaica, Trinidad, and the Guianas. As different peoples came together, cultural mixing occurred. For example, an Afro-Trinidadian might have a Spanish surname, belong to the Presbyterian Church, possess a Hindu love charm, enjoy English literature, and favor Chinese food. People of Asian or Middle Eastern ancestry have sometimes headed Latin American or Caribbean governments.

Despite the newcomers, Latin America remained more conservative than North America in social structure. The cre-

ole elite dominated most countries while European and Asian immigrants and mixed-descent people constituted the middle class. Many mulattos and most blacks and Indians remained in the lower class. Indians in countries such as Mexico, Guatemala, Peru, Bolivia, and Colombia often withdrew into their village communities and limited contact with the national society. In 1865 a Mexican described the wide gap between whites and Indians: "The white is the proprietor; the Indian the worker. The white is rich; the Indian poor and miserable."[21]

Because of its large populations of European, African, and mixed-descent people, Brazil developed a society and culture different from those of other Latin Americans countries. Brazilians wrote of their nation's unique, multiracial society, which they considered to be less obsessed by skin color than other countries. Unlike in the United States, economic class and skin color did not always coincide, and marriage and cultural mixing between members of different groups was common. For instance, millions of Brazilians of all backgrounds blended African religions with Catholicism, creating new sects. Yet blacks were also more likely than whites to experience prejudice and to be poor, a fact reflected in Rio de Janeiro's largely black hillside shantytowns.

Latin American and Caribbean Cultures

Latin American and Caribbean societies created diverse forms of culture. Latin Americans struggled to reconcile indigenous with imported cultural traditions and debated how much to look to Europe for inspiration. Rejecting European models, novelists focused on social themes. For example, Euclides da Cunha (KOO-nyuh) (1866–1909) helped create a modern, realistic Brazilian literature concerned with describing the life of the country's poor (see Profile: Euclides da Cunha, Brazilian Writer). The Chilean essayist Francisco Bilbao was even more radical, praising freedom and rationalism and denouncing slavery, Catholicism, and the expansionism of the United States. In contrast, the cosmopolitan, well-traveled Nicaraguan poet Ruben Dario (1867–1916) rejected the expression of ideas in art in favor of escapist and fantastic images and a stress on beauty as an end in itself. But he also expressed unease at growing U.S. political and economic power in the region.

Especially creative cultural innovations came in music and dance. For example, the sensuous dance called the tango emerged in the bars and clubs of poor neighborhoods in Buenos Aires, which had over 1,600,000 people by 1914, and it became the most popular music in Argentina and Uruguay. The tango reflected a mixing of African and European traditions, since the music was based partly on rhythms derived from the drumming of African slaves and featured the accordion-like *bandoneon,* invented in Germany and carried to Argentina by Italian immigrants. The tango became a symbol of lower-class identity, as much a philosophy of life as an entertainment. By the early 1900s it had become popular in the ballrooms and nightclubs of Europe.

Brazil's unique music blended European melody and African rhythms. The abolition of slavery and the migration of Afro-Brazilians from Bahia State in the northeast to Rio de

EUCLIDES DA CUNHA,
BRAZILIAN WRITER

Euclides da Cunha (1866–1909) was one of Latin America's greatest writers, respected for his prose style, and the spokesman for a rising Brazilian nationalism. Born near Rio de Janeiro to a family originally from Bahia in the northeast, Cunha grew up at a time of great social change and political turmoil, when Brazilians abolished slavery and the Brazilian empire became a republic. He attended a military college to study engineering but rebelled against the rigid discipline. After angrily hurling down his sword in front of the Minister of War, he left the college before graduating to work as a journalist. Cunha was also a scientist interested in geography and a sociologist interested in people. A man of many skills, later in life he worked as a sanitary engineer and surveyor as well as a professor of logic. He lived most of his life in Rio de Janeiro and São Paulo.

Cunha's generation of urban Brazilian intellectuals, influenced by European writers, sought political democracy, national unity, and an end to violence and racial prejudice. A voracious reader, Cunha came to passionately share these progressive views. Cunha also wanted Brazilians to free themselves from slavish imitation of European philosophical and intellectual trends and make Brazil rather than Europe their spiritual home. Perhaps because of his unhappy military school experience, he became antimilitarist, writing that war is "a monstrous thing, utterly illogical." Nonetheless, Cunha rejoined the army for a while to defend the new republican government that had replaced the conservative imperial state. But the republic's inability to maintain democracy proved demoralizing, and he left the army to work as a civil engineer before returning to writing.

Cunha's greatest literary contribution was his book *Rebellion in the Backlands*, published in 1902, which is often called the bible of Brazilian nationality and a major work of world literature. Cunha's book challenged the nation's conscience and stimulated other authors to question accepted political wisdom. The book examined a rebellion, the Canudos War of 1896–1897, in an impoverished and parched rural region of Bahia State in the northeast, where most people worked on cattle ranches. Cunha's somber book recounted the powerful story of a rural mystic, Antonio Conselheiro, who, preaching a primitive Christianity that rejected private property, gathered a fanatic group, numbering in the thousands, to oppose Brazil's republican government. Federal officials responded with force, brutally crushing the uprising and killing most of the rebels. The book was a sociological analysis that reads like fiction.

Cunha called his searing account of the struggle a "cry of protest" against an "act of madness" by the government, an attack on the barbarity of the "civilized" against the weak. He portrayed sympathetically the mestizo backwoods people, detailing their customs, occupations, joys, diversions, and sorrows. For example, he described their "multitude of extravagant" beliefs, a mix of Christian and African traditions, and their ceremonies to revere the dead: "It is a charming sight to see a backwoods family at nightfall kneeling before their rude altar, by the dim

Euclides da Cunha   Euclides da Cunha was one of the major writers and social critics of late nineteenth-century Brazil.   (Courtesy, Fundacao Biblioteca Nacional, Rio de Janeiro)

light of oil lamps, praying for the souls of their loved ones who have died or seeking courage against the storms of this life."

Few urbanites knew anything about the northeast backlands people, who were alien to urban Brazilians. "It was not an ocean which separates us from them," Cunha wrote, "but three whole centuries." Cunha portrayed the confrontation between two cultures, the coast and interior, a theme that became popular in Latin American literature. The deeply religious backlanders could not comprehend the antireligious, rationalist ideas popular in the major cities, while the urbanites could not understand why rural people did not want the modern vision of political and social progress offered them. Cunha admired the rural men who had thrown off European culture and desired to be left alone, finding in the northeastern cowboy "the very core of our nationality." He believed that mestizos, blacks, and Indians were all part of the nation but that bringing the urban and rural people together in one nation would take many years.

Cunha's writing laid the groundwork for artists, writers, and scholars in Brazil and the rest of Latin America to explore new topics. Sadly, Cunha himself would not live to see his influence spread. In 1909 he was a victim of the violence he deplored. Discovering that his wife was having an affair with an army officer, Cunha rashly confronted the rival and was mortally wounded in the ensuing exchange of gunfire.

THINKING ABOUT THE PROFILE

1. How did Cunha's ideas reflect the Brazil of his era?

2. How did he view the backlanders and their role in the Brazilian nation?

Note: Quotations from Euclides da Cunha, *Rebellion in the Backlands*, translated by Samuel Putnam (Chicago: University of Chicago Press, 1957) pp. xiii, v, iii, 112, 161, xvi.

Janeiro gave rise to **samba**, a popular music and dance developed by Bahian women, known as the *tias,* or "aunts," who settled in Rio's hillside shantytowns. The tias mixed the African traditions of Bahia with the popular music styles favored by Rio's whites. The result, samba, became an integral part of Carnival, the three-day celebration before the long Christian period of fasting and penitence known as Lent, which was first organized in Rio de Janeiro in the 1890s. Samba emerged as the soul of Brazil, popular with all classes.

Like Brazilians, Caribbean peoples also mixed African and European influences to produce distinctive cultures, but often in defiance of colonial restrictions. On Trinidad, the British colonial officials, who feared the black majority, passed laws to prohibit African-based musical forms, but they found them difficult to enforce. Two traditions emerged to reflect Afro-Trinidadian identity and defiance of British rule. The first was **calypso**, a song style that often featured lyrics addressing daily life and topical subjects and that eventually became the major popular music in the English-speaking islands of the eastern Caribbean. The second tradition was the pre-Lent Carnival, which, as in Brazil, became a major festival and assumed great social significance for average people while providing a forum for calypso. Calypso songs performed during Carnival often questioned colonial policies. A song in the 1880s protested colonial restrictions on music during Carnival: "Can't beat my drum, In my own native land. Can't have Carnival, In my native land."[22] Informal calypso presentations in makeshift theaters evolved by the 1920s into elaborate, heavily rehearsed shows. Nationalists adopted calypso and carnival in their anticolonial struggle.

The United States in Latin America

Latin Americans faced challenges from the increasingly powerful United States, a nation they both envied and feared, whose citizens and military forces occasionally intervened in Central America and the Caribbean. For example, in 1856 William Walker, an American adventurer financed by influential U.S. businessmen interested in acquiring natural resources and markets, invaded Nicaragua with a well-armed mercenary force of three hundred Americans and temporarily seized the country. Walker proclaimed himself president, and, despite opposition by Central American leaders, the United States granted his government diplomatic recognition. Walker introduced slavery and tried to make English the official language before being forced out in 1857, becoming a hated symbol in Central America of what Latin Americans often called Yankee imperialism.

The Spanish-American War led to U.S. domination in Cuba, which became a U.S. neocolony. The Platt Amendment to the Cuban constitution, imposed by the United States in 1901, integrated the Cuban and U.S. economies and required that the United States Congress approve any treaties negotiated by Cuban leaders. The American military governor summarized the consequences of the Platt Amendment: "There is little

---

samba A Brazilian popular music and dance.

calypso A song style in Trinidad that often featured lyrics addressing daily life and topical subjects.

or no real independence left to Cuba. She is absolutely in our hands, a practical dependency of the United States."[23] U.S. businessmen soon owned much of Cuba's economy, including railroads, banks, and mills, and the United States acquired a naval base at Guantanamo (gwahn-TAH-nuh-moe) Bay. Later Cuban nationalists blamed Cuba's squalid condition not on the often despotic Cuban governments but on the United States. The Platt Amendment was finally repealed in 1934.

In the early 1900s the United States became more deeply involved in Central America and the Caribbean. To build a canal across Central America linking the Pacific and Atlantic Oceans, the United States helped Panama secede from Colombia in 1903. Now essentially a U.S. protectorate, Panama leased a 10-mile-wide zone across the isthmus in perpetuity to the United States for the canal. Several thousand workers from Panama and various Caribbean islands died in the ten arduous years of construction. In 1914 the Panama Canal, 51-miles long, was completed, one of the great engineering feats of history and a boon to maritime commerce and travel. U.S. and other ships could now sail between the Atlantic and Pacific Oceans safely and conveniently.

Americans also intervened elsewhere. In 1912 the United States overthrew the president of Nicaragua, who was suspected of inviting the British to build a rival canal across his country. But the unrest that followed prompted the United States to send in a military force, which remained until 1933. U.S. soldiers also occupied Haiti (1915–1933) and the Dominican Republic (1916–1924) to quell unrest or maintain friendly governments. These interventions set the stage for a more active U.S. imperial policy in Latin America and the Caribbean.

SECTION SUMMARY

- After gaining independence from Spain, Latin American nations were plagued by instability, undemocratic governments, and socioeconomic inequality along racial lines.

- After a disastrous period as a republic, a brief occupation by the French, and a probusiness dictatorship, a long, violent revolution finally led to political stability in Mexico.

- Latin American economies tended to focus on the export of one or two natural resources, which created instability and made them susceptible to foreign domination.

- The abolition of slavery in Latin America did not greatly improve the economic conditions of former slaves, and millions of immigrants from Europe, India, Japan, and elsewhere flowed into Latin American countries.

- The tango developed in lower-class Buenos Aires, and samba was a result of cultural mixing in Rio de Janiero, while Caribbean calypso was a legacy of resistance to British efforts to stamp out African-based music on Trinidad.

- The United States repeatedly intervened in Latin American affairs, most directly in Cuba, whose diplomatic affairs it dominated for three decades, and Panama, through which it built the Panama Canal.

New Societies in Canada and the Pacific Basin

Why did the foundations for nationhood differ in Canada and Oceania?

The United States became the most powerful and, in this era, most prosperous of the societies founded in the Americas and Oceania by European settlers, but it was not the only one to build a democratic nation and foster growing economies. To the north of the United States, Canada also expanded across the continent to the Pacific and formed a federation of states. During this era Western nations also located and colonized the island societies scattered around the Pacific Basin. Meanwhile, in Australia and New Zealand, Britain established settler colonies, the British immigrants bringing with them their political institutions, ways of earning a living, and cultural traditions, which helped to transform these South Pacific territories.

Making a Canadian Nation

France originally colonized most of what is today eastern Canada, but by 1763 the British had defeated the French forces and gained control of this large region, including the main French colony, Quebec (see Chronology: Canada and the Pacific Basin, 1750–1914). The victorious British now had to forge a stable relationship with 80,000 French-speaking people, most of them in Quebec, who resisted assimilation into British culture and instead maintained their language, culture, and identity. By 1774 the British pragmatically recognized the influential role of the Catholic Church and French civil law in Quebec. Meanwhile, British colonists settled chiefly in the Atlantic coastal region, known today as the Maritimes, as well as west of Quebec in what became Ontario. Although the British governed Quebec and the largely English-speaking regions separately until 1841, relations between British and French Canadians, with different cultures and languages, remained uneasy, causing a British official in the 1830s to conclude that Canada was "two nations warring in the bosom of a single state."[24] The influence of France in North America ended in 1803, when the United States acquired the vast Louisiana territory, including the Mississippi River Basin long coveted by Americans.

Whatever their ethnic backgrounds, Canada's peoples had to deal with the ambitions of the United States, whose leaders hoped that Canada might eventually join the Union. In a U.S.-British treaty in 1783, the United States recognized British control north of the Great Lakes and the Saint Lawrence River. After the American Revolution, many Loyalists, who had supported continued British rule, moved north to Canada, increasing the English-speaking population substantially, especially in what became Ontario. Although Loyalists opposed the United States republic, they nevertheless imported its democratic ideals to Canada, promoting democratic reforms and representative assemblies.

The relations between the United States and British-ruled Canada remained tense for years. Americans feared that their northern neighbors were aiding the Native Americans who resisted U.S. expansion in the Ohio region. For example, Americans suspected that, from their Canada base, the British supported the powerful and charismatic Shawnee chief Tecumseh (teh-CUM-sah) (1768–1813), who gathered a large alliance of tribes to drive the white settlers out of Ohio and reinvigorate Indian ways. Tecumseh's forces repeatedly fought the United States Army. When conflict between the United States and Britain led to the War of 1812, Tecumseh served with the British. During the war Americans repeatedly invaded Canada with hopes of annexing the territory but were repulsed. The war ended U.S. attempts to expand north and also stimulated a sense of distinctiveness among Canadians, laying the seeds for a national identity separate from the United States and Britain. In 1846 another treaty fixed the U.S.-Canada boundary in the west.

Canadians could now turn to building a diverse society and democratic nation in peace while working to modify British control. Canada welcomed 800,000 British immigrants between 1815 and 1850, many of whom settled in Ontario. Growing popular sentiment prompted the British to consider reforms that eventually brought a unified Canada and an elected national parliament, and British influence over the Canadian government waned. But Canadians rejected complete

CHRONOLOGY
Canada and the Pacific Basin, 1750–1914
1763 British defeat of French forces in Canada
1774 British recognition of French culture and laws in Quebec
1770s Cook expeditions to Polynesia, New Zealand, and Australia
1788 First British penal colony in Australia
1792 First British settlers in New Zealand
1812–1814 U.S.-British War of 1812
1840s–1900s Western colonization of Pacific islands
1850 Treaty of Waitangi
1851 Discovery of gold in Australia
1867 Canadian Confederation
1885 Canadian transcontinental railroad
1901 Formation of Australian Commonwealth
1907 New Zealand self-government

Along the Canadian Pacific Railroad During the late nineteenth century both native-born Canadians and immigrants from many lands—British, Dutch, Germans, Poles, Russians, Scandinavians—followed the Canadian Pacific Railroad to settle the newly opened lands of the midwestern prairies and western mountains. Some people set up temporary tent villages by railroad stops before taking up farming, mining, logging, trade, or fishing. (Library and Archives Canada, #PA 38667)

independence in favor of self-rule within the British Empire as a strategy to help Canada maintain stability, settle the west, foster economic development, and resist U.S. power. In 1858 Canadians built a national capital at Ottawa, safely located well north of the U.S. border along the Ontario-Quebec boundary. In 1867 leaders from Ontario, Quebec, and New Brunswick and Nova Scotia in the Maritimes negotiated a Canadian Confederation that was largely independent of Britain in domestic affairs and that guaranteed strong provincial rights and preservation of the French language wherever it was spoken. Under this arrangement Canada became a **dominion**, a country having autonomy but owing allegiance to the British crown.

The confederation soon faced new challenges. Expansion of white settlement and political power to the west fired resentment among Indians and people of mixed descent, the French-speaking Metis (may-TEES), which sometimes led to violence. The combative Metis leader, Louis Riel (ree-EL) (1844–1885), who had once studied to be a Catholic priest, led two rebellions before being executed for treason, thus becoming a martyr to those who opposed domination by English Canadians. Eventually, however, Manitoba and British Columbia joined the confederation and the federal government promised to build a transcontinental railroad. Canada's first prime minister and Riel's chief opponent, Scottish-born John MacDonald (g. 1867–1873, 1878–1891), hoped the railroad would transform the 4 million Canadians into a unified nation. Crossing over 2,000 miles of forests, prairies, and high mountains, the railroad was completed in 1885. The government negotiated treaties with Native Americans, allocating reservations to many of them. Although they faced some resistance from Indians, white settlers increasingly moved to the

western provinces, and towns sprung up along the railroad. By 1905 Canada included all the present provinces except Newfoundland.

The Canadian economy and ethnic structure were transformed between the 1860s and 1914. Beaver fur and fish had been the major exports of Canada since the 1600s, but now wheat grown in the Great Plains surpassed fur as the major export. Gold strikes in the Yukon and the offering of free land in western Canada attracted immigrants from many lands, including the United States. From 1896 until 1911 over 2 million British and other European immigrants arrived, often settling in the west, where many built sod houses and grew wheat. Immigrants from eastern and southern Europe as well as newcomers from China and Japan enriched the ethnic mosaic. Increasingly critical of British imperialism in the world, by 1911 Canadians took control of their own foreign affairs and diplomacy. Over the next several decades Canada fostered increased industrialization and established warmer relations with the United States while maintaining the British monarch as symbolic head of state.

Exploration and Colonization of the Pacific Islands

The peoples who lived on the small mountainous islands and flat atolls scattered across thousands of miles in the vast Pacific Ocean Basin were the last to experience European expansion, but when it came, the impact was significant. The Spanish colonized Guam, in the Marianas, in 1663 but otherwise there had been little European contact with Pacific islanders during the Early Modern Era. By the mid-1700s the British and French had begun a race to explore what they considered the last frontier, the Pacific Ocean. Eventually these two countries, along with Spain, Germany, Russia, and the United States, had colonized all the inhabited islands.

---

dominion A country having autonomy but owing allegiance to the British crown.

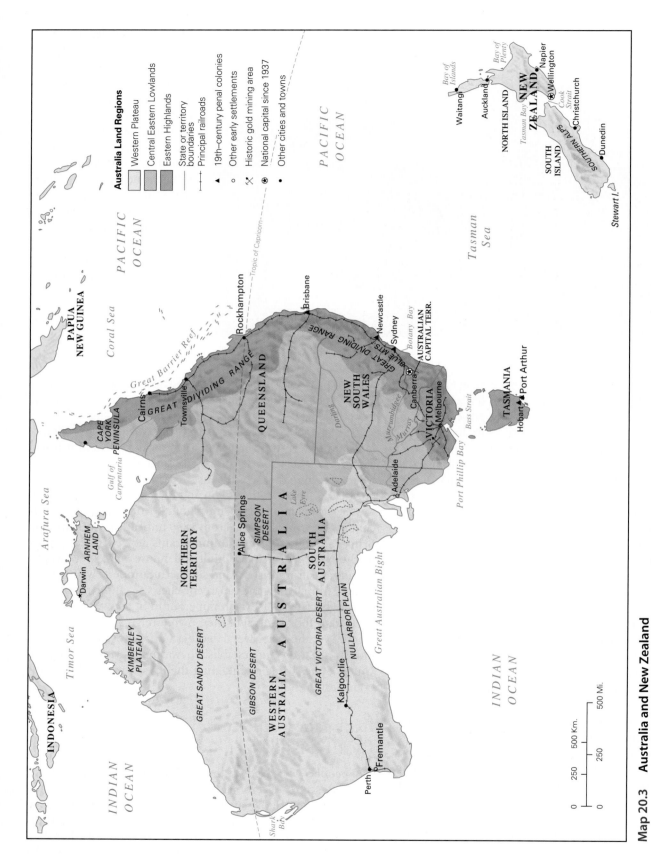

Map 20.3   Australia and New Zealand
The British colonized and gradually settled Australia and New Zealand between the late 1700s and 1914. In 1901 the six Australian colonies became a federation, with a capital eventually built in Canberra.

The English captain James Cook (1728–1779), the self-made son of an agricultural laborer, led some of the most extensive explorations, greatly aided by the learned Polynesian high priest, Tupaia (ca. 1725–1771). Cook reached the eastern Polynesian island of Tahiti in 1769, where he recruited Tupaia, who came from a family that had been sailing around Polynesia for generations and whose skills as a navigator and speaker of several Polynesian languages greatly aided the expedition. A scientist with Cook concluded that Tupaia knew more of Polynesia's geography, produce, religion, laws, and customs than anyone else. Tupaia drew up the charts that helped Cook map Polynesia, including New Zealand, and the coast of Australia, but then died on Java of fever. Cook made two more expeditions to the Pacific in the 1770s; after becoming the first known person to circumnavigate Antarctica, he located the Hawaiian Islands in 1778 and then sailed to Alaska. His early reports created an image of the South Sea islands as paradise, a "Garden of Eden" with amiable people, an image that still survives in popular culture, but Cook himself was killed in Hawaii after antagonizing local leaders, and some explorers who encountered hostility developed negative views of the Pacific islanders.

European explorations eventually led to economic exploitation and Christian missionary activity. In the late 1700s the Russians established a foothold in Alaska and the Aleutian Islands as a base for hunting seals and sea otters for their fur. By the 1850s both animals had been hunted to near extinction, and thousands of Aleuts had died from exposure to European diseases. Deep-sea whaling lasted longer, attracting Western sailors, especially British and Americans, as well as Polynesians in search of sperm whales. Western traders also visited the Pacific islands, seeking resources such as sandalwood, greatly valued in Asia for building furniture. It took only ten years to cut and export all of Fiji's sandalwood. Meanwhile, Protestant and Catholic missionaries went to the islands seeking converts, with varied results. The Samoans welcomed the missionaries, often adopting Christianity. Fijians initially rejected missionaries but later, desiring trade with the West, tolerated them. Fijian converts often pragmatically mixed Christianity with their own traditions. One chief, Ratu Tui Levuka, reportedly said that his right hand was Methodist, his left hand Catholic, and his body heathen. Some peoples were hostile to outside influences. For instance, the New Hebrides people killed the first missionaries who reached the islands.

Traders and missionaries opened the way for colonization, and between the 1840s and 1900 Western powers colonized all of the Pacific societies. Between the 1840s and 1870s the French gained domination over many island chains, such as the Society Islands, which included Tahiti, and the Marquesas, while the British colonized various others, among them the Fijian archipelago. By 1898 the Germans and Americans had divided up Samoa, and the British imposed a protectorate over the kingdom of Tonga. By 1900 the Germans had acquired most of Micronesia, and Britain and France controlled much of Melanesia. Hawaii's experiences with the West mirrored those of other Pacific societies. Hawaii was home to some 150,000 Polynesians in 1778. By 1875 the smallpox, measles, and venereal diseases introduced by Western visitors and settlers had reduced it to 50,000. The Western arrivals gradually gained economic power and political influence, but Hawaii remained a Polynesian kingdom until 1893, when American settlers seized control.

The Rise of Australia and New Zealand

The British colonized the continent they named Australia and the two large islands they called New Zealand, landmasses in the western Pacific whose human histories long predated the arrival of Europeans (see Map 20.3 and Chapter 9). European settlement in Australia began when the British began transporting convicts, often Irish, from overcrowded British jails to a penal colony they founded at Botany Bay on the southeast coast in 1788. Eventually more penal colonies were founded in fertile southeastern and southwestern Australia. Settlements formed around the fine harbor at Sydney, just north of Botany Bay, and eventually former convicts and discharged soldiers began settling the land. Agriculture, ranching, and mining became the basis for the modern economy. The British divided the continent into six colonies, with New South Wales and Victoria in the southeast having the largest populations.

British colonization came at the expense of the Aborigines, peoples completely different from the Pacific islanders in language, culture, and ways of life. The Aborigines' ancestors had lived on the continent for thousands of years. Divided into hundreds of scattered tribes and numbering somewhere between 500,000 and 3 million in 1750, Aborigines lived chiefly by fishing and nomadic hunting and gathering. The European settlers considered the Aborigines to be an inferior people with a primitive way of life. Adding to these negative feelings, many Aborigines resisted encroachments on their land by raiding British settlements. In the early 1800s the British settlers killed as many as 20,000 Aborigines. As was the case for Native Americans and Pacific islanders, diseases brought by Europeans such as smallpox and influenza were responsible for killing the majority of the Aboriginal population. By 1875 only 150,000 Aborigines remained, and many were further destabilized by having their land forcibly settled by white newcomers. Eventually, to survive, many Aborigines had little choice but to move to cities, where they faced unfamiliar ways of life, or to work on European cattle and sheep ranches. However, large numbers remained on tribal reservations, mostly in the interior and along the northern coast, where they maintained many of their traditions and beliefs.

Creating a common Australian identity and nationhood took over a century. Throughout the 1800s Europeans clung to the coastal regions suitable for farming and ranching and avoided the desert interior, which to them was inhospitable because, unlike the Aborigines, they lacked the skills to exploit it. The discovery of gold in southeastern Australia in 1851 attracted settlers from Europe, and by the 1860s over a million whites lived in Australia. Gold mining also prompted Chinese and other Asians to seek their fortunes in Australia, creating resentments among the Europeans. In 1899 one European leader charged that Asians "will soon be eating the heart's blood out of the white population."[25] Violence between Europeans and Asians, especially in the mining camps, led to laws restricting Asian immigration, which ended only in the later twentieth century. Tensions between Europeans, Asians, and Aborigines were not the only social challenge, however. White women struggled for influence in the male-dominated Australian society. By the 1880s white women's movements were pressing for moral reform and suffrage, and white women gained the right to vote in 1902, but women still enjoyed little political power at the local or national level. Aborigines only gained the right to vote in 1962.

Gradually Australia became a nation. By 1890 Britain had turned all six of its Australian colonies into self-governing states (see Map 20.3). Worried that disunity threatened their long-term security, the states formed the Commonwealth of Australia in 1901, with the British monarch remaining symbolic head of state. Like Canada, Australia became a self-governing, democratic dominion and maintained close political links with Britain, but it gradually formed its own identity. A transcontinental railroad system, completed in 1917, connected the vast country. Even with the railroad, however, the white population of the interior remained small; the majority of the 4 million Australians lived in or near five coastal cities. In 1908 Canberra, midway between the two largest cities, Sydney and Melbourne, became the nation's capital. Distance from European supplies fostered some local manufacturing, including steel production, and white Australians enjoyed prosperity.

The British also colonized the two large mountainous islands of New Zealand, 1,200 miles east of Australia, at the expense of the Polynesian Maori people. The Maori had lived on the islands, which they called Aotearoa, for a millennium, gradually dividing into sometimes warring tribes headed by chiefs and surviving by hunting, fishing, and horticulture. In 1792, when the first British settlers arrived, the Maori numbered around 100,000. Some Maori took advantage of the British newcomers for their own purposes. For example, one Maori chief, Hongi Hika (ca. 1772–1828), befriended a Protestant missionary, who took him to England. Returning to New Zealand with guns, Hongi and his warriors raided rival tribes, who soon began acquiring their own firearms from the British. Maori intertribal warfare became more deadly, killing many thousands by 1850, and made it harder for the rival tribes to cooperate against the British.

As more British settlers came, territorial disputes with the Maori increased. The Treaty of Waitangi in 1850 between the British and five hundred Maori chiefs seemingly confirmed the Maori's right to their land while acknowledging British sovereignty. But the Maori were unaware that the English-language and Maori-language versions of the treaty differed. Maori chiefs thought they still had authority over their lands and people, while the British asserted the treaty gave them political and legal power. Disagreement over the treaty provisions and the occupation of more Maori land by British settlers led to a series of wars that ended only in the 1870s and resulted in an even sharper decline in the Maori population. The British skillfully exploited Maori tribal rivalries and had the military

advantage of heavy artillery and armored steamships. Eventually Maori resistance subsided, leading to an 1881 peace agreement that accorded Maori control over some districts.

Gradually the European identity in New Zealand grew stronger. The discovery of gold in 1861 stimulated European immigration, mostly from Britain, so that by 1881 the Maori accounted for only 10 percent of the half-million population. Immigrants were attracted by higher living standards than they enjoyed in Europe, to a colonial economy based on farming and sheep raising, and to a growing government welfare system. New Zealand prospered after 1882, when steamships acquired refrigerated holds to carry lamb and dairy products from the islands to Europe. A parliamentary government including Maori representatives was formed in 1852, and by 1893 both men and women of all communities enjoyed universal suffrage. New Zealand gained self-government as a British dominion in 1907, but it continued a close alliance with Britain as a guarantee of security and proudly remained an outpost of the British Empire well into the twentieth century.

SECTION SUMMARY

■ Canada had to contend with the challenge of forming a unified country that included French and English speakers, as well as with the threat of the neighboring United States.

■ Over time, Canada became increasingly independent of Britain and stretched across the continent, and wheat eventually surpassed beaver fur as the country's top export.

■ Western nations, starting with Britain and France but later including Russia, the United States, and Germany, colonized the Pacific islands and exploited their natural resources.

■ Starting as penal colonies, British settlements in Australia expanded and pushed the native Aborigines off their land and then clashed with Asians who came to mine gold.

■ British colonizers of New Zealand clashed repeatedly with the native Maori, ultimately deceiving them into signing away the rights to their land in the Treaty of Waitangi, which led to a series of wars that ended only in the late nineteenth century.

Online Study Center ACE the Test

◆ Chapter Summary

During the Modern Era European societies and cultures were reshaped by industrialization, revolutions, and new ideologies such as nationalism and socialism. Populations grew and millions of people migrated within Europe or emigrated to the Americas and Oceania. More people lived in cities, where social problems and poverty increased. The industrial system influenced the relations between men and women, as family life changed and European women lost status, fostering feminist movements. Reacting to political and social turbulence, some European thinkers abandoned Enlightenment ideas, and writers and artists addressed the explosive forces around them with new styles. The pace of scientific and technological innovation also increased.

Across the Atlantic, the new democratic republic in the United States gradually became a regional and then world power with a diversified economy and distinctive culture. The United States expanded westward toward the Pacific, eventually incorporating large sections of North America, some of it acquired after war with Mexico. As Americans moved west and settled the frontier, they subdued Native Americans and fostered new social patterns. The Civil War temporarily divided the nation and abolished slavery. In the aftermath, economic growth and industrialization spurred massive immigration from Europe and social movements to improve the lives of workers and women. Industrial capitalism also motivated Americans to increase their influence in the wider world, eventually leading to the Spanish-American War. The U.S. victory in that conflict made the United States a world power.

Other new nations arose in the Americas and Oceania during the Modern Era. By the 1820s most of Latin America had gained independence from Spain and Portugal, but the new republics remained authoritarian and fostered little economic or social change. Latin American and Caribbean economies remained monocultures geared to the export of raw materials and under foreign domination. While millions of European immigrants arrived, most blacks and Indians remained poor. Social inequalities produced tensions and, in Mexico, a revolution. Latin American and Caribbean societies created unique cultures that reflected the mix of peoples from around the world. The United States also played an increasing role in the region, fostering resentments that have lingered into the present. Despite a division between French and English speakers, Canada expanded to the Pacific and became a nation with a self-governing democracy. Meanwhile European powers colonized the Pacific islands. Europeans settled in Australia and New Zealand and, like Canadians, elected to remain tied to Britain even while developing their own democratic nations.

Online Study Center **Improve Your Grade** Flashcards

Key Terms

feminism	protectionism	gauchos
suffragettes	Manifest Destiny	samba
romanticism	sphere of interest	calypso
modernism	caudillos	dominion
impressionism		

Suggested Reading

Books

Christensen, Carol and Thomas. *The U.S.-Mexican War*. San Francisco: Bay Books, 1998. Well-illustrated survey for the general public.

Costa, Emilia Viotti da. *The Brazilian Empire: Myths and Histories*. Chicago: The Dorsey Press, 1985. A study of the nineteenth century by a Brazilian historian.

Dubofsky, Melvyn. *Industrialization and the American Worker, 1865–1920*. 3rd ed. Wheeling, Ill.: Harlan Davidson, 1996. A good summary of the Industrial Revolution and its impact.

Fischer, Steven R. *A History of the Pacific Islands*. New York: Palgrave, 2002. A recent overview including New Zealand.

Foner, Eric. *The Story of American Freedom*. New York: W. W. Norton, 1998. A provocative examination of how Americans have pursued the dream of a free society.

Keen, Benjamin, and Keith Haynes. *A History of Latin America*. 7th ed. Boston: Houghton Mifflin, 2004. A good general survey.

Knight, Alan. *The Mexican Revolution*. Cambridge: Cambridge University Press, 1986. A readable synthesis of this major uprising.

Kraut, Alan M. *The Huddled Masses: The Immigrant in American Society, 1840–1921*, 2nd ed. Wheeling, I.L.: Harlan Davidson, 2001. Brief survey.

Longley, Lester D. *The Americas in the Modern Age*. New Haven: Yale University Press, 2004. Relates recent relationships to developments around the hemisphere since the mid-1800s.

Nile, Richard, and Christian Clerk. *Cultural Atlas of Australia, New Zealand, and the South Pacific*. New York: Facts on File, 1996. A comprehensive and readable overview of history and cultures.

Paterson, Thomas G. et al. *American Foreign Relations: A History*. 6th ed. Boston: Houghton Mifflin, 2005. A fine survey.

Riendeau, Roger E. *A Brief History of Canada*. Toronto: Fitzhenry and Whiteside, 2000. A short work covering 400 years of Canadian development.

Smith, Bonnie G. *Changing Lives: Women in European History Since 1700*. Lexington, Mass.: D.C. Heath, 1989. A comprehensive study of women's lives and their roles in public life.

Stearns, Peter N., and Herrick Chapman. *European Society in Upheaval: Social History Since 1750*. 3rd ed. New York: St. Martin's, 1991. A readable survey with lively material.

Stephanson, Anders. *Manifest Destiny: American Expansion and the Empire of Right*. New York: Hill and Wang, 1995. A readable brief analysis of this important American doctrine and its consequences.

Websites

WWW-VL: History: United States (http://vlib.iue.it/history/USA/). A virtual library that contains links to hundreds of sites.

Internet Resources for Latin America (http://lib.nmsu.edu/subject/bord/laguia/). An outstanding site with links to many resources.

Latin American Resources (http://www.oberlin.edu/faculty/svolk/latinam/htm). An excellent collection of resources and links on history, politics, and culture.

Modern History Sourcebook (http://www.fordham.edu/halsall/mod/modsbook.html). A very extensive online collection of historical documents and secondary materials.

The World of 1898: The Spanish-American War (http://www.loc.gov/rr/hispanic/1898). A Library of Congress site that provides excellent documents and resources.

CHAPTER 21

Africa, the Middle East, and Imperialism, 1750–1914

Online Study Center

This icon will direct you to interactive activities and study materials on the website: college.hmco. com/pic/lockard1e

Tomb of Muhammad Ahmad in Khartoum Muhammad Ahmad ibn 'Abd Allah, known to history as the Mahdi ("Divinely Guided One"), used Islamic appeals to recruit a large army and lead opposition to the joint British and Egyptian rule in Sudan. He died soon after routing the British forces in 1885, but his tomb remains a popular place of pilgrimage and a symbol of Muslim resistance to Western power. (Tim Beddow/Eye Ubiquitous)

The power of these Europeans has advanced to a shocking degree and has manifested itself in an unparalleled manner. Indeed, we are on the brink of a time of [complete] corruption. As for knowing what tomorrow holds, I am blind.

MOROCCAN HISTORIAN AHMAD IBN KHALID AL-NASRI, 1860s[1]

resh from his victories in Italy and Austria, in 1798 the French general Napoleon Bonaparte vowed to add his name to the list of illustrious European conquerors who had achieved glory and riches before him in the Middle East, the region encompassing North Africa and western Asia. In the fourth century B.C.E. Alexander the Great had conquered Egypt and Persia, and later Roman and Byzantine emperors had controlled the eastern Mediterranean and the lucrative trade routes that passed through it. Medieval Christian crusaders had also established temporary footholds in western Asia. A student of history, Bonaparte admired the earlier military commanders and coveted the rich lands they had gained. In his mind, Europe was a mere "molehill," hardly a match for his talents when the rich, Muslim-dominated lands of the Middle East beckoned. First he planned to invade Egypt, and then he intended to reduce the Ottoman Turks and Persians to French vassals. Eventually he hoped to reach India and found a new religion.

With an armada of four hundred ships carrying 50,000 soldiers, Bonaparte quickly established control over northern Egypt. He also took with him some five hundred French scholars to gather valuable information on Egyptian history, society, language, and environment. Near a town in the Nile River Delta they discovered the Rosetta stone, a tablet made in 196 B.C.E. that contained writings in several languages. Since one of those languages was Greek, scholars for the first time could translate ancient Egyptian hieroglyphics into Western languages. This development sparked the beginning of Egyptology as a field of study.

Bonaparte acted like a Muslim ruler and even hinted that he might embrace Islam. In a bid for popular support, the French general confidently announced: "People of Egypt, I come to restore your rights; I respect God, His Prophet and the Quran. We are friends of all true Muslims. Happiness to the People!"[2] He also claimed to have liberated the people from Egypt's repressive Mamluk (MAM-look) rulers, and he organized representative councils to promote self-government. Indeed, the Mamluks were widely disliked despots, but Bonaparte's policies soon alienated Egyptians, who came to see the French as even worse. Conquest soon proved a burden. The French army, small and ill-equipped, withered in the desert heat. An attempt to conquer Syria having failed, Bonaparte left for Paris in 1799, becoming just another example of a western society unsuccessfully attempting to control Muslim peoples.

Although unsuccessful, the French invasion of Egypt provided a harbinger of more invasions of the kind feared by the Moroccan historian Ahmad ibn Khalid al-Nasri, through which Europe would extend its domination in the world. Although the French were soon chased away, Bonaparte's expedition was a turning point in Western relations with sub-Saharan Africa and the Middle East, the cutting edge of a European thrust that also overwhelmed India, Southeast Asia, and the Pacific islands. The Industrial Revolution and capitalism in Europe had greatly accelerated Europe's need for natural resources that could be processed into industrial and commercial products, as well as for new markets to consume these goods. These economic factors combined with European political rivalries and a powerful industrial and military technology to launch a ruthless policy of incorporating territories in sub-Saharan Africa and the Middle East.

For sub-Saharan Africans and the Arabs and Berbers of North Africa, the most common form of Western imperialism was colonialism, political control of another country. This colonialism generally lasted for only a century or less, during which time sub-Saharan and North Africans often resisted Western power. Some scholars argue that this era was too short to permanently transform societies with rich histories and traditions. Yet the power of Western governments, technologies, and ideas reshaped African societies and their economies, cultures, and political systems. Colonialism also linked these regions more closely to a European-dominated world economy. Western Asian societies experienced less disruption than the peoples of Africa, but the Ottomans lost their North African and European territories, and the Ottoman and Persian states struggled to meet the challenges posed by increased European power.

FOCUS QUESTIONS

1. How did various Western nations obtain colonies in sub-Saharan Africa?
2. How did white supremacy shape South Africa?
3. What were some of the major consequences of colonialism in Africa?
4. What political and economic impact did Europe have on the Middle East?
5. How did Middle Eastern thought and culture respond to the Western challenge?

◆ The Colonization of Sub-Saharan Africa

How did various Western nations obtain colonies in sub-Saharan Africa?

During the nineteenth century various Western nations colonized most of sub-Saharan Africa. Although Europeans had established a few small, scattered outposts in West Africa and colonized coastal regions of Angola, Mozambique, and South Africa in the sixteenth and seventeenth centuries, the full-blown quest for colonies began only with the end of the trans-Atlantic slave trade and the spread of the Industrial Revolution in Europe in the mid-1800s. At this time European imperial ambitions fostered what a British newspaper called the "scramble for Africa," during which the European powers divided up the African continent among themselves, often against fierce resistance, and commenced the full-scale economic penetration of Africa. By 1914, when World War I began, the colonization process was complete.

CHRONOLOGY

	Sub-Saharan Africa	The Middle East
1800		**1805–1848** Rule of Muhammad Ali in Egypt
		1840 French colonization of Algeria
1850	**1870** Ending of trans-Atlantic slave trade	**1859–1869** Building of Suez Canal
	1874–1901 British-Ashante wars	**1882** British colonization of Egypt
	1884–1885 Berlin Conference on colonialism	
	1899–1902 Boer War	

The End of the Slave Trade

For over three centuries the trans-Atlantic slave trade (1520–1870) dominated relations between Africa, Europe, and the Americas, but growing opposition in all three regions eventually brought it to an end. Humanitarian as well as economic concerns spurred the abolition movement. In the West, especially in Britain, abolitionists hoped to open Africa to both Christian missionaries and free trade in commodities other than slaves. Many abolitionists were prompted largely by religious and moral outrage at slavery, and Protestant churches were active in the movement. Other abolitionists were influenced by the Enlightenment vision of human equality. One sympathizer wrote that people "are not objects. Everyone has his rights, property, dignity. Africa will have its day."[3]

Africans and African Americans also struggled against slavery. For example, Olaudah Equiano (oh-LAU-duh ay-kwee-AHN-oh) (1745–1797), an Igbo captured by slave raiders in Nigeria at the age of ten and taken to Barbados and then Virginia, eventually purchased his freedom and then actively campaigned in Europe for abolition. Equiano published a bestselling book in the 1780s that chronicled his own horrific experiences as he was shifted from owner to owner. In this book he pointed out the contradiction in self-proclaimed devout Christians mistreating and devaluing the humanity of their slaves. Slave revolts in the Americas, including the successful revolution in Haiti (see Chapter 19), as well as attempts by slaves to seize control of slave ships conveying them to the Americas, indicated the willingness of many slaves to risk their lives for freedom and also forced many Europeans to rethink their views on slavery. The British abolitionist movement was spurred by the tragic experience of Henry Williams, a slave who was badly beaten in Jamaica in 1829 for trying to assert his equality by attending a white church on the island. American and European opposition to slavery was also fueled by the widely read poetry and Christian writings of Phyllis Wheatley (ca. 1753–1785), a Senegal-born slave in Boston who learned Latin and Greek and eventually won her freedom. Her published writings, and those of others, undermined the notion widespread among whites that people of African ancestry were incapable of sophisticated thought.

Another force working against slavery was the Industrial Revolution, which made slavery uneconomical. Overseas markets for factory-made goods became more desirable than cheap labor for plantations. Furthermore, so many colonies produced sugar that the market was flooded and the price fell, making the plantations less profitable at the same time that African states were charging more to provide slaves. By 1800 British bankers could make more money investing in manufacturing than in plantations and the slave trade.

As a result of this combination of moral and economic factors, the slave trade from Africa to the Americas and the slavery era came to an end in the Atlantic world in the nineteenth century. The slave trade was first outlawed in Denmark in 1804, then in Britain in 1807, and then in all British-controlled territories, including their plantation-rich Caribbean colonies, in 1833 (see Chronology: Sub-Saharan Africa, 1750–1914). The British government declared war on the slave traders, intercepting slave ships in the Atlantic and returning the slaves to Africa. Many Latin American nations and Haiti outlawed slavery in the early 1800s, forcing planters to shift to free labor. By 1842 most European and American countries had made it illegal to transport slaves across the Atlantic, although some illicit trafficking continued until 1870. The Civil War ended slavery in the United States in 1865, and in the later 1880s Brazil and Cuba also finally outlawed slavery.

The East African trade that sent slaves to the Middle East and the Indian Ocean islands, run chiefly by Arabs from the eastern Arabian state of Oman, continued longer than the trans-Atlantic trade. In 1835 the Omani leader, Sayyid Sa'id (SIGH-id SIGH-eed) (r. 1806–1856), moved his capital to Zanzibar, an island just off the coast of modern Tanzania, and built a commercial empire that flourished for forty years procuring and shipping ivory to India, China, and Europe and shipping slaves to India, the Persian Gulf, and South Arabia. During the 1860s East African ports such as Zanzibar exported some 70,000 slaves a year. The Omanis also profited from growing Indonesian cloves on slave plantations on Zanzibar.

To obtain slaves and ivory, Omani and Swahili merchants opened or expanded overland trade routes through Tanzania into the eastern Congo River Basin. In 1873 the British convinced the Zanzibar sultan to close the island's slave market, and as compensation Britain imported vast amounts of ivory, which the British used for making piano keys, billiard balls, and cutlery handles. While fewer slaves were now exported from the coast, slavers still raided African villages to acquire the labor needed

CHRONOLOGY

Sub-Saharan Africa, 1750–1914

1804	Launching of Fulani jihads by Uthman dan Fodio
1804	Abolition of slave trade by Denmark
1806	British seizure of Cape region from Dutch
1807–1833	Abolition of slave trade in Britain and its territories
1816	Beginning of Shaka's Zulu Empire
1838	Great Trek by South African Boers
1842	Ending of trans-Atlantic slave trade by most European nations
1847	First American freed slave settlement in Liberia
1874–1901	British-Ashante wars
1878	Belgian colonization in Congo
1884–1885	Berlin Conference
1886	Discovery of gold in South Africa
1898	French defeat of Samory Toure
1899–1902	Boer (South African) War
1905	Maji Maji Rebellion in Tanganyika
1912	Founding of African National Congress in South Africa

to carry the huge ivory tusks to the coast for export, often in well-armed caravans of up to a thousand people. The British gained control of Zanzibar in 1890, but some slave trading continued on a modest scale in parts of East and Central Africa until the early 1900s.

Freed Slaves, Adventurers, and Traders

Between the later 1700s and later 1800s the diminishing importance and then ending of the trans-Atlantic slave trade gradually changed the relationship between Africans and Europeans, fostering several new African societies, exploration of Africa by Western adventurers, and increased commerce between Europeans and Africans. The Western impact on Africa had been uneven during the slave trade, which had integrated Africa into the world economy chiefly as a supplier of human beings. While it lasted, the slave trade had impeded most other trade between Europeans and Africans. The willingness of some African states to sell slaves for transport to the Americas also reduced the European appetite for territorial con-

quest to obtain this resource. But, as the demand for slaves waned, Europeans became more interested in acquiring African agricultural and mineral resources.

New African Societies Even before slavery was abolished in the Americas, freed slaves there who chose, or were pressured, to return to Africa from the Americas had established several West African states and port cities. The black founders of these states, and the whites who helped finance them, had both humanitarian aims and commercial goals, wanting to give the freed slaves opportunities to run their own lives while also setting up new centers of Western trade. Thousands of freed slaves also settled in coastal towns of the Gold Coast (modern Ghana), Nigeria, and Dahomey, where some became merchants engaged in trade with the Americas.

The two largest settlements of freed slaves emerged in Sierra Leone and Liberia. Spurred by abolitionists such as Olaudah Equiano, in 1787 the British settled four hundred former slaves around the fort at Freetown, which became the core of their colony of Sierra Leone. Over the next few decades the British shipped more former slaves to Freetown. Some came from the West Indian colonies, while others came from British-ruled Canada, where they had settled to escape retaliation for supporting the Loyalist cause during the American Revolution. Freed slaves from the United States were first shipped to Liberia in 1847, and they were joined by others after the Civil War. Although Liberia remained an independent state governed by the descendants of former slaves, its economy was dominated by U.S.-owned rubber plantations. In both Sierra Leone and Liberia, the local Africans often resented the freed slave settlers from the Americas, who were mostly English-speaking Christians, because they occupied valuable land, often dominated commerce, and held political power. In recent decades conflicts between the two groups have torn apart both countries.

Both Sierra Leone and Liberia produced reformers, such as West Indian-born Edward Blyden (1832–1912), one of the first African nationalists. Denied admission to universities in the United States because he was black, he emigrated to Liberia. Blyden believed that, given the racism in the Americas and Europe, people of African ancestry could realize their potential only in Africa. But he encouraged Africans to blend their traditions, such as the emphasis on the community rather than the individual, with Western ideas, such as Christianity and science.

Explorations and Encounters The decline of the trans-Atlantic slave trade, which had caused turmoil and made travel dangerous in parts of Africa, also made Africa more accessible to Western explorers. Europeans wanted to discover whether the great African rivers such as the Nile and the Niger were navigable for commercial purposes. The Scottish explorer Mungo Park (1771–1806), a doctor for an English trading company in West Africa who traveled along the Niger, hoped to open to British "ambition and industry new sources of wealth, and new channels of commerce."[4] Adventurers were obsessed with finding the source of Africa's greatest river, the Nile, and they finally located Lake Victoria in 1860. The most famous explorer, David Livingstone (1813–1873), a Scottish cotton mill worker turned medical missionary, spent over two decades traveling in eastern Africa, where he collected information and opened the region to Christian missionary activity and trade with the West.

Park, Livingstone, and other European adventurers claimed to have "discovered" inland African societies and geographical features, but these European explorers discovered little that Africans and Arabs did not already know, and they usually followed long established trading routes and used local guides. The ethnocentric stereotype of intrepid white explorers struggling in hardship through virgin territories is a myth, but it shaped Western views. Explorers publicized their findings and spread the notion of "Darkest Africa," which was seen as awaiting salvation by Christian missionaries and Western traders.

With Africa more open in the 1800s, European traders began to obtain various raw materials needed by the West, such as peanuts, palm oil, gold, timber, and cotton. In pursuing this goal they had to contend with dynamic West African merchants who, with the end of the slave trade, had set up cash crop plantations, many of which grew the trees that produced palm oil, the main lubricant for industrial machinery in Europe before the development of petroleum. For example, the Efik (EF-ik) and Ijo (EE-joe) merchants of coastal Nigeria, who had been active slave traders, now prospered from providing palm oil. To avoid these middlemen, British traders traveled up Nigeria's rivers to buy palm oil directly from the producers, especially the Igbo (EE-boh) people. With superior financial resources and the support of their governments, European companies eventually gained the upper hand over West African merchants, undermining states that were reluctant to grant trade concessions to Europeans and outcompeting their African rivals. As a result, by 1890 in the trading port of Lagos, once a center of African commerce, only one rich African merchant was still able to compete with British merchants.

African Muslim Warrior While Western pressure on coastal societies increased, several Muslim peoples expanded their influence in the West African interior. Some military forces, having acquired Western arms in exchange for slaves and gold, conquered regional empires that flourished for a century or more. [From John H. Hanson, *Migration, Jihad, and Muslim Authority in West Africa* (Bloomington and Indianapolis: Indiana University Press)]

Islamic Resurgence

Some major developments within Africa in this era derived largely from forces within African societies rather than from relations with the West. Among these forces were tensions within the Islamic societies of the Sudan that fostered militancy and political expansion. The most notable example, the Fulani jihad (holy war), was part of a larger religious ferment in West Africa that had begun in the Intermediate Era when expanding Islam encountered African traditions. Many West Africans had embraced Islam, but they also often blended the religion with their own customs and sometimes animist beliefs. Conflicts between those who wanted to purge Islamic practice of pre-Islamic customs and those who mixed Muslim and African traditions broke out sporadically in parts of West Africa in the seventeenth and eighteenth centuries. Often these conflicts involved the Fulani, a pastoral and trading people who lived in communities scattered across the western and

central Sudan from Senegal east to Chad. Some Fulani were devout Muslims, some nominal Muslims, and some animists.

By the 1790s the religious conflicts had spread to the Fulani in the prosperous Hausa states of northern Nigeria. One of these Fulani, Uthman dan Fodio (AHTH-mun dahn FOH-dee-oh) (1754–1817), a respected Muslim scholar and ardent follower of Sufi mysticism, criticized the tolerant attitude of many Hausa rulers toward religion, called for the conversion of non-Muslim Fulani, and proclaimed the goal of making Islam and the Quran central to Sudanic life. His magnetic personality and Islamic zeal soon attracted a Fulani and Hausa following. A follower said: "people trusted him. He spread knowledge and dispelled perplexity."[5] Uthman's attacks on high taxes and social injustice, and his promise to build a government that would spread Islam and purify it of animist beliefs, alarmed Hausa rulers, who feared the unrest he was causing and tried to restrict his activities. After an attempt was made on his life, Uthman mobilized his followers and launched a jihad in 1804. After conquering the Hausa states and then nearby territories, he created the Sokoto (SOH-kuh-toh) Caliphate, based in the city of Sokoto, and ruled much of what is today northern Nigeria. Uthman divided his empire into small, Fulani-led states led by governors, known as *emirs*, who were subordinate to Sokoto.

Uthman's jihad, and the vision of a purified Islam he offered, sparked others to take up his cause, and during the early 1800s several other jihadist states, often led by Fulani religious scholars turned state builders, formed in the Sudan. The Islamic revival sparked by the jihads, which continued into the 1880s, allowed a more orthodox Islam to spread widely. As a result, just as Western influence was increasing in some parts of Africa, the Sudan was becoming even more Islamic. But by the later 1800s, as leaders entrenched their powers and forgot Uthman's reformist vision, the Fulani states declined and Sokoto's power waned. A Hausa poet complained that the Fulani rulers forcibly seized possessions from the peasants and left them with nothing except the sweat of their brows. The Fulani resisted French and British expansion but eventually were unable to stop it. Nevertheless, Islam remained a vital cultural and political force in the Sudanic zone, and it still is today.

European Conquest

European interest in African resources accelerated in the late 1800s, when Britain, France, Germany, Spain, Belgium, and Italy all acquired African colonies, often by intimidating African leaders through warfare or the threat of force (see Map 21.1). Several factors propelled and made possible the Europeans' conquest. First, Western companies sought government help to compete with African traders and to pressure states to admit Western merchants. Second, advances in tropical medicine, especially the use of quinine for malaria, freed Europeans from high tropical mortality rates. Third, the invention of more powerful weapons gave Europeans a huge military advantage over African forces, which were armed only with rifles or spears. When possible, Europeans achieved conquest peacefully by using deceptive treaties, offering bribes, dividing up states, and convincing African leaders that resistance was futile. When faced with resistance, however, Europeans used ruthless force.

King Leopold of Belgium took the lead in colonization. In 1878 he hired Henry Stanley (1841–1904), a Welsh-born American and former Confederate soldier and journalist. As a journalist working for a New York newspaper, Stanley had earlier searched successfully in East Africa to find David Livingstone, who had lost touch with Europe, and then explored the Congo River Basin, which King Leopold now commissioned Stanley to acquire for Belgium.

Soon other European powers joined the scramble to obtain colonies. In 1884–1885 the colonizing nations held a conference in Berlin to set the ground rules for colonization. For a claim to be recognized, the colonizer had to first give notice to the other Western powers of its intent and then occupy the territory with a military presence. Agents of European governments, such as Stanley working for Belgium, asked African chiefs, most of whom knew no Western languages, to sign treaties of friendship in these languages, but the treaties actually gave the land to European countries. African chiefs usually had no right to sign over land, since it was owned by the people. To Africans the Westerners' concept of private ownership was alien, making it easy for European agents to manipulate them. If chiefs refused to sign, they were threatened with war. Fearing a slaughter and hoping to manipulate conditions for their own benefit, many chiefs signed. The king of Buganda reflected the Africans' distress when he concluded that, in his view, the Europeans were coming to eat his country. A Nigerian writer lamented in 1891 that the slavers' forcible possession of Africa's people had only been replaced by the European governments' forcible possession of Africa's land.

Europeans achieved domination for several reasons. First, the colonial scramble came at a time of famine when rains failed, and also when epidemics of smallpox and cholera were killing millions, especially in eastern Africa. One French missionary reflected the despair: "wars, drought, famine, pestilence, locusts, cattle-plague! Why so many calamities in succession? Why?"[6] For most Africans these were bitter years indeed.

The military disparity in weapons and tactics also played a role. For example, the British had the Gatling gun, which could fire 3,000 rounds per minute, and the Maxim gun, a totally automatic machine gun invented in 1884, while rifles were the most effective weapons available to Africans. Using these and other powerful weapons, Westerners willingly slaughtered thousands. Some of the worst atrocities occurred in Southwest Africa (today's Namibia), where the Germans killed all but 15,000 of the 80,000 Herero (hair-AIR-oh) people after a rebellion in 1904. In Kenya, British military expeditions attacked villages for chasing away tax collectors or for ambushing Western military patrols that were sent as a show of force to intimidate potential resisters. A British officer in Kenya wrote home in 1902 about punishing a Gikuyu village containing several hundred people because an Englishman had been killed nearby. The officer boasted about giving orders that every living thing, except children, should be killed without mercy. As a result, every adult villager was either shot or bayoneted, and the British burned all the huts and then razed the banana farms to the ground. The British called their policy of establishing law and order from the Kenya coast to Uganda, often by force, the "Pax Britannica," or British peace.

Finally, after centuries of rivalries and slave wars, Africans could not unite for common defense, and Europeans took advantage of the political instability and rivalries between societies, pitting state against state and ethnic group against ethnic group. For example, for many centuries the region that became Nigeria had been the home of various independent kingdoms, such as those of the predominantly animist Yoruba and the Muslim Hausa-Fulani, as well as village-based stateless societies such as the Igbo. Some of these societies were already unstable by the mid-1800s, and, partly because of conflicts generated by the trans-Atlantic slave trade, the Yoruba had engaged in a bitter civil war for much of the century. Capitalizing on these divisions, between 1887 and 1903 the British conquered or otherwise annexed these diverse societies, creating the artificial political unit they called Nigeria because it occupied both sides of the lower Niger River.

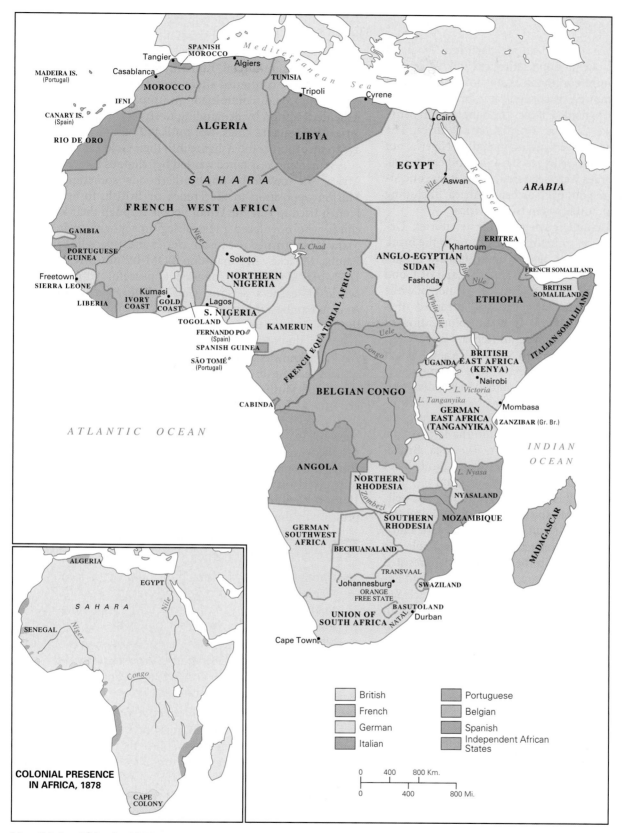

Map 21.1 Africa in 1914

Before 1878 the European powers held only a few coastal territories in Africa, but in that year they turned to expanding their power through colonization. By 1914 the British, French, Belgians, Germans, Italians, Portuguese, and Spanish controlled all of the continent except for Ethiopia and Liberia.

Online Study Center **Improve Your Grade** Interactive Map: Africa in 1878 and 1914

Partition and Resistance

The conquest of Africa resulted in its partition. By 1914 European powers, by drawing boundaries and staking claims, had divided up the entire continent except for Ethiopia and Liberia. The French empire was concentrated in North, West, and Central Africa and extended across the Sahara from Senegal in the west to Lake Chad in North-Central Africa. The British had four colonies in West Africa, including Nigeria, but they built most of their empire in eastern and southern Africa. The four German colonies were scattered, while Italy concentrated on the Horn region of Northeast Africa, including Somalia and Eritrea, and on Libya in North Africa.

European nations competed fiercely for territories. Despite the Berlin Conference, sometimes they came to the brink of war over rival claims, which had to be arbitrated. Britain wanted to control the whole region from the Cape of Good Hope at the southern tip of Africa to Cairo in the north, while the German chancellor, Otto von Bismarck, dreamed of a German empire in Central Africa. German colonization of Tanganyika inspired Britain to move into Kenya, Uganda, and Zanzibar, partly to block Germany. In South Africa, the brash British imperialist Cecil Rhodes (1853–1902), a clergyman's son who had made millions in the South African diamond mining industry, wanted to push British power north, outflanking the Portuguese and Germans. Rhodes was largely responsible for extending British influence into the territory he arrogantly named Northern and Southern Rhodesia. British settlers migrated to Southern Rhodesia (today's Zimbabwe) and Kenya, solidifying the British hold on the region.

While many Africans had little hope of repulsing the well-armed Europeans, others offered spirited resistance to European conquest and occupation. As a result, it took decades for Europeans to conquer and occupy some territories. For example, the Mandinka leader Samory Toure, in the western Sudan, resisted for decades (see Profile: Samory Toure, Mandinka King and Resistance Leader). Similarly, the British had to conquer each Yao village in today's Malawi one by one, and many people in Sokoto, the Fulani state founded by Uthman dan Fodio, chose to join their leaders and die in battle against the British in 1903 rather than surrender. Ethiopia, fortified in high mountains difficult to penetrate, was not conquered until the 1930s. In 1896 Emperor Menelik (MEN-uh-lik) II (1844–1914), a reformer, easily defeated an invasion force of 10,000 Italian troops with a French-trained army of 80,000 men.

In the West African region known as the Gold Coast (today's Ghana), the Ashante kingdom offered particularly strong political and military resistance. The Ashante, like many African states, expanded in the early 1800s. The British, seeking to protect their coastal forts, repeatedly clashed with the prosperous, powerful Ashante during this time, with both sides claiming some victories. In 1874, after more British-Ashante conflict over the coastal settlements, the British dispatched a large force against Ashante and secured control of the coastal zone. However, effective Ashante resistance prevented the British from pushing very deep into the interior. The British then deliberately fomented a civil war in the remaining Ashante territories to undermine the state, but the Ashante king continued to refuse British ultimatums to surrender. In 1896 three thousand well-armed British troops finally occupied the Ashante capital, Kumasi, and exiled the king. However, resistance continued after rebels captured the British governor, who had committed an unpardonable offense to Ashante tradition by demanding to sit on the golden stool reserved for Ashante kings. Not until 1901 did the British manage to incorporate the Ashante into their Gold Coast colony.

Sometimes resistance was led by religious leaders. In West Africa, the mystical Sufi brotherhoods sometimes rallied Muslim opposition to the French or British. In Senegal the French tried to rule the Wolof people through their kings and chiefs, who now faced a loss of legitimacy with their people. Many Wolof turned to Muslim clerics and especially to Amadu Bamba Mbacke (AH-mah-doo BOM-ba um-BACK-ee) (ca. 1853–1927), who had founded a peaceful Sufi order, the Murids ("learners seeking God"). The French considered Amadu Bamba a threat, exiling him for many years. Eventually they realized that they could only rule Senegal with the cooperation of the Murids and reached a compromise: Amadu Bamba acknowledged French administration but was free to expand the Murids, which remain a powerful influence among Senegalese Muslims. Religion also sparked resistance in southern Africa. The Shona and Ndebele (EN-deh-BAY-lee) people in Southern Rhodesia, although historic enemies, both resented the loss of their land and cattle to the British and joined to rally around Mlimu, an animist spirit who they believed spoke through a human medium. Believing that Mlimu had ordered a mass uprising, the Shona and Ndebele rose up in 1896–1897, killing many British. But the result was bloody repression by the British.

SECTION SUMMARY

■ Opposed by many Europeans on humanitarian and religious grounds, African slavery became less profitable than manufacturing as the Industrial Revolution gained momentum, and it was phased out by the end of the nineteenth century.

■ With the end of the slave trade, Europeans began to explore Africa's interior and to take advantage of its vast store of natural resources.

■ At the same time, tensions increased between purist and moderate West African Muslims, and Uthman dan Fodio, who led the Fulani jihads, established the Sokoto Caliphate, which became a strong presence in the Sudan.

■ European nations rapidly colonized Africa by engaging in deceptive negotiations, by threatening and often carrying out acts of violence, and by exploiting existing rivalries among groups of Africans.

■ By 1914, all but a small portion of Africa had been divided up among the European powers, which sometimes feuded over control of various territories and sometimes met fierce resistance from Africans such as the Ashante.

SAMORY TOURE, MANDINKA KING AND RESISTANCE LEADER

Samory Toure (1830–1900) was an effective resistance leader in West Africa and a powerful empire builder. He grew up an animist in a Mandinka village in what is today Guinea. Samory's mother was an animist Mandinka, and his father was a farmer descended from the Dyula, a Muslim merchant caste with branches throughout West Africa. His father's family had earlier abandoned Islam, but their connections to the Dyula trading world gave Samory links to a broader community and an understanding of both merchant and farmer concerns. The growing Atlantic trade brought prosperity to the Dyula and firearms to the interior, at a time when regional Islamic movements were energizing Muslims and fomenting conflict between varied Muslim and animist groups.

Samory began his career as a foot soldier and eventually became an inspirational military commander. By 1870 he had recruited a large, well-armed, well-trained, and intensely loyal force from many Mandinka groups. Skillfully exploiting divisions among his opponents while maintaining connections to both Muslims and animists, Samory built a large state, Kankan, in the Guinea highlands and western Niger River basin. He personally adopted Islam, perhaps chiefly for political reasons, and earned Dyula support by keeping open the trade routes. Islamic revivalism in West Africa influenced Samory to view Islam as a unifying force that could hold his ethnically diverse empire together, and in 1884 he transformed the kingdom into an Islamic state. However, the required conversion of animists led to rebellion. In a pragmatic move that showed his willingness to ignore Islamic scruples to further his political goals and personal ambitions, Samory abolished the theocracy and replaced it with a state based not on Islam but on personal loyalty and national unity.

A political rather than a religious figure, Samory was aware of the traditions of Mandinka empires going back to the great Mali Empire founded by Sundiata in the thirteenth century, and he became the architect of a revived Mandinka Empire modeled on Mali. His later admirers viewed him as an early nationalist trying to maintain a Mandinka state. Samory recruited friends and relatives to form an advisory council, and its members became ministers responsible for specialized tasks such as supervising the treasury, the system of justice, religious affairs, and relations with Europeans. At the same time, Samory also respected the authority of local chiefs. In addition, he gained merchant support by seeking a stable and crime-free order where, as he said, "a woman alone should be able to travel as far as Freetown" in Sierra Leone without facing assaults or robberies.

Samory spent his last ten years defending his state against the French. He had long avoided conflict with Europeans, but his state posed a barrier to French expansion into the interior, and in the 1880s French forces began to move into the gold-rich area. After being defeated by Samory's army, they sent a larger force but again faced stiff resistance and were forced to

Samory Toure   Samory Toure, the ruler of a Mandinka state, led a military force that resisted French incursion into their West African region in the late nineteenth century, but was eventually captured by the French. This photo shows him (front, left) in custody. (Roger-Viollett/Getty Images)

negotiate a truce. During the 1890s the two sides fought a war for seven years. To oppose the French effort, the British in Sierra Leone gave Samory firearms in exchange for slaves and gold, and Samory built workshops to maintain and make muskets and rifles. His army of 30,000 men included mostly foot soldiers and an elite core of cavalry. A clever military strategist who made good use of guerrilla tactics, Samory also developed an effective system of intelligence throughout the villages to detect French movements. Asked how he repeatedly discovered French movements without giving away his own, he replied, "It is because I eat alone" (thus keeping his secrets).

But the French had more and better weapons, including heavy artillery and machine guns. Samory was also disadvantaged by not being able to unite with rival African states after years of conflict. The French gradually pushed Samory eastward, where he forged a new empire in today's northern Ivory Coast and Ghana. As they retreated into the interior, Samory's forces carried out a scorched earth policy that devastated the inhabitants and cost him popular support. In 1898 the French finally defeated Samory's brave but exhausted and hungry army, captured the ruler, and exiled him to the new French colony of Gabon in south-central Africa, where he died.

THINKING ABOUT THE PROFILE

1. What does Samory's career tell us about Sudanic politics in this era?

2. How was Samory able to resist the French for decades?

Note: Quotations from *The Horizon History of Africa* (New York: American Heritage, 1971), p. 431; and Robert W. July, *A History of the African People,* 5th ed. (Prospect Heights, Ill.: Waveland, 1998), p. 207.

✦ The Making of Settler Societies

How did white supremacy shape South Africa?

While this era saw Europeans advancing in both Asia and Africa, only in Africa did Europeans take over large tracts of land as settlers. The largest settler colony, South Africa, experienced an unusual history: over three centuries of white supremacy introduced by the Dutch colonizers and perpetuated by the British. The first Dutch settlement, Cape Town, was established at the Cape of Good Hope in 1652. Over the next two centuries Dutch control gradually expanded along the coast and into the interior at the expense of the indigenous Bantu-speaking African peoples, who strongly resisted. South Africa's political, social, and economic system reshaped life for both Europeans and Africans. European immigrants also settled in British East Africa, the Rhodesias, and the Portuguese colonies. Asian migrants joined them, often as traders.

Europeans and South Africans

From the beginning, South Africa was shaped by conflicts between European settlers and the African peoples whose ancestors had lived in the region for centuries. The Dutch settlers, known as Boers (Dutch for "farmers"), established a system in South Africa based on white rule over nonwhites that enforced as much physical separation of the groups in all areas of life as possible. The system of white supremacy became even more rigid among those Boers who boarded wagon trains and migrated east along the coast and into the interior, a journey they called trekking, to find good farming land and to escape government policies they saw as inhibiting their freedom of action.

Trekking led to chronic conflict between the migrating Boers and the Bantu-speaking Xhosa (KHO-sa) people, farmers and pastoralists who already lived in the eastern Cape region. The two groups collided in the late 1700s and fought for nearly half a century. Many thousands died, mostly Xhosa. When fearing attack, trekkers pulled their wagons into a circle, known as a **laager**, a tradition that symbolized Boer resistance to new ideas and their desire for separation from other peoples.

The trek became the common way for Boers to flee restraints by any government. In 1806 the British annexed the Cape Colony, giving the Boers even more reason to migrate into the interior. The Boers and the British spoke different languages and shared few values. Boers viewed white supremacy as sanctioned by their strict, puritanical Calvinist Christian beliefs, and the system also ensured them a cheap labor supply for their farms and ranches. By ending South African slavery,

laager A defensive arrangement of wagons in a circle. Used by the Boers in South Africa in the eighteenth and nineteenth centuries to guard against attacks by native Africans.

the British harmed the Boer economy, which depended on thousands of slaves of African and Asian origin. Later, the British granted the right to vote and hold office to Africans and mixed-descent people, known as coloreds, privileges that the Boers considered heresy.

While the Boers at the Cape had to deal with the British, the migrating Boers had to contend with the largest Bantu-speaking South African group, the Zulus. In the early 1800s some Zulu peoples began a military expansion under an ambitious military genius, Shaka (ca. 1787–1828), who overcame the disadvantage of being born out of wedlock in a minor Zulu clan to gain fame as a courageous warrior. His exploits in war allowed him to become a powerful chief. Planning to gain dominance over the whole region, he united various Zulu clans in Natal (nuh-TALL), the region along South Africa's Indian Ocean coast, into a powerful nation. Shaka organized a disciplined army of some 40,000 warriors and invented effective new military tactics, such as dividing his troops into regiments armed with short, stabbing spears. In 1816, to build his empire, he began invading other groups' territories, and the resulting wars killed thousands of Africans, both Zulus and non-Zulus, and wreaked widespread disruption. A French missionary reported the "desolate countryside. On every hand we saw human bones whitening in the sun and rain."[7] After conquering much of the interior plateau, Shaka grew more despotic and was assassinated by his brother. This event undermined Zulu military effectiveness, and eventually the Zulu empire fell to the Boers.

Historians still debate Shaka's wars. Some suspect that the scale of fighting and the number of victims were exaggerated by Zulu enemies, both the Africans who fought the Zulus and the Boers who coveted the land being contested. Estimates of the dead vary widely. Soil exhaustion, severe drought, population growth in the region, and fears of potential Boer migration may all have been factors provoking Zulu expansion. Ironically, by depopulating large areas of the mineral-rich interior plateau, the wars made it easier for the Boers to later move in.

Some leaders of Bantu-speaking groups found effective ways to avoid conquest by the Zulus and Boers. Perhaps the most successful was Moshoeshoe (MOE-shoo-shoo) (b. ca. 1786), who created a kingdom for his branch of the Sotho (SOO-too) people. With the region in turmoil from warfare because of the Zulu and Boer expansion, Moshoeshoe moved his people to an easily defended flat-top mountain in 1824. There he strengthened his community by taking in African refugees regardless of their ethnic origin and integrating them into his people. The king emphasized not only military defense but also diplomacy, preferring peaceful negotiation to warfare; for example, he offered tribute, such as cattle, to his African rivals. Moshoeshoe also skillfully cultivated friendship with the British as a counterweight to the Boers. To gain British sympathy, he invited Christian missionaries to his state and used them to acquire guns and horses. While neighboring Africans fell under Boer rule, British support for Moshoeshoe allowed his Sotho kingdom to remain independent until 1871, when it was absorbed into the British-ruled Cape Colony.

British-Boer Conflict and White Supremacy

In the decades after British annexation of the Cape, conflict between the Boers and the British intensified, eventually leading to political change in South Africa. In 1838 about one-fifth of all the Boers, alienated by British policies in the Cape Colony, began what they called the Great Trek, boarding their wagons and, with their sheep and cattle, heading in well-armed caravans of several hundred families north into the interior. After many hardships, including fighting with Zulus, they moved into the high plateau of what is now northern South Africa and created two independent Boer republics, Transvaal (TRANS-vahl) and the Orange Free State. Although the Bantu peoples battled the Boers for decades, Boer military superiority ultimately prevailed. After conquering the Africans, the Boers seized their cattle and forced them to work on Boer farms.

As the Boers consolidated control over Bantu societies and their lands, their ideas of keeping themselves separate from Africans and upholding what one Boer leader called the proper relations between white "master" and African "servant" grew stronger. The evolving Boer ideology considered black Africans an "inferior race" unable to benefit from modernity and hostile to European values. Devaluing Africans and despising the British, the Boers committed themselves to maintaining their identity and culture whatever the cost.

However, the discovery in the Boer republics of diamonds in 1867 and gold in the 1880s spurred the British to seek control over Boer territories, and their attempts to annex the Boer republics led to the South African War (1899–1902), often called the Boer War. The war culminated in British victory but also created chronic Boer resentment of the British. During the war, the Boers employed guerrilla tactics, acting as civilians by day and raiding British targets at night. To eradicate local support for the Boer commandos, the British burned Boer farms, destroyed towns, and interned thousands of Boers, including women and children, in concentration camps, where 26,000 died of disease and starvation. These brutalities discredited the war in Britain. Moreover, the British relied on African troops for victory, and thousands of Africans died fighting the Boers in hopes that the British would be less oppressive. But, when the war ended, Africans found they had merely exchanged one set of white masters for another.

After the Boer War, British and Boer leaders worked out a compromise in which the South African government became essentially a collaboration between the two groups, restoring Boer rights and strengthening white supremacy policies. To win Boer cooperation, the British extended discriminatory Boer laws, restricting African civil and political rights and putting many Africans on reserves, rural lands with few resources from which workers desperate for jobs could be recruited while their families stayed behind. Africans were valued chiefly as cheap unskilled labor for the white-owned economy. The British instituted laws to limit Africans' movement and conduct and reserved the more desirable neighborhoods and jobs only for whites. These policies became a constant source of humiliation and tension for Africans. Continued African resistance gradually led the British to build a police state to enforce their racial policies. Furthermore, despite the political compromises they had made, British-Boer tensions simmered as thousands of British settlers arrived, eventually becoming a third of the white population. Asserting their long-established position in the country, the Boers began to style themselves Afrikaners (people of Africa) and their Dutch-derived language Afrikaans.

The Great Trek Many Boers migrated into the South African interior in wagon trains. These migrants, known as Trekkers, endured hardships but also eventually subjugated the local African peoples, taking their land for farming, pasturing, and mining. (MuseuMAfricA Johannesburg/ISOKO Museums)

South African Cultural Resistance

Domination by the Boers and the British reshaped South African life and culture in the later 1800s and early 1900s. Africans were recruited into the white-owned economy and often became Christian. Thousands of Africans moved to cities, especially the Transvaal mining center of Johannesburg, thus becoming temporarily or permanently removed from their farming villages and transformed into salaried workers. They experienced dreadful work conditions on white-owned factories and farms, but nowhere were conditions as bad as in the mines. There, where safety regulations were few, hundreds of miners died each year. The Zulu poet B. W. Vilakezi described the miner's life in the early 1900s:

> Roar, without rest, machines of the mines,
> Roar from dawn till darkness falls.
> To black men groaning as they labor,
> Tortured by their aching muscles,
> Gasping in the fetid air,
> Reeking from the dirt and sweat.
> The earth will swallow us who burrow.
> And, if I die there, underground,
> What does it matter?
> All round me, every day,
> I see men stumble, fall and die.[8]

Africans often resisted Western domination by adapting their cultural forms to changing conditions. For example, Zulu warriors reworked dance tunes and turned them into songs to protest white military incursion. The Sotho people gradually transformed their tradition of poetry praising influential people and ancestors into songs expressing the fears and experiences of male migrants working in the mines and the women left behind in the villages.

Educated urban Africans, who formed a middle class of professionals and traders, also found ways to oppose white supremacy. One of these, the Johannesburg lawyer Pixley ka Isaka Seme, a graduate of Columbia University in New York, helped found the African National Congress in 1912 to promote African rights and spur Africa's cultural regeneration. Some Bantu composers creatively mixed Christian hymns with traditional Xhosa or Zulu choral music. The African National Congress adopted one such hymn, "God Bless Africa," as their official anthem. Later the song, with its uplifting message of hope, became the anthem of black empowerment:

> Bless the youth, that they may carry the land with patience. Bless the wives and young girls. Bless agriculture and stock raising. Banish all famine and diseases. Fill the land with good health. Bless our effort, of union and self-uplift, of education and mutual understanding.[9]

European Settlers and Asian Traders

Like South Africa, several other colonies restricted African civil and economic rights, particularly Portuguese-ruled Angola and British-ruled Kenya and Southern Rhodesia. These colonial governments reserved for immigrant white farmers not only the best land, such as the fertile Kenyan highlands once dominated by the Gikuyu people, but also the most lucrative crops. For example, in Kenya coffee could be grown only on white-owned farms. African farmers also faced barriers in obtaining bank loans to compete with white farmers. The whites in these colonies participated in government, perpetuating their supremacy by preventing Africans from gaining any political power. The settler colonies erected rigid color bars to limit contact between whites and Africans except as employers and hired workers.

Asian minorities also became part of colonial societies. Beginning in the 1890s Indians arrived to build railroads, work on sugar plantations, or become middle-level retail traders. Indians became the commercial middle class of East Africa and occupied a key economic niche in South Africa, the Rhodesias, Mozambique, and Madagascar. Cities such as Nairobi in Kenya, Kampala in Uganda, and Durban in South Africa had substantial Indian populations, and their downtowns were dominated by Indian stores and Hindu temples. Indians also operated shops and restaurants in the towns of these colonies. In West and Central Africa, Lebanese occupied the middle levels of the economy as shopkeepers in cities and towns. The growing influence and wealth of the Asian immigrants, resented by black Africans, led after independence to many governments restricting Asian economic power. However, while the Europeans themselves disliked the Asians, they also recognized their value in perpetuating divide and rule since Africans often focused their resentment on the Asian traders they dealt with directly rather than the more remote European officials.

SECTION SUMMARY

■ Dutch settlers of South Africa, called Boers, pursued a policy of white supremacy in spite of more liberal British policies.

■ South Africa was also shaped by the conquests of Shaka, a Zulu leader.

■ The Boers fled inland to escape British control, but when diamonds and gold were discovered in the Boer republics, the British instigated and won the South African War, after which they agreed to enforce white supremacist policies in order to gain Boer cooperation.

■ Blacks suffered greatly in white-dominated South Africa, but many resisted through poetry, music, dance, and political organizations such as the African National Congress.

■ Whites dominated other African colonies as well, reserving the best resources and all political power for themselves, while Indians came to form the middle class in many African societies.

The Colonial Reshaping of Sub-Saharan Africa

What were some of the major consequences of colonialism in Africa?

The experience of living under Western colonial domination from the 1880s to the 1960s reshaped sub-Saharan Africans' politics, society, culture, and economy. The trans-Atlantic and East African slave trades had devastated parts of Africa for four centuries, but the colonial conquests that began in 1884 undermined the autonomy of all African societies. Colonialism created artificial states and transformed Africans into subject peoples who enjoyed few political rights. It also allowed Western business interests to penetrate the continent and integrate Africa into the global system as a supplier of valuable raw materials.

Colonial Governments

The colonial policies devised in London, Paris, Berlin, Lisbon, and Brussels introduced new kinds of governments in Africa, as each colonizing power sought the best way to achieve maximum control at minimum expense. The French grouped their colonies into large federations such as French West Africa that were headed by one governor, while the British preferred to handle each colony, such as the Gold Coast and Nigeria, separately. While the types of government varied, Europeans usually supervised administration and always held ultimate political authority. Africans had to abide by decisions made by European bureaucrats who often had little understanding of or interest in African culture.

The colonizers practiced two broad types of administration, direct rule and indirect rule. Under **direct rule** the administration was largely European, even down to the local level, and chiefs or kings were reduced to symbolic roles. Under **indirect rule** the Europeans gave the traditional leaders of a district, the kings or chiefs, considerable local power but kept them subject to colonial officials. In general, indirect rule, which left much of the original society intact, caused less disruption than direct rule. But even under indirect rule African leaders faced restrictions and were required to consult with the local European adviser on many matters. The advisers enforced colonial law and order, collected taxes, and supervised public works. Since Europeans lacked enough officials to administer a large colony such as Nigeria or Tanganyika, this form of rule was inspired by pragmatism. However, it did not

benefit African society. In order to work with local leaders, Europeans sometimes strengthened weak chiefs or appointed chiefs where none previously existed, undermining village democracy.

Nigeria, an unwieldy colony that contained some 250 distinct African ethnic groups, provided an example of both kinds of administration. Indirect rule was taken to its fullest extent in northern Nigeria. As the British struggled to keep the largely Muslim north pacified, they needed the collaboration of the region's Hausa and Fulani rulers. Lord Lugard, the British governor, proclaimed that every ruler "will rule over the people as of old time but will obey the laws of the [British] Governor."[10] Under this system the British left the traditional Hausa-Fulani courts and social structure largely undisturbed.

By contrast, the British governed southern Nigeria chiefly through direct rule, with the result that greater change occurred in the south, including the introduction of Christian missions and cash crop farming. Peoples such as the Igbo and Yoruba successfully adapted to these changes that transformed their regions. The Igbo, who were particularly receptive to culture change and Christianity, became prominent in Nigeria's educated middle class. The Yoruba successfully blended aspects of their indigenous culture, such as a rich artistic tradition and polytheism, with imported cultural traditions, such as English literature and Christianity, maintaining a high degree of tolerance for divergent views. They described their culture as a river that is never at rest, caught up within swift-moving currents that can either run deep and quietly or be turbulent and overpowering. Rejecting fate and helplessness, the Yoruba emphasized the obligation to make one's life meaningful by drawing upon creative capacities.

However, many changes were aimed at politically handicapping the Africans. Supporters of colonialism defended Western rule as providing "a school for democracy," but the rationale clearly differed from reality. By 1945 fewer than 1 percent of Africans enjoyed political rights or access to democratic institutions. Such access for Africans was largely limited to a few urban merchants and professionals in British Nigeria and the Gold Coast who could vote for and serve on city councils, and to males in French Senegal, who elected the members of the colonial council and a representative to the French parliament. Meanwhile, even the traditional African leaders, the chiefs and kings, served European interests if they wanted to keep their positions. They were expected to remain loyal to colonial rule and help implement such policies as cash crop agriculture, as well as recruit people for labor and war. Africans viewed these privileged and wealthy leaders as little better than paid agents of colonialism.

Colonial States and African Societies

The boundaries that European colonizers drew up to partition Africa into colonies created artificial countries that often ignored traditional ethnic relationships. Modern countries such as Nigeria, Ghana (the former Gold Coast), Congo, and Mozambique were colonial creations, not nations built on shared culture and

direct rule A method of ruling colonies whereby a largely European colonial administration supervised all activity, even down to the local level, and native chiefs or kings were reduced to symbolic roles.

indirect rule A method of ruling colonies whereby districts were administered by traditional (native) leaders, who had considerable local power but were subject to European officials.

identity. Colonizers ignored the interests of local people, sometimes dividing ethnic groups between two or more colonial systems. For example, the Kongolese, once masters of a major African kingdom, were split between Portuguese Angola and the Belgian and French Congos. At the same time, rival societies were sometimes joined, creating a basis for later political instability. For instance, in Nigeria the tensions between ethnic groups, including the Igbo, Yoruba, and Hausa-Fulani, have fostered chronic conflict, including a civil war, since the end of British rule. Other countries have also experienced ethnic conflicts that have sometimes led to violence.

To maintain their privileged position, Europeans also imposed a color bar that kept Africans out of clubs, schools, and jobs reserved for Europeans. Europeans typically considered African culture irrational and static, having no history of achievement. An ethnocentric British scholar argued in 1920 that "the chief distinction between the backward and forward peoples is that the former are of colored skin."[11] This prejudice translated into the demeaning and self-serving idea that Africans were unfit to rule themselves and badly in need of Western leadership. Such views ignored several thousand years of African governments, ranging from centralized kingdoms to village democracies, as well as participation in Eastern Hemisphere trade networks from ancient times. Racist ideology spawned the French and Belgian idea of the "civilizing mission," which viewed Africans as children who could attain adulthood only by adopting French language, religion, and culture.

The colonizers often misunderstood African societies and ethnic complexities. For example, to simplify administration and census data, the British tended to identify people of similar culture and language as "tribes," such as the Yoruba of Nigeria and Gikuyu of Kenya, even though these peoples were actually collections of subgroups without much historical unity. Despite loose cultural homogeneity, the Yoruba were traditionally divided into several competing states, each with its own king, while the Gikuyu had few political structures higher than the village. In reality, African peoples such as the Yoruba, Gikuyu, Igbo, Xhosa, and Mandinka were ethnic groups, not unlike the politically divided Italians, Irish, and Poles of early-nineteenth-century Europe or the Javanese and Malays of Southeast Asia.

Christian Missions and African Culture

Christian missionaries, whose primary goal was to reshape African culture and religious life, played a key role in colonial Africa. Christian missions established most of Africa's modern hospitals and schools. Both institutions helped Africans but also reflected Western views. Mission doctors practiced Western medicine and denounced African folk medicine. Mission schools taught new agricultural methods, simple mathematics, reading, writing, and Western languages, thus giving a small group of educated Africans the skills they could use in the colonial economy and administration. Critics complained that the mission schools taught not only Western values but also European history, ignoring African history, and held up European culture as superior while deriding African beliefs as su-

perstition. Some African nationalists, themselves products of mission schools, charged that these schools, as an Igbo writer put it, "miseducated" and "de-Africanized" them, perpetuating their status as "hewers of wood and haulers of water"[12] who were unable to challenge their subservience to Europeans. Furthermore, the Africans who attended mission schools and adopted Western ways often became divorced from their village societies. The individualism encouraged in mission schools conflicted with traditional African community, loosening the social glue of African societies.

Despite the mission schools, modern education reached only a small minority of Africans. Before 1945 only 5 percent of children attended any government or mission school. The schools typically produced clerks in governments and businesses or cash crop farmers, although a few graduates became teachers, doctors, lawyers, and journalists. The first modern African college was established in Sierra Leone in 1827. But before 1940 the few Africans who could attend a university had to do so usually in Europe or the United States.

Millions of Africans adopted Christianity, but Christian beliefs and practices varied widely. Some Africans became devout Catholics or Protestants, while others only partially embraced Christianity, adopting those beliefs they liked while rejecting others. For instance, Africans often emphasized Bible passages that seemed to call for justice and the equality of all people. In 1908 Elliott Kamwana in British Nyasaland (now Malawi) founded the Watchtower Sect, preaching that Jesus would soon return to liberate Africa from colonization. These views led to his arrest by alarmed colonial officials. Some African churches combined Christian doctrines with African practices and beliefs. Hence, in 1901 some Nigerians left the Anglican Church to form their own church, which condoned men having more than one wife. Yorubas, tolerant of diverse religious beliefs, often just added the Christian and Muslim gods to their polytheistic pantheon.

Christianity impacted women's lives. It marginalized the female dieties and shamans who had been common and influential, reducing women's religious roles. Promoting monogamy, Christian leaders sometimes asked men to give up multiple wives, leaving these women without support or their children. Yet, women often welcomed monogamy and favored Christian social values such as promoting education for girls.

Africans in the World Economy

The transformation of African economic life was at least as significant as the political reorganization. Extracting wealth from a colony required tying its economy more closely to that of the colonizer. For this reason, businessmen from colonizing countries came to control the top level of the economy, including the banks, import-export companies, mines, and plantations. In addition, colonial economic policies tended to undermine African societies. For example, colonial taxation forced changes on farmers and prompted others to migrate.

Colonial governments also imposed economic policies to transform Africans into producers for the world market, hence rejecting the subsistence agriculture that, while having sustained Africans for centuries, now could not produce enough revenues for the government or investors. Requiring taxes to be paid in cash promoted a shift from food cultivation to growing cash crops such as cotton, cocoa, rubber, and palm oil or mining copper, gold, oil, chrome, cobalt, and diamonds. If taxation did not work to induce Africans to shift from subsistence farming, authorities sometimes resorted to forced labor, most notoriously in the Belgian Congo, where much of the African population was reduced to near slavery and required to grow rubber for Belgian planters. If Congolese failed to cooperate, they were shot or mutilated. An American missionary reported in 1895 that the Belgian policies "reduced the people to a state of utter despair. Each town is forced to bring a certain quality [of rubber]. The soldiers drive the people into the bush. If they will not go they are shot down, and their left hands cut off. The soldiers often shoot poor helpless women and harmless children."[13] Over half of the Congo's population died from overwork or brutality over a twenty-year period.

Through such measures as these, colonial Africa became linked to the West and the world economy, but often this global economy left Africans vulnerable. For example, African livelihoods became subject to the fluctuations in the world price for the commodities they produced, a price determined largely by the whims of Western consumers and corporations. Colonies also became markets for Western industrial products, which displaced village handicrafts. Many Africans lost their economic self-sufficiency, becoming exporters of cash crops they did not consume, such as cocoa and rubber, and importers of goods they did not produce. Even many of the major cash crops that dominated African lives had been introduced from outside. For example, peanuts and rubber were brought from South America, and cocoa was brought from Mexico. With the growth of an automobile culture in the West, an oil-drilling industry also emerged along the West African coast from southern Nigeria to northern Angola, making these societies dependent on oil exports. In all such ventures, Western businesses and planters exercised considerable influence over governments.

Colonies often became economic monocultures dependent on the export of one or two major commodities, such as copper from Northern Rhodesia (now Zambia), cocoa from the Gold Coast, peanuts from Senegal, and cotton from Sudan. The dependence of Ghanaians on growing and selling cocoa was well described in a local popular song from the 1960s: "If you want to send your children to school, build your house, marry, buy cloth [or] a truck, it is cocoa. Whatever you want to do in this world, it is with cocoa money that you do it."[14] Many colonial policies made it difficult for Africans to diversify their economies.

The opportunities and demands of the colonial economy touched nearly everyone in some way, profoundly affecting the lives of both men and women. As men were frequently recruited or forced to migrate to other districts or colonies for mining or industrial labor, a permanent pattern of labor migration became established. For example, the white-owned farms and mines of South Africa recruited thousands of workers from Mozambique and British Central Africa on renewable one-year contracts, and men from the Sahel migrated to the cocoa estates of the Ivory Coast and Gold Coast. This migration

IN THE RUBBER COILS.

Rubber Coils in Belgian Congo The Belgians colonized the Congo hoping to exploit its resources. This critical cartoon, published in the British satirical magazine *Punch* in 1906, shows a Congolese ensnared in the rubber coils of the Belgian king Leopold in the guise of a serpent. Rubber was the major cash crop, introduced by the Belgians to generate profits. (Punch Cartoon Library & Archive)

disrupted family and village life, helping to further destabilize African society. The male migrants often lived in crowded dormitories or huts that offered little privacy, enjoyed few amenities other than drinking beer in makeshift bars, and were able to visit their families back home for only a few days a year.

African women faced a different combination of hardship and opportunities. In many African societies women had long enjoyed considerable autonomy, playing a major role as traders and farmers. Now, however, as men migrated for work or took up cash crop farming, women were left with all food production, which was less lucrative than the men's work and which increased their workload. For example, the agricultural workweek for women in the German-ruled Cameroons went from forty-five to seventy hours. The Baule women of Ivory Coast, who had long profited from growing cotton and spinning it into thread, lost their position to Baule men when cotton became a cash crop and textiles an export item. Many women traders who had dominated town markets now faced competition from Indians or Lebanese. Some women responded with self-help organizations. Ashante market women in Kumasi organized themselves under elected leaders later known as market queens to promote cooperation and settle disputes among themselves. Thanks to education, self-help, and ambition, some African women gained skills to support themselves as teachers, nurses, and merchants, lessening their dependence on men. But many poor women were overwhelmed by the challenges of trying to preserve their families while fulfilling their new responsibilities.

African Adaptiveness and Resistance

Africans responded to colonialism in various ways. The Igbos of Nigeria capitalized on change by taking up lucrative cash crop farming or using education to forge careers as professionals or clerks. Other Africans dealt with change by enriching traditional ways. The imaginative Yoruba artist Olowe of Ise (oh-LO-way of ee-SAY) (ca. 1875–1938), while emphasizing Yoruba themes and ideals in the woodcarvings, elaborately carved doors, and other objects he sculpted for Yoruba kings, also expressed his personal style by creating richly textured surfaces and the illusion of movement in his art. Some Africans negotiated change by mixing Western and African ideas. The Black Zion movement in South Africa had Christian overtones, as in the belief that Jesus was African, but it also promoted African pride and traditions such as faith healing.

Many Africans, however, chose noncooperation. Tax evasion and other forms of passive protest were rampant, especially in rural areas, while other Africans chose a more activist strategy and formed labor unions. Although unions were usually illegal in colonial systems that protected Western-owned businesses, strikes were common, especially among mine workers, who protested unsafe working conditions or long hours. The strike leaders were arrested and added to the growing number of political prisoners rotting away in colonial prisons.

Africans also used their traditional cultural forms both to protest colonialism and to address problems within their own societies. For example, in Nigeria, Igbo women used a unique combination of dance and theater to exercise influence in their individualistic but also patriarchal society, dancing and singing their grievances. In a strategy known as "sitting on a man," the dance performances were sometimes used to encourage noncooperation with colonial demands, such as increased taxes, or with excessive male Igbo chauvinism. The dances served to move people toward social action. When local leaders ignored the dance messages of dissatisfaction, the women were prepared to take stronger action, including rioting.

Sometimes distress and anger led to more drastic resistance. Rebellions sparked by unpopular policies, such as new taxes or forced labor, punctuated colonial rule. The Maji Maji Rebellion, for example, broke out in German-ruled Tanganyika in 1905 and was suppressed only after a bitter two-year struggle. Maji Maji began as a peasant protest against a new cotton-growing scheme that worked poorly because the people forced to work in the cotton fields earned only 35 cents a month. The disenchanted Africans preferred to be subsistence farmers and grow their own food rather than be commercial farmers. These feelings led to a new religious cult known as Maji Maji ("water medicine"), which used magic water in hopes of better crops. Maji Maji sparked a rebellion involving thousands. The rebels occupied some towns and sprinkled their bodies with magic water in hopes it would make them immune from bullets, but the Germans, using machine guns against rebels armed only with spears, soon regained the towns. Finally in 1907 the Maji Maji were defeated, at the cost of 26,000 African lives; however, the resistance caused the Germans to end forced labor.

The Legacy of Colonialism for Africans

Whether colonialism stimulated modern development or retarded and distorted it is one of the central questions of modern African history. Some historians contend that colonialism increased the productive capacity of the land, built cities and transportation networks, brought advances in technology, stimulated Africans to produce more wealth than they ever had before, and created rich opportunities for beneficial trade with the outside world. Other historians, however, question the purpose and beneficiaries of the globalization of the African economies in this era. They argue that colonial rulers stole land, exploited labor, gained profitable access to raw materials, shifted profits back to Europe, limited Africa's economic growth, and created artificial, unstable countries.

Although economic growth occurred, colonial Africa enjoyed little development or balanced growth that benefited the majority of the people. One observer in the early 1900s noted that in Portuguese-ruled Mozambique a man "works . . . all his life under horrible conditions to buy scanty clothing for his wife and daughters. The men and boys can rarely afford proper clothing."[15] Moreover, while any benefits brought to Africa by colonialism may be debated, it is clear that colonialism imposed an economic system that discouraged diversified growth, with the result that many of the former colonies are economically vulnerable today. Some of the profits from plantations and mines supported European industrialization and enriched European businesses, but the African peoples supplying the resources benefited little. For example, seventy-five years of Belgian colonialism in the Congo failed to build any paved road system linking the major cities or to establish more than a handful of schools and medical clinics for the millions of Congo's people. As a result of such policies transferring wealth from Africa to Europe, sub-Saharan Africa was the most impoverished region of the world at the end of the colonial era, a legacy difficult to overcome.

SECTION SUMMARY

- African colonial governments served the interests of the colonizers, though the colonizers' involvement in local affairs varied between forms of direct and indirect rule.

- Colonizers divided Africa into countries with artificial boundaries, sometimes splitting an ethnic group into more than one country and sometimes throwing rival groups into a single country, thus creating lasting tensions.

- Christian missionary schools provided a small minority of Africans with skills they could use in the white world but largely ignored and often damaged the native African culture.

- As African economies came to depend on a single commodity desired by Europeans, colonized Africans lost their subsistence skills, were sometimes forced into near slavery, and were often forced to work far from home.

- Some Africans took advantage of opportunities offered by colonization, others enriched their traditional ways, and a few, such as the Maji Maji, openly rebelled, though never successfully.

- While some historians think that colonization brought beneficial development to Africans, economic growth benefited mainly the colonizers, did little to materially improve African lives, and prevented Africans from building diversified and strong economies.

◈ Imperialism, Reform, and the Middle Eastern Societies

What political and economic impact did Europe have on the Middle East?

Between 1750 and 1914 most Muslim societies suffered repeated challenges from the growing power of western Europe and Russia. The Ottoman Empire remained the only significant Muslim power and, despite a remarkable ability to rejuvenate itself, fell behind the industrializing West. Expanding European empires ate at the fringes of Persia and the shrinking Ottoman domain, and European economic penetration and cultural influences reshaped Middle Eastern life. The response of Muslims to these changes differed from society to society.

Challenges to the Ottoman Empire

For a thousand years Islamic influence had spread throughout much of Afro-Eurasia. Muslims dominated the trade routes connecting sub-Saharan Africa, southern Asia, and the Mediterranean world until the 1500s, and they still played key roles in interregional trade in the 1800s. During the Early Modern Era large Islamic states stretched from Morocco to Indonesia. The Ottoman Turks forged a huge empire in southeastern Europe and western Asia, as well as gaining a strong influence across North Africa, while Safavid Persia and Mughal India also exercised regional power. Since many Muslims viewed the Ottoman sultan as the caliph, the successor to the Prophet and leader of the Islamic community, Ottoman leaders had enormous prestige in the Muslim world. But the rising influence of western Europeans posed a threat to the Islamic states. By 1750, as a result of both Western pressure and internal problems, the Ottoman power had diminished, the Safavids had fallen, the Mughals had lost most of India, and the Dutch ruled much of Indonesia. After 1750 the Islamic world faced new challenges. However brief, Napoleon Bonaparte's conquest of Egypt, discussed in the chapter opening, sent shock waves through the Middle East and suggested dangers ahead.

In the nineteenth century rising pressure from European nations, especially Russia, undermined the Ottoman Empire and its more than 60 million people (see Map 21.2). Since the 1500s the Russians had been slowly expanding south toward the Black Sea, and in 1768 they defeated Ottoman forces and gained control over part of the northern Black Sea coast. Between 1792 and 1812 they extended this control to include the Crimean peninsula, and in 1829 they took over the largely Christian Caucasus state of Georgia (see Chronology: The Middle East, 1750–1914). In 1853 Czar Nicholas I characterized the weakening Ottoman Empire as "the sick man of Europe," a reputation that would stick.

Perceiving Ottoman decline, the major European powers schemed to outflank each other while building up their influence in the weakening empire. With European support, the

CHRONOLOGY	
The Middle East, 1750–1914	
1792–1812	Russian control of northern Black Sea lands
1794–1925	Qajar dynasty in Persia
1798–1799	French occupation of Egypt
1805–1848	Rule of Muhammad Ali in Egypt
1829	Greek independence from Ottoman Empire
1840	French colonization of Algeria
1859–1869	Building of Suez Canal
1882	British colonization of Egypt
1890s–1915	Turkish genocide against Armenians
1897	First Zionist conference
1899	British protectorate over Kuwait
1905–1911	Constitutional revolution in Persia
1908	Young Turk government in Ottoman Turkey
1907–1921	Russian and British spheres of influence in Persia
1908	Discovery of oil in Persia
1911–1912	Colonization of Libya and Morocco

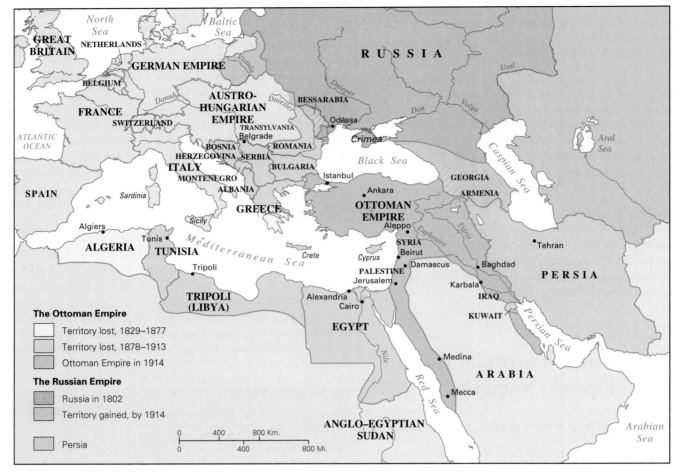

Map 21.2 The Ottoman Empire and Persia, 1914
The Ottoman Empire once included much of southeastern Europe, western Asia, and North Africa.
By 1914, after losing most of its European, Caucasian, and North African territories, it was restricted
largely to parts of western Asia.

Greeks, Serbs, Romanians, and Bulgarians rebelled and threw off Ottoman power in the 1800s. The Greek revolt, which enjoyed support from Britain, France, and Russia, revealed Ottoman weaknesses (see Chapter 19). A combined Ottoman-Egyptian force had nearly defeated the Greeks when an Anglo-French fleet and the Russian army intervened, shifting the military balance. The 1829 treaty that ended the war recognized Greek independence and gave autonomy to the Ottoman territories of Serbia and Moldavia.

Along with military setbacks, the Ottoman state also faced growing internal problems. Weakened by military losses, the central government had more difficulty satisfying the desires of the empire's multiethnic population. The Turks had long benefited from the empire's ethnic diversity, using the varied peoples to enrich their state. Non-Muslim minorities played major roles in Ottoman commerce, the professions, and government. Moreover, the Ottomans had generally been tolerant of ethnic and religious minorities such as Kurds (mostly Sunni Muslims), Jews, and Arab Christians. To respect minority cultures and keep the minorities from combining politically, the Ottomans allowed each group to basically rule itself through

its own religious establishment, such as the Greek Orthodox Church. Christians and Jews felt particularly secure in the major Ottoman cities, which commonly had large minority communities, and Jews in much of the empire enjoyed more security and prosperity than they did in Europe. Multiethnic Istanbul was described in 1873 as "a city not of one nation but of many. Eight or nine languages are constantly spoken in the streets and five or six appear on the shop fronts."[16] Various small religious sects also settled in the Lebanon mountains, where they maintained their traditions.

But in spite of the accommodation to ethnic diversity, some ethnic minorities became restless. Deteriorating Turkish relations with the Christian Armenians in eastern Turkey and the Caucasus led to a conflict between the two groups. Armenians had generally remained loyal Ottoman subjects, and some held high positions in the government. But during the 1800s the nationalist and socialist ideas percolating in Europe filtered into the Armenian communities and influenced some Armenians to want their own state where they could make their own laws. Acting on these nationalistic feelings, Armenians founded their own schools, colleges, libraries, hospitals, presses, and charitable organizations and looked to Europe and North America for financial and moral support.

Armenian-Ottoman conflict intensified, with deadly consequences for the Armenians. In the 1890s and early 1900s the Ottoman government responded to increasing Armenian assertiveness, including terrorist attacks on Ottoman targets, by seizing Armenian property, killing over 100,000 Armenians, and exiling thousands more. Many Armenians moved to North America to escape the persecution. In 1915, during World War I, the Ottoman government charged Armenians with supporting Russia and used the charge of treason to begin removing Armenians from eastern Anatolia, where in response Armenian nationalists declared a republic. During the turmoil the Ottoman army, aided by local Turks and Kurds, killed around a million Armenians. Many historians consider the violent assault a genocide, the singling out of one group for mass killing, but Turkish nationalists view it as an incidental side effect of war. The mass killings still complicate Armenian-Turkish relations. The surviving Armenians formed a small republic in the Caucasus, Armenia, that was absorbed by Russia in 1920.

Ottoman Reform and Modernization

Growing internal problems, combined with military setbacks, spurred Ottoman efforts to reform and modernize in order to match Western power. To survive, Ottoman sultans tried hard to build a strong, modern, and more secular government. They believed this required renewed centralization; however, because many interest groups benefited from weak central authority, this was no easy task. The various groups included the Islamic religious leaders, the privileged military force known as Janissaries, local officials in Anatolia, and governors of distant Arab provinces, who were virtually independent.

Gradually the system changed as Ottoman leaders and thinkers recognized the need to obtain knowledge and aid from the Christian West. One of the first reformist sultans, Mahmud II (MACH-mood) (r. 1808–1839), tried to reestablish central authority over local leaders. He also had to eliminate the Janissaries, who had once been an effective fighting force but who resisted change and had become a costly and ineffective burden. Mahmud recruited a new military force that attacked and crushed the Janissaries, and then he slowly built a modern state and an army trained by Prussian officers. His successors set up new schools that taught European learning and languages, and by 1900 the University of Istanbul had become the Muslim world's first modern institution of higher education. The Ottomans also replaced many older Islam-based laws with laws based on the French codes introduced during the French Revolution. Increasingly the Ottoman rulers marginalized Islam and treated Islamic knowledge as irrelevant, and Islamic leaders and institutions lost standing, demoralizing conservatives.

The growth of a more centralized government and a modern, secular Ottoman nationality continued through the 1800s, aided by the introduction of railroads and telegraphs. To foster a national identity, in 1846 Ottoman rulers declared all citizens equal before the law regardless of their ethnicity and religion, announcing that "the differences of religion and sect among the subjects is something not affecting their rights of citizenship. It is wrong to make discriminations among us."[17]

But attempts to involve the people in government largely failed, and the reforms proved inadequate, instead fostering rebellion and eventually the dissolution of the Ottoman Empire. In the 1880s a modernizing group known as the **Young Turks** emerged in the military and the universities. Their goal was to make Turkey a modern nation with a liberal constitution, and by 1908, when the Young Turks led a military coup that deposed the old sultan, Islam had faded as a political influence. The Young Turks espoused Turkish nationalism, and hoped to spread the Turkish language into Arab provinces, and unite all Turkish peoples in western and central Asia. Under the facade of parliamentary government, they ruled as autocrats and military modernizers. During World War I, as an ally of Germany and Austria-Hungary, the Young Turks embraced a Turkish ethnic identity, secularization, and closer ties to the Western world at the expense of Islamic connections. After their defeat in World War I, the Ottoman Empire was dissolved and the Arab peoples once ruled by the Ottomans fell under British or French rule. By 1920 the Turks were struggling to hold on to their Anatolian heartland.

Egypt: Modernization and Occupation

The most extensive effort to deflect Western pressure through modernization came in Egypt, but only after Ottoman influence was minimized. The Ottomans, who occupied Egypt in 1517, had governed the province through the Mamluks, a Muslim caste of Turkish origin, but by the later 1700s Egyptians considered the Mamluks corrupt, oppressive, and unable to deal with the repeated famines and epidemics that killed millions of Egyptians. Mamluk misrule gave French general Napoleon Bonaparte an excuse to invade the country. While claiming to liberate the Egyptians, Bonaparte hoped to revitalize Egypt's usually productive agriculture to provide grain for France. When Bonaparte abandoned his Egyptian adventure in 1801, Egypt came under the rule of Muhammad Ali (r. 1805–1848), a Turkish-speaking Albanian who had led the Ottoman forces that helped eject the French. Muhammad Ali encouraged innovations but ultimately these did not succeed in staving off British colonization.

Muhammad Ali's Egypt After being appointed viceroy by the Ottoman sultan, Muhammad Ali moved to centralize his power in what was effectively now an independent country. However, he was forced by the European powers, who feared his ambitions, to officially remain loosely bound to the weakening Ottoman state. The charming sultan impressed Europeans with his talents: "If ever a man had an eye that denoted genius, [he] was the person. Never dead nor quiescent, it was fascinating like that of a gazelle; or, in the hour of storm, fierce as an eagle's."[18]

Young Turks A modernizing group in Ottoman Turkey that promoted a national identity and that gained power in the early twentieth century.

Muhammad Ali Meets European Representatives Muhammad Ali, the Egyptian sultan who tried to modernize his state, cultivated ties with Western nations. This painting shows the sultan in 1839 meeting with representatives from several European governments. (Mary Evans Picture Library)

Muhammad Ali introduced ambitious reforms to transform Egypt into a European-style state with an effective army. He increased trade and moved to foster an industrial revolution by using government revenues from increased agricultural exports to establish textile, sugar, and glass factories, as well as foundries and shipyards. The Egyptian leader established a conscript army trained by Western instructors, formed a navy, and created an arms industry. He also replaced Islamic with French legal codes, as the Ottoman sultans had done, sent Egyptians to study technical subjects in Europe, encouraged the establishment of the first Arab newspapers, and laid the foundation for a Western-influenced state educational system to train people for the military and bureaucracy. These changes have led historians to credit Muhammad Ali with founding Egypt as a modern nation-state.

However, while Muhammad Ali's programs added to Egypt's power and wealth, they did not ultimately protect Egyptian independence and foster development, a failure that in time invited British interference. Some hurdles could not be overcome. For example, unlike European nations, Egypt lacked iron and coal, and the work force, not used to industrial regimentation, failed to care for their machines. In addition, as Muhammad Ali and his successors welcomed Western investment, the Egyptian economy became more shackled to European finance. In 1838 the British obtained free trade within Ottoman domains. The resulting influx of cheap British commodities stifled Egypt's textile industry and its cottage handicraft manufacturing. Although the Egyptian cotton industry was stimulated in the 1860s by the American Civil War, which cut exports from the United States to Europe, Europeans were more interested in procuring Egyptian raw cotton for processing in their own mills than they were in buying finished textiles.

Following the European model, Muhammad Ali turned to seeking resources and markets through the conquest of neighboring societies. Egyptian armies moved south into Nubia and the eastern Sudanic lands along the Nile River, which they made into an Egyptian colony, and also into the Ottoman territories of Arabia, Palestine, Syria, and Greece. But a northern thrust alarmed the European powers, and they intervened to push the Egyptians back. The British sought to destroy Egypt as a rival in order to have more influence in the region and to gain control of the Suez Canal, which was built as a French-Egyptian collaboration between 1859 and 1869. The 100-mile-long canal, a magnificent technological achievement whose construction had cost the lives of thousands of Egyptian workers, linked the Mediterranean and Red Seas, greatly decreasing the shipping time between Europe and Asia. British merchant and naval ships became the canal's major users, and in the end Britain also gained control of the canal by capitalizing on the failure of Muhammad Ali and his successors to transform Egypt. In 1875 Egypt's sultan Ismail, Muhammad Ali's grandson, was forced by his country's skyrocketing national debt to sell Egypt's large share in canal ownership to the British government.

The British in Egypt Eventually, to preempt the ambitions of other European powers, the British decided to seize Egypt using military force. By the 1870s Egypt was bankrupt and deeply in debt to European financiers and governments. In addition, the country's political and commercial elite, including many Coptic Christians, were oriented toward Western ideas and committed to modernization; indeed, many Copts, fearing Muslim nationalism and familiar with Western sciences and languages, welcomed the British. But most Egyptians, being chiefly influenced by conservative Islamic ideas and leaders, opposed the growing Western influence. In 1882 increasing local unrest and threats to European residents provided an excuse for the British to bombard Egypt's major port, Alexandria, and then invade the country. Thus, several decades after Muhammad Ali's death, Egypt became part of Britain's growing worldwide empire.

Soon after gaining control of Egypt, the British had to deal with a challenge coming from the Sudanic region straddling the Nile River to Egypt's south (today the nation of Sudan), which the Egyptians had seized between the 1820s and 1860s. In 1881 a militant Arab Muslim in the Sudan, Muhammad Ahmad (1846–1885), the son of a shipbuilder, declared that he was the Mahdi (MAH-dee) ("the Guided One") and pledged to restore Islam's purity and destroy the Egyptian-imposed government, which he accused of corruption, lax morality, and subservience to European advisers. He recruited an army that defeated the Egyptian forces and their British officers, after which he formed an Islamic state. However, the Mahdist government wasted money in wars with neighbors, and in 1898 British and Egyptian forces defeated the Mahdists and formed a new state known as the Anglo-Egyptian Sudan, which was effectively a British colony.

Persia: Challenges and Reforms

Persia, increasingly known as Iran, had long played a central role in the Islamic world, but in the 1700s it faced new problems. After the Safavid collapse in 1736 and the following decades of turmoil, in 1794 one Persian tribe, the Qajars (KAH-jars), established control over much of Persia from their base in Tehran and ruled uneasily until 1925. The Qajars took over an impoverished country that suffered from deserted villages, desolated cities, and much reduced trade after years of civil war and anarchy. The early Qajar rulers, presiding over a weak central government, were unable to resolve most of Persia's problems and became noted instead for greed, corruption, and lavish living. One particularly extravagant shah married 158 wives, fathering nearly 100 children, and was survived by some 600 grandchildren.

Under the Qajars, Persia was more a diverse collection of tribes, ethnic groups, and religious sects than a nation, a condition that fostered conflict. The majority of Persia's people, including the Qajar rulers, were Shi'ites, but the population also included Christian Armenians, Jews, Zoroastrians, and Sunni Kurds, all of whom sought to increase their autonomy. Shi'ite clerics, however, exercised great influence, controlling education, law, and welfare and enjoying vast wealth from landholdings and tithes. Independent of any government, the top Shi'ite clerics engaged in power struggles with the Qajar shahs, arguing that a virtuous and learned Shi'ite scholar should rule Persia and that few Qajar rulers fit that description. Meanwhile, Shi'ites persecuted as heretical the **Bahai** (buh-HI) religion. Founded in 1867 by the Persian Bahaullah (bah-hah-oo-LAH)

(1817–1892) as an offshoot of Persian Shi'ism, Bahai called for universal peace, the unity of all religions, and service to others. Shi'ites killed many Bahais and forced their leaders into exile.

Persia also faced continuous pressure from Russia and Britain. By the 1870s Russia had gained territory on both sides of the Caspian Sea, including the Caucasus, and between 1907 and 1921 it asserted a sphere of influence in northern Persia. Meanwhile, capitalizing on the Suez Canal, British power steadily grew in the Persian Gulf and along Arabia's Indian Ocean coast. The British, who wanted a strong Persia to keep the Russians away from the Persian Gulf and India, asserted a sphere of influence in southeastern Persia, which gave them a foothold at the entrance to the Persian Gulf. British entrepreneurs controlled a monopoly on Persian railroad construction, banking, and oil. The Anglo-Iranian Oil Company (later British Petroleum), which struck oil in 1908, became Persia's dominant economic enterprise, but profits went chiefly to Britain. Persians disliked the powerful British economic role, which they considered a humiliation.

The weakness of the central government, combined with foreign pressure, led to political reforms. Some Qajar shahs provided an opening for change when they attempted to restore central government power. In the later 1800s they rebuilt an army, set up a Western-style college, introduced a telegraph system, and gave Christian missionaries the right to establish schools and hospitals. Some celebrated the changes. The Persian writer Mirza Malkum (1834–1898) marveled in 1891 that all manner of new ideas were astir to shake a society needing change. However, these Qajar reforms also threatened the conservative Shi'ite clergy, who hoped to thwart modernization.

From 1905 to 1911 Persia enjoyed a constitutional revolution, unique in the Middle East, that fostered a brief period of democracy. The more liberal Shi'ite clergy, allied with merchants in the capital, Tehran, Armenians, and Western-educated radicals, imposed a democratic constitution that sought to curb royal power by setting up a parliament elected by several major groups and granting freedom of the press. Soon over four hundred newspapers were published. When a conservative, pro-Russian shah took power in 1907 and attempted to weaken the parliament, liberal newspapers, writers, and musicians lampooned him and his allies. Troubadours sang songs about the love of country, democracy, freedom, justice, and equality.

The progressive direction did not last, however. Britain and Russia formed an alliance and increased pressure on Persia to grant them more influence, straining the progressive leadership. As a result, the constitutionalist forces soon split into pro-Western nationalists seeking separation of religious and civil power, land reform, and universal education, and Shi'ite clerics and nobles who favored slower change. Many clergy had become alarmed at the secular direction. As violence increased in 1911, the conservative royal government closed down the parliament and ended the democratic experiment. Aref Qazvini, a popular pro-revolution songwriter, lamented the setback: "O let not Iran thus be lost, if ye be men of truth."[19] By then, however, Britain and Russia, stationing troops in southern and northern Persia, respectively, had reduced Persia's political and economic independence.

Bahai An offshoot of Persian Shi'ism that was founded in 1867; Bahai preached universal peace, the unity of all religions, and service to others.

Ottoman Syria, Lebanon, and Iraq

Declining Ottoman power, combined with growing Western activity, eventually had an impact on the Arab provinces of the eastern Ottoman Empire. Syria and Lebanon, which the Ottomans governed as one province, were particularly affected. Despite their diverse ethnic and religious mosaic, which included Arab and Armenian Christians, Sunni and Shi'ite Arabs, and Sunni Kurds, the peoples of these two adjacent territories had mostly lived in peace under Ottoman rule. By recognizing the autonomy of each community, the Ottoman government had promoted some degree of religious tolerance. A British writer commented on the generally stable conditions and social harmony in the late 1700s, writing that in Lebanon "every man lives in a perfect security of life and property. The peasant is not richer than in other countries, but he is free."[20]

However, in the 1850s poverty and a stagnant economy began to foster occasional conflicts in Syria and Lebanon, and as a result the densely populated region around Mount Lebanon came under the influence of several Western powers. For example, the French developed a special relationship with the Maronites (MAR-uh-nite), Arab Christians who sought a closer connection with the Roman Catholic Church, and American Protestant missionaries established a college in the main Lebanese city, Beirut, in 1866 that spread modern ideas. By the later 1800s the weak economy had also encouraged emigration from Syria and Lebanon. The majority of emigrants were Lebanese Christians, who often left as families for the United States. Other Lebanese Christians and Muslims moved to other parts of the Middle East or to West Africa, Latin America, or the Caribbean. By 1914 perhaps 350,000 Arabs from Syria and Lebanon had emigrated to the Americas.

Change also came to Ottoman-ruled Iraq, the heart of ancient Mesopotamia, which had spawned the first cities and states and had later become the center of a great Islamic empire. Under Ottoman rule, however, Iraq lacked political unity and had not prospered. The Ottomans divided Iraq into three provinces: a largely Sunni Arab and Kurdish north, a chiefly Sunni Arab center, and a Shi'ite Arab–dominated south. The Ottomans had difficulty collecting taxes in the south. Iraqis suffered from major floods and repeated epidemics of plague and cholera. A British official described Iraq as "a country of extremes, either dying of thirst or of being drowned."[21] Iraq also lacked order, foreign capital, and a transportation system such as railroads or steamships on the rivers. Pirates attacked shipping in the Persian Gulf, and Bedouin tribes raided land caravans. Although gradually more schools were founded in the later 1800s, the literacy rate remained extremely low.

Although the challenges were daunting, Western interest in this Ottoman backwater grew. European travelers were unanimous that Iraq had great economic potential: navigable rivers, fertile land, a strategic location, access to the Persian Gulf, and minerals. To gain a foothold in the region, in 1899 the British established a protectorate over the small neighboring kingdom of Kuwait (koo-WAIT) at the east end of the Persian Gulf. This relationship preserved the royal government but allowed the British to station troops and agents. But Iraq remained of more interest, particularly as both the British and Germans came to believe that it might have considerable oil, and in the early 1900s the Ottomans and foreign investors poured money into Iraq. However, World War I temporarily halted Western efforts to discover Iraqi oil.

European Colonization in Northwest Africa

Northwest Africa also experienced European colonization. The Arabic-speaking societies along Africa's Mediterranean coast from Libya to Algeria had never been under firm Ottoman control, and their proximity to Europe made them natural targets for colonization. In 1840 the French embarked on full-scale colonization of Algeria, in part to divert the French public from an unpopular home government. Abd al-Qadir (AB dul-KA-deer), an energetic Algerian Muslim cleric, used Islamic appeals to unite Arab and Berber opposition to the French. His resourceful followers quickly learned how to make guns. The French captured Abd al-Qadir in 1847, but the fighting continued for years. Facing determined resistance, the French attempted to demoralize the Algerians by driving peasants off the best land and selling it to European settlers. To diffuse opposition, they also relocated and broke up tribes. Yet various anti-French revolts, often spurred by appeals to Islamic traditions, erupted until the 1880s. The ruthless French conquest and suppression of rebellions cost tens of thousands of French and hundreds of thousands of Algerian lives.

French policy reshaped Algerian society. The French intended, as an official wrote in 1862, to impose French culture, settlers, and economic priorities on the Arabs. General Bugeaud, the conqueror of Algeria, conceded in 1849 that "the Arabs with great insight understand very well the cruel revolution we have brought them; it is as radical for them as socialism would be for us."[22] Between the 1840s and 1914 over a million immigrants from France, Italy, and Spain poured into Algeria, erecting a racist society similar to South Africa. The European settlers eventually elected representatives to the French parliament as Algeria was incorporated into the French state. The mainstay of the settler economy, vineyard cultivation and wine production, displaced food crops and pasture, an economic change that mocked Islamic values prohibiting alcoholic beverages.

Gradually European power in Northwest Africa increased. In Morocco, a coastal country west of Algeria, Sultan Mawlay Hassan (r. 1873–1895) skillfully worked to preserve the country's independence by playing the rival European powers off against each other. However, the French and Spanish, attracted by Morocco's economic potential and strategic position, by 1912 had divided the country between them. Tunisia, just east of Algeria, had long enjoyed considerable autonomy under Ottoman rule, and the port city of Tunis prospered as a center of trade and piracy. Coveting this trade, in 1881 France sent in troops to occupy Tunisia. Libya, a sparsely populated, mostly desert land between Tunisia and Egypt, was conquered by the

Italians in 1911 and 1912. The country's Islamic orders led repeated resistance efforts, and the resulting conflicts killed one-third of Libya's people. European colonialism now dominated the whole of North Africa.

SECTION SUMMARY

- After 1750, the Ottoman Empire's power began to wane under pressure from Russia and western Europe and also from the Armenians, who exerted pressure from within the empire for greater autonomy.

- The Ottomans modernized their army, adopted French-style laws, and became increasingly secular, but their decline continued until the empire was broken apart in World War I.

- After Napoleon left Egypt, an Ottoman-appointed governor, Muhammad Ali, attempted an ambitious and somewhat successful program of modernization; ultimately, however, Britain gained control of the Suez Canal and made Egypt a colony.

- Persia, fragmented under the rule of the Qajars, came to be dominated economically by Britain, and interference by both Britain and Russia helped to end a brief period of progressive rule.

- Westerners became increasingly influential in Syria and Lebanon, as well as in Iraq, which was backward and undeveloped but attracted Western attention because of its abundant resources, particularly oil.

- Europeans colonized Northwest Africa: first Algeria, where settlers established a racist society; then Morocco, which was shared by France and Spain; and finally Tunisia and Libya.

◆ Middle Eastern Thought and Culture

How did Middle Eastern thought and culture respond to the Western challenge?

West Asian and North African societies responded to the challenges facing them in three ways. One response was to form vibrant Islamic revivalist movements that promoted a purer version of Islamic practice rooted in early Muslim tradition. The second response involved reform movements that attempted to combine Islam with modernization and secularization. The early stirrings of Arab nationalism constituted a third response. While governments stagnated or struggled, revivalist, reform, and nationalist movements pumped fresh vitality into Islamic culture and religious life, influencing social and cultural patterns. But none of these movements offered an effective resistance to Western economic and military power.

Islamic Revivalism

Political crises in the Middle East helped spark influential movements of **Islamic revivalism**, which sought to purify Islamic practices by reviving what their supporters considered to be a purer vision of Islamic society than the existing one. Revivalists wanted to return to the earliest form of Islam for guidance and embraced what they regarded as God's word in the Quran and the sayings of the Prophet Muhammad. They also reaffirmed the ideal of the theocratic state of the early caliphs in Mecca, which blended religion and government.

The revivalists rejected what they considered the corruption of true Islam, criticizing the scholarly and mystical additions that had resulted from encounters with Persian, Hindu, Indonesian, African, and European cultures over the centuries. For example, in many African and Southeast Asian societies, Muslims still consulted shamans skilled in magic and healing, revered Sufi saints, and permitted women to engage in trade and reject veiling. Muslim revivalists despised Sufism and its mystical practices, such as music and dance, which had developed centuries after the founding of Islam. Heeding this criticism, several Sufi brotherhoods eventually moved away from mystical beliefs toward an emphasis on the original teachings of the Prophet Muhammad.

While political leaders lost prestige and authority, religious leaders allied to merchant and tribal groups seized the initiative to spread revivalist thought. Groups seeking to impose revivalist goals on others sometimes used violence, interpreting the early Muslim idea of jihad, or struggle for the faith, as a call to wage holy war against those Muslims who blended Islamic and local traditions. The Fulani jihads in West Africa led by Othman dan Fodio and the Mahdist army in Sudan, both discussed earlier in the chapter, were notable examples of Muslims waging war on other Muslims because of disagreements over faith.

Carried by scholars, merchants, and missionaries, revivalist Islam spread from the Middle East to societies in every other part of the Islamic world, fostering debates over the role of Islam and how to meet the Western threat. Many sub-Saharan African, Indian, and Southeast Asian Muslims visited, studied, or sojourned in the Middle East, often embracing the revivalist ideas. During the 1800s revivalist movements stiffened resistance against French colonization in Algeria and West Africa, British colonization in Sudan, and Dutch colonization in Indonesia.

The Rise of the Wahhabis

Revivalism had its greatest impact in Arabia, where it spurred a militant movement in the 1700s known as **Wahhabism** (wah-HAH-bi-zuhm). The movement's founder, Muhammad Abd

---

Islamic revivalism   Arab movements beginning in the eighteenth century that sought to purify Islamic practices by reviving what their supporters considered to be a purer vision of Islamic society.

Wahhabism   A militant Islamic revivalist movement founded in Arabia in the eighteenth century.

al-Wahhab (al-wah-HAHB) (1703–1792), led a long campaign to purify Arabian Islam. Al-Wahhab had left his home in central Arabia to study Islamic theology in Medina and Iraq, where he adopted a strict interpretation of Islamic law. Returning home, he preached against those who were lax in their religious practice and promoted intolerance toward all alternative views, such as Sufism and Shi'ism. In 1744 his campaign gained a key ally, Muhammad Ibn Saud (sah-OOD), a tribal chief who took an oath to help al-Wahhab spread his views. Together al-Wahhab and Ibn Saud put together a fighting force to expand their influence.

Wahhabi power ebbed and flowed. During the later 1700s the Wahhabis used military force to take over parts of Arabia and then advanced into Syria and Iraq, where they occupied the Iraqi city of Karbala (KAHR-buh-luh), the major Shi'ite holy site; to demoralize the Shi'ites, they destroyed much of the site. By 1805 the Wahhabis controlled Mecca and Medina, Islam's two holiest cities, where they horrified non-Wahhabi Muslims by massacring the residents and trying to destroy all sacred tombs in order to prevent saint worship. Their actions represented a major threat to conventional Islam. In response, Muhammad Ali, the governor of Egypt, used his European-style army and modern weapons to push the Wahhabis back from the holy cities. Despite these setbacks, however, Wahhabi ideas, puritanism, and zeal spread widely during the 1800s as Western power undermined Middle Eastern governments. Yet many Muslims condemned Wahhabi intolerance, extremism, and such practices as the forced veiling of women.

In 1902 the still-allied descendants of al-Wahhab and Ibn Saud launched a second great expansion. The head of the Saud family, Abdul Aziz Ibn Saud (1880–1953), sent Wahhabi clergy among the Bedouins to convince them to abandon their nomadic ways and join self-sufficient farming communities that mixed military and missionary goals. The Wahhabi Bedouin communities adopted extreme asceticism and a literal interpretation of the Islamic legal code, the Shari'a, expecting everyone to conform to their strict beliefs. For example, Wahhabi clergy beat men for arriving late for prayers, and Wahhabi

men pledged to die fighting for their beliefs. In 1925 the Saud family established Saudi Arabia, a state based on the Shari'a, and discovery of oil in 1938 gave the Saud family and their Wahhabi allies the wealth to maintain their control.

Online Study Center **Improve Your Grade**
Primary Source: The History and Doctrines of Wahhabis

Modernist Islamic Thought

Islamic revivalism as reflected in the Wahhabi movement was only one of several strands of Islamic thought that emerged during the Modern Era. Some Muslim thinkers, rejecting a rigid, backward-looking vision of Islam such as Wahhabism, promoted modernization as a strategy for transforming Islamic society in response to the challenges of rising Western power and weakening Muslim governments. While Wahhabis were rejecting the modern world, modernist ideas grew stronger among Muslim intellectuals, who argued that Muslims should reject blind faith and reconcile Islam with modernization by welcoming fresh ideas, social change, and religious moderation.

Modernists detested many conservative Muslim traditions, including the restricted role of women. For example, Qasim Amin (KA-sim AH-mean), a French-educated Egyptian lawyer, argued in 1898 that the liberation of women was essential to the liberation of Egypt, that acquiring their "share of intellectual and moral development, happiness, and authority would prove to be the most significant development in Egyptian history." Women reformers such as Bahithat al-Badiya (buh-TEE-that al-buh-DEE-ya) echoed these sentiments (see Witness to the Past: Egyptian Women and Their Rights). A few modernist men and women were even more radical on gender issues. The male Iraqi poet Jamil Sidqi az-Zahawi, like some other liberal intellectuals, identified the veil as the symbol of female exclusion, imploring women to "unveil yourself for life needs transformation. Tear it away, burn it, do not hesitate. It has only given you false protection!"[23]

Muslim modernists believed that introducing change would be a straightforward process. Leaders such as Muhammad Ali in Egypt thought that all they had to do was translate the technologies and institutions that made Europe strong to their own societies. They believed that by buying weapons and machines they could strengthen their armies and industries to deflect Western pressure, enrich their countries, and avoid domestic unrest. But

Cairo Opera House Hoping to demonstrate modernization, Egyptian leaders built an opera house in Cairo in the 1860s. One of the first pieces staged was an opera by Italian composer Giuseppe Verdi to celebrate the opening of the Suez Canal in 1869. (*Hulton/Getty Images*)

One of the leading women writers and thinkers in early twentieth-century Egypt, Bahithat al-Badiya (buh-TEE-that al-buh-DEE-ya) (1886–1918), advocated greater economic and educational rights for women in a rapidly changing society. She wrote at a time when Egyptian nationalists were demanding independence from Britain and a modern state and intellectuals were debating the merits of modernity as opposed to tradition. In 1909, in a lecture to an Egyptian women's club associated with a nationalist organization, Bahithat offered a program for improving women's lives. Struggling against male and Islamic opposition to women's rights, she sought a middle ground between Islamic conservatism and European secular liberalization.

Ladies, I greet you as a sister who feels what you feel, suffers what you suffer, and rejoices in what you rejoice. . . . Complaints about both men and women are rife. . . . This mutual blame which has deepened the antagonism between the sexes is something to be regretted and feared. God did not create man and women to hate each other but to love each other and to live together so the world would be populated. . . . Men say when we become educated we shall push them out of work and abandon the role for which God has created us. But isn't it rather men who have pushed women out of work? Before, women used to spin and to weave cloth for clothes, . . . but men invented machines for spinning and weaving. . . . In the past, women sewed clothes . . . but men invented the sewing machine. . . . Women . . . [made bread] with their own hands. Then men invented bakeries employing men. . . . I do not mean to denigrate these useful inventions which do a lot of our work. . . . Since male inventors and workers have taken away our work should we waste our time in idleness or seek other work to occupy us? Of course, we should do the latter. . . .

Men say to us categorically, "You women have been created for the house and we have been created to be breadwinners." Is this a God-given dictate? . . . No holy book has spelled it out. . . . Women in villages . . . help their men till the land and plant crops. Some women do the fertilizing, haul crops, lead animals, draw water for irrigation, and other chores. . . . Specialized work for each sex is a matter of convention, . . . not mandatory. . . . Women may not have to their credit great inventions but women have excelled in learning and the arts and politics. . . . Nothing irritates me more than when men claim they do not wish us to work because they wish to spare us the burden. We do not want condescension, we want respect. . . .

If we had been raised from childhood to go unveiled and if our men were ready for it I would approve of unveiling those who want it. But the nation is not ready for it now. . . . The imprisonment in the home of the Egyptian woman of the past is detrimental while the current freedom of the European is excessive. I cannot find a better model [than] today's Turkish woman. She falls between the two extremes and does not violate what Islam prescribes. She is a good example of decorum and modesty. . . . We should get a sound education, not merely acquire the trappings of a foreign language and rudiments of music. Our education should also include home management, health care, and childcare. . . . We shall advance when we give up idleness.

THINKING ABOUT THE READING

1. How does Bahithat evaluate women's roles and gender relations in Egypt?
2. What does her moderate advice to Egyptian women suggest about Egyptian society and the power of patriarchy?

Source: Bahithat al-Badiya, "A Lecture in the Club of the Umma Party, 1909," trans. by Ali Badran and Margot Badran, in *Opening the Gate: A Century of Arab Feminist Writing,* ed. by Margot Badran and Miriam Cooke, (Bloomington: Indiana University Press, 1990), pp. 228–238. Copyright © 1990 by Indiana University Press. Reprinted with permission of the publisher Indiana University Press.

---

their dreams proved impractical. The visionaries were ahead of their largely conservative populations.

By the later 1800s the challenges increased as Western technical and economic capabilities grew. Like European Enlightenment thinkers they often admired, some Muslim modernists struggled with how to reconcile faith and reason. They worried that the reforms needed to spur modernization required adopting Western philosophical and scientific theories, which were often contrary to Islamic beliefs about society, God, and nature. For example, capitalism undermined the Quranic prohibition against charging interest on loans, and the concept of human rights challenged slavery, still widespread in the nineteenth century Muslim world. Belief in equality contradicted the low status of Muslim women, and the Western notions of popular sovereignty and the nation troubled those who believed that only God could make laws or establish standards, which the state must then administer. Some reformers doubted whether Islam, with its universalistic idea of a multiethnic community guided by God, was compatible with nationalism, which emphasized the unity of one group of people defined by a common state. An Indian Muslim poet warned that, in the West, politics had dethroned religion. The Moroccan historian Ahmad ibn Khalid al-Nasri, quoted at the beginning of the chapter, feared that Western ideas tainted reforms. Writing of military cadets being trained in Western weapons and tactics, he worried that "they want to learn to fight to protect the faith, but they lose the faith in the process of learning how."[24] What role, the modernizers wondered, could clerics and the Shari'a have in a world of machines and nations?

Egypt-based thinkers took the lead in arguing the compatibility of Islam with modernization. The Persia-born activist and teacher Jamal al-Din al-Afghani (1838–1895), for example, preached innovative concepts of Islam. Al-Afghani favored modern knowledge and believed that reason and science were not contrary to Islam. In his view, rigid interpretations of Islam combined with the weight of local traditions contributed to Arab backwardness and stifled science. He lamented that, partly because of intolerance to new ideas, "the Arab world still remains buried in profound darkness."[25] Rational interpretations of Islam, he argued, would free Islamic societies for positive change in all areas of life. But al-Afghani also promoted resistance to Western power. His strong criticisms of British activity in Egypt and Persia as well as of Arab leaders he viewed as puppets led to his exile to Paris, where he published a weekly newspaper that promoted his views.

Another major modernist thinker, Muhammad Abduh (AHB-doo) (1849–1905), wanted to reform his native Egypt, to which he returned after some years in Beirut and Paris, and rejuvenate Islam. Although opposed to wholesale Westernization, Abduh admired major European thinkers; since Islam was reasonable, he argued, no knowledge, whatever its origin, was incompatible with the faith. In 1899 he was appointed to a top Islamic legal position, from which he promoted modernist Islam at Al-Azhar University, the most influential institution of higher education in the Middle East.

The Roots of Arab Nationalism

During the 1800s an Arab national consciousness developed in response to foreign domination by the Ottoman Turks and then by the British and French. There was even talk of a pan-Arab movement that would unite Arabs from Morocco to Iraq in a common struggle for political and cultural independence. But Arab identity was murky, divided by differences in religious and group affiliation. Arabs were predominantly Sunni Muslims, but some, particularly in the Persian Gulf and southern Iraq, were Shi'ites, and others, especially numerous in Egypt, Lebanon, and Syria, were Christians. They did not all have the same agenda or face the same problems. Even within the same society, Arabs were often divided into feuding patriarchal tribes that sometimes disliked rival tribes as much as they disliked Ottoman or European overlords, and some tribal leaders collaborated with such overlords to protect their own group. Indeed, many Arabs remained loyal to Ottoman rule. Furthermore, in 1876, hoping to defuse ethnic nationalism, the Ottomans introduced a new constitution and gave the Arabs seats in the legislature based on their large population in the empire. Thus a pan-Arab or pan-Muslim movement remained unrealistic.

Yet, some thoughtful Arabs began to envision self-governing Arab nations free of Ottoman or Western domination. Arab nationalism emerged from a literary and cultural movement in Syria in the later 1800s. Some of the pioneering writers were Lebanese Christians, one of whom published a poem calling on Arabs to "arise and awake." The writings of modernist Muslim scholars were also influential, although they posed a conflict between a pan-Islamic approach and a stress on Arab identity and language. Arab nationalist groups formed all over the Ottoman Empire in response to Ottoman centralization. For example, Abd-al-Rahman al-Kawabiki

(1849–1903), a Syrian who had studied in Egypt and Mecca, wrote witty books that criticized Ottoman despotism as contrary to Islam and suggested that Arabs should take leadership of their societies. Known for his hatred of intolerance and injustice and for making friends with Christians and Jews, al-Kawabiki had a pan-Arabist position. But before World War I the nationalist groups were small and had little public influence.

The Zionist Quest

While Middle Eastern societies struggled to respond to the Western challenge, the Zionist movement (see Chapter 19) introduced another challenge. In the Jewish ghettoes of eastern Europe, especially Poland and Russia, some thinkers began a quest for a homeland for their long persecuted people, who had been living in a diaspora scattered around the world since being forced by the Romans to leave Palestine nearly two millennia earlier. Prayers in Jewish synagogues for worshiping "next year in Jerusalem," the ancient Hebrew capital in Palestine, had endured for centuries. In fact, few European Jews spoke Hebrew, and many rejected Zionism, identifying instead with the country where they lived. But for others, Zionism functioned like nationalism, offering promises of a Jewish state. Looking deep into history, the first Zionist conference, held in Basel, Switzerland, in 1897, identified Palestine, then under Ottoman rule, as the potential Jewish homeland. For centuries some Jews had visited or settled in Palestine, and perhaps 20,000 lived there in 1870, but the Ottomans refused Zionist leaders permission to organize a massive settlement of Jews because many would likely come from the Ottomans' bitter enemy, Russia. This setback prompted the Zionist leader, the Hungarian-born journalist Theodor Herzl (1860–1904) to propose accepting a British offer for a temporary home in East Africa, but this plan was rejected by Russian Zionists.

Soon militant Zionists began promoting Jewish migration to Palestine without Ottoman permission or the support of European governments. By 1914 some 85,000 Jews, most of them newcomers from Russia and Poland, lived in Palestine alongside some 700,000 Arabs. Committed to creating a socialist society, the immigrants established dozens of Jewish collective farms, each known as a **kibbutz**, whose members shared their wealth and promoted Hebrew rather than a language such as the German-based Yiddish widely spoken by central and east European Jews. Immigrants also built the first largely Jewish city, Tel Aviv. Settlement in Palestine was funded by several international Zionist organizations, who bought land from absentee Arab and Turkish landowners. The Zionists had a flag, an anthem, and an active Jewish press. However, since Jewish aims and institutions had no legal recognition in Palestine, the stage was set for future conflict with Palestinian Arabs, who resented the newcomers and their plans to acquire more land for a Jewish state.

---

kibbutz A Jewish collective farm in Palestine that stressed the sharing of wealth.

SECTION SUMMARY

- One response to European pressure was Islamic revivalism, which advocated a pure form of Islam, favored a theocratic state, and sometimes used violence.

- Revivalism was most influential in Arabia, where militant followers of al-Wahhab and Ibn Saud took over a number of cities and eventually formed Saudi Arabia.

- Some intellectuals tried to modernize their religion, but modern European ideas such as equality continued to clash with Islamic practices such as slavery and the subjugation of women, and Western nationalism was at odds with the idea of a universal brotherhood under God.

- Some tried to inspire Arab nationalism, but religious divisions and rivalries made this a difficult task.

- Muslims were also challenged by European Zionists, who moved to Palestine in spite of Ottoman objections and also in spite of the Palestinian Arabs, setting the stage for future conflict.

 *Online Study Center* **ACE the Test**

 *Online Study Center* **Improve Your Grade** Flashcards

purify the religion and reject Western influence, while modernist reformers sought to adapt secular Western ideas to Islam in order to energize Muslim societies. Arab nationalist movements also arose but remained weak before World War I. Finally, Jewish Zionists posed a threat to Palestinian Arabs by beginning to settle in Palestine, where they hoped to build a Jewish state.

Key Terms

laager	Young Turks	Wahhabism
direct rule	Bahai	kibbutz
indirect rule	Islamic revivalism	

Suggested Reading

Books

Cleveland, William L. *A History of the Modern Middle East*, 2nd ed. Boulder: Westview, 2000. One of the best surveys of the era.

Hochschild, Adam. *King Leopold's Ghost: A Story of Greed, Terror, and Heroism in Colonial Africa.* Boston: Houghton Mifflin, 1998. A study of the Belgian Congo.

MacKinnon, Aran S. *The Making of South Africa: Culture and Politics.* Upper Saddle River, N.J.: Prentice-Hall, 2003. A comprehensive, readable survey.

Marsot, Afaf Lufti al-Sayyid. *Egypt in the Reign of Muhammad Ali.* New York: Cambridge University Press, 1984. An excellent study.

Northrup, David. *Africa's Discovery of Europe, 1450–1850.* New York: Oxford University Press, 2002. A sweeping survey.

Palmer, Alan. *The Decline and Fall of the Ottoman Empire.* New York: Barnes and Noble, 1992. A readable narrative.

Robinson, Francis. *The Cultural Atlas of the Islamic World Since 1500.* Oxford: Stonehenge, 1992. A useful compilation of materials.

Rodney, Walter. *How Europe Underdeveloped Africa.* Washington, D.C.: Howard University Press, 1982. Influential and controversial critique of the West in Africa by a Guyanese scholar.

Shillington, Kevin. *History of Africa,* rev. 2nd ed. New York: Palgrave Macmillan, 2005. A standard text with good coverage of this era.

Wheatcroft, Andrew. *The Ottomans.* New York: Viking, 1993. A lively discussion with particular attention to the governing elites.

Websites

Africa South of the Sahara (http://www-sul.stanford.edu/depts/ssrg/africa/). A valuable site that contains links relevant to African history.

History and Cultures of Africa (http://www.columbia.edu/cu/lweb/indiv/africa/cuvl/cult/html). Provides valuable links to relevant websites on African history.

Internet African History Sourcebook (http://www.fordham.edu/halsall/africa/africasbook.html). Contains useful information and documentary material on Africa.

Internet Islamic History Sourcebook (http://www.fordham.edu/halsall/islam/islamsbook.html). A comprehensive examination of Islamic history and culture.

Middle East Studies Internet Resources (http://www.columbia.edu/cu/lweb/indiv/mideast/cuvlm/index.html). A useful collection of links.

✦ Chapter Summary

Both sub-Saharan Africa and the Middle East underwent extensive change between 1750 and 1914. The ending of the trans-Atlantic slave trade opened Africa to exploration and trade by Europeans, and industrial Europe's need for resources and markets fostered a "scramble for Africa" as various Western nations colonized African societies, sometimes by military force against protracted resistance. The French colonized a vast area of West and Central Africa; Britain forged a large empire in West, Central, and East Africa; and the Germans, Belgians, and Italians also acquired African colonies. European settlers flocked to colonies in southern and eastern Africa, most notably South Africa, where they established white supremacist societies that exploited the African population. Colonialism created artificial, multiethnic countries. It also replaced subsistence agriculture with cash crop farming, plantations, and mineral exploitation while enmeshing Africa in the world economy as a supplier of natural resources. Africans mounted strikes and rebellions against colonial enterprises and governments, but all such efforts were eventually defeated.

The Middle East also experienced European imperialism. The Ottoman Empire attempted to stall its decline with Western-style reforms, but it still lost territory and influence over some provinces. Egypt attempted an ambitious modernization program, but it proved inadequate to prevent British colonization. In Persia, Western economic and political influence sparked reforms that were later rejected by Persian conservatives. After suppressing resistance, France and Italy colonized North Africa, and French settlers displaced Algerians from valuable land. In response to these changes, some Muslims, most notably the Wahhabis, pursued a revivalist strategy to

CHAPTER 22

South Asia, Southeast Asia, and Colonization, 1750–1914

Online Study Center

This icon will direct you to interactive activities and study materials on the website: college.hmco.com/pic/lockard1e

Dipenegara This painting shows Prince Dipenegara, a Javanese aristocrat who led a revolt against the Dutch colonizers in the 1820s, reading, with several attendants at hand.
(Universiteits-Bibliotheek, Leiden. Snouk Hurgronje Collection, Codex Orientales 7398)

Rice fields are littered with our battle-killed; blood flows or lies in pools, stains hills and streams. [French] Troops bluster on and grab our land, our towns, roaring and stirring dust to dim the skies. A scholar with no talent and no power, could I redress a world turned upside down?

PROTEST BY VIETNAMESE POET NGUYEN DINH CHIEU AGAINST
FRENCH CONQUEST, LATE NINETEENTH CENTURY[1]

Frustrated by the Vietnamese emperor's refusal to liberalize trade relations with Western nations and protect Christian missionaries, the French, seeking to expand their empire in Asia, attacked Vietnam with military force in 1858 and over the next three decades conquered the country against determined resistance. A blind Vietnamese poet, Nguyen Dinh Chieu (NEW-yin dinh chew) (1822–1888), became a symbol of the Vietnamese resistance to the French when he wrote an oration honoring the fallen Vietnamese soldiers after a heroic defense in a battle in 1862: "You preferred to die fighting the enemy, and return to our ancestors in glory rather than survive in submission to the [Westerners] and share your miserable life with barbarians." The French retaliated by seizing Chieu's land and property. The poet remained unbowed, refusing to use Western products such as soap powder and forbidding his children to learn the romanized Vietnamese alphabet developed by French Catholic missionaries. In verse spread by word of mouth and painstakingly copied manuscripts distributed throughout the land, Chieu rallied opposition. He heaped scorn on his countrymen who collaborated with the French occupiers and advised them to maintain the struggle for independence: "I had rather face unending darkness, Than see the country tortured. Everyone will rejoice in seeing the West wind [colonialism], Vanish from [Vietnam's] mountains and rivers."[2]

Chieu had the talents and background to rally the Vietnamese against a French occupation. The son of a mandarin in southern Vietnam, he overcame the handicaps of blindness to become a physician, scholar, teacher, and renowned writer and bard, famous for his epic poems sung in the streets. These poems extolled the love of country, friendship, marital fidelity, family loyalty, scholarship, and the military arts. Chieu earned admiration for his loyalty to family, king, and country even if his blindness prevented him from taking up arms. He rejected the French offer of a financial subsidy and the return of his family land if he would rally to their cause. Today the Vietnamese continue to revere the stirring poems Chieu composed to aid the resistance to the French.

By providing deadly new weapons and increasing the need for resources and markets, the Industrial Revolution in Europe and North America (see Chapters 19–20) set in motion an intensive Western penetration of other regions, including India (the major society of South Asia) and Southeast Asia. With enhanced military, economic, and technological power to assert their will, a few Western nations brought all southern and eastern Asia under direct colonial or indirect neocolonial control, with the single exception of Japan. Western domination destroyed traditional Asian political systems, reoriented Asian economies, and posed challenges for societies and their world-views, including the Vietnamese whom Nguyen Dinh Chieu attempted to rally.

Between 1750 and 1914 the principal colonizers in Asia were Britain, France, the Netherlands, and the United States, following the Portuguese and Spanish, who had established footholds in the Early Modern Era. The British, expanding their influence around the world, had by 1850 completed their conquest of India, and during the 1800s Britain, France, and other Western powers, after scrambling for colonies in Southeast Asia, eventually ruled all the societies except for Siam (Thailand). Since Western domination occurred while Western Europeans were at the high point of their military and industrial development and at the peak of their cultural arrogance, colonialism proved a transforming experience. It linked these regions more closely than ever to a European-dominated world economy and transmitted to the colonies the ideas and technologies of Western life. In turn, Asian workers produced resources that spurred Western economic growth.

Asians struggled with some success to reshape their relationship with the West. The unyielding resistance to imperialism exemplified by Nguyen Dinh Chieu gave hope to colonized people in Africa and the Middle East. Furthermore, the exchange of ideas was not all one way: Asian religions and arts attracted interest in the West and even developed a small following there. While European power was too great to be overthrown in this period, resentment against colonialism simmered for decades, and eventually the Indians, Vietnamese, and Filipinos, among others, used the Western concept of nationalism to assert the rights of their peoples for self-determination. After World War II the colonial systems finally ended, and the peoples of South and Southeast Asia regained their independence.

FOCUS QUESTIONS

1. How and why did Britain extend its control throughout India?
2. How did colonialism transform the Indian economy and foster new ideas in India?
3. How did the Western nations expand their control of Southeast Asia?
4. What were the major political, economic, and social consequences of colonialism in Southeast Asia?

◆ Forming British India

How and why did Britain extend its control throughout India?

By the early 1700s the Muslim Mughals who ruled much of India (see Chapter 18) were in steep decline, challenged by both Indians and Europeans. In the sixteenth and seventeenth

centuries the splendor of the Mughal court and India's valuable exports had attracted the Portuguese, Dutch, and British. As the Mughals lost power, the British took advantage of a fragmented India and began their conquest of the subcontinent in the mid-1700s, thus beginning the era of Western dominance throughout Asia. By the mid-1800s Britain controlled both India and the island of Sri Lanka. British conquest was in keeping with the history of South Asia, which had often

C H R O N O L O G Y		
	South Asia	**Southeast Asia**
1750	**1757** Battle of Plassey	**1788–1802** Tayson rule in Vietnam
1800	**1802** British colonization of Sri Lanka	**1819** British colony in Singapore
		1824–1886 Anglo-Burman Wars
1850	**1850** Completion of British India	**1858–1884** French conquest of Vietnam
	1857–1858 Indian Rebellion	**1898–1902** United States conquest of Philippines
	1885 Indian National Congress	
1900		

been conquered by outsiders from Western and Central Asia. But unlike the Asian invaders, who often became assimilated into Indian society by adopting Hinduism or Buddhism or spreading Islam, the British maintained their own separate identity and cultural traditions.

Indian Trade, the West, and Mughal Decline

Europeans had long coveted South Asia for its spices and textiles, which had been a part of regional commerce for millennia. Even today, small, single-masted sailing barges ply the coastline between western India, the Persian Gulf, and East Africa, continuing the ancient exchange of merchandise with the coming and going of monsoon winds. The Portuguese were the first Europeans to trade directly with India. In 1498 they established a base at Goa (GO-uh), and for a century they sought to control the trade from India and Southeast Asia to the West.

Soon other European traders arrived, and between 1500 and 1750 European powers controlled some of the Indian Ocean maritime trade; however, they conquered or gained control of only a few scattered outposts in South Asia. The Dutch challenged the Portuguese for domination of regional trade and eventually destroyed Portuguese power in South and Southeast Asia, although Goa remained a Portuguese colony until 1961. The Dutch concentrated on Sri Lanka and, farther east, Indonesia. The British also became active in South Asia. By 1696 the British East India Company possessed three fortified trading stations in India: at the towns of Calcutta in Bengal, Madras (today known as Chennai) on the southeastern coast, and Bombay (today called Mumbai) on the west coast. Meanwhile, the French formed a small colony in Pondicherry, a town near the British base at Madras, and became involved in regional politics.

Europeans encountered a fragmenting India. By 1750 the Mughals were corrupt and weak since many Indians had already broken away from Mughal control. Emperors might sit on the spectacular Peacock Throne in Delhi's Red Fort—a huge complex of royal apartments, government offices, factories, and military barracks and home to thousands of officials, servants, royal concubines, and royal family members—but the Mughal rulers had little actual power, often consoling themselves with the large royal harem or smoking opium. During the later 1700s Mughal factions quarreled and different rivals claimed the throne, but the Mughal government controlled little beyond Delhi, and the countryside became increasingly disorderly. Without a powerful imperial state to control it, Indian society, with its diverse cultures, castes, languages, regions, and religions, lacked strong national cohesion and was unable to effectively resist European encroachments.

With the Mughals losing their grip, groups like the **Marathas** (muh-RAH-tuhs) and the Sikhs built powerful new states. The Marathas were a loosely knit confederacy led by Hindu warriors from west-central India, and the Sikhs were a religious minority in northwest India; both of these groups competed with new Muslim states that were often set up by Mughal governors whose allegiance to the Mughal emperor was nominal. By 1800 the Marathas ruled much of western India, and the Sikhs, under their leader, the dynamic Ranjit Singh (RUN-ji SING) (1780–1839), had conquered the Punjab and Kashmir in the northwest. Mounted on sturdy ponies, the Marathas developed an appetite for plunder and became feared for their quick raids deep into central India against helpless Mughal armies. The various Indian states employed Europeans to train and lead their armies. In southern India, the Mughal collapse left a power vacuum that both Britain and France attempted to fill by supporting their respective Indian allies in the struggle for regional advantage. Ultimately, however, none of the rising Indian states, including the Marathas and Sikhs, gained enough power, acquired enough weapons, or forged enough cooperation to repulse the West.

Marathas A loosely knit confederacy led by Hindu warriors from west-central India; one of several groups that challenged British domination after the decline of the Mughals.

The Founding of British India

The British posed the gravest challenge to India, especially in Bengal, India's richest and most populous region. Bengal was ruled by Muslim governors who mostly ignored the Mughal government in Delhi. When local Indian governments resisted an expansion of the British presence into their lands, the British resorted to military force. In the mid-1700s the Bengali ruler, Aliverdi Khan (r. 1740–1756), had left British trade unmolested. But his successor, Siraja Dowlah (see-RAH-ja DOW-luh) (ca. 1732–1757), considered the British bothersome leeches on his land's riches. Soon after becoming ruler, Dowlah alienated Western merchants and even his own more cautious officials, and in 1757 he rashly attacked British trading stations. After capturing the main station, Calcutta, Dowlah's forces placed 146 captured British men, women, and children in a crowded jail known as the **Black Hole of Calcutta**. The next day only 23 staggered out, the rest having died from suffocation and dehydration. Siraja Dowlah was blamed for the atrocity, though he may not have been personally responsible for it.

Their rage and determination now fired, the British dispatched a force under Robert Clive (1725–1774) to regain Britain's holdings. A former clerk turned into a daring war strategist, the ambitious Clive and his 3,200 soldiers defeated some 50,000 Bengali troops at the Battle of Plassey in 1757 and recaptured Calcutta, marking the dawn of the British epic in India (see Chronology: South Asia, 1750–1914). Clive allied with Hindu bankers and Muslim nobles unhappy with Siraja Dowlah, who was executed, and by 1764 he controlled Bengal.

The British government, following a policy of mercantilism to acquire wealth for the state, allowed the British East India Company (often known as "the Company") to govern Bengal and other parts of India, as they were acquired, and to exploit the inhabitants while sharing the profits with the British government. The British showed a lust for riches equal to that of the Spanish conquistadors in the 1500s. As governor of Bengal (1758–1760, 1764–1767) for the Company, Clive launched an era of organized plunder, allowing British merchants and officials gradually to drain Bengal of its wealth while Company officials, including Clive, lived like kings in Calcutta. Praised by British political leaders and celebrated in the press and schoolboy stories, Clive became the idol of every young Englishman who dreamed of marching to glory and wealth via India's battlefields and bazaars. After 1760 the cry of "Go East," inspired by Clive's rags-to-riches story, fueled British imperialist ambitions. As they expanded their control of more Indian territory, the British became a new high caste, and, much like the former Mughal rulers, expected the Indians to serve them. Eventually the British Parliament accused Clive

Black Hole of Calcutta A crowded jail in India where over a hundred British prisoners of a hostile Bengali ruler died from suffocation and dehydration in 1757. This event precipitated the beginning of British use of force in India.

CHRONOLOGY

South Asia, 1750–1914

1744–1761	Anglo-French struggle for Coromandel coast
1757	Battle of Plassey
1764	British acquisition of Bengal
1774–1778	Warren Hastings governor of Bengal
1793	New land policy in Bengal
1799	British defeat of Mysore
1802	British colonization of Sri Lanka
1816	British protectorate over Nepal
1819	British occupation of all Maratha lands
1820s	Beginning of British Westernization policy
1839–1842	First Anglo-Afghan War
1849	British defeat of Sikhs in Punjab
1850	Completion of British India
1857–1858	Indian rebellion
1858	Introduction of colonial system in India
1877	Founding of Muslim college at Aligarh
1878–1880	Second Anglo-Afghan War
1885	Formation of Indian National Congress
1903	British invasion of Tibet
1906	Formation of Indian Muslim League

of corruption and fraud. Although cleared of the charges, a depressed Clive committed suicide at the age of forty-nine.

To transform the economic chaos left by Clive into a more profitable order and to consolidate the British position, the Company appointed Warren Hastings to serve as governor-general (1774–1778) of Bengal. Hastings redesigned the revenue system, made treaty alliances, and also pursued outright annexations to safeguard the British bases. A scholarly man who was influenced by Enlightenment thought, he also had sympathy for India. Hastings saw his task as a holding operation of limited ambitions, arguing that he hoped to never see the whole of India colonized. In contrast to other British officials, Hastings respected the people he governed, advising one of his successors that, like the English, many Indians had a strong intellect, a sound integrity, and honorable feelings and should be treated as participants in society, enjoying the same equal rights as the English colonizers. His successors, however, often disregarded his advice.

Clive Meets Indian Leaders
In this painting, Robert Clive meets the new Bengali official, Mir Jafir, after the British victory in the 1757 Battle of Plassey. Clive supported Mir Jafir's seizure of power from the anti-British leader, Siraja Dowlah.
(National Portrait Gallery, London)

Expanding British India

Success in Bengal fueled further British expansion in the subcontinent. In 1773 the British government gave the Company authority to administer all British-controlled Indian territories. Nonetheless, the Company still saw its role as mainly commercial. In 1794 the British Parliament forbade further annexation and declared territorial expansion to be repugnant to the honor and the policy of the nation. But despite the ban, governor-generals after Hastings continued to authorize the occupation of more areas of India, often against opposition, to prevent trade disruption or to counteract rival European nations. Some imperialists talked about Britain's sacred trust to reshape the world, viewing the extension of British authority—and with it British culture, Christianity, and free trade policies—as a great blessing for Asians.

The reality, however, was often something other than a blessing. In acquiring more Indian territory, the British mixed military force, extortion, bribery, and manipulation. Because India contained much political, linguistic, and religious diversity, British agents and merchants could play off one region against another, Hindu against Muslim. The British were aided by Indian collaborators, especially businessmen eager to increase their connections to the world market. Employing superior weapons and disciplined military forces, the British placed the resistance, however spirited, at a huge disadvantage. From India's warrior and peasant castes, mostly Hindus but also

some Muslims, they recruited mercenary soldiers, known as **sepoys**, under the command of British officers. By 1857 there were nearly 200,000 sepoy troops in the Company military force, greatly outnumbering the 10,000 British officers and soldiers.

The French initially provided the major European roadblock to British expansion in India. European wars involving the British and French were extended into an imperial contest for India that focused on India's southeastern Coromandel coast from 1744 to 1761. Victory there over the French soon led the British into actions against Indian states outside their control. One of the most formidable foes was Mysore (my-SORE), a mostly Hindu state in south-central India. Mysore gained prominence under Haidar Ali Khan (r. 1761–1782), a devout Muslim and French ally who modeled his army on Western lines. A brilliant military strategist of guerrilla war, Haidar warned the British, "I will march your troops until their legs swell to the size of their bodies. You shall not have a blade of grass, nor a drop of water."[3] Only in 1799, after twenty years of bloody wars, was Mysore defeated.

During the late 1700s and early 1800s the British imposed their control over much of western, central, and northern India. The Maratha confederacy, which controlled much of western and central India, was divided by rivalries. In 1805 the

---

sepoys Mercenary soldiers recruited among the warrior and peasant castes by the British in India.

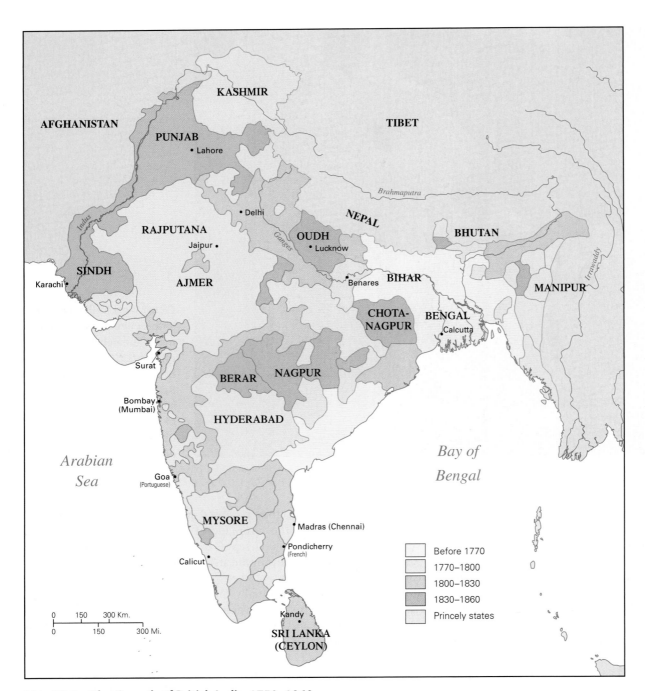

Map 22.1 The Growth of British India, 1750–1860
Gradually expanding control from their bases at Calcutta, Madras, and Bombay, the British completed
their military conquest of the final holdout states by the 1850s.

Online Study Center **Improve Your Grade** Interactive Map: India, 1707–1805

British occupied the Marathas' northern territories and entered Delhi, where they deposed the aged and powerless
Mughal emperor. They took the remaining Maratha lands in
1819. They then turned their attention to the states of northwest India, which were dominated by rajputs (RAHJ-putz) and
Sikhs. The rajputs, a Hindu warrior caste, were no longer the
feared fighters they had been in earlier centuries and now
signed treaties giving Britain claims on their lands. Only the

Sikhs remained a threat to the British. But the death of the Sikh
leader, Ranjit Singh, in 1839 shattered the Sikhs' unity and undermined their powerful military state. In 1849, after a series of
bloody British-Sikh wars, Britain finally triumphed. Britain
then stationed troops in the many small independent princi-
palities scattered around India, thus turning them into de-
pendencies. By 1850, the British ruled all Indians directly or
through princes who collaborated with them (see Map 22.1).

Britain and India's Neighbors

British expansion in India eventually led to interventions in neighboring societies, including Sri Lanka, the large, fertile island just south of India that the British called Ceylon. Fearing that the French might establish a base there, the British pursued a more aggressive policy in Sri Lanka. In 1796 they acquired the territory the Dutch had held since the 1630s, and in 1802 they declared their Sri Lankan holdings a crown colony. However, they only controlled the entire island after conquering the last remaining Sri Lankan kingdom, Kandy, in 1815. The British transformed Sri Lanka, seizing rice-growing land from peasants to set up coffee, tea, and rubber plantations and recruiting Tamil-speaking workers from southeast India as laborers. Cultivating crops such as rubber and tea was enormously time-consuming, and the Tamil workers on the Sri Lankan estates were poorly paid and enjoyed little time for leisure. By 1911 the Tamil laborers and their families made up 11 percent of the Sri Lankan population. Largely isolated on plantations, the Tamils maintained their own customs, language, and Hindu religion and had little contact with Sri Lanka's majority population, the Buddhist Sinhalese. By the end of the 1800s some educated Sinhalese, having turned to nationalism, considered both the British and the Tamils unwanted aliens. Sinhalese-Tamil tensions simmered and, after independence, led to a long civil war in Sri Lanka.

Fearing that the Russians, who were conquering Muslim Central Asia, intended to expand into South Asia by land, the British also attempted to secure India's land borders. First they turned to Nepal, a kingdom just north of India in the Himalayan Mountains. Nepal's Hindu ruling caste, the gurkhas (GORE-kuhz), were fierce fighters who had sometimes invaded north India. British victory over the gurkhas in 1814–1816 turned Nepal into a British protectorate, in which the British served as advisers to the government while the gurkha monarchy remained in power. Soldiers recruited from Nepal, also known as gurkhas, became a special military force for Britain and were employed on battlefields around the world in support of British objectives.

Afghanistan, a mountainous region just west of India, seemed the most vulnerable to Russian expansion. An ethnically diverse region that had enjoyed only short periods of political unity, Afghanistan seemed an unlikely candidate to become a viable independent state. However, Afghans, among them the devoutly Islamic Pashtun tribes in the south, possessed the fighting skills to oppose Europeans bent on conquest. To establish some political influence, the British twice invaded Afghanistan and occupied the major eastern city, Kabul, but they faltered against fierce resistance by Pashtun fighters. In the first Afghan War (1839–1842), Pashtuns massacred most of the 12,000 retreating British and sepoy troops and the British civilians, including women and children, who had accompanied them on what they naively thought would be a long-term occupation. Undeterred, the British fought the second Afghan War (1878–1880) and replaced a Pashtun leader who favored the Russians with one who was pro-British and who gave Britain control of Afghanistan's foreign affairs. With an ally as ruler, the British concluded that Afghanistan could not be annexed by military force.

India Under the East India Company

The British East India Company gradually tightened its control of India and began to impose Western values on Indians. After Hastings, the Company shifted from sharing government with local rulers to becoming the sole power and administering India through British officials. In typically arrogant colonial language that ignored centuries of Indian achievements, Sir Thomas Munro, governor of Madras from 1820 to 1827, explained the imperial mission to nurture a new India. He claimed that the British must maintain their rule until the

British East India Company Court
This painted wood model shows an Indian court presided over by an official of the British East India Company. (Courtesy of the Trustees of the Victoria & Albert Museum)

Indians, sometime in the distant future, abandoned their "superstitions" and became "enlightened" enough to govern themselves. Reflecting these views, the Company promoted a policy of **Westernization**, a deliberate attempt to spread Western culture and ideas, which led to some challenges to Indian culture and imposed economic policies that affected rural society.

Westernization

The Company policy of Westernization to change India began in the 1820s. Protestant movements were especially influential in Britain in this era, and Christian evangelism influenced the reform ideas proposed for India. One devout Company director argued that Britain must diffuse Christian teachings among Indians, whom he described as sunk in darkness and misery. British officials, often disregarding Indian religious and cultural sensitivities, encouraged Christian missions and tried to ban customs they disliked. Many Indians rejoiced when they banned *sati*, the northern custom of widows throwing themselves on their husband's funeral pyre. But there was less Indian enthusiasm for British attempts to tinker with Muslim and Hindu law codes that were rooted in religious beliefs.

The British also established schools that taught in English rather than an Indian language. This policy was spurred by Lord Macaulay (1800–1859), a reformer and firm believer in Western cultural superiority who considered it pointless to teach Indian languages, declaring in 1832 that "a single shelf of a good European library is worth the whole native literature of India and Arabia." Consequently, Macaulay, reflecting racist views then current in the West, proposed creating "a class of persons Indian in blood and color but English in taste, opinions, morals and intellect."[4] Indians often criticized the insistence on English as the language of education and considered it a threat to both Hindu and Muslim customs. Yet some Indians welcomed the English-medium schools because they opened Indian students to a wider world, and it was Indians themselves who formed the first English-medium institution of higher education, the Hindu College in Calcutta, in 1818.

Not all the British in India found Indian culture to be backward. Some British admirers of Indian culture, reflecting what came to be called **Orientalism**, showed a scholarly interest in India and its history and attempted to gain further knowledge about the Hindu classical age. Warren Hastings, for example, encouraged the study of Indian culture, languages, and literature. A scholar as well as an administrator and soldier, he preferred reading the European and Asian languages he had mastered—Greek, Latin, Persian, and Urdu—to pursuing his official duties. One of his officials, William Jones (1746–1794), who mastered Arabic, Persian, and Sanskrit, became the most influential Orientalist scholar, but his views,

however respectful of India, often reflected an attempt to fit India into Western concepts of history and religion. Knowing that Christians and Jews considered the Bible to reflect historical truth, Jones treated Vedic texts from ancient times as an accurate historical record rather than as religious teachings and argued that Sanskrit was the original source for other Indo-European languages. He also claimed that the classical Greeks, such as the mathematician Pythagoras and the philosopher Plato, derived their theories from the same ancient source as the classical Indian sages. Jones's ideas shaped European scholarly understanding of Indian history for generations. In addition, several religious movements based on Hindu concepts, such as reincarnation, gained a small following in the West, especially in Britain. Yet by the later 1800s Orientalist cosmopolitanism and respect had largely been replaced by British nationalism and intolerance.

The encounter between India and the West, as well as the British reforms, also fostered a Hindu social reform movement and philosophical renaissance under the brilliant leadership of the Bengali scholar Ram Mohan Roy (1772–1833). After seeing his sister burn to death on a funeral pyre, and concerned about what he saw as the harmful side of customs such as *sati* and caste divisions, Roy began a British-Indian dialogue in hopes of adopting certain Western ways to reform and strengthen Hinduism. To better understand the world by studying non-Hindu religions, Roy mastered their source languages—Hebrew and Greek for Christianity, Arabic and Persian for Islam—and thus became the world's first modern scholar of comparative religion. Roy and his followers attempted to create a synthesis of the best in Hinduism and Christianity. Roy also founded secondary schools, newspapers, and an organization working for reform of Hindu society and beliefs. Viewing the British positively as promoters of knowledge and liberty, Roy wanted Britain to promote modernization while also seeking Indian advice.

British Land Policy

In order to make India more profitable, the British East India Company built roads, railroads, and irrigation systems; most significantly for rural Indians, they revised the land revenue collection, the principal source of public finance, a change that reshaped peasant society. The British viewed Indian rural society as stagnant, unable to provide the tax revenues needed to support British administration. In precolonial times, most Indians, living in self-sufficient villages that were governed by the family and caste, had enjoyed a measure of social stability. Despite high taxes, bandits, and sometimes warfare, Indian villages generally provided psychological and some economic security by promoting cooperation among their residents. Land belonged to the royal families, but peasants had the hereditary right to use it. British observers recognized the village system as self-sufficient and stable over time. One wrote that "the village communities [have] everything they want within themselves. They seem to last when nothing else lasts. Dynasty after dynasty tumbles down; but the village communities remain the same."[5]

Westernization A deliberate attempt to spread Western culture and ideas.

Orientalism A scholarly interest among British officials in India and its history that prompted some to rediscover the Hindu classical age.

Indian Railroad Train   The railroads built during British rule carried both resources and passengers. This lithograph shows a Sikh signalman at the station and a train conveying Indian women and a European.   (Courtesy of the Trustees of the Victoria & Albert Museum)

Yet, while admiring this stability, Company officials decided that a different form of land ownership would provide the easiest way to gain revenues. They therefore began collecting taxes from farmers in money rather than, as had been common for centuries, a portion of the crop. In 1793 British officials in Bengal, inspired by the propertied aristocracy that once owned much of England's land, converted the Mughal revenue collectors, or **zamindars**, into landlords, who, in addition to their other tax obligations, were given the rights to buy and sell land on the understanding that they paid additional high taxes whenever they did so. Under this system, peasant farmers became tenants to landlords and were denied their hereditary rights to use the land. Many landlords sold their land rights at a good profit to businessmen, often city dwellers, who became absentee landlords and grew rich from the crops grown by the peasants. In Madras, however, a somewhat different system appeared. The Madras governor, Sir Thomas Munro, mistakenly believed that the peasants were or could be converted into profit-seeking individualists like English farmers. In his system the peasant farmer dealt directly with the government but had to pay tax in cash and could be evicted for nonpayment.

Under both systems, the village economy was changed from a barter economy, in which villagers such as barbers, carpenters, and farmers agreed to exchange their services or products with each other for their mutual benefit, to a money economy. Since some villagers earned more money, the cash-based system sacrificed a large measure of the stability and security peasants had once enjoyed. The emphasis on money benefited a moneylender caste that came to control much of the land. The Company also encouraged a switch from food crops to cash crops such as opium, coffee, rubber, tea, and cotton, often grown on plantations rather than peasant farms.

zamindars   Mughal revenue collectors that the British turned into landlords who were given the rights to buy and sell land.

Resistance: The 1857 Revolt

In spite of Indian reform movements such as Roy's, Indians usually resented the British East India Company's Westernization and its associated economic policies. Many once prosperous families had lost land or become indebted as a result of British land policies and the courts that enforced laws based on British traditions, and these losses fueled hostility. Even some British officials recognized that land sales and the revenue system were destroying the peasant class. As a result of such grievances, local revolts punctuated British rule. Furthermore, sepoys increasingly resented the aggressive attempts of British officers to convert them to Christianity. The sepoys stationed in Bengal were particularly offended by new army rifle cartridges, which had to be bitten off with the teeth before being rammed down the gun barrel. What outraged the soldiers was the rumor, probably true, that the cartridges were greased with beef and pork fat, violating the religious dietary prohibitions of both cow-revering Hindus and pork-avoiding Muslims.

In 1857 one revolt, sparked by sepoy outrage, spread rapidly and offered a serious challenge to British authority. The British called it the Indian Mutiny, and Indian nationalists later termed it the first War of Independence. The revolt began among sepoys in the army and was soon supported by peasant and Muslim uprisings. A few members of Hindu and Muslim princely families also joined the rebel cause. Among them was the widow of the Maratha ruler of Jhansi, a small state recently annexed by the British. The Rani (queen) of Jhansi led her troops into battle dressed as a man. Historians still debate whether the revolt was truly "national," since it was confined largely to north and northeast India. Because no rebel leaders envisioned a unified Indian nation, British observers argued that the rebels had limited and selfish goals. But broad groups of the population had perceived their customs and religions threatened by British policies. Some rebel leaders attempted to unite Hindus and Muslims by calling for a joint defense of their religions against their common British enemy.

The rebels captured Delhi and besieged several cities, but they could not hold them for long. The desperate struggle involved ruthless tactics; both sides committed massacres. For example, rebels murdered a thousand British residents when they occupied the city of Kanpur. On the other side, when British troops recaptured Delhi, they became berserk and engaged in widespread raping, pillaging, and killing. The Muslim poet Ghalib mourned: "Here is a vast ocean of blood before me. Thousands of my friends are dead. Perhaps none is left even to shed tears upon my death."[6] The rebellion had also attracted some conservatives who hoped to restore the old Mughal order. The anti-British sentiment was not widespread enough, however, to overcome the rebels' problems: inadequate arms, weak communications, and lack of a unified command structure. In addition, the rebels received no support from people in other parts of India, and they had no strategy for a national revolt. Linguistic, religious, cultural, and regional fragmentation made a united Indian opposition impossible. When the British captured the last rebel fort, held by the Rani of Jhansi, in 1858, she was killed and the rebellion collapsed, although a few small rebel groups fought skirmishes with the British until 1860.

SECTION SUMMARY

- Fragmented after the decline of the Mughals, India was unable to resist encroachment by the Portuguese, Dutch, British, and French.

- In reaction to the Black Hole of Calcutta, the British under Robert Clive took over Bengal and proceeded to plunder its riches; though his successor, Warren Hastings, was more respectful, many governor-generals disregarded Indians' rights.

- Though initially opposed by the French, the British East India Company gradually expanded its control over India by employing local collaborators and playing groups off against each other, and by 1850 Britain controlled all of India.

- The British expanded into Sri Lanka, where they imported Tamils to work on the tea plantations; into Nepal, where they recruited effective soldiers; and into Afghanistan, where they met fierce resistance but ultimately installed a friendly ruler.

- Many British tried to make Indians more Western by abolishing customs they considered backward, while others became interested in studying traditional Indian teachings.

- By having peasants pay their taxes in cash rather than in crops, the British began to shift India from a barter economy to a money economy, a change that undermined centuries of rural stability.

- Though some Indians supported Westernization, periodic revolts occurred, and in 1857 the sepoys began a large rebellion that led to much bloodshed and eventually Indian defeat.

The Reshaping of Indian Society

How did colonialism transform the Indian economy and foster new ideas in India?

The 1857 revolt prompted the British to replace the British East India Company government with direct colonial rule. The British felt betrayed by the rebels, but some officials understood the causes of the revolt, viewing the troubles as symptoms of deeper discontents that needed to be addressed. To move in that direction, the 1858 Government of India Act transferred sovereignty to the British monarch. In 1876 Queen Victoria was proclaimed Empress of India, head of the government known as the British *Raj*, named for the ancient title of Hindu kings. India became the brightest "jewel in the imperial crown," a source of fabulous wealth. The policies pursued by the British Raj reshaped Indian society, sparking new economic, intellectual, and social patterns and eventually inspiring movements reflecting a new sense of the Indian nation.

Colonial Government and Education

The British Raj bore many similarities to the Mughal system it had replaced. The top British officials, the viceroys, lived, like Mughal emperors, in splendor in Delhi. The British made efforts to win Indian support by pomp and circumstance, including Mughal-style ceremonies and building a new capital at New Delhi, next to the old Mughal capital of Delhi, with gigantic architecture dwarfing even the monuments of the Mughals. The British built palatial mansions, museums, schools, universities, and city halls. Yet, while they usually lived well, many British residents also faced health problems from the tropical heat and from diseases such as malaria. After 1857 British officials mistrusted Indians but, like the Mughals before them, also viewed the traditional princes, both Hindu and Muslim, as sources of support whose positions had to be preserved. The princes were allowed to keep their privileges and palaces in exchange for promoting acceptance of British policies.

Borrowing Mughal practices, the British ruled through a mix of good communications, exploitation of Hindu-Muslim rivalries, and military force. The British connected India with a network of roads, bridges, and railways, and by 1900 India had over 25,000 miles of track, the fourth largest rail system in the world. The British also deliberately pitted the Hindu majority against the Muslim minority by favoring one or the other group in law, language, and custom. For example, Hindus protested that the main Muslim language, Urdu, was used in many North Indian courts and that Muslim butchers were allowed to kill cows, considered sacred animals by Hindus. The British divide-and-rule policy helped maintain British power but also exacerbated hatreds that remain today. Local revenue supported a huge army of 200,000 men, mostly Indian volunteers, who were needed to keep the peace in India and fight British battles abroad.

In their efforts to rule, the British also introduced policies at variance with Mughal practice, among them discrimination against Indians. The British typically believed that Western colonialism improved Asian and African societies. Rudyard Kipling (1865–1936), a Bombay-born, Britain-educated English poet and novelist, reflected this view in his writings: "Take up the White Man's burden—Send forth the best ye breed— Go, bind your sons in exile. To serve your captives' need."[7] Some policies reflected racism. Much like colonized Africans, Indians were excluded from European-only clubs and parks as well as high positions in the bureaucracy, and enjoyed no real power or influence. Recognizing the pervasive discrimination, the Raj announced but did not always implement reforms.

Colonial Britain also concerned itself with border security and Russian ambitions. Frontier policy often relied on diplomacy but sometimes involved military aggression. For example, as part of what Kipling called the "Great Game" of strategic rivalry with Russia, Britain invaded Tibet in 1903, prompting Tibetan leaders to agree not to concede territory to Russia or any other foreign power. Lord Curzon (viceroy from 1899 to 1905) remarked that "we do not want their country. It would be madness for us to cross the Himalayas and to occupy it. But it is important that no one else should seize it, and that it should be turned into a sort of buffer state between the Russian and Indian Empires."[8]

The Raj continued the Westernization policy of the British East India Company, promoting British and often Christian values through an expanded English-medium education system. Thanks to these schools, English became the common language for educated Indians. However, only a privileged minority, mostly drawn from higher-caste Hindus, could afford to send their children, mostly boys, to the English schools. By 1911 only 11 percent of men and 1 percent of women were literate in any language.

Nonetheless, the schools fostered change by introducing new ideas. A small minority of Indians (less than 2 percent) had converted to Christianity by 1911. More importantly, an English-educated middle class emerged, with a taste for European products and ideas. These Indians sent their sons and a few daughters to British universities, where their children often studied, for the first time, Indian history and also learned about the ideas of Western political liberalism. Notions like "freedom" and "self-determination of peoples" learned in European universities stood in sharp contrast to conditions in India. The returning students asked why the British did not practice such ideas in their colony. As a result, British educational and political institutions fostered an Indian nationalist movement. The growing British-educated professional class organized social, professional, and political bodies concerned with improving Indian life and acquiring more influence in government.

Economic Transformation

The British also transformed the Indian economy. Before 1700 Mughal India had been an economic powerhouse and manufacturing center, and the world leader in producing cotton textiles. India still produced a quarter of all world manufactured goods in 1750. The disparity between urban and rural wealth was narrower than in most societies. However, two centuries later, conditions had changed. Many historians believe that British policies, which were designed to drain India of its wealth to benefit Britain, harmed the Indian economy. In their view, British land policies commercialized agriculture while tax and tariff policies diminished the existing manufacturing.

As already mentioned, British land policies greatly affected the rural economy and peasant life. The land tax system first introduced by the British East India Company in parts of India exploited the peasantry. By turning once self-sufficient peasants into tenants, the British planted the roots of one of contemporary India's greatest dilemmas, inequitable land distribution. As peasants lost their land rights and came to depend on the whims of landlords, they often fell hopelessly into debt. Furthermore, required now (as in Africa) to pay taxes in cash, peasants had to grow cash crops such as cotton, jute, pepper, or opium rather than food. As a result, famine became more common, killing millions as food supplies and distribution became more uncertain.

Other changes also affected rural life. The introduction of steamships freed shipping routes and schedules from the vagaries of monsoon winds, and the opening of the Suez Canal in 1869 made it easier and much faster to ship raw materials from India to Europe, increasing the demand for these resources. The return ships brought to India cheap machine goods, which undermined the role of village craftsmen such as weavers and tinkers. As imported goods displaced artisans and farmers shifted to cash crops, the village economy came to be based not, as it had been for millennia, on a symbiotic exchange of goods and services but on cash transactions. The quest for revenues and the priorities of commerce, which included felling forests and ploughing grassland to grow more cash crops, also placed massive pressure on the physical environment.

Some historians argue that the decline of Indian manufacturing was another key result of British rule. Hoping to find new markets abroad for Britain's industrial products, especially textiles, the British parliament denied India tariff protection for its more expensive handmade products and excluded Indian manufactured goods from Britain. The British also discouraged Indian manufacturing by taxing Indian-made goods passing between Indian states and by prohibiting the import of industrial machinery. Meanwhile, as often occurred in colonial Africa and Southeast Asia, British products flooded the country, destroying the livelihood of many skilled craftsmen. For example, textile imports increased sixfold in value between 1854 and 1913, ruining millions of Indian weavers. They, along with metalworkers and glass blowers, had little choice but to become farm laborers. A British report in 1909 stated that the only way for the Indian weavers to compete with British goods was to lower the price of their products, but this strategy left insufficient income for maintaining families.

Industrial activity did not disappear from India between 1815 and 1914, and, despite many barriers, a few Indians found ways to prosper. British entrepreneurs established the world's largest jute-manufacturing industry while Indians continued to compete with British imports by manufacturing cotton textiles and initiated a modern iron and steel sector. For example, the Gujerati industrialist Jamsetji N. Tata (1839–1904) built cotton mills, while his son, Sir Dorabji Tata (1859–1932), founded the Indian steel industry in 1907. Unable to get British funding, they raised money among Indian investors. They used their wealth to promote scientific education and found technical colleges.

By the late 1800s the limits on India's industries became a subject of heated controversy. Indian critics of British policies alleged that tariffs protected British industries while strangling Indian industries that might have competed with them. While the British claimed that their rule improved India, the gap between British and Indian wealth grew. By 1895 the per capita income in Britain was fourteen to fifteen times higher than India's, a much greater gap than existed two hundred years earlier. Indian scholars attacked what one called "The Drain" of wealth and argued that British policies gave India "peace but not prosperity; the manufacturers lost their industries; the cultivators were ground down by a heavy and variable taxation; the revenues were to a large extent diverted to England."[9] Defenders of British policies replied that British rule brought investment, imported goods, railroads, and law and order. But critics questioned whether these innovations benefited most Indians and fostered overall development or rather resulted in more systematic exploitation by increasingly prosperous British merchants and industrialists, as well as the Indian businessmen and landlords who cooperated with them. Whatever the merits of the arguments on both sides, by 1948, after two centuries of British rule, most Indians remained poor.

Population Growth and Indian Emigration

The plight of the peasant was worsened by population growth. Despite the deadly famines, under British rule the Indian population rose from perhaps 100 million in 1700 to 300 million by 1920. The British removed the traditional restraints on population growth posed by war and disease by imposing peace and improving sanitation and health; in addition, by encouraging agricultural productivity, they provided economic incentives to have more children to help in the fields. A similar population increase occurred in Europe at the same time, although for different reasons, but growing numbers of Europeans could be absorbed by industrialization or emigration to the Americas and Australia. Unlike Europe, India enjoyed neither an industrial revolution nor an increase in farm productivity. Indian landlords had a stake in the cash crop system and wanted no innovations that might threaten their dominance. As a result, the number of people far outstripped the amount of available food and land, creating dire poverty and widespread hunger.

As these problems mounted, millions of desperately poor Indians were recruited to emigrate to other lands. After the abolition of slavery in the Americas, African American workers often left the plantations. The need to replace them created a market for Indian labor in Trinidad, British Guiana (today's Guyana), and Dutch Guiana (now Suriname). Plantations in Sri Lanka, Malaya, Fiji, the Indian Ocean island of Mauritius,

and South Africa also wanted Indian labor. Many Indians saw no alternative to leaving, but travel was hazardous. For example, in 1884 a family of low-caste landless laborers, who faced starvation in the north Indian state of Bihar, boarded a sailing ship at Calcutta bound for the distant Fiji Islands in the South Pacific. The family was led by Somerea, a fifty-year-old widow, and included her two sons, a daughter-in-law, and four grandchildren ranging from ten years to fourteen months in age. The ship they boarded carried 497 adults and children. After three months of travel the ship arrived in the islands but, thanks to cases of cholera, dysentery, and typhoid and a shipwreck in Fijian waters, 56 passengers had died during the trip. Somerea's family apparently survived the journey, but their fate in Fiji is unknown.

Indian emigrants fell into several categories. Most, including Somerea's family, were destined for plantations growing cash crops such as sugar, tea, or rubber and were indentured, meaning they had signed contracts that obligated them to work for a period of years (usually three to five) in order to repay their passage. Somerea's family probably worked on a sugar plantation. The indenture contracts also stipulated the number of days per week (six) and hours per day (usually nine to ten) that must be worked. In addition to indentured workers, many Indian merchants, moneylenders, and laborers also emigrated, flocking to British Burma, Singapore, Malaya, and East Africa. Between 1880 and 1930 around a quarter million people a year, both men and women, left India. Few returned. The mortality rates for the indentured workers were so high and the indenture terms so unfavorable that critics considered the system another form of slavery. The pay was so low—a few pennies a day—and loss of income due to illness so common, that many Indians could never pay off their contracts.

The resulting diaspora made Indians one of the most recognizable global societies. Cities such as Nairobi in Kenya, Rangoon in Burma, and Port of Spain in Trinidad had large Indian neighborhoods. Indians now had key economic roles in many countries. Indian trade networks, usually based on family or caste ties, reached around the Indian Ocean and Pacific Rim. The future leader of the Indian nationalist movement, Mohandas Gandhi (GAHN-dee), then a young law school graduate, experimented with his ideas of nonviolent resistance to illegitimate power while working among Indians in South Africa. Today people of Indian ancestry make up half or more of the populations of Mauritius, Trinidad, Guyana, Suriname, and Fiji and are substantial minorities in Sri Lanka, Malaysia, Singapore, Burma, Kenya, and South Africa. However, although many Indian emigrants succeeded in business or the professions, large numbers in Southeast Asia, Sri Lanka, South Africa, Fiji, and the Caribbean still labor on plantations growing cocoa, rubber, tea, or sugar.

Indian Thought and Literature

In the later 1800s Indian intellectuals responded to British rule and ideas in several ways. A small group of well-educated Indians, in the tradition of Ram Mohan Roy during the early 1800s, wanted to combine the best of East and West. They sought reforms of customs, such as the ban on widow remarriage, that they saw as corruptions of Hinduism. But their influence waned after 1900. Another group, hostile to Western ways, sought to revive Hindu culture, calling attention to the glories of the past and arguing that India needed nothing from the West.

One thinker, Swami Vivekananda (SWAH-me VIH-vee-keh-NAHN-da) (1863–1902), was particularly influential in his concern for ending both British cultural and political domination: "O India, this is your terrible danger. The spell of imitating the West is getting such a strong hold upon you. Be proud that thou art an Indian, and proudly proclaim: 'I am an Indian, every Indian is my brother.'"[10] Swami Vivekananda was a reformer, condemning the oppression of untouchables and inspiring devotion to the needs of the poor. For inspiration, he turned to the traditions of popular Hinduism. His writings and lectures gave Indians great pride in their own culture.

Swami Vivekananda also became involved in the spread of Hindu thought to the West. In 1893, on a visit to New York, he formed the Vedanta Society, which promoted a philosophical view of Hinduism based on the ancient *Upanishads*. Vedanta thought portrayed the Hindu holy books, the Vedas, compiled over 2,500 years ago, as the supreme source of religious knowledge, although not necessarily authored by either God or humans. Even earlier, in the 1870s, Vedanta ideas had contributed to another North American and European movement, **Theosophy**, that attracted some Western followers by blending Hindu ideas with Western spiritualist and scientific ideas. Founded by Ukrainian-born Helena Blavatsky (1831–1891), Theosophy promoted the idea that India was more spiritual than other societies.

Like Hindus, Muslims were forced to rethink their values and prospects, and several currents of thought emerged. The British left many Muslim institutions, including the schools, untouched. But Muslims resented Christian missionaries setting up schools and trying to make converts, an effort that was supported by British officials openly critical of Islam. To Muslims, India seemed increasingly dominated by European and Hindu values and ideas. In response, some Muslims traveled to the Middle East in pursuit of Islamic knowledge and came home with Islamic revivalist ideas. The most dogmatic and militant form of Islamic revivalism, Wahhabism (see Chapter 21), became popular in the northwest frontier and Bengal. Opposed to modernization, especially progressive ideas such as women's rights, the revivalists clashed with other Muslims, Christians, Sikhs, and Hindus. Some revivalists opened schools to spread their version of Islam.

In contrast to revivalists, Muslim modernists, led by the cosmopolitan Sayyid Ahmad Khan (1817–1898), wanted Muslims to gain strength to achieve power. Khan argued that "the more worldly progress we make, the more glory Islam gains." He wanted to show that Islam was compatible with modern science, and in 1877 he founded a college at Aligarh (AL-ee-GAHR) that offered Western learning within a Muslim context. Trained for jobs in government service and politics, Aligarh students studied many subjects in English, and graduates, often not devout, typically learned how to play the British game of cricket and then went on to study at top British universities. A satirist observed the secular atmosphere at Aligarh, whose leaders "neither believe in God, nor yet in prayer. They say they do, but it is plain to see, What they believe in is the powers that be."[11] Aligarh graduates dominated Muslim political activity in India until independence.

Indian literature during this period included some with a nationalist bent. For example, the Tagore family, Hindus from Calcutta, were pioneers in the movement to awaken national pride and find literary outlets for self-expression. The most significant writer of the era, Rabindranath Tagore (RAH-bin-drah-NATH ta-GORE) (1861–1941), was a poet, educator, patriot, and internationalist whose writings won him the Nobel Prize for literature in 1913 (see Witness to the Past: Challenging British Imperialism with Spiritual Virtues). Writing of the romantic patriotism of his wealthy family in the 1870s, he recalled that they adopted foreign customs but also nurtured a pride in the Indian nation. Tagore sought a new and freer India, "where the mind is without fear and the head is held high; Where knowledge is free; where the clear stream of reason has not lost its way into the dreary desert sand of dead habit; Into that heaven of freedom, let my country awake."[12]

Social Life and Gender Relations

British policies also affected Indian social patterns, including the caste system. Some historians argue that caste has for centuries been an active, continually changing part of Indian life, providing a structure to separate people of higher status from those of lower status, especially untouchables. Others question whether the elaborate caste system of modern times was common in earlier centuries, arguing that the modern system reflected the views of colonial era officials seeking to classify Indians for administrative and census purposes. A case can be made for this argument. Before the colonial era, Hindus in Bengal, Punjab, and south India generally saw the formal differences among varied castes as of only moderate importance for groups and individuals. From the early 1800s, however, and owing partly to British attempts to win support from high-caste Hindus by emphasizing their elite status in the caste hierarchy, the caste system became more rigid. British policies sharpened caste identities, classifying people largely through their caste affiliations. Furthermore, as different Indians increasingly came into contact with one another, causing confusion about status, some Indians sought firmer social and moral boundaries by further dividing castes from each other. In the nineteenth century, much of India became more caste-conscious than ever before, with upper castes stressing their uniqueness and lower castes wanting to emulate the upper castes to improve their social status.

By the early 1900s caste had acquired even more meaning in the lives of Indians, but, as in precolonial times, it remained fluid and diverse, differing from region to region. Envying the highest

Theosophy A nineteenth-century North American and European movement that blended Hindu thought with Western spiritualist and scientific ideas.

Challenging British Imperialism with Spiritual Virtues

On the last day of the nineteenth century Rabindranath Tagore wrote a poem in Bengali protesting the brutal imperialism of the war Britain was waging against the Boers in South Africa, driven, Tagore believed, by British nationalism. The poem suggested that the patient cultivation of the "spiritual virtues" of India and the East would become a force in the world after the reckless power of Western imperialism, sparked by nationalism, had lost its control over humankind. In this, he echoed the views of many Hindu nationalists and reformers that Hinduism and India had a special devotion to peace and spiritual insights that could benefit the Western world. For this poem and other influential writings, Tagore won the Noble Prize for literature in 1913.

> The last sun of the century sets amidst the blood-red clouds of the West and the whirlwind of hatred.
>
> The naked passion of self-love of Nations, in its drunken delirium of greed, is dancing to the clash of steel and the howling verses of vengeance.
>
> The hungry self of the Nation shall burst in a violence of fury from its own shameless feeding, for it has made the world its food.
>
> And licking it, crunching it, and swallowing it in big morsels, It swells and swells,
>
> Till in the midst of its unholy feast descends the sudden shaft of heaven piercing its heart of grossness.
>
> The crimson glow of light on the horizon is not the light of thy dawn of peace, my Motherland.

> It is the glimmer of the funeral pyre burning to ashes the vast flesh—the self- love of the Nation—dead under its own excess.
>
> The morning waits behind the patient dark of the East, Meek and silent.
>
> Keep watch, India.
>
> Bring your offerings of worship for that sacred sunrise.
>
> Let the first hymn of its welcome sound in your voice and sing.
>
> "Come, Peace, thou daughter of God's own great suffering.
>
> Come with thy treasure of contentment, the sword of fortitude, And meekness crowning thy forehead."
>
> Be not ashamed, my brothers, to stand before the proud and the powerful, With your white robe of simpleness.
>
> Let your crown be of humility, your freedom the freedom of the soul.
>
> Build God's throne daily upon the ample barrenness of your poverty.
>
> And know that what is huge is not great and pride is not everlasting.

THINKING ABOUT THE READING

1. How does Tagore perceive nationalism?
2. How does he believe India should respond to Western power?

caste, brahmans (priests), other castes adopted brahman rituals and ideas, such as vegetarianism. For example, some untouchable leather workers, at the bottom of the social hierarchy, joined a movement that opposed the caste system but, like Brahmans, respected cows and avoided eating meat. In response to attempts by lower castes to improve their status, higher castes hoped to preserve their privileged positions by demanding that members of lower castes be excluded from government jobs. Hindu thinkers were divided about the caste system. Some social reformers called for abolishing caste, while defenders of Hindu culture praised the ideals of conduct and morality embedded in the caste system. Still others, such as Swami Vivekananda, took a middle ground, arguing that caste had its bad side but that its benefits outweighed its disadvantages.

Gender relations also changed during colonial times. Traditionally women and men had performed separate but interdependent roles within a household governed by men. Ploughing was men's work; transplanting and weeding were shared duties; and women did the house and garden. But both men and women in farming families faced a loss of work as

land came under the control of absentee landlords who emphasized growing cash crops rather than food. Lower-caste men in north India who sought to emulate the upper castes often placed more restrictions on their women, including forcing some into purdah, or seclusion. At the same time, however, new opportunities arose for other women. More girls attended school, and many became teachers, nurses, and midwives. The first women doctors graduated in the 1880s. By the 1870s women were publishing biographies of their experiences and struggles as women. Like boys, some girls now enjoyed social gatherings separate from their families. For centuries girls had been married early and had little choice in the matter. Now Indians began to speak of the "new women," a small minority in Indian cities who led more independent lives than had their mothers and married later, in their twenties or thirties, or sometimes did not marry at all.

Indian men and women also debated changes in gender relations, some taking strong positions. Indian and British reformers sought to improve the lives of Indian women and foster greater equality between the genders. A new marriage act in 1872 provoked controversy by providing for both civil marriage and marriage across caste lines. The British tried incremental reforms, such as banning sati, allowing widow remarriage, and raising the age of female consent from ten to twelve. Both British and Indian reformers tended to support the idea of marriage as based on love but also encouraged wives to show their husbands and children self-sacrificing devotion. This was not enough progress for some women, however. The first Indian feminist, Pandita Ramabai (1858–1922), whose writings urged women to take control of their lives, came from a prominent brahman family. Her father, a noted social reformer, declined to marry her off as a child. Her knowledge of Sanskrit won her the reputation of *Saraswati*, after the Hindu goddess of wisdom. She married a lawyer of low-caste background, a shocking move for a brahman woman, and then traveled to England, where she became a Christian. Upon returning to India, Ramabai opened a school for girls, especially child widows, and later a refuge for female famine victims. She also invited controversy by supporting girls who refused to enter arranged marriages.

The Rise of Nationalism

British rule inevitably produced a nationalist reaction. The Western idea of the "nation," defined by a feeling of inclusiveness among people living within the same state (see Chapter 19), was new for Indians, who tended to think of themselves as joined by a common Hindu or Muslim culture rather than a centralized state. Nonetheless, by establishing political unity in India under the Raj, educating Indians in European ideas, including nationalism, but then largely excluding Indians from administration, Britain fostered national feelings and bitterness. Furthermore, by 1900, Indians were publishing six hundred newspapers in various languages, which reported on world events such as the Irish struggle for independence from England, the Japanese defeat of Russia in war, and the U.S. conquest of the Philippines, all of which inspired Indians to oppose British rule.

Nationalist activity blossomed. In 1885 nationalists formed the Indian National Congress, which worked for peaceful progress toward self-government. But the Congress, as it came to be known, mostly attracted well-educated professionals and merchants, especially Bengalis, of brahman backgrounds and had few working class or peasant members. British officials were scornful of the Congress, doubting the possibility of Indian unity in such a diverse society. Constitutional reforms in 1909 brought a measure of representative government, but Indians still lacked true legislative and financial power.

Growing frustrations led impatient members to form a more aggressive nationalist faction within the Congress. By 1907 this radical group, led by a former journalist of Maratha background, Bal Gangadhar Tilak (1856–1920), transformed the Congress from a gentleman's pressure group into the spearhead of an active independence movement. A fierce opponent of Western influences, Tilak defended Hindu orthodoxy and custom, using religion as a vitalizing force for the nationalist movement. But many politically aware Indians disliked Tilak and remained wary of the Congress. Some feared that democratic values threatened their aristocratic privileges.

Muslims perceived the Hindu-dominated Congress, particularly radical leaders like Tilak, as anti-Muslim. As Hindu-Muslim tensions increased, new Muslim organizations were formed. In 1906 the All-India Muslim League was founded with the goal of uniting a population scattered in pockets all over the country. Hindus constituted 80 percent of India's population; Muslims were a majority only in eastern Bengal, Sind, north Punjab, and the mountain districts west of the Indus Valley. The Muslims' minority status led the influential Muslim reformer and educator Sayyid Ahmad Khan to oppose majority rule in 1887, arguing that "it would be like a game of dice, in which one man has four dice and the other only one."[13] The Muslim League's first great victory came in 1909, when British reforms guaranteed some seats in representative councils to Muslims, setting a precedence for minority representation. The Congress was enraged, charging divide and rule. Hindu-Muslim rivalries continued to complicate the nationalist movement throughout the twentieth century, eventually leading to separate Hindu- and Muslim-majority nations, India and Pakistan, in 1949.

SECTION SUMMARY

- After 1857, the British monarchy ruled India through the British Raj, which built palatial buildings, a large railroad system, and an expanded English-language school system, thereby educating Indians about Western ideals such as nationalism and sowing the seeds for an Indian revolution against Britain.

- Britain stifled Indian industry by using India as a market for British industrial products, and it turned Indian peasants into tenants who had to grow cash crops for Britain rather than their own food, thus destroying the centuries-old village economy and exacerbating famine and poverty.

- As the Indian population increased, many poor Indians were driven to work all over the world in indentured servitude, while other Indians emigrated to work as laborers, merchants, and moneylenders.

- While some Hindus wanted to combine the best in British and Indian culture, others, such as Vivekananda and Tagore, sought to revive more traditional Hindu traditions, while a Muslim college at Aligarh trained Muslims in English government and science.

- The caste system became more rigid under British rule, with lower castes imitating upper castes, upper castes trying to strengthen their privileges, and women facing greater restrictions in some cases and expanded opportunity in others.

- As Indian nationalists began to unite in their opposition to the British, the Hindu majority formed the Indian National Congress in 1885, but it was opposed by some aristocrats who feared losing their privileges and by Muslims, who formed the All-India Muslim League in 1906.

◆ Southeast Asia and Colonization

How did the Western nations expand their control of Southeast Asia?

Like Indians, Southeast Asians also had colonization imposed on them by Western military force. Arising on the Asian mainland and islands east of India and south of China, Southeast Asian societies had long flourished from trade and had formed strong, often dynamic, states, but by the 1700s most faced increasing political and economic challenges from Western powers. During the 1800s the challenges became more threatening, and by 1914 all the major Southeast Asian societies except the Siamese had come under Western colonial control. The major changes came in Indonesia, Vietnam, and Burma, where the Dutch, French, and British, respectively, increased their power, and in the Philippines, which by the end of the 1800s was controlled by the United States. Thus Southeast Asian societies became tied, more than ever before, to the larger world but lost their political and economic independence.

Dutch Colonialism in Indonesia

Between 1750 and 1914 the Dutch expanded their power in the Indonesian archipelago. They already controlled the Spice Islands (Maluku) of northeast Indonesia and the large island of Java, territories that supplied them with great wealth. In 1799 the Dutch government abolished the Dutch East Indies Company, which had governed the Dutch holdings, because of debts and corruption and replaced it with a formal colonial government charged with reenergizing the administration of the scattered Dutch-controlled territories and making Java even more profitable (see Chronology: Southeast Asia, 1750–1914). The Dutch colonial regime concentrated its economic exploitation in Java and Sumatra.

In 1830 Dutch administrators introduced the **cultivation system**, an agricultural policy that forced farmers on Java to grow sugar on their rice land. The government profited by setting a low fixed price to pay peasants for sugar, even when world prices were high. The cultivation system enriched the Dutch but ultimately impoverished many peasants. A Dutch critic of the system described the results: "If anyone should ask whether the man who grows the products receives a reward proportionate to the yields, the answer must be in the negative. The Government compels him to grow on *his* land what pleases *it*; it punishes him when he sells the crop to anyone else but *it*."[14] Dutch-owned plantations growing sugar and other cash crops replaced the cultivation system in the 1870s.

In the later 1800s the Dutch turned their attention to gaining control of, and exploiting the resources of, the Indonesian islands they had not already conquered, such as Borneo and

cultivation system An agricultural policy imposed by the Dutch in Java that forced Javanese farmers to grow sugar on rice land.

CHRONOLOGY	
Southeast Asia, 1750–1914	
1786	British base at Penang Island
1799	Abolition of Dutch East Indies Company
1788–1802	Tayson rule in Vietnam
1802	Nguyen dynasty in Vietnam
1819	British base at Singapore
1823–1826	First Anglo-Burman War
1830–1870	Cultivation system in Java
1851–1852	Second Anglo-Burman War
1858–1884	French conquest of Vietnam
1868–1910	Kingship of Chulalongkorn in Siam
1869	Opening of Suez Canal
1885–1886	Completion of British conquest of Burma
1897	Formation of Federation of Indochina
1898–1902	U.S. conquest of Philippines
1908	Dutch defeat of last Balinese kingdom

Sulawesi (see Map 22.2). In some areas the Dutch resorted to violence to impose their rule and suppress resistance. For example, they sent in armed forces between 1906 and 1908 to crush the small kingdoms on Bali, an island just east of Java. After the valiant Balinese resistance failed, the royal family of the largest Balinese kingdom committed collective suicide, walking into the guns of the Dutch forces rather than surrendering, shaming the Dutch and depriving them of any sense of victory. The Dutch created Indonesia as a country by uniting the thousands of scattered societies and dozens of states of this vast, diverse archipelago into the Dutch East Indies. But the colony, governed from Batavia (now Jakarta) on Java, promoted little common national feeling and remained a collection of peoples with diverse languages and distinctive cultures. Later this diversity made it difficult to build an Indonesian nation with a common identity.

The Making of British Malaya

At the same time as the Dutch were expanding their power, the British became more politically and economically active in the southern part of the Malay Peninsula, later known as Malaya, and eventually they subjugated the varied Malay states. British Malaya originated in coastal port cities. Seeking a naval base in the eastern Indian Ocean, the British East India Company purchased Penang (puh-NANG) Island, off Malaya's northwest

smaller number of Indians came to work in Malayan rubber plantations.

■ Economic changes due to colonization forced women to grow food for their families and eliminated the market for their handmade textiles, thus taking away their traditional ability to earn an income.

■ Education in colonies included both Western-style and more traditional schools, and cultural and artistic interchange between Westerners and colonized peoples produced new cultural forms, such as kronchong music.

✦ Chapter Summary

Change was more obvious than continuity in South and Southeast Asia during the decades between 1750 and 1914. Gradually Britain extended its control over the Indian subcontinent, using military force but also outmaneuvering rivals, forging alliances, and intimidating small states into accepting British domination. By 1850 the British East India Company controlled all of India directly or indirectly. The Company introduced policies to reshape India's economy and culture, including a Westernizing education system. The rebellion in 1857, suppressed with great difficulty, shocked the British into replacing the Company with colonial government rule. The new British Raj allowed little Indian participation in government. British policies transformed the Indian economy by favoring landlords at the expense of peasants and by suffocating traditional industries to benefit British manufactures. Population growth and poverty fostered emigration. The encounter with the West also prompted Indian thinkers to reassess their cultural traditions. Some Indians adopted Western influences, some rejected them, and others tried to mix East and West. Unpopular British policies generated a nationalist movement that challenged British rule.

While the British were consolidating control of India during the nineteenth century, they and other European powers finished colonizing Southeast Asia. Using military force or threats, the Dutch became dominant throughout the Indonesian archipelago, reaping its wealth in part by compelling Javanese to grow cash crops. Britain gained control of Burma through warfare but needed less force in Malaya, which proved profitable as a source of minerals and cash crops. Against strong resistance the French occupied Vietnam, exploiting and reshaping rural Vietnamese society. The Americans displaced the Spanish as the colonial power in the Philippines after suppressing a nationalist revolution. The Americans maintained the cash crop economic system in the Philippines but also fostered some political participation. Only Siam, led by perceptive kings, avoided colonization. Colonialism reshaped social patterns, undermining the economic activities of women, fostering urbanization, and promoting the immigration of Chinese, who later became the commercial class. Southeast Asians responded by forming creative schools and unique cultural activities.

Key Terms

Marathas	Westernization	cultivation system
Black Hole of Calcutta	Orientalism	plural society
	zamindars	can vuong
sepoys	Theosophy	

Suggested Reading

Books

Bayly, C. A. *Indian Society and the Making of the British Empire.* New York: Cambridge University Press, 1988. A masterly scholarly synthesis of research on the Company era.

Bayly, Susan. *Caste, Society and Politics in India from the Eighteenth Century to the Modern Age.* New York: Cambridge University Press, 1999. A major scholarly study.

Bose, Sugata, and Ayesha Jalal. *Modern South Asia: History, Culture, Political Economy,* 2nd ed. New York: Routledge, 2004. A recent brief survey text.

Brown, Ian. *Economic History in South-East Asia, c. 1830–1980.* Kuala Lumpur: Oxford University Press, 1997. A detailed but readable scholarly assessment.

Brown, Judith M. *Modern India: The Origins of an Asian Democracy,* 2nd ed. New York: Oxford University Press, 1994. A detailed study of India since 1750, especially strong on politics.

Forbes, Geraldine. *Women in Modern India,* rev. ed. New York: Cambridge University Press, 1999. A scholarly study since 1750.

Karnow, Stanley. *In Our Image: America's Empire in the Philippines.* New York: Ballantine, 1989. A readable survey.

Marr, David G. *Vietnamese Anticolonialism, 1885–1925.* Berkeley: University of California Press, 1971. A scholarly examination of the resistance to French colonization.

Owen, Norman G., et al. *The Emergence of Modern Southeast Asia: A New History.* Honolulu: University of Hawaii Press, 2005. The best survey, comprehensive and readable.

Tandon, Prakash. *Punjabi Century, 1857–1947.* Berkeley: University of California Press, 1968. A personal view of a century of change.

Tarling, Nicholas, ed. *The Cambridge History of Southeast Asia,* vol. 2. New York: Cambridge University Press, 1992. Contains interpretive essays on varied topics by major scholars.

Wyatt, David K. *Thailand: A Short History,* 2nd ed. New Haven: Yale University Press, 2003. The best general survey.

Websites

Asian Studies (http://coombs.anu.edu.au/WWWVL-AsianStudies.html). A vast Australian metasite.

East and Southeast Asia: An Annotated Directory of Internet Resources (http://newton.uor.edu/Departments&Programs/AsianStudies-Dept/general.html). This site offers many links.

Internet Indian History Sourcebook (http://www.fordham.edu/halsall/india/indiasbook.html). An invaluable collection.

Virtual Library: South Asia (http://www.columbia.edu/cu/libraries/indiv/area/sarai/). A major site on India.

WWW Southeast Asia Guide (http://www.library.wisc.edu/guides/SEAsia/). An easy-to-use site.

CHAPTER 23

East Asia and the Russian Empire Face New Challenges, 1750–1914

Online Study Center

This icon will direct you to interactive activities and study materials on the website: college.hmco. com/pic/lockard1e

Treaty Between Japan and China After an industrializing Japan defeated a declining China in a war over Japanese encroachments in Korea (1894–1895), diplomats from both nations met to negotiate a peace treaty. This painting shows the Chinese and Japanese representatives, easily identified by their different clothing styles, discussing the terms. (Visual Connection Archive)

The sacred traditions of our ancestors have fallen into oblivion. Those who watch attentively the march of events feel a dark and wonderful presentiment. We are on the eve of an immense revolution. But will the impulse come from within or without?

<small>A CHINESE OFFICIAL, 1846[1]</small>

n 1820 Li Ruzhen (LEE Ju-Chen) (1763–1830) published a satiric novel that boldly attacked Chinese social conditions, knowing that it would expose him to criticism from conservatives who favored the status quo. Set in the Tang dynasty a millennium earlier, *Flowers in the Mirror* was a complex novel that explored, among other themes, a sensitive topic that had been only superficially discussed by earlier male Chinese writers: the relationship between the sexes. In one section of *Flowers*, Li describes a trip by three men to a country in which all the gender roles followed in China for centuries have been reversed. In this country, it is men who suffer the pain of ear piercing and footbinding and who endure hours every day putting on makeup, all to please the women who run the country. One of the men, Merchant Lin, is conscripted as a court "lady" by the female "king":

> *In due course, his [bound] feet lost much of their original shape. Blood and flesh were squeezed into a pulp and then little remained of feet but dry bones and skin, shrunk to a dainty size. Responding to daily anointing [with oil], his hair became shiny and smooth. His eyebrows were plucked to resemble a new moon. With blood-red lipstick, and powder adorning his face, and jade and pearl adorning his coiffure and ears, Merchant Lin assumed, at last, a not unappealing appearance.[2]*

Li seemed an unlikely man to address so starkly and sympathetically the low social status and daily challenges faced by women. A conventionally educated Confucian scholar who had failed the civil service examinations and never qualified for a government position as a mandarin, Li became a writer on various nonfiction subjects, including language, political philosophy, mathematics, and astrology. But because Li's China was now awash in problems, he no longer felt bound to continue treating these more traditional subjects. Growing Western pressure to open China's borders to foreign trade, unchecked population growth, domestic unrest, political corruption, and growing opium addiction spurred Chinese scholars such as Li to reassess the relevance of Chinese traditions, such as outmoded civil service examinations, the inequality of wealth, and women's footbinding, for a changing world. In *Flowers* Li addressed the social inequities that he believed kept women from actively participating in China's regeneration. The growing dissatisfaction with China's practices that Li's provocative book represented, combined with Western intervention in China, set the stage for the immense revolution, predicted by the official in the chapter opening quote, that would eventually transform this ancient society.

A major world society for over two millennia, China was still powerful in the late 1700s. But in the 1800s, Western military, economic, and political pressure on China to open its doors to Western trade, combined with mounting domestic problems, contributed to three military defeats, a devastating rebellion, and increasing poverty for millions of Chinese. In response, the imperial government supported some reforms, but these did not foster the modernization, especially of military technology and government, that China needed to control foreign influence or to prevent the rise of revolutionary movements. Eventually these movements overthrew the imperial system.

Like the Chinese, the Japanese also faced challenges, even before Western ships forced the nation open in the 1850s. Soon the old system fell, and in the 1870s Japan's new leaders began an all-out program of modernization in an effort to prevent Western domination. By 1900 the Japanese had heavy industry, a modern military, and a comprehensive educational system. Emulating the Western imperialist countries, they also sought their own resources and markets abroad and soon colonized their neighbor, Korea, which had not modernized.

Although historically linked more closely to Europe than to Asia, Russia also became a factor in Asian politics after it expanded across Siberia to the Pacific. Perched on the borders of Europe, East Asia, and the Islamic Middle East and Central Asia, Russia engaged with societies in each of these regions through trade, warfare, and conquest. After it became dominant in parts of eastern Europe, pushed its borders southward into Ottoman territories, and conquered the Central Asian states, Russia was the largest territorial power in Eurasia.

FOCUS QUESTIONS

1. What were the causes and consequences of the Opium War?
2. Why did Chinese efforts at modernization fail?
3. What factors aided Japan in the quest for modernization?
4. How did the Meiji government transform Japan and Korea?
5. What factors explain the expansion of the Russian Empire?

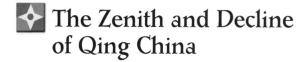

The Zenith and Decline of Qing China

What were the causes and consequences of the Opium War?

Established by the Manchus, pastoralist invaders from Manchuria, the Qing (ching) (1644–1912) was the last dynasty in China's long history, the final phase of China's 2000-year-old imperial system (see Chronology: China, 1750–1915). After reaching its zenith in the eighteenth century, Qing China experienced decay in the nineteenth. The challenges facing the Qing in the early and mid-1800s were particularly severe. Several catastrophic wars resulted in unequal treaties with the

West that increased Western penetration, and dynastic decline fostered major rebellions. Meanwhile, China's economy underwent changes, Christian missionaries posed a challenge to Chinese culture, and increasing poverty prompted millions of Chinese to seek their fortunes abroad. Although the Qing survived into the early 1900s, it had lost much of its strength. This decline in world standing had as much to do with Europe's rise as with China's failures.

Qing China in the 1700s

In the eighteenth century, Qing China was still one of the world's largest, most powerful, most prosperous, and most technologically sophisticated societies, largely self-sufficient

C H R O N O L O G Y		
China	**Japan and Korea**	**Russia and Central Asia**
1800		
1839–1842 Opium War		
1850		
1850–1864 Taiping Rebellion	**1853** Opening of Japan by Perry	**1800–1870s** Russian conquest of Turkestan and Caucasus
	1867–1868 Meiji Restoration	
1900		
1911 Chinese Revolution	**1910** Japanese colonization of Korea and Taiwan	**1905** First Russian Revolution

and very self-centered. But troubling signs of decay developed. Although the Manchus had followed the political example of earlier Chinese dynasties, they were more despotic. Manchus dominated the top government positions and forbade intermarriage with the Chinese. While the Chinese accepted Manchu rule, as they had tolerated alien rule in the past, they resented the ethnic discrimination. There were other problems as well. Like various earlier dynasties, the Qing had built a great empire by occupying predominantly Muslim Xinjiang (shin-jee-yahng), a mostly desert region just west of China; conquering the Mongols; annexing Tibet; and adding to the empire the fertile island of Taiwan (tie-WAN), to which thousands of Chinese migrated. Although this expansion consolidated China's borders, it also stretched Qing military power and proved economically costly.

Despite the challenges, the Qing generally maintained domestic prosperity and a growing economy for nearly two centuries. Chinese opened new lands for settlement. Taking advantage of trade with the West, they also introduced crops from the Americas that provided additional food sources, such as corn, sweet potatoes, and peanuts. Cash cropping of cotton and tea, both traditional crops, and of tobacco from the Americas expanded, although this agricultural growth also led to a growing concentration of land ownership. The volume of domestic trade grew in the 1700s, spurred by new textile factories, increased copper mining, and more money in circulation in the world's largest commercial economy. In 1830 China still accounted for a third of world manufacturing, and in the 1850s a British observer called the Chinese the world's greatest manufacturing people. Some historians suggest that the mid-Qing economic trends, such as a highly commercialized economy, resembled the patterns that sparked economic change in western Europe in the Early Modern Era.

As a result of its prosperity and agricultural growth, China's population doubled from 150 million in 1700 to 300 million by 1800, and then rose to 432 million by 1850. Peasants responded to population pressure by finding additional marginal land to farm and expanding their use of irrigation and fertilizer. But population growth still outstripped the growth of the food supply, straining resources and fostering corruption, which increased Chinese resentment of the Qing government. Although in the 1700s living standards in the more developed regions of China were probably comparable to those of the more affluent parts of western Europe, in the 1800s they deteriorated, partly because of overpopulation.

While the economy thrived, Chinese culture and society became more conservative. In 1783 the Qing government prohibited books and plays that it considered treasonable to the Manchu state or subversive to traditional Chinese values. Some scholars, considering these works immoral and arguing that moral laxness caused the fall of dynasties, applauded the crackdown. They worried particularly about fiction and other creative forms composed by both men and women, such as sung poetry, which often had an erotic, sometimes homosexual, focus. The Qing introduced harsher laws against unconventional behavior, such as homosexuality, which Chinese governments had generally tolerated for centuries, and increased social pressures on women to conform to such gender expectations as refusing to remarry after they became widows.

The Qing mandated that public meetings be held every month in which an imperial edict be read out. It emphasized

C H R O N O L O G Y	
China, 1750–1915	
1644–1912	Qing dynasty
1839–1842	Opium War
1842	Treaty of Nanjing
1856–1860	Arrow War
1850–1864	Taiping Rebellion
1894–1895	Sino-Japanese War
1898	100 Days of Reform
1900	Boxer Rebellion
1911	Chinese Revolution
1912	Formation of Chinese Republic
1915	Japan's 21 Demands on China

Confucian notions of moral virtue, heaping honor on filial sons, loyal officials, philanthropists, and faithful wives. Since increasing numbers of women were literate, the government published instructional books containing historical writings, some of them over two millennia old, on female obligations. Women were advised not to look around when walking, laugh aloud, talk loudly, or sway their skirts when standing. Yet, women also read and probably enjoyed popular literature, such as the satirical novel *Flowers in a Mirror,* discussed in the opening vignette. And, in a few districts in central China, peasant women wrote their observations and communications in a secret script, *nuxu* (noo-shoe), that may have been first developed by and for women centuries earlier.

Qing China in an Imperial World

China's problems during the later Qing can be traced to both internal decay and foreign pressure. Internally, by 1800 the Qing began to show clear signs of dynastic decline, such as increasing poverty and administrative corruption. For example, greedy officials in the court as well as in remote towns took bribes to allow the smuggling and sale of narcotic drugs, and sometimes they even participated in these illegal activities. Local rebellions against the Qing were suppressed, but the costs of defeating them added to increasingly severe economic problems.

As political, economic, and social conditions deteriorated at home, European nations exerted pressure on the Qing government to grant them more privileges. China had experienced pressure from Western adventurers and traders already in the sixteenth and seventeenth centuries. The Portuguese had established a base at Macao on the southern coast in 1557 and gradually turned it into a colony. The Russians, too, forged direct contacts as they expanded their influence in eastern Siberia and established trading posts along the Amur River separating Siberia from Manchuria. In the 1700s Dutch and English traders were granted permission to trade at the southern port of Guangzhou (gwahng-jo) (known to the British as Canton). Britain had become the most powerful European nation in the 1700s. Westerners wanted increased access, including freedom to travel inside China.

The Chinese debated how much contact with the West to allow. Chinese merchants in coastal cities, who had long traded with Southeast Asia, often supported contact because they could make fortunes by trading with the Europeans. From the early 1700s to the mid-1800s some merchants benefited from **Chinoiserie**, a Western vogue for Chinese artistic products such as ceramics, painting, lacquer ware, and decorative furniture. This trend grew after Europeans found themselves unable to produce porcelain duplicating the quality of China's. Western merchants and diplomats commissioned Chinese artists in Guangzhou to paint Chinese people, costumes, and city scenes using Western artistic techniques, especially watercolor. In the early 1800s a merchant's guild called the **Co-hong** had a monopoly on Guangzhou's trade with the West, and its head, Howqua (How-kwah) (1769–1843), became one of the world's richest men. Howqua was famous in China for his spectacular pleasure garden and lavish mansion, which employed a staff of five hundred servants.

Nevertheless, being largely self-sufficient in food and resources, China did not need foreign trade, and Qing emperors were unwilling to make concessions to the more open trade system desired by the Europeans. Before 1800 the Qing restricted trade to a few ports such as Guangzhou and Siberian outposts, and they refused diplomatic relations on an equal basis with the West. In the 1600s Catholic missionaries were expelled for their bickering and intolerance toward Chinese traditions, and thereafter Christian missionaries were prohibited from working in China. The Chinese knew little of the Western world and were confused by the diverse nationalities of the European peoples, whom they disparagingly called "foreign devils." Chinese leaders viewed European merchants as barbarians bearing tribute, and they required visiting diplomats to perform the humiliating custom of *kotow,* in which they prostrated themselves before the emperor.

Chinese and European world-views were also incompatible. The British righteously saw themselves as benefiting China by opening the country to free trade. A British official wrote in 1821 that governments should let the stream of commerce flow as it will. The Chinese differed. China's attitude toward foreign trade and the outside world was well exemplified in a letter written by the Qing emperor Qianlong (chee-YEN-loong) (r. 1736–1795) to King George III of Britain following a British trade mission in 1793 requesting more access. The emperor denied Britain permission to establish an embassy but commended the king for his respectful spirit of submission and humility in sending tribute: "Our dynasty's majestic virtue has penetrated into every country under heaven. Our celestial empire possesses all things in prolific abundance. It behooves you, O king, to display ever greater devotion and loyalty in the future, so that by perpetual submission to our throne, you may secure peace and prosperity for your country hereafter."[3]

The Opium Trade and War

Half a century after Emperor Qianlong blithely dismissed the British request with these words, the tables were turned. Two wars in the mid-1800s, in which Qing China suffered humiliating defeats, forcibly jarred the Chinese from their complacency and made clear that the world was changing. The first war, resulting from an increasing trade in opium centered in Guangzhou, granted new rights to the West, while the second expanded those rights. These wars forced China to open its doors and to rethink traditional values and institutions.

Chinoiserie An eighteenth- and nineteenth-century Western vogue for artistic products of China such as painting, ceramics, lacquer ware, and decorative furniture.

Co-hong A nineteenth-century Chinese merchant's guild that had a monopoly on Guangzhou's trade with the West.

Guangzhou During the eighteenth century, the Western traders in China were restricted to one riverside district in Guangzhou (Canton), where they built their warehouses, businesses, and homes in European style. (Photograph Courtesy Peabody Essex Museum, E79708 View of Guangzhou ca. 1800)

The Opium Trade In the late 1700s the British, taking the lead in the China trade, badly wanted more Chinese silk and tea, which had become valued revenue sources for British merchants. But China, desiring little from the West, accepted only precious gold and silver bullion as payment. Between the 1760s and 1780s the import of silver into China increased over 500 percent, presenting a serious balance of payments problem for Western economies. Seeking a marketable product that would solve this unfavorable trade disparity, the British found it in opium, an addictive drug that was grown in India and the Middle East. European sailors had first introduced opium into China in the 1600s, and it was first used as a painkiller. In the 1720s, however, the Chinese discovered that they could smoke opium for pleasure by mixing it in a pipe with tobacco. By the later 1700s businesses known as opium dens, where people could buy and use opium, began to appear. The drug gave users a dreamy, relaxed experience that temporarily relieved boredom, stress, physical pain, and depression. Opium appealed to bored officials, wealthy women cooped up at home, busy clerks, anxious merchants, nervous soldiers, and overworked peasants. A highly addictive drug, it produced severe withdrawal symptoms such as cramps and nausea.

The British, who began to grow opium as a cash crop in the Bengal region of India in the 1700s, soon found foreign markets around Asia, and British enterprises such as the British East India Company were greatly enriched by this trade. In fact, the sale of opium, chiefly obtained from the British, became an important revenue source for all the European colonial governments in Southeast Asia. U.S. traders also participated, shipping opium from Ottoman Turkey to East Asia. Eventually British and American traders began smuggling opium into China. The Western drug smugglers and the governments that supported them, being concerned only with profits, were indifferent to the terrible moral and social consequences of their enterprise. Between 1800 and 1838 opium imports to China increased sixfold, and by 1838 there were 5 to 10 million Chinese addicts. The opium trade destroyed the country's social fiber and impoverished thousands of families. One Chinese official concluded that "opium is nothing else but a flowing poison [which] utterly ruins the minds and morals of the people, a dreadful calamity."[4] Another argued in 1838 that opium smokers should be strangled and the pushers and producers beheaded.

The corrupt opium trade system at Guangzhou fostered conflict. China outlawed the opium trade in 1729, and the emperor issued decrees forbidding the marketing, smuggling, and consumption of the drug. British, American, and other Western traders were then forced officially to trade through the Co-hong merchant's guild, but this restriction did not limit the opium trade; the British found that officials could be bribed to overlook opium smuggling. To continue bringing in their huge profits from this trade, during the 1830s the British doubled opium imports while also pressing for reform of the trading system.

Chinese leaders responded by further isolating the Western traders and mounting an attack on the opium trade. The emperor appointed the mandarin Lin Zezu (lin tsay-shoe) (1785–1850) to go to Guangzhou as commissioner and end the opium trade. Lin, an incorruptible Confucian moralist, concluded that if the opium traffic was not stopped, China would become poorer and its people weaker. He wrote to Britain's Queen Victoria: "Suppose there were people from another country who carried opium for sale to England and seduced your people into buying and smoking it. Certainly you would be bitterly aroused."[5] Lin ordered his officials to raid the Western warehouses, where they seized and destroyed 20,000 chests of opium worth millions of dollars.

Online Study Center **Improve Your Grade**
Primary Source: Letter to Queen Victoria, 1839

The Opium War Lin's seizure of opium outraged Western traders, and Britain declared war. In the following Opium War (1839–1842), as the British called it, Western military power proved disastrous for China. The British fleet raided up and down the Chinese coast, blockading and bombarding ports, including Guangzhou. The Chinese fought back, often resisting against hopeless odds, but they lacked the weapons to triumph. Although China had one of the world's most formidable military forces in 1600, since then Europeans had greatly surpassed China in naval and military technology. The British won most of the battles of the war.

With defeat certain, dozens of Qing officers committed suicide. The lost battles also forced the Chinese to assess the Western threat. A few alarmed officials were concerned with the inadequacy of Chinese technology. Commissioner Lin wrote to a friend that China badly needed ships and guns like the British had, but he did not broadcast his views fearing the hostile reaction from his more conservative government colleagues. Unlike Lin, most officials and other educated Chinese rejected such ideas and remained scornful of all things Western. One official wrote to the emperor that "the English barbarians are a detestable people, trusting entirely to their strong ships and large guns." Average Chinese reacted with rage. One placard in Canton in 1841 was addressed to "rebellious barbarian dogs. If we do not completely exterminate you we will not be manly Chinese able to support the sky over our heads. We are definitely going to kill you, cut your heads off, and burn your bodies in the trash."[6]

In 1841, when the British made preparations to blow down the walls of the major city of Nanjing, along the Yangzi River in central China, the Qing were forced to negotiate for peace. In 1842 they signed the Treaty of Nanjing, the first of a series of humiliating unequal treaties that nibbled away at Chinese sovereignty. The treaty gave Britain permanent possession of Hong Kong, a sparsely populated coastal island downriver from Guangzhou; opened five ports to British trade; abolished the Co-hong and its trade monopoly; set fixed tariffs so that China no longer controlled its economic policy; and gave the British **extraterritoriality**, or freedom from local laws. The Chinese were also forced to pay Britain the war costs. Soon other Western countries signed treaties with China that gave them the same rights as the British. Each successive treaty expanded foreign privileges.

The Treaty System

The Opium War became to the Chinese a permanent symbol of Western imperialism. The debacle of the Opium War soon led to other wars and a treaty system that opened China to the West. After the Opium War, Westerners, especially the British, remained dissatisfied with the amount of trade, and the Chinese sought to evade their obligations. These factors ensured that another conflict would develop, and the one that did is often known as the Arrow War (1856–1860). China had imprisoned some Chinese sailors for suspected piracy aboard a Chinese ship, *The Arrow*, registered in Hong Kong, which the British were building into a key trading port, and Britain used this event as a pretext to attack China. France also entered the war, using the mysterious murder of a French priest as an excuse. Facing two formidable powers, China was again defeated and forced to sign new treaties that favored the West. This treaty opened more ports on the coast and along interior rivers to Western traders, established foreign embassies in Beijing, and permitted Christian missionaries to enter the Chinese interior. Again forced to pay the war costs, China fell deeper into debt. The Arrow War also undermined China's position as a regional power. China was forced to give up its claim to Vietnam, a longtime vassal state being colonized by France, and to acquiesce in the Russian takeover of eastern Siberia.

By restricting China's control of its economy and limiting Chinese power to make rules for Western residents, the treaty system deprived China of some of its autonomy. It also led to the formation of **international settlements**, zones in major Chinese cities set aside for foreigners in which no Chinese were allowed. They were in effect foreign cities with foreign governments in major ports such as Guangzhou and Shanghai. For example, a small island on the riverfront adjacent to downtown Guangzhou, and accessible only by a footbridge, became the home of Western merchants, officials, and missionaries. It boasted mansions, warehouses, clubs, and churches built by and serving the largely British, American, and French population. Some historians question whether the popular notion that signs in the international settlement in Shanghai warning "no dogs or Chinese allowed" really existed, but Chinese were clearly unwelcome except as servants.

The Opium and Arrow Wars and the treaty system they fostered forced the Chinese to debate how best to respond to the new dangers the country faced. Some Chinese officials and other scholars understood the need for China to learn from the West, to examine Western books and build modern ships and guns in order to meet the Western challenge. A few scholars argued that the Chinese should seriously study science, mathematics, and foreign languages. These views influenced the provincial official and reformer Zeng Guofan (zung gwoh-FAN) (1811–1872), who recommended making modern weapons and steamships. But, failing to see the magnitude of the challenges, few mandarins showed interest. One conservative mandarin rejected

---

extraterritoriality Freedom from local laws for foreign subjects.

international settlements Special zones in major Chinese cities set aside for foreigners, where no Chinese were allowed; arose as a result of China's defeat in the Opium and Arrow Wars.

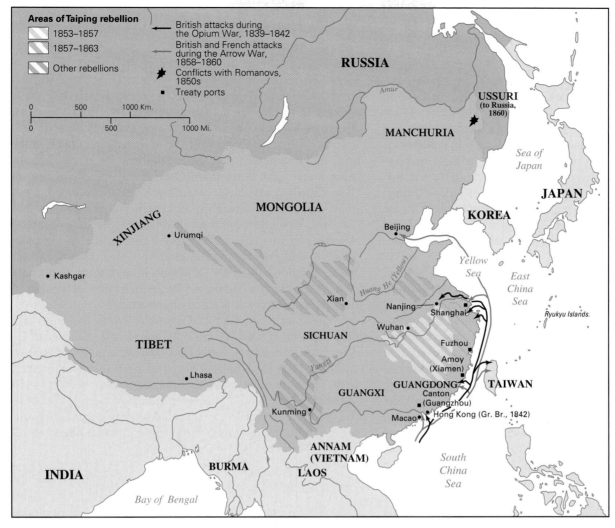

Map 23.1 Conflicts in Qing China, 1839–1870

During the mid-1800s Qing China experienced repeated unrest, including several major rebellions. The largest and most destructive, the Taiping Rebellion, engulfed a large part of southern and central China between 1850 and 1864.

Online Study Center **Improve Your Grade** Interactive Map: Conflicts in the Qing China, 1839–1870

Western knowledge because, he argued, Western sciences were based largely on earlier Chinese discoveries. In fact, Chinese discoveries had contributed to Western science and technology for centuries, but by the 1800s the West held the creative edge.

While scholars debated, China's problems multiplied, especially in the coastal provinces. To pay for the wars, the government had to raise taxes, causing many peasants to lose their land. The dispossessed often turned to begging or banditry. Natural disasters further demoralized the country. Between 1800 and 1850 the Yellow River flooded twenty times and then changed course, wiping out hundreds of towns and villages.

As a result of the treaty system, Western cultural influence—to Chinese critics just another form of imperialism—increased. Much of this influence spread through Christian missionaries from the United States and Britain. The missionaries opened most of China's Western-type schools and hospitals, providing educational and health benefits to those Chinese who had access to them. By the 1920s there were 2,500 American missionaries in China, some of them attached to the thirteen American-operated and funded colleges. However, Christian

missionaries posed a challenge to Chinese religions and provoked negative opinions. The Chinese knew that missionaries often lived well and were protected by Western military power. The missionaries and other Western residents, often ethnocentric and seeing themselves as the cutting edge of what they considered to be a superior Western and Christian civilization, tended to view the Chinese as depraved heathens and mocked their culture. Chinese generally distrusted not only the Christian missionaries but also the several hundred thousand Chinese who became Christian.

The Taiping Rebellion

Deteriorating conditions, government corruption, and the increasing Western presence eventually generated the Taiping Rebellion (1850–1864), the most critical of several midcentury upheavals against the Qing (see Map 23.1). Guangdong (GWAHNG-dong) province, on the southeast coast, experienced particularly severe social and economic dislocations that increased popular unrest. Officials reported that peasant families had no food surplus and were reduced to eating the chaff of the wheat. The rebellion began in a remote area and was fueled by economic insecurity, famine, loss of faith in government, and a desire for social change. The leader, Hong Xiuquan (hoong shee-OH-chew-an) (1813–1864), who had failed to pass the civil service examinations and had also studied with Christian missionaries, believed that God had appointed him the new Son of Heaven to exterminate evil. Impressed by Western military power but also proudly Chinese, Hong preached a doctrine blending Christianity and Chinese thought, a response to Western disruption, mixing local and Western ideas, that was typical in Asia and Africa in the nineteenth and twentieth centuries.

Hong wanted a new form of government and social system. He promoted an equal distribution of goods, communal property, and equality between men and women. The puritanical Hong also prohibited opium use, polygamy, footbinding, prostitution, concubinage, and arranged marriages. Hong established a sect, the Taipings (Heavenly Kingdom of Great Peace), that rejected Confucian traditions and envisioned a God-oriented utopia where all people would be equal. Many of the Taiping men and women were, like Hong himself, Hakkas, a dialect group in south China whose women never bound their feet and were raised to be assertive. These traditions no doubt influenced Taiping gender policies although male Taiping leaders did not always follow these liberal ideas. Hong organized an army, and in 1850 he launched a rebellion, invoking Chinese nationalism: "We raise the army of righteousness to liberate the masses for the sake of China."[7] Soon he had attracted millions of supporters from among the poor and disaffected.

The Taipings enjoyed early success, but ultimately their efforts failed and weakened China. Taiping armies conquered large parts of central and southern China, but the Taipings suffered from conflicts within their leadership, and their hostility to traditional Chinese culture cost them popular support. Some historians suspect that conservative Confucians especially disliked the Taiping espousal of women's rights, which they saw as a threat to the patriarchal family system. Intellectuals accused them of subverting Chinese society and opening China to Westernization. Ultimately most of the educated elite rallied to the Qing and organized provincial armies to oppose the Taipings. Westerners often sympathized with the Taipings because of their Christian influences and progressive social message but knew that a Qing victory would benefit Western nations. The Taipings, Westerners believed, threatened to establish a strong new dynasty, whereas a weak Manchu government meant more Western ability to continue exploiting China. Hence, various Western nations aided the Qing with money, arms, mercenary soldiers, and military advisers. The Taipings were defeated, and the process of dynastic renewal was aborted.

The conflict left China in shambles. Many provinces had been devastated, and 20 million Chinese had been killed. An American missionary described the destruction: "Ruined cities, desolated towns and heaps of rubble still mark their path. The hum of busy populations had ceased and weeds and jungle cover the land."[8] The Qing were now deeper in debt to the West and compelled to adopt even more conciliatory attitudes. The imperial government also lost some power to regional leaders.

Economic Change and Emigration

China's encounters with the West generated several economic changes. The extension of Western businesses into the interior stimulated the growth of the Chinese merchant class and small-scale Chinese-owned industries, such as match factories and flour mills. The Chinese merchants, however, disliked Western economic domination and the Qing government, which offered

Rattan Factory in Guangzhou This photo, taken around 1875, shows Chinese men and women workers, mostly of peasant background, in a factory making rattan, along with the factory's European owners. (Courtesy, Daniel Wolf Collection, NY)

little resistance to Western imperialism. Gradually a new working class, including women, labored in mines, factories, railways, and docks. The gulf between peasants in the interior and the merchants and workers in the coastal cities was vast.

The unequal treaties enabled Western economic penetration into China, increasing the incorporation of China into a world economy dominated by the West, and China's economy became increasingly geared to Western rather than Chinese needs. Westerners often ran Qing government agencies, banks, railroads, factories, and mines and guarded them with Western police. Western goods, entrepreneurs, and capital came into China. By 1920 foreign companies controlled most of China's iron ore, coal, railroads, and steamships, and Western businessmen became inspired by the notion of the vast China market. One U.S. firm launched an advertising campaign to put a cigarette in the mouth of every Chinese man, woman, and child. As happened in Southeast Asia, imported British textiles frequently displaced Chinese women from textile production, which peasant women had done for centuries to supplement family incomes. Local spinning was eliminated, and although women continued to weave, they earned lower incomes than before.

Historians debate whether this foreign economic penetration helped or hindered China's own economic development. Some scholars view economic imperialism as a spur to the growth of China's domestic economy. Others argue that Western competition ruined Chinese industries such as cotton spinning and iron and steel production, hurting China's ability to compete with the West. Western businesses had the advantages of greater capital and the support of Western governments and military power. Standard Oil's kerosene from the United States, for instance, replaced locally produced vegetable oil in the lamps of China. China's traditional exports also declined because of competition with other Asian countries. By 1900 India and Sri Lanka had become the world's largest producers of tea and Japan the largest producer of silk. The Qing, already deeply in debt to Western governments and banks, had little money left for building China's economic institutions.

Deteriorating economic, social, and political conditions in hard-hit coastal provinces, combined with natural disasters, prompted millions of Chinese to emigrate between the 1840s and 1920s, usually to places where Western colonialism and capitalism were opening new economic opportunities. Emigration accelerated in the later 1800s. Between 1880 and 1920 several hundred thousand people a year left from southern ports, usually headed for Southeast Asia but also, in many cases, bound for Pacific islands such as Hawaii and Tahiti or for Australia, Peru, Cuba, North America, and South Africa (see Chapters 20 and 22). The Chinese who emigrated to join relatives in their business enterprises, or to establish new ones, formed the basis for local middle-class Chinese business communities. The majority left China as part of the notorious "coolie trade," a labor system known as such because Westerners called the emigrant workers, whether Chinese or Indian, "coolies," a derogatory term. Under this system, desperate Chinese, usually peasants, were recruited or coerced to become indentured workers in faraway places, signing contracts that required them to labor for years on plantations or in mines, or to

work building railroads to repay their passage. Those laborers who survived the difficult voyages in crowded ships faced discrimination and harsh working conditions in alien lands.

Chinese had migrated to Southeast Asia for centuries, but the increased emigration now greatly enlarged the Chinese diaspora to a global scale. The societies where Chinese settled, especially in Southeast Asia, became more closely connected to China through economic and social networks than ever before. For example, Chinese businesses in Southeast Asia often had branches and labor recruitment offices in China, and families in China maintained ties to family members or their descendants living abroad. Chinese emigrants often returned to their native villages with wealth earned abroad, but others remained poor, never earning enough money to return to China as they originally hoped. Others who saved enough after years of hard work to establish small businesses often settled permanently abroad. Most emigrants were men, who sometimes supported wives and children in China or brought family members to their overseas homes. Chinese men also married local women, often non-Chinese. The emigrants and their descendants, while often sustaining Chinese culture and language, also mixed Chinese and local customs. Today some 30 million people of Chinese ancestry live outside of China, the large majority of them in Southeast Asia. They constitute a major source of investment capital for China, helping to finance businesses, industries, and educational institutions in their ancestral homeland.

SECTION SUMMARY

- In the eighteenth century, Qing China was still thriving on the strength of its agriculture, trade, and manufacturing, but its rapidly growing population began to produce internal problems such as poverty and corruption.

- In the nineteenth century, China faced increasing problems as well as pressure from Westerners for greater trade opportunities, but the Qing refused to allow an open trading system, thus creating a severe trade imbalance between the West and the East.

- To solve this imbalance, the British began smuggling opium into China, and when China resisted the British defeated China in the Opium War and forced the Chinese to agree to highly unfavorable terms that allowed the British to trade in China.

- After another war, China was forced to set aside special areas exclusively for Westerners, called international settlements, and to also allow Christian missionaries into the country.

- Economic insecurity, famine, and Western interference eventually led to the Taiping Rebellion, a widespread and devastating revolt that was ultimately put down by the Qing with help from Western powers.

- China's economy was increasingly penetrated and transformed by Western powers, and millions of Chinese emigrated throughout the world, some to be indentured workers and others to go into business.

From Imperial to Republican China

Why did Chinese efforts at modernization fail?

The rebellions, government stagnation, poverty, and growing Western demands brought about a crisis for the Qing. Some Chinese still concluded that China should reaffirm its traditional ways and reject the West. But other Chinese increasingly recognized the need to evaluate Western technologies and assess the severity of the Western challenge. For centuries China had absorbed invaders to survive, and a growing number of reformers now wanted to also adapt useful Western technologies to Chinese ways. As challenges mounted and China lost a war with Japan, some gave up on reform and organized revolutionary movements. In the early 1900s, revolutionaries overthrew the imperial system to form a republic, but these developments did not solve China's problems.

Conservatives and Liberals

China's educated elite divided over how much China should modernize its society: conservatives argued against borrowing Western models, while liberals wanted moderate reforms. The conservatives, who dominated the bureaucracy, advised that China hold fast to traditions, protecting itself with Confucian moral conduct. Believing China could learn nothing from Westerners, they opposed railroads, underground mines, and other innovations because these disrupted the harmony between humanity and nature, disturbed the graves of the ancestors, and put boatmen and cart drivers out of work. One conservative wrote that it was "better to see the nation die than its way of life change."[9] Conservatives asked how the Chinese could change some aspects of their life without changing others, since new technologies undermined social, economic, and even political values.

Liberals, believing China had to adopt certain Western ideas to survive, sponsored impressive government innovations. They streamlined central and regional governments, set up a foreign ministry, formed a college to train diplomats, and sent some students to schools in the West, especially to the United States. Several provincial governments established industries. A few bold reformers argued that Confucius had supported the idea of democratic government and favored reforms, and they questioned customs that exalted the ruler and demeaned his subjects and that favored the male over the female. Few liberals, however, wanted radical transformation, preferring to protect the core of Chinese tradition by simply grafting on some technological innovations. As one noted, "China should acquire the West's superiority in arms and machinery, but retain China's superiority in Confucian virtue."[10] Perhaps naively, liberals believed they could adopt Western tools while rejecting Western ideas and institutions. To them, Western ideas such as political democracy and nationalism were too foreign to easily adapt to China's family-centered society, which was defined in cultural rather than political terms.

Liberals also sought to modernize military forces. Chinese leaders perceived Western strength as essentially one of ships and guns, not of the dynamic and aggressive Western culture. Military reformers in the provinces, calling themselves "self-strengtheners," aimed to strengthen China to protect it. In the late nineteenth century these self-strengtheners built arsenals and shipyards. By 1894 China had a better-trained army and sixty-five warships. But this was still insufficient against a fully industrialized enemy.

The reforms failed to save the Qing because the technological innovations themselves generated new problems. The Chinese built warships but then needed coal to make steam to power them, which meant they needed improved coal-mining technology. Railroads had to be built to move the coal, and they in turn required telegraphs to communicate train movements. Technical schools were needed to train workers for these new enterprises. In addition, the new working class hired by the companies and factories did not fit into Confucian social categories, which divided society into scholars, peasants, artisans, and merchants. China also employed Western advisers to help set up and run the new industries, and it developed government departments such as the post office and maritime customs. But the new enterprises were often poorly run. The innovations were also expensive, further complicating the economic problems of a Chinese government forced to pay war reparations and to finance a growing debt to Western nations and banks.

China's problems grew less manageable. China was too large and overpopulated, its surplus wealth was too small for investment, and it was too saddled with a poorly led, bureaucratic, and overly conservative government to make any radical changes. From 1861 to 1908 the imperial government was dominated by the Empress Dowager Ci Xi (zoo shee) (1835–1908), a concubine of the old emperor; on his death Ci Xi had become the regent of the child emperor who replaced him. Forceful and intelligent, she was also covetous and irresponsible. For example, she diverted money intended to build a modern navy, spending it instead on constructing the magnificent Summer Palace, just outside Beijing, for her imperial retreat. Some historians identify the ineptitude and selfish policies of Manchu leaders such as Ci Xi as a major factor in China's failure to rapidly modernize. China's inability to deflect the growing challenges fostered escapism among many thoughtful Chinese, expressed by a poet official: "I'll drink myself merry, Thrash out a wild song from my lute, And let the storms rage at will."[11]

Foreign Pressures on Late Qing China

Historians have often emphasized external rather than internal factors in China's decline. They view late Qing modernization as impressive but thwarted by foreign economic and political domination that placed constraints on what China could accomplish. The foreign pressures, these historians argue, put Chinese leaders into a siege mentality. Indeed, by the late 1800s

Chinese Study Maxim Gun   After the Taiping Rebellion, the Qing emperor sent two Chinese mandarins to England to examine and purchase new weapons. In this photo, they examine a Maxim gun, one of the first machine guns that gave Western nations a great military advantage.   (Peter Newark's Military Pictures)

China lacked full autonomy: Western gunboats patrolled its rivers, international settlements existed in the major cities, Christian missionaries challenged Chinese values, and Westerners exerted influence on the imperial government, and also had partial control of the economy. Some foreign powers dominated particular regions as spheres of influence, such as Britain in Guangdong and the Germans in Shandong, acquiring resources, establishing enterprises, and manipulating local governments.

The United States, Britain, France, and Germany exercised their power over China through **gunboat diplomacy**, the use of superior firepower to impose a country's will on local populations and governments. The term comes from the use of Western gunboats to patrol some of China's rivers and seacoasts in the late 1800s and early 1900s, interceding to protect Western businessmen, missionaries, and diplomats whose activities generated Chinese hostility. The most notorious was a U.S. naval force known as the Yangzi Patrol, a group of shallow-draft gunboats, often supplemented by a half-dozen destroyers and cruisers, that patrolled the hundreds of miles of the Yangzi River between Shanghai and central Sichuan province between 1890 and World War I. According to a patrol commander, the mission of the Yangzi Patrol was "to make every American feel perfectly safe in coming into the valley to

live or to transact business, until such time as the Chinese themselves are able to afford these guarantees."[12] Sovereign Chinese rights and the people's outrage at foreign intrusion counted for little. But gunboats were only part of the story. Americans also promoted free trade, generously funded Christian missionaries, and donated to humanitarian causes such as flood relief and orphanages.

Despite the limits on its autonomy, China never became a full Western colony such as India or Vietnam, perhaps because too many foreign powers were involved. The United States, which had become one of the most powerful and prosperous Western nations in the late 1800s, discouraged full colonization by promoting what it termed an "Open Door" policy that allowed equal access by all the foreign powers to China's vast markets and resources. The Open Door enabled the Western nations and, eventually, Japan to avoid conflict among themselves and to acquire the economic fruits of empire without the high political and military costs of conquering and governing China.

Late Qing Reforms and Wars

Between 1890 and 1916 the growing foreign challenge now included Japan, which was rapidly industrializing. In search of resources and markets to exploit, in the 1890s Japan began intervening in Korea, long a vassal state of China. The Koreans sent pleas for help to China, and the resulting Sino-Japanese War (1894–1895) ended in a humiliating defeat for China. In

---

gunboat diplomacy   The Western countries' use of superior firepower to impose their will on local populations and governments in the nineteenth century.

the treaty ending hostilities, China was forced to pay an in-demnity and to recognize Korean independence, and in 1910 Korea became a Japanese colony. The Qing were also forced to cede the large island of Taiwan, populated largely by Chinese, to Japan, the island becoming a Japanese colony in 1910, and to acknowledge Japanese control of the Ryukyu (ree-OO-kyoo) Islands, between Japan and Taiwan, whose Japanese-speaking people had an independent state and a long-stand-ing tributary relationship with China. The Manchus had already lost influence over other tributary states, such as Viet-nam (to France) and Burma (to Britain). The defeat by Japan proved a blow to Chinese pride and to the credibility of the Qing rulers.

These crises brought a group of progressive reformers to the attention of the young Manchu emperor, Guangxu, and, in 1898, under their influence, he called for dramatic changes, later known as the 100 Days of Reform, which included a crash pro-gram of economic modernization. But the Empress Dowager Xi Ci and her conservative allies blocked the proposals, arrested the reformers, and placed the emperor under house arrest. Xi Ci and the reactionaries reclaimed power, promoted an antiforeign at-mosphere, and encouraged the Chinese to organize antiforeign militias.

The ensuing tensions led to the Boxer Rebellion, a popular movement in 1900 that aimed at driving the foreigners out of China but that resulted in an even stronger Western presence. The Qing gave strong backing to the Boxers ("Righteous Har-mony Fists"), an anti-Western, anti-Christian secret society comprising mostly poor peasants. To spread their cause, the Boxers wrote jingles promising that when all the foreigners were expelled from China, the Qing would bring peace to the land. The Boxers attacked foreigners in north China, occupied Beijing, and besieged the foreign embassies. The Qing declared war on all the foreign powers with which it had been forced to sign unequal treaties. In response, the British, Americans, French, and other powers put aside their differences and or-ganized an international force that routed the Boxers, occupied Beijing, and forced the Qing to pay another huge indemnity and to permit foreign military forces to stay in China. The Europeans talked openly of dismantling China, and the Russians used the rebellion as an excuse to occupy Manchuria.

The string of defeats generated final frantic efforts at re-form and modernization, setting the stage for more dramatic transitions. Fearing China might soon be divided into colonies, the chastened Manchus now began more serious reform ef-forts, looking to Japan for models. The Qing abolished the Confucian examination system, established two millennia earlier, set up modern, Western-style schools, and sent 10,000 students to Japan. By 1911 some 57,000 state schools enrolled 1,600,000 students, though this was in fact only a fraction of China's school-age children. The Qing also formed new gov-ernment departments, allocated more money to the military, and strengthened provincial and local governments. Reformist ideas also sparked movements among women. Some women studying in Japan formed the Encompassing Love Society, with the goal of uplifting Chinese women and making them full participants in society. Other women, including some Chris-

tians, strived to raise female literacy and expand economic op-portunities. The feminist Zhang Zhuzhun encouraged Chi-nese women to emulate Western women role models such as the British nurse Florence Nightingale and the American anti-slavery crusader Harriett Beecher Stowe.

Liberals who had criticized the Qing reformers for going too slowly now became more influential. Many reformers had read and even translated European literature and scholarship, including that of Enlightenment writers, and were deeply im-pressed by Japan's modernization in the later 1800s. The lead-ing liberal reformer, Liang Qichao (1871–1929), represented change within tradition. A scholar and journalist, Liang pro-moted a modernization that blended Confucian values and Western learning. He also believed China should industrialize, form a constitutional government, and focus on the idea of na-tion instead of culture. Liang's colleague and teacher, Kang Youwei (1858–1928), envisioned a world government, the end of nationalist strife and gender discrimination, and a welfare state to nurture humanity. Both men promoted women's edu-cation, and Kang founded the anti-footbinding movement to stop the longtime Chinese practice of forcing women to com-press their feet to please men's taste. Footbinding severely hampered women; as a song passed among illiterate women put it, "Your body is so heavy a burden for your feet that you fear you may stumble in the wind."[13]

Chinese Nationalism and Revolutionary Movements

For some Chinese inspired by nationalism, most importantly Sun Zhong Shan, better known as Sun Yat-Sen (soon yot-SEN), the fiasco of the Boxer Rebellion showed the futility of trying to change China by reform from above and prompted them to organize a revolution from below that could sweep the Manchus from power. Inspired by the Taipings, Meiji Japan (see next section), and the West, Sun (1866–1925) mixed tradi-tion and modernity. Unlike the liberal reformers such as Liang and Kang, Sun did not come from an upper-class mandarin background. He knew little of the Confucian classics and had no commitment to the traditional system. He identified with the poor and downtrodden, writing that he was a coolie and the son of a coolie. Born near Guangzhou to a peasant family that had supported the Taipings, Sun moved to Hawaii at age thirteen to join an elder brother. There he studied in an Anglican high school and became a semi-Christian. He then received a medical degree in British-ruled Hong Kong. Influ-enced by Western thought, he began dressing in Western clothes and visited England, where he learned that Westerners often criticized their own systems and sometimes favored socialism. Convinced that the Qing system was hopeless, Sun decided to devote his life to politics and became the chief architect of the Chinese Revolution.

In 1895 Sun founded an anti-Manchu secret society dedi-cated to replacing the imperial system with a Western-style re-public, and branches were set up in China, Japan, and Hawaii (see Witness to the Past: Planning a Revolutionary New

class. Hiroshige produced some 5,500 different prints, sold individually or in collections such as the *53 Stations of the Tokaido* and *One Hundred Views of Famous Places in Edo*. However, his personal life was often troubled. Hiroshige never prospered financially and was often pressed to finance his beloved nightly cup of rice wine. He married several times and sired several children. His eldest daughter's husband, known as Hiroshige II (1826–1869), continued Hiroshige's artistic tradition. At the age of sixty Hiroshige became a Buddhist monk, not an unusual step for aging Japanese men. He died at age sixty-two in 1858 of cholera during a great epidemic. On his deathbed, he discouraged his family from holding a lavish funeral by reciting an old verse: "When I die, Cremate me not nor bury me. Just lay me in the fields, to fill the belly of some starving dog."

Hiroshige was the last of the major Japanese print masters. Shortly after he died, Westerners opened up Japan, ending the secluded world that had nourished the woodblock prints and the artists who produced them. But Hiroshige prints continued to be traded around the world, giving foreigners their most vivid impressions of Japan. When Europeans imported the pictures in the late 1800s, they proved a revelation to artists looking for new ways to portray landscapes. Hence woodblock prints, born of isolation, became one of the first major cultural links between Japan and the outside world.

THINKING ABOUT THE PROFILE

1. How did Hokusai and Hiroshige's prints differ from earlier Japanese prints?

2. What do Hiroshige's life and art tell us about late Tokugawa Japan?

Note: Quotation from Julian Bicknell, *Hiroshige in Tokyo: The Floating World of Edo* (San Francisco: Pomegranate Artbooks, 1994), p. 50.

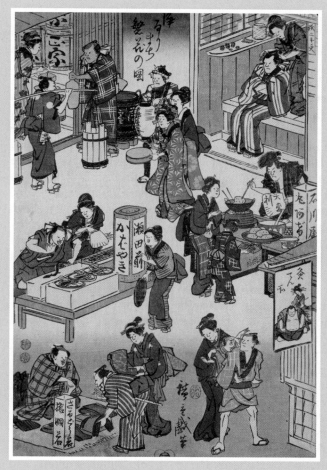

Street Stalls and Tradesmen in Joruricho   This print by Hiroshige portraying the street life in Edo reveals the artist's sympathy for common people, such as the peddlers, barbers, and food-sellers shown at work and their customers.
(Courtesy of the Trustees of the Victoria & Albert Museum)

Tokugawa arts were also vigorous, producing creations that achieved renown worldwide. Japanese artistic products that were prized in the West, such as ceramics, jewelry, and furniture, enriched the Dutch traders at Nagasaki who controlled the export trade. The late 1700s and early 1800s was a great age for painting and woodblock prints, some of it influenced by Western ideas. The two greatest artists blended Japanese and imported art styles. Katsushika Hokusai (HO-koo-sie) (1760–1849) produced tens of thousands of paintings and drawings, but he was most famous for landscape prints such as the *Thirty-six Views of Mount Fuji*. He strove to improve his craft, predicting that "by ninety I will surely have penetrated the mystery of life. At one hundred, I will have attained a magnificent level and at one hundred and ten, each dot of my work will vibrate with life."[17] Ando Hiroshige (1797–1858) concentrated on Tokyo scenes and landscapes emphasizing nature (see Profile: Ando Hiroshige, Japanese Artist). The treatment of atmosphere and light in Japanese color prints influenced the French impressionist painters of the later 1800s, who empha-

sized the effect of light and color in momentary scenes (see Chapter 20). Both Japanese prints and French impressionism asked the viewer to look at an everyday scene in a new way. The influential European artist Vincent Van Gogh admitted that he strove to emulate Japanese landscape painting.

Growing Problems and Reform

Despite these advantages, by the early 1800s some Japanese sensed internal decay. Japanese of all classes increasingly blamed the Tokugawa for the nation's growing domestic problems: inflation, increasing taxes, and social disorder. In addition, there was the gradual impoverishment of the samurai. Over the years the daimyo families, burdened with heavy expenses, had cut the salaries of the samurai, who were trained as warriors but often worked as bureaucrats in daimyo domains. With their income declining, and finding it harder to support their families, the samurai borrowed money and became indebted to merchants. In the 1830s Japan was also experiencing widespread famine and starvation. The growing social tensions and resentments reached a breaking point, fostering urban riots, peasant revolts, and various plots to depose the Tokugawa shogun.

While worried about domestic unrest, Japanese officials were more concerned about the growing Western presence in the region, which they correctly perceived would impact Japan. They knew that Russians had been active in Siberia and the North Pacific since the 1700s and that British ships had sailed along Japan's coast. In 1825 the shogun ordered that whenever a foreign ship was sighted approaching the coast, the samurai should fire on it and drive it away. After China's defeat in the Opium War, Japan's shocked leaders encouraged the samurai to develop new, more effective weapons and contemplated starting a navy. The Japanese considered the Westerners money-grasping barbarians who did not understand the proper rules of social behavior and who would contaminate the national spirit. As the samurai vowed to fight to the death to resist Western invasion, this feeling of nationalism grew, putting pressure on the shogun to deal firmly with the Western threat.

Japanese leaders responded with reforms to strengthen the country. The Tokugawa reforms implemented at the national level, such as breaking up merchant monopolies, establishing a bureau to translate Western books, and reducing the number of government officials to save money, were largely unsuccessful in energizing the system. But some provincial governments, especially in the southwest, attempted more daring and creative changes. They recruited men of talent to their local administrations, emphasized mastery of "Dutch studies," and even sponsored industrial experiments, including the construction of an electric steam engine in the 1850s. Samurai in several of these domains learned how to cast better guns and to produce iron suitable for making modern cannon.

The Opening of Japan

The need for change was made urgent by external forces that arose in the 1850s. Spanish and Portuguese merchants and missionaries had introduced Western influence into Japan in the 1500s, but their aggressive behavior and antagonizing of Japanese leaders had caused the Tokugawa to end the cultural and economic exchange. The Dutch presence at Nagasaki, which benefited both the Dutch and the Japanese, was the legacy of Japan's earlier encounter with the West. By the 1850s, however, Japan faced a new threat to its seclusion policy.

The most dramatic attempt to break down Japanese seclusion came from the Americans. American ships had occasionally visited the Dutch base at Nagasaki to trade, and by the early 1800s, besides trade, U.S. leaders also wanted Japan to protect shipwrecked sailors and provide fresh water and coal to ships making the long trip between California and China. In 1853 a fleet of eleven U.S. warships commanded by Commodore Matthew Perry sailed into Tokyo Bay and delivered a letter from the U.S. president, Millard Fillmore, to the shogun. The letter demanded that the Japanese sign a treaty opening the country or face war when Perry returned the following year. The three U.S. steamships with the expedition, known as

the "black ships," shocked the Japanese with their ability to move against the wind and tide. The shogun, remembering the Opium War and more realistic than his critics, granted Perry's demands in the Treaty of Kanagawa (1854) and then accepted the blame for the nation's humiliation. The treaty opened two ports to U.S. trade and allowed for the stationing of a U.S. consul. By 1856 American diplomats demanded a stronger commercial treaty, the opening of more ports, extraterritoriality, and the admission of Christian missionaries. The shogun reluctantly agreed; he soon signed similar treaties with the Dutch, British, French, and Russians.

Like China, Japan experienced a forcible intrusion from the West that held the seeds of potential colonization. Although the changes still limited the Westerners' movement in Japan, most Japanese leaders saw that Japan was the loser in these dealings. Western merchants soon arrived, flooding the nation with cheap industrial goods to create a market and destroy the native industries, as they had done earlier in China and India. International settlements restricted to foreigners were established in Japan's major port cities. Westerners enjoyed ever increasing economic and legal privileges, and escalating domestic disunity held the potential for enhancing Western power.

The Tokugawa Government in Crisis

Western encroachment provoked a crisis for the Tokugawa government and a national debate about how Japan should respond to its challenges. Some Japanese believed accommodation was preferable to war and favored either a complete or a limited opening to the West. One prominent Westernizer, Fukuzawa Yukichi (1835–1901), traveled in the West and became a strong proponent of Western liberalism, rationalism, and political freedom. Another group advocated complete defiance and the use of force to expel the intruders. One such advocate wrote that the Americans had dishonored Japan and that every Japanese needed to help stop the nation from becoming enslaved by other nations. Turning against the ineffective Tokugawa shoguns but not the powerless emperor who symbolized the nation, one faction proclaimed, "Revere the Emperor, Expel the Barbarians."

Shaken by the Western presence, the Tokugawa government launched efforts at modernization. It established a shipbuilding industry, promoted manufacturing, hired two hundred Western teachers, sent a few Japanese students abroad, established an institute of Western studies, and expanded the study of foreign languages. The Japanese who had already become interested in Western science and technology, however, saw these innovations as too little and too late.

Despite the reforms, the Tokugawa shogun was now widely perceived as weak. Aware of Japan's military disadvantage, the shogun always chose negotiation rather than defiance, even when the Westerners badly misused their power and retaliated for any attacks on Western residents. The shogun's strategy of avoiding confrontation led a respected poet to complain angrily: "You, whose ancestors in the mighty days, Roared at the skies and swept the earth, Stand now helpless to drive off wrangling foreigners—How empty your title, 'Queller of the Barbarians.'"[18] Furthermore, the Western powers continually made new demands. By the 1860s the Japanese seemed to be repeating the experience of China, gradually losing control of their political and economic future.

Challenges to the Korean Kingdom

Like Tokugawa Japan, Korea, though faced with growing problems in this era, had also chosen relative isolation. From ancient times the peoples of the mountainous Korean peninsula had been shaped by their location between powerful China and Japan. Over the centuries Koreans had mixed China's religions, political structure, and writing system with their own customs. Still, the Koreans maintained a strong national identity and learned how to balance close links to China with their political independence. Like China, Korea became a unified state presided over by a series of family dynasties ruling with a Confucian ideology.

The last of the Korean dynasties, the Yi (YEE) (1392–1910), ruled the state they called Choson (choh-SAN) for over five centuries, favoring powerful landlord families. By officially closing off Korea from the outside world after the Manchus invaded and pillaged the capital in the early 1600s, the Yi earned Choson the label of "the Hermit Kingdom." However, as in Tokugawa Japan, seclusion from the outside was not absolute. Korea still traded with China. Better irrigation technologies and new strains of rice from China increased agricultural productivity. Korean scholars also visited China and on their return some wrote books favorably contrasting Chinese society with what they considered Korea's overly rigid and inequitable social system. A few Koreans met Westerners in China and found their philosophies, political ideas, and technologies of interest.

Korean seclusion did not result in cultural stagnation. Several strong kings in the 1700s fostered a renewed culture of learning, including the printing of encyclopedias and historical records. Knowledge of writing in Korean spread more widely. Educated aristocratic women wrote memoirs, diaries, and stories of court life, and even some commoners wrote stories and novels. Literature, philosophy, painting, and ceramics flourished. Some thinkers, to promote justice, examined social conditions by studying the peasants.

However, by the early 1800s Choson, like Qing China and Tokugawa Japan, began to succumb to stress. As in Japan, the rigid social structure crumbled as the economy grew. Korea's population doubled to some 9 million between 1669 and 1800, increasing pressure on the land. With Buddhism losing influence, some Koreans turned to Christianity. Although officially prohibited, a few French and Chinese Christian missionaries nevertheless illegally entered Korea and spread their message. During the 1800s Korea also experienced recurrent famines and increased political instability, including peasant uprisings. The Choson government blamed and hence persecuted Christians and Western missionaries for undermining society and causing turmoil. One official told the French missionaries he was expelling that they had no right to tell Koreans to abandon their ancient teachings and accept those of alien cultures.

The challenges to Korea and its neighbors caused Koreans to reflect on and deal with the threats. As in China and Japan, Korean intellectuals debated the value of Western learning, and some pushed for reforms of the traditional political and social system. With the Yi refusing direct commercial negotiations with the West, Korean military forces drove away French and American ships seeking to open Korea to Western trade, and in 1871 they repulsed a U.S. naval force. The Yi also worried about Russian expansion to the north, in eastern Siberia. By the later 1800s Korea seemed in need of rejuvenation.

SECTION SUMMARY

■ Japan was better able than China to deal with foreign pressures because of its compactness and homogeneity, its openness to outside ideas, its balance of power between groups of elites, its strong merchant class, and its sensitivity to the threat posed by foreigners.

■ Late Tokugawa Japanese culture was vigorous, open to Western learning, and marked by thriving urban centers and ambitious artists.

■ Internal decay in Japan led to riots and revolts, but officials, more concerned with external threats, embarked on reforms designed to strengthen the country and enable it to withstand pressure from Westerners. However, when faced with a choice between war and opening Japan to American trade, the Japanese shogun chose trade, which led to trade agreements with other Western nations, a flood of cheap manufactured goods, and special privileges for Westerners in Japan.

■ For hundreds of years, the Yi dynasty had closed Korea off from the rest of the world, earning for itself the label "the Hermit Kingdom," and when Korea experienced famine and instability in the 1800s, its leaders blamed the influence of Christian missionaries.

The Remaking of Japan and Korea

How did the Meiji government transform Japan and Korea?

The ultimate Japanese response to Western intrusion was radically different from China's, allowing Japan to avoid the shackles of colonialism and become the only non-Western nation to successfully industrialize and achieve Western standards of living before World War II. This transition owed much to a revolution that ended Tokugawa rule in 1868 and created a new government that fostered dramatic reforms that helped Japan resist the West. By the early 1900s a powerful Japan had increased its influence in the wider world. Meanwhile, Korea was forced to abandon several centuries of isolation and eventually became a Japanese colony.

Tokugawa Defeat and the Meiji Restoration

By the 1860s the deteriorating situation in Japan led to a revolution against the Tokugawa shogunate, known as the **Meiji Restoration** (1867–1868) because it was carried out in the name of the emperor, whose reign name was Meiji (MAY-gee). The revolution that overthrew the Tokugawa resulted from a conspiracy by regional leaders, especially the progressive daimyo and younger samurai from the southwestern part of Japan. The anti-Tokugawa leaders, united mostly by their hatred of the status quo, had varied goals and perspectives. Some were avid Westernizers, others extreme nationalists. Most were ambitious outsiders of samurai background who were alienated from the Tokugawa power structure. Although they came from privileged families, they were unafraid to ally with commoners, especially merchants. They were generally pragmatic men who understood that protecting Japan from foreign domination required radical change.

As public respect for the shogun faded, Japanese dissidents turned to the relatively powerless Meiji emperor as an alternative. While the shoguns had exercised power from Edo, the imperial family had lived in seclusion in Kyoto two hundred miles to the south. In 1868 anti-Tokugawa leaders, backed by military force, seized the imperial palace in Kyoto and convinced the emperor to dismiss the shogun and decree the restoration of his own rule. The decree ousted the Tokugawa family from their land and positions, opened the government to men of talent, appointed the rebels as advisers to the emperor, and announced that "all matters shall be decided by public discussion" and "the evil customs of the past shall be broken off. Knowledge shall be sought throughout the world."[19] The Tokugawa family and their supporters fought back, sparking a bitter one-year civil war that cost many lives. Ultimately, however, the rebel forces prevailed and crushed all armed resistance.

The new regime took shape early. Among the major changes introduced by the new leaders, Japan joined the world community and agreed to honor all treaties. As a symbolic attack on centuries of tradition and an affirmation of a new beginning, the imperial residence was moved from Kyoto to Tokyo (formerly Edo), a much larger and more dynamic city. Perceiving change as a necessary evil, the Meiji leaders had no master plan but pragmatically sought ways to achieve national unity, wealth, defense, and equality with the West.

Meiji Government and the Military

The Meiji regime's crash program of modernization lasted for thirty years. Although influenced by Western political and economic models, Meiji reformers also incorporated Japanese traditions in building a distinctive form of industrial society, in the process defusing the threat of colonialism and neocolonialism. Despite its flaws, the system introduced by the Meiji proved both productive for Japan and, in recent decades, an attractive model for the rapidly industrializing nations in East and Southeast Asia.

Meiji Restoration A revolution against the Tokugawa shogunate in Japan in 1867–1868, carried out in the name of the Meiji emperor; led to the successful modernization of Japan.

Meiji leaders needed to establish an effective governmental structure and secure the loyalty of the population. One of their first acts was to form a State Council to advise and control the emperor. They then moved to defuse potential opposition by recruiting both samurais and commoners into the new bureaucracy while convincing the regional daimyo families to give up control of their land, and the peasants living on it, in exchange for appointment as regional governors with guaranteed salaries. Freeing the peasants made it easier for them to move to cities in search of manufacturing or service work, something illegal under the Tokugawa. The government employed thousands of Western advisers, teachers, and even workers, who gave advice but were required to train Japanese assistants to replace them when their contracts expired. Because it financed these programs through tax revenues, Meiji Japan did not need foreign loans, hence avoiding the debt trap that ensnared most Latin American and Middle Eastern societies as well as China.

The new political system had democratic trappings, but reformers were divided on how much democracy to foster. The Japanese had no tradition of political freedom and had to invent a new word for the concept. A small group of leaders made most of the key decisions until after the turn of the century. Nonetheless, responding to a growing movement for more popular participation in decision making, in 1889 the Meiji leaders wrote the first constitution in Japanese history and formed a constitutional monarchy symbolically headed by the emperor. The constitution introduced an independent judiciary and a two-house parliament that was elected by the 450,000 men who were tax-paying property holders. Parliament chose members for the cabinet, which made policy and supervised the government apparatus. The first political parties, led mostly by former samurai, were formed in the 1880s, but they remained factionalized and weak as a political force.

Using the slogan "rich country, strong army," the government stressed industrial development and enhanced communications by building railroads and telegraphs, in part to aid the construction of a modern military force to protect the nation. Anxious about Western imperialism in Asia, the Japanese concluded that military power was necessary to assert national interest in the modern world. To build up the armed forces, including a modern navy, Meiji leaders drafted commoners as soldiers, once a profession limited to samurai. By breaking down the former distinction between samurai, merchant, and peasant, the military draft promoted social leveling. Furthermore, military service fostered literacy and nationalism among the peasants who joined.

Compared with China, the Meiji leaders enjoyed more freedom of action to reshape their society to strengthen the nation. Since pressure from the West gradually diminished, Japan had time to improve its military. Japan was also a much less inviting target for the West than China or Southeast Asia, since it had few natural resources that could be profitably exploited. Westerners viewed Japan as a market for their goods, but China had many more potential consumers. The various Western powers, largely preoccupied elsewhere, saw Japan mainly as a potential ally against each other.

- Russian expansion brought it control of eastern Siberia, Muslim Central Asia, and the Caucasus states, although some peoples, such as the Chechens, fiercely resisted.

- Russia's economy expanded along with its territory, creating a discontented proletariat while many Russian thinkers embraced Western ideals, the Slavophiles argued for the superiority of traditional Russian culture.

- Russians increasingly discontented with the demands of empire-building and autocratic rulers joined terrorist groups and supported a revolution in 1905, which, while put down, led to reforms

Online Study Center **ACE the Test**

◆ Chapter Summary

Between 1750 and 1914 China faced daunting challenges from the Western powers. Qing China had long been able to rebuff Western demands for more trade, but the government and economy were declining by the early 1800s. China's attempts to halt British opium smuggling led to the Opium War, and its defeat in that war resulted in an unequal treaty system that gave Western nations greater access to China and its resources. Increasing poverty and rebellions further undermined Qing power. Attempts at modernization failed because of China's vast size, conservative opposition, and fears of radical culture change. In 1911 revolution ended the imperial system, but the new republic soon collapsed in civil war.

While the Western challenges progressively undermined China, they prompted Japan to transform its society. Tokugawa Japan faced increasing problems by the early 1800s. The arrival of American ships demanding that Japan open itself to the West forced the issue and undermined the shogunate, which gave in to Western demands. The shogunate then lost power in the 1868 Meiji Restoration, a short revolution led by progressive daimyo and younger samurai. Capitalizing on dynamic merchants, high literacy rates, a tradition of cultural borrowing, and national loyalties, the Meiji government launched a crash program to modernize Japan's government, military, economy, and social patterns, importing Western ideas and institutions. By 1900 the Meiji had industrialized Japan, deflected Western ambitions, and turned Japan into a world power. This power allowed Japan to defeat China and Russia in two wars and to colonize Korea.

Russian expansion into Asian power brought it into conflict with China and Japan, but Russia was shaped more by its proximity to Europe and Muslim Asia. Despotic Russian leaders pushed Russian control across Siberia and into eastern Europe and colonized Central Asia and the Caucasus. By the later 1800s Russia dominated large parts of Eurasia, forming the world's largest contiguous land empire. But maintaining an empire against restless colonized societies strained Russian capabilities. Russia also industrialized and promoted social change, but repression of the Russian peasants ultimately brought dissent and revolutionary movements.

Online Study Center **Improve Your Grade** Flashcards

Key Terms

Chinoiserie	gunboat diplomacy	Burakumin
Co-hong	Meiji Restoration	Russification
extraterritoriality	state capitalism	Slavophiles
international settlements	zaibatsu	

Suggested Reading

Books

Allworth, Edward, ed. *Central Asia: 130 Years of Russian Rule*, 2nd ed. Durham, N.C.: Duke University Press, 1994. A collection of essays.

Chang, Hsin-Pao. *Commissioner Lin and the Opium War*. New York: W. W. Norton, 1964. The classic account.

Ebrey, Patricia Buckley, Anne Walthall, and James B. Palais. *East Asia: A Cultural, Social, and Political History*. Boston: Houghton Mifflin, 2006. A recent, balanced survey.

Evtuhov, Catherine, et al. *A History of Russia: Peoples, Legends, Events, Forces*. Boston: Houghton Mifflin, 2004. A detailed survey.

Fahr-Becker, Gabriele, ed. *Japanese Prints*. New York: Barnes and Noble, 2003. A well-illustrated introduction to this wonderful art.

Madariaga, Isabel de. *Russia in the Age of Catherine the Great*. London: Phoenix Press, 1981. Reprint of a well-balanced and panoramic examination of Catherine and her era.

Matsunosuke, Nishiyama. *Edo Culture: Daily Life and Diversions in Urban Japan, 1600–1868*. Honolulu: University of Hawaii Press, 1997. A fascinating look at popular culture during the Tokugawa era.

McClain, James L. *Japan: A Modern History*. New York: W. W. Norton, 2002. An excellent survey of events since 1600.

Schirokauer, Conrad, and Donald N. Clark. *Modern East Asia: A Brief History*. Belmont, Calif.: Thomson/Wadsworth, 2004. A survey of China, Japan, and Korea in this era.

Smith, Richard J. *China's Cultural Heritage: The Ch'ing Dynasty, 1644–1913*, 2nd ed. Boulder, Colo.: Westview Press, 1994. A readable and comprehensive study.

Spence, Jonathan D. *The Search for Modern China*, 2nd ed. New York: W. W. Norton, 1999. A provocative examination.

Websites

East and Southeast Asia: An Annotated Directory of Internet Resources (http://newton.uor.edu/Departments&Programs/AsianStudies-Dept/general.html). Links on history, culture, and politics.

The Floating World of Ukiyo-e: Shadow, Dreams, and Substance (http://www.loc.gov/exhibits/ukiyo-e/). Introduces the Japanese prints at the Library of Congress.

Internet Guide to Chinese Studies (http://www.sino.uni-heidelberg.de/igcs/). An excellent collection of links, maintained by a German university.

Internet East Asian History Sourcebook (http://www.fordham.edu/halsall/eastasia/eastasiasbook.html). Sources and links on China, Japan, and Korea.

Russian History Index: The World Wide Web Virtual Library (http://vlib.iue.it/hist-russia/Index.html). Useful links.

CHAPTER 24

World Wars, European Revolutions, and Global Depression, 1914–1945

Online Study Center

This icon will direct you to interactive activities and study materials on the website: college.hmco.com/pic/lockard1e

Global Communism The Communist leaders of the Soviet Union hoped that their revolution in Russia in 1917 would inspire similar revolutions around the world, ending capitalism and imperialism. This poster reflects the dream of a triumphant communism.   (Museum of the Revolution, Moscow/The Bridgeman Art Library International)

My beautiful, pitiful era. With an insane smile you look back, cruel and weak, like an animal past its prime, at the prints of your own paws.

OSIP MANDELSTAM, RUSSIAN POET[1]

By April 1917 the French army had been fighting the Germans for over two and a half years. World War I was creating growing casualty lists and inflicting tremendous hardship on soldiers on both sides. The French officers were divided between those who favored a more aggressive strategy, likely to result in many more deaths, and those who wanted a more defensive approach. The latter group included a new French commander, General Philippe Pétain (peh-TANH) (1856–1951), who implemented a strategy to minimize French casualties. A peasant's son with the demeanor of an aristocrat, Pétain was noted for his sweeping white moustache and his passion for romance, including many love affairs with other men's wives. Pétain regarded his soldiers as more than cannon fodder, a view that made him popular with the fighting men.

At first Pétain was overruled, and the French launched another frontal assault on the well-fortified German lines. The result was a military disaster that caused perhaps 120,000 deaths and broke the fighting spirit of the French troops. Mutinies broke out in the units, ranging from minor infractions of code to violent disturbances. Some soldiers even proposed a protest march on Paris, and 20,000 deserted. Most mutineers were loyal to their nation, but they protested the slaughter resulting from a futile military strategy of suicidal assaults. The army executed about 50 mutineers but also made concessions to the frontline troops, granting them more leave, better food, and more generous rations of wine. Mutinies and an overwhelming war-weariness occurred among all the combatant nations. Pétain muttered that France should immediately consider peace negotiations. He emerged from World War I as a French hero, but he later lost his hero status when he served as the nominal head of the French government under hated Nazi occupation in World War II. Pétain died in prison, a broken man looking back on three tumultuous decades that had brought so much distress and destruction to the world.

Those three decades between 1914 and 1945 included not only two great military struggles involving many nations, but also a mighty revolution in Russia, a terrible economic depression with worldwide consequences, and the rise of new ideologies. The Russian Jewish poet Osip Mandelstam, reflecting on the turbulent decades beginning with World War I—an era full of achievements and atrocities, heroism and hardship—aptly described them as a "beautiful, pitiful era."

In the years before World War I some Europeans had believed that the world was poised for a new age in which the ideals of Western democracy might be achieved throughout the world and the horrors of war would be ended forever, bringing an era of international cooperation. Liberals even hoped World War I would be the war to end all wars, a goal it spectacularly failed to achieve. Indeed, the hopes of the idealists were dashed by two world wars, fought partly in Europe, that challenged the Western world-view of liberalism and rationalism that had captured the European imagination since the Enlightenment; and the faith in progress was shattered by dictatorship in Russia, economic collapse, and organized slaughter. The disarray in Europe, combined with the spread of new ideologies and technologies, helped undermine Western political influence in the world, except for that of the rising Western power, the United States.

FOCUS QUESTIONS

1. What was the impact of World War I on the Western world?
2. How did communism prevail in Russia and transform that country?
3. How did the Great Depression reshape world politics and economies?
4. What were the main ideas and impacts of fascism?
5. What were the costs and consequences of World War II?

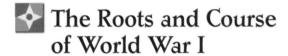

The Roots and Course of World War I

What was the impact of World War I on the Western world?

In August 1914, war broke out between the major powers of Europe. As the fighting began, the British foreign secretary remarked, "The lights are going out all over Europe. We shall not see them again in our lifetime."[2] The conflict pitted two alliances. Britain, France, and Russia formed the Triple Entente, which later included Serbia, Japan, Italy, Portugal, Romania, Greece, and eventually the United States. These nations, also known as the Allies, faced the Central Powers: Germany, Austria-Hungary, the Ottoman Empire, and Bulgaria. Although most of the military action took place in and around Europe, the leaders of the countries involved saw the conflict as nothing short of a struggle to control the global system, with its industrial economies and colonial empires. The Great War, as many Europeans called it, was history's first total war, an armed conflict between industrialized powers that lasted four terrible years. The war brought down empires and dynasties, made the United States a world power, and weakened western Europe's hold over the colonial world. And the end of the conflict made a second major war almost inevitable.

European Societies in the Early 1900s

In the early 1900s, before World War I began, Europeans enjoyed affluence, social stability, and growing democracy; there were few signs of a major war involving the key European powers. The productive European economies benefited from their links to each other and their access to resources and markets in other

parts of the world. Some thinkers of the time believed nations tied by interlocking transnational economies and commercial interdependence would never wage war against each other. European nations cooperated in many things besides trade. For example, they agreed on treaties binding their nations to protect the right of workers to pensions and health insurance while restricting child labor. Furthermore, culture often transcended borders. Whatever their nationality, educated Europeans shared a love for the music of the eighteenth-century Austrian composer Wolfgang Amadeus Mozart and the novels of the nineteenth-century Russian writer Leo Tolstoy. Europeans frequently spoke two or three languages, traveled in other countries, and were often citizens of countries whose royal families had intermarried. In 1899 European nations met in the Netherlands and agreed to limit armaments and create the International Court to settle disputes between nations. Although submitting disputes was voluntary and the court was seldom invoked, these European nations hoped it would discourage a sudden outburst of war.

Europeans looked to the future with confidence, felt superior to the rest of the world, and enjoyed their prosperity. Thanks in part to imperial expansion, which had acquired resources in colonized Africa and Asia, Europeans now consumed new products such as chocolate and rubber tires, and rising populations expanded markets. Between 1880 and 1910 the population grew 43 percent in Germany, 26 percent in Britain, and over 50 percent in Russia. European emigration to the Americas and Australia increased markets there for European goods, and improved transportation, such as automobiles and large ships, made it easier to move people, natural resources and manufactured products over long distances. European capital financed South African gold and diamond mines, Malayan rubber plantations, Australian sheep stations, Russian railways, and Canadian wheat fields, not to mention every sector of the growing U.S. economy.

at home, Germany was forced to agree to peace in November 1918. Kaiser Wilhelm II and the Austro-Hungarian emperor both abdicated, ending two long-standing European monarchies. The Allies dictated the peace terms.

Consequences of World War I

World War I undermined the power of Germany and shifted more influence to the victors: Britain, France, and the United States. It reshaped Europe politically and rearranged the colonial empires. World War I and its aftermath also affected the societies of Asia and Africa, destroying their hopes for achieving independence or self-rule. Although powerful Western nations still dominated world politics and the world economy, the war also changed the old global order and began a new one.

A New Europe The Paris Peace Conference of 1919, held in the former royal palace in the Paris suburb of Versailles (vuhr-SIGH), reshaped Europe and resulted in the Treaty of Versailles. The U.S. president, Woodrow Wilson, went to Paris hoping to use his prestige and his nation's growing power to sell an agenda, known as the Fourteen Points, to skeptical British and French leaders. Favoring political freedom and stability, Wilson also proposed conciliatory treatment of Germany because he worried that a humiliated, crippled Germany would become chaotic and seek revenge. However, Wilson had to compromise with the hardline French, who wanted to divide Germany. Although the final treaty did not divide Germany, it required Germany to partly dismantle its military; abandon its Asian, African, and Pacific colonies; and shift land to its European neighbors, leaving 3 million ethnic Germans outside of Germany in countries such as Czechoslovakia and Poland. The Treaty of Versailles also forced Germany to pay huge annual payments, known as reparations, to the Allies to compensate for their war costs. In short, Germany was left virtually disarmed and bankrupt. Ultimately the treaty failed to create a lasting settlement, instead planting the roots for future problems, as Wilson had feared. The new German leader, Fridrich Ebert, had a foreboding about Germany's troubled future: "The armistice will not produce a just peace. The sacrifices imposed on us must lead to our people's doom."[7]

The war had taken an appalling human toll on both sides, causing Europeans to reflect on what had happened. Altogether 9 to 10 million soldiers died, including 2 million Russians, 2 million Germans, 1.5 million French, and 75,000 Americans. Since some 10 million civilians died, the total killed was around 20 million. The war also had a social and political impact on Europe. The brutality and waste radicalized many workers and peasants, especially in eastern Europe. Leftist political parties—Socialists and Communists—gained strength. In 1914 Europeans had gone to war with patriotic enthusiasm, but by 1918 some philosophers and writers feared that the initial enthusiasm for war meant the rejection of Enlightenment rationality, and they concluded that the slaughter had destroyed the Western claim to moral leadership in the world. Pacifist, antiwar sentiments grew. The French writer

Henri Barbusse, a soldier himself, reflected these sentiments in these words: "The work of the future will be to wipe out the present. Shame on military glory, shame on armies, shame on the soldier's calling that changes men by turns into stupid victims and ignoble brutes."[8]

The war destroyed several old states and created new ones. The fall of centuries-old imperial houses brought political instability that worsened the social and economic dislocations. Four empires—the Russian, Ottoman, Austro-Hungarian, and German—collapsed. As a result of the Russian Revolution of 1917, Communists gained power in Russia, launching a new political and economic system. Elsewhere, Wilson, believing that ethnically homogeneous nation-states could prevent nationalist rivalries, promoted the self-determination of peoples in Europe. Wilson's efforts proved persuasive: the Paris Peace Conference redrew national boundaries to give ethnic minorities their own states. In eastern Europe, Poland, Czechoslovakia, Yugoslavia, and Finland were carved out of the ruins of the German, Austro-Hungarian, and Russian Empires. These countries later became pawns in the struggle for influence between Germany and Russia that helped launch World War II. But most of the new states placed various ethnic groups within arbitrary boundaries. For example, the country that became Yugoslavia included varied peoples—Orthodox Serbs, Catholic Croats and Slovenes, and Muslim Slavs and Albanians—who had fought each other for centuries and did not share a common national identity. The sacrifices of war, and the appeal of national independence, also led to changes within the British Empire. Britain faced uprisings and civil war in its longtime colony, Ireland, and in 1921 it was forced to grant most of the island special status within the British Empire as the self-governing Irish Free State. In 1937 Ireland became completely independent of the British crown, finally realizing the centuries-old dream of Irish nationalists.

Global Consequences The victorious powers ignored the principle of self-determination for their colonies. Woodrow Wilson advocated democracy and human rights, but in seeking to strengthen the main U.S. allies, Britain and France, he decided to support the preservation of their colonies in Asia, Africa, the Pacific, and the Caribbean. The peace settlement transferred Germany's African colonies to Britain, France, Belgium, and South Africa and its Asian and Pacific territories to Britain, France, Australia, New Zealand, and Japan. Furthermore, Britain and France also gained control of the Middle Eastern societies formerly ruled by Ottoman Turkey. The peace settlements of World War I, by ignoring the political struggles of colonized peoples, thus spurred opposition to the West in Asia and Africa. The death of thousands of Asian and African colonial subjects conscripted or recruited to fight for Britain, France, or Germany in World War I sparked even deeper resentments. Thus World War I was one of the key factors in the rise of nationalism, the desire to form politically independent nations, in the colonies between 1918 and 1941 (see Chapter 25).

The global system shaped by colonial empires and Western economic power survived, but European prestige and influence weakened. The war undermined European economies, allowing the United States to leap ahead of Europe. Like British leaders in the nineteenth century, Wilson, now president of the world's largest, most productive economy, wanted free trade and an open world economy in which American industry could assert its supremacy. Since European nations had borrowed money from the United States to finance the war, they now owed the United States $7 billion. This war debt allowed the United States, long a debtor nation, to become a creditor nation. By 1919 it was producing 42 percent of all the world's industrial output, more than all of Europe combined, and had replaced Britain as the banker and workshop of the world.

Wilson also proposed and helped form a League of Nations, the first organization of independent nations to work for peace and humanitarian concerns. But Wilson could not persuade the U.S. Congress, controlled by the largely isolationist Republican opposition, to approve U.S. membership in the league. Hence, the only nation with the power and stature to make the league work stayed outside, leaving Britain and France alone to deal with European and global issues.

SECTION SUMMARY

- The early 1900s in Europe were marked by great affluence and stability, expanding markets, and shared notions of culture, justice, and human rights.

- Many factors contributed to the start of World War I, including Germany's resentment of British and French colonial holdings, which led to a military buildup on both sides; competing claims on Bosnia-Herzegovina; and a few governments' desire to divert attention from domestic problems.

- Sparked by the assassination of Austrian archduke Franz Ferdinand in Sarajevo, the war soon involved Austro-Hungary, Germany, Britain, France, and Turkey, all of which employed unprecedented military technology that caused millions of deaths.

- In 1917, Russia left the war and Germany seemed on the verge of victory when the United States entered the fighting, in part because of pressure by business interests that provided goods to France and Britain and in part because of outrage over German submarine attacks on U.S. ships.

- The United States helped the French and British win the war, but U.S. president Woodrow Wilson could not prevent the French from dictating harsh settlement terms that required Germany to partially dismantle its military, abandon its colonies, give up some of its territory, and pay heavy reparations.

- The horrors of World War I led to the radicalization of many Europeans; a growth of antiwar sentiment; the breakup of the Ottoman and German Empires, much of which were colonized by Britain and France; the breakup of much of the Russian and Austro-Hungarian Empires, which were carved into new countries; and the world dominance of the United States.

The Revolutionary Path to Soviet Communism

How did communism prevail in Russia and transform that country?

The Russian Revolution, a major consequence of World War I, was a formative event of the twentieth century, shaping European and world history, politics, and beliefs. In the wake of the revolution, Russia provided a testing ground for a radical new ideology, communism, which fostered a powerful state that reshaped Russian society and provided an alternative to the capitalist democracy dominant in North America and western Europe.

The Roots of Revolution

The Russian Revolution had deep roots in Russian society and its history under the czars, the hereditary rulers (see Chapter 23). Controlling a huge Eurasian empire, Russia had enjoyed some industrialization under the despotic czarist governments. However, vested interests, including the powerful and wealthy landed aristocracy, opposed further industrialization. Socially and economically, Russia was still a somewhat feudalistic country. Although serfdom had been legally abolished in the nineteenth century, peasants often remained subject to the dictates of landowners and enjoyed little social mobility or wealth. Only revolution could forge a decisive change in Russian society.

Growing discontent among intellectuals, the floundering middle class, underpaid industrial workers, and peasants who wanted more control over their lives fomented radical movements. All of these groups hated the autocratic czarist system and the privileges enjoyed by the hereditary aristocracy. In 1905 a revolution broke out, only to be brutally crushed by the government, but it left a revolutionary heritage for the **Bolsheviks**, the most radical of Russia's antigovernment groups, who transformed the revolutionary socialist views promoted by Karl Marx in the mid-1800s into a dogmatic communist ideology. The Bolsheviks started as one faction of a broader socialist movement that split into several rival parties in 1903. The founder and leader of the Bolsheviks, Vladimir Lenin (LEN-in) (1870–1924), who was born into a middle-class family and trained as a lawyer, was humorless and uncompromising but a clever political strategist who recruited supporters with his passionate beliefs and persuasive speeches. Lenin's mission in life changed after reading the works of Karl Marx. He was further radicalized when the government executed his older brother for having joined an assassination plot against the czar. Most of the Bolshevik leaders, including Lenin, had spent time as political prisoners in harsh Siberian labor camps for opposing the gov-

Bolsheviks The most radical of Russia's antigovernment groups at the turn of the twentieth century, who embraced a dogmatic form of Marxism.

Lenin The Bolshevik leader Vladimir Lenin stirred crowds with his fiery revolutionary rhetoric, helping to spread the Communist message among Russians fed up with ineffective government, war, and poverty. (Sovfoto)

The Bolshevik Seizure of Power

By 1917 the Russian people were sick of war and seeking change, sparking two revolutions. The first revolution, which came in March, toppled the czar, imprisoned the imperial family, and set up a provisional government (see Chronology: Russia, 1917–1938). The unplanned March revolution erupted while riots and strikes caused by food shortages and other problems were paralyzing the cities. Working women had begun the protests by swarming the streets of the capital, St. Petersburg, demanding relief and food, and they soon gained support from the soldiers sent to control them. The new provisional government leaders, such as the teacher's son and lawyer Aleksandr Kerensky (kuh-REN-skee) (1881–1970), who had often defended political dissidents in court, were well-meaning urban liberals who wanted reform and Western-style democracy, but they had no roots among the mass of the population. They failed because they refused to provide the two things most Russians wanted: peace and land. Because of their commitments to the Allies, they vowed to continue fighting the highly unpopular war. They also declined to redistribute land from the old aristocracy to the peasantry until the war ended and elections could be held for a planned Constituent Assembly to form a new, more representative, Russian government.

The political situation became chaotic. While the increasingly discredited provisional government asked for

ernment, and they were embittered toward the czarist system. To avoid another arrest Lenin had lived in exile elsewhere in Europe since 1907, organizing his movement.

The Bolsheviks, inspired by the Marxist vision of a revolution that would bring about a transition to a classless communist society, espoused a goal of helping the downtrodden workers and peasants redress the wrongs inflicted upon them by the rich and privileged. A new society, forged by revolutionary violence, could bring about, Bolsheviks claimed, a more equitable distribution of wealth and power throughout the society. In his book *What Is to Be Done* (1902), Lenin advocated organizing a professional core of activists to lead the revolution. The Bolsheviks favored a small, disciplined revolutionary organization that would work for workers' interests but would include only full-time revolutionaries. All members had to abide by the decisions made by the leaders, a system known as the party line.

When World War I broke out, the Russian people and even most opposition political parties rallied around the unpopular czarist government, seeing it as a patriotic war of defense against the hated Germans, the longtime rivals for dominion in eastern Europe. Only the Bolsheviks opposed the war, which they saw, with some justice, as an imperialistic struggle over markets and colonies. But the war soon lost its allure as Russian military forces collapsed in the face of German armies. Russia lacked the economic power and military and political leadership to compete in the war.

C H R O N O L O G Y	
Russia, 1917–1938	
1917	March revolution
1917	October revolution
March 1918	Brest-Litovsk Treaty
1918–1921	Russian Civil War
1922	Formation of Soviet Union
1924	Death of Lenin
1928	Beginning of Five-Year Plans
1929–1953	Stalin's dictatorship
1936–1938	Stalin's Great Purge

time, radicals organized **soviets**, local action councils that enlisted workers and soldiers to fight the factory owners and military officers. The soviets represented a grassroots movement for change that undermined government authority. The strongest soviet, in the capital, St. Petersburg, had between 2,000 and 3,000 members and was headed by an executive committee. As the soviets and the government jockeyed for control of St. Petersburg, the Germans, hoping to undermine the Russian provisional government, helped Lenin, in exile in Switzerland, to secretly return to Russia hidden in a railroad box car. Using the slogans of "peace, bread, and land" and "all power to the soviets," Lenin rapidly built up Bolshevik influence in the soviets. The provisional government, increasingly discredited, tried to prevent leftist extremism, such as the peasants seizing land, but government control was weak.

In October 1917, the Bolsheviks and their 240,000 party members staged an uprising and grabbed power from Kerensky's crumbling provisional government. Aided by the soviets, the Bolsheviks seized key government buildings in St. Petersburg, including the czar's Winter Palace. With a fragile hold on power, the Bolsheviks had to allow diverse parties to freely contest elections for an assembly, which met in January 1918. After the assembly refused to support a Bolshevik bid for leadership, however, the Bolsheviks used troops to disperse the assembly and take over the national and city governments, pushing other parties aside and terrorizing or executing opponents. The Bolshevik's rivals, the moderate, prodemocracy Socialists, some of whom had served in the provisional government, were consigned, in the words of a Bolshevik leader, to the dustbin of history. Lenin claimed his goal for Russia was to transfer power from the capitalists to the working class. Defending the violence, he asserted that chefs cannot make an omelet without breaking eggs. The Bolsheviks renamed themselves the Communist Party. In one of its first moves, the Communists gained popular support by pulling Russia out of the war. In the Treaty of Brest-Litovsk, negotiated with Germany in March, 1918, Russia gave up some of its empire in the west to Germany, abandoning the Ukraine, eastern Poland, the Baltic states, and Finland. They also moved the capital from St. Petersburg, which they renamed Leningrad, to Moscow.

Communist International and Civil War

Once in power, the Communist regime had to develop a strategy for dealing with the wider world. In 1919, Lenin, hoping to protect Russia's revolution by promoting world revolution, organized the Communist International, often known as the Comintern, a collection of Communist parties from around the world. It would battle the U.S. vision, articulated by Woodrow Wilson, of promoting capitalism and democracy. Before World War II, however, the United States had the greater success in spreading its influence, partly because it

helped stabilize postwar Europe with economic, political, and food assistance to promote procapitalist, anti-Communist governments. The prospect of world revolution that would foster the spread of communism soon faded.

The Russian Revolution sparked the Russian Civil War (1918–1921) (see Map 24.2). The conservative, anti-Communist forces, who called themselves White Russians in contrast to the Communists' military force, the Red Army, included the czarist aristocracy (among them large landowners), generals who were angry at losing their dominance, and a few pro-Western liberals favoring democracy. Heavily funded and armed by Western nations, which were alarmed by the Revolution, the White Russian armies fought the Communist forces in the fringe areas of the Russian Empire in the three years following World War I. In mounting their defense, the Communists capitalized on the disunity among White Russian leaders and their Western backers. The cohesion and leadership of the Communist Party and the brilliant military leadership of the Red Army also helped. Most crucially, the Communists received growing support from the working class and the peasants, who feared the return of the hated landowners with a White Russian victory. Although the Communists initially looked vulnerable, they eventually gained the advantage, defeating the White Russians and even reclaiming some of the territory lost in the Brest-Litovsk Treaty, including the Ukraine.

The outside intervention added an international flavor to the Russian Civil War. This intervention had come chiefly from Japan, Britain, France, and the United States. Japan, which concentrated on eastern Siberia, and Britain sent the largest number of troops into Russia—60,000 and 40,000, respectively. The possibility of a permanent Communist government in Russia also worried the liberal idealist Wilson, who sent two separate American military forces to Russia in 1918 to roll back the Communist regime and, he claimed, spread democratic values. Five thousand American troops went to northern Russia to battle the Red Army for control of two port cities. But the episode proved disastrous for Americans: brutal winter weather, poor provisions, and 500 American casualties drove the U.S. troops to near mutiny. Another contingent of 10,000 Americans entered eastern Siberia. Soon recognizing the whole intervention effort as a quagmire, Wilson lamented that it was harder to get out than it was to go in. U.S. and other Western troops were finally removed in 1920, in some cases after soldiers mutinied. The Western intervention helped to solidify the Communist government, which was widely seen by Russians as fighting a nationalist war against foreign powers seeking to restore the old discredited czarist order.

Lenin and a New Society

By 1922 the Communist Party controlled much of the old Russian Empire, but it faced severe challenges. The civil war had left the country devastated and its people starving, as well as making good relations with the capitalist democracies impossible. The civil war had also reinforced the paranoid, authoritarian, and militaristic attitudes of the Communists. Crediting

---

soviets   Local action councils formed by Russian radicals before the 1917 Russian Revolution that enlisted workers and soldiers to fight the factory owners and military officers.

Map 24.2   Civil War in Revolutionary Russia (1918–1921)
The Communist seizure of power in Russia in 1917 sparked a counteroffensive, backed by varied
Western nations and Japan, to reverse the Russian Revolution. The Communists successfully
defended the Russian heartland while pushing back the conservative offensive.

Karl Marx as the key inspiration, the party had forged the world's first state based on Communist ideas; committed to world revolution, it inspired the growth of Communist groups in other countries. Russia's leaders renamed their nation the Union of Soviet Socialist Republics (USSR), in theory a federation of all the empire's diverse peoples—such as Kazakhs, Uzbeks, Armenians, and Ukrainians—but in actuality largely controlled by Russians, and hence, to opponents, essentially a continuation of the Russian Empire built by the czars. Soon the USSR turned from world revolution to building what the leaders termed "socialism in one country"—the USSR—using coercion against reluctant citizens if necessary. Yet party leaders did not yet have a blueprint for transforming Russian society.

Since they had no model of a Communist state, the Soviet leaders experimented while using their secret police to eliminate opponents, including those they called enemies of the working class, among them liberals and moderate socialists. The basis for Soviet communism was **Marxism-Leninism**, a mix of socialism (collective ownership of the economy) and **Leninism**, a political system in which one party holds a monopoly on power. Lenin initially favored centralization and nationalization of all economic activity, but he was forced by peasant opposition to adopt the **New Economic Policy** (NEP), a pragmatic approach that mixed capitalism and socialism. The NEP brought economic recovery and included limited capitalism in agriculture, allowing peasants to sell their produce on the open market. However, since the economy produced few consumer goods, the peasants had no incentive to sell their produce for profit because there was little to buy with the money they earned.

Lenin was dissatisfied with the results of the revolution, which he called socialist in appearance but not substance: "czarism slightly anointed with Soviet oil."[9] He criticized the bloated bureaucracy and warned, accurately, that his probable successor, Joseph Stalin (STAH-lin) (1879–1953), had dictatorial tendencies. Decades later Lenin's assessment of his government's failures remained accurate, since the USSR never became the egalitarian Communist society envisioned by Karl Marx. Lenin himself, who combined ruthless authoritarianism with concern for the poor and exploited, deserves some of the blame. While Lenin and other Soviet rulers constructed myths about the mass nature of their revolution and what they termed the "dictatorship of the proletariat," led by the Communist Party, the ties between the political leaders and the Soviet masses remained weak. The instability and divisions caused by World War I and the Russian Civil War made the Communist leaders even less willing to trust the people or allow dissent, which they feared would provoke unrest.

The long Russian tradition of authoritarian, bureaucratic government under the czars and an obedient population provided a foundation for Communist dictatorship. The Communists were a small party, and most party leaders were, like Lenin, intellectuals from urban middle-class backgrounds who knew little of Russia's largest social class, the peasants. To regenerate the economy, they eventually adopted not popular control of farms and enterprises by workers and peasants but a top-down managerial system staffed by officials chiefly of middle-class origin. Peasants and workers became just employees, not partners. Increasingly the Communist Party and state became bureaucratic. The middle class was now largely composed of state employees, managers, and bureaucrats with salaries and privileges that were denied the masses and dedicated not to fostering social change but to maintaining their own power. They made policies without consulting the people. Lenin hoped to reform the party but died in 1924.

Stalinism, Industrialization, and One-Man Rule

Lenin's successor was a master bureaucrat, Joseph Stalin (1879–1953), who reshaped Soviet communism and Russia. Born in the Caucasus province of Georgia, the son of a shoemaker, he studied to be a Russian Orthodox priest before being expelled from the seminary. After joining the Bolsheviks, he adopted the name Stalin ("Man of Steel"). Aided by his control of the Communist Party apparatus, Stalin outmaneuvered his party rivals to succeed Lenin. Stalin came to power as the peasants increasingly turned away from the Communist Party because they no longer feared the return of the landlords. Viewing the peasants as self-indulgent, Stalin urged a hard line against those who resisted state policies, eliminated all his competition in the party, and became a dictator. The system he imposed, known today as **Stalinism**, included state ownership of all property, such as lands and businesses, a planned economy, and one-man rule.

In 1928 Stalin ended Lenin's NEP and introduced an economic policy based on an annual series of plans for future production, known as Five-Year Plans, formulated by state bureaucrats. The Five-Year Plans produced basic industrial goods, such as steel and coal, but few consumer goods. Stalin also launched a massive crash industrialization program and withdrew the country from the global political and economic system. Under Stalin, the Soviet Union mobilized its own resources, refusing foreign investment. In order to introduce machines, such as tractors and harvesters, to increase farm production, Stalin strengthened the party's grip on the rural sector by collectivizing the land and turning private farms into commonly owned enterprises, in the process destroying the wealthier small farmers, the *kulaks*, as a class. Peasants who refused to join the collective farms were often exiled to Siberia.

Marxism-Leninism   The basis for Soviet communism, a mix of socialism (collective ownership of the economy) and Leninism.

Leninism   A political system in which one party holds a monopoly on power, excluding other parties from participation.

New Economic Policy (NEP)   Lenin's pragmatic approach to economic development, which mixed capitalism and socialism.

Stalinism   Joseph Stalin's system of government, which included state ownership of all property, such as lands and businesses, a planned economy, and one-man rule.

and Lorenz Hart, George and Ira Gershwin, Irving Berlin, Jerome Kern, and Cole Porter buoyed the spirits of people in North America and Europe. Porter's song, "Anything Goes" (1934), chronicled changing fashions: "In olden days a bit of [women's] stocking, was looked on as something shocking. Now, heaven knows, anything goes." By contrast, other popular songs of the 1930s, such as "The Boulevard of Broken Dreams" and "Brother, Can You Spare a Dime?," addressed harsh reality.

Cultural vistas expanded in other ways. Painters, poets, and novelists settled in a few run-down Paris neighborhoods and produced work that brought them fame. The best painters, vigorously breaking from older traditions, enlarged the world's sensibility. The innovative and versatile Pablo Picasso (pi-KAH-so) (1881–1973), a Spaniard who settled in Paris, shifted his style in the early twentieth century as he helped invent **cubism**, a form of painting that rejected visual reality and emphasized instead geometric shapes and forms that often suggested movement. Critics accused the Cubists of promoting revolutionary politics and contempt for tradition. Soon Picasso, who later joined the Communist Party, abandoned representational art entirely and sought visual experience as transformed by the artist in his mind. At the same time, literature explored the inner world of thought and feelings. For example, the Irishman James Joyce (1882–1941), who had enjoyed no formal education but became close to many of the nation's leading thinkers and writers, broke traditional rules of grammar, and his books were often banned for using obscenity. In England Virginia Woolf (1882–1941) converted the novel from a narrative story into a pattern of internal monologues, a succession of images, thoughts, and emotions known as stream of consciousness. Her 1929 novel, *A Room of One's Own*, championed women's growing economic independence.

The social and natural sciences also developed during the first half of the twentieth century, allowing for a greater understanding of human behavior and the physical world. Sigmund Freud (FROID) (1856–1939), an Austrian Jewish physician, developed the field of psychoanalysis, a combination of medical science and psychology, and shocked the world by arguing that sex was of great subconscious importance in shaping people's behavior. In physics, Albert Einstein (1879–1955) radically modified the Newtonian vision of physical nature and rejected the absolutes of space and time. Time, he argued, depended on the relative motion of the measurer and the thing measured. Einstein had fled the anti-Jewish atmosphere of Nazi Germany for the United States, where he helped convince President Roosevelt to sponsor research on atomic weapons that eventually produced atomic bombs. Einstein spent the rest of his life seeking a unifying theory to explain every physical process in the universe. He failed, but some of the ideas he developed contributed to ongoing attempts by physicists to explain the universe.

SECTION SUMMARY

- After the war Germany experienced rapid inflation because of its postwar debt, Europe lost economic ground to the United States and Japan, and women entered the work force and the political sphere.

- Many Japanese benefited from postwar economic growth, though some rural Japanese had to move to cities or emigrate, while Japan played a larger role in world affairs and clashed with the United States over its treatment of Japanese immigrants and Japanese ambitions in Asia.

- American fear of communism led to the "Red Scare," a harsh crackdown on dissidents and union organizers, while the split widened between the poor, who suffered under government policies, and the affluent, who enjoyed the "Roarin' 20s."

- Among the factors contributing to the Great Depression were America hoarding its profits, American tariffs against European imports, risky investment practices (which helped cause the stock market crash of 1929), and uneven distribution of income.

- With millions of Americans jobless, homeless, and hungry, radical movements grew in power and President Franklin Delano Roosevelt instituted the New Deal, a sweeping series of programs that put people to work, provided pensions, and protected against future depressions.

- The Great Depression hit Europe and Japan even harder than the United States, rendering Germany unable to pay its heavy debts and causing Japan to become more authoritarian and expansionist, while Scandinavian nations emerged in better condition by combining socialism and democracy.

- The United States took the lead in developing the new mass media of radio and motion pictures, painters such as Picasso broke radically with earlier forms, and Freud and Einstein did pioneering work in psychoanalysis and physics.

✦ The Rise of Fascism and the Renewal of Conflict

What were the main ideas and impacts of fascism?

By devastating the economies of Germany and Japan, the Great Depression helped spread a new ideology in these countries. Although its form varied from country to country, this ideology, **fascism**, typically involved extreme nationalism, hatred of ethnic minorities, ruthless repression of opposition

---

cubism A form of painting that rejected visual reality and emphasized instead geometric shapes and forms that often suggested movement.

fascism An ideology that typically involved extreme nationalism, hatred of ethnic minorities, ruthless repression of opposition groups, violent anticommunism, and authoritarian government.

Benito Mussolini gradually developed an ideology for his movement that appealed to the Italian people's nationalistic emotions. The following excerpt comes from an essay under Mussolini's name that was published in an Italian encyclopedia in 1932. In fact, the true author was a Mussolini confidant, the philosopher Giovanni Gentile. The essay reflected Mussolini's vision of fascism as the wave of the future, in which the individual would subordinate her or his desires to the needs of the state.

Fascism, the more it considers and observes the future and the development of humanity quite apart from political considerations of the moment, believes neither in the possibility nor the utility of perpetual peace. It thus repudiates the doctrine of Pacifism—born of the renunciation of the struggle and an act of cowardice in the face of sacrifice. War alone brings up to its highest tension all human energy and puts the stamp of nobility upon the peoples who have the courage to meet it. . . . Fascism [is] the complete opposite of . . . Marxian Socialism, the materialist conception of history. . . . Above all Fascism denies that class-war can be the preponderant force in the transformation of society. . . .

After Socialism, Fascism combats the whole complex system of democratic ideology, and repudiates it, whether in its theoretical premises or in its practical application. Fascism denies that the majority, by the simple fact that it is a majority, can direct human society; it denies that numbers alone can govern by means of periodic consultation. . . . The democratic regime . . . [gives] the illusion of sovereignty, while the real effective sovereignty lies in the hands of other concealed and irresponsible forces. . . .

But the Fascist negation of Socialism, Democracy, and Liberalism must not be taken to mean that Fascism desires to lead the world back to the state of affairs before 1789 [the French Revolution]. . . . Given that the nineteenth century was the century of Socialism, of Liberalism, and of Democracy, it does not . . . follow that the twentieth century must also be the century of Socialism, Liberalism, and Democracy: political doctrines pass, but humanity remains. . . .

The foundation of Fascism is the conception of the State, its character, its duty, and its aim. Fascism conceives of the State as an absolute, in comparison with which all individuals or groups are relative, only to be conceived of in their relation to the State. . . . The Fascist state is itself conscious, and has itself a will and a personality. . . . The Fascist state is an embodied will to power and government, the Roman tradition is here an ideal of force in action. . . . Government is not so much a thing to be expressed in territorial or military terms as in terms of morality and the spirit. It must be thought of as an Empire— . . . a nation which directly or indirectly rules other nations. . . . For Fascism the growth of Empire, . . . the expansion of the nation, is an essential manifestation of vitality, and its opposite a sign of decadence. . . . But Empire demands discipline, the co-ordination of all forces and a deeply felt sense of duty and sacrifice; this fact explains many aspects of the practical working of the regime, the character of many forces in the State, and the necessarily severe measures which must be taken against those who would oppose this spontaneous and inevitable movement of Italy in the twentieth century, and would oppose it by recalling the outworn ideology of the nineteenth century.

THINKING ABOUT THE READING

1. Why does fascism reject pacifism, socialism, and liberal democracy?

2. What role does the state play under fascism?

Source: B. Mussolini, "The Political and Social Doctrine of Fascism," *Political Quarterly,* IV (July–September, 1933), pp. 341–356. Copyright © 1993 by Blackwell Publishing. Reprinted with permission by Blackwell Publishing.

groups, violent anticommunism, and authoritarian government. Fascist movements also often included a party with a large membership, such as the Nazis (National Socialist German Workers), that was headed by a charismatic leader and that supported military expansion. Fascism was an assault on the liberal values and rational thinking of the Enlightenment. It came to power in Italy, Germany, and Japan and also influenced China and several eastern European and Latin American nations.

Roots of Fascism

First emerging in Italy in 1921 in the aftermath of World War I, fascism was a response to the inadequacies, corruption, and instability of democratic politics there, as well as to the economic problems caused by World War I. Domestic unrest increased as Italy's peasants sought a more just society, workers demanded the right to form unions, and the economy slumped. Fascism arose from a pragmatic alliance of upper-class conservatives in the military, bureaucracy, and industry with discouraged members of the middle class who faced economic hardships. Both groups feared the possibility of Communist revolution. The middle class chiefly furnished the mass support for fascism. Benito Mussolini (MOO-suh-LEE-nee) (1883–1945), a blacksmith's son, one-time teacher and journalist, and former socialist and World War I veteran, founded the Italian fascist movement, which advocated national unity and strong government.

Mussolini and his movement soon forged a new Italy. A spellbinding orator, Mussolini had a talent for arousing mass enthusiasm by promising a vigorous and disciplined Italy. He especially attracted war veterans with his nationalistic rhetoric, accusing socialists of being unpatriotic and using an ancient Roman symbol, the *fasces*, a bundle of sticks wrapped around an ax handle and blade, to symbolize the unity and power he wanted to bring Italy. Landowners and industrialists funded his movement because it battered labor and peasant organizations. The upper classes viewed Mussolini as a bulwark against the radical workers. Mussolini also won the support of the Italian king, the Catholic Church, and the lower middle class, from which the fascists organized a uniform-wearing paramilitary group, the Blackshirts, who violently attacked and intimidated opponents, assaulting socialists and striking workers and murdering antifascist politicians. In 1922 the king asked Mussolini to form a government. By 1926 Mussolini had killed, arrested, or cowed his opponents, turned Italy into a one-party state with restricted civil liberties, and created a cult of personality around himself. He also began to formalize his concept of fascism (see Witness to the Past: The Doctrine of Fascism). Despite the brutality, many Italians believed Mussolini was restoring social order. Furthermore, they appreciated that the government was efficient; for example, the trains ran on time, a rare experience under democratic Italian regimes.

Nazi Germany

Fascism became dominant in Germany after the Depression undermined the moderate, democratic Weimar Republic. Since the country had lost its empire after World War I, Germany had no colonies to tap for resources and markets that might aid recovery. The liberal Weimar leaders could not solve the severe problems. Even before the Great Depression, some Germans had advocated wars of territorial expansion against other Europeans to help the economy. The German people, who had an authoritarian political tradition and an economy in shambles, also shared a widespread resentment of the penalties imposed after World War I, especially the reparation payments, which drained the treasury. Many Germans, preferring security to freedom, were willing to listen to a charismatic leader who offered simplistic answers to complex problems. As in Italy, the German upper and middle classes feared working-class socialism.

The Nazi Party, led by Adolph Hitler (1889–1945), offered a strategy for regaining political and economic strength and efficiency and for keeping workers under control. Hitler was an Austrian-born social misfit and frustrated artist of modest origins who had made a precarious living painting signs and doing other odd jobs before joining the German army in World War I. Already at this time Hitler nurtured a hatred of Jews, or extreme anti-Semitism, and labor unions. After the war he became involved in rightwing German politics and, in 1920, helped form the Nazi Party, which promised to halt the unpopular reparations payments imposed by the Treaty of Versailles.

Hitler and the Nazis capitalized on the Great Depression to increase their strength. With economic collapse, the industrial workers moved left toward the Communists while the middle classes moved right toward the growing Nazi movement, financed by big industrialists. Germany was becoming a polarized society, with a shrinking political center. Many Germans were willing to believe, as Hitler claimed, that Germany's problems could be blamed on unpopular minorities, especially the Jews, and foreign powers. Hitler understood propaganda and how to use a few basic ideas, such as anti-Semitism, and he made up "facts" to gain support. In his book

Hitler's Motorcade   In this photo from 1938, Adolph Hitler, standing stiffly in his car, salutes members of a paramilitary Nazi group, the Brownshirts, who parade before him at a Nazi rally in Nuremburg. (Time Life Pictures/Getty Images)

Mein Kampf (My Struggle), written in 1924, he argued that "all effective propaganda has to limit itself to a very few points and to use them like slogans. A political leader must not fear to speak a lie if this might be effective."[18] Hitler developed a catchy slogan: "one people, one government, one leader."

The Nazis won the largest number of seats in the 1932 elections, garnering nearly 14 million votes, and, with support from non-Nazi conservatives, Hitler became Chancellor (the equivalent of prime minister) in January, 1933. Even though the Nazis won only 44 percent of the vote in the 1933 elections, Hitler tightened his grip on power and moved immediately to impose dramatic changes. His goals included a thorough purging of the educational system, theater, cinema, literature, and press so that his government could use them for its own purposes. The Nazis outlawed leftist parties, suspended civil liberties, imposed ideological conformity and heavy censorship, mobilized youth, told women to stay at home and take care of their husbands and children, and expanded the army. They also regeared the economy toward rearmament, thus solving the terrible unemployment problem. Massive government work-creation schemes eradicated unemployment by 1936. By 1939 Germany's GNP was 50 percent higher than it had been in 1929, mainly because of the manufacture of heavy machinery and armaments.

Beginning in 1933 Hitler introduced laws to reshape Germany. The Nazi myth about maintaining a pure German people—what Hitler termed the Aryan race, after the ancient Indo-Europeans who settled Europe, Persia, and India—led to anti-Semitic laws between 1933 and 1938. Hitler banned marriage and sexual relations between Jews and so-called Aryan Germans. He also excluded the half million Jews, many of them assimilated into German culture, from the civil service and varied occupations, pushing them back into the Jewish ghettos of German cities, where they could be watched. New laws also deprived the Jews of citizenship. The Nazis also enacted harsh laws against homosexuals and the Romany, or Gypsies, another unpopular, vulnerable minority.

Japanese Militarism and Expansion

During the 1930s Japan and Germany came to resemble each other fairly closely, even if their forms of fascism were very different. Although Japan never developed a mass-based Fascist Party like the Nazis, Japanese politics turned increasingly nationalistic and imperialistic. Japanese leaders often blamed foreign nations, especially the United States and the USSR, for Japan's problems. As in Nazi Germany, big business supported military expansion to gain resources and markets for exploitation. Groups of military officers assassinated liberal politicians and also fomented violence in the Chinese province of Manchuria to increase Japanese influence there. Manchuria, controlled only loosely by the Chinese government, was rich in natural resources, especially minerals such as coal and iron, and had open land on which to settle Japanese not needed at home.

Soon Japan turned more aggressive and authoritarian. In 1931 it invaded and gained control of Manchuria. The League of Nations imposed no stiff penalties on Japan, a failure that helped to discredit that organization. The Japanese military, in alliance with big business and bureaucratic interests, now played a key role in the Japanese government. By 1936 the military controlled Japan and, as in Nazi Germany, imposed a fascist government that promoted labor control, censorship, the glorification of war, police repression, and hatred of foreign powers (the West). The schools and media indoctrinated the population in obedience, patriarchy, and the sacred origins of the Japanese people while attacking Western values such as individualism and democracy. In 1937 a military skirmish outside Beijing provided an excuse for Japan to launch a full-scale invasion of China, which prompted the United States to impose an oil embargo on Japan. By 1938 Japan controlled most of eastern China. When Japan signed a pact with Germany and Italy in 1940, the United States and Britain introduced stronger economic sanctions, including an oil embargo. Japan now faced economic collapse or war.

The Road to War

During the later 1930s the European nations moved toward war, and various alliances formed. The United States, Britain, and France, known as the Allies, led a group of western European democracies that wanted to preserve the European state structure, the global economy, and the Western colonial system in Asia and Africa. The fascist countries, led by Germany, Italy, and Japan, known as the Axis Powers, sought to change the political map of Europe and Asia and gain dominance in the world economy. The prelude to another world war was also marked, as it had been for World War I, by diplomatic problems caused in part by a massive arms buildup all over Europe.

The big problem for the Allies was dealing with the imperialism of the Axis nations. Hitler pursued an aggressive foreign policy to dominate eastern Europe, arguing that Germany needed living space and colonies in order to prosper again. By doing this, Hitler sought to unite the several million ethnic Germans living in eastern and southeastern Europe, the legacy of centuries of migration and shifting state boundaries. In 1936 Hitler's troops occupied the Rhineland, German territory west of the Rhine River demilitarized after World War I. Demonstrating how fascism had made Italy a strong power, in 1935 Italy invaded and brutally conquered the last independent African kingdom, Ethiopia. The League of Nations voted ineffective sanctions against Italy. Hitler and Mussolini forged a close alliance in 1936, but the later Tripartite Pact of 1940, linking Germany and Italy with Japan for mutual defense, was a marriage of necessity, strained and wary. The Japanese did not view their interests as identical with those of the European fascists and pursued the pact partly to warn the United States that opposing Japanese aggression in Asia also meant facing the Germans and Italians.

Civil war in Spain heightened European tensions by drawing in foreign intervention and pitting competing ideologies against each other. Liberals and conservatives had struggled for two centuries to shape Spanish politics, and by the 1930s Spain was polarized between left and right. During the 1936 elections, Spain's Republicans, a leftwing coalition of liberals, socialists, and communists promising reforms, edged out the National Front of conservatives, monarchists, and staunch Catholics. British observer George Orwell wrote of the Republicans that they felt they had "suddenly emerged into an era of equality and freedom, not as cogs in the capitalist machine."[19] Alarmed, the right rallied around the fascist military forces led by General Francisco Franco (1892–1975), launching the Spanish Civil War (1936–1939). The Loyalist government forces, aided by the USSR, ultimately lost to Franco's fascists at a huge cost in lives on both sides. The war had an international flavor. Germany and Italy helped the Spanish fascists with weapons and advice, and several thousand volunteers from North America and varied European nations fought for the Loyalist cause. But the governments of the Western Allies refused to support the Loyalists, whom they viewed as too radical. The German bombing of Guernica (GWAR-ni-kuh), a village in northern Spain inhabited largely by Basque people, caused an international outcry and prompted Pablo Picasso to paint a celebrated testament to the atrocity. Spain endured Franco's fascist dictatorship until 1975.

In the late 1930s the Allies led by Britain followed a policy of appeasement toward fascist aggression. They were not yet prepared for war, and the catastrophe of World War I, in which several million young British and French men had died, had hung over the succeeding decades. Many in the Allied nations saw another war as too terrible to contemplate, even, as one British leader believed, the end of civilization. Some historians have considered the appeasement policy and the concessions it made realistic, the best of the available options, especially since public opinion in most countries opposed war,

while others view it as a shameful betrayal that only whetted fascist appetites and postponed the inevitable conflict.

War became inevitable. In 1938 Hitler turned his attention to eastern Europe. He succeeded through threats in merging Austria, a German-speaking nation with many pro-Nazi citizens, into Germany and then stimulated riots by German minorities in western Czechoslovakia and launched a claim to the territory. Czechoslovakia was handed over and occupied by German troops. As the war clouds approached, Hitler declared: "We shall not capitulate—no never! We may be destroyed, but if we are, we shall drag a world with us—a world in flames."[20] In August, 1939 Hitler and Stalin signed the Nazi-Soviet Pact, a nonaggression agreement. In September, with the Soviet threat temporarily removed, Hitler launched an invasion of Poland, forcing France and Britain to declare war against Germany (see Chronology: World War II, 1939–1945).

SECTION SUMMARY

- The Italian fascists, led by Benito Mussolini, appealed to those upset by instability, corruption, and economic problems and viciously fought communists and any others who opposed them.

- A new ideology, fascism, that developed out of economic collapse, stressed extreme nationalism, an authoritarian state, and hatred of minorities and leftists.

- Suffering from the Depression, resentful of post–World War I reparations, and fearful of socialism, many Germans supported Adolph Hitler's Nazi Party, which blamed problems on minorities such as the Jews and revived the economy through a military buildup.

- Japan became increasingly nationalistic and imperialistic, blamed its problems on foreigners, took over most of eastern China, and signed a pact with Germany and Italy.

- Tensions rose as Italy invaded Ethiopia, Fascists took over Spain, and Germany took over Austria and Czechoslovakia; France and Britain declared war after Germany signed a nonaggression pact with the Soviet Union and invaded Poland.

CHRONOLOGY

World War II, 1939–1945

1939	Beginning of war in Europe
June 1941	German invasion of Soviet Union
December 1941	Japanese bombing of Pearl Harbor; invasion of Southeast Asia
1942	Battle of Midway
1944	Allied landing at Normandy
July 1944	Bretton Woods Conference
February 1945	Yalta Conference
April 1945	Allied invasion of Germany
August 1945	U.S. bombing of Hiroshima and Nagasaki

◆ World War II: A Global Transition

What were the costs and consequences of World War II?

Historians have sometimes viewed the years from 1914 to 1945 as one continuum, with World War II a continuation and amplification of World War I. Both wars shared some of the same causes, including nationalist rivalries, threats to the European balance of power, and a struggle to control the global economic system. But there were differences, too. For one, World War II also involved a three-way ideological contest

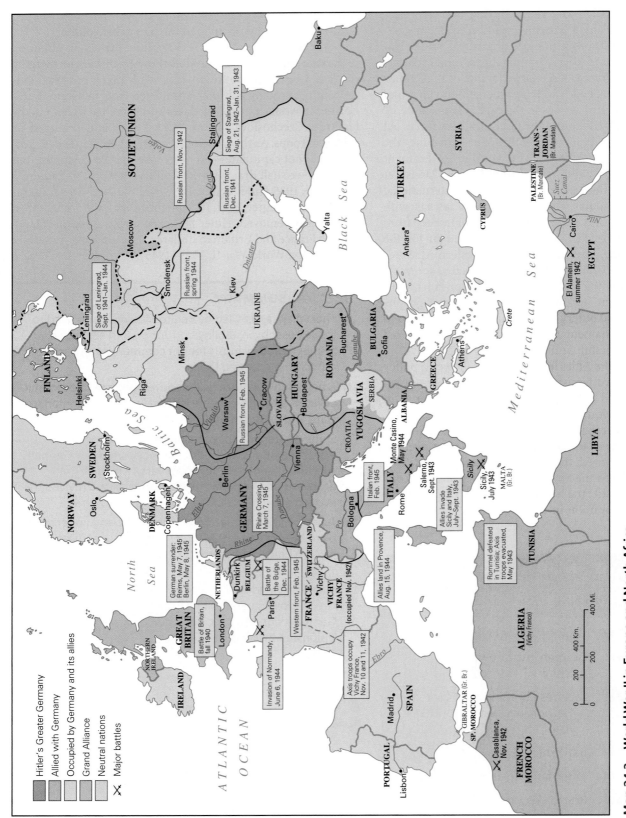

Map 24.3 World War II in Europe and North Africa

The Axis Powers, led by Germany and Italy, initially occupied much of Europe, and in 1941 they invaded the Soviet Union, but they were unable to hold their gains against the counteroffensive of the United States, Britain, the Soviet Union, and the Free French forces.

Bombing of Nagasaki
This photo shows the awesome power of the atomic bomb dropped by the United States on the Japanese city of Nagasaki in August, 1945, three days after the atomic bombing of Hiroshima. Some 60,000 Japanese died in the Nagasaki bombing. (Courtesy of the Trustees of the Imperial War Museum)

years, while Germany was temporarily divided into sectors controlled by Russia, Britain, France, and the United States. But the Allies gave the defeated nations massive aid and guidance to speed economic recovery. The war also fostered political changes in Asia. Chinese, Korean, and Vietnamese communists took advantage of Japanese occupation to gain support for their movements, and Western colonial rule was undermined throughout Southeast Asia, the Japanese having displaced the West in power. Furthermore, Indian nationalists who had been jailed because they opposed the British use of Indian troops in the war were even more embittered against British rule (see Chapter 25).

Allied leaders also developed new political institutions and links for the postwar world. In February 1945, Roosevelt, Churchill, and Stalin met at a conference at Yalta (YAWL-tuh), in Russia's Crimean peninsula, to determine the postwar political order. The conference agreed to set up a world organization, the United Nations, and proposed goals, an institutional structure, and a voting system for the new organization. The Yalta Conference also divided Europe into anticommunist and communist spheres of interest. Western leaders, drained by war and seeking postwar stability in Europe, reluctantly agreed to Stalin's demand that the Soviet Union be allowed to dominate eastern Europe by stationing troops there and influencing its governments.

The aftermath of war also fostered a new rivalry between the two emerging superpowers, the United States and the USSR, that complicated the new global political order. The United States, which had not fought on its own soil, emerged from the war not only much less devastated than any other major combatant but also politically and economically stronger, becoming the dominant world power. As a result, the United States took the lead in protecting a global system in which it held the strongest cards. But the USSR emerged from the war as a military power with imperial ambitions. U.S.

Woods, New Hampshire, to establish the postwar world economic order, including a system of international monetary cooperation to prevent the financial crises that caused the Great Depression. The Bretton Woods Conference set up the International Monetary Fund and the World Bank, both dominated by the United States, to provide credit to states requiring financial investment for major economic projects. Bretton Woods also fixed currency exchange rates and encouraged trade liberalization, both policies that benefited the United States most.

World War II also transformed world politics. It removed the twin threats of German Nazism and Japanese militarism. In contrast to World War I, the victorious Allies were more generous toward the vanquished. Germany, Italy, and Japan lost their colonies and were required to adopt democratic forms of government. U.S. forces occupied Japan for several leaders realized their nation would have to help reconstruct Europe and Japan to restore political stability and thwart Soviet ambitions there.

The political history of the world between 1945 and 1989 revolved around the conflict between these two competing superpowers, which had very different governments and economies. Rapidly rebuilding after the war, the USSR replaced Germany as the dominant power in eastern Europe and installed communist governments, including one in the eastern part of Germany under Soviet occupation. Indeed, World War II increased the appeal of communism worldwide and led to the establishment of communist regimes in Yugoslavia and North Korea. Both Soviet and U.S. leaders tended to look at the world through the lens of their World War II experience. For the USSR that meant paranoia about any threat from the West and the need for military power. Americans tended to find a repeat of Hitler's aggression anywhere in the world they experienced a political threat, such as a nationalist or communist-inspired revolution in Asia or Latin America; and they often sought to assert their power to reshape the world. The U.S.-Soviet rivalry created a world very different from that existing before World War II.

SECTION SUMMARY

- Germany rapidly took over most of Europe and used it as a source of raw materials, but the British withstood extended bombing and Germany wasted valuable resources on an ultimately unsuccessful invasion of the Soviet Union.

- Nazi Germany deliberately killed 6 million Jews and a half million Gypsies in death camps, along with millions of others; historians are divided on how much the German people knew about the death camps and how responsible they were for them.

- After Japan attacked Pearl Harbor, the United States entered the war in both Asia and Europe, and many women and blacks found work in professions that had until then been closed to them, while Japanese Americans were put in internment camps.

- After the United States entered the war, the Allies slowly began to win the war in Europe, and in the spring of 1945, with U.S. forces advancing from the west and the Soviets from the east, Hitler committed suicide and Germany surrendered.

- After Japan refused to agree to a total surrender despite serious setbacks, the United States dropped atomic bombs on Hiroshima and Nagasaki, killing, injuring, and sickening scores of thousands; historians still debate whether these bombs were necessary.

- World War II killed 50 million military personnel and civilians, but in its aftermath, Germany, Italy, and Japan were aided rather than punished, and the United States and Soviet Union emerged as the world's dominant powers.

Online Study Center **ACE the Test**

◆ Chapter Summary

The years between 1914 and 1929 in the industrialized Western nations were dominated by war and its aftermath. Growing tensions between European powers led to World War I, in which industrial technology produced new weapons that killed millions of civilians and soldiers alike. The terrible losses fostered widespread disillusionment and brought major political changes to Europe and the wider world. New nations were carved out of the German, Russian, Austro-Hungarian, and Russian Empires, while the United States emerged as a major world power. During the war the communist Bolsheviks seized power in Russia and created the Soviet Union. Lenin forged a one-party state, and his successor, Stalin, imposed a brutal dictatorship under which he collectivized the economy, used Five-Year Plans to encourage industrialization, and modernized the society.

During the 1920s much of Europe, the United States, and Japan experienced liberal democracy and middle-class prosperity. However, Europe changed dramatically in the 1930s. The Great Depression brought economic collapse, a sharp decline in world trade, and millions of unemployed workers. A few wealthy nations, especially the United States, pursued recovery through liberal reform and government spending, sustaining democracy despite the economic hardship. But for Germany, Italy, and Japan, economic disaster fostered fascism, an ideology that favored an authoritarian state, extreme nationalism, and repression of minorities. The increasing aggression of the fascist nations, in search of lands to exploit for their resources and markets, led to World War II. During the war, Nazi brutality led to genocide against the Jews and other minorities. Germany initially dominated eastern Europe and occupied much of western Europe, while Japan invaded China and Southeast Asia. With the entry of the United States into the war, however, the Allies eventually won. The war cost 50 million lives and devastated Europe and much of Asia. The United States emerged as the world's major superpower, with the Soviet Union as its major rival.

Online Study Center **Improve Your Grade** Flashcards

Key Terms

Bolsheviks	gulags	cubism
soviets	socialist realism	fascism
Marxism-Leninism	Great Depression	Holocaust
New Economic Policy	Dust Bowl	
Stalinism	New Deal	

Suggested Reading

Brendon, Piers. *The Dark Valley: A Panorama of the 1930s.* New York: Alfred A. Knopf, 2000. A readable account of this decade in both Europe and North America.

Doughty, Robert A., et al. *World War II: Total Warfare Around the Globe.* Lexington, Mass.: D.C. Heath, 1996. A brief account emphasizing military history.

Dower, John. *War Without Mercy: Race and Power in the Pacific War.* New York: Pantheon, 1986. Provocative look at the U.S.-Japan conflict.

Fitzpatrick, Sheila. *The Russian Revolution*, 2nd ed. New York: Oxford University Press, 2001. A provocative, concise, and readable account of developments from 1917 through the 1930s.

James, Harold. *Europe Reborn: A History, 1914–2000.* New York: Longman, 2003. An excellent survey of the period.

Kitchen, Martin. *A World in Flames: A Short History of the Second World War in Europe and Asia, 1939–1945.* New York: Longman, 1990. A readable narrative.

Lee, Stephen J. *European Dictatorships, 1918–1945*, 2nd ed. New York: Routledge, 2000. An interesting study of the major dictatorships and their leaders.

Lewin, Moshe. *The Soviet Century.* New York: Verso, 2005. Provocative and critical overview of the Soviet Union and Soviet Communism.

Lyons, Michael J. *World War I: A Short History*, 2nd ed. Upper Saddle River, N.J.: Prentice-Hall, 2000. A readable and comprehensive overview.

Mann, Michael. *Fascists.* New York: Cambridge University Press, 2004. Detailed but readable study of European fascism in this era.

Martin, Russell. *Picasso's War: The Destruction of Guernica and the Masterpiece That Changed the World.* New York: Plume, 2002. Examines the era through the artist and his most famous painting.

McClain, James L. *Japan: A Modern History.* New York: W. W. Norton, 2000. A very readable recent account with good coverage of these decades.

Moss, George Donelson. *America in the Twentieth Century*, 5th ed. Upper Saddle River, N.J.: Prentice-Hall, 2003. A readable survey of the United States in this period.

Neiberg, Michael S. *Fighting the Great War: A Global History.* Cambridge: Harvard University Press, 2005. A scholarly analysis of the conflict.

Parrish, Michael E. *Anxious Decades: America in Prosperity and Depression, 1920–1941.* New York: W.W. Norton, 1992. An examination of this era in the United States.

Sato, Barbara. *The New Japanese Women: Modernity, Media, and Women in Interwar Japan.* Durham: Duke University Press, 2003. A fascinating scholarly study.

Wilkenson, James, and H. Stuart Hughes. *Contemporary Europe: A History*, 10th ed. Upper Saddle River, N.J.: Prentice-Hall, 2004. A comprehensive general survey.

Websites

The Great War
(http://www.pitt.edu/~pugachev/greatwar/ww1.html).   A useful site on World War I with many essays and links.

WWW-VL: History: United States
(http://vlib.iue.it/history/USA/).   A virtual library, maintained at the University of Kansas, that contains links to hundreds of sites.

Russian History Index: The World Wide Web Virtual Library
(http://vlib.iue.it/hist-russia/Index.html).   Contains useful essays and links on Russian history, society, and politics.

Modern History Sourcebook
(http://www.fordham.edu/halsall/mod/modsbook.html).
A very extensive online collection of historical documents and secondary materials.

CHAPTER 25

Imperialism and Nationalism in Asia, Africa, and Latin America, 1914–1945

✦ Online Study Center

This icon will direct you to interactive activities and study materials on the website: college.hmco.com/pic/lockard1e

The Arsenal This portion of a famous mural, painted by Mexican artist Diego Rivera on a courtyard wall at the Ministry of Education in Mexico City in 1928, celebrates average Mexicans gathering weapons at an arsenal during the Mexican Revolution. (Reproduced with permission of Instituto Nacional de Bellas Artes, Mexico City. Courtesy, Banco de Mexico.)

What unhappiness strikes the poor, Who wear a single worn-out, torn cloth. Oh heaven, why are you not just? Some have abundance while others are in want.

PEASANT FOLK SONG PROTESTING COLONIALISM IN VIETNAM[1]

I n 1911 Nguyen Tat Thanh, a young man from an impoverished village in French-ruled Vietnam, signed on as a merchant seaman on a French ship; he would not return to his homeland for another thirty years. Nguyen hated colonialism and was dreaming of an independent nation of Vietnam. While a seaman he visited various ports in North Africa and the United States, and while touring several U.S. cities he developed both a distaste for America's white racism and an admiration for its freedom, which was born of revolution. After working as a cook in London, Nguyen moved to Paris and worked chiefly as a photo retoucher, all the while seeking to develop an anticolonial movement among the Vietnamese exiles in France. Adopting a new alias, Nguyen Ai Quoc ("Nguyen the Patriot"), he spent his free time reading books on politics and working with Asian nationalists and French socialists to oppose colonialism, especially in Vietnam but also wherever imperialism had imposed direct or indirect power over weaker countries.

Nguyen Ai Quoc became famous among Vietnamese exiles in Europe for his efforts to address the delegates at the Paris Peace Conference after World War I about the self-determination of peoples. Determined to force the issue of independence for colonized peoples, he attempted to enter the meetings and to present a moderate eight-point plan for changes in France's treatment of its Southeast Asian colonies, through which he hoped to gain personal basic freedoms, representation in government, and release of political prisoners. But the major Western powers, unwilling to consider any change in their colonial domains, refused to permit his entry. Becoming disillusioned with Western democracy, the Vietnamese exile helped found the French Communist Party, which promised to abolish the French colonial system. He then moved to the Soviet Union and later, under a new name, Ho Chi Minh ("He Who Enlightens"), the former seaman led the Communist forces in Vietnam in their long struggle against French colonialism and then against the Americans seeking to reshape the country. While nationalists and Communists did not necessarily share the same goals, Ho concluded that communism was the most effective strategy for promoting nationalism. Ho became a worldwide symbol of national assertion, opposition to Western imperialism, and sympathy for the plight of peasants, who were often negatively affected by colonial policies in Vietnam and elsewhere.

Between 1914 and 1945 nationalistic Asians such as Ho Chi Minh challenged the imperialism that had reshaped Asian and African politics and economies in the late nineteenth and early twentieth centuries. Rapid, often destabilizing change sparked political and cultural nationalism aimed at escaping Western domination or control, especially after World War I weakened the European powers. In response to economic dislocations and colonial repression, nationalist forces were awakened in colonies from Indonesia to Egypt to Senegal, becoming especially strong in India and Vietnam. Similar trends were also at work in independent countries such as Siam (now Thailand), Persia (now Iran), and particularly China. The Great Depression and World War II unsettled the world even more. In some societies in these regions, those seeking to overturn the status quo, such as Ho Chi Minh, mobilized large followings from discontented people. Despite frequent uprisings and protests against them, the Western powers were able to retain their empires until after World War II. During and after that war, however, nationalist movements became even stronger, making a return to the world of the 1930s impossible.

FOCUS QUESTIONS

1. What circumstances fostered nationalism in Asia, Africa, and Latin America?
2. How and why did the Communist movement grow in China?
3. What were the main contributions of Mohandas Gandhi to the Indian struggle?
4. How did nationalism differ in Southeast Asia and sub-Saharan Africa?
5. What factors promoted change in the Middle East and Latin America?

◆ Western Imperialism and Its Challengers

What circumstances fostered nationalism in Asia, Africa, and Latin America?

The events that rocked the industrialized nations between 1914 and 1945—two world wars, the Russian Revolution, and the Great Depression—also affected the nonindustrialized societies of Asia, Africa, and Latin America, who enjoyed little power in the global system. But the developments in the nonindustrialized societies also owed much to local dynamics. In particular, some of the local social and economic changes resulting from colonialism proved destabilizing. Many disenchanted Asians and Africans adopted nationalism and Marxism to struggle for power in their own societies and against Western colonizers.

The Impact of Colonialism

The colonialism imposed by Western nations on most Asians, Africans, and West Indians between 1500 and 1914 had a major impact on these peoples. World War I, for instance, fought chiefly among Western nations, had indirect effects in the colonies. The slaughter of millions of people during the war undermined Western credibility and whatever moral authority Western peoples claimed to possess. Adding to the resentment was the death of thousands of colonial subjects conscripted in Asia and Africa as soldiers and workers to support the colonial powers in the war effort. Both France and Germany drafted men, often through harsh and arbitrary methods similar to forced labor, from their African colonies, while Britain sent Africans and Indians. Some 46,000 Kenyans died fighting for Britain, and at least 25,000 West Africans perished helping France on the front lines. British and French officials had muted African resistance to the draft by promising democratic reforms and special treatment for war veterans, but these promises were not carried out. Few of the families of dead African soldiers ever received any compensation for their loss.

Colonialism also reshaped societies, often with harmful political, economic, and social results. As discussed in Chapters 21 and 22, colonization had resulted in the creation of artificial states that often ignored the ethnic composition of the territory or the historical configuration and economic bases of states in the region. As a result, colonies such as Dutch-ruled Indonesia, British Nigeria, and the Belgian Congo incorporated diverse and often rival ethnic groups who had little sense of national unity.

To cover the costs of managing the colonies, the colonial governments used a variety of methods that increased resentment, including higher taxes and forced labor. Forced labor was common in the African colonies. For instance, in Portuguese-ruled Mozambique, men and women who had no cash to pay the required taxes were assigned to work on plantations or in

CHRONOLOGY

	Asia	The Middle East and Africa	Latin America
1910	**1916–1927** Warlord Era in China		
1920	**1928–1937** Republic of China	**1920–1922** Nationalist unrest in Kenya	
		1922 Formation of Turkish republic	
		1925–1979 Pahlavi dynasty in Iran	
1930	**1930** Indochinese Communist Party		**1930–1945** Estado Novo in Brazil
	1935–1936 Chinese Communist Long March		**1934–1940** Cardenas presidency in Mexico
1940	**1941–1945** Japanese occupation of Southeast Asia		
	1942 Gandhi's Quit India campaign		

mines in a system not unlike slavery. After months of labor they often received little more than a receipt saying they had met their tax obligation for the year. Among the worst abuses by colonial regimes in Southeast Asia were their opium and alcohol monopolies, which provided revenues for governments. For example, in French-ruled Vietnam all villages were required to purchase designated amounts of these products to enrich government coffers. By 1918 opium sales accounted for one-third of all colonial revenues in Vietnam, and some Vietnamese became addicted to opium. Moreover, villages that bought too little alcohol or were discovered making their own illicit alcoholic beverages were fined, even though Vietnamese peasants had long made their own rice wine.

Another problem was that rising birth rates and declining death rates, abetted by colonial economic policies and, in some cases, improved health and sanitation, fostered rapid population growth in colonies such as India, Indonesia, the Philippines, and Vietnam. This population growth outstripped economic resources, exacerbating poverty and, for Indians and Indonesians, stimulating emigration. Furthermore, most of the colonies developed economies that locked them into the almost exclusive production and export of one or two primary commodities, such as rice and rubber from Vietnam, sugar from Barbados and Fiji, copper from Northern Rhodesia, and oil from Trinidad and Iraq. These economic limitations put a brake on later economic diversification, as many Latin American nations had discovered after gaining independence in the early 1800s.

Colonized peoples also disliked the arrogance of the Western colonizers. Europeans and North Americans assumed that their societies were superior, above those of other peoples of the world. This ethnocentric, often racist attitude was enshrined in the Covenant for the

Exporting Resources from Indonesia Small boats brought cash crops grown in eastern Java, part of the Dutch East Indies, to the port of Surabaya, from where they were shipped to Europe. (Royal Commonwealth Society Collection, Cambridge University Library Y30333/A9)

new League of Nations formed after World War I, which considered the colonized peoples not yet able to govern themselves in the modern world. Exploiting their unequal power, the Western officials, businessmen, and planters in the colonies commonly lived in luxury—with mansions, servants, and private clubs—while many local people lived in dire poverty, often underfed and malnourished.

At the same time, colonial governments built a modern communications and economic infrastructure that often spurred economic growth. The governments of British India, Dutch Indonesia, and British East Africa financed railroads that facilitated the movement of goods and people. Colonialism also fostered the growth of cities. For example, in 1890, to service their new East African Railroad from the Kenyan coast to Uganda, the British opened a settlement with a hotel and bar at Nairobi, a Gikuyu village in the Kenyan highlands. The British later made Nairobi, with its cool climate, the colonial capital. By 1944 Nairobi had grown to over 100,000 people. Port cities founded by Western colonizers, such as Hong Kong on the China coast, Jakarta in Indonesia, Singapore at the tip of Malaya, Bombay (today's Mumbai) in India, and Cape Town in South Africa, became key hubs of world trade. However, while defenders of colonialism boasted of their contributions, critics questioned how much they benefited Asians and Africans.

Capitalism

The capitalism introduced by the West also spurred resentment and anticolonial nationalism. Some non-European merchants, such as the Chinese in Southeast Asia and the Lebanese in West Africa, did profit from the growing economic opportunities. But colonial social and economic policies that promoted the spread of the capitalist market, expanded communications, and eroded traditional political authority also destabilized rural villages, fomenting opposition to these policies. The disruptions of capitalism also laid the groundwork for the rise of revolutionary responses in countries like Vietnam.

A radical innovation for many societies, capitalism reshaped rural life. The commercialization of agriculture transformed traditional, often communal, landowning arrangements into money-based private property systems. Rural societies were disrupted by the introduction by colonial officials or Western traders of competitive attitudes and policies that converted land into a commodity to be exploited on the free market. In many colonies, among them British India, French Vietnam, and Portuguese Angola, a powerful landlord class flourished at the expense of once self-sufficient peasant farmers. Even if peasant farmers held on to their land, they had no control over the constantly fluctuating prices paid for their crops. Lacking the money or connections to influential people to compete, many peasants fell into dire poverty. A Vietnamese peasant later recalled the bitter years of hardship under French colonization: "My father was very poor. He and my mother, and all of my brothers and sisters, had to pull the plow. In the old days, people did the work of water buffalo."[2]

The Great Depression of the 1930s brought economic catastrophe to many nonindustrialized societies as demand for their resources in the industrialized nations plummeted. The damage was widespread. For example, collapsing prices for rubber, sugar, and coffee crops harmed Southeast Asians. In Latin America, Argentina saw the livestock and wheat prices collapse, and Cuba was staggered by falling sugar prices. The Brazilians threw their nearly worthless sacks of coffee beans into the sea. To deal with the economic collapse while protecting Western investors, international agreements restricted rubber growing to large plantations, causing distress to many small farmers, rubber workers, and the shopkeepers who serviced them in colonies such as Malaya, Sri Lanka, and the Belgian Congo. As the marketing of the main exports declined, colonial revenues also fell. For instance, because rubber and tin provided the bulk of tax revenues in British Malaya, the price collapse in these commodities necessitated huge budget cuts, which in turn undermined such activities as education and road building.

Unequal landowning, growing mass poverty, limited economic opportunities for displaced peasants, and foreign control of the economy produced political unrest and activism. For example, the economic devastation of the Caribbean island of Trinidad, a British colony, by the Great Depression led to strikes, labor unrest, and increased efforts to organize opposition. The calypso singer Growling Tiger asked the colonial government in song not to ignore human suffering: "The authorities should deal much more leniently with the many unemployed in the colony; work is nowhere to be found but there is rent to pay while the money circulation decreases by the day."[3] But most colonial regimes, including Trinidad's, harassed and jailed protest leaders.

Nationalism and Marxism

As a result of these hardships, ideologies of resistance, including nationalism and Marxism, grew in influence in the colonized world. In time movements for change became movements for independence. Since colonial governments repressed nationalism and jailed or exiled the leaders, nationalists had to organize underground. Nationalism became especially popular among the educated middle class—lawyers, teachers, merchants, and military officers—who faced white racism and often found the doors to higher education closed to them. University and secondary school students were also drawn to nationalist movements. Colonial powers set up few universities, but those that existed offered a venue for nationalist-government conflicts and campus protests. In British Burma (today's Myanmar) during the 1920s and 1930s, for instance, nationalist students, both men and women, at the University of Rangoon repeatedly went on strike to protest British policies. After a major strike in 1936, student leaders were expelled, but the administration also met some student demands, such as introducing scholarships for poor students and allowing student representation on the university board.

To anticolonial leaders, nationalism promoted a sense of belonging to a nation, such as Indonesia or Nigeria, that transcended parochial differences such as social class and religion. But the "nation" sometimes existed only in people's imagination: in the multiethnic colonies of Africa, Southeast Asia, and the Caribbean, it was difficult to overcome ethnic antagonism and rivalries to create a feeling of nationhood. Nationalism also seemed a vehicle for addressing social problems. Whereas colonialism had uprooted people from their villages, families, customs, and traditions, nationalists sought to foster stability and help the poor. A main concern was capitalism, which was identified with foreign control.

Whether colonized or not, some Asians, Africans, and Latin Americans who sought radical change, such as Ho Chi Minh, mixed nationalism with Marxism, the ideas of socialism and revolution advocated by the nineteenth-century German Karl Marx. For them, Marxist ideas provided an alternative vision to colonialism, capitalism, and discredited local traditions and leaders. Young Asians, Africans, and West Indians studying in Europe and North America often adopted Marxism after facing bleak employment prospects and political repression back at home. Some of them gravitated to the most dogmatic form of Marxism, the communism imposed on and practiced in the Soviet Union by the Bolsheviks (see Chapter 24), which offered a dynamic approach to addressing social inequality and political powerlessness under the leadership of a centralized revolutionary party.

Radical nationalists, especially in Asia, also adopted revolutionary ideas developed by the Russian Communist leader, Vladimir Lenin. Lenin blamed the poverty of the colonial and neocolonial societies on the industrialized nations that had imposed a capitalist system on subject peoples. He saw the world as divided between imperial countries (the exploiters) and dominated countries (the exploited). Lenin's view appealed to radical nationalists who sought to make sense of their subjugation to the West. For example, an Indian nationalist observed in the 1930s that younger Indian men and women who used to read about, and admire, Western democracies now read about socialism and communism and found inspiration in Soviet Russia. Although Communist nations, among them the Soviet Union, also proved capable of blatantly imperialistic policies, during the first four decades of the twentieth century Lenin's theory of capitalism-based imperialism seemed to offer validity.

Lengthening the Imperial Reach

At the same time that anti-imperialist feelings were rising between 1900 and 1945, powerful nations were expanding their imperial reach and continuing to intervene in less powerful nations. For example, after World War I and the defeat of Germany and its Ottoman ally, Britain and France took control of the former Ottoman colonies in western Asia and the German colonies in Africa. Some of these societies, such as oil-rich Iraq, had valuable resources. Likewise, Australia and Japan occupied the German-ruled Pacific islands. Supported by colonial governments, Europeans continued to settle in Algeria, Angola, Kenya, South Africa, and Southern Rhodesia and to dispossess local people from their land. Moreover, while the war had ended, Western military conquests in Africa had not. In 1935–1936 Italy invaded and brutally conquered the last independent African state, Ethiopia, killing some 200,000 Ethiopians. The Ethiopian forces faced a fully mechanized and mobile Italian army, and, despite their spirited defense of the mountainous terrain, they succumbed to superior Italian aerial bombing and firepower. Italy's fascist dictator, Benito Mus-

solini, argued that it was a war to spread "civilization" and "liberate Africans"; in fact, he hoped to settle Italians in Ethiopia.

Meanwhile, the major Western power after World War I, the United States, continued to exercise influence in the Americas. For example, President Woodrow Wilson sent thousands of U.S. troops into Mexico during the Mexican Revolution to restore order and thereby protect large U.S. investments. Americans owned a large share of the Mexican economy, including most of the oil industry. American attitudes favoring the spread of democracy and capitalism in the world also played a role in the interventions, with Wilson arguing that he would teach the Latin American republics to elect good leaders. The longest U.S. intervention came in Nicaragua, where the U.S. Marines overthrew a government hostile to the United States and then remained there from 1909 to 1933, often fighting an anti-U.S. peasant resistance led by Agusto César Sandino (san-DEE-no) (1895–1934), who became a hero to nationalist Central Americans. The United States' desire to protect U.S. investments by maintaining stability in Central America meant supporting the governments led by landowners and generals, such as the notoriously corrupt Nicaraguan president, Anastasio Somoza (1896–1956). President Franklin D. Roosevelt defended the U.S. government's long relationship with Latin American dictators by maintaining that "they may be SOBs, but they're our SOBs."[4] Repeated U.S. interventions in the region left an aftertaste of local resentment against what Central Americans called "Yankee imperialism."

SECTION SUMMARY

- World War I affected colonies in Asia, Africa, and the Caribbean as thousands of colonial subjects were forced to fight and die for France, Germany, and Britain, and promises of democratic reforms and special treatment for war veterans were not carried out.

- Colonial governments imposed heavy taxes and hard labor on the colonial peoples, who often lived in poverty while their Western counterparts lived in luxury, a state of affairs that was defended by the Western idea that the colonial peoples could not yet govern themselves.

- Western capitalism disrupted traditional rural life in many colonies, placing formerly self-sufficient farmers at the mercy of landowners and the world economy, which led to misery, political unrest, and activism during the Great Depression.

- Nationalism appealed to many frustrated colonial subjects, though many multiethnic colonies struggled to develop a sense of nationhood, and Marxism appealed to many, such as Vietnam's Ho Chi Minh, as an alternative to exploitative capitalism.

- Despite local opposition, Western nations expanded their colonial reach between 1900 and 1945: Italy brutally conquered Ethiopia, France and Britain took over former Ottoman colonies, and the United States continued to meddle in Central America.

✦ Nationalism and Communism in China

How and why did the Communist movement grow in China?

The Chinese Revolution of 1911–1912, which ended the 2,000-year-old imperial system (see Chapter 23), had led to a republic that Chinese hoped would give the nation renewed strength in the world, but these hopes were soon dashed (see Chronology: China, 1911–1945). China lapsed into warlordism and civil war, with a central government in name only, nominally independent but nonetheless subject to pressure from the West and Japan. Alarm at China's domestic failures and continuing Western imperialism sparked movements that fostered a resurgent nationalism that was more influential than in most nonindustrialized countries, as well as the formation of a communist party and China's eventual reunification.

Warlords, New Cultures, and Nationalism

During the demoralizing Warlord Era (1916–1927), China was divided into territories controlled by rival **warlords**, local political leaders that had their own armies. The warlords extracted revenue as their armies terrorized the local population. They were a mixed lot. Some called themselves nationalists and reformers and were interested in promoting education and industry. A few social reformers prohibited prostitution, gambling, and opium in their domains. Still others took bribes to carry out policies favoring merchants or foreign governments. Meanwhile, high taxes, inflation, famine, accelerating social tensions, and banditry made life difficult for most Chinese.

Radical new currents arose out of the people's despair. Cities became enclaves of revolutionary ideas, fostering new intellectual, social, cultural, and economic thought that helped set new agendas for China. New schools and universities opened, though students were frustrated at China's failure. Schools for girls became more common. Between 1910 and 1919 the number of these schools increased from 40,000 to 134,000, and the enrollments from 1.6 million to 4.5 million girls, although vastly more boys enjoyed access to formal education. Thanks to the schools, by the 1920s many women worked as nurses, teachers, and civil servants, especially in cities, but few rural women became literate or enjoyed these new opportunities. Exposure to Western ideas in universities, especially those run by Western Christian groups, led some Chinese students to question their own cultural traditions. For instance, women activists and sympathetic men campaigned successfully against footbinding, which largely disappeared except in remote rural areas by 1930. New social and economic groups, including industrialists and a working class, formed chambers of commerce and labor unions.

warlords Local political leaders with their own armies.

CHRONOLOGY	
China, 1911–1945	
1911–1912	Chinese Revolution
1915	Beginning of New Culture Movement
1916–1927	Warlord Era
1919	May Fourth Movement
1926–1928	Northern Expedition to reunify China
1927	Guomindang suppression of Communists
1927–1934	Mao Zedong's Jiangxi Soviet
1928–1937	Republic of China in Nanjing
1931	Japanese occupation of Manchuria
1935–1936	Long March by Chinese Communists
1937–1945	Japanese invasion of China

During this time Chinese intellectuals supported the **New Culture Movement**, which sought to wash away the discredited past and sprout a literary revival. The movement originated in 1915 at Beijing University, China's intellectual mecca that dared to hire radical professors, some of them educated in Europe or Japan, and that encouraged a mixing of Chinese and Western thought. There a group of professors began publishing the literary magazine *New Youth*, which became the chief vehicle for attacking China's traditions, including Confucianism, which they believed were irrelevant to the modern world and kept China backward by promoting conformity and discouraging critical thinking. Seeking answers for China's problems, the magazine's editor, Chen Duxiu (chen too-shoe) (1879–1942), wanted a new culture based on republican government and science. Contributors to the magazine, while detesting Western imperialism, admired the liberal, open intellectual atmosphere in Western nations and viewed modern science as liberation from superstition. Essays asked youth to destroy the old society, derided the traditional Chinese family system as contrary to individual rights and ambitions, and advised women to seek equality with men. *New Youth* and similar progressive magazines were popular among both young men and women.

Chinese rage against Western and Japanese imperialism increased in the aftermath of World War I. During that war China had remained neutral, but Japan, allied with Britain, had occupied the German sphere of influence in the Shandong peninsula of eastern China. In 1919, with the war over, Japan

New Culture Movement A movement of Chinese intellectuals started in 1915 that sought to wash away the discredited past and sprout a literary revival.

presented China with 21 Demands, including control of Shandong, increased rights in Manchuria, and appointment of Japanese advisers to the Chinese government. The 21 Demands and the decision by the Western allies to allow Japan to take over Shandong provoked a radical nationalist resurgence, known as the **May Fourth Movement**, that opposed imperialism and the ineffective, warlord-controlled Chinese government. The students and workers, many of them women, supporting the movement mounted mass demonstrations, strikes, and boycotts of Japanese goods. Shouting that China's territory could not be given away, the protestors also decried social injustice and government inaction. Merchants closed their businesses in sympathy. Capitulating to the protests, the Chinese government refused to sign the Versailles treaty that followed World War I. The new Communist government running the Soviet Union openly sided with China and renounced the special privileges that had been obtained by the czars in the 1800s, winning admiration among the Chinese.

Some Chinese also began studying communism, finding in it new promise for organizing change. In 1921 professors and students at Beijing University, many of whom had been active in the New Culture and May Fourth Movements, organized the Chinese Communist Party (CCP). Some of the party founders, such as the first secretary general, the *New Youth* editor, Chen Duxiu, were European- or Japanese-educated reformers who admired Western science and culture. Others were nationalists who despised Western models and believed the Chinese people, including the peasantry, had the ability to liberate China from imperialism if they were mobilized for revolution. Soviet advisers encouraged the party to organize among the urban working class but otherwise largely neglected the Chinese Communists as unlikely to become influential. The Communists recruited support by forming peasant associations, labor unions, women's groups, and youth clubs, and the party grew slowly; by 1927 it had enrolled some 60,000 members.

The Communist Party was only one strand of a resurgent nationalism that sparked new attempts to end the political drift and reunify China. Sun Zhongshan, better known as Sun Yat-sen (soon yot-SEN) (1866–1925), who had led the revolutionary movement that overthrew the Qing dynasty but had then been forced into exile (see Chapter 23), began to rebuild his nationalist forces, the Guomindang (gwo-min-dong), or Nationalist Party. Receiving no help from the Western nations, who benefited from China's disarray, Sun forged closer ties to the Soviet Union, which sent advisers and military aid. In the mid-1920s Sun's Guomindang and the Chinese Communists worked together, in an alliance known as the United Front, to defeat warlordism and prevent foreign encroachment. However, Sun's ideology grew less democratic and more authoritarian, and he came to believe that China's 400 million people—in his view just "loose sand"—were not ready for democracy. Sun died in 1925, and the new Guomindang leader, Sun's brother-in-law, Jiang Jieshi (better known in the West as Chiang Kai-

shek) (1887–1975), was more conservative. Chiang, who came from a wealthy landowning family, was a pro-business soldier and a patriot but indifferent to social change. He began developing a close relationship with the United States while building a modern military force.

The Republic of China

Between 1926 and 1928 the Guomindang forces and their Communist allies reunified China with a military drive known as the Northern Expedition, during which they defeated or co-opted the warlords. Thus in 1928 one national government finally replaced the series of warlord regimes, which had been impotent in the international community. The foreign powers recognized Chiang's new Republic of China. However, during the drive, tensions had grown between leftwing and rightwing political factions, which had different goals. Whereas Communist and leftist Guomindang leaders sought social change and mobilization of workers, the right wing, led by Chiang, was allied with the antiprogressive Shanghai business community. Chiang expelled the Communists from the United Front in 1927, even before the nation's reunification had been completed, and began a reign of terror against the leftists, killing thousands of them; those who survived went into hiding or fled into the rural interior or abroad.

From 1928 to 1937 Chiang's Republic of China, based at Nanjing (nahn-JING) along the Yangzi River in east-central China, launched a program to modernize China. The Republic's leaders, many of them Western-educated Christians, fostered economic development and forged a modern state. They built railroads, factories, a banking system, and a modern army, streamlined the government, fostered public health and education, and adopted new legal codes. New laws promoted monogamy and equal inheritance rights for women, though Chiang's government had little power to carry them out. The regime also negotiated an end to most of the unequal international treaties imposed by the Western nations and Japan in the 1800s. The U.S. government, closely allied with Chiang's regime, and private Americans provided generous political and financial support for Chiang's modernization efforts. Spurred by the idealistic desire to help the Chinese by reshaping them along American lines, Americans felt a paternalistic responsibility for China and funded schools, hospitals, orphanages, and Christian missionary activity. In 1940 a prominent U.S. senator, reflecting the notion that Americans could enrich and Westernize China, proclaimed: "We [Americans] will lift Shanghai up, ever up, until it is just like Kansas City."[5]

Yet the Republic faced domestic challenges. While the urban elite in big coastal cities prospered, Chiang was unable or unwilling to deal with the growing poverty of the peasantry. Commercialization of agriculture gradually shifted more land to landlords, and by 1930 about half of China's peasants lacked enough land to support their families. Adding to the problems, Chiang also tolerated government corruption and rewarded his financial backers in the merchant and banking sector. As unhappiness with the government grew, Chiang, influenced by European fascism, expanded the repression used against the

---

May Fourth Movement A radical nationalist resurgence in China in 1919 that opposed imperialism and the ineffective, warlord-controlled Chinese government.

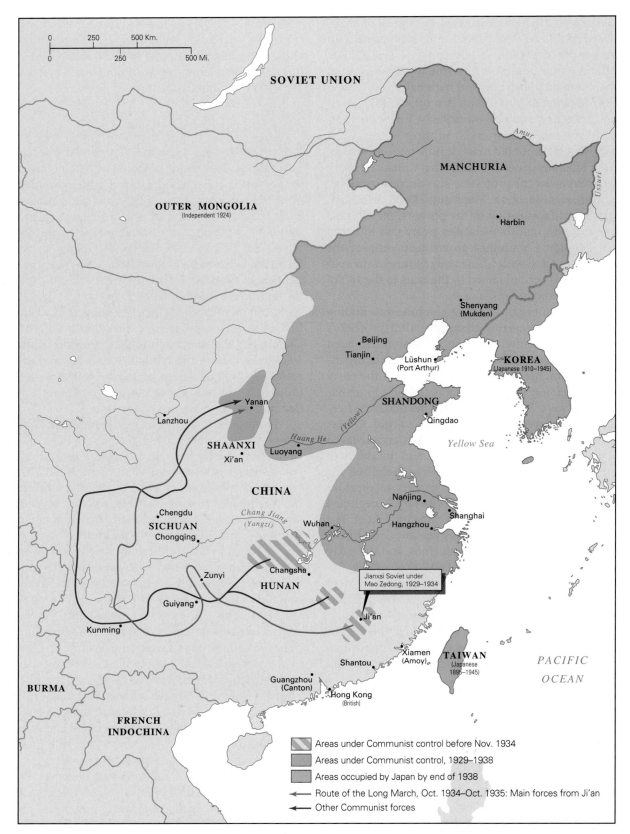

Map 25.1 Chinese Communist Movement and Chinese-Japanese War
Japan occupied much of northern and eastern China by 1939. In 1935–1936 the Chinese Communists made the famous 6,000-mile Long March from their base in Jiangxi in southern China to Yan'an in northwest China.

Communists and built an authoritarian police state that brutally repressed all dissent.

China also faced problems with Japan. In 1931 Japanese forces seized Manchuria, the large northeastern region rich in mineral resources and fertile farmland, and set up a puppet government under the last Manchu emperor, Henry Pu Yi (1906–1967) (see Map 25.1). Japan gradually extended its military and political influence southwest toward the Great Wall that separated Manchuria from northern China. Unable to match Japanese military power, Chiang was forced to follow a policy of appeasement. His attempts to strengthen the Chinese military diverted scarce resources from economic development, and his reluctance to fight Japan left him open to charges that he was unpatriotic.

During the years of warlordism and then the Republic, the challenges facing China were reflected in cultural life. Disillusioned by China's weakness in the world and continued political despotism, many intellectuals lost faith in both Chiang's regime and Chinese traditions. For example, the writer Lu Xun (LOO Shun) (1881–1936) had expanded his horizons by studying in Japan and becoming proficient in several foreign languages. On his return to China, he published satires on what he considered the failures of Chinese to grasp the challenges of the modern world. Lu Xun later formed a leftist writers' group and supported the Communists, but he never joined the Communist Party. In criticizing both imperialism and greedy Chinese leaders, he argued, "Our vaunted Chinese civilization is only a feast of human flesh prepared for the rich and mighty, and China is only a kitchen where these feasts are prepared."[6]

Ding Ling (1904–1985) was one of China's first feminist writers. She had fled her native village to avoid an arranged marriage, had participated in the May Fourth Movement, and lived a liberated city life. Her early novels and short stories focused on women's issues and featured passionate, independent modern women unable to find emotional or sexual satisfaction. Ding became alienated from the Republic when the Guomindang killed her politically activist husband. After this she dedicated her writing to the revolutionary cause, but she was later persecuted by the Communists for the feminism in her writing and her reluctance to follow the party line.

Chinese Communism and Mao Zedong

As the Communists who survived Chiang's terror worked to rebuild their movement, one of the younger party leaders, Mao Zedong (maow dzuh-dong) (1893–1976), pursued his own strategy to mount the revolution he now saw as necessary to replace the Chiang regime and reshape China. From a peasant family led by a domineering father who badly abused Mao's mother, Mao had run away from home to attend high school. In 1918 he moved to Beijing to work in the Beijing University Library, where he came to embrace communism. Over the next decade he edited a radical magazine, became an elementary school principal, and organized workers and peasants. In 1927, as Chiang attempted to eliminate Communists,

Mao fled to the rugged mountains of Jiangxi (kee-ON-see) province in south-central China, where he set up a revolutionary base, known as the **Jiangxi Soviet** after the political action groups of early twentieth-century Russia (see Chapter 24). There he organized a guerrilla force to fight the Guomindang. Rejecting the advice of Soviet advisers to depend on support from the urban working class, as the Communists had done in Russia in 1917, Mao opted instead to rely on China's huge peasantry, arguing that without the peasants no revolution could succeed.

In Jiangxi, Mao built an army out of peasants, bandits, and former Guomindang soldiers and mobilized the local population to provision and feed the army. Mao believed that violence was necessary to oppose Chiang, having earlier written that "a revolution is not a dinner party, or writing an essay, or painting a picture, or doing embroidery; it cannot be so refined, so leisurely and gentle. A revolution is an act of violence by which one class overthrows another."[7] Between 1928 and 1934 Mao expanded the Jiangxi Soviet by setting up Communist-led local governments and redistributing land from the rich to the poor. He got little help from the Soviet Union, however. As Chiang's repression intensified, top Chinese Communist Party leaders, who had once scorned Mao, moved to the Jiangxi Soviet. Increasingly alarmed by Mao's growing base and Communist inroads in other parts of China, Chiang had his army blockade the Jiangxi Soviet to keep out essential supplies. This move forced Mao to reluctantly abandon his base.

In 1935 Mao and 100,000 soldiers and followers broke through the blockade and, in search of a safer base, began the **Long March**, an epic journey, full of hardship, in which Mao's Red Army fought their way 6,000 miles on foot and horseback through eleven provinces. During the one-year venture, the Communists crossed eighteen mountain ranges, forded twenty-four rivers, and slogged through swamps, averaging seventeen miles a day; they lost 90 percent of their people to death or desertion. Finally in late 1936 the ragtag survivors arrived in a poor northwestern province, where they moved into cavelike homes carved into the hills around the dusty city of Yan'an (YEH-nan). The Long March saved the Communists from elimination by Chiang, making Mao the unchallenged party leader. Mao celebrated the achievement: "The Long March is the first of its kind in the annals of history [and has] proclaimed that the Red Army is an army of heroes."[8] But the Communists were still vulnerable to Chiang's larger, better-equipped forces.

The Communists would be saved by the decision of the Japanese to invade China in 1937. This decision, which was motivated by the desire for more resources to survive in the Great Depression, forced Chiang to shift his military priorities

Jiangxi Soviet A revolutionary base, established in 1927 in south-central China, where Mao Zedong organized a guerrilla force to fight the Guomindang.

Long March An epic journey, full of hardship, in which Mao Zedong's Red Army fought their way 6,000 miles on foot and horseback through eleven Chinese provinces to establish a safe base.

The Long March This painting glorifies the crossing, over an old iron chain bridge, of the Dadu River in western Sichuan province by the Communist Red Army during the Long March. This successful crossing, against fierce attacks by Guomindang forces, was a key event in the Communists' successful journey to northwest China. (Private Collection)

from attacking the Communists at Yan'an to fighting the Japanese. These developments gave the Communists an opportunity to regroup and spread their message of change against a weakened Chiang in wartime China.

Japanese Invasion and Communist Revolution

The Japanese invasion of China in 1937 and the disastrous Chinese-Japanese war that followed altered China's politics as Chiang had to divert money from modernization to the military. Mao captured the patriotic mood of the country by proposing a united front against Japan and Chiang had little choice but to agree, relieving pressure on Mao's Yan'an base. The Japanese soon occupied the major cities of north China and the coast, and by the end of 1938 Japanese forces had swept over most of the eastern seaboard and controlled the best farmland and the industrial cities. War and occupation affected the rival Chinese parties in opposite ways: it undermined Chiang's government, and it allowed the Communists to recruit support for their revolution, thus setting the stage for major changes in Chinese politics in the later 1940s.

The Republican Decline The Japanese invasion forced Chiang's government to relocate inland to Chongqing (CHUNG-king), a city protected by high mountains on the Yangzi River in west-central China. This move was followed by a mass migration of Chinese fleeing the Japanese. Unlike the modern, cosmopolitan coastal cities, Chongqing was a city with no bright lights or French restaurants and a depressing climate of fog and humidity. Fatigue, cynicism, and inflation discouraged the Guomindang and its followers. Virtually broke, Chiang's government had to squeeze

the peasants in the areas they still controlled for tax revenues to support an army of 4 to 5 million men.

Gradually many Chinese lost faith in the Republic. Militarily ineffective, politically repressive, and economically corrupt, Chiang's government offered limited resistance to the Japanese, killed and imprisoned opponents of Guomindang rule, and put the personal gain of its leaders above the economic well-being of China's people. The United States supported Chiang as an ally in the struggle against imperial Japan, but it was able to supply the Guomindang-held areas only by difficult, mountainous routes from Burma and India. Chiang often ignored U.S. advice in military and political matters. As the war wore on, Chiang, unable to push the Japanese out of China, also lost some of his popular support.

Yan'an Communism Although facing challenges, the Communists at Yan'an were able to improve their prospects. Used to poverty, they had a more disciplined army than Chiang's with a higher morale. While Chiang's much larger forces had the main responsibility to fight the Japanese, the Communists concentrated on mobilizing the people behind their revolution by forging a close relationship with the peasantry in north China and by mounting guerrilla bands, mostly peasants, to harass the Japanese. These guerrillas engaged in an unconventional struggle, which Mao called "**people's war**," that combined military action and political recruitment. In Mao's strategy of guerrilla war, "the enemy advances, we retreat; the enemy halts, we harass; the enemy retreats, we pursue."[9] On the political side of "people's war,"

---

people's war An unconventional struggle combining military action and political recruitment, formulated by Mao Zedong in China.

Communist activists set up village governments and peasant associations and encouraged women's rights, punishing abusive husbands. The Communist message of social revolution, now blended with nationalism, offered hope for a better life to the downtrodden. Thousands of Chinese, including students, intellectuals, writers such as Ding Ling, and workers, flocked to Yan'an to join the Communist cause. By 1945 the party had 1.2 million members.

The experiences of the Communist leaders at Yan'an, marked by war and popular mobilization to support revolution, fostered the development of what later came to be known as **Maoism**, an ideology promoted by Mao that mixed ideas from Chinese tradition with Marxist-Leninist ideas from the Soviet Union. Mao emphasized the subordination of the individual to the needs of the group (a traditional Chinese notion), the superiority of political values over technical and artistic ones, and belief in the human will as a social force. Mao also contended that political power grows out of the barrel of a gun (the military) and that the Communist Party must command the gun. To combat elitism, Mao introduced mass campaigns in which everyone engaged in physical labor that benefited villages, such as building dams and roads. As part of this effort, the Communists sent intellectuals into villages to teach literacy and also to learn from the peasants. Mao expressed faith that the Chinese people, armed with political understanding, had the collective power and creativity to triumph over nature, poverty, and exploitation to build a new society.

During the Japanese occupation Mao's Communists built the foundation for revolution by gaining domination over much of rural north China, where Mao's ideas on new forms of community, social change, and economic justice had gained popular support. Hence, when the war ended in 1945, the Chinese Communists had improved their prospects for fostering revolution while Chiang's Guomindang, although still a superior military force, was beset with problems resulting from its inability to defeat the Japanese and maintain popular support. As a result, the Communists were able to succeed in their revolutionary efforts: in the late 1940s they won a bitter civil war, and in 1949 they established a Communist government.

SECTION SUMMARY

■ After the end of the imperial system, rival warlords controlled China during a period of civil war, and intellectuals formed the New Culture Movement, which called for a modernized China that fostered individualism and equality rather than traditions such as Confucianism.

■ Japan's aggressive demands after World War I enraged the Chinese, and some were attracted to communism but Sun Yat-sen's successor, the pro-business Chiang Kai-shek, allied the nationalist movement with the United States.

Maoism An ideology promoted by Mao Zedong that mixed ideas from Chinese tradition with Marxist-Leninist ideas from the Soviet Union.

■ Chiang Kai-shek's Republic of China launched a modernization program, but it was hampered by a split with the Communists, persistent rural poverty, and the Japanese seizure of Manchuria.

■ Mao Zedong organized peasants into a Communist revolutionary army and then led them on the punishing Long March in search of safety from Chiang Kai-shek's far stronger army, which might have triumphed had it not been diverted by a 1937 Japanese invasion.

■ The Chinese people lost faith in Chiang's government as it squeezed them for taxes to support a failing war against Japan, while Mao's Communists instilled hope through guerrilla attacks on the Japanese and a promise of equality and progress through shared sacrifice.

◆ British Colonialism and the Indian Response

What were the main contributions of Mohandas Gandhi to the Indian struggle?

In India, as in China, resentment of Western imperialism, despotic government, and an inequitable social order sparked a powerful nationalist movement. Like the Chinese, Indians did not benefit from the reshaping of world political arrangements following World War I. Those who hoped that war would bring them self-determination could see that the British rhetoric about democracy and freedom did not apply to India. Growing organized opposition to British colonialism, spurred by the Indian National Congress formed in the later 1800s, led to unrest that forced the British to modify some of their colonial policies. At the same time, growing nationalism set the stage for the turmoil that eventually created separate Hindu and Muslim nations after World War II.

British Policies and the Nationalist Upsurge

Nationalist opposition to the British Raj, which had been building for decades, was spurred by the severe dislocations caused by World War I. To pay for the war, the British raised taxes and customs duties on Indians, policies that sparked several armed uprisings. In addition, over 1 million Indian soldiers fought for Britain in France and the Middle East, and 60,000 of these were killed. Many Indians expected a better future because of the sacrifices they had made in a war they did not start or want—a reward of self-government similar to that of Australia and Canada, former colonies where the British political presence was now largely symbolic. But the British dashed all hopes of major political change by declaring in 1917 that they would maintain India as an integral part of the British Empire. However, British prestige suffered from the losses incurred by war; by war's end, Britain, whose power was

MOHANDAS GANDHI, INDIAN NATIONALIST

Few individuals have had as much impact on history as Mohandas Gandhi (1869–1948), who became the leading figure of Indian nationalism in the 1920s by formulating ideas of nonviolent opposition to repressive colonial rule that influenced millions both inside and outside India. Gandhi was born into a well-to-do family of the vaisya caste in the western state of Gujerat; although vaisyas were commonly involved in commerce, his father was a government official. His parents maintained traditional attitudes, and his mother was a devout Hindu. Like many Hindu families, they arranged for him to marry young. The thirteen-year-old Mohandas married Kasturbai Kapada (KAST-er-by ka-PO-da) (1869–1948), the daughter of a rich merchant. Kasturbai proved a courageous helpmate in his later political activities.

Gandhi wanted to study law in London, but his family feared he would be corrupted there because his young wife, now with a son, had to stay in India. To gain their approval, he vowed to live a celibate life in England and never to touch meat or wine. In England he expanded his knowledge by reading Indian works such as the *Bhagavad Gita* and Western books such as the Christian Bible. His three years in London also gave him contact with Western nationalism and democracy, as well as a law degree.

At first unable to find a suitable position back in India, in 1893 Gandhi was hired by a large Indian law firm to work in South Africa, where the racist government and white minority mistreated not only Africans but also the thousands of Indians who had been recruited as laborers and plantation workers. With his wife's encouragement, he turned to helping the local Indians assert their rights, for which he was jailed, beaten by mobs, and almost killed by angry opponents, both white and Indian. The British who ruled South Africa raised taxes on Indians, shut down Indian gatherings, and refused official recognition of Hindu marriages. In response, and influenced by Kasturbai's advocacy of justice and nonviolence, Gandhi began developing his strategy of nonviolent resistance against oppressive rule, ideas that later inspired admirers throughout the world and that were used by Dr. Martin Luther King, Jr., in the U.S. civil rights movement of the 1950s and 1960s.

Between 1906 and 1914 Gandhi carried on his fight for justice for Indians in South Africa, spreading ideas of nonviolence. He led hunger strikes, public demonstrations, and mass marches, in which thousands of Indians resisted oppression by willingly risking beating or arrest for their cause. In 1914 the colonial regime bowed to the constant pressure and lifted the worst legal injustices against the Indians. Gandhi was forty-five years old when the triumph in South Africa earned him fame and the respected title of *Mahatma* (Great Soul) among Indians in South Africa and at home.

With the outbreak of World War I in Europe, Gandhi, Kasturbai, and their four children left South Africa to return to India. In 1915 he established a spiritual center near the Gujerat capital, Ahmedabad, where he trained followers in his ideas of nonviolence. Though Gandhi was deeply religious, he also believed that everyone had to reach truth in his or her own way, writing that "there are innumerable definitions of God, because His manifestations are innumerable. But I worship God as Truth only. I have not yet found Him, but I am seeking after Him." Moved by the poverty and suffering of the Indian masses, he also took up their cause. To identify with their plight, the high-caste Gandhi adopted the dress of the simple peasant and always traveled third class.

The British massacre of Indian protesters at Amritsar in 1919 shook Gandhi's faith in British justice. In 1920 he became the leader of India's major nationalist organization, the Indian National Congress, and over the next three decades he was at times a religious figure and at other times the consummate politician, crafty and practical. Needing mass support to build a policy of massive noncooperation, he launched three great campaigns of civil disobedience, in 1920, 1930, and 1942. Each time the British jailed him for long periods. His self-discipline was reflected in his practice of fasting to protest oppression, which added to his saintly image.

In his personal life, Gandhi was also troubled. His wife, Kasturbai, aided in his campaigns, but Gandhi was gone for long periods, neglecting her and their four children. One embittered

once believed unchallengeable, was no longer the imperial giant it had formerly seemed.

Growing problems, including a severe economic slump after the war, heightened Indian discontent and alarmed the British, causing them to clamp down on dissent and political activity and to maintain the laws that had been imposed during the war. The repression reached its height in 1919. In the Punjab city of Amritsar, British officers, fearing a mass uprising, ordered their soldiers, without warning, to open fire on an unarmed crowd at an unauthorized rally held in a walled field where escape was difficult (see Chronology: South Asia, 1914–1945). The attack killed 400 protesters and wounded 1,000, including women and children. The shooting stopped only when the troops ran out of ammunition. Throughout India, the Amritsar massacre was greeted with outrage. The anger intensified when the British hailed the officer in command, General Dyer, as a national hero. Dyer further enraged Indians by defending his action as the least amount of firing that would produce the necessary effect of intimidating potential Indian resistance. Prominent Indians, many once pro-British, were appalled at the cruelty, which shook their faith in British rule. The Nobel Prize–winning writer Rabindranath Tagore (tuh-GAWR) (1861–1941) wrote, "The enormity of the measures taken up for quelling some local disturbances had, with a rude shock, revealed to our minds the helplessness of our position as British subjects in India."[10]

Gandhi Addressing Calcutta Meeting
Mohandas Gandhi addressed some of his followers—many women as well as men—on a lawn following a meeting with British officials in Calcutta in 1931. (Bettman/Corbis)

son rejected his father entirely. When Gandhi took a lifelong vow of chastity in 1906, Kasturbai did also. Both kept their vows. Although both were born into affluent families, the Gandhis agreed to live simply. Critics accused Gandhi of sometimes humiliating his wife by, for example, asking her to do menial tasks such as cleaning toilets. Arrested during Gandhi's "Quit India" campaign, Kasturbai, in failing health, died in her husband's lap in prison in 1944. Before she passed away, she noted that they had shared many joys and sorrows and asked that she be cremated in a sari (dress) made from yarn he had spun.

Gandhi helped lead India to independence from Britain. Shortly thereafter, when trying to end accelerating Hindu-Muslim violence in 1948, he was assassinated by a Hindu fanatic who opposed Gandhi's tolerant approach (see Chapter 31). India's first prime minister, Jawaharlal Nehru, called Gandhi's death the loss of India's soul: "The light has gone out of our lives and there is darkness everywhere."

THINKING ABOUT THE PROFILE

1. How did Gandhi's South African experiences shape his political strategies?

2. How did Gandhi's ideas and activities have a great influence in the world?

Note: Quotations from Judith M. Brown, *Modern India: The Origins of an Asian Democracy,* 2nd ed. (New York: Oxford University Press, 1994), p. 211; and Rhoads Murphey, *A History of Asia,* 4th ed. (New York: Longman, 2003), p. 437.

C H R O N O L O G Y	
South Asia, 1914–1945	
1919	Amritsar massacre
1930	Gandhi's Great Salt March
1931	London Conference
1935	Government of India Act
1937	Provincial elections
1942	Gandhi's Quit India campaign

Gandhi: Nonviolent Resistance and Mass Politics

The unrest brought to the fore new Indian nationalist leaders, the most outstanding of whom was Mohandas K. Gandhi (GAHN-dee) (1869–1948). Gandhi developed unique ideas and exhibited eccentric personal behavior that generated bitter opponents and sometimes frustrated even his devoted allies (see Profile: Mohandas Gandhi, Indian Nationalist). After getting his law degree in Britain, Gandhi lived for twenty-two years in South Africa, where the British colonial regime practiced racial segregation and white supremacy (see Chapter 21). To assert the rights of the Indian immigrants in South Africa, Gandhi developed tactics of **nonviolent resistance**, noncooperation with unjust laws and peaceful confrontation with illegitimate authority. After returning to India, in 1920 he became the president of the main nationalist organization, the Indian National Congress. Gandhi's message of resisting the colonial regime nonviolently led him to mount mass campaigns against British political and economic institutions. Inspired by his example, huge numbers of ordinary people—factory workers, peasants, estate laborers—joined his movement, shaking the foundations of British colonial rule.

Gandhi's Ideology Influenced by his pacifist wife, Kasturbai, Gandhi developed a doctrine of nonviolence based on ideas against taking life that had been introduced 2,500 years earlier by the Jains and Buddhists, two of India's religious groups, and that were also promoted by the Quakers, a pacifist Christian movement Gandhi had encountered in England. Nonviolence—Gandhi often called it passive resistance—was, he wrote, "a method of securing rights by personal suffering; it is the reverse of resistance by arms."[11] Gandhi believed that violence, embodying hate and irrationality, was never justified. The enemy was to be met with reason, and if he responded with violence, this had to be endured in good spirit. Gandhi's approach required severe self-discipline.

Gandhi made mass civil disobedience, involving such tactics as marches, sit-ins, and boycotts, the most effective expression of nonviolence. He perfected the tactics of the boycott of British government institutions and businesses. Disobedience also involved hunger strikes, peaceful violation of law, and refusal to pay taxes. Gandhi's Congress colleague, Jawaharlal Nehru (JAH-wa HAR-lahl NAY-roo), placed Gandhi's strategy in perspective: "Gandhi was like a powerful current of fresh air that made us stretch ourselves and take deep breaths, like a Whirlwind that upset many things but most of all the working of people's minds."[12]

At the same time, some of Gandhi's ideas were outside the mainstream of nationalist thought, confounding allies. For instance, Gandhi opposed the global economic system because it was marked by competitive capitalism and trade between societies with unequal power and wealth. To escape that economy, he believed that India should reject Western capitalist models and return to the self-sufficient, village-based economy of precolonial times, where everyone could spin their own cloth. He called industrialization "a machinery which has impoverished India. India's salvation consists in unlearning what she has learned during the past fifty years. The railways, telegraphs, hospitals, [and] lawyers have all to go."[13] Critics considered Gandhi's ideal of a nation of self-sufficient villages living in simplicity a utopian fantasy, out of touch with the modern world, that prevented the development of more practical policies to improve people's lives.

Gandhi had other controversial views. He insisted that Indian society's lowest social group, the untouchables, be included in political actions, much to the distress of high-caste Hindus. Gandhi considered untouchability a religious and moral rather than a social and economic problem. He coined the term *harijans* (children of God) as a more dignified label to replace *pariahs*, the centuries-old name for untouchables. Gandhi did not entirely reject the caste system as a way of organizing society, but he wanted all people to enjoy the same dignity. In his conception, harijan toilet cleaners would have the same status as brahmans, members of the priestly caste, but would go on cleaning toilets. Even untouchable leaders often considered Gandhi's views unrealistic and patronizing.

Mass Campaigns Thanks to Gandhi's efforts, during the 1920s the Congress developed a mass base that was supported by people from all of India's cultures, religions, regions, and social backgrounds. The Congress sponsored strikes by factory workers, walkouts of workers on tea estates, and tax boycotts by peasants. Gandhi compared massive civil disobedience to an earthquake that could shut down a government. His tactics bewildered the British, who, while claiming to uphold law, order, and Christian values, clubbed hunger strikers, used horses to trample nonviolent protesters, and arrested Gandhi and other leaders. One of Gandhi's Indian critics told British officials in 1930 that the Congress "has undoubtedly acquired a great hold on the popular imagination. On roadside stations where until a few months ago I could hardly have suspected that people had any politics, I have seen demonstrations and heard Congress slogans."[14] Each campaign led to British concessions and a growing realization that Britain could not hold India forever.

The Great Depression that began in 1929 and lasted around the globe through the 1930s lowered the standard of living for most Indians, intensifying the nationalist unrest. The prices earned for India's major cash crops were cut in half, and this collapse, combined with a collapse of rural credit, caused distress and suffering. The suffering led to a new Gandhi-led campaign in 1930, beginning with what Gandhi called the Great Salt March. During this event, Gandhi and several dozen followers marched to the west coast, where they produced salt from the Indian Ocean seawater. In so doing they broke British laws, since salt production was a lucrative government monopoly. Gandhi's action and arrest caught the popular imagination, setting off a wave of demonstrations, strikes, and boycotts against British interests. In quelling the unrest, the British killed 103, injured 420, and imprisoned 60,000 resisters. They released Gandhi a few months later, and he agreed to halt civil disobedience campaigns if the British would promote Indian-made goods and hold a conference to discuss India's political future.

Hindu-Muslim Division

While these events were proceeding, a growing Hindu-Muslim division posed a problem for Indian nationalism. Although some Muslims supported the Indian National Congress, the fact that it was mainly Hindu sparked concerns among Muslims and other minorities about their role in India. While

---

nonviolent resistance Noncooperation with unjust laws and peaceful confrontation with illegitimate authority, pursued by Mohandas Gandhi in India.

Gandhi respected all religions and welcomed Muslim support, Muslim leaders, fearing that India's independence would mean Hindu domination, mounted their own nationalist organizations, separate from the Congress, to work for a potential Muslim country of their own. In 1930 student activists in Britain called their proposed Muslim nation Pakistan, meaning "Land of the Pure" in the Urdu language spoken by many Indian Muslims. Accounting for some 20 percent of British India's population and largely concentrated in the northwest and Bengal, Muslims occupied all niches of society but were divided themselves by social status, ancestry, language, and sect. The great majority were Sunni but some were Shi'a.

While Muslim leaders often focused on the need for a state that enshrined their religious values, Congress leaders were chiefly Western-oriented Hindu intellectuals who wanted a secular state that was neutral toward religion and, in contrast with Gandhi, a modern India. The forty-year-old Jawaharlal Nehru (1889–1964), who succeeded Gandhi as Congress leader in 1929, was the strongest advocate of a secular, modern India. Born into a wealthy brahman family and endowed with unusual charisma and rare public speaking skills, Nehru was an aristocratic, Marxist-influenced product of an elite Western education with a passion for the welfare of the common people. Nehru, like Gandhi, demanded complete freedom from British domination. But while Gandhi wanted to reshape colonial society, Nehru and other Congress leaders focused more on political independence. Few of the Indian nationalists, whether Hindu or Muslim, shared the Chinese Communist goal of radical social transformation as a necessary part of economic development.

By the 1930s the main rival to the Congress was the Muslim League, led by the Western-educated Bombay lawyer Muhammed Ali Jinnah (jee-NAH) (1876–1948), a dapper figure in his tailored suits who always spoke English and never learned Urdu. Jinnah promoted a Two Nations Theory, arguing that Islam and Hinduism were different social orders and that it was a naive Congress dream that the two groups could ever forge a common nationality. Jinnah developed the Muslim League into a mass political movement in competition with the Congress. His claim to speak for all Muslims outraged the Congress, which had over a hundred thousand Muslim members—some secular, some devout—and saw itself as a national party representing all religions and castes. But it faced a skilled foe in Jinnah, who cultivated good relations with the British and convinced regional Muslim leaders, some once pro-Congress, to support the Muslim League. The Congress tried to marginalize the Muslim League and refused to form a coalition with it, which proved to be a mistake in the long run.

The competing visions of the Congress and the Muslim League complicated British efforts to introduce representative government institutions. The two rival organizations clashed in 1931, when, as a result of Gandhi's agreement to suspend civil disobedience, Indian leaders and British officials met in London to discuss expanded elections. Represen-tatives of various minorities, including Muslims, Sikhs, and untouchables, demanded separate electorates to ensure that their groups gained representation. Seeing this as a tactic that would allow the British to divide and rule, Congress objected, but the minorities won electoral rights in India's many provinces.

The electoral agreement also did not end anticolonial unrest and counterviolence by the British. However, in 1935, their power in retreat, the British introduced a new constitution that allowed some 35 million Indians who owned property, including 6 million women, to vote for newly formed provincial legislatures. In the first provincial elections, in 1937, the Congress won 70 percent of the popular vote and the majority of seats, defeating the Muslim League even for seats reserved for Muslims. More Indians also rose to leadership positions in the army, police, and civil service. However, British officials argued that the communal divisions necessitated the continuation of British rule to maintain order, and Jinnah, battered but not broken by the disappointing Muslim League electoral performance, redoubled his efforts to unite Muslims against the Congress.

Social Change: Caste and Gender Relations

Nationalist politics, economic dislocations, and the stresses posed by rapid population growth also had an effect on India's social structure. India's population grew from 255 million in 1871 to 390 million in 1940. The trends that had reshaped the caste system beginning in the 1800s continued, including the adoption by lower castes, anxious to improve their status, of high-caste practices such as vegetarianism, and more awareness of caste identities than had existed in earlier centuries. These caste trends affected the untouchables, the most disadvantaged and powerless group in Hindu society and perhaps a fifth of India's population. Although Gandhi, a high-caste Hindu, urged fair treatment for all groups, increasing attention to caste identities often resulted in more discrimination against untouchables, which encouraged untouchable leaders to mount movements promoting the rights of their community.

The largest such movement was led by Dr. Bhimrao Ramji Ambedkar (BIM-rao RAM-jee am-BED-car) (1893–1956). Ambedkar rose from one of the lowest groups, the sweepers who cleaned village streets, to earn a Ph.D. and a law degree from major U.S. and British universities. On his return to India he started schools, newspapers, and political parties. Ambedkar rejected Gandhi's policies as patronizing and inadequate for real change. He successfully lobbied the government to promote upward mobility for the untouchables by offering them government jobs and scholarships for higher education. Later in life, believing untouchables could never flourish within Hinduism, Ambedkar led thousands of followers to abandon Hinduism and adopt Buddhism, which by then had only a small following in India.

Attitudes toward women were also changing. Hindus increasingly favored widow remarriage, once forbidden, to help offset what they believed to be the higher Muslim birthrate.

The trends, however, including greater emphasis on what traditionalists considered proper female conduct, largely favored male authority. Yet, while the feminist movement remained weak and had little support among Muslim and peasant women, many women joined the Congress and some demanded a vote equal to men for representative institutions, such as provincial legislatures. With British assent, all the legislatures granted women the franchise between 1923 and 1930. Educated women published magazines. Some were daring in challenging male authority. For example, Rokeya Hossain (1880–1932), a Bengali Muslim raised in seclusion who had opened girls' schools and campaigned for equal rights, published, with her liberal husband's support, a utopian short story, "Sultana's Dream," that portrayed men confined to seclusion because of their uncontrolled sexual desires while women governed. Gandhi's views on women were mixed. He advocated social equality between men and women and encouraged women's participation in politics and the rest of public life. He also urged women to abandon seclusion and join the nationalist cause in a women's corps known as "servants of the nation." But, once involved in the women's corps, women were usually offered the more menial tasks such as picketing and cooking. Gandhi himself, unable to escape patriarchal attitudes, promoted women's traditional roles as wives, mothers, and supporters of men. Impressed by his wife Kasturbai's advocacy of nonviolence, Gandhi believed women were especially suited to passive resistance. He wrote paternalistically that women were nobler than men, the embodiment of humility, sacrifice, and silent suffering. But some women with a more militant vision of change joined men in terrorist organizations aimed at undermining colonialism. For example, Pritilata Waddedar (1911–1932), a brilliant Bengali university graduate, led and died in an armed raid on a British club that reportedly boasted a sign: "Dogs and Indians not allowed."

Towards Two Nations

World War II was the deciding event in the path to Indian independence, but it also reshaped the nationalist dialogue by increasing the Hindu-Muslim divide. The British committed Indian troops to the war without consulting Congress leaders, who protested that cooperation must be between equal partners and by mutual consent. In 1942 Gandhi, fearing that the British had no intention of ending their colonial rule, mounted a campaign calling on the British to "Quit India." In response, the British arrested Ghandi, Nehru, and the entire Congress leadership and 60,000 party activists, jailing many of them for the duration of the war. World War II harmed the rural poor and urban workers, as prices for essential goods soared. At the same time, famine in Bengal killed 3 million to 4 million people. In response to these hardships, Nehru's main rival for Congress leadership, the militant Bengali Marxist Subhas Chandra Bose (1895–1945), allied with imperial Japan, Britain's fascist enemy along with Nazi Germany. With Japanese backing, Bose organized an Indian National Army, recruited largely from among Indian soldiers in the British Indian army and Indian emigrants in Southeast Asia. His army invaded India from Japan-held Burma to attack the British. The invasion failed, but many Indians saw Bose and other Indian National Army leaders as national heroes.

Meanwhile, the arrest of Congress leaders had left a vacuum that allowed for Jinnah to completely sever his Muslim League from the Congress. Seeking Indian support, the British cultivated Jinnah, who joined the government and consolidated the power of the Muslim League. Jinnah demanded the creation of a separate Muslim state, Pakistan, based on the provinces where Muslims were the majority. Rejecting Muslim separatism, the jailed Gandhi urged Muslims to resist what he termed the suicide of partition. But Gandhi's plea was futile, and British efforts to bring the factions together also failed. After World War II, the struggle between Indian nationalists and the British, and between Hindus and Muslims, resumed, leading to the end of British rule and the creation of two separate independent nations, predominantly Hindu India and a chiefly Muslim Pakistan carved out of the Muslim majority areas of British India.

SECTION SUMMARY

■ In the aftermath of World War I, in which tens of thousands of their people died, Indians were angry that Britain denied them greater autonomy and imposed higher taxes to pay for the war, and resentment peaked with the massacre of hundreds of peaceful protesters at Amritsar.

■ Mohandas Gandhi, the foremost Indian nationalist leader, promoted nonviolent resistance to British rule, including strikes, boycotts, and refusal to pay taxes, and won a massive popular following for the Indian National Congress.

■ While even his Indian supporters considered some of Gandhi's ideas naive and utopian, campaigns such as the Great Salt March were highly effective in winning concessions from the British.

■ Feeling threatened by the predominantly Hindu National Congress, the Muslim League, led by Jinnah, argued that Indian Muslims should have a country of their own, which they called Pakistan.

■ Leaders of the untouchables, the lowest Hindu caste, pushed for and obtained greater opportunities, and women were allowed somewhat more freedom, though many Indian men, including Gandhi, did not see them as entirely equal to men.

■ The British jailed tens of thousands of Indian National Congress activists after Gandhi objected to Indian troops being forced to fight in World War II, a Bengali Marxist led a failed invasion of India, the Muslim League grew increasingly independent, and eventually, after the end of World War II, both Pakistan and India gained independence from Britain.

◆ Nationalist Stirrings in Southeast Asia and Sub-Saharan Africa

How did nationalism differ in Southeast Asia and sub-Saharan Africa?

As in India, the challenges posed by European colonialism were also being addressed by nationalist movements and protests in Southeast Asia and sub-Saharan Africa, though few of them were as influential as the Indian National Congress. In 1930 the Indonesian Nationalist Party, struggling against Dutch colonialism, urged Indonesians to be zealous in the cause of national freedom and building a new nation. The plea symbolized the nationalist response in several other Southeast Asian colonies, especially French-ruled Vietnam. Although in sub-Saharan Africa organized nationalist movements, often based on ethnicity, were weaker than comparable movements in India or Southeast Asia, African nationalism was strongly expressed in cultural developments.

Changing Southeast Asia

Nationalism proved as influential a force in parts of Southeast Asia as in China and India, and stronger than in Africa, during this era. The first stirrings of Southeast Asian nationalism came in the Philippines in the late 1800s, but the revolution was thwarted by first Spain and then the United States. In the Philippines the U.S. promise of eventual independence and the co-optation of nationalist leaders into the colonial administration tended to reduce radical sentiments. By 1941 nationalism also had a large following in Vietnam, British Burma, and parts of Indonesia, all places that had suffered particularly oppressive colonial rule and where independence would come only through revolutionary war or the threat of armed force. Compared to these colonies, nationalism was weaker in French-ruled Cambodia and Laos and in British Malaya, all colonies that had experienced less social, economic, and political disruption.

One of the stronger nationalist movements arose in Burma (today's Myanmar). Despite limited self-government by the 1930s, including an elected legislature, the colony's majority ethnic group, the Burmans, viewed British rule as oppressive and resented British favoritism toward ethnic minorities who became Christian. They also resented the large, often wealthy Indian community, which had immigrated to Burma when the British combined the colony with British India and who dominated the economy. These resentments fostered the rise of nationalism among university students and graduates. The colony's schools, whether run by the government or by Christian missions, encouraged their students to adopt Western ways, including Western clothing styles, and devalued Buddhist traditions. The nationalists used Theravada

CHRONOLOGY	
Southeast Asia and Africa, 1912–1945	
1912	Formation of African National Congress in South Africa
1912	Formation of Islamic Union in Indonesia
1920	Formation of Indonesian Communist Party
1920–1922	Nationalist unrest in Kenya
1926–1927	Communist uprising in Indonesia
1927	Formation of Indonesian Nationalist Party
1928–1931	Peasant rebellions in the Congo region
1930	Founding of Indochinese Communist Party
1932	Nationalist coup in Thailand
1935–1936	Conquest of Ethiopia by Italy
1941	Formation of Viet Minh in Vietnam by Ho Chi Minh
1941–1945	Japanese occupation of Southeast Asia

Buddhism, the faith of most Burmese, as a rallying cry to press for reform, and some favored women's rights. When the Japanese invaded Burma in 1941, many Burmans welcomed them as liberators.

Although Siam (today's Thailand) was not a colony, nationalism grew there out of tensions between the aristocratic elite and the rising middle class of civil servants, military officers, and professionals; the latter groups wanted more influence in a political system dominated by the royal family and other aristocrats. This middle-class discontent was further fueled by the Great Depression, which forced salary and budget cuts. In 1932 military officers of middle-class background, who called themselves nationalists, took power in a coup against the royal government (see Chronology: Southeast Asia and Africa, 1912–1945). The Siamese king, whose family had ruled the country since the late 1700s, agreed under pressure to become a constitutional, mostly symbolic monarch. Military leaders then ran the government through the 1930s, pursuing nationalist policies, renaming the country Thailand ("Land of Free People"), and urging the Thai people to live modern lives, including dressing in a modern Western fashion, with hats and shoes. During the late 1930s Thailand forged an alliance with the rising Asian power, imperial Japan, and introduced features of a fascist regime, militarizing the schools and suppressing dissent.

Vietnamese Nationalism and Resistance

The most powerful nationalist movement in Southeast Asia emerged in Vietnam as a result of its destabilization during French colonial rule, when peasant lands were seized. The earliest nationalists seeking an end to French rule were led by the passionately revolutionary Phan Boi Chau (FAN boy chow) (1867–1940). Phan was born into a family of mandarins who had served the Vietnamese emperors as officials for generations, and he was educated in Confucian learning, like his paternal ancestors in a society strongly influenced by Chinese thought. By the time of his death in a French prison, Phan had inspired Vietnamese patriotism and resistance. As he wrote in his prison diaries, "It has been but a yearning to purchase my freedom even at the cost of spilling my blood, to exchange my fate of slavery for the right of self-determination."[15]

But the older Confucian scholars, such as Phan, gradually lost their nationalist leadership to the younger, urban, French-educated intellectuals of the Vietnamese Nationalist Party, which, against the well-armed French, had few options other than terrorism: they assassinated colonial officials and bombed French buildings. A premature uprising sparked by the group in 1930 brought about a French reign of terror against all dissidents. French repression destroyed the major nationalist groups except for the Vietnamese communists and, by eliminating noncommunist nationalist movements, unwittingly became a turning point in Vietnamese history.

The rise of Vietnamese communism during the repression owed much to Ho Chi Minh, a mandarin's son and former sailor turned leftwing political activist, as described at the start of the chapter. Ho had spent many years organizing the communist movement among Vietnamese exiles in Thailand and China. Ho came to believe that revolution, not reform, was the answer to economic exploitation, cultural stagnation, and political repression in Vietnam. Ho also favored equality for women and improving the lives of the peasants and plantation workers. Marxism provided an alternative to the discredited imperial system, an unjust society, and French rule. In 1930 Ho and his colleagues established the Indochinese Communist Party, which united anticolonial radicals from Vietnam, Cambodia, and Laos.

Vietnamese Marxists linked themselves to the patriotic traditions of the earlier Vietnamese rebels, who for 2,000 years had led resistance first to Chinese conquerors and then to the French. One of Ho Chi Minh's best-known poems examined the long history of Vietnam and praised the men and women who struggled against foreign aggression and for an equitable society. Another Vietnamese Marxist, writing in 1943, exemplified the links with the past: "And, so it seems we are not lost after all. Behind us we have the immense history of our people. There [are] still spiritual cords attaching us."[16] Remembering Vietnam's long history of resistance to foreign occupation, Vietnamese communism took on a strongly nationalist flavor. During the 1930s the Indochinese Communist Party, led by Ho, brought together all nationalist forces in a Marxist-led united front that worked toward revolution and independence.

In 1941 Ho established the **Viet Minh**, or Vietnamese Independence League, a coalition of anti-French groups that waged war against both the French colonizers and the Japanese, who occupied Vietnam during World War II.

Indonesian Nationalism

Southeast Asian nationalist activity emerged in the Dutch East Indies in the early twentieth century. Diverse organizations sought freedom from Dutch control while seeking ways to unite the diverse population, which included hundreds of ethnic groups with distinct languages. One strategy was to adopt a unifying language. Malay was the mother tongue for many peoples in the western Indonesian islands, while elsewhere in the archipelago it served as a trading language in the marketplace. Its wide use in trade made Malay a **lingua franca**, a language widely used as a common tongue among diverse groups that also had their own languages. Nationalist intellectuals began using Malay as a unifying national language and called it Indonesian, which gradually became the language of magazines, newspapers, books, and education.

Nationalist ideas competed with and sometimes reshaped Indonesian religious traditions. For example, some Muslims, impressed with but also resenting Western economic and military power, sought to reform and purify their faith by purging it of practices based on older pre-Islamic influences, such as mysticism and the sharp division between aristocrats and commoners, which they believed held Indonesians back by promoting cultural and social conservatism. *Muhammadiyah* ("Way of Muhammad") and its allied women's organization, *Aisyah*, criticized local customs and promoted the goal of an Islamic state. The organizations stressed the five pillars of Islam, devalued the writings of religious scholars after Muhammad, and favored the segregation of men and women in public, a custom long ignored by most Indonesians. In 1912 Javanese batik merchants who mixed these reformist religious ideas with nationalism established the colony's first true political movement, the Islamic Union, which by 1919 had recruited 2 million members.

As Marxism became an influence in Indonesia after the Russian Revolution, some Indonesians began working with Dutch Communists living in Indonesia. The colonial government responded by arresting Marxists. The more radical Marxists, bent on revolution, established the Indonesian Communist Party in 1920, which grew rapidly by attracting support chiefly from nondevout Muslim peasants and labor union members in Java. Overestimating their strength, the Communists sparked a poorly planned uprising in 1926. The government crushed the uprising with massive force and executed the Communist leaders.

Viet Minh   The Vietnamese Independence League, a coalition of anti-French groups established by Ho Chi Minh in 1941 that waged war against both the French and the Japanese.

lingua franca   A language widely used as a common tongue among diverse groups with different languages.

Sukarno, the fiery Indonesian nationalist, was skilled at articulating his criticisms of colonialism. A splendid orator, he attracted a large following through his use of Indonesian, especially Javanese, religious and cultural symbols and frequent historical references in his speeches. Arrested by the Dutch in 1930, Sukarno delivered a passionate defense speech, known as "Indonesia Accuses," at his trial that became one of the most inspiring documents of Indonesian nationalism. Sukarno stressed the greatness of Indonesia's past as a building block for the future.

The word "imperialism" . . . designates a . . . tendency . . . to dominate or influence the affairs of another nation, . . . a system . . . of economic control. . . . As long as a nation does not wield political power in its own country, part of its potential, economic, social or political, will be used for interests which are not its interests, but contrary to them. . . . A colonial nation is a nation that cannot be itself, a nation that in almost all its branches, in all of its life, bears the mark of imperialism. There is no community of interests between the subject and the object of imperialism. Between the two there is only a contrast of interests and a conflict of needs. All interests of imperialism, social, economic, political, or cultural, are opposed to the interests of the Indonesian people. The imperialists desire the continuation of imperialism, the Indonesians desire its abolition. . . .

What are the roads to promote Indonesian nationalism? . . . First: we point out to the people that they have had a great past. Second: we reinforce the consciousness of the people that the present is dark. Third: we show the people the pure and brightly shining light of the future and the roads which lead to this future so full of promises. . . . The P.N.I. [Indonesian Nationalist Party] awakens and reinforces the people's consciousness of its "grandiose past," its "dark present" and the promises of a shining, beckoning future.

Our grandiose past? Oh, what Indonesian does not feel his heart shrink with sorrow when he hears the stories about the beautiful past, does not regret the disappearance of that departed glory! What Indonesian does not feel his national heart beat with joy when he hears about the greatness of the [Intermediate Era] empires of Melayu and Srivijaya, about the greatness of the empire of Mataram and Madjapahit. . . . A nation with such a grandiose past must surely have sufficient natural aptitude to have a beautiful future. . . . Among the people . . . again conscious of their great past, national feeling is revived, and the fire of hope blazes in their hearts.

THINKING ABOUT THE READING

1. What is Sukarno's evaluation of imperialism?

2. How does he think Indonesians should capitalize on their past?

Source: Harry J. Benda and John A. Larkin, eds., *The World of Southeast Asia: Selected Historical Readings* (New York: Harper and Row, 1967), pp. 190–193. Copyright © 1967 Harper and Row. Reprinted with permission of John A. Larkin.

The destruction of the Communists left an opening for other nationalists. For example, organized women's groups arose originally with the goal of improving Indonesian women's lives, and in 1928 the Congress of Indonesian Women began openly advocating independence. More influential politically, the Indonesian Nationalist Party, led mostly by Javanese aristocrats who rejected Islamic reform ideas, was established in 1927. This party promoted a new national identity. Sukarno (soo-KAHR-no) (1902–1970), the key founder, was born into a wealthy aristocratic Javanese family. After studying engineering, he dedicated his life to politics and to achieving a free Indonesia. Sukarno loved the shadow puppet stories, often based on Hindu epics from India, that had been popular on Java for centuries, in which the same characters might be heroes and villains at the same time. Like the characters in those stories, Sukarno (who had no first name) had a way of bringing together ideas that might appear contradictory, such as Islamic faith and atheistic Marxism. The mass popularizer of Indonesian nationalism, he created a slogan: "one nation—Indonesia, one people—Indonesian, one language—Indonesian." He even designed a flag and wrote the national anthem for the independent Indonesia he favored. The Dutch authorities arrested Sukarno in 1929 and exiled him to a remote island prison for the next decade, making him a nationalist symbol and increasing his popularity (see Witness to the Past: Sukarno Indicts Dutch Colonialism). With the best-known nationalist leader, Sukarno, in jail, the Indonesian Nationalist Party and the nationalist vision grew slowly throughout the 1930s.

Japanese Occupation: The Remaking of Southeast Asia

The occupation of Southeast Asia by Japanese forces during World War II from 1941 to 1945 boosted nationalism and weakened colonialism. Before 1941 colonial authority had remained strong. Only Vietnamese nationalism enjoyed widespread popular support and posed a serious threat to colonial rule. Then, in a few weeks in late 1941 and early 1942, everything changed. Japan had already bullied Thailand and the French colonial regime in Vietnam, which now took orders from the pro-Nazi Vichy government in France (see Chapter 24), to allow the stationing of Japanese troops. Then the bombing of Pearl Harbor in 1941 was quickly followed by a rapid Japanese invasion of Southeast Asia. With superior naval and air strength, the Japanese easily overwhelmed the colonial forces. Within four months they controlled major cities and heavily populated regions, shattering the mystique of Western invincibility. As an Indonesian writer later remembered, the Japanese occupation "destroyed a whole set of illusions and left man as naked as when he was created."[17] European and American officials, businessmen, planters, and missionaries were either in retreat or confined in prison camps. The Japanese talked of "Asia for the Asians," and some Japanese officers with anticolonial sentiments sympathized with Southeast Asian nationalists. But this rhetoric also masked the Japanese desire for resources, especially the rubber, oil, and timber of Indonesia, British Borneo, and Malaya. Japanese rule, whose impact varied from place to place, did not endure.

The Impact of Occupation

Japanese domination was brief, less than four years, yet it led to significant changes. For example, in many places, conflicts between ethnic groups increased because of selective repression. In Malaya, Japanese policy that favored the majority Malays allowed Malay government officials to keep their jobs while members of the Chinese minority often faced property seizures and arrest, creating antagonism between Malays and Chinese that persisted long after the war. By destroying the link to the world economy, the occupation also caused economic hardship. Western companies closed, causing unemployment, while Japanese forces seized natural resources and food. By 1944 living standards, crippled by severe shortages of essential goods such as food and clothing, were in steep decline. Southeast Asians suffered also from harassment by the Japanese police, who treated even minor violators of occupation regulations, such as breaking curfews or hoarding food, with brutality. In addition, the Japanese forcibly conscripted thousands of Southeast Asians: Javanese men became slave laborers and Filipinas, called "comfort women" by the Japanese, served the sexual needs of Japanese soldiers. As their war effort against the United States faltered, the desperate Japanese resorted to even more repressive policies to keep order and acquire resources.

Although often harsh for local people, Japanese rule also offered some political benefits for Southeast Asians. For instance, since they needed experienced local help, the Japanese promoted Southeast Asians into government positions once reserved for Westerners. These Indonesians or Burmese were often better educated and more able than the Europeans they replaced. In addition, the Japanese, seeking to purge the area of Western cultural influences, closed Christian mission schools, encouraged Islamic or Buddhist leaders, and fostered a renaissance of indigenous culture and an outpouring of literature, especially fiction that examined life under Japanese rule.

The Japanese also promoted Southeast Asian nationalism, at least indirectly, because of their recruitment of Southeast Asian leaders to lend legitimacy to their rule. Under colonialism most nationalists had been in jail or exile and hence powerless. The Japanese freed nationalist leaders such as Sukarno from jail and gave them official positions, if little actual power. The nationalists enjoyed a new role in public life and used the Japanese-controlled radio and newspapers to foster nationalist beliefs. The Japanese also recruited young people into armed paramilitary forces, and these became the basis for later nationalist armies in Indonesia and Burma that resisted the return of Western colonialism after World War II.

Japanese Defeat and Political Change

Some Southeast Asians dared to actively oppose Japanese rule, especially in Vietnam. Vietnamese communism might never have achieved power so quickly had it not been for the Japanese occupation, which marginalized and therefore discredited the French administration and imposed great hardship on most of the population, a fact that the communists used to advantage. The Viet Minh, led by Ho Chi Minh, were now armed and trained by American advisers, who, after the United States entered the war and needed local allies, had been sent to help anti-Japanese forces. In 1944 the Viet Minh moved out of their bases along the Chinese border and expanded their influence in northern Vietnam, attracting thousands of poor peasants to the anti-French nationalist cause while attacking the Japanese occupiers with guerrilla tactics. The Viet Minh rapidly gained popular support and recruits, thanks partly to a 1945 Japanese policy that exported scarce food to Japan while a famine killed 2 million Vietnamese. To establish a political presence, the Viet Minh organized local village administrations led by peasants who sympathized with their movement.

Japanese fortunes waned as the United States gained the upper hand in the war, opening the way for political change in Southeast Asia. U.S. bombing of Japanese installations in Southeast Asia alerted local people that the regional balance of power was changing. Fearing the return of Western power in Asia, the Japanese encouraged Southeast Asians to resist Western attempts to reestablish colonial control. In Indonesia, Japanese officials helped set up a committee of nationalists to prepare for Indonesian independence, and Sukarno told the members that together the united Indonesian people would renew their struggle to end forever Dutch colonialism. Japanese officials allowed Burmese nationalists to establish a government. As Japanese power diminished, some Southeast Asian nationalists began secretly working with the Western Allies. Changing sides, the Burmese nationalist army helped push Japanese forces out of Burma.

Tired of economic deprivation and repression, few Southeast Asians regretted Japan's defeat, and some, especially in Malaya, British Borneo, and the Philippines, even welcomed the return of Western forces. Before World War II the United States had promised to grant independence to the Philippines and did so in 1946, turning the country over to pro-U.S. leaders. But often the returning Westerners faced growing political volatility. The end of war set the stage for dramatic political change in Vietnam, Indonesia, and Burma, as nationalist forces resisted any return to the prewar status quo and successfully struggled for independence in the late 1940s and early 1950s.

Nationalism in Colonial Africa

The roots of the African nationalist struggle had been planted in the decades before World War II, although nationalist protests were less disruptive in Africa than in Southeast Asia and India, and African nationalist organizations also lacked the mass base of the Vietnamese and Indian nationalists. African nationalists tried with only limited success to overcome a major barrier to fostering widespread popular support: the creation by colonial powers of artificial national boundaries that enclosed ethnically diverse, often rival groups within a common administrative structure. Another obstacle was that usually imperial regimes did not prepare their colonies for political and economic independence by permitting African participation in government or opening enough schools to produce a large educated class that could assume the responsibilities and burdens of nationhood.

The artificial division of Africa was a major hindrance to nationalist organizing. All over Africa the colonial regimes, by using divide-and-rule strategies to govern the diverse ethnic groups, had made it difficult to create viable national identities. Without a national identity, an anticolonial nationalist movement that would unite all people within a colony against Western rule faced an uphill struggle. For example, Nigeria, in West Africa, was an artificial creation, the result of the late-nineteenth-century British colonization of diverse and often rival ethnic groups. While some Pan-Nigerian nationalists sought unity, most of the Nigerian nationalist organizations found their greatest support only among particular regions or ethnic groups within Nigeria. In the 1940s a prominent leader of one of the major ethnic groups, the Yoruba, expressed the common fear that no Nigerian nation was really possible:

> Nigeria is not a nation [but] a mere geographical expression. There are no "Nigerians" in the same sense as there are "English" or "French." The word "Nigerian" merely distinguish[es] those who live within the boundaries of Nigeria from those who do not.[18]

West African nationalist currents were strongest in the growing, usually multiethnic cities, such as Lagos in Nigeria, Accra in the Gold Coast, and Dakar in Senegal. These became the breeding grounds of new ideas. City life, which offered a wide range of economic activities, also encouraged the growth of trade union movements, which sponsored occasional strikes to protest colonial policies or economic exploitation. Hence, market women in Lagos, Nigeria, protested taxation, zealously protected their control of the local markets, and demanded the right to vote. During World War II they refused to cooperate with price controls, forcing the British to back down. However, rural people, especially farmers, also asserted their rights. For example, during the 1930s cocoa growers in the British-ruled Gold Coast held back their crops from the government to protest low prices.

African nationalism was sparked by World War I and the unfulfilled expectations for better lives in its aftermath. During the war the British, French, and Germans had all drafted or recruited men from their African colonies to fight on European battlefields, where thousands died. When the survivors returned home, the promises the colonial powers had made to them about land or jobs proved empty. Africans were further embittered when taxes were raised. For example, Kenyan soldiers came back from the war to find that British settlers had seized their land. In response Harry Thuku (THOO-koo) (ca. 1895–1970), a middle-class Kenyan and member of Kenya's largest ethnic group, the Gikuyu, created an alliance of diverse Kenyan ethnic groups in 1920 to confront the British. When the British arrested Thuku in 1922, rioting broke out led by Gikuyu women and the British fired on the rioters, killing over twenty of them. Anticolonial protests were common in the Belgian Congo too, where they led to rebellions by peasant farmers upset at Belgian demands that they undertake unpaid labor. Women were often in the forefront of resistance. During World War II, for instance, Aline Sitoe Diatta (1920–1944) led an uprising in Senegal when the French conscripted her village's rice supplies. She was exiled and later executed. In Nigeria in 1929, tens of thousands of Igbo women, particularly the local palm oil traders, rioted to protest taxes on them. When the rioters attacked a district office, the British opened fire, killing thirty-two of them. The protests escalated and it took months to restore order.

Inspired in part by Harry Thuku's movement, organized nationalist organizations developed in various colonies in the 1920s and met with occasional success, especially in West Africa. These urban-based organizations were formed in part to press for more African participation in local government. They were led by Western-educated Africans who sought democracy and eventual political freedom. Among these was J. E. Casely Hayford (1866–1930), a lawyer and journalist in the British Gold Coast (today's Ghana) who was influenced by Gandhi. Some Africans, including Casely Hayford, favored a Pan-African approach and sought support across colonial borders; they did not view colonial boundaries as the basis for nations. Both nationalists and Pan-Africanists were unable to overcome the divide among rival ethnic groups within each colony and, unlike the Indian and Vietnamese nationalist leaders, the gap between the cities and the villages. Hayford, for example, had little understanding of rural life and criticized the traditional chiefs who often exercised considerable power outside the cities. Furthermore, some African merchants, chiefs, and kings profited from their links to the colonizers and discouraged protests. For all these reasons, the urban nationalists were unable to capitalize on unpopular Western actions, such as the brutal Italian invasion and occupation of Africa's last independent country, Ethiopia, in 1935–1936, and had little influence before World War II, and most African states would not achieve their independence until the 1960s.

Though Africans did not mount an organized resistance to the Western powers, colonial rule generated new cultural trends that allowed people to express their views, often critical, about colonial African life. For instance, during the 1930s a musical style arose in the Gold Coast and soon spread into other British West African colonies. It was carried chiefly by guitar-playing sailors, including Africans who had visited the Americas and West Indies who regularly crossed the Atlantic.

African Jazz Band Jazz from the United States had a wide following in the world in the 1920s, 1930s, and 1940s. Jazz especially influenced the music of black South Africans, some of whom formed jazz groups such as the Harmony Kings. (Courtesy, National Library of South Africa)

This widely popular new style, **highlife**, was an urban-based mix of Christian hymns, West Indian calypso songs, and African dance rhythms. Later West African musicians added musical influences from Cuba, Brazil, and the United States, especially jazz, indicating the continuing cultural links between West Africa and the Americas. Although the music was closely tied to dance bands and parties, some highlife musicians began addressing social and political issues, and this trend grew with nationalism. The very term *highlife* signified both an envy and disapproval of the Western colonizers and rich Africans, who lived in luxury in mansions staffed by servants. Highlife songs dealt with the problems of everyday life, such as work, poverty, marital distress, and death. Many highlife songs were sung in **pidgin English**, the form of broken English that developed during the colonial era. This language, a mix of African and English words and grammar, spread throughout British West Africa as a marketplace lingua franca among ethnically diverse urban populations.

South African Nationalism and Resistance

The racial inequality and white supremacy established by the Dutch in South Africa and largely maintained by the British remained in place during most of the twentieth century, sparking nationalism that led some to resist oppression. The early South African nationalists, such as the founders of the African National Congress (usually known as the ANC, established in 1912), came from the urban middle class. The ANC encouraged education and preached African independence from white rule but did not directly confront the government until the 1950s. However, more militant African resistance also flourished, especially in the mining industry, where strikes

were endemic throughout the twentieth century despite severe government repression.

Given a white supremacist government anxious to suppress dissent, resistance was often subtle, involving noncooperation with the authorities or affirmation of African cultural forms. Protest was often expressed in music, although usually veiled to avoid arrest. Even hymns in African churches had a protest element, since they were sung using African rather than Western vocal traditions. Knowing that few whites understood lyrics sung in African languages, African workers filled the mining camps and labor movements with political music, offering messages such as "we demand freedom" and "workers unite." Many work songs bemoaned the ills of white rule. For decades, road gangs worked to songs such as "We Say: Oh, the White Man's Bad." Zulu and Swazi workers blended their own traditions with Western influences to create new dances performed by men. Virile, stamping dancers laced their performances with provocative songs: "Who has taken our land from us? Come out! Let us fight! The land was ours. Now it is taken. Fight! Fight!"[19]

In the cities jazz became a form of resistance to the South African regime. A potent vehicle for protest, this music, adapted from African Americans, reflected the African rejection of the culture of the conservative and racist Afrikaners, the descendants of Dutch settlers and the largest white ethnic group in South Africa. African American musicians such as the trumpeter Louis Armstrong (1901–1971) and the pianist Duke Ellington (1898–1974), who led a famed big band, were particularly popular in the 1930s and influenced the formation of South African jazz bands and new jazz-based musical styles. Educated urban Africans who loved jazz envisioned a modern African culture and sometimes rejected African traditions, as one Johannesburg resident proclaimed:

Tribal music! Chiefs! We don't care about chiefs! Give us jazz and film stars, man! We want Ellington, Satchmo [Louis Armstrong], and hot dames! Yes, brother, anything American. You can cut out this junk about [rural home-

---

highlife An urban-based West African musical style mixing Christian hymns, West Indian calypso songs, and African dance rhythms.

pidgin English The form of broken English that developed in Africa during the colonial era.

steads] and folk-tales—forget it! You're just trying to keep us backward![20]

The preferred music of the small, educated black professional and business class, jazz ultimately became a symbol of black nationalism in South Africa.

SECTION SUMMARY

- Southeast Asian nationalism was strong in places such as Burma, which experienced harsh colonial rule, and even emerged as a rallying cry in Siam, which was never colonized but where a military coup of middle-class background overthrew the royal government.

- Vietnamese resistance to French rule dated back to the late nineteenth century and was continued by the terrorist Vietnamese Nationalist Party, which the French harshly repressed, and the Viet Minh, a coalition led by the communist Ho Chi Minh.

- A variety of groups representing Muslims, women, and communists worked toward independence for the Dutch East Indies, and of these the Indonesian Nationalist Party, which was led by Sukarno and incorporated both Islam and Marxism, was most influential.

- Southeast Asians suffered greatly under Japanese occupation, but Japanese control of Southeast Asia during World War II also showed that Westerners could be defeated and primed the colonized peoples to resist recolonization by Westerners after the war was over.

- Although African nationalist movements were hampered by the existence of rival ethnic groups within artificial colonies, anger over the poor treatment of Africans who had fought in World War I inspired many, especially in cities, to work for independence.

- In South Africa, nationalists opposed the repressive white supremacist government through education, strikes, and, most pervasively, music.

✦ Remaking the Middle East and Latin America

What factors promoted change in the Middle East and Latin America?

The peoples of both the Middle East (the chiefly Muslim societies of North Africa and western Asia) and of Latin America, while having different histories, cultures, and political systems, were influenced by nationalism between 1914 and 1945. While North Africans, like sub-Saharan Africans and Southeast Asians, experienced Western colonial rule, Arabs in much of western Asia had been controlled for five hundred years by the Ottoman Turks, and under their rule the region was stagnating economically by the 1800s. European influence intensified after World War I, when the Ottoman colonies in western Asia were transferred to Britain and France, sparking nationalist resentment among the western Asian Arabs. Latin Americans, mostly Christians, achieved their independence in the nineteenth century and shared few recent experiences with colonized Arabs, Africans, and Southeast Asians, but two world wars and the Great Depression in the twentieth century caused turmoil, fostered dictatorships, and, as in other regions, spurred feelings of nationalism.

The Ottoman Territories

World War I was a watershed for Middle Eastern societies because it dismantled the region's major state, the Turkish-dominated Ottoman Empire, and reshaped Arab politics. In the war the Turks favored their longtime ally Germany because it shared their hatred of Russia, which had long hoped to control the narrow body of water that bisected the Ottoman capital city, Istanbul (formerly Constantinople), and provided access between the Black and Mediterranean Seas. The Ottoman Turks also dreamed of liberating Russian-controlled lands in the Caucasus and Central Asia that were inhabited largely by Turkish-speaking peoples. However, the Ottomans and their European allies lost the war, and the resulting breakup of the Ottoman Empire led to the emergence of a new, very different Turkish nation.

The Fall of the Ottoman Empire The hardships during World War I spurred Arab nationalism against Ottoman rule. Unrest in Syria brought on fierce Ottoman repression, as the Ottomans sent nationalist dissidents into exile and hanged others for treason. The most serious challenge to Ottoman rule came in Arabia, where Sharif Hussein ibn Ali (1856–1931), the Arab ruler of the Hejaz, the western Arabia region that included the Muslim holy cities of Mecca and Medina, shifted his loyalties in the war from the Ottomans to the British, who promised to support independence for the Arabs in Ottoman territory. In 1916, at British urging, Sharif Hussein launched an Arab revolt against the Turks (see Chronology: The Middle East, 1914–1945). British officers, including the flamboyant Lt. T. E. Lawrence (famous as "Lawrence of Arabia"), advised Sharif Hussein's tribal forces, which attacked Ottoman bases and communications. The British invaded and occupied southern Iraq, an Ottoman province, which had a strategic position between Arabia, Syria, and Iran and was thought to have oil.

The end of World War I brought crushed dreams and turmoil to the Middle East. The Arab nationalists such as Sharif Hussein did not know that during the war the eventually victorious European Allies—Britain, France, and Russia—had made secret agreements for dismantling the Ottoman Empire that ignored Arab interests. The czarist Russians had planned after the war to incorporate Istanbul and nearby territories into their empire while Britain and France agreed to partition the Ottoman provinces in western Asia between them, despite British promises to Sharif Hussein about Arab independence. The Russian plans had to be modified after the Communists

CHRONOLOGY

The Middle East, 1914–1945

1916	Arab revolt against the Turks
1917	Balfour Declaration
1919	British withdrawal from Iran
1919–1922	Turkish Revolution by Ataturk
1921	Formation of Iranian republic by Reza Khan
1922	Formation of Turkish republic
1922	End of British protectorate in Egypt
1925	Formation of Pahlavi dynasty by Reza Khan
1928	Formation of Muslim Brotherhood in Egypt
1930	Independence for Iraq
1932	Formation of Saudi Arabia
1935	Discovery of oil in Saudi Arabia
1936	Britain-Egypt alliance
1936–1939	Civil war in Palestine

took power in Russia in 1917 and signed a peace treaty with Germany that allowed the Caucasus region, once under Ottoman rule but occupied by the Russians in the 1800s, to be returned to Germany's Ottoman ally. When the war ended, British troops occupied much of Iraq and Palestine, and French troops controlled the Syrian coast.

World War I caused great suffering to diverse Ottoman societies. The Caucasus peoples, especially the Christian Armenians, desired independence. Suspecting them of aiding Russia, the Turks turned on the Armenians living in eastern Anatolia (see Chapter 21). More than a million Armenians were deported, chiefly to Syria and Iraq, while perhaps another million died of thirst, starvation, or systematic slaughter by the Ottoman army. These sufferings created a permanent Turkish-Armenian hostility. After the war the Russians regained control of the Caucasus, including Armenia. In a different context, hunger and disease also affected millions of Arabs in the Ottoman Empire, with 200,000 dying in Syria alone during the war.

The Versailles treaty that ended World War I brought major political change, including dismemberment of the Ottoman Empire (see Map 25.2). Turkey's neighbors—the Greeks, Italians, and Armenians—made claims on Anatolia and adjacent islands, and European Zionists asked for a Jewish national home in Palestine (see Chapter 21). The Allies ended Ottoman control of Arab territories and gave autonomy and the option

of eventual independence to the Kurds, a Sunni Muslim people, distinct from both Arabs and Turks, who inhabited a large, mountainous region of Western Asia and were also the dominant ethnic group in southeast Turkey. Both Syria and Iraq declared their independence from the Ottoman Empire. However, the League of Nations, dominated by Western countries, awarded France control over Syria and Lebanon, and Britain control over Iraq, Palestine, and Transjordan (today Jordan), under what the League called mandates. In theory mandates were less onerous for local people than colonies because they allowed for administrative assistance for a limited time.

Instead of mandates, which they viewed as a new form of colonialism, Arabs often wanted to build their own governments and shape new social systems. Arab nationalists in Syria proposed a democratic government, and some favored granting women the vote, a daring idea; indeed, few Western nations had granted women voting rights. Ignoring Syrian Arab views, French forces quickly occupied Syria and, after facing armed but futile resistance, exiled nationalist leaders. The Allies also ignored the desire of the Kurdish people for their own nation. Despite British proposals for such a change, the Kurds remained divided between Turkey, Persia (Iran), Iraq, and Syria, thus becoming the world's largest ethnic group without their own state.

A New Turkey While all the former Ottoman territories experienced change after World War I, the heart of the empire, Turkey, saw the most revolutionary changes. The disastrous defeat in the war and the humiliating agreements that followed left the Turks helpless and bitter, as well as facing a Greek invasion and Arab secession. But under the leadership of the daring war hero and ardent nationalist later known as Kemal Ataturk (kuh-MAHL AT-uh-turk) (1881–1938), the Turks enjoyed a spectacular resurgence. In 1919 Ataturk began mobilizing military forces in eastern Anatolia into a revolutionary organization to oppose the Ottoman sultan, who was discredited by defeats, and to restore dignity to the Turks. Ataturk accepted the loss of Arab lands but wanted to preserve the Turkish majority areas and the eastern Anatolia districts inhabited chiefly by Kurds.

After establishing a rival Turkish government in the central Anatolia city of Ankara, Ataturk led his forces in fighting both the sultan's government in Istanbul and the foreign occupiers, especially the Greek forces that had moved deep into Anatolia. He finally pushed the Greeks back to the Aegean Sea, and eventually Turkey and Greece agreed to a population transfer in which many Greeks living in Turkish territory moved to Greece and the Turks dwelling in Greek lands moved to Turkey. In 1922 Ataturk deposed the Ottoman sultan and set up a republic with himself as president.

Ataturk was a controversial figure among Turks. He violated Muslim customs by pursuing sexual promiscuity and drinking heavily in public; devout Muslims also suspected his morality because of his agnostic stance. In addition, being a Turkish nationalist who glorified the pre-Islamic Turkish past, Ataturk dismissed Islamic culture as an inferior mix of age-old

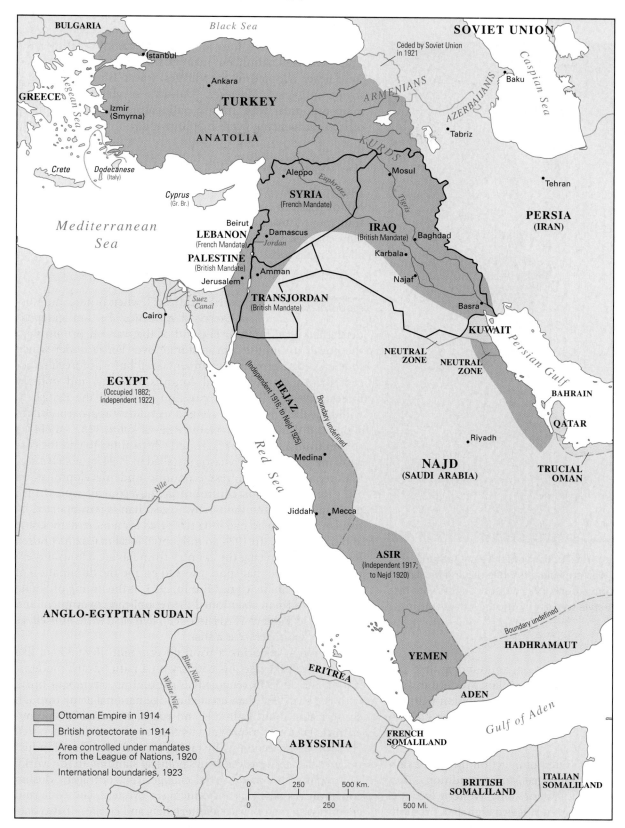

Map 25.2 Partition of the Ottoman Empire

Before 1914 the Ottoman Turks controlled much of western Asia, including western Arabia. After World War II the League of Nations awarded Iraq, Transjordan, and Palestine to Britain. Syria and Lebanon were given to France, and western Arabia was ruled by Arabs. Eventually the Saudi family, rulers of the Najd, expanded their rule into western Arabia and created Saudi Arabia.

Online Study Center **Improve Your Grade**
Interactive Map: The Disintegration of the Ottoman Empire, 1829–1914

Ataturk Wedding Dance The Turkish leader Kemal Ataturk promoted and adopted Western fashions while defying Muslim customs. In this photo from around 1925, Ataturk dances with his daughter at her Western-style wedding. (Hulton Archive/Getty Images)

mentalities. He favored modernization, announcing that "our eyes are turned westward. We shall transplant Western institutions to Asiatic soil. We wish to be a modern nation with our mind open, and yet to remain ourselves."[21] Ataturk claimed that secularization and the emancipation of women were the Turkish tradition.

In the 1920s these ideas were put in action through a dazzling series of reforms that challenged Muslim traditions. They included revamping the legal system along Western lines, replacing Arabic-based script with a Western alphabet, prohibiting polygamy, and granting women equal rights in divorce, child custody, and inheritance. Ataturk abolished Islamic religious schools and courts, and he removed reference to Islam as the state religion from the constitution. He also pushed Western-style clothing and banned the brimless hats popular with Muslim men, such as the *fez*, turban, and skullcap. His government resembled a parliamentary democracy, but he exercised near dictatorial power and alienated the Kurdish mi-

nority by suppressing their language and culture. Ataturk left a deeply changed nation, but many of the reforms he introduced were never adopted in the villages, where Islam remained a strong influence. However, Ataturk's secular approach remained popular with Turkish nationalists, including military officers, influencing Turkish politics today.

Modern Iran, Egypt, and Iraq

During this era major changes also occurred in the other major Middle Eastern countries. Like Turkey, Persia, later known as Iran, moved toward modernization, though with fewer permanent changes, and Egyptians and Iraqis turned toward nationalism in response to British attempts to maintain power in those countries.

Modernizing Iran Before World War I, when Britain and Russia exercised influence, Persian independence had been limited. The end of the war left Britain with the power to impose a protectorate over Persia under which the Persian government was maintained but was forced to accept British loans, financial controls, advisers, and military forces. Growing Persian opposition prompted the British to withdraw their troops in 1919 and seek a new approach. Britain supported General Reza Khan (REE-za kahn) (1877–1944), a soldier from a modest background who wanted to end the corrupt, ineffective royal dynasty, installed in 1794, establish a secular republic, and address economic underdevelopment. In 1921 Reza Khan took control of the government with British backing, ending the monarchy. Reza Khan was supported by secular Shi'ites, who had long struggled for a more democratic and open society. In 1924 an influential local magazine praised Reza Khan for freeing the country from having a king and expressed the hope that soon it would escape the domination of the powerful Shi'ite clergy. But in 1925, at the urging of Shi'ite clerics, Reza Khan abandoned the republican government and formed the Pahlavi (PAH-lah-vee) dynasty, with himself as king (known in Persia as a shah).

Although restoring a royal government, Reza Khan, like Ataturk in Turkey, set his country on a path toward modernization and, in 1935, renamed his nation Iran, a symbolic break with the past. The shah created a large national army through conscription, built railroads and roads, and established government factories to produce textiles, sugar, cement, and steel. He spurred the economy by taking control over the oil industry, an act that improved Iran's political standing in the world. The regime also made social changes that outraged Muslim conservatives, such as introducing a Western law code and encouraging men to wear Western hats and clothes. It also outlawed the veiling of women in public, which had the unintended effect of forcing women who wanted to wear the veil to stay home. But while the modernists, merchants, and middle class supported Reza Khan's policies, there was little improvement for poor Iranians, who mostly despised the government. Reza Khan expanded the landlord class at peasant expense.

The shah admired Ataturk's reforms but, lacking Ataturk's charisma and education, had less success in transforming Iran.

During World War II Reza Shah favored Germany. This position prompted an Anglo-Russian occupation of Iran, which the Allies needed as a supply route. Humiliated by the foreign intervention, Reza Shah abdicated in favor of his twenty-two-year-old son, Muhammad Reza Pahlavi (REH-zah PAH-lah-vee) (1919–1980), and went into exile. The son ruled until 1979.

Egypt, Iraq, and the British

British control of Egypt and Iraq and Arab resistance to that control fostered nationalist feeling in those countries. In Egypt during World War I the British had imposed martial law and drafted peasants to build roads and railroads and dig trenches in war zones. Egyptians resented these policies and the thousands of British soldiers stationed in their country during the war. A peasant song of the period castigated British officials for carrying off the peasants' corn, camels, and cattle and pleaded to be left alone. After the war nationalists unsuccessfully sought an end to British domination. The leading nationalist party, the *Wafd*, was led by Saad Zaghlul (sod ZOG-lool) (ca. 1857–1927), who had studied theology under Islamic modernists and then earned a French law degree. The Wafd was a secular movement seeking independence, representative government, civil liberties, and curtailed powers for the pro-British monarchy.

British missteps led to political change. In 1919 the British arrested Zaghlul and other Wafd leaders. Enraged Egyptians responded with strikes, student demonstrations, sabotage of railroads, and the murder of British soldiers. The anti-British movement united rich and poor, Muslims and Coptic Christians, men and women. The turmoil forced the British to release Zaghlul, who then went to the Paris Peace Conference to plead for national self-determination but, like Vietnam's Ho Chi Minh, was ignored. Upon returning to Egypt, Zaghlul was arrested again, but the resulting unrest forced Britain to grant Egypt limited independence in 1922, which nationalists saw as a sham, since Britain still controlled Egypt's defense and foreign affairs. In 1936 Britain officially ended its occupation and established an alliance with Egypt. But Britain still kept thousands of troops along the Suez Canal, which connected the Mediterranean and Red Seas through northeast Egypt, and it also shared with Egypt the administration of Sudan, the territory bordering Egypt on the south. Resentment of the continuing British presence increased during World War II.

The British also struggled to control Iraq, an artificial creation that united three Ottoman provinces, each dominated by a different group: Sunni Kurds, Sunni Arabs, and Shi'ite Arabs. Describing their occupation as a "liberation," the British promised to bestow on the Iraqis an efficient administration, honest finance, impartial justice, and security; in reality they planned to discourage self-government. To give the appearance of popular support, they held a plebiscite, but they manipulated the results to suggest pro-British sympathies. British occupation soon embittered many Iraqis. In 1920 Shi'ite clerics seeking an Islamic state proclaimed a holy war against the British, prompting various Shi'a and Sunni tribes to rise in rebellion. The British suppressed the rebellion, but at a great cost in money and lives: some 10,000 Iraqi and 400 British died in the fighting. The British kept their own casualty lists low by relying heavily on aerial bombing, which flattened whole villages.

Shaken by the fierce resistance, the British changed direction in Iraq. They introduced limited self-government that allowed Iraqi participation in an appointed Council of State. The skilled diplomacy of a pro-Arab British archaeologist, writer, and diplomat, Lady Gertrude Bell (1868–1926), defused tensions. Seeking a king for Iraq who would be content to "reign but not govern," as Bell put it, in 1921 Britain installed a member of the Hashemite (HASH-uh-mite) royal family of Mecca, Sharif Hussein's son Faisal (1885–1935). In 1930 Faisal convinced Britain to grant Iraq independence, but only after he agreed to accept continued British military bases and government advisers. By then the British had found oil in Iraq, making them unwilling to cut their ties. Many Arabs considered Faisal and his Hashemite successors to be British clients serving British interests, but Iraqi politics after 1930 was shaped by a series of Sunni Arab military strongmen, autocrats who dominated the kings and strongly influenced government policies, more than the kings themselves.

Islam and Zionism

The stranglehold of European power and Western culture remained concerns of most Middle Eastern societies during the era. Although various colonized peoples struggled to free themselves, nationalist success came slowly. Some movements tried, with limited success, to unite Arabs or Muslims across national borders. In the absence of political success, religion became a focus of attention. Arabs debated the merits of Westernization, the role of Islam in their societies, and the challenge posed by Zionism, an encounter that fostered a long-term hostility between Muslims and Jews.

Struggles over Westernization and Islam

Middle Eastern leaders and thinkers debated how or whether to emulate the powerful Western nations. They envied Western economic development, such as industrialization and a wealth of consumer goods, but disagreed about how many Western cultural, political, and social patterns, such as freethinking, parliamentary democracy, and women's rights, should be adopted. Some sought wholesale transformation; some favored Islamic tradition; and still others sought a middle path between the two, such as mixing Western and Islamic laws. Between 1923 and 1930 Western-style constitutions, which provided for civil liberties and an elected parliament, were adopted in Egypt, Iraq, Lebanon, Transjordan, and Syria. But these parliaments were limited in their duties and unrepresentative. Real power usually remained in the hands of European officials or powerful kings, and most Arab politicians had little respect for civil liberties. Inspired by Western ideals of modernity, Arabs made progress in education, public health, industrialization, and communications, but change came slowly. The Egyptian literacy rate rose from 9 percent in 1917 to only 15 percent in 1937.

Some women also asserted their rights and sought social change. One of these was the Egyptian Huda Shaarawi (HOO-da sha-RAH-we) (1879–1947). From a wealthy Cairo family, Huda had been married off at age thirteen to a much older cousin. Finding the marriage confining, Huda organized nonviolent anti-British demonstrations by women after World War I and then publicly removed her veil in 1923, shocking Egyptians. She founded and led the Egyptian feminist movement, which succeeded in raising the minimum marriage age for girls to sixteen and increasing educational opportunities for women.

The debates over Westernization fostered new intellectual currents in the Islamic world, some pro-Western, others anti-Western. Representing the former approach, a blind Egyptian, Taha Husayn (1889–1973), educated in traditional Islamic schools but also at the Sorbonne in Paris, became the key figure of Egyptian literature in the era. In his writings he challenged orthodox Islam and, in 1938, proclaimed that Westernizing Arab culture, which he favored, would fit with Egypt's traditions, which he described as a mix of Pharaonic, Arab, and Western cultures. "I want," he wrote, "our new life to harmonize with our ancient glory." In contrast, the popular reaction against Westernization came with a new Egyptian religious movement, the **Muslim Brotherhood**, founded in 1928 by schoolteacher Hasan al-Banna (1906–1949). Al-Banna despised Western values, arguing that it "would be inexcusable for us to turn aside from the path of truth—Islam—and so follow the path of fleshly desires and vanities—the path of Europe."[22] The Brotherhood followed a strict interpretation of the Quran and the hadiths, though it also accepted modern technology and was open to a more active public role for women. Expressing a widespread resentment against Western influence, such as films, bars, and modern, figure-revealing women's fashions, the Brotherhood soon developed a following in Sudan and western Asia.

The most extreme anti-Western reaction was that of the puritanical Wahhabi movement, which eventually dominated Arabia. The Wahhabis sought a return to a supposedly pristine version of Islam uncorrupted by centuries of change. They were opposed to shaving beards, smoking tobacco, and drinking alcohol. Wahhabi influence grew with the success of a tribal chief, Abdul Aziz Ibn Saud (sah-OOD) (1902–1969), who expanded the power of the Saudi family, which ruled much of central and eastern Arabia (a region known as Najd) (see Chapter 21). By 1932 his forces had taken western Arabia and the Islamic holy cities of Mecca and Medina from the Hashemites and formed the country of Saudi Arabia. As king, Abdul Aziz began strictly enforcing Islamic law by establishing Committees for the Commendation of Virtue and the Condemnation of Vice to police personal behavior. Policemen used long canes to enforce attendance at the five daily prayers, punish alcohol use and listening to music, and harass unveiled women. At the same time, the Saudis welcomed material innovations from the West, such as automobiles, medicine, and telephones. In 1935 oil was discovered in Saudi Arabia, which contained the world's richest oil reserves. The oil wealth chiefly benefited the royal family and their allies, the Wahhabi clergy.

Zionism and Palestine

The roots of a long-term problem for Arab nationalists were planted in Palestine. Before World War I Palestine was part of Ottoman-ruled Syria and had a largely Arab population. The British took over Palestine from the Ottomans after World War I. Meanwhile, the Zionist movement, which sought a Jewish homeland for the Jewish people, had been formed in the Jewish ghettoes of Europe (see Chapters 19 and 21). The Zionist slogan—"a land without a people for a people without a land"—offered a compelling vision: take the long persecuted Jewish minorities and return them to the homeland in Palestine from which they had been expelled by the Romans two millennia earlier. Zionist leaders cultivated the British government, which in 1917 issued the **Balfour Declaration**, a letter from the British foreign minister to Zionist leaders giving British support for the establishment of Palestine as a national home for the Jewish people. But the Zionist slogan had a flaw: Palestine was not a land without a people. Palestinian Arabs had lived there for many centuries, building cities, cultivating orchards, and herding livestock. A Zionist leader later conceded that Jewish settlers, under the impression that the land was largely uninhabited, were surprised to find people there. In Arab eyes, Jewish immigrants were European colonizers planning to dispossess them.

In the 1920s and 1930s, thousands of European Jews migrated to Palestine with British support, some of them fleeing Nazi Germany. By 1939 the Palestine population of 1.5 million was one-third Jewish. Although Jewish settlers established businesses, industries, and productive farms that contributed greatly to Palestine's economic development, Arabs did not see many benefits and feared they would become a vulnerable numerical minority in what they considered their own land. Land became a contentious issue. Zionist organizations began buying up the best land from absentee Arab landlords who disregarded the customary rights of villagers to use it, uprooting thousands of Arab peasants.

As tensions increased, violence spread, bewildering the British. Sometimes hundreds of Arabs and Jews were killed in armed clashes. In 1936 a major Arab rebellion fostered a three-year civil war. All Arab factions united to demand an end to Jewish immigration and land sales to Jews and to oppose plans for establishing an independent Palestine. Concluding that the Arab-Jewish divide was unbridgeable, Britain proposed a partition into two states and the removal of thousands of Arabs from the Jewish side. Both groups rejected the proposal. In 1939, worried about alienating Egypt and Iraq as Europeans prepared for World War II, Britain placed a limit on Jewish immigration and banned land transfers. But the Holocaust against the Jews in Europe during World War II spurred a more militant Zionism, reinforcing the Jewish desire for a homeland where they could govern themselves.

Muslim Brotherhood An Egyptian religious movement founded in 1928 that expressed popular Arab reaction to Westernization.

Balfour Declaration A letter from the British foreign minister to Zionist leaders in 1917 giving British support for the establishment of Palestine as a national home for the Jewish people.

Politics and Modernization in Latin America

While Islamic societies grappled with colonialism and the encounter with the West, Latin America, with economies reliant on a few natural resource exports such as beef, copper, coffee, and sugar, became more vulnerable to global political and economic crises. Sometimes this resulted in foreign interventions and domination, as when military forces from the United States occupied Nicaragua from 1909 to 1933 and Haiti from 1915 to 1934. Latin Americans paid a price for their openness to the world economy as foreign investment fell and foreign markets closed during the Great Depression in the 1930s, cutting the foreign trade of some countries by 90 percent. By 1932 Latin America as a whole was exporting 65 percent less than it had in 1929. Economic downturns led to political instability, which paved the way for governments led by military dictators, known as caudillos.

During the Great Depression dictators came to power all over the region (see Map 25.3). In 1930–1931 armed forces overthrew governments, among them elected ones, in a dozen Latin American nations, including large countries such as Peru, Argentina, and Brazil (see Chronology: Latin America and the Caribbean, 1909–1945). Some of the new governments, such as those in Argentina and Brazil, were influenced by European fascism. In Argentina one fascist military leader who took power announced boldly that there were no more political parties, only the Argentine people. Dictators often increased their governments' role in the economy, such as by beginning industries to provide products normally imported. They also used their power to amass huge fortunes for themselves and to repress dissent. In El Salvador, for example, President Maximiliano Hernandez Martinez massacred 30,000 protesting Indian peasants. He put a "positive spin" on poverty by saying that people who went barefoot could better receive the "beneficial vibrations" of the earth than those with shoes. Some dictatorships continued for years. For instance, Cubans suffered under brutal dictatorships for most of the era. The repressive Cuban rightwinger Gerardo Machado (r. 1925–1933) was forced out of office when the collapse of sugar prices generated a massive strike, temporarily bringing less autocratic leftwing nationalists and Socialists to power. But the United States disliked the new government, which challenged the U.S. claim of special privileges in Cuba and implemented labor and social reforms that hurt influential American and Cuban business interests. In 1934 the United States encouraged a coup by Sgt. Fulgencio Batista (fool-HEN-see-o bah-TEES-ta) (1901–1973), who dominated Cuba for the next twenty-five years as a rightwing dictator.

The challenges of the era also affected Chile, one of the most stable and open Latin American nations. Chileans typically accepted participatory government, claiming that Chile was "the England of Latin America." Although the military had occasionally seized power for short periods, Chile had generally enjoyed elected democratic governments and highly competitive elections involving several parties. The dislocations of the Great Depression helped the more reformist political par-

CHRONOLOGY	
Latin America and the Caribbean, 1909–1945	
1909–1933	U.S. military force in Nicaragua
1930–1931	Military governments throughout Latin America
1934	Fulgencio Batista Cuban dictator
1930–1945	Estado Novo in Brazil
1934–1940	Presidency of Lazaro Cardenas in Mexico

ties and social movements to gain support, and the squabbling leftist and centrist parties, all of which supported democratic processes, united in a Popular Front that came to power in the 1939 elections. Their reformist government, supported by labor unions, sponsored industrialization.

During the 1930s a growing women's movement that was allied with Chile's political left brought once forbidden ideas into the political debates of patriarchal, strongly Catholic Chile. Demanding respect for Chilean women and an end to what one organization called "compulsory motherhood," they lobbied for prenatal health care, child-care subsidies, and family planning, including birth control and the right to abortion, which was illegal but widely practiced. But while women won some basic legal rights, they still struggled for voting rights and could not get most of their social agenda, including abortion rights, approved, in part because of opposition by conservative Chilean women.

As elsewhere in Latin America, Brazil experienced political change that was often tinged with nationalism. In the 1920s middle-class reformers challenged domination by a corrupt ruling class that they felt did not listen to the common people or assert Brazil's national interests in the world. The reformers sought economic transformation. Their proposals for a more liberal society included official recognition of labor unions, a minimum wage, restraints in child labor, land reform, universal suffrage, and expansion of education to poor children. Worker unrest aided the growth of labor unions, but a chronic labor surplus limited the rise in organized labor's power.

Eventually the Great Depression reshaped Brazilian politics, prompting a civilian-military coup by Getulio Vargas (jay-TOO-lee-oh VAR-gus) (1883–1954) in 1930. A former soldier, lawyer, and government minister, Vargas launched the **Estado Novo** ("New State"), a fascist-influenced, modernizing dictatorship that ruled until 1945. A businessman who opposed Vargas described him as "intelligent, extremely perceptive, but also a demagogue who knew how to manipulate the masses."[23] Vargas's fascism was reflected in his use of torture and censorship

Estado Novo ("New State") A fascist-influenced and modernizing dictatorship in Brazil led by Getulio Vargas between 1930 and 1945.

Map 25.3 South and Central America in 1930
By 1930 Latin America had achieved its present political configuration, except that Britain, France, and Holland still had colonies in the Guianas region of South America, and Britain controlled British Honduras (today's Belize) in Central America.

to repress opponents. But the Estado Novo also sponsored modernizing reforms that made Vargas widely popular with the lower classes. He nationalized the banks, financed industrialization, introduced the vote for literate eighteen-year-olds and working women, and also introduced social security, an eight-hour workday, a minimum wage, and the right to strike. Gradually the dictator became more populist and nationalist. He was deposed by the army in 1945 after he had begun moving to the left. Acute tensions between rightwing and leftwing Brazilians remained.

Mexico After the Revolution

As in Chile and Brazil, strongly progressive and nationalist ideas emerged in Mexico. After the turmoil of the decade-long Mexican Revolution (see Chapter 20), which ended only in 1920, Mexico badly needed funds for reconstruction but faced sharply reduced export earnings and a deepening economic slump. A popular song from 1920 noted the hardship on common Mexican men and women: "The scramble to be president is one of our oldest haunts. But to eat a peaceful tortilla is all the poor man wants."[24] President Plutarcho Elias Calles (KAH-yays) (r. 1924–1928) put the political system on a solid footing by creating a new party that brought together various factions. Yet many Mexicans saw little improvement in their lives. For example, despite their sacrifices during the Mexican Revolution, women remained largely excluded from public life and were viewed by men as unfit to manage their own lives, let alone assume public positions of responsibility.

In 1934 Mexicans launched a new era by electing Lazaro Cardenas (car-DAYN-es) (r. 1934–1940), an army officer with socialist leanings, as president. Peasants had grown cynical about the promises by leaders during the Mexican Revolution to supply them with land. Cardenas fulfilled this promise by assigning land ownership to the *ejidos* (eh-HEE-dos), the traditional agricultural cooperatives, who now apportioned land to their members. As a result, some 800,000 people realized their dream. Cardenas hoped the ejidos would build schools and hospitals and supply credit to farmers, uplifting Mexico's poorest social class. But agricultural production for the market fell, and the money and services the government had promised never materialized.

Cardenas also introduced reforms that made him wildly popular with other Mexicans. Wooing the urban workers, he encouraged the formation of a large labor confederation. With this organization, the working class enjoyed a higher standard of living and more dignity. Cardenas also followed a nationalist economic policy. U.S. firms owned much of the oil industry, which was one of the world's largest. After these companies ignored a Mexican Supreme Court order to improve worker pay, Cardenas nationalized the industry, spurring celebrations in Mexico and outraging U.S. leaders. Workers gained a role in managing both the oil industry and the railroads. The president also supported women's rights, arguing that working women had the same right as men to participate in electoral struggles. In addition, Cardenas reorganized the ruling Party of Revolutionary Institutions around four functional groups: peasants, organized labor, the military, and the middle class. Organizing these groups allowed for more government control. Cardenas gave the Mexican Revolution new life, while the wealthy Mexican landowners and merchants, as well as U.S. political and business leaders, hated him.

Online Study Center **Improve Your Grade**
Primary Source: Speech to the Nation

Cardenas was followed by more moderate leaders who reversed support for the ejidos, favoring instead individual farmers, and ignored women's rights. Mexican women could not vote until 1953. These leaders also cooperated with the United States on immigration issues. Poor Mexicans had moved to the United States for decades. During World War II Mexico and the United States signed an agreement to send more Mexican workers north to fill the job positions in industry, agriculture, and the service sector left vacant by drafted American men. The flow northward of poor Mexicans, legal and illegal, became a floodtide after the war.

Cultural Nationalism in Latin America and the Caribbean

Cultural nationalism greatly affected Latin American and Caribbean societies. For example, a Brazilian literary trend known as Modernism sought to define a distinct national expression by exploring the country's rich cultural heritage. Rather than emulating European literary trends, modernist writers used forms and ideas reflecting Brazil's uniqueness. For instance, the poet, novelist, and critic Mario de Andrade (1893–1945) mixed words from various regional dialects and Native American, African, and Portuguese folklore into his work. Some modernists had a more internationalist outlook. Oswald de Andrade (1890–1954) saw Brazil as a creative consumer of world culture. He argued that Brazilians should mix ideas from all over the world and turn them into something distinctively Brazilian.

Nationalism, including the use of folk traditions, shaped Brazilian music. The prolific and unconventional composer Heitor Villa-Lobos (vee-luh-LO-bose) (1890–1959) developed a music to express the national character that was inspired by Afro-Brazilian and Indian religious rites and urban popular music. The popular music and dance known as *samba* became not only a world symbol of Brazilian society but also a way for the otherwise voiceless Afro-Brazilian lower classes to express themselves. Samba began as a street music and dance associated with the annual pre-Lenten carnival, a raucous celebration, in Rio de Janeiro. In 1928 professional samba groups organized into diverse schools that competed for prizes awarded by a jury, thus making samba a major social activity of the city's shantytowns. Samba infused the annual carnival processions, which grew increasingly extravagant, featuring elaborate floats, flamboyant costumes, and intricate group choreography.

The progressive spirit of the times also spurred literary and artistic movements throughout Latin America. In Chile writers combined radical politics with cultural renaissance. For example, the work of Marxist-influenced Chilean writers such as the poet Pablo Neruda (ne-ROO-duh) (1904–1973) bristled with anger over economic inequalities. Sometimes governments retaliated against dissident artists; Neruda wrote some of his greatest poetry while in hiding or exile. Meanwhile, Mexican culture reflected the currents of the revolution as it glorified the country's mixed-descent, or mestizo, heritage and addressed the poverty and powerlessness of the remaining Native American communities. Mexico produced several great artists who painted, usually on walls of public buildings, magnificent murals, showing the life of Mexico's people. Among them was Diego Rivera (rih-VEER-a) (1885–1957), a Marxist, who became one of the most famous artists in the Western Hemisphere. His huge, realistic murals depicted the common people, especially peasants and workers, struggling for dignity. Some of his murals depicting Mexican history emphasized the conflicts between the indigenous peoples and the Spanish colonizers. His wife, Frida Kahlo (KAH-lo) (1907–1954), the daughter of a German Jewish immigrant, specialized in vivid, even shocking paintings that often expressed the physical and psychological pain suffered by women, thus reflecting her own

stormy personal relationships and lifelong struggle against illness.

A cultural renaissance also occurred in the Caribbean, where intellectuals sought to create an authentic West Indian identity. In part this involved overcoming the negative attitudes, especially those held among the political and economic elite, toward acknowledging influences from Africa, the ancestral home of most West Indians. Adopting British and French racist stereotypes, West Indians had often associated Africa with the uncivilized. In contrast, Afro-Caribbean intellectuals such as the Trinidadian Marxist C. L. R. James (1901–1989) sought to rebuild Afro-Caribbean pride by celebrating African roots, which he argued were a major contributor to the distinctive West Indian culture. James also wanted to link cultural nationalism with political nationalism by using literature, art, and music to challenge Western colonialism. James was a well-traveled historian, prolific writer, political theorist, critic, skillful cricket player, and activist in Trinidad politics who was equally at home in the Caribbean, Europe, Africa, and North America. His ability to combine Afro-Caribbean nationalism with an internationalist perspective inspired intellectuals around the world.

Diego Rivera, *Sugar Cane* Diego Rivera, the greatest of the Mexican mural painters, was noted for art with an historical and political focus, often showing political leaders, cruel overlords, and suffering peasants and workers. This painting, *Sugar Cane*, pictures a Spanish overseer ordering black and Indian workers to cut, bind, and carry the sugar cane. [Diego Rivera, *Sugar Cane*, 1931. Philadelphia Museum of Art, Gift of Mr. and Mrs. Herbert Cameron Morris (1943-46-21)]

SECTION SUMMARY

- In the post–World War I breakup of the Ottoman Empire, lands such as Iraq, Syria, and Lebanon that sought freedom were instead colonized by Britain and France, but Turkey revived under the leadership of Ataturk, who modernized the country and minimized the role of Islam.

- Reza Khan, the British-supported shah of Persia, attempted to modernize his country as Ataturk had Turkey, though with less success, while Britain, in reaction to violent opposition, granted Egypt and Iraq increasing measures of autonomy and independence.

- Arab leaders debated how to balance modernization with Islam; the most puritanical form of Islam, Wahhabism, came to dominate Saudi Arabia; and the return of Jews to Palestine caused great tensions with the Arabs who had lived there for centuries.

- Vulnerable Latin American economies were greatly damaged during the Great Depression, which led to instability and the rise of military dictators in many countries, while in Chile, instability led to a progressive, prolabor government.

- Impoverished and frustrated after a long revolution, many Mexicans were pleased by the rule of Lazaro Cardenas, who gave land to agricultural cooperatives, nationalized industries, and supported women's rights, but who was followed by less progressive leaders.

- Latin American and Caribbean artists, musicians, and writers worked to produce art that expressed their unique cultural perspectives.

Online Study Center **ACE the Test**

Chapter Summary

During this era, in the face of major world changes, nationalism became a strong force in the Western colonies and other dominated societies of Asia, Africa, and Latin America. The global transitions of two world wars and the Great Depression had destabilized local economies, capitalism had reshaped rural life for millions of peasants, and many Asians and Africans resented the activities of the Western powers. In response, nationalism, often blended with Marxism, gained support as a strategy to oppose Western domination.

Nationalism became particularly influential in China and India. Nationalists reunified China after two decades of fragmentation and warlord violence but could not improve rural life or halt Japanese expansion, providing an opening for the Chinese Communists under Mao Zedong to gain support by offering a program to transform society. In India, nationalism in response to repressive British colonialism gained a mass following. Mohandas Gandhi mounted massive, nonviolent campaigns of civil disobedience, which undermined British rule.

But Gandhi and other nationalist leaders, mostly Hindus, could not prevent the minority Muslims from seeking a separate nation.

Nationalism had an uneven history in Southeast Asia, sub-Saharan Africa, and the Middle East. In Vietnam, Ho Chi Minh organized an effective Communist resistance to the French, while in Indonesia, Sukarno led opposition to Dutch rule. During World War II nationalists in Vietnam, Indonesia, and Burma organized to oppose a resumption of Western colonialism when the war ended. While political nationalist organizations developed in Africa and black South Africans resisted white domination, nationalism was often more influential as a cultural force, especially in music. World War I left the Middle East in turmoil, as Britain and France extended their power into Arab societies once ruled by the Ottoman Empire. But the Turks, led by Kemal Ataturk, and Iran developed modern states open to Western influences. Muslim intellectuals debated whether to adopt Western ideas or maintain Islamic traditions. Arab conservatives, including the Wahhabis, used Islam to oppose any social or cultural changes. The rise of Zionist immigration to Palestine posed another challenge to the Arabs. In many Latin American nations, while progressive social and literary movements proliferated, economic problems intensified and dictators gained power. Some Latin American governments, especially in Mexico and Brazil, tried to help the poor. Nationalism permeated literary, musical, and artistic expression in both Latin America and the Caribbean.

Online Study Center **Improve Your Grade** Flashcards

Key Terms

warlords	people's war	pidgin English
New Culture Movement	Maoism	Muslim Brotherhood
May Fourth Movement	nonviolent resistance	Balfour Declaration
Jiangxi Soviet	Viet Minh	Estado Novo
Long March	lingua franca	
	highlife	

Suggested Reading

Books

Bogle, Emory C. *The Modern Middle East: From Imperialism to Freedom, 1800–1958.* Upper Saddle River, N.J.: Prentice-Hall, 1996. An overview of the region during this era.

Brown, Judith M. *Gandhi: Prisoner of Hope.* New Haven: Yale University Press, 1989. One of the key studies of this seminal nationalist leader and thinker.

Brown, Judith M. *Modern India: The Origins of an Asian Democracy,* 2nd ed. New York: Oxford University Press, 1995. A strong introduction to modern Indian history.

Cleveland, William L. *A History of the Modern Middle East,* 2nd ed. Boulder: Westview Press, 2000. One of the best surveys.

Erlmann, Veit. *African Stars: Studies in Black South African Performance.* Chicago: University of Chicago Press, 1991. Essays on South African music and nationalism in this era.

Findley, Carter Vaughn, and John A. M. Rothney. *Twentieth Century World*, 6th ed. Boston: Houghton Mifflin, 2006. A comprehensive survey of this era.

Freund, Bill. *The Making of Contemporary Africa: The Development of African Society Since 1800*, 2nd ed. Bloomington: Indiana University Press, 1999. An excellent discussion of the colonial era and the changes it brought.

Huynh Kim Khanh. *Vietnamese Communism, 1925–1945*. Ithaca: Cornell University Press, 1982. A valuable scholarly study of this topic.

Keen, Benjamin, and Keith Haynes. *A History of Latin America*, 7th ed. Boston: Houghton Mifflin, 2004. A comprehensive account with considerable coverage of these decades.

Marlay, Ross, and Clark Neher. *Patriots and Tyrants: Ten Asian Leaders*. Lanham, Md.: Rowman and Littlefield, 1999. Sketches of Asian nationalists such as Gandhi, Nehru, Ho, Mao, and Sukarno.

Martin, Cheryl E. and Mark Wasserman. *Latin America and its People*. New York: Longman, 2005. A readable introduction with much on this era.

Owen, Norman G., et al. *The Emergence of Modern Southeast Asia: A New History*. Honolulu: University of Hawai'i Press, 2005. The best survey of modern Southeast Asian history, comprehensive and readable.

Sheridan James E. *China in Disintegration: The Republican Era in Chinese History, 1912–1949*. New York: Free Press, 1975. Dated but still the standard work on this period in China.

Spence, Jonathan D. *The Gate of Heavenly Peace: The Chinese and Their Revolution, 1895–1980*. New York: Penguin, 1982. A masterful account of China in this era through the eyes of artists, thinkers, and writers.

Stavrianos, Leften S. *Global Rift: The Third World Comes of Age*. New York: William Morrow, 1971. A provocative, innovative, and readable study that provides a global context.

Wolf, Eric R. *Peasant Wars of the Twentieth Century*. New York: Harper and Row, 1969. A pathbreaking study of the revolutions in China, Vietnam, Algeria, Cuba, and Mexico.

Websites

History of the Middle East Database (http://www.nmhschool.org/tthornton/mehistorydatabase/mideastindex.htm).   A useful site on history, politics, and culture.

Internet African History Sourcebook (http://www.fordham.edu/halsall/africa/africasbook.html). This site contains useful information and documentary material on Africa.

Internet East Asian History Sourcebook (http://www.fordham.edu/halsall/eastasia/eastasiasbook.html). An invaluable collection of sources and links on China, Japan, and Korea from ancient to modern times.

Internet Indian History Sourcebook (http://www.fordham.edu/halsall/india/indiasbook.html). An invaluable collection of sources and links on India from ancient to modern times.

Internet Islamic History Sourcebook (http://www.fordham.edu/halsall/islam/islamsbook.html). A comprehensive examination of Islamic societies and their long history, with many useful links and source materials.

Internet Modern History Sourcebook (http://www.fordham.edu/halsall/mod/modsbook.html).   An extensive online collection of historical documents and secondary materials.

Latin American Resources (http://www.oberlin.edu/faculty/svolk/latinam.htm).   An excellent collection of resources and links on history, politics, and culture.

WWW Southeast Asia Guide (http://www.library.wisc.edu/guides/SEAsia/).   An easy-to-use site.

Global Imbalances in the Modern World, 1750–1945

A world traveler in the nineteenth century could not help but notice the imbalances in wealth and power between the world's societies, imbalances that became even wider in the early twentieth century. One of these travelers, the American writer Mark Twain, author of beloved novels about Tom Sawyer and Huckleberry Finn, became a critic of the imperialism that increased these imbalances. Returning to the United States after lengthy travels in the South Pacific, Asia, Africa, and Europe, Twain blasted U.S. policies in Asia, including the costly military occupation of the Philippines as part of the Spanish-American War, writing in 1900 that "I left these [American] shores a red-hot imperialist. I wanted the American eagle to go screaming into the Pacific. But I have thought more, since then. [Now] I am opposed to having the eagle put its talons on any other hand."[1] His travels had convinced him that, despite Western stereotypes, most peoples, including Filipinos, were capable of governing themselves and that efforts to impose U.S. models on others were doomed to failure.

The imbalances that Twain had observed in his travels or gleaned from news accounts were part of the modern world, which was shaped in part by revolutions and innovations in western Europe and North America. In these Western societies, capitalism and industrialization fostered wealth and inspired new technologies, such as the steamships and railroads that conveyed travelers like Twain, resources, and products over great distances. But the new technologies also included deadly new weapons, such as repeating rifles and machine guns, that enabled the Western conquest of Asian and African societies, reshaping the world's political and economic configuration. Just as Spain and Portugal controlled Latin America until the early 1800s, a half-dozen Western nations ruled, or influenced the governments of, most Asian, African, and Caribbean peoples by 1914. Western domination of the global economy fostered investment but also facilitated a transfer of vast wealth to the West.

While several Western societies exercised disproportionate power in this era, other societies were not passive actors, simply responding to the West. In whatever part of the world they lived, people were linked to a global system that, however imbalanced in terms of political and economic power, promoted often useful exchanges between distant societies. Societies borrowed ideas, institutions, and technologies from each other, though redefining them to meet their own needs. Societies such as Siam (later Thailand), Persia (later Iran), Turkey, and, most spectacularly, Japan successfully resisted colonialism and, borrowing Western models, introduced some modernization. In fact, resistance to Western power was endemic in the global system. Even in colonized societies such as Vietnam, Indonesia, India, and South Africa, local peoples actively resisted domination and asserted their own interests. The movement of products, thought, and people, on a larger scale than ever before,

transcended political boundaries, connecting distant societies. Europeans avidly imported Asian arts, Africans embraced Christianity, and peasants from India settled in the South Pacific and the West Indies. By the 1930s people around the world, often using borrowed Western ideas such as nationalism and Marxism, were challenging Western political and economic power.

IMPERIALISM, STATES, AND THE GLOBAL SYSTEM

The world's governments changed greatly during the Modern Era, fostering new types of empires and states. A more integrated international order, dominated by a few Western nations and, eventually, also by Japan, was built on the foundation of the varied Western and Asian empires that had been the main power centers during the Early Modern Era. Societies worldwide grappled with the global political trends that affected people's well-being and livelihoods.

Global Empires

Powerful societies had formed empires since ancient times, but over the centuries successive empires grew larger and more complex. In the mid-1700s over two-thirds of the world's people lived in one of several large, multiethnic empires whose economies were based largely on peasant agriculture. These empires stretched across the Eastern Hemisphere from Qing China and the Western colonies in Southeast Asia, such as Dutch Java and the Spanish Philippines, to the Ottoman, Russian, and Habsburg Empires. In the Americas the huge Spanish Empire, Portuguese Brazil, and British North America all resembled the Eurasian empires in their multiethnic populations and agrarian base, although much of the agriculture was done by unfree

Queen Victoria as Seen by a Nigerian Carver This wood effigy of the British monarch was made by a Yoruba artist in just-colonized Nigeria in the late nineteenth century. (Pitt Rivers Museum, Oxford University)

labor. In addition to empires but smaller, there were also strong states such as Tokugawa Japan, Siam, and the Ashante kingdom in West Africa. All empires and states depended on a command of military power, especially gunpowder weapons. Great Britain and the Netherlands differed from the other strong states mainly in their greater reliance on world trade.

Many of the empires of the mid-1700s had crumbled by the early twentieth century. The Spanish, Portuguese, and British lost most of their territories in the Americas, and the Habsburg and Ottoman Empires were dismantled after World War I. In their place, modern empires had emerged. Between 1870 and 1914, Britain and France established overseas empires on a grander scale than ever before in history, ruling colonies in Africa, Asia and the Pacific, and Russia now controlled a vast expanse of Eurasia. On a smaller scale, Germany, Japan, and the United States also forged territorial empires. A huge portion of the globe, divided up into colonies or spheres of influence by the West, was incorporated into a Western-dominated world economic system. The influential British imperialist and author Rudyard Kipling summarized the rationale for exercising imperial power: "That they should take who have the power, And they should keep who can."[2]

Like empires throughout history, modern imperial states, whatever their democratic forms at home, punished dissent in their colonies. Sometimes protests, such as those led by Mohandas Gandhi in India, forced Western colonizers to modify their policies; more commonly, protest leaders, such as Gandhi, Harry Thuku in Kenya, and Sukarno in Indonesia, were jailed or exiled. Some observers recognized the failure of democratic countries to encourage democracy in their own colonies. For example, British critics condemned the repressive colonial policies of their government, especially the harsh treatment designed to discourage rebellion in Ireland against Britain. A nineteenth-century English wit charged that "the moment the very name of Ireland is mentioned, the English seem to bid adieu to common feelings, common prudence and common sense, and to act with the barbarity of tyrants and the fatuity of idiots."[3]

Nations and Nationalisms

Whether parts of empires or not, all over the world societies struggled to become nations, enjoying self-government and a common identity. But Western peoples formed the most powerful nations. Many European nations were formidable forces because of their strong government structures and democratic practices that fostered debate; they also enjoyed economic dynamism, possessed advanced weapons, and engaged in fierce rivalries with each other. Across the Atlantic most Latin American nations struggled to achieve prosperity and internal unity, but the United States matched European capabilities and shared similar imperial ambitions by the later 1800s, much to the disgust of anti-imperialists such as Mark Twain. Americans believed in the tenets of Manifest Destiny, articulated by an influential U.S. politician: "God has marked the American people as his chosen nation to finally lead in the regeneration of the world."[4] By contrast, few people in the colonies shared any sense of common identity, let alone a national mission; colo-

nial governments were unpopular and usually viewed by the colonized as illegitimate. By drawing up arbitrary colonial borders, often without regard to ethnic connections or economic networks, the British created Nigeria, the Dutch created Indonesia, the French created Laos, and the Belgians created the Congo, all colonies lacking any national cohesion. The ethnic diversity of most colonies—Indonesia and the Congo each contained several hundred ethnic groups—inhibited nationalist feeling and thus the formation of nationalist movements.

Still, despite the barriers, nationalism spread, often encouraged by travel, exile, or education. Giuseppi Garibaldi (gee-you-SEP-ee gare-a-BALL-dee) (1807–1882), for instance, who helped unify Italy, was born in France of Italian parents and nursed a love for his ancestral homeland during his years living in South America and then the United States before he returned to Italy. The Venezuelan Simon Bolivar, the Filipino Jose Rizal (rih-ZALL) (1861–1896), and the Vietnamese Ho Chi Minh (1890–1969), all disenchanted with colonial restrictions, embraced a nationalist agenda while living in Europe. Indian students discovered the writings of the English-born American revolutionary and exponent of liberty Tom Paine and wondered why their British rulers had ignored Paine's "rights of man" in India. Yan Fu, a Chinese student living in England in the 1870s, recalled spending "whole days and nights discussing differences and similarities in Chinese and Western thought and political institutions."[5] He perceived how Europeans became powerful by combining military aggression, well-defined national states, growing commerce, and a culture approving of political and religious debate. Back in China, Yan Fu translated the work of liberal British thinkers and used it to spread nationalism and other Western ideas in China. But nationalists seeking to confront Western power did not all look to the West for inspiration. By 1900 Japan was a role model of nationalism and modernization for many Asians, and the Vietnamese anticolonial leader Phan Boi Chau (fan boy-CHOW) (1867–1940) advised his countrymen to look east to Japan.

But nationalism was not always an imported sentiment. Many Asians had a sense of identity similar to nationalism long before the nineteenth century. People in Korea, Japan, and Vietnam, for example, had long enjoyed some national feeling based on shared religion, a common language, bureaucratic government, and the perception of one or more common enemies. African kingdoms such as Ashante (ah-SHAN-tee), Oyo (OH-yo), and Buganda (boo-GONE-da) enjoyed some attributes of nationhood. Reflecting such national feeling, in 1898, Hawaii's last monarch, Queen Liliuokalani (luh-lee-uh-oh-kuh-LAH-nee), pleaded with the United States not to colonize the islands, since her people's "form of government is as dear to them as yours is precious to you. Quite as warmly as you love your country, so they love theirs."[6] U.S. leaders ignored her pleas and annexed Hawaii. To protect their position, colonizers labored hard to crush these traditions and to counter anticolonial nationalism through the use of divide-and-rule strategies, such as the British encouragement of the Hindu-Muslim divide in India. Formerly well-defined states, such as Ashante and Buganda in Africa, lost their traditional cohesion as they now became parts of larger colonies. To resist colonial strategies, nationalists sought ways to regain the initiative and achieve sovereignty. The Indian nationalist Jawaharlal Nehru expressed the search for a successful anticolonial strategy: "What could we do? How could we pull India out of this quagmire of poverty and defeatism, which sucked her in?"[7]

Nationhood Through Revolutions

Some societies needed major rebellions and revolutions to transform old discredited orders and create new nations. The American and French Revolutions of the later 1700s began an Age of Revolution and inspired people elsewhere to take up arms against unjust or outdated governments. In the U.S. case, disgruntled colonists overthrew British rule, and key American revolutionaries, such as Thomas Jefferson and English-born Tom Paine, became known around the world as exponents of political freedom. During the mid-nineteenth century the Taiping (TIE-ping) Rebellion against China's Qing dynasty and the Indian Rebellion against the British East India Company, although they ultimately failed, provided fierce challenges to established governments in the world's two most populous societies. Like these upheavals, the rebellion by the southern states of the United States against the federal government, which resulted in some 600,000 deaths during the American Civil War did not succeed. Nonetheless, the struggle reshaped American society by allowing President Abraham Lincoln to abolish slavery and forge a stronger national government. Early in the twentieth century, other revolutions overturned old governments and built nations in Mexico, Turkey, and China; the Chinese revolution ended 2,000 years of imperial control and established the foundation for a modern republic. The Russian Revolution of 1917 installed the world's first Communist government, inspiring Communist movements and revolutionary nationalists around the world.

The aftermath of World War I brought new revolutionary upheavals and ideologies. Old states collapsed in eastern Europe, fascism spread in Germany and Japan in the economic shambles caused by the Great Depression, and Spain erupted in civil war. In 1914 Marxism, the revolutionary socialist vision developed by Karl Marx (1818–1883), had relatively little influence outside of Germany and Russia, but by 1945 the ideology had mass support in many societies. Communist revolutionary movements percolated in China, Korea, Indonesia, and Vietnam. Karl Marx had supplied the critique of the old society, which he saw as shaped by class struggle and capitalism. Now the Russian leader, Vladimir Lenin (1870–1924), forged a revolutionary party and strategy to overthrow that society, and the Chinese Communist leader Mao Zedong (maow dzuh-dong) (1893–1976) contributed a vision of a new, unselfish socialist society. Unlike Lenin, Mao believed that revolutionaries must work closely with the local people, writing that "the people are the sea, we [Communists] are the fish, so long as we can swim in that sea, we will survive."[8] By combining communism with nationalism, the Vietnamese revolutionary Ho Chi Minh provided a workable model to overthrow colonialism. The ideas of Lenin, Mao, and Ho made Marxism a major vehicle for change after World War II.

Change in the Global System

During the Modern Era the global system expanded and changed as Western influence increased. Networks of trade and communication linking distant societies grew in number and extent. However, because some Western nations came to enjoy more political and military power than other societies, they benefited more from their exchanges with the rest of the world. Aided by this power, Western culture dominated local traditions, especially in Western colonies. For example, textbooks in French colonial schools, where the students were of African, Afro-Caribbean, Asian, or Pacific islander descent, celebrated the history of the French—"our ancestors the Gauls"—while children in the U.S.-ruled Philippines, a tropical and predominantly Catholic land, learned English from books showing American youngsters throwing snowballs, playing baseball, and attending Protestant church services. In some cases this deliberate Westernization reshaped beliefs and ways of life, as occurred among the Filipinos and the Igbos of southern Nigeria. However, Western cultural influence was weak in other colonized societies, especially Muslim ones such as Egypt, the Hausa of northern Nigeria, and the Achehnese of Indonesia.

Countries gained or lost power in the global system, depending on their wealth, type of government, and access to military power (see Historical Controversy: Modernization or World-System?). In 1750, Western overseas expansion, including military conquests, had already reshaped the Americas and some regions of Africa and southern Asia. Chinese, Indians, and western Europeans were the richest peoples at this time, the Chinese accounting for a third and India and western Europe each accounting for a fourth of the world's total economic production. Collectively they accounted for 70 percent of all the world's economic activity and 80 percent of its manufacturing. China remained the greatest engine of the world economy. Britain was the rising political and economic European power, but it faced challenges from France, Russia, Spain, and the Ottoman Empire. The more economically developed districts and the major cities within the two wealthiest countries, Britain and China, apparently enjoyed similar living standards, such as abundant food and long life spans, until at least 1800. As late as the 1830s British observers reported that residents of Britain's capital, London, and the key Chinese trading city of Guangzhou had a roughly comparable material life.

By 1914, however, after a century and a half of Western industrialization, imperial expansion, and colonization, the global system had become more divided than ever before into rich and poor societies. India was now among the poorer countries, and China had succumbed to Western military and economic influence, falling well behind the West. Meanwhile, a few Western nation-states—especially Great Britain, the United States, Germany, and France—had grown rich and powerful, enjoying substantial influence around the world and over the global economy. Because of their unparalleled military power, all four of these nations ruled colonial empires, from which they extracted valuable resources; played a leading role in world trade; and tried to spread, with some success, their cultures and ideas. Also among the richest nations, but having less international power, were a few other western European countries,

Modernization or World-System?

Historians and social scientists in the West have vigorously debated which theories best explain the modern world, especially how it became interconnected. One influential approach uses the concept of modernization and focuses on individual societies. The other approach, world-system analysis, emphasizes the links between societies. This second approach has often interested world historians.

THE PROBLEM

Historians and historically-oriented social scientists have sought to understand societies and their changes over time. These efforts have spawned new intellectual approaches in the past several decades. Scholars have asked why some societies in the modern world, such as the United States, Britain, and Japan, became rich and powerful while others, such as Mozambique, Haiti, and Laos, remained poor and weak. Have societies developed as they did because of their own traditions or because of their connections to the larger world? Should we study societies as separate units, as the modernization approach advocates? Or should societies be examined as part of a larger system of exchange and power, or a world-system? Or are both of these approaches inadequate?

THE DEBATE

During the 1950s and 1960s modernization theory was developed in the United States by scholars such as C. E. Black and W. W. Rostow. In their classification, most societies were traditional, retaining centuries-old political and economic institutions and social and cultural values. These societies had despotic governments, extended family systems, and fatalistic attitudes. In contrast, a few dynamic societies became modern by adopting liberal democracy, secularism, flexible social systems, high-consumption lifestyles, and free market capitalism. This modernization began in Europe between 1500 and 1750 and reached its fullest development in the United States by the mid-twentieth century. All societies, these theorists asserted, were moving, rapidly or slowly, in the same direction toward U.S.-style modernization—some enthusiastically, others reluctantly—and this modernization was desirable.

Modernization theory was influential in the United States for several decades, but by the 1970s it began losing considerable support among historians. While the notion of modernity seemed helpful, critics found many flaws in the theory of modernization. They argued that it centered history on the West as the dynamic nursery of modernization and neglected other politically and economically successful societies, such as Qing China, Tokugawa Japan, Siam (today's Thailand), Ottoman Turkey, Morocco, and the Ashante kingdom in Africa. Although these societies had all either collapsed or struggled against Western imperialism during the nineteenth century, they had once flourished and fostered economic growth despite having few of the characteristics associated with moder-

nity. Furthermore, by emphasizing the individual trees (societies) at the expense of the larger forest (the global context), the theory failed to explain the interconnections of societies through various international networks and processes that created global imbalances, such as the transfer of wealth and resources—Indonesian coffee, Iraqi oil, West African cocoa, Latin American silver, Caribbean sugar—from colonies to colonizers.

Modernization theory generally reflects the views of scholars who believe that U.S.-style individualism, democratic government, and free enterprise capitalism are the best strategies to promote personal freedom and economic growth, and who want to export these ideas to the world. Modernization theorists such as Rostow have considered challenges to U.S. influence and to capitalism, from Marxists and radical nationalists, to be diversions leading to despotic governments and an economic dead end. While agreeing that political and economic freedom were valuable ideas that generally benefited Western peoples, critics doubt these are the foundation of modernity or applicable everywhere. By characterizing traditional societies as "backward" and blaming them for being this way, modernization theory, critics contend, reflects Western prejudices about the world, such as the French "civilizing mission" and the U.S. notion of "Manifest Destiny," and supports the expansion of Western political power and economic investment into Asia and Africa on the grounds that it fosters "progress." Furthermore, critics argue, most societies are a mix of "traditional" and "modern" traits. For example, the "modern" United States has been a highly religious society from its beginning, arguably less secular than "traditional" China. Nor have Asians and Africans always found Western social and cultural models, such as nuclear families and Christianity, to be more appealing or useful than their own traditions; some, often inspired by Western ideas, have hoped to reform Muslim, Hindu, Confucian, or Buddhist traditions, but most continued to find meaning in the beliefs and customs of their ancestors.

Challenging modernization theory's neglect of connections, scholars led by the American sociologist Immanuel Wallerstein developed the concept of the "world-system," a network of interlinked economic, political, and social relationships spanning the globe. To Wallerstein the world-system, originating in Europe in the 1400s and based on a capitalist world economy, rival European states, and imperialism, explains growing Western global dominance after 1500. By 1914 Western military expansion, colonialism, and industrialization had enriched Europe and brought other societies into the modern world-system. An Africa specialist, Wallerstein views the modern world-system as more widely spread than the more limited networks, such as those of the Mongols and Arabs, that linked Afro-Eurasian societies prior to the 1400s.

In this view, modernization involves not only changes within societies but also their changing relationship to the dominant political powers and the world economy. For example, the Ashante kingdom became a West African power in the 1700s by trading slaves to the West, but, in the late 1800s, it was conquered and absorbed into the British colony of the Gold Coast (modern Ghana). Under British rule, the Ashante chiefly grew cocoa for export and thus were dependent on the fluctuations of the world price for cocoa. To understand modern Ghana, then, requires knowledge of the Ashante relations to both British colonialism and the world economy.

To describe the world political and economic structure, Wallerstein divided the world-system into three broad zones, or categories of countries: the *core*, *semiperiphery*, and *periphery*. In 1914 the core included the rich and powerful nations such as Britain, France, and the United States, which all benefited from industrialization, growing middle classes, democracy, a strong sense of nationhood, and political stability. They sometimes used their armies and financial clout to assert power over other societies, even independent ones such as China, where Western powers established spheres of interest patrolled by their gunboats. By 1914 Wallerstein's middle category, the semiperiphery, included countries such as Japan, Russia, and Italy, which were partially industrialized, politically independent nation-states but less prosperous and powerful than the core nations. Finally, the largest group in 1914, the periphery, comprised the colonized societies, such as French Vietnam, British Nigeria, and the U.S.-ruled Philippines, and the neocolonies such as Brazil, Thailand (Siam), and Iran (Persia). These societies were burdened with export economies based on natural resources, little or no industrialization, massive poverty, little democracy, and domination by more powerful core nations. Colonialism transferred wealth from the periphery to the core, which used the wealth for its own economic development. As Wallerstein acknowledges, the world-system is not rigid, and a few societies shifted categories over the centuries. For example, the United States was semiperipheral in 1800, but by 1900 industrialization and territorial expansion had propelled it into the core. By contrast, once powerful China fell into peripheral status after 1800. But even with some movement up or down, Wallerstein argues, the core-semiperiphery-periphery structure still characterizes the world-system today.

If modernization theory predicts an increasing standardization around the world toward a Western-influenced pattern, world-system analysis suggests that the core and periphery, serving different functions in the world economy, have moved in opposite directions, toward wealth on the one hand and poverty on the other. Since the economic exchange between them was unequal, the periphery became dependent on the core for goods, services, investment, and resource markets, giving core societies, which exploited the resources of the periphery, great influence. For example, the Gold Coast's cocoa growers needed British markets, and British companies provided consumer goods to the shopkeepers, often Lebanese immigrants, who served these communities. The wealth and power of a country, then, reflect its political and economic position in the world-system.

Like modernization theory, world-system analysis has provoked controversy. Some scholars embrace a world-system approach but disagree with Wallerstein's version. Whereas Waller-

A Japanese View of America   This Japanese print records the impression of the United States and its wealth and power by a Japanese trade mission in 1860. It shows an American man and woman posing with symbols of modern technology, a pocket watch and a sewing machine.   (Private Collection)

stein believes a world-system began only around 1500, Christopher Chase-Dunn and Thomas Hall emphasize a longer history with diverse intersocietal networks that can be called world-systems beginning in ancient times. Andre Gunder Frank and Barry Gills identify one single world-system existing for 5,000 years, since, they argue, some form of capitalism began with the earliest states, such as Sumeria, in Afro-Eurasia. Some critics accuse Wallerstein, like the modernization theorists, of overemphasizing the West and underestimating the key roles played by Asians in the Afro-Eurasian economy.

Other critics are harsher. Some charge that Wallerstein's stress on exchange between countries downplays inequitable economies and class structures within countries—such as rapacious landowners, privileged aristocrats, tyrannical chiefs, and greedy merchants—hence shifting the blame for poverty to the world economy. Others, such as Daniel Chirot, question whether exploitation of the periphery explains the economic growth of the core. Critics also wonder whether terms such as *core* and *periphery* constitute a more sophisticated version of "modernity" and "tradition," marginalizing and perhaps demeaning poor societies. Finally, some think Wallerstein's focus on economic factors neglects politics and cultures, including religion, and places so much stress on the forest that it misses the trees.

EVALUATING THE DEBATE

The modernization and world-system theorists launched an ongoing debate about how world history can be understood, but neither approach fully explains modern history. World historians widely agree that the once dominant modernization theory is inadequate for understanding the world as a whole. Some are attracted to one or another version of world-system analysis. While many details of Wallerstein's approach are open to challenge, the general concept of a global system, divided into several categories of countries each with common features, helps understand relations between societies and the exchanges within the world economy. Situating societies within an interlinked world helps explain the impact of colonialism, the background to military interventions by more powerful countries, and the political turbulence of the poorer states today. While each society has unique characteristics that shape its history, perceiving some sort of global system or systems that rise and fall over time helps us understand large-scale, long-term change and explains how thousands of small hunting and gathering bands 12,000 years ago became the contemporary global community of nation-states.

THINKING ABOUT THE CONTROVERSY

1. How do modernization and world-system approaches explain the modern world and its diverse societies differently?

2. What are the major advantages and problems of each of the two approaches?

EXPLORING THE CONTROVERSY

Among the major works of modernization theory are C. E. Black, *The Dynamics of Modernization: A Study in Comparative History* (New York: Harper and Row, 1966); and W. W. Rostow, *The Stages of Economic Growth: A Non-Communist Manifesto* (Cambridge: Cambridge University Press, 1960). Immanuel Wallerstein has summarized his ideas in *The Capitalist World-Economy* (New York: Cambridge University Press, 1979) and *World-Systems Analysis: An Introduction* (Durham, N.C.: Duke University Press, 2004). Alternative versions of the world-system concept include Christopher Chase-Dunn and Thomas D. Hall, *Rise and Demise: Comparing World-Systems* (Boulder, Colo.: Westview Press, 1997); and Andre Gunder Frank and Barry K. Gills, eds., *The World System: Five Hundred Years or Five Thousand?* (New York: Routledge, 1996). Daniel Chirot takes issue with world-system analysis on many issues in *Social Change in the Modern Era* (New York: Harcourt Brace Jovanovich, 1986). Excellent summaries and critiques of world-system analysis and competing ideas can be found in Thomas R. Shannon, *An Introduction to the World-System Perspective* (Boulder, Colo.: Westview Press, 1989); Alvin Y. So, *Social Change and Development: Modernization, Dependency, and World-System Theories* (Newbury Park, Calif.: Sage, 1990); Stephen K. Sanderson, ed., *Civilizations and World Systems; Studying World-Historical Change* (Walnut Creek, C.A.: AltaMira Press, 1995); and Thomas D. Hall, ed. *A World-Systems Reader: New Perspectives on Gender, Urbanism, Cultures, Indigenous Peoples, and Ecology* (Lanham, M.D.: Rowman and Littlfield, 2000). For a provocative critique of these debates and the rise of the world economy by an Indian scholar, see Amiya Kumar Bagchi, *Perilous Passage: Mankind and the Global Ascendancy of Capital* (Lanham, M.D.: Rowman and Littlefield, 2005).

including the Netherlands, Belgium, and Switzerland. A middle category of countries—Canada, Japan, and European nations such as Russia, Italy, Portugal, and Spain—had a weaker economic base and less military power than those of the richest nations, but they still enjoyed economic and political autonomy. A third category of countries were those that were economically poor and militarily weak, either ruled directly as Western colonies, such as India, Indonesia, Nigeria, or Jamaica, or under strong political and economic influence as neocolonies, such as China, Thailand, and Iran. Economically, Latin American countries, relative to the rich North American and western European nations, were also poor.

Living conditions and governments in the rich countries differed dramatically in 1914 from those in the poor societies. Capitalism fostered growth in Europe and North America, although it took many decades for the benefits to reach the common people. The rich countries, such as Britain and the United States, were highly industrialized and enjoyed well-diversified economies and large middle classes. Many of their people lived in cities and, owing to mass education systems, became literate. These countries also boasted efficient, well-financed, constitutional governments. Rich countries were typically democratic, with their governments being chosen by voters (though usually only men) through regular elections. These governments generally tolerated an independent mass media, including newspapers and magazines, and diverse political opinions, such as those represented by socialist and feminist movements. These patterns were also common in the less powerful Western nations and in Japan.

By contrast, the poor societies, especially Western colonies in Asia and Africa, where many people worked the lands owned by foreign landlords or planters, were not industrialized and people earned meager wages. Economic growth was often determined by foreign investment and markets rather than by local needs. For example, rather than growing food for the local community, farmers in Honduras, in Central America, grew bananas for the U.S. market while farmers in French-ruled Senegal, in West Africa, raised peanuts for export. Politically, a small upper class—African chiefs, Indian princes, Javanese aristocrats—played a political role by cooperating with Western rulers. Only a small minority of people had access to formal education. A tiny middle class and low rates of literacy made democracy difficult, even if it had been allowed, but most Western colonies also prohibited or limited voting or officeholding by anyone who was not white and European.

Their general poverty and lack of economic and political options did not mean that people in poor societies were always miserable. For many generations, and through successive governments, they had learned how to make the best of poverty. Celebrating their survival skills in the early 1900s, the Indian writer and thinker Rabindranath Tagore (rah-BIN-dra-NATH TUH-gore) (1861–1941) found both triumphs and tragedies in Indian peasant life through the ages, which "with its everyday contentment and misery, has always been there in the peasants' fields and village festivals, manifesting their very simple and abiding humanity across all of history—sometimes under Mughal rule, sometimes under British rule."[9]

In the colonies, heavy Western cultural influence, such as the policies the French called their "civilizing mission" in Vietnam and West Africa, by which they tried to impose French ways on people they regarded as culturally inferior, was combined with psychological trauma as once proud peoples succumbed to foreign rule and its racist restrictions. An anti-imperialist African organization complained in 1927 that colonialism had abruptly cut short "the development of the African people. These nations were later declared pagan and savage, an inferior race."[10] Although Western Christian missionaries often found eager converts, as in Vietnam, Nigeria, and Uganda, nationalists frequently criticized the well-funded Christian missions, accusing them of undermining traditional beliefs. Western domination, however, did not preclude cultural and scientific achievements by colonized people. For example, although their country was a British colony, various Indian mathematicians, biochemists, and astrophysicists won international renown. In Calcutta the experiments of Sir Chandrasekhara Raman (CHAHN-dra-SEE-ker-ah RAH-man) (1888–1970) led to significant advances in the theory of the diffusion of light, for which he won the Noble Prize for physics in 1930.

Between 1914 and 1945 the global system underwent further changes. Wars were now sometimes world wars, fought on a greater scale than ever before and on battlefields thousands of miles apart. The United States became the world's richest, most powerful nation. Because of its military defeat in World War I, Germany temporarily lost wealth and power. Germany, Italy, and Japan—all middle-ranking nations by the 1930s—challenged the rich nations—Britain, France, and the United States—during World War II. Several Latin American nations and Turkey enjoyed enough economic growth and stability of government to move into the middle-ranking category by the 1940s. Yet most of the societies of Asia, Africa, Latin America, and the Caribbean remained poor colonies or neocolonies, exercising little diplomatic and economic influence in the global system.

THE WORLD ECONOMY

Even before the Western overseas expansion that occurred between 1500 and 1914, trade had taken place over vast distances. Chinese, Indian, Arab, and Armenian merchants had long dominated the vigorous Asian trade, and for centuries Chinese silks and porcelains and Southeast Asian and Indian spices had reached Europe, the Middle East, and parts of sub-Saharan Africa. European explorers wished to locate the source of these riches, and after 1500 the Portuguese, Dutch, and British played key roles in this trade, beginning the rise of the world economy. European influence on the world economy increased in the 1700s and 1800s when Western traders, supported by their governments, sought new natural resources and markets in the tropical world, thereby creating a truly global economic exchange. By 1914 the entire world was enmeshed in a vast economic exchange that particularly benefited the more powerful nations. People often produced resources or manufactured goods—Middle Eastern oil, Indonesian coffee, British textiles—for markets thousands of miles away. Europe's Industrial Revolution, which provided manufactured goods to trade for resources, dramatically reshaped the Western economies in the 1800s but only slowly spread to other regions.

The Inequality of Global Economic Exchange

Economic exchange between societies within the world economy did not proceed on an even playing field. As had been the case for empires throughout history—Assyrian, Roman, Chinese, Inca, Spanish, Dutch—imperialism and colonialism remained the means for transferring wealth to the imperial nations, which used that wealth to finance their own development. The imperial powers, seeking to enhance the value of their colonial economies, also used their control of world trade to shift cash crops indigenous to one part of the world to another. For example, Europeans introduced South American peanuts and rubber to colonized Africa, and coffee from Arabia became a major cash crop in Brazil and Indonesia. This transfer benefited colonial treasuries and plantation owners but also sometimes earned income for the small farmers who started growing these crops.

Gearing economic growth chiefly to the needs of the imperial powers impeded economic development that might have benefited everyone. Many colonies developed economies that produced and exported only one or two primary resources, such as rice and rubber from French Vietnam, sugar from Spanish Cuba, and cocoa from the British Gold Coast. Most of these resource exports were transformed into consumer goods, such as rubber tires and chocolate candies, and sold in stores in Western nations, to the profit of their merchants. For instance, chocolate, whose use for over two millennia was confined to elites in Mexico, became popular among wealthy Europeans after 1500. During the nineteenth century European chemists figured out how to produce chocolate bars, and soon chocolate products gained an eager market among all classes throughout the Western world. Meanwhile, the Western manufactured goods exchanged for these resources, especially textiles, found markets in Africa, Asia, and Latin America. Although much of this exchange was largely at the expense of the colonized peoples, some of them, including a few women, managed to capitalize on it. For example, Omu Okwei (OH-moo AWK-way) (1872–1943), an Igbo, made a fortune trading palm oil for European imported goods, which she distributed widely in Nigeria through a vast network of women traders.

Societies specializing in producing one or two natural resources were especially vulnerable to a changing world economy. To take one case, British Malaya was a major rubber exporter, but most of its rubber plantations, worked chiefly by poorly paid Indian immigrants, were British-owned, and Malayans had little influence over the world price of rubber, which was determined largely by demand in the West. And the prices of agricultural and mineral exports fluctuated more than the prices for industrial goods, which were produced largely in the West. Furthermore, the rise and fall of rubber prices affected not only the rubber tappers and their families but also the shops, often owned by Chinese immigrants, who sold them goods or extended credit to them. Thus the livelihoods of people all over the world increasingly became subject to chronic fluctuations in the world prices of the resources they grew or mined. These prices rose or fell depending on the whims of Western consumers and decisions by the corporations who controlled the international trade.

The world economy widened the wealth gap between societies. In 1500 the differences in per capita income and living standards between people in the richer regions—China, Japan, Southeast Asia, India, Ottoman Turkey, and western Europe—had probably been minor. And these peoples were roughly only two to three times better off materially than the farmers and city folk of the world's poorest farming societies. By 1750, however, while China, western Europe, and British North America enjoyed similar levels of economic production, the wealth gap between them and others was increasing. By 1900 the wealth gap between the richest and poorest societies had grown to about 10 to 1. This trend accelerated throughout the twentieth century, in part because the wealth produced in Western colonies seldom contributed to local development. For example, by the 1950s, after seventy-five years of Belgian colonialism that produced vast wealth for Belgian corporations, mine owners, and rubber planters, the Belgian Congo still lacked all-weather roads linking the major cities and had only a few schools and health clinics for its millions of people.

Unequal economic exchange also fostered conflict. Wars erupted as one country threatened another's access to markets and resources. For example, British free trade policies caused the Opium War against China in the mid-1800s. The Qing government worked to end both the legal and illegal opium trade, but, as the leading opium supplier, Britain needed to protect the opium exports to China from British India, which earned 20 percent of its colonial revenues from charging duty on opium. Britain's defeat of China hastened Chinese decline. In the first half of the twentieth century, World War I was at least partly caused by the bitter competition between European nations for resources in Asia and Africa.

The Spread of Industrialization

The Industrial Revolution, which began in Britain in the late 1700s, was not just a Western development. China and India had once been the world's leading manufacturing countries, and knowledge of Chinese mechanical devices probably stimulated several British inventions. Between 1750 and 1850, however, Britain took the lead in industrialization, and by the mid-1800s it produced about half of the world's manufactured goods while China and India fell behind. Various other European nations, the United States, and Japan industrialized in the later 1800s. Only these few nations increased their resources and weapons as a result of industrialization, and hence only a few became world powers. Some of the profits from colonialism and other overseas activities stimulated or furthered European industrialization. For example, the Dutch based some of their industrial and transportation growth on profits earned from selling coffee and sugar grown by peasants in their Indonesian colony. But even in Europe agriculture and other nonindustrial activities, such as trade, remained economically important. By 1881 only 44 percent of the British, 36 percent

EUROPE

Although western Europe recovered quickly from World War II, the imperial Western states were unable to maintain control of their colonies. The western European nations forged stable welfare states, providing a social safety net, and moved toward close cooperation and economic unity among themselves. The Soviet Union became a global superpower, controlling eastern Europe, but at the end of the 1980s it and its Communist satellites collapsed. Germany, divided after World War II, was reunified, and Russia sought a new role in the world.

WESTERN ASIA

Nationalists gained control of the western Asian nations but faced new challenges. Israel, a new Jewish state in Palestine, won wars against Arab neighbors, and Arab-Israeli hostilities have remained a source of tension. Some nations, such as Turkey, pursued modernization. An Islamic revolution reshaped oil-rich Iran, which fought oil-rich Iraq in the 1980s. Saudi Arabia and several Persian Gulf states flourished from oil wealth. After 2001 U.S.-led forces invaded and occupied Afghanistan and Iraq but, while removing despotic governments, struggled to restore stability.

EASTERN ASIA

Coming to power through revolution in 1949, Communists transformed China, creating a socialist society and fighting the United States during the Korean War. After 1978 new Communist leaders mixed free markets with socialism and fostered modernization, turning China into an economic powerhouse. Japan recovered rapidly from World War II, embracing democracy and becoming an economic giant. Borrowing Japanese models, South Korea and Taiwan industrialized. North Korea remained a repressive Communist state.

ARCTIC OCEAN

RUSSIA

BRITAIN
GERMANY
EUROPE
FRANCE
Danube
ITALY
TURKEY

ASIA

KOREA JAPAN

IRAQ IRAN
CHINA
ALGERIA
PAKISTAN
Ganges R.
HIMALAYAS
SAUDI
ARABIA
TAIWAN
Nile
INDIA
Niger R.
AFRICA
Mekong R. VIETNAM
THAILAND
NIGERIA
BANGLADESH
Congo R.
MALAYSIA

*ATLANTIC
OCEAN*
INDIAN OCEAN
INDONESIA

ANGOLA

AUSTRALIA

SOUTH
AFRICA

NEW ZEALAND

AFRICA

As Arab and African nationalism grew stronger, colonies became independent nations, sometimes, as in Algeria and Angola, through revolution. In North Africa, Egypt promoted Arab nationalism and became a regional power but faced economic problems. Most of the new sub-Saharan African nations, which were artificial creations of colonialism, struggled to maintain political stability and foster economic development, but South Africans finally achieved black majority rule.

SOUTHERN ASIA AND OCEANIA

Britain granted independence to predominantly Hindu India but also to largely Muslim Pakistan, which eventually split when Bangladesh seceded. India enjoyed democracy and economic progress, but Pakistan and Bangladesh often fell under military rule. In Southeast Asia, the U.S. and British colonies gained independence peacefully while Indonesians triumphed through revolution. Vietnamese Communists first defeated the French and then the United States. Malaysia, Singapore, and Thailand developed economically. Australia and New Zealand established closer links to Asia, and most of the Pacific islands gained independence from Western colonialism.

The Remaking of the Global System, Since 1945

Online Study Center

This icon will direct you to interactive activities and study materials on the website: college.hmco. com/pic/lockard1e

"Our World Is not for Sale" In 2004 tens of thousands of activists from all over the world, under the banner of "Our World Is not for Sale," marched on the streets of Mumbai (formerly Bombay), India's largest city, to protest economic globalization, racial and caste oppression, and the United States-led war in Iraq. The march reflected the globalization of social movements and political protests in the contemporary world.   (AP/Wide World Photos)

One heart, one destiny. Peace and love for all mankind.
And Africa for Africans.

BOB MARLEY, REGGAE SUPERSTAR[1]

In April 1980, when the new African nation of Zimbabwe (zim-BAHB-way) (formerly Southern Rhodesia) celebrated its independence from British rule, Bob Marley, a reggae music star from Jamaica and a symbol of black empowerment, performed at Zimbabwe's national stadium. Marley's experience there reflected many of the politcal and cultural trends of the later-twentieth-century world. Marley had been invited to appear in part because his songs, such as "Catch a Fire," "Stir it Up," and "Get Up Stand Up," often dealt with issues such as poverty, racial prejudice, and asserting one's rights, realities for thousands of Zimbabweans in the audience, who had lived for decades under an uncaring British colonial and then white minority government. But Marley's concert was disrupted by the local police, mostly whites who had enjoyed a privileged position under British rule. Fearing a riot and vandalism against white-owned property, they used tear gas to disperse thousands of black Zimbabweans who gathered outside the overcrowded stadium. The next night Marley ignored threats of violence against him by local white racists, who opposed Zimbabwe's rapid shift from white to black rule, and gave a free concert for 40,000 Zimbabweans, many of them unemployed. Although the free concert encountered no major problems, the violence of the previous night and the threats to his life had shown Marley that the social ills and ethnic hatreds he knew in Jamaica occurred elsewhere in the world as well. In Zimbabwe, where these ills ran particularly deep, they would not be solved by the nation's newly won independence under a black majority government.

An eloquent advocate of political and cultural freedom whose music was enjoyed by millions of fans around the world, Marley was an obvious choice to entertain people who had suffered through decades of white minority rule. Although he came from the slums of a small island of barely 2 million people, Marley and his music touched hearts and minds across racial, political, religious, class, and cultural barriers. Reggae itself was a truly world music, an intoxicating mix of African, Caribbean, and North American traditions. To the world, Marley personified reggae's progressive politics and spiritual quest. As Judy Mowatt, another reggae star, noted: "His music has caused people all over the universe to be enlightened, happy, dancing. His spirit is really touching all nationalities."[2] However, Marley failed to convince the racists among Zimbabwe's white minority to accept blacks as their equals.

Marley's career reflected a world interconnected as never before in history and, largely because of that connectedness, in great flux. Some 2,500 years ago ancient thinkers such as the Buddha in India, Daoists in China, and the Greek philosopher Heraclitus had argued that nothing was permanent except change; the world was in perpetual transition. Never, it seemed, was this more true than in the second half of the twentieth century. Since World War II the pace of change quickened and the global economy grew dramatically. Economic and cultural networks linked societies ever more closely while ideas, technologies, and products flowed across porous borders, affecting the lives of people everywhere. World politics were turbulent, reflecting the conflict between the United States and the Soviet Union (USSR), the world's two most powerful nations, and the struggle of African, Asian, and Latin American countries for decolonization and development. Since 1989, when the Soviet bloc collapsed, the world has groped toward a new political configuration while dealing with mounting economic and environmental problems and combating international terrorism.

FOCUS QUESTIONS

1. How did decolonization change the global system?
2. What roles did the Cold War and superpower rivalry play in world politics?
3. What were some of the main consequences of a globalizing world economy?
4. How did growing networks linking societies influence social, political, and economic life?

Decolonization, New States, and the Global System

How did decolonization change the global system?

The contemporary world derived both from Western imperialism in the five centuries before 1945 and from the resistance waged against it. After World War II Asia, Africa, and Latin America became the major battlegrounds between the United States and the Soviet Union; these two nations had so much military, political, and economic might in comparison to other countries that they were known as superpowers. The struggle of Asian, African, and Latin American societies to end domination by Western nations and to develop economically also shaped the postwar era. Nationalist movements proliferated, some seeking deep changes through social revolution. In some cases these nationalist and revolutionary struggles led to interventions by Western powers or the USSR anxious to preserve their political and economic influence. The former colonies also became part of a dynamic global system marked by continued imbalances in wealth and power.

Nationalism and Decolonization

The nationalism that spread through Europe and the Americas in the 1800s became a powerful force in the colonized world in the 1900s (see Chapter 19). Three basic types of nationalist movements developed between the early 1900s and the 1960s. In the first type, which occurred in most colonized societies, the nationalist goal was the end of colonial rule but not necessarily major social and economic change. Colonial powers were often willing to grant political independence where nationalist leaders, in countries such as Nigeria, Uganda, and the Philippines, accepted continued Western control of mines, plantations, and other resources. The second type of nationalist movement, mounted by social revolutionaries inspired by Marxism, wanted not only political independence but also a new social order free of Western economic domination. In China, for example, the Communist movement led by Mao Zedong sought to reorganize Chinese society while limiting contact with the world economy and the United States. Making up a third type were the nationalist movements by long repressed nonwhite majorities in white settler colonies such as Algeria and Zimbabwe. Struggling against domination by the minority whites, who owned most of the land and resources, they faced stiff

CHRONOLOGY

	International	Eurasia	The Americas
1940	**1945** Formation of the United Nations **1946–1975** Decolonization in Asia, Africa, and Caribbean **1946–1989** Cold War	**1950–1953** Korean War **1959–1975** U.S.-Vietnam War	
1960	**1968** Widespread political protests		**1962** Cuban Missile Crisis
1980		**1989–1991** Dismantling of Soviet bloc and Soviet Union	
2000			**2001** Al Qaeda attack on United States

resistance. Whatever the type of nationalist movement, the dislocations caused by the Great Depression and World War II intensified anti-Western and anticolonial feelings.

Colonialism gradually crumbled, often after confronting nationalist resistance led by charismatic figures such as Mohandas Gandhi in India and Sukarno in Indonesia, in the three decades after World War II. By the 1950s most of the Western colonizers realized that the increased military force required to maintain their political control against growing nationalist protests, strikes, and peasant unrest was too expensive. In 1946 the United States began the decolonization trend by granting independence to the Philippines (see Chronology: Global Politics, 1945–1989). Weary of suppressing nationalist resistance, in the later 1940s the British gave up their rule in India and Burma, and the Dutch abandoned Indonesia. Whatever the nationalist strategy, either peacefully or through the treat of violence, between 1946 and 1975 most of the Western colonies in Asia, Africa, and the Caribbean achieved independence (see Map 26.1).

Some colonizers accepted decolonization only after attempts to quell nationalist uprisings had failed. The Dutch intended to regain their control of Indonesia, a source of immense wealth, after World War II but faced a violent resistance by a nationalist army. In 1950, after losing many soldiers and anticipating more violence ahead, the Dutch granted Indonesia independence. Similarly, the French had no plans to abandon their profitable colonies in Vietnam and Algeria, but uprisings by revolutionaries in these colonies forced them to leave. In Vietnam, the Communist forces led by Ho Chi Minh fiercely resisted French power, and heavy U.S. aid to the French could not prevent a humiliating French defeat in 1954. The ultimately successful anticolonial struggles by the Indonesian, Vietnamese, and Algerian nationalists had electrifying global effects, giving hope to colonized peoples elsewhere that they could also overthrow Western domination and warning the Western powers that they would pay a heavy cost for opposing decolonization.

Both superpowers sought to capitalize on the nationalist surge. The Soviet Union generally supported nationalist movements, sometimes supplying arms to revolutionaries. The Soviets also offered economic aid and diplomatic support to Asian and African countries that achieved independence and had strategic value because of their size or location, such as India and Egypt, or valuable resources, such as oil-rich Iran and Indonesia. The most powerful Western nation, the United States, followed a mixed policy on decolonization. Wanting access to trade and outlets for investment in Asia and Africa, the

CHRONOLOGY

Global Politics, 1945–1989

1945	Formation of United Nations
1946–1975	Decolonization in Asia, Africa, Caribbean
1946–1989	Cold War
1949	Communist victory in China
1950–1953	Korean War
1954	Vietnamese defeat of French
1955	Bandung Conference
1959–1975	U.S.-Vietnam War
1959	Communist victory in Cuba
1962	Cuban Missile Crisis
1968	Widespread political protests
1975	End of Portuguese Empire

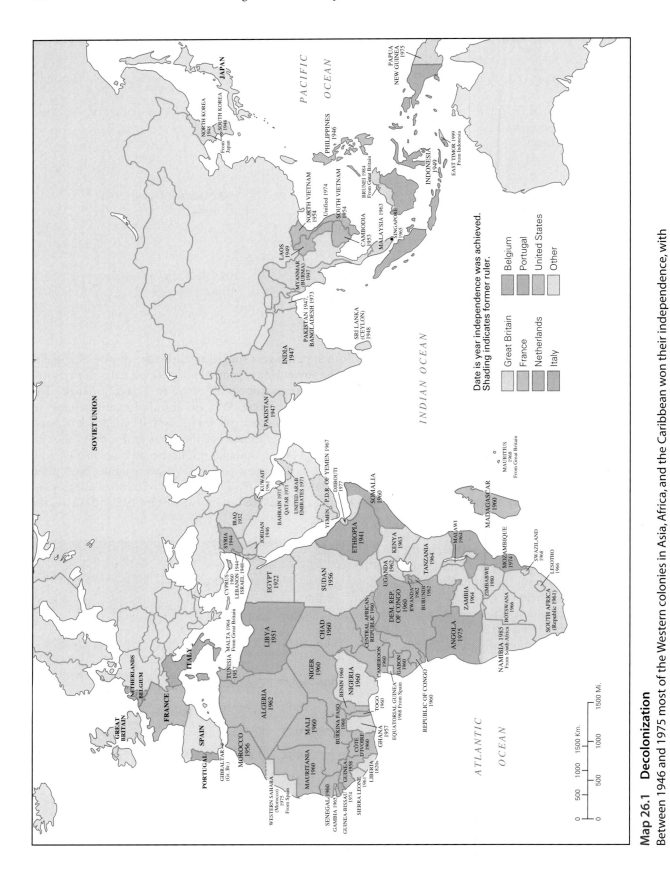

Map 26.1 Decolonization
Between 1946 and 1975 most of the Western colonies in Asia, Africa, and the Caribbean won their independence, with the greatest number achieving independence in the 1960s. The decolonization reshaped the political map, particularly of Africa, South Asia, and Southeast Asia.

Online Study Center **Improve Your Grade** Interactive Map: Decolonization and Independence, 1947 to 1997

United States encouraged the Dutch to leave Indonesia and urged independence for some British colonies in Africa. But Americans also opposed communism and the spread of Soviet influence. Consequently, where nationalism was led by communists or had a leftist orientation, as in French-ruled Vietnam and Portuguese-ruled Mozambique, the United States supported continued colonial power, no matter how unpopular among the colonized people, and helped finance the French and Portuguese military efforts to suppress the revolutionaries. With U.S. aid, Portugal stubbornly resisted decolonization until festering African rebellions, growing demoralization at home, and the toppling of its fascist dictator forced it to abandon its African empire in 1975.

Colonialism did not completely disappear. By the 1980s one major territorial empire, the USSR, remained, and it strained to repress the nationalist demands of the Baltic, Caucasus, and Central Asian peoples it ruled. The Soviet Empire was largely dismantled between 1989 and 1991, when the Soviet Union's Communist system collapsed, although Russians still controlled some unwilling subjects, such as the Chechens, a Muslim people in southern Russia. At the beginning of the twenty-first century Britain, France, and the United States controlled small empires. Britain and France, who once ruled huge empires, retained direct control of a few islands, mostly in the South Pacific, South Atlantic, and the Caribbean, and some outposts, notably British Gibraltar, a strategically valuable naval base on the Spanish coast at the entrance to the Mediterranean Sea, and French Guiana, on the northeast coast of South America. The territories, mostly self-governing, linked to the United States included Puerto Rico and the Virgin Islands in the Caribbean and a few Pacific islands such as American Samoa and Guam.

Decolonization often resulted in neocolonialism, a continuing strong political and economic influence by the former colonizers. This happened in the Philippines, where Americans maintained a major role in the economy, Philippine governments loyally supported U.S. foreign policies, and Filipinos avidly consumed American products and popular culture such as music, films, and fashions. Similarly, the French controlled much of the economy and advised the government in the African nation of Cote d'Ivoire (COAT dee-VWAHR) (better known as Ivory Coast), and many Ivoirians favored French cuisine, literature, and language. A West Indian–born writer offered a radical nationalist view of why most former colonies accepted neocolonialism: "The colonial power says, 'Since you want independence, take it and starve' [after economic aid ends]. Other countries refuse to undergo this ordeal and agree to [accept] the conditions of the former guardian power."[3] This view simplified complex relationships but was often shared by Asian and African nationalists. Disenchantment with the continuing strong Western presence prompted some Asian and African intellectuals to advocate "decolonizing the mind," to escape what Bob Marley called a "mental slavery" that kept formerly colonized people in awe of Western power, wealth, and culture. Instead he offered "songs of freedom." "Decolonizing the mind" sometimes meant building a nationalist culture reflecting local traditions or abandoning the use of

African Independence   In 1961 the British monarch, Queen Elizabeth II, made an official visit to newly independent Ghana, the former British colony of the Gold Coast. Here she walks under a ceremonial umbrella with the Ghanaian president, Kwame Nkrumah.   (UPI/Bettmann/Corbis)

Western languages in people's writing. For example, the Kenyan novelist Ngugi wa Thiongo switched from writing in English to writing in his native Gikuyu.

Social Revolutionary States

During the twentieth century, revolutionary activity erupted in Asia, Africa, and Latin America, intensified by the drive to end colonialism and other forms of Western domination. In most cases this revolutionary activity engaged peasants, who were often impoverished by the loss of their lands or the declining prices for the cash crops they grew. Revolutionary intellectuals, often spurred by a Marxist vision, capitalized on this unhappiness to mobilize support, although those who joined their movements did not always embrace the more radical ideas. Understanding this, Amilcar Cabral (AM-ill-car ka-BRAWL) (1924–1973), the revolutionary leader in Portugal's West African colony of Guinea Bissau (GIN-ee bi-SOU), advised his Marxist colleagues to "always bear in mind that the people are not fighting for ideas, for the things in anyone's head. They are fighting to win material benefits, to live better, and in peace, to see their lives go forward, to guarantee the future of their children."[4] Between

1949 and 1980 social revolutionary regimes came to power through force of arms not only in Algeria and Vietnam but also in several other countries, such as China, Cuba, and Mozambique. Opposed by the United States and often mistrusted by western European regimes, these states necessarily looked to the USSR for political, economic, and military support. Revolutionary movements with some popular support were also active, although ultimately frustrated, in a dozen other countries, mostly in Latin America and Southeast Asia.

The fruits of revolution were subject to debate. Thinkers and activists around the world, such as the West Indian–born psychiatrist and writer Frantz Fanon (1925–1961), who joined the anti-French movement while working in colonial Algeria, often romanticized the revolutionaries' promise to create more just societies. Yet scholars of politics disagreed as to whether revolutions ultimately achieved their stated goals of improving life and righting injustice or instead fostered tyranny and economic stagnation. While social revolutionary governments often substantially raised living standards for the poor and gave them more influence in their communities, they also commonly became bureaucratic, despotic, and intolerant of dissent, and they frequently compiled poor human rights records. But although often disappointed in the new society, most people in these revolutionary societies welcomed the end of the uncaring, often repressive governments the revolutions replaced.

Social revolutionary states had uneven relations with the world economy and the capitalist nations. Influenced by Stalinism, which fostered state-directed economic growth in the USSR in the 1930s, these states usually chose to withdraw from the world economy, partially or completely, in order to limit outside interference, renounce foreign debts, and assume control of their economic direction. They created planned economies in which economic decisions, such as allocation of food and investment capital, were made centrally, by governments, rather than through free markets, as in capitalist societies.

Social revolutionary approaches brought mixed results. Some countries saw their goals sidetracked by civil wars or by rebellions supported by Western powers. For example, in Angola, a country in southwest Africa, South Africa and the United States provided financial and military support to rebels who fought the Marxist-dominated government for over two decades. The civil war cost over 200,000 lives, ruined much of the country, and forced the Angolan government to devote most of its resources to the military rather than to improving people lives with schools and clinics. After the fighting ended in the late 1990s, the Marxists still held power, but the country's people were poorer than ever: half of the nation's children suffered from malnutrition. In contrast to Angola's woes, between 1949 and 1978 Communist-run China was able to increase its economic potential and reduce social problems, but at a heavy cost in repressing dissent and limiting personal freedom. After 1978 China dramatically modified its socialist economy with market forces, such as by allowing foreign investment and free enterprise, which sparked even more rapid growth. The shift of China, followed by Vietnam, toward market economies and greater participation in the world economy

in the 1980s suggested that revolution may have helped nations to gain control of their resources but was ultimately insufficient to raise living standards to the levels of the richer nations. Yet, China and Vietnam also found that capitalism and free markets could create more wealth than socialism but did not necessarily lead to an equitable distribution of wealth, fostering explosive social tensions.

A New Global System

A new global system, differing in many respects from that of the 1930s, formed after 1945. The prewar world had been dominated by a few great Western powers, led by Britain and France, ruling over vast empires encompassing large parts of Asia, Africa, and the Caribbean, but decolonization, the rise of the United States and Soviet Union to superpower status, and other trends modified this pattern. During the later twentieth century, observers often divided the world into three categories of countries, each one having a different level of economic development. One category, the **First World**, comprised the industrialized democracies of western Europe, North America, Australia-New Zealand, and Japan. The **Second World** referred to the Communist nations, led by the USSR and China. The **Third World** was made up of most societies in Asia, Africa, Latin America, and the Caribbean that were marked by mass poverty and a legacy of Western colonization or neocolonialism. Some experts added a fourth category, the **Fourth World**, or the poorest societies, which had very small economies and few exploitable resources, such as Laos, Bangladesh, Haiti, and Mali.

The notion of different worlds of economic development helped bring to light the roles played by different countries in global politics and economics between 1945 and the late 1980s, when the Western nations and the Communist bloc, both wealthy and powerful compared to other societies, competed for influence in the rest of the world. However, critics argued that lumping the world's societies—with their very different histories, cultures, and global connections—into a few categories was highly misleading. Furthermore, during the 1980s and 1990s the global system was changing, complicating attempts to categorize nations. Countries such as Malaysia, South Korea, Dubai (doo-BYE), and Chile, once grouped with the Third World, achieved rapid economic growth, and the Communist systems that had defined the Second World often collapsed.

At the economically developed end of the global system, most Western nations and Japan enjoyed new heights of prosperity from the 1960s through the 1980s. After World War II the dominant and wealthiest world power, the United States,

---

First World   The industrialized democracies of western Europe, North America, Australia-New Zealand, and Japan.

Second World   The Communist nations, led by the USSR and China.

Third World   Societies in Asia, Africa, Latin America, and the Caribbean, which were shaped by mass poverty and a legacy of colonization or neocolonialism.

Fourth World   The poorest societies, with very small economies and few exploitable resources.

offered generous aid to its allies; this aid promoted further economic growth in industrialized countries that already had literate, skilled, and mostly urban populations, well-funded governments, and diversified economies. U.S. aid and investment also helped western Europe and Japan recover from the ashes of World War II and stabilize and prosper. Japan's economy increased fivefold between 1953 and 1973, the fastest economic growth in world history. As Western and Japanese businesses invested heavily around the world, international trade soared. Japan and West Germany became the second and third largest capitalist economies. By the 1970s several Western nations, such as West Germany, Sweden, Canada, and Australia, had standards of living similar to those in the United States. In addition, most of these nations had far less inequality in the distribution of wealth and income than did the United States.

Although economic growth rates often slowed after 1990, Western prosperity relative to the rest of the world continued. By 2004, the Human Development Report, an annual study by the United Nations that rates the quality of life of the world's 177 nations by examining per capita income, health, and literacy, ranked, in order, Norway, Sweden, Australia, Canada, and the Netherlands as the most livable nations; following these were Belgium, Iceland, the United States, Japan, and Ireland. A hundred years earlier Norway, Sweden, and Ireland had been among the poorest European countries. Now Sweden achieved the world's lowest poverty rate (7 percent). Swedish poverty decreased largely because the Swedish state provided each citizen with free education, subsidized health care, and other welfare benefits, and the Swedish economy grew steadily. The report ranked thirty-six nations, mostly in sub-Saharan Africa, as having a low quality of life—massive poverty, inadequate health care, and low rates of literacy—even though their people may have enjoyed rich cultures and rewarding social relationships. Tanzanian president Julius Nyerere (nye-RE-re) put the gap between rich and poor nations in perspective: "While the United States is trying to reach the moon, Tanzania is trying to reach its villages."[5]

Some nations had more resources and advantages to secure their citizens' lives. The nations enjoying a higher quality of life boasted not only wealth but also political stability. Richer nations usually benefited from democracy and allowed voters to freely choose their leaders. They were also nation-states where the large majority shared a common culture and language. Some of these nations did contain restless ethnic or religious minorities. For example, the Basques in northern Spain, a people with a language and identity completely different from the Spanish majority, sought autonomy or independence from Spain. By and large, however, democratic governments controlled social tensions and generous welfare systems prevented mass poverty. Many western European states, Canada, and New Zealand adopted ambitious welfare systems, including comprehensive national health insurance. The European welfare states promoted a high degree of social justice and equality.

Poorer nations, often with highly diverse populations, small budgets, and competition among citizens for limited resources, faced greater challenges in building stable nation-states. Violence, such as the repeated ethnic conflicts in Yugoslavia in the 1990s, occurred in nations that had abandoned communism and its safety net of free or low-cost education, health care, and housing. The fighting between Yugoslav groups sometimes resulted in brutal atrocities and the forced expulsion of minorities. Only a few non-European nations, such as Sri Lanka and oil-rich Brunei and Saudi Arabia, tried to mount welfare states with free education and health care, but they struggled to pay for them.

SECTION SUMMARY

- Between 1946 and 1975, most Western colonies achieved independence, in many cases as a result of violent opposition movements, though the United States continued to oppose Communist anticolonial movements and the Soviet Union's vast colonial empire endured until 1989.

- Western nations maintained a great deal of influence over the economy and culture of many of their former colonies, which led some intellectuals to call for "decolonizing the mind."

- Revolutionary regimes, often inspired by Marxism, came to power in a number of Asian, African, and Latin American nations, though they met with mixed economic success and in some cases were embroiled in long-term civil war.

- The division of the world's nations into First, Second, and Third Worlds grew blurry as some Third World nations developed First-World-level economies and the Soviet Union collapsed, though democratic countries tended to be more stable and offer more support to their citizens.

✦ Cold War, Hot Wars, and World Politics

What roles did the Cold War and superpower rivalry play in world politics?

A new global political configuration emerged after World War II: two major superpowers, the United States and the Soviet Union, each developed a system of allies in their competition for international influence, while other nations struggled to carve their own paths. The confrontation between the two superpowers fostered the **Cold War**, a conflict lasting from 1946 to 1989 in which the United States and the USSR competed for allies and engaged in occasional warfare against their rival's allies rather than with each other directly. The United States enjoyed much greater influence than the USSR in the

Cold War A conflict lasting from 1946 to 1989 in which the United States and the USSR competed for allies and engaged in occasional warfare against their rival's allies rather than each other directly.

global system and boasted more allies. While the Cold War did not lead to a military conflict in which U.S. and Soviet military forces fought each other, it produced chronic tensions between the superpowers. The rivalry also led to covert and military interventions around the world by each of the superpowers seeking to block gains by the other.

The Cold War: A Divided World

During the Cold War the world took on a bipolar political character. Nations practicing capitalism and often democracy, led by the United States, fell on one side, and often called themselves the Free World; those marked by Socialist authoritarianism, led by the USSR and known as the Soviet bloc, were on the other. For over four decades U.S.-USSR relations, and the struggle of each superpower to gain an advantage over its rival, were a major factor in international affairs. While seeking to contain the spread of communism, the United States enhanced its own influence, while the USSR worked to protect its interests by spreading communism and undercutting American influence. Various other countries, in Asia, Africa, and Latin America, sought to forge a third bloc, asserting their interests while navigating the dangerous shoals of superpower demands. Leaders of nations such as Egypt, India, and Indonesia promoted nonalignment with either superpower. In 1955 leaders from twenty-nine nonaligned Asian and African countries held a conference in Bandung, Indonesia to oppose colonialism and gain recognition for what they called a Third World bloc, but they had trouble maintaining unity in the decades to follow.

Although Britain had been the world's leading economic, political, and military power in the nineteenth century, the United States became the world's most powerful nation in the twentieth, enjoying far greater wealth, military power, and cultural influence than any other nation, including the USSR. In 1945, the United States already had 1,200 warships, 3,000 bombers, and the atomic bomb; produced half of the world's industrial output; and held two-thirds of the gold. Americans seemed willing to bear a heavy financial and military burden to sustain their leading role in world affairs and to promote U.S. economic growth. U.S. President Dwight D. Eisenhower (g. 1953–1961) defended his nation's foreign policy, which included interventions against unfriendly governments, as necessary to obtain raw materials and preserve profitable markets.

Online Study Center **Improve Your Grade**
Primary Source: The Long Telegram

After World War II, U.S. concern shifted from opposing Nazi Germany and imperial Japan to countering the USSR. Americans now perceived their wartime ally as a rival for influence in a world, especially in the Western colonies that were experiencing tumultuous changes and frequent unrest. By 1948 the Soviets controlled all of eastern Europe and were allied with Communist governments in Mongolia and North Korea. The U.S. policy of preventing the emergence of Communist regimes, which would be probable Soviet allies, became globalized: first, Americans tried unsuccessfully to prevent Commu-

nists from coming to power in China in the late 1940s; then they became involved in the Korean War (1950–1953) to fight successfully the North Korean effort to forcibly reunify the Korean peninsula. Yet, in spite of U.S. efforts, Communist regimes came to power in China in 1949, North Vietnam in 1954, and Cuba in 1959. Furthermore, waging the Cold War and seeking to contain communism with military force, including a long war in Vietnam, financially burdened the United States, costing it $4 trillion or $5 trillion and some 113,000 American lives, mostly soldiers, between 1946 and 1989.

Superpower Conflict in the Cold War

The Cold War fostered misunderstandings and tensions between the superpowers. Historians debate whether the USSR actually posed a serious military threat to the United States and how much both sides misinterpreted their rival's motives and actions. Remembering centuries of invasions from the west, Soviet leaders occupied eastern Europe as a buffer zone and considered the United States and its western European allies a lethal danger; their combined military power greatly exceeded that of the USSR. American leaders mistrusted the USSR and despised communism, which excluded two of America's most treasured values, democracy and market economies. Americans viewed themselves as protecting freedom, while the Soviets claimed that they were helping the world's exploited and impoverished masses and acting as the beacon of anti-imperialism.

Some historians believe the Cold War brought a long period of peace and stability, while others point to some eighty wars, often related to superpower rivalry, between 1945 and 1989 that resulted in 20 million deaths and perhaps 20 million refugees. The Cold War rivalries also transformed world politics by dragging in emerging nations, already damaged by their long, humiliating subservience to Western colonialism and military power, and led to upheavals in some of them that bankrupted economies and devastated entire peoples. In place of a USSR-U.S. war, a series of smaller conflicts occurred involving surrogates, governments, or movements allied to one superpower and fighting the troops from the other superpower. During two of the major conflicts, in Korea and Vietnam, U.S. troops battled not Soviet armies but allied Communist forces that were Soviet surrogates. In Vietnam, the Soviets sent military supplies and advisers to help the Vietnamese Communists, led by Ho Chi Minh, fight first the French and then the United States, which had helped install and then supported a pro-Western government in South Vietnam after the French defeat. The Communists gained control of the entire country in 1975. Americans also used surrogates, such as when they supplied Islamic groups fighting the Soviets in Afghanistan in the 1980s.

In this warfare, rebels often used low-technology weapons and military strategies if those methods provided the most practical options available. Insurgencies became common in which people resorted to unconventional warfare, such as sniping, sabotaging power plants, and planting roadside bombs, to struggle against a government or occupying force.

Insurgents fighting superpower forces often resorted to **guerrilla warfare**, an unconventional military strategy of avoiding full-scale direct confrontations in favor of small-scale skirmishes. In Vietnam, for example, Communist guerrillas staged hit-and-run attacks on American patrols and field bases and planted land mines, explosives that detonated when stepped on, on trails used by American troops.

The Cold War fostered interventions—both covert and military—by both superpowers to protect their interests. The USSR sent military forces into Poland, Hungary, and Czechoslovakia to crush anti-Soviet movements and into Afghanistan to support a pro-Soviet government. Sometimes Soviet invasions proved disastrous; this was the case in Afghanistan, where the heavy Soviet losses and humiliating withdrawal in 1989 contributed to the collapse of the Soviet system. The Soviets, Chinese, and Cubans also gave aid to communist movements around the world. Communist parties and other leftist groups established a strong presence in nations such as Indonesia, India, and Chile, where they participated openly in politics, and they also launched insurgencies against governments in several countries, such as Peru, Malaysia, and the Philippines. But these Communist insurgencies failed to mobilize enough local support and were crushed.

For its part, the United States actively sought to shape the political and economic direction of Asian, African, and Latin American societies. It often did this by giving generous U.S. aid and promoting human rights. Americans were generous in donating food, disaster and medical assistance, offering technical advice, and supporting the growth of democratic organizations. But other efforts destabilized or helped overthrow governments deemed unfriendly to U.S. business and political interests, including left-leaning but democratically elected regimes in Brazil, Chile, and Guatemala.

The earliest U.S. intervention came in 1953 in oil-rich Iran, which was governed by a nationalist but non-Communist regime that had angered the Americans and British by nationalizing British- and U.S.-owned oil companies operating in Iran, companies that sent most of their huge profits abroad, paid their Iranian workers less than fifty cents a day, and offered them no health care or paid vacations. Most of the workers lived in shantytowns with no electricity. In response to the nationalization, Britain and the United States imposed an economic boycott on Iran, making it hard for Iran to sell its oil abroad. American agents recruited disaffected military officers and paid Iranians to spread rumors and spark riots that paralyzed the capital, forcing the nationalists from power and leading to a pro-U.S. but despotic government. The deposed Iranian leader argued that he faced U.S. wrath for trying to remove "the network of colonialism, and the political and economic influence of the greatest empire on earth [the U.S.] from this land."[6] For the first time ever the United States had organized the overthrow of a foreign government outside the Western Hemisphere. One result was the long-term hatred of the United States by ordinary Iranians.

To critics, the U.S. actions and other superpower interventions constituted a new form of imperialism. The interventions often proved costly as well. In Vietnam, for example, the Communist-led forces achieved a military stalemate that cost the United States vast sums of money, killed some 58,000 Americans, and forced it to negotiate for peace and withdraw, harming U.S. prestige in the world. The war also had spillover effects: it created economic problems in the United States and reduced the U.S. willingness to exercise military power for several decades. But the conflict in Vietnam also cost the lives of several million Vietnamese on all sides and required the USSR and China to spend scarce resources to supply their communist allies.

The Nuclear Arms Race and Global Militarization

The arms race between the superpowers and increasing militarization around the world became major components of the Cold War. Both superpowers developed **nuclear weapons**, explosive devices that owe their destructive power to the energy released by either splitting or fusing atoms. These weapons were the most deadly result of the technological surge that can be traced back to Albert Einstein, Sir Isaac Newton, and the scientific discoveries of the seventeenth and eighteenth centuries. A nuclear explosion produces a powerful blast, intense heat, and deadly radiation over a wide area. The nuclear weapons era began when the United States built the first atomic bombs and dropped two of these bombs from airplanes on the Japanese cities of Hiroshima and Nagasaki to end World War II. In the following decades, both the United States and the USSR developed even more deadly nuclear warheads that could be placed on the tips of missiles. The growth of nuclear arsenals was only the most dangerous part of a larger trend toward increased militarization, the expansion of war-making ability by many nations.

Both superpowers and the rest of the world feared the devastating power of nuclear weapons of mass destruction. Since 1945 the world has lived in the shadow of nuclear weapons; a small number of them could reduce whole countries to radioactive rubble. Many scientists believe that even limited use of such weapons could produce a nuclear winter, radically altering global weather patterns by producing pollution that might cool the earth. Einstein fretted that the unleashed power of the atom, which he helped foster, would change everything save peoples' ways of thinking, and he worried that leaders would create a global catastrophe by rashly using the new technologies.

Fortunately these weapons were never used after 1945, although the world was close to a nuclear confrontation on several occasions. For example, in the early 1950s, as French colonial forces were losing the fight against Communist-led insurgents in Vietnam, the Eisenhower administration in the United States offered atomic bombs to the French, who wisely

---

guerrilla warfare An unconventional military strategy of avoiding full-scale direct confrontations in favor of small-scale skirmishes.

nuclear weapons Explosive devices that owe their destructive power to the energy released by either splitting or fusing atoms.

declined the offer. In 1962, after discovering that the USSR had secretly placed nuclear missiles in Cuba, just 90 miles from Florida, President John F. Kennedy (1917–1963) demanded they be removed but vetoed a U.S. invasion that might have sparked all-out nuclear war. Some of Kennedy's advisers recommended that he attack Cuba with nuclear weapons. Kennedy rejected this advice but his firm stance against missiles in Cuba created a tense crisis, ultimately forcing the Soviets to withdraw them. However, before that withdrawal, the confrontation had nearly turned disastrous. In response to a U.S. attack on his boat during the crisis, a Soviet submarine commander armed a missile which carried a nuclear weapon and aimed it at the United States, but he was talked out of firing it by other Soviet officers.

Nuclear weapons shaped global politics. The Cold War fostered a balance of terror, with both superpowers unwilling to use the awesome power at their command for fear the other would retaliate. Historians debate whether the nuclear arms race helped preserve the peace by discouraging an all-out U.S.-USSR military confrontation or instead unsettled international politics and wasted trillions of dollars. Various other countries, including Britain, France, China, India, and Pakistan, also constructed or acquired nuclear bombs, while countries like Iran and North Korea began programs to do the same. In 1987 the two superpowers negotiated their first treaty to reduce their nuclear arms. Nevertheless, more nations sought a nuclear capability, provoking concerns about nuclear proliferation, especially that North Korea or Pakistan could sell bombs to other countries or perhaps to terrorist groups. But some outside the West argued that the monopoly on such weapons by a few powerful nations was unfair, and Middle Eastern leaders worried about Israeli nuclear efforts; a nuclear weapon would give Israel a decisive military advantage in any regional conflict.

The proportion of total world production and spending devoted to militaries grew dramatically during the Cold War. By 1985, the world was spending some $1.2 trillion annually on military forces and weapons, more than the combined income of the poorest 50 percent of world countries. The two superpowers together, with 11 percent of the world population, accounted for 60 percent of military spending, 25 percent of the world's armed forces, and 97 percent of its nuclear weapons; both the U.S. and USSR had stockpiles of thousands of nuclear weapons. They both also sold conventional weapons to other countries with which they had friendly relations. The world's weapons, from rifles and land mines to non-nuclear bombs, were often used in the era's many wars and conflicts.

Whether or not related to Cold War rivalries, the varied wars caused enormous casualties, with civilians accounting for some three-fourths of the dead. Two million people died during the Chinese civil war (1945–1949), 800,000 during the violent partition of India (1948), 2 million during the American-Vietnamese War (1959–1975), 1 million during the Nigerian civil war (1967), and more than 2 million in the Cambodian violence from 1970 to 1978. Millions of these deaths resulted from genocide, the deliberate killing of whole groups because of their ethnic or religious origin. Genocide, practiced for cen-

turies, had reached its most organized campaign with the Nazi holocaust against the Jews during World War II (see Chapter 24). In the later twentieth century genocides continued. For example, in the 1990s members of the Hutu majority slaughtered people belonging to the Tutsi minority in Rwanda (roo-AHN-duh), a Central African country, while extremist Serb Christians, seeking to maintain their political power, killed Bosnian and Albanian Muslims in Yugoslavia, in a policy they called "ethnic cleansing." The Yugoslav killings were finally stopped when the United States and western European nations sent in troops to restore order and punish the worst violators of human rights.

Global Organizations and Activism

During the Cold War, more than ever before in history, public and private organizations emerged with a global reach and mission to promote political cooperation and address various causes. The largest attempt by most of the world's sovereign nations to cooperate for the common good, the United Nations, was founded in 1945, in the burning embers left by World War II, with fifty-one members and became a key forum for global debate and an agency for improving global conditions. The founding United Nations Charter enumerated the organization's principles: "To develop friendly relations among nations based on respect for the principle of equal rights and self-determination of peoples and to take other appropriate measures to strengthen universal peace." Furthermore, the founding members agreed that the United Nations came about to "save succeeding generations from the scourge of war, reaffirm faith in fundamental rights, and respect international law."[7] The United Nations endorsed human rights and dignity. As colonies gained independence and joined, the organization grew to over one hundred members by the mid-1960s and to nearly two hundred by 2000. Pursuing cooperation on humanitarian aims, it developed agencies, such as the World Health Organization, that monitored diseases, funded and fostered medical research, and promoted public health, as well as the United Nations Children Fund, or UNICEF, which promoted children's welfare and education around the world, especially in poor countries, earning it the Nobel Peace Prize in 1965. U.N.-sponsored health and nutrition programs helped increase average life expectancy from 45 in 1900 to 75 in 2000, and greatly reduced the risk of mothers dying in childbirth. Yet, critics believed that political differences among member states often obstructed the U.N.'s humanitarian work.

The United Nations influenced international relations by discouraging, although not preventing, states from using force whenever they desired. To gain support for a possible military action, nations often felt it necessary to make their case before, and endure criticism in, the policymaking Security Council; sometimes they received support, as when the United States led a United Nations military force to prevent a North Korean conquest of South Korea. However, nations determined to go to war often ignored widespread disapproval by the organization's members, as the United States did when it invaded Iraq in 2003.

The Security Council sometimes voted to send peacekeeping troops into troubled countries, especially in Africa. Built on the ashes of the doomed League of Nations, the United Nations gave each of the five major powers of 1945 (the United States, China, Britain, France, and the USSR) permanent seats with veto power in the Security Council. Both superpowers vetoed decisions that challenged their national interests. For instance, the United States often vetoed resolutions aimed at penalizing its ally, Israel, and also blocked, for over two decades, the Chinese Communist government from occupying China's seat in the United Nations. Western nations found it more difficult to shape United Nations policies after Afro-Asian nations became the majority in the organization.

Since World War II, groupings of nations also cooperated to improve global conditions by forging international agreements and treaties. For example, most nations ratified an agreement banning biological weapons, such as deadly diseases like anthrax, in 1972. In 1997, 132 nations signed an international treaty to ban the production, use, and export of land mines, which continued to kill and injure civilians years after the end of the conflicts for which they were intended. In 1997 most nations signed the Kyoto Protocol, pledging to begin reducing the harmful gases that contribute to global warming. In 2002 a treaty establishing an International Criminal Court went into effect, with the goal of prosecuting the perpetrators of genocide, war crimes, and crimes against humanity. But the United States and several other industrial nations impeded international cooperation by refusing to approve the modest efforts made by these agreements to reduce weapons, promote environmental stability, and establish accountability for international crimes.

Private organizations and activists, chiefly based in western Europe, also worked for issues of peace, social justice, health, refugees, famine, conflict resolution, and environmental protection. Organizations such as Doctors Without Borders, which sent medical personnel to societies facing famine or epidemics, and Amnesty International, which worked to free political prisoners, were supported chiefly by private donations. In addition, leaders from different religious faiths worked for world peace, justice, and humanitarian concerns. For example, the Dalai Lama (DAH-lie LAH-ma) (b. 1935), the highest Tibetan Buddhist spiritual leader, won the Nobel Peace Prize in 1989 for his efforts—through speeches, writings, and conferences—to promote human rights, nonviolent conflict resolution, and understanding among different religions. In 1997 the Dalai Lama pleaded, "We all have a special responsibility to create a better world. No one loses, and everyone gains by a shared universal sense of responsibility to this planet and all living things on it."[8] Similarly, the Aga Khan IV (b. 1936), the spiritual leader of a largely Indian Shi'ite Muslim sect, funded charitable activities, such as schools and clinics, all over the world. Among Christian groups, the World Council of Churches, supported by diverse Protestant and Eastern Orthodox churches, encouraged interfaith cooperation and international understanding between Christians and non-Christians. Several Catholic popes favored inter-faith dialogue but their denouncing of war, birth control, abortion, and capital punishment were more controversial.

U.N. Peacekeepers in Congo
The United Nations has regularly sent peacekeepers into troubled countries such as the Congo. This photo, from 2003, shows U.N. troops from Uruguay guarding a U.N. office while a Congolese woman and her four children, displaced from her village by factional fighting, seek U.N. help. (AP/World Wide Photos)

World Politics Since 1989

Between 1989 and 1991 the Soviet bloc disintegrated and the communist regimes in eastern Europe and the former USSR collapsed, ending the Cold War and the bipolar world it had defined (see Chronology: Global Politics Since 1989). Historians disagree as to whether any particular leaders or nations deserve credit for ending the Cold War. Many scholars concur with long-time State Department official George Kennan (KEN-uhn) (1904–2004), the architect of the U.S. policy to contain communism in the 1940s, who concluded that no country or person "won" the Cold War because it was fueled by misconceptions and nearly bankrupted both sides. Other nations, especially Japan and West Germany, both protected from potential enemies by U.S. military bases, had gained the most economically from the conflict, at least in the short term, by investing heavily in economic growth rather than their own defense. Both U.S. and Soviet leaders deescalated tensions between the two superpowers in the later 1980s. When the Cold War ended, the United States became the sole superpower. By 2001 it had a larger annual military budget than the ten next largest military spenders, including Russia, China, and Britain, combined and was the major supplier of arms to the rest of the world. Yet, U.S. power was not absolute. Some observers perceived a tripolar system in which the U.S. had to share political and economic leadership with Western Europe, whose nations now cooperated closely, and several Asian nations, especially China and Japan.

The first major post–Cold War challenge for the United States came from Iraq's brutal dictator, Saddam Hussein (sah-DAHM hoo-SANE) (b. 1937), who ordered his army to invade and occupy Iraq's small, oil-rich neighbor, Kuwait. The United States had supported Saddam and provided his military with weapons in the 1980s, when Iraq was fighting a war against Iran, whose Islamic government the United States opposed. Now the United States organized an international coalition, funded chiefly by Arab nations, and, in the Gulf War of 1991, rapidly defeated the Iraqis and pushed them out of Kuwait. In the aftermath of the quick victory over Iraq, U.S. president George H. W. Bush proclaimed a "new world order"—a new global system, led by the United States, that was based on American values and faced no powerful challenge from communism. He envisioned the United States as a world policeman, with no superpower rival to check its power.

The end of the long, costly rivalry between capitalist countries and Communist societies, however, did not result in universal peace and stability or the triumph of American political values. Instead of a new world order, the 1990s saw what some observers called a new world disorder. Ethnic and nationalist conflicts exploded in massive violence in Yugoslavia, eastern Europe, and Rwanda in central Africa. States with weak or dysfunctional governments, such as Haiti in the Caribbean, Liberia and Sierra Leone in West Africa, and Somalia in Northeast Africa, also experienced chronic fighting and civil war. Rising tides of religious militancy, usually fundamentalist, or conflict between rival faiths complicated politics in countries such as India, Indonesia, Algeria, and Nigeria. Militant Islam demonstrated its potency in Iran, Sudan, and Afghanistan and led some extremists to form terrorist groups to fight moderate Islamic regimes,

Israel, and Western nations. By the early 2000s Islamic radicals posed a greater challenge in Southeast Asia and the Middle East than the declining Communist movements. The ambitions of aggressive dictators, such as Iraq's Saddam Hussein, and the Communist regime in North Korea, which limited contact with the outside world, fostered regional tensions. The new world order promise of a peaceful world moving, with U.S. support, toward democracy foundered on the shoals of proliferating regional, nationalist, religious, and ethnic conflicts that, combined with uneven economic growth, produced a context for violence.

CHRONOLOGY

Global Politics Since 1989

1989–1991	Dismantling of Soviet bloc and empire
1997	Kyoto Protocol on climate change
2001	Al Qaeda attack on United States
2003	U.S. invasion of Iraq

SECTION SUMMARY

- During the Cold War, the United States and the USSR struggled for world control, with the United States generally favoring democracy and capitalism but also seeking access to resources and foreign markets, and the USSR supporting emerging communist regimes and movements.

- Though the United States and the USSR never fought directly, they were involved in dozens of wars in other countries, such as Vietnam, Korea, and Afghanistan, in which millions died, and they intervened in countries such as Guatemala, Iran, Poland, Hungary, and Czechoslovakia.

- The United States and the USSR participated in a massive arms race, spending trillions of dollars on nuclear weapons, which led to widespread fear of mass destruction, though some argue that this fear helped prevent all-out war.

- The United Nations was formed with the goal of promoting world peace and human rights, and various agreements have been signed to ban biological weapons and land mines, to prevent global warming, and to facilitate an international justice system, though they have encountered opposition by the United States and some other industrial nations.

- When the Soviet Union collapsed, the United States was the sole superpower, with a military budget dwarfing that of other countries and dreams of a peaceful democratic world, but religious extremism and ethnic and nationalist conflicts have ensured continuing conflict.

Globalizing Economies, Underdevelopment, and Environmental Change

What were some of the main consequences of a globalizing world economy?

In the decades after 1945, the world economy was increasingly characterized by **globalization,** a pattern in which economic, political, and cultural processes reach beyond nation-state boundaries. This trend reduced barriers between countries and turned the world into a more closely integrated whole. Globalization transformed the world through worldwide commercial markets, finance, telecommunications, and the exchange of ideas. It also allowed for more collaboration between nations and the spread of new ideas. However, it came with some major problems. One was the widening inequality of nations. Another was the environmental consequences of industrialization and economic growth, including ever increasing pollution and a warming climate. In response to population growth and economic policies, people expanded agriculture into semidesert areas and cut down rain forests, causing widespread environmental deterioration.

The Transnational Economy

Globalization has increased the interconnectedness between societies; events occurring or decisions taken in one part of the world affect societies far away. For example, rising or falling prices on the Tokyo or New York stock exchanges quickly reverberate around the world, influencing stock markets elsewhere. Similarly, the decision by U.S. or British governments to sell supplies of stockpiled rubber, hence depressing world prices, affects the livelihood of rubber growers, and the businesses that supply them, in Malaysia, Sri Lanka, Brazil, and the Congo. Not all the transnational economic activity has been legal, especially the flow of narcotics. Heroin and cocaine sold in North America and Europe, creating millions of addicts, originates largely in Asia and Latin America and is smuggled by transnational criminal syndicates, some of them linked to corrupt politicians. Whatever the problems, economic globalization became a fact of contemporary life and had numerous impacts on the world's societies.

A World in Flux The roots of globalization are old: a world economy that links distant societies has been developing over the past 2,500 years. As a measure of this growth, the world's production of goods and services was 120 times higher in 2000 than it had been in 1500. Average personal income grew fourfold between 1900 and 2000. After World War II economic globalization involved the spread of

market capitalism as well as flows of capital, goods, services, and people. The United States, now the axis of the world economy, has been the major proponent of globalization, with its leaders arguing that open markets and conditions favorable to investment and trade foster prosperity. By 2000 the United States produced nearly a third of the world's goods and services; Japan, with the next largest economy, accounted for around a sixth. International observers described the impact of U.S. leadership metaphorically: when the United States sneezes, the rest of the world catches cold.

In spite of the growth of the world economy, globalization has had its critics. They charge that it promises riches it does not always deliver, distributing the benefits unequally. Economic growth in a country does not, by itself, improve the living conditions of the majority of people; better conditions also require well-functioning governments, secure legal and political rights, and health and education services available to all. The visionary Indonesian diplomat Soedjatmoko (so-JAHT-mo-ko) (1922–1989) argued that economic development, as opposed to economic growth, could only be understood as part of a larger process that reshaped societies and improved people's lives.

Globalization also brought more advantages to some nations, and some people within nations, than to others. By the 1990s two nations, the United States and China, were gaining the most from the trend toward removing trade barriers and fostering competitive markets worldwide. Both sucked in investment capital, aggressively acquired natural resources from around the globe, and supplied diverse products to growing foreign markets. China became the world's third largest economy, rapidly gaining ground on the second largest, Japan. Chinese factories turned out clothing, housewares, and other consumer goods to sell in both rich and poor countries. As they expanded their global connections, the Chinese even began investing in Africa, Latin America, and the Middle East and buying U.S.-based companies. However, not all Chinese benefited. China's state-owned enterprises, established before the shift to a market economy, were less efficient than private ones and often closed down, laying off workers, while peasants protested as their farmland was bulldozed to build foreign-owned factories, private housing developments, and golf courses for affluent Chinese.

Impacts of Globalization Globalization's impact has been uneven. By the early twenty-first century a few other nations, such as India, Ireland, Singapore, and South Korea, had, like the United States and China, also capitalized on globalization, fostering economic growth and becoming centers of high technology. But not all countries enjoyed such success. By the 1990s even Japan and some European nations, such as France and Germany, struggled to compete in the globalizing economy, while many Asian, African, and Caribbean nations fell deeper into poverty. As United Nations Secretary General Kofi Annan (KO-fee AN-uhn), a Ghanaian, put it in 2002: "Our challenge today is to make globalization an engine that lifts people out of hardship and misery, not a force that holds them down."[9]

---

globalization   A pattern in which economic, political, and cultural processes reach beyond nation-state boundaries.

Although experiencing occasional setbacks, the Western industrial nations and Japan have generally maintained a favorable position in the global economy. They control most of the capital, markets, and institutions of international finance, such as banks, and their corporations also own assets in other nations. For example, U.S. citizens control businesses, mines, and plantations in Latin America, Japanese operate factories in Southeast Asia, and the French maintain a large economic stake in West Africa. The capitalist systems in the industrialized nations have ranged from the laissez-faire approach, featuring limited government interference, common in the United States, to the mix of free markets and welfare states in western Europe, to the closely linked government-business relationship in Japan and South Korea. These contrast with the economies in many former colonies, especially in Africa, where power holders, often closely linked to foreign or domestic business interests, preside over largely poor populations. For instance, in the former Belgian Congo, corrupt national and local leaders work to protect the interests of the Belgian-owned and local corporations who fund them.

Some once-poor countries have exploited the transnational economy to their advantage, achieving spectacular growth. If revenues are not stolen by corrupt leaders, as has happened in some countries, such as Iraq and Nigeria, possession of oil, a natural resource in high world demand, provides an economic foundation for national wealth. A few oil-rich nations, such as the Persian Gulf states of Kuwait and the United Arab Emirates, use oil revenues to improve the material lives of their citizens. Although lacking vast oil reserves, various Asian countries, much like Japan in the late 1800s, have combined capitalist market economies, cheap labor, and powerful governments to orchestrate industrialization. At the same time they have ensured political stability and attracted foreign investment by repressing political opposition and harassing or arresting dissidents. These countries have favored export-oriented growth, producing consumer goods—clothing, toys, housewares—for sale abroad, especially in the richer, consuming nations of Europe and North America. This strategy has fostered high growth rates and the import of industrial jobs from other, often Western, countries; at the same time, however, these countries have held political prisoners, exploited labor, and suppressed strikes and labor unions.

Asian countries using this development strategy improved their position in the global system. In the 1980s and 1990s China, South Korea, Taiwan, Malaysia, Thailand, and Singapore fostered the fastest-growing economies in the world and considerable prosperity, their major cities boasting well-stocked malls, freeways, diverse restaurants, and luxury condominiums. Often the growing middle class and labor leaders have demanded a larger voice in government and political liberalization. By the 1990s Indonesians, South Koreans, Taiwanese, and Thais had replaced dictatorships with democratic governments that were chosen in free elections. The Asian systems became models for successful development by mixing capitalism, which is useful for creating wealth, with socialism, which can distribute wealth equitably. The Asian economic resurgence had the potential to restore the leading role some Asian societies had enjoyed in the world economy for many centuries before 1800. But in the late 1990s the economies of many Asian nations, except for China's, crashed, and Indonesia experienced political turmoil, posing at least a temporary setback to Asian resurgence.

International Economic Institutions

Various institutions shaped the transnational economy. The international lending agencies formed by the World War II anti-Fascist allies in 1944 to aid postwar reconstruction played crucial roles, especially the World Bank, which funded development projects such as dams and agricultural schemes, and the International Monetary Fund (IMF), which regulated currency dealings and helped alleviate severe financial problems. Most Asian, African, Caribbean, and Latin American governments, dependent chiefly on exporting natural resources, did not earn enough income from selling these resources to buy food and medicine, import luxuries, or finance projects such as building dams and improving ports. To get these funds, governments, emulating consumers, took out loans, mostly from the World Bank or the IMF, both institutions closely linked to the United States. The IMF, which had the right to dictate economic policies to countries borrowing from it, favored Western investment and free markets, often at the expense of government funding for social services such as schools and health clinics. Borrowers failing to make these changes risked loss of IMF loans. Especially in Latin America and Africa, countries fell deeply into debt, often having to devote 40 to 50 percent of their foreign income just to pay the interest on their loans.

Trade agreements and trading blocs also shaped the world economy, reflecting an economic connectedness between nations unprecedented in world history. In 1947, twenty-three nations established the General Agreements on Trade and Tariffs (GATT), which set general guidelines for the conduct of world trade and rules for establishing tariffs and trade regulations (see Chronology: The Global Economy and New Technologies). The inauguration of the World Trade Organization (WTO) by 124 nations in 1995 marked a new phase in the evolution of the postwar economic system, replacing GATT. By the early twenty-first century several Communist nations with market economies, including China and Vietnam, had joined the WTO. The WTO had stronger dispute-resolution capabilities than GATT, and a member country could not veto a WTO decision that declared one of its regulations, such as environmental protection, to be an unfair restriction on trade. Various regional trading blocs also formed. For example, the European Common Market (now the European Union) eventually included most European nations.

Giant business enterprises, known as **multinational corporations** because they operate all over the world, gained a leading role in the global marketplace. Some 300 to 400 companies, two-thirds of them U.S.-owned, dominated world

---

multinational corporations Giant business enterprises that operate all over the world, gaining a leading role in the global marketplace.

The Global Economy Cambodian Buddhist monks, following ancient traditions, collect their food from the devout in the capital city, Phnom Penh, while advertising for American cigarettes entices Cambodians into the global economy, despite government concerns about the health danger posed by tobacco products. (AP/World Wide Photos)

production and trade. By the early 1980s the multinationals had together become the third largest economic force in the world, exercising great influence over governments. By 2000 half of the world's 100 biggest economic entities were countries and half were multinational corporations, the largest being four U.S. companies—General Motors, Wal-Mart Stores, Exxon-Mobil, Ford Motor Company—and the Germany-based Daimler-Chrysler automobile company.

The multinational corporations set the world price for various commodities, such as coffee, copper, or oil, and could play off one country against another to get the best deal. They also could easily switch manufacturing and hence jobs from one country to another. Multinationals have created millions of jobs in poor countries. Increasingly women, willing to work for lower wages than men and less likely than men to challenge managers, have become the majority of the labor force in what economists called the global assembly line: factories producing for export. Supporters argue that moving jobs from high-wage to low-wage countries, a pattern known as outsourcing, fosters a middle class of managers and technicians and offers work to people, especially young women, with few other job prospects. Indeed, some impoverished African nations with high unemployment would probably welcome such globalization. Critics reply that most of these jobs pay low wages, require long hours, and often offer little future. For example, the U.S.-based Nike Corporation, praised for creating needed jobs by making shoes in Vietnam, is also criticized because the Vietnamese employees, mainly women, work in unhealthy conditions, face sexual harassment from their male supervisors, and are fired if they complain.

The Spread of Industrialization

The industrialization that had transformed Europe and North America in the nineteenth century spread to other parts of the world, especially to Asia and Latin America, during the later twentieth century. Entrepreneurs or state agencies in countries such as China, India, South Korea, Brazil, and Mexico built textile mills, steel mills, and automobile plants, primarily to produce goods for local consumption and later for export. Chinese textiles, Indian steel, and South Korean cars found markets around the world. Increasing competition from Asia and Latin America challenged Western and Japanese dominance in industrial activity. For example, the U.S. share of world industrial production fell from 50 percent in 1950 to below 30 percent in the late 1980s. Americans built over 75 percent of all cars in 1950 but less than 20 percent by the early 1990s. Consumers worldwide now had more choice. Malaysian car buyers, for example, could test-drive Volvos made in Sweden, Hyundais made in South Korea, Toyotas made in Japan, and Proton Sagas manufactured locally.

Technological innovations since 1945 spurred economic growth. The so-called **Third Industrial Revolution** came

CHRONOLOGY

The Global Economy and New Technologies

1947	Formation of GATT
1947	Invention of transistor
1958	Invention of silicon microchips
1995	Formation of World Trade Organization

Third Industrial Revolution The creation since 1945 of unprecedented scientific knowledge of new technologies more powerful than any invented before.

about through the creation of unprecedented scientific knowledge of new technologies more powerful than any invented before. These new technologies made the creations of the first Industrial Revolution, which began in the late 1700s, and the second Industrial Revolution of the later 1800s seem obsolete. With the new innovations, traditional smokestack industries such as steel mills in industrialized nations were displaced by nuclear power, computers, automation, and robotry. The technological surge also brought rocketry, genetic engineering, silicon chips, and lasers. Space technology produced the first manned trips to the moon and unmanned crafts exploring the solar system. In 2005 a probe from one of these crafts astounded the world by landing on Saturn's large, mysterious, cloud-covered moon, Titan, and sending back photographs of the surface. The increased knowledge of the solar system, and, owing to more powerful telescopes, of the universe, including the discovery of planets circling other stars, produced insights and gave earthlings a complete glimpse of their planet for the first time. The British poet Archibald MacLeish observed that the astronauts on the space capsules circling the planet did not perceive national boundaries or international rivalries, but only oceans and lands containing people with a common planetary home: "To see the Earth as we now see it, small and blue and beautiful in that eternal silence [of space] where it floats, is to see ourselves as rulers on the Earth together."[10]

The Third Industrial Revolution has had potentially dramatic consequences for people around the world. For example, the **Green Revolution** has fostered increased agricultural output through the use of new high-yield seeds and mechanized farming, such as gasoline-powered tractors and harvesters. Farmers with the money to take advantage of these innovations can shorten the growing season, thus raising two or three crops a year. Between 1965 and 1978, one village in India, using high-yield seeds, increased its food output by 300 percent. Once poor, the village now gained a paved road, regular bus service, and electricity while its people built bigger homes. But not all farmers benefited from the Green Revolution. In countries such as India, the Philippines, and Mexico, the Green Revolution, which requires more capital for seeds and machines but fewer people to work the land, has often harmed poor peasants whose labor was no longer needed or who could not afford the investment. Agriculture, however, was not the only economic sphere to feel the impact of new technology. In many industries, such as automobile manufacturing, automation has taken over production, allowing companies to fire workers.

Industry and other economic activities have also become globalized. By the 1990s over two hundred export processing zones, industrial parks occupied largely by foreign-owned factories paying low taxes and wages, and making goods of all kinds for the global economy, had been established around the world. For example, factories in northern Mexico, usually U.S.-owned, made goods, such as clothing, largely for the U.S. market and employed nearly half a million workers, mainly women. But not all the new jobs were in factories. During the

later twentieth century, the service and information exchange industries also grew. More people worked in service enterprises, such as fast-food restaurants, while others established transnational computer networks, such as AOL and Google, to help people use the Internet for communication and knowledge acquisition. By the 1990s India, responding to these trends, was graduating each year thousands of people fluent in English and skilled in computer technology, becoming a world center for offshore information and technical services. Increasingly consumers calling North American companies for computer technical support, product information, or billing questions reached Indians working in cubicles in cities such as Bangalore and Bombay (known in India as Mumbai).

Yet, the opportunities of industrialization and its globalization have come with risks. Hoping to better compete in the world economy, businesses have moved factories to countries with low wages and costs. Some Western and Japanese businesses have shifted operations to South Korea or Taiwan, where the average worker earns in a month what a U.S. or German worker earns in a week or ten days, yet produces as much. Others have established operations in Asian, African, Latin American, or Eastern European nations where workers earn even less. As North American and western European companies have sought more profits, they have outsourced, or relocated, the jobs once held by several million workers to foreign countries with cheap labor costs and eager workers, such as India and Mexico. As an example of how outsourcing has affected some people negatively, in 1990 the U.S. clothing maker Levi Strauss closed its plant in San Antonio, Texas; laid off 1,150 workers, most of them Mexican American women; and relocated the operation to Costa Rica. Viola Casares, one of the fired workers, expressed the despair: "As long as I live I'll never forget how the white man in the suit said they had to shut us down to stay competitive."[11] Between 1981 and 1990 Levi Strauss, losing markets to lower-priced competitors, closed fifty-eight U.S. plants with over 10,000 workers while shifting half of its production overseas. While some, such as these Americans, lost jobs, other people now had better economic opportunities.

Underdevelopment

Uneven economic growth contributed to a growing gap between rich nations and poor nations, often described as underdeveloped or developing. The gap was already wide in 1945, since colonialism often did little to raise colonial people's general living standards. A Guyanese historian concluded that "the vast majority of Africans went into colonialism with a hoe and came out with a hoe."[12] Outraged that they gain little from the polluting oil wells around them, local people in Nigeria's main oil-producing region have sabotaged operations and kidnapped foreign oil workers. Many Asian, African, and Latin American economies grew rapidly in the 1950s and 1960s, when the world economy boomed. In the 1970s and 1980s, however, as the world economy soured and the world prices for many exports collapsed, the growth rates of these economies declined. Then the world economy revived for a few years, only to experience a dramatic downturn in the later 1990s and early

---

Green Revolution Increased agricultural output through the use of new high-yield seeds and mechanized farming.

2000s. Despite economic growth, some countries remained underdeveloped, while women and children in these countries often faced more problems than did men.

Growth and Development Economic growth has not always fostered development, growth that benefited the majority of the population. With economic globalization growing, rich countries pressure or encourage other nations to open their economies to foreign corporations and investment. Some nations, especially in East and Southeast Asia, have prospered from this investment, earning money to build schools, hospitals, and highways, but elsewhere Western investment often has done little to foster locally owned businesses and instead encourages the nation to rely on exporting one or two resources. In Nigeria, for example, as in colonial times, British-owned enterprises have controlled banking, importing, and exporting, and foreign investment has gone mainly into cash crops and oil production, controlled largely by Western companies, such as Royal Dutch Shell. Furthermore, in countries like Nigeria and Congo, foreign investment and aid has often been misused to support projects favored by influential politicians or siphoned off to line the pockets of corrupt leaders, bureaucrats, and military officers.

Scholars debate how poor countries can better profit from their connections to the world economy and spur local efforts at development. One of the most influential scholars, the Indian economist Amartya Sen (b. 1933), had helped run evening schools for illiterate rural children as a youth. This experience laid a foundation for his studies of global poverty, for which he won the Nobel Prize in economics in 1998. Sen believes that the main challenges were how to use trade and technology to help the poorest people and improve their lives by addressing famine, poverty, and social and gender inequality. Influenced by his first wife, a prominent Indian writer and political activist, Sen began focusing on the role of women in development, wanting to enhance not just their well-being but also their abilities to improve their lives. Sen argues that women's literacy and employment are the best predictors of both child survival and fertility rate reduction, prerequisites for fostering development in poor villages. His views on poverty and gender inequality influenced the United Nations when, in 2000, that body developed an agenda to address the world's pressing problems, such as the kind Sen studies, by 2020 (see Witness to the Past: An Agenda for the New Millennium). However, without outside financial support, few poor countries have sufficient resources to seriously combat widespread poverty or promote women's empowerment.

While some nations have become richer, others have become poorer. Most poor nations have suffered from some combination of rapid population growth, high unemployment, illiteracy, hunger, disease, corrupt or ineffective governments, and reliance on only a few exports, chiefly natural resources. A United Nations conference on the Environment and Development in 1997 bluntly concluded: "Too many countries have seen economic conditions worsen, public services deteriorate, and the total number of people in the world living in poverty has increased."[13] By the 1990s the richest fifth of the

Rich and Poor in Brazil The stark contrast between the wealthy and the poor in many nations can be seen in the Brazilian city of Rio de Janeiro. Seeking jobs in expanding industries, millions of migrants flock to the city, building shantytown slums and squatter settlements in view of luxury high-rise apartment and office buildings. (Stephanie Maze/Woodfin Camp & Associates)

world's people received 80 percent of the total income while the poorest fifth earned less than 2 percent. For example, in the Central American nation of Guatemala, 90 percent of people lived below the official poverty line, and nearly half had no access to health care, indoor plumbing, piped water, or formal education. A fifth of the world's people earned less than $1 per day. By 2000 the world's three richest persons owned more assets than the forty-eight poorest nations together, and 358 billionaires had a combined net worth equal to that of the bottom 45 percent of the world's population combined. Furthermore, the policies of rich countries often penalized poor countries. Despite preaching the benefits of free trade, rich nations have often blocked or restricted food and fiber exports from poor nations into their own markets while heavily subsidizing their own farmers. Hence, wheat farmers in the West African country of Mali, however industrious, cannot compete with French or U.S. wheat farmers, who can sell their crops at much lower prices because of the financial support from their governments.

An Agenda for the New Millennium

In 2000 the United Nations called together the 188 member states for a summit at its headquarters in New York City to discuss the issues facing the world during the new millennium. In the following document, distributed before the summit, the United Nations secretary general, Kofi Annan of Ghana (GAH-nuh), laid out his vision for the organization and the challenges it faced in a world that had changed dramatically since the organization's formation over five decades earlier.

If one word encapsulates the changes we are living through, it is "globalization." We live in a world that is interconnected as never before—one in which groups and individuals interact more and more directly across State frontiers. . . . This has its dangers, of course. Crime, narcotics, terrorism, disease, weapons—all these move back and forth faster, and in greater numbers, than in the past. People feel threatened by events far away. But the benefits of globalization are obvious too: faster growth, higher living standards, and new opportunities—not only for individuals but also for better understanding between nations, and for common action.

One problem is that, at present, these opportunities are far from equally distributed. How can we say that the half of the human race which has yet to make or receive a phone call, let alone use a computer, is taking part in globalization? We cannot, without insulting their poverty. A second problem is that, even where the global market does reach, it is not yet underpinned by rules based on shared social objectives. In the absence of such rules, globalization makes many people feel they are at the mercy of unpredictable forces. So, . . . the overarching challenge of our times is to make globalization mean more than bigger markets. To make a success of this great upheaval we must learn how to govern better, and . . . how to govern together. . . . We need to get [our nations] working together on global issues—all pulling their weight and all having their say.

What are these global issues? . . . First, freedom from want. How can we call human beings free and equal in dignity when over a billion of them are struggling to survive on less than one dollar a day, without safe drinking water, and when half of all humanity lacks adequate sanitation? Some of us are worrying about whether the stock market will crash, or struggling to master our latest computer, while more than half our fellow men and women have much more basic worries, such as

where their children's next meal is coming from. . . . I believe we can halve the population of people living in extreme poverty; ensure that all children—girls and boys alike, particularly the girls—receive a full primary education; and . . . transform the lives of one hundred million slum dwellers around the world.

The second main [issue] is freedom from fear. Wars between States are mercifully less frequent than they used to be. But in the last decade internal wars have claimed more than five million lives, and driven many times that number of people from their homes. . . . We must do more to prevent conflicts from happening. Most conflicts happen in poor countries, especially those which are badly governed or where power and wealth are very unfairly distributed between ethnic or religious groups. So the best way to prevent conflict is to promote [fair representation of all groups in government], human rights, and broad-based economic development.

The third [issue] is . . . the freedom of future generations to sustain their lives on this planet. Even now, many of us have not understood how seriously that freedom is threatened. We are plundering our children's heritage to pay for our present unsustainable practices. We must stop. We must reduce emissions of . . . "greenhouse gases," to put a stop to global warming. . . . We must face the implications of a steadily shrinking surface of cultivable land, at a time when every year brings many millions of new mouths to feed. . . . We must preserve our forests, fisheries, and the diversity of living species, all of which are close to collapsing under the pressure of human consumption and destruction. . . . We need a new ethic of stewardship to encourage environment-friendly practices. . . . Above all we need to remember the old African wisdom which I learned as a child—that the earth is not ours. It is a treasure we hold in trust for our descendants.

THINKING ABOUT THE READING

1. What does Annan see as the major global issues of the new millennium?

2. How are the problems he outlined connected to each other?

Source: United Nations, *The Millennium Report* (**http://www.un.org/millennium/sg/report/state.htm**). Reprinted with permission of the United Nations.

Despite the challenges they have faced since World War II, the nations outside of Europe and North America can boast of achievements. Between 1960 and 2000 they reduced infant mortality by half and doubled adult literacy rates. China, Sri Lanka, Malaysia, and Tanzania have been particularly successful in providing social services, such as schools and clinics, to rural areas. Various countries have developed their own locally based development strategies. In sub-Saharan Africa, for instance, some countries, such as Burkina Faso (buhr-KEE-nuh FAH-so) and Niger (nee-jer), have moved away from big, expensive prestige projects—such as building large dams to supply hydroelectric power—to small-scale labor-intensive projects that aid the environment, such as tree-planting campaigns and hand-built dams to supply water for growing food crops in a small area. In these countries local cooperative banks have provided credit to farmers and stored grain for later consumption by villagers. However, these food supplies did not last long when severe drought caused major famine, as occurred in 2005, bringing widespread starvation.

Women and Development Women and their children have faced the harshest problems as modern economic growth has destroyed the traditional cycles of peasant life and undermined the handicrafts that once provided incomes for women. It has also fragmented families: men sometimes have to find work in other districts or countries, leaving their wives to support and raise the children. For example, in Africa, men migrate each year from Burkina Faso to the cocoa plantations and logging camps of the Ivory Coast, and from Mozambique to the mines of South Africa. Meanwhile, migrant work is becoming more feminized. Women leave India, Sri Lanka, and the Philippines to work as domestic servants for rich Arabs in the Persian Gulf states and Saudi Arabia, some facing sexual harassment or cruel employers. Asian and Latin American women are also recruited to work in homes and businesses in North America and Europe, some of them ending up in sweatshops or brothels. Furthermore, women often face social customs that accord them little influence at home and, in case of divorce, award the children to the father. A folk song in north India expressed the bitterness of powerless village women who, after marriage, have no claim on their birth family's property: "To my brother belong your green fields, O father, while I am banished afar."[14]

Experts once assumed that schemes to foster economic development would benefit both genders. But women have generally been left behind because of their inferior social status, relative invisibility in national economic statistics, and minimized role in local decision making. According to United Nations studies, women do 60 percent of the world's work and produce 50 to 75 percent of the world's food, yet they own only 1 percent of the world's property and earn 10 percent of the world's income. While many poor women earn money from growing food, engaging in small-scale trade, or working as domestic servants, most of women's labor—food preparation, cleaning, child rearing—is unpaid and done at home. This housework is often demanding. For example, in Senegal, in West Africa, a typical rural sixteen-year-old girl, married at a young age, gets up at 5 A.M. to pound millet, the staple food, for an hour. She then walks a few hundred yards or perhaps several miles to get water from a well, makes breakfast for the family, goes to the village shop, makes the family lunch, takes food to her mother-in-law working in the fields, does laundry for six adults and a child, makes supper, and then pounds millet again before bed. Some days she also has to find wood for cooking. Older women have to combine all this with farm work.

Some nations have fostered economic development that helps women and children through bottom-up policies relying on grassroots action: the efforts of common people. The Grameen (GRAH-mean) Bank in Bangladesh, which promotes a philosophy of self-help, provides an outstanding model. The founder, the economist Muhammad Yunus (b. 1940), felt that the conventional economics taught in universities was hollow and ignored the poverty and struggles occurring in his nation's villages. He credited this insight to a chance meeting with a poor woman who told him that, after repaying the loan for the cane she wove into mats, she earned only four cents a day. Learning that conventional banks did not make loans to the poor, in 1983 Yunus opened the Grameen Bank, which makes credit available on cheap terms to peasants, especially women, for small-scale projects such as buying the tools they needed to earn a living. For example, a borrower might buy a cell phone that villagers could use to make business or personal calls, paying the borrower for each call, or purchase bamboo to make chairs and use the profits from selling the chairs to buy more bamboo. The bank eventually made loans of less than $100 to over 2 million people. Only less than 2 percent of borrowers defaulted. The newly empowered women, earning an income for their families, now enjoyed higher social status. Rather than jeopardize their income by having more children, 40 percent of the women began using contraceptives, helping lower the Bangladesh birthrate from 3 to 2 percent a year.

Population, Urbanization, and Environmental Change

Rapid population growth and overcrowded cities became manifestations of global imbalance. With too many farmers competing for too little land, rural folk often had to abandon the livelihoods that had sustained their ancestors. They often ended up in crowded cities—Jakarta in Indonesia, Calcutta in India, Cairo in Egypt, Mexico City—where they survived any way they could, often living in shantytowns or, for the even less fortunate, on the sidewalks. Population growth and the resulting expansion of settlement into marginal lands posed unprecedented environmental challenges and increased competition for limited resources, such as oil, timber, and tin. These trends and the enormous surge of economic activity fueled by the use of energy based on fossil fuels have changed the world's environment.

People and Cities During the past fifty years the world's population has grown faster than ever before in history (see Map 26.2). Two thousand years ago the earth had between 125 and 250 million people. It took roughly 10,000 generations for the world to reach 1 billion in 1830. At the end of World War II the population had risen to 2.5 billion, and by 2006 it had more than doubled to 6.5 billion people. Some experts talked of a "population bomb" overwhelming the world's resources—water, food sources, forests, minerals—and a population of perhaps 12 billion by 2100, which the earth's resources could not support. But fertility rates began dropping in much of the world during the late twentieth century, with the biggest declines occurring in industrialized nations. The reasons for the decline were the introduction and widespread use of artificial birth control, such as contraceptive pills, which allowed women to decide if and when they wanted to become pregnant; better health care; and larger numbers of women entering the paid work force. By 1990 over half of the world's couples with

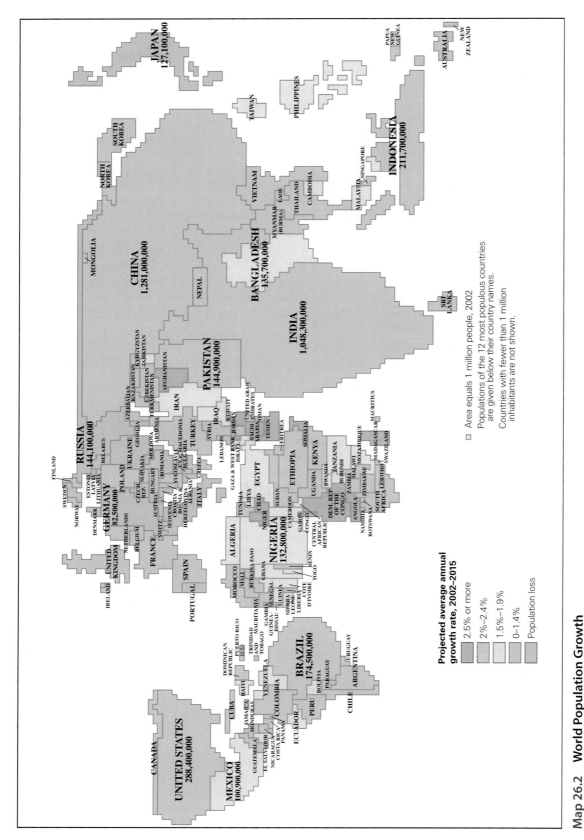

Map 26.2 World Population Growth
This map shows dramatically which nations have the largest populations: China, India, the United States, Indonesia, and Brazil. It also shows which regions experience the most rapid population growth: Africa, South Asia, and Central America.

women of reproductive age practiced some form of contraception to prevent births. Nonetheless, in the 1990s nearly 100 million people were born each year. Demographers now envision a world population of some 9 to 9.5 billion by 2050, which will still impose a heavy burden on countries to supply food and services. Some experts fear such major population growth could lead to increasingly severe social, economic, and environmental problems for the world. They argue that overpopulation, and the ensuing competition for limited resources, probably contributed to civil wars in crowded countries such as Rwanda and El Salvador in the later twentieth century.

Population growth has been more rapid in some world regions than in others. Most of it has occurred in Asia, Africa, and Latin America. By 2000, three of the five countries with the largest populations were in Asia; China and India had the highest number, with around a billion people each. While Asia has continued, as it has for millennia, to house at least 60 percent of humanity, Europe's share of population fell from a quarter in 1900 to an eighth. Because of their falling birthrates, various European nations and Japan have declining and aging populations, which put a growing burden on those of working age to produce more wealth to support elderly populations. Italy and Spain, both predominantly Roman Catholic nations that once had high birthrates, now have the world's lowest fertility rates. North American birthrates have also dropped, but the decline has been offset by immigration.

Nonetheless, the Western nations and Japan, enjoying high rates of resource consumption, have done more harm to the environment than countries with large populations but low consumption rates. For example, owing to heavy use of energy and metals-dependent innovations—air conditioners, central heating systems, gasoline-powered vehicles, refrigerators—the average American or Canadian consumes some twenty times, and the average Australian, German, or Japanese ten to fifteen times, the resources of the average Pakistani or Peruvian.

Population growth has diminished the possibility for economic development in overcrowded nations already struggling with a scarcity of food, health care, housing, and education for their people. For instance, in countries such as the Philippines, Pakistan, and Uganda, the population of school-age children has expanded faster than the resources needed to build new schools and hire teachers. By 2000, over 1 billion people around the world were desperately poor and unable to obtain basic essentials, such as adequate food. The Green Revolution, sparking dramatic increases in food production, averted mass famine, but by the 1990s harvests reached a plateau, producing only small food increases or sometimes even decreases in food supplies. Furthermore, by the 1990s fish catches were declining steeply, partly because of overfishing by Western and Japanese fleets using high-technology equipment. Feeding the new mouths has also required massive clearing of forests for new cropland. Twentieth-century advances in health and welfare could be reversed unless nations find ways to slow population growth that outstrips the ability of governments to solve social and economic problems.

The most effective tool to slow population growth, birth control, has been controversial, especially when this involves abortion, which is condemned as taking life by varied religious groups. Predominantly Islamic and Roman Catholic nations often discourage birth control as contrary to their religious beliefs, which oppose artificial curbs on pregnancy and favor large families. Prompted by these religious objections, some nations, including the United States, have opposed international family planning organizations. But other nations have pursued vigorous population control programs, thereby increasing their economic potential. For example, Thailand cut its birthrate by a fifth between 1980 and 2000. Using harsher means, overcrowded China dramatically reduced fertility, especially in the cities, through policies that promoted one child only per family; couples who flouted the laws faced stiff fines or, sometimes, forced abortions.

The most successful campaigns to limit growth have targeted women by giving them better education, health care, and a sense of dignity independent of their roles as mothers. For countless generations, many people viewed children—expected as adults to support their parents—as insurance for old age. This was true especially in societies with high infant mortality rates, where people expected that not all their children would survive into adulthood. In Mali, in West Africa, for example, the average woman had seven children, of which four survived to adulthood. Economic development, however, including better health care for women to lower infant mortality, often changed these attitudes. Most evidence suggests that increasing affluence reduces birthrates. Thus, as rural women in Bangladesh opened small businesses, which contributed to family incomes, they had fewer children.

During the twentieth century people increasingly lived in cities, where populations grew thirteenfold. In 1900 cities held some 10 percent of the world population. That figure rose to 50 percent by 2000. Cities often grew into vast metropolises. Thus Cairo, Egypt, grew from under 900,000 in 1897 to 2.8 million in 1947 and 13 million in 1995. In 1950 Western cities, headed by New York, dominated the list of the world's ten largest cities; fifty years later the rankings had changed dramatically as Asian and Latin American cities dominated the list. Tokyo, the world's largest city with 28 million people, was followed by Mexico City, Bombay (India), São Paulo (Brazil), and Shanghai (China). Huge traffic jams made driving in Bangkok, Tokyo, Mexico City, and Lagos a nightmare. Struggling to provide needed services, cities usually dumped raw sewage into bays and rivers. By the early twenty-first century cities are responsible for 75 percent of the world's resource consumption and produced 75 percent of its trash. City life has also reshaped traditional ways, to the distress of some. In a pop song from Peru in 1970, a boy who migrated to the capital city, Lima, but upheld rural values, complained that his girlfriend had abandoned these values: "You came as a country girl. Now you are in Lima you comb your hair in a city way. You even say, 'I'm going to dance the twist' [a popular dance from the United States]."[15]

Environmental Destruction Industrialization, population growth, and urbanization have also affected environments, including soils, air, waters, and plant and animal organisms, and contributed to a warmer, drier global climate. Over the twentieth century societies increased

WANGARI MAATHAI, KENYAN ENVIRONMENTAL ACTIVIST

Wangari Maathai (wahn-GAHR-ee muh-THIGH), who won the 2004 Nobel Peace Prize for her environmental activism, was born in 1940 and grew up in Nyeri, a small village in Kenya, East Africa. As a young girl, Wangari fetched water from a small stream. She grew fascinated by the creatures living in the stream and loved the lush trees and shrubs around her village. But over the years the stream dried up, silt choked nearby rivers, and the once green land grew barren. She lamented the assault on nature. Girls in rural Kenya in the 1940s and 1950s commonly spent their youth preparing for marriage and children. But a brother convinced Wangari's parents to send the inquisitive girl to the primary school he attended.

After graduating from a Roman Catholic high school, Wangari was awarded a scholarship to study in the United States, where she earned a B.A. in biology from a small Kansas college in 1964 and then completed an M.A. at the University of Pittsburgh in 1966. She credited her U.S. experience, including her observations of anti–Vietnam War protests, with encouraging her interest in democracy and free speech. Returning home, she earned a Ph.D. at Nairobi University in 1971, the first East African woman to achieve that degree, and then joined the faculty to teach biological sciences. She became a dean and joined a local organization that coordinated United Nations environmental programs.

Throughout her life Wangari has faced and overcome gender barriers, including in her marriage. Wangari married Mwangi Maathai and had three children, but their relationship soured and they divorced after he was elected to parliament in 1974. She attributed the breakup to gender prejudice: "I think my activism may have contributed to my being perceived as an [un]conventional [woman]. And that puts pressure on the man you live with, because he is then perceived as if he is not controlling you properly."

To stop the spread of desert in Kenya by planting trees, the dogged Wangari founded the Greenbelt Movement on Earth Day, 1977. She got the idea for the movement from talking to women when she served on the National Council of Women. Women told her they needed clean drinking water, nutritious food, and energy. She realized trees could provide for all these needs. Trees stop soil erosion, help water conservation, bear fruit, provide fuel and building materials, offer shade, and also enhance the beauty of the landscape. Over 10,000 Kenyans, largely women, became involved, planting and nurturing more than 30 million trees. For each tree planted, the members earned a small income. The movement showed Kenyans that the health of their forests and rivers mattered for both their immediate well-being and their future.

Realizing that logging contracts enriched leaders of corrupt governments, including Kenya's repressive regime, Wangari began to see the link between environmental health and good governance. As a result, the Greenbelt Movement launched programs of civic education, linking human rights, ecology, and individual activism and helping thousands of women gain more control of their lives. Women took on local leadership roles, running tree nurseries and planning community-based projects. Thanks to the movement, she said, "women have become aware that planting trees or fighting to save forests from being chopped down is part of a larger mission to create a society that respects democracy, the rule of law, human rights, and the rights of women."

their industrial output twentyfold and their energy use fourteenfold. Western industrial nations and Japan faced the environmental consequences, such as air and water pollution, for several generations. Once poor nations that became richer, such as China, South Korea, and Malaysia, paid the cost in noxious air, toxic waste, stripped forests, and warmer climates. Furthermore, many forests in North America and Europe have sickened or died from the acid rain produced by industrial pollution. Some environmental disasters have devastated large populations. For example, in 1957 an explosion in a nuclear waste dump in Russia killed some 10,000 people, contaminated 150 square miles of land, and forced the evacuation of 270,000 people. Meanwhile, by the 1990s scientists were reporting a massive die-off among varieties of frogs and some ocean species, a catastrophe perhaps due to pollution and ecological instability and suggesting that diverse environments are increasingly dangerous to life. Hence, sea turtle populations decreased drastically in regions as far apart as Southeast Asia, the Persian Gulf, and Central America.

Deforestation provides one sign of environmental destruction. In the twentieth century half of the world's rain forests were cut down, as commercial loggers obtained wood for housing, farmers sought to convert forests into farms, and poor people obtained firewood. This destruction continues at a furious pace today; an area larger than Hungary is cleared each year. Between 1975 and 2000 a quarter of the Central American rain forest was turned into grasslands, where beef cattle, raised chiefly to supply North American fast-food restaurants, now graze. Already most of the world's remaining tropical rain forest survives in only three nations: Brazil, Congo, and Indonesia. In tropical regions clearing the land exposes the thin topsoil to leaching of the nutrients by rains, so that often the cleared land can be farmed only for a few years before it becomes unusable desert.

Deforestation has had enormous long-term consequences, ranging from decreasing rainfall to loss of valuable pharmaceuticals, including those that might cure cancer or other illnesses. Millions of species of plants and animals have disappeared in recent decades, and by 2000 more than 11,000 species of plants and animals were threatened with extinction. Some scientists estimate that a quarter to half of all current species could disappear by 2100. The destruction of forests, which absorb the carbon dioxide that heats up the atmosphere, has contributed to the global warming, accelerating over the

people, migrating for short periods to other Southeast Asian nations and the Middle East and more permanently to North America. Some 8 million Filipinos lived abroad by 2002. Moving to a faraway, alien society is often traumatic, for both the migrant and the family members left behind. A poem by a Moroccan woman whose husband worked in Europe and rarely returned home captured the distress: "Germany, Belgium, France and Netherlands, Where are you situated? I have never seen your countries, I do not speak your language. I am afraid my love forgets me in your paradise. I ask you, give him back to me."[17]

Political turbulence, wars, genocides, and government repression have created some 20 million refugees. Desperate people have fled nations engulfed in political violence, such as Sudan, Guatemala, Afghanistan, and Cambodia, and drought-plagued states such as Ethiopia and Mali. For instance, by 2006 over 2 million African Muslims from the Darfur region of Sudan had fled genocidal attacks by Arab militias—attacks that already killed 200,000 people—for refuge in Chad, an equally impoverished nation. Cubans, Chinese, Laotians (lao-OH-shuhnz), and Vietnamese, among others, have fled Communist-run states that restricted their freedoms. Others, such as Haitians, Chileans, and Congolese, have escaped brutal rightwing dictatorships or corrupt despotisms. Millions of refugees have remained for decades, even generations, in squalid refugee camps, often fed and housed by international aid organizations. For example, many Palestinians who fled conflict in Israel have lived in refugee camps in neighboring Egypt, Jordan, and Lebanon (LEB-uh-nuhn)—sometimes welcomed, sometimes resented by local Arabs—for over five decades. Refugees such as the Cubans, Vietnamese, and Palestinians have nurtured resentments against the governments whose policies they escaped from or who forced them out, and citizens in countries offering refuge have often resented the refugees. Facing increasing numbers of people seeking refugee status, by the 1990s many nations, especially in Europe, became more cautious in granting political asylum.

The Global Spread of Disease

Diseases, whether confined chiefly to a local area or traveling the routes of trade and migration, have produced major pandemics, or massive disease outbreaks, throughout history. Today, although modern medicine has eliminated diseases that had long plagued humanity, such as smallpox, leprosy, and polio, other diseases, such as cholera and malaria, still bedevil people with little access to health care. Cholera, a bacterial disease that easily crosses borders, still kills several thousand people a year in poor countries, and malaria, spread by mosquitoes, debilitates millions of people in tropical regions. In the early twenty-first century experts worried about a possible global spread of several viral diseases, perhaps killing millions of people, that passed from birds and poultry to humans. Both United Nations agencies and private organizations, such as Doctors Without Borders, have worked hard to reduce health threats and treat victims. But the travel of migrants, tourists,

business people, armies, truck drivers, sailors, and others continues to spread diseases.

The most deadly contemporary scourge affecting nations rich and poor, autoimmune deficiency syndrome, better known as AIDS, is caused by a virus known as HIV. AIDS is partly spread through the increased trade and travel associated with globalization, including migrant and transportation labor. The disease spreads through sexual contact, needle sharing by drug addicts, and selling or receiving blood. Poverty, which forces many women into prostitution, is also a factor in the spread of AIDS. For instance, long-distance truck drivers who visit prostitutes along their routes often spread the infection, especially in Africa and India. By 2005 some 42 million people around the world were infected with either HIV or AIDS, and 3.1 million died annually from AIDS, about a fifth of them children and one-third adult women, who were often infected by their husbands. In some African districts parental deaths left some 30 percent of children orphans, and as much as 30 percent of the adult population of some African nations was HIV positive. By contrast, the disease is less catastrophic in countries with less poverty and better health care and communications. Only 0.2 percent of Americans were infected, and the rate was even lower in Europe. The pandemic, compared by some experts to the Black Death seven centuries earlier, has presented an obstacle to economic development and has proved to be a particular disaster in India, Southeast Asia, and east, central and southern Africa.

Because most AIDS victims are in their twenties and thirties, in the worst affected countries the disease has killed or incapacitated the most highly trained and economically active section of the population. Treating AIDS patients also puts an added stress on the limited resources available for health care. Only a few African and Asian governments, however, among them Uganda and Thailand, have mounted education campaigns to convince people to take precautions to avoid getting the disease or to seek treatment. In some heavily affected nations, such as China, India, and Zimbabwe, governments fearing bad publicity and not wanting to devote resources to the afflicted have often hid the problem from public scrutiny. AIDS victims are often rejected by their families and communities, dying alone and neglected by society.

Cultures and Religions Across Borders

The spread of cultural products and religions across national borders and the creative mixing of these with local traditions have been hallmarks of the modern world. These trends have developed within the context of a global system in which people and ideas meet. The contacts between societies have produced new forms of entertainment. In societies around the world, popular culture, commonly produced for commercial purposes and spread by the mass media, such as radio, television, and films, has become a part of everyday life for billions of people. Spurred by globalization, religions have struggled for relevance but also found new believers and adapted to new environments.

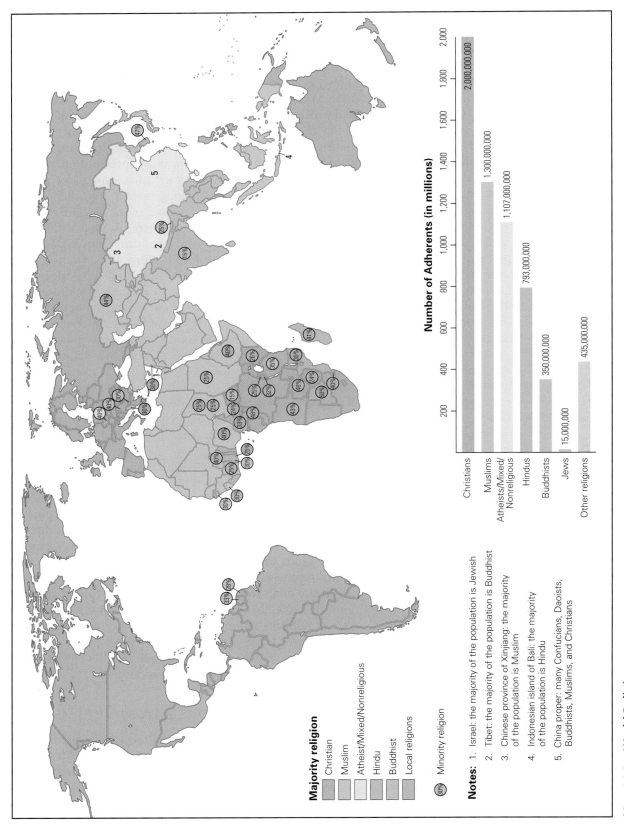

Majority religion
- Christian
- Muslim
- Atheist/Mixed/Nonreligious
- Hindu
- Buddhist
- Local religions

30% Minority religion

Notes:
1. Israel: the majority of the population is Jewish
2. Tibet: the majority of the population is Buddhist
3. Chinese province of Xinjiang: the majority of the population is Muslim
4. Indonesian island of Bali: the majority of the population is Hindu
5. China proper: many Confucians, Daoists, Buddhists, Muslims, and Christians

Number of Adherents (in millions)

Group	Number
Christians	2,000,000,000
Muslims	1,300,000,000
Atheists/Mixed/Nonreligious	1,107,000,000
Hindus	793,000,000
Buddhists	350,000,000
Jews	15,000,000
Other religions	435,000,000

Map 26.3 World Religions

Christianity has the most believers and is the dominant faith in the Americas, Oceania, Europe, Russia, and central and southern Africa. Most people in the northern half of Africa, western Asia, and Central Asia embrace Islam. Hindus are concentrated in India, and Buddhists in East and Southeast Asia.

Popular Cultures Societies have long exchanged cultural influences that have enriched local traditions. In the modern era, Western influences have been pervasive; yet, some of the modernization around the world that seems to reflect Westernization has remained superficial. Western videos, pop music recordings, jeans, and shopping malls that encourage consumption and present new options have attracted some youth in Asia, Africa, and Latin America, but their influence on the broader society, especially in the rural areas, is often more limited. No common world culture has emerged in this era. At the same time, Western technologies sometimes have served local needs. India, for instance, developed the world's largest film industry, producing some 1,000 films a year by 2002, three times more films than the next largest producers, the United States and Japan. And cheap, often pirated, audiocassettes in the 1970s, videocassettes in the 1980s, and DVDs in the 1990s enabled even many more poor people around the world to enjoy music and films while also enabling political or religious groups to spread their messages easily.

Modern media have reshaped people's lives, especially in cities, giving many societies a certain common denominator of experience. One observer in the 1990s noted the global popularity of television:

> Take a walk down any street, in any city or village, as the twilight fades and the darkness comes over the scene. Whether you are in London or Tokyo, Cairo or New York, Buenos Aires or Singapore, a small blue light will flicker at you from the unshuttered windows. These lights are the tiny knots in the seamless web of modern media.[18]

The mixing of cultures and the increasing role of the mass media have been reflected in popular music. Some popular musical styles, such as American jazz and Brazilian samba, emerged well before World War II, but most appeared after 1945. Anglo-American pop music styles, such as rock, jazz, and rap, all African American forms though having African roots, have found audiences all over the world. Vaclav Havel (vah-SLAV hah-VEL), the leader of the movement that overthrew Czech communism, credited the U.S. rock musician Frank Zappa with inspiring him to become an activist. Indeed, Havel had earlier in his life written songs for a Czech rock group. The South African leader, Nelson Mandela, enjoys listening to jazz, while rebellious youth in Manila and São Paulo use rap to express their feelings. Through the global reputations they often enjoy, and using the power of the mass media, Western pop stars also mount concerts to address issues such as racism, political prisoners, famine, and African poverty. Bono, the lead singer for the Irish rock band U2, uses his worldwide popularity to campaign among political leaders for causes such as debt relief for poor nations.

In the 1990s a British pop star who adopted an American Indian performance name, Apache Indian, demonstrated the creativity of transnational music by mixing West Indian reggae with American hip hop and *bhangra*, a folk music carried to Britain by immigrants from India and transformed into a distinctive pop music. Born into an Indian immigrant family in England, Apache Indian idolized both the American rocker Elvis Presley, popular in the 1950s, and the Jamaican reggae star Bob Marley. Apache Indian's often political songs express South Asian youth identity, criticize racism, and bridge tensions between blacks and South Asians in Britain. His songs also challenge caste and sexual attitudes in India. As he put it, "I want to speak on things that haven't been talked about before. I want to bring [problems] out in the open for discussion."[19]

Many forms of music have mixed indigenous and imported influences, often from outside the West. For example, Congolese popular music, which borrowed Latin American dance rhythms, gained audiences throughout Africa and Europe in the 1980s. Indian film music and Arab folk music have influenced the popular music of Southeast Asia and East Africa. Even pop music that does not cross borders can reflect a creative blending of traditions. A good case of this was *dangdut*, an Indonesian popular music that originated as a fusion of Western rock, Indian film music, and local folk music. The major dangdut star, Rhoma Irama (ROW-muh ih-RAH-muh), has sometimes faced arrest for offering political protests in songs that address poverty, human rights abuses, the struggle of the underdog, and the betrayal of the nationalist promise. Beginning in the 1970s he developed a huge following among poor rural folk and urban youth, who agree with the message of one of his more famous songs: "The rich get richer and the poor get poorer." Rhoma's music, which has a strong Islamic quality and promotes Muslim moral teachings, helped inspire the Islamic revival in Indonesia, but conservative Muslims have often condemned other dangdut singers for their erotic lyrics and suggestive performances.

Religious Dynamism Although in the modern era secular thought has become more popular than ever before in history, over three-quarters of the world's people identify with one or another universal religion with roots deep in the past. By 2000, the world contained almost 2 billion Christians, 1.3 billion Muslims, 800 million Hindus, and 350 million Buddhists. Nearly 900 million practiced a local faith, such as animism or Daoism, or professed no religion (see Map 26.3). Religion sometimes has become the basis for national identity, as in chiefly Roman Catholic Poland and Ireland and in Muslim Bangladesh and Pakistan.

Religious leaders have debated how much, if at all, their faiths need to change to better engage the contemporary world. Serious efforts at reform came, for instance, in the Catholic Church; in the 1960s Pope John XXIII (pope 1958–1963) engaged with the modern world by liberalizing church practices, such as having the mass in a vernacular language rather than Latin, and encouraged a more active dialogue with other churches and religions. Meanwhile, a movement arose among Catholic clergy and laypeople in Latin America, called liberation theology, that cooperated with socialist and communist groups to improve the lives of the poor. Catholic leaders disagreed on whether to support it. Muslim liberals and militants also confronted each other over which directions Islam should take, arguing over such issues as the role of women, relations with non-Muslims, and whether states with Muslim majorities should make Islamic law the basis of their legal systems. In sub-Saharan Africa and Southeast Asia, where Sunni Muslims are often nominal in their faith and tolerant toward other beliefs, some people have become more devout, and more men from these regions have gone to Cairo or Saudi Arabia to study religion, often returning home with more militant views.

The easy spread of ideas in the globalized world has worked to the advantage of portable creeds that are not dependent on one culture or setting. In many places, notably Africa, religions tied to local culture, usually some form of polytheism or animism, have faded while two universal religions, Christianity and Islam, fortified by missionary impulses, have gained wider followings. Protestants have evangelized and gained ground in predominantly Catholic Latin America. Protestants and Catholics have also competed with each other, and often with Muslims, for followers in Africa, Southeast Asia, and East Asia. Christian and Muslim missionaries have appealed to the downtrodden, suggesting that adopting their faith could lead not only to spiritual health but also to material wealth, and have recast their messages to recognize local cultural traditions.

At the same time, organized religion and its influence have declined in East Asia and much of the West. The Communists discouraged religious observance in China while increasing numbers of Japanese found neither their traditional faiths nor imported religions relevant to their lives. Meanwhile, Christian churches in Europe, Canada, and Australia competed with widespread lack of belief. Church attendance and membership in these societies fell dramatically between 1960 and the early twenty-first century. Traditional church attitudes have also competed with changing social attitudes. Even predominantly Catholic nations in Europe have legalized abortion and moved toward equal rights for homosexuals, policies opposed by the Catholic Church. Both the Netherlands, once a center for a puritanical form of Protestantism, and Spain, before the 1970s one of the staunchest Catholic nations, have approved same-sex marriage, as did Belgium and Canada.

Long a source of conflict, religion has now brought new tensions between members of different faiths. Sparked by political differences and sometimes traditional hostilities, some Christians and Muslims violently attacked each other in Indonesia, the Philippines, Yugoslavia, and West Africa. For example, hundreds of people were killed or wounded in Nigeria when rival Christians and Muslims, spurred by local political rivalries and increasing religious militancy, sporadically battled for control of several cities, leaving hundreds dead. Meanwhile, tensions between Muslims and Hindus sparked violence in India. Catholics and Protestants opposed each other in Northern Ireland and Uganda, while Sunni and Shi'a Muslims fought in Pakistan and western Asia. Governments controlled by Sunni Muslims sometimes discriminated against or persecuted Shi'ites. In Iraq, where some 60 percent of the population is Shi'a, the Sunni dictator, Saddam Hussein, restricted Shi'ite religious holidays, executed Shi'ites who opposed his regime, and allowed few Shi'ites into the government. After his regime was toppled by the U.S. invasion, conflicts between Shi'ites and Sunnis erupted, complicating U.S. efforts to restore political stability.

Religious militancy has grown among some believers. Some Muslim militants have turned the old notion of *jihad*, or struggle within believers to strengthen their faith, into a campaign for holy war, or physical combat in God's name, against unbelievers and countries or groups they consider anti-Muslim, and for the remodeling of secular states into Islamic ones. The militants, often known as Islamists or jihadis, appeal especially to the young and poor, who are often unemployed and embittered toward their governments and the West. Many Muslims oppose market capitalism, which they view as supporting the power of large, politically well-connected corporations, and Western cultural influence. The more puritanical Muslims despise the revealing clothing styles, open romantic behavior, independent women, and rebellious youth portrayed in Western television programs and movies, fearing that exposure to these influences will corrupt their children. Some Christians, especially in the United States, Latin America, and Africa, have turned to literal interpretations of the Bible, an approach labeled as fundamentalist, and formed proselytizing churches. These churches have often opposed secular culture, rejected scientific findings they deemed incompatible with biblical accounts, and condemned leftwing political and social movements, particularly those promoting socialism, feminism, legalized abortion, and homosexual rights. Christian and Islamic militancy has sparked similar movements in Buddhism, Hinduism, and Judaism, pitting the zealous believers against those with moderate, tolerant views.

Global Communications

A worldwide communications network has been a chief engine of globalization. The introduction of radio in the early 1900s and then tape recording and television in midcentury laid the basis for this network. These were followed by the invention of the transistor by three American physicists in 1947, which allowed for the miniaturization of electronics. In 1953 portable transistor radios became available and soon reached even remote villages, opening them to the news and culture of the wider world. Even villages without electricity could use transistor radios and cassette players. For example, by the 1960s in central Borneo, a densely forested island divided between Indonesia and Malaysia, isolated villagers, few of whom understood much English, listened to radio broadcasts from the United States, Britain, and Australia, and village youth enjoyed and could often sing the songs of Western pop musicians such as the British rock group the Beatles.

Technological breakthroughs provided the foundation for more rapid and widespread communications. For decades, U.S., British, and German engineers had been gradually building a foundation for computer technology. The first general purpose computers were built in 1948. In 1958 the first silicon microchips began a computer revolution that led several decades later to the first personal computers. By 2000 the world had more than 150 million personal computers with

Internet access, 330 million Internet users, and 1.6 billion web pages, all part of a vast network often termed the information superhighway. Every minute, 10 million electronically transmitted messages, or e-mail, are dispatched via computer. E-mail allows people in different countries, however distant, such as Canada and Malaysia, to communicate instantly with each other, exchanging views, sharing jokes, and forwarding articles, essays, and other writings or even music and films. An interested reader in Hong Kong, Ghana, or Finland can access online versions of newspapers, such as the *New York Times*, *Al Ahram* in Cairo, or the *Deccan Herald* in India. Along with computers, the rise of 24-hour cable news networks able to reach worldwide audiences, such as U.S.-based CNN (Cable News Network) and the Arab-language Al Jazeera, based in the Persian Gulf state of Qatar, widened access to diverse views. These trends have enriched people's understanding of the wider world.

The rapid evolution of media and information technology has had many consequences. For one, the development of fax communications, orbiting communications satellites, portable phones, electronic mail, and the worldwide computer web means that information can be transmitted around the globe beyond the reach of governments, undermining their power to shape their citizens' thinking. Repressive states seeking to limit information flow, such as Iran and Cuba, have banned satellite dish receivers and tried to jam access to controversial websites, including those used by political dissidents, but these efforts were only partly successful. In 2006 some U.S.-based Internet providers faced criticism for helping repressive governments such as China control the information flow and identify dissidents. Another major consequence is that technologies, especially the World Wide Web, have enhanced the value of education and of English, which has gradually become a world

language, like Latin in the Mediterranean zone 2,000 years ago and Arabic in the Islamic world 1,000 years ago. By 2004 some three-quarters of all websites were in English. Perhaps a quarter of the world's people know some English, and Asian countries with educated people fluent in English, such as India and Singapore, have an advantage in competing for high-technology industries. Both of these major trends have also enhanced the global exchange of scientific ideas. But in the poorest nations, only a lucky few have satellite dishes, fax machines, and networked computers, and these promising technologies have not changed the lives of peasants and low-wage workers. Furthermore, many nations resented the strong U.S. influence over the Internet, including the power to allocate web addresses and domains.

Global Movements

The increasing links between far-flung peoples have allowed for social and political movements originating in different countries and independent of governments to transcend borders and link to other movements with similar interests. A wide variety of transnational organizations has emerged to promote issues such as the treatment of political prisoners, women's rights, and antiracism. As an example, Amnesty International, based in Britain, publicizes the plight of people imprisoned solely for their political views and activities, such as the Burmese opposition leader Aung San Suu Kyi (AWNG sahn soo CHEE) and, during the Cold War, the Soviet dissident scientist Andrei Sakharov (SAH-kuh-RAWF), around the world, organizing letter writing and pressure campaigns to seek their release. Other movements have addressed globalization. For instance, the World Social Forum was formed in 2001 and has met annually in Brazil. This group brings together

Internet Cafe in Thailand In this photo, a waiter at a cyberspace café, operated by the Swiss multinational ice cream company, Häagen Dazs, in Bangkok, Thailand, helps a young Thai woman navigate one of the café's computers. (AP/Wide World Photos)

nongovernment organizations and activists who oppose globalizing free market capitalism and what they view as the imperialism of industrialized nations. They believe globalization undermines workers' rights and environmental protection.

As the world became more closely linked, social or political movements or upheavals in one nation or region sometimes spread widely. For example, during the 1960s, students, workers, and political radicals in various nations organized protests against the U.S. war in Vietnam, racism, unresponsive governments, capitalism, and other concerns. In 1968 demonstrations, marches, and strikes intensified around the world. These movements were not coordinated and addressed largely local grievances, but young protesters were often influenced by the same writers, music, and ideas. The more radical protesters revered Marxist icons, for example, wearing t-shirts celebrating Che Guevara (guh-VAHR-uh) (1928–1967), an Argentinean-born revolutionary who helped Fidel Castro take power in Cuba; Guevara became a communist martyr when he was killed while organizing a guerrilla army in Bolivia. However, other protesters looked to noncommunists or even anticommunists, such as the dissidents—often devout Catholics—who opposed the communist regime in Poland, such as the labor leader Lech Walesa (leck wa-LEN-za). To varying degrees the turbulence affected over a dozen countries, from the United States and Mexico to France, Czechoslovakia, and Japan. Not all governments, however, tolerated the activism. For instance, when thousands of demonstrators shouting "Mexico, Freedom" took to the streets of Mexico City to demand democracy and protest police brutality, the police opened fire, killing dozens of protesters. "There was a general stampede," noted one student protester, "because all hell broke loose and a hail of bullets started raining down on us from all directions."[20] In the wake of the 1968 activism, environmental, peace, workers' rights, homosexual rights, and feminist movements grew, chiefly but not only in industrialized nations.

Women have been particularly active in seeking to expand their rights. Although most women's organizations work within national boundaries, some activists have placed women's issues on the international agenda. The United Nations periodically sponsors global conferences on women's issues such as gender equality and eliminating violence against women. However, women who attend international conferences, divided by culture and by whether they come from a rich or poor country, do not always agree on goals and strategies. In the United Nation's fourth World Conference on Women, held in China in 1995, the 40,000 delegates divided sharply on priorities. Delegates from rich nations wanted to expand women's employment options, social freedom, and control over their bodies, while Asian, African, and Latin American delegates were often chiefly interested in making their families more healthy and economically secure. One delegate from India described the goals of U.S. delegates as irrelevant to Indian women: "They ask for abortion rights. We ask for safe drinking water and basic health care."[21] While abortion remained a controversial issue in most of the world, strongly opposed by many religious groups, it became legal in most Western and many Asian nations. In Latin America, which, despite stringent laws against it, has the world's second highest rate of abortion after eastern Europe, women's groups pushing for legalization were gaining support in several nations by the early 2000s. Women also won the right to vote in most democratic or semidemocratic nations.

Yet, despite disagreements, women have worked across borders on issues affecting all societies, such as preventing violence against women. For example, women activists and their male supporters from Muslim and Western nations fought, among other practices, the tradition common in some conservative Muslim societies of jailing or killing women for adultery while exonerating the man responsible. In 2005 Mukhtaran Bibi (MOOK-tahr-an BIH-bee), an illiterate woman from an impoverished Pakistani village without electricity, gained worldwide sympathy for her resistance to male brutality. As part of a village dispute involving her family, the tribal council had ruled that she be gang-raped to punish her family. Instead of following custom by ending the "disgrace" through suicide, however, she bravely pursued the rapists, men from another family, in court. They were convicted, and she used the money awarded her by the court to start two village schools, one for boys and one for girls. When a higher court then overturned the men's convictions, her courageous refusal to accept the verdict, a dangerous step in her patriarchal society, caused an international outcry. While the Pakistan government tried to suppress the controversy and forbade Mukhtaran from traveling abroad, men and women around the world, alerted by news accounts and Internet appeals, donated money and made her a symbol of the need for women's rights. Mukhtaran Bibi inspired millions everywhere with her courage and faith in education and justice.

Global Terrorism

Terrorism, small-scale but violent attacks aimed at undermining a government or demoralizing a population, intensified in the late twentieth and early twenty-first century, expanding to global dimensions and reshaping world politics. Terrorism, which has often targeted civilians as well as government officials and soldiers, has a long history, going back many centuries, and became common in the twentieth century. At the end of the century terrorist networks had formed which threatened the global order.

The Rise of Terrorism

For centuries various groups and states used terrorism to support their goals. For example, in the 1920s Vietnamese nationalists tossed explosives and shot at the residences, offices, and police stations used by the French colonizers. After 1945 Palestinians under Israeli control, Basque nationalists in Spain, and Irish nationalists in Britain, among others, engaged in terrorism for their causes. Some states also carried out or sponsored terrorism against unfriendly governments or political movements. For example, South Africa's white minority government organized

---

terrorism Small-scale but violent attacks aimed at undermining a government or demoralizing a population.

or financed insurgencies that opposed the Marxist governments of Angola and Mozambique, resulting in thousands of civilian deaths. Similarly, the United States sponsored terrorism against leftist-ruled Nicaragua in the 1980s, helping form a military force, known as the *Contras,* that often attacked civilian targets, such as rural schools, day care centers, and clinics operated by the government.

While terrorism has often remained local in scope, an increasingly interconnected world has spurred some terrorist organizations to operate on a global level, forming networks that have branches in many countries. The most active of these networks, formed by militant Islamists, have exploited communication and transportation networks to operate across national borders, capitalizing on widespread Muslim anger at Israel and U.S. foreign policies. Muslim terrorist groups became increasingly active during the 1970s and 1980s in Egypt, Algeria, and Lebanon. Aiming to undermine Israel, their own secular governments, and these governments' Western backers, the terrorists attacked politicians, police, Western residents and tourists, and Israeli and U.S. targets.

As a result, terrorism became a growing threat to life in the Middle East. For example, the *Hezbollah* movement in Lebanon, formed by Shi'ite Arabs opposed to the U.S.-backed Lebanese government and to U.S. support for Israel, used suicide bombers driving explosive-filled trucks to destroy the U.S. Embassy and a Marine Corps base in Beirut, killing several hundred Americans. Later, to oppose Israeli occupation of Arab lands and demoralize Israelis, Palestinian militants strapped explosives to their bodies and detonated them in Israeli buses and businesses. Outraged by the killing and wounding of hundreds of Israeli civilians—both Jewish and Arab—the Israelis responded with force, killing or arresting Palestinians and expelling families of suspected militants from their homes, often bulldozing the houses into rubble. The poet Hanan Ashrawi (HA-non uh-SHRAH-wee), a Christian Palestinian nationalist, condemned the suicide bombings but also lamented the earlier Israeli destruction of her family's property, which had been seized and allocated to Jewish settlers: "Have you seen a stone house die? It sighs, then wraps itself around its gutted heart and lays itself to rest."[22] Divided by politics, Israelis and Palestinians have shared the bitter experience of grieving for those lost in the chronic violence, among them innocent women and children.

Terrorist Networks The Soviet military intervention in 1979 to support a pro-Soviet government in mostly Muslim Afghanistan provided the spark for forming a global network of Islamist terrorists. Islamic militants from the Middle East and Pakistan flocked to Afghanistan to assist the Muslim Afghan insurgents resisting the Soviets. In 1988 the most militant of the foreign fighters began to come together in a jihadi organization known as *Al Qaeda* ("The Base"). Al Qaeda's main leader was the Saudi Osama bin Laden (b. 1957), who came from an extremely wealthy family—his Yemen-born father had made billions in the Saudi construction industry—and had been trained as an engineer. Bin Laden used his wealth to support the Afghan rebels, mostly devout Muslims, who

were also funded and armed by the United States as part of its Cold War rivalry with the USSR. After the Soviets abandoned Afghanistan in 1989, bin Laden used his supporters among the foreign fighters to set up Al Qaeda cells in Saudi Arabia, whose government he viewed as corrupt, and to target Egypt and Iraq, whose secular regimes suppressed Islamic militants. To recruit, support, and communicate with members, Al Qaeda used the instruments of the information superhighway, publicizing their cause by setting up websites, using e-mail and satellite phones, and releasing videotapes to cable news networks of bin Laden's messages.

Eventually Al Qaeda looked beyond the Middle East for targets. In the mid-1990s the Afghanistan-based bin Laden, a ruthless man willing to kill innocent people in pursuit of his goals, began to plot terrorist efforts against his former ally in the Afghan resistance, the United States, whose military bases in Saudi Arabia, support for repressive Arab governments, and close alliance with Israel enraged many Arabs. Viewing the U.S. command of vast economic and military power as the greatest barrier to his ambition of revitalizing the Islamic world by spreading the Islamist agenda and enhancing his own power, bin Laden argued that "to kill the Americans and their allies is an individual duty for every Muslim who can do it in any country in which it is possible to do so."[23] Most Muslims rejected such violent views. Al Qaeda or related groups sponsored attacks on U.S. targets, such as the embassies in Kenya and Tanzania, causing hundreds of casualties.

On September 11, 2001, Al Qaeda members hijacked four U.S. commercial airliners and crashed them into New York's World Trade Center and the Pentagon near Washington, D.C., killing over 3,000 people, mostly civilians. The attacks shocked Americans, unused to terrorism at home, as well as people everywhere who opposed indiscriminate killing. U.S. president George W. Bush responded by declaring a war on terrorism. U.S. forces attacked Al Qaeda bases in Afghanistan, and then occupied the country, whose government, controlled by Islamists who had fought the Soviets, shielded bin Laden, but the United States failed to capture bin Laden and still faced resistance from Islamic militants.

In 2003 the United States, claiming that Saddam Hussein's Iraq was closely linked to Al Qaeda and possessed weapons of mass destruction, invaded Iraq, removed Saddam's brutal, despotic government, and imposed a U.S. military occupation. Britain provided the chief support for the U.S. effort. The U.S. troops, however, found no evidence of any Saddam ties to Al Qaeda or any weapons of mass destruction. The occupation sparked an insurgency, including suicide bombings and unleashed sectarian divisions that hindered the U.S. efforts—supported by many Iraqis—to stabilize and rebuild Iraq. While most of the insurgents were Iraqis, mostly Sunni Muslims fearing domination by the Shi'ite majority, Islamists from other countries flocked to Iraq to attack Americans and help destabilize the country. The U.S. invasion and occupation, and the resistance to it, killed tens of thousands of Iraqi civilians, resulted in over 15,000 U.S. casualties, and kept a large U.S. military force tied down in Iraq. Whether the war in Iraq helped or harmed the U.S.-led war against terrorism remained subject to debate. The war alienated many

U.S. allies and, like the earlier U.S. conflict in Vietnam, was unpopular around the world. Meanwhile, capitalizing on anti-U.S. sentiments among Muslims, Al Qaeda spawned loosely affiliated terrorist groups, often operating without direct Al Qaeda guidance.

Terrorism by militant Muslims had direct and indirect consequences for societies around the world. Al Qaeda or related groups launched terrorist attacks on several continents, from Spain and Britain to Indonesia, Kenya, and Morocco. Nations with despotic governments, such as China, Egypt, and Uzbekistan, used the threat of terrorism as a reason to restrict civil liberties. Human rights concerns faded amid the Western obsession with terrorism. In 1993 a German historian had correctly predicted the challenges ahead in the post–Cold War world: "We are at the beginning of a new era, characterized by great insecurity, permanent crisis and the absence of any kind of *status quo*. We must realize that we find ourselves in one of those crises of world history."[24]

SECTION SUMMARY

- In the new global village, millions of people have immigrated to foreign countries seeking greater economic opportunity or an escape from insufferable conditions at home, including political repression, famine, and civil war.

- Modern medicine has eliminated many diseases, but cholera and malaria are still a serious problem, and AIDS has seriously affected India and areas of Southeast Asia and Africa.

- Western consumer culture has spread around the world, while musical forms from different cultures have mingled and musicians and performers have expressed political and often controversial views.

- The world's major religious traditions have remained numerically strong, and some have worked to adapt to the modern world; while representatives of rival religions have fought for control of various areas and many Muslims and Christians have grown more fundamentalist.

- Worldwide communication was facilitated by technologies such as radio, television, and the Internet, making a vast array of information available, even in countries such as Iran and Cuba, whose governments attempted to limit its availability.

- Increased global communication led to political movements that transcended conventional borders, such as Amnesty International, the 1968 youth protests, and women's rights movements.

- Terrorism, which had been used throughout the twentieth century by groups such as the Palestinians, the Basques, and the Irish, became more deadly, culminating in the radical Muslim group Al Qaeda's 2001 attack on the United States.

Online Study Center   ACE the Test

Chapter Summary

The later twentieth century proved turbulent. Nationalism spread outside of Europe and the Americas, leading to decolonization. During the 1950s and 1960s most of the Western colonies gained their independence through negotiations, the threat of violence, or armed struggle, and social revolutionaries gained power in some nations. However, the West maintained a strong economic presence in many former colonies. The rivalry between the United States and the USSR also shaped the global system, generating a Cold War in which the two superpowers faced each other indirectly or through surrogates. The powerful United States had a large group of allies and sometimes intervened in Asian and Latin American nations, while the USSR occupied eastern Europe. The collapse of the Communist bloc and then the USSR allowed the United States to become the world's lone superpower.

The world was also shaped by the increasing forces of globalization, with its unprecedented flow of money, products, information, and ideas across national borders. The global economy grew rapidly but did not spread its benefits equally. As industrialization spread, most Western and some Asian and Latin American nations prospered, but poor nations struggled to escape underdevelopment and raise living standards. A billion people remained mired in deep poverty. Meanwhile millions of people migrated, social and political movements addressed local and global problems, universal religions gained new converts, and the information superhighway and other technological innovations linked millions of people in new ways. Terrorists also took advantage of globalism, as new international terrorist networks challenged governments and prompted a reshaping of world politics.

Online Study Center   Improve Your Grade   Flashcards

Key Terms

First World	nuclear weapons	Green Revolution
Second World	globalization	desertification
Third World	multinational	global village
Fourth World	corporations	terrorism
Cold War	Third Industrial	
guerrilla warfare	Revolution	

Suggested Reading

Books

Ali, Tariq. *The Clash of Fundamentalisms: Crusades, Jihads and Modernity.* London: Verso, 2003. A controversial but powerful examination, by a London-based Indian writer, of Western policies and Islamic movements around the world.

Axford, Barrie. *The Global System: Economics, Politics and Culture.* New York: St. Martin's, 1995. A comprehensive, thoughtful review by a British scholar of approaches to understanding the global system.

Crossley, Pamela Kyle, et al. *Global Society: The World Since 1900.* Boston: Houghton Mifflin, 2004. A comprehensive survey.

DeFronzo, James. *Revolutions and Revolutionary Movements.* Boulder, Colo.: Westview Press, 1991. Useful surveys of revolutions and the societies they made, with case studies of Russia, China, Vietnam, Cuba, Nicaragua, Iran, and South Africa.

Enloe, Cynthia. *Bananas, Beaches and Bases: Making Feminist Sense of International Relations*, 2nd ed. Berkeley: University of California Press, 2001. A provocative examination of women's experiences in global politics.

Ehrenreich, Barbara and Arlie Russell Hochschild, eds. *Global Women: Nannies, Maids, and Sex Workers in the New Economy.* Provocative look at the feminization of the migrant work force.

Hunt, Michael H. *The World Transformed, 1945 to the Present.* Boston: Bedford/St. Martin's, 2004. A readable and up-to-date survey.

Kechner, Frank J. and John Boli. *World Culture: Origins and Consequences.* Malden, M.A.: Blackwell, 2005. Examines the impact of globalization on world culture.

LaFeber, Walter. *America, Russia and the Cold War, 1945–1992*, 9th ed. New York: McGraw-Hill, 2002. An excellent examination of the Cold War around the world.

Mazlish, Bruce, and Akira Iriye, eds. *The Global History Reader.* New York: Routledge, 2005. A provocative set of essays on global trends in the twentieth century, from the information revolution and environmental change to human rights and terrorism.

McNeill, J. R. *Something New Under the Sun: An Environmental History of the Twentieth-Century World.* New York: W. W. Norton, 2000. An outstanding examination of the interface between societies and environmental change.

Ponting, Clive. *The Twentieth Century: A World History.* New York: Henry Holt, 1998. A valuable thematic examination by a British scholar.

Reynolds, David. *One World Divisible: A Global History Since 1945.* New York: W. W. Norton, 2001. A comprehensive survey.

Sen, Amartya. *Identity and Violence: The Illusion of Destiny.* New York: Norton, 2006. An influential Indian economist's views on globalization, freedom, violence, and other global issues.

Wang, Gungwu, ed. *Global History and Migrants.* Boulder: Westview, 1997. Essays on recent population movements.

Weiss, Thomas G. et al. *The United Nations and Changing World Politics,* 3rd ed. Boulder: Westview, 2001. Examines the history and roles of the United Nations.

Westad, Odd Arne. *The Global Cold War.* New York: Cambridge University Press, 2005. Provocative study by a Norwegian scholar.

Websites

Global Problems and the Culture of Capitalism (**http://faculty.plattsburgh.edu/richard.robbins/legacy/**). An outstanding site, aimed at undergraduates, with a wealth of resources.

The Globalization Website (**http://www.emory.edu/SOC/globalization/**). A useful site with many resources and essays on globalization.

Human Rights Watch (**http://www.hrw.org/wr2k3/introduction.html**). The website of a major human rights organization that reports on the entire world.

Modern History Sourcebook (**http://www.fordham.edu/halsall/mod/modsbook.html**). A very extensive online collection of historical documents and secondary materials.

United Nations Environment Program (**http://www.unep.org/geo2000/ov-e/index.htm**). Provides access to United Nations reports on the world's environmental problems.

CHAPTER 27

East Asian Resurgence, 1945–Present

CHAPTER OUTLINE

- Mao's Revolutionary China
- Chinese Modernization
- The Remaking of Japan
- The Little Dragons in the Asian Resurgence

▪ PROFILE
Xue Xinran, a Chinese Voice for Women

▪ WITNESS TO THE PAST
A Japanese Generation Gap

Online Study Center

This icon will direct you to interactive activities and study materials on the website: college.hmco.com/pic/lockard1e

The China Stock Exchange The East Asian nations enjoyed an economic resurgence in this era. Since the 1980s, China has boasted the world's fastest growing economy and a booming stock exchange. (Wally McNamee/Corbis)

Once China's destiny is in the hands of the people, China, like the sun rising in the east, will illuminate every corner with a brilliant flame, and build a new, powerful and prosperous [society].

MAO ZEDONG, CHINESE COMMUNIST LEADER[1]

On October 1, 1949, after some two decades of directing brutal warfare against the Japanese invaders and the Chinese government, Mao Zedong (maow dzuh-dong) (1893–1976), the Chinese Communist leader, was driven into downtown Beijing, China's capital, accompanied by a dusty band of soldiers from the Communist military force, the People's Liberation Army. Mao, fifty-five years old, the son of a peasant family, had never been out of China and had spent the previous twenty-two years living in remote rural areas. Ahead of Mao's car rolled a Sherman tank, built in Detroit and originally donated by the United States to the Republic of China, the government headed by Jiang Jieshi (better known in the West as Chiang Kai-shek) (1887–1975), to help crush Mao's Communist forces. But Chiang's army had lost to Mao's troops, and the president had fled to the large offshore island of Taiwan. Wearing a new suit, Mao climbed to the top of the Gate of Heavenly Peace, the entrance to the Forbidden City of the Qing emperors overlooking Beijing's spacious Tiananmen Square. Mao probably enjoyed this moment of triumph. He and his comrades had sacrificed much to reach this pinnacle of power. Millions of Chinese jammed the square to hear their new ruler announce the founding of a new Communist government, called the People's Republic of China. Referring to a century of corrupt governments and humiliation and domination by Western nations and Japan, Mao thanked all those who, starting with the Opium War fought against the British in the mid-1800s, had "laid down their lives in the many struggles against domestic and foreign enemies," finally proclaiming: "The Chinese people have stood up. Nobody will insult us again."[2]

The formation of the People's Republic marked a watershed in the history of China, the rest of East Asia, and the world. The new government brought to an end a century of severe social and political instability, caused in part by the activities of foreign nations and China's inability to defend itself against imperialism. Its Communist leaders were committed to the revolutionary transformation of the society while making China respected abroad once again. Given China's size and a population—1.3 billion by 2005—greater than that of North America, Europe, and Russia combined, any major transition there had global significance. By the early twenty-first century Mao was long gone and many of his policies discarded, but China, with a booming economy, had reclaimed some of the political and economic status it had lost two centuries earlier.

But Chinese were not the only East Asians to enjoy a resurgence with a global impact. In the 1980s East Asian and outside observers referred to the **Pacific Rim**, the economically dynamic Asian countries on the edge of the Pacific Basin: China, Japan, South Korea, Taiwan, and several Southeast Asian nations. These observers also predicted that the twenty-first century would be the **Pacific Century**, marked by a shift of global economic power from Europe and North America to the Pacific Rim, whose export-driven nations seemed poised to dominate a post–Cold War era where economic power outweighed military might. Reflecting this view, an Australian study concluded that the center of gravity of world economic life, for centuries located in the eastern half of Eurasia, had shifted away as Europe and the Atlantic economy rose, and then in the 1990s had moved back toward a resurgent Asia, poised to dominate the modern world economy. Economic crises, especially an Asian financial collapse in 1997, and changing world politics have challenged the Pacific Century concept, but China, Japan, and their neighbors have remained major players in the global system.

FOCUS QUESTIONS

1. How did Maoism transform Chinese society?

2. What factors explain the dramatic rise of Chinese economic power in the world since 1978?

3. How did Japan rise from the ashes of defeat in World War II to become a global economic powerhouse?

4. What policies led to the rise of the "Little Dragon" nations and their dynamic economies?

 Mao's Revolutionary China

How did Maoism transform Chinese society?

The Chinese Revolution that brought the Chinese Communists to power in 1949 was one of the three greatest upheavals in modern world history. The first, the French Revolution (1789), destroyed the remnants of feudalism throughout western Europe and its leaders extolled the rights of the common people. The second, the Russian Revolution of 1917, charted a noncapitalist path to industrialization. Both events swept away old social classes and ruling elites. China's revolution joined these in remaking a major world society while restoring China's status as a major country. The Communists built a strong government that made China the most experi-mental nation on earth, veering from one innovative policy to another in an attempt to renovate Chinese life and resolve problems of underdevelopment. The People's Republic of China created a new model of economic development different from both Western-dominated capitalism, adopted by most poor nations, and the highly centralized Soviet Communism. But the path was littered with conflict and repression. Furthermore, the Chinese, like all societies, were products of their history. Even under Communist rule China remained partly an ancient empire and partly a modern nation, and its leaders often behaved much like the emperors of old in their autocratic exercise of power.

The Communist Triumph

The U.S. defeat of Japan in 1945 removed the common enemy of both of China's major political factions, Mao's Communists and Chiang Kai-shek's nationalist government, sparking a fierce civil war between them for control of China. Chiang disdained Mao as an unpolished peasant with earthy language, while Mao despised Chiang, from a wealthy landlord family, for favoring the rich, yet both men shared some personality traits, such as patriotism, an autocratic style, and hunger for power. Chiang's 3.7-million-man army vastly outnumbered

Pacific Rim   The economically dynamic Asian countries on the edge of the Pacific Basin: China, Japan, South Korea, Taiwan, and several Southeast Asian nations.

Pacific Century   The possible shift of global economic power from Europe and North America to the Pacific Rim in the twenty-first century.

	China	**Japan**	**Korea and Taiwan**
1940	**1945–1949** Chinese civil war **1949** Chinese Communist triumph	**1946–1952** U.S. occupation of Japan	**1950–1953** Korean War
1960	**1960** Sino-Soviet split **1966–1976** Great Proletarian Cultural Revolution **1978** Four Modernizations policy	**1960s–1989** Rapid economic growth	
1980			**1997** Asian financial collapse

the 900,000 Communist troops. The United States lavished military aid on Chiang and provided planes and trucks to transport his soldiers in order to occupy as much Chinese territory as possible. The Communists, aided by the Soviet Union (USSR), concentrated on north China and Manchuria. In trying to block Mao's forces, however, Chiang overstretched his supply lines. Chiang's Republic experienced, among other problems, a rapid decline in the value of Chinese currency that demoralized the population. The Chinese sought change, especially a less corrupt government, and many of them came to view the Communist movement as a more honest alternative to Chiang's Nationalist Party.

In the villages that they controlled, the Communists promoted a social revolution, known as the "turning over," by encouraging villagers to denounce local landlords, transferring land from richer to poorer peasants, replacing government-appointed leaders with elected village councils, and protecting battered wives. For example, encouraged to air their grievances by "speaking pains to recall pains" in village meetings, women warned abusive men to mend their ways or face punishment or arrest. Inevitably the release of pent-up rage against violent husbands or greedy landlords who mistreated tenants led to excesses, such as angry crowds beating them to death.

The military and political tide turned against the Republic. In 1948 Chiang's troops in Manchuria surrendered to the Communists. To revive Chiang's prospects, the United States pressured him unsuccessfully to broaden his political base with democratic reforms. Some American leaders demanded that the United States send troops to help Chiang, but others concluded that his regime had lost too much popular support to win the conflict. Through 1949 the Communists took the major cities of north China and pushed Chiang's army south. Finally Chiang fled to the island of Taiwan, along with thousands of troops and 2 million supporters. On Taiwan, with massive U.S. aid, the leaders of the relocated Republic of China developed a successful capitalist strategy for economic growth. Meanwhile, mainland China's history now moved in a direction very different from that of Chiang's Republic of China.

A New Economy and Government

The key question confronting the Chinese Communists after 1949 was how to achieve rapid economic development in an overpopulated, battered country. Two decades of war had ruined the economy, leaving little capital for industrialization. Unlike Britain and France in the nineteenth century, China had no overseas empire to exploit for economic resources. The new leaders did not want loans and foreign investment that might reduce their independence and lead to a debt trap. Furthermore, they faced a powerful enemy: propelled by alarm at Mao's policies and anti-Communist Cold War concerns, the United States launched an economic boycott to shut China off from international trade, refused diplomatic recognition, and surrounded China with military bases. Isolated, China created its own models of economic and political development.

Development Models Between 1949 and 1976 China followed two different models of economic development, each with its own priorities and consequences. The first, Stalinism, a system based on the Soviet model of central planning, heavy industry, a powerful bureaucracy, and a managerial system, dominated the early years (1949–1957) (see Chronology: China Since 1945). China received some Soviet aid in the 1950s, but otherwise the Chinese Communists financed development before the late 1970s through self-reliance. This meant withdrawal from the global system. As in Japan in the late nineteenth century and the Soviet Union in the early twentieth, the state took the lead, emphasizing austerity and acquiring capital from the people by making them work hard for low wages, in hopes that future generations would live better. In the Stalinist years the Communists abolished private ownership of business and industry and transferred land to poor peasants. Soon they began collectivizing the rural economy into cooperatives, in which peasants helped each other and shared tools. As in the Soviet Union, the emphasis on state directive fostered the rise of a new privileged

CHRONOLOGY

China Since 1945

1945–1949	Chinese civil war
1949	Chinese Communist triumph
1949–1957	Stalinist model
1950	Occupation of Tibet
1950	New marriage law
1950–1953	Korean War
1957–1961	First use of Maoist model
1958–1961	Great Leap Forward
1960	Sino-Soviet split
1966–1976	Great Proletarian Cultural Revolution
1972	Nixon's trip to Beijing
1976	Death of Mao Zedong
1976	Arrest of Gang of Four
1978	Four Modernizations policy
1978	Normalization of U.S.-China diplomatic relations
1978–1989	Market socialism
1978–1997	Deng Xiaoping era
1989	Beijing Massacre
1989	Introduction of market Leninism
1997	Return of Hong Kong to China

elite in the government and in the ruling Communist Party, which cracked down on dissent.

By the late 1950s Mao, growing disenchanted with Stalinism, introduced a second model of development based on a unique synthesis of Marxism and Chinese thought, known as Maoism, that emphasized the mass mobilization of the population. Under Maoism, which was China's guiding ideology from 1957 to 1961 and then again from 1966 to 1976, the Chinese people were mobilized for development projects, such as building dams. Pest elimination also became a priority. For instance, everyone was issued fly swatters and asked to kill as many flies as possible in hopes of reducing disease. The Communists also tried to reverse the ecological instability of recent centuries through massive tree-planting campaigns. However, Mao rejected the notion that China's fast-growing population was harming the environment.

Mao reorganized the rural economy into **communes**, large agricultural units that combined many families and villages into a common administrative system for pooling resources and labor. A commune could build and operate a factory, secondary school, and hospital, which would be impractical for a single village to have. The communes raised agricultural productivity, especially of grain crops such as rice and wheat, eliminated landlords, and promoted social and economic equality. Mao located industry in rural areas, thus keeping the peasants at home rather than fostering movement to cities, as happened in other countries. He held up a commune in the mountainous northwest as the model of self-reliance and revolutionary zeal; the commune claimed that, inspired by Mao's vision, it had increased agricultural production fivefold. Years later Chinese learned that the production figures had been inflated and that the commune had insufficient food.

The most radical Maoist policy was the **Great Leap Forward** (1958–1961), an ambitious attempt to industrialize China rapidly and end poverty through collective efforts. Farmers and workers were ordered to build small iron furnaces in their backyards, courtyards, and gardens and to spend their free time turning everything from cutlery to old bicycles into steel. The slogan "Achieve More, Better, Faster" swept through the nation. But the poorly conceived campaign, pushing the people too hard, nearly wrecked the economy and, along with disastrous weather, caused 30 million people to starve. One of Mao's critics in the Communist Party leadership charged: "Grains scattered on the ground, potato leaves withered; Strong young people have left to smelt iron, only children and old women reaped the crops; How can they pass the coming year?"[3] These failures undermined Mao's influence, bringing moderate policies in the early 1960s.

Chinese Politics   As in the USSR, the Communist Party, led by Mao as chairman, dominated the political system; party members occupied all key positions in the government and military down to village leaders. Using the slogan "Politics Takes Command," the Communists emphasized ideology, making political values pervasive. All Chinese were required to become members of political discussion groups, which met regularly in village or community centers. While people were supposedly free to voice their opinions, party activists monitored the discussions and reported dissenters. Political education was integrated into the schools, work units, and even leisure activities. Students often spent their school vacations working in factories or on farms. The party also sought to eradicate inequalities and to alter thought patterns and attitudes, emphasizing the interests of the group over those of the individual. To eliminate class distinctions, officials and intellectuals had to perform physical labor, such as

---

communes   Large agricultural units introduced by Mao Zedong that combined many families and villages into a common system for pooling resources and labor.

Great Leap Forward   Mao Zedong's ambitious attempt to industrialize China rapidly and end poverty through collective efforts.

Honoring Chairman Mao Since the beginning of Communist rule in China in 1949, this giant portrait of Mao Zedong, the chairman of the Chinese Communist Party, has hung on the Gate of Heavenly Peace, the entrance to the Forbidden City of the Qing dynasty emperors, in the heart of Beijing. (Peter Guttman/Corbis)

laying bricks for house construction or spreading manure to fertilize farm fields, so that they would understand the experience of the workers and peasants.

Mao's system required massive social control, enabled by a vast police apparatus; millions suspected of opposing the Communists were harassed, jailed, exiled, or killed. Even Communist sympathizers, such as the outspoken feminist writer Ding Ling (1902–1986), were purged after falling out of official favor: in 1958 Ding was sent to a remote labor camp to raise chickens and was also imprisoned between 1970 and 1975. In exchange for accepting its policies, the state promised everyone the "five guarantees" of food, clothes, fuel, education, and a decent burial. But thousands of people, wanting more personal happiness than the system allowed, fled to British-ruled Hong Kong over the years.

Maoist China in the World

The Communists restored China's status as a major world power (see Map 27.1), with only some setbacks, and remembering the domestic chaos between the 1830s and 1940s, pursued a foreign policy that maximized stability at home. Mao reasserted Chinese sovereignty in outlying areas of China and in 1950 sent armies to occupy Tibet, whose people, although conquered and incorporated into China by the Qing dynasty in the 1600s, were culturally and historically distinct from the

Chinese and had broken away from China in 1912. Most Tibetans, however, opposed Chinese rule, sparking periodic unrest. The Chinese suppression of a Tibetan revolt led the highest Tibetan Buddhist leader, the Dalai Lama (DAH-lie LAH-mah) (b. 1935), to flee to India in 1958. Devout Tibetans revered the Dalai Lama as both a spiritual and political leader, the reincarnation of previous Dalai Lamas and therefore someone to be worshiped. In exile the Dalai Lama became a defiant symbol of Tibetan resistance to Chinese rule, traveling the world to rally support for the Tibetan cause while promoting Buddhist ethics and world peace, for which he won the Nobel Peace Prize in 1989. China failed to reclaim another former Qing-ruled territory, Mongolia, which in 1924 had become a Communist state allied to, and protected by, the USSR.

China faced major challenges in foreign affairs. In 1950 China, which supported the Communist North Korean government installed in 1948, was drawn into the Korean War between the USSR-backed North Korea and United Nations forces led by the United States, sent to defend pro-U.S. South Korea. When the United Nations forces pushed the North Korean army toward China's border, despite Chinese warnings to stay away, and the U.S. commander, General Douglas MacArthur, talked recklessly of occupying North Korea and carrying the offensive across the Yalu River into China, the Chinese, feeling endangered, entered the conflict. Mao caught U.S. leaders by surprise by dispatching 300,000 troops into Korea, and the Chinese

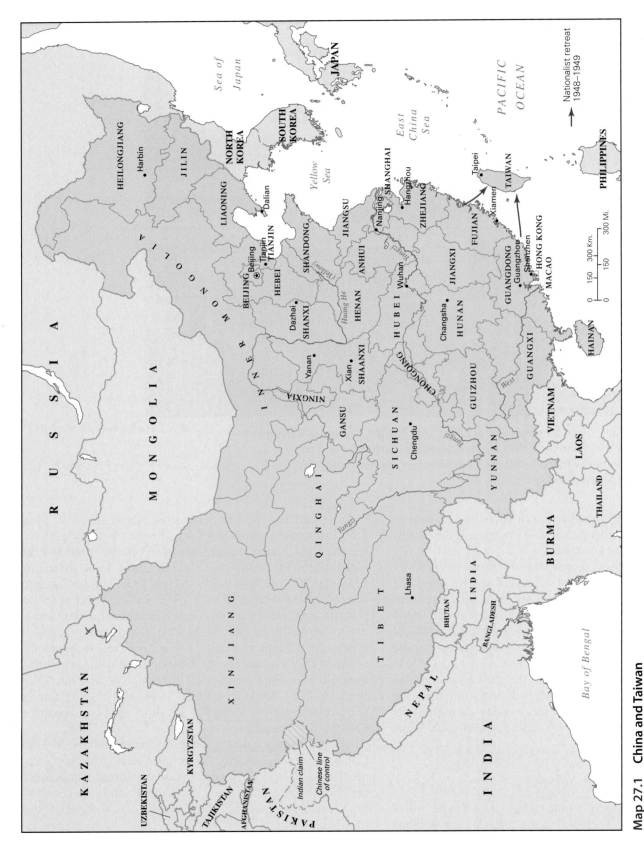

Map 27.1   China and Taiwan
China is a huge country, divided into many provinces, and occupies a large part of eastern Eurasia. In 1949 the government of the Republic of China, defeated by the Chinese Communists, moved to the island of Taiwan, off China's Pacific coast.

forces pushed United Nations troops back south. The war produced huge casualties on both sides, including several hundred thousand Chinese, and reinforced the hostility and mutual fear between China and the United States. When the Korean War ended in a stalemate in 1953, the United States, seeking to halt Communist expansion, signed a mutual defense treaty with Chiang Kai-shek's regime on Taiwan. The substantial U.S. forces stationed in Taiwan and South Korea joined the thousands of U.S. troops that had remained in Japan, Okinawa, and the Philippines after World War II, while the U.S. navy patrolled the waters off China, making for a formidable U.S. military presence in East Asia.

The Chinese Communists felt encircled, and Mao used the paranoia to mobilize the population around his programs. The ability to achieve a stalemate in Korea with the powerful United States improved China's international position, but the United States continued to veto the Chinese Communist effort to take China's United Nations seat from the Nationalist government in Taiwan. During the 1950s China, allied with the USSR, basically withdrew from the global system to consolidate the domestic revolution, maintaining limited trade with only a handful of Western nations. Meanwhile, many countries allied to the United States recognized the Republic of China, now based on Taiwan, as the official government of China.

China adapted to changing global politics. In the late 1950s tensions between China and the USSR grew. Chinese leaders did not share the Soviet view that what was good for the USSR was necessarily good for international communism. The Soviet policy of "peaceful coexistence" with the West enraged Mao, who labeled the United States "a paper tiger." Mao also opposed the 1956 decision of the Soviet leader, Nikita Khrushchev (KROOSH-chef), to reveal the excesses of Stalinist police-state rule in Russia, raising the issue of abuse of power by Communist dictators. By 1960 the Sino-Soviet split was official; the USSR withdrew advisors and technicians, even the spare parts for the industries they had helped build. Accusing the Soviet leaders of deviation from true Marxism-Leninism, Chinese leaders painted a new world future: "On the debris of a dead imperialism, the victorious [socialist] people would create very swiftly a civilization thousands of times higher than the capitalist system and a truly beautiful future for themselves."[4] The Chinese built up their military strength, tested their first atomic bomb, and occasionally clashed with Soviet forces on their border. To counterbalance the power of the United States and the USSR, China sought allies and influence in Asia and Africa. Yet, despite fierce anti-U.S. and anti-Soviet rhetoric, Chinese leaders generally followed a cautious foreign policy.

During the 1970s Chinese foreign policy changed dramatically. The change was symbolized by U.S. president Richard Nixon's trip to Beijing in 1972, the first official contact between the two nations since 1949. The two nations shared a hostility toward the USSR; moreover, the bitter U.S. experience fighting Communist forces in Vietnam and the gradual withdrawal of U.S. forces from that country had opened the door to foreign policy rethinking in both the United States and China. Chinese leaders perceived the United States as stepping back from

Asian military and political commitments, and hence as a diminishing threat. The United States now agreed to quit blocking Chinese membership in the United Nations and, in 1978, normalized diplomatic relations with China. Meanwhile, the Chinese developed better relations with non-Communist nations in Southeast Asia and Africa.

Mao's Cultural Revolution

Mao was a complex figure. He was, for example, a self-proclaimed feminist who promoted women's rights but also a sexually promiscuous man who married several times and had many lovers, but who also seldom bathed or brushed his teeth. A poor public speaker with few close friends, he could nevertheless inspire millions to follow his lead. A poet and philosopher but also power hungry and ruthless, he made many enemies, even within the Communist Party leadership. Although many of his initiatives ultimately failed or resulted in misery for millions of people, he played a powerful role in modern world history, leading the Communists to victory, reunifying China, focusing public attention on rural people, and placing his stamp on the world's most populous nation.

Mao's stamp was particularly strong when Maoism was China's guiding ideology. Dissatisfied with China's development and his eclipse by the early 1960s, in the mid-1960s Mao sought to regain his dominant status by resurrecting Maoism and offering a vision of a new society that comprised unselfish, politically conscious citizens. Maoism emphasized human will: people working together were capable of anything if they had confidence in their collective power. In Mao's vision of a disciplined society, individuals, inspired by the slogan "Serve the People," subordinated their own needs to the broader social order. His allies emphasized the cult of Mao and his revolutionary thoughts. Newspapers reported that, illuminated by Mao's ideas, factory workers discovered better techniques for galvanizing, the manager of a food store doubled his sales of watermelons, and farmers learned to judge exactly the right amount of manure to fertilize their plots. This campaign laid the foundation for a major social movement inspired by Mao's thoughts.

For a decade, between 1966 and 1976, massive turmoil generated by Mao convulsed and reshaped China like a whirlwind. The **Great Proletarian Cultural Revolution**, as it was called, was a radical movement that represented Mao's attempt to implant his vision, destroy his enemies, crush the stifling bureaucracy, and renew the revolution's vigor. The movement's major supporters, young workers and students known as **Red Guards**, roamed around cities and the countryside in groups, smashing temples and churches and attacking and arresting anti-Mao leaders. Mao's supporters created revolutionary

---

Great Proletarian Cultural Revolution A radical movement in China between 1966 and 1976 that represented Mao Zedong's attempt to implant his vision, destroy his enemies, crush the stifling bureaucracy, and renew the revolution's vigor.

Red Guards Young workers and students who were the major supporters of the Cultural Revolution in Mao's China.

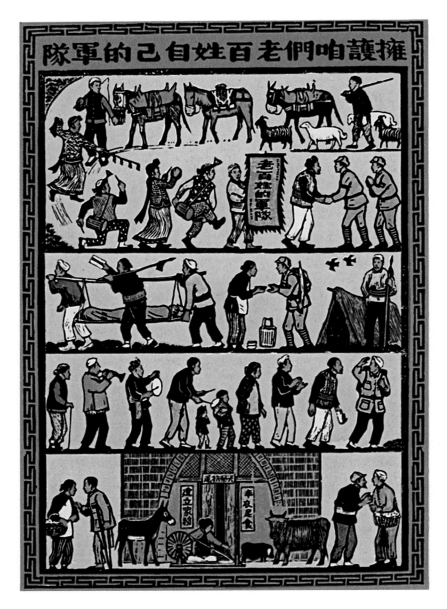

Chinese Political Art   This woodcut, carved during the Chinese civil war of the late 1940s, was typical of the political art made by the Communists to rally popular support for their cause, a hallmark of Mao's era. Entitled "Support Our Common People's Own Army," the woodcut shows Chinese peasants working together with the Communist military forces. (Woodcut by Ku Yuan, from Mei-shu, 1944)

sent to remote rural areas to experience peasant life. Anti-Mao officials, intellectuals, and people with upper-class backgrounds faced public criticism, followed by punishment if they failed to admit their political crimes. A Chinese journalist whose grandparents were capitalists, and hence identified as class enemies, remembered the attacks on her family: "Red Guards swarming all over the house and a great fire in our courtyard onto which were thrown my father's books, my grandparent's precious traditional furniture and my toys. The fire burned away everything."[6] Soon even Mao was dampening down the radical fervor.

Society, Gender, and Culture in Mao's China

Aiming to reshape Chinese society, the Communist movement in many ways succeeded. Mao prodded everyone to get involved in political and economic activities. He also promoted a model of social equality, known as the **Iron Rice Bowl**, in which the people, especially in the villages, shared resources—food, draft animals, farm equipment—and the peasants enjoyed status and dignity. Maoism generally improved life for the poorer Chinese, especially in the thousands of villages. An emphasis on preventive medicine included the training of villagers as paramedics. These peasants, known as barefoot doctors, were given skills to address the everyday health care needs of their communities, such as distributing medication and setting broken bones. As a result, most Chinese now enjoyed decent health care where once famine and disease were dominant. Mass education raised literacy rates to the levels of those in industrialized nations. Peasants often appreciated the changes. In 1971 an elderly peasant told visiting Western scholars what he had gained: "Now we are free to work full-time, have a secure home, eat enough food, have complete medical care, receive education—and take our future in our hands."[7]

The Communists also tried to overturn centuries-old, Confucian-influenced hierarchical relationships, including

committees, led by students, workers, and soldiers, to run cities, factories, and schools. Mao told them to destroy the party and government headquarters and that rebellion was justified. A Mao personality cult spread. The students carried copies of a little red book containing short quotations from Mao's writings, such as his claim that Marxism cannot be understood through books alone but also requires contact with the workers and peasants. One observer noted that "giant portraits of [Mao] now hung in the streets, busts were in every chamber, his books and photographs were everywhere on display."[5]

Online Study Center   **Improve Your Grade**
Primary Source: "One Hundred Items for Destroying the Old and Establishing the New"

The turmoil affected everyone. The chaos of these years caused serious economic problems, disrupting industrial and agricultural production and closing most schools for two years. The upheaval also resulted in thousands killed, jailed, or removed from official positions, and millions of others were

---

Iron Rice Bowl   A model of social equality in Mao's China in which the people, especially in the villages, shared resources and the peasants enjoyed status and dignity.

patriarchy, by raising the status of women. Mao praised women, who he said "held up half the sky," as a force in production. Two changes profoundly affected women's lives. First, a new marriage law in 1950 abolished arranged marriages, forbade men from taking concubines, and made divorce easier. Second, a land reform empowered women economically by expanding their property rights. Women now enjoyed legal equality with men and greater access to education. Consequently, women played a stronger public role, often leading local organizations, and women more often worked for wages. Yet few women held high national positions. Mao's last wife, Jiang Qing (chang ching) (1914–1991), a former film actress, wielded great power during the Cultural Revolution, but her radical policies made her unpopular. In 1976, after Mao's death, Jiang and her top party allies, the "Gang of Four," lost a power struggle and were imprisoned.

While many women no longer depended solely on men, they still faced obstacles. In conferences and periodicals, women debated the proper balance between housekeeping and paid work and whether they should devote their energies to the revolution as well as to their husbands and children. The rural areas remained more conservative than the cities in social matters. In general, however, communism changed the family system, often to the advantage of both women and men. Women activists worked to eliminate patriarchy, which they viewed as a relic of the past, and to build in its place a democratic family. An emphasis on love matches rather than arranged marriages fostered closer emotional ties between husbands, wives, and children, lessening male domination. Fathers spent more time with their children and their wives than had been common a generation earlier.

As with social patterns, the Communists often undermined traditional beliefs and culture. Calling religion a bond enslaving people, Mao moved to control religious behavior and marginalize religious institutions such as Christian churches, Buddhist monasteries, and Islamic mosques. By the 1970s only a small minority of Chinese openly practiced religion. Only Buddhist, Christian, and Muslim leaders who cooperated with the state maintained their positions. Determined to use the arts as a weapon in the class struggle, Mao sought to break down elitism and to foster a "people's art" created by and for the common people. He wrote, "In the world today all culture, all literature and art belongs to definite political lines. Art for art's sake, art that stands above the class and party do not exist in reality."[8] Critics argued that art that strictly served revolutionary goals reduced it to political propaganda.

Government policies broadened popular participation in creating art, literature, and music. For example, during the Great Leap Forward, party activists went out to collect literature written by common people and to encourage peasants and workers to compose poetry and songs. In Shanghai alone 200,000 people produced 5 million poems. Peasants painted scenes of people at work, often in bright, cheerful colors conveying an optimistic tone. Part-time writers got a day off from the factory to work on literary projects. Everyone was urged to work hard for a better future and a new society. A 1958 poem proclaimed: "Labor is joy, how joyful it is, Bathed in sweat and two hands full of mud. Like sweet rain, my sweat waters the land."[9]

The politicization of the arts reached its peak levels during the Cultural Revolution, when elitism came under fierce attack. Red Guards sang new songs in praise of change and Chairman Mao, such as "The East is red, the sun has risen. China has produced a Mao Zedong; He is the great savior of the people."[10] Opera and ballet became central for the new revolutionary art. Militant operas had a strong political message based on contemporary themes, such as the dignity of peasant life or Communist party history. Rejecting Western-style ballet as decadent, dancers composed revolutionary ballets that integrated Chinese martial arts, such as kung fu, folk dances, and Russian ballet. For example, *The Red Detachment of Women* portrayed the experiences of a women's company of Communist soldiers during the civil war against the Chiang's Republic.

The End of the Maoist Era

After Mao died in 1976, the Chinese took stock of Mao's legacy. The Communists could claim many achievements. They had restored China to great power status and renewed the confidence of the people after thirteen decades of imperialistic exploitation and invasion by Western nations and Japan. China was no longer a doormat; it even had nuclear weapons. As they had for two millennia before the disasters of the nineteenth century, the Chinese once again envisioned themselves as the Middle Kingdom exercising influence in the world. The Communists also took much of the sting out of poverty. Most Chinese, though enjoying little material surplus, could satisfy their basic food, housing, and clothing needs. During the 1940s impoverished Chinese had often had to resort to begging or prostitution to survive; by the 1970s few Chinese faced this dilemma. The economy in 1976 was healthier and more broadly based than in 1949, and food was more evenly distributed. Public health and literacy rates had risen substantially.

Mao's policies, however, had also resulted in failures and political repression. China may have gained control of its economic destiny but was still poor by world standards. Mao had discouraged free enterprise and individual initiative. On city streets few private cars interfered with the bicycles that most Chinese used to get to work or go shopping. Chinese wanted material benefits, such as better housing and more consumer goods, now rather than in a distant future. With few consumer luxuries or diversions available, life was dull. In addition, the fierce punishment of dissenters and the turmoil of the Great Leap Forward and Cultural Revolution had ruined numerous lives. Government coercion and corruption were also resented. The unfulfilled promises, and the chaos of the Cultural Revolution, disillusioned the youth. Bitter disagreements had ripped the Communist Party leadership apart. The Chinese often blamed Mao and his radicalism for the problems. Reformers in the party charged that, in his later years, Mao, isolated and clinging to unworkable utopian theories, had lost touch with common people's lives. Furthermore, the often erratic policies made people cynical, willing to give only passive cooperation to government policies and avoiding commitment to a particular line. Many Chinese were ready for change.

SECTION SUMMARY

■ After Japan was defeated in World War II, Chinese Communists and nationalists fought a civil war in which Mao Zedong's Communists triumphed by appealing to people's frustration with the corruption of Chiang Kai-shek's Nationalists.

■ To develop its economy, China first employed Stalinism, which featured central planning dominated by a bureaucratic elite, and then shifted to Maoism, which emphasized mass mobilization of the people to industrialize and maximize output, but under Maoism millions starved to death and many suffered under political repression.

■ China reasserted itself as a world power, reclaiming Tibet, becoming involved in the Korean War, ultimately splitting with the USSR, and reestablishing formal relations with the United States in the 1970s.

■ Frustrated with China's development, Mao led a decade-long cultural revolution, a period of radical upheaval in which young Red Guards attempted to destroy Mao's enemies and obstacles to progress, which caused great economic problems and brought misery to many.

■ Mao reshaped Chinese society, improving literacy rates and health care, especially for rural people, expanding the rights of women, opposing traditional religious institutions and elitism, and encouraging the people to produce their own literature and art.

■ While Mao restored China as a world power and brought many out of poverty, after his death in 1976 many Chinese wanted to join the modern world and gain increased access to material benefits.

✦ Chinese Modernization

What factors explain the dramatic rise of Chinese economic power in the world since 1978?

With Mao gone, Deng Xiaoping (dung shee-yao-ping) (1904–1997), a longtime Communist Party leader who had often clashed with Mao, came to power in 1978 and changed China's direction. Deng and his allies rejected Mao's view of a self-sufficient, ideologically pure China outside the world economy, concluding that collectivized agriculture had failed to raise productivity enough to substantially improve rural living standards or finance a jump into the high technology that Deng believed China needed to modernize the economy enough to make China a major power. In 1978 Deng, portraying China as at a turning point in history, announced the policy of Four Modernizations: the development of agriculture,

industry, military, and science and technology to turn China into a powerful nation by 2000. After Deng's death his replacements generally followed his pragmatic policies, which transformed China into an economic powerhouse and reshaped its society.

Market Socialism

From 1978 to 1989 Chinese leaders pursued **market socialism**, a mix of free enterprise, economic liberalization, and state controls that produced economic dynamism. This pragmatic approach, unlike Mao's, was more concerned with economic results than socialist values. Twice purged for opposing Mao, Deng was fond of a Chinese proverb: "It doesn't matter whether a cat is black or white, only if it catches mice." Deng used the market to stimulate productivity. China reentered the world economy, but on its own terms, to obtain capital investment to spur manufacturing for the global market. Like Meiji Japan in the late 1800s, China began to import technology, foreign expertise, and capitalist ideas. Deng believed that China had reached a plateau; to move to the next levels required wider international participation. Hence, he improved ties with the United States, Japan, western Europe, and non-Communist Southeast Asia. Dazzled by China's huge potential market of, as Western experts put it, 1 billion toothbrushes (for toothpaste) and 2 billion armpits (for deodorant), Western companies promoted increased trade.

Introducing capitalist ideas, such as offering workers material incentives rather than ideological slogans, Deng's reforms sparked dramatic changes. At first the government allowed small private enterprises, then it allowed larger ones, and ultimately both private and state-owned enterprises were competing with each other. In agriculture, Deng replaced Mao's communes with the contract system in which peasants could bid on and lease (but could not buy) land to work it privately. In many districts this free market led to soaring productivity and prosperity, with per capita income in rural areas rising fourfold in the first decade. Tapping a skilled, industrious, but cheap labor force, hundreds of Western and Asian companies set up manufacturing operations, producing goods such as shirts, underwear, and toys chiefly for export. China became a consumer society in the 1980s; even in small cities, shops stocked Japanese televisions and Western soft drinks. Over the next twenty-five years the economy quadrupled in size and foreign trade increased ten times over.

Deng also loosened political and cultural controls, arguing that liberation of thought and open-mindedness were essential for progress. Western popular culture, especially films, rock music, and discos, won a huge audience; books and magazines from around the world became available; and foreign travelers backpacked in remote areas. Chinese were even able to listen to popular music from Taiwan. The sentimental recordings of Taiwan's top female singer, Deng Lijun (deyn lee-choong), better

---

market socialism A Chinese economic program used between 1978 and 1989 that mixed free enterprise, economic liberalization, and state controls and that produced economic dynamism in China.

known to her millions of fans in Hong Kong, Japan, and Southeast Asia as Teresa Teng, were so widely played in Chinese homes and restaurants that people said that "the day belongs to Deng Xiaoping but the night belongs to Deng Lijun."[11] Intellectuals and artists enjoyed greater freedom; people long silenced or imprisoned were heard from again. The press was enlivened and the scope for public debate widened. Deng also increasingly tolerated religion, allowing Buddhist temples, Muslim mosques, and Christian churches to reopen.

Cultural figures, cowed during Mao's time, tested the limits of free expression. Novels and short stories revealed the depth of suffering during the Cultural Revolution. Writers reflected a widespread public cynicism about politics; popular writers developed massive audiences for stories daring to use sexual themes. Also demonstrating a new openness, Chinese-made films won international acclaim, while creative directors associated with semi-independent film studios skirmished with wary government censors, who decided whether films could be shown in China. Their films explored forbidden themes, portraying China as anything but a Communist paradise. Rock musicians, especially Cui Jian (sway jen), a former trumpeter with the Beijing Symphony, became a major voice for alienated urban youth. Dressed in battered army fatigues and a coat style favored by Mao, Cui sang: "This guitar in my hands is like a knife. I want to cut at your hypocrisy till I see some truth." Cui's songs were indirect in their criticism, focusing more on bureaucratic corruption, social problems, and young people's frustrations than on national politics, but Chinese youth easily read between the lines for the hidden meanings. One fan commented that "Cui Jian says things we all feel, but cannot say."[12]

Reform and Repression

Although Chinese often applauded the ideological loosening and the growing economic options, the dramatic changes under Deng Xiaoping showed a dark underside in the later 1980s. Many districts had seen few benefits from the reorganization of rural life. Chinese authorities imposed one policy for the vast nation rather than allowing districts and villages to find a policy—stressing the individual, the collective, or both—that worked for them. Under Deng's market socialism, some villagers, because of their better land, local leadership positions, or entrepreneurial skills, benefited more than others, opening a gap between newly rich and poor villagers. Prices rose rapidly. A widely shared street poem charged that "Mao Zedong was bad, so bad, But if you had a dollar you knew what you had. Deng Xiaoping is fine, so fine, But a dollar's only worth a lousy dime."[13] Corruption increased as bureaucrats and Communist Party officials lined their own pockets.

Public dissension mirrored divisions at the top. Within the party, Stalinists and Maoists viewed economic liberalization as undermining one-party rule and the commitment to communism. The fall of communism in eastern Europe and the USSR in 1989 alarmed hardliners. But dissidents and some reformers, seeing strong controls as inhibiting initiative, pushed democracy as "the fifth modernization." In response, party leaders opposed to liberalization called for cracking down, arresting dissidents. The most famous dissident, the outspoken Wei Jingsheng (way ching-sheng) (b. 1950), a former Red Guard who became a democracy activist while working as an electrician at the Beijing Zoo, spent years in jail.

In 1989 the tensions in Deng's China reached a boiling point, generating massive protests and government repression of them. Thousands of protesters, led by university students and workers, took over downtown Beijing, calling for the resignation of the most unpopular hardline leaders, an end to government corruption, and a transition to a fully open, democratic system. The party hardliners, in alliance with Deng, purged the moderate party leaders and ordered the army to clear out the demonstrators in what became known as the Beijing Massacre. Sending in tanks, the army killed hundreds and arrested thousands, while millions around the world watched the violence on television. The courageous Beijing protesters had not only underestimated the government reaction but had also overestimated their popular support. Since many Chinese outside the cities, valuing stability more than vague promises of a better world, applauded the government crackdown, the protesters had also miscalculated the prospects of democracy in a country with an authoritarian political tradition.

Economic Change and Political Challenge

After the Beijing Massacre the Communists modified market socialism into **market Leninism**, a policy whereby the Chinese state, obsessed with stability, asserted more power over society while also fostering an even stronger market orientation in the economy than had existed under market socialism. The Communist leadership reestablished control in political, social, and cultural spheres, tolerating less dissent than they had in the 1980s, but the economy became further privatized. China now did not fit either the Communist or the capitalist model. Eventually the party labeled the mixed system a socialist market economy. It benefited from the fact that, remembering the chaos of the Cultural Revolution and the 1989 unrest, Chinese often valued political stability over individual rights, especially at a time of overheated economic growth.

However, the control of the Leninist, or one-party, state was not absolute. In some local elections Communist officials did permit competition between candidates, allowing nonparty members to run for office. Many dissenters were able to spread their message. For example, opponents of the environmentally damaging Three Gorges Dam project, constructed to control the Yangzi (yahng-zeh) River and provide electrical power, publicized their views, although they had little success in halting the expensive project, which forced several million people to move from their homes along the river. However, the Chinese state, dominated by the Communist Party and often

market Leninism A policy followed after the Beijing Massacre in 1989 whereby the Chinese Communist state asserted more power over society while also fostering an even stronger market orientation in the economy than had existed under market socialism.

arbitrary in its actions, became warier of relaxing ideological controls and used the military and police to intimidate dissidents. Assertive political dissidents faced arrest, and public debate was dampened. China may execute more than 100,000 people a year, mostly criminals but including some accused of economic misbehavior or political opposition. Anxious to preserve national unity, China's leaders also suppressed dissent in Tibet and among Muslim Turkish groups in Xinjiang (shin-jee-yahng), in far western China. In both places people sought autonomy from China, greater religious freedom, and limits on Chinese immigration, which was overwhelming the local population.

After 1980, despite the ebb and flow of party domination, China enjoyed the fastest economic growth in the world, often 10 percent a year, abetted by a "get rich quick mentality" among many Chinese. Deng claimed that to get rich is glorious. Under Mao the Communist Party lionized Lei Feng, a soldier who loved everyone but himself and gladly served the people. Now they praised the rich, regardless of their motives or character. China's exports increased fifteenfold between 1980 and 2000. After 1989 the Communist leadership sought popular support by offering consumer goods and wealth rather than political reform, providing shops with ample consumer goods and households with spending money. In the early days of reform people aspired to the "three bigs": bicycle, wristwatch, and sewing machine. By 2000 they wanted televisions, washing machines, and video recorders. As a result of the economic growth, the urban middle class grew rapidly. By 2005 China had already moved ahead of Germany into the number 3 position in the world economy, with the size of its economy trailing only the United States and Japan. Some experts have argued that the United States and China are the two countries that have most benefited from the mobility of capital and products with economic globalization. If the economy maintains the high annual growth rates experienced since the 1980s, China will have the world's largest economy by 2015.

Although the economic reforms beginning in 1990 have improved living standards for many Chinese, they have also produced numerous downsides. Economic dynamism has occurred largely in a few coastal provinces and special economic zones, where living standards approach those of China's more highly developed neighboring countries, Taiwan and South Korea. Towering skyscrapers and huge shopping malls with upscale shops dot the landscape of cities such as Shanghai and Shenzen. Elsewhere, however, conditions have often deteriorated. Unemployment grows dramatically as state enterprises close or become uncompetitive and inflation skyrockets. Although laws make it illegal to migrate to another district without government permission, millions of peasants seeking jobs or a less rustic life have nonetheless moved to cities, where they struggle. Another problem is that, as China has developed, the Chinese have become even greater users of world resources, such as oil and coal, and major polluters of the atmosphere. China has become the number two producer of greenhouse gases that cause global warming, although its output, about one-eighth of the world total, is only half that of the United States. Water supplies have become badly overstretched, and,

with private cars clogging the city streets where bicycles once dominated, smog blankets the cities. Land and energy grow more expensive.

Political and economic changes have influenced other areas of Chinese life. In the cities, the newly rich entrepreneurs—enjoying luxury cars, access to golf courses, and vacations abroad—live lives alien to most Chinese. By 2004, some 236,000 Chinese were millionaires. Even the middle class, chiefly working in business, can aspire to some of these benefits. With money concentrated in the private sector, teachers, professors, and doctors leave their low-paying state jobs to open businesses or join foreign corporations. Some village leaders use their power to amass wealth and power. The wealthy flaunt their affluence, and the poor resent it. Street songs in towns and villages have often mocked the powerful: "I'm a big official, so I eat and drink, and I've got the potbelly to prove it. Beer, spirits, rice wine, love potions—I drink it all."[14] By 2005 peasant protests against seizure of village land to build polluting factories, luxury housing, and golf courses had become frequent, numbering in the thousands and resulting in the arrests of protest leaders. Meanwhile, the shift to market forces leaves millions unable to afford medical care and schooling for their children. Thanks to the decline in health care, especially in rural areas, experts estimate that between half a million and 1.5 million Chinese have HIV or AIDS. Poorer Chinese, forgetting his failures, long fondly for Mao and the dismantled Iron Rice Bowl. Yet, despite reduced job security and social services, people are now freer than before to travel, change jobs, enjoy leisure, and even complain.

As the Chinese society and economy have rapidly changed, the Communist Party has faced problems Mao could never have anticipated. A Communist Party that once viewed itself as the protector of the working class and poor peasants welcomes wealthy businessmen and professionals into its ranks. Yet, after Deng's death in 1997, the party, formerly the surest path to success, split between hardliners and younger reform-minded leaders and lost legitimacy; it now needs to organize karaoke parties to recruit new members. Powerful provincial leaders whose first priority is economic growth increasingly ignore Beijing. Many Chinese now enjoy materially improved lives and suffer less interference than they had known under Mao. But the rapid economic growth raises questions as to whether Chinese leaders can resolve the increasing inequalities and spread wealth more equitably to check the growth of social tensions. Some pessimists forecast more conflicts between rich and poor Chinese, or civil war between rich and poor regions. Critics also worry that the Chinese economy might overheat and then collapse, taking down much of the world economy with it.

Social Change, Gender, and Culture

Given growing tensions and the rich-poor gap, the government struggles to maintain social stability. Popular attitudes favor stability. Chinese usually define human rights in terms of the right to property, food, and housing rather than the freedom of individuals to do as they like. One Chinese observer, a prominent woman journalist, argues that "ideals such as happiness and equality are luxuries for the poor. First they want clean water and electricity; then washing machines and fridges."[15] Popular participation in government and unfettered free speech are lower priorities for average Chinese.

Nonetheless, various developments undermine social stability. Economic growth and the quest for wealth have led to a rapid increase in crime and links between criminal groups and government officials. The close connection between government and business corruption, underworld activity, and financial success has led to Chinese talking about the "Five Colors," or surest roads to riches: Communist Party connections, prostitution, smuggling, illegal drug dealing, and criminal gangs. Mao's China had been one of world's safest countries, but after 1978 desperate people turned increasingly to crime as the way to get ahead; drug dealing became rampant once again, serving the growing number of people, especially youth, who used narcotics for escape. Maintaining Confucian and Maoist attitudes, Chinese often view wealth as corrupting and mistrust rich business interests.

The recent economic and social changes have offered women opportunities but also posed problems. Women's economic status has often improved, but many still face restricted gender expectations. The feminist journalist Xue Xinran (shoe shin-rahn) wrote that "Chinese women had always thought that their lives should be full of misery. Many had no idea what happiness was, other than having a son for the family"[16] (see Profile: Xue Xinran, a Chinese Voice for Women). Scholars consider the common stereotype of the long-suffering, submissive Chinese woman misleading, noting that modern Chinese women are often strong-willed and resourceful. However, rural women may feel more intimidated by men than urban women. In contrast to Mao's era, women now receive little support from government policies, which are aimed at economic growth, not gender equality. Rather than remaining in their villages, millions of rural women prefer to migrate to the cities for industrial and service jobs. They provide much of the labor force for the new factories that have helped turn China into an economic giant. Wherever they live, women commonly work long hours, and few women occupy high positions in the national government, Communist Party, top business enterprises, or in rural communities.

Women have also faced other new hardships. Since by the 1980s China already had 1 billion people, a fifth of humankind, Deng Xiaoping introduced a one-child-per-family policy to try to stabilize the population. Officials enforced the policy because they hoped to limit growth toward a maximum population of 1.4 billion in 2010. Critics of the one-child policy complained that children without siblings were pampered and self-centered. Furthermore, the policy encouraged and sometimes mandated abortion and, since traditional attitudes favoring sons remained, also resulted in widespread killing of female babies. With more boys than girls being born and raised, an imbalance in numbers between the sexes developed, resulting in a growing trade in the abduction and sale of women to desperate men unable to find wives.

Because of China's growing contacts with the larger world economy, Chinese society is affected by global entertainment and consumer culture. Western popular culture, which spread to China in the 1980s, has become a powerful force among youth. Cui Jian and other rock musicians who had participated in the Beijing student protest movement later resumed their musical careers, competing for a youth audience with heavy metal, punk, and rap musicians. Every city has discos and clubs offering Western music, and Chinese imitators of Anglo-American boy bands and girl groups have found a vast teen audience. In 2005 more than 8 million Chinese voted for three finalists in a hugely popular Chinese television program, *Super Girl,* a local version of the popular U.S. television program, *American Idol.* Television offers U.S. series dubbed in Chinese, such as *The X-Files* and *Baywatch*, and in Shanghai a theme park very similar to Disney World features a Wild West Town. Chinese consumers in many places indulge their desires as they are served by numerous McDonald's outlets (one near Mao's mausoleum), Hard Rock Cafes, Wal-Marts, and some 85,000 Avon agents selling American cosmetics and beauty products. Partly due to greater contact with the outside world, homosexuals, who faced discrimination under Mao, have been slowly coming out, especially in the cities, where gay bars are common, and even have hundreds of their own websites. But Western culture is not the only outside influence. South Korean popular culture and consumer products—music, clothing, television dramas, movies, cosmetics—became very fashionable among young Chinese in the early 2000s, and much of the conversion of millions of Chinese to evangelical Christianity is due to the thousands of South Korean Protestant missionaries in the country.

Those Chinese with enough money to afford satellite dishes, fax machines, and personal computers linked to the Internet have gained access to ideas around the world. More than 100 million Chinese are Internet users. To restrict the free flow of information and exposure to dissident writings, state officials have tried to crack down on cyberspace, passing laws restricting Internet use. They sometimes close down some of the thousands of Internet cafes and prevent local Internet providers from allowing access to banned websites. Western Internet providers seeking a larger role in Chinese cyberspace have faced criticism in the West for cooperation in these restrictions and sometimes allowing the government to identify dissidents. But websites and blogs—some 14 million are available to Chinese—proliferate rapidly, making monitoring difficult. The government sometimes shuts down newspapers and magazines whose reporting is too daring, but brave journalists and officials have risked punishment by openly criticizing micromanagement of the media. Another source of knowledge about Western ideas comes from the several hundred thousand Chinese, including the children of high officials, who have studied in Western universities.

Policies toward religion have been inconsistent. After temples and churches reopened in the 1980s, the government tolerated millions of Chinese turning to the faith of their ancestors: Buddhism, Christianity, Daoism, or Islam. But the government has cracked down on movements that are deemed a threat or that refuse to register and accept official restrictions. For instance, it has arrested leaders and members of the assertive, missionary *Falun Gong* meditation sect, a mix of

XUE XINRAN,
A CHINESE VOICE FOR WOMEN

Xue Xinran The Chinese journalist, Xue Xinran, explored the lives of Chinese women on her radio program and in her writings. (Courtesy, Asia Society, AustralAsia Centre)

In the 1980s Xue Xinran (shoe shin-rahn), known professionally as Xinran, began working for a radio network and went on to become one of China's most successful and innovative journalists. A radio call-in show that she launched in 1989 featured hundreds of poignant and haunting stories by women. The huge audience the show attracted and her sensitive handling of the callers made Xinran a role model and heroine for Chinese women. Her own life and career also revealed women's experiences in contemporary China.

Born in Beijing in 1958, Xinran had a difficult childhood that was complicated by the turmoil of the Cultural Revolution. Her mother came from a capitalist, property-owning family. But Xinran's grandfather, although he cooperated with the Communists, lost his property and was imprisoned during the Cultural Revolution. Her mother joined the Communist Party and army at sixteen but was occasionally jailed or demoted in purges of those from capitalist class backgrounds. Xinran's father was a national expert in mechanics and computing but, like her mother, also from a once wealthy family. He too had been imprisoned. Xinran had been sent to live with a grandmother when she was one month old and seldom saw her parents during her childhood. Reflecting on her family, she wrote that, like many Chinese, her parents endured an unhappy marriage: "Did [my parents] love each other? I have never dared to ask." While working as an army administrator, Xinran married, had a son, PanPan, and later divorced.

Eventually she became a radio journalist. But she had to persuade the station to let her begin a nightly call-in program, *Words on the Night Breeze*. Since 1949 the media had been the mouthpiece of the Communist Party, ensuring that it spoke with one identical voice. However, Xinran said, "I was trying to open a little window, a tiny hole, so that people would allow their spirits to cry out and breathe after the gunpowder-laden atmosphere of the previous forty years." In starting her call-in program, the question that obsessed her was, What is woman's life really worth in a China where footbinding was a recent memory but women now lived and worked alongside men? Xinran's compassion and ability encouraged callers to talk freely about feelings. For eight groundbreaking years, women called in and discussed their lives, and Xinran was shocked by much of what they said. Broadcast all over China, the program offered an unflinching portrait of what it meant to be a woman in modern China, including the expectations of obedience to fathers, husbands, and sons. Women from every social status—daughters of wealthy families, wives of party officials, children of Cultural Revolution survivors, homeless street scavengers, isolated mountain villagers—called in stories, often heartbreaking tales of sexual abuse, gang rape, forced marriages, and enforced separation of families.

The stories Xinran heard did not fit the image promoted by the Communist Party of a happy, harmonious society. She told, for instance, of Jingyi and her boy friend, Gu Da,

university classmates who fell passionately in love but were sent by the government to work in different parts of the country. They had planned to eventually marry but lost touch during the chaos of the Cultural Revolution. For forty-five years Jingyi had first longed for and then searched for Gu Da. When they finally had a reunion in 1994, Jingyi was devastated to discover that Gu Da, despairing of ever seeing Jingyi again, had married another woman. Their saga provided a window on the disrupted personal and family lives common in China after 1949.

In Xinran's view, "When China started to open up [to the outside world], it was like a starving child devouring everything without much discrimination. But China's brain had not yet grown the cells to absorb truth and freedom." In 1997 the conflict between what Xinran knew and what she was permitted to say caused her to give up her career and leave for Britain, where she hoped to find a freer life and reach a global audience. In Britain, after mastering English, she first taught at the University of London and then became a columnist for a national newspaper, *The Guardian*. She published several nonfiction books based on the stories she learned in China. In *The Good Women of China: Hidden Voices* (2002), she opened a window revealing the lives of Chinese women to the outside world. Her reports revealed strong, resourceful characters who offered insights into China's past and present. Another book, *The Sky Burial* (2004), told the extraordinary story of an intrepid Chinese woman who spent thirty years searching rugged Tibet, a thousand miles from her home city, for her beloved husband, an army doctor who was reported killed. In 2002 Xinran married an Englishman, the literary agent Toby Eady. Every year she returns to China for visits and reporting.

THINKING ABOUT THE PROFILE

1. Why did Xinran achieve such fame in China?
2. What does her journalism tell us about the experiences of Chinese women?

Note: Quotations from Xue Xinran, *The Good Women of China: Hidden Voices* (New York: Anchor, 2002), pp. 126, 3, 227.

Daoist, Buddhist, and Christian influences, and has tried to close down rapidly proliferating Christian churches that have remained independent by not seeking government approval. While the Chinese remain a largely secular people, both Falun Gong and the independent churches have millions of followers who seek a deeper spiritual existence and sense of community.

China in the Global System

China's relations with the wider world have been colored by its historical experiences. In the nineteenth century this once powerful society suffered national humiliation as it lost wars to aggressive Western powers and Japan. Foreign gunboats patrolled China's rivers, and foreign interests controlled large swaths of Chinese territory. Years of civil war and Japanese invasion from the 1920s through the 1940s wrought devastation, but also left hope for a new future. Eventually Chinese saw their nation stand tall, strong and increasingly rich. In 1997 they celebrated the peaceful return of Hong Kong, which comprised several small islands and a peninsula on the southern coast, from British colonial control, which they saw as rectifying the loss of that territory during the Opium War of the mid-1800s. Hong Kong, a prosperous enclave whose towering skyscrapers, bustling shopping malls, and dynamic film industry made it a symbol of East Asian capitalism, was incorporated under the policy of "one nation, two systems." But critics charge that China's occasional interference in Hong Kong politics and its attempts to curb democracy have broken a pledge to respect the territory's special character and political freedoms. Nonetheless, a vocal pro-democracy movement in Hong Kong keeps these issues alive and can attract thousands of supporters to demonstrations. In 1999 Portugal also returned its small coastal colony of Macao, which it had first occupied in the 1500s, to Chinese control. Macao's economy is based on gambling casinos, a lucrative enterprise the once puritanical Communists now seem happy to tolerate.

Since 1976 China has pursued a pragmatic foreign policy designed to win friends and trading partners but to also avoid entangling alliances. China has exercised regional influence by trading extensively with neighbors. It gradually improved relations with the United States and USSR, and it cultivated diplomatic ties with other nations but avoided close ties that might limit its options. It also became increasingly active in the world community, a far cry from the isolationism of Mao's era. China joined international organizations such as the World Trade Organization, which regulated global economic exchange. To enhance China's competitive stance, some 200 million children study English.

The post-Mao foreign policy enhanced national power while accepting the constraints imposed by the global system. By the twenty-first century China enjoyed tremendous influence in the world economy, importing vast amounts of capital and natural resources, such as Zambian copper and Venezuelan oil, while exporting industrial products of every kind. Taking advantage of a cheap but resourceful labor force, thousands of foreign investors have come from the West, Japan, Southeast Asia, South Korea, and even Taiwan, opening factories and ne-

gotiating joint ventures with Chinese firms. Meanwhile, China has supported the U.S. economy, becoming the major buyer of the treasury bonds that financed the growing U.S. national debt in the early 2000s. As the Japanese and Americans did in the later 1900s, Chinese enterprises have begun buying up companies based on manufacturing and natural resources in other nations. Thus China has become the world's most successful newly industrializing economy, buttressed by a vast resource base and a huge domestic market.

Yet China has met roadblocks in enhancing its global power, among them uncertain relations with its neighbors. The Chinese government, still claiming Taiwan as an integral part of China, continues to threaten that island with forced unification if the Republic of China on Taiwan, which has ruled the island since 1949 and enjoys a defense agreement with the United States, tries to declare a permanent break from China. Although economic and social links between China and Taiwan developed unofficially beginning in the 1980s, few in the island nation, which enjoys democracy and a much higher standard of living, want a merger with the mainland in the near future. Meanwhile, Chinese relations with Japan ebb and flow. The two nations need each other economically and have close economic ties—thousands of Japanese businessmen are based in China—but are also natural rivals, the Chinese remaining resentful of Japanese brutality during World War II and antagonistic to contemporary Japanese nationalism. In contrast to sporadic Chinese-Japanese tensions, China has improved political and economic relations with once bitter enemies such as South Korea and anti-Communist countries such as Malaysia, the Philippines, and Australia. The leaders of these countries, seeing China as the future regional power, maintain friendly relations with China. In many of them, as well as in some African countries, large numbers of people are learning Chinese. In South Korea, for example, a close U.S. ally, as many people study Chinese as English. And some 90,000 foreign students study in China. Nonetheless, historical resentment of Japan and the West provides a strong foundation of Chinese nationalism, which sometimes provokes anti-Japan or anti-U.S. protest demonstrations. This resentment causes concern, for while by the early 2000s China only ranked fifth among the world's nations in defense spending, its neighbors have feared Chinese military power.

China's tremendous size, population, natural resources, military strength, national confidence, and sense of history have placed it in an unusual position of being a major global power while still having a much lower overall standard of living than that of North America, western Europe, Japan, and several industrializing Asian nations. Using such factors as literacy, life expectancy, and per capita income, the 2004 United Nations Human Development Report placed China only 94th out of 177 nations in overall quality of life. Nonetheless, China has been returning to its historical leadership as the Asian dragon and a major engine of the global economy. Experts debated whether either China or India might replace the United States as the major world power by 2050 or 2100. Some argued that India had some advantages over China, including democracy, a free press, and a sounder financial system, while others thought China had the better prospects, especially if the growing middle class fosters a more open political system, as happened in South Korea and Taiwan. Still others doubted that a decline of U.S. power was imminent. As during the long period of Chinese power and prosperity between 600 and 1800 C.E., China is once again a major force in world affairs.

SECTION SUMMARY

- Under Deng Xiaoping, China opened up to Western economic ideas and investment, gradually introducing private ownership and competition, as well as to political, religious, and cultural currents that had been suppressed under Mao.

- Although many supported Deng's reforms, they led to increasing corruption and a growing gap between rich and poor, especially in rural areas, and, in 1989, a violent suppression of prodemocracy dissidents in the Beijing Massacre.

- Under market Leninism, the Chinese state increased political and social control while continuing to privatize the economy, which grew briskly, though there was stagnation in many rural areas and environmental damage in others.

- The growth of China's economy has improved access to consumer goods but has also led to increased crime and drug use, and an effort to limit population has led to many abortions and the killing of female babies.

- China has become more open to Western culture, though its government has attempted to restrict the free flow of information.

- China has enjoyed a great recovery and return to world prominence in recent decades, though it still has uncertain relations with Taiwan and Japan, and its living standard remains much lower than many of its rivals.

◈ The Remaking of Japan

How did Japan rise from the ashes of defeat in World War II to become a global economic powerhouse?

Japan rose from the shambles of World War II to economic dynamism (see Map 27.2). In August 1945, Japan lay in ruins, its major cities largely destroyed by U.S. bombing and its economy ruined. Having no concept of military defeat or occupation, the Japanese people were psychologically devastated. Yet, within a decade the country had recovered from the disaster of World War II. After several decades of the highest economic growth rates in world history, Japan became one of the world's major economic powers, and by the 1980s it was challenging the United States for world economic leadership. A system stressing cooperation rather than individualism provided the basis for economic and social stability in an overcrowded land. But by the 1990s Japan was experiencing political and economic uncertainty.

Occupation and Recovery

The post–World War II occupation by the United States aided Japan's recovery. In the wake of defeat the Japanese people felt disoriented. The emperor, Hirohito (here-o-HEE-to) (1901–1989), still a revered figure, asked them to cooperate with the Allied occupation forces, and by and large they did. Japan was placed under a U.S.-dominated military administration, the Supreme Command of Allied Powers (SCAP), which was tasked with rebuilding rather than punishing Japan. The victorious World War II Allies also broke up Japan's empire. Japan lost Korea, Taiwan, and Manchuria, while the United States took control of the Ryukyu Islands, which were returned to Japan in the 1970s, and Micronesia. SCAP's mission was to demilitarize and democratize Japan, using the United States as the model, and to aid economic recovery. For their part, Japanese leaders hoped to win in peace what they had lost in war. SCAP dismantled the Japanese military, removed some civilian politicians, and tried and hanged seven wartime leaders as war criminals. Fearing that punishing the emperor, a member of an imperial family over 1,500 years old, would destabilize Japan, U.S. officials did not charge Emperor Hirohito with war crimes, but he was forced to renounce his godlike aura and become a more public figure. Scholars still debate his responsibility for Japanese wartime actions.

SCAP fostered political and social changes; some, including a thriving political democracy, took root. Sustaining democracy required a more egalitarian society in which once disadvantaged people shared in the economic progress. A new constitution guaranteed civil liberties and weakened the central government. It also had a unique feature: the document stated that, since they aspired to promote international peace and order, the Japanese people forever renounced war as the nation's sovereign right. The first democratic elections, held in 1946, involved various competing political parties. For the first time in Japanese history, all adult citizens, including women, could vote. Women gained status, including legal equality in society and marriage, but were only partly freed from the expectations of a patriarchal society. In education, new universities were opened, giving Japanese youth greater access than ever before to higher education. U.S. officials hoped to foster even greater political and social democratization, but, after the Communist victory in China and the outbreak of the Korean War, the United States shifted its emphasis from restructuring Japanese society to integrating Japan into the anti-Communist Western alliance, symbolized by the signing in 1951 of a formal U.S.-Japan peace treaty. U.S. military bases have remained in Japan ever since as part of a mutual defense treaty.

Under SCAP the economy gradually recovered, using the same sort of quasicapitalist system—a mix of government intervention and free markets—that Japan had had between the 1870s and the early 1930s. Land reform heavily subsidized the peasantry, making them strong government supporters and bringing unprecedented prosperity to the rural areas. SCAP also attempted to break up entrenched economic power, but these efforts were less successful; as before World War II, large industrial-commercial-banking combinations, or conglomer-

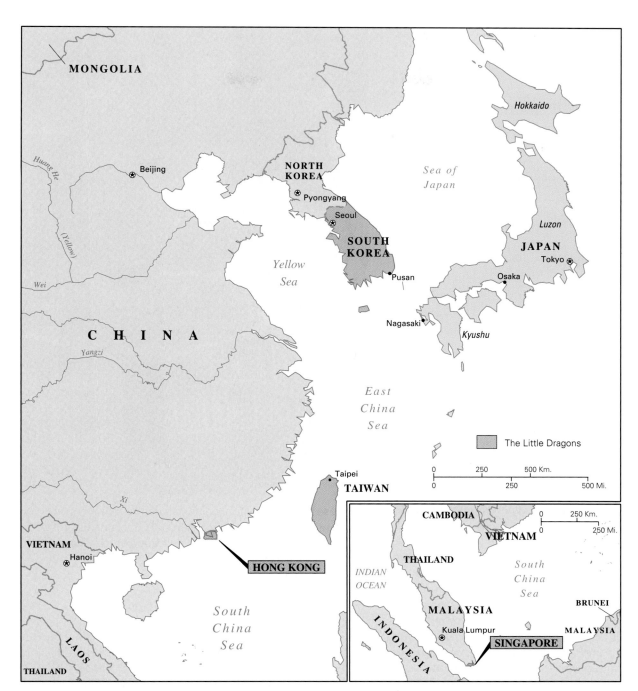

Map 27.2   Japan and the Little Dragons
Japan fostered the strongest Asian economy through the second half of the twentieth century, but in recent decades the Little Dragons—South Korea, Taiwan, Hong Kong, and Singapore—also have had rapid economic growth.

Online Study Center   **Improve Your Grade**   Interactive Map: Japan, 1800–1998

ates, still dominated business, especially manufacturing and foreign trade, making Japan more competitive in the world economy. But workers gained the right to unionize.

The policies implemented during the SCAP occupation, which officially ended in 1952, were most successful where U.S. and Japanese desires coincided or when the policies fit with the nation's traditions (see Chronology: Japan Since 1945). For

example, democratic government fit both criteria. The Japanese had enjoyed several decades of democracy, with competing political parties, before the Great Depression, and many Japanese longed for a return to this system, supported also by SCAP. Borrowing from abroad also fit with Japanese tradition. For several millennia the Japanese had been open to acquiring ideas, such as Buddhism, and technologies, such as textile manufacturing,

CHRONOLOGY

Japan Since 1945

1946–1952	SCAP occupation of Japan
1946	First postwar Japanese elections
1951	U.S.-Japan peace treaty
1960s–1989	Era of rapid Japanese economic growth
1989	Beginning of Japanese economic downturn
1993	Fragmentation of Liberal Democratic Party
1997	Asian financial collapse

from outside and adapting them to their own traditions. In the late 1940s they were again receptive to importing Western culture. With conditions stabilized, Japanese leaders embarked on a strategy of capitalizing on peace to strengthen the nation.

Politics in a One-Party Democracy

Despite stresses, Japan's democratic political system flourished. As in many western European countries, a variety of political parties, including socialists, Communists, liberals, Buddhists, and rightwing nationalists, competed for parliamentary seats. But since the early 1950s one major party, the center-right Liberal Democratic Party (LDP), has dominated Japanese politics, applying generally conservative, probusiness, and pro-U.S. policies. The electoral system imposed by SCAP gave greater weight to rural voters, the conservative backbone of LDP support, rather than the more liberal urban voters. Prime ministers, usually LDP leaders, learned to negotiate with varied opposition parties as well as with the diverse factions within the LDP. Nonetheless, critics believe that a political system dominated by one party and a few wealthy kingpins, who face little criticism from a press and media largely owned by huge corporations, is at best a partial democracy.

However, the need to finance political careers and raise money for elections fostered political corruption. Powerful corporations and criminal gangs were leading financial contributors. Bribery scandals sometimes forced political leaders to resign. For example, Prime Minister Tanaka Kakuei (ta-NAH-ka KAH-koo-ay) (1918–1983), who rose from rural poverty to become one of the most powerful LDP kingpins, was arrested in 1976 and later convicted for accepting payments from the U.S.-based Lockheed Corporation. In 1993 the LDP fragmented in factional disputes, and various opposition parties gained support for several years. But in 2001 the LDP returned to power under a reform leader, though it faced challenges from opposition parties.

Japanese Protest Political demonstrations are common in Japanese cities. During this protest in 2001, liberals and leftists criticized new middle-school textbooks, approved by the Education Ministry, that, the critics claimed, distorted history by emphasizing nationalist viewpoints and downplaying Japanese atrocities in World War II. (Getty Images)

To protect its shores, Japanese leaders forged a military alliance with the United States, but the alliance brought Japan problems as well as benefits. Thanks to this alliance, which allowed U.S. bases in Japan, Japan's military spending remained meager compared to that of the United States and the USSR: under 1 percent of total spending on goods and services. This ability to devote more resources to the civilian economy was a major reason for Japan's rapid economic growth. While the Cold War superpowers invested in weapons and armies, Japan devoted its economic surplus largely to industrial development.

Despite these benefits of the military alliance with the United States, the Japanese debated the value of the treaties and bases. Leftist parties, labor unions, and militant student groups long opposed the U.S. military presence, which they viewed as neocolonialism. Japanese also feared that the U.S. military interventions in places such as Vietnam and Iraq made Japan a potential target for U.S. enemies. Remembering the horrors of World War II, especially the atomic bombings of Hiroshima and Nagasaki that killed some 200,000 Japanese, many Japanese favored pacifism and believed that Japan's economic strength protected them from attack. Student protests have periodically broken out against the U.S. military bases and defense umbrella. Yet, with U.S. support, Japan began increasing its military spending in the 1980s, and by 2001 it had the fourth largest military budget in the world, ahead of China. The decision of Japanese leaders in 2004 to send soldiers to support, in noncombat activities, the U.S. war effort in Iraq was widely unpopular in Japan and, to critics, violated the constitutional ban against engaging in war.

The Japanese Economy

Adapting capitalism to its own traditions, Japan has achieved phenomenal economic growth: its goods were in demand on every continent only a century after it opened to the outside world. Wartime destruction had required the rebuilding of basic industries using the latest innovations. Investing in new industries and high-tech fields, the Japanese became the world leaders in manufacturing products such as pianos, oil tankers, and automobiles, as well as electronics products such as watches, televisions, and cameras. As a result, from the 1960s through the 1980s Japan's annual growth rate was three times higher than that of other industrialized nations. Now an industrial giant possessing an advanced technology and distinctive economic and industrial structure, in 2000 Japan produced some 16 percent of the world's goods and services, half the U.S. percentage but twice that of third-place Germany.

Economic Growth What observers often called Japan's economic miracle was particularly impressive considering the country's lack of natural resources, including those that produce energy. Unlike the United States, western Europe, and China, Japan has few mineral resources, limited productive farmland, and no major rivers to produce hydroelectric power. Consequently, the Japanese must import minerals needed for industry, such as iron ore, tin, and copper. Oil obtained from Alaska, Southeast Asia, and the Middle East powers Japan's transportation.

The Japanese became known for innovative technologies and high-quality products. Among those technologies was its magnificent mass transit system, including the state-of-the-art bullet trains that whisked passengers around the country at 125 to 150 miles per hour and were always on time. The most advanced trains skimmed along the 225 miles between Tokyo and Kyoto in one hour. Some high-tech goods made in Japan found a large world market. Electronics manufacturers such as Sony, Atari, and Nintendo invented entertainment-oriented products, among them video and handheld game systems, that became part of life on every continent, especially for youth. In addition, millions of people, from Boston to Bogotá to Bombay, drove Toyotas, Hondas, and other Japanese-made cars.

By the 1980s the Japanese enjoyed living standards equal to those of most western Europeans. With unprecedented affluence, the Japanese became Western-style consumers; everyone now sought to own cars, televisions, washing machines, and air conditioners. The Japanese also enjoyed the world's highest average life expectancy: seventy-nine or eighty years. A more varied diet, including more meat and dairy products than their ancestors had, produced taller, healthier children. Western foods and beverages became popular and coffeehouses and bars dotted most streets in commercial and entertainment districts. Western fast-food outlets such as McDonald's, introduced in 1971, proved a great success. By 1994 McDonald's had over 1,000 restaurants in Japan, most of them hugely profitable, that served the same items popular in the West as well as dishes adapted to local taste, such as teriyaki burgers and Chinese fried rice. The rural areas now also shared in the prosperity, although life there remained harder than in the cities and most rural youth left their villages for the more exciting life of the cities. Furthermore, there was an underside to Japanese economic success. Many workers had to make do with part-time jobs offering few benefits, and a small but growing underclass of people had no permanent jobs or homes.

Japanese Capitalism Japan's capitalist economy has differed in fundamental ways from those of other industrial nations. It was a form of mercantilism, a cooperative relationship between government and big business that became known as **Japan, Inc.** (Japan Incorporated). Under this system, the national government and big business worked together to manage the economy. The government regulated business, setting overall guidelines, sponsoring research and development, and leasing the resulting products or technologies to private enterprise. Most Japanese businesses accepted the government guidelines because they took a longer-term view of profitability than was common among Western business leaders. But government-business cooperation occurred chiefly in international trade, the country's lifeblood, and it was made easier by the economic dominance of large Japanese conglomerates, most of which owned diverse enterprises such as factories, banks, and department stores. As in many other countries, the government aided Japanese businesses by erecting protectionist barriers and bureaucratic hurdles that impeded foreign businesses in the Japanese market.

Economic growth, which relies on a dedicated labor force, has generated new problems. As in the West, industrialization has fostered wealth but also harmed the environment. As cities grew, developers cleared farmland and forests. Pollution of rivers and bays wiped out coastal fishing. Smoggy air, produced by automobile exhaust mixing with pollutants from smokestacks, is so bad that city residents sometimes cover their noses and mouths with masks to avert respiratory difficulties. Thousands of people have died or been made ill by toxic waste dumped by factories. In addition to declining environmental health, many younger people resent the long hours and sacrifices expected of both white-collar and blue-collar employees in Japanese companies, especially since a high standard of living has already been achieved.

Japan, Inc. The cooperative relationship between government and big business that has existed in Japan after 1945.

Japan's business and factory life has played a role in Japanese success. The system takes advantage of Japanese cultural values, such as conformity, hard work, cooperation, thrift, and foresight, but has added new innovations. The 30 percent of workers employed in larger Japanese companies have often enjoyed lifetime job security and access to generous welfare benefits offered by their employer, such as health insurance, recreation, housing, and car loans. Some companies sponsor group tours abroad or own vacation retreats, in the mountains or at the seashore, that employees and their families can use. When a corporation has faced financial trouble, top managers usually accept responsibility for the problems, cutting their own pay rather than firing workers. Most workers remain with the same employer for life, though, by the 1980s, it became more common to change jobs. To encourage workers to feel a part of the corporate family, employers often gather the employees together to sing the company anthem each morning before they head for their workstations.

Japanese companies emphasize working in teams and "bottom-up" decision making through quality control circles and work groups, such as a factory team that installs a car engine; these groups decide how best to undertake their tasks and suggest improvements to management. Business offices tend to be organized around large tables, where white-collar employees work collaboratively, rather than around the small cubicles common in North America. Along with the worker participation in decisions, however, businesses and factories have also expected their employees to put company over personal interests, including regularly working overtime.

Japanese Society

Urbanization and affluence have contributed to social change. Sixty percent of Japanese now live in cities of over 100,000. With nearly 30 million people, Tokyo is the world's largest city. With car ownership so popular, Tokyo and other cities have become jammed with traffic. Some of Tokyo's legendary traffic jams take police several days to untangle. The city subways are convenient but overcrowded. Rush hour has evolved into "crush hour," with city employees equipped with padded poles pushing commuters into overflowing cars to enable subway train doors to close. Yet, despite Mafia-like organized crime syndicates, Japan's cities are the safest in the world; experts attribute low rates of violent crime in part to strict gun control.

The economy has changed men's lives, especially in the growing middle class. University-educated men typically want to become salaried white-collar office workers for major corporations. Japanese observers describe the **salaryman**, an urban middle-class male business employee who commits his energies and soul to the company, accepts assignments without complaint, and takes few vacations. The cover of a local book on the salaryman pictures a harried middle-aged man eying

the sundry items that define his work life: a computer, newspaper, lunch box, demanding boss, and subway strap. Many men working in white-collar jobs are also known as "7-11 husbands" because they leave for work at 7 A.M. and do not return until 11 P.M. After work they and their office mates socialize in restaurants, bars, and nightclubs while their wives take care of the home. In the 1980s one wife complained, "I don't know why Japanese men marry if they are never going to be home."[17]

Meanwhile, while earning more money, gaining legal protections, and enjoying greater freedom from traditional restraints, women still struggle for full social and economic equality in a hierarchical society obsessed with patriarchy and seniority, with older men dominating most institutions, including the family. Most women are expected to marry and then retire from the work force in their early twenties to raise children, even though they often remain in paid work. According to one young woman, when she and other women graduated from a top Japanese university, "our bright appearance [for the graduation ceremonies] in vividly colored kimonos [traditional robes] was deceiving. Deep in our hearts we knew that our opportunities to use our professional education would be few."[18] As single women often discovered they could support themselves, the average age of marriage for women rose from twenty-two in the 1950s to twenty-seven in the 1990s. Indeed, in recent years, many women have avoided marriage altogether, preferring to concentrate on their careers or leisure interests. Accordingly, marriage rates have declined, alarming politicians.

Despite the popular, contemporary image of the timid Japanese female, women have become more assertive than women in previous generations. Working against the patriarchal grain of society, feminist organizations and several prominent women's leaders have publicized women's issues, and working women have lobbied companies for equal treatment and pay. Some women have moved into middle management or prestige occupations, such as law, journalism, college teaching, and diplomacy. Yet, women also largely remain outside political and economic power, and only a few attain positions of political leadership. Women aspiring to gender equality admire activists such as Ichikawa Fusae (ee-CHEE-kah-wah foo-SIGH) (1893–1981), a former schoolteacher and journalist who had organized the women's suffrage movement in the 1920s and served in the parliament as a political independent for twenty-five years after World War II, campaigning for women's equality and human rights.

Family life has gradually changed. Although the traditional arranged marriage remains common, increasing numbers of men and women select their own spouse. Also reflecting a rise in personal freedom, more Japanese get married late or opt to end unhappy marriages in divorce, a rare decision before World War II. Studies have suggested that, while many wives are lonely and resentful with their husbands seldom home, the majority prefer spending their growing leisure time away from their husbands. In fact, husbands and wives generally lead separate social lives. Meanwhile, children in middle-class families do not expect to see much of their fathers

---

salaryman An Japanese urban middle-class male business employee who commits his energies and soul to the company, accepts assignments without complaint, and takes few vacations.

Learning from their defeat in China, and using generous U.S. aid, the Republic's leaders promoted rapid industrial and agricultural growth and a more equitable distribution of wealth, implementing the land reform they had neglected on the mainland. With land ownership and access to credit facilities, the peasantry prospered. As in South Korea and Meiji Japan, the economy mixed capitalism and foreign investment with a strong government role, including extensive planning and sizeable state investment. Light industry and manufacturing eventually accounted for half of Taiwan's economic production and the bulk of exports, with electronics constituting the leading edge. Taiwan became the world's third largest producer, after the United States and Japan, of computer hardware. Between the early 1970s and the late 1990s it enjoyed more years of double-digit growth than any other nation. Taiwanese companies set up operations in Southeast Asia, China, Africa, and Latin America. By the 1980s the economic indicators far surpassed those on the mainland, including a per capita annual income of $8,000, 99 percent of households owning a color television, 92 percent literacy, and a life expectancy of seventy-five. In the late 1990s Taiwan businessmen built the world's tallest skyscraper, 1,667 feet high, in the capital city, Taipei. Rapid development, however, has brought severe problems, among them environmental destruction, traffic congestion, political corruption, and a severe economic slowdown in 1997. Concrete high-rise buildings increasingly displace the lush greenery of the mountains around Taipei.

Modernization has challenged Chinese values and traditions. The small roadside cafes selling noodle soup and meat dumplings, a beloved mainstay of local life for generations, often close, unable to compete with U.S. fast-food restaurants and convenience stores selling Coca-Cola, hamburgers, and ice cream. Rampant materialism concerns those who believe life should offer more than the quest for luxury goods and money. While Confucian values, such as the emphasis on hard work, have fostered the material success of the Little Dragons, some Taiwanese have worried that Confucian ethics, including respect for parents and concern for the community rather than the individual, are threatened. Agreeing with them, the Taiwan government has supported traditional Chinese culture and religion by mandating the teaching of Confucian ethics in the schools. Despite the modernization, traditional Chinese culture remains stronger in Taiwan than in the mainland. Over 90 percent of the people describe themselves as, like their ancestors, Buddhists, Daoists, Confucianists, or a mix of the three ancient traditions. Some 5 percent of Taiwan's people have adopted Christianity, and several million others are comfortable with secularism, only infrequently attending temples or churches.

Politics on Taiwan Like South Korea, Taiwan until the later 1980s followed the authoritarian Little Dragon political model. For several decades Chiang Kai-shek and his family controlled the island with a police state, which held numerous political prisoners. Favoring eventual reunification with the mainland whenever Communist rule there ended, Chiang made it illegal to advocate making Taiwan permanently independent of China. Both the Nationalist leaders on Taiwan and the Communists on the mainland believed in one China, of which Taiwan was one part. Both opposed those who advocated two separate Chinese nations. However, they disagreed on which party should rule this unified China. For four decades Chiang's political party, the Nationalists, ruled as the sole legal party, but in 1989, nudged by a growing middle class seeking liberalization, they permitted opposition candidates to run in elections. Gradually the regime recognized civil liberties, including the freedom of speech and press. The 2000 elections swept into office the Democratic Progressive Party (DPP), largely supported by the native Taiwanese; many party leaders, reflecting widespread Taiwanese opinion, advocated that Taiwan become a separate nation, a stance that angered both the Nationalist leaders on Taiwan and the Communist leaders on the mainland. However, Taiwan's voters seemed less eager to confront China by 2005, when elections showed reduced support for the DPP.

China has remained Taiwan's permanent challenge. Fearing an invasion to forcibly annex the island, Taiwan lavishly funded its military, kept a large standing army, and bought the latest fighter jets and gunboats, at the same time maintaining a defense alliance with the United States and allowing U.S. bases. But in 1978 the United States recognized the People's Republic as China's only government, embraced the one-China policy, and withdrew diplomatic recognition from its longtime ally, the Republic of China on Taiwan. However, the United States has maintained a strong informal economic presence and repeatedly reaffirms a commitment to defend the island from attack. In the later 1980s Taiwan and China began informal talks about improving relations. As a result, informal trade between the two countries has grown substantially and many people from Taiwan have visited the mainland, to do business or look up relatives. However, doubts about whether China will move toward political liberalization and allow for free speech, competing parties, and democracy, as well as alarm at occasional Chinese military exercises being conducted near Taiwan, have precluded any serious negotiations on reunification. For several decades China's leaders have threatened military action to prevent any move by Taiwan for permanent independence. Such action would alarm Japan, which has close ties to Taiwan, and might draw in the United States because of its commitment to defend Taiwan. Thus Taiwan's political future remains an open question, fiercely debated by Taiwanese and their several competing political parties.

The Little Dragons in the Global System

The rise of the Pacific Rim, including China, Japan, and the Little Dragons, in the late twentieth century reshaped the global system. The quarter of the world's population living along the western edge of the Pacific Basin established policies that allowed them to outpace the West and the rest of the world in economic growth while maintaining political stability. A global economy that had been based on the tripod of the United States, western Europe, and Japan now has to accommodate China and the Little Dragons. In the Little Dragons, high annual economic growth rates helped them industrialize, with both the benefits and the problems that entailed. By the 1990s the Little Dragons had diversified into high technology, making computers and other electronics products and thereby posing an economic challenge to Japan and the West. Meiji Japan in the late 1800s had established the economic model by mixing capitalism and state investment with strong government authority. The Little Dragons successfully used that model to develop and compete with Japan and the West.

Some economic trends suggested that the Pacific Rim nations were becoming an Asian counterpart to the European Community, the free trade zone formed by western European nations, thus foreshadowing, some scholars argued, the Pacific Century, in which Asian nations would dominate the world economy. Many of the East and Southeast Asian nations forged closer economic cooperation, with Japan and China forming the hubs. But in 1997 an economic meltdown hit South Korea, Taiwan, Japan, and the industrializing economies of Southeast Asia. As businesses closed, unemployment soared. By the early 2000s South Korea and Taiwan had regained some of their dynamism but still faced challenges. The uncertainty in the Pacific Rim and the continuing global power of the United States suggested that a Pacific Century would not materialize in the near future, and China and Japan will undoubtedly play major roles in the years to come. Yet in many respects, East Asia had returned to its historical role as a key engine of the world economy.

SECTION SUMMARY

- After World War II, Communist North Korea, assisted by the USSR and China, fought a war with South Korea, assisted by a U.S.-dominated United Nations force, that caused thousands of deaths and economic devastation and ended with the same border that existed at the start of the war.

- South Korean governments have grown more tolerant of internal dissent and more open to relations with former enemies such as Communist North Korea and China, though their primary emphasis has been on economic growth.

- After the Korean War, North Korea recovered with support from the USSR and China and was ruled as a repressive Communist dictatorship with a centrally planned economy whose shortcomings led to widespread food shortages in the 1990s.

- With the Communists ruling mainland China, the nationalists took over Taiwan, which they ruled as a police state and turned into an economic powerhouse, but relations with mainland China have continued to be tense.

- China and the "Little Dragons" (Taiwan, South Korea, Singapore, and Hong Kong) grew rapidly in the late twentieth century, leading to predictions of a coming "Pacific Century," but a slowdown in the 1990s dampened such expectations.

 *Online Study Center* ACE the Test

 # Chapter Summary

In the decades after World War II, East Asia experienced revolutionary upheavals and dramatic economic development that led to a resurgence of the region's influence in the world. The Communist triumph in China began the process of change. After experimenting with a Soviet-style Stalinist development model, China's leader, Mao Zedong, imposed his own version of communism. Emphasizing collective efforts, political values, and mass mobilization, Mao reorganized the rural economy into communes. He also sparked the Cultural Revolution, which attacked the bureaucracy and those who opposed his political and economic vision but also created turmoil. After Mao's death, Deng Xiaoping led China in a new direction; his market socialism energized the economy but led to tensions and then repression. During the 1990s market Leninism continued the economic reforms, providing a basis for rapid growth. China became a world economic power, but the growing inequalities of wealth have threatened to destabilize the nation.

The experiences of Japan and the Little Dragons differed from those of China. After the World War II defeat and U.S. occupation of Japan, the nation rapidly rose to become an economic powerhouse, based on a system mixing political democracy and a form of capitalism in which government and business worked together. The Japanese rebuilt their industries and fostered new forms of business and production. But social change came slowly, leaving Japan hierarchical. The Little Dragon nations of South Korea and Taiwan achieved industrial growth and prosperity by borrowing the Japanese model and mixing free markets with government intervention, eventually fostering democracy, while North Korea chose Stalinism and isolation from the world. The dynamism of most East Asian nations suggests that they have recovered from the disasters they experienced from the mid-1800s to the mid-1900s as a result of Western imperialism, Japanese expansion, and war, but their overall role remains unclear for the twenty-first century.

 *Online Study Center* Improve Your Grade Flashcards

Key Terms

Pacific Rim	Great Proletarian	market Leninism
Pacific Century	Cultural Revolution	Japan, Inc.
communes	Red Guards	salaryman
Great Leap Forward	Iron Rice Bowl	Little Dragons
	market socialism	

Suggested Reading

Books

Benson, Linda. *China Since 1949.* New York: Longman, 2002. Brief overview.

Cumings, Bruce. *Korea's Place in the Sun: A Modern History*. New York: W. W. Norton, 1997. A provocative and readable account emphasizing the years since World War II.

Dietrich, Craig. *People's China: A Brief History*, 3rd ed. New York: Oxford University Press, 1998. A fine study of China's Communist era.

Dreyer, June Teufel. *China's Political System: Modernization and Tradition*, 5th ed. New York: Longman, 2005. One of the best surveys of contemporary China.

Ebrey, Patricia Buckley, Anne Walthall, and James B. Palais. *East Asia: A Cultural, Social, and Political History*. Boston: Houghton Mifflin, 2006. A readable, comprehensive survey.

Gamer, Robert E., ed. *Understanding Contemporary China*, 2nd ed. Boulder, Colo.: Lynne Rienner, 2002. An excellent collection of essays on all aspects of Chinese society.

Kingston, Jeffrey. *Japan in Transformation, 1952–2000*. New York: Longman, 2001. A useful study of Japan's recent history.

McCargo, Duncan. *Contemporary Japan*, 2nd ed. New York: Palgrave, 2004. Provocative survey by a British scholar.

Reischauer, Edwin O., and Marius B. Jansen. *The Japanese Today: Change and Continuity*, 2nd ed., enlarged. Cambridge: Harvard University Press, 2004. A classic examination of Japanese society.

Schirokauer, Conrad, and Donald N. Clark. *Modern East Asia: A Brief History*. Belmont, Calif.: Wadsworth, 2004. Extensive coverage of China, Japan, and Korea in this era.

Schoppa, R. Keith. *Revolution and its Past: Identities and Change in Modern Chinese History*, 2nd ed. Upper Saddle River: Prentice Hall, 2006. Recent study offering an historical perspective.

Spence, Jonathan. *Mao Zedong*. New York: Viking, 1999. One of the best, most readable biographies of this major Chinese leader.

Stueck, William, ed. *The Korean War in World History*. Lexington: The University Press of Kentucky, 2004. A recent reassessment from multiple perspectives.

Tao Jie, et al., eds. *Holding Up Half the Sky: Chinese Women Past, Present, and Future*. New York: Feminist Press, 2004. Interesting essays on many aspects of women's lives in China today.

Terrill, Ross. *The New Chinese Empire*. New York: Basic Books, 2003. A readable recent study that places China's rise in historical context.

Yahuda, Michael. *The International Politics of the Asia-Pacific*, 2nd ed. New York: Routledge Curzon, 2004. Comprehensive study of the changing roles of China, Japan, Russia, and the U.S. in East Asia and the world.

Websites

Asian Studies
(**http://coombs.anu.edu.au/WWWVL-AsianStudies.html**). A vast metasite maintained at Australian National University, with links to hundreds of sites.

China-Profile: Facts, Figures, and Analyses
(**http://www.china-profile.com**). Offers useful information on China today.

East and Southeast Asia: An Annotated Directory of Internet Resources
(**http://newton.uor.edu/Departments&Programs/AsianStudies-Dept/asianam.html**). A superb set of links, maintained at the University of Redlands.

Internet East Asian History Sourcebook
(**http://www.fordham.edu/halsall/eastasia/eastasiasbook.html**). An invaluable collection of sources and links on China, Japan, and Korea from ancient to modern times.

Internet Guide to Chinese Studies
(**http://www.sino.uni-heidelberg.de/igcs/**). An excellent collection of links, maintained at a German university.

CHAPTER **28**

Rebuilding Europe and Russia, Since 1945

Online Study Center

This icon will direct you to interactive activities and study materials on the website: college.hmco. com/pic/lockard1e

Fall of the Berlin Wall In 1989, as Communist governments collapsed in eastern Europe, peaceful protesters climbed on top of the Berlin Wall, which had already been decorated with graffiti. The wall, which divided Communist East and democratic West Berlin, was soon torn down.   (AP/Wide World Photos)

This [united] Europe must be born. And she will, when Spaniards say "our Chartres," Englishmen "our Cracow," Italians "our Copenhagen," and Germans "our Bruges." Then Europe will live.

**J**acques Delors (deh-LOW-er) faced a challenge. Born in 1925, this French banker's son turned socialist politician had lived through a tumultuous and divisive modern European history, including the Great Depression, World War II, and the Cold War. Now, after holding high economic positions in the French government, he had dedicated himself to building a united Europe. In 1985 he became president of the European Commission, established to further European political cooperation. His goal was to reconcile national loyalties with support for a united Europe. In December 1991, Delors convened the leaders of twelve European nations, already closely linked through a common economic market, in the Dutch city of Maastricht. Calling on all his formidable diplomatic skills and communicating his sense of mission, he prodded them to conclude a historic agreement for increased cooperation. The Maastricht meeting realized a dream of European unity that had been percolating among European visionaries, such as the Spanish writer quoted above, for decades. Now Europeans, chastened by centuries of conflict, seemed ready to subordinate national interests to a common good.

Delors asked the national leaders meeting at Maastricht to transform the economic and political alliance begun in the late 1940s and expanded in the 1950s into a more comprehensive union. This meeting on Europe's future took place in the same month that the Soviet Union (USSR) dissolved. With their biggest Communist rival no longer a threat, European leaders hoped to link their countries to ensure a stable and peaceful future. They planned to invite some states formerly allied with the Soviet Union to join their union. In theory the new European Union, as the grouping was called, would stretch from the Atlantic to the western frontier of Russia, allowing people to cross borders between member states without passports and permitting trade goods to pass freely from country to country. A single currency, the *euro*, would also unite these states. Persuaded by Delors, conference leaders signed the Maastricht Treaty, and it was later ratified by voters in all member nations, though debates continued as new members joined. While facing bumps in the road, the European Union, given the centuries of European strife that was now fading, was nonetheless a huge achievement, for which Delors can claim some of the credit.

From 1945 until 1990 three themes dominated European history: (1) the Cold War shaped by the United States and the USSR, the world's rival superpowers, each with a political and military power vastly exceeding that of other nations; (2) the rebirth of western European wealth and power; and (3) the movement toward European unity represented by the Maastricht Treaty. After World War II, which had left most European countries in shambles, Europe became divided by the Cold War into mutually hostile political and military blocs. However, while eastern Europe came under Soviet domination in the later 1940s, enduring authoritarian Communist governments and struggling economically, much of western Europe recovered its prosperity, ensuring freedom, peace, and the well-being of citizens. The trauma of two world wars had fostered a drive for unity by consensus of the nation-states involved rather than through military might. This movement accelerated after 1989, when the governments allied to the USSR collapsed and communism was largely abandoned, opening the way for a new, interconnected Europe that had to forge a new direction in a post–Cold War world in which the United States held the dominant power.

FOCUS QUESTIONS

1. What factors fostered the movement toward unity in western Europe?
2. How did the rise of welfare states transform western European societies?
3. What factors contributed to political crises in the Soviet Union and eastern Europe?
4. How did the demise of the Communist system contribute to a new Europe?

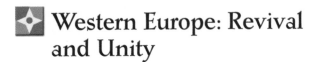

Western Europe: Revival and Unity

What factors fostered the movement toward unity in western Europe?

Western Europe emerged from the ashes of World War II economically and morally bankrupt, yet, made a rapid recovery with aid from the United States. Most western European societies reestablished working multiparty democracies that accorded personal freedom to their citizens. Beginning in 1947, however, Europe was split into two mutually hostile camps, western and eastern Europe, each with a different model of postwar reconstruction and rival military forces. Gradually West Germany, France, and Britain served as the core of a rebuilt, increasingly unified European community and were able to regain influence in the world. The combination of economic prosperity and new opportunities blunted the appeal of radicalism in western Europe.

Recovery from War

World War II had left western Europe devastated in the later 1940s. The war had cost some 50 million lives. Large-scale air raids had reduced major cities to rubble and destroyed bridges, tunnels, and roads; Europe's economic potential was cut by some 50 percent. Transportation, food, housing, and fuel were in short supply. The chaos of war and the redrawing of political boundaries after the war had displaced people from their home countries, including 10 million Germans who were forced to leave eastern Europe, where many had lived for generations, and move to Germany. Emotionally traumatized by the war and the atrocities that had been committed, Europeans also saw their prestige in tatters around the world. War crimes trials held by the victorious Allies in Nuremberg, Germany, in 1946 condemned Nazi leaders to death and declared crimes against humanity, especially genocide, indefensible. A Dutch thinker wrote that the old Europe was dead and beyond redemption. A fresh start was needed.

Economic growth provided the foundation for a new Europe. In 1947 the U.S. secretary of state, former general George Marshall (1880–1959), who had directed the U.S. army through World War II, proposed that, in order to achieve European stability and guarantee peace, the United States assist in restoring the economic health of the world, especially Europe. This initiative, the **Marshall Plan**, created a recovery program aimed at preventing Communist expansion and spreading liberal economic principles, such as free markets. Recognizing that economic problems had helped spark World War II, between 1948 and 1952 the United States offered $13 billion in aid, about half going to Britain, France, and West Germany. In exchange, American business enjoyed greater

---

Marshall Plan A recovery program proposed for western Europe by the United States that aimed to prevent Communist expansion and to spread liberal economic principles.

CHRONOLOGY	Western Europe	Russia	Eastern Europe
1940	1946–1989 Cold War 1949 Formation of NATO 1957 European Common Market	1955 Warsaw Pact	1945–1948 Formation of Communist governments
1960		1979–1989 Soviet war in Afghanistan	
1980	1991 Maastricht Treaty	1991 Breakup of Soviet Union	1989 End of Communist governments

access to European markets. The Marshall Plan restored agricultural and industrial production while bolstering international trade. The rapid economic resurgence from 1948 to 1965, unmatched in world history except for Japan's recovery in the same years (see Chapter 27), also owed much to liberal democracy, modern production and managerial techniques, advances in science and technology, and changes in power generation, transportation, and agriculture.

The British leader Winston Churchill (1874–1965), who served twice as prime minister (1940–1945, 1951–1955), prophecied the new trends for Europe. First, speaking in the United States in 1946 with U.S. president Harry S Truman at his side, Churchill predicted the coming Cold War, warning that his wartime ally, the Soviet Union, was expansionist and required the concerted action of many nations to stop. In words that lived for years afterward, he said that "an iron curtain" had descended across Europe, dividing western Europe from eastern Europe and pro-Western, capitalist West Germany from Communist East Germany. This Cold War division, however, as Churchill also predicted, helped stimulate a western European movement for cooperation. When eight hundred delegates met at the Hague, in Holland, in 1948, where they called for a democratic European economic union and the renunciation of national rivalry, Churchill urged them to "proclaim the mission and the design of a United Europe, where men and women of every country will think of being European as of belonging to their native land, and wherever they go in this wide domain they will truly feel 'Here I am at home'"[2] (see Chronology: Western Europe, 1945–1989). The Hague Congress proposed practical steps toward unity, such as creating a European assembly and a court of human rights, and generated what soon became the "European Movement."

The Remaking of European Nations

After the war, the western European governments and politics changed. Europeans made a commitment to sustain parliamentary democracy. This was true for both the republics and the surviving constitutional monarchies, including Belgium, Britain, the Netherlands, and the Scandinavian nations, where kings and queens remained symbols of their people but enjoyed little power. Four major states—France, Italy, West

CHRONOLOGY	Western Europe, 1945–1989
1946–1949	Greek civil war
1947–1989	Cold War
1947–1969	De Gaulle era in France
1948	Hague Congress on European unity
1948–1949	Berlin crisis
1948–1952	Marshall Plan
1949	Formation of NATO
1951	Formation of European Coal and Steel Community
1957	Formation of European Common Market
1969	West German ostpolitik policy

Germany, and Britain—were the most influential in postwar western Europe. Throughout Europe, new leaders and parties rose to power. Longtime dictators opposed to change were overthrown and replaced by democrats in Spain, Portugal, and Greece in the 1970s. The end of colonial empires, and the loss of revenues from them, also reshaped European politics.

New Politics New European political alignments emerged. Given the frequent conflicts between France and Germany in the past, political stability in western Europe depended on improved relations between these two nations, as well as on German recovery from war. Some leaders sought to reverse these old hostilities. Charles De Gaulle (1890–1970), the crusty general and proud nationalist who largely dominated French politics between 1947 and 1969, imagined France, as he put it, "like the princess in the fairy stories, as dedicated to an exalted and exceptional destiny."[3] But overcoming centuries of hatred, he made French-German reconciliation the cornerstone

Basque Terrorism The extremist Basque nationalist movement, the ETA, has waged a terrorist campaign against the Spanish government for decades. They have assassinated dozens of people and exploded bombs at government targets in cities and towns, resulting in the sort of destruction shown here after one attack. (AP/Wide World Photos)

of French policy. Similarly, the West German leader, Konrad Adenauer (ODD-en-HOUR) (1876–1967), sought a more cooperative relationship with France. Germany's reconciliation with France and its other neighbors was furthered in the 1960s by West German chancellor Willy Brandt (1913–1992), a fervent anti-Nazi who, in the 1930s, had moved to Norway and then Sweden to escape Adolph Hitler's government. Brandt accepted German responsibilities for the war and the new borders imposed after the war, which awarded a large chunk of German territory to Poland.

The improved French-German relationship also owed much to economic growth. Because of its sheer size and central location, West Germany's economy, which rapidly recovered in the 1950s and 1960s, lay at the heart of western European recovery. By 1960 West Germany, now firmly allied with France, accounted for a fifth of the world's trade in manufactured goods, surpassing Britain, which had been dominant in world trade in the 1800s.

New political parties and movements took shape. On the right, parties calling themselves Christian Democrats, which had been closely tied to the Catholic Church before World War II, freed themselves from clerical patronage. Still emphasizing Christian values and protecting the traditional family, these conservative parties either formed governments or led the opposition in a half dozen countries, including West Germany and Italy. But eventually some Christian Democratic leaders became corrupt: scandals arose especially in West Germany and Italy, and the parties had lost considerable support by the 1990s.

At the same time, parties on the left competed for support. Most influential, the social democratic parties, which favored generous welfare programs to provide a safety net for all citizens, acquired more clout than they had enjoyed in the prewar years. Social democratic governments came to power in several countries, including Britain and France, soon after the war and

moved toward state ownership of large industries such as steel and railroads. Eventually most of the social democratic parties, such as the British Labor Party, abandoned state ownership and economic planning for free markets. Meanwhile, the western European Communist parties, with whom the social democrats had largely avoided cooperation, declined rapidly, maintaining a substantial following only in France, Italy, Portugal, and Spain. Seeking popular support in these democratic nations, they often embraced **Eurocommunism**, a form of communism in western Europe that embraced political democracy and free elections and that rejected Soviet domination. Despite the shift to Eurocommunism, however, the Communist parties lost most of their support in the 1990s, often fragmenting into small feuding parties. By the 1980s a new political movement had had an impact, especially in West Germany. This movement, the **Greens**, rejected militarism and heavy industry and favored environmental protection over economic growth. Women such as Petra Kelly (1947–1992) were prominent in the West German Green Party leadership, helping it appeal to women voters and win seats in the West German parliament.

Western Europe was not immune to dissident movements and other forms of political unrest. For instance, a civil war raged in Greece between 1946 and 1949, where conservatives supporting the monarchy, aided by the United States, defeated revolutionaries who wanted to end the monarchy and establish a Communist state. Elsewhere, the desire of ethnic minorities for their own nations spurred unrest, and sometimes terrorism by extremists. A chronic ethnic conflict embroiled Spain, where the Basque people, who live mostly in the north and speak a language completely different from Spanish, have long sought either autonomy within, or independence from, Spain. An underground Basque independence movement, known as ETA (for "Basque Homeland and Freedom"), has carried out assassinations, bombings, and other terrorist acts against peo-

---

Eurocommunism A form of communism in western Europe that embraced political democracy and free elections and that rejected Soviet domination.

Greens A political movement in western Europe that rejected militarism and heavy industry and favored environmental protection over economic growth.

ple linked to the Spanish government. Similarly, for decades in Northern Ireland, also known as Ulster, a territory that occupies a quarter of the island of Ireland but remains a part of Great Britain, the Catholic minority have sought freedom from British rule and the ability to merge the province with the largely Catholic Irish republic, while the majority Protestants have wanted to remain a British province. Over the past half century extremist Catholic and Protestant paramilitary groups have attacked each other and, at times, fought the British army, causing thousands of deaths, including those of many innocent civilians caught in the crossfire.

Dismantling European Empires   In the thirty years after World War II, most European colonizers abandoned their efforts to quell nationalist movements in Asia and Africa and started to leave their colonial territories. For example, the British, whose empire had occupied an area 125 times larger than Great Britain, realized that imperial glory was only memory. In 1947 they bowed to the demands of Indian nationalists and recognized the independence of India, and they started a process of decolonization elsewhere as well. The Dutch, facing a determined nationalist resistance, reluctantly followed the British example and abandoned their lucrative colony, Indonesia, in 1950. By the mid-1960s the British had turned over most of their colonies in Africa, Asia, and the Caribbean to local leaders. By the 1990s they retained control of only a few tiny outposts, such as Gibraltar, a strategically valuable peninsula on the southern coast of Spain, and a few Caribbean, South Atlantic, and South Pacific islands. While postimperial Britain sought to balance a special relationship to the United States, forged in the fires of two world wars, with closer links to Europe, it also continued financial assistance and capital investment to many former colonies and maintained a more formal connection with them through the **British Commonwealth of Nations**. The Commonwealth, which the British established in 1931 and which comprised fifty-three states by 2000, provided a forum for the member states to cooperate politically and discuss issues of mutual interest.

By contrast to the British, the French and Portuguese only grudgingly recognized the inevitable. In the mid-1940s nationalist rebellions broke out in French-controlled Algeria and Vietnam, which France attempted to quell at the cost of much bloodshed. In his criticism of France's use of torture against rebels in Algeria, the French philosopher Jean-Paul Sartre, an outspoken opponent of colonialism, wrote: "We are sick, very sick. Feverish and prostrate, obsessed by old dreams of glory and the foreboding of its shame. France is struggling in the grip of a nightmare it is unable either to flee or to decipher."[4] In 1954, unable to defeat Communist-led rebels, the French withdrew from Vietnam, and in 1962 they left Algeria, causing 800,000 European settlers, many embittered toward the French government for its withdrawal from Algeria, to flee to France.

Although it retained a few small Caribbean, Pacific, and Indian Ocean islands and French Guiana, France, like Britain and the Netherlands, had to define its role in regard to its former colonies. Eventually France established close relations with most of its former colonies, including an enduring economic connection that critics considered a form of neocolonialism, or indirect domination, since French business interests and advisers remained prominent in these areas. Portugal wasted lives and wealth violently resisting decolonization against nationalist movements but, after democrats overthrew the longstanding fascist dictatorship, granted its African colonies independence in 1975.

Europe and NATO in the Cold War

Beginning in 1946, the Cold War, shaped by rivalry between the two superpowers, the United States and the USSR, influenced European politics and the various European nations' roles in the world. The USSR helped install Communist governments in eastern Europe and East Germany. Meanwhile, the other superpower, the United States, assumed the burden for protecting western Europe militarily. In 1947 the U.S. president, Harry Truman (president 1945–1953), formed a policy, known as the **Truman Doctrine**, that asserted that the United States was the leader of the free world and was charged with defending countries, such as Greece and Turkey, that were threatened by Communist movements or Soviet pressure.

Strong European and U.S. fears of possible Soviet attack led to the formation in 1949 of the North Atlantic Treaty Organization, commonly known as **NATO**, a military alliance that linked nine western European countries with the United States and Canada. NATO allowed coordination of defense policies against the USSR and the Communist states allied with it, known as the **Soviet bloc**, to repulse any potential Soviet military attack across the "iron curtain" frontier. To discourage any Soviet expansion, permanent U.S. military bases were set up in NATO countries, especially West Germany. The Soviets responded in 1955 by forming the **Warsaw Pact**, a defense alliance that linked the Communist-ruled eastern European countries with the USSR (see Map 28.1). By the 1980s senior officers in NATO and the Warsaw Pact had spent their careers preparing for a war that, partly because both sides possessed nuclear weapons and were reluctant to risk having their own territories destroyed, never came. Like Russians and Americans, western Europeans were alarmed by nuclear weapons, which could obliterate their cities in minutes, and worried that a nuclear conflict between

---

British Commonwealth of Nations   A forum, established by Britain in 1931, for discussing issues of mutual interest with its former colonies.

Truman Doctrine   A policy formed in 1947 that asserted that the United States was the leader of the free world and was charged with protecting countries like Greece and Turkey from communism.

NATO (North Atlantic Treaty Organization)   A military alliance, formed in 1949, that linked nine western European countries with the United States and Canada.

Soviet bloc   The Soviet Union and the Communist states allied with it.

Warsaw Pact   A defense alliance formed in 1955 that linked the Communist-ruled eastern European countries with the USSR.

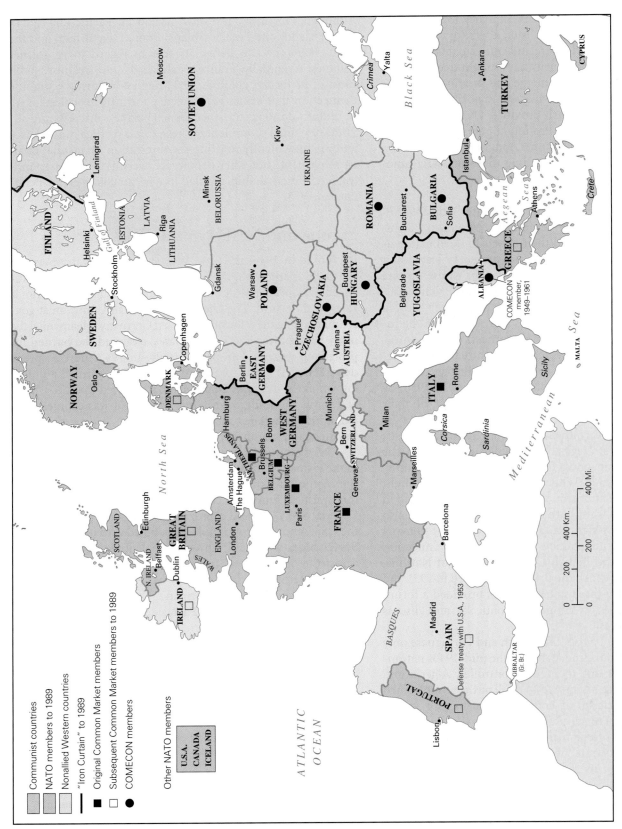

Map 28.1   Military Alliances and Multinational Economic Groupings, 1949–1989
Post–World War II Europe was divided by Cold War politics into Communist and non-Communist blocs. Most western European nations joined the NATO defense alliance. Western Europeans also cooperated in economic matters. By 1989 the Common Market had expanded from six to eleven members. The Soviet bloc counterpart, COMECON, had eight members.

the United States and the USSR would inevitably destroy Europe as well.

The Cold War and NATO were partly a response to the postwar division of Germany. Each of the four World War II allies—the United States, Britain, France, and the USSR—had an occupation zone in Germany and had also divided up the pre-1945 German capital, Berlin. In 1948 the three Western powers united their occupation zones. Angered by this move, the USSR blockaded Berlin to prevent supplies from reaching the city's Western-administered zone by land through Soviet-controlled East Germany. For a year the allies supplied the city by airlift to the Berlin airport; each day the allied cargo planes landed with 8,000 tons of food and fuel for 2 million Berliners. In 1949 the USSR stopped the blockade and allowed the creation of the Federal Republic of Germany, or West Germany, while forming its own allied government, the German Democratic Republic, or East Germany. By 1954 West Germany was fully sovereign and soon joined NATO.

In the 1960s, Cold War fears slackened in Europe as the danger of actual war faded, leading western Europeans to reappraise their policies toward both the United States and the Soviet bloc. Some Europeans, especially in Britain, were strong Atlanticists and promoted the U.S. alliance, while others emphasized what French president Charles De Gaulle called a "European Europe" and placed the United States at arm's length. Many Europeans grew to resent U.S. power and what they considered irresponsible U.S. foreign policies. Most Europeans opposed the American war in Vietnam, which American leaders justified as an effort to stop the spread of communism in Asia, as well as U.S. interventions to overthrow left-leaning governments in Latin America, such as Guatemala (1954) and Chile (1973). The West German chancellor Willy Brandt, a Social Democrat, began the rethinking of Cold War attitudes in 1969. Although Brandt was strongly anti-Communist, his policy of **ostpolitik** ("eastern politics") sought a reconciliation between West and East Germany and an expanded western European dialogue with the USSR. This policy led to a thaw in West Germany's relations with the Soviet bloc and gave hope to eastern Europeans who wanted more freedom. Gradually western Europeans, by building their own military forces, became less reliant on U.S. power and played a larger role in NATO. Despite the differences between Europeans and Americans, however, the Western alliance and NATO remained strong because of mutual interests during the Cold War.

From Cooperation to European Community

As a result of wartime economic destruction, increasing U.S. political and economic power, and the costs of suppressing nationalism in the Western colonies, western Europe's role in the global economic system changed. Between 1800 and 1914 Europe had energized the world economy, supplying goods, services, capital, and people to the rest of the world. Between the two world wars Europeans still owned enterprises all over the globe, including Indian tea plantations, Malayan rubber estates, African mines, and South American railroads. But during the 1940s Europeans lost influence to the United States. The Bretton Woods agreement on international monetary cooperation, negotiated by representatives of forty-four countries in 1944, reshaped the world economy by making the U.S. dollar, pegged to the price of gold, the staple currency of the Western nations.

Faced with declining economic influence in the world, Europeans concluded they had no choice but to cooperate with each other. In 1949 ten western European nations formed the Council of Europe, which sought to operate on the basis of a shared cultural heritage and democratic principles. In 1950 the Council produced the European Convention on Human Rights, the root of a Europe-wide justice system and court. But some leaders wanted more. The two most notable were Jean Monnet (MOAN-ay) (1888–1979), a French economist, financier, and former League of Nations official who was often called the "Father of United Europe," and French prime minister Robert Schuman (1886–1963), whose wartime service against the Nazis made him a strong proponent of French-German reconciliation; the two men wanted to make further war in Europe not only unthinkable but impossible. To encourage better economic coordination, they devised a plan for a European Coal and Steel Community (ECSC), which was finally formed with the signing of the Treaty of Paris in 1951. They hoped that the ECSC, which brought together six nations, including France and Germany, would be a first step to build a framework for unity and encourage peace in Europe. Indeed, the ECSC promoted European economic stabilization. But some European nations, including Britain, feared loss of economic independence and declined to join.

Building on the foundation of the ECSC, the Common Market, later known as the European Community (EC), was formed in 1957 with six members: France, Italy, West Germany, the Netherlands, Belgium, and Luxembourg. The new organization included a customs union to remove tariff barriers between members, thus opening frontiers to the free movement of capital and labor. The members also set a plan for preserving peace and liberty by pooling economic resources, and they called upon other Europeans to join in their efforts. Soon others did. The EC added Britain, Ireland, and Denmark in 1973.

The EC created unprecedented economic unity in the world's largest free trade zone, but it only slowly generated political unity. The founders, such as Monnet and Schuman, dreamed of a united Europe: societies that depend on one another, they reasoned, won't go to war. But European nationalism occasionally flared up. The EC weathered many disagreements as the member nations squabbled to get the best deal for their own farmers or businesses, and the British, an island people proud of their distinctive traditions and always wary of continental Europeans, periodically threatened to quit the grouping. Every member economy had to adapt to the laws of the marketplace, dumping uncompetitive industries. Some doubters, the "Euro-skeptics," believed cooperation had gone too far. Yet the EC greatly reduced old national tensions. The members eventually established an elected European Parliament, based in

---

ostpolitik ("eastern politics") A West German policy, promoted by Chancellor Willy Brandt, seeking a reconciliation between West and East Germany and an expanded dialogue with the USSR.

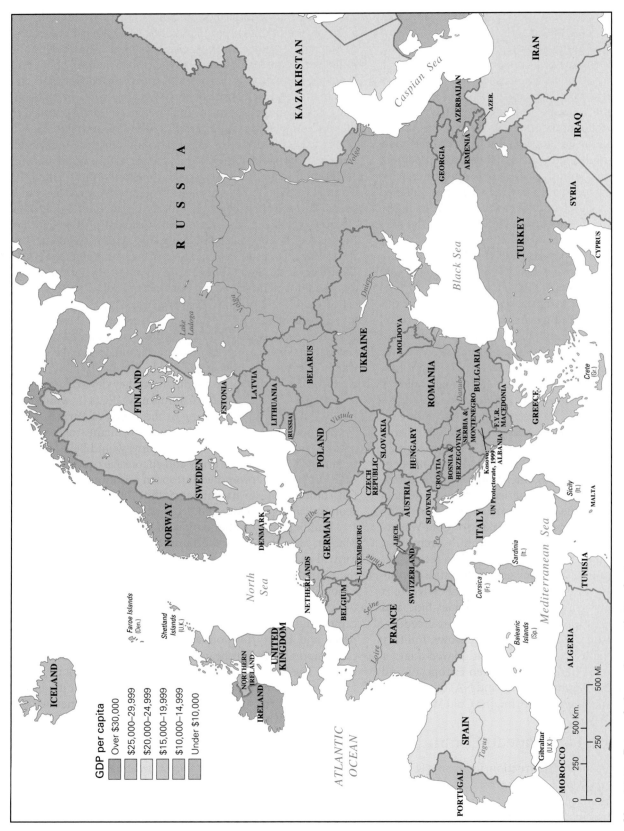

Map 28.2 Europe's Gross Domestic Product

The gross domestic product, or the official measure of the output of goods and services in a national economy, provides a good summary of a nation's economic production. In the early twenty-first century, Norway, Ireland, and Switzerland were the most productive European countries on a per capita basis, while former Soviet bloc nations had the weakest performance.

Brussels, Belgium, to discuss shared issues and to make policies that encouraged cooperation and standardization.

The European Community fostered unprecedented economic growth, creating a consumer society in western Europe (see Map 28.2). The prosperous 1960s spurred the rapid expansion of European and world trade. With higher wages, greater purchasing power, and more available consumer products, families bought automobiles, washing machines, refrigerators, and televisions. More people worked in the service sector and fewer in agriculture. The middle classes grew rapidly, while blue-collar workers shared middle-class aspirations. Consumer markets reached from Europe's sprawling cities into remote villages, transforming them. A journalist's description of an old French village in 1973 revealed the change: "The last horse trod its streets in 1968. The water mill closed down in 1952. The washing machine replaced the wash house—and broke up the community of women—in the 1960s."[5] Europeans invested in railroads using the latest technologies, high speed turnpikes to link peoples together, and mass transit—subways and commuter trains—to make city life more convenient. Yet prosperity did not eliminate all poverty or regional disparities. For example, industrialized northern Italy remained much wealthier than largely agricultural southern Italy.

Despite the growing cooperation and the successes it fostered, western Europe still faced mounting economic problems. Europeans were hurt by decisions by U.S. leaders that led to the dismantling of the Bretton Woods international monetary system. In 1971, with the U.S. economy undermined by the war in Vietnam, President Richard Nixon devalued the U.S. dollar, the staple currency of the Western nations, and ended its parity with gold. These moves destabilized world trade, triggering soaring prices and trade deficits. Then in 1973 European economies were brought to a standstill by a quadrupling of oil prices, followed by a short embargo on oil exports by the major oil-producing nations, which were angered by Western support of Israel. The frustrated motorists waiting in long lines at gas stations showed how vulnerable prosperity could be in the global system. Western Europe also faced the environmental problems common to all industrial societies, such as noxious air, toxic waste, and lakes and forests dying from acid rain, the apparent price of industrialization.

Cooperation also could not avert other economic problems deriving from global economic patterns. The end of cheap energy and growing competition from industrializing Asian nations and Japan hurt local European industries and workers. Factories built a century or more earlier, often decaying and inefficient, scaled back operations or closed, causing high unemployment in industrial cities such as Birmingham and Manchester in England. Jobless young people, living in bleak row houses or apartments and surviving on welfare payments, hung out on street corners, some turning to drugs or crime. By 1983 unemployment rates in western Europe had risen to 10 percent, posing a special problem to those just out of school, women, and immigrants. Some Europeans, blaming their problems on immigrant workers, especially the Arabs and Turks who competed with local people for jobs, sought to have immigration curbed. These feelings gave a boost to rightwing, anti-immigrant parties. Capitalizing on the economic problems, free market conservatives often regained political power, and once in power, they penalized striking workers and weakened labor unions.

SECTION SUMMARY

- World War II devastated western Europe's population, infrastructure, and economy, but it enjoyed a remarkable period of growth, aided by extensive U.S. funding under the Marshall Plan.

- After World War II, Germany and France overcame centuries of mutual hatred, rightwing Christian Democrat parties competed with leftist social democrats, and the Greens agitated for environmental protection over economic growth.

- A wave of decolonization followed World War II, though the British Commonwealth maintained connections between Great Britain and its former colonies, and France, after struggling to maintain its colonies, maintained economic ties with its former holdings.

- The Cold War shaped European politics, with eastern Europe allied with the USSR and western Europe allied with the United States, but over time some European leaders distanced themselves from U.S. policies and advocated dialogue with the USSR.

- Having been surpassed economically by the United States, European countries joined together in the European Community, which became the world's largest free trade zone and led to increased prosperity; however, the 1970s brought hard times, and European unity sometimes threatened to give way.

 ## Western European Societies and Cultures

How did the rise of welfare states transform western European societies?

In the ashes of World War II the wartime British prime minister, Winston Churchill, wrote, "What is Europe? A rubble heap, a charnel house, a breeding ground for pestilence and hate."[6] Seeing the need for change, western European nations embarked on various experiments to reshape their societies and improve the quality of life for all their citizens. The main experiment was the blending of capitalism and socialism. The economic boom from the late 1940s to the 1970s allowed most western European states, influenced by socialism, to construct welfare programs that fostered political stability, ensured public health, and eliminated poverty for most citizens. Gender relations, family life, and sexual attitudes were also reshaped, while musicians, philosophers, and churches addressed the changes of the times.

Social Democracy

The rise of western European **welfare states**, government systems that offer their citizens a range of state-subsidized health, education, and social service benefits, and the high quality of life they fostered, owed much to an influential political philosophy called social democracy. Social democracy derived from socialists in the early 1900s who favored evolutionary rather than revolutionary change, eventually promoting a mixing of liberal democracy, market economies, and a safety net for workers. Since 1945 social democratic parties have governed or been the dominant opposition in many Western countries. They have usually controlled the governments in the Scandinavian nations of Denmark, Finland, Norway, and Sweden and have often governed in several other nations, including Britain, France, and West Germany. They have also been influential in Australia, Canada, and especially New Zealand.

Welfare States Since the 1940s social democracy has meant welfare programs, a mixed capitalist-socialist economy, a commitment to parliamentary democracy and civil liberties, support for labor unions, and the goal of moderating the extremes of wealth and poverty. As a result of these priorities, workers in northern and central Europe have gained more rights and protections than workers enjoy anywhere else in the world. In West Germany, for example, they received generous pensions and gained seats on the boards of directors of the enterprises that employ them. Whatever their occupation, Europeans have often valued leisure at the expense of work. Europeans boast that they work to live while Americans, who on average earn more, live to work. Surveys showed that less than half of Europeans considered it important to make lots of money. By the 1990s both white-collar and blue-collar Europeans worked fewer hours each year than their counterparts in the United States and Japan. The 35-hour workweek became the norm in France and West Germany. By 2000, the average German spent around 400 fewer hours a year on the job than the average American. Depending on the European society, the average paid vacation has averaged four to six weeks a year. During the most popular vacation month, August, the beach and mountain resorts are jammed, and, with their employees gone, stores often offer limited services. Social democracies remain free market economies, but capitalism is mixed with government regulation.

Citizens in nations influenced by social democracy have received generous taxpayer-funded benefits from the state. Europeans tend to define welfare not just as assistance to the poor, as Americans do, but as protections to ensure that everyone enjoys better living standards and opportunities. Free education through the university level (but with stiff university entrance exams) has helped people from working-class and farming backgrounds to move into the middle and upper classes. Generous unemployment insurance removes the pain of job loss. Governments also subsidize housing for the elderly, while inexpensive, widely available day care allows mothers to work outside the home for wages. Whether married or single, custodial parents receive child support payments from the welfare state. Adding to these benefits, extensive mass transit makes travel and commuting affordable for all. Meanwhile, socialized medicine, such as the British National Health Service, which opened in 1948, has removed the fear of serious illness, providing inexpensive prescription drugs and guaranteeing medical care to all. These benefits have greatly improved public health. Where Europeans had looked to the extended family for support in the early 1900s, now they expect the welfare state to care for the elderly and incapacitated. In addition, northern European nations have the most equitable distributions of income in the world and have nearly eliminated slums and real poverty.

The Scandinavian nations, poor a century ago, have claimed both the strongest social democratic governments and the world's most prosperous societies. Norway has achieved the highest standard of living in the Western world, thanks to North Sea oil and a generous welfare state. The annual Human Development Report, issued by the United Nations, ranked Norway and Sweden as having the highest quality of life in the world in 2004, followed by three other countries in which social democracy has been influential: Australia, Canada, and the Netherlands. In 2005 the Scandinavian nations were also ranked, along with countries such as Ireland, the Netherlands,

Swedish Father and Child Swedes have been the most innovative Europeans in social policy, including adopting in 1975 a law requiring employers to grant parental leave. While women mainly take advantage of the law, some men, including this man with his child, take off the full allotted time. (B.O. Olsson, photographer)

---

welfare states Government systems that offer their citizens a range of state-subsidized health, education, and social service benefits; adopted by western European nations after World War II.

and Switzerland, as having the most press freedom in the world, with the least government interference in the free flow of information. Sweden has been Europe's most creative country in experimenting with social change. Women, youth, and even animals have more rights and protections there than elsewhere. Swedish citizens enjoy housing subsidies, free hospitalization, and a pension that pays two-thirds of their salary upon retirement. By providing child care in kindergartens and preschools, the Swedes attract women into the work force. While Sweden has achieved the world's most level playing field and lowest poverty rate, its services have not dampened economic growth. Indeed, after the 1970s, Sweden has often enjoyed the most dynamic economic growth in Europe. The other Scandinavian nations have also generally enjoyed strong economies.

Economic Challenges Although the welfare states help create political and social stability, when economic growth rates level off they cannot meet all the fresh demands placed on them. Funding the welfare programs has required high taxes, often half of a citizen's annual income, and worker protections make it hard for companies to fire workers, prompting companies to hire fewer people. Workers have enjoyed so much security that they have not needed to strive harder. Thus the shift from focusing on work to focusing on leisure has an economic cost. Furthermore, many people with modest incomes, especially immigrants, live in drab apartment blocks or houses, often far from potential jobs and the best schools.

Beginning in the 1980s the welfare states experienced more problems related to a downturn of the world economy and the resulting recession. For decades governments had paid for social services by borrowing against future exports, a strategy known as deficit spending. The falling export profits that resulted from the economic downturn thus placed the welfare systems under strain, forcing cutbacks in benefits, and also prompted nations to cut spending for military defense. To enhance their competitiveness, companies began downsizing, thus putting pressure on generous unemployment programs. In some countries, conservative parties gained power and began to modify the welfare systems. For example, in Britain, the government led by Prime Minister Margaret Thatcher (governed 1979–1990), a free market enthusiast, reduced health services, with the result that people had to wait longer to receive medical attention. But the conservative regimes did not dismantle welfare state institutions such as national health insurance, which remained hugely popular.

The economic problems, unlike those caused by the Great Depression of the 1930s, did not bring violence or political instability. While occasionally a political party with an anti-immigrant or anti–European Union platform has gained a following, extremist rightwing and ultranationalist forces have remained weak in most countries. For example, the French National Front, led by the paratrooper turned lawyer Jean-Marie Le Pen (b. 1928), won 10 percent of the national vote in 1986 with a platform calling for expulsion of Arab and African immigrants and secession from the European Community, but

since then Le Pen's appeal has faded. The welfare state, which allows even the unemployed to receive their basic necessities, provides stability because it diminishes workers' fear of job competition from immigrants. Hence, even most free market conservatives have accepted the broad framework of the welfare state, although they want to make it more efficient and cost-effective.

Social Activism, Reform, and Gender Relations

Western European societies changed dramatically in the decades since 1945. Although most people have seemed satisfied with their lives, occasional student and worker protests against capitalism and materialism have erupted. During the 1960s leftist activism was especially pervasive. Social movements helped spur new trends in other areas of life.

Social Protests and Movements A serious challenge to mainstream society came in 1968, when youth protests broke out in France that were aimed at the aging, autocratic president Charles De Gaulle, an antiquated university education system, and the unpopular U.S. war in Vietnam, France's former colony. Protest posters urged students to "be realistic—ask for the impossible." Soon university students went on strike, hundreds of them were beaten by police, protesters blocked traffic in parts of Paris, and activists fought pitched battles in the streets with police, who responded with teargas. As public sentiment shifted toward the protesters, industrial workers, demanding higher wages and more say in decision making, called a general strike, bringing some 10 million workers into the streets. Although De Gaulle outmaneuvered the protesters by rallying conservatives, raising workers' wages, and calling for a new national election, the protests begun in Paris soon spread to Italy and West Germany, where students resented conservative governments, staid bureaucracies, rigid university systems, and powerful business interests. Lacking strong public support, however, Europe's student protests soon fizzled; governments did not fall or need troops to restore order. However, De Gaulle resigned a year later after the public rejected, in a referendum, his proposals to reorganize the French government.

Europeans also dealt with social problems common to all industrialized nations, such as drug and alcohol abuse and high divorce rates. But European attitudes and responses to the problems were often different from those in other countries. In contrast to the United States, for example, which has harshly punished drug use and trafficking, by the 1980s western European legal systems generally treated drug use and minor drug sales as social and medical issues rather than criminal ones. Some European countries even decriminalized use of less dangerous drugs, such as marijuana. Other laws in Europe also differed from those elsewhere in the world. Europeans generally opposed and abolished capital punishment, and most European nations enacted strict gun control laws, often banning handguns. The scarcity of guns fostered low rates of violent crime.

Social Patterns Attitudes toward marriage and gender relations also shifted in Europe. After World War II, governments tried to revitalize traditional attitudes toward marriage and the family, such as the view that women were chiefly homemakers and that families should have many children. But in the 1960s and 1970s the changing attitudes toward sexual activity, often known as the sexual revolution, fostered in part by a general access to artificial means of birth control, began to undermine conventional practices. The contraceptive pill, which remained illegal in some Catholic countries until much later, gave women control over their reproduction and sexuality. The sexual revolution upset those with traditional values, such as the rural Spanish woman who ruefully observed the ease of pursuing sex outside of marriage: "If a boy wants to be alone with a girl there's no problem; they go off alone and whatever fires they have can burn."[7] Changing social attitudes also eliminated or moderated the social shame of divorce, extramarital sex, and unmarried cohabitation. All these activities, which had been around for centuries, now became open, a challenge to legal restrictions and cultural taboos. Although sex scandals involving politicians are not unknown, especially in Britain, in many countries political leaders have little fear of public criticism for openly having extramarital relationships or children out of wedlock. Pornography and obscenity laws were relaxed, allowing long banned work to be published, such as the racy 1920s novel *Lady Chatterly's Lover* by the British author D. H. Lawrence. British poet Philip Larkin satirized the times: "Sexual intercourse began, in nineteen sixty-three (Which was rather late for me)—Between the end of the *Chatterly* ban, And the Beatles' first LP."[8]

Inspired by feminist thinkers such as the French philosopher Simone de Beauvoir (bo-VWAHR) (see Profile: Simone de Beauvoir, French Feminist and Philosopher), women's movements grew in strength across Europe and, by the 1970s, pressed their agendas more effectively. An English women's group hoped that "a world freed from the economic, social and psychological bonds of patriarchy would be a world turned upside down, creating a human potential we can hardly dream of now,"[9] a change that might benefit both men and women. Feminists in general wanted legal divorce, easier access to birth control, the right to abortion, and reform of family laws to give wives more influence. Feminists had their most success in Protestant countries, which often adopted their agenda, such as legal abortion. In 1973 Denmark, which had legalized some limited abortions in the 1930s, became the first nation to allow abortion on request. The feminist movements also made headway in Catholic nations. Although Pope John Paul II (pope 1978–2005) reiterated the long-standing church ban on contraception, abortion, and divorce, many Catholics ignored the conservative teachings of their church on these matters. Whether dominated by Protestants or Catholics, governments wrestled with the abortion issue for years. During the 1970s and 1980s most Catholic nations, including Italy and Spain, followed the earlier examples of France, Britain, and Germany and, defying the Catholic Church, legalized both divorce and abortion.

The lives of both men and women were affected by the changes in work, politics, and family life that the women's movements helped foster. Men and women now shared the responsibility for financially supporting their families. By the 1980s women were half the work force in Sweden, a third in France and Italy, and a quarter in conservative Ireland. Women moved into the professions, business, and even politics, no longer male monopolies. At various times women headed governments in nations such as Britain, France, Iceland, and Norway. Even Ireland, where patriarchy remained strong, in 1991 elected its first woman president, social democrat Mary Robinson (b. 1944), who was an outspoken law professor, feminist, single parent, and supporter of homosexual rights. Women political activists made their voices heard. For instance, in 1976 two Northern Ireland mothers, Mairead Corrigan (b. 1944) and Betty Williams (b. 1943), jointly shared the Nobel Peace Prize for their efforts to bridge the Catholic-Protestant divide and bring peace to their troubled land. As they became wage earners, women became less dependent on men. Yet, some changes came slowly. So few women had been able to achieve high business and industry positions even in egalitarian Norway that, in 2006, Norway's social democratic government outraged corporate leaders by requiring that 40 percent of the board members of large private companies must be women.

As a result of less rigid gender roles, marriage patterns also gradually changed. In the 1970s the popular culture still held up the model of the married heterosexual couple, and even rock stars known for their live-in girlfriends, such as Mick Jagger of the Rolling Stones, a popular British group, married, surrounded by celebrities. Some celebrities, such as French rock star Johnny Halliday, apparently enjoyed weddings so much that they changed spouses frequently. But by the 1980s more men and women than before remained single. In 1998, 15 percent of women and men between twenty-five and twenty-nine years old in western Europe lived on their own. In Scandinavia and Germany, the singles accounted for between a quarter and a third of the adult population. Increasing personal independence and mobility fostered small nuclear families instead of the large extended families of old, especially in northern Europe. As unhappy couples no longer needed to stay married for economic survival, the rates of divorce around Europe more than doubled between 1960 and 1990.

Women increased their political power in part because they had won the right to vote and constituted a majority of the electorate. In some nations, such as Belgium, France, and Italy, female suffrage came only in 1945, as the ashes left by war discredited the old politics. Influenced by churches, until the 1970s women tended to be more conservative voters than men. But as once powerful institutions such as the military and church, whose leaderships were both dominated by men, declined in influence, more and more women voted for socialist and liberal parties supportive of the welfare state that guaranteed them and their children inexpensive health care and education.

Homosexuals also began to enjoy equal rights. Homosexual subcultures in Europe, especially in major cities such as Berlin and Paris, had been active since World War I. Organizing to change discriminatory laws and attitudes, reform movements

SIMONE DE BEAUVOIR, FRENCH FEMINIST AND PHILOSOPHER

Few thinkers have had more influence on the study of women and on contemporary women's movements than Simone de Beauvoir (1908–1986), the first systematic feminist philosopher and a prolific writer of novels, essays, and autobiographical works. She was born in Paris to a middle-class family. Her father, a lawyer, and a devout mother with very traditional values sent her to fashionable Roman Catholic girls' schools that taught her, she remembered, "the habit of obedience." She believed that God expected her "to be dutiful." Her classmates aimed at marriage rather than careers. But when World War I impoverished de Beauvoir's family, Simone was pushed toward a career. During her teens she battled her parents for more freedom to leave the house on her own and alarmed her parents by becoming an atheist.

Simone loved the liberating intellectual atmosphere at the Sorbonne in Paris, the most prestigious French university, but found that, to succeed in her studies there, she had to overcome gender stereotypes: "My upbringing had convinced me of my sex's intellectual inferiority. I flattered myself that I had a woman's heart and a man's brain." Graduating at the top of her class, she then supported herself, first as a high school teacher and then as a writer. De Beauvoir began a romantic and intellectual partnership with Jean Paul Sartre, later to become Europe's most acclaimed philosopher, whom she had met at the Sorbonne, and became a vital contributor to Sartre's ideas and books. The two maintained an intense free union, and their lifelong connection provided a model of an adult relationship between a man and woman without wedlock or exclusive commitment. Both had lovers on the side.

De Beauvoir's life reflected the transformation of a privileged woman into a feminist icon. By the late 1940s she was the most famous female intellectual of the day. Throughout her life she enjoyed the new opportunities gained by women as French society liberalized, offering women legal equality, educational opportunities, the vote, and diverse economic roles, but she also saw the limits to these freedoms. Sartre suggested she write about what difference being a woman had made in her life. The result was the pioneering 1,200-page study *The Second Sex* (1949), which challenged conventional thinking on women's issues, becoming perhaps the most influential book on women ever written. The study ranged through biology, history, mythology, sociol-ogy, and Marxist and Freudian theory to conclude that all women were oppressed by the attitudes of society. It critically analyzed Western culture as dominated by males and argued that women are not born inferior but are made to view themselves as such. De Beauvoir showed how girls saw their future different from that of boys and had their choices, such as in careers, restricted. Men took themselves as the model: "There is an absolute human type, the masculine. He is the Absolute—she is the Other." In her view, marriage denied women's individuality, becoming a contract of subjugation rather than an equal partnership. Her writings greatly influenced the North American and European feminist movements. Later she addressed aging, including the way society dictated roles for the elderly.

Disillusioned by the slow pace of change in gender relations, in 1972 de Beauvoir became a feminist activist, acknowledging her solidarity with other women and arguing that they had to fight for an improvement in their social condition. She became president of the French League of Women's Rights and editor of journals that called attention to problems of violence, sexual assault, and lack of easily available contraception in Europe and the world. In 1976 she addressed the International Tribunal of Crimes against Women, noting, "You are gathered here to denounce the oppression to which women are subjected. Talk to the world, bring to light the shameful truths that half of humanity is trying to cover up." Admired by millions, de Beauvoir died in 1986 at age seventy-eight.

THINKING ABOUT THE PROFILE

1. How did de Beauvoir's personal life affect her ideas?

2. What were de Beauvoir's main arguments about how history and society shaped perceptions of gender?

Note: Quotations from Bonnie S. Anderson and Judith P. Zinsser, *A History of Their Own: Women in Europe from Prehistory to the Present*, vol. 2 (New York: Harper, 1988), pp. 204, 169, 422; and Bonnie G. Smith, *Changing Lives: Women in European History Since 1700* (Lexington, Mass.: D.C. Heath, 1989), p. 519.

Simone de Beauvoir and Jean Paul Sartre The French feminist thinker Simone de Beauvoir and her partner, the philosopher Jean Paul Sartre, were frequent visitors to the cafés of European cities and influential participants in the lively intellectual life of post–World War II Europe. (Time Life Pictures/Getty Images)

began in Switzerland in the 1930s and, after World War II, in several other countries. Nonetheless, in the 1950s many governments continued to prosecute homosexuals, some of them respected figures in the arts, for consensual sexual activity. For example, in West Germny between 1953 and 1965 some 99,000 men were convicted, and frequently jailed, under still existing Nazi-era laws prohibiting homosexual activity. Laws opposing homosexual behavior began to be reformed or eliminated during the 1960s and 1970s, but combating prejudice took longer. Hence, in 1974 a conservative Christian Democrat leader in Italy, opposing social change, warned that "if divorce is allowed, it will be possible to have marriages between homosexuals, and perhaps your wife will run off with some pretty young girl."[10] As late as 1979 the West German government excluded homosexuals from legislation that paid compensation to minorities, such as Jews, that had been singled out for Nazi persecution. However, most societies developed more tolerant attitudes. Denmark recognized domestic partnerships for homosexuals in 1989. By 2001 most of northern Europe had such laws providing legal protection, and discrimination against homosexuals had ebbed. Several nations, including the Netherlands, Belgium, and Spain, legalized homosexual marriage in the early twenty-first century. Openly homosexual politicians, men and women, served as high government officials or political leaders in nations as socially different as the liberal Netherlands and conservative Ireland.

Immigration: Questions of Identity

Population movements had been a feature of western European history for centuries, but in the later twentieth century this pattern took a new turn as several million immigrants settled in various European countries as "guest workers." In response to economic growth that created labor shortages in northern Europe and Britain in the 1950s and 1960s, people from poorer southern Europe, especially Italians, Greeks, and Portuguese, migrated north in search of better jobs and pay. They were soon joined by Turks, Algerians, Moroccans, and people from West Africa and the Caribbean, who were fleeing even harsher poverty. Meanwhile, many Indians, Pakistanis, and Bangladeshis sought a better life in their former imperial power, Britain, while emigrants left the former Dutch colonies of Indonesia and Suriname (formerly Dutch Guiana) for the Netherlands. By 1974, 10 percent of the working population of France and West Germany were foreign-born. Middle Eastern immigrants worked in Scandinavia, Italy, and Spain.

The immigration reshaped European societies. By the early twenty-first century immigrants constituted 10 percent of the population of Germany, 6 percent in France, and 5 percent in Britain. Major European cities such as Paris, London, and Berlin took on an international flavor. By 2006 London's population was 40 percent nonwhite. Paris became a center of Arab and African culture, including a large recording industry churning out music by Arab and African musicians, often for export to their homelands. Islamic culture flourished in cities such as Hamburg (Germany) and Marseilles (France), where

Arab- and Turkish-language radio stations had large audiences. As in North America, immigrants contributed much to European societies. For example, small neighborhood grocery stores run by Arabs served vital functions in French urban life. The Indian and Pakistani sundry goods and grocery shops and restaurants became features of English city life. Observers remarked that the favorite British food was now Indian curry, ironically a dish developed by mixing Asian and Portuguese cuisines, mostly spicy sauces poured over rice, in colonial India for British residents there that then spread widely around the world. People of Asian and African descent were elected to parliaments in countries such as Britain and the Netherlands..

The immigration also posed problems of absorption into European society, especially fostering tensions between whites and the nonwhite immigrants. Over the years, as Turks, Arabs, Africans, and Pakistanis arrived to do the low-paying jobs nobody else wanted and then settled down, they and even their local-born children faced discrimination and sometimes violent attack by rightwing youth gangs and others favoring their expulsion. For example, neo-Nazis in Germany sometimes set fire to immigrant apartment buildings, and young toughs in England boasted of "Paki-bashing," or beating up people from the Indian subcontinent. In response, many immigrants retreated into their own cultures. A British scholar of the Asian and West Indian settlers noted their preference for "the novels that document the idiocies of English social snobbery, the musical forms that sustain the separate immigrant lifestyles, the ghetto life that builds up defense-mechanisms."[11] However, while older immigrants often clung to the cultures and attitudes they brought from their Asian or Middle Eastern village, such as a husband's authority over his wife and the preference for arranged marriages, their children struggled to reconcile the contrasting expectations of their conservative parents and religious traditions with the materialistic, individualistic, secular societies of Europe.

Tensions between immigrants and local-born Europeans mounted further after 1989. Vanishing jobs put both the immigrants and the local people on the unemployment rolls or in competition for scarce work. Despite the economic problems, illegal immigration also increased. In 2001 perhaps 700,000 people fleeing extreme poverty or harsh repression illegally entered the European Union. Since the mid-1990s anti-immigrant (especially anti-Muslim) movements have emerged even in famously tolerant countries like Denmark and the Netherlands, especially after the terrorist attacks against the United States in 2001, which shocked Europeans. For their part, to express their alienation from European society, young people of Middle Eastern, South Asian, and African-Caribbean background have often turned to musical forms from their countries of origin, such as Algerian *rai* for Arabs and Jamaican dancehall and reggae for Afro-Caribbeans. Some immigrant youth have adapted African American rap to their needs, writing lyrics in their own languages. Hence, in France the Senegal-born M. C. Solaar achieved popularity for songs commenting on the lives of young people of African ancestry. Facing particular hostility since 2001, some Muslims, rejecting

Western culture as immoral and criticizing the Islam brought by their parents from North African, Turkish, or South Asian villages as corrupted by Sufi mysticism, have become more devout and rigidly orthodox than their parents. The most alienated Muslim youth, seeking a purpose in life, have turned to militant Islamic groups for direction.

Reshaping Cultures

Enriched by imports from cultures around the world, western Europeans enjoyed a resilient cultural life. The influence of mass culture from the United States became more widespread than before the war. American cigarettes, Coca-Cola, and chewing gum symbolized postwar fashions, while American films and music, especially jazz and rock, reshaped cultural horizons. African American jazz musicians often settled in Europe, especially in France and Scandinavia, in the 1950s and 1960s to escape racism at home; their music appealed especially to middle-aged, middle-class Europeans. North American and British cultural forms, such as popular music, that were linked by a common language tended to mix, prompting European governments to try to protect their languages and culture industries from the powerful Anglo-American challenge by, for instance, mandating how much foreign music could be played on government radio stations. Young people also enjoyed popular entertainments from outside of North America, such as Caribbean reggae music, Latin American dances, and Japanese animated films. Yet Europeans often treasured entertainers who reflected local culture, such as the waiflike French singer Edith Piaf (1915–1963), who was known for her sad, nostalgic songs of lost love and lost youth.

Rock music helped define youth cultures, allowing young people to embrace an exciting, edgy music that their parents often disliked. After rock emerged in the United States in the mid-1950s, it rapidly gained a huge following in Europe, where American rock stars such as Buddy Holly, Elvis Presley, and Chuck Berry enjoyed massive popularity. By the 1960s European musicians inspired by U.S. rock and blues, such as Francois Hardy in France and the Beatles and Rolling Stones in Britain, had reshaped the local music scenes. The Beatles, young working-class men from Liverpool, a cosmopolitan port city, matured as musicians while playing clubs in West Germany and became the symbols of youth culture for a decade. Beatlemania, as their impact was called, reached around the world. Rock became known as "yeah yeah" music in nations as different as Brazil and Malaysia, after the Beatles lyric "she loves you yeah yeah yeah." The music and fashion, such as clothing and hair length, of the Beatles and other rockers represented an assertion of youth identity. But eventually rock music introduced more personal reflection and social commentary, as reflected in such top-selling Beatles albums as *Revolver* (1966), which lambasted the taxman, greedy for revenues, and introduced Eleanor Rigby, a fictive woman who died alone, ignored by society. The Beatles 1967 album, *Sgt. Pepper's Lonely Hearts Club Band*, became the prototype of the concept album, with a linking theme, cross-cultural musical explorations (including use of Indian instruments), and provocative lyrics, influencing popular musicians around the world for decades after.

By the mid-1970s a new style of rock, called punk, appeared that expressed social protest. Although it gained a presence in North America and continental Europe, punk became especially influential in Britain, where working-class youth faced limited job options. The provocative songs of a leading British punk group, the Sex Pistols, deliberately insulted the monarchy and offended the deeper values of British society, much to the delight of their fans. As a leading punk magazine asserted: "[Punk] music is a perfect medium for shoving two fingers up at the establishment."[12] As punk's energy dissipated, it was replaced in the 1980s by escapist dance music. But punk provided a foundation for creative new forms of rock in the 1990s in Europe and North America.

Cultural forms from Asia and Africa also influenced European culture. For example, in Britain the popular **bhangra** music emerged from a blending of Indian folk songs with Caribbean reggae and Anglo-American styles, such as rock, hip hop, and disco. Using a mix of Indian and Western instruments, bhangra became a lively dance music, popular with both white and Indian youth in Britain. By the 1980s bhangra had spread to the Indian diaspora communities in continental Europe, North America, and the Caribbean, sustaining Indian identity and encouraging Indian youth to have fun. The music also developed an audience among young people in India and Pakistan. By the early 2000s bhangra's appeal had widened, becoming a truly world music.

Cultural life was influenced not only by the wave of cultural imports but also by local developments, especially political liberalism and a growing mass media such as television and cinema. These loosened conventional restraints and encouraged a wide variety of views. The creative cinema of France, Italy, and Sweden developed a global audience by depicting the humblest lives and psychological and social dilemmas common to people in a rapidly changing world. Literature also reflected political change. Writers known as postcolonialists sought to escape the world-view shaped by Western colonialism and dominance. For example, the India-born British writer Salman Rushdie (b. 1947), a Cambridge University–educated former actor and advertising copywriter from a Muslim family, confronted Western ethnocentrism. Remembering the prejudice he faced in British schools, Rushdie criticized Western society, especially the Western treatment of Asian peoples. At the same time, however, he challenged what he considered the antimodern sensibilities of Islamic culture. His books *Shame* (1983), a satire on Pakistan's history, and especially *The Satanic Verses* (1988), a critical look at Islamic history, created an uproar among conservative Muslims. Some Muslims, such as the rulers of Iran, issued death threats, forcing Rushdie to go into hiding and hire bodyguards.

---

bhangra A popular music that emerged in Britain from a blending of traditional folk songs brought by Indian immigrants with Caribbean reggae and Anglo-American styles, such as rock, hip hop, and disco.

Thought and Religion

Philosophy flourished, continuing a secularizing trend that had been strong in Europe for over a century. For several decades after World War II Europeans struggled to understand the horrors of that war, which seemed to contradict the emphasis on rational thought and tolerance that had been building in Europe since the Enlightenment of the seventeenth and eighteenth centuries. In seeking answers some turned to new philosophies while others struggled to reconcile religious faith and modern life.

Modern Philosophy **Existentialism**, a philosophy whose speculation on the nature of reality reflects disillusionment with Europe's violent history and doubt that objectivity is possible, and Marxism, which envisions a noncapitalist future for societies, became the most influential schools of secular thought. At the same time organized religion declined as churches struggled to remain relevant in an increasingly secular society.

The French philosopher Jean Paul Sartre (SAHRT) (1905–1980) and the French feminist thinker Simone de Beauvoir (1908–1986), his longtime partner, transformed existentialism from a little known Scandinavian and German approach into a philosophy with wide appeal. Sartre argued that women and men are defined by a reality that they tend to view as the work of fate or imposed by others. He advised people not to let others determine their lives. Rather, people must find their own meaning, whatever society's values. They cannot banish uncertainty about the world and their place in it, but they can overcome it. In his view, people must accept responsibility for their actions, and this should lead to political engagement to create a better society in which people have wider choices. Sartre himself became active in leftwing political movements, such as those promoting world peace and banning nuclear weapons. To ensure peace and freedom, he encouraged the movement toward European unity. Sartre provided a philosophy that every individual could act upon and that reached across political boundaries. During his life Sartre achieved fame unusual for a philosopher; when he died in 1980, thousands of people attended his funeral.

Meanwhile, like existentialism, other influential philosophies debated the nature of reality. Marxism fostered an understanding of social class and gender inequality, but as a political philosophy it lost many followers after the 1960s. In contrast to Marxism, which offers a certitude about truth and the workings of society, an approach called deconstruction, pursued by the Algeria-born Frenchman Jacques Derrida (DER-i-dah) (b. 1930), claimed that all rational thought could be taken apart and shown to be meaningless. Derrida questioned the entire Western philosophical tradition and the notion, still popular in Europe and North America, that Western

civilization was superior to other cultures and occupied a special place in world history. Inspired by Derrida's questioning of accepted wisdom, by the 1990s literature and scholarship were influenced by the intellectual approach known as **postmodernism**, which contends that truth is not absolute but constructed by people according to their society's beliefs. For example, a society's notions of different male and female aptitudes or of the superiority of one literary work over another are not objective but merely subjective attitudes acquired by people as they grow up in that society. Even scholars, postmodernists argue, cannot completely escape the prejudices of their gender, social class, ethnicity, and culture. Other thinkers, among them many Marxists, rejected the postmodernist notion that truth is relative and objectivity impossible.

Christians, Jews, and Muslims While philosophy flourished, organized religious life went into decline. The horrors of World War II and postwar materialism had destroyed many people's faith. Churchgoing ceased to be the social convention it once was, leaving churches in many cities semideserted. Polls in the 1990s showed that, whereas some two-thirds of Americans had a moderate or strong religious faith, less than half of western Europeans did. While 40 percent of Americans regularly attended church, only 10 percent of western Europeans did. Scholars wrote of a "seasonal conformity," in which people attended church only at certain times such as Christmas or weddings. Meanwhile, conflicts between rival Christian churches, once a source of tension, lost their intensity. Protestants and Catholics no longer lived in separate worlds, and ecumenical cooperation among all church denominations increased. Formed in 1948, the World Council of Churches, based in Switzerland, brought together the main Protestant and Eastern Orthodox churches. Appalled by the Holocaust perpetrated by the Nazis against the Jews, Christian thinkers began acknowledging their faiths' relationship to Judaism by referring, for the first time in history, to Europe's *Judeo-Christian* heritage. Although the Jewish population in Europe decreased sharply because of the Holocaust and post–World War II emigration to Israel and the Americas, Jews remained a key religious minority there. Christians had also to deal with another faith: by 2000 immigration and conversions had made Islam the second largest religion in France, Belgium, and Spain after Roman Catholicism.

In northern Europe, Protestant churches struggled to maintain their influence in increasingly secular societies. Often churches paid a price for their close ties to the state. Governments often subsidized state churches, as in Scandinavia and Britain, and church-operated schools, as in West Germany, but many observers believed this government financial support only undermined religious devotion in societies where people increasingly found traditional values irrelevant. Churches funded partly by the state, these observers reasoned, did not need to actively solicit support from believers and so were un-

---

existentialism A philosophy, influential in post–World War II western Europe, whose speculation on the nature of reality reflects disillusionment with Europe's violent history and doubt that objectivity is possible.

postmodernism A European intellectual approach contending that truth is not absolute but constructed by people according to their society's beliefs.

wealth to gain control of major segments of the Russian economy. At the same time, Yeltsin faced secession movements within the Russian federation, especially in Chechnya, a largely Muslim Caucasus territory that Russia had annexed in the 1870s. In 1994 this oil-rich region declared independence. Although oil was also produced elsewhere in Russia, Yeltsin feared that recognizing Chechnya's independence would encourage other secession movements. Using military force, he therefore tried to crush the Chechen separatists, sucking the Red Army into a quagmire with thousands of casualties on both sides.

The economic pain of the Russian people was widespread. Millions of workers lost their jobs as inefficient, obsolete Soviet industries closed. More women than men lost their jobs, costing women income and social status. Some male leaders reemphasized the Soviet era ideal of men as soldiers and women as working mothers. Arguing that the Communists had destroyed the family by encouraging women to work, conservatives advocated that women stay at home and tend to family obligations rather than taking jobs. With the end of free higher education, families preferred to devote their limited money for schooling on their sons. Some desperate women turned to prostitution for survival. Even when their enterprises did not close, factory workers, miners, and state employees, such as teachers, were often not paid for years. Yeltsin dismantled parts of the welfare state. As a result of reductions in health care, declining incomes, and the increasing tendency, especially among men, to escape worry through heavy drinking and illegal drug use, public health deteriorated and men's life expectancy dropped from sixty-four in 1990 to fifty-nine in 2002. By 1992 inflation was 2,500 percent, devastating people who lived on pensions and fixed incomes. According to a popular local joke, "All the good things the Communists said about communism were false, but all the bad things they said about capitalism were true."

Russia Today In 2000, with the Russian economy near collapse and free markets discredited, Yeltsin resigned in disgrace and was replaced by Vladimir Putin (b. 1952), who ended shock therapy and changed the nation's direction. A former secret police colonel who kept a portrait of the modernizing eighteenth-century czar Peter the Great in his office, Putin supported capitalism and democratic reforms, including multiparty elections, but also pursued policies that were more authoritarian and nationalist than Yeltsin's. Political liberalism faded as Putin took control of much of the media, seizing or muffling opposition newspapers and television stations, and prosecuting some oligarchs for corruption. The state has also taken over many large private companies, turning the economy into a form of state capitalism not unlike Meiji Japan. Company managers profit while the public pays for losses. The economy made a modest recovery because of improved tax collection and higher prices for two leading Russian exports, oil and natural gas. Putin outmaneuvered rivals, including the discredited pro-U.S. free market advocates, the rebuilt Communist Party, and extreme rightwing nationalists.

Putin brought back stability after fifteen years of turbulence, fostering a Russia that mixed the old autocratic government with a new, more outward-looking attitude. The Russian Orthodox Church, for centuries closely connected to Russian national identity and political power, regained some of the influence it had lost under communism. Within the church leadership, liberals promoted a tolerant and ecumenical view while conservatives largely denounced ecumenism. The extreme church conservatives supported anti-Semitic, anti-Muslim views and a return of the Russian monarchy. Yet, in many parts of Russia, Muslims—some 15 percent of the nation's population—and Christians have peacefully adapted to each other, living in harmony. Putin also sought good relations with Germany, France, the United States, and China. In Putin's Russia, however, the contrasts between rich and poor became stark. While elegantly dressed men and women in Moscow cavorted in fine restaurants and glitzy casinos, towns often went without heat and power. Corruption, poverty, unaccountability, weak legal institutions, and the festering war in Chechnya stifled development. Russia still had the world's third largest military budget, but it was only a fifth that of the United States. Polls showed that a majority of Russians preferred the Communist years, especially under Leonid Brezhnev, to the new Russia, and many people expressed nostalgia for Stalin and Lenin. In surveying the post-Soviet era, a respected Russian historian harked back to Peter the Great and Catherine the Great, advising Russians, "Our future lies in openness to the entire world and in enlightenment."[19] It remained unclear whether Russia would follow that path.

The New Eastern Europe

The changes in the USSR resonated throughout eastern Europe. In the late 1980s the Soviet leader, Mikhail Gorbachev, who admired the Hungarian market socialism model, had begun promoting reform in eastern European countries, since the USSR could no longer afford to rescue their stagnant economies. When it became clear that the USSR was no longer willing to protect the corrupt, largely unpopular eastern European Communist governments, they began to fall like dominoes. Democratic movements once underground surfaced. Hungary adopted a democratic system, Solidarity came to power in Poland, and East Germans voted with their feet by streaming across the border into West Germany, an exodus that led to the dismantling of the Berlin Wall. People around the world could watch on television as Berliners gleefully knocked down the Berlin Wall, the symbol of Cold War division, and carried off its bricks as souvenirs. Soon the East German regime and the other east European Communist governments had collapsed or been overthrown. In Czechoslovakia, the playwright and former rock group lyricist, Václav Havel (vax-LAV hah-VEL) (b. 1936), who had been frequently arrested for his prodemocracy activities and whose hero was the eccentric American rock star Frank Zappa, was elected president after massive demonstrations forced the Communist leaders to resign in a largely peaceful transfer of power known as the "Velvet Revolution." Havel announced, "Your government, my people, has been returned to you."[20]

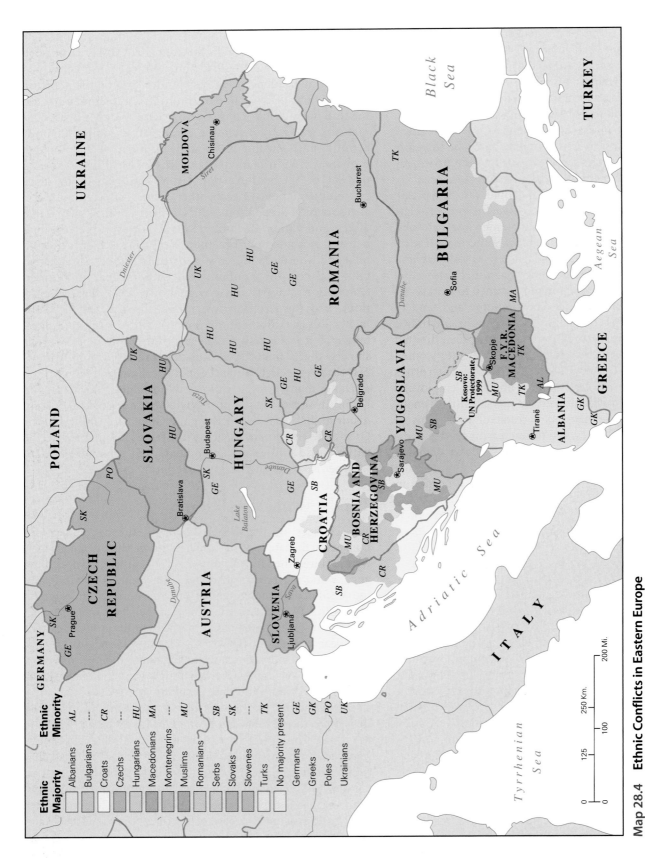

Map 28.4 Ethnic Conflicts in Eastern Europe
Many of the nations in central and eastern Europe contain substantial ethnic minorities, and tensions between various groups have often led to conflict. In Yugoslavia, the conflicts between the major ethnic groups—Serbs, Croats, Bosnian Muslims, and Albanians—led to violence and civil war at the end of the twentieth century.

Ethnic Majority / **Ethnic Minority**

Albanians	AL
Bulgarians	---
Croats	CR
Czechs	---
Hungarians	HU
Macedonians	MA
Montenegrins	---
Muslims	MU
Romanians	---
Serbs	SB
Slovaks	SK
Slovenes	---
Turks	TK
No majority present	
Germans	GE
Greeks	GK
Poles	PO
Ukrainians	UK

Democratic or semidemocratic governments were installed, seeking to replace centralized planned economies with market forces. Allowed to elect their governments, east Europeans took up voting enthusiastically. Yet they also experienced the negatives of change, especially when reformers did not anticipate the results of their policies. As in the former Soviet Union, the end of communism uncorked ethnic hatreds and rivalries going back centuries. For example, Slovaks seceded from the Czechs, forming their own country, while Romanians repressed the large Hungarian minority. Several countries persecuted or avoided providing services, such as schools, to the Romany (Gypsies), and prejudice against Jews intensified.

The rapid move to capitalism, while providing abundant consumer goods, also proved destabilizing. Critics wrote of shock without therapy. Millions were thrown out of work as obsolete factories closed; western European or North American companies bought many of the remaining enterprises. Dazzled by the Western consumer goods just over the border, east Europeans may have misunderstood the risks that came with Western-style capitalism. Shops were full of attractive goods, but few people had the money to buy them. Only Poland and the Czech republic enjoyed robust economic growth. In addition, certain protections of the Communist welfare system, such as free education, health care, and subsidized housing, were removed, causing misery. Finally, by 2000, salaries caught up with prices some places, but pockets of high unemployment remained and the rich-poor gap widened.

The political environment changed. Diverse political parties competed for power. Capitalizing on a widespread desire for rebuilding the social safety net, former Communist Party members who now called themselves reform Communists, although their views resembled social democracy, won some national elections, especially in Poland and Hungary. They competed for power with free market advocates, pro-Western liberals, and rightwing nationalists. In a striking repudiation of the Soviet legacy, reform Communists often supported joining the European Union and even the NATO military alliance. Anti-Communists had few regrets of the changes since 1989, however jarring they were. For example, Adam Michnik, a leader of Polish Solidarity, reflecting on the struggles against communism, concluded that "without the slightest hesitation it is much better to live in a country that is democratic, prosperous and thus boring"[21] than in other types of countries.

The greatest instability came to Yugoslavia, a federation of states that self-destructed in bloody civil wars between ethnic groups (see Map 28.4). Created artificially for political convenience by diplomats after World War I, Yugoslavia contained antagonistic ethnic and religious groups. The largest, the nationalistic Orthodox Serbs, wanted to dominate the federation, while the Catholic Croats and Slovenians and the Bosnian and Albanian Muslims wanted independence for the regions they dominated. After the long-term federal leader, Tito, the product of a mixed Croat-Serb marriage whose autocratic policies limited dissent and kept the lid on ethnic hatreds, died in 1980, Yugoslavia became a seething cauldron of ethnic conflict.

The Velvet Revolution Protesters took to the streets in Prague, Czechoslovakia, to protest Communist government and demand democracy. These protests, known as the Velvet Revolution for their peaceful nature, were led by Václav Havel, pictured on the poster carried by a protester. (Peter Turnley/Corbis)

The violence began in 1991, when the Serb-dominated Yugoslav army tried to stop two states, Slovenia and Croatia, from breaking away from the federation. In response, the United Nations sent in peacekeeping troops to secure their independence. In 1992 the Muslim majority in another Yugoslav state, Bosnia, declared independence, a move opposed by the minority Serbs and Croats in the state. Bosnian Serb militias, aided covertly by the largest Yugoslav state, Serbia, massacred thousands of Muslims, introducing a new term for genocide, "ethnic cleansing," and leading the United Nations to send more peacemakers. As the violence continued, U.S. air strikes under NATO auspices forced the Serbs to accept a peace treaty in 1995. The Bosnia conflict had killed 200,000 people and generated 4 million refugees. In 1999 violence returned when the Albanian majority in Kosovo, the southern region of Serbia, revolted and the Serbs responded with ferocity, prompting another NATO imposed settlement in 2000. Thousands of NATO troops remained in Bosnia and Kosovo, a symbol of eastern Europe's unresolved challenges.

Toward European Unity

Two themes have dominated western Europe in the years after 1989. One was the reunification of Germany. With the fall of communism and the Berlin Wall, the East German state collapsed and Germany was quickly reunified in 1990, but the financial costs proved burdensome and the results have satisfied neither West nor East Germans. Despite Germany's problems, Europeans have continued to move toward unity, a second theme. Yet, the movement has also faced setbacks.

The European Union   The hasty German reunification disappointed its proponents. For many East Germans, merging with the prosperous West Germany promised access to a materially comfortable life they could only dream of before. But reunification cost billions and threw the German economy into a tailspin. Before reunification West Germany had enjoyed a long boom. A decade later, however, the reunified nation of 80 million people, suffering from Europe's slowest economic growth, was stuck in deep recession. Since Germany has western Europe's largest economy, the engine of the European Community, the German slump has dragged down the rest of Europe. Many workers in the former East Germany have lost jobs as obsolete factories have been closed or sold to West Germans, who often downsize the work force to make them more profitable. By 2004 the unemployment rate in the east was twice as high as in the west. Some disillusioned youth have turned to rightwing, often neo-Nazi, groups to express their anger. These extremist young people often favor local heavy metal rock groups whose songs promote hatred of foreigners and immigrants they see as taking jobs and maintaining alien cultures.

Worried by Germany's problems, western European leaders believed that hastening unification was the best strategy to stabilize post-Communist Europe. The Maastricht Treaty, discussed in the chapter opener, which recognized a single currency, the euro, and a central bank, set a goal of achieving economic and monetary union by 2000. It required budgetary and wage restraint as a prelude to monetary union. The treaty pledged to promote balanced and sustainable economic progress by strengthening economic and social cohesion. By 2002, eleven of fifteen signers of the treaty had adopted the euro as their currency, an index of unity. European unity was also aided by other factors. Millions of Europeans were multilingual, moving easily between cultures, and young Europeans often studied in other European countries. The cosmopolitanism in turn influenced the arts. For instance, the popular Greek singer Nana Mouskeri (NA-na mouse-KUR-ee) gained a large international audience by recording in English, French, German, and Spanish. The Eurotunnel, which stretched ninety-four miles under the English Channel and made possible a three-hour train ride from London to Paris, symbolized the decline of both political and cultural borders.

The European Union (EU) doubled its membership from twelve nations in 1993 to twenty-five in 2004. In 1995 Sweden, Finland, and Austria joined, followed in 2004 by various eastern European nations, including the Czech Republic, Poland, and Hungary. The Danish prime minister told prospective new EU members: "In 1989 brave and visionary people brought about the collapse of the Berlin Wall. They could no longer tolerate the forced division of Europe. Today we are giving life to their hopes."[22] With the new members the EU became a bloc of nearly 400 million people encompassing most of Europe and enjoying a combined economic power equal to that of the United States. Some of the members, such as Norway, Sweden, and Ireland, once one of Europe's poorest countries but now often known as the Celtic Tiger because its rapid growth resembled that of the "Little Tiger" nations of Southeast Asia (see

European Economic Power   Business and political leaders from India and the European Union met in a summit in 2005 to increase trade relations, reflecting the growing economic power of both India and western Europe. (AP/Wide World Photos)

Chapter 31), have continued to show steady economic growth. Conducting a quarter of the world's commerce, the EU became one of the three dominant economic forces in the world, along with the United States and Japan. Some observers spoke of a tripolar world led by the United States, the EU, and East Asia (especially China and Japan).

Challenges to Unity However, the European Union hit several major road bumps. Critics had long called the EU a faceless bureaucracy with innumerable rules that compromised national independence and threatened national traditions. Indeed, two of Europe's most prosperous nations, Norway and Switzerland, declined membership, fearing the loss of national identity and the cost of subsidizing poorer members. The EU leaders have been cautious in admitting those former Soviet bloc states that have weak economies and autocratic leaders. Turkey, a largely Muslim nation, has long sought membership, fostering a EU debate about how to define Europe and whether non-Christian nations have a role in it. This debate spilled over into the effort by European diplomats to prepare a constitution for the Union. Amid much controversy, the constitution proposed in 2004 rejected any mention of Europe's Christian heritage, a reflection of the changes affecting European societies during the twentieth century. But the voters in each member nation had to approve the document. In 2005 voters in two of the most pro-unity countries, France and the Netherlands, fearing loss of control to the EU bureaucracy, shocked EU leaders by rejecting the constitution. This rejection raised questions about the EU's future.

Increasing unity did not resolve, and may have contributed to, political, economic, and social problems caused by a changing global economy. The economic austerity policies of the 1990s unsettled welfare states and provoked government changes. Social democrats, who had governed eleven of the sixteen western European nations in the early 1990s, now jockeyed with centrists, free market conservatives, Greens, anti-immigrant nationalists, and the fading Communists for power. Attempts to roll back social benefits sometimes set off massive protests and long strikes. While many Europeans preferred to maintain what they termed the social market economy, meaning the welfare state and an economic system that guaranteed generous leisure time, even at the cost of slower economic growth, both the German and French governments replaced the 35-hour workweek with the 40-hour workweek to increase their economic competitiveness. Yet, some large companies continued to downsize and cut or export jobs. In 2006 thousands in France rioted against loosening job protections. Some observers compared Europe's social market economies and their sluggish growth unfavorably with the dynamic U.S. economy and predicted Europe would continue to lose ground and sink into irrelevance. Others disagreed, noting that many European nations have nearly as high a per capita income as the U.S., less inequality, a greater commitment to sustainable development and quality of life for all, and, collectively, a larger Gross Development Product, the total production of goods and services.

Europeans also faced other challenges. By 2000 Europe, a century earlier overcrowded and the world's greatest exporter of people, had a declining population, due mainly to the world's lowest birthrate: 1.2 children per woman. Yet, concerned about a much higher birth rate among Muslims, Europeans became increasingly hostile to immigration from the Middle East. Tensions simmered and in 2005 rioting and vandalism by young Arab and African residents in France, many of them unemployed, caused much damage and raised the issues of what sort of integration of immigrants into European societies was possible. The European population decline also posed a long-term economic problem, since, with more people retiring from than entering the work force, younger workers had more responsibility for financing government services, such as pensions and health care, for the growing population of elderly. The problems contributed to widespread political disenchantment. By the early twenty-first century an anti-incumbent mood and strong anti-U.S. sentiments had taken hold, often causing voters to reject the governing parties. Anti-immigrant parties became more influential, even in the most tolerant nations, Denmark and the Netherlands. Thus Europeans still struggled to define their place in a changing world.

Europe and Russia in the Global System

With the end of the Cold War, Russia, western Europe, and the former Soviet bloc states searched for new roles in the world. Russia sought to maintain good relations with the EU, the United States, China, and the nearby Islamic nations, such as Iran, but also, like most nations, continued to act in its own self-interest. Sometimes this meant opposing U.S. or EU policies. NATO also needed to redefine its mission. By 2004 it had added many of the former Warsaw Pact nations, discomforting Russia. Western Europeans seemed more reluctant than Americans to devote vast sums to the military or to send their armed forces into combat. The crises in Yugoslavia showed European weakness, with the United States pressing NATO for intervention and then leading the effort to end the killing and restore order.

European relations with its military ally and main trading rival, the United States, became complicated. Various European nations, as part of a NATO commitment, sent troops to Afghanistan after the 2001 terrorist attacks on the United States and shared the goal of combating international terrorism. But most Europeans mistrusted the U.S. desire to invade oil-rich Iraq in 2003, believing it had little to do with fighting terrorism and fearing it would destabilize the Middle East. As a result, major European nations such as France and Germany criticized the U.S. invasion and occupation. Although their people strongly opposed the war, some close U.S. allies, such as Italy, Poland, and Spain, sent small token forces, but only Britain had a sizeable military presence in Iraq.

Europeans also disagreed on how best to respond to international terrorism, especially the threat posed by militant Islamic groups. The substantial Muslim immigrant populations in Europe complicated European nations' policies on the Middle East. By 2000, 19 million immigrants, including 13 million Muslims, made up 6 percent of the total EU population. Islamic militancy spread among some people of Arab or South Asian ancestry in Europe, especially among unemployed youth. The major terrorist network, Al Qaeda, had a presence in several nations. Indeed, some of the men who perpetrated the 2001 attacks on the United States had studied in Europe, especially in Germany, where they were recruited by Islamic militants. Deadly terrorist attacks on commuter trains in Madrid in 2004 and the London subway in 2005, which killed several hundred people, showed the potential for terrorist violence in Europe but also convinced many Europeans that Western military interventions in the Middle East might increase rather than diminish the terrorist threat. In 2006 shocked Europeans found how tense Muslim-Western relations had become when offensive cartoons insulting or satirizing the Islamic prophet Muhammad, published by a rightwing, anti-immigrant Danish newspaper to test the limits of press freedom and stimulate controversy, caused massive riots and demonstrations, often fomented by extremists, around the Muslim world, resulting in hundreds of deaths and attacks on Danish and other European embassies and business interests.

Europeans still played key roles in resolving world problems. Polls in the early 2000s showed that Europeans identified global warming as the major world problem. European nations took the lead in developing international treaties on issues such as climate change, biological and chemical weapons, international criminal courts, and genocide. U.S. opposition to these treaties built resentment. European workers also led movements against the economic globalization they saw as costing jobs and livelihoods. Saying the world is not for sale, French farmer José Bové set fire to a McDonald's outlet to protest against the large global corporations that often displace local enterprises, becoming a hero to those Europeans opposed to globalization and the institutions, such as the World Trade Organization (see Chapter 26), that promote it.

With the move, symbolized by the EU, toward closer political and economic integration, Europe became much more than a geographical expression and a collection of separate countries sharing certain cultural traditions and history. A few European leaders have even envisioned a political federation, or united states of Europe, but many hurdles would have to be overcome first. Europe is no longer the colossus it had been in the nineteenth century, but its peoples are carving out a new place in the world.

SECTION SUMMARY

- The collapsing Soviet bloc and Soviet decay created problems for Gorbachev, and he was replaced by Boris Yeltsin, who allowed independence for all the non-Russian Soviet republics, some of which ended up with authoritarian governments, and pursued a rapid shift to capitalism.

- However, as a result of this "shock therapy," a small group of former Communist Party officials became extremely wealthy while most Russians suffered economically, and Yeltsin was replaced by the more authoritarian Vladimir Putin, who brought back some stability and pursued good relations with Europe and the United States.

- With the fall of the USSR, formerly Communist eastern Europe became more democratic, though many countries struggled economically and others suffered political upheaval, especially Yugoslavia, which experienced violent civil war and "ethnic cleansing."

- German reunification, celebrated at first, yielded mixed results, while the European Union grew to include twenty-five nations by 2004 but faced questions over whether to admit non-Christian nations and over what form its constitution should take.

- European nations struggled to navigate the evolving world economy, to deal with Islamic terrorism, and to work out relations with each other and with the United States, whose 2003 invasion of Iraq was generally unpopular in most countries.

 *Online Study Center* **ACE the Test**

◆ Chapter Summary

Emerging shattered from World War II, western Europeans were determined to build a new Europe. Although the Cold War divided Europe, western Europeans rebuilt democracies and began a movement to foster unity. Sparked by French-German reconciliation, Europeans established institutions for economic cooperation. Eventually these became the European Union, which established a single currency and a European parliament. Stability also resulted from the rise of welfare states, which guaranteed all citizens fair access to housing, health care, and education. Social democratic parties took the lead in creating the safety net, but supporting it became more costly with growing economic problems and unemployment rates. Gradually family and gender relations changed, while millions of immigrants reshaped European societies.

The Soviet Union maintained a government and economy very different from those in western Europe. A powerful state dominated life and work. The Soviets installed Communist governments in eastern Europe and brutally repressed opposition, but they failed to realize much economic dynamism and lost ground in the Cold War to a more powerful U.S.–western Europe alliance. By the 1980s the Soviet system and the Soviet bloc needed reform. Communism thus fostered modernization and improved living standards, but ethnic minorities were restless, the bureaucracy was stifling, and the economy remained stagnant. The unsettling reforms resulted in the collapse of communism and the dismantling of the Soviet Empire in 1991. Since then the former Communist nations have struggled to introduce capitalism and liberal democracy. Meanwhile, by 2004 most of the European nations had joined the European Union, the world's third largest economic power. Germany struggled to make reunification work, Russia debated a new role in the world, and the European Union sought the appropriate mix of cooperation and national sovereignty.

Online Study Center **Improve Your Grade** Flashcards

Key Terms

Marshall Plan	NATO	existentialism
Eurocommunism	Soviet bloc	postmodernism
Greens	Warsaw Pact	Brezhnev Doctrine
British Commonwealth	ostpolitik	glasnost
of Nations	welfare states	perestroika
Truman Doctrine	bhangra	oligarchs

Suggested Reading

Books

Bridenthal, Renate, et al., eds. *Becoming Visible: Women in European History,* 3rd ed. Boston: Houghton Mifflin, 1998. Offers readable essays.

Crockatt, Richard. *The Fifty Years War: The United States and the Soviet Union in World Politics, 1941–1991.* New York: Routledge, 1995. A detailed study of the Cold War and U.S.-Soviet relations.

Evtuhov, Catherine, et al. *A History of Russia: Peoples, Legends, Events, Forces.* Boston: Houghton Mifflin, 2004. A readable, up-to-date survey.

Gleason, Gregory. *The Central Asian States: Discovering Independence.* Boulder: Westview, 1997. A study of the peoples and modern history of Turkestan.

James, Harold. *Europe Reborn: A History, 1914–2000.* New York: Longman, 2003. A survey of the period.

McCormick, John. *Understanding the European Union: A Concise Introduction,* 3rd ed. New York: Palgrave Macmillan, 2005. A broadranging introduction to European integration.

Pagden, Anthony, ed. *The Idea of Europe: From Antiquity to the European Union.* New York: Cambridge University Press, 2002. An interesting collection of essays on European unity through the ages, including the contemporary era.

Rifkin, Jeremy. *The European Dream: How Europe's Vision of the Future is Quietly Eclipsing the American Dream.* New York: Tarcher/

Penguin, 2004. A provocative, sympathetic examination by an American scholar.

Roskin, Michael G. *The Rebirth of Eastern Europe,* 4th ed. Englewood Cliffs: Prentice Hall, 2001. A provocative survey emphasizing politics and economics.

Ryback, Timothy W. *Rock Around the Bloc: A History of Rock Music in Eastern Europe and the Soviet Union.* New York: Oxford University Press, 1990. A fascinating examination of the role of rock music in the Communist bloc.

Smith, Bonnie G. *Changing Lives: Women in European History Since 1700.* Lexington, Mass.: D. C. Heath, 1989. A readable introduction with good coverage of the twentieth century.

Suny, Ronald Grigor. *The Soviet Experiment: Russia, the USSR, and the Successor States.* New York: Oxford University Press, 1998. An excellent overview of Soviet history and the aftermath.

Tipton, Frank B. and Robert Aldrich. *An Economic and Social History of Europe: From 1939 to the Present.* Baltimore: Johns Hopkins University, 1987. Accessible and comprehensive introduction.

Vinen, Richard. *A History in Fragments: Europe in the Twentieth Century.* Cambridge: Da Capo Press, 2000. A provocative, wide-ranging narrative by a British historian.

Wilkenson, James, and H. Stuart Hughes. *Contemporary Europe: A History,* 10th ed. Upper Saddle River, N.J.: Prentice-Hall, 2004. One of the best, most comprehensive general surveys.

Websites

EUROPA—Gateway to the European Union (http://europa.eu.int/index_en.htm). Provides information on many topics.

European Union in the US (http://www.eurunion.org/states/home/htm). Provides a wealth of data on the European Union.

Internet Resources on Russia and the CIS (http://www.ssees.ac.uk/russia.htm). A British site with a collection of links on many aspects of Russia and the Soviet Union.

Internet Modern History Sourcebook (http://www.fordham.edu/halsall/mod/modsbook.html). A very extensive online collection of historical documents and secondary materials.

Russian History Index: The World Wide Web Virtual Library (http://vlib.iue.it/hist-russia/Index.html). Contains useful essays and links on Russian history, society, and politics.

CHAPTER 29

The Americas and the Pacific Basin: New Roles in the Contemporary World, Since 1945

Online Study Center

This icon will direct you to interactive activities and study materials on the website: college.hmco.com/pic/lockard1e

A Naturalization Ceremony Seeking political freedom or economic opportunities, immigrants flock to the United States and many become citizens. At this ceremony, 800 residents, representing 88 countries, took the oath of citizenship in Columbus, Ohio, in April, 2005. (AP/Wide World Photos)

It's curious. Our generals listen to the [U.S.] Pentagon. They learn the ideology of National Security and commit all these crimes [against the Argentine people]. Then the same [American] people who gave us this gift come and ask, "How did these terrible things happen?"

The women appeared one day in the historic Plaza de Mayo, adjacent to the presidential palace in downtown Buenos Aires, Argentina. It was 1977, and for several years the military regime running the country had been waging a bloody campaign to eliminate dissidents, killing or abducting some 30,000 people and arresting and torturing thousands more. Some of those targeted may have belonged to outlawed leftist groups, but many simply held progressive political ideas or were friends with regime critics. Initially only the feared secret police paid attention to the dozen or so frightened women who came once a week, standing in silent protest. Soon the women's ranks swelled to over a hundred at each weekly vigil, making them impossible to ignore. A year later the peaceful protesters numbered more than a thousand. Wearing kerchiefs on their heads and sensible flat shoes on their feet, the mothers and grandmothers pinned to their chests photographs of missing family members, victims of the state's terror. They all asked the same question: Where were their missing children, husbands, pregnant daughters, and grandchildren, some of them newborn infants?

The "Mothers and Grandmothers of the Plaza de Mayo," as they came to be known, dared to challenge one of Latin America's most brutal tyrannies. Whether rich, poor, or middle class, most were housewives taking to the street, as one put it, to fight the vicious armed forces, spineless politicians, complicit clergy, muzzled press, and co-opted labor unions, and to find their family members. Their courageous protest inspired others in Argentina and around the world with hope and moral outrage at repression by military forces. The gatherings continued weekly until 1983, when the regime fell and a civilian government could investigate the disappearances. Most of the women never learned the fates of their loved ones.

The protest by the Plaza de Mayo women illustrates how some Latin Americans addressed the authoritarian governments under which they lived, sometimes for decades, since World War II. Latin American countries often shifted back and forth between dictatorship and democracy, neither of which fostered widespread economic prosperity nor sustained stability amid the stark contrasts between rich and poor. Many Latin Americans also resented the United States, which, as Raul Alfonsin (b. 1927), the democratically elected Argentine

901

president who replaced the military dictatorship, noted, often supported the Latin American military regimes and other despotic governments that repressed their people while welcoming U.S. investment.

The United States remained the hemisphere's dominant power during this period while gradually expanding its global influence. Wars in Korea and Vietnam were part of the U.S. effort to shape the global system while also opposing the expansion of communism. U.S. president Harry Truman (president 1945–1953) argued in 1947 that American political and business practices could only thrive at home if foreign countries also embraced similar practices. After World War II the United States became the global workshop and banker, preacher and teacher, umpire and policeman. It enjoyed unrivaled supremacy, a combination of military might, economic power, and political-ideological leadership that was contested only by the Soviet Union between 1946 and 1989. After 1989 the United States became the world's only remaining superpower. U.S. society increasingly differed from those of its North American neighbor, Canada, and the Pacific Basin countries of Australia and New Zealand. The three northernmost nations—Canada, Mexico, and the United States—shared a border and intertwined histories but had each developed different world-views and sometimes struggled to understand each other. Similar misperceptions often shaped relations between the English- and Spanish-speaking nations.

FOCUS QUESTIONS

1. How did the Cold War shape U.S. foreign policies?
2. How and why are the societies of the United States, Canada, and Australia similar to and different from each other?
3. Why have democracy and economic development proven to be difficult goals in Latin America?
4. How have Latin American and Caribbean cultures been dynamic?

◈ The United States as a Superpower

How did the Cold War shape U.S. foreign policies?

By virtue of its size, power, and wealth, the United States has played a major role in the world. The Americans helped Europe and Japan to regain their footing after World War II, espoused and often promoted human rights and freedom, have lavished aid on various allies or potential allies, and have provided leadership in a politically fragmented world. During the Cold War (1946–1989), U.S. policies were shaped by competition with the Soviet bloc for allies and strategic advantage, and these policies in turn influenced the world's perceptions of the United States (see Chronology: North America and the Pacific Basin, 1945–Present on page 904). Soviet domination of eastern Europe, the Communist victory in China, and the Korean War all convinced Americans that communism was on the march. While millions of people around the world admired American democratic ideals, prosperity, and technological ingenuity, the U.S. drive to oppose Communist expansion led to wars, interventions, support for often authoritarian allies, frequent neglect of human rights, and the globalization of capitalism that fostered widespread hostility toward the United States. After the Cold War, the United States and its allies faced new challenges, especially the rise of international terrorism.

The Postwar United States and the Cold War

World War II was a watershed for the United States, a rallying cry that forged Americans' vision of world politics. The war had accelerated political centralization and economic growth in the United States; at the same time, it had encouraged Americans to accept international involvements and thus promoted an activist foreign policy. By the later 1940s observers began referring to both the United States and the USSR as

CHRONOLOGY

	North America	Pacific Basin	Latin America and the Caribbean
1940	**1946–1989** Cold War **1950–1953** Korean War		**1959** Cuban Revolution
1960	**1963–1975** U.S. war in Vietnam	**1962–1990** Decolonization of Pacific islands **1973** End of "white Australia" policy	**1964–1985** Military government in Brazil **1973–1989** Military government in Chile
1980	**1994** Formation of NAFTA		
2000	**2001** Al Qaeda terrorist attacks in United States		

superpowers because of their unrivaled political, economic, and military might. The end of the war also placed the United States in the position of global powerbroker and policeman. As U.S.-Soviet rivalry increased, the two superpowers sought to outmaneuver each other and sometimes to block each other from gaining influence in other countries.

The American Century The victory over Nazism and Japanese militarism reinforced American confidence and sense of mission. In 1941, Henry Luce, the publisher of one of the most influential news magazines in the U.S., *Time*, declared that the twentieth century would be the American Century, and that Americans, citizens of the world's most powerful nation, must accept their duty and opportunity to exercise influence in the world, by whatever means they could. Luce believed that America's idealistic Bill of Rights, magnificent industrial products, and technological skills would be shared with all peoples. His view, while arrogant, reflected Americans' longtime belief in the exportability of their country's values and institutions, that their nation was the shining "City Upon a Hill," as a seventeenth-century colonist put it, and the world's model. But U.S.-style capitalism and democracy proved difficult to implant where they had no roots.

American leaders planned to take a leading role in the postwar world. In 1941, even before the nation entered World War II, a conference of influential Americans recommended a policy that emphasized strengthening U.S. economic influence around the globe. After the war the U.S. government pursued the strategy, rebuilding defeated Germany and Japan, establishing global financial networks, lavishing aid on western Europe to help stabilize it under democratic governments, and using U.S. military forces to protect U.S. allies in Asia. The United States also opposed radical nationalist movements, especially Communist-led revolutionary groups, in Asia, Africa, and Latin America. In these ways, it took the lead in maintaining a global system in which it held the strongest position.

For several decades, as the U.S. economy soared, the notion of an American Century seemed realistic. Americans believed that they were destined to lead and inspire the world. But the economic superiority of the United States in the 1940s and 1950s was founded on unusual conditions, since many rival nations had been devastated by world war. Among the great powers, only the United States had not been bombed or financially drained, and therefore it was able to keep intact a modern industrial system. The United States alone could produce, on a large scale, the consumer goods needed by others. In 1950, it accounted for 27 percent of total world economic output. By supplying the world, Americans experienced an economic boom that lasted until the late 1960s and helped finance an activist U.S. foreign policy.

The United States became not just the supplier but also the engine of the world economy. Americans forged close trade links with Canada, western Europe, and Japan while sponsoring large-scale foreign aid programs and investment, especially in Asian and Latin American countries. Such foreign aid and investment benefited western European nations after World War II, helping to spark their economic renaissance and ensure their political stability. Other nations in East Asia, especially Japan, and some in Latin America also benefited from U.S. aid and investment. However, in these regions the aid and investment often supported cash crop agriculture and mining, reinforcing the economic dependence of developing nations on producing natural resources for the world economy and, as a result, promoting unbalanced economic growth. Later, U.S. investment developed light industry, especially textile factories, that utilized cheap labor in countries such as Mexico and Thailand. This investment and trade became very profitable for U.S. corporations. Asian, African, and Latin America countries became key U.S. markets, acquiring over a third of American exports by the 1990s. However, American consumption of ever more foreign imports, from Japanese cars to Middle Eastern oil, contributed to a chronic trade imbalance, as Americans spent more for foreign products than they earned from exports. By 2005 imports were 57 percent larger than exports as Americans lived beyond their means and globalization led to outsourcing of manufacturing and jobs.

The Cold War　The Cold War shaped U.S. foreign relations, especially with the USSR. American leaders saw the Soviet Union as pursuing global aggression and fostering political unrest. Although they had good reason to worry about the Soviet state, which was headed by a ruthless dictator, Joseph Stalin, and possessed formidable military might, U.S. leaders and intelligence analysts often overestimated the Soviet threat. George Kennan, the State Department official who constructed the anti-Soviet policy in the late 1940s and early 1950s, later admitted that the popular view held by Americans

of the USSR poised to attack the West was based more on imagination than on hard evidence. The Cold War produced an expectation of permanent conflict between two competing ideologies: communism and capitalist democracy. Given this assumption, the U.S. government became obsessed with secrecy and control. Two key U.S. institutions carrying out the anti-Soviet strategy, the Central Intelligence Agency (CIA) and the National Security Council, both established in 1947, operated in top secrecy, with little congressional oversight and ever larger budgets, reaching a total of $40 billion per year for all intelligence agencies by the 1980s. By the early 1950s the **domino theory**, which envisioned countries falling one by one to communism, became a mainstay of U.S. policy.

Anticommunism intensified within the United States after U.S. senator Joseph McCarthy (1909–1957), a hard-drinking former judge, and his allies charged, without offering proof, that Communists had infiltrated the U.S. government and shaped foreign policy. During the early and mid-1950s a campaign, known as McCarthyism, to identify suspected Communists in the government, the military, education, and the entertainment industry led to the firing or the blacklisting of not only a handful of secret Communists but also of thousands of Americans who held leftwing or other unpopular political views, which were condemned as "un-American." (Blacklisting prevented people from working.) For example, high school teachers were fired for suggesting that, to better understand communism, their students read *The Communist Manifesto*, by Karl Marx, and university experts on Asia lost their positions for criticizing U.S. Asian policies. McCarthy called hundreds of people, from movie actors to State Department officials, before his Senate committee, where he questioned them about their political activities or the political views of their friends. In 1954 the U.S. Senate censured McCarthy for recklessly charging top military leaders with treason. To critics, McCarthy's investigation, which ruined many innocent people, was a witch-hunt that violated the Bill of Rights, a Cold War–driven hysteria that generated accusations against people who held largely harmless political opinions.

For much of the Cold War era, American leaders largely agreed on foreign policy goals. A broad consensus emerged around opposing the spread of communism and Soviet power. To pursue these goals, most American leaders favored an activist foreign policy, including the use of military power. However, U.S. leaders disagreed as to which approach was most effective in achieving the goals. Some leaders pursued **multilateralism**, an approach in which the United States sought a common front and a coordination of foreign policies with allies in western Europe, Japan, and Canada, avoiding activities that might enflame world opinion against the United States. In contrast, most policymakers, and the presidents they

---

domino theory　A theory that envisioned countries falling one by one to communism and that became a mainstay of U.S. policy.

multilateralism　A foreign policy in which the United States sought a common front and a coordination of foreign policies with allies in western Europe, Japan, and Canada, avoiding activities that might enflame world opinion against the United States.

served, favored **unilateralism**, a foreign policy in which the United States acted alone in its own perceived national interest even if key allies disapproved, as they did with the U.S. war in Vietnam. Unilateralism often led to support of repressive dictatorships allied to the United States, such as in the Philippines and the Congo. The Cold War–driven consensus stifled those who questioned the rationale, tactics, and cost of an activist policy. Ultimately the costly interventions abroad, especially the frustrating war in Vietnam, provoked a debate about the goals, operation, and impact of U.S. foreign policy. By the later 1960s, this debate had undermined the consensus and provoked increasing dissent within the nation.

The main U.S. strategy, known as **containment**, was aimed at preventing Communists from gaining power, and the USSR from getting political influence, in other nations. Containment resulted in wars, as in Korea and later Vietnam, and to briefer interventions to shape governments, especially in countries that were gaining independence from Western colonialism or seeking to weaken Western economic domination. An influential, top secret government report, known as NSC-68, prepared by the National Security Council in 1950, provided the rationale for activist policies by painting a bleak picture of the USSR's search for world supremacy: "The issues that face us are momentous, involving the fulfillment or destruction not only of this [U.S.] Republic but of civilization itself."[2] NSC-68 sanctioned any tactics, including assassination, in the anticommunism struggle. It remained a key basis for U.S. military and intelligence policies abroad until the mid-1970s.

Rising U.S. Power Containment policy led to a massive, expensive military buildup. NSC-68 had called for a huge defense budget and expansion of the nuclear weapons arsenal as a deterrent, to be paid for by tax increases and major reductions in social welfare spending. Security, the document argued, was to take precedence in the national budget, at the expense of all other priorities. The Soviets matched the U.S. military buildup, creating a constant escalation of military spending and ever more sophisticated weapons on both sides. Under a policy known in the United States as **Mutually Assured Destruction**, or MAD, the United States and the USSR used the fear of nuclear weapons to deter each other. Some historians believe that MAD prevented a direct military confrontation between the two rivals that might have sparked World War III. Americans reacted to the threat of nuclear war in the 1950s by often building bomb shelters in their basements or backyards and having schools hold mock air raid drills. During these drills millions of American students learned to "duck

and cover," jumping under their desks to protect themselves from a hypothetical nuclear attack.

Defense spending reshaped the U.S. economy. Despite the warning of U.S. president Dwight Eisenhower (g. 1953–1961), a chief commander during World War II, to guard against the growing influence on U.S. foreign and domestic policy of what he termed the military-industrial complex, an alliance of military leaders and weapons producers, defense became an enormous business. It employed a fifth of the U.S. industrial work force and a third of scientists and engineers by the 1960s, while costing U.S. taxpayers hundreds of billions a year. The United States also sold weapons to allied nations, among them despotic regimes, some of which, such as Argentina and Thailand, both ruled by military dictatorships, used the weapons against their own population or their neighbors; the United States also trained these regimes' military officers and police forces, who often used the tactics they learned to eliminate dissidents.

Between 1945 and 1975 U.S. power was unmatched in the world, and the United States maintained military bases on every inhabited continent and in dozens of countries around the world (see Map 29.1). Both the United States and the USSR intervened directly or indirectly in civil wars and revolutions to outflank the other. The United States employed military force, as in the long war in Vietnam and the invasion of the Dominican Republic in 1965, and covertly aided governments to suppress opposition or, as in Chile in 1973, to overthrow governments considered unfriendly to U.S. economic or political interests, even if, as in Chile, these governments were democratic and had been freely elected. Some foreign observers applauded U.S. efforts to suppress leftwing governments and movements that might have favored the USSR or Communist China, while others were hostile to U.S. power and criticized the United States for superpower imperialism. The rivalry between the United States and the USSR persisted until the collapse of the Communist regimes in 1989.

U.S. power, especially its economic leadership, was less dominant between the mid-1970s and the early 1990s. Reasons for this change included the rise of a rebuilt western Europe and Japan to economic power, the military strength of the USSR, the economic challenge from industrializing nations such as South Korea and China, and the damage done to the U.S. economy and prestige by the unsuccessful, widely unpopular war in Vietnam. Also a factor was the economic price Americans paid for global power. The increasing extension and cost of U.S. military commitments caused the nation's economic creativity to sag and industries to become obsolete as heavy defense spending diverted U.S. wealth away from the domestic economy. Over four decades the Cold War cost the U.S. government around $4 trillion, money that did not go to improving education and health care or meeting other needs. The growing U.S. defense budgets of the 1980s did help undermine the Soviet Union, which was unable to match the lavish spending on expensive weapons, such as unproven antimissile systems, but it also transformed the United States from a creditor nation into the world's largest debtor nation, leaving Americans with ballooning federal budget deficits. Only in the

---

unilateralism A foreign policy in which the United States acted alone in its own perceived national interest even if key allies disapproved.

containment The main U.S. strategy aimed at preventing Communists from gaining power, and the USSR from getting political influence, in other nations during the Cold War.

Mutually Assured Destruction A policy, known as MAD, in which the United States and the USSR used the fear of nuclear weapons to deter each other.

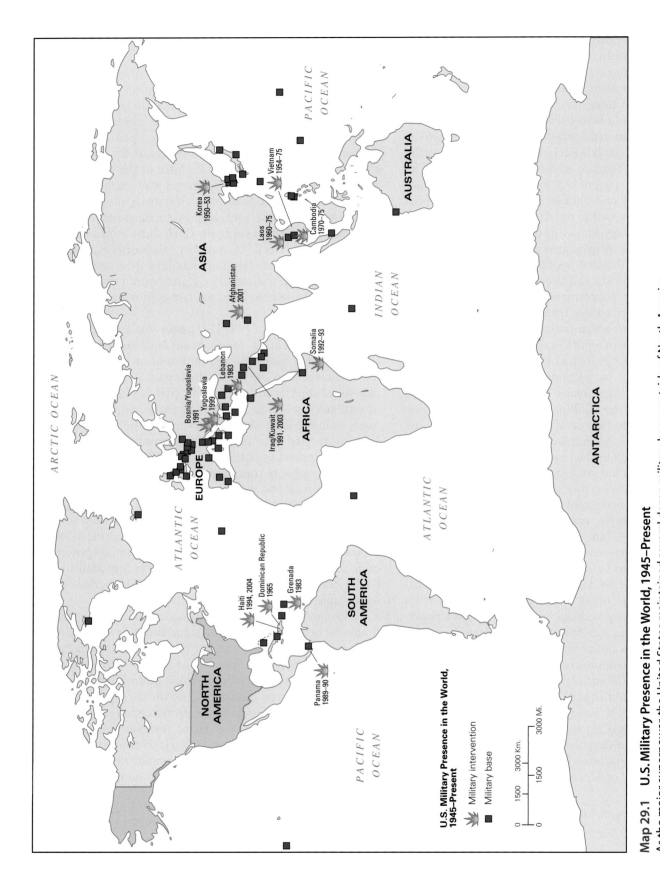

Map 29.1   U.S. Military Presence in the World, 1945–Present
As the major superpower, the United States maintained several dozen military bases outside of North America while engaging in military operations in Latin America, Africa, Asia, the Middle East, and Europe. This map shows some of the major U.S. bases and military conflicts.

Online Study Center   **Improve Your Grade**   Interactive Map: The Cold War

1990s, under President Bill Clinton (g. 1993–2001), did the U.S. government eliminate the budget deficits that had accelerated between the 1960s and the 1980s to pay for the Cold War.

Wars in Korea and Vietnam

In 1949 the Chinese Communist victory in China, a country whose longtime government had been allied with and armed by the United States (see Chapter 27), escalated U.S. concern about the expansion of communism. Communist expansion, and the U.S. determination to halt it, led to the Korean War. The decision to send U.S. troops to Korea, under the auspices of the newly formed United Nations, signaled the U.S. adoption of an interventionist foreign policy. The Korean War (1950–1953) was followed a decade later by a more massive U.S. intervention in another Asian society, Vietnam, which resulted in the longest war the United States had ever waged (1963–1975).

The Korean War was sparked when North Korea, ruled by a brutal Communist regime allied to the USSR, invaded South Korea, a U.S. ally, with the goal of forcibly reunifying the Korean peninsula (see Chapter 27). The U.S. president, Harry S Truman, viewed the North Korean invasion in the light of his World War II experience: as a second coming of Nazi aggression. The anti-Communist mood in the United States, already inflamed by the Communist victory in China, made it politically unthinkable for Truman not to oppose the North Korean thrust. Truman never consulted the U.S. Congress, which had the constitutional responsibility to declare war, and his approach to entering Korea thereafter made presidents supreme in decisions to go to war. Officially Korea was a police action under U.N. sponsorship rather than a war, a precedent that allowed future presidents to commit U.S. military forces without congressional approval. Scholars credit Truman's Korean intervention with contributing to the centralizing of power in the executive branch. Furthermore, the Soviet support of North Korea with arms and advice, and the intervention of the Communist Chinese on the North Korean side,

deepened American fear of an expanding communism, especially in Asia. However, despite the 38,000 Americans killed and over 100,000 wounded, the war ended not in victory for the United States and the U.N. forces it led but in stalemate. For the first time since the War of 1812, the United States had failed to decisively win a major military conflict.

The U.S. intervention in Korea reflected not only Cold War anticommunism but also the desire of idealistic Americans to spread democracy and free market capitalism around the world. An American economic adviser to the South Korean government reported the hope of his more idealistic American colleagues that South Korea "will institute a whole series of necessary reforms which will so appeal to the North Koreans that their army will revolt, kill all the nasty Communists, and create a lovely liberal democracy to the everlasting credit of the U.S.A.!"[3] North Korea, however, remained a rigid Communist state and South Korea did not become a democracy until the 1980s, over three decades after the war.

The domino theory, which predicted a Communist sweep through Southeast Asia, and the desire to maintain military credibility and keep valuable Southeast Asian resources, such as tin and tungsten, in friendly hands provided the rationale for financing the French effort to maintain colonial control (1946–1954) in Vietnam and, when that effort failed, increasing U.S. involvement, leading eventually to the U.S. military fighting Vietnamese Communist forces armed by the USSR and China (see Chapter 31). Misunderstandings hurt the U.S. effort. Few U.S. leaders comprehended the historical and cultural factors, such as anti-Western nationalism and the examples of resistance to foreign invaders over the centuries, that sparked the Vietnamese Communist movement they were fighting. As a growing Communist-led insurgency, backed by North Vietnam, challenged a widely unpopular, U.S.-supported South Vietnamese government, the United States sent thousands of military advisers to South Vietnam.

By the mid-1960s, as the unpopular South Vietnamese regime lost ground and support, the U.S. president, Lyndon B. Johnson (g. 1963–1969), committed military forces and launched an intensive air war against targets in North and South Vietnam and later in neighboring Cambodia and Laos. U.S. troop totals topped off at 550,000 by 1967. The domino theory rhetoric often exaggerated the Communist threat. In escalating the Vietnam conflict, Johnson asserted that "if we don't stop the [Communists] in South Vietnam, tomorrow they will be in Hawaii and next week they will be in San Francisco,"[4] very unlikely scenarios given the limited Chinese and Vietnamese naval and air power. Between 1963 and 1975,

On Patrol in Vietnam U.S. soldiers sought out National Liberation Front fighters and supporters in the villages, rice fields, and jungles of South Vietnam. They could not easily tell friend from foe and warily dealt with local people. (Corbis)

2.5 million Americans served in Vietnam; 58,000 died and 300,000 were wounded there.

As support within the United States for the war ebbed with military stalemate and increasing casualties in what seemed a quagmire, Johnson's successor, President Richard Nixon (g. 1969–1973), gradually withdrew U.S. forces and negotiated a political settlement with North Vietnam. But a policy through-out the war of spending lavishly on both "guns and butter"—military and domestic needs—generated huge budget deficits and other economic problems with which the United States struggled from the later 1960s into the 1990s. The war in Vietnam ultimately cost U.S. taxpayers around $1 trillion. Furthermore, the lack of a military victory despite the high cost in lives made Americans temporarily wary of supporting other military interventions that might become Vietnam-like quagmires.

The United States and the Developing Nations

Decolonization, nationalism, the U.S.-Soviet struggle, and per-sistent poverty combined to make the Asian, African, and Latin American societies prone to crises, sometimes drawing in the United States. The United States often favored decolonization that presented opportunities to U.S. business; for example, it successfully pressured the Dutch to abandon Indonesia and the British to grant independence to most of their African colonies. However, it opposed independence for colonies, such as French-ruled Vietnam and Portuguese-ruled Mozambique, where Communists or other leftists dominated the nationalist movements. After decolonization, Americans offered generous aid to friendly nations and to victims of famine or natural ca-tastrophes. U.S. assistance also sparked the Green Revolution in agriculture, which led to improved food production in coun-tries such as India, Mexico, and the Philippines. However, Cold War challenges often involved the United States in long-term confrontations with Communist-led revolutions, as in China, Vietnam, and Cuba, and also sparked interventions to help U.S. allies suppress leftist insurgencies and to oppose left-leaning, though non-Communist, governments, such as in Iran, Chile, and Guatemala. But some U.S.-installed or supported govern-ments lacked widespread popular support or lost their credibil-ity, often surviving only by repressing domestic opposition, sometimes killing thousands of their own citizens.

In some U.S. interventions, presidents dispatched troops to overturn a government or to support one side in a civil war or revolutionary situation. U.S. leaders used the threat of com-munism as the rationale for these actions, but some interven-tions removed democratic governments, as in Guatemala and Chile, or suppressed democratic movements. For example, President Lyndon Johnson, claiming that Americans would not permit another Communist government alongside Fidel Castro's Cuba in the Western Hemisphere, dispatched 20,000 U.S. Marines into the Dominican Republic in 1965 to sup-port a military government under attack by the democrati-cally elected leaders they had recently overthrown. However,

Johnson had consulted no other Latin American governments, the Dominican Communist movement was tiny, and the democratically elected leaders, while left-leaning, were non-Communist reformers who had wide popular support. Former Dominican president and the leader of the antimilitary move-ment, Juan Bosch (1909–2001), declared that "this was a dem-ocratic revolution smashed by the leading democracy in the world."[5]

In addition to military interventions, the United States also provided friendly governments or antileftist groups with weapons and other assistance. Instead of troops, presidents sent military advisers, intelligence agents, and funding. For example, the United States aided a pro-Western but often repressive gov-ernment combating a leftist insurgency in El Salvador during the 1970s and 1980s. In Laos from 1960 to 1975, during what was known as the CIA's "secret war" because the U.S. role, while widely known in Southeast Asia, was kept hidden from Con-gress and the U.S. public, Americans recruited an army from among hill peoples to fight Communist Laotian and North Vietnamese forces (see Chapter 31).

A final type of intervention involved covert destabiliza-tion, which involved American agents working underground to help undermine or spark the overthrow of governments seen as hostile to U.S. interests. Covert actions included hiring local people to spread misinformation about government policies, subsidizing opposition political parties, providing weapons to the military, and arranging for assassinations of government leaders. For example, U.S. clandestine activity, which undermined elected left-leaning democratic govern-ments in Iran in the 1950s and Thailand and Chile in the 1970s, brought brutal dictatorships to all three countries. U.S. Secretary of State Henry Kissinger defended the U.S. encour-agement of a military coup against the democratically elected, leftist Chilean government—a democratic government that respected civil liberties—by explaining, "I don't see why we need to stand by and watch a country go Communist due to the irresponsibility of its own people."[6] This attitude that the United States knows best what is in their interest has often in-furiated people in other nations. Only in the mid-1970s, with congressional hearings on covert activities, did Americans learn of the U.S. role in Chile and other interventions. This awareness forced debate of the question, still unresolved today, of whether engaging in secret operations and foreign interven-tions unknown to the public is compatible with democracy and open, accountable government.

The United States in the Global System After 1989

The demise of the Soviet bloc in 1989 and the dissolution of the USSR in 1991 left the United States the dominant world power, although the European Union and the rising East Asian nations (especially China and Japan) also enjoyed great influence in the global system. But the lack of a rival superpower did not mean the end of challengers, among them international terrorists. The United States used its unsurpassed military and economic power to maintain a global presence and intervene in several countries, but Americans also paid a price in blood and treasure for activist foreign policies and global leadership, what some called the *Pax Americana* ("American Peace").

A New World Disorder

The United States now struggled to find a new role in a world characterized by what observers called a "New World Disorder" because of an outbreak of small, deadly conflicts. During the early 1990s, for example, President Bill Clinton (g. 1993–2001) sent a small number of U.S. troops, under United Nations auspices, to stabilize Somalia, a famine-racked northeast African state involved in a civil war. The intervention turned out badly, however, when the forces of a local warlord paraded the mutilated bodies of dead U.S. soldiers through the streets, forcing a U.S. withdrawal. In the aftermath, the reluctance to assert power in other turbulent states like Rwanda, Liberia, and Sierra Leone, all places where civilians were being slaughtered by the thousands, suggested that the United States lacked the political will to intervene to stop ethnic conflicts, genocides, or revolutions in small nations. However, working with European allies, Clinton sent U.S. forces to help end the deadly civil wars in the former Yugoslavia. Furthermore, the United States continued to try to resolve other foreign policy problems. For example, after being forced out of Vietnam in 1975, it refused diplomatic recognition and imposed a strict trade embargo against the Communist-ruled country. However, in the 1990s the Clinton administration established diplomatic ties and lifted the embargo, which it viewed as punitive and counterproductive for U.S. business, forging better relations with Vietnam.

Cold War policies sometimes came back to haunt the United States. In the 1980s it had given military and financial aid to the Islamic rebels fighting Soviet troops and the pro-Soviet government in Afghanistan (see Chapter 30). Some of this aid went to Arab volunteers, among them the Saudi militant Osama bin Laden (b. 1957), who were fighting alongside the rebels. After the Soviets left Afghanistan in defeat in 1989, Muslim militants, the Taliban, defeated the other factions and took power. The Taliban imposed a rigid Islamic state and offered a base for Islamic groups to form into the global terrorist network known as Al Qaeda ("the Base"), which was led by bin Laden. Al Qaeda now plotted terrorist attacks against the United States, sometimes using leftover U.S. weapons (see Chapters 26 and 30). Further west, Iraq's ruthless dictator, Saddam Hussein, used weapons acquired from the United States, his ally against Iran in the 1980s, to threaten Iraq's neighbors and repress dissident groups. In 1991 the United States led a coalition of nations that pushed invading Iraqi forces out of Kuwait during the Gulf War and then later protected the Kurds in northern Iraq from Saddam's reprisals. The intervention in oil-rich Kuwait was part of a consistent U.S. policy over the decades to protect the flow of oil from the Middle East, especially the Persian Gulf, to the West.

9/11 and Its Aftermath

Americans had long been insulated from terrorist violence, including bombings and airplane hijackings. However, the terrorist attack launched by Al Qaeda on the World Trade Center in New York and the Pentagon in Washington, D.C., in September, 2001, which killed nearly 3,000 Americans, shocked the nation and led to a reshaping of both domestic and foreign policies. The new U.S. president, George W. Bush (b. 1946), introduced policies, such as preventive detention and monitoring of libraries, designed to prevent possible domestic terrorism but that critics believed went too far, infringing on civil liberties. By attacking buildings that symbolized often unpopular U.S. economic and military power to people around the world, the terrorists, young Muslim fanatics mostly from two close U.S. allies, Egypt and Saudi Arabia, hoped to capitalize on widespread anti-U.S. feelings. However, people in most countries, even if they disliked the United States and its power, deplored the bombings and the loss of innocent life.

The attacks prompted President Bush to declare a war on international terrorism using military force. But unlike the USSR during the Cold War, whose leaders had to be cautious, terrorist networks had no clear command structure or military resources and could not be influenced by diplomacy. With international support, the United States invaded Afghanistan to destroy Al Qaeda terrorist bases and displace the militant Islamic government that tolerated their presence. Bush announced a new doctrine of **preemptive war** that sanctioned unilateral military action against potential threats (see Witness to the Past: Justifying Preemptive Strikes), and he named Iraq, Iran, and North Korea as states at the core of an "axis of evil" that threatened their neighbors and world peace. The Bush doctrine advocated that the United States maintain overwhelming military superiority over all challengers. Critics perceived the Bush doctrine as a recipe for acquiring an American empire through military action, a violation, they charged, of international law and the United Nations charter.

The concern with international terrorism led to a resumption of unilateralist U.S. foreign policies, in which the United States acted without widespread international support. Rejecting opposition from the United Nations and key U.S. allies, among them Canada and Germany, in 2003 the Bush administration, claiming, based on faulty or manipulated intelligence, that Iraq possessed weapons of mass destruction and aided Al Qaeda, organized an invasion and occupation of Iraq, ending Saddam Hussein's brutal regime. But the U.S. forces found no weapons of mass destruction or evidence of a Saddam–Al Qaeda link; furthermore, the Bush administration had planned poorly for restoring stability in Iraq, a nation rich in oil but troubled by ethnic and religious divisions that threatened to explode into civil war and complicated U.S. attempts to foster democracy. A mounting insurgency by Iraqis and suicide bombings largely linked to foreign terrorists, who now flocked to Iraq to fight Americans, caused thousands of U.S. casualties and complicated political and economic reconstruction, making an early withdrawal of U.S. forces difficult. By 2006 basic services, such as electricity, and oil production had still not been restored to prewar levels and the streets in many

---

preemptive war A U.S. doctrine, triggered by the 2001 terrorist attacks, that sanctioned unilateral military action against potential threats.

In the wake of the shocking terrorist attacks on the United States in September 2001, the administration of President George W. Bush produced a document, the National Security Strategy of the United States, that restated the U.S. desire to spread democracy and capitalism while announcing that the United States would act preemptively, striking first, unilaterally if necessary, against any hostile states that the Bush administration believed might be planning to attack U.S. targets. Depending on the observer, the document either reflected or exploited Americans' fear of terrorist attacks. In 2003 Bush used the preemptive strike rationale to order a military invasion and occupation of Iraq, which he claimed had weapons of mass destruction. After Saddam's fall, Bush offered a new mission: fostering democracy in Iraq as an example for the Middle East. To critics, however, the failure to find such weapons, the faulty intelligence about them, and the huge financial and human costs of the resulting occupation for both Americans and Iraqis all suggested the dangers of a preemptive strategy. Furthermore, they argued, many presidents before Bush had claimed to promote democracy abroad but had rarely done so, especially when they used military force to install a pro-U.S. government in another country.

The great struggles of the twentieth century between liberty and totalitarianism ended with a decisive victory for the forces of freedom—and a single sustainable model for national success: freedom, democracy, and free enterprise. . . . Only nations that share a commitment to protecting basic human rights and guaranteeing political and economic freedom will be able to unleash the potential of their people and assure their future prosperity. . . . Today, the United States enjoys a position of unparalleled military strength and great economic and political influence. In keeping with our heritage and principles, we do not use our strength to press for unilateral advantage. We seek instead to create a balance of power that favors human freedom. . . . We will extend the peace by encouraging free and open societies on every continent.

Defending our Nation against its enemies is the first and fundamental commitment of the Federal Government. Today, that task has changed dramatically. Enemies in the past needed great armies and great industrial capabilities to endanger America. Now, shadowy networks of individuals can bring great chaos and suffering to our shores for less than it costs to purchase a single tank. Terrorists are organized to penetrate open societies and to turn the power of modern technologies against us. To defeat this threat we must make use of every tool in our arsenal. . . . The war against terrorists of global reach is a global enterprise of uncertain duration. . . . America will hold to account nations that are compromised by terror, including those who harbor terrorists—because the allies of terror are the enemies of civilization. . . . Our enemies have openly declared that they are seeking weapons of mass destruction. . . . The United States will not allow these efforts to succeed. . . . And, as a matter of common sense and self-defense, America will act against such emerging threats before they are fully formed. . . . We must be prepared to defeat our enemies' plans. History will judge harshly those who saw this coming danger but failed to act. In the new world we have entered, the only path to peace and security is the path of action. . . .

The struggle against global terrorism is different from any other war in our history. It will be fought on many fronts against a particularly elusive enemy over an extended period of time. . . . New deadly challenges have emerged from rogue states and terrorists. . . . Rogue regimes seek nuclear, biological, and chemical weapons. . . . We must be prepared to stop rogue states and their terrorist clients before they are able to threaten or use weapons of mass destruction against the United States and our allies. . . . The United States can no longer solely rely on a reactive posture as we have in the past. . . . We cannot let our enemies strike first. . . . We must adapt the concept of imminent threat to the capabilities and objectives of today's adversaries. . . . The greater the threat, the greater the risk of inaction—and the more compelling the case for taking anticipatory action to defend ourselves, even if uncertainty remains as to the time and place of the enemy's attack. To forestall or prevent such hostile acts by our adversaries, the United States will, if necessary, act preemptively.

THINKING ABOUT THE READING

1. How does the document reflect the tendency of U.S. leaders to claim a national goal of spreading U.S. political and economic models in the world?

2. What does the document offer as the rationale for preemptive actions?

Source: The National Security Strategy of the United States (**http://www. whitehouse.gov/nsc/print/nssall.html**).

regions remained unsafe, demoralizing Iraqis. The spiraling costs of the Iraq occupation and other expenses, combined with large tax cuts, ballooned U.S. budget deficits that could not be sustained long term without serious damage to the U.S. economy. The ever expanding appetite of Americans for oil contributed to the interventions in the Middle East and support for often corrupt, dictatorial regimes, and caused critics to charge that the Iraq war was also about oil. The Iraq war, unpopular in much of the world, charges that the U.S. tortured suspected terrorists, and the U.S. rejection of several international treaties, such as that on global warming, further alienated Western allies. Yet, the United States also earned praise for generous assistance to the victims of a catastrophic tidal wave in South and Southeast Asia in 2005.

Because of its unparalleled economic and military might, the United States had assumed heavy burdens, sending troops to Afghanistan, Iraq, and elsewhere while maintaining military bases in several dozen countries and islands around the world. While western Europeans and East Asians have generally concentrated on trade relations with other nations, Americans have attempted to balance trade and other nonterrorism issues with confronting the nations they perceive as dangerous. By 2004 the United States accounted for half of all military spending worldwide, spending as much on its military and weapons as all other nations combined, and it also accounted for about half of all arms sales to the world's nations. The United States plays a vital role in world governance through its diplomatic engagements, vast military deployments, and buttressing of the global economy, a fact appreciated by many nations because the cost is largely borne by U.S. taxpayers. As a result, while anti-U.S. sentiments grew steadily in the early twenty-first century, no coalition of nations has come together to oppose the U.S. role. However, the budget deficits that now pay for it, helping to double the national debt between 2000 and 2006, are only possible because Asian investors, especially the Chinese, Japanese, and South Koreans, finance around half of the debt and must eventually be repaid, giving these countries leverage with the United States in the future. Scholars debate whether the United States will retain its dominance in the years ahead or whether the growing burdens will overwhelm the economy and reduce U.S. power as other nations, perhaps China or India, surge ahead. Whatever the case, since the Romans two millennia ago, no other nation has been as dominant in military, economic, political, and social realms as the United States has been after 1990. This dominance has forced Americans to debate, as the Romans and, before them, the Athenians did, whether democracy and imperial power are consistent.

SECTION SUMMARY

- For several decades after World War II, the United States enjoyed a period of economic growth and lavished economic aid on western Europe and Japan, where it helped those countries to recover, and later on developing nations, where it was not used as effectively.

- During the Cold War, McCarthyism led to the persecution of many U.S. citizens for supposed Communist sympathies, U.S. presidents aimed to contain the spread of communism through unilateral action, the two superpowers followed the Mutually Assured Destruction policy (which may have helped prevent a nuclear war), and defense spending became a key factor in the U.S. economy.

- On the basis of the domino theory, which argued that if communism wasn't stopped it would take over the world, the United States adopted an interventionist foreign policy and fought Communists in Korea and Vietnam, but neither war achieved U.S. goals and the Vietnam War severely crippled the U.S. economy.

- During the Cold War, the United States opposed not only Communist movements but also non-Communist leftist movements in several countries, in many cases helping to replace them with brutal military dictatorships.

- In response to the terrorist attacks of September 11, 2001, U.S. president George W. Bush proclaimed a policy of preemptive war and led the country to war in Afghanistan and then in Iraq, the second of which was fought despite United Nations disapproval and has been very controversial.

The Changing Societies of North America and the Pacific Basin

How and why are the societies of the United States, Canada, and Australia similar to and different from each other?

In the years following World War II, the United States and Canada in North America and Australia and New Zealand in the southwestern corner of the Pacific Basin—all originally settled by people from the British Isles—shared a general prosperity, similar social patterns, and many cultural traditions, but they also played different roles in the world. Besides exercising more political, economic, and military power than these other nations, the United States had a stable democracy and a rapidly changing society. The United States, Canada, and Australia all attracted millions of immigrants from around the world, helping to globalize their cultures and link them more closely to other nations.

Prosperity, Technology, and Inequality in the United States

Living in the world's richest nation, many Americans benefited from a growing economy and widespread affluence. During the nation's most prosperous decade, the 1960s, the production of goods and services doubled, and per capita income rose by half. Many Americans moved into new automobile, aerospace, service, and information technology industries. By 2000 the United States accounted for a third of the world's total production of goods and services, over twice as much as second-place Japan, and enjoyed a median annual family income of over $40,000. As per capita producers of wealth, Americans exceeded everyone except the people of Luxembourg, Norway, and Switzerland. Americans also owned the majority of, and profited from, the giant multinational corporations, such as General Motors and Wal-Mart, that played ever larger roles in the globalizing world economy. However, there were downsides to this growth. With 6 percent of the world population, Americans also consumed around 40 percent of all the world's resources, such as oil and iron ore, and produced a large share of the chemicals, gases, and toxic wastes that pollute the atmosphere, alter the climate, and destroy the land. The United States lagged in environmental protection; a major world study in 2005 ranked the nation twenty-eighth in meeting sustainable environmental goals, well behind most of western Europe, Japan, Taiwan, and several developing nations, such as Chile and Malaysia. Americans also worked longer hours than any industrialized people except the Japanese.

The rise of high technology and the decline of smokestack industries, such as steel production, reshaped the economy and workplace. Americans celebrated innovations in medicine, space research, transportation, and particularly electronics. Space satellites greatly improved weather forecasting, communications, and intelligence gathering. Computers revolutionized life with their convenience and versatility, since these machines could, as *Time* magazine concluded, "send letters at the speed of light, diagnose a sick poodle [and] test recipes for beer."[7] By the twenty-first century Americans often carried with them pocket-sized devices, once the stuff of science fiction novels, that could make telephone calls, send text messages, play music, and access news and weather.

Beginning in the 1970s, a growing economy improved the lot of some people, especially those trained in the new technologies, but it hurt millions of others, including unskilled workers, younger workers, and children in single-parent households. As computers and robots increased efficiency, they also replaced many workers. In the 1980s, a third of industrial jobs disappeared. Industrialists won corporate bonuses for relocating factories and exporting jobs to Latin America or Asia, devastating factory-dependent American communities. By the early 2000s, although life for the majority of Americans remained comfortable compared to that in most other nations, unemployment for men was the highest it had been in five decades and millions of men and women had to work two jobs to support their families. Some economists referred to a "winner-take-all economy" that produced ever more millionaires—over 2 million of them by 2005—but also a struggling middle class and, at the bottom of the social ladder, more homeless people sleeping in city streets and parks. Except for the richest 1 percent of Americans, whose earnings skyrocketed, average incomes fell between 2001 and 2006. Yet, when surveyed, most Americans, often including people with modest incomes, identified themselves with the middle class and its aspirations rather than, as Europeans often did, with the working class.

In contrast to western Europe, Canada, Australia, and New Zealand, the United States never developed a comprehensive welfare state. As a result, despite federal government efforts at abolishing poverty, a widening gap separated the richest third and the poorest third of Americans. The inequality of wealth in the United States grew dramatically after 1980, and by 1997 the top 1 percent of the population owned 20 percent of all the wealth. By 2004, 12.5 percent of Americans lived below the poverty line, the highest poverty rate in the industrialized world. Today the gap between the richest 20 percent and the poorest 20 percent of Americans is three times wider than in Japan, the Netherlands, Sweden, or Germany, and millions of

Americans today have no health insurance, a striking contrast to western Europe and Canada, where social democratic policies prevail. A devastating hurricane that caused massive damage and flooding in the Gulf Coast in 2005, ruining New Orleans, rendering millions homeless, and killing several thousand people, starkly revealed the gap; most of the people who died or were only rescued days later were black and poor, unable to afford transportation out of the area. Partly because of the inequalities in wealth and health care, the United States ranked eighth—behind several European nations, Canada, and Australia—in overall quality of life in the 2004 United Nations Human Development Report.

Changes in the economy went hand in hand with the suburbanization of American life, deepening the inequalities. In the decades following World War II, families with young children wanted affordable housing. Millions of people sought a better life in suburbia, the bedroom communities on the edges of major cities. Suburbs, occupied typically by white Americans, built shopping malls, offered well-funded schools, and seemed immune from city violence. Governments supported the suburban trend by subsidizing real estate developers. William Leavitt, who built vast suburban tracts, known as Leavittown, around New York City, argued that no person who owned his or her own house and yard could be a Communist because he or she was too busy keeping up, and working to pay for, his or her property. The two-car, multitelevision family became a common symbol of affluence. The automobile, increasingly affordable for the middle class, combined with government-funded freeway and highway construction, made long commutes from the suburbs to jobs in the central city possible. Later, as the jobs often moved to the suburbs, the city cores were increasingly dominated by the local-born poor, often nonwhite, or immigrants. Furthermore, increasing use of fossil fuels for gasoline, electricity, and heating caused pollution while clearing land for housing and business development harmed the environment.

American Political Life: Conservatism and Liberalism

Americans have tended to alternate between conservatism and liberalism in their political life, a pattern that continued in the decades after World War II. For most of these years, political conservatives, commonly allied with both big business groups favoring low taxes and opposed to government welfare programs and religious groups who disliked social and cultural liberalization, such as legal abortion and homosexual rights, dominated the presidency and often the United States Congress and the judiciary. Liberals played a key role in U.S. political life chiefly in the 1960s and, to a lesser extent, the 1990s; they were generally supported by labor unions and groups that sought social change and a stronger government safety net, such as women's and civil rights organizations. Each political philosophy was also reflected in society and culture.

The widespread desire for stability after the great Depression and a calamitous world war encouraged both a political and social conservatism throughout the 1950s. Prosperous, the middle and upper classes rarely questioned their government or the prevailing social arrangements. Americans who criticized U.S. foreign policy or favored radical social change faced harassment, expulsion from job or school, arrest, or grillings by congressional committees who accused them of being "un-American." Whatever their social class, more Americans than ever before married, producing a "baby boom" of children born in the years following the war. The mass media portrayed women as obsessed with bleaching their clothes a purer white and content in a world defined by kitchen, bedroom, babies, and home. Society expected homosexuals to remain deep in the closet, and those who did not faced taunting, beatings, or arrest. At the same time, the growing consumer economy emphasized pleasure and leisure time activities, such as cocktail parties, backyard barbecues, and baseball games. Like their parents, teenagers became consumers, creating a market for youth-oriented clothes and music.

American politics and society were reshaped again during the 1960s, becoming open to new ideas and lifestyles as liberalism became influential. The era saw many achievements, including the first people to walk on the moon and the idealism that created the Peace Corps, an agency that sent young Americans to help communities in developing nations, chiefly as teachers, health workers, and agricultural specialists. Presidents John F. Kennedy (g. 1961–1963) and Lyndon B. Johnson (g. 1963–1969) launched government programs to address poverty and racism. But the 1960s was also a decade of doubts, anger, and violence. Three national leaders were assassinated, including Kennedy, who was shot in the head while riding in a motorcade in 1963. The war in Vietnam, the civil rights movement for African Americans, and issues of environmental protection and women's empowerment divided the nation. The country's social fabric fragmented as prowar "hawks" and antiwar "doves" competed for support. Riots and demonstrations punctuated the decade.

During the 1960s a large segment of young people, chiefly middle class, rebelled against the values of their parents and established society. The folksinger Bob Dylan (b. 1941), who had a very large following, sung: "Come, mothers and fathers, throughout the land, And don't criticize what you can't understand. Your sons and your daughters are beyond your command, Your old world is rapidly aging'. Please get out of the new one if you can't lend your hand, For the times, they are a-changing."[8] Some youth, especially high school and university students, worked to change society and politics, registering voters, holding "teach-ins" to discuss national issues, and going door to door to spread their cause. Other youth forged what they called a counterculture that often involved using illegal drugs, such as marijuana, and engaging in casual sex. Supporters of social change emblazoned the slogan "Make love, not war" on bumper stickers, posters, and buttons. The Summer of Love in 1967, during which young people from North America and elsewhere gathered in San Francisco to hear rock music and share comradery, and the Woodstock rock music festival of 1969, which attracted over 300,000 young people to a New York State farm field to hear some of the most popular rock

musicians, marked the zenith of both the youth counterculture and political activism.

In the 1970s, with the winding down of the war in Vietnam and widespread concern at the excesses of the decade, the nation returned to more conservative values and politics. With the exception of the 1990s, when the moderate Bill Clinton (g. 1993–2001) held the presidency, conservatives have maintained their dominance of American politics and the social agenda, including a vigorous campaign to punish illegal drug use. Religion has also remained a powerful force, with Americans being more likely to attend churches and profess strong Christian beliefs than Canadians or most Europeans. While many Protestants, Catholics, and Jews supported liberal causes, by the 1980s Christian conservatives, both Catholics and evangelical Protestants, became influential in politics and public life, helping elect political conservatives to office. Some experts attributed the rise of Christian conservatism to a rejection of the Enlightenment and its emphasis on reason and tolerance. In this view, believers sought certainty and timeless rules. Others pointed to the search for a personal spiritual experience to help people withstand the stresses of modern life. Many churches stressed membership in a supportive community of believers while others preached a philosophy of self-help. While Americans avidly consumed new technologies, such as cell phones and portable music players, polls showed that, because of religious conservatism, substantial numbers also mistrusted science, for example, rejecting scientific explanations for the origins of the universe and human evolution in favor of biblical accounts.

Observers found much to deplore and much to praise in U.S. politics. On the negative side, in contrast to the political activism of the 1960s, fewer Americans now participated in the democratic process, with barely half of eligible voters bothering to vote in presidential elections. Americans voted in lower numbers than people in other industrial democracies. Money from big corporations and other special interests increasingly played a major role in politics, fostering corruption and widespread political apathy. However, on the positive side, a free media exposed government corruption, including abuse of power by presidents. President Richard Nixon, facing impeachment, resigned in 1973 for sanctioning and then covering up illegal activities by his subordinates. The presidencies of both Ronald Reagan (g. 1983–1989) and Clinton were marred by congressional hearings examining their misdeeds. After the controversial, bitter 2000 and 2004 elections, Americans were sharply divided between the two major political parties and the divergent policies they supported.

American Society

American society was different from what it had been before World War II. For example, suburbanization influenced social patterns. Most suburbs lacked ethnic and cultural diversity and isolated residents from the stimulation, as well as the problems, of big city life. Suburban living also intensified the trend, begun before World War II, toward two-parent, single-breadwinner nuclear families that lived apart from other relatives. By moving people farther away from city jobs, it encouraged mothers to stay at home. From World War II to the mid-1960s the image, conveyed in the media and advertising, of the fashionably dressed, stay-at-home suburban housewife, smiling proudly as she served breakfast to her husband and children, remained ingrained in the culture, even as women increasingly found it necessary to undertake paid work, especially after 1960. Critics lambasted the conformity of life in the standardized suburban tract houses, which, according to a song from the 1950s, resembled "little boxes. There's a green one, a pink one, a blue one and a yellow one. And they're all made out of ticky-tacky, And they all look just the same."[9] Changing city life affected both ethnic and gender relations.

Ethnic Relations   The changing American society affected ethnic minorities, families, women, and men. Throughout the decades since World War II Americans addressed racial issues. As they had since the end of slavery, African Americans, over 10 percent of the population, continued to experience much higher rates of poverty than whites and faced various forms of discrimination. The southern states maintained strict racial segregation, forcing blacks to attend separate schools and to even use different public drinking fountains than whites. Racism and poverty often encouraged African Americans in northern industrial cities to concentrate in run-down inner-city neighborhoods, known as ghettos.

The civil rights movement, organized by African Americans in the 1950s, eventually forced courts, states, and the federal government to introduce reforms. For example, in 1954 the Supreme Court outlawed segregated schools. A year later, in Montgomery, Alabama, Rosa Parks (1913–2005), a seamstress and community activist, bravely refused to follow the local law

and give up her front seat on a bus to a white man, sparking a mass movement for change. A black minister, Reverend Martin Luther King, Jr. (1929–1968), led a bus boycott to protest her arrest and fine. Using the strategy of nonviolent resistance pioneered by Mohandas Gandhi in South Africa and India in the early twentieth century, King led a protest movement all over the South. While leading the 1963 March on Washington to demand equal rights for nonwhites, he presented his vision: "I have a dream. When we let freedom ring, all of God's children will be able to join hands and sing in the words of that old spiritual, 'Thank God almighty, we are free at last!'"[10] King's assassination by a white racist in 1968 shocked the nation, but by then the African American struggle for equal rights had inspired similar struggles by nonwhites elsewhere in the world, including black South Africans, Afro-Brazilians, and Australian Aborigines. Thanks to the efforts of King, Parks, and many others, African Americans gradually gained legal equality, and many became able to move into the middle and upper classes, although by the twenty-first century African Americans were still far more likely than whites to live in poverty, face unemployment, and be imprisoned.

Americans boasted that they lived in a "melting pot," a society where ethnic groups merged and lost their separate identity, which was often the case for people of European ancestry during the century before World War II. However, members of many ethnic groups, especially non-whites, often maintained their separate identities and cultures so that in the later twentieth century Americans faced an increasingly multiracial, multicultural society. By 2006 the U.S. population of 300 million, the third largest total in the world after China and India, was more diverse than ever, and over 10 percent were foreign-born. American life took on a cosmopolitan flavor as Latin American

Martin Luther King, Jr.   An Atlanta minister, Dr. Martin Luther King, Jr., led many peaceful demonstrations for African American civil rights. In this photo, Dr. King (center front, with his wife, Coretta Scott King, to his right) leads a 1963 March on Washington for Jobs and Freedom, attended by some 200,000 supporters.   (Corbis)

grocery stores, Asian restaurants, and African art galleries opened in communities throughout the country, and Spanish was widely spoken. Alaska and Hawaii, both with large non-white populations, became states in 1959, adding to the nation's diversity.

Ethnic groups grew through legal and illegal immigration. Millions of Latin Americans moved to the United States. By 2000 the Mexican American population alone numbered around 20 million and seemed poised to soon outnumber the 25 million African Americans. Several million Asians also relocated to the United States, especially from China, South Korea, India, and Southeast Asia. Immigrants also arrived from Europe, the Middle East, the Caribbean, and South Pacific islands, especially Samoans and Tongans. To survive, some immigrants, legal or illegal, have labored for meager wages in crowded sweatshops in big cities, where bosses often allow workers only one or two breaks during their shift and ignore city safety regulations. For example, Chinese sewed clothing in New York City and Mexicans did the same in Los Angeles. Immigration marginalized Native Americans even more than before. While many lived in cities, others remained isolated on reservations. Some of them joined movements to assert their rights, often seeking a return of lands seized by white settlers generations earlier, and a few tribes achieved prosperity by operating gambling casinos; however, most Native Americans remained poor.

Gender Relations Women's issues became more prominent than before in U.S. history. In the 1950s few women worked for high pay, colleges imposed strict quotas on female applicants, married women could not borrow money in their own names, there was no legal concept of sexual harassment, and men often joked of keeping women "barefoot and pregnant." By the early twenty-first century conditions had changed dramatically but it took a long struggle for gender equality. Beginning in the 1960s women often joined feminist movements demanding equal legal rights with men and improved economic status. In 1963 Betty Friedan's (1921–2006) passionate book, *The Feminine Mystique*, identified women's core problem as a stunting of their growth by a patriarchal society. Women often agreed with Friedan's message that housework was unfulfilling. With slogans such as "Sisterhood Is Powerful," women came together in groups, such as the National Organization for Women (NOW), founded by Friedan in 1966, to fight for expanded options and opportunities for girls and women. Thanks in part to feminists' efforts, the median income of women workers climbed from 62 to 70 percent of that of men, and the number of women with paid work more than doubled between 1960 and 2000. Women held governorships, served in Congress, and sat on the Supreme Court. By the twenty-first century more women than men finished secondary school and attended universities, some joining highly paid, traditionally male occupations such as law, university teaching, engineering, and medicine. While many young women rejected the feminist label by 2000, those that chose to pursue satisfying, well-paid careers, run for political office, and enjoy personal freedoms unimag-

inable to their great grandmothers owed their gains largely to the feminist movement and its male supporters. However, whether professionals or working class, most women with paid jobs struggled to juggle work with family and housekeeping responsibilities. One young mother of two complained in the 1990s that "it's like twenty-four hours a day you're working. My day never ends."[11] Sexual harassment, especially in the workplace, stalking, and rape remained serious problems.

Social and legal changes affected both women and men. Divorce became easier and more common; by the 1990s over half of all marriages ended in divorce. Single-parent households grew more frequent. Increasingly, as in Europe, men and women never married, often living with partners out of wedlock. Whatever their gender, Americans remained deeply divided on some women's issues, especially abortion, which was long common but illegal in the United States before being declared legal by the Supreme Court in 1973. Americans also disagreed about homosexuality. By the 1960s gay men and lesbians actively struggled to end harassment and legal discrimination, gaining greater acceptance in society. Yet the growing numbers who openly acknowledged their sexual identity still faced hostility. During the early twenty-first century Americans quarreled over allowing homosexuals to marry or establish legal partnerships, a pattern of acceptance common in Europe and Canada but opposed by many Christian churches in the United States.

American Popular Culture

Once importers of culture from Europe, Americans became the world's greatest exporters of popular culture products. U.S.-made films, television programs, books, magazines, and sports reached a global audience, and popular music had widespread influence. Various musical styles, including the Broadway musicals of songwriters such as Richard Rogers and Oscar Hammerstein, the blues of singer Billie Holiday and guitarist B. B. King, the jazz of saxophonist John Coltrane and trumpeter Miles Davis, and the country music of singer-songwriters Hank Williams and Dolly Parton spread far and wide.

But no music style had the power of rock, which in the 1950s and 1960s helped spark a cultural revolution, especially among youth, in the United States and gained a huge following abroad. The first exhilarating blasts of rock and roll, notably from the white singer Elvis Presley (1935–1977), whose suggestive, hip-swinging performances earned him the nickname "Elvis the Pelvis," and the inventive black guitarist Chuck Berry (b. 1926), defied the Eisenhower era's puritanical emphasis on social and political conformity, pleasing youth while often alarming adults. In the United States, and then throughout the world, rock music broke down social barriers by challenging sexual and racial taboos.

The first American popular music appealing across social class boundaries, rock was inspired by black music, chiefly rhythm-and-blues, but also by the country and gospel music of white southerners. Early rock made a powerful statement that young Americans were less divided by race than their parents. Rock became the heart of the youth movement of the 1960s, when albums by key rock musicians, such as the poetic

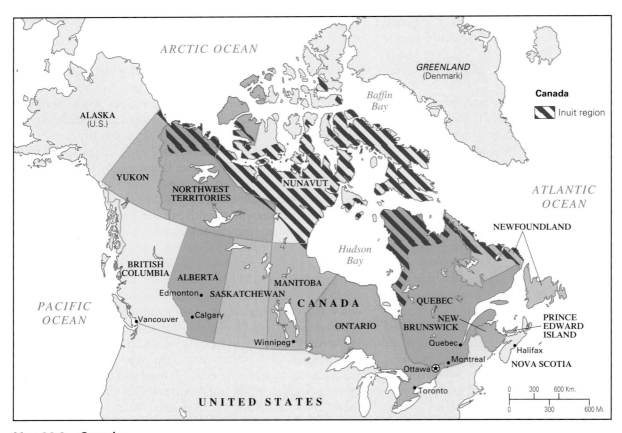

Map 29.2 Canada
The Canadian federation includes eleven provinces stretching from Newfoundland in the east to British Columbia and the Yukon in the west. In 1999 a large part of northern Canada, inhabited chiefly by the Inuit, became the self-governing region of Nunavut.

American singer-songwriter Bob Dylan and the British group the Beatles, seemed infused with messages that often shaped political awareness. After the 1960s rock lost its political edge but, evolving into forms such as punk, grunge, and heavy metal, remained at the heart of U.S. popular music.

The music created by African Americans, which has influenced all Americans and contributed to world culture, has also addressed problems of African American life. For example, the soul music in the 1960s, from artists like James Brown and Aretha Franklin, conveyed a message of black self-respect and unity parallel to the messages of the black pride movements of the era. In the 1980s and 1990s rap music emerged out of black ghettos to become the cutting-edge, politicized form of Western pop music. An eclectic mix of rock, soul, rhythm and blues, and Caribbean music, rap expresses the tensions of urban black youth yearning for independence, dignity, sex, and fun. The boastful, often angry tone highlights conflict between white and black, rich and poor, and male and female. Rap musicians have outraged segments of both white society and the black middle class, who fear the music threatens the social order. Musicians in nations around the world have adopted the rap style, often integrating it into their own traditions, but by the early twenty-first century rap's radical message was being watered down as it became mainstream in the United States and was embraced by more whites.

The Canadian Experience

Although they share cultural traditions and a democratic spirit with Americans, Canadians have remained proudly independent of their powerful southern neighbor while nurturing their political and social differences from Americans, such as by maintaining two official languages—English and French. Two parties, one liberal and one conservative, have dominated national elections, but, in contrast to the United States, smaller leftwing and rightwing parties also play key roles, often governing Canadian provinces. The Party Québécois (KAY-be-KWAH), for example, which supports French Canadian nationalism, has often won power in French-speaking Quebec, a province that contains a quarter of Canada's population, and periodically holds provincial votes, so far unsuccessful, on separating Quebec from Canada (see Map 29.2). In 1985 the federal parliament, hoping to preserve a united Canada, responded to French Canadians' resentments against Canada's English-speaking majority by recognizing Quebec as a distinct society within Canada and granting more autonomy to all the provinces. Canadians still debate how much power to allocate to the provinces and how much to the federal government.

Canadians, 33 million strong by 2005, cannot ignore their proximity to the United States, which has almost ten times

Canada's population and vastly more power in the world. Former prime minister Pierre Trudeau (troo-DOE) (g. 1968–1984), a French Canadian, complained that sharing a border with the United States was "like sleeping with an elephant. No matter how friendly or even-tempered the beast, one is affected by every twitch and grunt."[12] Most of Canada's people live within a hundred miles of the U.S. border and thus have easy access to the U.S. mass media and other cultural influences. Canada has also formed a major trading partnership with its southern neighbor. Americans own some 20 percent of the Canadian economy, prompting some Canadians to welcome U.S. investment as a spur to economic growth and others to resent U.S. domination. In 1994 the North American Free Trade Agreement (NAFTA) further bound the Canadian, Mexican, and U.S. economies. Yet, despite usually friendly U.S.-Canada relations, Canadians have often opposed U.S. foreign policies, including the wars in Vietnam and Iraq.

Despite occasional economic downturns, Canadians have enjoyed industrialization and prosperity, which in turn have fostered social stability. Agricultural, industrial, and natural resource exports have helped finance rising living standards; vast oil reserves have enriched western provinces. Canada has consistently ranked among the top five nations in the annual United Nations Human Development Index of quality of life. Unlike the more individualistic United States, over the years Canada, influenced by social democratic ideals, has built a strong social safety net for its citizens, including national health insurance. Also, like western Europeans, Canadians have generally been more liberal on social and economic issues than Americans. For example, in spite of strong opposition, Canadians have approved same-sex marriage, banned the death penalty, and, in some provinces, decriminalized marijuana use. As the society has become more secular, organized religion has had a declining influence in public life, in contrast to the United States. The secularizing trend has been especially notable in Quebec, where, a half century earlier, the Catholic Church had enjoyed great influence. By 2005 even openly homosexual politicians could gain popular support in Quebec and the province's birth rate, one of the world's highest in the 1940s, had fallen by over half to become one of the world's lowest.

Canadian society has become increasingly diverse. The nation has welcomed several million immigrants from all over the world, many from Asia and the Caribbean. In 2005 one of those Caribbean immigrants, Haitian-born Michaelle Jean, a television journalist in Quebec, became Canada's governor general, the nation's official head of state. Unlike Americans, who like to claim that they have become a "melting pot," the officially bilingual Canadians have adopted laws, especially the Multiculturalism Act of 1988, to allow ethnic minorities to maintain their cultures. But some Canadians, resenting the recognition of Portuguese Canadians or Chinese Canadians, have favored a melting pot of unhyphenated Canadians. Canadians have also recognized the rights of the indigenous Native Americans, known in Canada as the "First Nations," who have pressed land claims. To address the desire for autonomy of the Inuit, or Eskimo, people of the Arctic region, in 1999 the federal government transformed much of northern Canada into the self-governing territory of Nunavut (NOO-nuh-voot), whose 27,000 people are mostly Inuit. Canadians are still in the process of determining, as the Quebec journalist Alain Dubuc put it, how much to think of themselves as English or French or Inuit Canadians and how much to live comfortably with multiple identities.

The Pacific Basin Societies

The diverse societies scattered around the Pacific Basin experienced major changes during this era as they adjusted to a new world. In the two largest, most populous countries, Australia and New Zealand, the majority population, descended from European, mainly British and Irish, settlers, had long identified with western European society, building economies that closely resembled those of the industrial West. But the rise of Asian economies, which fostered increased trade, prompted Australia and New Zealand to cultivate closer ties with East and Southeast Asian nations. Meanwhile, many Pacific islands once ruled by Britain, France, or New Zealand became independent nations navigating in a globalizing world.

Australia and New Zealand During this era Australia became one of the world's most affluent nations, known to its people as the "lucky country" because of its abundant resources and high living standards. Thanks in part to a comprehensive system of social welfare, health care, and education, Australians have forged a quality of life that placed the nation third after Norway and Sweden in the United Nations Human Development Report for 2004. However, the nation has also faced economic and social problems, among them a chronic high unemployment rate and areas of persisting poverty. Feminists complain that men dominate most institutions, including government, business, and churches, and that Australian women are less influential than women in most Western nations. Nonetheless, the efforts of women's organizations have forged considerable gender equity.

With 20 million people by 2005, Australia has become an increasingly diverse nation. In 1973 the federal government, seeking better relations with Asian nations and reflecting changing Australian social attitudes, abandoned restrictions on nonwhite, especially Asian, immigration—known as the "white Australia" policy—that had been in place since 1901. The shift to a policy based on skills rather than ethnicity stimulated immigration from Asia and the Middle East, and predominantly Asian neighborhoods developed in major cities. Newcomers from Europe also continued to arrive. For example, one of major cities, Melbourne, boasted the world's largest Greek emigrant population. By 2001 nearly a quarter of Australia's people had been born abroad. Race relations improved as Aborigines, often poor and facing discrimination, gained some self-determination and land rights for their tribal territories. As a result, one group was able to block a dam project in the 1990s that threatened tribal land. Yet, those Aborigines living in cities, often in run-down neighborhoods, have struggled to find their place in the largely white-owned urban economy. Attacks on Arab immigrants by drunken

Lion Dance In recent decades, many Asians have settled in Australia. This Chinese lion's dance, in Melbourne's large Chinatown, celebrates the Chinese New Year. (Glenn Hunt/AAP)

white youth in Sydney in 2005 showed that racism had not been eliminated.

Changing global conditions have forced new economic thinking. With an economy based primarily on the export of natural and animal resources, such as minerals, wheat, beef, and wool, Australia needed secure outside markets. But the formation of the European Community and NAFTA threatened traditional markets in Europe and North America, raising questions about the nation's traditional link to Britain. In a 1995 referendum, 55 percent of Australians supported remaining a constitutional monarchy under the British queen. Yet, Britain was far away while Asia was, as Australians put it, the "near north." To secure markets and promote cooperation, Australians established closer trade links to nations in Southeast Asia, East Asia, and the Pacific islands. By 2000, Asian nations accounted for some 60 percent of Australia's export market. Australians saw themselves as suppliers and investors to the rising Asian and Pacific economies but also became consumers of Asian goods and investment.

Like Australians, New Zealanders had long cultivated their British heritage and depended on British patronage, but they now had to forge strategic and economic connections within the Asia-Pacific region. The nation's economy relied heavily on tourism and the export of agricultural products, mostly to Britain. Suffering from a stumbling economy and jolted by Britain's membership in the European Community, which diminished New Zealand's access to British markets, New Zealand cultivated especially close relations with the United States. However, these relations cooled after New Zealand refused to allow nuclear-armed U.S. ships to make visits to its ports. New Zealand then fostered economic cooperation with

nearby Asian and Pacific countries, and by 2000 these countries accounted for one-third of the nation's trade.

New economic directions affected New Zealand's society. While experiencing rising unemployment, New Zealanders were supported by an elaborate social welfare system. Owing in part to expanded educational opportunities, women gained new economic roles and served in politics. In 1999 Helen Clark (b. 1950), a former university professor, became the nation's first female prime minister. Closer ties to the Pacific region also resulted in increased immigration from Asia and the Pacific islands. Like Australians, New Zealanders became more comfortable with ethnic diversity. The government recognized the land rights of, and worked to end discrimination against, the native Maori minority, who sought to maintain their Polynesian culture while adding modern economic skills.

The Pacific Islands While Australians and New Zealanders had long enjoyed independence, the decolonization of the Pacific islands, spurred by the United Nations, had to wait till the 1960s. Between 1962 and 1980 nine independent Pacific nations were formed in Polynesia and Melanesia, and in 1990 the United States gave up control of some of its Micronesian territories. The new states ranged from republics such as Fiji to kingdoms like Tonga to voluntary groupings such as the Federated States of Micronesia. Not all Pacific islanders, however, became independent. Some French-ruled islands, such as Tahiti and New Caledonia, became overseas departments of France, with representation in the French parliament, but many islanders still resented what they considered a disguised French colonialism. Most independent islands retained close ties to their former colonizer, as the Federated

States of Micronesia did with the United States. Whether nation or colony, islanders usually remained dependent on fishing, tourism, and the export of mineral and agricultural products, mostly to Japan, the United States, Australia, and New Zealand.

Islanders cooperated on common issues. They formed regional organizations to promote everything from duty-free trade to art festivals. Together the islanders fought high-technology fishing fleets from industrialized nations, especially Japan, that threatened their own low-technology fishing. To oppose nuclear weapons testing, and the radiation it created, they joined with Australia and New Zealand to declare the Pacific a nuclear-free zone. The international Law of the Sea Treaty gave the islands more control of adjacent sea beds, and hence their minerals. However, some problems affecting islands have defied solution. Thanks to rising sea levels, which threaten low-lying atolls and coastal plains, many islanders will have to relocate over the next century. The Tuvalo islands in the central Pacific, home to 11,000 people and on average only three feet above sea level, will be inundated by 2050.

The Pacific islanders have held on to some indigenous traditions while also adapting to social and political change. While most islanders have become Christian, some pre-Christian, precolonial customs have remained important. For example, Western Samoa, first ruled by Germany and then by New Zealand, has an elected parliament, adopted from the West, but clan chiefs still govern the villages, as they have for centuries. But certain forces have undermined traditional village life. Poverty has fostered migration to island cities, such as Suva in Fiji and Pago Pago in American Samoa, and emigration to Australia, New Zealand, Hawaii, and the mainland United States. By 2000 more Samoans and Cook Islanders lived abroad than at home, and thousands of Tongans lived in California. The money sent back by migrants has become a valuable source of income for their home islands. Some islands have also experienced ethnic or regional conflict as groups compete for political power and scarce land. For example, occasional military coups have rocked Fiji, resulting from tensions between the descendants of Indian immigrants, who comprise nearly half of the population, and the native Fijians. The Fijians fear that the Indians, should they gain power, would diminish the role of traditional Fijian chiefs and challenge tribal rights to land.

SECTION SUMMARY

- On average, U.S. residents are among the wealthiest in the world, yet in recent decades many industrial jobs have been moved overseas and the gap between rich and poor has grown wider, with the former often living in suburbs and the latter left behind in inner cities.

- In the 1950s, political conservatism dominated the United States and a large number of children were born; in the 1960s, liberalism was prominent, especially among the rebellious youth; and since the 1970s, conservatism has been generally dominant, though the country is sharply divided politically.

- After 1945 more Americans lived in suburbs, African Americans gained legal rights through the civil rights movement, immigrants made America more diverse, women increasingly entered the work force, and gays and lesbians became more visible but still struggled for equal rights.

- American culture became popular around the world, particularly music such as rock, which energized youth in the 1950s and 1960s, and rap, which initially expressed the radical political sentiments of African Americans but became watered down in the twenty-first century.

- While Canada's culture and economy are strongly influenced by the United States, in many ways Canada resembles western Europe, with a strong social safety net and a more liberal attitude on social issues.

- Australia and New Zealand have maintained their traditional ties with Britain but have also traded increasingly with their Southeast Asian neighbors, while many Pacific islands have gained independence from former colonizers but still face challenges such as rising sea levels, poverty, and ethnic conflict.

✦ Political Change in Latin America and the Caribbean

Why have democracy and economic development proven to be difficult goals in Latin America?

The Latin American and Caribbean peoples (see Map 29.3) had a different experience than North Americans and the Pacific Basin societies. Social inequality, economic underdevelopment, and the demands for change often created a pressure cooker, generating revolutionary and progressive political movements in impoverished villages and shantytowns. Sometimes leftists gained power, launching reforms, though only in Cuba did they remain in power for decades. A few Latin American countries and most small Caribbean islands enjoyed a consistent democratic tradition; elsewhere, however, military leaders or autocratic civilians often dominated governments. In most cases governments, whether democratic or dictatorial, proved unable to eliminate their nation's major problems.

Despotisms and Democracies

Latin American governments struggled to find the right mix of policies to raise living standards and expand political participation. Early in the century the Mexican Revolution, for example, challenged the inequities in society and wealth but later lost most of its revolutionary vigor and ultimately failed to resolve Mexico's problems. At other times paternalistic but authoritarian reformers mobilized workers and peasants for change, but they also failed to empower the mass of the population or significantly improve their lives.

Map 29.3 Modern Latin America and the Caribbean
Latin America includes the nations of Central and South America and those Caribbean societies that are Spanish-speaking, including Cuba and the Dominican Republic. Brazil, Argentina, and Mexico are the largest Latin American nations. The peoples, mostly English or French speaking, of the small Caribbean islands also formed independent states.

The charismatic Juan Peron (puh-RONE) (1895–1974), a former army officer, admirer of the Italian fascist leader, Benito Mussolini, and hypnotic public speaker who was elected Argentina's president in 1946, was one of the major autocratic reformers (see Chronology: Latin America and the Caribbean, 1945–Present). Peron soon marginalized the legislature and crushed his opposition. With help from his hugely popular wife, Evita Peron (puh-RONE) (1919–1952), a radio and stage actress from a poor family and a proponent of social justice, the nationalistic Peron won the support of workers and the middle class by emphasizing industrialization and by having his government buy up banks, insurance companies, railroads, and shipping companies often owned by unpopular foreign interests. Meanwhile, Evita promoted women's issues, including voting rights. After Evita's death in 1952, Peron's popular support waned. Corruption, growing unemployment, inflation, strikes, and human rights abuses led to his overthrow in 1955. Peron returned to power briefly in 1973–1974, but otherwise the military ruled Argentina for most of the 1950s through early 1980s, often killing opponents. Yet Peron's followers sustained a Peronist movement with a working-class base that often governed the nation after the restoration of democracy in 1983.

Rightwing and leftwing forces, with vastly different goals, have jockeyed for power in Latin America. In the majority of countries from the 1950s through the late 1980s, rightwing military governments and despots ruled, suppressing labor unions, student protesters, and democracy activists to maintain stability. Some rightwing governments, especially in Central American countries such as El Salvador and Guatemala, organized informal armed units, known as death squads, to assassinate dissident peasants, liberal clergy, teachers, and journalists deemed threats to the regime. However, despite the repression, leftwing movements increased their strength. By 1979 the Sandinistas, a revolutionary movement led by Marxists, had mobilized enough popular support to defeat the dictatorship, in power since the 1920s, and gain control of Nicaragua. An even more radical movement, the Shining Path, emerged in Peru in 1970. The movement's leaders, half of them women, dismissed all other Latin American Marxists as sell-outs and mixed Maoist ideas with a call to emancipate the impoverished Indians of Peru. Their rebellion used terrorism to demoralize Peruvians and bring the country to its knees before finally being crushed in the early 1990s.

During the later 1980s, with rightwing authoritarian rule largely discredited because it was unable or unwilling to address mass poverty, many nations turned to democracy under centrist or moderate leftist leaders. But in most cases the free markets these democratic governments introduced were unable to resolve the severe problems or diminish social equalities, allowing both rightwing and extreme leftist forces to increase in strength. Some nations also faced racial and ethnic tensions. In particular, the large Indian communities in Bolivia, Peru, Colombia, Mexico, and Guatemala, often allied with the left, increasingly sought equal rights, a fairer share of the wealth, and recognition of their cultures, aspirations often opposed by whites. In 2005, for example, chronic resentment by Bolivia's Indian majority led to the

CHRONOLOGY	
Latin America and the Caribbean, 1945–Present	
1946–1955	Government of Juan Peron in Argentina
1954	CIA overthrow of Guatemalan government
1959	Triumph of Fidel Castro in Cuba
1962	Cuban missile crisis
1964–1985	Military government in Brazil
1973	Overthrow of Chilean government
1973–1989	Military government in Chile
1979–1989	Sandinista government in Nicaragua
1983	Restoration of Argentina's democracy
1990	U.S. invasion of Panama
1994	Formation of NAFTA
1998	Economic collapse in many nations
2000	Election of President Vicente Fox in Mexico
2002	Election of President Lula da Silva in Brazil

election, as president, of Evo Morales, a former small-town soccer player and trumpeter of humble origins who had led a movement of coca farmers fighting a white-dominated government and U.S. opposition to coca growing. At the ruins of an ancient temple, Morales took part in a spiritual ceremony steeped in the traditions of Tiwanaku, the state built by his Aymara Indian group that flourished centuries before the Incas. Walking barefoot up the pyramid steps, he donned a traditional tunic and cap and accepted a gold and silver baton from Aymara priests, then promised to "seek equality and justice" for the poor and do away with the vestiges of the Spanish colonial past.

By the later 1990s, as disillusionment with capitalism increased, the left was regaining the political initiative, working largely within a democratic context. Mobilizing workers and peasants, who had benefited little from the country's oil wealth, the former general Hugo Chavez was elected president of oil-rich Venezuela and introduced socialist policies that alienated the wealthy and middle class, who organized mass protests against his regime. However, these protests increased support for Chavez among poor Venezuelans, who supported his marginalization of the congress and control of the courts. Chavez called his policies the Bolivaran Revolution, linking them to the nineteenth-century, Venezuelan-born liberator. But the United States moved to isolate the dictatorial, pro-Cuba Chavez regime and support the opposition. During the early twenty-first century, voters, like those in Venezuela, who were desperate for more equitable economic and social policies also elected pragmatic leftist leaders in countries such as Argentina, Brazil, Chile, and Uruguay. These leaders often began the process, neglected by their cautious predecessors, of prosecuting the human rights violations that occurred years earlier under military rule. But whether imported economic ideas, whether from the left or the right, will work for Latin Americans remains to be seen.

The United States in Latin America

The United States has had a powerful economic and political presence in Latin America since the nineteenth century, and, as the world's major superpower, it had even more of an impact in the second half of the twentieth. Referring to longtime U.S. economic leverage over his country, a Nicaraguan leader critical of the United States claimed that his country's "function was to grow sugar, cocoa and coffee for the United States; we served the dessert at the imperialist dining table."[13] Not all Latin Americans took such a negative view, however. The U.S. role in the region was complex, with the country serving not only as the neighborhood bully at times—especially when it helped overturn governments—but also as a leading trading partner, a major source of investment capital, a supplier of military and economic assistance, and an inspiration to the region's democrats and free market enthusiasts. As a result, many Latin American leaders maintained close relations with various U.S. administrations and often supported U.S. foreign policies. U.S. popular culture, particularly films and music, has reached a huge audience, influencing local cultures. And several million people seeking a better life have moved to the United States legally or illegally. The United States gained favor in the region by transferring control over the Panama Canal, built by the United States in the early 1900s, to Panama in 1999; yet the agreement also allowed U.S. military bases to remain along the canal, a symbol of U.S. regional power.

The United States intervened in Latin American and Caribbean countries under the banner of anticommunism. These interventions aroused much local resentment, as was illustrated by the earliest intervention, in Guatemala in 1954. A force led by exiled Guatemalan military officers, covertly organized, armed, and trained by the U.S. Central Intelligence Agency (CIA), overthrew a democratically elected reformist government, led chiefly by liberals and socialists, that American leaders accused of being Communist, an unsupported claim. The government had angered U.S. business interests, especially the powerful United Fruit Company, by implementing land reform and encouraging labor unions, whose leaders were chiefly leftists. The United Fruit Company controlled much of the Guatemalan economy, especially the banana plantations, and had close ties to officials in the Eisenhower administration. The removal of the democratic regime cheered both wealthy Guatemalans, especially large landowners, and U.S. corporations with investments in Guatemala, but the new Guatemalan leaders proved to be murderous tyrants.

Forming death squads, they killed over 200,000 Guatemalans, especially poor Indian peasants and workers, over the next three decades. By 1990, 90 percent of Guatemalans still lived in poverty, and one-third of them lacked adequate food.

The successful ousting of the Guatemalan government encouraged U.S. leaders to use their power elsewhere to further Cold War foreign policy objectives. Americans offered military assistance and advice to maintain friendly governments in power against the challenge of revolutionary movements in El Salvador, Honduras, and Colombia. As in Guatemala, the United States also used covert operations to help undermine or overthrow governments deemed too left-leaning, for example, in Brazil (1964), Chile (1973), and Nicaragua (1989). The American public was often unaware of the covert U.S. activities until years later. Sometimes the United States resorted to sending in U.S. military force, as in the Dominican Republic (1965) and Grenada (1982). Not all interventions were inspired by anticommunism. In 1990 U.S. troops invaded Panama to remove and arrest the dictator Manuel Noriega (b. 1940), a longtime U.S. ally and well-paid CIA informant who was also implicated in human rights abuses in Panama and in smuggling narcotics into the United States, and in 1994 U.S. troops were sent to Haiti, the Western Hemisphere's poorest country, in support of a reform government that had replaced a brutal dictatorship. U.S. troops have remained in Haiti as leftwing and rightwing political forces intermittently battled for control, leaving Haitians poorer and more desperate.

The Mexican Experience

The Mexican Revolution in the early twentieth century had led to hopes of reducing social inequality, but the nation's leaders soon turned to emphasizing economic growth over uplifting the poor majority. As a result, even today, in a southern state where, nearly a century ago, the revolutionaries had promised to bring liberty and justice to the poor, peasant men, wearing traditional white cotton pants and shirt, still use a machete to cultivate their tiny plots of corn. Mexico's limited democracy offered regular elections and some civil liberties. But one party, the Party of Revolutionary Institutions, known as the PRI, controlled the elections and hence the government, often resorting to such electoral tricks as voter fraud. A coalition of factions ranging from left to right, the PRI was led by businessmen and bureaucrats. For decades its leaders fostered stability while deflecting challenges to their power monopoly. The PRI had typically either co-opted or arrested opponents, but in 1968 it shocked the nation by ordering police to open fire on a large demonstration, killing hundreds of university students and other protesters.

By the 1980s the PRI began to falter. Although leftist and rightwing parties struggled to overcome the PRI's vast power and wealth, they made some national gains. In the early 1990s a peasant revolt in a poor southern state, Chiapas, revealed starkly the PRI's failure to redress rural poverty. The election of a reformist, non-PRI president, Vicente Fox, a pro-U.S. free-market conservative, in 2000 ended the seven decades-long

PRI monopoly on federal power. However, Fox proved unable to foster much economic or social change. While the PRI lost some credibility, it still held power in many states and enjoyed a national power base. By 2005 a more open and pluralistic political system had emerged, with stronger leftist and rightwing parties contending with the PRI for support. Whether the democratic processes fostered by Fox, who failed to deliver on most of his promises but, unlike his predecessors, was not corrupt, can be consolidated and endure remained to be seen.

Mexico's economic system also gradually opened, but without diminishing poverty. For decades the PRI had mixed capitalism with a strong government role. However, the collapse of world oil prices in the 1980s damaged Mexico's development prospects, since Mexico's oil was the major foreign revenue source. In the late 1980s PRI leaders replaced protectionist policies with open markets. In 1994 the North American Free Trade Agreement (NAFTA) helped integrate the U.S. and Mexican economies, and many U.S.-owned factories opened on the Mexican side of the border that employed thousands of workers. The majority of these workers, however, have been poorly paid young women who are usually housed in crowded dormitories or flimsy shacks and often complain of harassment or assault by male workers or managers. Elsewhere Mexicans have lost jobs; peasant corn farmers, for example, unable to compete with highly subsidized U.S. farmers, have often been ruined. By 2000 half of the 100 million Mexicans lived on $4 a day or less, and the bottom 20 percent of Mexicans earned only 3.5 percent of the country's personal income. Even the urban middle class feels the economic pain as wages stagnate. In 1980 Mexico's economy was nearly four times larger than South Korea's; by 2005 a dynamic South Korea had pushed ahead of Mexico. In addition, Mexico's population quadrupled between 1940 and 2000, pressuring the nation's resources. Because of poverty and overpopulation, thousands of desperate Mexicans continue to cross the border to the United States each year, legally or illegally in search of a better life.

Online Study Center **Improve Your Grade**
Primary Source: Free Trade and the Decline of Democracy

Revolutionary Cuba

In contrast to Mexico's mix of authoritarian and democratic politics, public ownership and capitalism, Cuba, led by Fidel Castro (b. 1927), built a society dominated by a powerful Communist government. Castro, a onetime amateur baseball star nearly signed by a U.S. professional team who instead became a lawyer, came to power in 1959, the victor of a revolution against a repressive, corrupt dictator long supported by the United States. Although the son of a rich sugar planter, Castro allied with the Cuban Communist Party and promised to introduce radical change, prompting thousands of upper- and middle-class Cubans to flee to the nearby United States. In 1961 the United States moved to isolate and then overthrow his regime by organizing a military force composed of Cuban exiles that landed on a Cuban beach, known as the Bay of Pigs. But the invasion had been poorly planned and enjoyed little

popular support in Cuba. Castro's forces routed the invading exiles, a humiliation for the United States.

Needing a protector, Castro became a firm Soviet ally, thereby igniting even more opposition from an alarmed United States. The Cuba–USSR alliance soon precipitated a major crisis. In 1962 U.S. air surveillance of the island revealed Soviet ballistic missiles with a 2,000-mile range and capable of carrying nuclear warheads. The U.S. demand that the missiles be removed sparked what became known as the Cuban missile crisis, during which the United States imposed a naval blockade on Cuba and considered an invasion of the island. With the threat of nuclear confrontation looming, the Soviets backed down and removed the missiles, defusing the crisis. However, in the aftermath, the United States, hoping to bring down Castro's regime, imposed an economic boycott, strongly supported by Cuban exiles in the United States, that endured into the twenty-first century, cutting off Cuba from sources of trade and investment.

In the 1960s and 1970s Castro tried innovative socialist policies, often known as **Castroism**, to stimulate economic development in Cuba while also tightly controlling its population. Castro called capitalism "repugnant, filthy, gross, alienating because it causes war, hypocrisy and competition"[14]; yet his own policies generated little surplus food and few consumer goods. Despite valiant efforts, Cubans failed to diversify their sugar-based economy. Nonetheless, Castroism improved the material and social life of the working classes; the regime built schools and clinics, mounted literacy campaigns, and promoted equality for long-marginalized Afro-Cubans and women. In quality of life statistics, by the mid-1980s Cuba, with the lowest infant mortality and highest literacy rates and life expectancy, ranked well ahead of other Latin American nations. Cubans lived as long as North Americans and ten years longer than Mexicans and Brazilians. Cuba had nearly as many doctors per population as the United States and over twice as many as Mexico or Brazil. In addition, in contrast to some Latin American dictatorships, the Cuban government did not form death squads or sponsor murders of dissidents. However, it did attempt to control the Cuban people. Government agencies monitored citizens and their opinions, and Castro placed limits on free expression, jailing those who defied the ban. The jailed included brave writers, homosexuals, and those publicizing human rights violations and advocating free speech and elections. Seeking political freedom, better-paying jobs, or higher living standards, several hundred thousand Cubans have fled over the years, chiefly to the United States.

The Cuban Revolution, and the society it created, had international repercussions. Castro exchanged dependence on the United States for dependence on the USSR, which, to maintain the alliance, poured billions of dollars of aid into the country. With the collapse of the USSR in 1991, however, Castro lost his patron and benefactor. Since then Cuba has struggled. Because

---

Castroism Innovative socialist policies introduced by Fidel Castro to stimulate economic development in Cuba while tightly controlling its population.

Castro Addressing Crowd
A spellbinding orator, the Cuban leader, Fidel Castro, often recruits support for his government and policies by speaking at large rallies.
(Corbis)

of the U.S. embargo, the country has few markets or sources of capital. The social welfare system has cracked, and the economy has crumbled despite efforts to introduce some market forces. Yet, frustrating his opponents, Castro remains in power. Critics of U.S. policy, including most U.S. allies, have argued that the U.S. embargo helps Castro by reinforcing strong anti-U.S. feelings and discrediting pro-U.S. dissidents. Remembering the history of U.S. domination from 1898 to 1959, many Cubans, while desiring a freer, more productive system, do not necessarily want the United States to determine their fate.

Brazil: Dictatorship and Democracy

While Mexico and Cuba, despite some successes, have disappointed those who hoped they would become development models for Latin America, few Latin American nations have had as much promise and experienced as many problems as Brazil. Occupying half of the South American continent, and with a population in 2005 of some 186 million, Brazil is Latin America's colossus and has its largest economy. From the mid-1940s to the mid-1960s the nation had a democratic government, which persisted for two decades despite increasing tensions between left and right and periodic economic crises. In 1961 Joao Goulart (jao joo-LART) (1918–1976), a populist reformer supported by leftist groups, assumed the presidency. Under his rule, the economy stumbled and efforts to organize the impoverished peasants and rural workers antagonized powerful landlords. Seeking to halt change and impose order, the military overthrew Goulart in 1964 and ruled Brazil for the next two decades under a harsh military dictatorship, which arrested some 40,000 citizens. Viewing Brazil as ripe for a Communist takeover, the United States had encouraged the military coup. Brazilian industrialists, businessmen, planters, and affluent urbanites, fearing the nation faced turmoil, welcomed the change.

Between 1964 and 1985 authoritarian governments, headed by generals and supported by the United States, gave priority to economic growth and national security at the expense of social programs. Relying on brutal repression, the regimes imposed comprehensive censorship, outlawed political parties, and banned strikes and collective bargaining. Human rights abuses became rampant. Rightwing vigilante groups and death squads instilled terror, killing or torturing dissidents; one police squad assassinated over 1,000 people the government called "undesirables," among them labor leaders and shantytown residents. Death squads remained active into the 1980s, murdering up to 100 victims a month.

The generals imposed a capitalist economic model recommended by American advisers encouraging free markets and foreign investment. For a decade the economy boomed, eliciting foreign praise of the "Brazilian miracle" as annual growth rates averaged 10 percent between 1968 and 1974 and exports soared. The policies promoted a major shift in exports from natural resources, such as coffee, to manufactured goods. Industrialization relied heavily on foreign investment, technology, and markets. The United States and international lending agencies poured in $8 billion in aid. But the "miracle" depended on low wages and redistributing income upward to the rich and middle class, confirming the local saying that there is no justice for the poor. The top 10 percent of people enjoyed 75 percent of the income gain while half of all households lived below the poverty line. Less than half the labor force earned the minimum wage. While many people went barefoot and dressed in rags, Brazil made and exported shoes. Beginning in the 1960s, Brazilian governments encouraged land speculators and foreign corporations to open up the vast Amazon basin, the world's largest tropical rain forest and river system. The virgin forest was rapidly stripped for logging, farming, mining, and ranching, displacing many of the 200,000 Indians who lived off its resources.

By 1980 the "miracle" was fading as Brazil experienced an inflation rate of over 100 percent, a huge balance of payments deficit, a massive foreign debt, and sagging industrial production. Meanwhile, numerous sectors of society, including students, demanded democracy, and the Catholic Church criticized human rights violations and advocated for social justice. In 1985 the growing political liberalization climaxed with a return to democracy and the election of a civilian president. Under the successive democratic governments led by moderate reformers, however, many problems remained unresolved, since leaders feared that policies hurting big business might provoke a military coup. As economic problems increased, inflation soared to 2,500 percent by 1994. Responding to the gross inequality in rural land ownership, landless peasants seized land, but landowners hired gunmen to harass the militants. Social inequities such as school dropout rates, malnutrition, bankrupt public health services, homelessness, and debt slavery grew. Brazil maintained one of the world's most unequal income distributions: the wealthiest 1 percent of people earned the same percentage of national income as the poorest 50 percent. As a result, many Brazilians became disillusioned with democracy.

Although the economy revived in the later 1990s, Brazilians, wanting further reform, turned to the political left. In 2002 they gave leftist candidates 80 percent of the vote and elected as president Socialist labor leader Luis Ignacio da Silva (b. 1944), known as Lula, a former metalworker and longtime dissident. While Lula has fostered faster economic growth, and some observers compare Brazil to dynamic Southeast Asian nations such as Malaysia, Singapore, and Thailand, peasant and worker groups believe Lula's economic policies go too far in pleasing financial interests and international lenders. Despite the booming economy, by 2006 corruption scandals threatened to bring down the regime. Whatever their political fortunes, Brazilians have often shared an optimistic outlook because of the nation's size and economic potential, reflected in the saying that "God is a Brazilian." But a perennial local joke reflects cynicism: "Brazil, Country of the Future, but the future never comes."[15]

Chile: Reform and Repression

While Cubans sought to escape underdevelopment through revolution, Chileans, like Brazilians, tried a succession of strategies, from reform to dictatorship to democracy. Chileans enjoyed a long tradition of elected democratic governments sustained by a large middle class, high rates of literacy and urbanization, and mass-based political parties. Nonetheless, a wealthy elite of businessmen, military officers, and landowners held political power and suppressed labor unrest. Despite a growing manufacturing sector, Chile depended on the export of minerals, especially copper. By the 1960s it was divided politically between the right, center, and left, and a stagnant economy widened the gap between rich and poor. Two-thirds of Chileans earned under $200 a year.

Chile shifted direction with the 1970 elections. Six liberal, socialist, and Communist parties united in a left-leaning coalition, the Popular Unity, that was supported largely by small businessmen, the urban working class, and peasants. Their

winning presidential candidate, Salvador Allende (ah-YEN-dee) (1908–1973), who had developed compassion for the poor while working as a medical doctor, promised a "Chilean road" to socialism, with red wine and meat pies, through constitutional means in a parliamentary democracy. His regime took over, and paid compensation to, banks and a copper industry that had been dominated by powerful U.S. corporations. Land reform broke up underutilized ranches and divided the land among the peasant residents. Allende's government supported the labor unions and provided the urban shantytowns with health clinics and better schools. Both employment and economic production reached the highest levels in Chilean history. The Popular Unity was also committed to the creation of a Chilean cultural renaissance. Imported magazines, recordings, and films from abroad, especially from the United States, had become popular in Chile, especially among the middle class, marginalizing Chilean-produced cultural products. According to a pro-Allende cultural organization, "Our folklore, our history, our customs, our way of living and thinking are being strangled [by] the uncontrolled invasion [of the U.S. media and popular culture]."[16]

Democracy flourished and Allende enjoyed growing popularity, but the Popular Unity government also generated opposition. The rapid reforms produced shortages of luxury goods, fostering middle-class resentment. Allende's opponents controlled the mass media and judiciary and dominated the congress. At the same time, the U.S. president, Richard Nixon, worried about Allende's friendship with Cuba's Fidel Castro and feared that Allende's socialism without revolution could become a model for Latin America, threatening U.S. power and economic interests. The United States also mounted an international economic embargo on Chilean exports. The CIA undertook a disinformation campaign, such as spreading untrue rumors that Allende planned to conscript women into the military, cooperated in assassinating pro-Allende military officers, and organized strikes to paralyze the economy.

In 1973 a military coup supported by the United States overthrew Allende, who died while defending the presidential palace from an assault. The military imposed a brutal military dictatorship led by General Agusto Pinochet (ah-GOOS-toh pin-oh-CHET) (b. 1915). Pinochet launched a reign of terror, arresting some 150,000 Allende supporters and detaining and routinely torturing hundreds of political prisoners for years. The regime murdered thousands of dissidents, sometimes in front of other prisoners held in the national stadium, and buried the victims in unmarked mass graves. Thousands of Chileans fled the country. The junta forbade labor unions and strikes, prohibited free speech and political parties, restored nationalized U.S. property, and engaged in public burnings of books and records produced by leftist Chileans. Advised by U.S. economists, Pinochet shifted to a free enterprise economy, similar to military-ruled Brazil's, that generated growth and moderate middle-class prosperity purchased at the cost of a monumental foreign debt and environmental degradation. But little of this wealth trickled down to the poor, whose living standards deteriorated. By the later 1980s, unemployment had skyrocketed to 30 percent of Chileans, and some 60 percent of people were poor. Two observers wrote that Pinochet's Chile "remained a dual society of winners and losers. The rich, roaring through traffic in their expensive sedans, seemed to mock those left behind, trapped in fuming buses."[17]

However, a severe economic crisis that undermined the regime's legitimacy led to a return to a civilian-led liberal democracy. Escalating social tensions and political protests prompted the junta to hold an election and restore democracy in 1989. The resulting center-left governments struggled to maintain middle-class prosperity while promoting a more equitable distribution of wealth. They retained free enterprise while making additions to health, housing, education, and social spending. These policies chipped away at poverty. The population living in poverty has been reduced by half and unemployment has plummeted. Tax increases and increased welfare have not stifled the annual economic growth of about 10 percent. Chile has become the most prosperous Latin American economy, enjoying a stable democratic system. Chilean and U.S. officials have discussed the possibility of Chile joining NAFTA. Yet, many Chileans remain bitter toward the United States for having once helped install and perpetuate a brutal military regime.

SECTION SUMMARY

- In Latin America, rightwing and leftwing movements competed for power; rightwing movements were dominant from the 1950s through the 1980s, and moderates and leftists such as Venezuela's Hugo Chavez gained more power in the 1990s.

- Many Latin Americans resented U.S. interference in their economies and support for the overthrow of leftist governments, while others welcomed the U.S. example of democracy and free trade.

- The Mexican Revolution led to decades of single-party rule that failed to significantly help the poor, and a reformist president elected in 2000 also failed to improve their lot. Many Mexicans illegally crossed the U.S. border in search of a better life.

- Under Castro, Communist Cuba has attempted to control its people but has also provided excellent medical care and education; however, the withdrawal of aid from the USSR in 1991 and the U.S. embargo have left its economy struggling.

- Under a brutal U.S.-supported military dictatorship, Brazil enjoyed a period of impressive growth but then experienced extreme inflation and increasing gaps between rich and poor; democracy returned in the mid-1980s, and the economy recovered in the late 1990s.

- Alarmed by the popularity of a democratically elected leftist government in Chile, the United States supported a 1973 coup there as well as the brutal military dictatorship that resulted, which rewarded the wealthy and further impoverished the poor, and which was replaced by a democratic government in 1989.

 # Changing Latin American and Caribbean Societies

How have Latin American and Caribbean cultures been dynamic?

The societies of Latin America and the Caribbean, while facing daunting economic problems, have had social and cultural patterns different from those of North America and the Pacific Basin. Rather than balanced economic growth, Latin American and Caribbean nations have often emphasized export of traditional natural resources such as oil, sugar, coffee, bananas, wool, and copper. The Spanish-speaking nations, Portuguese-speaking Brazil, and the English- and French-speaking Caribbean societies, being derived from varied mixes of peoples and traditions, often have little in common with each other. But the regions' peoples have fostered dynamic cultural forms that have found international popularity.

Latin American Economies

Although often enjoying economic growth, no Latin American nations have achieved the level of prosperity found in the industrialized West. Latin Americans forged rising literacy rates, lowered infant mortality rates, and more people than ever now own televisions, even in poor neighborhoods. Nonetheless, the world price for most of their natural resource exports usually has declined every year, leaving less money for economic development. Most countries have experienced little growth in per capita income or productivity. To pay the bills and import luxury items, governments have taken out loans, eventually owing billions to international lenders. Rapidly expanding populations, growing at 3 percent a year, add to the social burden and cause environmental problems. Governments have tried to satisfy land hunger, mineral prospecting, and timber exploitation by treating indigenous peoples and the rain forests they inhabit as expendable resources.

As Brazil, Chile, and Mexico demonstrated, Latin America has also suffered severe income inequality. By 2000 the top 10 percent of the population earned half of all income, and 70 percent of the people lived in poverty. The rich have often evaded taxes, leaving states with little money for building schools and clinics. The small elite class drives Rolls Royces, while the poor lack bus service. In Brazil half of the people have had no access to doctors even while Rio de Janeiro has become the world's plastic surgery capital, with hundreds of cosmetic surgeons catering to wealthy Brazilians and foreigners. In Caracas, Venezuela's capital, one shopping mall that serves the affluent boasts 450 stores, an amusement park, two movie theaters, and a McDonald's. But any customers coming from a slum of open sewers and tin shacks, perched a few miles away on unstable hillsides, would have to pay half a day's wage for a Big Mac. To survive, poor peasants in some nations, especially after the decline of world coffee prices pushed coffee growers out of jobs, have often turned to growing coca and opium for making

U.S. Factory in Mexico Since the 1980s growing numbers of U.S. companies have relocated industrial operations to Mexico, building many factories along the Rio Grande River that separates Mexico from Texas. In this factory, in Matamoros, Mexico, the mostly female labor force makes toys for the U.S. market. (Keith Dannemiller/Corbis)

cocaine and heroin. But the drug trade, largely to the U.S. market, fosters political turbulence and government corruption and profits only a few drug kingpins.

Agriculture has remained a mainstay of most Latin American economies. Landholding is usually concentrated in a small group of aristocratic families and multinational corporations, such as the U.S.-based United Fruit Company. By the 1990s, 60 percent of all agricultural land was held in large estates and farmed inefficiently, contributing to food shortages and malnutrition. Modern agriculture requires large investments for machinery, fertilizers, pesticides, and fuel, but growing beans and corn to feed hungry peasants supplies inadequate revenue. As a result, vast tracks of rain forests and land that once grew food crops have been transformed into ranches, which often raise beef cattle for fast-food outlets in North America and Europe. Latin America remains a food importer, mostly from North America, and malnutrition causes half of all child deaths. In Peru's major city, Lima, hundreds of poor children, known as "fruit birds," desperately compete with stray dogs for spoiled fruit. In Mexico, beef cattle consume more food than the poorest quarter of people.

Life in rural areas has often been marked by hardship. A Brazilian novel captured the hopelessness of the rural workers in the drought-tortured northeast, where, in the 1980s, life expectancy was thirty years, eighty-five children died each hour, and only two-thirds of children attended school. The herder Fabiano understands that everything prevents his escape from endless poverty: "If he could only put something aside for a few months, he would be able to get his head up. Oh, he had made plans, but that was all foolishness. Ground creepers were never meant to climb. Once the beans had been eaten and the ears of corn gnawed, there was no place to go but to the boss's cash drawer [for a loan]."[18]

Unemployment and unprofitable farms have generated migration from rural areas to cities; by 2000 the region had become the world's most urbanized, with 75 percent of people living in cities and towns. The migrants fill cities with surplus people living in festering shantytowns and working as shoeshine boys, cigarette vendors, car washers, or in other poorly paid work. Half the urban population lack adequate water, housing, sanitation, and social services. But economic growth has also fostered growing middle classes, which have become a third of the population in Argentina, Chile, and Uruguay and a fifth in Brazil and Mexico.

Beginning in the 1980s many Latin American nations, hoping to emulate the success of the United States, adopted **neoliberalism**, an economic model, encouraged by the United States, that promoted free markets, privatization, and Western investment. The model generated growth for a decade, but more people than ever remained stuck in poverty. The neoliberal model failed to curb government corruption, install honest judicial systems, foster labor-intensive industries, or reduce the power of rich elites or dependence on foreign loans and investment. Free markets have often meant a few people enjoyed fabulous wealth while most people remained poor. The nation that most ardently adopted neoliberalism, Argentina, saw its economy collapse in 1998; unemployment soared and, by 2001, half of the people lived in poverty. The economy only revived after Argentineans elected pragmatic leftists into power in 2003. Since then the economy has grown by 9 percent a year and, in 2006, the nation paid back the money still owed to the International Monetary Fund, a rare occurrence in the world

---

neoliberalism An economic model encouraged by the United States in the developing world that promoted free markets, privatization, and Western investment.

and a symbol of recovery as well as of a turn to a more state-oriented economy and a paternalistic style of governing by President Nestor Kirchner, a Peronist. But although neoliberalism lost credibility, no other economic model, such as Cuban communism or Allende's socialism with democracy, had widespread support or a record of success in Latin America.

Latin America: Society and Religion

Political and economic change has modified social arrangements, especially in gender relations and family life. Although men dominate the governments, militaries, businesses, and the Catholic Church, women's struggles have managed to reduce gender inequality. Once considered helpless and groomed as girls to be a wife and mother, many women now go out to paid work, some fighting for recognition in male-dominated trades. Millions of women have earned money selling clothing, handicrafts, and food in small markets or from street stalls. Factories relocating from North America attract young women, who are preferred to men because they accept lower wages and have been raised to obey. As women have entered the work force, family life has undergone strains. By the 1990s far fewer people married, especially among the poor. But divorce, banned by the Catholic Church, has remained difficult or impossible in some nations, and men still enjoy a double standard in sexual behavior, with men's extramarital affairs being tolerated while women's are condemned. Although abortion is illegal everywhere in the region, Latin America has one of the world's highest abortion rates. Gay men and lesbians also struggle for acceptance. Homosexuality remains illegal in many nations, including Castro's Cuba, although Brazil and Costa Rica have fostered more tolerant climates.

As gender expectations have changed, women have become more active in politics. Between 1945 and 1961 women gained the right to vote. In 1974 Isabel Peron (b. 1931) of Argentina, a former dancer who married Juan Peron after Evita's death, succeeded her late husband to become the region's first woman president, but she was ousted in a military coup in 1976. In 1990 Violeta Chamorro (vee-oh-LET-ah cha-MOR-roe) (b. 1919), a newspaper publisher, was elected president of Nicaragua, and she served until 1996. In 2006 Chileans showed a willingness to expand their political horizons by electing as president the pediatrician turned socialist politician Michelle Bachelet (BAH-she-let), a divorced mother of three and avowed agnostic whose father was murdered while she and her mother were jailed and tortured during the Pinochet years. Leading the victorious center-left coalition, Bachelet struck a blow for gender equity by filling half of her cabinet positions with women, including the key defense and economy ministries. Men have often resented women's empowerment, and dictatorships have singled out women activists, such as Bachelet's mother, for torture. During military rule in Argentina, Brazil, and Chile, women political prisoners were kept naked and often raped. For instance, Doris Tijereno Haslam (b. 1943), an early member of the leftist Sandinista movement in Nicaragua who fought as a guerrilla commander, was twice arrested and badly tortured by the corrupt dictatorship of General Anastasio Somoza Debayle

(1923–1967). After the Sandinista victory in 1979 she headed the national police and served in the congress. Women fought back against discrimination and violence, as in Mexico, where the feminist movement challenged inequitable laws and social practices. In 1974 the Mexican legislature passed a law, similar to one proposed but never approved in the United States, guaranteeing women equal rights for jobs, salaries, and legal standing. In countries such as Argentina, Brazil, and Uruguay, liberal women's groups have made loosening the anti-abortion laws a top priority and have gained more public support for their cause.

Another traditional foundation for Latin American society, religion, also was subject to change. In the 1960s progressive Latin American Roman Catholics developed **liberation theology**, a movement to make Catholicism more relevant to contemporary society and address the plight of the poor. Priests favoring liberation theology, especially in Brazil, cooperated with Marxist and liberal groups in working for social justice until the Vatican prohibited the movement in the 1980s. On the whole, the Roman Catholic hierarchy remained conservative. While fewer Catholics attended church services, popular Catholicism still centered on fiestas, pilgrimages, and the family altar. Protestantism, chiefly evangelical or pentecostal, grew rapidly with increased missionary efforts, attracting converts with its participatory, emotional services. By the 1990s Protestants numbered nearly 20 percent of the population in Guatemala and 8 percent in Brazil and Chile. But their active evangelization, which often targeted Catholics, caused resentment among Catholic leaders. Nonetheless, the religious landscape of Latin America looked very different and was more diverse in 2000 than it had been a century earlier.

Brazilian Society

Latin America's largest nation, Brazil, has reflected both the region's social changes and its continuities during the era. Over the decades urbanization, population growth, industrialization, and the ebb and flow of politics have introduced new influences, yet long-standing social patterns have also persisted.

Between 1920 and 1980 urban population grew from about a quarter to three-fifths of Brazilians. Migrants jammed into shantytowns surrounding the central cities, such as the notorious hillside shacks of Rio de Janeiro. Poverty remained pervasive. By the 1980s three-fifths of breadwinners averaged under $100 per year in income, three-fourths of Brazilians were malnourished, a third of adults had tuberculosis, a quarter of the population suffered from parasitic diseases, and millions of abandoned or runaway children wandered city streets, living by their wits. Yet, despite the street people, the shantytowns were also well organized, led by community activists and filled with hard-working residents proud of their communities and seeking a better future for their children.

---

liberation theology   A Latin American movement that developed in the 1960s to make Catholicism more relevant to contemporary society and to address the plight of the poor.

Although Brazilians have increasingly tolerated racial and cultural diversity, race remains a central social category. Like the United States, Brazil has never become a true racial "melting pot." Afro-Brazilians often condemn what they view as a racist society steeped in prejudice and having a wide gap in racial income. Race has often correlated with social status: whites dominate the top brackets, blacks the bottom, and mixed-descent Brazilians fall in between. The flexible Brazilian concept of race, however, differs from the biological concept that North Americans have. Dark-skinned people can aspire to social mobility by earning a good income since, as a popular local saying claimed, "money lightens." Furthermore, Afro-Brazilian culture has had a growing influence, and many whites have embraced aspects of black culture. For example, over a third of Brazilians, often devout Catholics, have adopted or been influenced by one of the Afro-Brazilian faiths, formed decades ago, that link a West African god or other African traditions with a Roman Catholic saint and ceremonies.

For Brazil, as for most nations, professional sports have become a popular entertainment and diversion from social problems. For example, European football, or soccer, has been hugely popular in Brazil, as in most of Latin America, for decades, uniting Brazilians of all social backgrounds. From the late 1950s to late 1970s the storied career, fluid play, and magnetic personality of the superstar Pele (b. 1940), from a poor Afro-Brazilian family, did much to spread the popularity of soccer in the world. Brazilians are proud of the international success of their national team, which won the World Cup championships five times between 1958 and 2002 by employing a creative, teamwork-oriented strategy, known as "samba football," that Brazilians have identified with the national spirit. A playwright noted how his countrymen obsessively suspend their daily lives during the World Cup, which is held every four years: "The nation pauses, all of it. Robbers don't rob, ghosts don't haunt, no crimes, no embezzlements, no deaths, no adulteries."[19]

Latin American Cultures

Latin America has fostered creative cultural forms that have reached a global audience. The mass media have both shaped and reflected the prevailing cultures. Inexpensive transistor radios became widely available, and by the 1980s thousands of radio stations had sprouted all over the region. While most stations were privately owned, governments frequently sought to control their content. In 1950 television came to the main cities, eventually spreading widely. Immensely popular local television soap operas dominated prime time viewing, with those from Brazil and Mexico enjoying the widest popularity. They also gained a large market around the world.

Literature has also flourished, with writers often criticizing or describing social conditions and government failures. For instance, the popular Brazilian novelist Jorge Amado (HOR-hay ah-MAH-do) (1912–2001) blended fantasy, realism, and political commitment in ways that provided insight into life in his home region, Brazil's impoverished northeast. Former journalist Gabriel García Márquez (MAHR-kez) (b. 1928), a Nobel Prize–winning Colombian novelist, developed an international audience for imaginative books full of what literary scholars called "magic realism," the representation of possible events as if they were wonders and impossible events as commonplace. His most famous work, *One Hundred Years of Solitude* (1970), charts the history of a Colombian house, the family who live in it, and the town where it was located, through wars, changing politics, and economic crises.

Some writers tested the tolerance of governments for works critical of those holding power. For example, in Chile, the greatest epic poem of the leftist writer and former diplomat Pablo Neruda (neh-ROO-da) (1904–1973), *General Song*, published in 1950, portrays the history of the entire hemisphere, showing an innocent pre-Columbian America cruelly awakened by Spanish conquest. The poem romanticizes the Incas, extolls the liberators who ended Spanish rule, castigates foreign capitalists (often from the United States), who are depicted as exploiters, and identifies an emerging mass struggle to establish an America truly governed by and for the people rather than the rich. In 1971 Neruda won the Nobel Prize for literature, cheering his admirers around the hemisphere and distressing those who viewed him and his radical views as a threat to Latin American society.

Other art forms also developed a social consciousness. For instance, the Brazilian New Cinema movement, launched in 1955, tried to replace the influence of Hollywood films with films that reflected Brazilian life. One of the movement's finest films, *Black Orpheus* (1959), which gained an international following, employed a soundtrack of local popular music to examine the annual pre-Lenten Carnival in Rio de Janeiro's shantytowns and the extremes of wealth and poverty revealed in the different ways rich and poor celebrated Carnival.

Like other peoples, Latin Americans have mixed local cultural traditions with imported influences, but the local forms have often proved more inspiring. For example, a musical style known as **New Song**, based chiefly on local folk music and closely tied to progressive politics and protest, gained popularity in a half-dozen countries in the 1960s and 1970s, becoming especially influential in Chile. Seeking an alternative to the Anglo-American popular culture favored by elite Chileans, Chilean musicians have used indigenous Andean instruments and tunes. During the later 1960s Chilean New Song pioneers such as Violeta Parra and Victor Jara (HAR-a) wrote or collected songs that addressed problems of Chilean society such as poverty and inequality. Parra (1918–1967) served as the bridge between the older generation of folk musicians and the younger generation of singer-songwriters (see Profile: Violeta Parra, Chilean New Song Pioneer). Her protégé Jara put his goal of using music to promote his political goals in song: "I don't sing for the love of singing, Or to show off my voice, But for the statements, Made by my honest guitar."[20]

New Song A Latin American musical movement based chiefly on local folk music and closely tied to progressive politics and protest; became popular in the 1960s and 1970s, especially in Chile.

VIOLETA PARRA, CHILEAN NEW SONG PIONEER

Violeta Parra An influential Chilean musician, folklorist, and artist, Violeta Parra is credited with founding the folk-music-oriented New Song movement, influencing many musicians in Chile and throughout Latin America.   (Archivo, La Fundacion Violetta Parra)

Born in 1918 to a poor schoolteaching family, Violeta Parra was the key figure in the early development of New Song, a Chilean music based chiefly on local folk music, and a multitalented artist in many mediums, including poetry, film-making, tapestry, and painting. Despite her lower-middle-class background, the unconventional Parra lived and dressed like a peasant, wearing her hair long and almost uncombed. Restless and unsuited for marriage, she struggled to find the best outlet for her talents while supporting herself and her two children, Isabel and Angel (AHN-hell). After working as a commercial entertainer, she began collecting, writing, and singing folk music in the 1940s and eventually collected over 3,000 songs. She had clear musical goals: "Every artist must aspire to unite his/her work in a direct contact with the public. I am content to work with the people close to me, whom I can feel, touch, talk and incorporate into my soul." Yet, unlike her protégés, such as Victor Jara, who was deeply engaged in leftwing movements, she never became directly active in politics.

In the early 1950s Parra began Chile's first folk music radio program and recorded her debut album, with simple guitar-accompanied arrangements. She also taught briefly at a southern Chilean university. Parra and her children introduced Andean and African American folk music to Chile after a four-year sojourn in Paris, France, where they encountered musicians from various countries. Settling with her children in Chile's capital city, Santiago, she enjoyed cooking huge pots of beans for the young Chileans who gathered around her to drink wine, discuss Chilean affairs, and exchange songs and stories. A café the Parras opened in Santiago became a meeting place for performers and other Chileans interested in New Song and leftist politics. Parra greatly influenced younger urban musicians, who began learning from her how to play traditional Andean instruments while collecting or writing their own songs, and she provided a role model for other Latin American musicians. As Cuba's top New Song musician, Silvio Rodriguez, claimed: "Violeta is fundamental. Nothing would have been as it is had it not been for Violeta."

Parra's songs displayed two essential elements of later New Song: a base in folk music and concern with Chile's social, economic, and political problems. In "Look How They Tell Us About Freedom," she critiqued the Catholic Church establishment and her nation's ills: look how the nation's religious and political leaders brag about freedom, she sang, when they are actually keeping it from us; they boast about tranquility as their power tortures us. Her music attacked such issues as the brutality of the police, the inequalities of capitalism, the exploitation of Indians, and chronic conflict between Latin American governments. At the same time, her songs retained an intense, highly personal, and contemporary mood, which was both Chilean and universal.

Besides being held in contempt by the Chilean elite for her unconventional life and antiestablishment sympathies, Parra was plagued by poverty and increasing personal problems, including depression. Even her closest friends found her strong, often unpredictable personality difficult, and younger musicians began gravitating to Victor Jara and other New Song figures. Her later songs took on a more philosophical spirit. On her last album in 1966 she recorded her famous farewell, "Gracias a la Vida" (I Give Thanks to Life), a prayerlike expression of gratitude for the richness of life: "I am grateful for the life that has benefited me so much; It has given me both laughter and tears; because of this I can differentiate happiness from sadness; everybody's song is my own song." Not overtly political, the song reflected her identification with the common people and became the underground anthem of many Latin Americans living under dictatorships. As Parra's depression deepened, she committed suicide in 1967. But her career had built a bridge between an older, peasant-based folk tradition and the developing interest of younger musicians. She may have gone, but New Song flowered in Chile and around Latin America.

THINKING ABOUT THE PROFILE

1. Why did her peers consider Parra fundamental to the evolution of New Song in Latin America?

2. How did Parra's life reflect Chilean social and political conditions?

Notes: Quotations from *Studies in Latin American Popular Culture*, 2 (1983), pp. 177–178, and 5 (1986), p. 117; and Nancy E. Morris, *Canto Porque es Necesario Cantar: The New Song Movement in Chile, 1973–1983* (Albuquerque: Latin American Institute, University of New Mexico, Research Paper Series No. 16, July 1984), p. 6.

Because of its leftwing connections, New Song was vulnerable to changing political conditions. In 1970 Chilean New Song musicians had joined the electoral campaign of the leftist Popular Unity coalition, which sought to unseat a centrist administration. After the coalition's leader, Salvador Allende, won the presidency, he encouraged the media to pay more attention to New Song and less to popular music from the United States. For their part, New Song musicians promoted the new government's programs, such as land reform, and some toured abroad to foster foreign support for Allende's government. In 1973, the Chilean military seized power and arrested, executed, or deported most of the New Song musicians while making it illegal to play or listen to New Song. Before thousands of other detainees held in the national stadium, soldiers publicly cut off Victor Jara's fingers, which he had used to play his guitar, and then executed him, symbolizing the death of free expression in Chile and the government's fear of the power of popular culture.

Caribbean Societies and Cultures

With diverse populations of blacks, whites, and Asians, the Caribbean islands, like Latin America, offered an environment for creative cultural development, especially in religion and music. Jamaica, where slavery and colonialism had fostered a blending of African and European traditions, proved particularly fertile soil. **Rastafarianism**, a religion mixing Christian, African, and local influences, arose in Jamaica in 1930 and attracted urban slum dwellers and the rural poor by preaching a return of black people to Africa. The believers revered the emperor Ras Tafari of Ethiopia, the sole unconquered, uncolonized African state in 1930. Its followers, known as Rastas, adopted distinctive practices, including smoking ganja, an illegal drug, and sporting dreadlock hair, that outraged Jamaica's social and economic elite. The return to Africa became more a spiritual than a physical quest and was mixed with black nationalism. As a movement of the black poor, Rastafarianism became identified in Jamaica and other Caribbean islands with radical groups seeking to redistribute wealth.

The most influential popular music to come out of the Caribbean had similar mixed origins. In the 1960s Jamaican musicians created **reggae**, a style blending North American rhythm and blues with Afro-Jamaican traditions and marked by a distinctive beat maintained by the bass guitar. The songs of reggae musicians, who were often Rastas, promoted social justice, economic equality, and the freedom of people, especially Rastas, to live as they liked without interference by the police. The international popularity of reggae owed much

to Bob Marley (1945–1981), a Rasta, and his group, the Wailers. Marley became the first international superstar from a developing nation. His perceptions were shaped by the status of black people in Jamaica and the wider world, in particular the degrading conditions of the nonwhite poor. His explosive performances and provocative lyrics offered clear messages: "Slave driver, the table is turned; Catch a fire, you gonna get burned."[21] As New Song musicians did in Chile, Marley and other reggae musicians became involved in politics, and many musicians supported socialist Michael Manley (1924–1997), whose antibusiness policies as prime minister (1972–1978) prompted economically crippling sanctions by the United States that caused the Jamaican people hardship. After Marley's death from cancer in 1981, many reggae musicians watered down their message, leaving raunchy party music to dominate the Caribbean music scenes.

Latin America and the Caribbean in the Global System

The peoples of Latin America and the Caribbean, who remained major suppliers of natural resources to the world but also lived in the shadow of the United States, forged closer relations with one another. Over the years various leaders sought to increase regional economic cooperation. Commerce between Latin American nations, frequently joined in trade pacts, more than doubled between 1988 and 1994. For example, the Southern Cone Common Market, formed in 1996, included six South American nations with over 200 million people. Similarly, Caribbean countries cooperated in the Caribbean Community and Common Market, formed in 1973. Latin and North American leaders periodically met in summits to bolster hemispheric solidarity and enhance cooperation on immigration, tariff reduction, suppression of the illegal drug trade, and other issues, but these proved more symbolic than substantive. Some U.S.-Latin American issues remain contested. For instance, while people in the United States have blamed Latin American drug cartels for smuggling illegal drugs into the United States, Latin Americans have often resented the U.S. interventions and economic impositions they consider "Yankee imperialism." Latin American and Caribbean leaders have also feared being pushed aside in a world economy dominated by North American, European and, increasingly, Asian nations.

Globalization influenced Latin Americans and their economies. Asian nations, especially China, Japan, Taiwan, and South Korea, captured a growing share of Latin America's traditional overseas markets while also investing in Latin America and the Caribbean. In a globalized economy, a hiccup in Tokyo or New York caused a stomach ache in Ecuador or El Salvador. Since most Latin American and Caribbean economies followed the track of the U.S. economy, they were particularly vulnerable to change in the United States. When the 2001 terrorist attacks in the United States diverted U.S. attention to the Middle East, the sudden U.S. disinterest in Latin America and its problems sparked a regional economic downturn that reduced demand

---

Rastafarianism A religion from Jamaica that arose in 1930 and that mixed Christian, African, and local influences; Rastafarianism attracted urban slum dwellers and the rural poor by preaching a return of black people to Africa.

reggae A popular music style that began in the 1960s and that blended North American rhythm and blues with Afro-Jamaican traditions; reggae is marked by a distinctive beat maintained by the bass guitar.

for Latin American exports. The economic gains made in the mid-1990s slipped away, and the fifth of Latin America's 500 million people who lived in extreme poverty by 2000 faced an even grimmer future. Only a few nations, such as Brazil and Chile, had much hope of improving their status in the global system. Although U.S. exports to Latin America nearly matched those to Europe, by 2006 relations between the United States and Latin America were at their lowest point since the Cold War.

Buffeted by political changes and economic crises, Latin Americans search for their identity and role in a world dominated by other societies. Calling on leaders to recognize the needs of all the people, regardless of class, ethnicity, and gender, and for both North and Latin Americans to find common ground with each other, the salsa music star and lawyer Ruben Blades (blayds), who splits his time between his native Panama and the United States, ponders the hemisphere's destiny in song: "I'm searching for America and I fear I won't find her. Those who fear truth have hidden her. While there is no justice there can be no peace. If the dream of one is the dream of all let's break the chains and begin to walk. I'm calling you, America, our future awaits us, help me to find her."[22]

SECTION SUMMARY

- Latin American economies have been marked by overdependence on natural resources, extreme inequality of income, agriculture that deemphasizes production of foodstuffs for domestic consumption, increasing urbanization, and failed experiments with free trade.

- Though men continue to dominate Latin American society, more women have entered the work force, and several have become national leaders, while liberation theology, a Catholic movement addressing the plight of the poor, became popular for awhile but was outlawed by the Vatican and Protestantism gained a following.

- Brazil, Latin America's largest nation, became increasingly urban and suffered widespread poverty, with a racial divide between lighter- and darker-skinned people, but Brazilians have found escape from their problems through popular sports such as soccer.

- Latin American culture has flourished, with writers employing magic realism to explore their region's experience, others airing political views through poetry and music, and many preferring to use local traditions and forms rather than foreign ones.

- In the Caribbean, the Jamaican religion of Rastafarianism promoted redistribution of wealth and a closely related musical form, reggae, that frequently included calls for social justice and freedom from police interference.

- Latin American and Caribbean nations forged closer relations, signed several trade pacts, and shared an uneasy economic relationship with the United States, while Asian nations also became important competitors with and investors in their economies.

Online Study Center ACE the Test

◆ Chapter Summary

Having emerged from World War II as the dominant superpower, the United States soon engaged in a Cold War with the Soviet Union. The U.S. campaign to contain communism fostered the growth of a powerful military and a strong government. During the Cold War the United States lavished aid and investment on its allies and the developing nations and intervened in many nations, including some in Latin America and the Caribbean, to counter revolutionary movements or overthrow left-leaning governments. While the U.S. economy flourished for decades, American society and culture rapidly changed, as ethnic minorities and women struggled for equal rights. Although shaped, like the United States, by massive immigration from Europe, especially Britain, the societies of Canada, Australia, and New Zealand have more liberal attitudes on social issues and, unlike the United States, have extensive social welfare systems.

Latin American and Caribbean experiences differ from those in the United States and Canada and the Pacific Basin. Military dictatorships dominated many Latin American nations for decades. Most nations struggled to implement and sustain democracy, which became prevalent in the 1990s, and to find the right economic mix to foster economic development. Many people have remained in dire poverty. Women and nonwhites have worked to improve their status, with only modest success. The Latin American and Caribbean peoples have also fostered dynamic cultural forms, from innovative literatures to popular musical forms, that have often expressed protest and have gained worldwide audiences.

Online Study Center Improve Your Grade Flashcards

Key Terms

domino theory	Mutually Assured	neoliberalism
multilateralism	Destruction	liberation theology
unilateralism	preemptive war	New Song
containment	Castroism	Rastafarianism
		reggae

Suggested Reading

Books

Brown, D. Clayton. *Globalization and America Since 1945.* Wilmington, Del.: Scholarly Resources, 2003. A brief but useful study of the U.S. role in a globalizing world.

Chafe, William H. *The Unfinished Journey: America Since World War II*, 5th ed. New York: Oxford University Press, 2003. An outstanding, readable survey of the era.

Clayton, Lawrence A., and Michael L. Conniff. *A History of Modern Latin America*, 2nd ed. Belmont, Calif.: Wadsworth, 2005. A readable general history, with much on the contemporary era.

DePalma, Anthony. *Here: A Biography of the New American Continent.* New York: PublicAffairs, 2001. A U.S. jounalist's account of contemporary Canada, Mexico, and the United States.

Green, Duncan. *Faces of Latin America.* London: Latin American Bureau, 1991. An entertaining and provocative examination of Latin America's people and their vibrant cultures.

Hillman, Richard S., ed. *Understanding Contemporary Latin America,* 3rd ed. Boulder: Lynne Rienner, 2005. A valuable collection of essays.

Isserman, Maurice, and Michael Kazin. *America Divided: The Civil War of the 1960s.* New York: Oxford University Press, 2000. comprehensive history of this important era in U.S. history.

Kinzer, Stephen. *Overthrow: America's Century of Regime Change from Hawaii to Iraq.* New York: Times Books, 2006. A critical examination of U.S. interventions and forced regime changes abroad over the past century.

Page, Joseph A. *The Brazilians.* Reading, M.A.: Addison-Wesley, 1995. Readable examination of Brazilian society and culture.

Paterson, Thomas, et al. *American Foreign Relations,* 6th ed. Boston: Houghton Mifflin, 2004. A readable survey with much on this era.

Rosen, Ruth. *The World Split Open: How the Modern Women's Movement Changed America.* New York: Viking, 2000. One of the best studies of the women's movement in the U.S. since World War II.

Schaller, Michael, et al. *Present Tense: The United States Since 1945.* Boston: Houghton Mifflin, 2004. An up-to-date and informative survey.

Skidmore, Thomas E., and Peter H. Smith. *Modern Latin America,* 6th ed. New York: Oxford University Press, 2004. An excellent introduction to the recent history of the region and its nations.

Terrill, Ross. *The Australians.* New York: Touchstone, 1988. Readable introduction to Australian history and society.

Thompson, Roger C. *The Pacific Basin Since 1945,* 2nd ed. New York: Longman, 2001. An Australian scholar's broad examination of the East Asian, Pacific, Latin American, and North American societies and their relations.

Winn, Peter. *Americas: The Changing Face of Latin America and the Caribbean,* 3rd ed. Berkeley: University of California Press, 2006. A sweeping, highly readable examination of the region and its peoples.

Websites

WWW-VL: History: United States (http://vlib.iue.it/history/USA/). A virtual library, maintained at the University of Kansas, that contains links to hundreds of sites.

Internet Modern History Sourcebook (http://www.fordham.edu/halsall/mod/modsbook.html). Extensive online collection of historical documents and secondary materials.

Internet Resources for Latin America (http://lib.nmsu.edu/subject/bord/laguia/). This outstanding site, from New Mexico State University, provides information and links.

Latin American Network Information Center (http://lanic.utexas.edu/). Very useful site on contemporary Latin America, maintained at the University of Texas.

U.S. Diplomatic History Resources Index (http://faculty.tamu-commerce.edu/sarantakes/stuff.html). An index of sources on U.S. foreign policy.

CHAPTER **30**

The Middle East, Sub-Saharan Africa, and New Conflicts in the Contemporary World, 1945–Present

Online Study Center

This icon will direct you to interactive activities and study materials on the website: college.hmco. com/pic/lockard1e

Modern vs. Traditional Wearing traditional clothing, including veils and head scarves, Egyptian women walk through downtown Cairo in 1998 in front of billboards promoting popular entertainers. The scene illustrates the encounter between Islamic customs and modern ideas in many Middle Eastern nations. (AP/Wide World Photos)

I saw the Berlin Wall fall, [Nelson] Mandela walk free. I saw a dream whose time has come change my history—so keep on dreaming. In the best of times and in the worst of times gotta keep looking at the skyline, not at the hole in the road.

"YOUR TIME WILL COME" BY SOUTH AFRICAN POP GROUP SAVUKA, 1993[1]

The Nigerian writer Chinua Achebe (ah-CHAY-bay) (b. 1930) dissected the underside of African politics in a controversial 1987 blockbuster novel, *Anthills of the Savannah*, about a military dictatorship like the one he had experienced in his own country. *Anthills* portrays the problems faced by average people in Nigeria and throughout much of Africa and the Islamic world, mercilessly depicting the immorality, vanity, and destructiveness of dictatorship. Achebe did not have to look far for examples: the Nigerian military leaders who overthrew a civilian government in 1983 had first arrested people whose corruption was well known, a popular move, but then proceeded to jail anyone, including journalists, who questioned the regime's own economic mismanagement and human rights abuses. Achebe's satire on moral bankruptcy forewarns of the dangers of unaccountable, repressive power. Just as the black and white musicians in the South African pop group, Savuka, could sing of dreams changing history and a new era beginning with the end of white minority rule, Achebe also offered a powerful message about the need for people to hope for, and struggle to attain, a better life.

The political and economic realities of contemporary Africa and the Middle East are reflected in these regions' arts and literature. The candid Achebe has argued that the artist and society cannot be separated. He and other writers, musicians, and artists have used their art to spur political and social change. Achebe claims that no novel is ever politically neutral because even saying nothing about politics is a political statement that says everything is OK. *Anthills* argued eloquently that, in Achebe's view, everything is not OK. Like various other creative people, Achebe, who has specialized in urban satires attacking corruption, social injustice, the pretensions of politicians, and the destabilization brought by the West, has had to live in exile from intolerant governments.

Despite achievements in many areas of life, the problems vividly described by Achebe for Nigeria—corruption, economic stagnation, combustible social tensions, and failed promises of democracy—have applied to most other nations in sub-Saharan Africa and the Middle East. The triumph of nationalism and the resulting decolonization had reshaped Africa and the Middle East. Between 1945 and 1975 country after country became independent or escaped from Western political domination. In contrast to various East Asian, Southeast Asian, and

935

Latin American nations, however, African and Middle Eastern nations have often struggled just to survive. While innovative in areas such as music, literature, and other forms of culture, few of the nations have successfully resolved their social and economic problems. For some nations, Islam has become a rallying cry to assert political interests and preserve cultures. To serve their own ends, global superpowers have manipulated governments and intervened to shape the regions.

FOCUS QUESTIONS

1. How have Arab-Israeli tensions and oil shaped contemporary Middle Eastern politics?
2. What roles has Islam played in the contemporary Middle East?
3. What were the main political consequences of decolonization in sub-Saharan Africa?
4. What new economic, social, and cultural patterns have emerged in Africa?

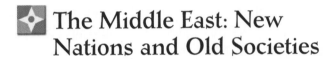

The Middle East: New Nations and Old Societies

How have Arab-Israeli tensions and oil shaped contemporary Middle Eastern politics?

Few world regions have witnessed more turbulence in the past half century than the Middle East, the predominantly Muslim nations stretching from Morocco eastward across North Africa and western Asia to Turkey, Iran, and Afghanistan. The major ethnic group, the Arabs, have dominated most of these nations, but Turks, Iranians, Kurds, and Israeli Jews also influence the region. After World War II the Middle Eastern societies ended Western colonization and asserted their own political interests, often under modernizing leaders. But within these societies, dictatorial governments have proliferated and chronic political instability has been common. Centuries old hostilities between Sunni and Shi'a Muslims simmer. Meanwhile, the Persian Gulf area, which contains much of the world's oil reserves, has made the Middle East crucial to the global system.

The Reshaping of the Middle East

In the decade after World War II nationalist governments in the Middle East replaced most of the remaining colonial regimes. The French abandoned control of Morocco, Tunisia, Lebanon, and Syria while the Italians left Libya. However, Muslim guerrillas fought 500,000 French troops for eight years to bring independence to Algeria, which had a large European settler population. Some 250,000 Algerians died in the conflict. Seeing no clear end to the struggle, the French granted independence in 1962 (see Chronology: The Middle East, 1945–Present). Some Middle Eastern nations, such as Egypt and Morocco, had a long history of national identity and thus unity, but many were fragile states. For example, after World War I the British had formed the new, artificial states of Iraq, Jordan, and Palestine with arbitrary boundaries, while Afghanistan, Turkey, Lebanon, and Syria included diverse and often feuding ethnic and religious groups.

Iran and Turkey, which had never been colonized, sought influential roles in the region and built formidable military forces. Both also abused their citizens' human rights, arresting dissidents and restricting ethnic minorities. Iran shifted from a secular, pro-Western royal government to a militant Islamic government. By contrast, Turkey, led largely by secular politicians and generals, looked increasingly westward, joining NATO (the North Atlantic Treaty Organization), hosting U.S. military bases, developing democratic institutions, and applying for membership in the European Union. But Turkey's governments, while generally promoting a modern version of women's rights, have also suppressed the culture and language of the largest ethnic minority, the Kurds, who chiefly live in southeastern Turkey, and, although the nation's 70 million people are largely Muslim, have limited political activity by groups favoring an Islamic state.

After decolonization the hopes for development throughout the Middle East were soon dashed as vested economic interests, such as large landowners, and most of the Muslim clergy opposed significant social and economic changes. Many people remained mired in illiteracy, poverty, and disease. Freewheeling and enduring multi-party democracy has been hard to establish or maintain but some have made the effort. Turkey shifted from military-dominated to democratically elected governments by the 1980s, but the military remained powerful and strict internal security laws resulted in the imprisonment of several thousand people for political offenses. Lebanese could choose between many competing warlord or religious-based parties, and a new constitution in 2002 allowed both men and women in the small Persian Gulf kingdom of Bahrain (BAH-rain) to elect a parliament with considerable power. In the early twenty-first century the Moroccan king, Muhammad VI, who claims descent from the prophet Muhammad,

C H R O N O L O G Y

	The Middle East	Sub-Saharan Africa
1940	**1948** Formation of Israel **1954–1962** Algerian Revolution	**1948** Apartheid in South Africa **1957–1965** African decolonization
1960	**1967** Arab-Israeli Six-Day War **1973** OPEC oil embargo **1979** Islamic revolution in Iran	**1975** Independence for Portuguese colonies
1990	**2003** United States invasion of Iraq	**1994** Black majority rule in South Africa

used a tolerant interpretation of Islam to try and modernize his nation, granting new rights to women and strengthening civil liberties and the role of an elected parliament. But in

C H R O N O L O G Y

The Middle East, 1945–Present

1948	Formation of Israel
1948–1949	First Arab-Israeli War
1951	Nationalist government in Iran
1952–1970	Nasser presidency in Egypt
1953	CIA overthrow of Iranian government
1954–1962	Algerian Revolution
1956	Suez crisis
1960	Formation of OPEC
1967	Arab-Israeli Six-Day War
1973	Arab-Israeli (Yom Kippur) War
1973	OPEC oil embargo
1978	Egypt-Israel peace treaty
1979	Islamic revolution in Iran
1979–1989	Soviet war in Afghanistan
1980–1988	Iran-Iraq War
1987	Beginning of Palestinian Intifada
1996–2001	Taliban government in Afghanistan
1993	Limited Palestinian self-government
2000	Renewed Israeli-Palestinian conflict
2001	U.S. invasion of Afghanistan
2003	U.S. invasion and occupation of Iraq

most countries elections were rigged, parliaments were weak, or governments made it hard for opposition candidates to run. Furthermore, the United States and the Soviet Union, attracted by the region's oil and strategic location along vital waterways, including the Persian Gulf and Suez Canal, soon filled the power vacuum created by decolonization. To become more influential in the world, Arabs talked about uniting across political borders, but pan-Arab nationalism, based more on Arabs' shared cultural and linguistic background than political interests, was never able to overcome political rivalries and meddling by the superpowers. Divided by rival Muslim sects and differing outlooks toward the West, Arabs floundered in their quest for unity. In addition, a number of post-1945 challenges have made the Middle East a highly combustible region subject to strains.

Arab Nationalism and Egypt

Confrontation between Arab nationalism and the world's superpowers, especially during the 1960s and 1970s, was acute in Egypt, a former British protectorate and the most populous Arab country, with 77 million people by 2005. In 1952 a charismatic Egyptian leader, General Gamal Abdul Nasser (NAS-uhr) (1918–1970), led a military coup that ended the corrupt pro-British monarchy. Although he was raised lower middle class in the cosmopolitan city of Alexandria, Nasser's frequent visits to his parents' impoverished farming village had sparked his sympathy for the poor and his resentment of rich landlords. Like many Egyptians, he also despised the British who dominated Egypt and the Egyptian leaders who collaborated with them. As a radical student and then army officer with a commanding personality, he had demonstrated a flare for politics and developed a vision of a new Egypt, free of Western domination and social inequality.

As Egypt's president, Nasser, a modernizer, preached socialism and unity, promising to improve the lives of the impoverished masses and to implement land reform, ideas that made him a hero in the Arab world. To generate power and improve flood control, Nasser's regime used Soviet aid to build the massive Aswan High Dam along the Nile, completed in 1970. But his nonaligned foreign policy antagonized a United States obsessed by the Cold War rivalry with the Soviet Union. Nasser's support of pan-Arab nationalism generated wars. Accusing the West of "imperialist methods, habits of blood-sucking and usurping rights, and interference in other countries,"[2] in 1956 Nasser's government took over ownership of the British-operated Suez Canal, a key artery of world commerce that was built through Egypt in the nineteenth century to allow ships to move between the Mediterranean and Red Seas. To Egyptians foreign ownership of the canal had symbolized their subjugation to foreign powers. To Europeans, the canal was the lifeline that moved oil and resources to the West from Asia. To protect that link Britain, France, and Israel sent in military forces to reclaim the canal from Egyptian troops, but diplomatic opposition by the United States, which disliked Nasser but feared regional instability, and the pro-Egypt Soviet Union forced their withdrawal. By standing up to the West, Nasser became an even greater Arab hero and a leader of the movement among developing nations for nonalignment, or neutrality, between the two rival superpowers. However, the Israeli defeat of Egypt and its allies in a brief 1967 war humiliated Nasser. Furthermore, although Nasser had introduced social and economic reforms, they fostered little economic development and gave Egypt no economic or military strength in the world.

Nasser's successors followed pragmatic, pro-U.S. policies and in 1978 signed a peace treaty with Israel brokered by the U.S. president, Jimmy Carter. But a shift to capitalism and heavy U.S. aid largely has failed to improve living conditions. Egypt's leaders reversed Nasser's land reform and dismantled the socialist economy, allowing a few well-connected capitalists to acquire state property and become fabulously rich while the poorest became even poorer. In the capital city, Cairo, the contrast between the glittering rich neighborhoods, featuring luxury apartments and mansions surrounded by high walls, and the poor, overcrowded neighborhoods, where the most desperate families live in huts on top of ramshackle apartment buildings, has grown more dramatic. Millions of Egyptians have sought work in oil-rich Arab nations. With no oil and few resources other than the fertile lands along the Nile, Egypt suffers from high malnutrition and unemployment, low rates of literacy and public health, and a huge national debt. While liberals seek more democracy, Islamic militants, feeding on these frustrations, challenge the secular but corrupt, repressive government. In 2005 other candidates were able to run against the long-entrenched president but were hampered in campaigning; Islamic parties won many parliamentary seats but the major liberal opposition leader was arrested after the election.

Israel in Middle Eastern Politics

The conflict between Israel and the Arabs, especially the Palestinians, became the Middle East's most insurmountable problem, sustaining tensions for over half a century. Under the influence of Zionism and its dream of a homeland for a long persecuted people, Jews had been emigrating from Europe to Palestine since the late 1800s, building cities and forming productive socialist farming settlements. The growing Jewish presence, however, especially the buying of land, triggered

occasional conflicts with the Palestinian Arab majority. Then the Nazis' murder of 6 million Jews during World War II spurred a more militant Zionism and Jewish desire for a homeland free of oppression, setting the stage for the birth of Israel. But the new nation never established a secure position or fostered allies within the region.

The Birth of Israel Israel emerged in a climate of violence. In the late 1940s Jewish refugees, traumatized by the Holocaust, poured into Palestine from post–World War II Europe. Moderate Jewish leaders negotiated with the British, sympathetic to the Zionist cause, for a peaceful transfer of power to them in Palestine. Meanwhile, Zionist extremists, impatient with negotiations, practiced "gun diplomacy," using terrorism, such as bombings and assassinations, against the British, Arabs, and moderate Jews. At the same time, Arabs, opposed to an Israeli state at their expense, resorted to violent attacks on Jews. Unable to maintain order, Britain abandoned the territory, referring the Palestine question to the new United Nations, then dominated by Western nations. As the British withdrew in 1948, Jewish leaders proclaimed the establishment of the state of Israel, based on the Zionist claim that Jews had a right to form their own sovereign state. By establishing a multiparty parliamentary democracy and seeking to rebuild shattered Jewish lives, the Israelis gained the strong support of Western nations and especially the United States, which pumped in several billion dollars a year in aid for the next five decades.

The establishment of a Jewish state in Palestine led to full-scale war in 1948–1949 between Israel and its Arab neighbors, to whom Israel was a white settler state and a symbol of Western colonialism (see Map 30.1). As Palestinian Arabs fled the fighting and continued terrorism against them by Jewish extremists, or heeded the calls of opportunistic Arab leaders to leave, Israelis occupied their farms and houses. The Israelis won the war against the disorganized Arabs and expelled 85 percent of the Palestinian Arabs from Israel. Palestinian refugees settled in overcrowded, squalid refugee camps in Egypt, Lebanon, Jordan, and Syria. While some Palestinian exiles became a prosperous middle class throughout the Middle East, most remained in the camps, nursing their hatred of Israel. They supported the Palestine Liberation Organization (PLO), a coalition of Arab nationalist, Muslim, and Christian groups led by Yasser Arafat (YA-sir AR-uh-fat) (1929–2004), an engineer and journalist from a wealthy Jerusalem family who was educated at Egypt's Cairo University. Arafat's pragmatic style united factions. However, neither the Western nations nor Israel officially recognized or would negotiate with the PLO until the 1990s, prompting it to resort to terrorism against Israel, such as by attacking public buses and rural settlements.

Israel remained in a state of confrontation with its Arab neighbors and the PLO. The Palestinians remaining in Israel participated in democratic politics but were disproportionally poor and often saw themselves as second-class citizens. Meanwhile, thousands of Jewish immigrants arrived, many from Middle Eastern countries where they had faced discrimination or retribution. The immigration intensified the divisions in

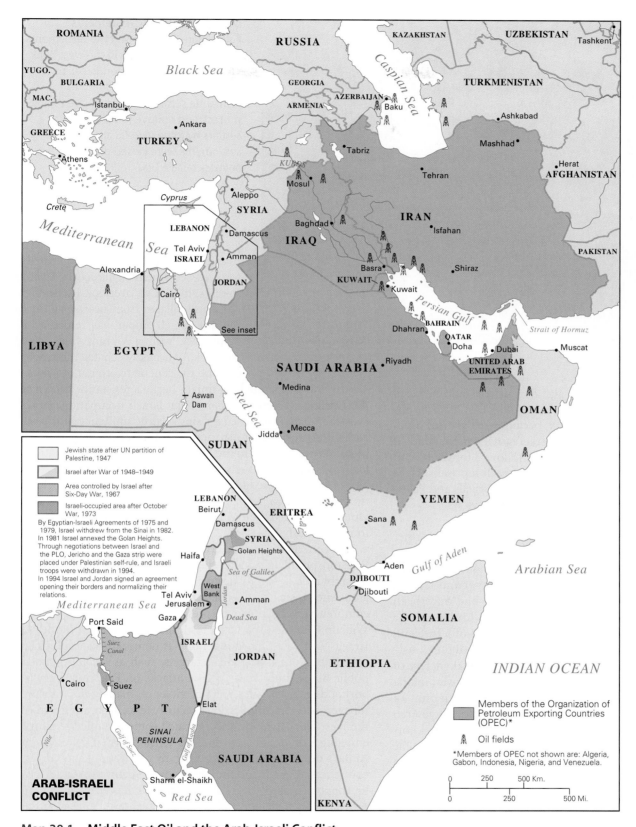

Map 30.1   Middle East Oil and the Arab-Israeli Conflict
Several Middle Eastern nations, including Saudi Arabia, Iran, Iraq, Libya, and the small Persian Gulf states, are rich in oil and active members of OPEC. Israel, founded in 1948, and the neighboring Arab countries of Egypt, Jordan, and Syria have been in chronic conflict that has resulted in four wars. Israel's victory in the 1967 war allowed it to take control of Gaza, the West Bank, and the Golan Heights.

Dismantling Israeli Settlements
Palestinians have viewed the settlements built by ardent Zionists in the West Bank and Gaza as a provocation. Israeli troops have sometimes been ordered to dismantle settlements, expensive to protect, and remove the enraged settlers by force. In 2005 all the Israeli settlements were closed down in Gaza. (AP/Wide World Photos)

Israeli society between secular and devout Jews and between Jews from Europe and those from the Middle East. Israelis, obsessed now with military security, became well armed, especially by the United States. Half of Israel's total national budget went to the military. A cycle of violence followed for years, with a PLO attack on Israelis followed by an Israeli reprisal such as the bombing of a refugee camp in Lebanon. Israelis and Palestinians could seldom comprehend each other's views.

Israel and the Arabs Since 1967

An Arab-Israeli War in 1967 further complicated regional politics, heightening conflict and reshaping Israeli society. Responding to an ill-advised attack led by Egypt and Jordan, Israel gained control of new territories that had once been part of Palestine: the West Bank, that part of Jordan on the western side of the Jordan River; the eastern half of Jerusalem, filled with both Jewish and Islamic holy places and previously governed by Jordan; the Gaza Strip, a small coastal enclave of Egypt; and the Golan Heights, a Syrian plateau overlooking northeast Israel. The Israeli victory doubled the amount of land controlled by Israel, but this land incorporated a large Arab population. Israel and the occupied territories combined now contained 3 million Jews and 2 million Arabs, a combustible situation. By 2005 Israel and the occupied territories contained some 5 million Jews and 4 million Arabs. Israel treated the Palestinians in the occupied territories as a colonized people, allowing them no political rights. In 1973 another Israeli war with Egypt and Syria proved costly to all sides.

Increasing Israeli control over the Palestinians in the occupied territories exacerbated the conflict. Although many Israelis wanted to trade occupied land for a permanent peace settlement, others hoped to permanently annex the occupied lands as part of biblical Israel. Ultranationalist Israelis, with government support, began claiming and settling on Arab land, creating an-

other problem: thousands of Jewish settlers, largely militant Zionists and religious conservatives, living amid hostile Arabs. Palestinians resent the heavily fortified settlements, guarded by Israeli soldiers, that often overlook Palestinian cities and villages from nearby hilltops. Because Israel proper has remained a democracy with a vibrant free press, Israelis have heatedly debated these policies and the general treatment of Arabs.

In 1987 desperate Palestinians began a resistance known as the **Intifada** (Uprising) against the Israeli occupation. However, the turmoil spawned a rising Islamic militancy in the occupied territories that alarmed both the secular Fatah movement, the main party in the PLO, and the Israelis. Negotiations led in 1993 to limited self-government under the PLO in some parts of the occupied territories, the basis for a possible Palestinian state, and a peace agreement between Israel and Jordan. Optimists hoped a permanent peace agreement might be found to satisfy both sides.

But in 2000 violence erupted again, returning the Israel-Palestine problem to center stage in Middle Eastern politics. Political blunders—a provocative visit to a disputed Muslim religious site by an Israeli leader and Yasser Arafat's rejection of a comprehensive peace deal presented by the U.S. president, William Clinton—sparked a resumption of conflict. Moderate Israelis and Palestinians lost hope as demoralizing Palestinian suicide bombings of civilian targets, such as restaurants and public buses, and Israeli reprisal attacks on Palestinian neighborhoods renewed fifty years of violence, making life insecure for everyone. Israel built a high security fence separating it from the West Bank that also incorporated some occupied territory, enraging Palestinians. Yet, in 2005 tensions eased. After Yasser Arafat's death, Fatah, bogged down by corruption, chose a less controversial leader and the Israeli government, with wide public support, closed the Israeli settlements in Gaza, which had proven costly to defend and also disbanded several illegal settlements in the West Bank. However, in 2006 the Palestinians, tired of Fatah's ineffective regime, gave the militant Islamic Hamas movement a majority of seats in the Palestinian parliament, alarming Israelis since Hamas had sponsored terrorist

Intifada ("Uprising") A resistance begun in 1987 by Palestinians against the Israeli occupation.

attacks and refused to recognize Israel's right to exist. Hamas owed its victory in part to its longtime social welfare activities and to hundreds of conservative Muslim women wearing head scarves who campaigned door to door for the party; six of them won seats, including the mother of three Hamas militants killed fighting Israelis. The future of Israeli-Palestinian relations remained uncertain. With only a third of the world's 14 million Jews living in Israel, the Zionist dream of a Greater Israel stretching from the Mediterranean coast through the West Bank to the Jordan River is fading. Nonetheless, with conflicting visions of how Israelis and Palestinians might coexist, no basis for ensuring long-term peace has yet emerged.

Online Study Center **Improve Your Grade**
Primary Source: Arab and Israeli Soccer Players Discuss Ethnic Relations in Israel, 2000

Islamic Revolution in Iran

Rich in oil and strategically located along the Persian Gulf, Iran, once known as Persia, had been buffeted between rival European nations for a century. Outside interference in Iranian affairs continued after World War II, when internal politics revolved around a conflict between the young king, Shah Mohammed Pahlavi (pah-LAH-vee) (1919–1980), and nationalist reformers opposed to foreign domination. In 1951 nationalists came to power, reducing the shah to a ceremonial role; because Iran had been receiving little of the revenue from the British-dominated oil industry, the nationalists also took ownership of that industry. In response Britain and its ally, the United States, which considered the nationalists to be sympathetic to communism and the USSR, cut off aid and launched a boycott to close oil markets, bringing Iran to near bankruptcy and fostering unrest. In 1953, American CIA agents secretly organized opposition among military leaders and paid disgruntled Iranians to riot against the nationalist government, undermining their authority. In the turmoil, royalists overthrew the nationalist government, imprisoned its leaders, and restored the unpopular shah to power, embittering many Iranians. Shah Pahlavi, a ruthless, pleasure-loving man who dreamed of restoring Persia as a great power and making Iran as industrialized as France, allied himself with the strongest superpower, the United States, and allowed U.S. companies to control the oil industry.

Along with the modernization, the shah's three and a half decades of rule also brought a huge military force built with oil revenues and political repression. What the shah termed his "white revolution," which promoted a market economy and women's rights while enlarging the middle class, was admired in the West but failed to improve living standards for most Iranians. While a corrupt elite siphoned off most of the money earmarked for development, including generous U.S. aid, and the royal family lived extravagantly, 60 percent of peasants remained landless. Seeing no future in the villages, people flocked to the cities, which became choked in traffic and smog. The population of Tehran, the capital, increased fivefold between 1945 and 1977. To increase national pride and attract Western tourists, the shah spent billions to renovate the splendid palaces and tombs of Persepolis, a city built for Persian kings 2,400 years ago, but few Iranians had the money to visit the city.

The shah's policies and the persisting inequalities fostered unrest. The absolute monarchy tolerated little dissent and the shah's secret police eliminated opposition. Political prisoners numbered in the thousands. The Iranian poetess Faruq Farrukhzad (fuh-ROOK fuh-ROOK-sad) wrote of how the intellectuals, cowed into submission by the shah, lost their voice, retreating into "swamps of alcohol [while] the verminous mice gnawed through the pages of gilded books, stacked in ancient closets."[3] Conservative Shi'ite leaders opposed the modernization, such as the unveiled women and crowded bars, which they viewed as Westernization and a threat to Muslim religion and culture. Then in 1979 the economy slumped. Strikes and protests forced the shah into exile in the United States and turned the United States and Iran into bitter foes.

With the shah's departure, an Islamic revolution began to reshape Iran. While some Shi'ite thinkers discouraged the clergy from political activism, others promoted clerical involvement in governing an Islamic state. The latter's views prevailed when militant Shi'ite clerics, led by the long exiled Ayatollah Ruhollah Khomeini (roo-HOLE-ah KOH-may-nee) (1902–1989), took power, eliminated leftists and moderate nationalists, and overturned the shah's modernization. Khomeini had long criticized the shah's secular policies, urging that they be replaced by the Islamic Shari'a, which devout Muslims considered the law of God. As Iran became an Islamic state, thousands of Iranians fled abroad, many settling in the United States. Among the new restrictions, women were forced to wear veils and prohibited from socializing with men from outside their families. The regime restricted personal freedoms, as reflected in a popular joke: "We used to drink in public and pray in private. Now we pray in public and drink in private." Like the shah, the clerics ruled by terror, suppressed ethnic minorities, such as the Kurds in the northwest, and executed opponents.

The Iranian Revolution fostered opposition from outside. The United States became bitterly opposed after Islamic militants, led by women students, seized the U.S. Embassy in Tehran in 1979 and held it and the U.S. diplomats for one year. The militants hated the United States for its long support of the shah. Iran's Arab neighbors, who had always feared Iran's territorial size, large population (68 million in 2005), military strength, and regional ambitions, were also alarmed. Now they had to worry about Islamic militancy aimed at their more secular governments. The tensions were fueled by centuries of animosity between the mostly Sunni Arabs and the mostly Shi'ite Iranians. An Iranian program to develop nuclear power and, many international observers believed, nuclear weapons also concerned the international community.

Eventually Iranian politics changed as the nation mixed theocracy with the trappings of democracy. A more open electoral process allowed opposition parties to win seats in parliament. Beginning in 1997, reformers gained a share of power. This, however, fostered a power struggle between moderate reformers, many of them clerics, and the hardline clerics who controlled the judicial and electoral systems. With the economy floundering, the reformers sought closer ties to the outside world, democratization, and a loosening of harsh laws but found the United States unwilling to improve relations. Young people, resenting clerical leadership and Islamic laws, often supported reform. By the early 2000s, people increasingly challenged restrictions on personal behavior. For example, young women, often unveiled or wearing fashionable head scarves, began socializing again with men. But the hardliners maintained overall political power, banning reformist newspapers and disqualifying reformist political candidates. At home the hardliners were distressed when Shirin Ebadi (shih-RIN ee-BOD-ee) (b. 1947), a feminist Iranian lawyer and human rights activist, won the Nobel Peace Prize in 2003 for bravely challenging the clerical leadership and favoring a reformist Islam. Ebadi contended that Iran would only have the rule of law when women enjoyed the same rights as men under the law. But in 2005 Iranians lost faith in the ineffective reformist leaders and elected a hardline, anti-reform president who pledged to increase the nation's nuclear capabilities and restore conservative values. One of his first acts was to ban Western music from radio and television.

Iraq and Regional Conflicts

Iraq proved a major source of regional instability. In 1958 the Iraqi army overthrew an unpopular monarchy and began over four decades of ruthless military dictatorships that crushed all opposition. These governments also fostered secular policies and some economic development, making Iraq one of the most prosperous Arab societies by the 1980s. These regimes were usually led by members of the **Ba'ath** ("Renaissance") Party, which favored socialism and Arab nationalism and strongly opposed Israel. Representing the Sunni minority of 20 percent, the Ba'ath ruled a nation with a restless Arab Shi'ite majority, located mostly in the south, and a disaffected Kurdish minority in the north. A rival Ba'ath group ran Syria. In 1979 Saddam Hussein (b. 1937), a landless peasant's son and army officer, took power in Iraq and proved even more brutal than his predecessors.

Alarmed by the Iranian Revolution, and hated by Ayatollah Khomeini, who considered Saddam's secular regime godless, in 1980 Saddam launched a war against Iran, using poison gas against Iranian soldiers, but he was unable to achieve victory. The war drew in outsiders because it threatened Persian Gulf shipping lanes and hence the world supply of oil. For example, the United States, with its vested interest in Iraq's oil—the world's second largest proven reserves—and hostility toward Iran, sided with Iraq, attacking Iranian shipping and arming Saddam's military. As the casualties mounted, both Iran and Iraq drafted teenagers to fight. The costs of war were staggering: over 260,000 Iranian and 100,000 Iraqi dead and grave damage to the Iraqi economy, including major destruction in Iraq's main port, Basra.

When the war ended in 1988 with no victor, Saddam's actions fostered regional tension. The United States government viewed Saddam as a useful strategic ally and continued providing him with weapons. But Iraqi leaders had long claimed that Kuwait, a British protectorate until 1961 that sits atop oil riches and blocks Iraq from enjoying greater access to the Persian Gulf, should be part of Iraq. In 1991 Iraq invaded prosperous Kuwait, ruled by an Arab royal family. The United States, worried that oil-rich Saudi Arabia might be next, formed a coalition and launched the Persian Gulf War (1991), which drove Iraqis from Kuwait and killed perhaps 30,000 Iraqi soldiers. The war restored Americans' faith in their military, undermined by the bitter defeat in Vietnam in 1975, but the euphoria proved short-lived. Saddam remained in power, persecuting dissidents and slaughtering Shi'ites and Kurds who rebelled, with U.S. encouragement, after the Gulf War defeat. At least 30,000 Shi'ites and many thousands of Kurds died from the fighting. But Saddam's war-making capabilities had been badly damaged and the U.S. and U.N. eventually gave the Kurds in the north some military and police protection, freeing them from Iraqi power and allowing them to set up a government with democratic trappings in their region; and sanctions imposed by the United Nations to restrict Iraq's foreign income and hence ability to buy weapons undermined Iraq's economy. Because of these sanctions and Saddam's economic mismanagement, the Iraqi people, who numbered 26 million by 2005, struggled to acquire food and medical supplies, and thousands died from the resulting shortages.

Saudi Arabia, Oil, and the World

The Persian Gulf War pointed up the close connection between Saudi Arabia, a kingdom built on the twin pillars of conservative Islam and oil, and the outside world, especially the United States, which had military bases and a strong economic stake in the kingdom. Comprising mostly bleak desert, Saudi Arabia possesses the world's largest known oil reserves. Beginning in the 1940s the nation's leaders used oil revenues to fund modernization projects, building highways, hospitals, and universities. By the 1980s the Saudis had achieved health and literacy rates that were high by the standards of Africa and the rest of the Middle East. Glittering shopping malls, which offered the latest Western fashions and electronic gadgets, have served affluent urbanites, who reach the malls in luxury cars often driven by chauffeurs. Yet, outside the cities, poor Saudis often still travel by camel and sleep in tents.

Despite the modernization, Saudi political and social life has remained conservative, with the royal family exercising power and living extravagantly while tolerating corruption and quashing dissent. They have used their power to maintain traditional customs and social patterns. Indeed, the country became a laboratory for the clash between modern institutions (like television) and a highly puritanical, patriarchal Islamic culture. With the acquiescence of the Saudi royal family, the Wahhabis, followers of the most rigid form of Islam, maintain a stranglehold on Islamic thought and practice and on religious education in the kingdom's schools. Wahhabis are hostile

---

Ba'ath ("Renaissance") A political party in the Middle East that favored socialism and Arab nationalism and strongly opposed Israel.

Oil Wealth Saudi Arabia contains the world's largest oil operations, mostly located on or near the Persian Gulf. A Saudi worker overlooks one of the nation's many refineries, which produces the oil exports that have brought the nation wealth. (Bill Strode/Woodfin Camp & Associates)

to Western and often any modern ideas; they believe, for example, that women should stay at home and be controlled by men. Hence, although some educated women wish to enjoy freedom, thanks to Wahhabi-influenced laws they still cannot legally drive or work alongside men. Armed with canes, a special police force patrols the streets and markets, including the city malls, to punish women for violating the strict dress codes, which require them to be covered head to foot. In the 1990s the religious police prevented unveiled female students from fleeing a school dormitory fire, causing dozens of the girls to burn to death. The Shi'ite minority, despised by the Wahhabis, have enjoyed few rights. These conflicts have fostered tensions. Saudi and Western critics believe that what they see as the narrow Islam taught in Saudi schools promotes extremism and anti-Western feeling.

Saudi Arabia's policies have strongly influenced world oil prices and availability. The kingdom was the major player in the formation in 1960 of **OPEC** (Organization of Petroleum Exporting Countries), a cartel designed to give the producers more power over the price of oil and leverage over consuming nations. OPEC's members range from Middle Eastern nations such as Algeria, Iran, and the United Arab Emirates to more distant countries such as Mexico, Nigeria, and Indonesia. In 1973 OPEC members, angry at Western support of Israel, reduced the world oil supply to raise prices, badly discomforting industrialized nations by causing long lines at gasoline stations. After the embargo ended the world price remained high, enriching

OPEC members. High prices also forced the U.S. and western Europe to find ways to conserve fuel, such as by designing more fuel-efficient cars. But in the 1980s reduced oil consumption broke OPEC's power and prices plummeted, damaging the economies of most OPEC members.

Saudi Arabia remained the world's largest exporter of oil, ensuring political support and profits from industrialized nations but not guaranteeing Saudi prosperity. Indeed, by the 1990s the Saudi economy had soured. Between 1980 and 2000 income levels fell by two-thirds, resulting in the cutting of government welfare benefits and climbing unemployment. Meanwhile, members of the royal family spent money lavishly and often violated Wahhabi restrictions with their high living abroad, cavorting in the nightclubs of Beirut and the casinos of Europe. Resentment of the royal family increased, as did dislike of the royal family's U.S. allies. Many Saudis oppose the U.S. military bases on Saudi soil, which symbolize U.S. support for the royal family and materialistic interest in the kingdom's oil. Seeing little future for themselves, frustrated young people often drink alcohol and have mixed-gender parties behind closed doors. In contrast, others have embraced militant Islam, a few joining terrorist groups such as Al Qaeda. Most of the young men who hijacked four U.S. airliners and crashed them into the Pentagon and World Trade Center in 2001 were Saudis, often well educated and from middle-class families. The Al Qaeda leader, Osama bin Laden (b. 1957), a militant Wahhabi from a large, wealthy Saudi family, had long raged against the presence of U.S. military bases in Saudi Arabia. Yet, Saudis also have been among the biggest investors in the U.S. and European economies, and many Saudis have studied in the West. Thanks to oil, Saudi Arabia and the industrialized nations,

OPEC (Organization of Petroleum Exporting Countries) A cartel formed in 1960 to give producers more power over the price of oil and leverage with the consuming nations.

especially the United States, have remained close allies despite vastly different social and political systems.

SECTION SUMMARY

■ After World War II, nationalist governments replaced many colonial regimes in the Middle East, but the region has failed to develop many working multiparty democracies.

■ Egyptian leader General Gamal Abdul Nasser became a hero when he threw off British influence, seized control of the Suez Canal, and pursued socialist policies, but neither Nasser nor his pro-American successors brought prosperity to Egypt.

■ Traumatized by the Holocaust, many Jews moved to Palestine after World War II and established the state of Israel, which led to a war between Jews and Arabs, a mass exodus of Palestinians into refugee camps, and enduring tensions.

■ After the 1967 Arab-Israeli War, Israel occupied lands with a large Arab population and severely limited their freedom, and, while Israelis debated how to achieve peace, Palestinians became increasingly militant in their opposition.

■ After nationalists overthrew the Iranian shah, the United States helped organize a coup that returned him to power and he ruled ruthlessly until 1979, when he was overthrown by Islamic fundamentalists.

■ From 1958 on, Iraq was ruled by ruthless military dictatorships dominated by the Sunni minority, and in 1979 Saddam Hussein came to power, launched a costly war against Iran, and then was attacked by the United States after invading Kuwait.

■ Saudi Arabia grew extremely wealthy from oil sales, but many citizens have remained poor, and Saudi society is dominated by extremely conservative religious leaders, some of whose followers resent the close relationship the Saudi royal family has forged with the United States.

✦ Change and Conflict in the Middle East

What roles has Islam played in the contemporary Middle East?

In 1979 the Islamic world celebrated thirteen centuries of Islamic history. For most of those centuries Muslims had made brilliant contributions to the world, fostering extensive trade networks, accommodating and introducing scientific knowledge, and founding powerful empires. By the nineteenth century, however, the European powers increasingly reconfigured the political and economic life of these societies, though the longer history and older traditions of Islam remained relevant into the present. Islamic societies also experienced social and cultural change. And new conflicts resulting from foreign interventions, Islamic militancy, and international terrorism unsettled the Middle East and world politics, reshaping the region's role in the global system.

Religion, Ethnicity, and Conflict

In parts of the Middle East ethnic and religious hostilities have fostered long-term conflict. In Lebanon, for example, a series of political crises and then a long civil war resulted from rivalry between a dozen rival factions, Christian and Muslim, for control of the small state and its resources. In this deeply fragmented land, a national government existed largely only in name during the 1970s and 1980s. Lebanon's main city, Beirut, once a prosperous, freewheeling mecca for trade, entertainment, and tourism, was devastated by factional fighting. Supporting various factions, Israel, Syria, and the United States were all sucked into the chronic conflict. Syria stationed troops in the north and east, and Israel did the same in the south. In the 1980s the United States intervened on behalf of a weak national government led by the largest, most pro-Western Christian faction. U.S. warships shelled areas around Beirut dominated by opposition, especially Shi'ite, factions while U.S. Marines secured the Beirut airport. The disastrous U.S. mission resulted in some five hundred U.S. deaths from suicide bombers and the holding of U.S. hostages. The intervention also made the United States a focus of Arab rage. In the 1990s the fighting ebbed, and Lebanon regained some stability but little national unity.

Elsewhere, in the Sudan, a huge country linking the Middle East and sub-Saharan Africa, the Arab Muslim-dominated government, which imposed an Islamic state, used military force to control the rebellious African Christians and animists in the south; this conflict resulted in 2 million deaths. In 2005 the two sides agreed to end the conflict, but by then the Arab-controlled Sudan government faced a rebellion in Darfur, an impoverished western region where African Muslim farmers competed for scarce land with Arab pastoralists. To regain control the government launched, with the aid of local Arab militias, a genocide against the Africans. Thousands of people died from military assaults on their villages or from disease and starvation after they fled, many into neighboring Chad.

Another longtime ethnic conflict concerned Kurds, a large ethnic group—over 20 million strong—inhabiting mountain districts in Iran, Iraq, Syria, and Turkey. Although deeply divided by clan and factional rivalries, Kurds had long sought either their own nation or self-government within their countries of residence. This desire brought them into constant conflict with central governments. Kurdish rebel groups were especially active in eastern Turkey, where the Turkish government, hoping to build a national identity based on Turkish identity and language, repressed Kurdish culture and language, banning Kurdish books, newspapers, and records. Kurds were also restless in oil-rich northern Iraq, where the dictator, Saddam Hussein, made Kurds a special target of his repression, launching military operations, including air raids and poison gas attacks, against Kurdish villages.

Gender Relations

Gender relations and family life have changed relatively little in the Middle Eastern societies. Although women have been elected prime ministers in the predominantly Muslim nations of Bangladesh, Pakistan, Indonesia, and Turkey, no Arab or Iranian women have reached this goal. In a few nations also, notably Turkey, Iraq, and Lebanon, urban women have expanded their economic opportunities by running businesses and entering the professions. But compared to women in the rest of the world, most Middle Eastern women remained in the home, often secluded from the outside world, with their lives as daughters, wives, and mothers controlled by the men of their families.

Male and female reformers have challenged women's subservient status for centuries, and a full-fledged feminist movement emerged in Egypt in the 1920s. Muslim liberals advocated improving women's lives through education, hence empowering them to change society. Turkey, Tunisia, and Iraq adopted Western-influenced family laws allowing civil marriages and divorce and according women rights in divorce and child custody. Blaming patriarchal cultural traditions rather than Islam for restrictions, some women activists argued that the Quran supported women's rights. Some women used such arguments to fight against controlling parents and spouses and to expand their options. But conservative Muslims opposed these liberal laws and prevented their enactment in other Middle Eastern societies. Devout women often opposed secular feminism, arguing that women were best protected by strict Islamic law, but this conservatism did not necessarily make them reluctant to become leaders and activists. For instance, Zainab Al-Ghazali (1917–2005) in Egypt founded an organization that built mosques, trained female preachers, and promoted an active women's role in public life; her staunch support of Islamic values upset not only liberal feminists but also Egypt's modernizing President Nasser, who had her jailed and tortured. The conflict between liberals and conservatives, modernizers and traditionalists, often resulted in gender role confusion, as an Egyptian writer noted: "Our mothers understood their situation. We, however, are lost. We do not know whether or not we still belong to the harem, whether love is forbidden or permitted."[4]

Liberal and conservative Muslims disagree on women's dress. Liberals sympathetic to modernization and feminism often see the veil as a symbol of female subjugation. Many women, especially from the urban middle and upper classes, have adopted Western dress. On the other hand, traditionalists have praised the veil as a part of female modesty. Since the 1960s, in secular nations such as Turkey and Egypt, women influenced by revivalist Islam have sparked political debates by lobbying to wear the veil or the less restrictive head scarf as a symbol of piety. This has been a major issue in Turkey, where the secular government, wary of Islamic militancy, has banned head scarves from schools. A young Egyptian reflected the views of many religious women who reject liberal views when she claimed that "being totally covered saves me from the approaches of men and hungry looks. I feel more free, purer, and more respectable."[5] Many independent-minded, well-educated Muslim women have not wanted to uncritically adopt Western ways. For instance, the liberal Moroccan sociologist and Quranic scholar Fatema Mernissi, a frequent visitor to the West who credited her illiterate grandmother's advice to travel with stimulating her curiosity about the world, argued that Western women face their own version of the veil through their obsession with physical appearance, which, she believed, limited their ability to compete with men for power: "I thank you, Allah, for sparing me the tyranny of the 'size six harem.' I am so happy that the conservative male elite [in the Middle East] does not know about it. Imagine the [Muslim] fundamentalists switching from the veil to forcing women to fit size 6."[6]

Attitudes toward homosexuality have generally become more repressive. For centuries Muslim societies often tolerated, although did not approve, homosexual activity, and writings sympathetically exploring homosexual experiences circulated widely. By the late nineteenth century this changed, forcing homosexuals into the closet. However, by the 1990s the taboo began to slowly diminish, at least in some cities. The strict gender segregation in countries such as Saudi Arabia, where people spend most of their time, and enjoy emotional bonds, with other people of the same sex and where touching and hand holding between friends of the same sex has been common for centuries, actually makes it easier for homosexual couples to escape notice. Yet, in many countries homosexual behavior, when discovered, frequently results in jail terms or even more severe punishments.

Religion and Culture

The clash between tradition and modernity in the Middle East has provided a fertile environment for creativity in religion, music, and literature. Islam has remained at the heart of Middle Eastern life, but, despite its message of peace, social justice, and community, it has often proved more divisive than unifying (see Map 30.2). Age-old divisions such as those between Sunni and Shi'a, liberal and conservative, secular and devout, Sufi and anti-Sufi, remain powerful, especially in western Asia. While many Middle Easterners have adopted a more conservative brand of Islam, musicians and writers often resist the trend toward puritanical practices and beliefs.

Varieties of Islam Antimodern, usually puritanical militants known as **Islamists**, who seek an Islamic state and are bitter rivals of secular Muslims, became increasingly influential, especially in Egypt, Algeria, Turkey, and Iran. Anti-Western revivalist groups such as the Muslim Brotherhood, founded in Egypt after World War I, spread around the region. The writings of the Iranian Ali Shariati (SHAR-ee-AH-tee) (1933–1977), educated in France but a critic of the West, influenced Shi'ites. He castigated Western democracy as

---

Islamists Antimodern, usually puritanical Islamic militants who seek an Islamic state.

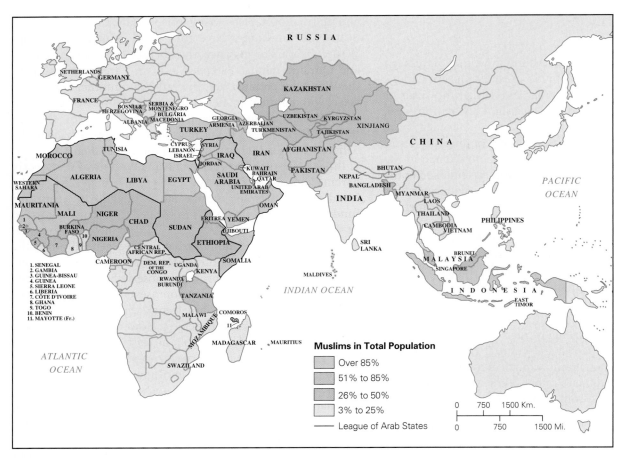

Map 30.2 The Islamic World
The Islamic world includes not only the Middle East—Western Asia and North Africa—but also countries with Muslim majorities in sub-Saharan Africa, Central Asia, and South and Southeast Asia. In addition, Muslims live in most other Eastern Hemisphere nations and in the Americas.

Online Study Center **Improve Your Grade** Interactive Map: Modern Islam, 2002

subverted by the power of money but also blamed Islamic tradition for reducing women to, as he put it, the level of a washing machine. Egyptian writer Sayyid Qutb (SIGH-eed ka-TOOB) (1906–1966) sparked political Sunni Islam and redefined *jihad* ("struggle") as violent opposition to the West rather than, as most Muslim thinkers had taught for centuries, personal struggle to maintain faith. Qutb lived in the United States for two years; he found Americans friendly but was appalled by the racism directed toward black Americans, as well as by the hedonism, such as heavy drinking and casual male-female romance, that he witnessed. Returning to Egypt, Qutb promoted an Islamic state and joined the militant Muslim Brotherhood. Inspired by thinkers like Qutb, the most extreme Islamists, known as *jihadists,* formed organizations that plotted violence against Muslims and non-Muslims they considered obstacles to imposing their rigid version of Islam.

While most people have rejected extremist groups, disillusionment with governments that repress opposition groups, dissatisfaction with lack of material improvement, and resentment of Western influence and world power have prompted a growing turn to Islam for moral support. When elections are allowed, Islamic groups with their large followings tend to tri-umph over secular parties, as happened in Iraq, Egypt, and Palestine in 2005, a reason why pro-Western modernists often fear democracy. In a troubled world the Islamic revival satisfies for millions a need for personal solace, a yearning for tradition, and a dream of a just political system as propounded by the earliest Muslims. During the past several decades Islamic influence has grown. For example, Islamic dress and practice became more common in Egypt after war losses to Israel, as well as in Iraq after the U.S. invasion of 2003, which overthrew Saddam Hussein and the secular Ba'athist government. These upheavals allowed local religious leaders to assert power. Shi'ite activists in Iraq have closed bars and harassed unveiled women, while Sunni militants attack followers of Sufi mysticism, which they view as heresy. Islamists in Algeria, Egypt, and Saudi Arabia have mounted movements aimed initially at challenging their governments; eventually, frustrated at home, they have become linked to international terrorist groups.

Music and Literature While Islamic militants have condemned music, dance, and other pleasures, many people—both the secular and the devout—have been fans of popular culture, especially popular music. While popular music has provided entertainment, the musicians often hope to encourage national unity or shape society, usually in a more liberal direction. Some musicians, among them the Egyptian singer Oum Kulthum (oom KAL-thoom) (1904–1975), have symbolized Arab people's feelings. Attracting a region-wide following with her emotional songs of abandonment and love, Kulthum dominated Middle Eastern popular music from the 1940s through the 1960s. At her height she was one of the two most popular figures among the Arabs all over the region, the other being her friend, Egypt's president Nasser. Her concerts attracted huge crowds and her recordings were always on the radio and in films. Popular music was also a unifying force that created a sense of community. Hence, the songs of peace and coexistence sung by hugely popular Lebanese singer Fairuz (fie-ROOZ) were sometimes credited with being the major symbol of hope in that turbulent, civil war–plagued land. Similarly Israelis revered Yemini-born Shoshana Damari (1923–2006), whose optimistic songs encouraged Israeli unity by extolling the nation and its military forces.

In religiously dogmatic or ethnically divided states, popular music has sometimes stirred controversy. The Islamic government of Iran, opposed to women performing in public, tried to silence all female singers, including especially the vocalist and film star Googoosh (GOO-goosh), whose melancholic Westernized pop music had a huge audience in Iran during the 1960s and 1970s. The clerics destroyed all the recordings, posters, and films they could locate, turning Googoosh into a popular symbol of opposition to clerical rule. Some music, such as the *arabesk* pop music of Turkey, which is rooted in the experiences of migrants to Istanbul from the country's largely Arabic- and Kurdish-speaking southeast, has derived from powerless subgroups. One observer noted that "arabesk describes a decaying city in which poverty-stricken migrant workers are exploited and abused, and calls on its listeners to pour another glass of wine and curse fate and the world."[7]

Some popular music styles blend Arab and foreign forms while addressing social problems. For example, the **rai** ("opinion") pop music of Algeria is based on local Bedouin chants, Spanish flamenco, French café songs, Egyptian pop, and other influences, and its improvised lyrics often deal with forbidden themes of sex and alcohol. By the 1970s synthesizers, drum machines, and electric guitars were added to the exciting mix. Rai holds great appeal to urban working-class youth in North Africa and to the offspring of Arab immigrants in France, but it is anathema to puritanical Islamic militants in Algeria, who have frequently forced singers into exile or even assassinated them. Rai musicians often move their base to Paris.

Middle Eastern writers have used their literature to express ideas forbidden in politics and religion. For instance, the novels of the Egyptian Naguib Mahfuz (nah-GEEB mah-FOOZ) (b. 1911), a merchant's son turned government official and

Arab Art The large monument of Revolution, in Baghdad, sculpted by a major modern Iraqi artist, Jawad Salim (1920–1961), occupies a central place in the city. Commissioned in 1958 after the overthrow of the monarchy, it celebrates the Iraqi struggle for justice and freedom and often provided a motif for Iraqi poets. (Monument to Revolution, Liberation Square, Baghdad. Artist: Jawad Salim)

journalist, have addressed social problems, such as poverty, and questioned conservative religious values and blind faith, which he believes keep individuals from realizing their full potential. Many of his writings have been banned in Egypt and other Islamic nations. But Mahfuz, strongly influenced by both Western and Arab writers, has achieved worldwide renown and in 1988 became the first Arab writer to win a Nobel Prize for literature. Iranian writers have often been anticlerical and have attacked religious hypocrisy. They have also risked punishment by satirizing the failings of governments and business. One famous Iranian novel recommended opportunism for career success: "Try to establish connections with the holders of high offices. Agree with everybody, no matter what his opinion is."[8]

---

rai ("opinion")   A pop music of Algeria based on local Bedouin chants, Spanish flamenco, French café songs, Egyptian pop, and other influences and featuring improvised lyrics that often deal with forbidden themes of sex and alcohol.

Turmoil in Afghanistan

Violence and extreme militant Islamic movements emerged in Afghanistan, fostering instability there for three decades. Afghanistan's diverse Muslim ethnic groups, further subdivided into rival tribes, have little sense of national unity in this landlocked land of harsh deserts and rugged mountains. From the early 1800s until 1978 kings from the largest ethnic group, the Pashtuns, loosely governed the territory. Some Afghan leaders advocated modernization, triggering revolts by conservative tribes. In 1978 pro-Communist generals seized power, forged close ties with the Soviet Union, and introduced radical social and economic reforms that challenged Islamic traditions. They implemented land reform, promoted women's education, and replaced Islamic law with a secular family law giving women more rights.

When conservative Islamic rebels, known as **mujahidin** ("holy warriors"), rebelled against the pro-Soviet regime, the Soviet Union invaded in 1979 to protect the regime, launching decades of turbulence. The mujahidin, while poorly armed and divided, won small victories against the 150,000 Soviet troops. Both sides resorted to ruthless brutality, attacking civilians suspected of aiding or supporting the enemy. Indiscriminate Soviet air attacks on the rebels created 5 million refugees and turned the population against the Soviet occupation. The United States, Pakistan, and Arab nations sent military and financial aid to the rebels, especially to extremist Pashtun factions, and Islamic volunteers such as the wealthy Saudi Osama bin Laden (b. 1957), a trained engineer turned Islamic militant. By the mid-1980s Afghanistan had become an unwinnable quagmire for the Soviet forces, which withdrew in 1989, a defeat which led to the ending of Soviet communism and the dismantling of the Soviet Empire. The pro-Soviet government collapsed, and rival mujahidin groups fought for control. With the USSR gone and the civil war over, the West offered little help to reconstruct the ruined country.

Afghanistan soon returned to global attention. As conflict between rival militias continued, a group of Pashtun religious students known as the **Taliban** ("Students"), many educated in Pakistan, organized a military force to impose order and stamp out what they considered immoral behavior, such as rape and drinking, among the tribal factions fighting each other to control the post-Soviet government. The Taliban conquered much of the Pashtun south and then seized the capital, Kabul, in 1996. Eventually they extended their influence into the north, where ethnic factions continued to resist the Taliban. The puritanical Taliban reversed the modernization of the pro-Soviet regime and introduced an especially harsh form of Islamic rule. Women in the capital, Kabul, who once wore jeans and T-shirts and attended universities, were now required to wear long black robes and stay at home. Education for women was banned and alcohol disappeared from stores. The Taliban banned pleasures such as music as sinful and executed people for even minor infractions. Under the Taliban the streets were safe but life offered no joy. Reflecting their intolerance and disdain for Afghanistan's pre-Islamic past, the Taliban also destroyed spectacular monumental Buddhas carved into a mountainside over a millennium ago, outraging the world.

International terrorist groups with a jihadist agenda and hatred for the West, especially for the United States, and for the Saudi royal family, began to form around Arab volunteers who had come originally to fight for the mujahidin cause and then, often facing jail in their own countries as radicals, remained. The Saudi Osama bin Laden became the leader and chief financial backer of the largest international terrorist group, Al Qaeda. Bin Laden called on Muslims to take up arms against the United States and other Western regimes, whom he called "crusaders" after those Christian knights who invaded the Middle East and fought Muslims during the Intermediate Era: "Tell the Muslims everywhere that the vanguards of the warriors who are fighting the enemies of Islam belong to them."[9] In the late 1990s these Islamic terrorist groups made Taliban-controlled Afghanistan their base, building camps to train more terrorists.

Islamic Militancy, Terrorism, and Western Interventions

The rise of international terrorism linked to Islamist groups and chiefly targeting Americans and Europeans soon resulted in a renewal of superpower intervention. After the Al Qaeda attacks on the United States in September 2001, the United States, with widespread world support, sent military forces into Taliban-ruled Afghanistan. Soon the United States and its allies among local anti-Taliban, mostly non-Pashtun groups, had displaced the Taliban, destroyed the Al Qaeda bases, and installed a fragile pro-Western government. Many Afghans and most Muslims outside Afghanistan, even in conservative Iran and Saudi Arabia, applauded the demise of the Taliban, but instability ensued in Afghanistan: tribal warlords controlled large territories; the major Taliban and Al Qaeda leaders, including bin Laden, evaded the U.S. troops and went into hiding; and the United States and western Europe struggled to foster development and support a fledgling democracy in a poor, largely tribal land. By 2005 a Taliban-led insurgency against the pro-Western regime was growing in strength.

The Afghan war was followed by a larger conflict in Iraq. Charging that Iraq's dictator, Saddam Hussein, had weapons of mass destruction and was linked to Al Qaeda, the U.S. president George W. Bush, supported chiefly by Britain, ordered an invasion and occupation of Iraq in 2003 without support from the United Nations, many Western allies, and regional allies such as Turkey and Egypt. Massive looting followed the quick U.S. victory, as museums, ancient historical sites, power plants,

---

mujahidin ("holy warriors")   Conservative Islamic rebels who rebelled against the pro-Soviet regime in Afghanistan in the 1970s and 1980s.

Taliban ("Students")   A group of Pashtun religious students who organized a military force in the 1980s to fight what they considered immorality and corruption and to impose order in Afghanistan.

others have been relatively open, even allowing some democratic choice among candidates for office. Some nations, such as Nigeria and Ghana, shifted back and forth between authoritarian military dictatorships and ineffective, corrupt civilian governments. Not all the despotic governments have brutally mistreated their own people, but some have become major violators of civil liberties and human rights. For example, during the 1970s in Uganda, then ruled by Idi Amin (EE-dee AH-meen) (1925–2004), a poorly educated former amateur boxing champion who rose to become a general, some 300,000 people suspected of opposing Amin were killed, and thousands more were jailed or fled into exile.

Western-style democracy has had little chance to flower in these artificial, multiethnic countries created by a colonialism that generally intensified ethnic hostilities. These countries typically have a tiny middle class and numerous poor people. And, given the deteriorating economic conditions of the past thirty years, governments have had little money to spend on containing ethnic tensions or for building schools, hospitals, and roads. Furthermore, the nationalist leaders and parties that have governed the new nations have often lost their credibility and mass support after a few years. For instance, Ghana's Kwame Nkrumah, once Africa's greatest hero, was overthrown for economic mismanagement and an autocratic governing style and died in exile.

African leaders have been a mixed lot. Some have been highly respected, farsighted visionaries, such as Tanzania's Julius Nyerere (NEE-ya-RARE-y) (g. 1962–1985) and Mozambique's Samora Machel (g. 1975–1986), and pragmatic problem solvers, such as South Africa's first black president, Nelson Mandela. While not all their initiatives have succeeded, they have used political office largely to improve society rather than enrich themselves. Others have disappointed or brutalized their people. Some, such as the Congo (Zaire) dictator Mobuto (g. 1965–1997) and the Nigerian military dictator Sani Abacha (g. 1993–1998), have been ruthless crooks, arresting or murdering opponents and plundering the public treasury to amass multibillion-dollar fortunes. When Abacha, hopped up on Viagra, died of a heart attack while he engaged in an orgy with prostitutes, few Nigerians lamented. Whether dictators or not, leaders have too often been reluctant to give up their power: even when their credibility has ended, they have rigged elections or had compliant parliaments declare them presidents for life.

Political instability, conflict, and social unrest have grown as people have struggled for their share of the dwindling pie. The blatant corruption, conspicuous consumption, and smuggling in government and the business sector have increased inequalities and deepened public frustrations. Sub-Saharan Africa has the world's highest rate of income inequality. In some countries, government officials have become known as "Mr. 10 Percent," a reference to the share of public budgets they grab. East Africans chastise the **wabenzi**—"people who

drive a Mercedes Benz"—a privileged urban class of politicians, high bureaucrats, professionals, military officers, and businessmen who manipulate their connections to amass wealth. Political, military, and business elites have often squandered scarce resources on importing luxuries, such as fancy cars and hard liquor, signs of the continuing hold of Western taste and consumer goods.

On the other hand, in some societies relations between governments and the governed have improved, offering wider participation in politics. New grassroots and other nongovernmental organizations have worked for issues such as human rights and the environment. Ordinary people, especially women, have demanded and sometimes gained greater responsibility for improving their lives. For example, by 2000 some 25,000 local women's groups in Kenya had pushed for improved rights and other issues of interest to women, such as environmental protection. The Kenyan women's rights and environmental activist, Wangari Maathai (wan-GAHR-ee MAH-thai), won the Nobel Peace Prize in 2005 (see Chapter 26). Since few Africans can afford health insurance, in countries such as Senegal poor people have come together to form small mutual health organizations, negotiating with local clinics to get an affordable group rate for health care. Strong support from women voters helped Liberian economist Ellen Johnson-Sirleaf (b. 1939), a Harvard-trained banker and former United Nations official admired by Liberians as tender but also tough, become the first woman president in Africa in 2005, as the country sought to recover from a long civil war and then a corrupt dictatorship. But she faced a monumental challenge to bring progress and stability to a maimed nation with no piped water or electric grid and few functioning schools and hospitals.

Political Violence The combination of artificial boundaries, weak national identity, and economic collapse has produced chronic turmoil in several African nations, resulting in what one discouraged African observer called the dark night of bloodshed and death. For example, Liberia and Sierra Leone, once among the more stable countries, disintegrated in the 1990s as ethnic-based rebel groups challenged their country's government for power. In both countries thousands fled the slaughter and the maiming of civilians, causing larger African nations like Nigeria to send in troops to bring stability. In drought-plagued Somalia, when longtime military rule collapsed in 1991, the country divided into regions ruled by feuding Somali clans with their own armies. As the Somali economy disintegrated, causing thousands to starve to death, the United Nations dispatched a humanitarian mission. But some Americans in the United Nations force were killed and the United Nations withdrew in 1994, unable to achieve a unified government. While the fighting lessened, Somalia remained a country in name only, controlled by warlords.

Sometimes hatreds have led to genocide, killing directed at eliminating a particular group. This happened in the small, impoverished, and densely populated state of Rwanda, most of whose population belonged to the majority Hutu and minority Tutsi ethnic groups. The German and then the Belgian colonizers had ruled through Tutsi kings. Soon after independence, the

---

wabenzi ("people who drive a Mercedes Benz") A privileged urban class in Africa of politicians, high bureaucrats, professionals, military officers, and businessmen who manipulate their connections to amass wealth.

Hutu rebelled against the Tutsi-dominated government, slaughtering thousands of Tutsi and forcing others out of the country. Those Tutsi who remained faced discrimination and repression. In 1994 the extremist Hutu government in Rwanda began a genocide against the remaining Tutsi and moderate Hutus, murdering over 500,000 people. Tutsi exiles based in Uganda then invaded Rwanda, forcing the Hutu leadership and its followers into the neighboring Congo. Over 2 million Hutu fled. The new Tutsi-led government continued to face militant Hutu resistance groups based in the Congo, leading to Rwandan military incursions into the Congo.

Nigeria: Hopes and Frustrations

The hopes and frustrations of contemporary Africa are mirrored in Nigeria, which in 2005 was home to some 130 million people, about a fifth of Africa's total population. Nigeria's ethnic diversity and natural wealth have been both a blessing and a curse. Like many African countries, Nigeria contains an extraordinary variety of ethnic groups, languages, religions, artistic traditions, and even ecologies. While some 250 ethnic groups live in Nigeria, about two-thirds of the people belong to the Hausa-Fulani, Igbo (Ibo), or Yoruba groups. Nigeria's oil wealth has brought income—80 percent of the nation's total revenues—but has also corrupted politics and increased social inequality.

Nigeria's history has frequently been punctuated by coups, countercoups, riots, political assassinations, and civil war rooted in regional and ethnic rivalries. Between 1967 and 1970 Nigeria endured a bloody civil war to prevent the secession of the Igbo-dominated and oil-rich southeast region. The religious divide between Christians, who dominate the south, and Muslims, who control the northern states, has also complicated politics. Following a Muslim revival among the Hausa-Fulani, northern states have often imposed strict Islamic law, antagonizing non-Muslims. Several Muslim women were sentenced to death by stoning for adultery while the men involved were not punished, causing an outcry in Nigeria and around the world. Sometimes severe Christian-Muslim fighting has broken out for control of religiously mixed cities or districts, causing the death of hundreds of people. The numerous destabilizing factors have often led to corrupt military rule, which brought stability by suppressing opposition but pushed the people hard, alternating with periods of corrupt civilian democracy, which increased political freedom but often caused ineffective government.

The Nigerian oil industry, while creating some prosperity, has also made Nigeria dependent on oil exports and spawned political and economic problems. A few politicians, bureaucrats, and businessmen have monopolized oil profits, fostering corruption, sometimes outright plunder of public wealth, and the inequitable wealth distribution resented by many Nigerians. By 2005 the top 20 percent of Nigerians received 56 percent of all the country's wealth while the bottom 20 percent got only 4.4 percent. People living in the southern districts producing the oil see few jobs or other benefits and watch sullenly as pipelines through their villages move oil to the coastal ports, from where tankers carry most of the oil to consumers in Europe and North America. Their sporadic protests, including sabotage of the oil pipelines, have been met with military force; protest leaders are accused of treason and sometimes executed. Disenchanted Nigerians refer to a "republic of the privileged and rich" and a "moneytocracy." Oil money created high expectations in the 1970s, but the economic boom turned to bust in the 1980s when world oil prices collapsed, increasing economic hardship and social unrest and forcing the nation to take on massive foreign debt to pay its bills. Nigeria's per capita income declined by three-quarters between 1980 and 1993.

In addition to the ethnic divisions and economic inequality, the debate about whether Nigeria should seek to adopt Western political, economic, and cultural models or attempt to retain its own indigenous traditions has never abated. The Nigerian writer Mabel Segun (SAY-goon) beautifully expressed the cultural dilemma in her poem "Conflict":

> Here we stand, Infants overblown, Poised between two civilizations [Europe and Africa], Finding the balance irksome, Itching for something to happen, To tip us one way or the other. Groping in the dark for a helping hand, And finding none. I'm tired of hanging in the middle way—But where can I go.[14]

The New South Africa

Another large country, South Africa, experienced conflict and inequality for over three centuries. From World War II to the early 1990s South Africa remained the last bastion of institutionalized white racism on a continent where white rule had once been widespread. The white population, some 15 percent of the total and divided between an Afrikaner majority (descendants of Dutch settlers) and an English minority, ruled the black majority (74 percent) and the Indians (2 percent) and mixed-descent Coloreds (9 percent). Aided by a ruthless police security system, the result was a nearly unparalleled cruelty, a chilling juxtaposition of comfort for whites and despair for blacks. Before things rapidly changed in the 1990s, the authoritarian government rendered public protest of any type dangerous.

Apartheid Society South African racial inequality and white supremacy, in place for several centuries, became more systematic after 1948, when Afrikaner nationalists won the white-only elections and declared full independence from Britain. A top nationalist leader claimed: "We [whites] need [Africans] because they work for us but they can never claim political rights. Not now, nor in the future."[15] Their new policy, **apartheid** (uh-PAHRT-ate) ("separate development"), set up a police state to enforce racial separation and passed laws requiring all Africans to carry ID ("pass") cards specifying the locations where they could legally reside or visit.

---

apartheid ("separate development") A South African policy to set up a police state to enforce racial separation.

Interracial marriage and sexual relations were also outlawed. The lives of nonwhites were controlled to a degree inconceivable in most other countries.

Apartheid expanded segregation to include designated residential areas, schools, recreational facilities, and public accommodations. Urban black men were commonly housed in crowded dormitories near the mines or factories where they worked or, often with their families, in shantytown suburbs of major cities, from where they commuted to their jobs. While white families usually lived comfortably in well-furnished apartments or houses with spacious yards and swimming pools, a typical house in Soweto, a dusty African suburb of Johannesburg, was bleak, with the residents using candles or gas lamps for lighting. Only a quarter of the Soweto houses had running water and perhaps fifteen in one hundred enjoyed electricity. Demoralized blacks, especially men, found escape in alcohol, frequenting the informal bars that dotted African urban neighborhoods.

Apartheid also created what white leaders called tribal homelands, known as **bantustans**, rural reservations where black Africans were required to live if they were not needed in the modern economy. The system allocated whites 87 percent of the nation's land and nonwhites the other 13 percent. Every year thousands of Africans were forcibly resettled to the impoverished bantustans, which contained too little fertile land and too few jobs and services, such as hospitals and secondary schools. Infant mortality rates in the bantustans were among the world's highest. Under this system black families were fractured as men and women were recruited on annual contracts for jobs outside the bantustans. Even if a husband and wife were both recruited for jobs in the same city, they could not legally visit each other if their ID cards restricted each of them to a different city neighborhood.

Rich in strategic minerals such as gold, diamonds, uranium, platinum, and chrome, South Africa became the most industrialized nation on the continent. But the wealth and its benefits were monopolized by the white minority. While whites enjoyed one of the world's highest standards of living, with access to well-funded schools and medical centers, Africans and also the Colored and Indian minorities enjoyed few benefits from the system. Spending on health, literacy, and education was imbalanced. Whites controlled over two-thirds of the nation's wealth and personal disposable income. By 1994 the ratio of average black to white incomes stood at 1:10, the most inequitable income distribution in the world. African unemployment reached 33 percent. Nonetheless, because of the country's mineral wealth and extensive foreign investment, the South African government enjoyed the open or tacit support of several powerful industrialized countries, including the United States, Britain, and Japan, who feared that unrest or black majority rule might threaten their billions in investments and access to lucrative resources.

bantustans Rural reservations in South Africa where black Africans under apartheid were required to live if they were not needed in the modern economy.

Despite the repression, Africans resisted and often paid a price for their defiance. South African leaders forged the world's leading police state, with the world's highest rate of execution and brutal treatment of dissidents. Among the victims was Stephen Biko (1946–1977), a former medical student who led an organization that encouraged black pride and self-reliance. Biko was beaten to death in police custody. Hundreds of Africans were arrested each day for "pass law" violations and held for a few days or weeks before being released. For example, a mineworker might be arrested for visiting his wife who was a live-in maid in a white household a few miles away. The police violently repressed protests and imprisoned thousands of dissidents, including numerous children, often without trial. Death squads of off-duty policemen sometimes assassinated black leaders, such as Victoria Mxenge (ma-SEN-gee), a lawyer who defended anti-apartheid activists. Defying the government, strikes, work interruptions, and sabotage became common. Resistance was often subtle, too; Nobel prize–winning white South African novelist Nadine Gordimer (b. 1923), a longtime critic of apartheid, described in her novel, *Something Out There*, how even domestic servants in white households could protest and assert their dignity in nonverbal ways:

> Every household in the fine suburb had several black servants—a shifting population of pretty young housemaids whose long red nails and pertness not only asserted the indignity of being undiscovered fashion models but kept hoisted a cocky guerrilla pride against servitude to whites.[16]

The African National Congress (ANC), long a voice for nonviolent resistance, emerged as the major opposition organization. The ANC remained multiracial, with some whites, Coloreds, and Indians serving in its leadership. In 1955, despairing of peaceful protest, a more militant ANC leadership had framed its inclusive vision in the Freedom Charter: "South Africa belongs to all who live in it, black and white."[17] But the ANC was declared illegal and government repression forced it underground, where it adopted a policy of violent resistance and trained young South Africans in exile how to use weapons. Several of its main leaders, including Nelson Mandela (man-DEL-uh) (b. 1918), spent as many as thirty years in prison for their political activities (see Profile: Nelson and Winnie Mandela, South African Freedom Fighters). Women, among them Mandela's wife, Winnie Mandela, played an influential role in the ANC, often, like the men, facing arrest and mistreatment.

Postapartheid Society

Ultimately, moderation and realism in both the ANC and the ruling National Party brought a more just and democratic society. International isolation, economic troubles, the increasing incompatibility between apartheid's restrictions and a need for more highly skilled black workers, and growing black unrest forced the government to relax apartheid and release Mandela from prison. The two parties agreed on a new constitution requiring "one man, one vote." In 1994 an amazed

NELSON AND WINNIE MANDELA,
SOUTH AFRICAN FREEDOM FIGHTERS

Courageous symbols of unbroken black determination, Nelson Mandela (b. 1918) and Winnie Mandela (b. 1934) made a mark on history in the struggle against apartheid, South Africa's policy of rigid racial separation, despite severe white supremacist repression. The inspirational Mandelas represented African ambitions for several generations.

Nelson Mandela was born in the Transkei reserve near South Africa's southeast coast, the son of a Xhosa (KHO-sa) chief. His middle name, Rolihlahla (ROH-lee-la-la), meant "troublemaker." Mandela was groomed to succeed his father as chief, but, after years of hearing stories about the valor of his ancestors in war, he wanted to help with the freedom struggle. After attending a Methodist school and then earning a B.A. from the only college for black South Africans, he qualified as a lawyer and opened the country's first black legal practice. He also joined the African National Congress (ANC), which had, for half a century, followed a policy of promoting education for blacks and cautiously criticizing rather than confronting the government. Mandela and his young colleagues transformed the ANC into an activist mass movement. In 1958 he married Winnie Madikizela (MAH-dee-kee-ZEH-la), a Xhosa nurse, but they had only a short life together before political repression separated them.

The white government tolerated little opposition. In 1960, after police opened fire on 20,000 peaceful black protesters, killing 69 of them (including women and children), the government banned the ANC and arrested black leaders. The ANC then became an underground movement committed to violence. In 1964, found guilty of sabotage and treason, Mandela was sentenced to life in prison. In his stirring statement to the court, Mandela articulated his goals: "During my lifetime I have dedicated myself to this struggle of the African people. I have fought against [both] white and black domination. I have cherished the ideal of a democratic and free society in which all persons live together in harmony and with equal opportunities. It is an ideal for which I am prepared to die."

Mandela spent most of the next three decades in the notorious Robben Island prison off Cape Town, where he was joined by dozens of other ANC leaders and members. He turned the prison experience into an ANC school, leading political discussions and studying other freedom fighters, such as Mohandas Gandhi and Jawaharlal Nehru in India. Over the years Mandela grew into an international hero. During his imprisonment, although jailed for a short time herself and then confined to a remote settlement, Winnie Mandela kept her husband's flame burning, gaining an international reputation as a freedom fighter. Returning to Johannesburg in 1985, Winnie campaigned ceaselessly for black rights and her husband's release, earning a reputation for courage and skill in negotiating a male-dominated society.

In 1990, after secret negotiations, a realistic new South African president, F. W. de Klerk, legalized the ANC and released Nelson Mandela from prison. In 1993 Nelson Mandela and de Klerk shared a Nobel Peace Prize. In 1994 the first all-race elections made Nelson Mandela the first black president of South Africa. At his inauguration, he told the people: "Out of the experience of an extraordinary human disaster that lasted too long must be born a society of which all humanity will be proud. Let there be justice [and] peace for all. We must act together as a united people, for the birth of a new world. God bless Africa!"

Forgiving and pragmatic, Mandela remained popular with most South Africans, white and black. His moderate, accommodationist style reassured whites but also disappointed some impatient blacks. Meanwhile his marriage to Winnie became strained, in part because of her controversial activities, legal problems, and political ambitions. Her popularity declined after 1988 when bodyguards she hired to protect her from

world saw white supremacy come to an end in the first all-race elections in South African history, which installed Mandela as president and gave the ANC two-thirds of the seats in Parliament.

The ANC government enjoyed massive goodwill but has also faced daunting challenges in healing a deeply fragmented society while restoring the pride and spirits of African communities destabilized by apartheid. Mandela worked to find the right mix of racial reconciliation and major changes to benefit the disadvantaged black majority. In 1999 Mandela left office, a still popular figure, and the ANC retained power in free elections. It improved services, such as electricity and water, in black communities, raised black living standards, and created opportunities for Africans, fostering a growing black upper and middle class. Yet millions of other blacks have felt neglected, wanting better land and services and complaining about corruption and mismanagement at the local level. Crime has rapidly increased, violent protests have broken out, and black unemployment has remained high, prompting some blacks to leave the ANC and join opposition parties, some of them also having many white supporters. South Africa has one of the world's highest rates of HIV/AIDS, with some 5 million South Africans infected. Nonetheless, given the long history of repression and fear, the rapid transition to multiparty democracy has been impressive. South Africa has become the model of progress for sub-Saharan Africa, and people all over the continent hope that the nation succeeds in healing racial wounds while spreading the benefits of its wealth to all its citizens.

Nelson Mandela A symbol of black South African aspirations for nearly thirty years in prison, Mandela led the African National Congress after his release and, in 1994, was elected the nation's first black president. (Corbis)

black and white foes were implicated in the kidnapping and murder of a black youth; Winnie herself was convicted of involvement in the kidnapping, but her sentence was commuted. In 1996 Nelson and Winnie Mandela divorced. Winnie remained active in the ANC, supporting a militant faction that mistrusted Nelson's conciliatory policy of bringing white and black South Africans together. Nelson later married Grace Machel, the widow of the respected Mozambique president Samora Machel, who had been killed in an airplane crash.

In 1991, at the age of eighty-one, Mandela voluntarily retired from politics and moved to his native village. In his autobiography, he wrote, "I have walked a long road to freedom. I have tried not to falter, I have made missteps along the way. After climbing a great hill, one only finds that there are many more hills to climb. With freedom come responsibilities. I dare not linger, for my long walk is not yet ended." The long walk taken by Nelson and Winnie Mandela changed history.

THINKING ABOUT THE PROFILE

1. Why did the Mandelas become international symbols of the freedom struggle?
2. How did the Mandelas change history?

Note: Quotations from Kevin Shillington, *History of Africa*, rev. ed. (New York: St. Martin's, 1995), p. 405; and Nelson Mandela, *Long Walk to Freedom: The Autobiography of Nelson Mandela* (Boston: Little, Brown, 1996), pp. 620, 625.

SECTION SUMMARY

- European colonial rulers had played rival ethnic groups in Africa against each other, but after World War II, pressures for independence became stronger and Ghana, under the leadership of Kwame Nkrumah, became the first colony to achieve independence.
- Most British colonies attained independence through peaceful means, but Kenya's transition was long and violent, as was that of the Belgian Congo, Angola, Guinea-Bissau, Mozambique, and Zimbabwe.
- After independence, many African nations were ruled by military dictatorships or corrupt civilians, many nationalist leaders lost favor over time, the gap between rich and poor widened, and some nations experienced ongoing violence, disorder, and genocide.
- Nigeria, home to rival ethnic and religious groups, has experienced civil war, coups, and corrupt military rule, and while its oil reserves have brought wealth to the elite, they have hardly benefited the poor, and dependence on them led to economic problems in the 1980s.
- Under apartheid, a white minority in South Africa viciously suppressed the black majority with laws restricting their political, economic, and physical freedom, but the African National Congress, led by Nelson Mandela, resisted fiercely and ultimately won control of the government in 1994.

Changing African Economies, Societies, and Cultures

What new economic, social, and cultural patterns have emerged in Africa?

In the decades since the 1960s, for many sub-Saharan African nations, achieving economic development and true independence has seemed a desperate struggle rather than an exhilarating challenge. African nations have tried various strategies to generate development to benefit the majority of people, but no strategy has proved effective over the long term. Economic problems have proliferated. But Africans have created new social and cultural forms to aid them in dealing with their political and economic problems.

Economic Change and Underdevelopment

Africa has experienced severe economic problems. As during colonial times, Africans have mostly supplied agricultural and mineral resources, such as cocoa and copper, to the global economy, but this has not brought widespread wealth. For example, in Kenya, small farmers encouraged to abandon subsistence food growing and take up tobacco planting found that their new crops brought in little money, required cutting down adjacent forests, and leached nutrients from the soil. In 2004 one of the farmers, Jane Chacha, who still lived in the same two-room, mud-and-thatch house she and her husband built fifteen years earlier, complained that "this is a hopeless dream. Growing tobacco has been nothing but trouble."[18]

Only a few countries have enjoyed consistently robust economic growth, been able to escape reliance on producing one or two resources, or substantially raised living standards. With a few exceptions, nations have fostered economic growth but little economic development that benefits the majority of people. Sub-Saharan Africa contained nineteen of the world's twenty poorest countries in 2004. With over 670 million people (almost 13 percent of the world population) by 2004, this region accounts for only 1 percent of the world's production of goods and services, about the same as one of the smallest European nations, Belgium, with 10 million people. Most sub-Saharan African countries have annual per capita incomes of under $1,000 per year, and some are under $500. Half of the people live in poverty, earning less than $1 per day, the highest rate of poverty in the world. Sub-Saharan Africa has also had the world's highest infant mortality rates and lowest literacy rates and average life expectancies.

The economic doldrums have been linked to other problems. The region's economies have generally grown by 1 to 2 percent a year, but its population increase is the world's highest, over 3 percent. Since 10 to 15 percent of babies die before their first birthday, parents have had an incentive to have many children to provide for old-age security. At current rates the population will double to 1.3 billion by 2025, but new jobs, classrooms, and food supplies will not keep pace. Only a few nations have enjoyed self-sufficiency in food production; most require food imports from Europe and North America. Women grow the bulk of the food, but the male farmers growing cash crops for export receive most of the government aid. Millions of Africans, perhaps a third of them children, are chronically malnourished, and as a result often have permanent brain damage. Several million children die each year from hunger-related ailments. Severe drought and the drying up of water sources is a chronic problem in many regions, resulting in numerous deaths from dehydration or starvation or in migration in search of a better life. Less than half of school-age children attend school, while millions of others work in the labor force. Many rural schools lack toilets for girls, discouraging their attendance. As a result, some 25 million girls receive no elementary education. Poverty means scraping by, physically and mentally exhausted by the struggle for survival. Many people face joblessness; for example, half of Kenya's secondary school graduates could not find paid work in the 1990s.

To achieve economic development, Africans have sought viable economic strategies. What scholars term "neocolonial capitalism," because it involved close economic ties to the Western nations and free markets of some sort, became the most common development model. The countries following this model favored the cash crops and minerals that had dominated the colonial economy, often at the expense of food production, and welcomed western European and U.S. investment and economic advice. Westerners, especially British and French, have managed or owned a substantial portion of the economies.

A few countries prospered with this strategy, at least for a awhile, but the political consequences were often negative. Ivory Coast (or Côte d'Ivoire) and Kenya were among the most hospitable to a Western presence, and in the 1960s and 1970s this policy paid off with high rates of growth and rising incomes. Ivory Coast remained a major exporter of coffee and cocoa, while Kenya, with world famous game parks, lived from tourism and the export of coffee, tea, and minerals. By the mid-1980s both had per capita incomes about double the African average. That success came at some cost, however. For example, the Ivory Coast timber industry rapidly cut down the once verdant rain forest, causing less rain. In addition, close relations with France resulted in more French living there by the 1990s than during colonial times, and the French and other non-Ivoreans owned most of the economy. But the successes also proved short-lived. Both countries eventually became one-party states that, while stable, grew despotic. Well-placed leaders plundered the economies. While the glittering major cities, Abidjan and Nairobi, had fancy restaurants, boutiques, and nightclubs, some rural people faced starvation. By the late 1990s, as world prices for coffee and cocoa collapsed, the economies experienced increasing stress, protesters demanded more democracy, the delicate ecologies became dangerously unbalanced, and crime rates soared. Economic development became a fading memory. By the early 2000s Ivory Coast was engulfed in civil war, while Kenyans had forced out a dictator and elected a reformist government that has failed to fulfill its promises to end corruption and maintain press freedom.

The most disastrous example of neocolonial capitalism was the Democratic Republic of the Congo (known as Zaire between 1971 and 1997). A huge country, with 60 million people, Congo enjoys a strategic location in the center of Africa, rich mineral resources, and good land. But it became Africa's biggest failure. Over the years the United States and Belgium poured billions of investment and aid into the Congo to keep President Mobuto Sese Seko in power. To the Congolese, however, Mobuto was unforgivingly corrupt, looting the treasury and foreign aid to amass a huge personal fortune—some 4 to 5 billion dollars—while repressing his opponents. Mobuto built palaces for himself all over the country and in Europe and hired top chefs from France to prepare his food, meanwhile spending little money on schools, roads, telephones, and hospitals. As a result of neglect, the Congo suffered one of the world's highest infant mortality rates, limited health care, and widespread malnutrition. In 1998 a long-festering rebellion gained strength, forcing Mobuto into exile, where he died. Rebels took over, but they have done little to foster democracy or development. The Congo was soon fragmented in civil war and interethnic fighting, and rebel groups controlled large sections of the sprawling country. Nearly 4 million Congolese died from the fighting and its side effect, the collapse of medical care, between 1998 and 2004, causing a humanitarian crisis.

The most recent showcases for economic success have been Ghana and Botswana. Once a symbol of failure, Ghana has made steady progress. For several decades after Kwame Nkrumah lost power the country had experienced a roller coaster of corrupt civilian governments interspersed with military regimes. In the 1990s the leaders gradually strengthened democracy and adopted certain policies of the Asian Little Dragons, such as Taiwan and South Korea, by mixing capitalism and socialism. Ghana became increasingly prosperous: by 2000 it enjoyed one of the continent's highest annual per capital incomes, $1,600, and a life expectancy of fifty-seven. Investment in schools resulted in one of Africa's most educated populations. Beginning as a failure like Ghana, Botswana, when it gained independence in 1966, exported nothing, was one of the world's poorest countries, and had an annual per capita income of $35. Gradually, however, using ethnic traditions as a foundation, Botswanans carved out a successful democracy; the economy, health care, education, and protection of resources all steadily improved, despite deadly droughts. By 2000 Botswanans had fostered living standards higher than those of most African and many Middle Eastern, Asian, and Latin American societies, boasting an annual per capita income of over $3,000, an economy growing by 11 percent a year, and a literacy rate of 70 percent. Unfortunately, the AIDs epidemic, which hit Botswana particularly hard, rapidly undermined economic and health gains.

African Socialisms

To foster development, some African nationalists have pursued revolutionary or reformist strategies. They have concluded that the political and economic institutions inherited from colonialism, such as large Western-owned businesses and plantations, could not spark economic development, since they were implanted to transfer wealth and resources to the West rather than to benefit Africans. After independence more wealth still flowed out of Africa than into it, and the disparity has increased every year. The radicals argued that, to empower Africans, it was necessary to reduce the colonial state to ashes and replace it with something entirely new.

Various social revolutionary regimes emerged from the long wars of liberation against entrenched colonial or white minority governments. Some Africans looked toward communist-ruled China or the USSR for inspiration. Marxist revolutionary governments came to power in Angola and Mozambique after the Portuguese left, but they struggled to implement socialism. To counter these governments, the white-ruled South African state sponsored opposition guerrilla movements, aided by a U.S. government wanting to overturn Marxist regimes, that kept these countries in civil war for several decades. During Angola's long civil war, over 1.5 million people died. Leaders on both sides exploited natural resources for their own gain. While the war eventually ended, Angola, blessed with coffee, oil, diamonds, and other minerals but plagued with corruption, still struggled to foster development. The civil war in Mozambique, one of the world's poorest nations, resulted in 1 million deaths and 5 million refugees. Since its war came to an end in 1992, the pragmatic Marxist leaders introduced free multiparty elections and liberalized the economy, raising the per capita income to $1,200.

One social revolutionary state, Zimbabwe, the former British colony of Southern Rhodesia, at first became Africa's biggest success story. The Marxist-influenced government, led by the liberation hero Robert Mugabe, a schoolteacher turned lawyer, proved pragmatic for over a decade, respecting democratic processes and human rights, encouraging the white minority to stay, and trying to raise living standards and opportunities for black Zimbabweans. The country became one of the few food-exporting nations on the continent. Zimbabwe eventually faced severe problems, however, including tensions between rival African ethnic groups. Continuing white ownership of the best farmland produced resentment among land-hungry blacks. During the 1990s Mugabe, succumbing to the allure of power and wealth, became more dictatorial and used land disputes to divide the nation. As his support among both whites and Africans waned, he rigged elections, harassed or jailed his opponents, and ordered the seizure of white-owned farms. By 2005 commercial agriculture had collapsed, the country was gripped by drought, life expectancy had dropped sharply, and Mugabe's police had demolished the homes and shops of poor blacks who favored the opposition, driving them out of the cities. The nation, once one of Africa's most promising, veered toward catastrophe.

Another African nation, Tanzania, experimented with a socialism compatible with African traditions, especially cooperation and mutual sharing of resources. Under its visionary president, Julius Nyerere (1922–1999), Tanzania opted for "African socialism," based on local traditions, which reorganized agriculture into cooperative villages and devoted resources to education and social services, with the goal of achieving local and national self-sufficiency. Nyerere encouraged some democracy in his one-party state by holding regular elections and allowing multiple candidates—all members of the ruling party—to run for each office or parliamentary seat. Nyerere's emphasis on building and funding schools and clinics improved literacy to 68 percent and health to well above African norms.

But Nyerere's dreams were dashed as the government became overly bureaucratic, the planning proved inadequate, and people often lost enthusiasm for socialism. Because Tanzania imported few luxury goods, life was austere compared to that available to affluent city residents in neighboring capitalist Kenya. Peasants often preferred their small family farms and individual effort to the collective villages they were encouraged, or forced, to join. As the economy slumped, Tanzania had to take more foreign loans. Tanzania's African socialism had produced as many failures as successes, and Nyerere, still admired by his people, retired in 1985, one of the few founding African leaders to voluntarily give up power. Nyerere's successors dismantled much of the socialist structure, promoted free enterprise, welcomed foreign investment and loans, and fostered a multiparty system and respect for civil liberties. Yet life for most Tanzanians has improved little, malnutrition has become widespread, and Tanzania remains a poor nation.

Cities, Families, and Gender

Modern Africa has seen rapid social change. Since the 1940s, more people have lived in cosmopolitan cities where traditional and modern attitudes meet, mix, and clash. Cities have grown rapidly. However difficult, city life offers more variety—jobs, department stores, movie theaters, nightclubs—than village life and so attracts rural people. While some older, precolonial cities have remained centers of trade and tourism, they have been largely eclipsed as economic centers and the seats of government by the cities that developed under colonial auspices, such as Nairobi (Kenya), Lagos (Nigeria), and Dakar (Senegal), which have grown nearly 5 percent a year since 1980. Between 1965 and 2000 the percentage of sub-Saharan Africans living in urban areas doubled, from 14 to 30 percent. But people concentrate in one or two key cities for each country. Hence, Abidjan in Ivory Coast and Luanda in Angola each contain a quarter of their country's population. With their modern office towers, theaters, and shopping centers, cities have become the centers for political and economic power as well as for cultural creativity and social change.

Cities have grown so fast that services such as buses, water, power, police, schools, and health centers cannot meet the needs of their populations. These problems are exemplified by Nigeria's largest city, Lagos, which grew from less than a million in 1965 to a megalopolis of some 10 million by 2000. A journalist described the urban chaos:

Lagos is a vast laboratory of helter-skelter expansion, a fount of confusion and frenzy. A tiny minority of people live extremely well, in villas or plush apartments, and they go to work in gleaming skyscrapers that sit awkwardly next to traditional marketplaces. A vastly larger number of people live in appalling slums, where open sewers may run under disintegrating floorboards. The traffic jam, or "go-slow," is a fact of life. Much of the everyday commerce occurs in this city through the windows of cars, trucks, and other vehicles.[19]

Social changes have been numerous. Interethnic mixing, even marriage, has become more common. Neighborhoods have developed their own slang, hairstyles, music, dance, art, and poetry. They forge their own institutions such as bars, churches, football (soccer) leagues, labor unions, women's clubs, and student movements. Many of these are voluntary associations that help migrants adjust by creating a new community to replace the village left behind. Small traders set up shop along the sidewalks, hawking everything from food and drinks to cheap clothes, religious items, and music cassettes. Sports has become a major activity. Various African nations have enjoyed international football success, and Ethiopians and Kenyans have dominated long-distance running in the Olympic Games. Africans have also played in the U.S. National Basketball Association and the National Football League.

The family, while remaining the primary social unit, has also changed. The extended family of the villages declined in the cities and was often replaced by the smaller nuclear family. Individualism increasingly challenged the communalism of the village tradition, where marriages were largely arranged by elders. In the cities, young people often arrange their own marriages, and love has become a major criterion for selecting a spouse. Traditionally village men had an economic incentive to take more than one wife, since women did most of the routine farm work, especially the planting, weeding, and harvesting of food crops that ensured family survival and gave rural women economic status. With no farming option, however, urban women have lost economic status and men no longer need several wives. Men enjoy more educational opportunities than women and hence dominate the remunerative wage labor in business and transportation. Sometimes governments erected barriers against women in the economy. Hence, President Mobuto in the Congo stressed an authoritarian male model and discouraged women from seeking paid work, and in the 1980s Nigeria's military regime blamed market women for high prices, raiding their stalls and beating them.

Gender roles have changed as women have become more independent and a growing number served in governments and parliaments. Indeed, sub-Saharan Africa ranks ahead of the rest of the developing world in the percentage of women (16 percent) in legislative positions. While women are educationally disadvantaged compared to men, some women use their skills to good advantage, achieving such positions as politicians, professors, lawyers, and company heads. For example, the Kenyan Grace Ogot (OH-got) (b. 1930) served in parliament while writing short stories in which her heroines confronted traditional values and change. Women have formed groups to work for society's improvement. For instance, the Nigerian Eka Esu-Williams (b. 1950), the daughter of a midwife, earned a Ph.D. in Immunology and pursued an academic career before forming Women Against AIDS in Africa in 1988, with the goal of educating and empowering women, more likely than men to get HIV, through workshops, schools, and support schools. Some women have become teachers, nurses, and secretaries, but these are poorly paid occupations. Women are usually left with self-employment in low-wage activity, such as the small-scale trade of hawking goods and keeping stalls in city markets, a female near monopoly for centuries; domestic work as maids, cooks, or nannies; or hairdressing. Women have formed organizations for work, savings, or worship. Meanwhile, many men spend long hours commuting to and from work and socializing with their friends after work in bars or at club meetings. Although homosexuals face severe intolerance in many African countries, homosexuality has been more open in South Africa, where the courts legalized homosexual marriage in 2005.

African Cultural Expression

Africans have reconstructed their cultures in creative ways. In the popular arts, especially music and literature, imported ideas are combined with African culture. Africans believe they have much to offer world culture. As the Senegalese writer and president Leopold Senghor (sah-GAWR) (1906–2001) has asked, "Who else would teach rhythm to the world that has died of machines and cannons?"[20]

Popular Music Urbanization, the growth of mass media, and the mixing of ethnic groups and outside influences have all created a fertile ground for mixed popular music styles that have reflected social, economic, and political realities. Exciting new musical genres have emerged as both male and female musicians have sought to make sense of their changing social identities, world-views, and lives. Miriam Makeba (muh-KAY-ba) (b. 1932), the South African jazz and pop singer forced by the apartheid government to spend

decades in exile, described her mission as follows: "I live to sing about what I see and know. I don't sing politics, I sing truth."[21]

Popular music has become a creative blending of local and imported influences. As one Ghanaian musician remarked: "In the 'new music' coming out of Africa, the rich spontaneity and color of African life are magnified a hundred times."[22] The new forms of musical expression have reflected the presence of hundreds of distinctive cultures in this vast region. The rise of varied African-based popular music styles has helped Africans adjust to change while affirming their spirit in the face of external influences and internal failures. For instance the *juju* music of the Nigerian Yoruba reflects Yoruba traditions and values while mixing local and Western instruments, such as electric guitars. Through the Africanization of musical ideas and technology coming from abroad, Africans have confronted the powerful influences emanating from the industrialized nations.

Musicians have been groping for a new Africa that can resolve its problems while successfully blending the old and the new, the indigenous and the foreign. African popular musicians also reach an international audience, performing and selling recordings around the world. Perhaps the greatest African superstar, the Senegalese Youssou N'Dour (YOO-soo en-DOOR) (b. 1959), travels all over the world and does collaborations with leading Western musicians. Yet, he remains true to his roots, living in Dakar and following his tolerant Sufi Muslim faith. Some musicians are highly political. The Nigerian Fela Kuti (1938–1997), whose music mixed jazz, soul, rock, and Yoruba traditions, used his songs as a weapon to attack the Nigerian government and its Western sponsors, and faced frequent arrest and beatings for his protests. Like Bob Marley, Bob Dylan, and Chile's Victor Jara, Fela gained worldwide fame for his use of music to attack injustice and influence politics. Women also used music to express their views. For instance, Oumou Sangare of Mali

African Cultural Expression Africans have developed diverse and vibrant popular music, often by mixing Western and local traditions. In Nigeria, juju music, played by bands such as Captain Jidi Oyo and his Yankee System in this 1982 photo, has been popular among the Yoruba people.
(Courtesy, Christopher Waterman, UCLA)

had a massive hit with her account of a young woman torn between pleasing her parents and her loved one.

A particularly influential African pop music developed in the Belgian Congo in the 1950s and spread rapidly. Congolese (Zairean) pop music, known widely as **soukous** ("to shake"), was shaped by dance rhythms from Cuba and Brazil, musical forms that were themselves African in origin. Soukous depends heavily on the guitar, imported from the West, as well as on traditional African songs and melodies. Congolese musicians, unable to make a living or speak freely in their troubled homeland, have often sought their fortunes in other African countries or Europe, hence enlivening the musical culture of other nations. Soukous became a major dance music throughout Africa and among African immigrants in Europe.

Literature   As with popular musicians, writers have produced distinctive literatures by combining old traditions with new influences to comment on modern society. African literature has questioned the status quo, asserted African identity, and attempted to influence political change and economic development. Major figures have often written in English or French to better develop an international reputation. For example, the Nigerian Wole Soyinka (WOE-lay shaw-YING-kuh) (b. 1934), a Yoruba poet, playwright, novelist, and sometime filmmaker who won the 1986 Nobel Prize for literature, has mixed Yoruba mysticism with criticisms of Western capitalism, racism, and cultural imperialism and of African failures, including the brutalities of Nigerian political life. A former political prisoner, Soyinka has denounced repressive African leaders, including Nigeria's, with as much venom as he attacks Western imperialists, chastising "Nigeria's self-engorgement at the banquet of highway robberies, public executions, public floggings and other institutionalized sadisms, casual cruelties, wanton destruction."[23] The powerful criticism of governments offered by Soyinka and his Nigerian colleague Chinua Achebe, discussed in the chapter opening vignette, has often forced both men to live in exile. Not all African writers accept Soyinka's and Achebe's highly critical view of African politics.

Writers and artists have also tried to find authentic African perspectives. **Negritude** is a literary and philosophical movement to forge distinctively African views that first developed in the 1930s. The Senegalese writer and later the first president of his country after independence, Leopold Senghor, a former professor of classics in France, was a major negritude voice, attempting to balance the Western stress on rational thought with African approaches to knowledge, such as mysticism and animism, long disdained by Europeans as superstition. To Senghor, Africans needed to assert, rather than feel inferior about, their black skins and cultural traditions. Negritude influenced French artists and writers, and the philosopher Jean Paul Sartre praised the approach as a key weapon against all forms of oppression.

One of the best-known writers in Francophone West Africa, Ousmane Sembene (OOS-man sem-BEN-ee) (b. 1923) of Senegal, was influenced more by Marxism than negritude. Drafted into the French army during World War II, Sembene, the son of a poor fisherman, fought in Italy and Germany. After the war he worked in France as a dockworker and became a leader of the dockworkers' union, and his first novel portrayed the stevedore's hard life. Eventually Sembene returned to Senegal. His writings, often set in the colonial period, show African resistance to Western domination and social inequality. Sympathizing with exploited people, his work also attacks Senegal's privileged elite, including greedy businessmen and government officials. Sembene also made films that gained international acclaim. Like his writings, some of the films satirize corrupt African bureaucrats and illustrate the struggle of the poor for breathing room in a system in which the rich exploit the poor.

English-language literature has also flourished in South Africa and East Africa. For example, Kenyan Ngugi Wa Thiongo (en-GOO-gee wah thee-AHN-go) (b. 1938), a former journalist turned university professor who did his graduate studies in England, has written several novels that explore the relationship between colonialism and social fragmentation, showing Gikuyu society struggling to retain its identity, culture, and traditions while adjusting to the modern world. Ngugi's heroes are alienated figures drifting back and forth between African and Western traditions. Once a devout Christian, Ngugi later rejected Christianity, which he viewed as a legacy of colonialism. His 1979 novel, *Petals of Blood*, portrays a Kenya struggling to free itself from neocolonialism but also beset with corruption. His attacks on the privileged local elite allied with Western exploitation earned Ngugi several terms in Kenyan jails.

Religious Change

Africans have maintained a triple religious heritage: animism/polytheism, Islam, and Christianity. All these faiths have many followers, although the older animism has lost influence, and the relations between the traditions are not always easy. With their links to wider worlds, Christianity and Islam are also globalizing influences, spreading Western or Middle Eastern political, social, and economic ideas. Africans often view religions in both theoretical and practical terms, refusing to divorce metaphysical speculation from everyday life. They adopt views that help them survive the changes of modern times, rejecting old ideas and adding new ones as needed. Religion has remained in constant flux.

Christianity became Africa's largest religion, attracting some 250 to 300 million followers by 2000, both the fervent and the nominal in faith. Some countries, such as Congo, South Africa, and Uganda, became largely Christian. Africans are prominent in the world leadership of the Anglican and Catholic churches. Christianity has proven a powerful force for social change. Many Christian churches prevent their followers from practicing traditional customs. Believers often favor the liberation of women, and mission schools have educated many African leaders, influencing their world-views. A growing num-

---

soukous ("to shake")   A Congolese popular music that was shaped by dance rhythms from Cuba and Brazil.

negritude   A literary and philosophical movement to forge distinctively African views.

ber of independent churches, some blending African traditions into worship and theology, have no ties to the older Western-based denominations. By promising to help members acquire wealth and happiness, some African churches have enjoyed spectacular growth, which has enabled them to build big urban churches that attract thousands of congregants each Sunday. In a reversal of historical patterns, several Nigerian churches even send missionaries to revitalize Christianity in the West, establishing branches in Europe and North America. Yet many other Africans have viewed Christianity as connected to Western imperialism. According to a popular nationalist saying: "When the missionaries came the Africans had the land and the Christians had the Bible. They taught us to pray with our eyes closed. When we opened them they had the land and we had the Bible."[24]

Over 200 million black Africans follow Islam. About a fourth of all sub-Saharan countries have Muslim majorities. Some revivalist and Wahhabi movements have gained influence, especially in northern Nigeria, where some states have imposed Islamic law, sparking deadly clashes with Christian minorities. Muslim-Christian clashes in Nigeria caused by Muslim outrage at cartoons published in Denmark in 2005 that mocked the prophet Muhammad left over one hundred people dead. But most Muslims and Christians remain moderate and inclusive. While politicians use religion as a wedge issue, and Christian-Muslim clashes have occurred in countries such as Ivory Coast, tolerance has more often marked relations among Christians, Muslims, and animists. Among the Yoruba, for example, members of each group mix easily and even intermarry. Ethnicity often divides people more than religion.

Africa in the Global System

African developments have occurred in a global context. During the Cold War, some African countries, especially their elites, benefited from the international rivalry between the USSR and the United States. It gained them aid but also fostered manipulation on the part of the superpowers. Countries such as Congo and Angola often became pawns in the Cold War, with the superpowers helping to support or remove leaders. But with the Cold War over, the Western world has largely ignored Africa, providing it with little aid and investment. Furthermore, the wealth gap between African countries and the Western industrialized nations has grown even wider than during colonial times. Today the gap between the richest Western nations and the poorest African countries is around 400 to 1.

Global conditions have often proven counterproductive for Africans. Only when the world economy boomed in the 1950s and 1960s did African economies show steady growth. Since the 1970s, however, as the world economy soured and the world prices for many African exports collapsed, African economic growth rates steadily dropped. Western experts have encouraged a policy known as "structural adjustment," in which international lenders, such as the International Monetary Fund (IMF) and the World Bank, loan nations money on the condition that these nations open their economies to private investment and, to balance national budgets, reduce government spending for health, education, and farmers. The result-

ing hardship on average people—from eliminating money for poor children to attend the village primary school to closing the local office that aids small farmers—increases unrest and resentment both of governments and of the Western nations that control the IMF and World Bank. This private investment also promotes a shift away from traditional farming, which mostly involves shifting cultivation and produces little food surplus, to modern agriculture, which is much more productive. But modern agriculture, with its reliance on tractors, chemical fertilizers, and new seeds, entails a large environmental and social cost: marginal land poorly suited to farming is often turned into desert, and small farmers, both men and women, do not have the means to buy the modern supplies.

To obtain the goods—cars, fashionable clothes, electronic gadgets—desired by the politically powerful urban middle and upper classes, African nations have taken out loans to pay for them. By 1998, as a percentage of total output, African countries had the largest foreign debts in the world: $230 billion. At the same time, the world prices for most of Africa's exports, such as coffee, cotton, and tobacco from Tanzania and cocoa from Ghana, have steadily dropped since the 1960s. Some exports now bring in a third of what they once did, leaving ever larger revenue gaps. And small farmers, such as the cotton growers in Mali, cannot compete with highly subsidized Western farmers and the tariff barriers erected in Europe, North America, and Japan against food and fiber imports from Africa. Increasingly desperate, countries such as Guinea-Bissau and Somalia have agreed to allow dangerous toxic waste, such as deadly but unwanted chemicals produced in the West, to be buried on their land in exchange for cash.

Africa's economic problems have had diverse roots. Some resulted from colonialism, which imposed economic policies that caused severe environmental destruction, such as desertification and deforestation, while incorporating the people into the world economy as specialized producers of minerals or cash crops for export rather than food farmers. Hence, Zambia relies on exploiting copper (87 percent of exports), Uganda coffee (72 percent), Malawi tobacco (72 percent), and Nigeria oil (95 percent). Nations have remained vulnerable to drops in world commodity prices for their exports. The colonial regimes also often failed to build roads, schools, and clinics. Since independence, bad policy decisions, poor leadership, corruption, unstable politics, and misguided advice from Western experts have also contributed to the economic crisis. In addition, the rapid spread of HIV/AIDS has ravaged African nations, killing and affecting millions (see Chapter 26). In some nations a third of the population has the HIV virus.

But although falling behind much of Asia and Latin America economically, Africans have had both successes and failures. Using foreign aid and their own resources, they have made rapid strides in literacy, social and medical services, including active birth control campaigns, and road construction. Some nations, such as South Africa and Uganda, have a feisty free press. Africans have also attempted to work together to resolve problems. The African Union, formed in 2000 with 54 members, has sent peacekeeping troops into violence-torn countries such as Sudan. But finding the right mix of African and Western ideas to promote economic progress, political stability, and democratic decision making has proved difficult. By the 1990s Africans had grown skeptical about the usefulness of Western models of development, which often depend on expensive high technology, and were also disillusioned with centralized governments controlling economic activity. Many nations have moved toward more democratic systems and private enterprise. However, political leadership has often failed to root out corruption, restructure existing institutions, and foster food production. Millions still live in poverty. Africa suffers a particularly acute "brain drain" as academics, students, and professionals, seeking a better life, move to Europe or North America.

African history is not only an authentic, dynamic saga of indigenous African development but also part of a larger global process. Over the past half century Western influence has remained strong, including outside manipulation of governments, economic power, and cultural and religious life. Hence, Africans have not enjoyed complete control of their destiny. The Ghanaian historian Jacob Ajayi (a-JAH-yee) laid out the challenge: "The vision of a new [African] society will need to be developed out of the African historical experience. The African is not yet master of his own fate, but neither is he completely at the mercy of fate."[25]

SECTION SUMMARY

- African countries have struggled economically, with many being forced to import food and others, like the Congo, to enter into neocolonial relationships with Western powers, but Ghana and Botswana have managed to significantly improve their economies.

- Marxist revolutionary governments, which appealed to many Africans who wanted to erase the colonial legacy, came to power in Angola and Mozambique, both of which then entered into long civil wars, as well as in Zimbabwe.

- African cities have grown rapidly and often lack necessary services, individualism has grown more common, and women have lost some of the economic value they had in agricultural villages, though some have become successful professionals.

- African musicians, writers, and artists have drawn on local traditions as well as influences from the West to create original forms, such as soukous, as well as works that criticize both Western encroachment and homegrown corruption.

- While animism has grown less influential in Africa, Christianity is the most popular religion and has undermined traditions and been seen by some as connected to Western imperialism, while Islam is followed by 200 million Africans.

- The economic gap between Africa and the industrialized West continues to grow larger, and Western attempts to help Africa through the IMF and the World Bank often include requirements that harm the environment and the poor and inspire resentment, as do tariffs against African imports and the enduring colonial legacy.

 *Online Study Center* ACE the Test

 # Chapter Summary

The Middle East and sub-Saharan Africa have shared certain experiences, including decolonization, mass poverty, reliance on exporting natural resources, political instability, and intervention by Western powers. Yet, while Islam had adherents in both regions, the societies and cultures of Africans and Middle Easterners have remained quite different.

The Middle East was reshaped by diverse developments since 1945. Arab nationalism, especially strong in Egypt, generated conflict with the West and with Israel, which became the major Arab enemy. The Arab-Israel conflict greatly destabilized the region, while ethnic and religious divisions fostered violent struggles within nations. Islam proved most potent as a revolutionary political force in Iran, long a battleground for international rivalries over its oil supplies. The Middle East, especially the Persian Gulf region, provided much of the world's oil, fostering wealth but also global attention as world consumption increased. Oil-rich Saudi Arabia forged an alliance with the United States. Most Middle Eastern societies remained conservative but also fostered cultural creativity. The rivalry between militants and secular Muslims has provided a major cleavage in many countries.

By the 1970s the long colonized African nations had achieved independence under nationalist leaders. But the hopes for a better life were soon dashed. Artificially created multiethnic nations have found it difficult to sustain democracy, and dictatorial governments have often gained power. Most nations have remained dependent on exporting one or two resources. Ambitious development plans have given way to economic stagnation and, as commodity prices fall, increasing poverty. Neither capitalism nor socialism has proved able to both stimulate growth and raise living standards for Africa's majority. But South Africa was finally transformed from a racist state to a multiracial democracy. Societies urbanized, redefined family life and gender roles, and created new music and literature. Africans still search for the right mix of imported ideas and local traditions to create better lives.

Online Study Center Improve Your Grade Flashcards

Key Terms

Intifida	mujahidin	wabenzi
Ba'ath	Taliban	apartheid
OPEC	pan-Africanism	bantustans
Islamists	Mau Mau	soukous
rai	Rebellion	negritude

Suggested Reading

Books

Anderson, Roy R., et al. *Politics and Change in the Middle East: Sources of Conflict and Accommodation*, 7th ed. Upper Saddle River, N.J.: Prentice-Hall, 2003. An introductory survey of politics and economies.

Bates, Daniel G., and Amal Rassam. *Peoples and Cultures of the Middle East*, 2nd ed. Upper Saddle River, N.J.: Prentice-Hall, 2001. A readable introduction to the social and cultural patterns of the region.

Clark, Nancy L. and William H. Worger. *South Africa: The Rise and Fall of Apartheid*. New York: Longman, 2004. A brief survey with documents.

Cleveland, William L. *A History of the Modern Middle East*, 3rd ed. Boulder, Colo.: Westview, 2004. A political overview of the region during this era.

Cooper, Frederick. *Africa Since 1940: The Past of the Present*. New York: Cambridge University Press, 2002. A brief overview of contemporary history.

Danielson, Virginia. *The Voice of Egypt: Umm Kulthum, Arabic Song, and Egyptian Society in the Twentieth Century*. Chicago: University of Chicago Press, 1997. A fascinating view of modern Egypt through the life and work of the Arab world's most famous pop singer.

Davidson, Basil. *The Black Man's Burden: Africa and the Curse of the Nation State*. New York: Times Books, 1992. Reflections on modern Africa and its challenges by an influential historian.

Esposito, John L. *Islam: The Straight Path*, 3rd ed. revised. New York: Oxford University Press, 2005. Detailed examination of modern Islam.

Gerges, Fawaz A. *The Far Enemy: Why Jihad Went Global*. New York: Cambridge University Press, 2005. A gripping account of the rise of Islamism, Al Qaeda, and terrorism by a Labanon-born, U. S.-based scholar.

Gerner, Deborah J. and Jillian Schwedler, eds. *Understanding the Contemporary Middle East*, 2nd ed. Boulder: Lynne Rienner, 2003. Useful collection of essays on varied aspects of the Middle East today.

Gordon, April A., and Donald L. Gordon, eds. *Understanding Contemporary Africa*, 3rd ed. Boulder, Colo.: Lynne Rienner, 2001. An excellent collection of essays on aspects of Africa.

Keddie, Nikki R. *Modern Iran: Roots and Results of Revolution*. New Haven: Yale University Press, 2003. Updating and revision of a major study.

Martin, Phyllis M., and Patrick O'Meara, eds. *Africa*, 3rd ed. Bloomington: Indiana University Press, 1995. Essays on African history, politics, culture, and economies.

Nugent, Paul. *Africa Since Independence: A Comparative History*. New York: Palgrave Macmillan, 2004. A recent, detailed survey.

Smith, Charles D. *Palestine and the Arab-Israeli Conflict: A History with Documents*, 5th ed. Boston: Bedford/St. Martin's, 2004. A comprehensive, balanced survey.

Tenaille, Frank. *Music Is the Weapon of the Future: Fifty Years of African Popular Music*. Chicago: Lawrence Hill, 2000. A recent overview of varied African pop musicians and musical styles.

Websites

Africa South of the Sahara
(http://www-sul.stanford.edu/depts/ssrg/africa/guide.html). A valuable gateway for links on many topics in African studies.

African Studies Internet Resources
(http://www.columbia.edu/cu/lweb/indiv/). Provides valuable links to relevant websites on contemporary Africa.

Arab Human Development Reports
(http://www.un.org/Pubs). The general United Nations site contains links to the reports, issued annually beginning in 2002 and available online, that assess the successes and challenges facing the Arab nations.

History of the Middle East Database
(http://www.nmhschool.org/tthornton/mehistorydatabase/mideastindex.htm). A useful site on history, politics, and culture.

Internet African History Sourcebook
(http://www.fordham.edu/halsall/africa/africasbook.html). Contains useful information and documentary material on Africa.

Internet Islamic History Sourcebook
(http://www.fordham.edu/halsall/islam/islamsbook.html). A comprehensive examination of Islamic societies and their long history, with useful links and source materials.

CHAPTER 31

South Asia, Southeast Asia, and Global Connections, 1945–Present

Commuting to Work Vietnam has largely recovered from its decades of war and has experienced increasing economic growth. These women in Hanoi are commuting to work by bicycle. (Mary Cross)

Online Study Center

This icon will direct you to interactive activities and study materials on the website: college.hmco.com/pic/lockard1e

This music sings the struggle of [humanity]. This music is my life. This is the revolution we have begun. But the revolution is only a means to attain freedom, and freedom is only a means to enrich the happiness and nobility of human life.

HAZIL, THE INDONESIAN REVOLUTIONARY NATIONALIST IN MOCHTAR LUBIS'S NOVEL *A ROAD WITH NO END* (1952)[1]

I n 1950 a small, idealistic group of leading Indonesian writers published a moving declaration promoting universal human dignity: "We [Indonesians] are the heirs to the culture of the whole world, a culture which is ours to extend and develop in our own way [by] the discarding of old and outmoded values and their replacement by new ones. Our fundamental quest is [helping] humanity."[2] These writers hoped that Indonesia could combine the most humane ideas of East and West to become a beacon to the world, open to all cultures and showing respect for the common people. The writers' beliefs had been shaped by their familiarity with Western Enlightenment intellectual traditions, including the ideals of democracy, free thought, and tolerance, and also by the Indonesian Revolution against the repressive colonial Dutch, a nationalist struggle, waged in the name of political freedom, that raged between 1945 and 1950 and had finally led to Indonesian independence. While delighted with independence, the writers warned against the dangers of a narrow nationalism that devalued other cultures.

The writers had been inspired by the irreverent Sumatran poet Chairul Anwar (CHAI-roll ON-war) (1922–1949), who believed the revolution had destroyed the old colonial society and opened up the possibility of building a new, open society. A true bohemian who was undisciplined in his personal life, Anwar had risen from poverty—his family was too poor to send him to secondary school—to master the Dutch, English, Spanish, and French languages. Influenced both by Western books and by an Indonesian sensibility, Anwar excited Indonesian writers with his pathbreaking poems that stretched the possibilities of the Indonesian language. But Anwar had died when just twenty-seven years old, sapped by his appetite for the pleasures of the flesh, and his death left it to others, among them the liberal Sumatran novelist and journalist Mochtar Lubis (MOKE-tar LOO-bis) (b. 1920), whose work is quoted above, to carry on the campaign. Their goal, as expressed in the 1950 writers' declaration, was to create a new society by blending widely admired ideas from abroad with Indonesian ideas, to foster change while also preserving continuity.

The declaration's noble aspirations and recognition of Indonesia's connection to the wider world reflected a new sense of possibility as walls of colonialism were being knocked down. But the writers' idealism was soon dashed by the realities of the early post–World War II years. While Indonesians, like other Southeast Asians, longed for human dignity, other, more immediate goals took precedence, including securing independence, building a new nation, and addressing problems of poverty and underdevelopment. The cosmopolitan values of Anwar, Lubis, and their colleagues even came to seem quaint and contrary to the dominant nationalist agenda. But despite false starts and conflicts, over the following decades Indonesians and other nations of South and Southeast Asia sought, and sometimes found, answers to their challenges while increasing their links to global networks.

The societies of South and Southeast Asia, which changed dramatically without destroying tradition, offer striking contrasts with the wider world as well as with each other. Except for East Asia, this is the most densely populated part of the world: well over 1.5 billion people live in the lands stretching eastward from Pakistan and India to Indonesia and the Philippines. It is also a very diverse area, containing a wide array of languages, ethnic groups, religions, world-views, governments, and levels of economic development. Some nations have experienced destabilizing conflict; others have achieved widespread prosperity. This region of contrasts between wealth and poverty, development and underdevelopment, has played an important role in the world for over four millennia and continues to be one of the cornerstones of the world economy.

FOCUS QUESTIONS

1. What factors led to the political division of South Asia?
2. What have been the major achievements and disappointments of the South Asian nations?
3. What were the causes and consequences of the wars in Indochina?
4. How did decolonization shape the new Southeast Asian nations?
5. What role do the Southeast Asian nations play in the global system?

 # The Reshaping of South Asia

What factors led to the political division of South Asia?

World War II undermined British colonial control and led to independence for the peoples of South Asia. The British, economically drained by the war and realizing that continued control of India would come only at a great cost in wealth and perhaps lives, handed power over to local leaders. The first prime minister of independent India, Jawaharlal Nehru (NAY-roo) (1889–1964), told his people: "A moment comes, which comes rarely in history, when we step from the old to the new, when an age ends and when the soul of a nation, long suppressed, finds utterance."[3] Yet Nehru's idealism about India's independence was tempered by the realities of the challenges ahead. India's long struggle for independence, marked by the nonviolent philosophy of Mohandas Gandhi (1868–1948), had ironically ended with Gandhi assassinated

and British India divided into several separate, often hostile countries, predominantly Hindu India and largely Muslim Pakistan. Two other major South Asian nations also gained independence: mostly Buddhist Sri Lanka and, in the 1970s, largely Muslim Bangladesh. Each of the four nations had its achievements and failures, but the geographically largest and most populous, India, has been the regional colossus and a major player in world affairs.

Decolonization and Partition

The religious divisions of South Asia undermined regional unity. During World War II relations between the British and the mainly Hindu leadership of the Indian National Congress ruptured (see Chapter 25). Taking advantage of this rupture, and fearing domination by the much larger Hindu community in India, the Muslim League pressed its case with the British for a separate Muslim nation, to be called Pakistan. After the war ended, negotiations to bring the Congress and the Muslim

CHRONOLOGY

	South Asia	Southeast Asia
1940	**1947** Independence for India and Pakistan **1948–1964** Nehru era in India	**1945–1950** Indonesian Revolution **1946–1954** First Indochina War **1948** Independence of Burma
1950		
1960		**1963–1975** U.S.-Vietnamese War **1966–1998** New Order in Indonesia
1970	**1971** Formation of Bangladesh	**1975** Communist victories in Vietnam, Cambodia, Laos
1980	**1984** Assassination of Indira Ghandi	
1990		**1997** Asian economic crisis

League together in a common vision broke down in 1946. As the tension increased, rioting broke out, and Muslims and Hindus began murdering each other, pulling victims from buses, shops, and homes. In Calcutta alone 5,000 people died. The rioting undermined any pretence of Hindu-Muslim unity, and the Muslim leader, Mohammed Ali Jinnah (1876–1948), announced that if India were not divided it would be destroyed. The rioting spread into the Ganges Valley and the Punjab. The Congress leaders and British officials now realized that some sort of partition was inevitable. In 1947 British negotiators reached an agreement with Congress and Muslim League leaders to create two independent nations, India and a Pakistan formed out of the Muslim majority areas of eastern Bengal and the northwestern provinces along the Indus River (see Chronology: South Asia, 1945–Present).

The two nations emerged in hopefulness. In a speech to his new nation, India, Prime Minister Nehru proclaimed: "Long years ago we made a tryst with destiny, and now the time comes when we shall redeem our pledge. At the stroke of the midnight hour, when the world sleeps, India will awake to life and freedom."[4] A similar mood of renewal struck people in Pakistan. But the euphoria in both new nations proved short-lived as a bloodbath ensued. Muslims and Hindus had often lived side by side, but partition sparked hatreds between local members of the majority faith, who felt empowered, and religious minorities, who feared discrimination. As violence flared, thousands of Hindus and Sikhs fled Pakistan for India, and thousands of Muslims fled India for Pakistan. Altogether some 5 million refugees crossed the India–West Pakistan border, and a million crossed the India–East Pakistan border. Religious extremists sometimes attacked whole villages or whole trainloads of refugees. About half a million refugees died from the religious violence.

The sixty-eight-year-old Mohandas Gandhi, who remarked that from his youth he had dreamed of communal unity, labored to stop the killing. Moving into the Muslim quarter of

CHRONOLOGY

South Asia, 1945–Present

1947	Independence for India and Pakistan
1948	Assassination of Mohandas Gandhi
1948	Sri Lankan independence
1950	Indian republic
1948–1964	Nehru era in India
1959	Sri Lanka's Sirimavo Bandaranaike first woman prime minister
1962	India-China border war
1971	Formation of Bangladesh
1975–1977	State of emergency under Indira Gandhi
1984	Assassination of Indira Gandhi
1988–1990	First Benazir Bhutto government in Pakistan
1993–1996	Second Benazir Bhutto government
1999	Military government led by Pervez Musharraf

Delhi, he toured refugee camps without escort, read aloud from the scriptures of all religions, including Islam's holiest book, the Quran, and confronted Hindu mobs attacking mosques. Finally, in desperation, and hoping to send a message to everyone in India and Pakistan, Gandhi, who weighed only 113 pounds, began a fast until all the violence in the city had stopped or he died. He quickly fell ill, but Gandhi's effort worked, allowing him to break off his fast. After the violence subsided, a substantial Muslim and Sikh minority remained in India and a Hindu and Sikh minority in Pakistan. But partition had been shattering. A Muslim poet spoke for many disillusioned people: "This is not that long looked-for break of the day. Where did that fine breeze blow from—where has it fled?"[5] Furthermore, Gandhi's support for Muslim victims of Hindu violence outraged Hindu extremists, who regarded Gandhi as a traitor to Hinduism. In January 1948, one of them gunned down Gandhi as he walked to a meeting, shocking the whole country.

Despite its bloody start, India was built on a solid political foundation. Britain bequeathed the basis for parliamentary democracy, a trained civil service, a good communications system, and an educated if Westernized elite committed to modernization. India became a republic with a constitution based on the British model, led by a prime minister chosen by the majority party in an elected parliament. However, given its huge ethnic, religious, and linguistic diversity (fourteen major languages and hundreds of minor languages), India has had difficulty building national unity. To accommodate the many religious minorities, regions, and diverse cultures, India adopted a federal system, with elected state governments, and was officially secular with complete separation of religion and state. Kashmir (CASH-mere), a mountainous Himalayan state

on the India-Pakistan border, presented a long-term problem because it had a Muslim majority but a Hindu ruler who opted to join India. Kashmir has remained a source of constant tension and sometimes war between India and Pakistan.

The new Pakistan confronted numerous problems. It was an artificial country, with two wings separated by a thousand miles of India. The nation's founding leader, Jinnah, died soon after independence, and his successor was assassinated. Before independence Muslims had been overrepresented in the British Indian military, and the army now played a stronger role in Pakistan's politics than in India's. The loss of top civilian leaders, lack of a balanced economic base, massive poverty, and geographical division made Pakistan more vulnerable than India to political instability and military rule. Pakistan and India quarreled over issues from water use to trade to ownership of Kashmir.

India During the Nehru Years

India's first prime minister, Nehru, a close associate of Gandhi and the son of a respected early Indian nationalist, dominated Indian politics for a decade and a half (1948–1964). A gifted speaker and brilliant thinker, Nehru was supported by the middle class, who saw him as the builder of a modern India, and by the mass of the people because he identified himself with issues of concern to the poor. The majority of Indians lived in overcrowded, unhealthy urban slums or dusty villages that lacked electricity and running water. Nehru promised to raise living standards and address the nation's overwhelming poverty. He believed firmly in democracy, emphasizing consent rather than coercion. While India lagged behind communist-ruled China in

Muslims Leaving India for Pakistan During Partition   As India and Pakistan split into two new nations in 1947, millions of Muslims and Hindus fled their homes to escape violence. This photo shows displaced Muslims, carrying a few meager belongings, jamming a train headed from India to Pakistan.   (Wide World Photos)

economic development, it nevertheless preserved a system of personal freedom. Believing in peaceful coexistence with neighbors and renouncing military aggression, Nehru became a major figure on the world stage, helping found the Non-Aligned Movement of nations, such as Egypt and Indonesia, unwilling to commit to either the U.S. or Soviet camps in the Cold War. Hoping to prevent a nuclear conflict between the superpowers, Nehru led the Congress Party to three smashing electoral victories.

Nehru's policies derived from his complex ideals. Although the British-educated lawyer admired Western politics, literature, and economic dynamism, he also respected India's cultural heritage. Nehru talked of India's moral strength, which, he believed, sanctioned his leadership of the non-aligned countries. Yet he opposed any narrow understanding of tradition and religion. Raised a Hindu, Nehru was nevertheless a secularist who believed that Congress should represent all religions and social groups and promote justice for all. Although himself a high-caste brahman, he distrusted the influence of the Hindu priests. Perhaps Nehru's greatest contributions came in addressing social problems. He shared Gandhi's opposition to restrictions imposed by the caste system and fought gender inequalities. In 1955, after years of struggle, Nehru convinced parliament to approve new laws on untouchability and women's rights that provided penalties for discrimination. The lowest-ranking social group, untouchables, acquired special quotas in government services and universities, while Hindu women gained equal legal rights with men, including the right to divorce, property rights, and equal inheritance. To discourage child marriage, Nehru set a minimum marriage age at eighteen for males and fifteen for females. But the laws, which challenged centuries of tradition, were often ignored, especially in rural areas.

Nehru's government built the framework for productive economic change. Nehru introduced a planning system to foster modern technology and mixed capitalism and socialism, private capital and a strong state sector. He left established industries in private hands but set up public ventures to, for example, build power plants and dams, which doubled power production, and irrigation canals, which increased agricultural yields by 25 percent. In the 1960s the Green Revolution, agricultural innovation marked by the introduction of new high-yield wheat and rice, fostered a dramatic rise in food production. Nehru employed five-year plans to make India independent of foreign suppliers for power, steel, basic commodities, and food. By the 1970s India was one of the world's ten most industrialized nations and nearly self-sufficient in food.

But the Nehru record was mixed. Some of his policies proved failures. Government control of the private sector through regulations gave bureaucrats great power, fostered corruption, and shackled private enterprise. Nehru failed to cultivate good relations with Pakistan or with China, and in 1962 Chinese troops humiliated Indian forces during a border dispute. Nehru also failed to recognize that a rapidly growing population, which rose from 389 million in 1941 to 434 million in 1961, would undermine most of India's economic gains. In addition, he only belatedly endorsed family planning, and the government built schools and universities but failed to substantially raise literacy rates. Yet, when Nehru died in 1964, millions mourned the end of an idealistic era that had earned India respect in the world. Furthermore, Congress had no leader of comparable stature to follow Nehru.

Nehru Opening a New Dam
As prime minister, Jawaharlal Nehru tried to build a modern India, devoting scarce financial resources to improving the economic infrastructure. In this photo, Nehru opens a new dam, which will generate power for commerce and industry. (Corbis)

Map 31.1 Modern South Asia

India, predominantly Hindu, is the largest South Asian nation and separates the two densely populated Islamic nations of Bangladesh and Pakistan. Buddhists are the majority in Sri Lanka, just off India's southeast coast. The small kingdoms of Bhutan and Nepal are located in the Himalayan mountain range.

Online Study Center **Improve Your Grade** Interactive Map: The Partition of India, 1947

The Making of Pakistan and Bangladesh

Pakistan faced greater challenges than did India. Jinnah had pledged to make the nation happy and prosperous, but the leaders who followed him had only limited success, in part because of differences, and sometimes tensions, between ethnic groups who shared an Islamic faith but often little else. From the beginning tensions flared between the nationalistic Bengalis, who dominated the east, and the Punjabis and Sindhis, who dominated the west. The two regions, although strongly Islamic, dif-

fered in language, culture, and outlook. The factionalized Pakistani parliament, whose members chiefly represented regions and ethnic groups rather than rival ideologies, proved unworkable, providing an excuse for military leaders to take over the government in 1958. By 1969 dissatisfaction with military dictatorship led to riots, prompting martial law.

At the end of the 1960s ethnic tensions came to a boil, eventually fracturing Pakistan into two nations, Pakistan and Bangladesh (Bengali Nation) (see Map 31.1). The Bengalis in East Pakistan had felt they did not get a fair share of the nation's resources and political power. After the **Awami League**, a Bengali nationalist party, won a majority of East Pakistan's seats in national elections, in early 1971 Pakistani troops arrested the party leader, Sheikh Mujiber Rahman (shake MOO-jee-bur RAH-mun) (1920–1975), in the middle of the night. Then, hoping to crush Awami League support, troops opened fire on university dormitories and Hindu homes, causing hundreds of casualties.

Inspired by Sheikh Mujiber, who asked his supporters to carry the message of independence to every rice field and mango grove in the country, the Awami League then declared independence. In response, troops from West Pakistan poured into East Pakistan, terrorizing the Bengali population with massacres, arson, and the raping of thousands of women. At least half a million Bengalis died at Pakistani hands. The civil war caused 10 million desperate, starving Bengali refugees to flee to India. World opinion turned against Pakistan. India appealed for world support of East Pakistan, armed the Bengali guerrillas, and, after an ill-advised Pakistani attack on Indian airfields, declared war and sent troops into both West and East Pakistan, rapidly gaining the upper hand. Fearful of India, Pakistan had long cultivated an alliance with China and the United States, both of which supplied it with military aid. The United States, where the administration of President Richard Nixon ignored the massive killing of Bengalis, and China threatened to intervene on behalf of Pakistan, but Soviet backing of India discouraged such a move. By the end of 1971 Pakistani troops in Bengal had surrendered to Indian forces, and the Awami League, led by Sheikh Mujibur, established a new nation, Bangladesh, in what had been East Pakistan.

The Indira Gandhi Era

Nehru had not only led India but had also fostered a family political dynasty. With the sudden death of Nehru's respected successor in 1966, the Congress selected Nehru's daughter, Indira Gandhi (1917–1984), to be the nation's first woman prime minister. She had worked closely with her father while her husband (no relation to Mohandas Gandhi) served in parliament. A shrewd campaigner, Mrs. Gandhi enjoyed a decade and a half in power. When her support waned in the 1967 elections, she responded aggressively with policies to win back the poor. Her status was elevated by India's smashing military victory over archenemy Pakistan. But Mrs. Gandhi's war triumph and mounting domestic problems also fostered her use of increasingly harsh policies, which often made matters worse. Powerful vested interests ignored her reforms, the economy faltered, and many Indians turned against the Congress.

Indian democracy faltered. In 1975 Gandhi declared a state of emergency, suspending civil rights, closing state governments, and jailing some 10,000 opposition leaders and dissidents. One arrested leader complained that those who were in jail should be out while those who were out should be in. While her actions were condemned, however, some of her policies

improved the economy. Meanwhile, her youngest son, Sanjay Gandhi (1946–1980), launched a controversial birth control campaign to forcibly sterilize any man with more than three children and implemented a slum-clearance program that forced thousands out of sidewalk shanties. Both programs became deeply unpopular. In 1977 Indira lifted the emergency and announced general elections. After thirty years in power, the Congress Party, and with it Indira Gandhi, was voted out of office and replaced by an uneasy coalition of diverse parties that included Hindu nationalists who wanted to end the secular approach of the Congress. But the coalition government solved few problems, and in 1980 it collapsed.

Indira Gandhi and the Congress returned to power in the 1980 elections, restoring the Nehru dynasty. But they also faced new problems. Nearly half the electorate had stayed away, disenchanted with cynical politics, and Mrs. Gandhi faced growing unemployment and unrest. In 1980 Sanjay Gandhi died in a plane crash, and Indira Gandhi elevated her eldest son Rajiv (1944–1991), an apolitical airline pilot, as her heir apparent. Violence in the Punjab, India's richest state, which had a heavy Sikh population, provoked Mrs. Gandhi's final crisis. The growing political consciousness of the Sikhs, whose religion mixes Hindu and Muslim ideas, had led to a desire for statehood. In 1983 armed Sikh extremists occupied the Golden Temple at Amritsar (uhm-RIT-suhr), the holiest shrine in the Sikh religion, and turned it into a fortress. They called for an independent Sikh homeland and murdered those, including moderate Sikhs, who opposed them. In 1984 the Indian army stormed the Golden Temple against fierce resistance. When the fighting ended, the temple was reduced to rubble and over a thousand militants and soldiers lay dead.

Violence had returned to Indian political life. The destruction of their holiest temple shocked the Sikhs and led to the shooting death of Indira Gandhi by two of her Sikh bodyguards. The assassination in turn generated rioting and attacks on Sikhs. Hindu mobs roamed Delhi, burning Sikh shops and killing Sikhs, often by pouring gasoline over them and setting them ablaze. The dead numbered in the thousands. Rajiv Gandhi, succeeding his mother at only forty years old, proved ineffective. In 1991, while campaigning in the southern city of Madras, he was blown up by a young Sri Lankan woman handing him flowers. The suicide bomber, who had the bomb hidden in her clothing, opposed India's support of the Sri Lankan government in its war against the secessionist group to which she belonged. Yet despite this tumult, India remained a functioning democracy and a thriving nation.

Awami League   A Bengali nationalist party that began the move for independence from West Pakistan.

SECTION SUMMARY

- After World War II, when majority Muslim Pakistan broke off from majority Hindu India, widespread religious violence broke out and a dispute over the territory of Kashmir set the stage for continued tension between the two countries.

- Nehru attempted to expand the rights of women and, through a mix of capitalism and socialism, vastly increased India's industrial and agricultural output, but the population expanded at a dangerously rapid rate and not all policies were successful.

■ East and West Pakistan were divided along ethnic lines, and a military crackdown on a Bengali nationalist party led to a bloody civil war in which India intervened on behalf of East Pakistan, which then became a separate country, Bangladesh.

■ Nehru's daughter, Indira Gandhi, was prime minister for over a decade, but she treated her opposition harshly and was assassinated in the midst of clashes between Hindus and Sikhs, and her son and successor, Rajiv Gandhi, was also assassinated.

South Asian Politics and Societies

What have been the major achievements and disappointments of the South Asian nations?

South Asian societies changed beginning in the 1970s, each forging its own political role in the region. With a little over 1 billion people by 2005 and 65 percent of the land in the subcontinent, the Republic of India rose to regional dominance. Indian governments began to liberalize the economy, stimulating growth. At the same time, growing Hindu nationalism has challenged the domination of India's Congress Party, threatening its secular vision. Meanwhile, India's neighbors in South Asia have struggled to achieve stability and economic development. Both Pakistan and Sri Lanka have experienced persistent ethnic violence, while India and Pakistan remain on bitter terms, building up military forces and nuclear weapons to use against the other. Whatever the political tensions that divide them, however, they also share some life patterns. In each South Asian nation ancient customs exist side by side with modern machines and ways of living; some of them, such as democratic forms, are imports from outside.

Indian Politics

When India celebrated its fiftieth jubilee of independence in 1997, the nation's president reminded his people that India's challenge was to achieve economic growth with social justice. That goal remains elusive; India has been unable to mount the sort of concerted attack on mass poverty found in China. However, Indians can boast that, in politics, their country has maintained one of the few working multiparty democracies outside the industrialized nation-states, one that fosters lively political debate and forces candidates to appeal to voters. An Indian novelist described the rhetoric of political campaigns leading up to elections: "The speeches were crammed with promises of every shape and size: promises of new schools,

clean water, health care, land for landless peasants, powerful laws to punish any discrimination."[6] While such grandiose promises usually proved difficult to fulfill, millions of people voted in these elections, and changes in state and federal governments have regularly occurred.

India rejected the revolutionary path of China, instead promoting civil liberties and constitutional democracy. However, scholars debate how that democracy has shaped India. To some observers, for example, democracy fosters national unity by providing a flexible system for accommodating the differing interests of the diverse population. Others, however, argue that democracy has intensified differences between groups. Certainly, tensions between Hindus and Muslims and between high-caste and low-caste Hindus, manipulated by opportunistic politicians, have complicated political life. There are also differences over how real the effects of democracy are in the presence of powerful economic and political elites. While voting is said to give the poor an opportunity to put pressure on elites, elites are seen as manipulating the democratic system to preserve their privileges. Some say that democracy has become only a safety valve for popular frustration, creating the illusion of mass participation that prevents a frontal attack on caste and class inequalities. Yet, lower caste voters do make their voice heard, sometimes forcing officials to meet their needs, such as by paving the pathways in their neighborhoods.

The Congress Party has remained nationally influential for over five decades but has had to contend with rivals. On the left, several Communist parties dominate politics in West Bengal in the northeast and Kerala in the southwest, repeatedly winning elections by promoting modernization and support for the poor within a democratic framework. On the right, several Hindu nationalist parties have opposed the secular Congress, but with limited success until the 1990s. In the southern Indian states various parties representing regional interests gradually gained strength, generally dominating state governments and becoming part of federal coalitions. These regional parties, often led by stars of the local film industries, have worked to protect local languages while preserving English, the only common language understood by educated people around the country, as a national language. All of India's parties have suffered from corruption, elected officials and the bureaucrats they hire often seeing public service as a way to enrich themselves.

Since 1989 Indian politics has become more pluralistic. The Congress lost several elections to coalitions that included Hindu nationalists. The major Hindu nationalist party, the **Bharatha Janata** (BJP), gained influence in north India with a platform of hostility to Muslims and of state support for Hindu issues, such as having schools teach Indian history in accordance with Hindu traditions and religious writings. The BJP slogan, "One Nation, One People, One Culture," confronts the Gandhi-Nehru vision of a tolerant multicultural state. By the late 1990s India suffered from rising political corruption, violent secessionist movements in border regions, caste conflict, religious hostilities, and fragmentation into several rival political factions. In 2002 major Hindu-Muslim violence broke

Bharatha Janata (BJP)   The major Hindu nationalist party in India.

out again, leaving over a thousand people dead and over 100,000 terrified Muslims, burned out of their cities, huddled in tent camps. In 2004 the Congress, led by Rajiv Gandhi's Italian-born, sari-wearing widow, Sonia Gandhi (b. 1946), a Roman Catholic who met Rajiv when both were students in England, capitalized on disenchantment among the poor and Muslims and, allied with leftist parties, unexpectedly defeated the ruling BJP-led coalition and form a new government committed to secularism and economic growth. A Pakistan-born Sikh economist, Manmohan Singh, became the first non-Hindu prime minister. Furthermore, a free press monitors politics. In 2005 an investigation of corruption by a television station forced several members of parliament to resign, indicating the continued vibrancy of Indian democracy.

Indian Economic Growth

India has struggled to resolve problems inherited from colonial times: economic backwardness, skyrocketing population growth, and crushing poverty for the majority. Nehru had sought to end ignorance, poverty, and inequality of opportunity. While his dream has not yet been realized, Indians can boast of many gains, especially after India changed directions economically in the 1970s. For example, in 1956 India had to import vital foodstuffs and manufactured goods. By the late 1970s it was a net exporter of grain and by 2000 was making and exporting its own cars, computers, and aircraft.

After 1991 Indian leaders dismantled the socialist sector of the economy built by Nehru while sparking economic revival. Reform, deregulation, and liberalization contributed to an economic growth rate of 6 to 7 percent a year by the late 1990s. Several cities, especially Bangalore and Bombay, became high-tech centers closely linked to global communications. Hundreds of North American and European companies, taking advantage of a growing, educated Indian middle class, especially university graduates fluent in English, have moved information and technical service jobs, such as call-in customer service and computer programming, from North America and Europe to India. India's boom has even prompted thousands of highly educated Indians living in North America and Europe to return to India and join its high-tech sector. These returnees—30,000 technology professionals in 2004 and 2005 alone—often move into spacious, newly built California-style suburbs with names like Ozone and Lake Vista. Even greater progress has been made in agriculture. Since 1947 India has doubled food production, thanks largely to the Green Revolution of improved seeds and fertilizers. The nation now grows enough wheat and rice to feed the entire population, but persisting social, economic, and regional inequalities have prevented equitable distribution of the food.

In spite of the economic revival, many Indians have yet to enjoy its fruits. Compared to China, Malaysia, and South Korea, India's economy has been less able to deliver a better life to the mass of the population. More than half of Indians still live below the poverty line, and 40 percent lack an adequate diet. While China nears universal literacy, only half of Indians can read and write. Meanwhile population growth eats away at the national resources. Every year 30 million Indians are born. By 2050 India will have 1.5 billion people, more than China and four times more than the United States. Ironically, success in doubling life expectancy contributes to overpopulation, which causes overcrowded cities, a lack of pure drinking water and adequate sanitation, and insufficient primary health care. India has half as many physicians per population and over twice as much infant mortality as China; Chinese live twelve years longer than Indians. Millions of Indians sleep on city sidewalks for lack of money and housing. While affluent Indians increasingly buy fancy imported cars to drive along newly built highways, many commuters ride on the roofs of jammed buses and trains. Yet, most quality-of-life indices place India ahead of most African nations.

The stark contrasts between the modern and traditional sectors of the economy have produced development amid underdevelopment and raised questions as to who benefits from the changes. The "haves" can afford to pay for services that strapped governments cannot provide: good schools, clean water, decent health care, efficient transport. Despite increased agricultural productivity, per capita calory consumption remains well below world averages. Ambitious birth control campaigns enjoy success in cities but less in the countryside. The Green Revolution has increased output but mostly benefits the big landowners, who can afford the large investments in tractors and fertilizers. Successive Indian governments have been unable or unwilling to challenge vested interests such as the powerful landlords. Meanwhile, poor peasants, unable to make a living from their small farms, fall further behind. Half the rural population has become landless. Poverty fosters growing urban crime and rural banditry, especially in several densely populated northern states. The population below the official poverty line lacks purchasing power to sustain local industry. Economic growth and poverty ravage the environment as cities encroach on farmland and people cut down trees for firewood. As in China, poor peasants protest, often violently, the taking of their land for building factories, often foreign-owned, and highways. The Chipko forest conservation movement, based on traditional and Gandhian principles and led mostly by women, is one of many groups working to protect the environment. A Chipko leader, the globetrotting Sunderlal Bahugana (SUN-dur-LOLL ba-hoo-GAH-na), stresses the place of people in the larger web of nature. The Congress-led government pledged to spend more on rural health care and education.

Indian Cities, Gender Patterns, and Cultures

In his will, India's first prime minister, Jawaharlal Nehru, asked that his ashes be scattered in the Ganges River, not because of the river's traditional religious significance to Hindus but because it symbolized to him India's millennia-old culture, ever changing and yet ever the same. Such a pattern has indeed characterized India's society and culture. Ancient traditions such as caste, gender stereotypes, and family practices have persisted but have also been modified, especially in the cities, and Indians make religion both central to their lives and a source of conflict.

Indians have also used literature, film, and other cultural forms to examine their society and place in the world.

The contrast between the villages, where 80 percent of Indians live, and the often modern cities remains stark. Unlike in the villages, in the cities the growing urban middle class—many millions strong by 2006—enjoy recreations and technologies, from golf to video games, that are available to the affluent around the world. As young people move around the country, often on the new national highway system, they identify less with their home region and more with India, becoming cosmopolitan. Whether they live in the Punjab, Calcutta, or Bangalore, educated urban young people often like the same music and buy the same consumer goods, a homogenization that conservatives see as a threat to local cultures. Practices that ensure strict divisions between castes, such as avoiding physical contact or sharing food, are harder to maintain in cities than in villages. City people often still pay attention to caste, but their approach to preserving it is different. For instance, high-caste families often place classified ads in national newspapers seeking marriage partners from similar backgrounds for their children, as in this example: "Suitable Brahman bride for handsome Brahman boy completing Ph.D. (Physics). Write with biodata, photograph, horoscope."[7] Caste remains much more firmly rooted in the villages. At the bottom of the caste system, the untouchables, some 20 percent of India's population, still live difficult lives, especially in the villages, even though government assistance and laws to improve their status have enabled some low-caste people to enter high-status occupations or succeed in politics. The grooves of tradition run deep, particularly in the rural areas, and changes can bring demoralization and disorientation as well as satisfaction.

However, in some regions, especially in cities, families have changed. Modern life has hastened the breakup of the traditional joint families, where parents lived in large compounds with their married and unmarried children and grandchildren; some Indians now live in smaller, nuclear families. New forms of employment, which can cause family members to move to other districts or countries, have undermined family cohesion. A traditional preference for male babies, however, has continued, and the ratio of females to males in the population has even declined. Today the ability of technology to determine the sex of a fetus has led many Indians who want male children to terminate pregnancies. Experts worry that a population that is becoming predominantly male will experience increasing social problems.

Nehru had believed that India could progress only if women played a full part in the nation. In response to such concerns, new laws banned once widespread customs such as polygamy, child marriage, and sati. Female literacy has risen, from 1 percent in 1901 to 27 percent in 2000, though it is still only half the male rate. But some changing customs have penalized women. For example, the practice of requiring new brides to provide generous dowries to their in-laws, once restricted to higher castes, has become common in all castes. As a result, especially in rural areas, reports have increased of families banishing, injuring, or killing young brides whose own families failed to supply the promised dowries. Notions of women's rights, common in cities, are less known in villages. In some towns the police harass unmarried couples in public parks for public displays of affection.

Some women have experienced more changes than others. Many Indian women have benefited from education, even becoming forceful leaders in such fields as journalism, business, trade unions, the arts, and government. Women have even been elected to parliament and serve as chief ministers of states, especially in south India. Outside the big cities, however, women have remained largely bound by tradition, expected to demonstrate submission, obedience, and absolute dedication to their husband. Women's organizations affiliated with the Hindu nationalist BJP downplay patriarchy, emphasizing women as mothers producing sons and portraying Muslim men as a threat to Hindu women. But an antipatriarchy women's movement, growing for a century, has become more active since the 1970s, suggesting that women's issues will remain on the nation's agenda. For instance, the Self-Employed Women's Association, founded by Ela Bhatt in 1972, has provided low-cost credit and literacy training to some of the poorest city women, the ragpickers and sidewalk vendors. By 2004 AIDS grew rapidly as a health problem, a result largely of women being forced into prostitution to serve the sexual needs of increasingly mobile male workers such as long-haul truckers. HIV infection has spread largely along the transportation networks.

Religion, like society, has changed, becoming intertwined with politics. As it has for millennia, religion still plays a key role in Indian life. Although Hindus form a large majority, India's population also includes 120 million Muslims, over 20 million Sikhs, and nearly 20 million Christians. Religious differences have become politicized. Some upper-caste Hindus, for instance, particularly in the BJP, have used the notion of a Hindu nation to marginalize Muslims and low-caste Hindus. Civil unrest involving violent attacks on Muslims by militant Hindu nationalists, often fundamentalists who interpret the ancient Hindu religious texts, or Vedas, literally, has caused political crises. Sometimes Muslims have initiated the violence. For instance, in 2006 Muslims protesting Danish cartoons offensive to Muslims rioted and attacked Hindu and Western targets. Tensions are fueled by mass poverty among all the religious groups. Yet, despite the tensions, Muslims occupy high positions in India's government, business, and the professions and play a key role in cultural expression, such as films and music. India's most famous modern artist, Tyeb Mehta (b. 1925), is a Shi'ite Muslim whose works, much of which address the Hindu-Muslim divide, sell all over the world.

Indians have also eagerly embraced modern cultural forms to express ideas. While Indian-born novelists such as Arundhati Roy (AH-roon-DAH-tee roy) and Salman Rushdie have achieved worldwide fame, a more popular cultural form in contemporary India has been film. India has built the world's largest film industry; it makes about a thousand movies a year, and many also find a huge audience among both Indian emigrants and non-Indians in Southeast Asia, Africa, Europe, and the Caribbean. The Bombay film industry, known as **"Bollywood,"** has become India's largest (see Profile: Raj Kapoor, Bollywood

Bollywood   The Bombay film industry.

RAJ KAPOOR,
BOLLYWOOD FILM STAR

Raj Kapoor As the most influential male lead and director in Indian films, Kapoor could attract the top actresses to star in his films. He made many films with Nargis, the two of them shown here in a 1948 musical, "Barsaat." (Dinodia Picture Agency)

Raj Kapoor (1924–1988) was a true pioneer: the first real superstar of Indian film, an accomplished actor, director, producer, and all-round showman. Kapoor skillfully combined music, melodrama, and spectacle to create a cinema with huge popular, even international, appeal, especially among the poor. He was born in Peshawar, the son of one of India's most distinguished stage and film actors, Prithviraj Kapoor, among whose hundreds of roles was that of Alexander the Great. The family settled in Bombay in 1929, when the Hindi-language film industry was in a formative stage (Hindi is the major language spoken in north India). At age twenty-two Kapoor entered an arranged marriage to Krishnaji. Although he had romances with actresses, the marriage endured and the couple had five children.

Handsome and vigorous, with a talent for comedy, music, and self-promotion, the young Kapoor formed his own film company in 1948 with hopes of appealing to the common person. Over the next three decades he starred in or oversaw dozens of films, many of them commercially successful. Kapoor's greatest success came during the Nehru years from the late 1940s to mid-1960s, when Indians were optimistic and looked outward. His films, often subtitled in local languages, brought him celebrity all over South Asia and in Southeast Asia, East Africa, the Middle East, the Caribbean, and the Soviet Union. He was largely responsible for the recognition of Indian cinema in the world. Songs from his films were sung or hummed on streets of cities and small towns thousands of miles from India. He and his female costars became popular pin-ups in the bazaars of the Arab world and folk heroes in the Soviet lands. Kapoor, like Nehru, believed that an Indian could be international, enjoying foreign products and influences, while also remaining deeply Indian. A song from his film *The Gentleman Cheat* in 1955 reflected the hero's transnational identity: "The shoes I'm wearing are made in Japan, My trousers fashioned in England. The red cap on my head is Russian. In spite of it all my heart is Indian."

Kapoor believed that some of his films achieved international success because "the young people of those countries saw in the films their own sufferings, the strivings to achieve, and their own triumph over a world in chaos." Fans saw in his characters youth, optimism about life, and revolt against authority, the little man straddling the great divides of wealth and poverty, city and village, sophistication and innocence. For example, in *The Vagabond* (1951) he portrays a rebellious youth and petty thief growing up on the streets, both daring and vulnerable, charming and reckless, surviving by his wits.

The themes of Kapoor's films often touched on social problems or politics and were filled with humanism and sensitivity. They cried out against destitution and unequal wealth, offering underdog heroes who were poor but also happy. These themes permeated some of his most popular films, such as *The Vagabond*, which broke box office records in the USSR and the Middle East, where it was dubbed into Arabic, Persian, and Turkish. An ardent fan of American comedians, especially

Charlie Chaplin, Kapoor, like Chaplin, often portrayed a deglamorized tramp, the little man at odds with the world and hiding his pain behind a smiling face, a figure he thought "had a greater identity with the common man."

Kapoor's romanticism was evident in his sympathetic treatment of women. The heroine, often played by the actress Nargis (NAR-ghis) (1929–1981), a Muslim whose mother was a famed singer, was always a central player in his films. Sometimes Kapoor's films presented women as strong and without flaws, as was his character's love interest, Nargis, in *The Vagabond*; at other times women were victims, exploited and tormented by religion and tradition. Kapoor argued, "We eulogize womankind as the embodiment of motherhood but we always give our women the worst treatment. They are burnt alive [in sati], treated as slaves [by men]." Yet, in spite of his concern for the sexual exploitation of women, Kapoor's films presented sensuous actresses and opened the way to more sexually explicit scenes, shocking social conservatives.

Kapoor's career faded in the 1970s, when his style of romantic hero became old-fashioned. The newer films focused on the angry young man, often a gangster, and turned away from Kapoor's adoring treatment of women. At the time of his death in 1988 he was making a film exploring the taboo subject of love across the India-Pakistan border, between a Hindu and a Muslim. His sons, all actors, tried to keep his banner alive, but Bollywood moved in new directions, centering stories on men and their challenges rather than balancing strong male-female roles as Kapoor had done.

THINKING ABOUT THE PROFILE

1. Why is Kapoor often credited with spreading Indian film to other countries?
2. What social viewpoints were expressed in his films?

Note: Quotations from Sumita S. Chakravarty, *National Identity in Indian Popular Cinema, 1947–1987* (Austin: University of Texas Press, 1993), pp. 138, 203; and Malti Sahai, "Raj Kapoor and the Indianization of Charlie Chaplin," *East-West Film Journal*, 2/1 (December, 1987), p. 64.

Film Star), churning out films in the major north Indian language, Hindi, but companies in other regions of India make films in local languages, such as Tamil in southeast India. Many films, especially musicals, have portrayed a fantasy world that enables viewers to forget the problem-filled real world. As one fan explains: "I love to sit in the dark and dream about what I can never possibly have. I can listen to the music, learn all the songs and forget about my troubles."[8] Religious divisions are muted in Bollywood, and the leading directors, writers, and stars often come from Muslim backgrounds. Because of their superstar status, film stars are often able to move into state and federal politics. For example, voters in southern India have long favored stars of the local film industry as state leaders. By the 1980s that trend had even spread to parts of north India.

Islamic Politics and Societies

South Asia's two densely populated Muslim countries, Pakistan and Bangladesh, have struggled to develop and to maintain stability. Both countries are divided between secular and devout Muslims, have alternated between military dictatorships and elected civilian governments, and have generally conservative cultures.

Pakistan Containing 150 million people, over 95 percent of them Sunni Muslims, Pakistan has had difficulty transforming its diverse ethnic and tribal groups into a politically stable, unified nation. The most long-lasting civilian leader, Zulkifar Ali Bhutto (zool-KEE-far AH-lee BOO-toe) (r. 1971–1977), a lawyer educated at top universities in Britain and California, came to power with great ambitions. Although from a wealthy landowning family, he pursued socialist policies unpopular with the wealthy. Accusing him of corruption, the army took power and later executed Bhutto. The Soviet occupation of Afghanistan in 1979 and the Pakistan-supported Islamic resistance to the Soviets that followed (see Chapter 30) distracted Pakistanis from their unpopular military regime and brought more U.S. military aid to Pakistan.

Pakistani politics has remained turbulent. In 1986 Bhutto's daughter, Benazir Bhutto (BEN-ah-ZEER BOO-toe) (b. 1953), a graduate of Britain's Oxford University, put together a movement to challenge the military regime. As unrest increased in 1988, Benazir Bhutto became prime minister and later became the first head of a modern Asian government to give birth to a child while in office. She was respected abroad but struggled to govern effectively. Accused of abuse of power, she was dismissed in 1990. The civilian who replaced her tried to strengthen Islamic practices. Benazir Bhutto returned to power after the 1993 elections but failed to resolve critical problems, including growing fighting between ethnic factions and attacks by militant Sunnis on the small Shi'a Muslim and Christian minorities. In 1996 she was once again removed.

In 1999 the military took over, installing as president Indian-born General Pervez Musharraf (per-VEZ moo-SHAR-uff) (b. 1943), whose family had fled to Pakistan during the partition of India in 1947. He faced the same challenge as his predecessors: to halt factional violence, punish corruption, collect taxes from the wealthy, restore economic growth, and balance the demands of both militant and secular Muslims. Although Musharraf allied with the United States after the 2001 terrorist attacks on the United States and the resulting U.S. invasion of Afghanistan, many Pakistanis prefer closer ties with the Middle East and resent the U.S. and the West, in part because the United States, while seeking Pakistani help in the war on international terrorism, is reluctant to remove high tariff barriers against Pakistani textiles, a major export that accounts for nearly half of all manufacturing jobs. Pakistanis make everything from shirts to sheets for Western companies, and experts argue that an expansion of this work might relieve the high unemployment rate and hence reduce the appeal of extremist Islam for desperate young men.

Pakistani society and culture have remained conservative. Pakistan's founding leader, Jinnah, a cosmopolitan British-educated lawyer, had favored more rights for women, arguing that it was a crime that most Pakistani women were shut up within the four walls of the house as prisoners. But national leaders who shared this view were reluctant to challenge the strong opposition to women's rights, especially in rural areas. In 1979 an Islamizing military government pushed through discriminatory laws that made women who were raped guilty of adultery, a serious offense. Women enjoyed far fewer legal rights than men and were more commonly jailed or punished than men for adultery. Women's groups who courageously protested in the streets were attacked by military force, prompting the feminist poet Saeeda Gazdar (SIGH-ee-da GAZ-dar) to write: "The flags of mourning were flapping, the hand-maidens had rebelled. Those two hundred women who came out on the streets, were surrounded on all sides, besieged by armed force, [repressed by] the enemies of truth, the murderers of love."[9] By the 1990s things had changed little: only 10 percent of adult women were employed outside the home, and fewer than 20 percent were literate. The United Nations ranked Pakistan near the bottom of nations in women's equality. In some districts Islamic militants succeeded in restricting women from voting or from attending school with males.

Serious problems persist in Pakistan. It remains a land of villages dominated by large, politically influential landowners. Life expectancy for Pakistanis improved from forty-three to sixty years between 1960 and 1997, but 40 percent of children in that period suffered from malnutrition. The attempts by Islamic leaders to prohibit the broadcasting of music by popular singers, especially women such as London-based Nazia Hassan, set off an ongoing debate about the role of Westernized popular culture and women entertainers.

Bangladesh Even more so than Pakistan, Bangladesh, over-crowded with 125 million people, has encountered barriers to development. Mostly flat plains, the land is prone to devastating hurricanes, floods, tornados, and famine. The nation's founder, Sheik Mujiber Rahman, had hoped that the nation he envisioned—secular, democratic, and socialist—would rapidly progress, but, after tightening his power, he was assassinated by the military. None of the succession of governments after him, whether military or civilian, has had much

Like Laos, Cambodia also became part of the Indochina conflict. Its first president, the multitalented Prince Sihanouk, ruled as a benevolent autocrat while also writing sentimental popular songs, playing the saxophone, directing films, and publicizing his political views in foreign newspapers. Sihanouk diplomatically maintained Cambodian independence and peace. But during the 1960s both the Vietnamese Communists, whose forces roamed the border area, and the United States, whose war planes bombed Communist positions in Cambodian territory, violated Cambodian neutrality. Sihanouk faced other problems as well. The **Khmer Rouge** (kmahr roozh) ("Red Khmers"), a Communist insurgent group seeking to overthrow the government and led by alienated intellectuals educated in French universities, built a small support base of impoverished peasants. In addition, although Sihanouk remained popular among the majority of peasants, military officers and big businessmen resented his dictatorial rule and desired to share in the U.S. money and arms flowing into neighboring South Vietnam, Laos, and Thailand.

In 1970 Sihanouk was overthrown by U.S.-backed generals and civilians, beginning a tragic era in Cambodian history. With Sihanouk in exile, U.S. and South Vietnamese forces soon invaded eastern Cambodia in search of Vietnamese Communist bases, and the resulting instability created an opening for the Khmer Rouge to recruit mass support. The pro-U.S. government lacked legitimacy and became increasingly dependent on U.S. aid for virtually all supplies, and the ineffective Cambodian army suffered from corruption and low morale. Meanwhile, to attack the Khmer Rouge, U.S. planes launched an intensive, terrifying air assault through the heart of Cambodia's agricultural area, where most of the population lived. The bombing killed thousands of innocent civilians. Rice production declined by almost half, raising the possibility of massive starvation. Amid the destruction, the Khmer Rouge rapidly enlarged its forces, recruiting from among the displaced and shell-shocked peasantry. From 1970 through 1975 between 750,000 and 1 million Cambodians, mostly civilians, perished from the conflict between the Khmer Rouge, who were brutal toward their enemies, and the U.S.-backed government. In 1975 the Khmer Rouge seized the capital, Phnom Penh.

Conflict and Reconstruction in Indochina

After years of war and destruction, Vietnam, Laos, and Cambodia began to rebuild and deal with lingering tensions resulting from the bitter divisions. The challenge was daunting. In the largest nation, Vietnam, socialist policies failed to revitalize the economy, and the reunification of North and South Vietnam proved harsh. Because of mismanaged political and economic policies, natural disasters, a long U.S. economic embargo, and the devastation of the war, between 1978 and 1985 half a million refugees, known as "boat people," risked

their lives to escape Vietnam in rickety boats, becoming easy targets for pirates. After spending months or years in crowded refugee camps in Southeast Asia, most of the refugees were resettled in North America, Australia, or France.

In the 1980s the Vietnamese government recognized its failures and introduced market-oriented reforms similar to those in China favoring private enterprise and foreign investment. These reforms increased productivity, fostered some prosperity in the cities, and ended the refugee flow. Emphasis on education more than doubled the 1945 literacy rates to 85 percent of adults. But the shift from rigid socialism also widened economic inequality, leaving most farmers living just above the poverty line. Vietnamese debated the appropriate balance between socialist and free market policies to resolve the rural problems. Politically, Vietnam, like China, remained an authoritarian one-party state, with little democracy, but restrictions on cultural expression loosened. Several former soldiers became rock or disco stars, and many writers addressed contemporary problems and the war's legacy in fiction. For example, "The General Retires," a short story by a former North Vietnamese soldier, caused a sensation by depicting the despair of an old soldier contemplating the emptiness of the new society.

After victory in the long struggle to end foreign domination, the Communists expanded ties to the West and the world economy. By the late 1990s, the United States and Vietnam had resumed diplomatic relations, and U.S. president Bill Clinton lifted the U.S. economic embargo. Bustling Saigon, now renamed Ho Chi Minh City, has enjoyed especially dynamic economic growth and prosperity. Consumers in the United States now buy shrimp and underwear imported from Vietnam while many Americans, including former soldiers and Vietnamese refugees, visit Vietnam. Hundreds of American veterans operate businesses or social service agencies in Vietnam, sometimes in partnership with former Communist soldiers. Still, the ruling Communists have to satisfy the expectations of the 80 million Vietnamese struggling to overcome the devastation wrought by decades of war.

Like the Vietnamese, Laotians also needed to deal with the divisions and destruction caused by the war. Many Laotians fled into exile to escape retribution or hard times, among them 300,000 Hmongs who settled in the United States. Since the 1980s Laotian leaders have sought warmer relations with neighboring Thailand and China as well as with the United States, but these relations have not fostered a more open society or energized the economy. Rigid Communists still dominate the one-party state. While several cities and districts have vibrant economies, attracting Western tourists, most Laotians remain poor. Looking across the Mekong at the busy freeways, neon lights, and high-rise buildings on the Thailand side, Laotians often suspect that capitalist, democratic Thailand offers a more successful model of development.

Cambodia has faced a far more difficult challenge than Vietnam and Laos, because war was followed by fierce repression. Agriculture had been badly disrupted by war, raising the specter of widespread starvation. When the Communist Khmer Rouge, hardened by years of brutal war, achieved power in 1975, they

Khmer Rouge ("Red Khmers") A Communist insurgent group seeking to overthrow the government in Cambodia during the 1960s and 1970s.

Honoring Ho Chi Minh These schoolgirls, dressed in traditional clothing and parading before Ho Chi Minh's mausoleum in Hanoi, are part of an annual festival to honor the leading figure of Vietnamese communism. (AP/Wide World Photos)

Khmer Rouge to the Thailand border. The Vietnamese invasion liberated the Cambodian people from tyranny and installed a less brutal Communist government. But military conflict continued for years as a Khmer Rouge–dominated resistance, subsidized chiefly by China and the United States, which both wanted to weaken Vietnam by forcing it to spend money in Cambodia, controlled some sections of the country. Cambodia proved to be for Vietnam what Vietnam had been for the United States, an endless sinkhole of conflict that drained scarce wealth and complicated Vietnam's relations with the West.

In the early 1990s a coalition government was formed under United Nations sponsorship that brought about change. The Khmer Rouge, which refused to take part, splintered and collapsed as a movement. While the resulting peace was welcomed by all, the government remained repressive and corrupt. The ruling party tolerated some opposition but controlled the voting. Sihanouk returned from exile to become king but had little power and served largely as a symbol of Cambodia's link to its past. Life for many Cambodians remained grim as they faced everything from the high price of fuel to poor education, problems that have spurred some people to organize in support of more democracy and attention to social problems. Nevertheless, the new government has transformed Cambodia, while still haunted by past horrors, from a traumatized to a functioning society, kept afloat largely by Western tourism and aid.

turned on the urban population with a fury, driving everyone into the rural areas to farm. The Khmer Rouge's radical vision of a propertyless, classless peasant society, combined with their violence against those believed to dissent or resist, led to the flight of thousands of refugees into neighboring countries and what survivors called the "killing fields": the Khmer Rouge executed thousands of victims in death camps and shot or starved many others, including both common people such as peasants and taxi drivers and Westernized and educated people such as doctors and artists. Ultimately the Khmer Rouge and their brutal leader, Pol Pot (1925–1998), in their attempt to create a new Communist society, were responsible for the death of 1 to 2 million Cambodians. Perhaps 500,000 were executed and the rest died from illness, hunger, and overwork, sparking comparisons with Nazi Germany.

The situation changed in 1978, leading to a new government. The Vietnamese, alarmed at Khmer Rouge territorial claims and the murder of thousands of ethnic Vietnamese in Cambodia, allied with an exile army of disaffected former Khmer Rouge, invaded Cambodia, and rapidly pushed the

SECTION SUMMARY

■ After World War II, the Communist Viet Minh, led by Ho Chi Minh, took partial control of Vietnam and declared independence, but the U.S.-supported French fought back in the First Indochina War, which ended in frustration for the French.

■ Instead of allowing an election to determine the future of South Vietnam, the United States installed Diem as president but he was opposed by the Communist National Liberation Front, setting the stage for the Vietnam War.

■ Using a questionable attack as a pretext, the United States went to war to rid Vietnam of communism, but despite vastly superior resources, the United States and its allies in South Vietnam could not triumph over the

Communists, who gained control of Vietnam two years after the U.S. pulled out its ground forces.

- In Laos the United States recruited Hmong hill people to fight the Pathet Lao revolutionaries, who took control of the country in 1975, while in Cambodia the United States bombed areas occupied by North Vietnamese and supported a weak, dependent government, which was overthrown in 1975 by the Khmer Rouge.

- Vietnam struggled after the war, but in the 1980s it opened up its economy and by the 1990s had reestablished ties with the rest of the world, including the United States.

- Many Laotians fled into exile, while the Communist-dominated government has opened somewhat to the world economy, and Cambodia endured vicious repression under the Khmer Rouge, who continued to wreak havoc even after a Vietnamese invasion pushed them out of power.

CHRONOLOGY	
Non-Communist Southeast Asia, 1945–Present	
1945–1950	Indonesian Revolution
1948	Independence of Burma
1963	Formation of Malaysia
1965	Secession of Singapore from Malaysia
1965–1966	Turmoil in Indonesia
1966–1998	New Order in Indonesia
1997	Economic crisis in Southeast Asia

 # New Nations in Southeast Asia

How did decolonization shape the new Southeast Asian nations?

In addition to the Indochinese countries, the nationalist thrust for independence from colonialism produced other new nations in Southeast Asia in the aftermath of World War II (see Map 31.3). But the euphoria of independence proved short-lived, and the building of states capable of improving the lives of their people had only just begun. Indonesia, the Philippines, Burma, and the other new nations, while often facing violent unrest, avoided the destructive warfare rocking Indochina but also had to overcome economic underdevelopment, promote national unity in ethnically divided societies, and deal with opposition to the new ruling groups. The years between 1945 and 1975 were marked by economic progress, but also by conflict and dictatorships. The leaders also had to forge new relationships with the former colonial powers and the new superpowers of a Cold War world—the United States and the Soviet Union—as well as with nearby China.

Indonesia: The Quest for Freedom and Unity

Indonesian independence came through struggle. The violent resistance to Dutch colonialism of the late 1940s, known as the Indonesian Revolution, was a bitter conflict in which the Dutch used massive violence to suppress the Indonesian nationalists, who fought back. In a short story about the brutal battle to control the east Javanese city of Surabaya, a nationalist writer noted that, for the revolutionary soldiers, "everything blurred: the future and their heart-breaking struggle. They only knew that they had to murder to drive out the enemy and stop him trampling their liberated land. They killed [the Dutch soldiers] with great determination, spirit and hunger."[17] The United States, fearing regional instability, pressured the Dutch to grant independence in 1950 (see Chronology: Non-Communist Southeast Asia, 1945–Present).

Indonesia still faced the challenge of fostering a unified nation. Given the diversity of islands, peoples, and cultures, Indonesian leaders became obsessed with creating national unity and identity. Their national slogan, however, "unity in diversity," expressed more a goal than a solid reality. During the 1950s and early 1960s Indonesia was led by the charismatic but increasingly authoritarian president Sukarno (soo-KAHR-no) (1902–1970), the son of a Javanese aristocrat and a Balinese mother and an inspirational nationalist. A spell-binding orator who was able to rally popular support and bring different factions together, Sukarno worked to create national solidarity and unite a huge nation in which villagers on remote islands and cosmopolitan city dwellers on Java knew little about each other.

Despite his efforts, however, Sukarno proved unable to maintain stability. The multiparty parliamentary system he headed in the 1950s became divisive. Regionalism grew as outer islanders resented domination by the Javanese, who constituted over half of Indonesia's population and, many outer islanders believed, were favored by Sukarno. Sukarno's nationalistic but poorly implemented economic policies contributed to a severe economic crisis by the early 1960s and deepened divisions between Communist, Islamic, and military forces. A pro-Communist Javanese novelist described the economic failures of the Sukarno years: "Jakarta [the capital city] reveals a grandiose display with no relationship to reality. Great plans, enormous immorality. [There are] no screws, no nuts, no bolts, no valves, and no washers for the machinery we do have."[18]

By 1965 Indonesia had become a country of explosive social and political pressures and was experiencing its greatest crisis as an independent nation. After a failed attempt by a small military faction with Communist sympathies to seize power, a group of discontented generals arrested Sukarno, seized power,

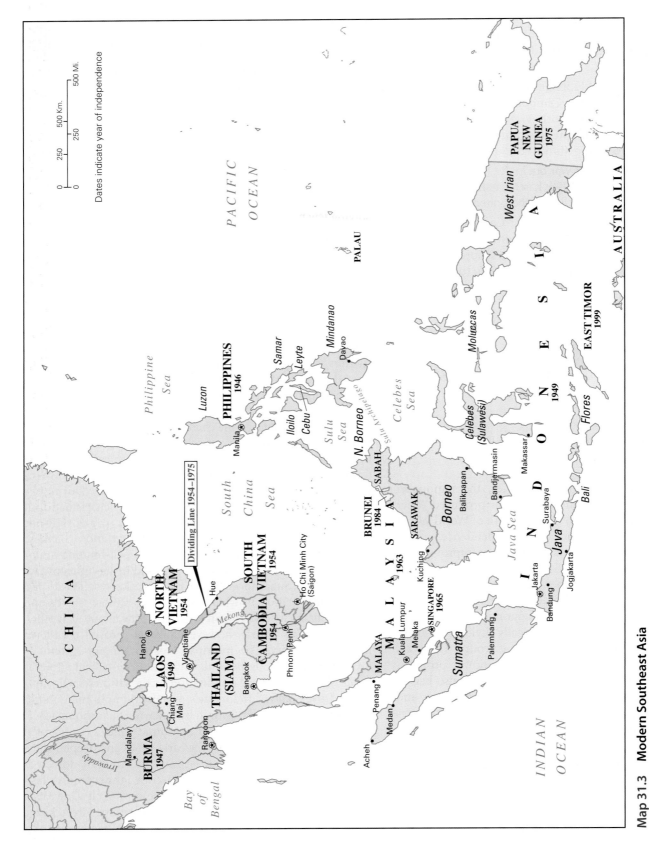

Map 31.3 Modern Southeast Asia

Indonesia, covering thousands of islands, is the largest, most populous Southeast Asian nation. Southeast Asia also includes four other island nations (including the Philippines and Singapore), five nations on the mainland, and Malaysia, which sprawls from the Malay Peninsula to northern Borneo.

and launched a brutal campaign to eliminate all leftists, especially those affiliated with the large Communist Party, which had built up its influence among poor peasants in Java. The resulting bloodbath, led by the army and Muslim groups, killed perhaps half a million Indonesians, including Communists and members of the large, unpopular Chinese minority. Most Communist leaders were killed or arrested; thousands of leftists were held in remote prison camps for years. Sukarno died in disgrace in 1970.

Making the Philippine and Malaysian Nations

The Philippines and Malaysia both became independent but troubled nations. In the sixteenth century the Philippines had been one of the first Southeast Asian societies to be colonized by a Western country, Spain. At the end of the nineteenth century, the United States replaced Spanish rule with its own. In the nineteenth century the British had colonized Malaya, on the Malay Peninsula, and also dominated the northern Borneo territories of Sabah (North Borneo) and Sarawak. The Americans and British both exploited their colonies' natural resources—cash crops and minerals—for export. However, the two ruling powers also treated the colonized people less harshly than the French did the Vietnamese or the Dutch the Indonesians. As a result, anti-Western nationalism in the Philippines, Malaysia, and British Borneo before World War II was weaker and less violent than in Vietnam and Indonesia.

The Philippines achieved independence from the United States on July 4, 1946, though the two countries remained bound by close political and economic links. The new nation soon faced problems sustaining democracy. A small group of landowners, industrialists, and businessmen who had prospered under U.S. rule manipulated elected governments to preserve their political and economic power and to protect U.S. economic interests. Free elections involved so much violence, bribery, and fraud that disillusioned Filipinos spoke of them as decided by "guns, goons, and gold."

Furthermore, nationalists often believed that continuing U.S. influence hindered the creation of a truly independent Filipino identity and culture. Several major U.S. military bases near Manila symbolized this influence, and the popular U.S. films, television programs, music, comics, and books helped to spread it. A prominent Filipina scholar wrote that her people "sing of White Christmases and of Manhattan. Their stereos reverberate with the American Top 40."[19] Outside influences—first Spanish and then American—on Filipino culture were often superficial, but Filipinos have struggled to create a clear national identity out of the diverse mosaic of local languages and regions.

Economic inequality and social divisions have fueled conflict. A Filipino poet portrayed the gap between the rich and poor: "[For the affluent] there's pleasure and distraction, fiesta and dancing, night-long, day-long; who dares whisper that thousands have no roofs above their heads; that hunger stalks the town."[20] The Communist-led Huk Rebellion from 1948 to 1954 capitalized on discontent among the rural poor. Only heavy U.S. assistance to the government suppressed the rebel-

lion. In the 1970s the Communist New Peoples Army (NPA) controlled many rural districts. Like the Huks, the NPA's promise of radical social and economic change attracted support from rural tenant farmers and urban slum dwellers. Religious differences have also led to conflict. While most Filipinos became Christian in Spanish times, the southern islands have large Muslim populations, who have often resented political domination by and favoritism toward Christians. As a result, several Muslim groups have taken up arms to fight for autonomy. In 1972 President Ferdinand Marcos (1917–1989) used the restoration of law and order as an excuse to suspend democracy, and from 1972 until 1986 he ruled as a dictator, resolving few problems.

Compared with the Philippines, governments proved more stable in Malaya after independence. After World War II the British sought to dampen political unrest in Malaya as Communist-led insurgents kept the colony on edge for a decade. In 1957, with the insurgency crushed, Malaya became independent as a federation of states under a government led by the main Malay party, **UMNO** (United Malays National Organization). However, the predominantly Chinese city-state of Singapore, a major trading center and military base, remained outside the federation as a British colony. In Malaya the majority ethnic group, the Malays, nearly all Muslim, dominated politics, but the Chinese, a third of the population, were granted liberal citizenship rights and maintained strong economic power. British leaders, seeing their colonial role in Singapore as well as in two northern Borneo states they controlled, Sabah and Sarawak, as burdensome, suggested joining them with Malaya in a larger federation, to be called Malaysia. This new, geographically divided Malaysia was formed in 1963.

In the years that followed Malaysia struggled to create national unity out of deep regional and ethnic divisions. Singapore withdrew from Malaysia in 1965 and became an independent nation. Given the need to reduce political tensions, sustain rapid economic growth, and preserve stability, the leaders of the key ethnic groups in Malaya—Malays, Chinese, and Indians—cooperated through political parties that allied in an UMNO-dominated ruling coalition, but below the surface ethnic tensions simmered. Street fighting between Chinese and Malays following the heated 1969 election led to a nationwide state of emergency. After 1970 Malay-dominated governments pursued policies designed to reshape Malaysia's society and economy.

Diversity and Dictatorship in Thailand and Burma

Thailand and Burma also struggled to create national unity and stability. Although historical rivals, the two countries have shared certain patterns. The majority ethnic groups, the Thais and the Burmans, are both Theravada Buddhists who assert authority over a variety of ethnic minorities, including various hill tribes, Muslim peoples, and immigrant trading communities,

UMNO (United Malays National Organization) The main Malay political party in Malaysia.

largely Chinese and Indians. Both countries also have experienced insurgencies by disaffected ethnic, religious, or political factions. However, while Burma had been an often restless British colony since the mid-1800s, Thailand (once known as Siam) was the only major Southeast Asian country to avoid colonization. As a result, Thais have had more control over their government, economy, and culture than other Southeast Asians have enjoyed.

In Thailand, leaders sought to build a national culture based on Thai cultural values, including reverence for Buddhism and the monarchy, which had little formal power but symbolized the nation. Thai culture promotes respect for those in authority and values social harmony. However, this conservatism has also fostered authoritarian governments and bureaucratic inertia. Ethnic and religious diversity has also posed political problems. Various communist and Islamic insurgent groups operated during the 1960s and 1970s in ethnic minority regions. Partly because of this unrest, Thailand's political history after 1945 was characterized by long periods of military rule, often corrupt and oppressive, followed by short-lived democratically elected or semidemocratic governments.

Not until the 1970s would a true mass politics develop in Thailand, as opposition movements challenged the long-entrenched military regime. Opposition gained sway in part from Thais' resentment of the United States, which supported the military regime and had military bases and some 50,000 troops in the country. The presence of free-spending American soldiers created a false prosperity while also posing a challenge to Buddhist morality. Staunch Buddhists were outraged by the sleazy bars, gaudy nightclubs, and brothels that often exploited poor Thai women and that served the Americans but also attracted eager Thai men.

In 1973 antigovernment feelings boiled over and the military regime was overthrown following student-led mass demonstrations that involved several hundred thousand people. The military strongman was forced to flee the country, having lost public support after his troops arrested protest leaders and killed or wounded over a thousand demonstrators. The collapse of military rule opened a brief era of political liberalization. For the first time in Thai history, democracy and debate flourished. The civilian government tolerated these activities, yet it proved fragile and unable to resolve major problems. Meanwhile, rightwing military officers and bureaucrats became alarmed at challenges to their power and privileges, and Thai society became increasingly polarized between liberals and conservatives. Finally, in 1976, bloody clashes between leftist students and rightwing youth gangs led to a military coup and martial law, which resulted in the killing or wounding of hundreds and the arrest of thousands of students and their supporters. The return of military power reestablished order, but the massacres discredited the military.

To the west of Thailand, Burma emerged from the Japanese occupation devastated, with whole cities blasted into rubble by Allied bombing. After the war the British returned to reestablish their colonial control. However, facing a well-armed Burmese nationalist army and weary of conflict, they elected to negotiate independence with the charismatic

nationalist leader Aung San (1915–1947). In 1948 the British left Burma, but newly elected Prime Minister Aung San was assassinated by a political rival. He was replaced by his longtime colleague, U Nu (1907–1995), an idealistic Buddhist who, like Aung San, supported democracy. Soon key ethnic minorities, fearful of domination by the majority Burmans, each declared their secession from Burma and organized armies. For the next four decades the central government rarely controlled more than half the nation's territory as the ethnic armies and communist insurgents fought each other and the Burmese army. To fund their armies the insurgents often relied on revenues from growing and exporting opium.

In 1962 the army deposed U Nu and seized control. Skeptical of democracy for a fragmented nation, military rulers suspended civil liberties, imposed censorship, and devoted most government revenue to the military. The military took over industries, banks, and commerce, and discouraged foreign investment. However, by the 1980s, as a result of the military keeping a tight control of the government and economy, economic stagnation and political repression had fostered dissent and the various secession movements continued, only to be largely suppressed in the 1990s.

SECTION SUMMARY

■ After a difficult fight for independence from the Dutch, Indonesia's wildly diverse population struggled to attain unity under Sukarno, but different groups became more divided and a group of generals cracked down harshly on leftists and removed Sukarno from power.

■ After attaining independence, the Philippines remained strongly influenced by the United States and struggled with economic inequality and a Muslim insurgency, while Malaysia experienced intermittent tensions between the politically dominant Malays and the economically strong Chinese.

■ Thailand alternated between long periods of military rule and short periods of democratic or semidemocratic rule, while Burma endured decades of factional fighting and, since 1962, brutal military domination.

 ## Tigers, Politics, and Changing Southeast Asian Societies

What role do the Southeast Asian nations play in the global system?

Southeast Asia changed dramatically after 1975, mixing influences from the past and from the wider world. The fast pace of change has reshaped societies and cultures in both cities and villages. Some nations have developed economically. Indonesia, Malaysia, Singapore, and Thailand, enjoying lively market economies geared to world commerce, have gained reputations as "tigers" because of their economic dynamism. At the same time, governments play a major role in stimulating economies and often have become authoritarian in an effort to ensure social stability.

The Resurgence of Southeast Asia

After the mid-1970s a shift of economic direction allowed several Southeast Asians to develop and play a greater role in the world economy. On the eve of this shift, in 1976, Indonesia, Burma, and Thailand were under military rule, a dictator governed in the Philippines, and only Malaysia and Singapore had at least partial democracies. Few of the countries had achieved impressive economic growth. But in the years to follow, and especially after 1980, the pace of change accelerated in every area of life. Leaders, inspired by the example of Japan's industrialization in the late nineteenth century and encouraging their people to "Look East," mixed capitalism and activist government to spur economic growth and industrialization. Local entrepreneurs of Chinese ancestry provided much of the initiative and capital for economic expansion. By the 1990s experts talked about a vibrant Pacific Rim that included the "tiger" nations as well as Japan, China, Taiwan, and South Korea (see Chapter 27). Some forecast a Pacific Century in which these nations would lead the world economically and increase their political strength.

Economic growth contributed to social and political change. Migrants crowding into cities brushed elbows with other peoples, encouraging cultural mixing. More schools were built, helping foster larger middle classes that sought more political influence. Yet, while nations were slowly being built in both institutions and people's minds, governments often abused their powers, squashing dissent and repressing personal liberties. There were also drawbacks to economic growth: industrial activity and the expansion of agriculture, mining, and logging caused widespread environmental destruction.

To promote economic growth and political stability, Southeast Asian countries began cooperating as never before. Founded in 1967 by Malaysia, Indonesia, Thailand, Singapore, and the Philippines, **ASEAN** (Association of Southeast Asian Nations) was a regional economic and political organization aimed at fostering economic exchange among the non-Communist Southeast Asian nations and coordinating opposition to Communist Vietnam. However, ASEAN's priorities shifted after the end of the wars in Indochina in 1975. As Vietnam, Cambodia, Laos, Burma, and the tiny, oil-rich state of Brunei, on Borneo, became members, ASEAN emerged as the world's fourth largest trading bloc. It also provided a forum for the various nations to work out their differences and deal with the wider world. In the early twenty-first century ASEAN, wanting regional stability, cultivated closer relations with the dominant East Asian nations, China and Japan.

Still, challenges demanded solutions. By 2000 there were some 550 million Southeast Asians, a huge increase over the 20 to 25 million four centuries earlier. Population growth outstripped economic growth, placing a greater burden on limited resources such as food and water, especially in the Philippines, Indonesia, and Vietnam. The impact of these conditions sometimes resulted in riots or even full-blown insurgencies. But despite occasional eruptions of violence and political upheavals, the destructive wars of the earlier years were not repeated. In some cases, dictatorships were eventually replaced by more open regimes.

In 1997 most Southeast Asian countries faced a severe economic crisis, part of a broader collapse among Asian and world economies. The widespread dislocations called into question the prospect of a forthcoming Pacific Century. The reasons for the troubles included poorly regulated banking systems, overconfident investments, and government favoritism toward well-placed business interests. The dislocations hit all social classes. By the early 2000s, however, as the crisis eventually bottomed out, several countries began to put their economies back on a rapid growth track.

Indonesia: New Order and Islamic Society

The colossus of Southeast Asia, Indonesia, with a rapidly growing population of 230 million that includes more than seven hundred ethnic groups, struggled to preserve political stability while developing economically. Between 1966 and 1998 the government, known as the **New Order**, headed by general-turned-president Suharto (b. 1921), a Javanese former soldier first in the Dutch colonial and then in the nationalist army, mixed military and civilian leadership to maintain law and order. For instance, Suharto used force to repress regional opposition to his Javanese-dominated central government, as in East Timor, a small, former Portuguese colony where the mostly Christian population sought independence, and in north Sumatra, where the fiercely Islamic Achehnese have sought independence for decades. However, although it limited political opposition, the New Order improved Indonesia's economic position and encouraged the rise of an educated urban middle class and a vibrant popular culture shaped by creative musicians, writers, artists, and filmmakers. Per capita income, life expectancy, and adult literacy increased, aided by an annual economic growth rate of nearly 5 percent by the 1990s, though a third of the population remained desperately poor, earning less than a dollar a day.

Yet, for all the economic productivity, the New Order also started some negative trends. During these years Indonesia became economically dependent on exporting oil, which represented 80 percent of foreign earnings. When the decline of world oil prices in the 1980s reduced funds for the national

---

ASEAN (Association of Southeast Asian Nations)   A regional economic and political organization formed in 1967 to promote cooperation among the noncommunist Southeast Asian nations; eventually became a major trading bloc.

New Order   The Indonesian government headed by President Suharto from 1966 to 1998, which mixed military and civilian leadership.

budget, Indonesia was forced to accumulate an enormous foreign debt. Adding to the problems, the rapid development of mining, forestry, and cash crop agriculture took a toll on the environment. Rain forests were clear-cut so rapidly for timber and to open space for plantations that forest fires became common, polluting the air and creating a thick, unhealthy haze every year that spread into neighboring nations. Furthermore, income disparities between classes and regions widened while political and business corruption became a major problem. One Indonesian fiction writer criticized a society in which government officials and predatory businessmen solicited bribes and grabbed public funds for themselves: "Indonesia, Land of Robbers. My true homeland stiff with thieves. In the future, I shall plunder while my wife shall seize."[21] Thanks to such corruption, the wealthy frolicked in nightclubs, casinos, and golf courses built across the street from slums or on land appropriated from powerless villages. Suharto, the son of poor peasants, became one of the world's most corrupt leaders, and he and his family acquired over $15 billion in assets from their business enterprises, which received government favoritism, and from access to public coffers.

Many Indonesians disliked the New Order. For some, Islam provided the chief vehicle for opposition. Some 87 percent of Indonesians are either devout or nominal Muslims, but few have supported militant Islamist movements like those in the Middle East and Pakistan. Suharto discouraged such Islamic radicalism as a threat to national unity in a country that also includes Christians and Hindus. However, devout Muslims have often opposed the government's secular policies and have desired a more Islamic approach to social, cultural, and legal matters. Muslim conservatives denounce gambling casinos, racy magazines and films, and scantily-clad female pop singers. At the same time, a progressive, democratic strand of Indonesian Islamic thought has favored liberal social and political reform. The Muslim liberals tap into the traditional Javanese emphasis on harmony, consensus, and tolerance that was incorporated into Indonesian, especially Javanese, Islam; they thus offer a stark contrast to the more dogmatic Islam common in countries such as Pakistan and Saudi Arabia. But, whether conservative or liberal, Muslims have blamed the government for poor living standards and massive corruption. Poets, novelists, musicians, and theater groups also addressed the New Order's problems.

By the 1990s Indonesian society was suffering from increasing class tensions, insecurities, student protests, and labor unrest, all of which set the stage for dramatic changes. When the economy collapsed, throwing millions out of work and raising prices for essential goods, riots throughout the country resulted to Suharto's resignation in 1998. With the longtime strongman gone, the country fell into turmoil, and protests and ethnic clashes proliferated. Many civilians, particularly among the urban middle class, wanted to strengthen democracy, and in 1999 free elections were held. Later, Megawati Soekarnoputri (MEH-ga-WHA-tee soo-KAR-no-POO-tri), the daughter of Indonesia's first president, Sukarno, became Indonesia's first woman president. Like her father, Megawati followed secular, nationalist policies but also showed little faith

in grassroots democracy and resolved few problems. By 2004 popular support for her regime had ebbed and she was defeated for reelection by a Javanese general.

The end of Suharto's New Order, and the disorderly democracy that replaced it, brought unprecedented freedom of the press and speech but also new problems. Removing New Order restrictions allowed long-simmering ethnic hostilities to reemerge. East Timor, for example, which had endured a long, unpopular occupation by Indonesia, finally achieved independence, but only after thousands of its people were killed by Indonesian troops and pro-Indonesian Timorese militias. Conflicts in Indonesia between Muslims and Christians and continuing regional rebellions, especially in Acheh, resulted in numerous deaths. Islamic militants capitalized on the instability to recruit support. Terrorist attacks in Indonesia, especially the bombing of popular tourist venues on Bali in 2003 and 2005, added to the growing tensions, raising questions about the long-term viability of Indonesian democracy. Complicating the political problems, in 2005 over 100,000 Indonesians perished from earthquakes and a deadly tidal wave, or tsunami, that destroyed cities and washed away coastal villages on Sumatra. Efforts to recover from these major setbacks further undermined the economy.

Politics and Society in the Philippines

Like Indonesia, the Philippines, a nation of 85 million people, also experienced political turbulence and social instability. In economic development the Philippines lagged well behind the most prosperous nations in Southeast Asia. During the fourteen years that Ferdinand Marcos ruled the nation as a dictator, economic conditions worsened, rural poverty became more widespread, the population grew rapidly, and political opposition was limited by the murder or detention of dissidents, censorship, and rigged elections. The dictator and his family and cronies looted the country for their own benefit, amassing billions. The government built high walls along city freeways so that affluent motorists would not have to view slums along the route. In the capital, Manila, a tiny minority lived in palatial homes surrounded by high walls topped with bits of broken glass and barbed wire, and with gates manned by armed guards. Across the street from the glittering pavilions of Manila's Cultural Center, whose landscaped gardens were a gaudy monument to Marcos splendor, homeless families slept in bushes. The majority of rural families were landless, and child malnutrition increased. A Filipino novelist described the unchanging rural society and its poverty, with villagers eking out a living on unproductive land: "Nothing in the countryside had changed, not the thatched houses, not the ragged vegetation, not the stolid people. Changeless land, burning sun."[22] To find work and escape poverty, Filipinos often migrated, temporarily or permanently, to other Asian nations, the United States, or the Middle East. Some 10 million Filipinos lived abroad by 2006, many being women who worked as nurses, maids, or entertainers. About 2,500 Filipinos leave the country every day for overseas work.

The failures of the Marcos years led to massive public protests in 1986 that brought down Marcos and restored

People's Power Demonstration in the Philippines In 1986 the simmering opposition to the dictatorial government of Ferdinand Marcos reached a boiling point, resulting in massive demonstrations in Manila. Under the banner of "people's power," businesspeople, professionals, housewives, soldiers, students, and cultural figures rallied to topple the regime.   (Corbis)

democracy. The opposition had rallied around U.S.-educated Corazon Aquino (ah-KEE-no) (b. 1933), a descendant of a Chinese immigrant, whose popular politician husband had been assassinated by Marcos henchmen. In a spectacular nonviolent revolution under the banner of "people's power," street demonstrations involving students, workers, businessmen, housewives, and clergy demanded justice and freedom. Marcos and his family fled into exile in the United States, which had long supported his regime. As Marcos and his family escaped by helicopter, thousands of demonstrators who broke into the presidential palace found that the dictator's wife, Imelda Marcos, a former beauty queen, had acquired thousands of pairs of shoes and vast stores of undergarments, symbolizing the Marcos's waste of public resources. Mrs. Aquino became president and reestablished democracy.

Yet the hopes that the nation could resolve its problems proved illusory and politics remained turbulent. The government, while open to dissenting voices, was, as had been true since independence, dominated by the wealthiest Filipinos, mostly members of the hundred or so landowning families who were favored during U.S. colonial rule; members of these families have held some two-thirds of seats in Congress. Mrs. Aquino, herself a member of one of these families, voluntarily left office at the end of her term in 1992. Her successors had rocky presidencies; one of these men, a former film star with a reputation for heavy drinking, gambling, and womanizing, was impeached for corruption and vote-rigging. In 2001 another woman, Gloria Macapagal-Arroyo (b. 1947), a Ph.D. in economics and the daughter of a former president, became president but also faced allegations of corruption. She was reelected in 2005 but faced constant challenges questioning her legitimacy. Two decades after the overthrow of Marcos the public seems disillusioned with the results. Many Filipinos also resented the continuing close ties to, and influence from, the

United States. A best-selling pop song reflected the opposition to what nationalists considered U.S. neocolonialism: "You just want my natural resources, And then you leave me poor and in misery. American Junk, Get it out of my bloodstream. Got to get back to who I am."[23]

Post-Marcos governments had successes and failures. Democracy returned, a free press flourished, and the economy improved after 1990, yet much of the economic growth was eaten up by the region's fastest population growth, since Filipinos maintained their preference for large families. And none of the governments successfully addressed poverty or seemed willing to curb the activities of influential companies exploiting marine, mineral, and timber resources, often harming the environment. A local Catholic priest noted how economic exploitation and environmental destruction have remained characteristic for decades: "A plunder economy, that's the post World War II Philippine history: plunder of seas, plunder of mines, plunder of forests."[24] Differences in access to health care, welfare, and related services continued to reflect the great gaps in income between social classes and regions.

Politics and Society in Thailand and Burma

Since the 1970s the contrasts between prosperous Thailand and stagnant Burma, both countries with histories and cultures very different from those of Indonesia and the Philippines, have been striking. In the early 1950s both nations had economies of similar size and growth rates, but the gap between them has become vast, with Thais enjoying the most success. Both nations have had a long history of military dictatorship, but only the Thais, finding the repressive atmosphere chilling, made a transition to more open government.

By the 1980s Thailand had turned away from military dictatorship and developed a semidemocratic system combining

Angkhan Kalayanaphong (AHN-kan KALL-a-YAWN-a-fong), born in 1926, the most popular poet in Thailand for decades, also gained fame as an accomplished graphic artist and painter. His poems often addressed social, Buddhist, and environmental themes. In his long poem, "Bangkok-Thailand," he examines Thailand and its problems in the 1970s and 1980s. The author pulls no punches in condemning Thai society for neglecting its heritage; he skewers politicians, government institutions, big business, and the entertainment industry. In this section, Angkhan pleads for Thais to save the forest environment being destroyed by commercial logging.

Oh, I do not imagine the forest like that
So deep, so beautiful, everything so special.
It pertains to dreams that are beyond truth. . . .
Dense woods in dense forests; slowly
The rays of half a day mix with the night.
Strange atmosphere causing admiration.
Loneliness up to the clouds, stillness and beauty.
Rays of gold play upon, penetrate the tree-tops
rays displayed in stripes, the brightness of the sun.
I stretch out my hand drawing down clouds mixing them
* with brandy.*
This is supreme happiness. . . .
The lofty trees do not think of reward for the scent of their
* blossoms. . . .*

Men kill the wood because they venerate money as in all
* the world. . . .*
The lofty trees contribute much to morals.
They should be infinitely lauded for it.
The trace of the ax kills. Blood runs in streams. . . .
You, trees, give the flattering pollen attended by scents.
You make the sacrifice again and again.
Do you ever respond angrily? You have accepted your fate
* which is contemptuous of all that is beautiful.*
But troublesome are the murderers, the doers of future sins.
Greedy after money, they are blind to divine work.
Their hearts are black to large extent, instead of being
* honest and upright.*
They have no breeding, are lawless. . . .
Thailand in particular is in a very bad way.
Because of their [commercial] value parks are 'purified,'
* i.e., destroyed.*
Man's blood is depraved, cursed and base.
His ancestors are swine and dogs. It is madness to say they
* are Thai.*

THINKING ABOUT THE READING

1. What qualities does the poet attribute to the forest?
2. What motives does he attribute to the loggers and businessmen who exploit the forest environment?

Source: Klaus Wenk, *Thai Literature: An Introduction* (Bangkok: White Lotus, 1995), pp. 95–98. Copyright © 1995 Klaus Wenk. Reprinted with permission of the publisher, White Lotus Co., Ltd.

---

traditions of order and hierarchy, symbolized by the monarchy, with notions of representative, accountable government. While most successful political candidates came from wealthy families, often of Chinese ancestry, the rapidly expanding urban middle class generally supported an expansion of democracy that would give them more influence. A new constitution adopted in 1997 guaranteed civil liberties and reformed the electoral system. A lively free press emerged.

Thailand has generally enjoyed high rates of economic growth since the 1970s. Despite a growing manufacturing sector, the export of commodities such as rice, rubber, tin, and timber remains significant. Although the Chinese minority, some 10 percent of the population, controls much of the wealth, Thais enjoy high per capita incomes and standards of public health by Asian standards. Indeed, hoping to save money, thousands of people from North America and Europe come to Thailand each year for medical treatment. Yet perhaps a quarter of Thais are very poor, especially in rural areas. The economic "miracle," as some have called it, has, in many respects, been built on the backs of women and children, many from rural districts, who work in urban factories, the service sector, and the sex industry. Millions of Thai women have identified with

the songs of popular singer Pompuang Duangjian (POM-poo-ahn DWONG-chen) (1961–1992), herself the product of a poor village, that often deal with the harshness of the lives of poor female migrants to the city, where they encounter predatory men: "So lousy poor, I just have to risk my luck. Dozing on the bus, this guy starts chatting me up. Say's he'll get me a good job, now he's feeling me up."[24] Pompuang herself had only two years of primary school education and worked as a sugar-cane cutter before starting a music career. With much of her money stolen by lovers, managers, and promoters, she died at age thirty-one unable to afford treatment for a blood disorder.

Problems besides widespread poverty and sexual exploitation also challenge Thais. The economic collapse of 1997 that affected much of Asia also threw many Thais out of work. The rapidly growing, overcrowded capital, Bangkok, is one of the most polluted cities in Asia, drenched in toxic matter from factories and automobiles despite efforts by local environmental groups to clean up the air. The nation's once abundant rain forests disappear at a rapid rate, a fact lamented by Thai musicians and poets (see Witness to the Past: A Thai Poet's Plea for Saving the Environment). Health issues have arisen too: the

AIDs rate skyrockets. Yet, despite their problems, Thais have reason for optimism. The people possess a talent for political compromise, and Buddhism teaches moderation, tolerance, respect for nature, and a belief in the worth of the individual. Thais have the basis for a democratic spirit, a more equitable distribution of wealth, and an environmental ethic.

Whatever Thailand's problems, they seem dwarfed by Burma's. Under Burma's harsh, corrupt military regime, few outside the ruling group have prospered despite the country's valuable natural resources of timber, oil, gems, and rice. By the 1980s Burma was ranked by the United Nations as one of the world's ten poorest nations. Sparked by economic decline and political repression, mass protests in 1988, led by students and Buddhist monks, demanded civil liberties. These protests ended, however, when soldiers killed hundreds and jailed thousands of demonstrators. The regime increased its repression. In 1990 Burma (now renamed Myanmar (myahn-MAH), under international pressure, allowed elections, though with restrictions. Taking advantage of the elections, and while most of its leaders were in jail, the opposition quickly organized and won a landslide victory. Aung San Suu Kyi (AWNG sahn soo CHEE) (b. 1945), daughter of the founding president and an eloquent orator, returned from a long exile in England to lead the democratic forces. But the military refused to hand over power, put Aung San Suu Kyi under house arrest, and rounded up hundreds of opposition supporters. Refusing to compromise in exchange for the regime ending her house arrest, Aung San Suu Kyi said that she did not consider herself a martyr because other Burmese had suffered much more than she had. A courageous symbol of principled leadership, she won the Nobel Peace Prize in 1991 for her role in Burmese politics.

Today the military regime remains in power and still detains opposition leaders, including Aung San Suu Kyi. The generals cleverly manipulate politics while slightly relaxing their grip. Although many Burmese still dream of democracy, and illicit cassettes of protest music and opposition messages are exchanged from hand to hand, others have accommodated themselves to military rule, valuing stability and worried about a possible civil war. To expand the economy and thus increase its own revenues, the government began welcoming foreign investment. Western, Japanese, and Southeast Asian corporations invest in Burma, especially in the timber and oil industries, diminishing the willingness of other countries to punish Burma for gross human rights violations.

Diversity and Prosperity in Malaysia and Singapore

Of all the Southeast Asian nations, Malaysia and Singapore, both open to the world as they have been for centuries, have achieved the most political stability and economic progress. The two nations, once joined in the same federation, have shared a similar mix of ethnic groups, though while Malays constitute slightly over half, Chinese a third, and Indians a tenth of the Malaysian population, around three-quarters of Singaporeans are Chinese. Both countries maintain democratic forms, but the ruling parties restrict the ability of opposition political groups to compete in elections on a level playing field and sometimes arrest or harass opposition leaders. After 1970 Malaysia has remained politically stable by maintaining a limited democracy and holding regular elections in which the ruling, modernizing Malay-led coalition of parties controls the voting and most of the media. The Chinese-dominated ruling party in Singapore has used similar strategies to maintain its hold on power. Since the print and broadcast media are controlled by the government or their allies in both nations, dissidents use the Internet to spread their views on their societies. Both countries have successfully diversified their economies and thus stimulated economic development, and they have also raised living standards and spread the wealth.

In Malaysia religion has remained vital, including in politics, which has often divided the Muslim majority from the Christian, Hindu, Buddhist, and animist minority. Conflict also occurs within religious traditions. For instance, Islamic movements with dogmatic, sometimes militant views have gained support among some young Malays, especially rural migrants to the city, who are alienated by a Westernized, materialistic society and looking for an anchor of certainty in an uncertain world. These movements, which discourage contact with non-Muslims, encourage women to dress modestly, and sometimes reject modern technology or products, often alarm secular Malays and non-Muslims who view the movements as taking Malaysia backward. In response, Malay women's rights groups use Islamic arguments to oppose restrictions favored by conservatives. They find some support among the numerous women holding high government positions. Hence, Sisters in Islam, founded in the 1980s by the politically well-connected academic, Zainab Anwar, espouses an Islam supporting freedom, justice, and equality and fights strict interpretations of Muslim family law. At the other extreme, aimless Malay youth mock the conventions of mainstream society, wearing long hair and listening to heavy metal music.

Supported by abundant natural resources, such as oil and tin, economic diversification, and entrepreneurial talent, Malaysia has become a highly successful developing nation, surpassing European nations like Portugal and Hungary in national wealth. High annual growth rates have enabled Malaysia to achieve a relatively high per capita income and to build light industry that employs cheap labor to make shoes, toys, and other consumer goods for export. Many of these workers are women; half of Malaysian women work for wages. The manufacturing sector has continued to grow rapidly: Malaysians even build their own automobiles. Timber and oil have become valuable export commodities. Malaysia recovered rapidly from the 1997 Asian economic collapse by imposing more government controls on the economy, ignoring Western economic advice. But economic growth comes at the price of toxic waste problems, severe deforestation, and air pollution.

Economic growth in Malaysia corresponds to social change. Violence between Chinese and Malays in 1969 resulted in the New Economic Policy; aimed at redistributing more wealth to Malays, it has fostered a substantial Malay middle class. Others also benefited from the prosperity. By the 1980s

Kuala Lumpur Dominated by new skyscrapers, including some of the world's tallest buildings, and a spectacular mosque, the Malaysian capital city, Kuala Lumpur, has become a prosperous center for Asian commerce and industry. Modern buildings gradually replace the older shophouses built decades ago. Yet, poor shantytowns have also grown apace to house the poor. (Corbis)

televisions, stereos, and videocassette recorders became nearly universal in the cities and increasingly common in the rural areas. Official poverty rates dropped from some 50 percent in 1970 to around 20 percent by 2000. As in other Asian nations and Latin America, many young women labor in electronics and textile factories. Nevertheless, the gap between rich and poor remains and may have widened. In the bustling capital city, Kuala Lumpur, jammed freeways, glittering malls, and high-rise luxury condominiums contrast with shantytown squatter settlements and countless shabbily dressed street hawkers hoping to sell enough of their cheap wares to buy a meal.

Restricted to a tiny island, Singapore, despite few resources, has done even better than Malaysia economically and has become among the world's most prosperous nations. The numerical and political predominance of Chinese, the descendants of immigrants during the past two centuries, makes Singapore unique in Southeast Asia. The Singapore government has mixed freewheeling economic policies with an autocratic leadership that tightly controls the 5 million people and limits

dissent. Singapore is run like a giant corporation, efficient and ruthless. People pay a stiff fine if caught spitting, littering, or even tossing used chewing gum on the street. Yet it is also one of the healthiest societies, enjoying, for example, the world's lowest rate of infant mortality. Singapore has devoted more of its national budget to education than other nations, and everyone studies English in school. The city has become a hub of light industry, high technology, and computer networking, in the vanguard of the information revolution. Businesspeople and professionals from around the world have flocked to this globalized city, just as they had flocked to the Straits of Melaka trading states of Srivijaya and Melaka centuries ago.

Southeast Asia in the Global System

Although Southeast Asians still export the natural resources they did in colonial times, some nations have seen major economic growth through industrialization and exploitation of other resources. The gold, pepper, and spices of earlier centuries have been largely replaced by oil, timber, rubber, rice, tin, sugar, and palm oil. With these exports the region's role in the world has also changed, fostering some of the fastest-growing economies in the world. Malaysia, Thailand, Singapore, and, to some extent, Indonesia and Vietnam have become major recipients of foreign investment. Meanwhile, workers produce manufactured goods like shoes, clothing, computer chips, and sports equipment for European and North American markets. To overcome underdevelopment, several countries elsewhere in Asia, Africa, and Latin America borrow economic models from the Southeast Asian "tigers." By the early twenty-first century the Southeast Asian nations were shifting their focus from the United States to China, which they viewed as the rising world power with which they must cooperate for regional stability.

Southeast Asians have also influenced politics worldwide. The Indonesian Revolution against the Dutch, for instance, had electrifying global effects because it forced a major colonial power to abandon its control while giving hope to colonized Africans. Similarly, Vietnamese communists under Ho Chi Minh, in their ultimately successful fifty-year fight against French colonialism, Japanese occupation, and then U.S. intervention, stimulated a wave of revolutionary efforts, from Nicaragua to Mozambique, to overthrow Western domination. The Vietnamese struggle for independence also inspired student activists in Europe and North America; a few of the more radical shouted slogans in praise of the Vietnamese communist leader, Ho Chi Minh, while protesting against war and inequality in the 1960s. Women have long played an influential role in Southeast Asia, and the political leaders Megawati Soekarnoputri in Indonesia, Corazon Aquino in the Philippines, and Aung San Suu Kyi in Burma have become inspirations to women worldwide.

Engagement with the outside world has shaped modern Southeast Asia. Global influences and economic development have increasingly modified lives. For example, the resident of an upscale suburb of Kuala Lumpur, Bangkok, or Manila, connected through her home computer to the information superhighway and working in a high-rise, air-conditioned office reached by driving a late-model sports car along the crowded freeways, has a way of life vastly different from that of the peasant villager whose life revolves around traditional society. The modern cities feature malls, supermarkets, boutiques, Hard Rock Cafes, and Planet Hollywoods. Even rural areas, while maintaining age-old traditions, have become more connected to wider networks by televisions, outboard motors, motor scooters, and telephones.

Yet change has often been superficial. In poor city neighborhoods restaurants may have compact disc players and cold beer, but they also feature traditional music and dance and serve up fiery hot curries. For every youngster who joins the fan club for a Western or local pop star, another identifies with an Islamic, Buddhist, or Christian organization, sometimes a militant one. Many people find themselves perched uneasily between the cooperative village values of the past and the competitive, materialistic modern world.

SECTION SUMMARY

- Beginning the late 1970s, Southeast Asia experienced rapid economic growth through a Japanese-style mix of capitalism and active government involvement, though a severe economic crisis hit the region in 1997.

- Under Suharto, the Indonesian New Order government repressed regional opposition and improved the economy, but Suharto was extravagantly corrupt and was forced to resign in 1997 amid widespread unrest and economic collapse.

- Under Marcos, the Philippines was divided between the very rich and the poor; Marcos was forced out after massive protests, and the democratically elected governments that followed were more open to dissent but still dominated by the wealthy.

- Since the 1980s, Thailand has developed a semidemocratic system and has grown economically, though it has endured widespread poverty and sexual exploitation, while Burma has been burdened with a corrupt regime that has failed to take advantage of ample natural resources and stifled its opposition.

- Malaysia has taken advantage of abundant natural resources to become highly successful, surpassing some European nations in wealth, while Singapore, with fewer resources, has been even more successful through a combination of economic freedom and political restriction.

- With their rapidly growing economies, the Southeast Asian "tigers" have inspired developing nations around the world, and while most of the region has joined the modern world, tradition thrives in them as well.

 *Online Study Center* ACE the Test

 Chapter Summary

After decolonization, the societies of southern Asia struggled to shape their futures. The traumas of World War II made a return to the imperial patterns of old impossible. Since Hindu and Muslim leaders could not agree on a formula for unity after independence, British India fragmented into two rival nations, predominantly Hindu India and mostly Muslim Pakistan. Under Nehru, India adopted democratic practices and modernizing policies. Indians generally sustained multiparty democracy, raised the legal status of untouchables and women, achieved a dramatic rise in food production, industrialized, and fostered high-technology enterprises. But they failed to transform rural society, distribute the fruits of economic growth equitably, and eradicate Hindu-Muslim conflict. Muslim-dominated Pakistan divided when Bangladesh broke away, and both Pakistan and Bangladesh have had difficulty maintaining democracy and generating economic development. India and Pakistan, both armed with nuclear weapons, have remained hostile neighbors.

Like South Asians, Southeast Asians also regained the independence they had lost under Western colonialism. Vietnamese Communists led by Ho Chi Minh launched a revolutionary war that eventually forced the French to leave, giving the Communists control of North Vietnam. The United States, influenced by Cold War thinking, supported anti-Communist South Vietnam and, in response to a growing Communist insurgency, sent American troops to South Vietnam. But the United States withdrew in 1975, unable to triumph over a determined foe. The conflict caused several million casualties and major environmental damage. With the war over, Vietnam, Cambodia, and Laos, all under Communist control, struggled for reconstruction. The rest of Southeast Asia also faced challenges after achieving independence. Some, such as Indonesia and Malaysia, worked to build national unity in a complex mosaic of peoples and cultures. Burma, Thailand, and the Philippines experienced chronic unrest that often led to military or civilian dictatorships. But eventually Malaysia, Singapore, Thailand, and Indonesia achieved rapid economic growth, supplying natural resources and manufactured goods to the world.

 **Online Study Center** Improve Your Grade Flashcards

Key Terms

Awami League	Tet Offensive	UMNO
Bharatha Janata	Pathet Lao	ASEAN
Bollywood	Khmer Rouge	New Order
National Liberation Front (NLF)		

Suggested Reading

Books

Abinales, Patricio N. and Donna J. Amoroso. *State and Society in the Philippines.* Lanham, M.D.: Rowman and Littlefield, 2005. Readable recent study with much on recent politics.

Beeson, Mark, ed. *Contemporary Southeast Asia: Regional Dynamics, National Differences.* New York: Palgrave Macmillan, 2004. Essays on varied topics.

Brown, Judith M. *Nehru.* New York: Longman, 1999. A readable biography of an important Asian leader.

Ganguly, Sumit, ed. *South Asia.* New York: New York University Press, 2006. Recent essays on the South Asian countries.

Ganguly, Sumit and Neal DeVotta, eds. *Understanding Contemporary India.* Boulder: Lynne Rienner, 2003. Accessible collection covering most aspects of Indian society.

Harrison, Selig S., et al., eds. *India and Pakistan: The First Fifty Years.* New York: Cambridge University Press, 1999. An excellent collection of essays covering many topics.

Karnow, Stanley. *Vietnam: A History,* 2nd ed. New York: Penguin, 1997. One of the better introductions to modern history and the Vietnam War.

Kingsbury, Damien. *South-East Asia: A Political Profile,* 2nd ed. New York: Oxford University Press, 2005. An up-to-date, comprehensive survey by an Australian scholar.

Lockard, Craig A. *"Dance of Life": Popular Music and Politics in Southeast Asia.* Honolulu: University of Hawaii Press, 1998. An examination of politics and societies through popular culture.

Marlay, Ross, and Clark Neher. *Patriots and Tyrants: Ten Asian Leaders.* Lanham, Md.: Rowman and Littlefield, 1999. Sketches of Asian nationalists, such as Gandhi, Nehru, Ho, and Sukarno.

Neher, Clark D. *Southeast Asia: Crossroads of the World,* 2nd ed. DeKalb: Center for Southeast Asian Studies, Northern Illinois University, 2004. A general, readable introduction to cultures and politics.

Olson, James S., and Randy Roberts. *Where the Domino Fell: America and Vietnam, 1945–1995,* 4th ed. St. James, N.Y.: Brandywine, 2004. An outstanding survey with an emphasis on U.S. policies and actions.

Stein, Burton. *A History of India.* Malden, M.A.: Blackwell, 1998. A detailed history with good coverage of the contemporary era.

Varshney, Ashutosh. *Ethnic Conflict and Civic Life: Hindus and Muslims in India,* 2nd ed. New Haven, C.T.: Yale University Press, 2003. A key study of Hindu-Muslim relations in three cities, including peacemaking and violence.

Vickers, Adrian. *A History of Modern Indonesia.* New York: Cambridge University Press, 2005. Quirky but fascinating study.

Websites

Asian Studies: WWW Virtual Library (http://coombs.anu.edu.au/WWWVL-AsianStudies.html). A vast metasite maintained at Australian National University, with links to hundreds of sites.

East and Southeast Asia: An Annotated Directory of Internet Resources (http://newton.uor.edu/Departments&Programs/AsianStudies-Dept/). A superb set of links on Southeast Asia, maintained at the University of Redlands.

Internet Indian History Sourcebook (http://www.fordham.edu/halsall/india/indiasbook.html). An invaluable collection of sources and links on India from ancient to modern times.

Virtual Library: South Asia (http://www.columbia.edu/cu/libraries/indiv/area/sarai/). A major site maintained by Columbia University.

WWW Southeast Asia Guide (http://www.library.wisc.edu/guides/SEAsia/). An easy-to-use site.

The Contemporary World, Since 1945

The world has changed dramatically since 1945. Some observers have described these years as the most revolutionary age in history, reshaping whole ways of life and worldviews. All regions of the world, opening to ideas and products from everywhere, have become, as some experts put it, part of a global village or global system. The Indonesian thinker Soedjatmoko (so-jat-MOH-ko), summing up the era's trends, described a world of collapsing "national boundaries and horrifying destructive power, expanding technological capacity and instant communication [in which] we live in imperfect intimacy with all our fellow human beings."[1] This interconnected and rapidly changing global society, and the people who shape it, have produced both great good and indescribable horrors.

The contemporary world has become a global unity within a larger diversity. Globalization has fostered or intensified networks of exchange and communication: international trade pacts and electronic fund transfers, jet-speed travel and fax machines. These networks link distant societies. Yet, even as they have become more closely linked, nations have not been able to work together to meet the challenges facing humanity, such as poverty and environmental distress. No clear international consensus has emerged on maintaining strong local cultures in the face of global influences, correcting the widening gap between rich and poor nations, and achieving a better balance between environmental preservation and economic development. Solving these problems requires complex strategies and the joint efforts of many nations. Ensuring a brighter future also requires examining how the patterns of the past and the trends of the present may shape the years to come.

GLOBALIZATION AND CULTURES

Over recent centuries the world's people have built a human web, or networked society—a global system that today encompasses most of the world's 6.5 billion people. All these terms imply transnational connections and the institutions that foster them, such as the World Bank, the Internet, and religious missionaries. Around the world people speak, with fear or enthusiasm, of globalization. Some observers see the trend as dangerous folly, others as a boon, and still others have mixed feelings. In recent decades, people have experienced global influences not only by, for some, frequent travel abroad but because these influences have reshaped the cities, towns, and villages where they live. The interaction between global influences and local traditions, such as religion and music, has become a force in the world, helping to shape cultures.

Globalization and Its Impacts

The roots of globalization go deep into the past. During the first millennium of the Common Era trade networks such as the Silk Road, which linked China and Europe across Central Asia and the Middle East, and the spread of religions such as Buddhism, Christianity, and Islam, connected distant societies. A thousand years ago an Eastern Hemisphere–wide economy based in Asia and anchored by Chinese and Indian manufacturing and Islamic trade networks represented an early form of globalization. The links between the hemispheres forged after 1492, during which Europeans competed with each other and with Asians for a share of the growing trade in raw materials, expanded the reach of this economy. In the nineteenth century the Industrial Revolution, which produced desirable trade goods, and European imperialism, which led to the Western colonization of large parts of the world, extended the connections even further, aided by technological innovations such as steamships and trans-oceanic cables.

The integration of commerce and financial services today is more developed than ever before. As the global system has become increasingly linked, societies have become more dependent on each other for everything from consumer goods and entertainments to fuels and technological innovations. For example, all over the world people consume Chinese textiles, U.S. films, Persian Gulf oil, Indian yoga, and Japanese electronics. Videoconferencing allows business partners in Los Angeles, Berlin, and Hong Kong to confer instantaneously with one another. During the early twenty-first century the world's most powerful nation, the United States, has become increasingly reliant on Asian nations, especially China, to finance its skyrocketing national debt. The debt has grown in part because of a costly U.S. military engagement in Iraq and an increasing economic imbalance as Americans import more from abroad than they export. Such interdependence, as well as the reach of political, cultural, and social events across distances, has had an increasing impact in a shrinking world. This reality was demonstrated in 2005 when some faraway African societies were affected indirectly by Hurricane Katrina, which devastated the Gulf Coast of the United States, disrupting the export of corn from the U.S. Midwest through the port of New Orleans. Japan, a major consumer of that corn, then turned to South Africa for supplies, which deprived people in Malawi of South African corn, causing widespread starvation in Malawi. Yet, while globalization affects every country to some degree, the great bulk of world trade and financial flow and activity is concentrated in, and has the largest impact on, the peoples of three huge interlinked blocs: North America, Europe, and a group of Asian nations stretching from Japan to India.

Furthermore, many observers believe that globalization is unmanageable. U.S. journalist Thomas Friedman writes:

Globalization isn't a choice. It's a reality, and no one is in charge. You keep looking for someone to complain to, to take the heat off your markets. Well guess what, there's no one on the other end of the phone. The global market today is an electronic herd of anonymous stock, bond and currency traders sitting behind computer screens. Sure, this is unfair [but] there's nobody to call.[2]

If governments are often somewhat powerless in the face of global economic trends, they need to adapt by educating their citizens, especially their young people, for a new, more competitive world. Various Asian nations, such as India, Taiwan, and Singapore, have adapted to these changes more rapidly than North American and European nations, pouring money into education, science, and high technology. The Western nations that have successfully adjusted to globalization are mainly those, especially in Scandinavia, that have combined open markets with strong societal and environmental protections.

This impersonal globalization, operating independent of governments, has had major impacts on societies, politics, economies, cultures, and environments. Whether they are seen as positive or negative consequences depends on the observer. For example, some Western free market enthusiasts celebrate a new global order in which everybody on the planet is in the same economy, offering entrepreneurs unparalleled opportunities for profit. But graffiti by disillusioned Poles in the 1990s took a different view, complaining that when Poland abandoned communism it asked for democracy but ended up with the bond market and domination by transnational corporations. Scholars and others energetically debate the value and scope of globalization (see Historical Controversy: Globalization: For and Against).

Global forces, symbolized by advertising for foreign-made goods and satellites miles up in the sky relaying information around the world, interact with local cultures, raising questions about national and local identity. As a result, local traditions and products sometimes get replaced, and imported and local cultures blend. An example of blending comes from France, where, with its large Arab immigrant population, Arab entrepreneurs have prospered by selling fast-food hamburgers and pizza prepared according to Muslim requirements and adapted to Arab taste. People around the world consume global products, from fast food to fashionable footwear to action films, but still enjoy cultural traditions that are distinctly local and popular with earlier generations. Examples include the unique Thai style of boxing in which combatants can attack with both hands and feet, sumo wrestling in Japan, and the African-influenced martial arts of Brazil.

To adapt and flourish in an interconnected world, people have had to become aware of international conditions. In North America, activists seeking to fight inequality or preserve the environment have urged people to think globally but act locally. Thinking globally, for example, would include understanding how rapid deforestation in the tropics—especially in the Amazon and Congo Basins, where rain forests recycle vast amounts of water into the air—diminishes rainfall around the world. Acting locally, Brazilian environmental and citizens' groups work to save their rain forests, while environmentally conscious North Americans and Europeans support organizations, businesses, and political leaders committed to improving the global environment. Others wonder, however, if this is

enough, arguing that, since the world is so interlinked, people must think and act both globally and locally—to embrace both a global citizenship and a local citizenship. But, despite greatly increased travel and migration, only a small minority of people have become true citizens of the world, comfortable everywhere. Few people have gone as far toward an ecumenical view as Australian Aboriginal writer Colin Johnson, who both embraced Hinduism, imported from India, and dedicated his first novel to the Jamaican reggae star Bob Marley and his Rastafarian faith. Moreover, world government remains a distant prospect at the beginning of the twenty-first century.

Cultural Imperialism: The Globalization of Culture

The inequitable relationship between the dominant West and the developing nations has compelled observers to examine global change. Arising from this effort has been the concept of cultural imperialism, in which the economic and political power of Western nations, especially the United States, enables their cultural products to spread widely. Some African writers have called this pattern a "cultural bomb" because, they believe, Western products and entertainments destroy local cultures. In this view, the developed countries export popular music, disco dancing, skimpy women's clothing, and sex-drenched films and publications reflecting these countries' own values and experiences. Other societies adopt these products, which modify or suffocate their own traditions. For instance, big budget Hollywood films attract large audiences while local films, made on small budgets, cannot compete, and the local film industries often die as a result. To survive, local filmmakers adopt the formulas used by successful Hollywood filmmakers: sex and violence. Critics of Western power argue that cultural exchange has been common throughout history but in the modern world has become largely a one-way street, leading to domination by Western, especially Anglo-American, culture.

Popular culture produced in the United States, entertaining but also challenging to traditional values, has emerged as the closest thing available to a global entertainment. The Monroe Doctrine—the early-nineteenth-century declaration by Congress that the United States would interfere in Latin American political developments—has now become, in the view of certain wags, the "Marilyn Monroe Doctrine," after the famous American actress who, for many non-Americans, symbolized U.S. culture in the 1950s. Other examples of American cultural influence were popular U.S. television programs, such as the drama series *Dallas,* the racy *Desperate Housewives,* and *The Muppet Show,* a variety show, which have been broadcast in dozens of nations.

Some American icons, from basketball star Michael Jordan to McDonald's, have become symbols of a new global modernity and capitalism. In 1989 two young East Germans crossed the Berlin Wall and discovered their first McDonald's restaurant. One of them remembered, "It was all so modern, the windows were so amazing. I felt like a lost convict who'd just spent twenty-five years in prison. I was in a state of shock."[3] Not even the Chinese, with one of the world's most admired cuisines, were immune to the appeal of modern U.S. marketing techniques and convenience for harried urbanites.

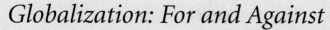

Globalization: For and Against

The first pictures taken from the moon in 1969, which showed the earth as a blue oasis in the middle of nowhere, made clear that humans share a single home. The pictures also suggested that this home is shared by an interlinked future. Different kinds of networks have increasingly connected peoples across distance and borders, and globalization—the interconnections between societies, the rise in cross-border exchanges, and the creation of one world—has become a major subject of debate. Often used vaguely and inconsistently, the concept became a metaphor to explain capitalism spreading throughout the world. But to many observers, the concept has deeper meanings, describing a process that both unites and divides, creates winners and losers, and brings both new possibilities and new risks. The debates on globalization cut across political leanings and national divisions.

THE PROBLEM

Globalization inspires passionate support and bitter opposition, generating immense discussion and disagreement. The debate focuses on four questions: When did globalization begin? What are the arguments in favor of it? What are some of the major opposing views? Is the trend leading the world into a troubled era of increasing conflict or greater cooperation?

THE DEBATE

The first question, the roots of globalization, remains disputed. Some scholars argue that its origins lie deep in the past, going back to the interconnections that slowly enveloped people from the dawn of cities and states. The German historians Jurgen Osterhammel and Niels Petersson, for example, trace it back a millennium or two to the silk trade between China and the Mediterranean region, the sea trade between the Middle East and India, and the caravans crossing the deserts of Africa, all activities that moved people, ideas, artwork, natural resources, goods, and coins. By contrast, Robbie Robertson, an Australian, argues that history changed dramatically only five hundred years ago, when the gradual linking of the world by European voyages of discovery transformed societies and economic activities. Still other scholars trace it no further back than the mid-nineteenth century, pointing to the first permanent transoceanic telegraph cable in 1866, global social movements such as feminism, and global regulatory bodies such as the Universal Postal Union. Some other writers claim that globalization did not affect most of humanity until the 1960s or later. Whatever the roots, by 2000 a global system defined by market capitalism, over two hundred nation-states, some four hundred international organizations, and 40,000 transnational corporations, existed with no central authority.

On the second and third questions, whether the effects are positive or negative, the debate has raged for years. Among the benefits attributed to globalization are higher living standards and the worldwide sharing of culture. British sociologist John Giddens identifies a worldwide trend toward democracy and intellectual freedom. Walter Anderson praises the opening of societies to one another, as reflected in communications satellites and the fiber-optic submarine cable system winding its way around the world. As a result, he notes, the Inuit people living in northern Alaska watch twenty-eight channels of satellite television, take courses through the Internet, and stay in touch with their families by cell phones. Free market enthusiasts, such as Indian-born, U.S.-based economist Jagdish Bhagwati, stress the fostering of economic freedom. Opposing antiglobalization movements as the misguided enemy of progress, all these thinkers complain that newspapers and television reports focus more on shuttered textile factories, as jobs move overseas, than on the African child at the computer. Bhagwati claims that when properly governed, globalization becomes a powerful force for social good, bringing prosperity to underdeveloped nations, reducing child labor, increasing literacy, and helping women by creating jobs that increase their income and status. Another enthusiast, Thomas Friedman, considers globalization the principal trend of the post–Cold War world, symbolized by the Lexus, a Japanese-made luxury car sold around the world. Yet, he argues, people often prefer to hold on to meaningful traditions, symbolized by the olive tree often found at the center of an Arab village, rather than embrace new ideas. The world, he argues, has gotten flat, and this level playing field has allowed over two billion Chinese, Indians, and Russians to contemplate eventually owning a car, house, refrigerator, and toaster, increasing competition and raising the demand for the world's resources dramatically.

The contrary views on globalization stress negative consequences. These consequences include a concentration of economic power, more poverty, and less cultural diversity. The challengers of economic globalization argue that powerful governments and multinational corporations bully the marketplace, control politics, and stack the deck in their favor. Walter LaFeber shows how U.S. basketball star Michael Jordan, whose games were broadcast all over the world, became an international phenomenon of great commercial appeal, benefiting the international corporations who used Jordan to create a demand for their expensive products, such as sneakers, often at the expense of local manufacturers making the same product. To LaFeber, the terrorist attacks on the United States, especially the World Trade Center in New York in 2001, must also be understood in the context of the growing opposition to globalization around the world as the rich become richer and the poor become poorer. Joseph Stiglitz, an ardent fan of capitalism and former World Bank official, believes that globalization can be positive but that misguided policies and the economic power of industrial nations have made free trade unfair for developing nations. Looking at other aspects of globalization, Cynthia

Kuwaiti Stock Exchange   Capitalism has spread widely in the world, and with it financial institutions such as investment banks and stock exchanges. The oil-rich, politically stable Persian Gulf sultanate of Kuwait has one of the most active stock exchanges.   (Corbis)

Enloe explores the often negative effects of tourism and U.S. military bases on women, who, enjoying fewer economic options than men, often need to sell their bodies to male tourists and soldiers to survive. James Mittelman argues that, experienced from below, globalization fosters the loss of local political control as power shifts upward and also a devaluation of a society's cultural achievements as foreign cultural products, such as music and films, become influential. All of these globalizing trends spur angry resistance, reflected in antiglobalization movements.

Experts also disagree about the fourth question, where globalization is taking the world. Some predict a growing divide both between and within societies. Benjamin Barber, for example, analyzes the conflict between consumerist capitalism (what he calls McWorld, after McDonald's) and tribalism or religious fundamentalism (what he terms jihad, after Islamic militants). Barber dislikes both trends: the dull homogeneity of McWorld, in which everyone, moved by capitalism and advertising, has the same tastes and ideas; and the balkanized world of jihad in which rival cultures, convinced of their own superior values and disdainful of others, struggle for dominance. Other scholars also predict tensions. John Giddens argues that the globalization of

information, symbolized by the World Wide Web, that puts people in touch with others who think differently will promote a more cosmopolitan world-view respecting cultural differences but will also generate a backlash among narrow nationalists and religious fundamentalists who see only one path to truth. Preventing conflict between the factions and lessening the growing divide between rich and poor nations require cooperation between nations. Bhagwati, for example, supports managed rather than unfettered globalization, with world leaders discussing how to foster equality as well as growth. Taking a different approach, Mittelman doubts that globalization can be managed and calls for people around the world, rather than leaders and governments, to work together to decentralize political and economic power to build a future of greater equity.

EVALUATING THE DEBATE

The globalization discussion, much more than an academic debate, is a disagreement about profound transformations in the world and about what ethical and institutional principles should be applied to better organize human affairs for a brighter future. Some authors engaged in the debate have proposed catchy ideas, such as the Lexus and the olive tree, jihad and Mc-World, but the reality of globalization is usually more complex. Both proponents and opponents make convincing points about the consequences of globalization; the truth may lie somewhere between. Globalization may indeed bring great benefits, at least to a section of the world's people. The free flow of ideas inspires some people to demand more political rights or social inequality, while many young women working long hours for low wages in foreign-owned factories may often prefer that life to the dead end of rural poverty. But improving the lives of those who do not benefit, as even globalization proponents Bhagwati and Friedman concede, will probably require action such as land reform to help poor peasants, more funding for schools, and stiffer environmental and worker protection laws to smooth the impacts on societies, cultures, and environments. Yet, the relations between business interests and their political supporters prompting globalization and the antiglobalization activists, often from worker or peasant backgrounds, remain tense. Local, national, regional, and global forces are intermingling in new and complex ways that may necessitate not just actions to remedy inequalities but also new ways of thinking.

THINKING ABOUT THE CONTROVERSY

1. When did globalization begin?
2. What are the positive arguments for globalization?
3. What main points do opponents make?

EXPLORING THE CONTROVERSY

Among the key historical studies are Robbie Robertson, *The Three Waves of Globalization: A History of a Developing Global Consciousness* (New York: Zed Books, 2003), and Jurgen Osterhammel and Niels P. Petersson, *Globalization: A Short History* (Princeton: Princeton University Press, 2005). Some of the major proponents are John Giddens, *Runaway World: How Globalization Is Reshaping Our Lives* (London: Routledge, 2000); Walter Truett Anderson, *All Connected Now: Life in the First Global Civilization* (Boulder, Colo.: Westview Press, 2001); Jagdish Bhagwati, *In Defense of Globalization* (New York: Oxford University Press, 2004); and Thomas L. Friedman, *The Lexus and the Olive Tree: Understanding Globalization* (New York: Anchor, 2000) and *The World Is Flat: A Brief History of the Twenty-First Century* (New York: Farrar, Straus, and Giroux, 2005). Writers questioning the benefits include Walter LaFeber, *Michael Jordan and the New Global Capitalism*, new and expanded ed. (New York: W. W. Norton, 2002); Joseph E. Stiglitz, *Globalization and Its Discontents* (New York: W. W. Norton, 1993); Cynthia Enloe, *Bananas, Beaches and Bases: Making Feminist Sense of International Politics*, updated ed. (Berkeley: University of California Press, 2001); and James H. Mittelman, *The Globalization Syndrome: Transformation and Resistance* (Princeton: Princeton University Press, 2000). For one view of future trends, see Benjamin R. Barber, *Jihad vs. McWorld* (New York: Times Books, 1995). On globalization generally, see David Held, ed., *A globalizing World? Culture, Economics, Politics* (New York: Routledge, 2000); Robert K. Schaeffer, *Understanding Globalization: The Social Consequences of Political, Economic, and Environmental Change* (Lanham, M.D.: Rowman and Littlefield, 1997); and Manfred B. Steger, *Globalization: A Very Short Introduction* (New York: Oxford University Press, 2003).

In 1993 a famous roast duck restaurant in China's capital, Beijing, sent its management staff to study the McDonald's operation in British-ruled Hong Kong and then introduced its customers to "roast duck fast food." The restaurant also faced a challenge from the growing number of McDonald's franchises in Beijing. Yet, Chinese restaurants flourish around the world.

Still, popular American entertainments often face opposition. Governments, from the Islamic clerics running Iran to the more democratic leaders of India, have attempted to halt or control the influx of what they consider destabilizing, immoral pop culture. In 1995 an Islamic political party in Pakistan even demanded, unsuccessfully, that the United States turn over to them American pop stars Madonna and Michael Jackson so that they could be placed on trial as "cultural terrorists" destroying humanity. In 2005, representatives of many nations, meeting under the auspices of the United Nations cultural organization, agreed that all nations had the right to restrict cultural imports, outraging American political and entertainment leaders. To maintain their cultural traditions and boost local artists many nations have mandated, as Portugal did in 2006, that a set percentage of music on radio and television must be locally made.

Forming New World Cultures

Whatever the real scope of cultural imperialism, a new world culture appears to be on the rise. The world is becoming one network of relationships as ideas, people, and goods move between its different regions. Similar cultural forms, often Anglo-American in origin, develop across national boundaries, transcending any one territory, society, or tradition. Yet the rising world culture is not uniform. No total homogenization of expression and meaning has occurred.

Anglo-American cultural forms are not the only ones to reach a global audience. Mexican and Brazilian soap operas, Indian (Bollywood) films, Nigerian novels, Arab, African, and Caribbean pop music, and Japanese comics and electronic games have been popular all over the globe. For example, thanks in part to the popularity of Jamaican singer/songwriter Bob Marley, reggae music spread around the world, as one observer marveled in the 1980s:

> In Papeete, Tahiti, the buses all have speakers the size of foot lockers, making them moving sound systems. Their routes are jumping with the rhythms of [reggae groups] Steel Pulse, Black Uhuru, and Bob Marley. Four thousand miles away in Tokyo, there is a reggae night spot called Club 69, where local youth wear dreadlocks and dance to the beats of the Wailers. Africa has its own reggae styles and hundreds of bands.[4]

The cultural traffic flow is not one way. In North America, western Europe, and Australia, people take up Indian yoga, Chinese *tai qi*, and other Asian spiritual disciplines; patronize Thai, Indian, Chinese, and Japanese restaurants; enjoy Brazilian and African pop music; learn Latin American dances; and master Asian martial arts, such as karate and judo. Even classical musicians in the West have embraced foreign influences. For instance, in 1998 the Chinese cellist Yo Yo Ma, born in Paris

and later a U.S. resident, founded the Silk Road Ensemble, which brings together Western, East Asian, and Middle Eastern musicians to tour the world playing music that mixes the instruments and traditions of both East and West.

The meeting of global and local cultures fosters hybridization, the blending of two cultures, a process that can be either enriching or impoverishing. Record stores in Western cities set aside some of their display space to sell a hybrid form called "world music," popular music originating largely outside of the West that mixes Western influences with local and other traditions. Some experts contend that world music reflects Western cultural imperialism, since Western influence—rock beats and electric instruments, for example—are often strong, and Anglo-American rock stars such as Peter Gabriel, Paul Simon, and Sting have promoted and sometimes appropriated some of the music. Yet world music has introduced Western and global audiences to a rich variety of sounds, often rooted in Asian, African, Caribbean, and Latin American traditions. While reshaping music for a global market, world music has also given Asian, African, and Latin American musicians a larger audience. Just like Western pop stars, some world musicians such as the Brazilian singer-songwriter Caetano Veloso, the Indian film diva Asha Bhosle (the most recorded artist in history: 20,000 songs in over a dozen languages), and the Senegalese Youssou N'Dour, the descendant of griots, who mixes guitars with West African talking drums, perform around the world.

INEQUALITY AND DEVELOPMENT

Globalization, resulting from interconnections transcending the boundaries of nations, benefits some people but not all equally. The gap between rich and poor nations, and rich and poor people within nations, has grown and remains one of the world's major problems. In 1960 the richest fifth of the world's population had a total income thirty times the poorest fifth; by 2000 the ratio had more than doubled. The former Soviet leader Mikhail Gorbachev, a keen student of world affairs, has asked: "Will the whole world turn into one big Brazil, into countries with complete inequality and [gated communities] for the rich elite?"[5] International and national leaders have addressed the challenges of development, considering a more equitable sharing of the world's diminishing resources.

The North-South Gap

With the changes in the global system since World War II, nations on every continent have improved their living standards, lowered poverty rates, and increased their stake in the global economy, which has more than quintupled in size since 1950. The average per capita income in the world grew 2.6 times in the same period, to some $5,000 per year. But the rising tide of the world economy has not lifted all ships, leaving some nations, especially in the southern lands near or below the equator, poor relative to the northern countries. The economies of these nations, known as underdeveloped nations, have stagnated or enjoyed only very modest growth, leaving the majority of their people in poverty. Over 1 billion people live in extreme poverty, with an income of less than $1 per day. Using a popular term for an underdeveloped nation, Jamaican reggae star Pato Banton reflected on the harshness of poverty in a 1989 song, "Third World Country":

> In a Third World country, the plants are green, it's a beautiful scene. Seems like a nice place for human beings. But there's people on the streets, no shoes on their feet. They gotta hustle to get a little food to eat. Things shouldn't be this way.[6]

The gap between the richest and poorest countries, often known as the North-South gap, has widened steadily (see map). For instance, the difference in average per capita incomes between industrialized and nonindustrialized nations grew from 2:1 in 1850 to 10:1 in 1950 to 30:1 by 2000. Today the industrialized North contains a quarter of the world's population but accounts for over three-quarters of its production of goods and services. Poor nations from Haiti to Sierra Leone have experienced civil war or insurgency as rival factions fight to control their limited resources and revenues.

The growing North-South gap has many aspects all documented in dry statistics that, however, represent real people. The disparity in consumption is striking. For example, while Americans, 5 percent of the world's population, consume 40 percent of the world's resources, people in a Bolivian valley consume few resources and experience an impoverished material life. According to a study of the valley: "In a man's lifetime, he will buy one suit, one white shirt, perhaps a hat and a pair of rubber boots. The only things which have to be purchased in the market are a small radio-record player, the batteries to run it, plaster religious figures, a bicycle, and some cutlery."[7] Food consumption also differs dramatically. On average, North Americans consume twice as many calories each day as Haitians and Bangladeshis. While overeating contributes to widespread obesity in industrialized nations, a sixth of the world's people are chronically malnourished, often suffering permanent brain damage because of it, and lack access to clean water. Fifteen million children die each year from hunger-related ailments.

There are also other indicators of difference in wealth. The 10 percent of people who live in the most industrialized nations consume two-thirds of the world's energy. Literacy rates range from a low of 14 percent in Niger, in West Africa, to a high of 99 percent in some twenty wealthy countries. Life expectancy ranges from a high of eighty in Japan to a low of thirty-seven in Sierra Leone, in West Africa. Over 60 percent of the world's poorest people are women, who often struggle to compete with men for resources or are often prevented by local custom from working outside the home.

Challenges of Development

Of course, the experiences of the Asian, African, and Latin American nations involve more than the bleak story of poverty and underdevelopment. Life expectancy worldwide has grown by nearly half and infant mortality has dropped by two-thirds since 1955. Some Asian and Latin American nations have achieved literacy rates comparable to those of some European nations. The number of countries the United Nations considers to have "high human development" grew from sixteen to fifty-five between 1960 and 2004. The rapidly industrializing nations of East and Southeast Asia have led the way: Singapore and South Korea achieved similar world economic rankings with such European nations as Italy, Greece, and Portugal. Several Latin American nations, Caribbean islands, and small oil-rich Persian Gulf states joined the top development category. Many rising nations—such as Malaysia, Thailand, India, and Brazil—formed a growing group of Newly Industrializing Countries (NICs) which, since the 1960s, have enjoyed high economic growth rates. Malaysia, for example, has dramatically reduced poverty rates, while India and Singapore have become centers of high technology. Nor is technological innovation restricted to the well educated. In India, for example, creative farmers have made their work easier by inventing cotton-stripping machines and modifying motorcycles into tractors.

While some countries are on the rise, however, others struggle to spur economic growth that benefits all the population. Valiant efforts have failed to substantially raise living standards or create wealth for everyone. For instance in much of Latin America the wealthiest 20 percent have enjoyed huge income increases while the poorest 40 percent have lost income. Capitalism supported by Western investment has helped a few countries, especially those that combine strong governments with social and economic reform, as in South Korea, Malaysia, and Thailand. But reliance on free markets and Western investment has often failed to sustain development. Little of the trickle down of wealth from the rich to the poor, predicted by Western economists who favor free enterprise, has occurred. Instead, the result has often been trickle out: the loss of a country's wealth to multinational corporations and international banks. Throughout the Contemporary Era, for instance, more wealth has flowed out of Africa and Latin America in the form of resources and profits than has flowed in through aid and investment.

At the same time, alternatives to capitalism have not necessarily brought improvement. Communist and other social revolutionary countries have experienced severe problems. Some of these countries, such as Fidel Castro's Cuba and Mao Zedong's China, did a good job of delivering education and health care but were unable to create much wealth. Some Communist countries, such as Angola and Vietnam, also sometimes faced civil wars and trade embargoes imposed by the West that drained their economies. Since in most cases neither capitalism nor socialism by itself proved the answer, most Communist regimes eventually introduced economic liberalization, such as allowing private companies and Western investment while still maintaining strong, centralized governments. Since adopting this model after the end of the Maoist era, China, for example, has generated the world's most rapid economic growth; in recent years Vietnam has tried to follow the same path. However, economic liberalization that dismantles government services has deprived millions of Chinese and Vietnamese, especially peasants, of the free education and health care they enjoyed under socialism, fostering unrest. The formula of mixing capitalism and socialism has worked well in much of East and

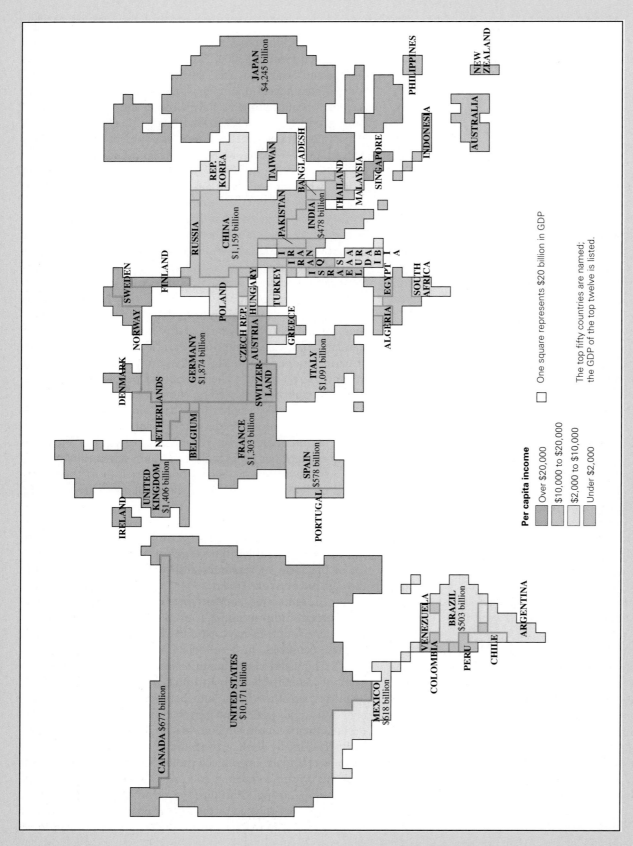

Global Distribution of Wealth The countries of North America, northern Europe, and Japan have the most wealth and the world's highest per capita incomes, averaging over $20,000 per year. At the other extreme, many people in South America and most people in the poor countries of sub-Saharan Africa, South Asia, and the Middle East earn under $2,000 per year.

Per capita income

- Over $20,000
- $10,000 to $20,000
- $2,000 to $10,000
- Under $2,000

☐ One square represents $20 billion in GDP

The top fifty countries are named; the GDP of the top twelve is listed.

Southeast Asia. In these regions, a dynamic, largely unfettered private sector has evolved along with government investment, planning, land reform, investment in education, and other public policies to benefit the common people.

Envisioning a New World Order

The challenge of development is only a part of a larger contemporary question: how societies, working together, can forge a new, more equitable world order. The old world order, built in the nineteenth century when powerful Western nations conquered much of Asia and Africa, was one in which a few rich nations politically and economically dominated most of the others. Even after World War II, decolonization, and the rise of revolutionary states such as China, a few nations, mostly in the West and East Asia, still held disproportionate power and influence. The United States has played the key role and borne the major costs in managing the global system through military alliances (such as NATO), trade pacts (such as GATT), and international organizations (such as the World Bank). However, since the 1960s experts and, often, leaders of underdeveloped nations have argued that fostering widespread economic development also requires addressing the inequalities within the global system, including adjusting power relations between the North and South, and spurring cooperation on international issues. The United Nations has been one major attempt at global cooperation but has had a mixed record.

The current world order contains many problems. The tensions resulting from governments unable significantly to raise living standards for the majority, to deal successfully with mounting social and economic problems, or to sustain hope for a better future have often led to political instability: coups, rebellions, and interventions by foreign powers. Conflicts in one nation then often spill over into neighboring nations, complicating international relations. Furthermore, people have experienced feelings of powerlessness in a world dominated by the governments, businesses, armies, and cultural influences of a few industrialized nations and the impersonal force of global markets. Leaders in the West have also expressed doubts about globalization. French president Jacques Chirac (g. 1995–present), for example, is suspicious of globalization, arguing that democracies "must tame it, accommodate it, humanize it, civilize it."[8]

The prospect of fostering a more equitable sharing of world resources raises questions about the availability of resources. Experts worry that the world's resources and environment could not support a Western standard of living for all the world. If every Chinese, Indian, Egyptian, and Peruvian, they argue, consumed the same products and calories as Americans, Swedes, or Japanese, world resources would quickly diminish. For all 6.5 billion people in today's world to live at a western European standard of living would require a 140-fold increase in the consumption of resources and energy. Present oil supplies would run out in one or two decades, assuming the oil could be pumped and refined into petroleum that fast. Furthermore, the world population is growing rapidly—4.4 people born every second—, and most of the growth is occurring in the developing nations, putting even more pressure on diminishing resources.

China's recent economic success shows the challenges ahead. By the early twenty-first century a China rushing toward development had become a huge consumer of the world's industrial, agricultural, and natural resources, energizing global trade but causing shortages elsewhere. For example, world oil prices have soared since 2000 in part because of China's increasing energy appetite as Chinese switch from bicycles to cars. If the Chinese consumed as much oil per capita as Americans their demand would exceed the present world production. By 2006 the Chinese consumed nearly twice as much meat and more than twice as much steel as Americans. China's living standards remain far below those of Japan and South Korea. Should they rise to that level, however, in the next decade or two, China will import vastly more resources than it does today, further stressing supplies. Assuming China does not experience a revolution, civil war, or economic collapse, all of which are possible, experts expect it to have the world's largest economy by 2035 or 2040, eclipsing the United States. As occurred in the industrializing West earlier, rapid Chinese development, including the growing use of polluting fossil fuels, has also led to environmental degradation, including dangerous air pollution. People in nations once poor but becoming developed, such as China and India, do not believe that the industrialized Western peoples have any more right to consume the world's resources than they do, and they want their fair share.

Resolving problems of underdevelopment, and the poverty it brings, requires change within individual countries, such as implementing land reform, curbing corruption, and reducing bureaucratic obstacles to enterprise. Many experts have advocated "bottom up" development that involves peasants, workers, and women, rather than bureaucratic elites, in decision making. Such decisions would include shaping policies that provide families with adequate economic security, hence reducing the desire among parents for many children to ensure their support in old age. The Grameen Bank in Bangladesh, which loans money to poor women, is an outstanding example of such a "bottom up" policy. The visionary Tanzanian leader Julius Nyerere argued that people cannot be developed by outsiders but must develop themselves, using their own efforts and visions to improve their lives. Self-development, however, requires more social and economic equality within societies so that the wealth can be shared more equitably.

International cooperation is hobbled because the leaders of rich and poor nations often disagree on how to address global inequality. For economic and strategic reasons, Western nations want to protect their access to and heavy consumption of resources such as oil and copper and also worry about trade competition from Newly Industrializing Nations. In democratic nations these leaders have had to answer to voters, who fear compromising their own prosperity. Beginning in the 1970s various conferences and movements have debated modifying the world economic order by, for example, stabilizing world prices for natural resource exports, which chiefly come from developing nations, so that governments could better anticipate annual revenues. Responding to a worldwide campaign to help poor nations, in 2005 the industrialized nations canceled the burdensome debts of the poorest nations. Yet critics wondered whether poor nations with corrupt, often dictatorial, governments would use increased revenues or aid wisely. Furthermore, several Western nations, including the United States, Britain, and France, have often opposed efforts to build a new economic order because such an order could threaten their powerful position in the world economy and transfer wealth to poor nations.

SUSTAINABLE ENVIRONMENTS

The decades since the mid-twentieth century were unusual for the intensity of environmental deterioration and the centrality of human effort in sparking it. The industrialized nations especially had become used to rapid economic growth and were dependent on abundant cheap energy and fresh water, needs that led to environmental destruction on an unparalleled scale. By the dawn of the twenty-first century the challenge of a changing environment became obvious. On every continent, but especially in Eurasia and North America, gas-guzzling vehicles, smoky factories, coal-fired power plants, and large farming operations produce large amounts of carbon dioxide and other pollutants, contributing to rising average temperatures that scientists call global warming. This climate change, if it continues, may have a greater impact—possibly catastrophic—on human life than any conventional war or other destructive human activities. Problems such as global warming raise the question of whether in the long term the natural environment can maintain itself and support plant, animal, and human life—a pattern known as sustainability.

Societies and Environmental Change

Experts have wondered whether the world's resources—minerals, wild plants, food crops, fresh water—could sustain present living standards on a long-term basis. For the past several decades scientists have been alarmed at the human consumption of natural resources faster than nature can replenish them. A major scientific study in the 1990s concluded that a devastating environmental crash would occur during the twenty-first century as resources become exhausted, forests disappear, plant and animal species die off, a warming climate makes certain regions uninhabitable, and pollution increases.

Human activity has altered environments since prehistory, sometimes with catastrophic results. Environmental collapse triggered by agricultural practices or deforestation helped undermine the Mesopotamians, Romans, and Maya, among others. But modern industrial societies and rapidly growing populations encroach on their natural settings even more heavily than did earlier societies. In the twentieth century people used more energy than had been used in all previous history. Between the 1890s and the 1990s the world economy grew fourteen times larger, industrial output twenty times, energy use fourteen times, carbon dioxide emissions seventeen times, water use nine times, and marine fish catches thirty-five times. These increases contributed to, among other pressing problems, air and water pollution, disposal of hazardous waste, declining genetic diversity in crops, and a mass extinction of plant and animal species. With their heavy economic production and consumption, people today are borrowing from tomorrow.

The atmosphere faces particular dangers, including a measurable warming. Earth's climate changed little, with only minor fluctuations, between the last Ice Age, which ended 10,000 years ago, and the end of the eighteenth century, when the Industrial Revolution began in Europe, but it has been changing fast over the past two centuries. The global temperature rose by one degree during the twentieth century. Since 1985, the world has experienced the highest average annual temperatures on record and unprecedented droughts. Scientists

Protesting Global Warming People in societies around the world became alarmed at the increasing environmental damage brought by modern economic activity and exploitation of resources. This demonstration by environmental activists concerned with global warming, a potentially dangerous trend caused by burning fossil fuels such as coal that produces more carbon dioxide, took place in Turkey. (AP/Wide World Photos)

now largely agree that global warming has been increasing, although they debate its causes and dangers. Without major efforts to curb warming, scientists forecast a rise of somewhere between an alarming 2.5 and a catastrophic 10.4 degrees by 2100, which, if it happens, will change human life dramatically. Referring to the enclosed buildings where warm-weather plants are raised in cold climates, scientists speak of a Greenhouse Effect, the overheating of earth from human-made pollutants. The main culprits are gases such as carbon dioxide, chlorofluorocarbons, and methane that accumulate in the atmosphere and trap heat. The amount of heat-trapping carbon dioxide in the atmosphere increased by a third between 1900 and 2000, mostly from burning coal and oil. The greenhouse gases come largely from factory smokestacks, coal-fired power plants, and gasoline-powered vehicle exhausts. The most industrialized nation, the United States, has become the major producer, accounting for some 25 percent of the carbon dioxide and up to 50 percent of the other polluting chemicals. Europe, Russia, Japan, and China produce much of the rest. Some pollutants also destroy the ozone layer, a gaseous region in the upper atmosphere that protects humans from the cancer-causing ultraviolet rays of the sun. Scientists discovered that the ozone depletion rate in the 1990s was twice as fast as was thought a decade earlier.

In the pessimistic scenarios, the consequences of rising temperatures for many of the world's peoples are devastating. Earth gets baked, rich farmland turns to desert, and forests wilt. Fresh water, already scarce, becomes even harder to find as lakes and streams dry up. Rising ocean temperatures damage fisheries and kill most protective coral reefs while also increasing the intensity of hurricanes, making them more often like the catastrophic storm that devastated New Orleans and the U.S. Gulf Coast in 2005. Tropical and subtropical nations find agriculture and life generally more difficult. In North America farming becomes tougher in the southern United States, though more productive in a warming Canada. As the ice on Greenland melts, pouring fresh water into the North Atlantic, the warming Gulf Stream may shift southward and bring harsher winters to Europe and eastern North America.

Some peoples might face even more daunting challenges. Global warming has reduced the ice covering the Arctic Ocean by half in recent years while thawing the adjacent land; these developments diminish the habitat for cold-adapted animals, such as polar bears, and threaten the livelihood and settlements of Arctic peoples. At the other end of the world, the West Antarctic ice shelf holds a vast amount of water and in some places has already begun to melt. If this trend accelerates, it will raise sea levels enough over the next two centuries to cover much low-lying coastal land. This will have disastrous consequences for regions such as the U.S. Gulf Coast and Florida, the Low Countries of northwest Europe, Bangladesh and eastern India, and small island nations already now barely above sea level, including Tonga, Tuvalu, the Bahamas, and the Maldives.

Environmental Issues and Movements

The environmental challenges, such as diminishing resources, global warming, and deforestation, reinforce the scientific concept, first popularized in the 1970s, of global ecology—of the world, including human societies, as a complex web in which all living things interact with each other and their surroundings. From earliest times, societies have had complex relations with the environment, including interdependence with it. The Industrial Revolution, which has reshaped the world over the past two centuries, often for the better, came at great costs to the environment. Yet the world's leaders cannot agree on ways to better balance economic growth, which all nations desire, with environmental protection.

The exploitation of the earth's resources for human benefit, which has accelerated since 1945, has undermined sustainability. While soil, forests, and fisheries are renewable resources if properly managed, which they often were not in the past century, mineral resources such as oil and copper cannot be replaced once used up. Oil experts disagree as to when all known recoverable oil reserves will become exhausted. Optimists think oil supplies will be adequate for 30 or 40 years before declining and becoming scarce well before the century ends. Pessimists, noting the increased demand by countries such as China and India, believe all easily exploitable sources will be gone within two or three decades, causing conflict as nations scramble for oil supplies. Anticipating future resource and energy shortages, experts have for years recommended that industrial nations conserve oil by reducing dependence on it as the main fuel while developing renewable energy resources, such as solar, tidal, and wind power. Some nations have turned toward building more nuclear power plants, which are expensive and potentially dangerous but do less damage to the climate than burning fossil fuels. So far a few developing nations and some European countries have shown the most commitment to conservation and developing renewable energies.

Scientific conclusions about global warming and the need to reduce dependence on oil have often challenged powerful economic interests and upset governments that favor economic growth and worry about economic competition from rival nations. For example, since the 1970s U.S. presidents and Congress, fearing possible negative effects on U.S. business, have often opposed environmental agreements, such as the Kyoto treaty of 1997, which was an effort, supported by most of the world's nations, to begin reducing greenhouse gases, as well as a European proposal seeking a 15 percent alternative energy use by 2010 (versus 1 percent today). Leaders of a few other powerful nations, including Japan, Russia, Britain, and China, have also been reluctant to cooperate with the world community on environmental issues. In 2005, 150 nations met in Montreal, Canada, and reaffirmed their commitment to the Kyoto treaty. To sustain environmental health, a Canadian statesman has argued, requires a "revolution in [our] thinking as basic as the one introduced by Copernicus who [in the 1500s] first pointed out that the earth was not the center of the universe."[9]

An environmental movement began in the West in the late nineteenth century, eventually sparking similar movements around the world. Yet environmental awareness grew slowly. In the 1940s, the American environmentalist Aldo Leopold called for an ethic that treats the land with respect because all life belongs to a community of interdependent relationships: "Land is a fountain of energy flowing through a circuit of soils, plants, and animals, a sustained circuit, like a slowly augmented revolving fund of life."[10] Such ideas did not gain a large following. By the 1970s, however, views had changed; organizations such as Greenpeace, Earth First!, and the Rainforest Action Network pressed for a global commitment to stop environmental destruction. In 1992 a United Nations–sponsored global conference in Rio de Janeiro issued a proclamation urging sustainable development: "Human beings are entitled to a healthy and productive life in harmony with nature."[11] But the realities of modern politics, national rivalries, and fierce economic competition continue to make such a change difficult.

GLOBAL PASTS AND FUTURES

The study of history helps us understand today's news and views as they are reported in daily newspapers, broadcast on radio and television, and disseminated on the World Wide Web. Historians often describe their work as involving a dialogue between past, present, and future. A few years ago French scientist René Dubos argued: "The past is not dead history. It is living material out of which makes the present and builds the future."[12] Current global problems have their roots in the patterns of world history: the rise of cities, states, and organized religions; the expansion of trade and capitalism to global dimensions; the unprecedented mastery and altering of nature represented by the scientific, industrial, and technological revolutions; the proliferation of competitive, unequal nations; and the myriad of social, economic, political, and cultural connections between peoples encompassed in the expanding global system. While seeking to understand how the past shaped the present, historians also speculate on how current trends may shape the future.

Understanding the Global Past

World historians offer several ways of understanding the world of yesterday, today, and tomorrow. One view is that contacts and collisions between different societies produce change. Whether through peaceful exchange or warfare or perhaps both, when societies encounter other societies they are exposed to different customs and ideas. For millennia after the transition to agriculture most of those contacts were with nearby peoples, but around two thousand years ago, thanks to advances in transportation and growing economies, increasingly mobile peoples began to encounter others much further away, laying the roots for a global system to emerge after 1450. Historians also emphasize continuity, the persistence of social, cultural, political, and religious ideas and patterns, as well as change, the transformations in ways of life, work, and thought. Continuities are common. For example, many Christians, Muslims, Jews, Buddhists, and Hindus still look at the world through the prism of traditional religious values forged millennia ago and still meaningful today. Hence, in 2004 over 400,000 Christian missionaries—many from countries like

Nigeria, the Philippines, and South Korea—were spreading the gospel around the world, at an annual cost of some $11 billion. Islam increased its following from 400 million people in 1960 to 1.3 billion by 2004. Yet changes, too, are everywhere. Thus most people, among them the devout followers of the old religions, also engage in activities, face challenges, and use forms of transportation and communication nonexistent a few generations ago. As a result, missionaries and clerics often use radio, television, and the Internet to spread their message. Another insight offered by global historians is that great transitions, such as the agricultural and industrial revolutions or, more recently, the rise of high technology, can turn history in new directions. Hence, thousands of years ago farming largely displaced hunting and gathering, two centuries ago industry transformed the world economy, and today instant communication and information bring distant peoples closer together. For instance, youngsters in Wisconsin can watch Australian-rules football matches from Melbourne on cable television while fans of Chinese rock and rap groups can hear their music on websites accessible from around the world.

As an example of the contacts and collisions that foster change, some scholars explain the changes of the past five hundred years in terms of the larger world's exposure and accommodation to the West, which led in turn to the political, economic, and military triumph of the West and often the adoption of its values and institutions. As a result of the spread of Western cultural influences, market economies, economic consumption practices, and individualistic values, they see a growing standardization of the world's societies. Many people welcome this standardization as a sign of progress, while others perceive it as a threat to local traditions. Still others consider the claim that societies and cultures are standardizing inaccurate, seeing instead a real increase in differences, especially the growing gap between rich and poor nations. In fact, living standards in the world have not been standardized. While people in the rich countries usually own several expensive electrical appliances, from washing machines to plasma televisions, millions of people in the poor nations do not even have electricity. Still, thanks to contacts between distant societies, the Western value of materialistic indulgence has became common, even if often out of reach for the poorest half of the world's people.

The experiences of most societies over the past half century reveal a mix of change and continuity. For example, Western ideas have gained even greater influence in the world since 1945 than they had before. People in different lands have adopted Western ideas of government, such as constitutions and elections, although not necessarily the substance of democracy, along with Western-rooted ideologies and faiths: capitalism, socialism, nationalism, and Christianity. Western pop culture, from rock music to soft drinks and blue jeans, has spread widely, leading to the "Coca-Colazation" of the world stemming from Western economic power, including advertising. Yet influences from the West are usually strongest in large cities and penetrate less deeply into the villages in Africa, Asia, and the Middle East, where traditional ways reflect continuity with the past. As a result, city youth in Malaysia or Tanzania may follow the latest recordings from Western pop stars, but these recordings may be unknown to their rural counterparts. Yet the urban youth may also share with rural youth traditional views about family and faith, and rural youth may, like their city counterparts, own motorcycles, boom boxes, and cell phones that make their lives different from those of their parents.

As a result of the transition to globalizing technology, culture, and commerce, the contacts between societies and their interdependence have vastly increased since 1945. In different ways nuclear weapons, multinational corporations, earth-circling satellites, World Cup soccer, and cable news networks draw people together, willingly or not. Imperialists once claimed proudly that "the sun never set on the British Empire." By the 1990s observers noted that "the sun never sets on McDonald's." Closer contact, of course, does not necessarily mean friendly relations and a less dangerous world; it can also bring collisions. Guided missiles and planes carrying bombs can reach 10,000 miles from their base. Over the past several decades over 60,000 Americans have died fighting in Vietnam, Afghanistan, and Iraq in support of U.S. efforts to reshape distant nations. On the other side, terrorist plots hatched in Afghanistan by Islamic militants who blame the United States for Middle Eastern problems killed Americans in New York City and Washington, D.C., in 2001. Some of the terrorists involved in planning or carrying out those and other attacks were once secular Muslims who went to Europe or the United States for college and, culturally disoriented and resentful of Western policies, became Islamic militants and then joined a terrorist organization with global reach and access to high technology such as satellite phones, computers, and the Internet. Experts also speak of cyberspace terrorism, in which political or religious extremists advertise their violent goals and deeds on websites. The same technologies that allow people to instantly access and share information around the world also allows governments to spy on citizens and criminals to use cyberspace for their own purposes. Meanwhile, hackers can live anywhere and disrupt computer operations all over the world. Technology also threatens governments. In 2005 the search engine company, Google, made available a program, Google Earth, that can be freely downloaded and allows a user anywhere to see aerial and satellite photos of any location in the world. Governments from Algeria to India to Russia protested unsuccessfully that this violated their laws and revealed data, such as the layout of military bases, that they did not want available to the general public.

The contacts, changes, and transitions since 1945 have created a global village, a single community of exchange and interaction. In some regions, such as Southeast Asia, even remote villages have become part of this global village. By the 1960s, for example, people living in the once isolated interior of the island of Borneo, divided between Indonesia and Malaysia, could access the outside world through battery-powered transistor radios and cassette players, and also by means of visiting traders, Christian missionaries, and government officials. Borneo's interior people also often left their remote villages to find work at logging camps, oil wells, or plantations as their rain forest environment and small farms rapidly disappeared, destroyed by international timber and mining operations that cut forests and stripped land to procure resources to ship to distant countries. As once remote peoples, like those in the Borneo interior, are brought into the global system, and ethnic minorities are incorporated into nations, they find it harder to maintain their cultures and languages. Half of all languages are in danger of dying out over the next several decades and less than one percent of languages are used on the Internet.

Towards the Future

Women and men created the present world from the materials of the past and are now laying the foundation for the future. As a Belgian scholar wrote a few years ago, "We cannot predict the future, but we can prepare it."[13] But this raises the questions of what kind of future. In 1974 the American economic historian Robert Heilbroner, asking what promise the future holds, doubted the permanence of modern industrial society and even democracy in the face of population explosion, environmental degradation, resource depletion, militarization, and the increasing economic desperation of people in the poorest countries. His question remains highly relevant in the early twenty-first century. For example, as industrialization spreads to other nations, the world requires more use of fossil fuels, which spurs more global warming. Heilbroner drew a gloomy picture of the future. He believed most people are not willing to sacrifice for the good of future generations. Like him, other experts often despair. The world's long history of war, inequality, and exploitation, even when seemingly offset by progress, does not foster optimism. Indeed, some respected experts predict human extinction if people do not adopt more sustainable ways, and scientific studies are more frequently pessimistic than optimistic about the future. Worried tht we face environment collapse, one study concludes: "Our generation is the first to be faced with decisions that will determine whether the earth our children inherit will be habitable."[14]

Yet, since World War II humanity has produced many green shoots of hope. Western Europe moved rapidly to political and economic unity, defusing centuries of conflict. Eastern Europeans and Russians overturned dogmatic communist regimes, ending the long Cold War between the superpowers. The Scandinavian nations, a hundred years ago among the poorest European societies, have virtually eliminated poverty, achieving the world's highest quality of life. Several Asian nations rapidly developed, dramatically improving living standards and national wealth. A century ago desperately poor, China has become not only able to feed and clothe its huge population but also to export industrial products to the world. Thanks in part to global efforts, black majority rule came to South Africa. Over two dozen nations, including some in Asia, Latin America, and the Caribbean, have elected women presidents or prime ministers, and women, making their voices heard, have increasingly gained more power over their lives in many countries. Despite some notable conflicts, wars have become less common than before. Unlike the Cold War years

International Women's Day 2005   Women around the world became more willing to assert their rights. Activists from diverse Indian nongovernmental organizations interested in women's rights marched in New Delhi, India's capital, in 2005 to mark International Women's Day.   (AP/Wide World Photos)

between 1946 and 1992, when fighting between and within nations was frequent, between 1992 and 2005 the number of wars with over 1,000 battle deaths a year declined by 80 percent.

Hopeful developments have also resulted from international cooperation. A large majority of nations have signed agreements to ban weapons of mass destruction, punish genocide, and reduce gases contributing to global warming. Drastic reductions in the arms race have diminished the threat of nuclear war. United Nations agencies have improved lives for children and women in many countries and spurred cooperation on environmental issues. Local nongovernmental organizations, often with international connections, have also become active, working for the rights of women, children, workers, and peasants and for a healthier environment. Human rights groups with chapters around the world have

worked courageously to promote civil liberties and the release of political prisoners. Encouraged by environmental activists abroad, brave tribal groups in tropical rain forests have resisted the logging and mining destroying their habitats. Not least in its effects, the growing information superhighway now instantly links millions of office or home computers with people, libraries, and other information sources around the world.

A history not only of cruelty and exploitation but also of compassion and sacrifice provides hope in navigating troubled times. Remembering when people behaved magnificently may foster inspiration to answer the challenges. The contemporary age offers ample examples of inspiring people: democracy activists such as Nelson Mandela, Vaclav Havel, Mohandas Gandhi, and Aung San Suu Kyi; social activists such as Wangari Maathai, Dr. Martin Luther King, Jr., Shirin Ebadi, and Mukhtaran Bibi; cultural figures such as Wole Soyinka, Violeta Parra, Simone de Beauvoir, and Cui Jian; and figures who have built links between societies such as Jean Monnet, Bono, and the Dalai Lama. Historians sometimes view the past as a stream with banks. The stream is filled with people killing, bullying, enslaving, and doing other things historians usually record, while on the banks, unnoticed, women and men build homes, raise children, tend farms, settle disputes, sing songs, whittle statues, trade with their neighbors, and chat with travelers from other lands. Historians often ignore the banks for the stream, but what happens on the banks may be more reassuring.

Some observers, believing that cultural differences will increasingly drive international politics, forecast a clash of civilizations, such as between the Christian West and Islam, which are seen as irreconcilably opposed in world-views. But simplistic formulas miss the complexity of the global order. None of the great religions and the cultures that they shaped are monolithic, the divisions among Christians or Muslims, Westerners or Middle Easterners, being as great as their differences with other traditions. No cultures have a monopoly on values such as peace, justice, charity, tolerance, public discussion, and goodwill. In any case, nations generally shape their foreign policies according to their national interests rather than ideology. Wars over resources, such as oil and water, some observers claim, are more likely to occur than wars over cultural differences. Other observers doubt that, whatever the tensions, any titanic military struggle like the two world wars of the twentieth century is inevitable; they expect that the world will cooperate on major issues and tolerate different concepts of economics, government, God, morality, and society for years to come. Furthermore, thanks to the many available information sources people can become informed about why past societies, such as the Mesopotamians and Maya, destroyed their environments and collapsed, and how countries blundered into wars or failed to develop cooperative relations with their neighbors that maintained peace. These insights, if acquired, may help people today to avoid repeating the mistakes of the past and construct a better future.

Four centuries ago, the English playwright William Shakespeare wrote that the past is prologue to the present. The study of world history allows us to ask questions about the global future because we understand the changing patterns of the global past, including the building of societies, their interactions through networks, and the great transitions that reshaped humanity. These have led to an increasingly connected world in the past 1,500 years. The contemporary age has been marked by a complex mix of dividing and unifying forces, unique societies differing greatly in standards of living but linked into a global system of exchange. People today cannot yet know with certainty where the path will lead, but they can help build it. Nineteenth-century British novelist Lewis Carroll (1832–1898) suggested a way of looking at the problem in his novel *Through the Looking Glass*, about Alice in Wonderland. Lost and perplexed in Wonderland, Alice asked the Cheshire Cat: "Would you tell me, please, which way I ought to go from here?" The enigmatic cat pondered the query for a few moments and then replied: "That depends a great deal on where you want to get to."[15] Societies, working together, must chart that course into the future.

SUGGESTED READING

BOOKS

Baylis, John, et al., eds. *The Globalization of World Politics: An Introduction to International Relations*, 3rd ed. New York: Oxford University Press, 2004. Essays on world politics by British scholars.

Brown, Lester. *Plan B 2.0: Rescuing a Planet Under Stress and a Civilizaion in Trouble.* New York: W. W. Norton, 2006. A survey of the world's environmental and resource challenges and some possible solutions.

Hannerz, Ulf. *Transnational Connections: Culture, People, Places.* New York: Routledge, 1996. Interesting essays on cultures and networks in the age of globalization by a Swedish scholar.

Held, David, ed. *A Globalizing World? Culture, Economics, Politics.* New York: Routledge, 2000. An excellent collection of essays and readings on various aspects of globalization, compiled by British scholars.

Hobsbawm, Eric. *On the Edge of the New Century.* New York: The New Press, 1999. Thoughts on the past, present, and future by a British historian.

Kennedy, Paul. *Preparing for the Twenty-First Century.* New York: Random House, 1993. A study of how population, technology, and the environment shaped the contemporary world and various regions.

Mayor, Federico, and Jerome Bindé. *The World Ahead: Our Future in the Making.* New York: Zed Books, 2001. A comprehensive study, prepared by European scholars for the United Nations, of political, economic, social, cultural, and environmental trends.

Mazrui, Ali. *Cultural Forces in World Politics.* London: Heinemann, 1990. A challenging examination of world-views and patterns by a distinguished African scholar.

Newland, Kathleen, and Kamala Chandrakirana Soedjatmoko, eds. *Transforming Humanity: The Visionary Writings of Soedjatmoko.* West Hartford, Conn.: Kumarian Press, 1994. Thoughtful essays on development, violence, religion, and other issues in the contemporary world by an influential Indonesian thinker.

Pieterse, Jan Nederveen, ed. *Global Futures: Shaping Globalization.* London: Zed Books, 2000. Provocative essays on world trends by scholars from around the world.

Sachs, Jeffrey. *The End of Poverty: Economic Possibilities for Our Time.* New York: Penguin, 2005. Controversial but stimulating discussion of global poverty issues.

Seager, Joni. *The Penguin Atlas of Women in the World,* revised and updated. New York: Penguin, 2003. Creative, indispensable examination of women around the world.

Sen, Amartya. *Identity and Violence: The Illusion of Destiny.* New York: W. W. Norton, 2006. Provocative critique by an India-born economist of the clash of civilizations idea.

Smith, Dan, and Ane Braein. *Penguin State of the World Atlas,* 7th ed. New York: Penguin, 2003. The latest edition of an invaluable map-based reference providing an overview of world conditions.

State of the World. New York: W. W. Norton. Informative annual surveys of the world's environmental health that are published annually by the Worldwatch Institute in Washington, D.C.

Taylor, Timothy D. *Global Pop: World Music, World Markets.* New York: Routledge, 1997. A fine study of the world music industry and major musicians.

WEBSITES

Global Problems and the Culture of Capitalism (http://faculty.plattsburgh.edu/richard.robbins/legacy/). An outstanding site, aimed at undergraduates, with a wealth of resources on many topics.

Globalization Guide (http://www.globalisationguide.org). A useful collection of essays and links.

The Globalization Website (http://www.sociology.emory.edu/globalization/). A very useful site with many resources and essays related to globalization.

United Nations (http://www.un.org). The pathway to the websites of the many United Nations agencies, operations, and ongoing projects.

The WWW Virtual Library (http://vlib.org). The homepage of a vast and indispensable British-based network of links on many topics and issues.

GLOSSARY

The glossary for *Societies, Networks, and Transitions: A Global History* is for the complete text, Chapters 1 through 31.

absolutism A system of strong monarchial authority in which all power is placed in a supreme authority, a king or queen. (*p. 445*)

Achaemenid The ruling family of the Classical Persian Empire (ca. 550–450 B.C.E.). (*p. 146*)

Age of Revolution The period from the 1770s through the 1840s when revolutions rocked North America, Europe, the Caribbean, and Latin America. (*p. 566*)

Ahura Mazda (the "Wise Lord") The one god of **Zoroastrianism**. (*p. 150*)

Aksum A literate, urban state that appeared in northern Ethiopia before the Common Era and grew into an empire and a crossroads for trade. (*p. 231*)

Allah To Muslims the one and only, all-powerful God. (*p. 274*)

animism The belief that all creatures as well as inanimate objects and natural phenomena have souls and can influence human well-being. (*p.15*)

apartheid ("separate development") A South African policy to set up a police state to enforce racial separation; lasted from 1948 to 1994. (*p. 956*)

Arianism A heretical Christian sect that arose in the fourth century C.E. that taught that Jesus was not divine but rather an exceptional human being. (*p. 218*)

Aryans Indo-European-speaking nomadic pastoralists who migrated from Iran into northwest India between 1600 and 1400 B.C.E. (see **pastoral nomadism**). (*p. 47*)

asceticism A system of austere religious practices, such as intense prayer, that was used to strengthen spiritual life and seek a deeper understanding of god; began to be used in the Christian church in the fifth and sixth centuries C.E. (*p. 218*)

ASEAN (Association of Southeast Asian Nations) A regional economic and political organization formed in 1967 to promote cooperation among the non-Communist Southeast Asian nations; eventually became a major trading bloc. (*p. 993*)

Atlantic System A large network that arose with the trans-Atlantic slave trade; the network spanned western and Central Africa, the east coast and southern region of English North America, the Caribbean Basin, and the northern and eastern coastal zones of South America. (*p. 473*)

audiencias Judicial tribunals with administrative functions that served as subdivisions of viceroyalties in Spanish America. (*p. 500*)

australopithecines Early **hominids** living in eastern and southern Africa 3 to 4 million years ago. (*p. 9*)

Awami League A Bengali nationalist party that began the move from independence from West Pakistan. (*p. 975*)

Ba'ath ("Renaissance") A political party in the Middle East that favored socialism and Arab nationalism and strongly opposed Israel. (*p. 942*)

Bahai An offshoot of Persian Shi'ism that was founded in 1867; Bahai preached universal peace, the unity of all religions, and service to others. (*p. 649*)

Balfour Declaration A letter from the British foreign minister to Zionist leaders in 1917 that gave British support for the establishment of Palestine as a national home for the Jewish people. (*p. 776*)

Bantu Sub-Saharan African peoples who developed a cultural tradition based on farming and iron metallurgy, which they spread widely through great migrations. (*p. 67*)

bantustans Rural reservations in South Africa where black Africans under apartheid were required to live if they were not needed in the modern economy. (*p. 957*)

baroque An extravagant and, to many, shocking European artistic movement of the 1600s that encouraged release from restraints of thought and expression. (*p. 451*)

Bedouins Tent-dwelling nomadic Arab pastoralists of the seventh century C.E. who wandered in search of oases, grazing lands, or trade caravans to raid (see **pastoral nomadism**). (*p. 270*)

benefices In **medieval** Europe, grants of land from lord to **vassal**. (*p. 391*)

Bhagavad Gita ("Lord's Song") A poem in the *Mahabharata* that is the most treasured piece of ancient Hindu literature. (*p. 51*)

bhakti Devotional worship of a personal Hindu god. (*p. 363*)

bhangra A popular music that emerged in Britain from a blending of traditional folk songs brought by Indian immigrants with Caribbean reggae and Anglo-American styles, such as rock, hip hop, and disco. (*p. 881*)

Bharatha Janata (BJP) The major Hindu nationalist party in India. (*p. 976*)

Black Hole of Calcutta A crowded jail in India where over a hundred British prisoners of a hostile Bengali ruler died from suffocation and dehydration in 1757. This event precipitated the beginning of British use of force in India. (*p. 660*)

Black Legend The Spanish reputation for brutality toward Native Americans, including the repression of native religions, execution of rebels, and forced labor. (*p. 502*)

bodhisattva ("One who has the essence of Buddhahood") A loving and ever compassionate "saint" who has postponed his or her own attainment of **nirvana** to help others find salvation through liberation from birth and rebirth (see **Buddhism, Mahayana**). (*p. 186*)

Boers Dutch farming settlers in South Africa in the eighteenth century. (*p. 470*)

Bollywood The Bombay film industry in India. (*p. 978*)

Bolsheviks The most radical of Russia's antigovernment groups in the early twentieth century, who embraced a dogmatic form of Marxism. (*p. 722*)

bourgeoisie The urban-based, mostly commercial, middle class that arose with **capitalism** in the Early Modern Era. (*p. 435*)

Brahman The Universal Soul, or Absolute Reality, that Hindus believe fills all space and time. (*p. 176*)

Brahmanas Commentaries on the **Vedas** that emphasize the role of priests (**brahmans**). (*p. 52*)

brahmans The priests, the highest-ranking caste in Hindu society. (*p. 50*)

Brezhnev Doctrine In the late twentieth century, an assertion by Soviet leaders of Moscow's right to interfere in Soviet satellites to protect Communist governments and the Soviet bloc. (*p. 886*)

British Commonwealth of Nations A forum, established by Britain in 1931, for discussing issues of mutual interest with its former colonies. (*p. 871*)

Buddhism A major world religion based on the teachings of the Buddha that emphasized putting an end to desire and being compassionate to all creatures. (*p. 178*)

Bunraku The puppet theater of Tokugawa Japan. (*p. 543*)

Burakumin ("Hamlet people") A despised Japanese subgroup who traditionally were restricted to poor neighborhoods and performed jobs considered unclean and undignified. (*p. 706*)

Bushido ("Way of the Warrior") An idealized ethic for the Japanese **samurai**. (*p. 322*)

caliphate An imperial state headed by an Islamic ruler, the caliph, considered the designated successor of the Prophet in civil affairs. (*p. 274*)

calligraphy The artful writing of words. (*p. 286*)

calypso A song style in Trinidad that often featured lyrics addressing daily life and topical subjects. (*p. 621*)

can vuong ("Aid-the-king") Rebel groups who waged guerrilla warfare for fifteen years against the French occupation of Vietnam. (*p. 675*)

capitalism An economic system in which property, exchange, and the means of production are privately owned. (*p. 430*)

caste system The four-tiered Hindu social system comprising hereditary social classes that restrict the occupation of their members and their relations with members of other castes. (*p. 50*)

Castroism Innovative socialist policies introduced by Fidel Castro to stimulate economic development in Cuba while tightly controlling its population. (*p. 923*)

caudillos Latin American military strongmen who acquired and maintained power through force between the early nineteenth and mid-twentieth centuries. *(p. 616)*

Centuriate Assembly A Roman legislative body made up of soldiers. *(p. 203)*

Chavín The earliest-known Andean urban society. *(p. 102)*

chinampas Artificial islands built along lakeshores of the central valley of Mexico and used by the Aztecs for growing food. *(p. 349)*

Chinoiserie An eighteenth- and nineteenth-century Western vogue for artistic products of China such as painting, ceramics, lacquer ware, and decorative furniture. *(p. 688)*

chivalry The rigid code of behavior, including a sense of duty and honor, of **medieval** European knights. *(p. 391)*

Clovis A Native American culture dating back some 11,500 to 13,500 years. *(p. 96)*

Co-hong A nineteenth-century Chinese merchant's guild that had a monopoly on Guangzhou's trade with the West. *(p. 688)*

Cold War A conflict lasting from 1946 to 1989 in which the United States and the USSR competed for allies and engaged in occasional warfare against their rivals' allies rather than against each other directly. *(p. 807)*

colonialism Government by one society over another society. *(p. 474)*

Columbian Exchange The transportation of diseases, animals, and plants from one hemisphere to another that resulted from European exploration and conquest between 1492 and 1750. *(p. 499)*

commercial capitalism The economic system in which most capital was invested in commercial enterprises such as trading companies, including the world's first joint-stock companies. *(p. 435)*

communes Large agricultural units introduced in China by Mao Zedong that combined many families and villages into a common system for pooling resources and labor. *(p. 838)*

Confucianism A Chinese philosophy based on the ideas of Confucius (ca. 551–479 B.C.E.) that emphasized the correct relations among people; became the dominant philosophy of East Asia for two millennia. *(p. 122)*

conquistadors The leaders of Spanish soldiers engaged in armed conquest in the Americas. *(p. 495)*

consuls Two **patrician** men, elected by the **Centuriate Assembly** each year, who had executive power in the Roman Republic. *(p. 203)*

containment The main U.S. strategy aimed at preventing Communists from gaining power, and the USSR from getting political influence, in other nations during the **Cold War.** *(p. 905)*

Coptic Church A branch of Christianity, based on **Monophysite** ideas, that had become influential in Egypt and became dominant in Nubia between the fourth and sixth centuries C.E. *(p. 231)*

Cossacks Tough adventurers and soldiers from southern Russia who were descendants of Russians, Poles, and Lithuanians fleeing serfdom, slavery, or jail. *(p. 484)*

Counter Reformation A movement to confront Protestantism and crush dissidents within the Catholic Church (see **Protestants, Reformation**). *(p. 441)*

courtly love A standard of polite relationships between knights and ladies that arose in the 1100s in **medieval** Europe. Courtly love was celebrated in song by wandering troubadours. *(p. 394)*

creoles People of Iberian ancestry who were born in Latin America. *(p. 500)*

Cro-Magnons The first modern, tool-using humans in Europe. *(p. 13)*

cubism An early-twentieth-century form of painting that rejected visual reality and emphasized instead geometric shapes and forms that often suggested movement. *(p. 735)*

cultivation system An agricultural policy imposed by the Dutch in Java that forced Javanese farmers to grow sugar on rice land. *(p. 672)*

cultural relativism The notion that societies are diverse and unique, embodying different standards of correct behavior. *(p. xxxi)*

cuneiform ("wedge-shape") A Latin term used to describe the writing system invented by the Sumerians. *(p. 36)*

Cynicism A Hellenistic philosophy, made famous by the philosopher Diogenes (fourth century B.C.E.), that emphasized living a radically simple life, shunning material things and all pretense, and remaining true to one's fundamental values (see **Hellenism**). *(p. 169)*

daimyo ("Great name") Large landowning territorial magnates who monopolized local power in Japan beginning during the Ashikaga period (1338–1568). *(p. 324)*

Daoism A Chinese philosophy that emphasized adaptation to nature; arose in the late Zhou era. *(p. 125)*

Dar al-Islam ("Abode of Islam") The Islamic world stretching from Morocco to Indonesia and joined by both a common faith and trade; arose between the eighth and the seventeenth centuries. *(p. 289)*

Darkest Africa Those areas of the African continent least known to Europeans but, in European eyes, awaiting to be "opened" to the "light of Western civilization." *(p. 465)*

deism Belief in a benevolent God who designed the universe but does not intercede in its affairs. *(p. 454)*

Delian League A defensive league organized by Greek cities in the fifth century B.C.E. to defeat the Persians. *(p. 161)*

desertification The transformation of once productive land into useless desert. *(pp. 65 and 823)*

devaraja ("God-king") The title used by Indianized Southeast Asian rulers, who wished to be seen as a reincarnated Buddha or **Shiva** worthy of cult worship. *(p. 370)*

development Growth in a variety of economic areas that benefits the majority of people; the opposite of **monoculture.** *(p. 507)*

direct rule A method of ruling colonies whereby a largely European colonial administration supervised all activity, even down to the local level, and native chiefs or kings were reduced to symbolic roles (see **colonialism**). *(p. 641)*

dominion A country that has autonomy but owes allegiance to the British crown; developed in the early twentieth century. *(p. 623)*

domino theory A theory that envisioned countries falling one by one to communism and that became a mainstay of U.S. policy during the **Cold War.** *(p. 904)*

Dravidian A language family whose speakers are the great majority of the population in southern India. *(p. 45)*

dreamtime In Aboriginal Australian mythology, the distant past when the spiritual ancestors gave order and form to the universe at the world's creation. *(p. 248)*

Dust Bowl Parts of the U.S. Midwest and Southwest during the 1930s where disappearing topsoil and severe drought threw agriculture badly out of balance. *(p. 733)*

dyarchy A form of dual government that began in Japan during the Nara period (710–784) whereby one powerful family ruled the country while the emperor held mostly symbolic power. *(p. 317)*

dynastic cycle The Chinese view of their political history, which focuses on dynasties of ruling families. *(p. 88)*

empiricism An approach that stresses experience and the testing of propositions rather than reason alone in acquiring knowledge. *(p. 454)*

enclosure Arising in Early Modern Europe, the pattern in which landlords fenced off common lands once used by the public for grazing livestock and collecting firewood. *(p. 455)*

encomienda ("Entrustment") The Crown's grant to a colonial Spaniard in Latin America of a certain number of Indians from whom he extracted tribute. *(p. 507)*

Enlightenment A philosophical movement based on science and reason that began in Europe in the late seventeenth century and continued through the eighteenth century. *(p. 453)*

Estado Novo ("New State") A fascist-influenced and modernizing dictatorship in Brazil led by Getulio Vargas between 1930 and 1945. *(p. 777)*

ethnocentrism Viewing others narrowly through the lenses of one's own society and its values. *(p. xxx)*

Eurocommunism A form of communism in western Europe in the later twentieth century that embraced political democracy and free elections and that rejected Soviet domination. *(p. 870)*

excommunicate To expel a person from the Roman Catholic church and its sacraments. *(p. 396)*

existentialism A philosophy, influential in post–World War II western Europe, whose speculation on the nature of reality reflects disillusionment with Europe's violent history and doubt that objectivity is possible. *(p. 882)*

extraterritoriality Freedom from local laws for foreign subjects. *(p. 690)*

G. Oxtoby, ed., *World Religions: Eastern Traditions* (New York: Oxford University Press, 1996), p. 230.

10. From "Kautilya's 'Artha-Sastra,'" in O. L. Chavarria-Aguilar, ed., *Traditional India* (Englewood Cliffs, N.J.: Prentice-Hall, 1964), p. 125.

11. Quoted in Rhoads Murphy, *A History of Asia*, 4th ed. (New York: HarperCollins, 2003), p. 74.

12. Quoted in Lucille Schulberg, *Historic India* (New York: Time-Life Books, 1968), p. 80.

13. Xuan Zang, quoted in David Christian, *A History of Russia, Central Asia, and Mongolia*, vol. 1 (Malden, Mass.: Blackwell, 1998), p. 254.

14. From McNaughton, *Light from East*, p. 377.

15. Quoted in John Keay, *India: A History* (New York: Atlantic Monthly Press, 2000), p. 145.

16. Kalidasa, quoted in Auboyer, *Daily Life*, p. 117.

17. Quoted in Stephanie W. Jamison, *Sacrificed Wife/Sacrificer's Wife: Women, Ritual, and Hospitality in Ancient India* (New York: Oxford University Press, 1996), p. 13.

18. Quoted in Barbara N. Ramusack, "Women in South and Southeast Asia," in *Restoring Women to History* (Bloomington, Ind.: Organization of American Historians, 1988), p. 9.

19. Quoted in A. L. Basham, *The Wonder That Was India: A Survey of the History and Culture of the Indian Sub-continent Before the Coming of the Muslims*, 3rd. revised ed. (New Delhi: Rupa and Company, 1967), p. 420.

20. From Harry J. Benda and John A. Larkin, eds., *The World of Southeast Asia: Selected Historical Readings* (New York: Harper and Row, 1967), pp. 3–4.

21. Quoted in Keith Taylor, "The Rise of Dai Viet and the Establishment of Thanglong," in Kenneth R. Hall and John K. Whitmore, eds., *Explorations in Early Southeast Asian History: The Origins of Southeast Asian Statecraft* (Ann Arbor: University of Michigan Center for South and Southeast Asian Studies, 1976), p. 153.

22. From Nguyen Ngoc Bich, ed., *A Thousand Years of Vietnamese Poetry* (New York: Knopf, 1975), p. 89.

Chapter 8 Empires, Networks, and the Remaking of Europe, North Africa, and Western Asia, 500 B.C.E.–600 C.E.

1. Quoted in Tim Cornell and John Matthews, *The Roman World* (Alexandria, Va.: Stonehenge, 1991), p. 51.

2. Quoted in Felipe Fernandez-Armesto, *Civilizations: Culture, Ambition, and the Transformation of Nature* (New York: Simon and Schuster, 2001), p. 365.

3. Livy, quoted in Frederick Gentles and Melvin Steinfield, eds. *Hangups from Way Back: Historical Myths and Canons*, vol. 1 (San Francisco: Canfield, 1974), p. 173.

4. Diodorus, quoted in Barry Cunliffe, *The Extraordinary Voyage of Pytheas the Greek* (New York: Penguin, 2002), p. 52.

5. From Plautus, *The Casket*, quoted in Henry C. Boren, *Roman Society: A Social,* *Economic and Cultural History*, 2nd ed. (Lexington: D.C. Heath, 1992), p. 88.

6. Frederick Gentles and Melvin Steinfield, eds., *Hangups from Way Back: Historical Myths and Canons*, Vol. 1, 2nd ed. (San Francisco: Canfield Press, 1974), p. 167.

7. From Plutarch, *Life of Antony*, in William S. Davis, ed., *Readings in Ancient History*, Vol. 2 (Boston: Allyn and Bacon, 1913), pp. 163–164.

8. Quoted in Jerome Carcopino, *Daily Life in Ancient Rome*, 2nd ed. (New Haven, Conn.: Yale University Press, 1968), p. 202.

9. Quoted in Norman Davies, *Europe: A History* (New York: Harper, 1998), p. 193.

10. Quoted in Lesley Adkins and Roy A. Adkins, *Handbook to Life in Ancient Rome* (New York: Oxford University Press, 1998), p. 276.

11. Diodorus Siculus, in Jo Ann Shelton, *As the Romans Did: A Sourcebook in Roman Social History* (New York: Oxford University Press, 1988), p. 175.

12. The quotes are from Boren, *Roman Society*, pp. 279, 219.

13. Quoted in Susan Whitfield, *Life Along the Silk Road* (Berkeley: University of California Press, 1999), p. 21.

14. Tacitus, *Agricola*, quoted in Moses Hadas, ed., *A History of Rome from Its Origins to 529 A.D. as Told by the Roman Historians* (Garden City, N.Y.: Doubleday Anchor, 1956), pp. 126–127.

15. Quoted in Neil Christie, *The Lombards* (Malden, Mass.: Blackwell, 1998), p. 2.

16. Matthew 22: 37–39, in *The Holy Bible*, King James Version (Chicago: Thomas Nelson, 1982), p. 957.

17. Quoted in Bonnie S. Anderson and Judith P. Zinsser, *A History of Their Own: Women in Europe from Prehistory to the Present*, vol. 1 (New York: Harper and Row, 1988), p. 76.

18. Quoted in Gillian Clark, *Women in Late Antiquity: Pagan and Christian Lifestyles* (Oxford: Clarendon, 1994), p. 124.

19. Quoted in Michael McCormick, *Origins of the European Economy: Communication and Commerce, A.D. 300–900* (New York: Cambridge University Press, 2001), p. 27.

20. From A. Atwater, trans., *Procopius: The Secret History* (Ann Arbor: University of Michigan Press, 1963), p. 8.

21. Quoted in Daniel Del Castillo, "A Long-Ignored Plague Gets Its Due," *Chronicle of Higher Education*, February 15, 2002, p. A22.

22. Quoted in Philip Sharrard, *Byzantium* (New York: Time-Life, 1966), p. 36.

23. Quoted in Touraj Daryaee, "The Persian Gulf Trade in Late Antiquity," *Journal of World History*, 14/1 (March 2003): p. 9.

24. Quoted in Patricia Crone, "The Rise of Islam in the World," in Francis Robinson, ed., *The Cambridge Illustrated History of the Islamic World* (New York: Cambridge University Press, 1996), pp. 4–5.

Chapter 9 Classical Societies and Regional Networks in Africa, the Americas, and Oceania, 600 B.C.E.–600 C.E.

1. From *The Horizon History of Africa* (New York: American Heritage, 1971), p. 207.

2. Ibn Battuta, quoted in Robert W. July, *Precolonial Africa: An Economic and Social History* (New York: Charles Scribner's, 1975), p. 183.

3. Quoted in Stanley Burstein, ed., *Ancient African Civilizations: Kush and Axum* (Princeton, N.J.: Markus Wiener, 1998), p. 41.

4. Quoted in Derek A. Welsby, *The Kingdom of Kush: The Napatan and Meroitic Empires* (Princeton: Markus Wiener, 1996), p. 40.

5. From *Horizon History*, p. 78.

6. Quoted in Basil Davidson, *African Kingdoms* (New York: Time-Life, 1966), p. 42.

7. Quoted in Graham Connah, *African Civilization. Precolonial Cities and States in Tropical Africa: An Archaeological Perspective* (Cambridge: Cambridge University Press, 1987), p. 78.

8. Quoted in Robert W. July, *A History of the African People*, 5th ed. (Prospect Heights, Ill.: Waveland, 1998), p. 45.

9. Rufinus, quoted in Burstein, *Ancient African Civilizations*, p. 95.

10. Quoted in Christopher Ehret, *An African Classical Age: Eastern and Southern Africa in World History, 1000 B.C. to A.D. 400* (Charlottesville: University of Virginia Press, 1998), p. 275.

11. From the *Popul Vuh*, quoted in Brian M. Fagan, *Kingdoms of Gold, Kingdoms of Jade: The Americas Before Columbus* (London and New York: Thames and Hudson, 1991), p. 94.

12. Father Bernardino de Sahagun, quoted in Richard E. W. Adams, *Prehistoric Mesoamerica* (Boston: Little, Brown, 1977), p. 110.

13. Frey Diego de Landa, quoted in T. Patrick Culbert, *Maya Civilization* (Washington, D.C.: Smithsonian, 1993), p. 23.

14. Quoted in Michael Wood, *Legacy: The Search for Ancient Cultures* (New York: Sterling, 1994), p. 166.

15. Frey Diego de Landa, quoted in Culbert, *Maya Civilization*, p. 22.

16. Fra Bernardino de Sahagun, quoted in Juan Schobinger, *The First Americans* (Grand Rapids, Mich.: William B. Eerdmans, 1994), p. 97.

17. Cieza de Leon, quoted in Fagan, *Kingdoms of Gold*, p. 192.

18. Quoted in Brian Fagan, *The Long Summer: How Climate Changed Civilization* (New York: Basic Books, 2004), p. 213.

19. Quoted in Judy Thompson and Allan Taylor, *Polynesian Canoes and Navigation* (Laie, Hawaii: Institute of Polynesian Studies, 1980), p. 32.

20. Quoted in Peter Bellwood, *The Polynesians: Prehistory of an Island People*, revised ed. (London: Thames and Hudson, 1997), p. 7.

21. Quoted in Peter Bellwood, *Man's Conquest of the Pacific: The Prehistory of Southeast Asia and Oceania* (New York: Oxford University Press, 1979), p. 300.

Societies, Networks, Transitions: Classical Blossomings in World History, 600 B.C.E.–600 C.E.

1. Quoted in Michael Wood, *Legacy: The Search for Ancient Cultures* (New York: Sterling, 1994), p. 192.

2. Quoted in Patricia Buckley Ebrey, *The Cambridge Illustrated History of China* (New York: Cambridge University Press, 1996), p. 46.

3. The quotes are from Felipe Fernandez-Armesto, *Ideas That Changed the World* (New York: DK, 2003), pp. 117, 119.

4. Quoted in Lindsay Allen, *The Persian Empire* (Chicago: University of Chicago Press, 2005), p. 43.

5. From Patricia Buckley Ebrey, ed., *Chinese Civilization: A Sourcebook*, 2nd ed., revised and expanded (New York: Free Press, 1993), pp. 57–58.

6. Quoted in Romila Thapar, *Asoka and the Decline of the Mauryas* (Delhi: Oxford University Press, 1997), p. 147.

7. Quoted in Robert P. Clark, *The Global Imperative: An Interpretive History of the Spread of Humankind* (Boulder: Westview, 1997), p. 3.

8. Quoted in Richard C. Foltz, *Religions of the Silk Road: Overland Trade and Cultural Exchange from Antiquity to the Fifteenth Century* (New York: St. Martin's, 1999), p. 62.

9. Tertullian, quoted in Erik Gilbert and Jonathan T. Reynolds, *Africa in World History: From Prehistory to the Present* (Upper Saddle River, N.J.: Prentice-Hall, 2004), p. 74.

10. Quoted in Kenneth R. Hall, *Maritime Trade and State Development in Early Southeast Asia* (Honolulu: University of Hawaii Press, 1985), p. 29.

11. Hou Han Shu, quoted in *Monks and Merchants: Silk Road Treasures from Northwest China* (http://www.asiasociety.org/arts/monksandmerchants/index/html).

12. Quoted in Frances Wood, *The Silk Road: Two Thousand Years in the Heart of Asia* (Berkeley: University of California Press, 2001), p. 66.

13. Quoted in Lionel Casson, *The Ancient Mariners: Seafarers and Sea Fighters of the Mediterranean in Ancient Times*, 2nd ed. (Princeton: Princeton University Press, 1991), p. 166.

14. From Basil Davidson, *African Civilization Revisited: From Antiquity to Modern Times* (Trenton, N.J.: Africa World Press, 1991), p. 64.

15. Quoted in Louis Crompton, *Homosexuality and Civilization* (Cambridge: Harvard University Press, 2003), p. 218.

16. Quoted in Peter N. Sterns, *Gender in World History* (New York: Routledge, 2000), p. 28

Chapter 10 The Rise, Power, and Connections of the Islamic World, 600–1500

1. From *The Muqaddimah: An Introduction to History*, translated by Franz Rosenthal and edited by N. J. Dawood (Princeton: Princeton University Press, 1967), pp. 25–27.

2. Quoted in Albert Hourani, *A History of the Arab Peoples* (Cambridge: Belknap Press, 1991), p. 3.

3. Quoted in Mohammed Munir, "The Birth of Islam in the Arabian Desert," in Claire Swisher, ed., *The Spread of Islam* (San Diego, Calif.: Greenhaven Press, 1999), p. 40.

4. Quoted in Jonathan Bloom and Sheila Blair, *Islam: A Thousand Years of Faith and Power* (New Haven, Conn.: Yale University Press, 2002), p. 29.

5. Quoted in Wiebke Walther, *Women in Islam* (Princeton: Markus Wiener, 1993), p. 104.

6. Quoted in Karen Armstrong, *Muhammad: A Biography of the Prophet* (San Francisco: HarperSanFrancisco, 1992), p. 160.

7. Quoted in Arthur Goldschmidt, Jr., *A Concise History of the Middle East*, 4th ed. revised (Boulder: Westview, 1991), p. 37.

8. Quoted in Francis Robinson, *The Cultural Atlas of the Islamic World Since 1500* (Oxford: Stonehenge, 1992), p. 180.

9. Quoted in Henry Bucher, *Middle East* (Guilford, Conn.: Dushkin, 1984), p. 19.

10. Quoted in Manuel Komroff, ed., *Contemporaries of Marco Polo* (New York: Horace Liveright, 1928), pp. 286–292.

11. Quoted in Alfred Guillaume, "Islamic Mysticism and the Sufi Sect," in Swisher, ed., *Spread*, p. 153.

12. "Baba Kuhi of Shiraz," translated by Reynold A. Nicholson. Quoted in Mary Ann Frese Witt et al., *The Humanities: Cultural Roots and Continuities*, vol. 1, 7th ed. (Boston: Houghton Mifflin, 2005), p. 270.

13. Quoted in Adam Goodheart, "Pilgrims from the Great Satan," *New York Times*, March 10, 2002, p. A12.

14. Quoted in Walther, *Women in Islam*, p. 40.

15. Quoted in Mervyn Hiskett, "Islamic Literature and Art," in Swisher, ed., *Spread*, p. 120.

16. Excerpted in John Yohannan, ed., *A Treasury of Asian Literature* (New York: New American Library, 1965), pp. 261–262.

17. Quoted in Jonathan P. Berkey, *The Formation of Islam: Religion and Society in the Near East, 600–1800* (New York: Cambridge University Press, 2003), p. 233.

18. Quoted in Bernard Lewis, *The Arabs in History* (New York: Harper and Row, 1960), p. 131.

19. Quoted in Hourani, *History of Arab Peoples*, p. 201.

20. Hariri, quoted in Fernand Braudel, *A History of Civilizations* (New York: Penguin, 1995), p. 71.

21. From *An Arab-Syrian Gentleman and Warrior in the Period of the Crusades: Memoirs of Usamah Ibn-Munqidh*, translated by Philip K. Hitti (Princeton: Princeton University Press, 1987), p. 195.

22. Ibn Al Athir, quoted in Mike Edwards, "Genghis Khan," *National Geographic* (December, 1996): p. 9.

23. Quoted in Francis Robinson, *The Cambridge Illustrated History of the Islamic World* (Cambridge: Cambridge University Press, 1996), p. 198.

Chapter 11 East Asian Traditions, Transformations, and Eurasian Encounters, 600–1500

1. Quoted in John Merson, *The Genius That Was China: East and West in the Making of the Modern World* (Woodstock, N.Y.: Overlook Press, 1990), p. 14.

2. Quoted in John A. Harrison, *The Chinese Empire* (New York: Harcourt Brace Jovanovich, 1972), p. 239.

3. Po Chu-I, quoted in William H. McNeill, *The Pursuit of Power: Technology, Armed Force, and Society Since A.D. 1000* (Chicago: University of Chicago Press, 1982), p. 28.

4. Quoted in C. P. Fitzgerald, *China: A Short Cultural History* (New York: Praeger, 1961), p. 336.

5. Quoted in Derk Bodde, *China's Cultural Tradition: What and Whither?* (New York: Holt, Rinehart and Winston, 1957), p. 31.

6. The Wang and Li poems are from Robert Payne, ed., *The White Pony: An Anthology of Chinese Poetry* (New York: Mentor, 1960), pp. 154, 174.

7. Du's poems are from Cyril Birch, ed., *Anthology of Chinese Literature from Early Times to the Fourteenth Century* (New York: Grove Press, 1965), pp. 240–241; and *Tu Fu: Selected Poems* (Peking: Foreign Languages Press, 1962), p. 100.

8. John Meskill, "History of China," in Meskill, ed., *An Introduction to Chinese Civilization* (Lexington, Mass.: D.C. Heath, 1973), pp. 127–128.

9. Yuan Tsai, from Patricia Buckley Ebrey, ed., *Chinese Civilization and Society: A Sourcebook* (New York: The Free Press, 1981), p. 96.

10. The quotes are from Dun J. Li, ed., *The Essence of Chinese Civilization* (Princeton, N.J.: Van Nostrand, 1967), p. 88; and James Zee-Min Lee, *Chinese Potpourri* (Hong Kong: Oriental Publishers, 1950), p. 319.

11. Quoted in H. H. Gowen and J. W. Hall, *An Outline History of China* (New York: D. Appleton, 1926), p. 142.

12. Quoted in H. D. Martin, *The Rise of Chingis Khan and His Conquest of North China* (Baltimore: Johns Hopkins University Press, 1950), p. 5.

13. R. E. Latham, trans., *The Travels of Marco Polo* (Baltimore: Penguin Books, 1958), pp. 184–187.

14. Quoted in Arthur Cotterell and David Morgan, *China's Civilization: A Survey of Its History, Arts, and Technology* (New York: Praeger, 1973), p. 190.

15. Quoted in Dun J. Li, *The Ageless Chinese: A History*, 2nd ed. (New York: Charles Scribner's, 1971), p. 283.

16. Zhang Tao, quoted in Timothy Brook, *The Confusions of Pleasure: Commerce and Culture in the Ming* (Berkeley: University of California Press, 1998), p. vii.

17. Quoted in Bruce Cumings, *Korea's Place in the Sun: A Modern History* (New York: W.W. Norton, 1997), p. 37.

18. Quoted in Yung Chung Kim, ed. and translator, *Women of Korea: A History from Ancient Times to 1945* (Seoul: Ehwa Women's University Press, 1977), p. 32

19. Quoted in Donald Keene, "Literature," in Arthur E. Tiedemann, ed., *An Introduction to Japanese Civilization* (Lexington, Mass.: D.C. Heath, 1974), p. 395.

20. Quoted in Ivan Morris, *The World of the Shining Prince: Court Life in Ancient Japan* (New York: Kodansha, 1994), p. 229.
21. Quoted in ibid., p. 204.
22. Quoted in Mikiso Hane, *Japan: A Historical Survey* (New York: Charles Scribner's, 1972), p. 56.
23. From Ryusaku Tsunoda et al., eds., *Sources of Japanese Tradition*, vol. 2 (New York: Columbia University Press, 1958), p. 236.
24. Quoted in Noel F. Busch, *The Horizon Concise History of Japan* (New York: American Heritage, 1972), p. 58.

Chapter 12 Expanding Horizons in Africa and the Americas, 600–1500

1. Quoted in Patricia W. Romero, *Lamu: History, Society, and Family in an East African Port City* (Princeton: Markus Wiener, 1997), p. 14.
2. The quotes are from Basil Davidson, *The Lost Cities of Africa* (Boston: Little, Brown, 1959), p. 151.
3. Quoted in Esmond Bradley Martin and Chryssee Perry Martin, *Cargoes of the East: The Ports, Trade and Culture of the Arabian Seas and Western Indian Ocean* (London: Elm Tree Books, 1978), p. 9.
4. Quoted in *Africa's Glorious Legacy* (Arlington, Va.: Time-Life Books, 1994), p. 90.
5. Quoted in E. Jefferson Murphy, *History of African Civilization* (New York: Dell, 1972), p. 120.
6. The quotes are from E. W. Bovill, *The Golden Trade of the Moors*, 2nd ed. (London: Oxford University Press, 1970), p. 95.
7. Leo Africanus, quoted in Kevin Shillington, *History of Africa*, rev. ed. (New York: St. Martin's, 1995), p. 105.
8. Quoted in Constance B. Hilliard, ed., *Intellectual Traditions of Pre-Colonial Africa* (New York: McGraw-Hill, 1998), pp. 311–312.
9. Quoted in John Iliffe, *Africans: The History of a Continent* (Cambridge: Cambridge University Press, 1995), p. 93.
10. The quotes are from Davidson, *Lost Cities of Africa*, p. 156.
11. Quoted in John Middleton, *The World of the Swahili* (New Haven, Conn.: Yale University Press, 1992), p. 40.
12. Duarte Barbosa, quoted in Derek Nurse and Thomas Spear, *The Swahili: Reconstructing the History and Language of an African Society, 800–1500* (Philadelphia: University of Pennsylvania Press, 1985), p. 83.
13. Quoted in Bovill, *Golden Trade*, p. 96.
14. Djeli Mamoudou Kouyate, quoted in D. T. Niane, *Sundiata: An Epic of Old Mali* (London: Longman, 1965), p. 1.
15. John Smith, quoted in Charles Mann, "The Pristine Myth," *The Atlantic Online,* March 7, 2002 (http://www.theatlantic.com/unbound/interviews/int2002-03-07.htm).
16. Quoted in Richard F. Townsend, *The Aztecs*, rev. ed. (New York: Thames and Hudson, 2000), p. 59.
17. Quoted in Brian M. Fagan, *Kingdoms of Gold, Kingdoms of Jade: The Americas Before Columbus* (London: Thames and Hudson, 1991), p. 7.

18. Friar Bernardino de Sahagun, quoted in Michael E. Smith, *The Aztecs*, 2nd ed. (Malden, Mass.: Blackwell, 2003), p. 113.
19. Quoted in Fagan, *Kingdoms of Gold*, p. 224.
20. Quoted in Robert M. Carnack et al., *The Legacy of Mesoamerica: History and Culture of a Native American Civilization* (Upper Saddle River, N.J.: Prentice-Hall, 1996), p. 415.
21. Quoted in Marysa Navarro, "Women in Pre-Columbian and Colonial Latin America," in *Restoring Women to History* (Bloomington, Ind.: Organization of American Historians, 1988), p. 6.
22. Quoted in *Incas: Lords of Gold and Glory* (Alexandria, Va.: Time-Life Books, 1992), p. 52.
23. Pedro Cieza de Leon, quoted in Terence N. D'Altroy, *The Incas* (Malden, Mass.: Blackwell, 2002), p. 3.

Chapter 13 South Asia, Central Asia, Southeast Asia, and Afro-Eurasian Connections, 600–1500

1. From L. S. Stavrianos, *The Epic of Man to 1500* (Englewood Cliffs, N.J.: Prentice-Hall, 1970), pp. 160, 162–163.
2. Quoted in Tansen Sen, *Buddhism, Diplomacy, and Trade: The Realignment of Sino-Indian Relations, 600–1400* (Honolulu: University of Hawaii Press, 2003), p. 11.
3. Quoted in A. L. Basham, *The Wonder That Was India* (New York: Grove Press, 1959), p. vi.
4. Al-Biruni, quoted in Romila Thapar, *Early India: From the Origins to AD 1300* (Berkeley: University of California Press, 2002), p. 437.
5. Quoted in Paul Thomas Welty, *The Asians: Their Evolving Heritage*, 6th ed. (New York: Harper and Row, 1984), p. 68.
6. Narenda K. Sethi, *Hindu Proverbs and Wisdom* (Mount Vernon, N.Y.: Peter Pauper Press, 1962), p. 5.
7. Nammalvar, quoted in Roberta Smith, "Where Gods Set Bronze in Motion," *New York Times*, December 6, 2002, p. B3.
8. Quoted in Lucille Schulberg, *Historic India* (New York: Time-Life Books, 1968), pp. 11–12.
9. Quoted in Debiprasad Chattopadhyana, *History of Science and Technology in Ancient India*, vol. 3 (Calcutta: Firma KLM Private Ltd., 1996), p. 60.
10. Minhaju-s Siraj, quoted in John Keay, *A History of India* (New York: Atlantic Monthly Press, 2000), p. 245.
11. Quoted in Hermann Kulke and Dietmar Rothermund, *History of India*, 3rd ed. (New York: Routledge, 1998), p. 119.
12. Stanley Wolpert, *A New History of India*, 5th ed. (New York: Oxford University Press, 1997), p. 113.
13. Quoted in Keay, *History of India*, p. 274.
14. Quoted in Richard Eaton, "Islamic History as Global History," in Michael Adas, ed., *Islamic and European Expansion: The Forging of a Global Order* (Philadelphia: Temple University Press, 1993), p. 21.

15. Quoted in Christopher Pym, *The Ancient Civilization of Angkor* (New York: New American Library, 1968), p. 118.
16. Quoted in David Chandler, *A History of Cambodia*, 2nd ed. updated (Boulder, Colo.: Westview Press, 1996), p. 74.
17. From Harry J. Benda and John A. Larkin, eds., *The World of Southeast Asia: Selected Historical Readings* (New York: Harper and Row, 1967), pp. 45–46.
18. From ibid., p. 41.
19. Ibn Muhammad Ibrahim, from Michael Smithies, *Descriptions of Old Siam* (Kuala Lumpur: Oxford University Press, 1995), p. 91.
20. Quoted in Ralph Smith, *Viet-Nam and the West* (Ithaca, N.Y.: Cornell University Press, 1971), p. 9.
21. Quoted in Anthony Reid, *Southeast Asia in the Age of Commerce, 1450–1680*, vol. 2 (New Haven: Yale University Press, 1993), p. 10.
22. Tome' Pires, quoted in Paul Wheatley, *The Golden Khersonese* (Kuala Lumpur: University of Malaya Press, 1961), p. 313.
23. Quoted in Kenneth R. Hall, *Maritime Trade and State Development in Early Southeast Asia* (Honolulu: University of Hawaii Press, 1985), p. 210.

Chapter 14 Christian Societies in Medieval Europe, Byzantium, and Russia, 600–1500

1. From a fourteenth-century legend, quoted in Amy G. Remensnyder, "Topographies of Memory: Center and Periphery in High Medieval France," in Gerd Althoff et al., eds., *Medieval Concepts of the Past: Ritual, Memory, Historiography* (New York: Cambridge University Press, 2002), p. 214.
2. Quoted in *What Life Was Like in the Age of Chivalry: Medieval Europe, AD 800–1500* (Alexandria, Va.: Time-Life Books, 1997), p. 17.
3. Quoted in James C. Russell, *The Germanization of Early Medieval Christianity* (Oxford: Oxford University Press, 1994), p. 186.
4. "Charlemagne's letter to Pope Leo III, 796," from C. Warren Hollister et al., *Medieval Europe: A Short Sourcebook*, 2nd ed. (New York: McGraw-Hill, 1992), p. 78.
5. Quoted in F. Donald Logan, *The Vikings in History*, 2nd ed. (New York: Routledge, 1991), p. 15.
6. Hugo of Santalla, quoted in Jerry Brotton, *The Renaissance Bazaar: From the Silk Road to Michelangelo* (Oxford: Oxford University Press, 2002), p. 195.
7. Quoted in John M. Hobson, *The Eastern Origins of Western Civilization* (New York: Cambridge University Press, 2004), p. 113.
8. Quoted in Jo Ann H. Moran Cruz and Richard Gerberding, *Medieval Worlds: An Introduction to European History, 300–1492* (Boston: Houghton Mifflin, 2004), p. 388.
9. Quoted in Eileen Power, *Medieval People*, new rev. ed. (New York: Barnes and Noble, 1963), p. 18.
10. Richard of Devizes, quoted in Jacques Le Goff, ed., *The Medieval World* (London: Postgate Books, 1997), p. 139.

11. The quotes are from Frederic Delouche, et al., *Illustrated History of Europe: A Unique Portrait of Europe's Common History* (New York: Barnes and Noble, 2001), p. 170; and Georges Duby, "Marriage in Early Medieval Society," in *Love and Marriage: The Middle Ages,* translated by Jane Dunnett (Chicago: University of Chicago Press, 1994), p. 11.

12. Quoted in Carolly Erickson, *The Medieval Vision: Essays in History and Perception* (New York: Oxford University Press, 1976), p. 73.

13. Quoted in Cruz and Gerberding, *Medieval Worlds,* p. 277.

14. Quoted in Clive Ponting, *A Green History of the World: The Environment and the Collapse of Great Civilizations* (New York: Penguin, 1991), p. 144.

15. Quoted in Thomas F. Madden, *A Concise History of the Crusades* (Lanham, Md.: Rowman and Littlefield, 1999), pp. 8–9.

16. Quoted in C. Warren Hollister, *Medieval Europe: A Short History,* 8th ed. (Boston: McGraw-Hill, 1998), p. 296.

17. Quoted in ibid., p. 273.

18. Quoted in Nicholas V. Riasanovsky, *A History of Russia,* 5th ed. (New York: Oxford University Press, 1993), p. 72.

19. Eustache Deschamps, quoted in J. Huizinga, *The Waning of the Middle Ages* (Garden City, N.Y.: Doubleday Anchor, 1954), p. 33.

20. Quoted in Delouche, *Illustrated History,* p. 168.

21. Quoted in Brotton, *Renaissance Bazaar,* p. 75.

22. Canon Pietro Casola, quoted in ibid., p. 38.

23. Quoted in Edith Simon, *The Reformation* (New York: Time-Life Books, 1966), p. 71.

24. Cadamosto, quoted in Peter Russell, *Prince Henry "the Navigator": A Life* (New Haven, Conn.: Yale University Press, 2000), p. 225.

Societies, Networks, Transitions: Expanding Horizons in the Intermediate Era, 600 B.C.E.– 600 C.E.

1. Quoted in Jack Turner, *Spice: The History of a Temptation* (New York: Vintage, 2004), p. 103.

2. Quoted in Fernand Braudel, *The Wheels of Commerce* (New York: Harper and Row, 1979), p. 127.

3. Abdul Kassim ibn Khordadbeh, quoted in Elmer Bendiner, *The Rise and Fall of Paradise* (New York: Dorset Press, 1983), p. 101.

4. Quoted in John M. Hobson, *The Eastern Origins of Western Civilisation* (New York: Cambridge University Press, 2004), p. 40.

5. Quoted in M. N. Pearson, "Introduction," in Pearson, ed., *Spices in the Indian Ocean World* (Aldershot, U.K.: Valiorum, 1996), p. xv.

6. Quoted in Philip D. Curtin, *Cross-Cultural Trade in World History* (New York: Cambridge University Press, 1984), p. 125.

7. Quoted in John Kelley, *The Great Mortality* (New York: HarperCollins, 2005), p. 2

8. Quoted in Peter N. Stearns, *Western Civilization in World History* (New York: Routledge, 2003), p. 52.

9. Al-Musabbihi, quoted in Heinz Halm, *The Fatimids and Their Traditions of Learning* (New York: I.B. Taurus, 1997), p. 73.

10. Leon Battista Alberti, quoted in Jeremy Brotton, *The Renaissance Bazaar: From the Silk Road to Michelangelo* (London: Oxford University Press, 2002), pp. 73-74.

11. Quoted in Peter N. Stearns, *Gender in World History* (New York: Routledge, 2000), p. 52.

12. Quoted in Anthony Reid, *Southeast Asia in the Age of Commerce, 1450–1680,* vol 1 (New Haven: Yale University Press, 1988), p. 1.

13. Quoted in Adriaan Verhulst, *The Carolingian Economy* (New York: Cambridge University Press, 2002), p. 48.

14. Ibn al-Athir, quoted in David R. Ringrose, *Expansion and Global Interaction, 1200– 1700* (New York: Longman, 2001), p. 22.

15. Quoted in Rene Grousset, *The Empire of the Steppes: A History of Central Asia* (New Brunswick: Rutgers University Press, 1970), p. 249.

16. Quoted in L. S. Stavrianos, *Lifelines from Our Past: A New World History,* revised ed. (Armonk, N.Y.: M. E. Sharpe, 1997), p. 58.

17. Quoted in Frederick F. Cartwright, *Disease and History: The Influence of Disease in Shaping the Great Events of History* (New York: Thomas Y. Crowell, 1972), p. 37.

18. Quoted in Brian Fagan, *The Long Summer: How Climate Changed Civilization* (New York: Basic Books, 2004), p. 224.

19. Peter Martyr, quoted in Turner, *Spice,* p. xi.

Chapter 15 Global Connections and the Remaking of Europe, 1450–1750

1. From "The Tempest," *The Riverside Shakespeare,* 2nd ed. (Boston: Houghton Mifflin, 1997), p. 1684.

2. Quoted in Edith Simon, *The Reformation* (New York: Time-Life Books, 1966), p. 74.

3. Franciscan friar Toribio de Montolinia, quoted in Marvin Lunenfeld, ed., *1492: Discovery, Invasion, Encounter: Sources and Interpretations* (Lexington, Mass.: D.C. Heath, 1991), p. 214.

4. Quoted in Carlo M. Cipolla, *Before the Industrial Revolution: European Society and Economy, 1000–1700,* 2nd ed. (New York: W.W. Norton, 1980), p. 270.

5. Quoted in Miriam Beard, *History of the Businessman* (New York: Macmillan, 1938), p. 239–240.

6. Quoted in H. O. Taylor, *Thought and Expression in the Sixteenth Century,* vol. 1 (New York: Macmillan, 1920), p. 175.

7. Quoted in Charles Blitzer, *Age of Kings* (New York: Time-Life Books, 1967), p. 11.

8. From "Hamlet," The Riverside Shakespeare, 2nd ed. (Boston: Houghton Mifflin, 1997), p. 1204.

9. Quoted in James Krokar et al., *Rhetoric and Civilization,* vol. 2 (Littleton, Mass.: Copley, 1988), p. 620.

10. Quoted in Frederic Delouche et al., *Illustrated History of Europe* (New York: Barnes and Noble, 2001), p. 244.

11. Quoted in *What Life Was Like During the Age of Reason* (Alexandria, Va.: Time-Life Books, 1999), p. 18.

12. P. P. Shafirov, quoted in Paul Dukes, *The Making of Russian Absolutism, 1613–1801,* 2nd ed. (New York: Longman, 1990), p. 77.

13. Quoted in Blitzer, *Age of Kings,* p. 119.

14. From Hobbes, *The Leviathan,* Chapter 13 (**oregonstate.edu/instruct/ph1302/texts/ hobbes/leviathan-c.html**)

15. Quoted in Martin Oliver, *History of Philosophy* (New York: Metro Books, 1997), p. 73.

16. Quoted in Norman Davies, *Europe: A History* (New York: Harper, 1996), p. 599.

17. Quoted in John M. Hobson, *The Eastern Origins of Western Civilisation* (Cambridge: Cambridge University Press, 2004), p. 194.

18. From Dena Goodman and Kathleen Wellman, eds., *The Enlightenment* (Boston: Houghton Mifflin, 2004), p. 167.

19. The quotes are from Christopher Hill, *The World Turned Upside Down: Radical ideas During the English Revolution* (Hammondsworth, England: Penguin, 1975), p. 107; and Delouche, *Illustrated History of Europe,* p. 247.

20. Quoted in Simon, *Reformation,* p. 30.

21. Quoted in Diarmaid MacCulloch, *The Reformation: A History* (New York: Penguin, 2005), p. 609

22. Quoted in Robert Wallace, *Rise of Russia* (New York: Time-Life Books, 1967), p. 140.

Chapter 16 New Challenges for Africa and the Islamic World, 1450–1750

1. Quoted in Ali Mazrui, *The Africans: A Triple Heritage* (Boston: Little, Brown, 1986), p. 11.

2. Quoted in Basil Davidson, ed., *African Civilization Revisited* (Trenton, N.J.: African World Press, 1991), p. 118.

3. Quoted in Robert W. July, *A History of the African People,* 5th ed. (Prospect Heights, Ill: Waveland, 1998), p. 74.

4. Quoted in Basil Davidson, *Africa in History* (New York: Touchstone, 1995), pp. 176–177.

5. Andre Alvares de Almada, quoted in George E. Brooks, *Landlords and Strangers: Ecology, Society, and Trade in Western Africa, 1000–1630* (Boulder, Colo.: Westview Press, 1993), p. 267.

6. Quoted in Derek Nourse and Thomas Spear, *The Swahili: Reconstructing the History and Language of an African Society, 800–1500* (Philadelphia: University of Pennsylvania Press, 1985), p. 82.

7. Quoted in Michael Pearson, *The Indian Ocean* (New York: Routledge, 2003), p. 119.

8. From Roland Oliver and Caroline Oliver, eds., *Africa in the Days of Exploration* (Englewood Cliffs, N.J.: Prentice-Hall, 1965), p. 111.

9. From Basil Davidson, ed., *The African Past: Chronicles from Antiquity to Modern Times* (New York: Grosset and Dunlap, 1964), p. 136.

10. Quoted in Kevin Shillington, *History of Africa,* rev. ed. (New York: St. Martin's, 1995), p. 216.

11. Malcolm Cowley and Daniel Mannix, "The Middle Passage," in David Northrup,

ed., *The Atlantic Slave Trade* (Lexington, Mass.: D.C. Heath, 1994), pp. 99, 101.

12. Quoted in Charles Johnson and Patricia Smith, *Africans in America: America's Journey Through Slavery* (New York: Harcourt Brace, 1998), p. 79.

13. Quoted in R. A. Houston, "Colonies, Enterprise, and Wealth: The Economies of Europe and the Wider World in the Seventeenth Century," in Euan Cameron, ed., *Early Modern Europe: An Oxford History* (New York: Oxford University Press, 1999), p. 165.

14. Quoted in Winthrop D. Jordan, "Slavery: Its Development in Colonial America," in Mildred Bain and Ervin Lewis, eds., *From Freedom to Freedom: African Roots in American Soil* (New York: Random House, 1977), p. 166.

15. Quoted in Halil Inalcik, *The Ottoman Empire: The Classical Age, 1300–1600* (London: Phoenix Press, 2000), p. 41.

16. Quoted in Arthur Goldschmidt, Jr., *A Concise History of the Middle East*, 4th ed. revised and updated (Boulder, Colo.: Westview Press, 1991), p. 129.

17. Quoted in Andrew Wheatcroft, *The Ottomans* (New York: Viking, 1993), p. 89.

18. Ibrahim Pecevi, quoted in Philip Mansel, *Constantinople: City of the World's Desire, 1453–1924* (New York: St. Martin's, 1995), p. 171.

19. Quoted in Inalcik, *Ottoman Empire*, p. 189.

20. From John J. Saunders, ed., *The Muslim World on the Eve of Europe's Expansion* (Englewood Cliffs, N.J.: Prentice-Hall, 1966), p. 35.

21. Quoted in Francis Robinson, *The Cultural Atlas of the Islamic World Since 1500* (London: Stonehenge, 1987), p. 49.

22. Quoted in Willem Floor, "The Dutch and the Persian Silk Trade," in Charles Melville, ed., *Safavid Persia: The History and Politics of an Islamic Society* (London: I.B. Taurus, 1996), p. 325.

Chapter 17 Americans, Europeans, Africans, and New Societies in the Americas, 1450–1750

1. Quoted in Michael C. Meyer and William L. Sherman, *The Course of Mexican History*, 2nd ed. (New York: Oxford University Press, 1983), p. 86.

2. From Lewis Hanke, ed., *History of Latin American Civilization: Sources and Interpretations*, vol. 1 (Boston: Little, Brown and Company, 1973), p. 64.

3. Quoted in Oliver Cox, "The Rise of Modern Race Relations," in William Barclay et al., eds., *Racial Conflict, Discrimination, and Power* (New York: AMS Press, 1976), p. 91.

4. Quoted in Herman J. Viola, "Seeds of Change," in Herman J. Viola and Carolyn Margolis, eds., *Seeds of Change: A Quincentennial Commemoration* (Washington, D.C.: Smithsonian Institution Press, 1991), p. 13.

5. Quoted in L. S. Stavrianos, *Lifelines from Our Past: A New World History*, rev. ed. (Armonk, N.Y.: M.E. Sharpe, 1997), p. 96.

6. Alonso de Zuazo, quoted in Kathleen Deagan and Jose Maria Cruxent, *Columbus's Outpost Among the Tainos: Spain and America at La Isabela, 1493–1498* (New Haven, Conn.: Yale University Press, 2002), p. 210.

7. Magá Lahen Hurao, quoted in Geoffrey C. Gunn, *First Globalization: The Eurasian Exchange* (Lanham, Md.: Rowman and Littlefield, 2003), p. 194.

8. Quoted in Jane MacLaren Walsh and Yoko Sugiura, "The Demise of the Fifth Sun," in Viola and Margolis, *Seeds of Change*, p. 41.

9. Louis Le Golif, quoted in David Cordingly, ed., *Pirates: Terror on the High Seas* (North Dighton, United Kingdom: JG Press, 1998), p. 37.

10. Quoted in Noble David Cook, *Born to Die: Disease and New World Conquest, 1492–1650* (Cambridge: Cambridge University Press, 1998), p. vi.

11. From Hanke, *History of Latin American Civilization*, p. 388.

12. Quoted in Jonathan C. Brown, *Latin America: A Social History of the Colonial Period* (Belmont, Calif.: Wadsworth, 2000), p. 146.

13. Fray Diego Duran, quoted in Rolena Adorno, "The Indigenous Ethnographer: The 'Indio Ladino' as Historian and Cultural Mediation," in Stuart B. Schwartz, ed., *Implicit Understandings* (New York: Cambridge University Press, 1994), p. 397.

14. Quoted in Felipe Fernandez-Armesto, *Millennium: A History of the Last Thousand Years* (New York: Scribner's, 1995), p. 300.

15. Quoted in Marysa Navarro and Virginia Sanchez-Korrol, "Latin America and the Caribbean," in *Restoring Women to History* (Bloomington, Ind.: Organization of American Historians, 1988), p. 23.

16. Gonzalo Fernandez de Oviedo, quoted in L. S. Stavrianos, *Global Rift: The Third World Comes of Age* (New York: William Morrow, 1981), p. 83.

17. Guzman Poma de Ayala, quoted in Brown, *Latin America*, p. 183.

18. Quoted in Robert Heilbroner and Aaron Singer, *The Economic Transformation of America, 1600 to the Present*, 3rd ed. (Fort Worth, Tex.: Harcourt Brace, 1994), p. 68.

19. Quoted in David Freeman Hawke, *Everyday Life in Early America* (New York: Harper and Row, 1988), p. 120.

20. Quoted in Salvador de Madariaga, *The Rise of the Spanish American Empire* (New York: Macmillan, 1947), pp. 90–91.

21. From Fray Toribio Motolinia, "The Ten Plagues of New Spain," in John Francis Bannon, ed., *Indian Labor in the Spanish Indies* (Boston: D.C. Heath, 1966), p. 45.

22. Quoted in Stuart B. Schwartz, "Brazil," in Seymour Drescher and Stanley L. Engerman, eds., *A Historical Guide to World Slavery* (New York: Oxford University Press, 1998), p. 101.

23. Gonzalez de Cellorigo, quoted in Jonathan Williams, *Money: A History* (New York: St. Martin's, 1997), p. 162.

Chapter 18 South Asia, Southeast Asia, and East Asia: Triumphs and Challenges, 1450–1750

1. Quoted in Anthony Reid, "Early Southeast Asian Categorizations of Europeans," in Stuart B. Schwartz, ed., *Implicit Understandings* (Cambridge: Cambridge University Press, 1994), p. 275.

2. Quoted in Om Prakash, *European Commercial Enterprise in Pre-Colonial India* (New York: Cambridge University Press, 1998), p. 4.

3. Quoted in Francis Robinson, *The Cultural Atlas of the Islamic World Since 1500* (London: Stonehenge, 1992), p. 39.

4. The quotes are from Rhoads Murphey, *A History of Asia*, 4th ed. (New York: Longman, 2002), p. 185; and Michael Edwardes, *A History of India* (New York: Farrar, Straus and Cudahy, 1961), p. 191.

5. Quoted in Edwardes, p. 190.

6. Quoted in John E. Wills, Jr., *1688: A Global History* (New York: W.W. Norton, 2001), p. 276.

7. Quoted in Geoffrey C. Gunn, *First Globalization: The Eurasian Exchange* (Lanham, Md.: Rowman and Littlefield, 2003), p. 214.

8. Quoted in Klaus Wenk, *Thai Literature: An Introduction* (Bangkok: White Lotus, 1995), pp. 14–16.

9. Joost Schouten, quoted in Michael Smithies, *Descriptions of Old Siam* (Kuala Lumpur: Oxford University Press, 1995), p. 19.

10. Quoted in Nicholas Tarling, "Mercantilism and Missionaries: Impact and Accommodation," in Colin Mackerras, ed., *Eastern Asia: An Introductory History*, 3rd ed. (Frenches Forest, NSW, Australia: Longmans, 2000), p. 115.

11. Quoted in David Joel Steinberg, *The Philippines: A Singular and a Plural Place*, 3rd ed. (Boulder: Westview, 1994), p. 82.

12. Pedro Chirino, quoted in Carolyn Brewer, "From Animist 'Priestess' to Catholic Priest: The Re/gendering of Religious Roles in the Philippines, 1521–1685," in Barbara Watson Andaya, ed., *Other Pasts: Women, Gender and History in Early Modern Southeast Asia* (Honolulu: Center for Southeast Asian Studies, University of Hawaii at Manoa, 2000), p. 69.

13. The quotes are from Felipe Fernandez-Armesto, *Millennium: A History of the Last Thousand Years* (New York: Scribner's, 1995), p. 324; and Alisa Zainu'ddin, *A Short History of Indonesia* (Sydney: Cassell Australia, 1968), p. 88.

14. Thomas Stamford Raffles, quoted in Anthony Reid, *Southeast Asia in the Age of Commerce, 1450–1680*, vol. 1 (New Haven, Conn.: Yale University Press, 1993), p. 164.

15. Quoted in Jonathan S. Spence, *Emperor of China: Self-Portrait of Kang-Hsi* (New York: Vintage, 1975), p. 29.

16. Quoted in Richard J. Smith, *China's Cultural Heritage: The Ch'ing Dynasty, 1644–1913* (Boulder, Colo.: Westview Press, 1983), p. 210.

17. Quoted in Francesca Bray, "Towards a Critical History of non-Western

Technology," in Timothy Brook and Gregory Blue, eds., *China and Historical Capitalism* (New York: Cambridge University Press, 1999), p. 184.

18. Quoted in John A. Harrison, *The Chinese Empire* (New York: Harcourt Brace Jovanovich, 1972), p. 335.

19. Jean-Baptiste DuHalde, quoted in Carolyn Blunden and Mark Elvin, *The Cultural Atlas of China* (Alexandria, Va.: Stonehenge, 1991), p. 144.

20. Quoted in Spence, *Emperor of China*, pp. 72–73.

21. Quoted in Joanna Waley-Cohen, *The Sextants of Beijing: Global Currents in Chinese History* (New York: W.W. Norton, 1999), p. 55.

22. Matsuo Basho, quoted in Noel F. Busch, *The Horizon Concise History of Japan* (New York: American Heritage, 1972), p. 64.

23. Quoted in Ronald P. Toby, "The 'Indianess' of Iberia and Changing Japanese Iconographies of Other," in Schwartz, *Implicit Understandings*, p. 326.

24. Quoted in Edward Seidenstecker, *Japan* (New York: Time Inc., 1961), p. 58.

25. Yamaga Soko, quoted in Conrad Totman, *A History of Japan* (Oxford: Blackwell, 2000), p. 221.

26. Quoted in Mikiso Hane, *Modern Japan: A Historical Survey*, 2nd ed. (Boulder, Colo.: Westview Press, 1992), p. 36.

27. Chikamatsu Monzaemon, quoted in *What Life Was Like Among Samurai and Shoguns* (Alexandria, Va.: Time-Life Books, 1999), p. 118.

28. The haiku are from Conrad Schirokauer, *A Brief History of Chinese and Japanese Civilizations*, 2nd ed. (San Diego: Harcourt Brace Jovanovich, 1989), p. 373; and Harold G. Henderson, *An Introduction to Haiku: An Anthology of Poets from Basho to Shiki* (Garden City, N.Y.: Doubleday Anchor, 1958), p. 40.

Societies, Networks, Transitions: Connecting the Early Modern World, 1450–1750

1. Francisco Lopez de Gomara, quoted in Roger Schlesinger, *In the Wake of Columbus: The Impact of the New World on Europe, 1492–1650* (Wheeling, Ill.: Harlan Davidson, 1996), p. 23.

2. Quoted in Peter J. Hugill, *World Trade Since 1431: Geography, Technology, and Capitalism* (Baltimore: Johns Hopkins University Press, 1993), p. vii.

3. Quoted in Roger Savory, *Iran Under the Safavids* (Cambridge: Cambridge University Press, 1980), p. 205.

4. Quoted in Gregory Blue, "China and Western Social Thought in the Modern Period," in Timothy Brook and Gregory Blue, eds., *China and Historical Capitalism* (New York: Cambridge University Press, 1999), p. 64.

5. Quoted in Kenneth Chase, *Firearms: A Global History to 1700* (New York: Cambridge University Press, 2003), p. 2.

6. Quoted in Patricia Risso, *Merchants and Faith: Muslim Commerce and Culture in the Indian Ocean* (Boulder, Colo.: Westview Press, 1995), p. 96.

7. Quoted in Robert B. Marks, *The Origins of the Modern World: A Global and Ecological Narrative* (Lanham, Md.: Rowman and Littlefield, 2002), p. 81.

8. Quoted in Christine Dobbin, *Asian Entrepreneurial Minorities: Conjoint Communities in the Making of the World-Economy, 1750–1940* (Richmond, United Kingdom: Curzon, 1996), p. 23.

9. Quoted in J. Donald Hughes, "Biodiversity in World History," in Hughes, ed., *The Face of the Earth: Environment and World History* (Armonk, N.Y.: M.E. Sharpe, 2000), p. 31.

10. Quoted in H. William Skinner, *Chinese Society in Thailand: An Analytical History* (Ithaca, N.Y.: Cornell University Press, 1957), p. 8.

11. Balthasar Barreira, quoted in George E. Brooks, *Landlords and Strangers: Ecology, Society, and Trade in Western Africa, 1000–1630* (Boulder, Colo.: Westview Press, 1983), p. 306.

12. Quoted in Annemarie Schimmel, *The Empire of the Great Mughals: History, Art, and Culture* (New Delhi: Oxford University Press, 2005), p. 113.

13. Quoted in Susan Mann, *Precious Records: Women in China's Long Eighteenth Century* (Stanford, Calif.: Stanford University Press, 1997), p. 108.

14. Quoted in Schimmel, *Empire of Great Mughals*, p. 130.

15. Juan Gimes de Sepulveda, in Marvin Lunenfeld, ed., *1492: Discovery, Invasion, Encounter: Sources and Interpretations* (Lexington, Mass.: D.C. Heath, 1991), pp. 219–220.

Chapter 19 Modern Transitions: Revolutions, Industries, Ideologies, Empires, 1750–1914

1. Quoted in Eric Hobsbawm, *The Age of Revolution, 1789–1848* (New York: New American Library, 1962), p. 44.

2. From Charles Dickens, *A Tale of Two Cities* (New York: Bantam, 1989), p. 1.

3. From David A. Hollinger and Charles Capper, eds., *The American Intellectual Tradition: A Sourcebook*, vol. 1, 2nd ed. (New York: Oxford University Press, 1993), p. 131.

4. Quoted in William Appleman Williams, *America Confronts a Revolutionary World, 1775–1976* (New York: William Morrow, 1976), pp. 15, 25.

5. Quoted in Peter N. Stearns, *Life and Society in the West: The Modern Centuries* (San Diego: Harcourt Brace Jovanovich, 1988), p. 164.

6. Quoted in Eric Hobsbawm, *Workers: World of Labor* (New York: Pantheon), p. 34.

7. Quoted in Michael Elliott-Bateman et al., *Revolt to Revolution: Studies in the 19th and 20th Century European Experience* (Manchester, England: Manchester University Press, 1974), p. 87.

8. Jose San Martin, quoted in Edwin Early, *The History Atlas of South America* (New York: Macmillan, 1998), p. 76.

9. Quoted in Carlos Fuentes, *The Buried Mirror: Reflections on Spain and the New World* (New York: Houghton Mifflin, 1992), p. 252.

10. Quoted in E. Bradford Burns and Julie A. Charlip, *Latin America: A Concise Interpretive History*, 7th ed. (Upper Saddle River, N.J.: Prentice-Hall, 2002), p. 75.

11. Quoted in John R. Gillis, *A World of Their Own Making: Myth, Ritual, and the Quest for Family Values* (New York: Basic Books, 1996), p. 65.

12. Quoted in Fernand Braudel, *The Perspective of the World: Civilization and Capitalism, 15th–18th Century* (New York: Harper and Row, 1984), p. 553.

13. Quoted in Peter Gay, *Age of Enlightenment* (New York: Time, Inc., 1966), pp. 105–106.

14. Quoted in Peter Hall, *Cities in Civilization* (New York: Fromm International, 1998), p. 310.

15. Quoted in Oliver Zimmer, *A Contested Nation: History, Memory and Nationalism in Switzerland, 1761–1891* (Cambridge: Cambridge University Press, 2003), p. 119.

16. Quoted in W. Raymond Duncan et al., *World Politics in the 21st Century*, 2nd ed. (New York: Longman, 2004), p. 311.

17. Quoted in Patrick Galvin, *Irish Songs of Resistance* (New York: Folklore Press, n.d.), p. 84.

18. Quoted in S. C. Burchell, *The Age of Progress* (New York: Time, Inc., 1966), p. 120.

19. Quoted in Reginald Nettel, *Sing a Song of England: A Social History of Traditional Song* (London: Phoenix House, 1969), p. 183.

20. Quoted in Robert A. Huttenback, *The British Imperial Experience* (New York: Harper and Row, 1966), p. 101.

21. Hillaire Beloc, quoted in Eric Hobsbawm, *The Age of Empire, 1875–1914* (New York: Vintage, 1987), p. 20.

22. Quoted in John Steele Gordon, *A Thread Across the Ocean: The Heroic Story of the Transatlantic Cable* (New York: Perennial, 2003), p. 215.

23. Quoted in Winnifred Baumgart, *Imperialism: The Idea and Reality of British and French Colonial Expansion, 1880–1914* (New York: Oxford University Press, 1986), p. 88.

24. Quoted in L. S. Stavrianos, *Global Reach: The Third World Comes of Age* (New York: William Morrow, 1981), p. 263.

25. Quoted in Baumgart, *Imperialism*, p. 52.

Chapter 20 Changing Societies in Europe, the Americas, and Oceania, 1750–1914

1. *Nostromo* (Garden City, N.Y.: Doubleday, Page, and Company, 1924), p. 77.

2. The Kume quotes are from Donald Keene, *Modern Japanese Diaries: The Japanese at Home and Abroad as Revealed Through Their Diaries* (New York: Columbia University Press, 1998), pp. 90–115.

3. Quoted in Frederic Delouche et al., *Illustrated History of Europe* (New York: Barnes and Noble, 2001), p. 312.

4. Quoted in Louise A. Tilly and Joan W. Scott, *Women, Work and Family* (New York: Holt, Rinehart and Winston, 1978), p. 64.

5. Quoted in Dorothy Marshall, *Industrial England, 1771–1851* (New York: Charles Scribner's, 1973), p. 135.

6. Quoted in T. W. C. Blanning, "The Commercialization and Sacralization of European Culture in the Nineteenth Century," in T. W. C. Blanning, ed., *The Oxford Illustrated History of Modern Europe* (Oxford: Oxford University Press, 1996), p. 147.

7. The quotes are from Alexis De Tocqueville, *Democracy in America and Two Essays on America* (New York: Penguin, 2003), pp. xxv, xxxiii.

8. Quoted in James Chase and Caleb Carr, *America Invulnerable: The Quest for Absolute Security from 1812 to Star Wars* (New York: Summit, 1988), p. 46.

9. From Peter Blood-Patterson, *Rise Up Singing* (Bethlehem, Pa.: Sing Out Publications, 1988), p. 246.

10. Quoted in Walter L. Williams, "American Imperialism and the Indians," in Frederick E. Hoxie, ed., *Indians in American History: An Introduction* (Arlington Heights, Ill.: Harlan Davidson, 1988), p. 233.

11. Quoted in Gabriel Kolko, *Main Currents in Modern American History* (New York: Pantheon, 1984), p. 47.

12. Quoted in Simon Serfaty, *The Elusive Enemy: American Foreign Policy Since World War II* (Boston: Little, Brown, 1972), p. 13.

13. Quoted in William Appleman Williams, *The Contours of American History* (Chicago: Quadrangle, 1966), p. 284.

14. Quoted in Robert Heilbroner and Aaron Singer, *The Economic Transformation of America, 1600 to the Present*, 3rd ed. (Fort Worth, Tex.: Harcourt Brace, 1994), p. 163.

15. The quotes are in Juliet Haines Mofford, ed., *Talkin' Union: The American Labor Movement* (Carlisle, Mass.: Discovery Enterprises, 1997), pp. 12, 24.

16. From Mark Van Doren, ed., *The Portable Walt Whitman* (New York: Penguin, 1973), p. 210.

17. Quoted in Lloyd Gardner, *Safe for Democracy: The Anglo-American Response to Revolution, 1913–1923* (New York: Oxford University Press, 1984), p. 26.

18. From Mariano Azuela's novel *The Flies*, quoted in Lesley Byrd Simpson, *Many Mexicos*, 4th ed. rev. (Berkeley: University of California Press, 1967), p. 298.

19. Quoted in Stanley J. Stein and Barbara H. Stein, *The Colonial Heritage of Latin America: Essays on Economic Dependence in Perspective* (New York: Oxford University Press, 1970), p. 151.

20. Quoted in E. Bradford Burns, *Latin America: A Concise Interpretive History*, 5th ed. (Englewood Cliffs, N.J.: Prentice-Hall, 1990), p. 213.

21. Quoted in Michael C. Meyer and William L. Sherman, *The Course of Mexican History*, 2nd ed. (New York: Oxford University Press, 1983), p. 416.

22. Quoted in Lloyd Braithwaite, "The Problem of Cultural Integration in Trinidad," in David Lowenthal and Lambors Comitas, eds., *Consequences of Class and Color: West Indian Perspectives* (Garden City, N.Y.: Anchor, 1973), p. 248.

23. General Leonard Wood, quoted in Saul Landau, *The Dangerous Doctrine: National Security and U.S. Foreign Policy* (Boulder, Colo.: Westview Press, 1988), pp. 80–81.

24. Quoted in Louis Hartz, *The Founding of New Societies* (New York: Harcourt, Brace and World, 1964), p. 248.

25. Quoted in Donald Denoon and Philippa Mein-Smith, *A History of Australia, New Zealand and the Pacific* (Malden, Mass.: Blackwell, 2000), p. 210.

Chapter 21 Africa, the Middle East, and Imperialism, 1750–1914

1. Quoted in Edmund Burke III, *Prelude to Protectorate in Morocco: Precolonial Protest and Resistance, 1860–1912* (Chicago: University of Chicago Press, 1976), p. xi.

2. Quoted in Alan Palmer, *The Decline and Fall of the Ottoman Empire* (New York: Barnes and Noble, 1992), p. 58.

3. Quoted in John Iliffe, "Tanzania Under German and British Rule," in B. A. Ogot, ed., *Zamani: A Survey of East African History*, new ed. (Nairobi: Longman Kenya, 1974), p. 301.

4. Quoted in Kevin Shillington, *History of Africa*, rev. ed. (New York: St. Martin's, 1995), p. 296.

5. Muhammad Bello, quoted in Robert W. July, *A History of the African People*, 5th ed. (Prospect Heights, Ill.: Waveland, 1998), p. 191.

6. Francois Coillard, quoted in John Iliffe, *Africans: The History of a Continent* (New York: Cambridge University Press, 1995), p. 208.

7. Quoted in Basil Davidson, *Africa in History: Themes and Outlines*, rev. ed. (New York: Touchstone, 1991), p. 272.

8. Quoted in Tom Hopkinson, *South Africa* (New York: Time Inc., 1964), p. 93.

9. The lyrics are in David B. Coplan, *In Township Tonite: South Africa's Black City Music and Theater* (London: Longman, 1985), pp. 44–45.

10. Quoted in Iliffe, *Africans*, pp. 200–201.

11. H. H. Johnston, quoted in M. E. Chamberlain, *The Scramble for Africa* (Harlow, U.K.: Longman, 1974), p. 96.

12. Nnamdi Azikiwe, quoted in Minton F. Goldman, "Political Change in a Multi-National Setting," in David Schmitt, ed., *Dynamics of the Third World: Political and Social Change* (Cambridge: Winthrop, 1974), p. 172.

13. Rev. J. B. Murphy, quoted in Shillington, *History of Africa*, pp. 333–334.

14. Quoted in Dennis Austin, *Politics in Ghana* (London: Oxford University Press, 1964), p. 275.

15. Quoted in Leroy Vail, "The Political Economy of East-Central Africa," in David Birmingham and Phyllis M. Martin, eds., *History of Central Africa*, vol. 2 (New York: Longman, 1983), p. 233.

16. Quoted in Andrew Wheatcroft, *The Ottomans* (New York: Viking, 1993), p. 146.

17. Quoted in Halil Inalcik, "Turkey," in Robert E. Ward and Dankwart A. Rostow, eds., *Political Modernization in Japan and Turkey* (Princeton: Princeton University Press, 1964), pp. 57–58.

18. Quoted in Afaf Lufti al-Sayyid Marsot, *Egypt in the Reign of Muhammad Ali* (New York: Cambridge University Press, 1994), p. 28.

19. Quoted in Yahya Armajani and Thomas M. Ricks, *Middle East: Past and Present*, 2nd ed. (Englewood Cliffs, N.J.: Prentice-Hall, 1986), p. 221.

20. Quoted in Charles Issawi, *The Middle East Economy: Decline and Recovery* (Princeton: Markus Wiener, 1995), p. 126.

21. Gertrude Bell, quoted in Emory C. Bogle, *The Modern Middle East: From Imperialism to Freedom, 1800–1958* (Upper Saddle River, N.J.: Prentice-Hall, 1996), p. 103.

22. Quoted in Eric R. Wolf, *Peasant Wars of the Twentieth Century* (New York: Harper and Row, 1969), p. 209.

23. The quotes are from Akram Fouad Khater, ed., *Sources in the History of the Modern Middle East* (Boston: Houghton Mifflin, 2004), p. 75; Wiebke Walther, *Women in Islam* (Princeton: Markus Wiener, 1993), p. 221.

24. Quoted in Burke, *Prelude to Protectorate*, p. 38.

25. From Khater, *Sources*, p. 34.

Chapter 22 South Asia, Southeast Asia, and Colonization, 1750–1914

1. From Huynh Sanh Thong, *An Anthology of Vietnamese Poems from the Eleventh Through the Twentieth Centuries* (New Haven, Conn.: Yale University Press, 1996), p. 88.

2. The poem excerpts are in Helen B. Lamb, *Vietnam's Will to Live: Resistance to Foreign Aggression from Early Times Through the Nineteenth Century* (New York: Monthly Review Press, 1972), pp. 134, 152.

3. Quoted in Sinharaja Tammita-Delgoda, *A Traveller's History of India*, 2nd ed. (New York: Interlink, 1999), p. 154.

4. The quotes are in Burton Stein, *A History of India* (Malden, Mass.: Blackwell, 1998), pp. 265–266.

5. Charles Metcalfe, quoted in David Ludden, *An Agrarian History of South Asia* (New York: Cambridge University Press, 1999), p. 161.

6. Quoted in Tammita-Delgoda, *Traveller's History*, p. 167.

7. Quoted in ibid., p. 173.

8. Quoted in Judith M. Brown, *Modern India: The Origins of an Asian Democracy*, 2nd ed. (New York: Oxford University Press, 1994), p. 134.

9. Dadabhai Naoroji and R.C. Dutt, quoted in Ainslee T. Embree, *India's Search for National Identity* (New York: Alfred A. Knopf, 1972), pp. 48–49.

10. Quoted in Clark D. Moore and David Eldridge, ed., *India Yesterday and Today* (New York: Bantam, 1970), pp. 154–155.

11. The quotes are in Francis Robinson, *The Cultural Atlas of the Islamic World Since 1500* (Oxford: Stonehenge, 1992), pp. 148–149.

12. From Rabindranath Tagore, *Gitanjali: A Collection of Indian Songs* (New York: Macmillan, 1973), pp. 49–50.

13. Quoted in John McLane, ed., *The Political Awakening of India* (Englewood Cliffs, N.J.: Prentice-Hall, 1970), p. 46.

14. Douwes Dekker, from Harry J. Benda and John A. Larkin, eds., *The World of Southeast Asia: Selected Historical Readings* (New York: Harper and Row, 1967), p. 127.

15. Quoted in Truong Buu Lam, *Resistance, Rebellion, Revolution: Popular Movements in Vietnamese History* (Singapore: Institute of Southeast Asian Studies, 1984), p. 11.

16. From Huynh, *Anthology of Vietnamese Poems*, p. 214.

17. The quotes are in Lamb, *Vietnam's Will to Live*, p. 229; Truong Buu Lam, *Patterns of Vietnamese Response to Foreign Intervention, 1858–1900*, Monograph Series No. 11, Southeast Asia Studies (New Haven, Conn.: Yale University Press, 1967), p. 8.

18. Quoted in David Joel Steinberg, 3rd ed., *The Philippines: A Singular and Plural Place* (Boulder, Colo.: Westview Press, 1994), p. 64.

19. The quotes are in Teodoro A. Agoncillo, *A Short History of the Philippines* (New York: Mentor, 1969), p. 93; and Mina Roces, "Reflections on Gender and Kinship in the Philippine Revolution, 1896–1898," in Florentino Rodao and Felice Noelle Rodriguez, eds., *The Philippine Revolution of 1896: Ordinary Lives in Extraordinary Times* (Manila: Ateneo de Manila University Press, 2001), p. 34.

20. Quoted in David Joel Steinberg et al., *In Search of Southeast Asia: A Modern History*, rev. ed. (Honolulu: University of Hawaii Press, 1987), p. 274.

21. Quoted in Daniel B. Schirmer, *Republic or Empire: American Resistance to the Philippine War* (Cambridge: Schenkman, 1972), p. 237.

22. The quotes are in David Howard Bain, *Sitting in Darkness: Americans in the Philippines* (Baltimore: Penguin, 1986), p. 2; and Gary R. Hess, *Vietnam and United States: Origins and Legacy of War* (Boston: Twayne, 1990), p. 25.

23. Quoted in Ngo Vinh Long, *Before the Revolution: The Vietnamese Peasants Under the French* (New York: Columbia University Press, 1991), p. v.

24. Tran Tu Binh, *The Red Earth: A Vietnamese Memoir of Life on a Colonial Rubber Plantation*, translated by John Spragens, Jr. (Athens, Ohio: Center for International Studies, Ohio University, 1985), p. 26.

25. Raden Ajoe Mangkoedimedjo, quoted in Norman Owen et al., *The Emergence of Modern Southeast Asia: A New History* (Honolulu: University of Hawaii Press, 2005), p. 197.

Chapter 23 East Asia and the Russian Empire Face New Challenges, 1750–1914

1. Quoted in Frederic Wakeman, Jr., *Strangers at the Gate: Social Disorder in South China, 1839–1861* (Berkeley: University of California Press, 1966), p. 126.

2. Quoted in Jonathan D. Spence, *The Search for Modern China*, 2nd ed. (New York: W.W. Norton, 1999), p. 148.

3. Quoted in Derk Bodde, *Chin's Cultural Tradition: What and Whither?* (New York: Holt, Rinehart and Winston, 1957), pp. 62–63.

4. Chu Tsun, quoted in Hsin-Pao Chang, *Commissioner Lin and the Opium War* (New York: W.W. Norton, 1970), p. 89.

5. Quoted in Mark Borthwick, *Pacific Century: The Emergence of Modern East Asia* (Boulder, Colo.: Westview Press, 1992), p. 97.

6. The quotes are from Franz Schurmann and Orville Schell, eds., *Imperial China* (New York: Vintage Books, 1967), p. 146; and Ssu-Yu Teng and John K. Fairbank, eds., *China's Response to the West: A Documentary Survey, 1839–1923* (New York: Atheneum, 1963), p. 26.

7. Quoted in Jean Chesneaux et al., *China: From the Opium Wars to the 1911 Revolution* (New York: Pantheon, 1976), p. 123.

8. S. Wells Williams, quoted in John A. Harrison, *China Since 1800* (New York: Harcourt, Brace and World, 1967), p. 42.

9. Hsu Tung, quoted in Joseph R. Levenson, *Confucian China and Its Modern Fate: A Trilogy* (Berkeley: University of California Press, 1968), p. 105.

10. Quoted in Earl Swisher, "Chinese Intellectuals and the Western Impact, 1838–1900," *Comparative Studies in Society and History*, 1 (October, 1958), p. 35.

11. Wang Pengyun, from Cyril Birch, ed., *Anthology of Chinese Literature* (New York: Grove Press, 1972), p. 294.

12. Quoted in Lloyd Gardner, *Safe for Democracy: The Anglo-American Response to Revolution, 1913–1923* (New York: Oxford University Press, 1984), p. 318.

13. Quoted in Ono Kazuko, *Chinese Women in a Century of Revolution* (Stanford, Calif.: Stanford University Press, 1989), p. 30.

14. Quoted in Jonathan D. Spence, *The Gate of Heavenly Peace: The Chinese and Their Revolution, 1895–1980* (New York: Viking, 1981), p. 52.

15. Otsuki Gentaku, quoted in Mikiso Hane, *Modern Japan: A Historical Survey*, 2nd ed. (Boulder, Colo.: Westview Press, 1992), p. 59.

16. Quoted in Patricia Fister, "Female *Bunjin*: The Life of Poet-Painter Ema Saiko," in Gail Lee Bernstein, ed., *Recreating Japanese Women, 1600–1945* (Berkeley: University of California Press, 1991), p. 109.

17. Quoted in Matthi Ferrer, *Hokusai* (New York: Barnes and Noble, 2002), p. 9.

18. Yanagawa Seigan, quoted in H. D. Hartoonian, *Toward Restoration: The Growth of Political Consciousness in Tokugawa Japan* (Berkeley: University of California Press, 1970), pp. 1–2.

19. Quoted in Paul Varley, *Japanese Culture*, 4th ed. (Honolulu: University of Hawaii Press, 2000), p. 238.

20. Quoted in Kenneth B. Pyle, *The Making of Modern Japan*, 2nd ed. (Lexington, Mass.: D.C. Heath, 1996), p. 101.

21. Fukuzawa Yukichi, quoted in Mikiso Hane, *Peasants, Rebels, and Outcasts: The Underside of Modern Japan* (New York: Pantheon, 1982), p. 33.

22. Quoted in Conrad Totman, *A History of Japan* (Malden, Mass.: Blackwell, 2000), p. 341.

23. The quotes are from Varley, *Japanese Culture*, p. 272.

24. Ch'oe Ik-hyon, quoted in Bruce Cumings, *Korea's Place in the Sun: A Modern History* (New York: W.W. Norton, 1997), pp. 146–147.

25. Quoted in L. S. Stavrianos, *Global Rift: The Third World Comes of Age* (New York: William Morrow, 1981), p. 344.

Chapter 24 World Wars, European Revolutions, and Global Depression, 1914–1945

1. Quoted in Anne Applebaum, *Gulag: A History* (New York: Doubleday, 2003), p. 3.

2. Quoted in S. L. Marshall, *World War I* (Boston: Houghton Mifflin, 1987), p. 53.

3. Quoted in Sir Michael Howard, "Europe 1914," in Robert Cowley, ed., *The Great War: Perspectives on the First World War* (New York: Random House, 2003), p. 3.

4. David Lloyd George, quoted in Holger H. Herwig, ed., *The Outbreak of World War I*, 6th ed. (Boston: Houghton Mifflin, 1997), p. 12.

5. The quotes are in Michael J. Lyons, *World War I: A Short History*, 2nd ed. (Upper Saddle River, N.J.: Prentice-Hall, 2000), p. 195; and Ian Barnes and Robert Hudson, *The History Atlas of Europe: From Tribal Societies to a New European Unity* (New York: Macmillan, 1998), p. 131.

6. From L. S. Stavrianos, ed., *The Epic of Modern Man: A Collection of Readings* (Englewood Cliffs, N.J.: Prentice-Hall, 1966), p. 354.

7. Quoted in A. J. Nicholls, *Weimar and the Rise of Hitler*, 2nd ed. (New York: St. Martin's, 1979), p. 11.

8. Quoted in Piers Brendon, *Dark Valley: A Panorama of the 1930s* (New York: Alfred A. Knopf, 2000), p. 6.

9. Quoted in L. S. Stavrianos, *Global Rift: The Third World Comes of Age* (New York: William Morrow, 1981), p. 499.

10. Quoted in Brendon, *Dark Valley*, p. 493.

11. Quoted in Kenneth B. Pyle, *The Making of Modern Japan*, 2nd ed. (Lexington, Mass.: D.C. Heath, 1996), p. 173.

12. Senator William Borah, quoted in William Appleman Williams, *American-Russian Relations, 1781–1947* (New York: Rinehart, 1952), p. 164.

13. *The Great Gatsby* (New York: Scribner's, 1925), p. 182.

14. Paul Reynaud, quoted in Brendon, *Dark Valley*, pp. 153–154.

15. Quoted in Robert Heilbroner and Aaron Singer, *The Economic Transformation of America, 1600 to the Present* (Fort Worth: Harcourt Brace, 1994), p. 289.

16. From Harold Leventhal and Marjorie Guthrie, eds., *The Woody Guthrie Songbook* (New York: Grosset and Dunlap, 1976), pp. 180–181.

17. Maurice Sachs, quoted in Brendon, *Dark Valley*, p. 168.

18. Quoted in Felix Gilbert with David Clay Large, *The End of the European Era, 1890 to*

the Present, 4th ed. (New York: W.W. Norton, 1991), p. 263.

19. Quoted in Harold James, *Europe Reborn: A History, 1914–2000* (New York: Longman, 2003), p. 139.

20. Quoted in Martin Kitchen, *A World in Flames: A Short History of the Second World War in Europe and Asia, 1939–1945* (London: Longman, 1990), p. vi.

21. Quoted in Stephen J. Lee, *European Dictatorships, 1918–1945*, 2nd ed. (London: Routledge, 2000), p. 207.

22. Quoted in George Donelson Moss, *America in the Twentieth Century*, 4th ed. (Upper Saddle River, N.J.: Prentice-Hall, 2000), p. 257.

23. The quotes are in James L. McClain, *Japan: A Modern History* (New York: W.W. Norton, 2002), p. 515.

Chapter 25 Imperialism and Nationalism in Asia, Africa, and Latin America, 1914–1945

1. Quoted in James C. Scott, *The Moral Economy of the Peasant: Rebellion and Subsistence in Southeast Asia* (New Haven: Yale University Press, 1976), p. 236.

2. Quoted in James W. Trullinger, *Village at War: An Account of Conflict in Vietnam* (Stanford, Calif.: Stanford University Press, 1994), p. 18.

3. Dick Spottswood, liner notes to the album *Calypsos from Trinidad: Politics, Intrigue and Violence in the 1930s* (Arhoolie 7004, 1991).

4. Quoted in Lester Langley, *Central America: The Real Stakes: Understanding Central America Before It's Too Late* (New York: Dorsey, 1985), p. 23.

5. Kenneth Wherry of Nebraska, quoted in John Brooks, *The Great Leap: The Past Twenty-five Years in America* (New York: Harper and Row, 1966), p. 327.

6. Quoted in *A Pictorial Biography of Luxun* (Beijing: Peoples Fine Arts Publishing House, n.d.), p. 157.

7. "Report on an Investigation of the Peasant Movement in Hunan," in *Selected Works of Mao Tse-Tung*, vol. 1 (Peking: Foreign Languages Press, 1965), p. 28.

8. Quoted in Stephen Uhalley, Jr., *Mao Tse-Tung: A Critical Biography* (New York: New Viewpoints, 1975), p. 55.

9. Quoted in John Meskill, "History of China," in John Meskill, ed., *An Introduction to Chinese Civilization* (Lexington, MA: D.C. Heath, 1973), p. 302.

10. Quoted in Sinharaja Tammita-Delgoda, *A Traveller's History of India*, 2nd ed. (New York: Interlink, 1999), p. 189.

11. From Clark D. Moore and David Eldridge, eds., *India Yesterday and Today* (New York: Bantam, 1970), p. 174.

12. Quoted in Martin Deming Lewis, ed., *Gandhi: Maker of Modern India?* (Lexington, Mass.: D.C. Heath, 1965), p. xii.

13. Quoted in Hermann Kulke and Dietmar Rothermund, *History of India*, 3rd ed. (New York: Routledge, 1998), pp. 135–136.

14. Sir T.P. Sapru, quoted in Judith M. Brown, *Modern India: The Origins of an Asian Democracy*, 2nd ed. (New York: Oxford University Press, 1994), p. 280.

15. "Phan Boi Chau's Prison Reflections, 1914," in Robert J. McMahon, ed., *Major Problems in the History of the Vietnam War: Documents and Essays* (Lexington, Mass.: D.C. Heath, 1990), p. 32.

16. Hoai Thanh, quoted in David Marr, "Vietnamese Historical Reassessment, 1900–1944," in Anthony Reid and David Marr, eds., *Perceptions of the Past in Southeast Asia* (Singapore: Heinemann, 1979), pp. 337–338.

17. Sitor Situmorang, quoted in Harry Aveling, ed., *From Surabaya to Armageddon: Indonesian Short Stories* (Singapore: Heinemann, 1976), p. vii.

18. Obafemi Awolowo, quoted in Chester L. Hunt and Lewis Walker, *Ethnic Dynamics: Patterns of Intergroup Relations in Various Societies*, 2nd ed. (Holmes Beach, Fla: Learning Publications, 1979), p. 277.

19. Quoted in Veit Erlmann, *African Stars: Studies in Black South African Performance* (Chicago: University of Chicago Press, 1991), pp. 95–96.

20. Quoted in Charles Hamm, "'The Constant Companion of Man': Separate Development, Radio Bantu and Music," *Popular Music*, 10/2 (May, 1991), p. 161.

21. Quoted in Hans Kohn, *A History of Nationalism in the East* (New York: Harcourt, 1929), p. 257.

22. The quotes are from Akram Fouad Khater, ed., *Sources in the History of the Modern Middle East* (Boston: Houghton Mifflin, 2004), pp. 167, 176.

23. Severino Fama, quoted in Robert M. Levine, *The History of Brazil* (New York: Palgrave, 1999), p. 107.

24. From Frederick B. Pike, ed., *Latin American History: Select Problems. Identity, Integration, and Nationhood* (New York: Harcourt, Brace and World, 1969), p. 319.

Societies, Networks, Transitions: Global Imbalances in the Modern World, 1750–1945

1. From Jim Zwick, ed., *Mark Twain's Weapons of Satire: Anti-Imperialist Writings on the Philippine-American War* (Syracuse, N.Y.: Syracuse University Press, 1992), pp. 3–5.

2. Quoted in L. S. Stavrianos, *Lifelines from Our Past: A New World History*, rev. ed. (Armonk, N.Y.: M.E. Sharpe, 1997), p. 114.

3. Rev. Sydney Smith, quoted in Frederic Delouche et al., *Illustrated History of Europe: A Unique Portrait of Europe's Common People* (New York: Barnes and Noble, 2001), p. 289.

4. Senator Albert Beveridge of Indiana, quoted in Henry Allen, *What It Felt Like Living in the American Century* (New York: Pantheon, 2000), p. 7.

5. Quoted in Benjamin Schwartz, *In Search of Wealth and Power: Yen Fu and the West* (New York: Harper Torchbooks, 1964), p. 29.

6. Quoted in Scott B. Cook, *Colonial Encounters in the Age of High Imperialism* (New York: Longman, 1996), p. 100.

7. From Clark D. Moore and David Eldridge, eds., *India Yesterday and Today* (New York: Bantam, 1970), p. 170.

8. Quoted in John A. Harrison, *China Since 1800* (New York: Harcourt, Brace and World, 1967), p. 161.

9. Quoted in Ranajit Guha, *History at the Limit of World-History* (New York: Columbia University Press, 2002), p. 91.

10. International Congress of the League Against Imperialism and Colonial Oppression, quoted in Clive Ponting, *The Twentieth Century: A World History* (New York: Henry Holt, 1998), p. 197.

11. Quoted in Richard H. Robbins, *Global Problems and the Culture of Capitalism* (Boston: Allyn and Bacon, 1999), p. 90.

12. Quoted in "Introduction," in Walter D. Wyman and Clifton B. Kroeber, eds., *The Frontier in Perspective* (Madison: University of Wisconsin Press, 1965), p. xviii.

13. Quoted in Pamela Scully, "Race and Ethnicity in Women's and Gender History in Global Perspective," in Bonnie G. Smith, ed., *Women's History in Global Perspective*, vol. 1 (Urbana: University of Illinois Press, 2004), p. 207.

14. Quoted in Ng Bickleen Fong, *The Chinese in New Zealand* (Hong Kong: Hong Kong University Press, 1959), p. 96.

15. Quoted in J. R. McNeill and William H. McNeill, *The Human Web: A Bird's-Eye View of World History* (New York: W.W. Norton, 2003), p. 217.

16. Quoted in Daniel R. Headrick, *The Tentacles of Progress: Technology Transfer in the Age of Imperialism, 1850–1940* (New York: Oxford University Press, 1988), p. 127.

17. Quoted in L. S. Stavrianos, "The Global Redistribution of Man," in Franklin D. Scott, ed., *World Migration in Modern Times* (Englewood Cliffs, N.J.: Prentice-Hall, 1968), p. 170.

18. Quoted in Daniel R. Headrick, *The Tools of Empire: Technology and European Imperialism in the Nineteenth Century* (New York: Oxford University Press, 1981), p. 116.

19. Quoted in Gordon Rohlehr, *Calypso and Society in Pre-Independence Trinidad* (Port of Spain: Gordon Rohlehr, 1990), pp. 80–81.

Chapter 26 The Remaking of the Global System, Since 1945

1. Quoted in Adrian Boot and Chris Salewicz with Rita Marley as Senior Editor, *Bob Marley: Songs of Freedom* (London:Bloomsbury, 1995), p. 278.

2. Quoted in Sean Dolan, *Bob Marley* (Philadelphia: Chelsea House, 1997), p. 113.

3. Frantz Fanon, *The Wretched of the Earth* (New York: Grove, 1968), pp. 97–98.

4. Quoted in Goran Hyden, *Beyond Ujamaa in Tanzania: Underdevelopment and an Uncaptured Peasantry* (Berkeley: University of California Press, 1980), p. 202.

5. Quoted in Jennifer Seymour Whitaker, *How Can Africa Survive?* (New York: Harper and Row, 1988), p. 13.

6. Mohammed Mossadeq, quoted in Michael H. Hunt, *The World Transformed, 1945 to the Present* (Boston: Bedford/St. Martin's, 2004), p. 283.

7. The quotes are in Choi Chatterjee et al., *The 20th Century: A Retrospective* (Boulder, Colo.: Westview Press, 2002), pp. 153, 306.
8. Dalai Lama, *My Land and My People* (New York: Warner Books, 1997), p. x.
9. Quoted in Peter Singer, "Navigating the Ethics of Globalization," *Chronicle of Higher Education*, October 11, 2002, p. B8.
10. Quoted in J. Donald Hughes, *An Environmental History of the World: Mankind's Changing Role in the Community of Life* (New York: Routledge, 2002), p. 206.
11. Quoted in Miriam Ching Louie, "Life on the Line," *The New Internationalist* (http://www.newint.org/issue302/sweat.html).
12. Walter Rodney, *How Europe Underdeveloped Africa* (London: Bogle-L'Ouverture, 1972), p. 162.
13. Quoted in Clive Ponting, *The Twentieth Century: A World History* (New York: Henry Holt and Company, 1998), p. 545.
14. Quoted in Hunt, *World Transformed*, p. 428.
15. Quoted in Eric Hobsbawm, *The Age of Extremes: A History of the World, 1914–1991* (New York: Pantheon, 1994), p. 365.
16. A. G. Hopkins, "Globalization: An Agenda for Historians," in Hopkins, ed., *Globalization in World History* (New York: W.W. Norton, 2002), p. 11.
17. From Hazel Johnson and Henry Bernstein, eds., *Third World Lives of Struggle* (London: Heinemann Educational, 1982), p. 173.
18. J. R. McLeod, "The Seamless Web: Media and Power in the Post-Modern Global Village," *Journal of Popular Culture*, 15/2 (Fall 1991), p. 69.
19. Quoted in Timothy D. Taylor, *Global Pop: World Music, World Markets* (New York: Routledge, 1997), p. 158.
20. Quoted in Chatterjee et al., *20th Century*, p. 222.
21. Quoted in David Reynolds, *One World Divisible: A Global History Since 1945* (New York: W.W. Norton, 2000), p. 491.
22. Quoted in Hunt, *World Transformed*, p. 409.
23. Quoted in Tariq Ali, *The Clash of Fundamentalisms: Crusades, Jihads and Modernity* (London: Verso, 2003), p. 280.
24. Michael Sturmer, quoted in Hobsbawm, *Age of Extremes*, p. 558.

Chapter 27 East Asian Resurgence, 1945–Present

1. Quoted in Jerome Chen, *Mao and the Chinese Revolution* (New York: Oxford University Press, 1967), p. 6.
2. The quotes are from Ross Terrill, *Mao: A Biography* (New York: Harper, 1980), p. 198.
3. Peng Dehuai, quoted in Craig Dietrich, *People's China: A Brief History*, 3rd ed. (New York: Oxford University Press, 1998), p. 130.
4. Quoted in Jonathan D. Spence, *The Search for Modern China*, 2nd ed. (New York: W.W. Norton, 1999), p. 558.
5. Quoted in Maurice Meisner, *Mao's China and After: A History of the People's Republic*, 3rd ed. (New York: The Free Press, 1999), p. 281.
6. Xue Xinran, *The Good Women of China: Hidden Voices* (New York: Anchor, 2002), p. 175.
7. Quoted in the Committee of Concerned Asian Scholars, *China! Inside the Peoples Republic* (New York: Bantam, 1972), p. 34.
8. From Timothy Cheek, *Mao Zedong and China's Revolutions: A Brief History with Documents* (Boston: Bedford/St. Martin's, 2002), p. 116.
9. Quoted in Hu Kai-Yu, *The Chinese Literary Scene: A Writer's Visit to the People's Republic* (New York: Vintage, 1975), p. 227.
10. Quoted in Orville Schell, *Discos and Democracy: China in the Throes of Reform* (New York: Anchor, 1989), p. 101.
11. Quoted in June Teufel Dreyer, *China's Political System: Modernization and Tradition* (New York: Paragon House, 1993), p. 345.
12. The quotes are in Andrew F. Jones, *Like a Knife: Ideology and Genre in Contemporary Chinese Popular Music* (Ithaca, N.Y.: East Asia Program, Cornell University, 1992), pp. 97, 148.
13. Quoted in Orville Schell, *Mandate of Heaven: A New Generation of Entrepreneurs, Dissidents, Bohemians, and Technocrats Lays Claim to China's Future* (New York: Simon and Schuster, 1994), p. 35.
14. Quoted in R. Keith Schoppa, *Revolution and Its Past: Identities and Change in Modern Chinese History* (Upper Saddle River, N.J.: Prentice-Hall, 2002), p. 433.
15. Xue Xinran, author Interview in *Random House: Reading Group for the Good Women of China* (http://www.randomhouse.co.uk/offthepage/guide.htm?command=Search&db=catalog/mai).
16. Ibid.
17. Quoted in James L. McClain, *Japan: A Modern History* (New York: W.W. Norton, 2002), p. 585.
18. Misuzu Hanikara, from Richard H. Minear, ed., *Through Japanese Eyes*, vol. 2 (New York: Praeger, 1974), p. 88.
19. Kenzaburo Oe, quoted in Patrick Smith, *Japan: A Reinterpretation* (New York: Pantheon, 1997), p. 238.
20. Quoted in Mikiso Hane, *Modern Japan: A Historical Survey*, 2nd ed. (Boulder, Colo.: Westview Press, 1992), p. 371.
21. Quoted in Frank Gibney, *The Pacific Century: America and Asia in a Changing World* (New York: Charles Scribner's, 1992), p. 231.
22. Cho Se-hui, quoted in Bruce Cumings, *Korea's Place in the Sun: A Modern History* (New York: W.W. Norton, 1997), p. 337.

Chapter 28 Rebuilding Europe and Russia, Since 1945

1. Quoted in Norman Davies, *Europe: A History* (New York: Harper, 1998), p. 1066.
2. Quoted in ibid.
3. Quoted in Felix Gilbert with David Clay Large, *The End of the European Era, 1890 to the Present*, 4th ed. (New York: W.W. Norton, 1991), p. 429.
4. Quoted in Harold James, *Europe Reborn: A History, 1914–2000* (New York: Longman, 2001), p. 248.
5. Quoted in Robert O. Paxton, *Europe in the Twentieth Century* (New York: Harcourt Brace Jovanovich, 1973), p. 576.
6. Quoted in Davies, *Europe*, p. 1065.
7. Quoted in Bonnie G. Smith, *Changing Lives: Women in European History Since 1700* (Lexington, Mass.: D.C. Heath, 1989), p. 509.
8. Quoted in Richard Vinen, *A History in Fragments: Europe in the Twentieth Century* (New York: Da Capo, 2000), p. 370.
9. Quoted in Bonnie S. Anderson and Judith P. Zinsser, *A History of Their Own: Women in Europe from Prehistory to the Present*, vol. 2 (New York: Harper Perennial, 1988), p. 334.
10. Amintore Fanfani, quoted in Vinen, *History in Fragments*, p. 493.
11. Gordon Lewis, quoted in Chester L. Hunt and Lewis Walker, *Ethnic Dynamics: Patterns of Intergroup Relations in Various Societies*, 2nd ed. (Holmes Beach, Fla.: Learning Publications, 1979), p. 316.
12. *Sniffin' Glue*, quoted in Peter Wicke, *Rock Music: Culture, Aesthetics and Sociology* (New York: Cambridge University Press, 1990), p. 148.
13. Quoted in Ronald Grigor Suny, *The Soviet Experiment: Russia, the USSR, and the Successor States* (New York: Oxford University Press, 1998), p. 387.
14. Quoted in James, *Europe Reborn*, p. 279.
15. Quoted in Timothy W. Ryback, *Rock Around the Bloc: A History of Rock Music in Eastern Europe and the Soviet Union* (New York: Oxford University Press, 1990), p. 35.
16. Quoted in Davies, *Europe*, p. 1102.
17. Quoted in James, *Europe Reborn*, p. 300.
18. Quoted in Elaine Mensh and Harry Mensh, *Behind the Scenes in Two Worlds* (New York: International Publishers, 1978), p. 313.
19. Dmitry Likhachev, quoted in Catherine Evtuhov et al., *A History of Russia: Peoples, Legends, Events, Forces* (Boston: Houghton Mifflin, 2004), p. 819.
20. Quoted in James Wilkenson and H. Stuart Hughes, *Contemporary Europe: A History*, 10th ed. (Upper Saddle River, N.J.: Prentice-Hall, 2004), p. 559.
21. Quoted in Vinen, *History in Fragments*, p. 520.
22. Quoted in Wilkenson and Hughes, *Contemporary Europe*, p. 590.

Chapter 29 The Americas and the Pacific Basin: New Roles in the Contemporary World, Since 1945

1. Quoted in James D. Cockcroft, *Latin America: History, Politics, and U.S. Policy*, 2nd ed. (Chicago: Nelson-Hall, 1996), p. 567.
2. Quoted in Marilyn B. Young, *The Vietnam Wars, 1945–1990* (New York: HarperCollins, 1991), p. 25.
3. Quoted in James Matray, *The Reluctant Crusade: American Foreign Policy in Korea, 1941–1950* (Honolulu: University of Hawaii Press, 1985), p. 3.
4. Quoted in L. S. Stavrianos, *Global Rift: The Third World Comes of Age* (New York: William Morrow, 1981), p. 712.

5. Quoted in Walter LaFeber, *America, Russia and the Cold War: 1945–1992*, 7th ed. (New York: McGraw-Hill, 1993), p. 248.

6. Quoted in Cockcroft, *Latin America*, p. 531.

7. Quoted in Walter LaFeber et al., *The American Century: A History of the United States Since 1941*, 5th ed. (Boston: McGraw-Hill, 1998), p. 519.

8. From Peter Blood-Patterson, ed., *Rise Up Singing* (Bethlehem, Pa.: Sing Out Publications, 1988), p. 219.

9. Folksinger Malvina Reynolds, quoted in Richard O. Davies, "The Ambivalent Heritage: The City in Modern America," in James T. Patterson, ed., *Paths to the Present: Interpretive Essays on American Society Since 1930* (Minneapolis: Burgess, 1975), p. 163.

10. Quoted in George Donelson Moss, *America in the Twentieth Century*, 4th ed. (Upper Saddle River, N.J.: Prentice-Hall, 2000), p. 409.

11. Quoted in James T. Patterson, *America Since 1941: A History*, 2nd ed. (Fort Worth, Tex.: Harcourt, 2000), p. 254.

12. Quoted in Wayne C. Thompson, *Canada 1997* (Harpers Ferry, Va.: Stryker-Post, 1997), p. 1.

13. Jaime Wheelock, quoted in Kyle Longley, *In the Eagle's Shadow: The United States and Latin America* (Wheeling, Ill.: Harlan Davidson, 2002), p. 291.

14. Quoted in Sebastian Balfour, *Castro*, 2nd ed. (New York: Longman, 1995), p. 167.

15. The quotes are in Thomas E. Skidmore and Peter H. Smith, *Modern Latin America*, 4th ed. (New York: Oxford University Press, 1997), p. 147; Joseph A. Page, *The Brazilians* (Reading, Mass.: Addison-Wesley, 1995), p. 5.

16. Quoted in David J. Morris, *We Must Make Haste—Slowly: The Process of Revolution in Chile* (New York: Vintage, 1973), pp. 270–271.

17. Pamela Constable and Arturo Valenzuela, *A Nation of Enemies: Chile Under Pinochet* (New York: W.W. Norton, 1991), p. 38.

18. Graciliano Ramos, *Barren Lives*, quoted in E. Bradford Burns, *Latin America: A Concise Interpretive History*, 5th ed. (Englewood Cliffs, N.J.: Prentice-Hall, 1990), p. 231.

19. Nelson Rodrigues, quoted in Warren Hoge, "A Whole Nation More Agitated than Spike Lee," *New York Times*, June 5, 1994, p. A1.

20. From Jara's song "Manifiesto." ("Manifesto"). The song and the translation can be found on Jara's album *Manifiesto: Chile September 1973* (XTRA 1143, 1974).

21. See Marley's album *Catch a Fire* (Island ILPS 9241, 1973).

22. Quoted in Jan Fairley, "New Song: Music and Politics in Latin America," in Francis Hanly and Tim May, eds., *Rhythms of the World* (London: BBC Books, 1989), p. 90.

Chapter 30 The Middle East, Sub-Saharan Africa, and New Conflicts in the Contemporary World, 1945–Present

1. See Savuka's album *Heat, Dust and Dreams* (EMI 9777-7-98795, 1993).

2. Quoted in Ian J. Bickerton and Carla L. Klausner, *A Concise History of the Arab-Israeli Conflict*, 2nd ed. (Englewood Cliffs, N.J.: Prentice-Hall, 1995), p. 131.

3. Quoted in James Alban Bill, *The Politics of Iran: Groups, Classes and Modernization* (Columbus, Ohio: Charles E. Merrill, 1972), pp. 76–77.

4. Latifa az-Zayyat, quoted in Wiebke Walther, *Women in Islam from Medieval to Modern Times* (Princeton: Markus Wiener, 1993), p. 235.

5. Quoted in Daniel Bates and Amal Rassam, *Peoples and Cultures of the Middle East*, 2nd ed. (Upper Saddle River, N.J.: Prentice-Hall, 2001), p. 235.

6. Fatema Mernissi, *Scheherazade Goes West: Different Cultures, Different Harems* (New York: Washington Square Press, 2001), p. 219.

7. Martin Stokes, *The Arabesk Debate: Music and Musicians in Modern Turkey* (Oxford: Clarendon Press, 1992), p. 1.

8. Sadiq Hidayat, in *Hajji Aqa*, quoted in Bill, *Politics of Iran*, p. 105.

9. From Akram Fouad Khater, ed., *Sources in the History of the Modern Middle East* (Boston: Houghton Mifflin, 2004), p. 362.

10. Naguib Mahfuz, quoted in Bates and Rassam, *Peoples and Cultures*, p. 199.

11. Quoted in Frances Robinson, *The Cultural Atlas of the Islamic World Since 1500* (Alexandria, Va.: Stonehenge, 1982), p. 158.

12. Quoted in Basil Davidson, *The People's Cause: A History of Guerrillas in Africa* (Burnt Mill, U.K.: Longman, 1981), p. 165.

13. A. Toure, quoted in Bill Freund, *The Making of Contemporary Africa: The Development of African Society Since 1800* (Bloomington: Indiana University Press, 1984), p. 192.

14. From James E. Miller et al., eds., *Black African Voices* (Glenview: Scott Foresman, 1970), p. 322.

15. Prime Minister John Vorster in 1968, quoted in L. S. Stavrianos, *Global Rift: The Third World Comes of Age* (New York: William Morrow, 1981), p. 759.

16. Quoted in Jean Comaroff, *Body of Power, Spirit of Resistance: The Culture and History of a South African People* (Chicago: University of Chicago Press, 1985), p. vi.

17. Quoted in Gwendolen Carter, "The Republic of South Africa: White Political Control Within the African Continent," in Phyllis Martin and Patrick O'Meara, eds., *Africa*, 2nd ed. (Bloomington: Indiana University Press, 1986), p. 353.

18. Quoted in Joe Asila, "No Cash in This Crop," in Wayne Edge, ed., *Global Studies: Africa*, 2nd ed. (Guilford, Conn.: Dushkin, 2006), p. 285.

19. Sanford Unger, *Africa: The People and Politics of an Emerging Continent* (New York: Simon and Schuster, 1985), pp. 131–132.

20. Quoted in Richard A. Fredland, *Understanding Africa: A Political Economy Perspective* (Chicago: Burnham, 2001), p. 139.

21. Quoted in John Follain, "Only the First Step for 'Mama Africa,'" *New Straits Times*, February 23, 1990.

22. Kenneth Goldstein and Saka Acquaye, Liner notes to Acquaye's album *Voices of Africa: High-Life and Other Popular Music* (Nonesuch 72026, n.d.).

23. Quoted in Tejumola Olaniyan, "Narrativizing Postcoloniality: Responsibilities," *Public Culture*, 5/1 (Fall 1992), p. 47.

24. Quoted in Chinweizu, *The West and the Rest of Us: White Predators, Black Slavers, and the African Elite* (New York: Vintage, 1975), p. 1.

25. Quoted in Jennifer Seymour Whitaker, *How Can Africa Survive?* (New York: Harper and Row, 1988), p. 197.

Chapter 31 South Asia, Southeast Asia, and Global Connections, 1945–Present

1. Mochtar Lubis, *Road with No End*, translated by Anthony Johns from 1952 Indonesian edition (Chicago: Henry Regnery, 1968), p. 9.

2. Quoted in Anthony Johns, "Introduction," in Lubis, *Road with No End*, p. 4.

3. Quoted in John R. McLane, ed., *The Political Awakening of India* (Englewood Cliffs, N.J.: Prentice-Hall, 1970), p. 178.

4. Quoted in B. N. Pandey, *The Break-up of British India* (New York: St. Martin's, 1969), p. 209.

5. Faiz Ahmed Faiz, quoted in Sugata Bose and Ayesha Jalal, *Modern South Asia: History, Culture, Political Economy* (New York: Routledge, 1998), p. 200.

6. Rohinton Mistry, *A Fine Balance* (London: Faber, 1996), p. 143.

7. Quoted in Susan Bayly, *Caste, Society and Politics in India from the Eighteenth Century to the Modern Age* (New York: Cambridge University Press, 1999), p. 315.

8. Quoted in Jeremy Marre and Hannah Charlton, *Beats of the Heart: Popular Music of the World* (New York: Pantheon, 1985), p. 150.

9. Quoted in Bose and Jalal, *Modern South Asia*, p. 232.

10. Quoted in Stanley Wolpert, *A New History of India*, 7th ed. (New York: Oxford University Press, 2004), p. 462.

11. Quoted in William J. Duiker, *Ho Chi Minh: A Life* (New York: Hyperion, 2000), p. 323.

12. Quoted in George Donelson Moss, *Vietnam: An American Ordeal*, 4th ed. (Upper Saddle River, N.J.: Prentice-Hall, 2002), p. 40.

13. Jacques Philippe Leclerc, quoted in James S. Olson and Randy Roberts, *Where the Domino Fell: America and Vietnam, 1945–1995*, 3rd ed. (St. James, N.Y.: Brandywine, 1999), p. 28.

14. Quoted in Thomas G. Paterson et al., *American Foreign Policy: A History Since 1900*, 3rd ed. rev. (Lexington, Mass.: D.C. Heath, 1991), p. 553.

15. Anh Vien, quoted in Arleen Eisen Bergman, *Women of Vietnam*, rev. ed. (San Francisco: Peoples Press, 1975), p. 123.

16. Quoted in Neil L. Jamieson, *Understanding Vietnam* (Berkeley: University of California Press, 1993), p. 290.

17. From Idrus, "Surabaya," in Harry Aveling, ed., *From Surabaya to Armageddon: Indonesian Short Stories* (Singapore: Heinemann, 1976), p. 13.

18. From Pramoedya Ananta Toer, "Letter to a Friend in the Country," in Aveling, *From Surabaya*, p. 72.

19. Doreen Fernandez, "Mass Culture and Cultural Policy: The Philippine Experience," *Philippine Studies*, 37 (4th Quarter, 1980), p. 492.

20. "The Kingdom of Mammon," in Amado V. Hernandez, *Rice Grains: Selected Poems* (New York: International Publishers, 1966), p. 31.

21. From Taufiq Ismail's story "Stop Thief!" in David M. E. Roskies, ed., *Black Clouds over the Isle of Gods and Other Modern Indonesian Short Stories* (Armonk, N.Y.: M.E. Sharpe, 1997), p. 97.

22. F. Sionel Jose, quoted in David G. Timberman, *A Changeless Land: Continuity and Change in Philippine Politics* (New York: M.E. Sharpe, 1991), p. xi.

23. "American Junk," by the Apo Hiking Society, quoted in Craig A. Lockard, *Dance of Life: Popular Music and Politics in Southeast Asia* (Honolulu: University of Hawai'i Press, 1998), p. 156.

24. Quoted in Robin Broad and John Cavanaugh, *Plundering Paradise: The Struggle for the Environment in the Philippines* (Berkeley: University of California Press, 1993), p. xvii.

25. Quoted in Pasuk Phongpaichit and Chris Baker, *Thailand: Economy and Politics* (Kuala Lumpur: Oxford University Press, 1995), pp. 413–415.

Societies, Networks, Transitions: The Contemporary World, Since 1945

1. Kathleen Newland and Kamala Chandrakirana Soedjatmoko, eds., *Transforming Humanity: The Visionary Writings of Soedjatmoko* (West Hartford, Conn.: Kumarian Press, 1994), pp. 186–187.

2. Quoted in Jan Pronk, "Globalization": A Developmental Approach," in Jan Nederveen Pieterse, ed., *Global Futures: Shaping Globalization* (London: Zed Books, 2000), p. 46.

3. Daphne Berdahl, quoted in James L. Watson, ed., *Golden Arches East: McDonald's in East Asia* (Stanford, Calif.: Stanford University Press, 1997), p. xvii.

4. Billy Bergman, *Hot Sauces: Latin and Caribbean Pop* (New York: Quill, 1985), p. 18.

5. Quoted in Hans-Peter Martin and Harald Schumann, *The Global Trap: Globalization and the Assault on Democracy and Prosperity* (New York: Zed Books, 1996), p. 163.

6. From Banton's album, *Visions of the World* (IRSD-82003, 1989).

7. Frank Cajka, quoted in Peter Worsley, *The Three Worlds: Culture and World Development* (Chicago: University of Chicago Press, 1984), p. xi.

8. Quoted in Robbie Robertson, *The Three Waves of Globalization: A History of a Developing Global Consciousness* (New York: Zed Books, 2003), p. 263.

9. Lester Pearson, quoted in Lester R. Brown, *World Without Borders* (New York: Vintage, 1972), p. ix.

10. Aldo Leopold, *A Sand County Almanac* (New York: Ballantine, 1966), p. 253.

11. Quoted in J. Donald Hughes, *An Environmental History of the World: Humankind's Changing Role in the Community of Life* (New York: Routledge, 2001), p. 230.

12. Rene Dubos, *So Human an Animal* (New York: Scribner's, 1968), p. 270.

13. Ilya Prigogine, quoted in Federico Mayor and Jerome Bindé, *The World Ahead: Our Future in the Making* (New York: Zed Books, 2001), p. 1.

14. Lester Brown et al., "A World at Risk," in *State of the World 1989* (New York: W.W. Norton, 1989), p. 20.

15. Lewis Carroll, "Alice's Adventures in Wonderland," in *The Complete Works of Lewis Carroll* (New York: Modern Library), pp. 71–72.

INDEX

Abacha, Sani (Nigerian leader), 955
Abacus, 133
Abbas, Shah, 481
Abbasid Caliphate, 279, 280–282 *and map*, 475; cities in, 280, 281; decline of, 281–282, 292; homosexuality in, 420; Mongols and, 282, 292,
Abbas (uncle of Muhammad), 280
Abbeys, 385. *See also* Christian monasteries
Abd al-Qadir (Algerian nationalist), 650
Abduh, Muhammad (Egyptian reformer), 654
Abed, Fazle Hasan (Bengali activist), 981
Abelard and Heloise, 400 *and illus.*
Abidjan (Ivory Coast), 962
Abolition (abolitionists), 606, 607, 631, 793; in Latin America, 618–619; in United States, 610, 611
Aborigines of Australia, 15, 16, 106, 247–248, 795, 1002; European colonists and, 625; land management and, 247, 917; rights of, 626, 914
Abortion, 15, 210, 821. *See also* Birth control; in China, 847; in Europe, 828, 878; women's movement and, 830; in Japan, 855; in United States, 915; in Latin America, 928
Abraham (Hebrew), 71, 73, 74; Islam and, 271, 272
Absolutism: in Africa, 465; in France, 445, 455; in Iran, 941
Abu Hureyra (Syria), 5, 18, 19*(illus.)*, 21
Abu-Lughod, Janet (historian), 417
Abu Simbel (Egypt), statues at, 54*(illus.)*
Academies: *See also* Schools and scholars; in Athens, 157; in China, 301
Acadia (Nova Scotia), 498, 503
Accra, Ghana, 471, 769
Achaemenids (Persia), 146, 223, 257. *See also* Persian Empire; decline of, 151–152; legacy of, 164
Achebe, Chinua (Nigerian writer), 935, 964
Aceh (Sumatra), 379, 529, 553; Islam in, 528, 531, 559, 993; rebellion in, 994
Achilles (Greek warrior), 77
Acid rain, 8
Acropolis, in Athens, 161 *and illus.*
Actium, Battle of (31 B.C.E.), 207
Acupuncture, 133
Adams, John Quincy, 607
Adenauer, Konrad (Germany), 870
Administration: *See also* Bureaucracy; Civil service; Government; in Assyrian Empire, 39; in Egypt, 59, 63; in China, 88, 130, 535; cities as centers of, 106; in Persian Empire, 150; in Mauryan India, 181, 182; in Teotihuacan, 242; empire and, 257; Inca, 352, 353; Swedish, 450; Ottoman, 476, 477; Spanish colonial, 496, 549; colonial Latin America, 500; in English North America, 509; Mughal India, 519, 521; in Siam, 528; colonial Africa, 641, 642, 769; Vietnamese village, 768
Adriaenz, Job (Dutch artist), 428*(illus.)*
Adshead, S. A. M. (historian), 416, 417
Adulis (modern Massawa), 232, 233, 237
Aeneid (Virgil), 212

Aeschylus (Greek playwright), 156, 158, 164
Afghani, Jamal al-Din al- (Persian modernist), 653–654
Afghanistan (Afghans), 165, 257; China and, 129; Greco-Bactrian kingdom, 166, 167 *and map*, 180, 184; Mauryan India and, 181, 183; Sassanian, 223; Islam in, 276; Arab armies in, 365; Delhi Sultanate and, 368; Mughal India and, 518, 520, 523; British war with, 663; Russia and, 663, 711; Pashtun tribes in, 663, 948; Soviet war with, 808, 809, 831, 886–887, 889, 948; refugees from, 825; invasion of, 897; Taliban rule of, 909, 948; Pakistan and, 980
Afghan Wars (1839–1880), 663
Africa (Africans). *See also* Bantu-speaking peoples; East Africa; North Africa; Sub-Saharan Africa; West Africa; human origins in, 8; migrations from (100,000 to 10,000 years ago), 9–10, 12*(map)*; Nok people, 68 *and illus.*, 69, 70; agricultural origins in, 65–66; 1500 B.C.E.–600 C.E., 230*(map)*; long-distance trade and, 227; chronology (400–1591), 329; Islam in, 286, 328–329, 331, 333; America states compared, 328; chronology (1482–1750), 461; Portuguese exploration of, 493; Europeans in, 547; American foods in, 556–557; hybrid social groups in, 558; art of, and European modernism, 604; European colonies in (1914), 593, 635*(map)*, 636; German colonies in, 753; chronology (1912–1936), 765; nationalism in, 634, 769–771; poverty in, 814; Western weaponry in, 795; debt of, 814; migrant workers within, 819; AIDS in, 825; desertification in, 823; labor migration from, 824; arts and literature of, 935; decolonization in, 871, 951–953; stateless societies in, 338
African Americans: mulatto children of, 500; cultures of, 512; in colonial North America, 567; in United States, 606; racial segregation and, 611–612; lynching of, 612, 732; railroads and, 613; in World War II, 743; music of, 606, 614, 770, 827, 916; civil rights movement and, 913, 914 *and illus.*
African National Congress (ANC), 640, 770; majority rule and, 957–958
African nationalism, 632, 634, 769–771, 935; decolonization and, 951–953
African slavery, 285, 420, 466, 556; in colonial Brazil, 505; in colonial North America, 503, 509; disease and, 499; intermarriage and, 557; maroon societies, 512; music and, 340; in plantation zone, 434, 488, 507–509, 510–512 *and illus.*, 550
African slave trade, 340–341, 461, 548–549; African societies and, 473–474; in Atlantic System, 506*(map)*, 510, 512–513; Dutch and, 470; middle passage and, 472–473 *and illus.*; mortality rates in, 472, 473; Portugal and, 467, 468–469, 470; women in, 558; end of, 631–632, 793; in Americas, 619, 791, 793

African Union, 965
Afrikaans language, 639
Afrikaners, 639, 770. *See also* South Africa
Afro-Asiatic languages, 57. *See also* Bantu; Semitic languages
Afro-Brazilians, 574, 598, 779, 914, 929; music and dance of, 619–620, 621
Afro-Caribbeans, 574, 780, 931
Afrocentrism, 255–256
Afro-Cubans, 598, 923
Afro-Eurasia: *See also* Eurasia; peoples of, 32; Ming China and, 313–315; Islam in, 460
Afro-Haitians, 574
Afro-Jamaicans, 931
Afterlife, belief in. *See also* Heaven and hell, concepts of; Reincarnation; Stone Age, 15; in ancient Egypt, 63–64; in Buddhism, 136; in Zoroastrianism, 150; in Islam, 272; in Japan, 323; in Chimu, 343
Agade (Mesopotamia), 31, 32, 37
Agamemnon (Aeschylus), 77, 158
Agamemnon (Greek king), 77
Age grades (generations), in Africa, 339
Agenda for the New Millennium, 818
Age of Reason, 453. *See also* Enlightenment
Age of Revolution. *See* Revolution, Age of
Aggase, Guillaume (French doctor), 397
Agriculture, 791. *See also* Cash crops; Farmers and farming; Plantation zone. *See also* Farmers and farming; Irrigation; Landowners (landownership); Peasants; Plows; Rural society (rural areas); *and specific crops;* Neolithic "revolution" in, 5, 18–24; origins of, 20*(map)*; shifting cultivation, 19, 66, 99, 235; origins of, in Mesopotamia, 33, 34; origins of, in Africa, 65–66; in ancient Egypt, 61, 62*(illus.)*; in early China, 83–84, 89, 120; in Korea, 94; Native American, 99; in Southeast Asia, 91, 92; as historical transition, 104; population growth and, 109; in India, 188, 977; Roman, 200; spread of Islam and, 278, 282; Mongols and, 292; in Korea, 321*(illus.)*; in Japan, 324; in sub-Saharan Africa, 340; Maya, 343; Inca, 353; shifting cultivation, 335, 340, 343, 346; terracing in, 340, 343; in Southeast Asia, 370; in Iceland, 388; in medieval Europe, 389–390 *and illus.*; manorialism, 391–392; in eastern Europe, 407; technology for, 417; in Southeast Asia, 526; Ming China, 534; in China, 537; in Japan, 541; mechanization of, 600; in Australia, 625; commercialization of, 667, 752, 755; in Japan, 705; Soviet collectivization of, 726–727; in Great Depression, 733; Mexican land reform and, 779; peasant-based, 783; communal, in China, 838; Chinese reform of, 844; shifting cultivation, 965; cooperative, in Tanzania, 961–962; Green Revolution in, 816, 908, 973, 977; in Latin America, 927; global warming and, 1011
Aguinaldo, Emilio (Filipino nationalist), 677

from, 825, 987–988; Vietnam War and, 984, 985(map)
Laotili footprints (Tanzania), 9(illus.)
Laozi (Lao Tzu), 125, 137, 253, 254 and illus.. See also Daoism
Lapis lazuli, 30(illus.), 31
Lapita culture (Pacific Islands), 93
Lapulapu (Filipino chief), 529
Larkin, Philip (British poet), 878
Las Casas, Bartolomé de (Spanish missionary), 502
Las Castas (Mexican painter), 486(illus.)
Lateen sails, 191, 291, 409, 433
Latin America, 598, 615–616, 920(map). See also Latin America, colonial; specific countries; colonial heritage, 573–574; Revolutions in, 575–577 and map; Catholicism in, 574, 616, 619; chronology (1823–1914), 599; abolition of slavery and social change in, 618–619; chronology (1861–1914), 616; dictatorships in, 616, 753, 777, 901, 902, 921; independence in, 615, 751; economic patterns in, 618, 926–928; in 1930, 778(map); chronology (1930–1945), 751; politics and modernization in, 777–779 and map; United States' interventions in, 732, 753, 922; cultural nationalism in, 779–780; nationalism in, 784; Japanese immigration to, 794; debt of, 814; Protestantism in, 828; abortion rights in, 830; Catholicism in, 827, 928; American investment in, 902, 903; chronology (1964–1989), 903; chronology (1945–present), 921; migration to United States, 915; poverty in, 789, 926, 927, 932; political change in, 919–932; globalization and, 931–932; wealth disparity in, 1007
Latin America, colonial, 488, 553; Catholicism in, 559; economic changes in, 505, 507; free blacks in, 512; mestizos (mixed-descent) in, 486(illus.), 557; women in, 500–502
Latin language, 215, 257, 384
Latins, 201, 202(map)
Latin West (Europe), 222. See also Medieval Europe
Latvia (Latvians), 744, 884, 887
Latvian language, 892
La Venta (Olmec center), 101
Law of the Retarding Lead, 417
Law of the Sea Treaty, 919
Lawrence, D. H. (British writer), 878
Lawrence, T. E. (British adventurer), 771
Laws (legal codes), 108; Hindu, 52; Mosaic (Hebrew), 38, 73, 74; Code of Hammurabi, 38, 39–41 and illus., 108, 109–110, 112; Persian Empire, 148; Code of Manu, 174, 188; empire and, 549; Roman, 203, 207, 209; Byzantine, 221; Islamic, 463; Islamic Shari'a, 278, 288; French, 571, 622, 647, 648; Ottoman reform and, 647; in Egypt, 648; Islamic, 652; Turkish reforms, 774
League of Nations, 722, 738, 752, 811; mandates in Middle East and, 772, 773(map)
Leavitt, William (American developer), 912
Lebanon (Lebanese), 475, 650, 775, 936, 945. See also Phoenicia (Phoenicians); cedars of,

23, 59, 76; in Latin America, 619; Christians in, 654; in African towns, 640, 752, 787; as merchants, 793; French control of, 772; terrorists in, 831; Palestinians in, 825, 938, 940; civil war in, 944; Shi'ite Islam in, 280
Le dynasty (Vietnam), 377, 378(illus.)
Lefkowitz, Mary (historian), 256
Legal codes. See Laws (legal codes)
Legalism, 125–126, 181, 257; Confucianism and, 129–130, 254
Lei Feng (Chinese model soldier), 846
Leisure pursuits, 27, 48, 110, 240. See also Art; Ballgames; Music; Sports; in China, 535; in Europe, post–World War I, 729
Le Loi (Vietnamese ruler), 377
Lemoinnier (French artist), 454(illus.)
Lenin, Vladimir, 722–723 and illus., 753, 785; New Society and, 724, 726
Leo Africanus (Arab traveler), 461
Leo III, Pope, 383, 386
Leopold, Aldo (environmentalist), 1011–1012
Leopold (Belgium), 634, 643(illus.)
Leo X, Pope, 439
Lepanto, Battle of (1571), 443
Le Pen, Jean-Marie (French politician), 877
Leprosy, 190
Lerner, Gerda (historian), 112
Levant, 33
Leveller movement (England), 455
The Leviathan (Hobbes), 451
Levi Strauss company, 816
Lewis, Sybil, wartime work of, 743
Liang Qichao (Chinese reformer), 696, 698
Liberal Democratic Party (Japan), 852
Liberalization: in China, 845; in South Korea, 860; in Taiwan, 863; in India, 977; in Thailand, 992; in former communist countries, 1007
Liberals (liberalism), 586; in China, 694, 696; in Russia, 723, 724; in United States, 605, 912–913
Liberation movements, in Africa, 953
Liberation theology, 827, 928
Liberia, 632, 909; civil war in, 955
Libertarian principles, 570, 586
Libraries: in Assyrian Empire, 39; in Sui China, 138; in Alexandria, 169; in Islamic Spain, 282, 287; in Il-Khanid Persia, 292; Timbuktu, 333; in Christian monasteries, 385; in Fatimid Egypt, 419; in Timbuktu, 461; in colonial Mexico, 501; Mughal India, 521; Carnegie's philanthropy and, 793
Libya: Egypt and, 60, 63; as Italian colony, 636, 650–651
Life expectancy, 110, 599; in Japan, 853; drop of, in Russia, 893; in Cuba, 923; in Arab countries, 950; in Pakistan, 980; in Sri Lanka, 981; North-South gap in, 1007
Light bulb, 612
Liliuokalani (Hawaii), 614, 784
Lima, Peru, 496, 505, 821
Lincoln, Abraham, 611, 785
Lindbergh, Charles, 732
Lineages: See also Clans; Matrilineal systems; in Africa, 336, 338; matrilineal societies, 461–462, 463, 505; patrilineage, 240, 247, 336, 338, 351, 378, 522

Lingua franca, 766, 770
Lin Zezu (Chinese mandarin), 689–690
Li Po (Chinese poet), 304–305
Li Ruzhen (Chinese novelist), 685
Li Si (first Chinese emperor), 126
Literacy, 26, 113, 789, 818. See also Education; Schools; in ancient China, 88, 90; in Europe, 433, 439; in Funan, 193; in Meroë, 230; Islam and, 286, 329; in Japan, 543, 549, 700, 857; in China, 688, 696, 842, 843; in Soviet Union, 727; in Egypt, 775; of women, 688, 696, 817, 978; spread of, 795; in Siam, 528, 549; in South Korea, 860; in Saudi Arabia, 942; in Arab countries, 950; in Africa, 960; in India, 973, 977, 978; in Sri Lanka, 981; in Vietnam, 987; North-South gap in, 1007
Literature, 113, 735. See also Drama; Libraries; Poets and poetry; Printing technology; Writing; Sumerian, 37, 41–42; in ancient Egypt, 63–64; Chinese, 131, 537, 685, 687, 688; Greek, 157–158; Indian, 48, 190, 668–669, 670, 978; Roman, 212; in Islam, 280–281, 286; Tang China, 304–305; Chinese novels, 311, 313; Heian Japan, 318–320; African oral tradition, 339; in Vietnam, 377; of Southeast Asia, 371, 969, 989, 991, 996; in medieval Europe, 401; medieval English, 405, 407; Italian Renaissance, 409; Safavid Persia, 482; Romanticism, 603; American, 614; Brazilian, 619, 620; Renaissance, 438–439; in Burma, 676; colonial Southeast Asia, 681; Japanese, 706, 730; Korean, 703; Russian, 712; Chinese feminists, 757; Egyptian, 776; Latin American, 779–780, 929; European postcolonialist, 881; Soviet Union, 885, 887; Nigerian, 935; in Middle East, 947; Negritude movement, 964;
Lithuania (Lithuanians), 403, 406(map), 435, 450, 484, 744, 891. See also Baltic region; Poland-Lithuania; Catholicism in, 404; serfdom in, 407; Russia and, 445, 570, 573; Soviet Union and, 884, 887
Little Dragons of Asia, 851(map), 858. See also Hong Kong; Singapore; South Korea; Taiwan; in global system, 863–864
Little Ice Age, 404, 423, 430–431, 491, 498, 556
Liu Xiang (Chinese scholar), 132
Liverpool, England, 513, 578
Living standards (quality of life), 807; in Africa, 960, 961; in Canada, 917; in China, 846, 849, 1009; in India, 972, 977; in Scandinavia, 876, 1013; in South Africa, 957; sustainability of, 1010; Western, 1009
Livingstone, David (British explorer), 633, 634
Llamas and alpacas, 23, 100, 245, 352
Loans. See also Credit; Debt; interest (usury) on, 41, 393, 395, 433, 435; to Europe, by United States, 728, 732, 734; to villagers, 819
Local culture, globalization and, 1004, 1006, 1012
Local development, world trade and, 790, 1002
Locke, John, 454–455, 503, 536–537, 586; American Revolution and, 568; Enlightenment and, 454–455, 503, 537
Lockheed Corporation, 852
Loess (soil), 83

governmental crisis in, 702–703; modernization in, 700, 702–703; opening of, 702; problems and reform in, 701–702; Qing China compared, 699–700; society and culture, 700–701; defeat of, 704

Tokyo (Edo), 795, 854, 857; street stalls and tradesmen in, 701(illus.); Tokugawa era, 542–543, 551, 700, 704; population growth in, 821

Toleration. See Religious toleration

Toleration Act (England), 449

Tolosa, Luis Mariano de (Brazilian planter), 510, 511

Tolstoy, Leo (Russian writer), 712, 716

Toltecs (Mexico), 246, 344, 347, 348(map); rise and fall of, 343

Tomatoes, 263, 500, 556

Tombs. See also Burials (cemeteries; graves); in ancient Egypt, 58, 59(illus.), 61, 62 and illus., 64; Mesopotamian, 38(illus.); in China, 87, 130; pilgrimages to, 284; in Khartoum, 628(illus.)

Tonga, 92, 93 and map, 249, 625, 918, 919, 1011

Tonghak Rebellion (Korea), 708

Tongmen Hui (Chinese Alliance Association), 697

Tools, 11, 96. See also Iron and steel industry; Technology; human capacity for using, 10, 13, 14; agriculture and, 18; early metalworking and, 24; stone, 10, 14, 96, 98, 489–490

Topiltzin (Toltec), 343

Topkapi Sarai palace (Istanbul), 479

Tordesillas, Treaty of (1494), 493

Tourism, 1004

Tours, Battle of (732), 276, 386

Toussaint L'Overture, Dominique (Haiti), 574

Towns. See Cities and towns

Toxic waste, in Africa, 965

Trade agreements, 814

Trade beads, 98 and illus.

Trade (commerce; trade networks), 488. See also Barter; Merchants (merchant class); Maritime trade (ships and shipping); Slave trade; Trade routes; and specific commodities. See also World economy (world trade); origins of long-distance, 26; Mesopotamian, 32, 35; Egyptian, 55, 59, 63, 75, 76, 108, 174; Nubian, 67; Central Asian, 89; in Americas, 97, 98, 100; cities and, 107–108; transportation and, 104, 106; Southeast Asia, 92; Carthaginian, 205, 235; Roman, 211; in Southern Africa, 236; Kushite, 228–229; Axial Age empires and, 257; cultural contact and, 262–263; in Mecca, 274; Mongols and, 292; Muslim-Christian, 295; imperial China, 299, 306 and illus., 315, 359, 375; government monopolies, 309; Japan and, 324, 541, 543; in sub-Saharan Africa, 327–328; East Africa and, 335, 336; in Sudanic Africa, 340; Pueblo Indians and, 344; Toltec, 343; Cahokia, 346; in Antwerp, 429; in early modern Europe, 430; in Southeast Asia, 371; Portuguese, 434; medieval Europe, 389, 393–394, 409; Viking, 403; capitalism and, 435; Dutch, 435, 447; in coastal Africa, 462(map), 464; interregional contact and, 412, 414; Ottoman, 477; Safavis Persia, 481–482; Pacific Islander, 494;

expansion of Islam and, 528; in Southeast Asia, 526; China, 537–539; emerging world economy and, 553, 555; in Korea, 541; British Empire and, 590; Indian, 659, 668; protectionism of, in United States, 605, 611, 612; Egyptian modernization and, 648; Singapore and, 673; Chinese, with Europe, 688; Islamic, 1001; of United States, in China, 695; of United States, in Japan, 702; Asian immigrants and, 793; Chinese, 844; Australian with Asia, 918; United States' imbalance, 903–904

Trade diaspora, 186, 263, 291, 415; Armenian, 481–482; Chinese, 693, 793; Indian, 520; in Latin America, 619

Trade embargo. See Trade sanctions (boycott, embargo)

Trade liberalization, 745. See also Free trade

Trade monopoly, 434, 531, 581, 690, 762

Trade routes, 23, 26, 413(map). See also Caravan trade and routes; Exploration (expeditions); Indian Ocean trade (maritime system); Silk Road; Trade; Trans-Saharan trade and caravan routes; in Australia, 16; Minoan and Mycenaean, 72(map), 75–76; Austronesian, 93; Phoenician, 76–77, 108, 149, 163; Persian, 146; Andean, 100, 243; Mediterranean, 108, 199; Byzantine, 221–222; Axial Age, 253, 257, 258(map); disease and, 261; Roman Empire, 211–212; Ptolemaic Egypt, 205–206; Aksumite, 232, 233; Maya, 239; Teotihuacan, 239, 242; North American Indians, 246; transportation and, 257, 259; spread of Islam and, 290–291 and map; Byzantium and, 402; Mongol Empire and, 420; Muslim domination of, 645

Traders. See Merchants (traders)

Trade sanctions (boycott; embargo), 1007; on Japan, 738; on Iran, 809; on China, 837; on Vietnam, 909; on Cuba, 923, 924; on Chile, 925; on Jamaica, 931; on Iraq, 942; on Iran, 941; on Vietnam, 987

Traditional culture: Japanese, 856; in Taiwan, 863; in Middle East, 949; Western pop culture and, 1012; globalization and, 1001, 1002, 1003, 1006, 1012

"Trail of Tears" (American Indian removal), 610

Transitions, concept of, xxxi

Transnational economy, 813

Transportation, 593. See also Canals; Roads and highways; Railroads; Ships and shipping; in China, 82, 132; Indian roads, 520, 978; in medieval Europe, 391; Ming China, 534; Mongol China, 310; steam power and, 590; trade networks and, 104, 106; trade routes and, 257, 259; in United States, 612–613; migration and, 791; communication and, 794–795, 1012

Trans-Saharan trade and caravan routes, 227, 230(map), 258(map), 330(map), 413(map), 555; camels for, 68, 227, 235, 328; Hausa states and, 333; slavery and, 341; sub-Saharan Africa and, 68, 235; Timbuktu and, 331, 461; Kanem-Bornu and, 463; slave trade and, 466, 472(map), 474

Trans-Siberian Railway, 711, 795

Transvaal (South Africa), 639, 640

Travel and travelers, 422, 488, 795. See also Exploration (expeditions); Pilgrims; Roads; Maritime trade (ships and shipping); Trade routes; Transportation; African (See Ibn Battuta, Muhammad ibn Abdullah); mapmaking and, 106, 149, 249(illus.); Arabs in East Africa, 327, 335; Herodotus in Persia, 148, 149, 150, 160, 162; Greeks, 173, 185, 199, 233, 237, 253; Marco Polo, 306, 311(map), 312, 380, 415, 491; maritime trade and, 291; Muslims in Africa, 329; in Southeast Asia, 380, 559; Zheng He, 314–315 and map, 380, 418, 423, 491, 539; in early modern world, 547; Japanese, 597–598; Europeans, in United States, 606; of Mark Twain, 783

Treatymaking, Egyptian-Hittite, 109(illus.)

Treaty system, in China, 690–691, 696, 698

Tree-planting campaigns, 818, 822–823; in China, 838; Chipko, in India, 823, 977

Trekking, in South Africa, 470, 638, 639(illus.)

Trench warfare, World War I, 719, 720(illus.)

Trent, Council of (1545–1563), 442, 456, 883

Tribal homelands, in Africa, 957

Tribal nomads, 27, 235. See also Nomadic peoples; Quraysh tribe specific tribes; in India, 47–48

Tribes, Afghan Pashtun, 663, 948

Tribunes of Rome, 203

Tribute system: Aztec, 496; China and East Asia, 534, 534(map), 696; Chinese, 129, 315, 320, 377; in colonial Latin America, 507; Assyrian, 146; Gupta India, 181(map); Persian Empire, 147, 163; Aztec, 347–348

Trieu, Lady (Vietnamese rebel), 195

Trigonometry, 185, 287

Trinidad, 493, 509, 512, 619, 668, 780; as British colony, 497; calypso music in, 621; Great Depression in, 752; oil from, 751

Tripartite Pact of 1940, 738

Triple Entente (Britain, France, Russia), 716, 718(map)

Triremes (Greek ships), 160

Tristan, Flora (women's rights activist), 587

Trojan War, 77, 158

Tropical agriculture, 553. See also Plantation zone; in Central America, 618

Tropics, environment of, 64. See also Rain forests; specific tropical region

Troubadours, 270, 282, 394

Troy (Anatolia), 76, 77, 158

Trudeau, Pierre (Canadian leader), 917

Truman, Harry S, 869, 902; fear of Communism, 871; Korean War and, 859, 907; Vietnamese independence and, 983

Truman Doctrine, 871

Trung sisters (Vietnamese rebels), 194, 195

Truth, Sojourner (abolitionist), 606

Ts'ai Shu (Chinese artisan), 81

Tswana (South Africa), 335

Tuberculosis, 346, 499, 705, 928

Tudor dynasty (England), 408

Tula (Toltec capital), 343, 344(illus.)

Tull, Jethro (English inventor), 453

Tunis, 276

Tunisia, 480, 945; as French colony, 650

Tupac Amaru II (Peruvian rebel), 500, 574

Tupaia (Polynesian priest), 625

and, 869–870; homosexuality in, 880; postwar reconstruction of, 868; as welfare state, 876; church-operated schools in, 882

West Indies. *See* Caribbean region

West Lake Poetry Society (China), 307

Westphalia, Treaty of (1648), 444

Whale hunting, 625

What Is to Be Done (Lenin), 723

Wheat: in Argentina, 752; in Canada, 623, 716; in China, 84; domestication of, 65; Egyptian export of, 205; government subsidies for, 817; in India, 43, 44, 45, 52; in medieval Europe, 390

Wheatley, Phyllis (African slave poet), 631

Wheelbarrow, 390, 414

Wheel of life, 176–177. *See also* Reincarnation

Wheels, 37, 106

White collar workers, 583

"White man's burden," 593, 667, 677

White Russians, 724, 725(*map*)

White supremacy: *See also* Racism; in South Africa, 470, 638, 640, 770, 956–957

Whitman, Walt (American poet), 614

Widow burning (sati), 188, 359, 361

Wilde, Oscar (Irish writer), 601

Wilhelm II, Kaiser (Germany), 719, 721

William and Mary (England), 449

William I, Kaiser (Germany), 584

William of Normandy, 391, 397

William of Orange, 443, 449

Williams, Betty (Irish activist), 878

Williams, Hank (American musician), 915

Williams, Henry (Jamaican slave), 631

Wilson, Woodrow, 615, 722, 732; World War I and, 720; Fourteen Points of, 721; Russian Communism and, 724; Mexico and, 753

Windmills, 390, 555; in Caribbean, 508(*illus.*)

Wine, 22, 48, 110; in China, 87, 88, 305; in Mediterranean region, 71, 75, 163, 200; in Algeria, 650; in Vietnam, 751

"Winner-take-all" economy, 912

Winthrop, John (Puritan leader), 503, 569

Witches, torture of, 456

Wolf, Eric (historian), 550

Wollstonecraft, Mary, 571, 602

Wolof people of Senegal, 339, 636

Wolsey, Cardinal of Canterbury, 408

Women. *See also* Family; Feminism; Gender relations; Marriage; Matrilineal societies; Sexuality; agriculture and, 21; pottery and, 19; as religious specialists, 24; as Sumerian priestesses, 35, 37; in African politics, 461–462, 463; Indian, 48; in ancient Egypt, 61, 63; in Minoan Crete, 75 *and illus.*; Arawak, 490(*illus.*); as shamans, in Korea, 94; property rights of, 35, 48, 61, 110; cloth production by, 14, 26, 61, 110, 111, 340; in early China, 87, 131–132; work of, 107; as prostitutes, 40, 159; as Vietnamese rebels, 194, 195; in Greece, 154, 158 *and illus.*; childbearing and childcare, 15, 24, 111, 159; in Japan, 140, 318–320, 323; as nuns, 137, 179, 218, 261, 407; early Christianity and, 217, 218, 222; property rights of, 188, 210, 221; Roman, 210, 263–264; Kushite queens, 229; Native American, 98, 240; Hindu, in India, 360–361; as African queens, 333, 338; Chinese footbinding of,

308, 311, 419, 536, 685, 696, 754; in Angkor, 374; in Korea, 317, 321; in imperial China, 302; in Inca royalty, 351; in Islam, 285–286 *and illus.*, 288, 369, 419; in Japan, 543; in American Revolution, 568; in markets, 531; in Mexican Revolution, 617 *and illus.*; in Mughal India, 519–520, 522, 523; African colonialism and, 643–644; "new women" in India, 670; Islamic modernization and, 652; Ottoman, 477, 480; sati (widow burning) and, 519, 558; in Siam, 528; as slaves, 510–511 *and illus.*, 512; in Southeast Asia, 528; in Spanish Americas, 500–501, 502–503; Vietnamese poets, 674; in Philippines' revolution, 677; birth control and, 819, 821; development and, 819; in Japan, 729–731; AIDS and, 825; Russian economic woes and, 893; in suburban United States, 914; protests by, 901; Islamic modernization and, 934(*illus.*), 943; Palestinian Muslim, 941; poverty of, worldwide, 1007

Women, education of: in Islam, 286; in Europe, 400 *and illus.*, 454; in Indonesia, 681, 682; in China, 536, 558–559, 688, 754; in Egypt, 653; in Korea, 703; in Japan, 543, 700, 854; in Russia, 712; reduced fertility and, 821; in Saudi Arabia, 943; in India, 978

Women, seclusion of (purdah), 670; in Africa, 461; in India, 522; in Middle East, 945; in Safavid Persia, 481, 482; in Saudi Arabia, 943; veiling and, 652, 943, 945

Women, work of, 729. *See also* Market women; in textile industry, 474, 502, 528, 532, 553, 601, 606, 612(*illus.*), 613, 680, 693, 705; in colonial Africa, 643–644, 790; market women, 643–644, 680, 769, 790, 928, 963; in World War II, 743; in Africa, 769, 963; multinational corporations and, 815; fertility rates and, 817; in China, 847; in Mexican border factories, 816, 923, 927(*illus.*); in Europe, 878; in Japan, 854, 855(*illus.*); in South Korea, 860; in Soviet Union, 887; in United States, 915; Mexican, 923, 927(*illus.*); in Latin America, 928; in Vietnam, 968(*illus.*); prostitution and, 893; in Malaysia, 997, 998; political leadership of, 982, 999, 1013

Women Against AIDS in Africa, 962

Women's movement, 830. *See also* Feminism; de Beauvoir and, 878, 879 *and illus.*; in India, 978; in Russia, 712

Women's rights, 221, 607, 796. *See also* Voting rights (suffrage) for women; French Revolution and, 571; in Latin America, 577, 921, 928; in United States, 569, 613–614; in Europe, 601–602; in Australia, 626, 917; in China, 692, 697, 755; in Egypt, 653, 775–776; in India, 669, 763–764, 973, 978; in Mexico, 618, 779; in Vietnam, 674; in Japan, 731, 850; in Nigeria, 769; in Turkey, 774; in Chile, 777; in Brazil, 779; in Africa, 822–823; in China, 837, 843, 848; in Morocco, 937; in Iran, 941, 942; Islam and, 945; in Afghanistan, 948; in Kenya, 955; in Bangladesh, 981; in Pakistan, 980; Islam in Malaysia and, 997; march for, in India, 1014(*illus.*)

Wong, R. Bin (historian), 551

Woodblock printing, 137, 303–304, 409; in China, 534, 842(*illus.*); in Japan, 543, 544(*illus.*), 700–701 *and illus.*, 796; in Korea, 316

Woodstock music festival (1968), 913

Woolen trade, in Europe, 394

Woolf, Virginia (British writer), 735

Work, gendered division of, 5, 14, 15

Working class, 420. *See also* Labor; Slaves; British industrialization and, 581–583; British protest, 586; Marxist proletariat, 587–588; European, 590, 729, 875; wages of, 600; sexuality and, 601; socialism and, 602; Chinese, 692(*illus.*), 693, 694; Japanese, 705, 731; in Nazi Germany, 737; Russian, 712, 722, 723, 724; Mexican, 779; European welfare states and, 876, 877; in United States, 731, 912; rock music and, 881; Argentina, 921; Cuban, 923

Working women. *See* Women, work of

World Bank, 745, 814, 965

World Conference on Women (1995), 830

World Council of Churches, 811, 882

World cultures, 1006

World Cup (football), 929

World economy (global trade), 547, 729, 784, 789–791. *See also* Globalization; African slave trade and, 474; Ottoman role in, 480; Java in, 532; China in, 537–539, 550, 693, 785, 802, 806, 844, 847; Southeast Asia and, 533, 678, 679–680, 992; Asia and Europe in, 553–555 *and map*; emerging, 551, 553–555; trading networks and, 553, 555; Latin America in, 505, 507, 618; British Empire and, 590; Africa in, 632, 642–644, 965; British Malaya and, 674; Vietnam and, 674; European influence on, 716, 789, 875, 877; Great Depression and, 732, 733, 734; Axis Powers and, 738; colonial ports in, 752; Gandhi's opposition to, 762; inequality in, 790; Western domination of, 783; world system and, 786, 788; spread of industrialization and, 790–791; underdevelopment and, 816–817; women in, 817; cosmopolitan cities and, 824; Japan in, 853, 857; North Korea's withdrawal from, 861; South Korea in, 860; United States' supremacy in, 722, 873, 903, 911; North-South gap, 1006; environmental sustainability and, 1010

World Health Organization, 810

World history, foundations of xxvii, 104–110. *See also* Historians; political, 108–109; social and cultural, 109–110; technological, 104–105; urban and economic, 106–108

World music, 1006

World politics, 812; changes in, 802

World Social Forum (Brazil), 829

World-system concept, 786–788

World Trade Center attack, 831, 909, 943, 1003

World Trade Organization (WTO), 814, 898; China and, 849

World War I, 715–722; European societies prior to, 716; preludes to, 717, 719; Armenian genocide in, 647; causes of, 790; colonialism and, 750, 952; course of,

GREENLAND
(DENMARK)

ICELAND

ALASKA
(U.S.)

CANADA

UNITED
KING

IRELAND

45°N

UNITED STATES

PORTUGAL
SPAIN

Azores

ATLANTIC OCEAN

MOROCCO

30°N

Bermuda

WESTERN
SAHARA
(MOROCCO)

AL

MEXICO

BAHAMAS

CUBA   DOMINICAN REP.
                    Virgin Is.
JAMAICA HAITI   ST. KITTS AND NEVIS
         Puerto Rico ANTIGUA AND BARBUDA
BELIZE   DOMINICA
HONDURAS   ST. VINCENT AND
           ST. LUCIA THE GRENADINES
GUATEMALA   BARBADOS
EL SALVADOR GRENADA
        NICARAGUA   TRINIDAD AND TOBAGO

MAURITANIA

MAL

CAPE
VERDE   SENEGAL
         GAMBIA
GUINEA-BISSAU
         GUINEA

BURKI
FASO

15°N

PACIFIC OCEAN

Hawaiian Is.

COSTA RICA

PANAMA

VENEZUELA   GUYANA
            SURINAME
COLOMBIA   FR. GUIANA

SIERRA LEONE

LIBERIA

IVORY
COAST

GHANA TO
EQUATORIAL GUIN

Equator

Galapagos Is.

ECUADOR

SÃO TOMÉ AND PRINC

R

0°

PERU

BRAZIL

15°S

ABBREVIATIONS

BOLIVIA

AUS.	AUSTRIA
BEL.	BELGIUM
B. H.	BOSNIA AND HERZEGOVINA
CR.	CROATIA
CZ.	CZECH REPUBLIC
DEN.	DENMARK
HUNG.	HUNGARY
LUX.	LUXEMBOURG
M.N.	MONTENEGRO
MAC.	FORMER YUGOSLAV REPUBLIC
	OF MACEDONIA
NETH.	NETHERLANDS
SERB.	SERBIA
SLK.	SLOVAKIA
SLN.	SLOVENIA
SWITZ.	SWITZERLAND

CHILE   PARAGUAY

30°S

URUGUAY

ARGENTINA

0   500 1000 1500 Km.

0   500   1000

45°S

Falkland Is.

60°S
        150°W 135°W 120°W 105°W 90°W   75°W   60°W   45°W   30°W   15°W

75°S

Conversion Factors and Relationships

Length

SI unit: meter (m)

$1\,m = 1.0936\,yd$
$1\,cm = 0.39370\,in$
$1\,in = 2.54\,cm\,(exactly)$
$1\,km = 0.62137\,mi$
$1\,mi = 5280\,ft$
$\quad\; = 1.6093\,km$
$1\,Å = 10^{-10}\,m$

Temperature

SI unit: kelvin (K)

$0\,K = -273.15\,°C$
$\quad\;\; = -459.67\,°F$
$K = °C + 273.15$
$°C = \dfrac{(°F - 32)}{1.8}$
$°F = 1.8\,(°C) + 32$

Energy (derived)

SI unit: joule (J)

$1\,J = 1\,kg \cdot m^2/s^2$
$\quad = 0.23901\,cal$
$\quad = 1\,C \cdot V$
$\quad = 9.4781 \times 10^{-4}\,Btu$
$1\,cal = 4.184\,J$
$1\,eV = 1.6022 \times 10^{-19}\,J$

Pressure (derived)

SI unit: pascal (Pa)

$1\,Pa = 1\,N/m^2$
$\quad\;\; = 1\,kg/(m \cdot s^2)$
$1\,atm = 101{,}325\,Pa$
$\quad\;\;\; = 760\,torr$
$\quad\;\;\; = 14.70\,lb/in^2$
$1\,bar = 10^5\,Pa$
$1\,torr = 1\,mmHg$

Volume (derived)

SI unit: cubic meter (m^3)

$1\,L = 10^{-3}\,m^3$
$\quad = 1\,dm^3$
$\quad = 10^3\,cm^3$
$\quad = 1.0567\,qt$
$1\,gal = 4\,qt$
$\quad\;\;\; = 3.7854\,L$
$1\,cm^3 = 1\,mL$
$1\,in^3 = 16.39\,cm^3$
$1\,qt = 32\,fluid\,oz$

Mass

SI unit: kilogram (kg)

$1\,kg = 2.2046\,lb$
$1\,lb = 453.59\,g$
$\quad\;\; = 16\,oz$
$1\,amu = 1.66053873 \times 10^{-27}\,kg$
$1\,ton = 2000\,lb$
$\quad\;\;\; = 907.185\,kg$
$1\,metric\,ton = 1000\,kg$
$\quad\quad\quad\quad\;\; = 2204.6\,lb$

Geometric Relationships

π	$= 3.14159\ldots$
Circumference of a circle	$= 2\pi r$
Area of a circle	$= \pi r^2$
Surface area of a sphere	$= 4\pi r^2$
Volume of a sphere	$= \dfrac{4}{3}\pi r^3$
Volume of a cylinder	$= \pi r^2 h$

Fundamental Constants

Atomic mass unit	1 amu 1 g	$= 1.66053873 \times 10^{-27}\,kg$ $= 6.02214199 \times 10^{23}\,amu$
Avogadro's number	N_A	$= 6.02214199 \times 10^{23}/mol$
Bohr radius	a_0	$= 5.29177211 \times 10^{-11}\,m$
Boltzmann's constant	k	$= 1.38065052 \times 10^{-23}\,J/K$
Electron charge	e	$= 1.60217653 \times 10^{-19}\,C$
Faraday's constant	F	$= 9.64853383 \times 10^4\,C/mol$
Gas constant	R	$= 0.08205821\,(L \cdot atm/(mol \cdot K)$ $= 8.31447215\,J/(mol \cdot K)$
Mass of an electron	m_e	$= 5.48579909 \times 10^{-4}\,amu$ $= 9.10938262 \times 10^{-31}\,kg$
Mass of a neutron	m_n	$= 1.00866492\,amu$ $= 1.67492728 \times 10^{-27}\,kg$
Mass of a proton	m_p	$= 1.00727647\,amu$ $= 1.67262171 \times 10^{-27}\,kg$
Planck's constant	h	$= 6.62606931 \times 10^{-34}\,J \cdot s$
Speed of light in vacuum	c	$= 2.99792458 \times 10^8\,m/s\,(exactly)$

SI Unit Prefixes

a	f	p	n	μ	m	c	d	k	M	G	T	P	E
atto	femto	pico	nano	micro	milli	centi	deci	kilo	mega	giga	tera	peta	exa
10^{-18}	10^{-15}	10^{-12}	10^{-9}	10^{-6}	10^{-3}	10^{-2}	10^{-1}	10^3	10^6	10^9	10^{12}	10^{15}	10^{18}

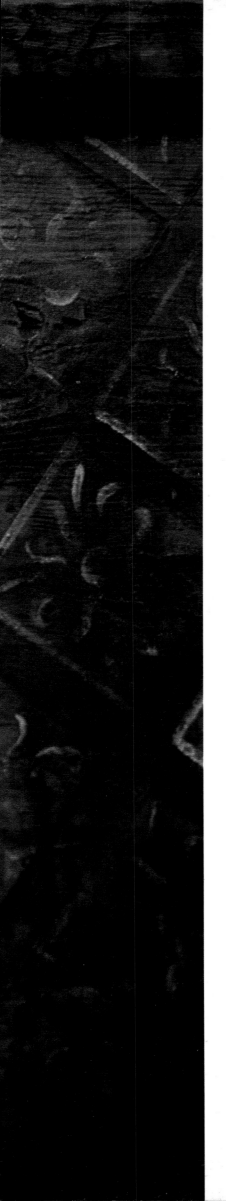

THE PRAGUE CASTLE
AND ITS TREASURES

Texts
Charles, Prince of Schwarzenberg
Ivo Hlobil, Ladislav Kesner, Ivan Muchka, Tomáš Vlček

Photography
Miroslav Hucek and Barbara Hucková

Design
Emil M. Bührer

English translation
John Gilbert

THE VENDOME PRESS • NEW YORK

Coordinating Editor
Irina Mirabaud, Lucerne

English Edition Editor
Madge Phillips

Colour separation by
Lanarepo, Lana

Typesetting and layout by
Avalon

Printed and bound in Italy by
Grafiche Lema,
Maniago PN

© 1992 Motovun (Switzerland) Co-Publishing
Company Ltd., Lucerne;
Barbara and Miroslav Hucek, Prague (photographs)

Published in the USA in 1994
by The Vendome Press,
1370 Avenue of the Americas,
New York, NY 10019

Distributed in the USA and Canada
by Rizzoli International Publications
through St. Martin's Press
175 Fifth Avenue, New York, NY 10010

Library of Congress Cataloging-in-Publication Data
Hradschin. English
    The Prague Castle and its treasures / by Prince Karl
von Schwarzenberg et al.: introduction by Václav Havel:
photographs by Miroslav Hucek and Barbara Hucková.
    p.   cm.
    ISBN 0-86565-952-4
    1. Art. Czeck — Czeck Republic — Prague.
2. Christian art and symbolism — Czeck Republic —
Prague. 3. Pražsky hrad. 4. Prague (Czech Republic)
— Buildings, structures, etc. I. Schwarzenberg Karl.
II. Hucek, Miroslav. III. Hucková, Barbara. IV. Title.
N6833.P72H7313 1994
728.8'1'0943712—dc20   94-3827
                                        CIP

Jan Žižka, military leader of the Hussites, with his
army. Jena Codex, before 1500.

'Ancient, sublime, shrouded in mystery,
like a precious jewel borne by a pauper woman,
unalterably beautiful beneath her wrinkles:
such is Prague in the hands of Bohemia'.

Pavel Kohout

Prague
stands at the crossroads of history,
where past and present converge,
as on a measureless stage that has seen
mighty political encounters and manoeuvres.
Here, the representatives of religious and worldly powers
have clashed with one another in argument and battle.
Here, on the stage of European diplomacy,
threads of intrigue have been woven,
stratagems have been laid,
and the drama of revolution has been enacted.
For in Prague,
history has seldom paraded as light-hearted entertainment,
burlesque or empty comedy.
Its constantly repeated themes are far more serious:
they have to do with the nation's very existence,
its striving for statehood and its claim to
its rightful place in Europe.

Václav Havel

Václav Havel

Bust of Charles IV by Peter Parler, placed in the triforium of St Vitus's Cathedral, a realistic representation of the emperor in old age. Of all monarchs, Charles IV was undoubtedly the best equipped to build the residence of the Czech and Germanic kings and emperors, and it was not by chance that the Czech people expressed their admiration for him by dubbing him "father of the country".

Pages 8-9: *view of Prague from the Strahov Gardens.* This view from the east shows the picturesque site of the town in the Vltava basin, dominated by the powerful towers of Prague Castle. On the right is the crest of Petřin Hill.

Below: *the Charles Bridge,* built in 1357, by order of Charles IV, on the site of the Romanesque Judith Bridge, destroyed by flooding. Resting on sixteen arches, the bridge is 520 m (1700 ft) long and 10 m (33 ft) wide. Between 1683 and 1714, it was decorated with 30 statues of saints.

Pages 12-13: *classic panorama of Prague Castle* reflected in the waters of the Vltava with, in the foreground, the Gothic bridge and its statues, and the Malá Strana quarter dominated by the Baroque St Nicholas's Church; behind are the harmonious façades of the castle buildings, above which are outlined the towers of St George's Basilica and St Vitus's Cathedral.

Pages 14-15: *general view of Prague Castle from the Malá Strana tower of the Charles Bridge*, with St Nicholas's and St Thomas's churches. It also shows an important historical monument, the Bishop's Court, originally the residence of the bishops of Prague, of which only one polygonal tower (lower right) survives.

ORIGINS AND HISTORY OF PRAGUE CASTLE

There is an engraving, dating back to the Baroque era, of Bohemia, shown as a rose with one hundred petals, at the heart of which is Prague. But the true heart of Bohemia always was, and still remains, Prague Castle. Its origins are veiled in mystery. At the end of the 11th century, Kosmas, the first Czech chronicler, resorted to legend: the daughter of the mythical king Krok, the aristocratic, gracious and chaste Princess Libuše, endowed with the gift of prophecy, had predicted the future to the elders of the nation in these terms:

'I see a great castle whose glory will reach to Heaven; it is located in a deep forest, bounded by the waves of the Vltava. There, a large rocky mountain called Petřín heaves like the back of a porpoise, the seahog, and winds towards the river. You will find there a man who is digging out a threshold. And because even the great noblemen must bow low before a threshold, you shall give the name Prague (*Praha*) to the castle that you shall found there. This castle shall then give birth to two golden olives whose tips shall reach the seventh heaven; and miracles and wonders shall light up the world. All those generations living in the Czech lands, and other peoples too, shall pay honour to them with gifts and sacrifices. The first olive shall be called *Více slávy* (*Svatý Václav*) ['Greater glory', St Wenceslas]; the second *Voje utěcha* (*Svatý Vojtěch*) ['Consolation of Voj', St Vojtěch = Adalbert].

Such was the prophecy of Libuše, whose marriage to the 'ploughman' Přemysl gave rise to the line of the Přemyslids which gradually came to dominate the whole of Bohemia.

What was the true origin of Prague Castle? Apparently, after its arrival in the country, the Slav tribe of the Czechs moved north towards the Elbe. Subsequently it set up one of its earliest fortresses, named Levý Hradec (now situated some 10 kilometres north of Prague), on a rocky promontory facing the Vltava. It was here, too, according to legend, that the first Christian church in Bohemia was built.

The tribe chose its headquarters in a place where the Vltava, until then hemmed in by steep hills, forms a meander, with a flat catchment basin that had been inhabited for centuries. There, almost in the very centre of the country, protected on all sides by mountain barriers, at the most convenient spot for fording the river, stood a crossroads of ancient trade routes which ran northward from the south and the west until they reached the sea, thence proceeding onward to the Near and Far East. To the north, the basin was defended by a string of prehistoric strongholds, the names of which are lost. To the south, on the river's left bank, stood the powerful castle of Děvín. On the opposite bank, a little higher up, the castle of Vyšehrad, regarded in Czech royal legend as the most ancient of princely seats, perched on a rock, surrounded by the Vltava and the Botič. Certainly, around the middle of the 12th century, the castle often served as the residence of Czech monarchs (who kept there the bast slippers worn by the first prince, Přemysl, to recall his peasant origins); and until the Hussite Wars, Vyšehrad, at various times, contained more shrines than Prague Castle itself.

In the middle of this protected basin, the mountain of Petřín (which must originally have been fortified as well) narrowed to form the legendary 'porpoise's back', shielded to the south by a sheer drop down to the river, and to the north by the steep valley of the Brusnice stream. So all that was needed for defence was a deep trench dug across the col formed by the mountain backbone (i.e. between the present Archbishop's Palace and the First Courtyard of the castle). The oldest stronghold was protected by ramparts with palisades and gates facing west, south and east; inside was the prince's residence and a raised area called Žiži, doubtless a tomb (apparently situated between the eastern end of the modern cathedral and St George's Basilica), which may have been used in a fire cult and, at the same time, as the stone base of the prince's throne.

Opposite page: *statue of St Wenceslas* on the cornice of the façade wall of the chapel dedicated to him in St Vitus's Cathedral. The principal patron saint of Bohemia is represented in a typical guise of the Middle Ages, as a knight, his shield emblazoned with a spread eagle. The statue, in marl, with precious traces of medieval polychromy, is by Peter Parler and Heinrich of Gmünd (1373).

The Czechs immediately adopted the Christian faith that had arrived from the West: in the year 845 fourteen Czech princes went to be baptised at Ratisbon (Regensburg). The second wave of Christianity, certainly much stronger, was of Eastern origin: in 863 Cyril and Methodius were sent as missionaries from Constantinople to Moravia, carrying relics of St Clement (Kliment). It was to this saint that the first churches of Levý Hradec, Vyšehrad and Stará Boleslav — but not Prague Castle — were dedicated. The earliest Christian church in Prague was built, in the late 9th century, in honour of the Virgin Mary.

During the first third of the 10th century, Prague Castle was the scene of a dramatic confrontation between the forces of paganism and the new faith. Before 921, Prince Vratislav had built St George's Basilica: the story of the saint's fight against the dragon was surely understood as being symbolic (the rotunda of Mount Říp is dedicated to the same saint and it was said that a dragon lived in the castle of Wawel at Cracow). According to Czech legends, the drama reached its culmination after the death of Prince Vratislav in 921, while his son Wenceslav (Václav) was still a minor. Vratislav's widow, Drahomíra, who must have been a staunch pagan, forced the Princess Ludmila (whom legends say was the grandmother of St Wenceslas) to flee to Tetín Castle, on the Berounka, and then sent assassins who strangled her. Later, Prince Wenceslas brought the body of Ludmila to St George's Basilica at Prague Castle. But because of the spring that gushed from the ground, the body could not be buried there, and it was only when the basilica was consecrated by the bishop of Ratisbon that it was permitted to lie in peace.

During the reign of Prince Wenceslas, when the Church of Cyril and Methodius was destroyed by the Hungarian invasion, Bohemia turned its spiritual gaze to the West. This is proved by contacts that already existed with the bishop of Ratisbon and, moreover, by the fact that the new church which Prince Wenceslas now built in Prague Castle was dedicated to St Vitus (Vít). He was a saint virtually unknown at home but venerated in Saxony (only a few historians have sought to associate this saint's name with the cult of Svantovít which flourished among the Slavs on the shores of the Baltic). Prince Wenceslas had obtained the shoulder of the saint from Emperor Henry I of Saxony and the rotunda of St Vitus subsequently became the foundation of the cathedral. The flames that appear on the eagle of St Wenceslas are said to refer to the importance of the saint and to the legend of his martyrdom.

In fact, the death of Wenceslas was the occasion for the third confrontation between the pagan and Christian faiths, from both west and east. In either 929 or 935 Wenceslas was invited by his brother Boleslav to the castle of Stará Boleslav for the festivities of St Comus (Kosma) and St Damian (Damián) on 27 September. These, together with the feast of St Michael (Michal) on 29 September, were the Christian replacements of the older pagan harvest and vintage festivals. Comus and Damian, two physicians from the east, already had their church at Stará Boleslav (the crypt had always been dedicated to them) and it was there that Wenceslas proposed a chivalric toast to St George. The next morning he was murdered by his brother near the door of the cathedral and Boleslav assumed power in Prague. The miracles that occurred at the tomb of Wenceslas caused his body to be transported, three years later, to Prague and buried in St George's Rotunda. The first golden olive of Libuše's legend had flourished and had been destroyed.

The second olive found its embodiment in the person of Bishop Vojtěch (Adalbert) of Prague. Prince Boleslav I the Cruel (d. 967) did his utmost to have a diocese created at Prague Castle and sent his daughter Mlada to Rome to conduct negotiations. In Rome Mlada learned of the existence of the Benedictine order; the pope consecrated her as abbess and she returned to Prague with a papal bull to found there, beside St George's Basilica, a convent of Latin liturgy 'not conforming to the rites of the Russian or Bulgar peoples or to the Slav language'. She died as mother superior of the convent, and of saintly reputation, in 994. The diocese had by then been established, in 973, during the reign of Boleslav II the Pious, and it owed obedience to the archbishop of Mayence. The Saxon

Coins: Bořivoj II, *c.* 1100, with a rider.
Vladislav I, *c.* 1109, with a warrior.

monk Dětmar (who knew the Slav tongue) became its first bishop: he had been enthroned in 975 in St Vitus's Cathedral while choristers sang the German canticle *Kriste Ginado*, to which the congregation gave the response of *Kyrie Eleison*, in the Czech phonetic form of *Krlèche*.

On the death of Dětmar, St Adalbert was proclaimed bishop by the great assembly of nobles and common folk held at Levý Hradec in 982. He was a member of the Slavník family which held sway over the whole of eastern Bohemia, and the hope was that his election as bishop would enable the Přemyslids to re-establish good relations with the rival dynasty. In fact, Adalbert became embroiled in incessant quarrels with the leading families of Prague and was compelled to return to Rome. During his second stay in Italy, in 995, on the anniversary of the death of St Wenceslas, his entire family was massacred at Liblice Castle. The bloodthirsty climax to the power struggle, imposing unification by force, terminated Adalbert's episcopal functions. He set off for the north as a missionary to the heathen Prussians and died there, a martyr, in 997. His body was brought to the Polish town of Gniezno which, as a consequence of this translation, became the metropolitan archdiocese of Poland.

This period, too, saw a radical change in the relations between Poland and Bohemia. Until then the Czechs had held Cracow, but in the year 1000 the Polish king, Boleslaw the Brave, not only captured the town but also proceeded soon afterwards to take Prague. Fighting continued, with various changes of fortune, until 1039, when Prince Bretislav I conquered Gniezno and preached a sermon to the rival factions, at the tomb of St Adalbert, enjoining them to observe the Christian faith, particularly in respect of marriages and burials and in the consecration of Sunday to God. He returned to Prague with the body of the saint and with

vast quantities of stolen treasures, burying the remains of St Adalbert in a chapel beside the entrance to St Vitus's Rotunda.

From 1050 Prague Castle was gradually and steadily transformed into a typical feudal stronghold. Stone fortifications were constructed and, next to St Vitus's Rotunda a great basilica with a three-aisled nave was built and placed under the patronage of St Vitus, St Wenceslas and St Adalbert; only the crypt retained its original consecration to St Comus and St Damian. The bishop was given his own residence and St George's Basilica was refitted. In 1198, the Czech princes obtained the hereditary title of king of Bohemia, reconstructed their palace, dug additional moats on the west side, raised towers over the gates and built All Saints Chapel.

The golden age of the castle began with the reign of Charles IV. After his return from France, in 1333, he decided to build a new palace and to strengthen the fortifications; and in 1342 he created a chapter at All Saints Chapel. In 1344 he succeeded in raising the diocese of Prague to the status of archdiocese and, soon afterwards, laid the foundation stone of the new St Vitus's Cathedral. Moreover, the establishment of a university at Prague and the enlargement of the town (by creating an extensive new quarter, Nové Město, the New Town) bear testimony to the fact that Charles IV was methodically rebuilding Prague with a view to its becoming the new capital of the Holy Roman Empire. He collected valuable saintly relics from all over Europe, embellishing them with gold, silver and precious stones, displaying most of them in the cathedral (where they still represent the most beautiful part of its treasure), and assigning the remainder to the castle of Karlštejn, then in course of construction.

Přemyslid through his mother, Luxembourg through his father, Charles IV adhered to the traditions of both dynasties. He had tombs carved in the cathedral for his Czech ancestors, adorned the sarcophagus of St Wenceslas with gold, and covered the walls of his chapel with semi-precious stones. He recalled his father's traditions by commissioning, for the palace, portraits of the emperors who had preceded him and transporting the remains of St Sigismund into the cathedral, where he built a chapel for them, facing that of St Wenceslas. He officially declared six national protectors: St Vitus, patron saint of the cathedral; Wenceslas the Přemyslid; Bishop Vojtěch (Adalbert); Ludmila the Přemyslid (whose carved tomb, in the new chapel of St George, he embellished); St Procopius, founder in the mid-11th century of a Slav convent in the Sázava region; and, finally, St Sigismund. All these saints are depicted on the mosaic of the cathedral's Golden Gate (south entrance), in the sculptures of the upper level of the triforium, and on the ex-voto of Archbishop Jan Očko of Vlašim. Adding a final and wholly modern touch, Charles IV immortalised his entire family, the archbishops, bishops and even the architects of the cathedral with marvellously realistic busts situated on the lower level of the cathedral's triforium.

There were various interrelated influences behind Charles IV's plan to build his new European capital. The impact of ancient Rome and papal Rome was evident in the portraits of the emperors, in the transfer of copies of the Virgin from the basilica of Sta Maria d'Aracoeli and of the Veraïkon of Christ; France and the age of chivalry were recalled in the construction of All Saints Chapel, a beautiful imitation of the Sainte-Chapelle in Paris; and the walls of St Vitus's Cathedral and of Karlštejn Castle, encrusted with semi-precious stones, harked back to wealthy Byzantium. Yet, although his work in Prague marks a peak of Gothic culture, his dream of making Prague the centre of the empire did not survive the emperor himself, who died in 1378. His son, Wenceslas IV, did not dare even to lay claim to the imperial crown, and embarked on a quarrel with Archbishop Jan of Jenštejn that reached its climax when he had the archbishop's vicar-general, John of Nepomuk, later to become the saint of Czech Baroque, tortured and drowned. He did not even manage to complete the cathedral, of which only the monumental torso of the choir and the powerful South Tower remain.

The national and social rivalries of the age soon plunged the country into the Hussite religious revolu-

tion. The fact that the newly elected (in 1458) Czech king, George of Poděbrady, did not take up residence at the castle, but in the so-called Royal Court in the Old Town (Staré Město) quarter, near the Powder Tower, demonstrates the rising power of the Hussites. It was not until 1485 that King Vladislav II, of the Polish Jagiello dynasty, restored the castle to its former glory. Above the palace of Charles IV he built the gigantic Vladislav Hall (from which the President today sets out for his election), as well as the Riders' Staircase leading to it. In the cathedral the foundations were laid of the North Tower and the Royal Oratory was incorporated. Finally, Vladislav built the fortification towers. Thus, as the Gothic age gave way to the Renaissance, the heroic era of Prague Castle came to an end.

The breakthrough of the Renaissance in Bohemia was linked with the accession of the Hapsburgs in 1526. In the castle it is represented by the charming summer pavilion known as the Belvedere, one of the purest Italian Renaissance-style buildings to appear north of the Alps. But before it was completed, in 1541 a terrible fire broke out in the castle: it destroyed a number of buildings (including Charles IV's All Saints Chapel), the new fittings in the cathedral and the Crown Jewels, as well as the property registers where for centuries the tenants of the lands belonging to the

Map: first map of Bohemia with Czech place names, drawn by Mikuláš Klaudián and dated 1518.

Trent (1545-63). The Catholic nobility, although few in number and in a minority, were nevertheless rich and influential: the immense Rožmberk (Rosenberg) Palace, which then occupied the entire eastern part of the castle's south front, bore witness to the power of the Catholic aristocracy. The papal nuncio and Spanish ambassador, along with the highest functionaries and their Spanish wives (whom they had met during their missions to Spain) formed a 'Spanish faction' which had a strong influence on policy. One of their actions was to arrange for the translation of the remains of St Procopius to All Saints Chapel (from the convent of the Sázava region which had been suppressed).

The emperor himself showed signs of ruling under constraint and coercion. He was mainly interested in his collections of paintings, statues, precious stones and curiosities of nature for which he built the magnificent Spanish Room. He invited to court the painters Giuseppe Arcimbolo, Hans von Aachen and Bartholomeus Spranger; the sculptors Hans Mont and Adriaen de Vries; the medallist Abondio and dozens of others. His lively interest in all the sciences kept him in touch with research throughout Europe. The scholar John Dee came from England to see him, together with the spiritualist Edward Kelley; the astronomer Tycho Brahe arrived from Denmark and Johannes Kepler soon joined him; and in the course of a journey across Europe, Giordano Bruno also passed through Prague. The famous Prague rabbi, Yehuda Löw ben Bezaliel, apparently gave the emperor a demonstration of the secrets of the camera obscura. All these astronomers, astrologers, mineralogists, botanists, mathematicians, geometricians, specialists in exact sciences and charlatans received a warm welcome at Rudolf's court.

The castle set a rare example of refined culture and artistic endeavour. Indeed, it became virtually the most influential centre of Mannerism north of the Alps. Of this richness little remains: the Royal Ball Court, the white marble mausoleum of the Czech kings, several tombs in the cathedral and a few paintings and statues. Meanwhile, the popular new radical trend persuaded the emperor to publish, in 1609, imperial letters that

nobility had been listed.

It was at this time, too, that the country rapidly veered towards Lutheranism under the influence of neighbouring Saxony; and there was even an attempt, in 1547, to defy the Catholic king. A religious compromise of a conciliatory nature was effected under Maximilian II (emperor from 1564 to 1576). But the accession of Rudolf II, his successor to the Czech throne in 1576, was already marked by a militant Catholicism reflecting the spirit of the Council of

21

granted freedom of conscience. But shortly afterwards, in 1611, the Czech Estates placed Matthias, brother of Rudolf II, on the royal throne of Bohemia, and the emperor, stripped of almost all his powers, died in the following year, isolated amid his precious collections. Events were soon to explode, irreversibly, into crisis.

The Catholic and Protestant nations of a divided Europe prepared for a struggle that actually began at Prague Castle, in 1618, when the Catholic lieutenant-governors were hurled out of the windows of their offices at court. The rebellious estates now chose Frederick, the elector Palatine, as their new Czech king; he displayed his Calvinist leanings shortly before Christmas 1619 when he 'cleansed' the cathedral of its altars, statues and 'idolatrous' paintings. It was a very ill-advised action in a country proud of its past. Thus, for the Catholics, the defeat of King Frederick at the battle of the White Mountain, in 1620, and his flight from Prague constituted a well-deserved punishment. Ferdinand II, the victorious emperor, now subjected the country to extremely harsh measures: the abolition of many social and economic rights, the outlawing of non-Catholic religions (which led to a massive exodus of the nobility, the middle classes and intellectuals), and the suppression of the Czech language. The Thirty Years' War, which broke out at Prague Castle, also ended there in 1648 when the city was captured by the Swedes. They made off with the magnificent collections of Rudolf II, some of them going back to Sweden, some being dispersed all over Europe and the rest being offered by Queen Christina, a Catholic convert, to the pope.

The organic life of the castle also came to an end with the Peace of Westphalia, in 1648. Only on exceptional occasions, and increasingly rarely, did the castle now receive imperial guests from Vienna. Apart from Joseph I, Joseph II and Franz Joseph I, monarchs continued to be crowned at Prague Castle, but they gradually lost interest in it as an imperial residence. The cathedral alone remained a living force, a proud symbol of the nation's faith and conscience. Matouš Ferdinand Sobek of Bílenberk, archbishop from 1668 to 1675, dreamed of endowing the country with a new

Slav saint. He made a bid to canonise St Ivan, a legendary hermit who had formerly lived not far from Ludmila's Tetín, but the attempt failed. He then resorted to a prophecy which predicted that whoever finished the building of the cathedral would go on to conquer the Turks. In 1673 massive columns were stacked in the cathedral's building yard, but war soon ended the work.

A close colleague of Archbishop Sobek was his vice-general, Tomáš Pešina of Čechorod, an ardent patriot who wrote histories of the land and of the cathedral. In 1673, in a work entitled *Phosphorus septicornis*, he drew up a thorough inventory of the cathedral's collection of jewels and relics, which he himself had meticulously arranged. Another patriotic friend of Pešina was Bohuslav Balbín, a fervent Jesuit, who besought the Virgin Mary to protect 'an already declining nation' and, in a desperate attempt to discover a saint who would restore past glory to the humiliated Czechs, wrote the legendary biography of the medieval doctor of canon law, John of Nepomuk.

In the ensuing decades there were repeated attempts to bring about John's canonisation. A commission, made up of professors of medicine from Prague University, examined his tomb in Prague Cathedral and found his tongue intact (recent inspection of the saint's remains, carried out in the 1980s, led to the astonishing discovery that some brain tissue had been preserved, testifying to the conscientious work of the 17th-century professors). Many miracles were witnessed at the site of the tomb. In 1721 John of Nepomuk was beatified, and finally, in 1729, canonised. The city of Prague had not known such festivities since the days of Charles IV.

Medal: representation of Emperor
Ferdinand II of Habsburg (1608-57), a
work by Alessandro Abondio.

The canonisation was celebrated with triumphal arches and illuminations, sermons and prayers, songs, music, theatrical performances and long processions converging on the saint's tomb. The cathedral now enjoyed a new lease of life as the glory of the saint was shared in neighbouring parts of Europe. In 1733 the tomb was enriched with an enormous silver mausoleum, paid for by the donations of grateful citizens. The canonisation of St John of Nepomuk coincided with the summit of the Baroque era in the cathedral. It also signalled a turning point in the country's life and fortunes. From then on, spurred by the continuing resistance of its heretics and the patient work of historians and philologists, the concept of liberation took root and prospered.

The accession to the throne of the Empress Maria Theresa, in 1740, coincided with the outbreak of the War of the Austrian Succession. The king of Prussia, Frederick the Great, besieged Prague and, with unnecessary brutality, deliberately pointed his cannons at the city's most important monuments. He bombarded the castle and, above all, the cathedral. The damage caused by the war eventually encouraged the empress to undertake a vast reconstruction of the castle. She refurbished the Rožmberk Palace and set up an institute for the daughters of the nobility. Then, in 1755, she commissioned the architect Niccolo Pacassi to unify the entire west part of the castle in a single block which, though monotonous in appearance, created a suitably monumental effect.

After 1780, the reign of her son Joseph II ushered in a series of radical reforms which granted social freedoms and liberty of conscience. But this had a negative impact on the castle, with the closure of churches, chapels and St George's Convent. Indeed, the emperor even envisaged turning the whole castle into a barracks. The tragic fate of the castle collections, sold by auction in 1782, was thus typical of the age. Even Přemysl's bast slippers were sold and the fate of the ancient Trojan torso (which had originally graced the gallery of Rudolf II) epitomises the manner and spirit in which these sales were handled. This 'marble cornerstone' failed to find a buyer but was eventually sold, as a last resort, in 1814, to the king of Bavaria for the ludicrous sum of 6,000 ducats.

At the beginning of the 19th century, Prague Castle was dead in every sense. 'Never before,' recalled one contemporary witness, 'had so many ghosts been about in Prague.' The castle survived as a cluttered lumber room for a succession of monarchs: l'Aiglon, the unhappy son of Napoleon and titular king of Rome, stayed there; Charles X, the destitute king of France, lived there; and, from 1845 to 1875, the emperor of Austria, Ferdinand I, ended his days there after his abdication. The changes that were made to the castle reflected the taste of the age: the rebuilding of All Saints Chapel in the Second Courtyard, around 1852-6, and the pseudo-Baroque renovation of the Spanish Room.

The completion of the cathedral, from 1843, posed a number of problems. In a spirit of strict historicism, the Baroque installations had been partially dispersed or destroyed, and not even the Gothic remains had been spared, subsequently proving difficult to rediscover in private collections or abroad. The existing part of the building, with its single high tower, and the Cyclops-like appearance of the transept with its enormous empty dome, still without windows, seemed to be an invitation to complete the cathedral in a spirit and style consonant with the nation's historic evolution. In 1859, a Union for the Completion of St Vitus's Cathedral was set up. Work commenced in 1873 and the building of the three-aisled nave and the west façade with its two towers was finished in 1929, in time to celebrate the millennium of the martyrdom of St Wenceslas. The amount of money collected for carrying out this work testifies to the nation's attachment to this monument and its proud place in popular tradition. The Union continued to exist even after the work's completion and was dissolved only by the Communists in 1954. Among modern developments, the stained glass windows, based on the designs of eminent Czech artists, once more flood the cathedral triumphantly with sunlight.

In Bohemia, the prophecy of Libuše was never commemorated more fervently than in 1848, which promised to be a year of rebirth and new hope for

23

many nations. The symbol of the castle, with its dim outlines of saints and Czech monarchs, was reflected once more in painting and sculpture. Josef Václav Myslbek carved a statue of Libuše, face turned towards the castle, for a new bridge in Prague; it was also his idea to build a monument of St Wenceslas for the busiest thoroughfare in the modern capital, Wenceslas Square (Václavské náměsti). The same symbolic fervour pervaded poetry and music: Smetana's opera *Libuše* celebrated the nation's resurrection; its blazing fanfares still sound today to announce the arrival of the Republic's president.

Yet for all the enthusiasm generated by the nation's 'awakeners', there was a reverse side to the coin. Certain politicians at the beginning of the present century criticised the castle as representing, above all, a monument to Austrian imperialism and the vanished power of the Church. One should not therefore be surprised at the embarrassment shown by the founder of the new Czechoslovakian state, Tomáš Garrigue Masaryk, when, after his election as president of the Republic, he was assigned the old imperial apartments as his residence. However, as a dedicated democrat, he managed to resolve the dilemma with his customary common sense. His plan was to make the castle more accessible to everyone, without in any way damaging its monuments. He entrusted the work in 1920 to the Slovenian architect Josip Plečnik, who was unburdened with the weight of history and local tradition. The granite monolith which he put up in the Third Courtyard for the tenth anniversary of the Revolution was, for Masaryk, the symbol of the castle's response to the new age.

The first Republic lasted no more than twenty years. On 15 March 1939, the German army entered Prague and, from a window in the castle, Adolf Hitler looked down on a subservient city. Despite that, in the hearts of the nation, Hradčany Castle remained throughout the war the emblem of hope and independence. It is hard to describe the three intoxicating years of freedom that followed 1945 when the second president of the Republic, Edvard Beneš, returned to take up residence in the castle, which took on a distinctly civic air and

promised to flourish anew. It was not to be. Significantly, after the Communist *coup d'état* of February 1948, President Beneš pointedly left the castle to take refuge in his summer residence. He resigned in the summer of the same year and died soon afterwards, in September.

The first so-called 'workers' president', Klement Gottwald, saw his entry into the castle as the symbolic victory for the 'working class' over the 'bourgeois democrats' and the feudal lords of yesteryear. It would nevertheless be unjust to underestimate the changes made to the castle during the forty years of Communist rule. Whereas, in the country at large, monuments deteriorated and disappeared, Prague Castle represented a cultural challenge for its new masters. Thanks to the work of the best architects of the time (Pavel Janák, who had already worked there before the war, Jaroslav Fragner, Josef Gočár and others), restoration was carried out on the Royal Ball Court and the Riding School; the burgrave's residence was converted into a children's home, and the castle's Art Gallery was installed in the old stables; St George's Convent was refurbished to accommodate the collection of ancient art from the National Gallery and, finally, an exhibition of the National Museum was opened in the Lobkowicz (Lobkovic) Palace. Major exhibitions were also held in the Vladislav Hall. Altogether the restorations were carried out with great sensitivity. But the general attitude of the regime was also evident in these new areas: the absence of organic links between the great art of the past and the *nouveau riche* aspect of contemporary utilitarian works of art could only arouse ridicule. At last, in November 1989, came the 'velvet revolution', opening new horizons for the nation and bringing liberation to the castle.

Prague Castle has stood as the centre of the tribe, of a nation, of the Holy Roman Empire; it has served as a residence for saints and iconoclasts; it has been the symbol of oppression and of intoxicating freedom. It has been transformed over the centuries and will continue to be so; change is inherent in its life, just as life among the people associated with the castle is also subject to endless change.

THE COURSE
OF HISTORY

According to legend, the founder of the Czech dynasty of the Přemyslids, the ploughman Přemysl, was summoned by Princess Libuše to share her power: The princess's envoys had found him ploughing a field. This scene is one of the **wall paintings** of St Catherine's Rotunda at Znojmo, which date from 1134.

LANDMARKS IN TIME

An overview of 1200 years of the history of Bohemia, of the city of Prague and its castle, as reflected in important local events and lives. The parallel selective list of dates sets these in the broader context of European and world history.

Opposite page, above: **973** *The diocese of Prague was created at the Romanesque St Vitus's Rotunda. The present Gothic cathedral of the archbishops of Prague has remained under the same patronage.* **Silver bust of St Vitus**, *dating from 1699, made after a model by František Preiss, in the Vlašim Chapel of St Vitus's Cathedral. The busts of the Czech patron saints are placed on an altar.*

First-century nasal helmet, known as the helm of St Wenceslas, *the most important archaeological discovery associated with the beginnings of history in Czech lands.*

PRAGUE & BOHEMIA

7th century: A Frankish merchant, Samo, reigns for some thirty years over a union of Slav tribes dedicated to fighting the Avars.

723: Legendary date of the foundation of Prague.

From 830 to 908: Foundation of the kingdom of Greater Moravia which, at its peak, comprises not only present-day Moravia but also Bohemia, Slovakia and Pannonia (part of modern Hungary and Austria). In 895 the Czech tribes scattered through Bohemia throw off the Moravian yoke and seek protection from the Frankish king. Greater Moravia is broken up in 908 by Hungarian raids.

845: Baptism of fourteen Czech princes at Ratisbon.

863: Constantinople sends two missionaries to Moravia, Constantine (better known by the name of Cyril, which he later assumed in Rome) and Methodius (who becomes the first bishop of Moravia in 869). The pope authorises the Slav liturgy, which he replaces with the Latin liturgy in 885.

870-874: The Moravian sovereign Svatopluk breaks with Byzantium and extends his possessions northward to Cracow.

874: Baptism of the Czech prince, Bořivoj I (-894), in Moravia. He builds the first Christian church in Bohemia at Levý Hradec and the first church of Prague Castle, dedicated to the Virgin Mary. According to the chronicle of Kosmas, the reigning Princess Libuše, daughter of the mythical King Krok, had married a simple labourer named Přemysl, thus founding the Přemyslid dynasty, of which Bořivoj is the first identifiable descendant.

894-921: Spytihněv I and Vratislav I (*c.* 888-921), the sons of Bořivoj, try to reconquer the Moravian territories, but these do not return to the Czech crown until the 11th century.

920: Vratislav builds St George's Basilica at Prague Castle.

EUROPE & THE WORLD

c.500: Salic Law of Succession. The oldest version of this law goes back to the time of Clovis (465-511). It is known mainly for a clause that excluded women from succeeding to the throne.

527: Justinian I (d. 565), codifier and legislator, becomes Byzantine emperor.

563: St Columba, missionary and abbot, founds a monastery on the Northumbrian island of Iona.

622: On 16 July, Mahomet flees from Mecca to Medina: this departure is the Hegira (the beginning of the Islamic calendar).

672-735: Venerable Bede, monk and theologian, author of the *Ecclesiastical History of the English Nation*.

696: Foundation of the state of the doges in Venice.

711: Beginning of the conquest of the Iberian peninsula by the Arabs who capture the Visigoth state. In 712 the Arabs occupy Samarkand.

732: Charles Martel (*c.* 688-741) checks the invasion of the Arabs, led by Abdal-Rahman, at Poitiers.

760: *Book of Kells*, Latin gospels, written in Ireland.

793: An attack on the English monastery of Lindisfarne marks the beginning of the age of the Vikings.

800: Charlemagne (742-814), king of the Franks since 768 and king of the Lombards, is consecrated as Western emperor in Rome. Emergence of the Carolingian Renaissance.

843: Treaty of Verdun, dividing the Carolingian empire into France, Germany and Italy with Lotharingia (Lorraine).

Early 10th century:
- Birth of Romanesque art.
- The caliphate of Cordova attracts scholars from the Islamic world.
- Beginning of Christian reconquest of Spain under Alfonso III of Castile.
- England is divided into shires, with county courts to protect civil rights.

PRAGUE & BOHEMIA

921: Princess Ludmila, widow of Bořivoj I, murdered on the orders of her daughter-in-law, Drahomira, opposed to Christianity. She later becomes the first Czech saint.

924: The remains of Ludmila transferred to St George's Basilica by her grandson Wenceslas (Václav) when he comes to power.

After 926: Wenceslas builds a rotunda with four horseshoe-shaped apses on the site of the castle, which he dedicates to St Vitus. Some historians believe his choice of this saint to have been a politically astute move: the Czech name (Vit) is similar, phonetically, to that of a pagan idol, Svantovit.

EUROPE & THE WORLD

910: Foundation of the Benedictine abbey of Cluny by William the Pious, duke of Aquitaine. Thanks to its exemption privileges, the abbey was never controlled by a bishop or a feudal lord but was responsible directly to the papacy. The golden age of the Cluniacs came in the early 12th century.

925: Henry I the Fowler, king of Germany from 919 to 936, founds the first Saxon dynasty and joins Lorraine to Germany. The Přemyslids recognise his sovereignty in 929.

937: The English king, Athelstan, defeats the Danes and the Scots at Brunanburh.

Right: **929** or **935** *According to legend, Prince Wenceslas was assassinated by his elder brother in front of the closed doors of the St Comus and St Damian Church at Stará Boleslav.* **Painting by Master IW** *on this subject, dating from 1543, in St Wenceslas's Chapel of St Vitus's Cathedral.*

Below: **1032 Old Slavic text of one of the Glagolitic fragments of Prague,** *written in Glagolitic characters (writing used in the kingdom of Greater Moravia) before the first half of the 11th century. A treasured relic of national and Slav culture, it was made for the convent of the Sázava region, where the mass was said in Slavic.*

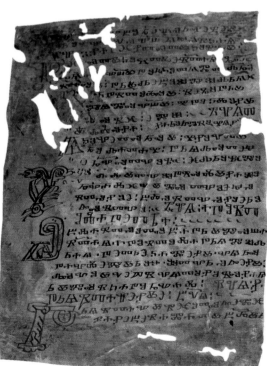

929 or 935: Prince Wenceslas, the first Czech martyr and saint, murdered on the orders of his brother, who reigns until 967 as Boleslav I the Cruel. His successors are Boleslav II the Pious (967-9) and Boleslav II the Red (999-1003).

962: Otto I the Great, son of Henry the Fowler and king of Germany from 939 to 973, founds the Holy Roman Empire.

966: St Oswald founds Worcester Cathedral.

976: Building of St Mark's, Venice, begins.

1125 Floor tile with the bust of the emperor Nero. *Part of the collections of the National Museum to be found in the historical exhibition at the Lobkowicz Palace, it comes from St Vavřinec's Basilica at Vyšehrad and dates from 1129 or 1130.*

1142 Romanesque bas-relief representing St Paul: *fragment of a sandstone tympanum from the middle of the 12th century, which came originally from the commune of Předhradí, near the ancient town of Poděbrady.*

PRAGUE & BOHEMIA

973: Creation of a bishopric at St Vitus's Rotunda (first bishop, Dětmar). Foundation of a Benedictine convent, the first in Bohemia, beside St George's Basilica.

993: Foundation of a Benedictine monastery, the first in Bohemia, at Břevnov.

995: Boleslav II the Pious consolidates the power of the Přemyslids in Bohemia by having the rival Slavnik family assassinated.

997: Adalbert (Vojtěch), second bishop of Prague from 983 to 995, is murdered during a journey as missionary to the pagans of Prussia. He later becomes one of the Czech patron saints.

1003: Boleslaw II the Brave of Poland captures Prague Castle and reigns for two years over a Polish-Czech kingdom.

1032: St Procopius (Prokop) establishes the mother house of Benedictine Slav-liturgy monasteries in the Sázava region. The monks are expelled in 1055 and settle in Hungary. The abbot's body is subsequently transferred to Prague Castle. In 1097 the monastery is taken over again by Latin-liturgy Benedictines.

1060: Prince Spytihněv II (1031-61), who succeeds his father Břetislav I in 1055, founds the basilica dedicated to St Vitus, St Wenceslas and St Adalbert at Prague Castle. It is consecrated in 1096.

1085: Prince Vratislav II concedes the non-hereditary title of king of Bohemia to the German emperor Henry IV.

1125: Death of the first known Czech chronicler, Kosmas (born *c.* 1045).

1135: Prince Soběslav II (died 1140) begins the Romanesque rebuilding of the castle and St George's Basilica. After a terrible fire ravages the castle in 1142, the rebuilding work continues until 1182.

1158: Frederick Barbarossa confers the hereditary title of king of Bohemia on Vladislav II, but refuses, in 1173, to recognise his son Bedřich.

EUROPE & THE WORLD

987: Hugh Capet, king of France, founds the Capetian line.

1000: Christianity reaches Iceland and Greenland.

1054: Schism within the Church. The Eastern (Orthodox) Church separates from the Western (Catholic) Church.

1066: Duke William of Normandy defeats the English king, Harold II, at Hastings and is crowned William I of England.

1096-1099: First Crusade, led by feudal princes of France and Italy.

1122: Concordat of Worms between Pope Calixtus and Emperor Henry V ends the investiture controversy by distinguishing temporal jurisdiction from the spiritual jurisdiction of the clergy.

c.1130: Birth of Gothic art. In France, the new Gothic style appears in the architectural renovation of St-Denis where, for the first time, ogives and ribbed vaults combine as supports.

1163-1182: Building work begins on Notre-Dame de Paris: the bulk of this is completed by 1245 but work continues until 1345; restoration by Viollet-le-Duc from 1845 to 1864.

1167: Foundation of Oxford University. The earliest colleges date from the mid-13th century.

1171: Saladin the Turk founds the Ayyubid dynasty in Egypt and captures Jerusalem in 1187.

1189: Third Crusade, led by Richard I of England, Philip II Augustus of France and the Holy Roman Emperor Frederick Barbarossa (drowned en route). Acre is captured in 1191.

1199: Introduction of inquisitorial procedure by Pope Innocent III: in his bull, *Vergentis in senium*, he equates heresy with the crime of treason.

1204: Armies of the Fourth Crusade capture and sack Constantinople and subsequently establish the Latin Empire.

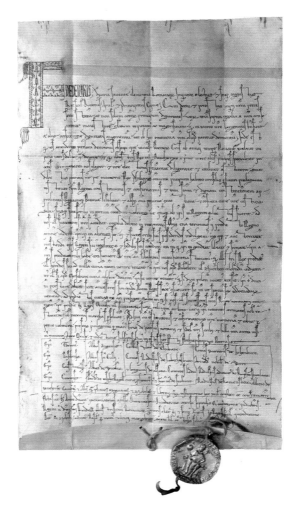

1212 *Under the terms of the* **Sicilian Golden Bull,** *the king of Sicily and the Germanic emperor Frederick II established the rights of the Czech state in relation to the Holy Roman Empire, confirming, among other things, the hereditary title of king of Bohemia on Přemysl Otakar I.*

Right: **1197-1230** *Charles IV commissioned sumptuous sarcophagi, similar to this* **tomb of Přemysl Otakar I** *in the Chapel of the Holy Sepulchre, a work by Peter Parler from 1376.*

Above: **1278-1305** *The opening of the Kutná Hora silver mines enabled coins to be struck, known from around 1300 as* **Prague grosche** *(3.86 g of silver).*

PRAGUE & BOHEMIA

1198: Emperor Frederick II of Sicily confers the hereditary title of king of Bohemia on Přemysl Otakar I (king from 1197 to 1230). In 1212 he confirms, by the Sicilian Golden Bull, this hereditary title and lists the rights and privileges attaching to it (the king of Bohemia, most importantly, becomes an elector of the Holy Roman Empire and, consequently, eligible as emperor).

1230-1253: Reign of King Wenceslas I (born 1206) who profits from the principle of primogeniture adopted in 1216.

1253-1278: Reign of Přemysl Otakar II, king of Bohemia, duke of Austria and elector of the Holy Roman Empire, killed at the battle of Moravské Pole (Marsfeld) fighting the Habsburg

Rudolf I, German emperor since 1273. Their differences mark the beginning of a power struggle that pits, with varying fortunes, the Přemyslids against the Habsburgs.

1278-1305: Reign of Wenceslas II (1271-1305), son of Přemysl Otakar II, who advantageously re-establishes the Polish Kingship and obtains the crown of Hungary for his son, the future King Wenceslas III.

1306: Assassination, at Olomouc, of Wenceslas III, last of the Přemyslids, who, after renouncing the Hungarian crown, lays claim to the crown of Poland but reigns for only one year.

1310: John of Luxembourg marries Elisabeth (Eliška), the last Přemyslid, and becomes king of Bohemia.

EUROPE & THE WORLD

1215: King John of England signs the Magna Carta at Runnymede. Definitively reissued by Henry III in 1225, this was the great charter of English civil liberties.

c.1220-c.1292: Roger Bacon, English philosopher, scientist and educational reformer, author of treatises on the sciences.

1228: Emperor Frederick II leads the Sixth Crusade and recovers Jerusalem.

1251-1259: Peak of Mongol power which, under the leadership of Mangu, conquers China.

1257: Foundation of the Sorbonne by Pierre de Sorbon. The University of Paris becomes the intellectual centre of continental Europe, rivalled by Oxford and Cambridge Universities in England.

1265-1321: Dante Alighieri: *The Divine Comedy*, 1307.

1271: Marco Polo (d.1324) sets out from Venice on his travels to the East. He reaches China and the palace of Kublai Khan in 1275, remaining there for seventeen years, returning to Venice in 1299 to dictate his adventures.

1304-1374: Francesco Petrarca (Petrarch), Italian humanist and lyric poet.

PRAGUE & BOHEMIA

1316: Birth of their eldest son, baptised Wenceslas (Václav), but who takes the name Charles (Karel) in Paris where he is brought up during adolescence at the royal court of his cousin, Charles V. His tutor is Pierre Roger de Beaufort, the future Pope Clement VI from 1342 to 1352. His father entrusts him to manage the affairs of the Czech kingdom in 1341 and he reigns as Charles IV from 1346 to 1378.

EUROPE & THE WORLD

1309: The French-born Pope Clement V settles in Avignon. Rome does not again become a papal seat until 1367.

1310-1375: Giovanni Boccaccio, Florentine novelist: *Decameron* 1349-51.

1314: Battle of Bannockburn, in which the Scots led by Robert Bruce rout the English under Edward II.

Right: **1321** *Cunegonde (Kunhuta), daughter of Přemysl Otakar II, died in 1321 after having been head of the Benedictine convent near St George's Basilica. The Passional of the abbess Cunegonde, dated between 1313 and 1321, is in the National Library of Prague. In the* **illumination,** *kneeling before the abbess, is the author of the text, the Dominican Kolda of Koldice, and the scribe and illuminator of the manuscript, Beneš, canon of St George's Basilica.*

1321: Death of Cunegonde (Kunhuta), abbess of St George's Convent, daughter of Přemysl Otakar II and author of a *Passional.*

1344: Foundation of the archbishopric of Prague, the first incumbent of which (until 1364) is Arnošt (Ernest) of Pardubice, a friend and counsellor of Charles IV. The foundation stone is laid of St Vitus's Cathedral at Prague Castle: the building commission is given to a French architect, Matthew of Arras.

1346: John of Luxembourg is killed at the batle of Crécy. Charles IV becomes the German king at Aix-la-Chapelle (Aachen) in 1349, then Holy Roman Emperor at Rome in 1355.

1315: Battle of Morgarten: in defeating the Austrians, the Swiss of the Three Cantons (Uri, Schwyz and Unterwalden) obtain their independence and renew their 'perpetual pact' of 1291.

1327: The Aztecs of Mexico reach the site of their capital Tenochtitlán.

c. 1320-1384: John Wycliffe, English religious reformer and inspirer of Jan Hus. He opposes the papacy, attacks some of the central doctrines of the Church and makes an English translation of the Bible.

1333 or 1337-after 1400: Jean Froissart writes his *Chronicles* in French; they cover the period 1325 to 1400.

1348 Letter patent of Charles IV, *confirming all the privileges previously accorded to the kings of Bohemia by the kings and emperors of the Holy Roman Empire.*

After 1370 Ex-voto of the archbishop of Prague, *Jan Očko of Vlašim, destined for the chapel consecrated in1371 of the castle of Roudnice on the Elbe, the archdiocesan residence. On the upper, "celestial" part, to the right of the Virgin Mary, is Charles IV, kneeling in prayer and, to her left, his son, the future Wenceslas IV. Behind Charles IV is his patron, St Sigismund, and behind the crown prince, St Wenceslas. In the lower "terrestrial" lower part, the donor kneels among the country's patron saints (from left to right, St Procopius, St Adalbert, St Vitus and St Ludmila). The painting is today kept in the gallery of St George's Convent.*

PRAGUE & BOHEMIA

1348: Charles IV founds at the Prague Carolinum a university that still bears his name. He builds Karlštejn Castle to accommodate the Crown Jewels. Prague becomes the third most important city of Europe, after Rome and Constantinople.

1356: Peter Parler is summoned to Prague to continue the construction of St Vitus's Cathedral, following the death of Matthew of Arras in 1353.

1364-1378: Jan Očko of Vlašim is the second archbishop of Prague.

1375: Death of Beneš Krabice of Weitmile, chronicler of the court of Charles IV.

1379-1396: Jan of Jenštejn is the third archbishop of Prague. He leaves for Rome (where he dies in 1400) following quarrels with Wenceslas IV which are resolved by the murder of John of Nepomuk, the future Czech saint of the Baroque era.

1382: King Wenceslas IV leaves Prague Castle to live at the royal court (Králův dvůr) in Prague's Old Town.

1385: The vault of the choir of St Vitus's Cathedral is set in place.

1399: Death of Peter Parler. His sons Václav and Jan continue his work in the cathedral.

Left: **1385** *Indications as to the foundation and progress of building work on the Gothic St Vitus's Cathedral are given on a* **commemorative plaque,** *dating from 1396, placed on the west pillar of the south door (the Golden Gate). Its author was apparently Václav of Radeč, the fifth works director. The vault of the choir was only built after its consecration "in honore beate Marie et Sancti Viti" ("in honour of the Blessed Virgin and St Vitus") by the archbishop of Prague, Jan of Jenštejn, on 1 October 1385.*

EUROPE & THE WORLD

1337-1453: The Hundred Years' War begins with the confiscation of Guienne by Philip VI and ends with the reconquest of Bordeaux by Charles VII. The English fleet defeats the French at the battle of Sluis in 1340; the English infantry and artillery crush the French at Crécy in 1346. The English take Calais in 1347 and hold it for two centuries. In 1415, the English beat the French at Agincourt. Then the tide turns in the French favour, with the period of Joan of Arc, followed by the recapture of Paris in 1436 and of Guienne from 1450 to 1453. But the Hundred Years' War only really ends with the Treaty of Picquigny, signed in 1475.

c. 1340-1400: Geoffrey Chaucer, English poet: *Troilus and Criseyde, Canterbury Tales,* etc.

1346-1349: The Black Death ravages Europe. A third of the population of England is killed.

1350: The English parliament divides into two chambers, the House of Commons and the House of Lords.

1361: The Danes capture the Hanseatic town of Visby.

1363: The building of the Kremlin is ordered by the grand duke, Dimitri Ivanovich Donskoi.

1378-1417: Great Schism in the Roman Catholic Church: there is one pope in Rome and another in Avignon; then, in 1409, there is a third in Pisa. Not until the Council of Constance (1415-18) is a single pope elected in 1417.

1390: Byzantines lose remaining possessions in Asia Minor to Turks.

1400:
- Beginning of the ascendancy of the Medicis in Florence.
- The Justinian Code finds increasing application throughout the Holy Roman Empire.
- Prosperity of craft corporations.
- Polychrome porcelain manufacture is initiated in China, near Nanking.

1415 *Jan Hus was burned alive as a heretic on 6 July 1415, at Constance — a tragic event in medieval Czech history. Later he was venerated as a saint by the Calixtins (Utraquists). The* **Gradual of Litoměřice,** *done prior to 1517, depicts the death and apotheosis of Jan Hus (donated by Wenceslas of Řepinice, burgomaster of Litoměřice).*

Below: **1424** *Jan Žižka of Trocnov, the one-eyed general of the radical Hussites, died on 11 October 1424, during a military campaign. This* **sculpted head,** *dating from 1516 and originally in the town hall of Tábor, is the oldest representation of Jan Žižka, although not necessarily an authentic portrait.*

PRAGUE & BOHEMIA

1415: On 6 July, Jan Hus is burned as a heretic at Constance. A supporter of the Reformation, Hus had committed the crime of preaching against the abuses of the Catholic Church and had demanded that the University accord the Czech language the same status as German, Latin and Serbo-Croat.

1419: The victims of the first defenestration in Prague, on 30 July, are the municipal counsellors of Nové Město (the New Town quarter of Prague), chosen from the anti-Hussite faction by Wenceslas IV. It sparks off the ensuing riots and violence. The king dies on 16 August at Kunratice. The work on the cathedral is interrupted.

1420: Sigismund, king of Bohemia, steals precious gold and silver artefacts from St Vitus's Cathedral.

1421: Hussite iconoclasts destroy paintings and statues in St Vitus's Cathedral. Konrád of Vechta, the seventh archbishop of Prague, accepts the demands of the Hussites and is excommunicated. The Prague archbishopric remains vacant for 140 years.

1424: Jan Žižka of Trocnov, military head of the Hussite faction of intransigents, dies of the plague.

1434: The battle of Lipány seals the victory of the Catholics over the radical Hussite wing. The conflict does not really end until 1436 after several pockets of resistance have been wiped out.

1437: Death of Sigismund, last king of Bohemia of the Luxembourg family.

1438-1439: Reign of Albert II of Habsburg as German emperor. Having married Sigismund's daughter, he is also king of Bohemia and Hungary (1437). His reign is marked by a diminution of royal powers.

1458-1471: Reign of George (Jiří) of Poděbrady who has run the country since 1448. He restores the state's economic and cultural power. He proposes the first plan for the unification of Europe, a union of Christian monarchs designed to restrict interference by the papacy in political affairs, to repel the Turkish threat and to bring peace to Europe. This plan falls through.

EUROPE & THE WORLD

c. 1422-1491: William Caxton, translator and first English printer, notably of French and English works, including Chaucer's *Canterbury Tales* and Sir Thomas Malory's *Morte d'Arthur*.

1431: Joan of Arc is burned at Rouen after a trial for heresy.

1434-1455: J. Gutenberg invents the printing press in 1434 and, in 1441, the ink that allows printing on both sides of the paper; in 1455 he prints the first Bible with metal characters.

1450:
- Florence, under the Medicis, is the hub of Renaissance culture and humanist thought.
- In the Near East and Europe, delicate, blue-decorated Chinese porcelain influences Islamic and European art (e.g. Delft pottery).

1453: The Turks take Constantinople: Greek scholars flee to Italy and help to initiate humanism. End of the Eastern empire.

1455-1487: The Wars of the Roses, fought between the armies of the houses of York and Lancaster and their allies for the English throne. The civil war ends at Bosworth Field (1485) in the defeat of the Yorkist Richard III by Henry Tudor, who as Henry VII establishes the Tudor dynasty.

c.1466-1536: Erasmus, Christian humanist and key figure of the northern Renaissance.

1469: Ferdinand of Aragon marries Isabella of Castile.

1472: Tsar Ivan III marries Sophia Paleologus. Russia is unified and looks westward to Europe.

1476: The Swiss Confederation, allied to Louis XI, defeats Charles the Bold at the battle of Morat.

1481: Ferdinand V of Spain ends the period of religious tolerance and sets up the Inquisition. The emigration of persecuted Moors and Jews ruins the country's industries.

1482-1499: Leonardo da Vinci (1452-1519) in Milan, where his masterpieces include the *Virgin of the Rocks*, the *Sforza Monument* and *The Last Supper*.

PRAGUE & BOHEMIA

1468: First book printed in the Czech language, *The Chronicle of Troy (Trojánská Kronika)*, followed twenty years later by the first Czech Bible, edited by Jan Pytlík.

1471-1516: Vladislav II (Vladislas), king of Poland and Hungary, is the first Czech king of the Jagiello dynasty. His reign ushers in a period of humanism and a blossoming of arts and culture.

EUROPE & THE WORLD

1492: Spanish conquer Moorish kingdom of Granada. Christopher Columbus discovers America.

1494: Treaty of Tordesillas signed, dividing the possessions of the New World between Spain and Portugal according to a longitudinal demarcation line 100 leagues west of the Cape Verde Islands.

Above: **1453-7** *Ladislav Posthumus, son of the Czech king and emperor Albert II of Habsburg, died suddenly at the age of eighteen. George of Poděbrady was suspected of having ordered his murder. On this* **page of**

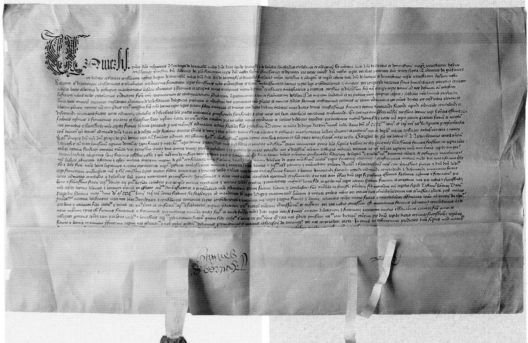

the missal of Ladislav Posthumus, *dating from after 1453, is a decorated initial with the young king kneeling.*

Above: **1468** *The oldest Czech incunabulum is the* **Chronicle of Troy,** *published at Plzeň (Pilsen) around 1468 by an unknown printer. It contains the translation in Czech of the Latin narrative of this classical subject by Guido della Collona.*

Above, right: **1458-71** *At the end of the Middle Ages, George of Poděbrady tried to form an alliance with other Christian kings — a sort of security system for Europe. This is a* **treaty signed with King Louis XI of France** *at Dieppe on 18 July 1464.*

Right: **1458-71** *Reign of George of Poděbrady: descended from the Czech branch of the lords of Kunštat, he was the only Czech king elected by the Czech nobility from its own ranks. This* **portrait,** *done later, is in the Chronicle of the Foundation of the Czech Nation by Martin Kuthen, 1539.*

1483: Following troubles in the city, Vladislav II re-establishes Prague Castle as a royal residence.

1486: Work begins on rebuilding Prague Castle in Late Gothic style. From 1490 it is apparently directed by Benedikt Ried (c. 1454-1534).

1493: The oldest 'view' of Prague is printed in *Liber Chronicarum (Book of Chronicles)* by Hartman Schedel. It is the work of the German engravers Michael Wolgemut and Wilhelm Pleydenwurff.

1502: Completion of the Vladislav Room and the Riders' Staircase at Prague Castle.

1506: Completion of the Louis (Ludvík) Wing.

1500-1506: Leonardo da Vinci paints the *Mona Lisa* and *Battle of Anghiari* in Florence.

1471-1516 The Czech king Vladislav II Jagiello, son of the Polish king Kazimierz IV, embarked on a large-scale restoration of the royal castle as soon as he arrived in Prague. **His monogram and blazon with the Czech lion** *were modelled, soon after 1490, by Hans Spiess, on the ceiling of the Vladislav Hall.*

Opposite page, above: **1559-63 Volumes from the Land Rolls.** *The Land Rolls, where changes in ownership of the lands of the Czech kingdom were registered, constitute an irreplaceable body of juridical documentation.*

Above: **1576 Medal of Rudolf II.** *Various artists and craftsmen played an important role at the court of Rudolf II. Medallists were represented mainly by Antonio Abondio and his son Alessandro, who made this medal around 1608.*

PRAGUE & BOHEMIA

1515: At the Congress of Vienna, the Jagiellos and the Habsburgs settle their disputes by the marriages of the grandchildren of Maximilian I of Habsburg to the successors of Vladislav II Jagiello. Bohemia and Hungary now come under Austrian domination.

1516-1526: Reign of Louis II, last of the Jagiellos on the Bohemian throne. Married to Mary of Habsburg (daughter of Charles V), he is killed at the battle of Mohács at the age of twenty, without issue. The Jagiellos hand over to the Habsburgs.

1518: Map of the kingdom of Bohemia made by Nicolas Claudián (Mikuláš Klaudián).

1526-1564: Ferdinand I, king of Bohemia and Hungary (1526), becomes king of the Romans in 1531 and Holy Roman Emperor in 1558. In 1521 Ferdinand marries Anna Jagiello, and his eldest brother, Charles V, recognises his right, in that same year, to the five Habsburg States (Edict of Worms), appointing him, in 1522, governor of southern Germany, Tyrol and Upper Alsace.

1538: Building work begins (for Queen Anna) on the pleasure pavilion known as the Royal Belvedere, an architectural jewel of the Renaissance.

1541: A catastrophic fire in Malá Strana spreads to the castle and the Hradčany quarter.

1545-1560: Construction of Pernštejn Palace.

1556-1597: Arrival in Prague of the Order of Jesuits which, in addition to the Clementium, create colleges at Olomouc, Brno, Český Krumlov, Chomutov, Jindřichův Hradec and Klodzko to resist the Reformation.

1559-1563: Reconstruction of the Diet Room.

1561: The archbishopric of Prague again has an incumbent: Antonín Brus of Mohelnice.

1563: Jan Kozel and Michal Peterle: first colour engraving of Prague.

EUROPE & THE WORLD

1509: Beginning of traffic in black slaves from Africa to America.

1513: Machiavelli (1469-1527) writes *The Prince* (not published until 1532).

1517: The Reformation begins in Germany as Martin Luther (1483-1546) posts his famous 95 theses on the door of Wittenberg Church: salvation by faith alone.

1519: Ulrich Zwingli (1484-1531), key figure of the Swiss Reformation, preaches at the Grossmünster in Zurich. His doctrine differs in some respects (e.g. on communion) from that of Martin Luther.
- Ferdinand Magellan sails on 20 September on his voyage to circumnavigate the world. He is killed on 27 August 1521.

1520-1566: Ottoman power in Europe reaches its peak under Suleiman the Magnificent.

1521: The Spanish conquistadors under Hernán Cortés sack Tenochtitlán and destroy the Aztec empire.

1525: Revolt of German peasants, led by Thomas Münzer, is suppressed.

c. 1525: Paracelsus (1493-1541) inspires developments in medicine and chemistry.

After 1530-40: Italian artists, on the invitation of Francis I, arrive in France and help transform French medieval castles from military strongholds into palaces (e.g. Amboise, Chambord, etc.).

1531: Henry VIII is recognised as Supreme Head of the Church in England. After divorcing Catherine of Aragon and marrying Anne Boleyn, he is excommunicated by the pope in 1533.

1533: John Calvin (1509-64) supports the Reformation. He publishes, in 1536, his *Institution de la religion chrétienne*, a summary of the most important principles of the reformed faith. In 1541 he settles in Geneva, where he imposes his scheme of reform ('Ecclesiastical Ordinances'). Calvinism spreads in France (the Huguenots), the Netherlands, England and Scotland.

Below: **1516-26** *Louis II Jagiello (1506-26) was killed while fleeing from a defeat by the Turkish armies of Suleiman the Magnificent. His death signalled the end of the Jagiello era on the Czech throne. The young king is depicted in this* **illumination in The Compilation of the Laws of the Town of Znojmo** *by the scribe Štěpán Vyškov, printed in 1523 by Wolfgang Frölich.*

PRAGUE & BOHEMIA

1564: Maximilian II (1527-76) succeeds Ferdinand I and becomes Holy Roman Emperor after being elected king of the Romans (1562), of Bohemia (1562) and of Hungary (1563). His reign is marked by fighting against the Turks and by a measure of religious toleration.

1569-1571: The larger Royal Ball Court is built.

1576: Rudolf II succeeds Maximilian II. In 1584, he decides to live permanently in Prague and transforms the city into a centre of arts and sciences. He provides the castle with a room for art treasures, a gallery for paintings and a room for sculptures (the future Spanish Room).

EUROPE & THE WORLD

1535: Sir Thomas More (b. 1478), English politician and humanist, author of *Utopia*, is executed during the unrest following Henry VIII's break with the Church of Rome.

1541: Michelangelo (1475-1564) completes his fresco of the *Last Judgement* (begun in 1536) in the Vatican's Sistine Chapel.

1543: A few days before his death, Copernicus (b. 1473) publishes the work containing his theory of the dual movements of the planets, turning on themselves and around the sun. This hypothesis is later proved by Johannes Kepler and Galileo Galilei.

1558: Accession of Queen Elizabeth to the English throne.

Below, right: **1593 Painting of a session of the Enlarged Supreme Court of Bohemia.** *Although the composition of the court is purely hypothetical, the picture does allude to a particular session, summoned to deliver judgement on Ladislav Lobkowicz and Sebastián Vřesovec, who had organised the Estates in opposition to Rudolf II in 1593. At the feet of the emperor sits the grand burgrave of Prague, Adam of Hradec. On the emperor's right are Jiří of Lobkowicz, grand steward of the Court, and Joachim of Kolovrat, burgrave of Karlštejn. To the left of the emperor sit Jan of Wallenstein (Valdštejn), grand chamberlain of the Court; Jiří Bořita of Martinic, the supreme judge; the grand chancellor and the president of the Aulic Council. (Until the 13th century, this*

PRAGUE & BOHEMIA

1592: Birth of Comenius (Jan Amos Komenský) in Moravia. Last bishop of the Bohemian Brothers (Hussites), this humanist thinker and teacher dies an exile in Amsterdam, in 1670.

c.1600: Creation of the Crown Jewels (sceptre and orb).

1601: Death of the astronomer Tycho Brahe, protégé of Rudolf II following his disgrace in Denmark.

EUROPE & THE WORLD

1572: Massacre of St Bartholomew's Day, in which more than two thousand French Protestants are murdered, including their leader, Admiral de Coligny.

1576-1596: Tycho Brahe, Danish astronomer, having discovered a 'new star' in Cassiopeia in 1572, works on the island of Hven, near Copenhagen, and founds an observatory there.

1577-1580: Francis Drake circumnavigates the world in the *Golden Hind.*

council was the country's supreme tribunal, but at the end of the 16th century it was no more than a tribunal of arbitration between the king and the nobility, mainly in matters relating to mortmain property.)

Above: **1592 Title page of the complete works of Comenius (Jan Amos Komenský).** *In this engraving by David Loggan, dated after 1657, and based on a portrait by Crispin de Passe, Comenius is seated at his table; behind him are the different spheres of human activity, such as he described in his "Orbis pictus".*

1608: Rudolf II grants his brother Matthias the crown of Hungary, Moravia and Austria.

1609: Rudolf II publishes a royal decree guaranteeing freedom of conscience and worship to the Protestants and the Czech Brothers.

1611: Rudolf II abdicates the throne of Bohemia in favour of his brother who becomes Holy Roman Emperor in 1612 as Matthias II on the death of his elder brother.

1588: The 'invincible' Spanish Armada, despatched by Philip II to conquer England, is defeated and scattered by the English fleet commanded by Lord Howard of Effingham.

1596-1650: René Descartes, French philosopher and mathematician, who reduces knowledge to the principle of 'Cogito ergo sum' ('I think, therefore I am'). Pointing the way to 17th- and 18th-century rationalism, his principal works are the *Discours de la Méthode* and the *Méditations Philosophiques.*

Tycho Brahe

PRAGUE & BOHEMIA

1601 Portrait of the Danish astronomer Tycho Brahe *by A. Niederhofer. Under Rudolf II, Prague became a centre of scientific research. Brahe lodged close to the castle, at Pohořelec, and carried out his astronomical observations from Queen Anna's Summer Pavilion.*

1614: This date, on the Matthias Gate, marks the end of the work, during Rudolf's reign, on Prague Castle.

1618: Second defenestration of Prague: Czech Protestants throw two royal stewards, Martinic and Slavata, out of the castle windows, an act that is instrumental in sparking off the Thirty Years' War.

1619: The Protestant Elector Palatine Frederick becomes king of Bohemia when Ferdinand II, successor to Matthias II, is removed by the Czech Estates.

1620: The Czech Estates are defeated at the battle of the White Mountain. Frederick V, the elector palatine, 'king for a winter', is forced to flee, and Ferdinand II then regains his throne (Habsburg rule in Bohemia is to last until 1918). This defeat marks the beginning of enforced Catholicism in the land and the suppression of the Czech language.

1621: Execution, in the square of the Old Town, of twenty-seven Czech aristocrats, heads of the mutiny by the Czech Estates. Non-Catholics are mercilessly persecuted, their properties and wealth are confiscated and redistributed among the Austrian, German, French and Spanish nobility allied to Ferdinand II. Hundreds of thousands of Protestants are forced to escape abroad.

1627: Succession of the Habsburgs to the Bohemian throne becomes hereditary. Catholicism is proclaimed the official state religion. German becomes the country's administrative language, along with Czech.

1631: Prague and its castle are temporarily occupied by the Saxon army in the course of the power struggle between the Habsburgs and the other electoral princes.

EUROPE & THE WORLD

1601-1612: William Shakespeare (1564-1616) follows his comedies and historical plays with his great tragedies and last plays, notably *Hamlet*, *Othello*, *King Lear*, *Macbeth*, *Antony and Cleopatra*, *The Winter's Tale* and *The Tempest*.

1603: James VI of Scotland crowned James I of Great Britain and Ireland.

1607: The first English colony is established in Virginia. In 1620 102 emigrants, including 41 Puritan 'pilgrims', land from the *Mayflower* near Cape Cod and create the colony of New England.

1634: Cardinal Richelieu, minister to Louis XIII, founds the Académie Française.

1642-1649: English Civil War between Cavalier supporters of King Charles I and the Roundheads (Parliamentarians) commanded by Oliver Cromwell. Charles is executed on 30 January 1649 and England declared a Commonwealth.

1648: The Peace of Westphalia brings the Thirty Years' War to an end. Germany emerges politically and economically weakened.

1660: English monarchy restored under Charles II.

1661: Louis XIV (1643-1715) reigns as absolute monarch in France.

1665: Great Plague of London rages for four months.

1666: Great Fire of London (2-9 February).

1667: *Paradise Lost* by John Milton (1608-74).

1675: Foundation of the Greenwich Observatory.

1688: James II is forced to flee and William of Orange is invited to England (the 'Glorious Revolution'). In 1689 he is crowned William III and reigns jointly with his wife Mary.

1687: Publication of *Philosophiae Naturalis Principia Mathematica* by Sir Isaac Newton (1642-1727), English physical scientist and mathematician.

1611 The army of Passau entering Prague. *Illustration from the Memoirs of Jindřich Hýrzl of Chody, officer of the imperial army. The army of the emperor's cousin, Archduke Leopold, bishop of Passau (Bavaria), coming to Rudolf II's rescue, entered Malá Strana by the Újezd Gate.*

1634 Engraved portrait of Albrecht of Wallenstein, duke of Friedland, *whose life inspired Schiller's dramatic trilogy* Wallenstein *(1798-9). In this engraving by Peter of Iode, dating from the second half of the 17th century, it is noted that it was based on a portrait by Antony van Dyck, which has not survived.*

Right: **1648 Engraving of the siege of Prague by the Swedes** *during the Thirty Years' War. The town is seen from the east, with the Hradčany quarter and Petřin in the background.*

Below: **1729** *John of Nepomuk was priest of the St Havel Church in the Old Town and chancellor of the archbishop of Prague, Jan of Jenštejn. He paid dearly for his dissent against Wenceslas IV and the archbishop: on the orders of the king, he was arrested, tortured and finally thrown from a bridge into the Vltava. Well before his canonisation, a statue of* **John of Nepomuk** *was erected on the Charles Bridge, with bas-reliefs showing various episodes from his life, a work by Matthias Rauchmiller.*

PRAGUE & BOHEMIA

1634: Albrecht of Wallenstein, Ferdinand II's military chief, is assassinated at Cheb on suspicion of having made contact with the Protestants.

1637: Emperor Ferdinand III (1608-57) succeeds his father, Ferdinand II.

1638-1642: The architect Giuseppe Matei draws up plans for the 'empress's wing' and the 'ladies' wing'. These plans include the building of the castle's Third Courtyard.

1648: General Königsmark and the Swedish army occupy part of Prague, notably Malá Strana and the castle. They make off with Rudolf II's art collections.

1657: Leopold I (1640-1705) succeeds his father, Ferdinand III.

EUROPE & THE WORLD

1701: The elector of Brandenburg becomes king of Prussia as Frederick I.

1701-1713: The War of Spanish Succession to determine dynastic claims to the Spanish throne by Bourbons and Habsburgs. Maritime Powers, under the Duke of Marlborough and Prince Eugene of Savoy, defeat the French and Bavarians at Blenheim (1704), followed by further victories at Ramillies (1706), Oudenaarde (1708) and Malplaquet (1709). Spain cedes Gibraltar to England under the Treaty of Utrecht (1713).

1715-1774: Age of Enlightenment in France. Regency (1715-23), then the reign of Louis XV (1723-74).

1721: Peter I (the Great) proclaimed Emperor of Russia.

1673: Fruitless attempt to complete the building of St Vitus's Cathedral.

1694: The Winter Riding School, designed by Jean-Baptiste Mathey, is built.

1705: Emperor Joseph I (1678-1711) succeeds his father, Leopold I.

1755: Foundation of the first Russian university in Moscow thanks to the patronage of the Empress Elisabeth.
- Samuel Johnson (1709-84) completes the *Dictionary of the English Language*, begun in 1747.

1756-1791: Wolfgang Amadeus Mozart, Austrian composer.

1740 Empress Maria Theresa with her family. *This painting, from the studio of Martin van Meytens, was probably done before the death (in 1765) of Francis of Lorraine, husband of the empress. It shows the four sons and seven daughters of Maria Theresa; missing from the group are Charles Joseph (d. 1761) and John Gabriel (d. 1762).*

1743 Coronation of Empress Maria Theresa *as queen of Bohemia in St Vitus's Cathedral in 1743. Maria Theresa's coronation in Prague inspired many contemporary writers and artists. Johann Joseph Dietzler and the engraver M. Tyroff recorded all the stages of the procession, which left from the Nová Město quarter and crossed Prague by the "Royal Way" to reach the cathedral.*

PRAGUE & BOHEMIA

1711: On the death of Joseph I, his brother, Charles VI (1685-1740) becomes emperor of Germany and king of Bohemia and Hungary. In 1713, he issues the 'pragmatic sanction', assuring the succession of the Habsburgs through the female line.

1729: Canonisation of John of Nepomuk who, according to legend, was drowned in 1393 for having refused to divulge the secret of the queen's confession for the benefit of King Wenceslas IV.

1730: Kilián Ignác Dientzenhofer is named court architect.

1733-1736: A funerary monument to John of Nepomuk is built in St Vitus's Cathedral, on the plans of Johann Emmanuel Fischer von Erlach.

1740: Charles VI dies without a male descendant. First and only beneficiary of the 'pragmatic sanction' (1713), his daughter, Maria Theresa (1717-80), becomes empress of Austria and queen of Bohemia and Hungary.

1741-1743: In pursuit of the Prussian army of Frederick II the Great, a Franco-Bavarian army occupies Bohemia and Prague, and the electoral prince, Charles Albert, becomes king of Bohemia as Charles VII.

1743: Maria Theresa ejects this Franco-Bavarian army and has herself crowned queen of Bohemia.

1753-1755: General rebuilding of Prague Castle according to the plans of Niccolo Pacassi.

1756-1763: Seven Years' War between Austria and Prussia, which sees many changing alliances.

1757: Battle of Kolín on the Elbe; Prussian bombardments ravage the Royal Garden of Prague Castle.

1780: Accession of Joseph II (1741-90), son of Maria Theresa.

1781: Joseph II proclaims an edict of tolerance and abolishes slavery and forced labour. Later he institutes civil marriage, organises the secular clergy and carries out a series of other reforms.

EUROPE & THE WORLD

1756-1763: The Seven Years' War ends with British expansion of empire in Canada and India.

1759: *Candide*, by François-Marie Arouet Voltaire (1694-1778), French writer and philosopher.
- British Museum opened at Montagu House, London.

1762: *Du contrat social* by Jean Jacques Rousseau (1712-78), French-Swiss moralist.

1770-1827: Ludwig van Beethoven, German composer.

1770-1831: Friedrich Hegel, German philosopher, founder of dialectics.

1772: Captain James Cook (1728-79), English navigator and explorer, sails on second of his three great voyages of discovery in the southern hemisphere.

1776-1781: American Declaration of Independence is followed by American Revolution, culminating in British surrender at Yorktown.

1782: James Watt (1736-1819), Scottish engineer, invents the double-action steam engine.

1789: French Revolution, storming of the Bastille, *Declaration of the Rights of Man and the Citizen*.

1793: Execution of Louis XVI and Marie Antoinette.

1796: Napoleon Bonaparte (1769-1821) launches his campaign in Italy, followed by the invasion of Egypt in 1798.

1798: William Wordsworth (1770-1821) and Samuel Taylor Coleridge (1772-1834) publish *Lyrical Ballads*, one of the starting points of the Romantic movement in English poetry, as exemplified by Lord Byron (1788-1824), Percy Bysshe Shelley (1792-1822) and John Keats (1795-1821).

1755-75 Entrance gate of the Court of Honour. *The monograms of Maria Theresa and her son Joseph II are interlaced above the entrance gate to the Court of Honour, as a symbolic expression of the fact that during the reign of the empress the castle took on its definitive appearance, in both architectural and artistic terms.*

PRAGUE & BOHEMIA

1790: Leopold II (1747-1792) succeeds his brother. Alarmed by the repercussions of the French Revolution, he retracts some of Joseph II's reforms.

1792: Francis II succeeds his father, Leopold II. He is the last Holy Roman Emperor (1792-1806) and the first hereditary emperor of Austria (1804-35) under the name of Francis I. In 1815, he becomes president of the German Federation and adheres to the Holy Alliance.

1805: Victory of Napoleon I at Austerlitz (Slavkov): it forces Francis II to abdicate, on 6 August 1806, his title of German emperor.

1814-1815: Congress of Vienna. The members of the Holy Alliance, victors over Napoleon, proceed to reorganise Europe.

1826-1834: The lithographer Antonín Langwell makes a scale model of Prague: it is displayed today in the National Museum (at the top of Wenceslas Square).

1835: Accession of Ferdinand I of Austria (1793-1875), emperor of Austria, king of Hungary and Bohemia (under the name of Ferdinand V the Debonair).

1841-1845: Arrangement of Queen Anna's pleasure pavilion, designed by the architect Bernard Grueber, for the use of the Society of the Patriotic Friends of the Arts.

1848: At the end of this year of revolution in Europe, Emperor Ferdinand I (King Ferdinand V of Bohemia) abdicates in favour of his nephew, Franz-Joseph I (1830-1916). Ferdinand dies in Prague in 1875. The new Austrian emperor reigns over Bohemia.

1852: Alexander Bach, advocate of absolutist centralisation, becomes state chancellor to Franz-Joseph I. He is dismissed in 1860 and, in that same year, the emperor promulgates the October Charter, whereby he renounces absolutism and recognises the historic rights of Bohemia. One year later, the Czech candidates win the Prague municipal elections against the Germans and take control of the city.

EUROPE & THE WORLD

1804-1815: Napoleon Bonaparte, initially first consul (1799-1804) is emperor. French land victories at Austerlitz (1805) and Jena (1806). French invasion of Russia (1812) ends in retreat and rout. Following his abdication and banishment to Elba, Napoleon is defeated by Wellington and Blucher at Waterloo, 18 June 1815.

1808: Part I of *Faust* by Johann Wolfgang von Goethe (1749-1832), who together with Friedrich Schiller (1759-1805) inaugurates the *Sturm und Drang* ('Storm and Stress') movement in reaction against rationalism and classicism.

1824: National Gallery of London founded.

1825: Opening, on 27 September, of Stockton-Darlington railway, the first passenger train, drawn by a locomotive built by George Stephenson (1781-1848), English inventor and founder of railways.

1831: Discovery of electromagnetic induction by Michael Faraday (1796-1867), English physicist and chemist.
- Cholera pandemic from India spreads through Central Europe.

1834: Invention of the 'analytical engine' (forerunner of the modern computer) by English mathematician Charles Babbage (1792-1871).

1837: Samuel Morse (1791-1872), American artist and inventor, exhibits his electric telegraph in New York.

1848: Karl Marx (1818-83) and Friedrich Engels (1820-95) jointly publish *The Communist Manifesto* and *Das Kapital* (first volume 1867, Marx; second and third volumes, 1885 and 1894, Engels).

1854-1856: Crimean War, in which Russia is defeated by the combined forces of Great Britain, France and Turkey.

1859: Publication of *On the Origin of Species by Means of Natural Selection* by English naturalist Charles Darwin (1809-82).

1836 The Coronation of Ferdinand V, *painting by Leopold Bucher. This scene of the crowning of Ferdinand V the Debonair as king of Bohemia in St Vitus's Cathedral is signed "Leopold Bucher pinx. 1847". Ferdinand V (emperor of Austria under the name of Ferdinand I) kneels before the high altar, then surmounted by the painting by Jan Gossaert, known as Mabuse, of St Luke Painting the Holy Virgin. Dozens of political personalities of the time are faithfully portrayed in this coronation scene, albeit in miniature.*

1867 Renaissance coats-of-arms of the lands of the Holy Roman Empire *in the choir of St Vitus's Cathedral. Included are the blazons of most central and European countries, whose destinies, as in the case of Hungary, were inextricably linked.*

PRAGUE & BOHEMIA

1859: Creation of the Union for the completion of St Vitus's Cathedral.

1866-1868: Rebuilding of the Spanish Room and the gallery of Rudolf II in neo-Renaissance style, designed by Ferdinand Kirschner and Heinrich von Ferstel.

1867: The Austro-Hungarian compromise, signed in February, brings the Austrian empire to an end and creates the Austro-Hungarian 'dual monarchy'. Bohemia is disappointed not to have been included in the compromise.

1916: Death of Franz-Joseph I. His grandnephew Charles I (1887-1922) succeeds him for two years as emperor of Austria and king of Hungary.

1918: Creation of a Czech Republic which includes Bohemia, Moravia, Slovakia and sub-Carpathian Russia. Its founding father, Tomáš Garrigue Masaryk, is its first president. Prague Castle is the presidential residence.

1920: New building work begins on Prague Castle, directed by the Slovenian architect Josip Plečnik.

EUROPE & THE WORLD

1861-1865: American Civil War. Defeat of seceding Confederacy by Union forces of the North paves way for abolition of slavery in South.

1870: French Impressionist school of painting, so named from Monet's *Impression, soleil levant* (1864).

1876: Alexander Graham Bell, American physicist, invents the telephone.

1888: Suez Canal internationalised (Constantinople Convention).

1889: Universal Exhibition in Paris, for which Gustaf Eiffel builds his famous tower in the Champ de Mars.

1895: First public film show in Paris by Lumière brothers, inventors of cinematography. Eight years later, they invent the polychrome plate, the first commercial process of colour photography.
- Invention of X-rays by Wilhelm Conrad Röntgen (1845-1923) who wins the Nobel Prize for physics in 1901.

1900: *The Interpretation of Dreams* by Sigmund Freud (1856-1939), founder of psychoanalysis.

1901: Gugliemo Marconi (1874-1937), Italian physicist, transmits first telegraphic radio messages from Cornwall to Newfoundland.

1903: On 17 December Orville and Wilbur Wright make the world's first successful sustained flight in a powered airplane near Kitty Hawk, North Carolina.

1905: Albert Einstein (1879-1955) publishes his *Theory of Relativity*.

1914-1918: First World War, following the assassination in Sarajevo of the Archduke Ferdinand of Austria.

1917: October Revolution in Russia. Lenin, Trotsky and Zinoviev create Soviet Russia, which becomes the USSR (Union of Soviet Socialist Republics) in 1922.

1919: Prohibition in the USA: it is not lifted until 1933.

Above: **1918 The standard of the president of the Republic**: *in the centre of this large blazon are the coats-of-arms of all the territories formerly belonging to the Czech crown. The device "Pravda vitězí" means "truth conquers" (although in times of difficulty, to keep hopes high, people always said: "Pravda zvitězí", "truth will conquer".)*

PRAGUE & BOHEMIA

1935: Death of President Masaryk, aged eighty-five. Edouard Beneš (1884-1948) becomes the second president of the Republic.

1938: The Munich Agreement, signed by Germany, Italy, France and Great Britain, forces Czechoslovakia to cede the Sudeten frontier region to Germany.
President Beneš leaves for England and sets up, in 1941, a Czechoslovak government in exile. Judge Emil Hácha assumes presidency of the Republic.

1939: On 15 March, Hitler enters Prague. The Wehrmacht occupies Bohemia and Moravia, which become German protectorates. Slovakia becomes an independent state governed by Jozef Tiso, who places it under German protection.

1944: Slovak nationalist uprising put down in October by the Germans.

1945: Uprising in Prague, 5 May: the Soviet army reaches the capital on 9 May, and the American army halts at Plzeň, near the country's western border.
Czechoslovakia is reconstituted, with the exception of sub-Carpathian Russia, annexed by the USSR. Edouard Beneš is once more president.

1948: The February coup enables the Communists to grab power. The president of the Communist party, Klement Gottwald, replaces Edouard Beneš.

1951: The architect Otto Rothmayer, who continues Plečnik's work at Prague Castle, rebuilds the 'angled corridor' in front of the Spanish Room.

1952-1955: Restoration of the Royal Belvedere and reconstruction of the parterre in front of the building.

1953: Death, on 15 March, of Klement Gottwald, after catching a chill at Stalin's funeral. He is replaced as president of the Republic by Antonín Zapotocký, a politician with a trade union background. Antonín Novotný becomes leader of the Czechoslovak Communist Party.

1957: Antonín Novotný replaces Zapotocký as president of the Republic and carries out his duties under the direction of the Communist Party.

Left: **1918** *The university professor* **Tomá[š] Masaryk** *became first president of the fre[e] state because of his important contributio[n] towards the ideal of independence. This sta[t]ue is by Jan Štursa, a leading sculptor of th[e] first half of the present century.*

Above: **1939 Entry of the German arm[y] into Prague, 15 March 1939.** *This phot[o]*

graph by Karel Novák sums up the despair, the grief and the bitterness felt by the Czech people in the face of enemy occupation.

Below: **1968** *On the night of 20 August, troops of the Warsaw Pact invaded Czechoslovakia.* **Soviet tanks** *line the quays of the Vltava.*

PRAGUE & BOHEMIA

1960: Czechoslovakia becomes a 'socialist' republic, the intials ČSR being changed to ČSSR.

1965: Opening of the gallery of painting at Prague Castle.

1968: The 'Prague Spring', as reforming Communists try to liberalise the regime. On 5 January, Novotný is replaced as head of the Communist Party by Alexander Dubček who, in April, hands over the presidency of the Republic to General Ludvík Svoboda. On 21 August Czechoslovakia is invaded by five member-nations of the Warsaw Pact, which brings to an end this attempt at 'socialism with a human face'. The 'temporary' occupation by Soviet troops is to last until June 1991.

16 January 1969: On 16 January the student Jan Palach burns himself to death at the foot of the St Wenceslas statue in protest against Soviet intervention and occupation.

1969: Czechoslovakia becomes a federal state comprising Bohemia-Moravia on the one part, and Slovakia on the other. In April, Gustav Husák replaces Alexander Dubček as head of the party; after several months of 'stabilisation' he proceeds to 'normalisation'.

1969-1975: Renovation of St George's Convent to accommodate the permanent exhibition of the paintings and sculptures from the National Gallery's department of ancient Czech art.

1971: End of the restoration of the Royal Ball Court (the work began after World War Two and continued intermittently).

1975: President Svoboda, aged eighty, is replaced by the head of the Communist party, Gustav Husák, who combines the two functions.

1977: Birth of the 'civic initiative' known as Charter 77, bringing together citizens of various shades of opinion: opposition to the regime thus comes out into the open, specifically denouncing the excesses of 'normalisation' and proposing democratic reforms. The persecution that ensues leads to the formation of the VONS (Committee for the Defence of Persons Unjustly Harassed) which publicly condemns the government policy. Among the founders is dramatist Václav Havel.

EUROPE & THE WORLD

1920: Creation of the League of Nations in Geneva and of the Nansen passport for displaced persons.

1929: Stock market crash precipitates the collapse of the American economy.

1936-1939: Spanish Civil War. Supported by Hitler and Mussolini, the nationalist insurgents, led by General Franco, are victorious.

1939-1945: Second World War. Nazi Germany surrenders on 9 May 1945 and the atomic bombs dropped on Hiroshima and Nagasaki lead to the surrender of Japan on 14 August.

1945: The conference between Churchill, Roosevelt and Stalin at Yalta agrees on occupation zones in Germany.

1946-1954: War in Indochina. France withdraws after the Geneva agreements.

1947: The Marshall Plan brings American economic aid to Europe. Adoption of the universal declaration of human rights by the United Nations (UNO): abstention by the USSR and the five people's democracies. UNO partitions Palestine into a Jewish and an Arab state, the prelude to Israeli-Arab conflicts.

1948: Assassination of Mahatma Ghandi.

1949: On 1 September Mao Tse-Tung proclaims the People's Republic of China in Peking, recently captured by the Communists.

1952: The USSR and the Eastern Communist regimes create their military organisation by signing the Warsaw Pact.

1956: Polish and Hungarian uprisings are crushed by the invasion of Hungary by Soviet troops.

1959: Fidel Castro overthrows the Batista regime in Cuba.
- The Dalai Lama flees to India.

1960: John Fitzgerald Kennedy president of the United States. He is assassinated in 1963.

1961: Building of the Berlin Wall.
- First man in space: the Soviet cosmonaut Yuri Gagarin.

1989 *On 29 December 1989* **Václav Havel** *was solemnly elected president of the Republic by deputies of the two houses of the Federal Parliament, sitting in the Vladislav Hall of Prague Castle. It was in this historic room, with its hallowed connotations for the Czech people, that he took the oath. Behind him, on the left, Alexander Dubček, elected president of the Federal Parliament in December 1989, proclaims Havel's election.*

PRAGUE & BOHEMIA

Late 1988-1989: Large-scale Catholic demonstrations against state control of the Church, the commemoration, on 16 January, of the suicide of the student Jan Palach in 1969, and a series of civil initiatives that include a petition for democratic reforms (supported by many intellectuals and artists who, until then, have not sided openly with the opposition) culminate in the silent demonstration on 17 November 1989 in Prague (harshly suppressed) and to other mass demonstrations that come to constitute the 'velvet revolution'. On 19 November, the opposition regroups as the Civic Forum (Občanské forum).

On 24 November, the leadership of the Communist Party resigns en bloc. On 28 December, Alexander Dubček is elected president of the Federal Parliament which next day elects Václav Havel head of state.

1990: The country is renamed the Czech and Slovak Federal Republic, and the initials ČSSR are replaced by ČSFR.

On 8 June the first free legislative elections since the end of World War Two are held, with the Civic Forum emerging victors. The new parliament re-elects Václav Havel as president of the Republic for two years, the time needed to re-establish normal, pluralist politics prior to organising new and genuinely democratic elections.

1991: On 21 February, Czechoslovakia becomes the twenty-fifth member of the Council of Europe. A multitude of political parties and lesser groups see the light. In Slovakia, independent voices are heard. In Bohemia, there is a clear rejection of left-wing views.

1992: The major victors of the June elections embark on a process of partitioning Czechoslovakia. They are Ladislav Klaus (Democratic Civic Party, ODS), ex-minister of finance and new head of the Czech government, and his Slovak counterpart, Vladimír Mečiár (Movement for a Democratic Slovakia). On 3 July, the nationalist Slovak deputies, backed by the Communists and extreme right-wing Czechs, prevent the re-election of Václav Havel, who resigns on 20 July.

1993: The Czech parliament re-elects Václav Havel as president.

EUROPE & THE WORLD

1965-1973: War in Vietnam, with heavy commitment of US armed forces. The occupation of Saigon by North Vietnamese troops in April 1975 ends almost thirty years of civil warfare.

1968: Assassination of Martin Luther King and Robert Kennedy.

1969: American astronaut Neil Armstrong is the first man to walk on the Moon.

1973: Watergate scandal: American President Richard Nixon is forced to resign the following year.

1980: The first free trade union in an eastern-block country, 'Solidarity', led by Lech Walesa, is established in Poland.

1981: The Shah of Iran is overthrown. An Islamic republic is set up under the Ayatollah Khomeini.

1984: Assassination of Indian Prime Minister Indira Ghandi. Her son Rajiv later suffers the same fate.

1985: Mikhail Gorbachev comes to power in the USSR. He tries to lead the country towards democracy (*perestroika* and *glasnost*).

1989: Destruction of the Berlin Wall. End of the Cold War between West and East.
- In China, demonstrations by students in favour of democracy are ruthlessly suppressed.

1990: Reunification of Germany.
- Occupation of Kuwait by Iraq in August leads to the Gulf War, which lasts until February 1991.

1991-1992: Collapse of the USSR. Gorbachev resigns. Boris Yeltsin takes over power. Break-up of the former Soviet Union awakens nationalism.
- Disintegration of Yugoslavia as civil war erupts.

1992: Maastricht Treaty as a step towards European union. Conference of the Earth at Rio.

THE CASTLE

THE CASTLE SITE: ITS PLACE IN THE CITY'S LIFE AND LANDSCAPE

Prague is indisputably one of the most spectacular cities of Europe. Not only is it embellished by its remarkable, centuries-old architecture, but it enjoys a privileged position in an extraordinary landscape. The city is situated in a broad basin formed by a bend of the Vltava and fringed by gently sloping hills. The highest of these hills is on the left bank of the Vltava, its spurlike summit dominating the river valley; on the other side, the hill is blocked by the gorge of the Brusnice stream. Over the centuries, the summit of the hill has been the principal scene of building activity and the focal point of political influence. It was here, in the Middle Ages, on the foundations of a Slavic stronghold, that a castle was built. This castle was destined to become the heart of the kingdom and later of the Holy Roman Empire. And at intervals, as rebuilding and renovation altered its appearance, it was the centre of political power, of science and of art, its cultural activity always indissolubly linked with the life of the city below.

Although, in the course of its growth over more than a thousand years, Prague Castle was never isolated, either culturally or politically, from the rest of the city, it nevertheless retained its special and individual identity. At all times, however, the bond between the castle and the city has remained indisoluble.

Today the castle gives the overall impression of having been built on an island. The terrain is actually a narrow spur, which the first chronicler, Kosmas, at the very end of the 11th century, compared to the back of a porpoise. Over the centuries new buildings were erected, the fortifications were strengthened and the various palaces were linked by courtyards and passages to form a coherent whole. The castle owed very much of its importance and charm to the unique character of its site, which made it a favourite subject of paintings and engravings from the 15th to the 18th century.

During the 19th and 20th centuries, Prague Castle attracted many writers and artists, not only Czechs but also Germans, who were inspired by it as a magical place still haunted by its dramatic past, but one that nurtured untold possibilities and as yet unrealised hopes for the future.

The cathedral towering over the ramparts gives the castle an unworldly appearance which, at the dawn of the modern age, corresponded precisely to the romantic concept of an idealised spot graced by nature itself — often represented in art by an island or a mountain — and doubly blessed by its sacred architecture. Writers of the 19th and early 20th century glimpsed, in the themes associated with Prague Castle, a reflection of the human mystery and the modern world: this is exemplified in the works of Jan Neruda, Julius Zeyer, Gustav Meyrink, Max Brod and Franz Kafka.

In the verses of Apollinaire's poem *Zone*, dating from the early 1910s, the influence of Prague Castle on the poet is evident: this pioneer of European avant-garde literature and art saw in the hallowed stones of St Wenceslas's Chapel in St Vitus's Cathedral the portents of his own destiny. The theme of Prague Castle recurs in many other avant-garde works, for example, the verses of Vítěslav Nezval and Jaroslav Seifert or the paintings of Antonín Slavíček and Oskar Kokoschka, and continues to spur the imagination of writers and artists to this day. The geographical location of the castle, its architectural diversity, its eventful history — spanning catastrophe and triumph, despair and faith — combine to give Prague Castle the semblance of a microcosm of human destiny.

The imposing silhouette of the castle is an ever-present symbol to the people of Prague and remains an unforgettable memory for visitors. In fair and foul weather, it floats majestically against the skyline, most spectacularly at sunset. And this powerful visual impression is reinforced by the interior of the castle, with its multiplicity of styles in the course of over a thousand years of continuing historical development.

THE ROYAL PALACE AND THE MEDIEVAL BUILDINGS OF PRAGUE CASTLE

Archaeological research, carried on for more than a century, has shown that the first building of Prague Castle dates back to the second half of the 9th century. This was the stronghold of Prince Bořivoj, comprising a mound of earth that served as a rampart and wooden constructions inside enclosing walls. This stronghold stood on the top of the spur, in the area between the wing that nowadays separates the Second and Third Courtyards and the eastern end of St George's Convent. To the west and east, a ditch completed the fortifications, marking out on the periphery of the narrow spur the line of the foundations of the future castle.

Whereas the architectural plan of the castle had been determined, for several centuries, by considerations of defence, its later development was notable for the construction of sacred buildings, in advance of their time and important for the entire region. They were among the first buildings in local masonry. The oldest was the Church of the Virgin Mary, situated in the western bailey of the stronghold. Here were found tombs identified as those of Prince Spytihněv I, who died in 915, and his wife.

The other sacred buildings from the beginning of the 10th century are St George's Basilica and St Vitus's Rotunda. As for the original appearance of the prince's palace, we know only that it stood in the centre of the future princely and royal palaces, near the south wall, almost in the middle of the fortress and perhaps opposite the episcopal palace. The bishopric had been created in 973 and the episcopal palace was built soon after the year 1000. This was the dramatic period when the Czech state was founded, on the basis of Christian ideals, in the course of wars and invasions involving the mightiest rulers and dynasties of Central Europe.

In 1003 Prague Castle was captured by King Boleslaw the Brave of Poland and later, in 1041 by Emperor Henry III. Nevertheless, the Přemyslid princes who reigned at Prague Castle were never completely vanquished and continually rebuilt the castle as their centre of power. In the 11th century they began to improve the defences. After 1041 Prince Břetislav proceeded to reinforce the earth ramparts with an enclosing wall of stone. His successor, Spytihněv II, then began to rebuild St Vitus's Rotunda in order to make it a basilica. In the reign of Vratislav II, Spytihněv's successor, the question of the primacy of the Church exacerbated the differences between the ruler and Bishop Jaromir, forcing Vratislav to move to another castle stronghold in Prague, Vyšehrad, where the Czech princes resided until 1135. Later, Vratislav's successor, Soběslav I, returned to live at Prague Castle and embarked on a large-scale programme of reconstruction, replacing the earth ramparts with a marl-brick wall. This powerful surrounding wall reached a height of 14 metres (45 ft) in certain places, as can be seen from the remains of the south ramparts which served as the basis of the later transformations of the Royal Palace.

The fortification works of Soběslav also included the erection of three gate towers giving access to the castle. In the south-west section of the wall he built the White Tower, today part of the wing situated between the Second and Third Courtyards. In front of the princely palace he built the South Tower and at the eastern end the Black Tower, which still stands today. A gateway in the west wall of the fortifications completed these three gate towers.

Work on rebuilding the Royal Palace was begun in 1253, the year that saw the death of Wenceslas I and the accession of Otakar II. A new wing was raised at right angles to the main building. New vistas opened up during the reign of Přemysl Otakar II, whose political influence was such as to make him the strongest contender for the crown of the Holy

46

Roman Empire. The fortifications were further strengthened and were extended on the south side of the castle with the ramparts of Malá Strana.[1] Přemysl's other projects never saw the light of day because of his tragic death on 26 August 1278 in the battle of Moravské Pole against Rudolf of Habsburg.

Wenceslas II, still a minor when he succeeded and under threat during the regency, re-established political power and even extended it for a brief time to include the crown territories of Poland and Hungary, but he did not make any notable contribution to the building of Prague Castle. It was only under the Luxembourg dynasty, following the accession of John of Luxembourg to the Czech throne in 1310, that fresh work began.

Even in John's reign such work was limited in scope, but under his son, later Charles IV, whom he had summoned to Bohemia in 1333, the entire castle site hummed with renewed activity. In his autobiography, *Vita Caroli*, Charles IV described the state of the castle, as he found it on his arrival: 'Prague Castle had been so devastated, demolished and dilapidated that, since the reign of King Otakar, it had been wholly destroyed down to the ground level.' Charles, who represented his father at the castle, had embarked on its restoration by rebuilding the Royal Palace. On the north side, he enlarged its Romanesque foundations with arcades to support the apartments and ceremonial rooms of his new palace. To the west he extended the palace so as to include the Romanesque tower of the south gate. The heart of the palace was a reception hall which stood on the site of the present Vladislav Hall. But Charles IV's work on the castle was likewise concentrated essentially on its sacred buildings: St Vitus's Cathedral and St George's Basilica, and plans for the reconstruction, on the model of Sainte-Chapelle, of All Saints Chapel adjoining the Royal Palace. Charles's dream was to rebuild the

1. Quarter of Prague, situated on the left bank, which begins at the Charles Bridge and climbs the hillside to the Hradčany quarter and Prague Castle.

entire castle. He broadened the fortifications and built forward enclosing walls in front of the existing Romanesque ramparts. He also restored the gates of the entrance towers which had recently been crowned by roofing in gilded lead, as testimony to the importance that he attached to Prague and its castle as the symbolic heart of his imperial power.

Yet the ambitious work on which he embarked was still incomplete at his death, in 1378, and remained so during the reign of his successor, Wenceslas IV. The latter also wished to decorate the Royal Palace and the castle in the prevailing artistic style. He modified Charles IV's work by replacing the beamed ceilings with rib vaulting.

A legacy of the building activity of Wenceslas IV is the Hall of Columns, situated in the western part of the palace, a work in the Flamboyant Gothic style, which in Bohemia and Moravia attained its pinnacle in various artistic fields. After the work initiated by Wenceslas, all building activity at Prague Castle was interrupted for a considerable time. With the death of the king and the onset of the Hussite Wars, royal power, as symbolised by his actual presence in the castle, began to disintegrate, since Wenceslas's brother Sigismund, Holy Roman Emperor and king of Hungary, was only represented there by a military garrison.

THE CHANGES TO PRAGUE CASTLE FROM THE LATE GOTHIC TO THE BAROQUE

After Wenceslas IV, the castle remained abandoned for more than sixty years. It only recovered its traditional importance, in a new guise, during the period of transition in Europe from medieval to modern times: between the last flickerings of Late Gothic and the heyday of the Renaissance. This was a time when inherited patterns of temporal power came under challenge from innumerable individual, economic, political and cultural initiatives, coinciding with the spiritual clash between the supporters of the Reformation and the adherents of the established faith. It was this interaction of old and new that inspired the next sequence of developments at Prague Castle, around 1500, inaugurating one of the most significant achievements in contemporary European architecture.

This occurred during the reign of Vladislav II Jagiello, elected king of Bohemia on 27 May 1471 at Kutna Hora. Very shortly after he was crowned, to strengthen his political position Vladislav chose Prague Castle as the central symbol of his power. Apparently inspired by the example of the rebuilt castle of the dukes of Saxony at Meissen (where a historic landmark had been renovated in order to epitomise the economic prosperity of the new Saxe-Wittenburg territories), the Bohemian king entrusted the reconstruction of Prague Castle to the master craftsman Benedikt Ried of Piesting[2]. In all probability, Ried was in contact with the office in charge of the rebuilding work from 1484, and within the next few years gradually came to play a leading role in the vast reconstruction project for the Royal Palace and the modernisation of the castle fortifications. Ried concentrated his principal activity on the building of the hall designed for coronations and ceremonies, and the area adjoining it, given over both to official royal functions and to the monarch's private life.

The changes that Ried brought to the castle were wholly individual, based on architectonic principles that were astonishingly audacious for their time. Rebuilding work had already begun before he was called in: a corridor already linked the palace to the oratory in the south part of the cathedral close by. Evidently this oratory was also the work of another architect, as was the 'green room', adjacent to the corridor, which has retained its characteristic Late Gothic stellar vault: according to most recent studies, this was the work of Hans Spiess of Frankfurt.

2. Known also in Bohemia under the name of Rejt.

Fortunately, Benedikt Ried's grandiose plan for the castle was not interrupted by the accession of King Vladislav II Jagiello to the throne of Hungary in June 1490. Ried's work includes, above all, the Vladislav Hall, the Riders' Staircase, the old Diet Hall and the beginning of the perpendicular Gothic south wing, known as the Louis Wing.

The Vladislav Hall was built on the foundations of the Romanesque palace and the Gothic palace of Charles IV, the two floors of which form its base. Ried unified the area and did away with parts of the old palace, including the chapel, to make a large hall 16 metres (52 ft) wide, 62 metres (203 ft) long, 13 metres (43 ft) high. Its dimensions were appropriate to the changes that had come about in the life of the castle, and it met with the enthusiastic approval of Prague's nobility. The large size and majestic appearance of the Vladislav Hall made it eminently suitable, in due course, for important ceremonial occasions, including coronations, tournaments, receptions and even as a marketplace for exclusive merchandise, as during the first industrial exhibition in Bohemia. It is used, too, for the election of the Republic's president. Here, in the Vladislav Hall, Václav Havel was elected president and made his address to the nation and Parliament.

In many ways, Ried's design of the Vladislav Hall harmonised with the rest of the castle. He also developed a number of structural and functional elements of Charles IV's architecture, giving them a new appearance and dimension. His work was thus a synthesis of Late Gothic motifs, principally derived from Danubian architecture, but he attained a level of expressiveness quite beyond the existing range of local architects, schools and workshops. For Ried, the most important element of such a building was the vault; and he embellished it with the most picturesque features of Late Gothic to create a wholly original design in which his personal vision blended with an impersonal rhythm that unified an area divided into five bays of vaulting. The historian of Czech art, Václav Mencl, has described Ried's work as follows: 'The surface of the vault,

perfectly balanced, seems to ripple with the softest movement, summit and base merging in a long, vibrant, luminous surface, virtually imperceptible to reason and imprecise in form, yet full of melody and music, where the supple forms of the space are imparted to the material of the vault and where the rigid structural frontier between matter and space is completely obliterated.'

By applying the discoveries of Late Gothic to a vast area and by exhibiting them in the context of continuously changing surfaces, Ried modelled

himself on Peter Parler, elaborating the theme of transformation and continuity of the surface in space, with results that were further developed, locally, only in the work of that genius of Baroque, Santini Aichel. The hall built by Ried is justly regarded as one of the architectural masterpieces of Central Europe around the year 1500 and was already recognised as such in his time. Václav Hájek, the 16th-century Czech chronicler, wrote of it: 'There was not, in the whole of Europe, a similar construction, unsupported by pillars, of such width, length and height.' Hájek went on to describe the Vladislav Hall as the 'jewel of the Czech kingdom'.

In many respects, Ried's work is testimony to his remarkable insight into the traditions of Czech architecture, the characteristic features of which he was able to apply in a new manner. One is struck not only by the continuity of the interior space but also by the dramatic contrast between this interior and the façade of the building. This façade has the attributes of Italian Renaissance at its finest, as exemplified in its harmonious proportions, its restrained appearance and the sumptuous character of the different elements of the building, such as the windows and the main doorway. The combination of Late Gothic and Renaissance elements achieves a degree of syncretism that is typical not only of Central European art, but more specifically of the castle architecture as a whole, in which so many different styles are astonishingly reconciled and crystallised.

The interlinking of Late Gothic and Renaissance is equally characteristic of Ried's later work at Prague Castle, notably on the apartments in the Louis Wing, named after the son of Vladislav II Jagiello, who succeeded him in 1516 and in whose reign the wing was completed. This extraordinary synthesis of styles is evident, however, in all the architectural work on the castle. The architect experimented boldly and was able to manipulate conventional styles as if they were elements of a language that in combination could be used to create new expressions and patterns. This was the case, for example, in the composition of the door to the Riders' Staircase, where the Late Gothic saddleback motif of the architrave would be unthinkable in Renaissance architecture; or of the doorway leading from the Vladislav Hall to the Diet, where the Renaissance fluted pilasters are deliberately coiled in the form of a screw, while the overall plan of the doorway pays tribute to the purity and simplicity of the Renaissance style.

The new Renaissance motifs used by Ried for the windows and doorways of the palace found no other application in the construction and decoration work at Prague Castle. After the death of Louis II Jagiello, following his defeat by the Turks at the battle of Mohács (1526), there was a further interruption in work at the castle. In 1526 the Czech Estates elected Ferdinand of Habsburg king of Bohemia, he having promised them to live in Prague. During his reign, without touching the heart of the castle, all building work was concentrated on the northern buttresses, situated behind the Stag Moat. To gain access to this area and to reach its buildings, a new bridge had to be constructed in the northern wall. In this way the castle was opened out towards its gardens, creating a new horizontal focal point, undreamt of by those responsible for its medieval layout.

In 1541 a fire in a house in Malá Strana spread to Prague Castle and the entire Hradčany quarter, even affecting the buildings behind the Stag Moat. This event delayed all new building activity for more than ten years. The work was not resumed until the time of Ferdinand of Tyrol who, after the death of Queen Anna, represented the government of Ferdinand I of Habsburg in Bohemia (1547-63). Thanks to him, reconstruction of the castle continued and the Royal Garden was completed. To do this, Ferdinand of Tyrol created a Court Building Office, which at first was run by Paolo della Stella, then by Hans Tirol and, from 1556, by Boniface Wohlmut. The last-named completed the castle repairs, showing both good taste and an eye for beauty: he respected the work of his predecessors and carried out restorations in their spirit. Thus he built the vault of the Diet, leading to the Vladislav Hall, in Late Gothic style, modelling himself on Ried. He proved himself a champion of Palladianism in building the tribune of the chief clerk of the Land Rolls, which had been lodged at the Diet in 1564. After the fire which destroyed a whole series of buildings at Prague Castle, new opportunites presented themselves; and it was builders employed by the nobility — the Rožmberks and the Pernštejns — who were given

Wood engravings: Two views of the town and castle of Prague by Joris Hoefnagel, court painter to Rudolf III, in *Civitates Orbis terrarum*, a work in several volumes by Georg Braun, dating from 1595.

the responsibility. But in the palace itself, only the royal apartments adjoining the White Tower were rebuilt in the reign of Maximilian II, who had succeeded Ferdinand I in 1564.

Emperor Rudolf II, Maximilian's successor, settled permanently in Prague after his accession to the throne in 1576. He launched major building operations, decisive for the future of Prague Castle.

(Continued on page 81)

THE SITE
OF THE CASTLE

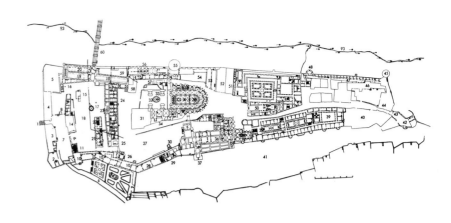

Copy of the plan of Prague Castle before its reconstruction during the reign of Maria Theresa of Austria (before 1755).

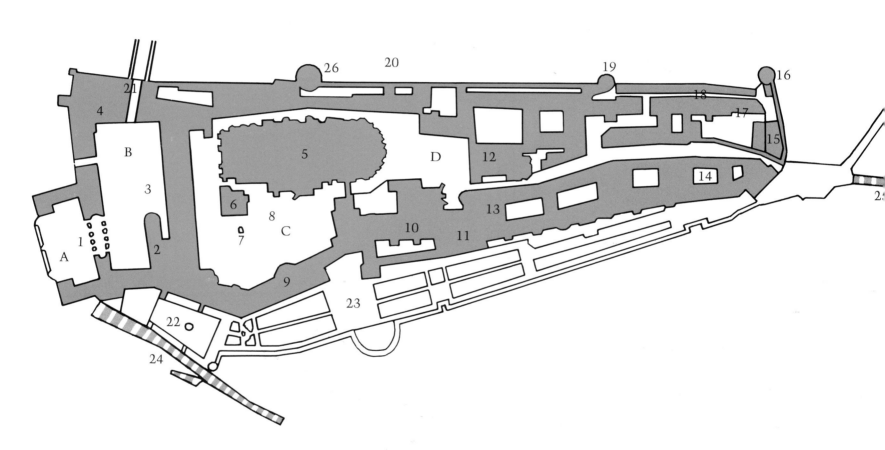

A First Courtyard
B Second Courtyard
C Third Courtyard
D George Square (Jiřské náměsti); also commonly known as St George's Square (Náměsti u svatého Jiří)
1 Matthias Gate
2 Holy Cross Chapel
3 Kohl Fountain
4 North wing of the castle, with the Spanish Room and Rudolf Gallery
5 St Vitus's Cathedral
6 Old Provost's Lodging
7 Monolith
8 St George's Fountain
9 South wing of the castle: offices of the president of the Republic and his chancellery
10 Louis Wing and Vladislav Hall
11 All Saints Chapel
12 St George's Basilica and Convent
13 Former Former Rožmberk Palace, later the Institute for Noblewomen
14 Pernštejn Palace, later Lobkowicz Palace
15 Black Tower
16 Daliborka Tower
17 Burgrave's House
18 Golden Lane
19 White Tower
20 Stag Moat
21 Powder Bridge
22 Paradise Garden
23 Ramparts Garden
24 New Castle Steps
25 Old Castle Steps
26 Mihulka (Powder) Tower

Putti playing with a lion: fragment of a sculpture by Ignác Platzer, dated 1770-1, part of the decorative railing separating the Court of Honour from Hradčany Square.

Below and right, p. 55: *The Fighting Giants*: sculptures by Ignác Platzer, dating from 1770-1, on the pillars of the entry gate to the Court of Honour.

Centre: *the Matthias Gate*: designed near the end of the reign of Rudolf II by Giovanni Mario Filippini and built in 1614 under Matthias II. Originally isolated, in the course of the reconstruction carried out by Niccolo Pacassi it was linked to the castle by the perpendicular wing, thus becoming the centrepiece of the Court of Honour and the main entrance gate to the castle. On the attic storey is an allegory of War and Peace, as well as war trophies (a work by the Platzer workshop).

55

HRADČANY SQUARE

View from the third floor of the west wing of the castle, with the gate and railings of the Court of Honour in the foreground:

On the left, in the foreground, is the *Salm Palace,* formed of three wings, with a courtyard opening onto the square. The palace was built from 1800 to 1810, on classical lines, by the architect František Pavíček for Prince Vilém Florentin Salm-Salm, archbishop of Prague from 1793 to 1810.

Behind it stands the *Schwarzenberg-Lobkowicz Palace,* one of the most impressive examples of the Renaissance style, built from 1545 to 1567 by the Italian architect Agostino Galli. The walls are decorated with diamond-point bossage and the façades surmounted by stepped gables and lunette cornices.

The *Thun-Hohenstein Palace* or Tuscan Palace, in the centre, was built in the Baroque style between 1689 and 1691 for Count Michal Oswald Thun. Its construction is attributed to the Burgundian architect Jean-Baptiste Mathey who, with Francesco Caratti, introduced the monumental Baroque style into Bohemia.

The *Archbishop's Palace*, on the right, has undergone several transformations. The ancient Gryspek Palace, dating from before 1538, was rebuilt from 1562 to 1564 by Ulrico Aostalli, to the designs of Boniface Wohlmut, for Archbishop Antonín Brus of Mohelnice who, from 1561, was the first incumbent of Prague's

archbishopric after the Hussite Wars. Jean-Baptiste Mathey renovated the palace in Baroque style from 1675 to 1694, slightly altering its structure, and Jan Josef Wirch adorned it with an elegant Rococo façade between 1763 and 1765.

THE CASTLE COURTYARDS

Second courtyard of the castle, north-east side. On the right is the northern end of the Holy Cross Chapel. The wing of the castle with the façade visible here was built by the architect Antonín Haffenecker from 1772 to 1775 in the context of the general reconstruction of the castle by Niccolo Pacassi for Empress Maria Theresa, his objective being to give uniformity to the whole site.

Centre: *view of the Third Courtyard,* from the south tower of St Vitus's Cathedral; the paving and the additions of the fountain and the monolith were the work of Josip Plečnik.

Right: *view of George Square (Jiřské náměsti)*, also known as St George's Square (Náměsti u svatého Jiří). This little square is dominated by the west front and towers of St George's Basilica. Behind is the Vltava, crossed by two bridges. The nearer is the Svatopluk Čech Bridge, built from 1906 to 1908 by Jiří Soukop and Jan Koula in the Secession style; it is an iron structure with transverse arches, adorned with elegant lampposts and flanked, at either end, by four marble columns topped by winged statues. In the distance is the Josef Hlávka Bridge, in reinforced concrete, built by Pavel Janák (1909-12), giving access to Štvanice Island, used since the 1980s exclusively for tennis.

59

THE CASTLE'S ROMANESQUE BUILDINGS

Right: lower floor of the Romanesque palace.

Opposite page: Romanesque barrel *vault* from the mid-12th century.

Below: *model* of the castle site seen from the west, around 1250, with the two towers of St Vitus's Romanesque basilica in the foreground, and the basilica of St George's Convent in the background.

THE GOTHIC PALACE

Together with the cathedral, *the Charles Room of the Royal Palace* is the most important architectural achievement of the reign of Charles IV.

Left: corner of the vaulting; on the walls are mouldings of Gothic statues from St Vitus's Cathedral.

Above: first Renaissance doorway leading to the Gothic part.

Opposite page: view of the Charles Room.

South front of the Louis Wing, with Renaissance windows designed by Benedikt Ried between 1502 and 1509. The obelisk with a cross, in Early Baroque style, was placed in the gardens laid out by Josip Plečnik as a monument commemorating the defenestration of the two pro-Catholic royal officials, Jaroslav Bořita of Martinic and Vilém Slavata of Chlum, on 23 May 1618.

Opposite page: *Renaissance doorway* in the Louis Wing, with a view of the Bohemian Chancellery, built to the plans of Benedikt Ried between 1502 and 1509.

Opposite page: *Wenceslas IV's Hall of Columns*, built around 1400 by the royal building workshop of Točník Castle. The hall is one of the most striking examples of Gothic architecture of the Luxembourg era, known as Flamboyant Gothic. An atmosphere of elegance and purity is conveyed by the use of space and the various structural elements , notably the optical contraction of the ribs of the vault, which spring directly from the smooth, rounded columns or from the walls.

Right and below: *the Diet Hall on the first floor of the Louis Wing*. The doors are decorated with marquetry; on the walls are portraits of the Habsburgs; on the left, a portrait of Philip V of Spain (copy of a Velasquez); in the centre, a painting by Ignác Raab, the *Siege of Prague by the Prussian Army*; and, in a corner of the hall, a 17th-century faïence stove. From the Middle Ages this was the room where negotiations were held between the king and his nobles, and it was, above all, the seat of the Aulic Council of the Czech kingdom, whose deliberations were entered in the Land Rolls registers.

THE OLD DIET HALL

Old Diet Hall: winged head and dragon in a springing of the vault, above the clerk's tribune.

Opposite page: during the reign of Ferdinand I, Boniface Wohlmut built, in a corner of the Diet Hall *a tribune* for the chief clerk of the kingdom, which was linked to the room where the new Land Rolls registers were kept. A throne dating from the 19th century placed in the Diet reflected the wish of Czech society to see the rights and institutions of the kingdom re-established.

Vault of the Diet, constructed in 1559-63 by Boniface Wohlmut after the vault built by Benedikt Ried around 1500 had been destroyed by a fire in 1541.

Wohlmut built a vault in which the semicircular arches were buttressed by a network of ribs, the flowing lines of which combine to create the overall impression of much greater size.

Detail: according to legend, Boniface Wohlmut intended to add his own bust opposite that of Ferdinand I, placed on a bracket above the throne.

71

Room of the new Land Rolls, decorated with the coats-of-arms of the officials in charge of them from 1561 to 1774. In the rooms adjoining the Vladislav Hall, where the Land Rolls were kept, the ornamentation was in strict order of precedence. Thus, beneath the Czech lion from right to left, were the blazons of the royal steward, the supreme judge and the chief clerk: on the lower row were those of the steward of the kingdom, the deputy supreme judge, the royal clerk, the agent of the Land Rolls, the deputy chamberlain and the clerk of the minor Land Rolls.

Opposite page: in 1737, the wing containing the rooms that housed the Land Rolls was extended to include another room for the safekeeping of the archives concerning the St Wenceslas Crown and, subsequently, the Crown Jewels.

THE VLADISLAV ROOM AND HALL

North wall of the Vladislav Hall: the upper part of the façade, built between 1490 and 1502 by Benedikt Ried, rests on the foundations of the Gothic palace of Charles IV.

Opposite page: with its Late Gothic stellar vault, the so-called *Vladislav Room* was one of the first to be built in the course of the castle reconstruction that commenced in 1486, during the reign of Vladislav II Jagiello. The architect of the vault is thought to have been Hans Spiess of Frankfurt.

The areas adjacent to the Vladislav Hall allowed Benedikt Ried to apply his creative talents and imagination and to convey a sense of movement to the stone vaulting, its spanning ribs and the bay of the vault surrounded by columns and walls.

Below: the stairs leading to the south-west corner of the Vladislav Hall.

Opposite page: *the Riders' Staircase*, giving competitors on horseback access to the tournaments held in the Vladislav Hall.

The Vladislav Hall: the most extensive enclosed space of the Royal Palace of Prague Castle represents one of the peaks of Late Gothic architecture. The hall was built above the Romanesque and Gothic storey. Benedikt Ried boldly joined together several rooms of Charles IV's old palace to create an area of impressive dimensions and harmonious proportions based on the juxtaposition of contradictory features of Gothic and Renaissance styles.

Over the centuries this hall has been used for the most important events in the political and social life of the Czech kingdom and of the Czechoslovak state, such as coronation banquets and gatherings of the Estates General. This is where constitutions were adopted and where, from 1918, the elections of the president of the Republic have been held. During the time of Rudolf II, the hall was also the setting for knightly tournaments and for sales of valuable works of art and expensive merchandise.

Left: the east wall of the Vladislav Hall, with the Mannerist doorway of Giovanni Gargioli, who linked the hall to All Saints Chapel: it was used by the highest functionaries of the realm and by witnesses to the swearing of oaths in the chapel.

Fresco: on the second storey of the
White Tower, where Rudolf II had his
armoury, Bartholomeus Spranger painted
a fresco reflecting the function of the
place, namely the armed Minerva with
Mercury.

During his reign Prague and its castle not only became the heart of the Holy Roman Empire but also a cultural centre of exceptional importance. Karel van Mander, painter and theorist, and one of the guests of the social and cultural court entourage, wrote in 1604: 'Whoever aspires today to do anything great need only come (if he can) to Prague, to the greatest patron of the contemporary world, the emperor Rudolf II; he will see there, in the imperial residence, as in the collections of other great art lovers, an extraordinary number of excellent and precious things, special, unusual and beyond price.'

Rudolf initiated the new architectural activity in 1576 by commissioning the Royal Steward's House, next to the White Tower. During the 1580s he gradually developed his idea of transforming Prague Castle into a royal residence comparable to the Spanish Escorial, but his grandiose scheme was only partly realised. A new and very spacious wing of the palace was started in 1589 on the north side of the castle and was not completed until the early 1610s. It is not known who was the principal designer. Apparently a succession of Italian artists and craftsmen in the emperor's service played a part in it: they included the Florentine architect Giovanni Gargioli (d. 1585), the stonemason Giovanni Antonio Broca and the architects Giovanni Maria Philippi, Martin Gamborina and Antonio Valladra de Codero. The ground floor of the new wing served as stables for the Spanish stud horses; above were large rooms, one of which was named the Spanish Room, while another became the Rudolf Gallery, designed to house the royal art collection. Even though Rudolf was unable to carry through his plan to build a monumental edifice comparable to the Escorial, the new wing was nevertheless one of the most sumptuous buildings of its kind in Central Europe, thanks largely to its interior decorations by the eminent court sculptors and painters, Adriaen de Vries, and Hans and Paul Vredeman de Vries. Unhappily, in the 18th and 19th centuries this wing was refurbished in such a manner that, apart from the entrance door and some of the engravings, nothing remains of its original décor.

The uncertainty as to which architects and craftsmen were responsible for the royal building activities during the reign of Rudolf II is in some measure due to the very fact that so many were employed on the castle, then enjoying such extraordinary pre-eminence as a centre of learning and culture. One new and unusual feature was the so-called 'mathematical' tower, which was fashioned from the old episcopal tower and provided with an interior spiral staircase, a project inspired by the theory and example of Andrea Palladio and Vincenzo Scamozzi. This tower was subsequently demolished in the course of the reconstruction of the central part of the castle under Empress Maria Theresa in the 1770s.

After the reign of Rudolf II, Prague Castle no

longer enjoyed the pride of place and favour accorded it by an emperor renowned for his interest in the arts and sciences. Although the new emperor, Matthias II, who succeeded his brother in 1611, continued the building work initiated by Rudolf, using architects who had already seen service at the castle or who had been drawn to Prague by the reputation of the court, the years of glory had departed. Among the visitors who now came to Prague was the remarkable Venetian architect Vincenzo Scamozzi, to whom the new building work in the west wing was originally, though incorrectly, attributed. Matthias planned this wing as a link, on the south side of the castle, between the royal apartments and the Spanish Room. Another of his initiatives was the gate on the western side of the castle, which effectively ended Rudolf's dream of a palace with a frontage extending almost to Hradčany Square. Dynamically heightened to accommodate the carriageway, and featuring a dramatic series of architectonic elements, this gate is the first example of Bohemian Early Baroque. Indeed, the local saying that Baroque in Bohemia entered by way of the Matthias Gate seems fully justified.

During the first decades of the 17th century, which saw the onset of profound cultural and political changes in Europe, Prague Castle was notable as one of the earliest sites to be affected by the Baroque style. More dramatically, it was the place where a political and religious crisis flared up, with the defenestration of the Catholic nobles Martinic and Slavata on 23 May 1618. As a result of ensuing political developments, with Catholicism sweeping the country, Prague Castle lost its capital position in European politics and art. As the crisis of the Thirty Years' War erupted, construction work on the castle came to a virtual halt, and the important collections that had made the castle one of the most remarkable places of the age were dispersed.

PRAGUE CASTLE, POLITICAL AND ADMINISTRATIVE CENTRE OF COUNTRY AND STATE: FROM REFORMED MONARCHY TO DEMOCRATIC REPUBLIC

It was not until the middle of the 18th century that Prague Castle once again came to play a key role in the plans of imperial Vienna and emerged as one of the political centres of the Habsburg monarchy. In 1755, Empress Maria Theresa sent a communication to the council of the Czech governor, issuing the order 'to transform, reconstruct and furnish our royal residential castle, so that it can be comfortably inhabited, in our Czech city of Prague'. Once the decision had been taken to make more frequent use of the castle, the services to be provided clearly had to be in keeping with the living standards and administrative needs of the imperial court.

These were the considerations that now determined the nature and style of the rebuilding programme

Under the direction of Niccolo Pacassi, the architect of the Viennese imperial court, the work began in 1755 with the construction of the south wing which led from the old Royal Palace to the Hradčany quarter. In 1759 the western part was tackled, linking the new south wing to the north wing built under Rudolf. The work terminated with the construction of the wing connecting the northern and southern parts of the palace — the heart of the building that effectively divided the central courtyard into two sections. In extending the south and north wings towards the Hradčany quarter, Pacassi also created an additional courtyard eminently suitable for court ceremonial. The First Courtyard is still used today for special occasions. Visually and spatially, it was a small but welcome apendage to the overall structure of Prague Castle as devised by Paccasi, for the architect's plans completely sacrificed the picturesque variety of the castle buildings. Pacassi modernised the castle from top to bottom, applying a uniform pattern to the façades. The scheme he adopted was strictly horizontal, with deliberate repetition of window and mullion elements, a far cry from the verticality and diversity of the former buildings, many of which dated from the Middle Ages or rested on medieval foundations.

It was Anselmo Lurago who carried out Pacassi's plans, aided by Anton Kunz, who had come from Vienna. In 1766, on Lurago's death, Kunz assumed control of the work and, on his own death in 1769, its direction was entrusted to Antonín Haffenecker, who completed the project in 1755. A number of Prague artists and craftsmen were involved: stucco workers, cabinet-makers, carpenters, painters and sculptors. The sculptor Ignác F. Platzer made an important contribution: he created the statues of the *Fighting Giants* flanking the piers of the entry gate of the First Courtyard, facing Hradčany Square. Pacassi's achievement was to have transformed Prague Castle into a centre responding perfectly to the requirements of the country's new administration. The castle was now an ideal place from which to exercise tutorial and, in due course, state policy.

Pacassi's uniform style introduced a new dimension to the architecture of Prague Castle, to which all earlier architectonic schemes on the site had to accommodate. The subsequent 19th-century alterations and additions were centred principally on the sacred buildings and, with the exception of the Chapel of the Holy Cross, the castle site itself remained untouched. Czech society was meanwhile undergoing radical change, influenced by the interconnected concepts of rationalism and national renewal, but even more by the country's economic development. Expansion of the capital brought hundreds of thousands of new inhabitants to Prague, and the many buildings needed to accommodate them completely transformed the face of the city. Yet Prague Castle, with its Baroque outlines, still looked down, unaltered, from its hill, ever the symbol of administrative centralism.

With the birth of the Czechoslovak state in the 20th century, it was felt that the fortunes of Prague Castle needed to be integrated with the life of the Republic. This was immediately recognised by the first president of the Czechoslovak Republic, Tomáš G. Masaryk, elected on 14 November 1918. In his philosophical and sociological works Masaryk had roundly criticised the alienated culture of modern times, justly condemning this tendency as represented by many features of Pacassi's architecture. With a view to giving democratic life and meaning to Prague Castle, Masaryk envisaged certain essential developments. In the course of his search for someone to undertake the task, Václav V. Štech, professor of art history, and Jan Kotěra, professor of architecture, introduced him to the Slovenian architect Josip Plečnik.

Plečnik, without doubt the most gifted student of Otto Wagner's school in Vienna, was already familiar with Prague, where he had successfully directed, since 1910, the architectural studio of the School of Decorative Arts. Masaryk recognised in him a man whose conception of art was extraordinarily akin to his own: both of them saw art as an essential component of life and longed to restore to it the status it had enjoyed during the period when the humanist tendency of European culture found expression in Greek classicism. Just as, for Masaryk, the work of the ancient Greek philosophers and, above all, of Plato was the source of his philosophical thinking, centred as it was upon the constituents of modern alienated culture, so, too, the classic elements of Greek and Mediterranean architecture had become the fundamental motifs of the work of Plečnik who, rejecting contemporary conventions, resorted to earlier styles as the inspiration, well in advance of his time, of his 20th-century architecture.

In 1920 Masaryk appointed Plečnik architect of Prague Castle and charged him with the replanning of the courtyards and surroundings. The president's spiritual legacy was to be formulated in the clearest terms in a testament of 1925, in which he recapitulated the key elements of his thinking, explained his choice of Plečnik and the directives he gave the latter for his work at the castle: 'I wish Professor Plečnik to be the builder of the castle and to take decisions on all the necessary repairs and alterations... the layout of the gardens and also the new buildings there... I wish the work done at the castle to be an example for the nation, both in its careful preparation and its reasoned approach, and in its choice of good materials and the excellence of its accomplishment. The overall programme should be carried out with due consideration and in stages... The reason for establishing these criteria is to make the castle the residence of a democratic president; all the appointments of the castle, both inside and outside, should convey a sense of simple, yet artistic nobility, symbolising the ideas of independence of the state and of democracy... The people look on the castle as a national concern and for that reason not only presidents, but also governments, should be interested in seeing the transformation of a castle that was planned and built from a monarch's standpoint into a castle that is truly democratic.'

Masaryk discussed his ideas about the castle both directly with the architect and through the intermediary of his daughter Alice. Once these ideas were jointly agreed, Plečnik proceeded to express them in the clearest and most cultivated architectural terms. His plans related both to the inside and outside of the castle.

Shortly before his official appointment as castle architect, Plečnik had made a study of the Paradise Garden, adjacent to the south front of the building, and it was here that he began his work. He suggested altering the lie of the land, without affecting the building that overlooked the garden. The changes he introduced to this corner of the castle, previously hemmed in and of comparatively little interest, converted it into an area of striking originality, one of the first to be encountered by visitors approaching the castle from Malá Strana. Plečnik boldly opened up the garden, setting a gate in the old surrounding brick wall and exposing the slope of the terrain; to give access he provided the monumental staircase that was to become its most remarkable feature. He planned to connect the garden with what remained of an abandoned landscaped park, with its shrubs and trees, by setting up various symbolic objects, notably an obelisk near the steps and an enormous granite vase in the lower part of the garden. Even though the obelisk idea never came to fruition, the staircase was to constitute the garden's key architectonic element, affording splendid views of the castle, the lawns and the city. The garden was completed in 1924, at the same time as a neighbouring garden, located a little to the east, known as the Ramparts Garden. If the Paradise Garden, with its simple yet masterfully realised forms, conveyed an impression of space, with the panorama of town and castle symbolically framed by huge vases, the Ramparts Garden incorporated various architectonic themes characteristic of the city, accentuating the links between town and castle.

The Ramparts Garden begins with a small parterre in the middle of which Plečnik placed a Baroque fountain taken from the Paradise Garden.

The garden extends eastward by way of a level path, encompassing a narrow, geometrically divided area with a long view from the Baroque fountain to the eastern ramparts. The lengthwise section described by paths running from east to west is intersected at right angles by other paths leading to pavilions and terraces that offer interesting viewpoints of Prague. To emphasise the interrelationship of town and castle, Plečnik lowered the level of the surrounding wall to reveal the gardens lying below the ramparts. It was from this point of the ancient bastions that he provided spectacular views of the dominant buildings and landmarks of Prague, exploiting the natural beauty of the city as an inherent feature of the garden itself. Thus, for example, the semicircular terrace in the centre of the garden affords a commanding view of St Nicholas's Church in Malá Strana. The church can also been seen along the axis of the staircase which leads from the Third Court into the garden through a boldly columned doorway — yet another feature underlining the historic links between the castle interior, the garden area and the town. This semicircular terrace is an eye-catching feature, both horizontally and vertically, of the garden plan, its position highlighted by the adjoining obelisk.

The singular arrangement of the individual constructions in the Ramparts Garden transforms its geometrical structure into a living and evocative architectonic ensemble. In addition to panoramic pavilions, balustrades, colonnades and pergolas, Plečnik gave pride of place to various symbolic objects, such as the columns, obelisk and pyramid, intended to reinforce the spiritual significance of the castle and its place in history. One monument, for example, recalls the site of the historic defenestration of Martinic and Slavata in 1618. And among the exceptional buildings of the garden are the Bellevue colonnade, the panoramic summer house and the Moravian bastion. Each is unique, not only because of its positioning, but also for the original conception of its elements, the happy choice of its constituent materials and its ideological integration into the overall scheme. Classic architectonic motives are here transformed and integrated with exquisite aesthetic sensibility.

The Paradise Garden and the Ramparts Garden linked the south face of the castle and the city in a novel manner. The doors of this sealed monolith of a building were literally flung open, thanks to the new access to the gardens, and the gardens themselves now formed a panoramic link with the historic city monuments in the immediate vicinity of the castle. For the rest, Plečnik's primary aim was to do away with the barracks-like uniformity which characterised the castle courtyards and interiors.

In 1921 he was offered and accepted the chair of architectonic composition at Ljubljana University. From then on he planned all his work during alternate stays in Prague and Ljubljana and through an exchange of correspondence with the president, his daughter Alice and his friends, including Jan Kotěra. The associations of Plečnik with Ljubljana seem to have reinforced the Mediterranean character of his work, as well as his expressive originality and individuality. He was conspicuously successful in applying the tasteful, cultivated southern European tradition to the space at his disposal. In his subsequent changes to the castle interior, Plečnik never lost sight of the surrounding areas, aiming at an interpenetration, at once spatial and ideological, of the enclosed block of buildings, the courtyards and the gardens.

Plečnik's reconstruction of the First Courtyard consisted essentially in repaving it and adding two flagpoles, 25 metres (82 ft) high, placed in front of the Matthias Gate. The alterations to the Bastion Garden, carried out from 1927 to 1930, were of greater significance. Plečnik built a new passage from the Second Courtyard into this garden, and enclosed it with a wall intended to effect a transition between the Late Baroque style of the Archbishop's Palace and the modern atmosphere he had created in the garden. This time, showing considerable inventiveness, he designed two semicircular flights of steps, one convex, the other concave, linking the two garden levels. At the front of the garden, facing Hradčany Square, he contrasted the stylised greenery of the existing conifers with the natural informality of the Stag Moat: the garden was joined to the moat by arcades, above which a railed path led over sloping ground to the Masaryk panorama, itself a new garden feature.

The refurbishing of the castle's three courtyards was a particularly challenging task. Plečnik gave a feeling of unity to all three by applying a geometrical structure to the pavements, and by using fairly large granite flagstones, the identical dimensions of which helped to create an overall impression of spaciousness and deliberate significance. For the flags, he utilised materials from different parts of the country, avoiding monotony thanks to the subtle colour nuances of the stone which enliven the whole composition and suggest yet another symbolic link between the castle and the various regions of the Republic.

The work carried out in the Third Courtyard of the castle (situated between the south wing of the Royal Palace, the perpendicular main building and the cathedral) was particularly arduous. There, too, Plečnik provided a link with the garden via a staircase, in the form of a closed pergola, emerging at the east corner of the courtyard. In the foreground, he introduced two objects of particular interest: at the corner of the Old Provost's Lodging he set up a granite monolith, 16 metres (52 ft) high, in memory of the Czechoslovak Legions and in honour of the democratic republic, and to the east of this monolith he set up a fountain, in the form of a Gothic equestrian statue of St George and the dragon. The fountain, on a massive block of granite, stands off-centre to the rectangular water basin beneath; and this, in turn, is placed off-centre to the circular railing that surrounds it. The monument testifies to Plečnik's masterly skill in combining selected materials (bronze, stone and water) to create a composition which observes the principles of asymmetry and harmony, which achieves a balanced horizontal and vertical division of space, and which constitutes, in

every detail, a pure work that in its materials and motifs is unashamedly respectful of historical tradition.

Inside the castle Plečnik embarked on a major project which was continued by his talented pupil Otto Rothmayer and by Pavel Janák, the immediate successor to Plečnik as architect of Prague Castle.

In some places, Plečnik did away with the separate levels which, in Pacassi's alterations, implied a distinction between the life of the imperial court and the administration. His most radical achievement was the building of the Hall of Columns in the west wing of the palace, facing the passage situated behind the Matthias Gate. It was here that Plečnik gave clearest expression both to the democratic idealism of the new state and to his own temperament and personal credo. He unified the verticality of the room with three superimposed horizontal rows of columns, set inside the enclosing wall of the palace. This balanced and dignified composition, so characteristic of southern classical architecture, was very rare in a Czech environment loyal to its Baroque tradition. The harmony of the colonnades was enhanced by the innovative use of a classical motif on the front wall, in the form of columns, an arch and a round window directly above.

Plečnik's plans, approved by Masaryk, for the private apartments and the library of the president were likewise attuned to the needs and tastes of a head of state who was imbued with the ideals of democracy and freedom.

In the block of buildings situated in the south wing of the castle, Plečnik found further opportunity to make a link between the presidential apartments, the courtyard and the garden. His solutions for the inside passages of communication and, in particular, the access corridor to the staircase and the lift were particularly ingenious. The lift and the spiral staircase surrounding the lift-shaft were likewise exceptional achievements. Plečnik placed the steps inside a barrel vault, the structure of which, like that of the walls, was thrown into relief by white pointing. It was a remarkably inventive example of a

geometrically structured curved surface in space, demonstrating, as in all his work, a thorough appreciation of the emerging principles underpinning an apparently simple construction.

Plečnik paid just as much attention to the reception rooms of the presidential apartment, particularly to the inner vestibule, situated beneath a light well deriving from an ancient skylight at the point where the wings of the historic palace intersected. He made no attempt to conceal the original purpose of this area: on the contrary, he emphasised it by making it the focal point of his new scheme. He covered the skylight of the vault with glass tiles, complementing the curvature with arches dividing the hall into sections, and placing directly below the well, in the centre of the room, a table with a vase full of water, its surface artificially lit. Thus the presidential apartment was furnished with a traditional motif of a Roman house — an atrium complete with impluvium — harmonising perfectly with its modern setting. And in his work on other parts of the private apartments and offices at Prague Castle, Plečnik displayed a similar insight into the values of past and present, with equally happy results.

Plečnik remained at Prague Castle only a little longer than the Republic's first president. In 1935 T.G. Masaryk resigned the presidency and in 1936 a new architect for Prague Castle was appointed, namely Pavel Janák, who had succeeded Plečnik to the chair of architecture at the School of Decorative Arts. In his study on Plečnik, Janák expressed respect for the extraordinary work of his predecessor and appreciation of the values that his inventiveness had brought to 20th-century architecture: '... [Plečnik] does not subscribe to the customary definitions and conventions of space or form; but impelled by deep inner feeling, he arranges his columns, his pillars and his materials, which are at once simple and innovative, in a manner that is strikingly original, yet wholly authoritative. He is in no sense a romantic classicist, but a complete man of his time, who has to justify everything to himself, to create everything.'

The true successor of Plečnik at Prague Castle, however, was not Janák, but Plečnik's pupil and colleague Otto Rothmayer. Having collaborated with Plečnik, Rothmayer was sufficiently in tune with his teacher's ideas and objectives to pursue the work in the same spirit, notably by reinforcing the bonds between the castle, the gardens and the city. Thus he built a graceful spiral staircase to link the Ramparts Garden with the Vladislav Hall. The staircase was placed against the wall of the south rampart, on a projection contiguous to the Vladimir Hall. Between 1947 and 1950, again using Plečnik as his model, Rothmayer designed and built a large hall in the west wing and a corridor joining this room to the historic areas of the castle's south wing. At the point where the corridor crossed the room, he set up two Ionic columns, clearly based on Plečnik's use of classic elements in a modern architectural context. Yet Plečnik's concept of architecture, as reflected in all his work, was unshackled by modern conventions. The judgement of the Czech architect Otakar Novotný puts it succinctly: 'In fact, Plečnik was opposed to all modern architecture. He was one of Wagner's best pupils, but it was in himself that he found true mastery, in his deep religious conviction, in his inflexible sense of truth and beauty...'

At Prague Castle, Rothmayer provided Plečnik's work with an epilogue worthy of his genius, fulfilling his teacher's ambition to revalue a thousand years of architectural tradition. Paradoxically, his work coincided with a period, from 1948 and for some forty years, when the ideals of democracy were silenced throughout the country, and all attempts to find meaning and inspiration in the new architectural heritage of Prague Castle were repressed. Today, once more, the castle is the object of appreciation, assessment and study. Its historic and recent achievements, particularly the work of Plečnik, are a challenge to the architecture, the art and the culture of the 20th century.

THE HABSBURG ROOM

Preceding and opposite pages: in all the royal residences or nobles' castles, one room was always devoted to ancestors. In Prague Castle, on the first floor of the south wing, there is a gallery of this nature, relatively restrained for its period, comprising twenty-two portraits of the family of Empress Maria Theresa, whose own portrait was given place of honour in the centre of the main wall. On her right is her husband, Francis of Lorraine, and on her left, her son Emperor Joseph II. The other large paintings (which from their style may be attributed to the court portraitists Martin van Meytens and Johann Karl Auerbach) are of the sons and daughters of the empress, each surmounted by a smaller portrait of their spouse. There are

also portraits of Maria Theresa's brother and sisters, hung between the windows, and two of children, one (above) of her grandson (1768-1835), who was to become emperor in 1792 under the name of Francis II (last ruler of the Holy Roman Empire). In order to enliven this series of portraits, some people are shown with the instruments of their hobby: Marie Caroline, future queen of Naples, holds painting implements, the Archduchess Marie Elisabeth sits at a spinet, etc. These portraits also constitute valuable historical and cultural documents inasmuch as they reproduce royal crowns, insignia of orders and various kinds of costume ornamentation.

THE BROŽIK ROOM

In the many reception rooms on the first
floor of the castle's south wing (reached by
a staircase situated the Matthias Gate) two
principal features are found: firstly, stucco
decorations on the walls and ceilings (some

from the time of Empress Maria Theresa
and others completed in the 19th century) as
well as furniture, all modelled on the interiors of the Schönbrunn Palace, which combine to give an impression of stylistic unity;
secondly, certain objects of an individual
nature which serve to differentiate the various rooms. Thus, the main drawing room is
distinctive for an immense painting by
Václav Brožík, done in Paris in 1878, with a
historical subject: the mission of the Czech
king, Ladislav Posthumus, to the court of
the French king, Charles VII. This picture,
originally in the imperial gallery in Berlin,
was bought for Prague Castle in 1922 and
has been hanging in its present position
since 1938.

The music room, its contours following those of the building, is one of the reception rooms designed by the court architect, Niccolo Pacassi, for the south wing of Prague Castle. In a niche is a copy of Matyaš Bernard Braun's sculpture, *Night*. The Rococo faïence stove is part of the original furniture.

Space on the first storey of the central building: this is one of the few areas of the old Renaissance palace that has been preserved, or rather reconstructed. It served as a passage between the king's private apartments, which extended from the south wing of the castle overlooking the town to the central or perpendicular wing containing the arts room and the corridors transformed into a painting gallery. The various bays of the vault are accentuated by the unobtrusive but artistically effective ornamentation of astragals.

Left: *tapestry of the Antony and Cleopatra cycle.* Certain series of tapestries from the Early Baroque period — notably those originating in the Brussels factories of celebrated tapestry makers like Geraert Peemans, Jan van Leefdael and others, devoted to subjects popular at the time, such as the different parts of the world, the months of the year, etc. — give some idea of the extraordinary quality of the original castle tapestries. They were subsequently dispersed, either because of the fortunes of war or because they were transferred to the imperial court in Vienna. The series of seven tapestries in the Antony and Cleopatra cycle, made around the middle of the 17th century by Jan van Leefdael and Geraert van der Strecken, includes this *Battle Under the Ramparts of Alexandria.*

97

THE GALLERY OF RUDOLF II AND THE SPANISH ROOM

Concealed behind the monotonously uniform façades of the castle's Second Courtyard are interiors quite different in character: the southern part was reserved for the private apartments of the king (and also for President Masaryk), while the north wing was used for exhibiting collections and, after these were dispersed, for official celebrations. This is more obvious on the north side of the castle, where the large windows of Rudolf II's Gallery open in a semicircle overlooking the Stag Moat. The emperor had this room built in 1597-8 as a picture gallery, but the present neo-Renaissance restoration, to the designs of Heinrich von Ferstel, dates only from 1866-8.

Pages 99-101: In the time of Rudolf II, the largest chamber, the Spanish Room, was devoted to the exhibition of sculpture. The statues were placed not only in the room itself, then divided by columns, but also in the niches, now hidden by large mirrors, in the south wall. From this period all that remains is the stucco decoration to be seen in the spandrels above the niches and windows and on the frieze that surrounds the room. As in Rudolf II's Gallery, most of the refurbishing was done in 1866-8, based on the designs of Ferdinand Kirschner, assisted by the court sculptor, Auguste le Vigne. Today this room has two functions: it is used by the president of the Republic for occasions of protocol (for example, the signing of a treaty with Germany in 1992), and it is thrown open to the public for concerts, conferences and social gatherings.

PLEČNIK'S HALL OF COLUMNS

This room was created in the perpendicular wing between the First and Second Courtyards and linked by a passage to the Matthias Gate. Plečnik removed Pacassi's interior floors to make an immense hall which would constitute an official entrance to the castle and stand as a symbol of the new democracy. By using three superimposed rows of columns with Ionic capitals, Plečnik divided the height and created a harmonious combination of vertical and horizontal lines, directing the eye upward. The architecture expressed Masaryk's endeavours to achieve a creative linkage between the modern Republic and its classical cultural heritage. The monumental columns, placed at the point where the hall (which extends to the wing situated behind it) intersects with the corridor, form, as it were, an epilogue to the ancient dream that is linked, here in the castle, with the names of Tomáš Masaryk and Josip Plečnik. The columns were designed by the architect Otto Rothmayer, who succeeded Plečnik at the castle and, ironically, completed the work in the 1950s, at the very moment when the democratic ideals of the First Republic were smothered by the totalitarian Communist regime.

THE CASTLE RESIDENCE OF THE PRESIDENT OF THE REPUBLIC

At the point where the south wing of the castle crosses the perpendicular wing (between the First and Second Courtyards) Josip Plečnik found the necessary space to build, in the 1920s, the private apartments and reception rooms of the residence of President Tomáš Masaryk.

Opposite page: *entrance hall*, created by covering a small inner court in the centre of the southern part of the castle.

Impluvium: Plečnik made the best possible use of this area below a skylight to express the spiritual values that President Masaryk considered to be the most important aspects of human life and society. Plečnik bounded the impluvium with pillars supporting the semicircles of the walls, and completed it with vases, creating a harmonious whole which, through the significance of forms and materials, conveyed a mystical impression.

The Golden Room or *Harp Room* was part of the residence of President Masaryk in the south wing of the castle. It was conceived by Josip Plečnik in the traditional spirit of the most important interiors of the Czech kingdom, notably St Wenceslas's Chapel in the cathedral and the Holy Cross Chapel of Karlštejn Castle. The fact that the walls and ceilings were decorated in gold is an allusion to these chapels. The Yugoslav sculptor Damian Pešan assisted with the ornamentation, and was responsible for the sculpture above of the door (*detail above*).

THE OFFICES OF THE PRESIDENCY

The mural painting and the entrance door are the work of the contemporary Czech painter Aleš Lamr. These rooms were arranged after the election of Václav Havel as president of the Republic in 1989. The large office is decorated with contemporary and older works of art. Plečnik was responsible for the spiral staircase, with panelling and a marble ramp, which links the private apartments of the president (situated on the ground floor) to the reception rooms on the first floor of the residence.

THE OFFICE OF PRESIDENT VÁCLAV HAVEL

Below: Secession-style objects on the president's desk.

The president's library.

Opposite page: The new office of President Václav Havel designed by Bořek Šípek, a Czech living in the Netherlands: between the windows, a painting by Josef Vyletal; behind the desk, Plečnik's two flagpoles intended for the presidential banner and the flag of the Republic. The bookcase has many photographs of head of states.

Below: View from the desk onto the room. The map attributed to Johann Müller is of Bohemia in the 18th century without Moravia and Silesia. The statue is by the Czech sculptor Olbram Zoubek.

Page 112: *winding staircase* built by Josip Plečnik around the lift shaft, in the presidential palace.

ST VITUS'S CATHEDRAL

Prague Castle, overlooked by St Vitus's Cathedral, is the dominating feature of the city landscape. Viewed from the river, Hradčany is one of the most sensational sights of Europe. Inseparable from the secular and religious life of Prague, the thousand-year-old castle is a potent symbol of the Czech nation and its history. St Vitus's Cathedral, the metropolitan church of the Czech lands, is, from the viewpoint both of art history and conservation, the most important of the state's sacred buildings.

The cathedral's origins date back to the reign of the three Luxembourg kings on the Bohemian throne. John of Luxembourg (reigned 1310-46), known as the Blind, began the actual construction, but it was Charles IV (reigned 1346-78) who determined its appearance, and Wenceslas IV (reigned 1378-1419) who completed the medieval part of the cathedral. Under the Luxembourgs the Czech lands acquired great political importance and a cultural reputation in marked contrast to the chaos that had followed the murder of Wenceslas III, last male heir of the Přemyslids — the original Czech dynasty — in 1306, at Olomouc.

Charles IV, historically the most influential of the three Luxembourg monarchs, came to the throne of Bohemia on the death of his father, John, killed at the battle of Crécy where, despite his blindness, he fought with the French against Edward III of England. Charles, whose mother was a Přemyslid, had been baptised Wenceslas, but had been raised in the French court, where he had acquired a rich cultural background. He returned to Prague in 1333, at the age of seventeen. During his reign, Prague became the capital of the Holy Roman Empire. Elected Roman king on 11 July 1346, Charles IV was crowned at Bonn the same year, then ceremonially enthroned at Aachen (Aix-la-Chapelle) in 1349. He was consecrated by the pope as Holy Roman Emperor, in Rome, in 1355. Nowadays Charles is remembered principally for having founded Prague University (1348), the oldest in central Europe, as well as the city quarter of

Nové Město in the same year. This New Town covered almost 360 hectares (900 acres), a huge area for that time. He was also responsible for building a stone bridge over the Vltava and the celebrated Karlštejn Castle, where the imperial Crown Jewels were to be safely housed.

Charles takes credit, too, for establishing the archdiocese of Prague and for building the city's cathedral. Enea Silvio de Piccolomini (1405-64), who became Pope Pius II in 1458, said that Charles IV 'would certainly have been a truly illustrious monarch if only he had not been more preoccupied with the Czech kingdom than with the Holy Roman Empire', and others were to echo this opinion. However, this view was emphatically rejected by the Czechs, who have always looked on Charles as the father of the country. The only native challenge to this assessment was to come from the rebellious Hussites. Both extremes of belief have to be taken into account, because Czech history from the Middle Ages to modern times has been moulded equally by the cultural and social advances that were initiated in Europe during Charles's time and by the Hussite resistance, based on the moral precepts of the Bible, to papal supremacy.

The present St Vitus's Cathedral was, in fact, the third church of the Prague diocese, which had been established in 975-6 at the site of the first ancient rotunda. Later, St Vitus's Rotunda was replaced by the Ottonian basilica of Prince Spytihněv II (reigned 1055-6). Completed by his successor, Vratislav II, it had been solemnly consecrated in 1096 by Kosmas, head of the chapter and the most important chronicler of the early Přemyslid state. The building of the new cathedral stemmed directly from the wish of the Czech kings to raise the diocese of Prague to the status of archdiocese. On 30 April 1334, this ambition was achieved when Pope Clement VI (Charles IV's former tutor from his Paris years) despatched a bull creating the archdiocese of Prague. The first archbishop was the king's counsellor and friend, Arnošt of Pardubice (1297-1364).

The foundation stone of the cathedral was ceremonially laid on 21 November 1344, after the archbishop's public enthronement. Beneš Krabice of Weitmile, chronicler of Charles's court, noted that 'the new archbishop of Prague, the king of Bohemia, his two sons John and Charles, and a large number of churchmen and nobles came out of the church and made their way to the place that had been dug and prepared to receive the new foundations. The archbishop, the king and his two sons descended to the site... and laid, with all due respect and piety, the first building stone of the new church... while the choir joyfully sang the *Te Deum Laudamus*.' At the same time, the king of Bohemia, together with his sons, made a donation towards the building of the church 'for eternity, of one-tenth of the royal revenues from taxes levied on the Kutná Hora silver mines'. Under an act dated 13 October 1341, kept in the archives of St Vitus's chapter, John of Luxembourg had already donated one-tenth of royal revenues of all the Bohemian silver mines, at that time highly profitable, for the building of the new cathedral.

John of Luxembourg had expressed the wish that the available finances should be used primarily to embellish the tombs of St Wenceslas and St Adalbert (Vojtěch), buried in St Vitus's Cathedral *'primo pro decore et exaltatione seu structura sepulchrorum beatorum Wenzeslai et Adalberti... cum argenteis tabulis et imaginibus deauratis cum gemmes et lapidibus pretiosis'*. This was undoubtedly to make good the wrong he had done in 1336 when he had removed from St Wenceslas's tomb the silver statues of the twelve apostles — statues that Charles had commissioned three years previously on his return to Bohemia. According to contemporary legend, this act could well have brought on the blindness that later afflicted King John.

In due course Charles IV enriched the treasure of St Vitus's Cathedral with an astonishing quantity of precious relics and reliquaries. The first and most important of these treasures was the huge gold St Wenceslas Crown, made for his coronation as king of Bohemia on 1-2 September 1347, and thenceforth kept in the cathedral. After being altered in 1354 and 1378, the crown weighed almost 2.5 kilos (5 lbs). It was studded with ninety-one precious stones (sapphires, spinels, emeralds and rubies) and twenty pearls. The crown itself was surmounted by a reliquary in the form of a cross, with a cameo containing one of the thorns of Christ's crown. Charles had dedicated his crown to St Wenceslas and since 1358 it had rested on the head of the saint's gold-encased bust. In response to Charles's request, a papal bull from Clement VI, dated 6 May 1346, was received, guaranteeing the St Wenceslas Crown special protection: the bull stipulated that the crown should not be removed from the saint's head except for coronations and, exceptionally, for 'ceremonies entailing the use of the royal crown, but only in Prague or its suburbs'. Anyone attempting to steal, sell or pawn the crown would be punished, among other ways, by excommunication. 'Whoever dares to do it or attempt it will incur the wrath of all-powerful God and of the saintly apostles Peter and Paul,' proclaimed a letter patent which was certainly intended to strike fear into the hearts of Charles's successors to the Czech throne. (Events during the following centuries showed that this protection was effective. Even today, the crown of the ancient Czech kings is displayed only on commemorative or special state occasions, and has never been exhibited in a museum.)

Among the most valuable gold objects in the cathedral treasure dating from the early part of Charles's reign, two deserve special mention. These are an onyx cup with an inscription that identifies it as a gift from Charles IV, dating from 1351, and a no less astonishing receptacle, 87 cm (34 in) high, containing many relics and Roman and Byzantine cameos. Made in 1354, it was originally destined for Karlštejn Castle. During his travels of 1354-5 to mark his coronation as Holy Roman Emperor, Charles acquired a large number of relics. At Pavia he obtained the head and body of St Vitus, patron saint of Prague's cathedral; at Einsiedeln he was

Bust of Wenceslas of Luxembourg.

given a large piece of the skull of St Sigismund, king of Burgundy in the 6th century, which Charles, himself crowned king of Burgundy, kept in order to propagate the cult. Then, in 1365, at St-Maurice d'Augane (diocese of Sitten in Switzerland) Charles was donated the body of St Sigismund, which he placed in a special chapel in the new cathedral. One year later, by a decision of the synod of Prague, St Sigismund became the national patron saint. Unfortunately, golden statues of the two saints on their columns subsequently disappeared.

One object in particular testifies to the quality of the goldsmiths' work commissioned by Charles IV during those years. It is a reliquary bust of Charlemagne in silver-gilt, surmounted by the crown of the Roman king, dating from 1349, cleverly made in Prague and now part of the treasure of

Aachen Cathedral. E. Poche has advanced the theory that the bust itself was originally kept in Prague, associating it with the sculpture of Peter Parler's early period. From 1350, during the Easter festivities, the most important relics and reliquaries given to the cathedral by Charles IV were exhibited to the crowds of pilgrims (up to 100,000 people) who gathered in the cattle market (now Charles Square) in Prague's Nové Město quarter. The vast majority of pilgrims were sure to visit the cathedral and expected to contribute towards the building of a new choir. Once the necessary money was found, work could proceed with the construction of the cathedral during the seventy-five years that followed the laying of the foundation stone.

Matthew of Arras (*primus magister fabrice*) was summoned from Avignon, in 1344 at the latest, to

115

direct the building of the new cathedral. Certainly, the choice of a French builder was not due entirely to the links that existed between the Luxembourgs and Pope Clement VI: it was mainly as a result of Charles's declared intention to transform Prague into a town modelled on those of the West, furnished with a cathedral in the prevalent French Late Gothic style. (After Prague, the only cathedral of the French type to be built abroad was in Milan, in 1387.)

In Prague, Matthew of Arras envisaged a complete cathedral plan: a raised choir, a hexagonal ambulatory surrounded by closed radiating chapels, a separate transept and a three-aisled basilica with a west front topped by twin towers. In 1352, on the death of Matthew, it became clear that such a project could never be realised. The parts that had been finished included the columns of the polygon and the ambulatory around the choir and its constituent chapels, up to the level of the triforium; in the northern section, the east wall of the sacristy was up, and in the southern section, Matthew had completed the first three side chapels, although the third, the Holy Cross Chapel (originally the St Simon and St Jude Chapel) is only partially attributable to him, by reason of an altered plan.

The creative art of Matthew of Arras is associated with the development of French architecture at the end of the 13th and beginning of the 14th centuries. The most characteristic feature of his architecture is the balanced, rhythmic effect of space, based on the repetition and breaking up of horizontal planes. A carefully devised system involving the use and juxtaposition of different architectonic elements gives a lively and dynamic overall effect to a style of architecture that does not abound in figurative or individual ornamental detail.

After the death of Matthias of Arras, the activities of the building workshop were directed for three or four seasons by one of his assistants, a foreman (*parlerius, parlier*) whose identity is unknown. The team now began to build (*construiere*) the first new altars, the scarce remains of which testify to the

sculptural talents of the workshop's stonecarvers: examples include the stone antependium in the Chapel of the Holy Relics (originally the St Adalbert and St Dorothea Chapel), made for Rudolf, duke of Saxony (d. 1356), and the antependium in St Wenceslas's Chapel (transferred from St Anne's Chapel), which was commissioned by Purchard, burgrave of Magdeburg (before 1358). Nevertheless, however important these works may be from the historical and iconographical viewpoint, their artistic worth is negligible in comparison with the remarkable quality of the later sculpture of St Vitus's Cathedral.

In 1356 Charles IV found a solution to this period of transition by calling upon a new German architect and sculptor from Schwäbisch Gmünd (*secundus magister fabrice, magister operis*). He was Peter Parler (son of Heinrich Parler of Cologne) who was then only twenty-three. Peter Parler took charge of the cathedral construction from 1356 until the end

Bust of Peter Parler.

of the century. Moreover, at the emperor's behest or with his express agreement, he created a number of other remarkable works in the Luxembourg Gothic style: the stone bridge over the Vltava; the choir of St Bartholomew's Church at Kolin, on the Elbe; All Saints Chapel in Prague Castle; and perhaps, in part, St Barbara's Church at Kutná Hora. Before coming to Prague, in addition to his apprenticeship in his father's workshop at Schwäbisch Gmünd while the Holy Cross Church was under construction, Peter Parler had already worked in Augsburg (on the east choir of the Cathedral of the Virgin Mary), at Nuremburg (in the Frauenkirche), and perhaps also in Cologne, the native town of his future wife, Gertrude.

Peter Parler was completely at home in Prague. From 1359 he was the owner of a house in the Hradčany quarter and he often sat on the municipal council. His salary as director of works at the cathedral was 56 Bohemian grosche per week (when ordinary labourers often earned no more than one grosch weekly). The building workshop of the cathedral which he set up employed highly qualified stonemasons from many different German-speaking lands and towns: among them were several of his relatives and, later, his own sons Wenzel and Johann. Charles could not have wished for a more brilliant architect and sculptor than Peter Parler to carry through his visionary schemes. Inventive in conception and pleasing in execution, Parler's works paved the way for the final period of European Late Gothic throughout the Czech and German territories and far beyond.

Several precise dates indicate the systematic manner in which work on the new choir of St Vitus's Cathedral progressed under Parler's supervision. In 1362 the north side of the sacristy was completed with two bays of stellar vaults and pendentives, the first of their kind in Bohemia. In the same year Archbishop Jan Očko of Vlašim consecrated the high altars of St Vitus and of the Virgin Mary. In 1373 Peter Parler built the triumphal arch (*arcus magnus*). In 1385 a great net vault, again the first of its kind in Europe, was constructed in the choir. In 1392 the foundation stone was laid of the three-aisled basilica, dedicated to the Visitation of the Blessed Virgin, to St Wenceslas and to the other patron saints of Bohemia. Subsequently, in 1396, Archbishop Olbram of Škvorec had the relics of St Adalbert and the Five Brother Saints (martyrs of the missionary journey of St Adalbert to Poland and Prussia),which had been brought from Gniezno to Prague in 1039, transferred from the old church to the eastern part of the new central nave, then under construction. Most of these donations, as well as others, are inscribed on the plaque, dated 1396, on the west pier of the cathedral's south doorway, the text of which is probably by Wenceslas of Radeč, who was then head of the workshop.

The architectural conception of Peter Parler, as seen in the cathedral choir, differs considerably from that of Matthew of Arras and his colleagues. Parler retained only fragments of the parts previously completed, and continued the work in his own fashion. Obviously in accord with the wishes of Charles IV and possibly also with those of the archbishops of Prague and the chapter (and thus in keeping with the direction of contemporary architecture, already far removed from the universality of Late Gothic cathedral building), Peter Parler abandoned the homogeneous conception of the choir for an indiviual conception of an entity of separate parts, each related to the other, yet each with its own significance and function. The carefully ordered geometrical plan of the basilica within the context of the ideal cathedral, as envisaged by Matthew, was no longer considered obligatory, any more than the latter's conception of the walls and the handling of space. Everywhere, new creative approaches were used to attain an original expressive effect. The striking changes affecting the volume and variety of architectonic elements hark back, in a sense, to the traditional forms of the 13th century. The details deriving from Romanesque art (such as the semicircular arches) juxtaposed, at the other extreme, with modern elements reminiscent of similar tendencies in mainland Europe and England (the airy interplay of vaults and the flamboyant motifs of rose windows) are altogether remarkable. Equally notable is the effect produced by the contrast between the lower level of the choir, relatively dark, given the nature of the material composing its walls, and its bright upper part, with the large windows of the triforium letting in plenty of natural light.

All the parts of the cathedral built by Peter Parler were planned independently of one another. This was particularly true of St Wenceslas's Chapel, especially revered as a place of worship and spiritual inspiration, being the chapel of the oldest Czech saint, that duke of Bohemia who was a distant Přemyslid ancestor of Charles IV himself. The key importance of this chapel arose from the fact that the original site of Wenceslas's tomb had been venerated since the translation of his remains, in 938, from Stará Boleslav, on the orders of his brother, Boleslav I, who had murdered him in either 928 or 935. Charles IV adhered to this tradition and did not place the remains of Wenceslas near the high altar, in 1358, which would have entailed changing the identity of the cathedral's original patron. However, as noted by Beneš Krabice of Weitmile, he commissioned for the saint a new 'funerary monument in pure gold, and had it adorned with the costliest of jewels and choice semi-precious stones, and embellished it in such a manner that its like could be found nowhere else in the world' (it vanished, after the brutal intervention of Emperor Sigismund at the beginning of the Hussite Wars). The veneration Charles IV showed to St Wenceslas is attested by his inscription on the monument: *Hystoria nova de sancto Wenceslao martyre, duce Bohemorum, per dominum Karolum, imperatorem Romanorum, regem Bohemie compilata.*

Constructed on an extensive square plan, St Wenceslas's Chapel extends into the south arm of the transept, in line with the chapels on the south side of the choir. Flanked by massive walls and lit only by small windows, this chapel was doubtless regarded originally, because of its valuable contents, as a treasure chamber. Nevertheless, its overall visual and emblematic effect was designed to convey a sense of other-worldly beauty, probably with the intention of representing, symbolically, celestial Jerusalem. The complexity of the stellar vaulting, supported on huge triangular-based pedestals, suggests a protective baldaquin spread high above the sacred tomb. In 1372 Peter Parler's stonemasons lined the chapel walls, under the projecting cornice of the surrounding vault, with flat semi-precious stones which, with their gilded stucco work, provide a rich frame for the eleven mural paintings of Christ's Passion, by the imperial painter Oswald. Above the altar is a Crucifixion, showing Charles IV kneeling with his third wife, Elizabeth of Pomerania. Unfortunately, Late Gothic repainting has altered the appearance of these works.

Other paintings by Oswald, which evidently played an important part in decorating the cathedral, are preserved in the Vlašim Chapel, originally dedicated to St Erhard and St Odile, and today to St Adalbert. On the east wall is the *Baptism of St Odile*, with the donor, Bishop Jan Očko of Vlašim (after 1370); and on the west wall is Jan Očko of Vlašim as cardinal (he had been consecrated on 27 September 1378), kneeling before Christ and the saints. Oswald's work is directly descended from that of Master Theodoric, who did the panel paintings in the Holy Cross Chapel at the imperial castle of Karlštejn. Belonging to a school allied to that of Oswald, Theodoric executed the mural painting representing the Adoration of the Magi in the St Adalbert and St Dorothea Chapel, the so-called Saxony Chapel, which also contained the ancient reredos of St Adalbert. He was also responsible for the painting of the Madonna and St Mary Magdalen in the chapel to this saint, also known as the Wallenstein (Valdštejn) Chapel.

From the original St Wenceslas's Chapel there still remains a large iron reliquary, in the shape of a tower, for which the master smith Wenceslas was paid 1200 Bohemian grosche. The small gilded doors of the wall custodial behind the altar is also a delicate piece of ironwork and locksmith's work, apparently from the same period. A Romanesque bronze door-knocker, in the form of a lion's head, emphasises the Romanesque character of the north door. According to legend, St Wenceslas clung to this door-knocker as he died a martyr's death in front of the church of Stará Boleslav.

Charles IV certainly regarded St Wenceslas's Chapel as a place of great religious and ideological importance. Peter Parler reiterated this belief by placing a stone statue of St Wenceslas outside the chapel in the wide space demarcated by the supporting pier above the chapel. The statue is two metres (just over six feet) high and bears on the pedestal Parler's personal inscription (since the end of the 19th century this has been a copy). Made in 1373 with the assistance of his nephew, Heinrich of Gmünd, it is one of Parler's masterpieces. To the left of the chapel, an open, two-newel winding staircase climbs towards the roof of the great transept vault:

dating from 1372, it is unique of its kind and among Parler's most remarkable achievements.

On the outside, the individual contribution of Peter Parler to the construction of the cathedral is shown in his emphatic treatment of the south front, flanked, on the transept side, by St Wenceslas's Chapel to the east and by a tall tower to the west. The importance given to the south façade was a consequence of its position, opposite the Royal Palace. The area between these two main buildings, symbolising temporal and spiritual authority and power, was sufficiently spacious to accommodate splendid assemblies and processions in keeping with the ostentation of the Luxembourgs. That was the reason why the doorway, known as the Golden Gate, leading to the south arm of the transept of the emergent cathedral was chosen to be the principal entrance to the new church, duly emphasised by its three-part portico. In 1367 Beneš Krabice of Weitmile noted *à propos* this subject: 'A fine work has just been completed and perfected: a great doorway and portico for St Wenceslas's Chapel, in the cathedral of Prague, a very sumptuous work of sculpture.' The statues that stood on the central and engaged piers have not survived. Judging by the number of empty plinths, they must have been of Christ and the twelve apostles, worshipped on either side by Charles IV and Empress Elizabeth of Pomerania, accompanied by pages, or possibly by Charles IV and Wenceslas IV with their wives.

From the start, St Vitus's Cathedral was intended to be used for coronations. At the request of John of Luxembourg, on 5 May 1344, Pope Clement VI granted the archbishops of Prague the right to crown the kings of Bohemia. On the eve of his own coronation on 1 September 1347, Charles IV drew up the *Ordo ad coronandum regem Boemorum*, a new set of regulations concerning the coronation of the Czech monarchs, established on the lines of the old, 10th-century Germanic ceremonial and completed by certain liturgical texts deriving from the French ceremonial of 1328. He took into consideration, too, ancient Přemyslid traditions. The cathedral also served as the royal burial place. Both coronation and funeral processions entered the cathedral by the Golden Gate, on which, in 1370-1, the symbol of heavenly protection was set, with a mosaic of the Last Judgement made by Venetians invited to Prague. Behind the wall with the mosaic was the original sacristy of St Wenceslas's Chapel, where the chapel's precious relics were kept, as well as the St Wenceslas Crown, at times when these were not on display. According to V. Kotrba, the terraced platform overlooking St Wenceslas's Chapel and the Golden Gate was intended for displaying relics and church treasures, but was not used for this purpose because of the death of the emperor in 1378 and the years of unrest that followed. Even the High Tower remained unfinished. Designed in Charles's time, but begun only later, it was to have accentuated even further the importance of the south front. The symbolic purpose of this tall landmark was to direct the cathedral, the castle, the city of Prague and the Czech kingdom towards heaven.

Peter Parler used his great talent and feeling for sculpture to enrich St Vitus's Cathedral with a large number of monumental works, created on a progressive iconographical pattern worked out by Charles IV himself. Many other figurative details, large and small, were added by the stonecutters of Parler's workshop, working under his orders. Parler's own importance as a creative sculptor derives from the sense of realism he brought to the Late Gothic style and, even more, from the new conception of form that he bequeathed to the ensuing period, the Flamboyant Gothic of the late 14th century. Mention has already been made of the vanished stone statues of the south portal, and the huge statue of St Wenceslas, considered to be one of the supreme original examples of this new style. The figurative brackets of the chapel's north portal are also of extraordinary quality. The left-hand one represents St Peter denying Christ, the right-hand one, occupying more space, the devil tearing out the tongue of Judas. The oldest funerary monument by Peter Parler in the cathedral is the sarcophagus of

Archbishop Jan Očko of Vlašim (1364-78) in St Adalbert's Chapel. In the parish of Klodsko he had already made the marl sarcophagus of Arnošt of Pardubice (d. 1364), Jan Očko's predecessor as bishop of Prague; and then, in Wroclaw Cathedral, he fashioned the tomb of Bishop Przeclaw of Pogorzel (d. 1376).

In December 1373, Emperor Charles IV gave orders for the translation 'of the bodies of the ancient Czech princes and kings who were buried in the new choir of the church of Prague' (Beneš Krabice of Weitmile). For six of them, stone sarcophagi had been built in three of the radiating chapels that surrounded the ambulatory. Placed face to face and in chronological order, the recumbent figures represented the Přemyslid monarchs with their emblems and armour: the princes Břetislav I (d. 1055), who had transferred the body of St Adalbert from Gniezno to Prague; Spytihněv II (d. 1061), founder of the episcopal basilica of St Vitus, St Wenceslas and St Adalbert; Břetislav II (d. 1100) and Bořivoj II (d. 1124); and the two Czech kings, Přemysl Otakar I (d. 1230) and Přemysl Otakar II, who died in 1278 at the battle of Moravské Pole (not far from the village of Dürnkrut in Lower Austria) fighting Rudolf of Habsburg. On 30 August 1377, on the emperor's orders, Peter Parler was paid the relatively large sum of 900 Bohemian grosche. The magnificent statue of Přemysl Otakar I is impressive for its sheer bulk and power. The king's face, evidently a very good likeness, expresses deep melancholy brought on by the burdens of life. The recumbent figure of Přemysl Otakar II is also certainly Peter Parler's work, whereas the statue of Spytihněv II is attributed to Heinrich Parler (of Gmünd). The other sarcophagi are the work of various stonecutters and sculptors from the workshop responsible for the construction of the cathedral.

The gallery of twenty-one busts in the cathedral triforium, above the nave arcades, is unrivalled. The busts, set in the wall, are in sandstone, originally polychrome, and almost life-size. They were not all done at the same time. The oldest of them, placed

Tomb: Among the many tombs of monarchs placed in the radiating chapels of the ambulatory, there is also the sarcophagus of a dignitary of the church, Jan Očko of Vlašim, archbishop of Prague.

on the pillars at the end of the polygon, represent Charles IV and the closest members of his family. On his left are his four wives: Elizabeth of Pomerania-Stolp (d.1393), Anne of Silesia-Schweidnitz (d. 1362), Anne of Bavaria (d. 1353) and Blanche de Valois (d. 1348). To the north of these are the busts of Charles's two brothers: John Henry, margrave of Moravia (d. 1375) and Wenceslas, duke of Luxembourg and Brabant (d. 1383), courtly poet and protector of Jean Froissart, the greatest French chronicler of the Middle Ages. On the south side, to the right of Charles IV, are the busts of his parents, John of Luxembourg and Elizabeth, last of the Přemyslids (d. 1330), of his eldest son, Wenceslas IV, king of Bohemia (d. 1419), and of Wenceslas's first wife, Joanna of Bavaria (d. 1386). The busts on the sides of the triforium date from the years 1379-80. These represent the first three archbishops of Prague and four work-masters (*directores fabrice*) of the cathedral;

the bust of the fifth, Wenceslas of Radeč, was added later.

To this gallery of the highest temporal and spiritual dignitaries of the kingdom of Bohemia, were added the busts of the two architects, Matthew of Arras and Peter Parler, each bearing on his chest a plaque with an identifying inscription. Their inclusion is most surprising for their time, but was undoubtedly intended as a mark of recognition of exceptional merits. Not all the triforium busts are by the same hand; they were done by several stonemasons from the workshop (which normally turned out little sculpture), under the direction of Peter Parler. Several are attributed to the architect, among them the one of Parler himself which, according to J. Homolka, is the 'first monumental self-portrait in Late Gothic sculpture'.

Some time ago, K.M. Svoboda deciphered the symbolic meaning of the arrangement, on three levels, of the monumental sculptures by Peter Parler and his workshop in St Vitus's Cathedral: the sequence expresses the continuity of the divinely protected Czech dynasty, from its ancient Přemyslid past (the sarcophagi of the dark lower floor) to the contemporary Luxembourg line (the busts in the well-lit triforium). Another series of busts, placed on the entablatures of the surrounding pillars, on the upper level of the triforium symbolises heavenly protection. They represent Christ, the Virgin Mary, foreign saints much venerated in the country: Vitus, Sigismund, Cyril, and Methodius; and the local saints: Wenceslas, Ludmila, Adalbert and Procopius. According to extant invoices dating from 1375, these ten busts were the work of the stonemason Hermann, the best-known sculptor of the period from the St Vitus's Cathedral workshop. They would have been executed, of course, under the direction and with the participation of Peter Parler and perhaps of his nephew and colleague, Heinrich of Gmünd. Hermann's art, probably French in tendency, brought a measure of naturalism to portraiture. He is likely to have influenced the artistic expression of Wenceslas and Johann, Peter Parler's sons, who subsequently made some of the busts, doubtless with other sculptors, on the sides of the lower triforium.

According to the inscription, dated 1386, on his own bust in the triforium, Peter Parler worked on the construction of the choir stalls, which had been covered and consecrated shortly before (the stalls were burned in 1541). The only surviving testimony to the high quality of sculpture in Peter Parler's workshop, and its tendency towards the Flamboyant Gothic style, is the aforementioned bust of Wenceslas of Radeč and the astonishing figurative brackets of the baldaquins on the central piers at the polygonal end of the choir, notably that of the south pier representing Adam and Eve before the Tree of Knowledge. The statues of the Virgin Mary and Christ the Saviour, which were positioned over the baldaquins, have long since been destroyed. It is thought that the panel painting of the St Vitus's Madonna in the Prague National Gallery is a surviv-

ing part of the original cathedral decorations: it may have been commissioned at the same time as its frame in relief by Archbishop Jan of Jenštejn to commemorate the laying of the cathedral's foundation stone in 1392.

Peter Parler supervised the building of the cathedral until his death. This occurred on 13 July 1399 according to the inscription on his funerary slab, discovered in 1928, at the same time as the epitaph of Matthew of Arras, near the north sacristy (the two slabs were placed in the St Mary Magdalen or Wallenstein Chapel). In 1397 Wenceslas, elder son of Peter Parler, succeeded his father for a short while; his younger son Johann then took charge from 1398 to 1406, followed by a certain Petr, known as Petrlík, whose family name is not known. The latter continued construction work on the cathedral until the start of the Hussite disturbances in 1419. It included the erection of the high South Tower and a connecting railing above the window arch of the south arm of the transept. The wealth of decorative motifs indicates that the stonecutters of the cathedral workshop had lost none of their creative flair. Even after Peter Parler's death, the high level of accomplishment of the figurative works of sculpture apparently did not decline. The mastery of overall composition, as well as the intricacy of detail, can be seen from the reliefs of the corner brackets above the gallery of the façade, on the first floor of the high South Tower. One has the fantastic appearance of a bat, another of a dragon. Albert Kutal, the eminent historian of Czech art, investigated the evidence that enables us to identify the three last 'workmasters' of St Vitus's Cathedral during the Luxembourg era as being landed proprietors of Prague, which continued to turn out painters, builders and stonemasons renowned throughout Europe until the end of the Middle Ages.

Even after the death of Charles IV (1378) additions were made to the already considerable cathedral treasure, of which detailed inventories were prepared in 1387, 1396 and 1413. This treasure also included the furnishings of the sixty-four altars of the pre-Hussite church, apparently stored in the two sacristies. Above the main sacristy, situated on the north side of the choir and comprising an altar dedicated to St Michael, there was a special room that served as a treasure chamber. It opened onto the nave by an entrance with a semicircular vault leading to 'a small balcony... where sacred objects were sometimes displayed' (Václav Hájek of Libočany). Among the reliquaries that survive, two dating from the last years of Charles IV deserve special mention: the so-called Pope Urban V reliquary, containing a fragment of the Holy Shroud, fashioned in gold in the shape of a cross and decorated with enamel and precious stones (height: 31.3 cm/13 in); and a beautifully-made reliquary in silver-gilt, struck with the mark of Peter Parler, probably donated to the cathedral by a member of the Parler family. The archives and precious books of the St Vitus chapter were apparently kept in the chamber above the chapter room, near the west wall of the South Tower. This vast collection of archives today constitutes the essential source of all documented study of St Vitus's Cathedral and Prague Castle: they are now kept, together with the rich chapter library, in the new palace situated in the Third Courtyard.

The Hussite uprisings that began on 30 June 1419 were in great part a reaction against the preceding era of profligacy, which had long been criticised by the reform movement. On 16 August of the same year, Wenceslas IV died and the insurrectionist Estates prevented his burial in St Vitus's Cathedral (it was not until 1424 that his remains could be transferred to the royal crypt). Historical events had tragic consequences for the cathedral itself. During his coronation as king of Bohemia performed on 28 and 29 July 1420, Sigismund of Luxembourg 'took possession, in the church of Prague and St George's Convent, of the heads, hands, monstrances and other gold and silver treasures, giving orders for them to be smashed, using them to pay the salaries of his army...' The following year, the people of Prague occupied the castle and, on 10 June 1421, at the instigation of the radical Hussite priest Jan Želivský, 'blasphemously burned the very beautiful pictures and precious triptychs of the altar... And had not a number of lords and other brave men intervened to prevent them, this bunch of good-for-nothings would have destroyed the castle, with the church of our patron saints,' noted Vavřinec of Březová, the most important historian of the Hussite period. And he asked this question: 'Who committed the gravest sin? Those who destroyed the paintings on wood or those who destroyed the silver effigies?'

But even before these tragic events, the building of the cathedral had been interrupted again and was not to be resumed for many years. The choir dating from the Luxembourg period (enclosed and separated from the triple nave, then under construction, by a temporary wall) and the shell of the uncompleted tower represent fragments of the cathedral as conceived by Matthew of Arras and Peter Parler. The generations to come inherited the challenge to complete the unfinished work.

(continued on page 141)

ST VITUS'S CATHEDRAL

Metropolitan church of Bohemia and Moravia, coronation and burial place of Czech kings, the cathedral is the dominant feature of Prague Castle. Founded in 1344 by John of Luxembourg and the Margrave Charles, the future Emperor Charles IV, it was erected on the site of the 10th-century rotunda dedicated to the same saint. The construction of the eastern medieval part of the cathedral (including the high South Tower) lasted until 1419. The three-aisled nave and the west front with its two towers were only completed between 1859 and 1929. The objects, furnishings and ornaments are from different periods, from 1350 to the 20th century.

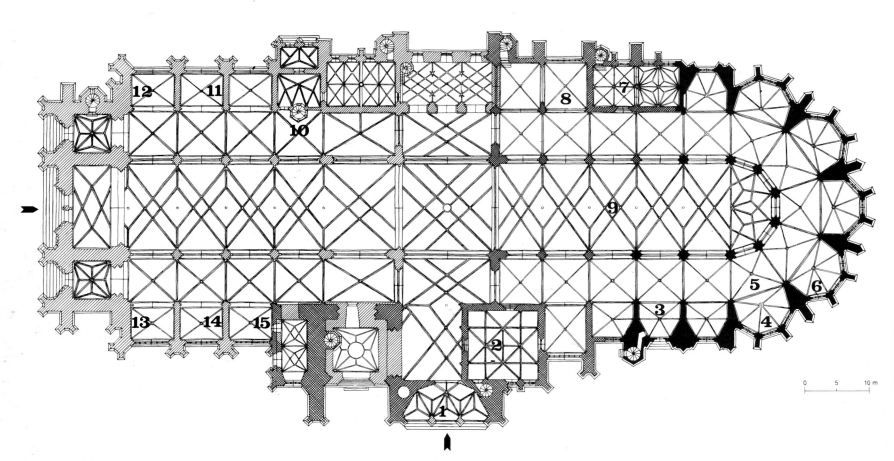

1. Golden Gate
2. St Wenceslas's Chapel
3. Royal Oratory
4. Chapel of St John of Nepomuk and St Adalbert
5. Tomb of St John of Nepomuk
6. Chapel of Holy Relics (Saxon Chapel)
7. Ancient Sacristy
8. St Sigismund's Chapel
9. Royal Mausoleum
10. Staircase leading to the Treasure Chamber
11. Schwarzenberg Chapel
12. Bartoň of Dobenín's Chapel
13. St Ludmila's Chapel
14. Holy Sepulchre Chapel
15. Thun Chapel

Period of building under the direction of Matthew of Arras, 1344-52

Period of building under the direction of Peter Parler, 1356-99

Period of building under the direction of Josef Mocker and Kamil Hilbert 1873-1933

Opposite page: *the neo-Gothic west front* (1873-1929) with the great rose window. In 1928 Jan Jareš made the stained-glass windows representing the creation of the world, based on the designs of František Kysela.

The tympanum of the central doorway of the west front: the Crucifixion and other scenes of the Passion by Ladislav Pícha, based on the models of Karel Dvořak (1893-1950).

Opposite page: the *South Tower.* Begun in 1396 by Peter Parler, its construction continued under other cathedral work-masters from 1398 to 1419. The architecture is of the Flamboyant Gothic late style of Peter Parler's workshop. It was completed by a Renaissance gallery and an onion-shaped dome, designed by Boniface Wohlmut (d. 1579) and renovated in 1770 by Niccolo Pacassi. Thanks to Kamil Hilbert, the cathedral was spared the attentions of neo-Gothic purists wishing to impose stylistic uniformity.

Pages 128-129: south view of *St Vitus's Cathedral* from the Third Courtyard of the castle. This shows the medieval façade of the church dating from the reign of Charles IV (d. 1378), with the Golden Gate leading to the south arm of the transept, the neo-Gothic lower storey of the tower and a part of the Gothic triple nave.

Below: *the flying buttresses* of the cathedral, like the pinnacles, show a high level of elaborate workmanship.

Opposite page: *spire on the roof of St Vitus's Cathedral*, above the point where the transept crosses the central nave. It is the dominant feature of the neo-Gothic roof, standing 26 metres (85 ft) high.

Console of the tabernacle of the south-eastern pillar at the end of the choir, with carvings on the theme of Original Sin, probably from 1385. A remarkable product of Peter Parler's workshop, it dates from the period when sculpture was evolving towards the Flamboyant Gothic style.

Opposite page, top to bottom: the emblem of the Czech kingdom (two-tailed lion), the crowned initial of King Vladislav II Jagiello, and his emblem (a crowned spread eagle) appear on a pendentive in the Royal Oratory.

Below: *the Oratory of Vladislav II Jagiello*, in the south nave of the choir, built by Hans Spiess from 1490 to 1493. With its wealth of ornamental and heraldic decoration in the naturalistic Late Gothic style, it is an important example of the development of the cathedral architecture under the Luxembourgs.

Opposite page, left: *sculpture of St John of Nepomuk* (canonised in 1729) on his Baroque silver sarcophagus at the south-eastern end of the ambulatory. This is a work by Antonio Corradini, dated 1733-6, after a model by Josef E. Fischer von Erlach.

Opposite page, right: *Apotheosis of St Sigismund* on the Baroque altar in this side chapel in the north nave, sculpted by František Ignác Weiss between 1735 and 1741. This example of the dynamic Baroque style found its way into the Gothic part of the cathedral following the victory of the Counter-Reformation in Bohemia and Moravia.

Below: *Baroque funerary monument of the Grand Chancellor Leopold Šlik* near the south pier of the ambulatory. It was made between 1723 and 1725 by Matyáš Braun, the most important Czech sculptor of the Late Baroque, and the assistants of his workshop.

Above: *the sarcophagus of Přemysl Otakar II,* dating from 1366-7 in the Chapel of Holy Relics (Saxon Chapel). One of Peter Parler's most celebrated works, the sarcophagus, with its recumbent figure, was commissioned by Emepror Charles IV in memory of the king who died tragically in the battle of Moravské Pole.

"The charm of Prague's Baroque night drew me like the stage of a theatre, invited me into its corridors, at once as actor and spectator. The towers of the cathedral, with their capitals and golden crosses, and the bold lines of the roofs of the palaces were, like an orchestra, in harmony with my inexpressible mood."

Alexandr Kliment: Trouble in Bohemia

Spiral staircase leading to the Treasure Chamber of the cathedral. Neo-Gothic in style, designed by Kamil Hilbert, it was built between 1905 and 1909 by the stonemasons of St Vitus's new workshop.

Opposite page: *view from the west of the central nave*, after the removal of the wall separating the choir from the modern neo-Gothic transept and the three aisles of the nave. The vault of the choir was designed in 1385 by Peter Parler and that of the central nave in 1903 by Kamil Hilbert. At the eastern end of the cathedral, there is a strong contrast between the dark zone of the ambulatory arcades (attributed to the first builder of the cathedral, Matthew of Arras, who died in 1352) and the highly luminous effect created by the skeletal architecture of the triforium and Peter Parler's windows.

THE TRIFORIUM
GALLERY OF BUSTS

A unique group from the Middle Ages: Charles IV; his mother Eliška, last of the Přemyslids, wife of John of Luxembourg (above); and his four wives, Anne of Silesia, Elizabeth of Pomerania-Stolp, Blanche de Valois and Anne of Bavaria. These life-size busts were carved in sandstone in 1374-5 by Peter Parler and other sculptors of his workshop. The Latin inscriptions engraved beneath the busts in 1389-92 were undoubtedly suggested by the director of the works, Václav of Radeč.

"In the end we returned to Bohemia after an absence of eleven years. We no longer found our mother alive; she had died several years previously... So it was that on our arrival in Bohemia, we found neither father, nor mother, nor brother, nor sister, nor even a friend."

Charles IV, in his autobiography

St Vitus's Cathedral: *view from the east of the choir* and its flying buttresses, the work of Peter Parler from 1371 to 1385. Behind is the Renaissance-style South Tower.

In 1421, because he had accepted the Four Articles of Prague that constituted the principal demands of the Hussites, the seventh archbishop of Prague, Konrád of Vechta, was anathematised. The archbishopric remained vacant for 140 years. Given the additional fact that after Wenceslas IV the Czech kings no longer resided in Prague Castle, little progress was made, in rebuilding the cathedral at the end of the revolutionary Hussite period, in 1434. A change of policy did not come about until the accession of the Catholic Vladislav II Jagiello, king of Bohemia from 1471 to 1516. For fear of disturbances among the Calixtin population of Prague, he took up residence at Prague Castle in 1483, and initiated a series of improvements, including the building of a new corridor linking the Royal Palace, by way of the Vladislav Hall, with the new Royal Oratory in the south nave of the cathedral (1490-3). The designer of this corridor was the Master Hans Spiess of Frankfurt-am-Main. The parapet of the oratory, in Late Gothic style and covered with a naturalist dead-branch pattern of ornament, bore many emblems of the Vladislav II Jagiello coat-of-arms. The creation of the Royal Oratory was the first building enterprise in the cathedral since the Hussite period. In 1509, Vladislav embarked on the even more ambitious scheme of completing the construction of the cathedral: work started on the foundations of the pillars of the church nave and of the North Tower, but it was abandoned after the third season.

Wishing to re-establish the tradition of Charles IV, by generous donations Vladislav II did much to replace the objects that had been destroyed. The cathedral treasury preserves the silver reliquaries in the form of busts of St Vitus (1484-6?), St Wenceslas and St Adalbert (1497-1500) which replaced the destroyed busts of the Luxembourg period. In the fine bust of St Wenceslas, J. Homolka has pointed to an early affinity, in the form and expression of the face, with Italian Renaissance sculpture. Like Charles IV, Vladislav II paid particular attention to St Wenceslas's

Chapel. He commissioned a mural painting of the Czech patron saints (probably in 1484-5) above the main altar. Among the group of saints are two angels on either side of Peter Parler's statue of St Wenceslas, placed on a bracket in the centre of the picture, after it had been transferred from its position outside (above the chapel, under a baldaquin). In 1502 the king donated a purple cloak specifically intended for this statue (*palium de purpura rubea supra imaginem s. Venceslai*).

The series of wall paintings relating the legend of the saint was doubtless part of the preparations for the ceremonial coronation of Louis II Jagiello as king of Bohemia in 1509 (while his father was still alive), in St Vitus's Cathedral. They were done by the Master of the Litoměřice Altar (the most expressive Late Gothic painter in Czech lands at a time of transition to the Renaissance style) and his assistants. The great scene of the miraculous reception of St Wenceslas at the imperial Diet by Emperor Henry I the Fowler (876-936), placed above the west entry to the chapel, is on two levels; the upper section beneath the vault recalls the ancient right of the kings of Bohemia to the first vote for the elector and, also without doubt, is an allusion to the agreement signed in 1507 for the marriage of Louis to the granddaughter of Maximilian I, Mary of Habsburg. Altogether, this scene, with its hierarchical organisation, is an elegant depiction of a court ceremony. It may be possible one day to identify more precisely each of the persons represented.

In this chapel and beneath this painting, so full of promise from the viewpoint of contemporary Czech aspirations, Ferdinand I was elected king of Bohemia on 24 October 1526. Founder of the reigning dynasty of the Habsburgs in Bohemia and Moravia (a dynasty that lasted until 1918), he succeeded his brother-in-law Louis II Jagiello, who died tragically after the defeat at Mohács without issue. So it was during the Habsburg era that the maltsters of Staré Město (the Old Town) made a donation to the cathedral, apparently to replace an object from the time of Charles IV, of a bronze candelabrum in Early Renaissance style, made in 1532 at Nuremburg by Hans Vischer. This gift was intended to commemorate the saving of the cathedral in 1421.

A disastrous fire gutted the cathedral and the rest of the castle on 2 June 1541. Its restoration, in Renaissance style, took twenty long years. Among the work undertaken was the erection of a new loft for the organ and choristers in the western part of the church: it was built by the Prague court architect Boniface Wohlmut, originally from Uberlingen, in Baden, who died in 1579 (in 1924 this loft was transferred to the north arm of the transept). From the architectural point of view, it employed, for the first time in Bohemia, superimposed Renaissance columns, on the model of Sebastiano Serlio. As a man of the north, Wohlmut accentuated the link with the tradition of Gothic architecture by covering the ground floor with a massive, ingeniously designed, rib vault. His is also the original form — a Renaissance onion-shaped dome — of the present-day spire of the high South Tower of the cathedral, which was far removed from the Gothic spirit. On the first floor is the great Sigismund (Zikmund) bell which is 2.03 metres (78 in) high, cast in 1549 by Tomáš Jaroš of Brno.

The fire of 1541 destroyed the marble sarcophagus of St Adalbert, on the west side of the triple nave of the church built in the 14th century. In 1556, on the orders of Emperor Ferdinand I, the pillared arcades were removed and the space thus gained was used as a tomb: above the tomb of the saint, the Italian Ulrico Aostalli built, in 1575-6, perhaps according to an old plan of Wohlmut, an oval decagonal chapel (destroyed in 1879). This chapel was undoubtedly erected in response to the wishes of Antonín Brus of Mohelnice (1561-80), the first post-Hussite archbishop of Prague. Around 1566, to honour the memory of his dead parents (Ferdinand I and Anna Jagiello), Maximilian II commissioned from the Dutch sculp-

tor Alexander Colin (of the court of Ferdinand I at Innsbruck) a huge marble mausoleum which was placed, as a last resort, in front of the choir, on the central axis of St Vitus's Cathedral. The work was not completed until 1589, after modifications to the original design at the behest of Rudolf II (king of Bohemia from 1576 to 1611). At his express wish,

example of Renaissance craftsmanship. The reliefs on the circular medallions represent the Annunciation and the Holy Trinity; the other figures on the outside of the bell are the patrons of the country and Ferdinand I and his wife.

a statue of Maximilian II was added to those of Ferdinand I and Anna Jagiello on the lid of the mausoleum, while medallions of Charles IV and his four wives, of Wenceslas IV and two other Czech kings, Ladislav Posthumous (king of Bohemia, 1453-7) and his successor, George of Poděbrady (reigned 1458-71), were attached to the sides. The protective grille of the tomb, considered to be the most important piece of ironwork of the time in Bohemia, was made (except for the few later additions) by Jiří Schmidthammer, an ironsmith from the Malá Strana quarter. Below the mausoleum was the royal crypt, built in 1589-90 by Ulrico Aostalli, again at the wish of Rudolf II, who was eventually buried there in a richly decorated tin coffin. Among the numerous non-royal, but historically important burials in the cathedral at this time, mention must at least be made of the marble sarcophagus of Vratislav of Pernštejn (d. 1582) and the tomb that the Spanish aristocrat Maria Manrique de Lara had made for her husband, the grand chancellor of the kingdom of Bohemia.

In 1619, the Czech Estates deposed Ferdinand II and elected to the throne of Bohemia the Elector Palatine Frederick V, who was the head of the Evangelical Union. Following this decision, fatal from the political point of view in that it marked, in fact, the beginning of the Thirty Years' War, calamity struck St Vitus's Cathedral for the third time: on 21 and 22 December 1619, Calvinists led by Abraham Scultety, preacher of the royal court, devastated the cathedral, intent on making it a Calvinist oratory. The cathedral was not surrendered to the Catholics until after the victory of the armies fighting for Frederick II at the battle of the White Mountain, on 8 November 1620. Doubtless it was to compensate for the damage done to the cathedral that Ferdinand II donated a new reredos for the high altar: a large painted triptych with, in the centre, *St Luke Painting the Virgin Mary and the Infant Jesus*. It was a work by the celebrated Dutch painter Jan Gossaert, known as Mabuse, certainly done around 1513, which hangs today in the

Prague National Gallery.

The progressive changes dating from the beginning of the Baroque period took place in the time of the cardinal-archbishop Arnošt of Harrach (1623-77). Caspar Bechteler, the court cabinetmaker, was responsible for the following works: in 1631, the throne; in 1630, the door in relief in the ground floor arcade of the organ loft, originally in the west wall of the choir; and also, after 1631, two large reliefs, on the south and north sides of the choir, representing, in strikingly epic terms, the destruction of the cathedral in 1619 and the flight from Prague of the King for a Winter, Frederick the Palatine, in 1620. An unfortunate soldier, but a great lover of art, Archduke Leopold William, who had been, among other things, bishop of Olomouc from 1632 to 1662, commissioned, in 1641, the design and casting in bronze of a new stand for the Romanesque candelabra, known as the Jerusalem Candelabra. This object, much prized in Czech history — it was reputed to have been the booty of a Czech duke at the capture of Milan — had been badly damaged by the Calvinists. Today, only four branches remain, with small busts of four patron saints of the kingdom, St Wenceslas, St Vitus, St Adalbert and St Methodius.

Inspired by local patriotism, Czech historians of the Baroque era drew heavily on the example of the old national patron saints and focused much attention on the religious history and monuments of the pre-Hussite period. The most important of these, the Jesuit Bohuslav Balbín (1621-88), as well as his colleagues, showed particular interest in St Vitus's Cathedral. Jan Tomáš Pešina of Čechorod (1629-80), then dean of the cathedral chapter and later titular bishop of Prague, published in 1673 a work entitled *Phosphorus septicornis, stella alias matutina (Seven-branched ray, otherwise morning star)*, one chapter of which was largely devoted to the relics of St Vitus's Cathedral. In the same year, G.D. Orsi, at the expense of Emperor Leopold I, king of Bohemia from 1657 to 1705, began digging again the foundations of the church nave — a nave wholly Baroque in conception, radically different from the Gothic choir, as can be seen from contemporary paintings. But the great uprising of the serfs (1679-80), the disaster of the plague (1680) and the breakthrough of the Turkish army towards Vienna (1683) rapidly brought this project to an end.

There are, nevertheless, a number of valuable Baroque works in the cathedral. František Preiss (*c.* 1660-1712) carved wood sculptures, in 1696, of eight Czech patron saints, slightly larger than life-size: these sculptures are today in the crossing of the transept, whereas originally they were placed on the piers of the choir. The same Prague sculptor was also certainly responsible for the moulds of the silver busts of St Wenceslas, St Adalbert, St Vitus and St Cyril, initially made for the high altar and subsequently transferred to the Chapel of St John of Nepomuk (previously the Chapel of St Erhard and St Odile). These had been donated to the cathedral by Jan J. Breuner, archbishop from 1694 to 1710. Between 1735 and 1741 the reredos of the St Sigismund altar, undoubtedly designed by Jan B. Fischer von Erlach, took on a Baroque appearance thanks to a figurative representation of the saint's apotheosis by František Ignác Weiss (*c.* 1690-1756). The highly elaborate sculptures on the tombstone of Leopold Šlik, grand chancellor of the Czech kingdom, with its pompous epitaph dated 1723-5, were the work of Matyaš B. Braun (1684-1738), the most important of Bohemia's Late Baroque sculptors, and of his studio. It is not of very high quality and certainly does not rank among his best works. The same is true of the painting *Baptism of Christ* (1722), hanging near the sacristy, done by Petr Brandl (1668-1735), a Czech Baroque artist of the time.

After the end of the Thirty Years' War and the victory of the Counter-Reformation, the cult of the most popular saint of the Czech Baroque, the cleric John Nepomuk, martyred on 20 March 1393 and buried in the south part of the ambulatory of St Vitus's Cathedral, steadily intensified. He was canonised by Pope Benedict XIII on 19 March 1729. In that same year, Jan F. Schor (1686-1757) proposed completing the cathedral, this time in the Gothic style, but not even this project was carried out. The great silver altar-tomb of the saint, surmounted by a ciborium, was a magnificent monument, the culmination of the cult of St John of Nepomuk in St Vitus's Cathedral during the Baroque period. Baldaquin included, it stood five metres (over 16 ft) high and was fashioned in stages, on the site of the original burial of the saint, between 1733 and 1771, at the expense of Emperor Charles VI (king of Bohemia from 1711 to 1740). It represents the apotheosis of St John Nepomuk, carried in his shroud to heaven by angels. The central scene was created in Vienna between 1733 and 1736, based on the design of Josef E. Fischer von Erlach; Antonio Corradini modelled it in wood and Jan Josef Würthle sculpted it in silver.

The numerous attempts to complete St Vitus's Cathedral were not realised until the 19th century, when the Romantic movement looked to the past for evidence of the nation's political, religious and cultural stature. In 1842, Cologne Cathedral was completed; two years later, at the third congress of German architects, in Prague, Canon Václav Pešina (1782-1859) demanded the same for St Vitus's Cathedral. But the opportune moment only arrived during the time of Bedřich J. Schwarzenberg (cardinal-archbishop from 1849 to 1885). In 1859 a Union for the Completion of St Vitus's Cathedral was formed, with Count Thun Hohenstein as its first elected president. To bring the project to a successful conclusion, a new builder of the cathedral was appointed, the architect Josef O. Kranner (1801-71), born in the Malá Strana quarter of Prague. His first assignment was to save and restore the remains of the medieval building, which were in a dangerous condition (as a result of dilapidation and the 1575 Prussian bombardment during the siege of Prague). The contemporary fashion for purity of style persuaded him to adopt the Gothic and to reject the later ornamentation. To replace the Renaissance triptych, with its central painting by

145

Jan Gossaert (Mabuse), which had been transferred in 1870 to the gallery of the Society of Patriotic Friends of Art, he designed a neo-Gothic high altar.

In 1866, because of the threat posed by the Austro-Prussian Seven Weeks' War, the Czech Crown Jewels were removed to Vienna. On their return, they were deposited in a new treasure chamber, built by Josef Kranner in the ancient sacristy above St Wenceslas's Chapel.

In 1873, on the 900th anniversary of the creation of the diocese of Prague, Cardinal Bedřich J. Schwarzenberg laid the foundation stone of the three-aisled nave; and in 1879 the St Adalbert (Vojtěch) Chapel, which had stood in the way of this project, was demolished. The work was directed by Josef Mocker (1835-99), the leading exponent of pseudo-Gothic building in Bohemia. He had studied at the Technology Institute and Academy of Fine Arts in Vienna, and had participated in some of the restoration work, from 1863 onward, at the St Stephen Cathedral in Vienna, directed by Friedrich Schmidt. On Mocker's recommendation, the three aisles were completed by a series of side chapels, and the distant view of the cathedral was highlighted by a new twin-towered west front. This academic approach, insensitive to local feeling, aroused criticism. Mocker was reproached for having obliterated the traditional panoramic effect of the old cathedral and for having 'destroyed the exclusively lateral orientation towards the town, which had been the hallmark of Peter Parler's building' (Josef Cibulka).

In the course of the 19th century the interior of the cathedral was considerably modified by the commissioning of new works in various styles imitating those of the past. Only a few of these can be mentioned. The altar-tomb of St Vitus, dating from 1840, situated in the centre of the ambulatory of the choir, was designed by Josef Kranner, and the statue of the saint executed by Josef Max (1804-55), chief representative of the Prague school of sculpture during the first half of the 19th century. Josef Kranner also designed the sandstone altar,

dated 1849, in St Ludmila's Chapel, which stood in the Chapel of the Virgin Mary until 1901. The carvings of this altar, including the statue of St Ludmila, in Carrera marble, were by Emmanuel Max (1810-1901), who had lived for some time in Vienna and Rome. The marl altar of St John the Baptist's Chapel was built in 1876 to the designs of Josef Kranner and Josef Mocker. Václav Levý (1820-70), who played an influential role in the development of Czech sculpture in the second half of the 19th century, did the terracotta statues for this altar, with one exception: the statue of St Methodius, made by Josef M. Myslbek (1848-1922) at the beginning of his career. Myslbek was the man who spearheaded the national revival of Czech sculpture, and he is represented in the cathedral by one of his most admired works: a monument cast in bronze, dating from 1891-5, in commemoration of Cardinal Schwarzenberg, 2.04 metres (80 in) high and standing in the north part of the choir. In the early 1980s it was still considered in Prague to be the most valuable Czech contribution to modern world sculpture (Antonín Matějček).

The rebuilding of the cathedral was nonetheless completed, as already planned, in neo-Gothic style, which thereby survived, in terms of general artistic development, far longer in Prague than in other parts of Europe. In 1903 the main nave was covered with a rib vault, on the lines conceived by Peter Parler. In 1909 a new sacristy was built in the northern side aisle; and over it a treasure chamber, which today once more houses the cathedral treasure. The great rose window of the west front dates from 1915. In 1924-5 a violent argument broke out between the supporters and opponents of a scheme to preserve the medieval wall separating the ancient and modern parts of the cathedral: the verdict went against those in favour of a strict conservationist approach, in keeping with the principles of Alois Riegl. Finally, to commemorate the millenary of the martyrdom of St Wenceslas, on 28 September 1929, the prayers of past generations were answered and the completed cathedral was opened to the public.

The decoration and furnishings of the new part of the cathedral were not based on any homogeneous principle. The contemporary view of art was encouraged, but stress was laid on observing the decorous expression of religious art. Even today, only a few works of this recent period can be mentioned. The bronze west door was executed in 1927-9 after the designs of the painter Vratislav H. Brunner and the models of Otakar Španiel. On the sides of the rose window of the west façade are stone busts of the cathedral builders by Vojtěch Ducharda (1929). A large number of people who made contributions to the building of the cathedral are represented by sandstone busts in the new triforium. They are the works of a number of eminent pre-war Czechoslovak sculptors: Josef Štursa, Bohumil Kafka, Ladislav Kofránek, Jan Lauda and Břetislav Benda.

Of exceptional interest is the remarkable collection of stained glass, done well after 1929. The window of the Thun Chapel, a work by František Kysela, founder of modern stained-glass window art, has for its subject the threats against human life and its defence (1927, the donation of the first Czech insurance company). At the time of the Secession, Alfons Mucha (1860-1939), that great patriot and internationally famous artist, designed the window of the Archbishops' Chapel representing the legend of Cyril and Methodius, which was completed in 1931. Max Švabinský (1873-1962) also carried out many stained-glass projects; professor of graphic arts at the Academy of Fine Arts, Prague, until 1927, he found ample scope for his talents in the cathedral. Most notably he created the great window of the south arm of the transept, which depicts the Last Judgement (1935-9), and the windows at the end of the choir representing the Holy Trinity (1939-49).

There are many visitors to the Royal Crypt, refurbished from 1928 to 1935 to the designs of the architect Kamil Roškot. Together with the sculptor

Ladislav Kofránek, he designed new tombs for the Czech monarchs buried there: Charles IV, Wenceslas IV, George of Poděbrady, and others. The work of embellishing St Vitus's Cathedral was resumed after the World War II and still continues.

Stained-glass window of the Archbishop's Chapel, in the north aisle of the nave. This Apotheosis of the evangelising saints Cyril and Methodius, with an allegory of the Slav people, is based on a design, inspired by Slav and Czeh patriotism, by Alfons Mucha, one of the best-known exponents of Art Nouveau.
The windows illustrated on the following pages are representative of the religious art of the Czechoslovak First Republic. All of them were created by Czech glass-makers based on the designs of painters from the Academy.

Stained-glass windows of the north and south aisles of the nave; left to right:

Schwarzenberg Chapel: history of the Schwarzenberg family and of St John of Nepomuk; at the sides, scenes from the life of Abraham. Design by Karel Svolinský, 1931.
St Ludmila's Chapel (baptistry): Descent of the Holy Spirit, made in 1935 by Jan Jareš, to a design by Max Švabinský.

Bartoň of Dobenín Chapel: allegories of the Beatitudes, made in 1934 by Jan Jareš, to a design by František Kysela.
Thun Chapel: an allegory of Threat and Protection by Jan Jareš (1927) to a design by František Kysela.

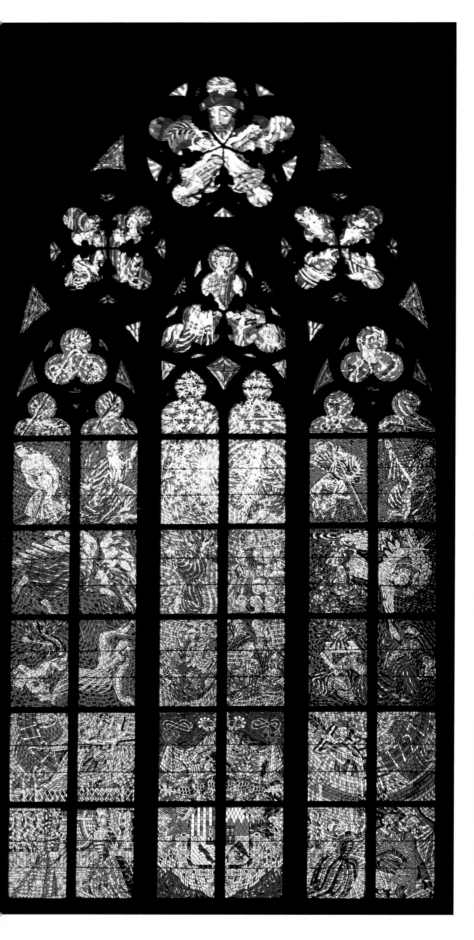

Pages 152-153: *the transept and central aisle of the nave*, with the great rose window of the west front, completed in 1929. In the foreground, left, is the royal mausoleum of Ferdinand I and Maximilian II, built in Innsbruck to the designs of the Dutch sculptor Alexander Colin. The pulpit, in Early Baroque style, was made in 1618 by Caspar Bechteler.

Missal of Jan IX of Středa, bishop of Olomouc: decorated initial representing the Annunciation and the donor (after 1364).This is one of the best-known illuminated manuscripts from the time of Charles IV, made on the orders of this royal councillor, known for his humanist leanings.

Right, below: *18th-century silk cover,* designed to protect a fragment of the *Gospel of St Mark,* dating from the 6th century, that Charles IV acquired in Italy. It is the oldest extant manuscript in Bohemia and bears an autograph of the emperor.

Opposite page, above: early Renaissance cover for an *Exegesis of the Apocalypse of St John*.

Below: *Latin Gradual*: manuscript on parchment with illuminations by Fabián Puleř, 1552; the decorated initial represents the Assumption of the Virgin Mary.

THE TREASURE CHAMBER

Crown of the Czech kings, known as St Wenceslas's Crown. Measuring 19 cm (7.5 in) high, it is made of gold and adorned with sapphires, spinels, pearls, emeralds and rubies. On top is a reliquary in the form of a cross containing a thorn of Christ's crown. Made for the coronation of Charles IV as king of Bohemia, in 1347, it underwent alterations between 1534 and 1587. It is the most important historical symbol of the medieval Czech state and a masterpiece of goldsmiths' work from the era of Charles IV.

Sceptre and Orb. These remarkable Renaissance works of art, were undoubtedly made around the 1550s in southern Germany. (A sword dating from 1346, and a cape and a stole from the 18th century, are

also among the Crown Jewels.) The orb, adorned with enamel, spinels, sapphires and pearls, is embellished with carved scenes: Adam before his Creator; the Entry to Paradise; the Creator warning Adam and Eve against eating the fruit of the Tree of Knowledge; the Anointing of David; and David fighting Goliath.

157

THE CATHEDRAL TREASURE

The origins of this treasure go back to the period of St Vitus's Rotunda, built on the same spot by order of Prince Wenceslas (d. 925 or 935). Charles IV (d. 1378) was one of the leading collectors of relics in the Middle Ages, as is attested by the cathedral inventories, the oldest of which dates from 1354. At the end of the 15th century, Vladislav II Jagiello tried to replace the precious reliquaries destroyed during the Hussite Wars (1419-34). The cathedral treasure was also greatly enriched over the following centuries. Not counting the valuable possessions of the chapter library, there are, in the Treasure Chamber, in the region of 350 objects, some of which are very famous.

Left to right: *Cross of Pope Urban V*: height 31 cm (12 in); gold with crystal, sapphires and spinels; 1368 (and *c.* 1370).

Reliquary of St Catherine in the form of a monstrance: height 45 cm (18 in); silver gilt and crystal; *c.* 1380.

Cross of Zaviš: height 80 cm (31.5 in); gold inlaid with precious stones and decorated with filigree and enamel; *c.* 1220-30; the base was made later; the cross comes from the Cistercian convent of Vyšši Brod.

Monstrance of the prior Jan Dlouhoveský: 17th century (without the Mannerist pendentives, from the early 17th century); the base dates from the 1750s.

Reliquary-bust of St Vitus: height 51 cm (20 in); silver; after 1480.

159

Large reliquary-cross, the so-called Coronation Cross: height 62.5 cm (24.5 in); gold adorned with 20 sapphires, one emerald, four spinels, 24 pearls, nine cameos, and containing precious relics; made after 1354 for Charles IV. The silver-gilt base, in Early Renaissance style, was probably commissioned by the Czech king Louis I Jagiello. Except for St Wenceslas's Crown, this is the most important example of the goldsmith's art to survive from the reign of Charles IV.

St Wenceslas's Chapel, view of the west wall: Early Renaissance mural paintings, done before 1509 by the Master of the Litoměřice Altarpiece. Their subject is the miraculous reception of St Wenceslas by the emperor at the imperial Diet, in the presence of the electors of the Holy Roman Empire. The purpose of this court scene, conceived in the epic manner, was to recall the historic position of the Czech sovereign, elector of the empire, by transposing it to the Jagiello period.

160

St Wenceslas's Chapel is the main shrine of the Přemysl prince and patron saint of his country. The chapel is a very individual, private place, covered with a stellar rib vault. Its massive walls and dim natural lighting combine with the overall decoration, especially that of the walls, to convey a wholly supernatural impression.

Below: on the north wall is a painting of *Christ before Pontius Pilate* part of a Passion cycle, by Master Oswald, painter to Charles IV, dating from 1372-3. The wall paintings are framed with amethysts, jasper and gilded stucco, part of the original decoration of the chapel.

Page 164: *Romanesque lion-headed doorknocker* of the north entrance door, made in the second half of the 12th century by a workshop of a Prague foundry. Originally it was in Stará Boleslav, where Prince Wenceslas was assassinated.

Opposite page: *the eastern part of St Wenceslas's Chapel.* In the foreground is the reliquary of St Wenceslas, made by Kamil Hilbert. The frontal of the altar table carved into the stone (and formerly in St Anne's Chapel) must have been made before 1358 by the cathedral workshop *(detail of the altar below).* Above the altar, on the cornice, is a statue of St Wenceslas, 2 m (6.5 ft) high *(see p. 16).* It is assumed to be one of the first

examples of the Flamboyant Gothic style. The mural paintings representing two angels and the patron saints of Bohemia were added later, around 1484-5. The large bronze chandelier was made in Nuremberg in 1532.

ST GEORGE'S BASILICA

The oldest church of Prague Castle, dedicated to the Virgin Mary, was founded by Prince Bořivoj I (baptised in 883 in Moravia). His son, Prince Vratislav I (*c.* 888-921) had a second church built: completed after his death, and was dedicated to St George. Its construction coincided with the upsurge of Christianity in Bohemia and the progressive establishment of the Přemyslid state. The original plan of St George's Basilica comprised three aisles which were incorporated into the east side of the present church. The later building of the south chapel is attributed to the translation, in 925, of the body of St Ludmila of Tetín.

The learned Mlada, sister of Prince Boleslav II the Pious (duke of Bohemia from 973 to 999), managed to win from Rome, in 973, certainly after tough negotiations, permission to create the diocese of Prague and, at the same time, her own consecration as abbess of the order of St Benedict under the name of Mary. The diocese was established at St Vitus's Rotunda, already built (by St Wenceslas, who died in 935), and Boleslav II had the Benedictine convent joined to St George's Basilica. A group of priests, the future canons of St George's, together with a provost father, recited mass. The Benedictine convent was the first monastic establishment in Bohemia, and the fact that it was founded by the Přemyslid family was to assure it of a privileged position in Bohemia and Moravia. In due course, the abbesses of St George's were granted the title of princess and the right to crown the Czech queens.

In response to the needs of the Mary-Mlada convent, the west side of St George's Basilica was enlarged: a separate choir for the nuns was built, as well as galleries over the side aisles. This 10th-century construction in Ottonian style was devastated in the castle fire of 1142. Under Bertha (abbess from 1145 to 1151), extensive rebuilding was undertaken in the prevalent Romanesque style of architecture, as used for St George's Basilica. From this period date the raised choir, still to be found on the east side of the basilica, the underlying three-aisled vaulted crypt, and a pair of twin, prism-shaped towers. The Chapel of the Virgin Mary was also rebuilt. The side aisles have since been covered with a vault and the galleries furnished with triplet windows. The three-aisled nave was again extended westward. Fragments of Romanesque paintings from this period are still preserved in the choir and northern side aisle. Under the abbess Agnes (1200-28), sister of Přemysl Otakar I, the raised St Ludmila's Chapel was built near the south side of the choir. The abbess and her royal brother are depicted on the walls by a three-part bas-relief, the central section of which represents the Virgin Mary in majesty, adored by the abbesses Mary and Bertha. This bas-relief, done during the time of Bertha, adorned the tympanum of one of the doorways, either of St George's Basilica or of the convent (the original is now in the Prague National Gallery). Dating from the same period are the wall paintings at the south end of the Chapel of the Virgin Mary and representing Christ in majesty and celestial Jerusalem.

A number of medieval manuscripts from St George's Convent have been preserved. The most precious is the Passional of the abbess Cunegonde (Kunhuta: 1265-1321), daughter of Přemysl Otakar II, who became abbess in 1302: it is now kept in the National Library of Prague. It was edited, calligraphed and painted between 1313 and 1321 by Beneš, canon and librarian of St George's. This manuscript, equally prized for its contents, is the most representative work of Czech culture from the first half of the 14th century.

In the centuries that followed, St George's Basilica underwent several changes. The effect of the alterations made during the reign of Charles IV is very evident, particularly in St Ludmila's Chapel. It was at this time, too, in 1371, that the high altar was again consecrated. The great south doorway of the basilica, in primitive Renaissance style and made by members of the royal castle workshop supervised by Benedikt Ried, undoubtedly dates only from 1510. The sculptures produced by this workshop were full of figurative detail, and this makes an extraordinary impact in the bas-relief of

This square *(Jiřské Náměsti)* is dominated by the west front of St George's Basilica (*c.* 1770). At the back are the Romanesque towers of the basilica; on the right is St John of Nepomuk's Chapel, added to the basilica in 1718-22; on the left is the ancient Benedictine convent (abolished in 1782), which now houses the National Gallery's collection of ancient Czech art. St George's Basilica was founded by Prince Vratislav (d. 921), and the Benedictine convent, established by the reigning Přemyslid dynasty, was created in 973. The interior of the basilica contains the best-preserved remains of Romanesque and pre-Romanesque religious architecture in Prague.

St George on the tympanum of the doorway (the original is now in the Prague National Gallery). The present vault of St Ludmila's Chapel and its Late Renaissance paintings date from the reconstruction that followed the fire of 1541.

In 1732 the Baroque staircase with two incurved flights leading to the raised choir was built. The outside appearance of the basilica was decisively altered as a result of the Early Baroque style of the west façade, undoubtedly dating from the 1670s, apparently designed by Francesco Caratti, originally from Bissone in southern Switzerland. Between 1718 and 1722 a small central chapel (Chapel of St John of Nepomuk) was added to the south side of the basilica by the architect František M. Kaňka (1674-1766). The fresco of the east dome was done by Václav V. Reiner (1689-1743), a notable Late Baroque Bohemian painter. During the reforms of Joseph II the convent was suppressed and St George's Basilica temporarily closed. The present appearance of this impressive building results from the restoration that lasted from 1888 to 1918. In 1962-3 the interior of the basilica was transformed into a museum, necessitating the removal of most of the furnishings.

St George's Basilica also has some historical importance as a burial place for the members of the ancient ruling dynasty of the Přemyslids. Two of them were provided with raised sarcophagi, of great artistic merit, which still exist today. To the southeast of the central aisle is the tomb of the basilica's founder, Prince Vratislav I (d. 13 February 921); inside is a lead reliquary in the form of a cist. Catherine of Lipoltice (abbess from 1378 to 1386) authenticated its contents after sealing it. The wooden piece of furniture, in the shape of a small house, above the sarcophagus is reminiscent in form of medieval reliquaries. Analysis of the painted ornaments, figurative and heraldic, indicates that this portion of the tomb was undoubtedly made between 1437 and 1442, evidently as part of a restoration.

The stone sarcophagus of St Ludmila, in the centre of the chapel added to the choir of the basilica, is much more important from the religious and historical points of view. Princess Ludmila, wife of Bořivoj I, was murdered at the castle of Tetín during the night of 15 or 16 September 921, on the orders of her daughter-in-law, Princess Drahomira. Ludmila, renowned for her virtuous nature and baptised, was the teacher of St Wenceslas. Her cult was deservedly propagated by St George's Convent. The sarcophagus contains St Ludmila's remains (clearly inscribed as such on a lead plaque) in a metal cist: it was undoubtedly made between 1350 and 1375 by at least three different craftsmen. The recumbent figure of St Ludmila (on the lid of the tomb), although badly damaged when the chapel vault was destroyed in 1541, is still a work of striking iconographic originality and great artistic quality. It was apparently done by one of the stonemasons of Peter Parler's workshop. The bas-reliefs on the sides, which depict the silhouettes of saints beneath baldaquins, testify to a fair amount of formal eclecticism but also, to some degree, a continuation of older styles, notably those of the stonecutters of the workshop of Matthew of Arras at St Vitus's Cathedral, dating from the 1350s. The head of St Ludmila was preserved in a silver-gilt reliquary-bust 34 cm (13 in) in height, also from the 1350s or later, which has been in the cathedral treasure since 1782.

THE HOLY CROSS
ROYAL CHAPEL

The Holy Cross Chapel, situated in the Second Courtyard of the castle, was built between 1756 and 1764 and reconstructed in classical vein from 1852 to 1856 for the ex-emperor of Austria, Ferdinand I (who lived in Prague, after his abdication, until his death in 1875). The statues of St Peter and St Paul, on the façade, are by Emanuel Max (1854). In the foreground is a sandstone Baroque fountain with sculptures by Jeroným Kohl (1686).

Above: *cartouche with the monogram of Emperor Leopold I*, on the Early Baroque fountain of the castle's Second Courtyard.

Opposite page: *the neo-Baroque interior of the Holy Cross Chapel*, dated *c.* 1855. The painting of the crucified Christ above the altar, dating from 1762, is by František Xaver Palko.

ALL SAINTS COLLEGIATE CHAPEL

THE HOLY CROSS ROYAL CHAPEL

In 1339 Charles IV (who was then merely margrave of Moravia) raised the chapel of the Royal Palace of Prague Castle to the status of collegiate church, generously providing it with a dean, a provost and eleven canons of the chapter. In addition he donated to the church 'a number of holy relics richly decorated in gold, silver and precious stones, as well as various priestly garments of high price, numerous chalices and monstrances, other objects of worship and everything necessary for the servicing and ornamentation... of a collegiate church' (Chronicle of Francis of Prague).

During the 1370s Peter Parler built, in place of the original chapel, a new church with a single nave, a very demanding project from the architectural viewpoint, which he decorated with no care for expense. Taking the Sainte-Chapelle in Paris as his model, Peter Parler produced a version in Prague which was wholly individual in style. As in the neighbouring cathedral, he made use of rib and net vaulting. The walls were encrusted with semi-precious stones, similar to those of Karlštejn Castle and St Wenceslas's Chapel. The lower floor was divided by stone stalls. The frames of the rose windows and the buttresses were treated in a special manner. This jewel of a church was completely destroyed in the castle fire of 1541. Its Renaissance-style reconstruction was not finished until around 1580; and in 1598 Giovanni Gargioli built the west door leading from the Vladislav Hall to the west organ loft.

On 28 May 1588 the remains of St Procopius (d. 1053) were placed in All Saints Chapel. This hermit of the Sázava region, who became abbot of the local Benedictine monastery using the Slav liturgy, had been canonised in 1204. The Baroque sarcophagus of the Czech saint, on the epistle side of the altar, was embellished in 1738 with sculptures by František Ig. Weiss. The legend of St Procopius was illustrated in the choir by a series of paintings, dating from 1669, by Kristian Dittman. The All Saints painting on the high altar was done in 1732 by Václav Vavřinec Reiner; the sculptures were the work of Richard J. Prachner (1750).

In the overall architectural reconstruction of Prague Castle as planned by Niccolo Pacassi, his successor, the Italian architect Anselmo Lurago (1701-56), built, in the Second Courtyard, a new chapel with a single nave, the Holy Cross Chapel, to adjoin the south wing of the palace. All that remains of the original building is the high altar of Ignác Fr. Platzer the Elder (1717-78), a Prague sculptor of the Baroque era, with a painting of *Christ on the Cross* by František A. Palko (1724-67).

Between 1852 and 1856 a neo-classical reconstruction of the chapel was put in hand, for the use of the old emperor of Austria, Ferdinand I (king of Bohemia under the name of Ferdinand V the Debonair), who had abdicated in 1848 in favour of his nephew Franz Joseph and who lived afterwards at Prague Castle with his wife Maria Anna, far from the Viennese court. The biblical frescoes on the ceiling are by Vilém Kandler, student of the Academy of Fine Arts in Prague, the stained-glass windows by Jan Z. Quast and the statues by Emanuel Max.

Opposite page: *the choir of All Saints Collegiate Chapel* originally the chapel of Charles IV's palace. It was built during the 1370s by Peter Parler and radically altered after the fire of 1541. The furnishings and decoration are Baroque.

THE NATIONAL GALLERY
ANCIENT CZECH ART AT ST GEORGE'S CONVENT

St George's Convent is situated in the small, intimate, gently sloping George Square (Jiřské náměsti), and is approached from the east either by climbing the original ancient street winding up to the castle (Na Opyši) or by taking the old Castle Steps and then up George Street (Jiřské ulice), which leads into the square. From the west, you have to pass St Vitus's Cathedral on your right, cross the Third Courtyard of the castle and take the narrow Vicar's Lane (Vikářská). Once in the square, if you face the choir of the cathedral, you see that the left side of the square is enclosed by a row of splendid buildings, notably the Vladislav Hall, the Old Diet, All Saints Chapel and the Institute of Noblewomen; on the right is the pseudo-Gothic New Provost's Lodging. Turn halfway round and you will see in front of you the entrance to the St George's Basilica, with its low façade adjoining St George's Convent, which accommodates the National Gallery's collection of ancient Czech art.

Opposite page: *statues of St Vitus and St John Nepomuk in the transept of St Vitus's Cathedral*. Carved in limewood and gilded, they stand 2.20 m (7.25 ft) high, and were executed in 1696 by František Preiss. The metropolitan canon Tobiáš Jan Becker donated them to the cathedral, along with statues of six other Czech patron saints.

HISTORY OF THE CONVENT

The original St George's Church, the first Christian sanctuary in the centre of the castle itself, was a short, three-aisled basilica, founded around 920 by Prince Vratislav I. Its present appearance, with its two characteristic white towers, dates from the time of the abbess Bertha (1145-51), following the castle fire of 1142. In 973, beside the original church, a Benedictine convent was founded (the oldest monastery in Bohemia and Moravia) by Prince Boleslav II and his sister Mlada, and endowed with a canonry. The convent church occupied a broad area between George Street and the north wall of the castle.

This convent (which as yet had no cloister) was demolished under Vladislav II in 1142, when the castle was besieged by Konrád of Znojmo. It was entirely destroyed by the fire, as were the basilica and other nearby buildings. It was the abbess Bertha who had the convent rebuilt, earning herself the title of 'second founder'. These changes gave St George's Basilica its present-day appearance, whereas the convent later underwent various modifications. In the course of the 14th century the convent saw a succession of improvements and alterations. But it was continually subjected to the changing fortunes of peace and war, of prosperity and vandalism, with little prospect of continuity or permanence.

The convent was restored and revived by its Renaissance-style reconstruction in the mid-16th century. Its present aspect and layout date essentially from 1671 to 1680, during the time of the abbess A.M. Schwenweisová. It was the architect Carlo Lurago who drew up the Early Baroque plans for this rebuilding project. For a century or so, the convent was again used for its original purpose. Then, after more than eight centuries, the reform programme of Joseph II brought its tragic and proud history to an end. The convent was closed on 8 March 1782. The building was used to accommodate clergy and then was turned over to the military and converted into a barracks. Finally, in 1969, plans were made to transform it into an adjunct of the National Gallery. After a complete archaeological survey, this project was realised between 1970 and 1975, based on the designs of the architects František Cubr and Josef Pilař. The collection of old Bohemian art, comprising paintings and sculptures from the 14th to 18th century, was installed on the three floors of the new museum. A permanent exhibition was opened to the public in 1976.

LAYOUT OF THE CONVENT

The site of the convent, including the basilica, is broadly in the form of a large rectangle extending east-west. Immediately beyond the entrance is the Paradise Courtyard; on the other side, at the end, is a smaller courtyard with the back entrance to the building (used only for the interior, it faces a small square leading into Golden Lane). Around the Paradise Courtyard are the four galleries of the cloister: the south and west galleries are mainly for access, the north and east ones forming part of the exhibition. The medieval collections are housed on the lower and ground floors, the Baroque on the first floor. Below the Paradise Courtyard are the extensive foundations of the convent, discovered in the course of archaeological digs and well preserved: although accessible, they are not open to the public.

It will be opportune at this stage to provide a brief guide to the layout of the convent and the arrangement of the various parts of the collection. Facing the entrance door is the long corridor of the south wing of the cloister, passing the foot of the tower; to the left of the entrance is the west corridor leading to the collection on the lower floor. Here are works dating from about 1350 to 1370, comprising paintings and sculptures, mainly of mid-14th-century Madonnas, by the Master of the Vyšší Brod

(Hohenfurth) Cycle, the Master of the Michle Madonna, Master Theodoric, etc.

On the ground floor is a large room, originally the old convent refectory, with a collection of work by the Master of the Třeboň Altarpiece. The north corridor contains works in the Flamboyant Gothic style and its followers, including the Master of the Rajhrad (Raigern) Altarpiece. In a small adjoining room is the Týn Tympanum. The north corridor leads directly to the north wing of the cloister with Late Gothic works of art. The exhibition then continues in the east wing, with the Master of the Litoměřice (Leitmeritz) Altarpiece and the Master of the Žebrák *Lamentation of Christ*, into the St Anne Chapel. Next to the chapel is a small room containing the sculptures of Master IP, the last room devoted to medieval art.

Visitors now take the stairs to the first floor, beginning with a small, select group of Mannerist works from the period of Rudolf II by Vries, Spranger, Aachen and others. The works of these foreign artists from Rudolf's court in Prague form a logical link between local Gothic and Baroque. On this floor, too, are Czech Baroque paintings and sculptures. The reconstruction of the building joined the north and south wings so as to form a number of impressively large rooms in which more than two hundred works are exhibited in chronological order. Some parts of this collection are devoted exclusively to religious subjects, but basically the three main rooms are designed to create an impression of size and space as a setting for the most important works of Czech Baroque art.

The first room is given over to Karel Skréta (1610-74); the second, and largest, to three Late Baroque painters, Braun, Brokoff and Brandl; and the third to Václav V. Reiner. This basic arrangement is completed by a series of smaller rooms and communicating corridors, displaying paintings by a number of other important artists, represented by works that are mainly of documentary interest: Willmann, Liška, Kupecký and minor figures of the Baroque such as Kern and Grund.

The second feature of the exhibition is the manner in which the space is divided rhythmically by a series of panels in a special stucco, either straight or curved in Baroque fashion, and in different colours: grey-black, red and russet. And as an additional touch, providing some relief and variation, there are showcases containing small works of sculpture and a modest selection of craft products of the 17th and 18th centuries.

A room on the west side of the first floor is devoted to temporary exhibitions, several of which are organised each year as an interesting supplement to the permanent collections. Behind this room are the offices and studios of the gallery's staff and specialists. The final treat for visitors, as they descend the staircase, is a fresco by Josef Kramolín, dating from 1782. Transferred here from the church of St Elisabeth's Convent, at Doupov in western Bohemia: it depicts angels with the attributes of the saint, with a cartouche inscribed *Cultui Divae Elisabeth oblatum.*

This gallery of paintings and sculptures was arranged chronologically to chart the course of the country's artistic development. However, this scheme is modified here and there by exhibits which are deliberately highlighted by reason of their symbolic or decorative effect within the context of the collection.

In the middle of the great Paradise Courtyard is a fountain: this is a contemporary classical work dominated by one of two angels by Matyáš Bernard Braun. This angel comes from a small town in central Bohemia and was carved in 1717-18; the other angel is in the Late Baroque room.

In the south wing of the cloister, just before the foot of the tower, is a sandstone sculpture of Vulcan, also by Braun, dating from 1714-16, which was originally on the attic storey of the Clam-Gallas Palace in Prague. In the smaller courtyard, another sandstone sculpture, by Ferdinand Maximilián Brokoff, dating from around 1710, shows Hercules fighting with Cerberus.

At the very start of the visit, at the basement entrance, there is a bas-relief fragment depicting an eagle which is the work of an unknown artist from St Vitus's Cathedral workshop in the second half of the 14th century.

Particularly beautiful, and open to visitors to the exhibition, is the chapel originally dedicated to the Virgin Mary, which underwent many transformations and was reconsecrated in the 17th century to St Anne. Although not very big, the reconstructed chapel displays characteristic examples, side by side, of three major art styles: one part, with its dressed stonework, is Romanesque; there is a Gothic high window; and the perfectly proportioned rose window and ornamental stucco vaulting are Renaissance. In addition, there are various Baroque features dating from the final period of alterations, around 1675.

The chapel is packed with rare objects relating to the history of the convent, either by reason of their provenance or because of their association with its religious purpose and mission. First of all there is a remarkable votive relief model of the court. Beside the remains of the abbesses (the engraved tomb of Cunegonde with a Baroque grille and, beyond that, the reputed remains of Mlada in a glass coffin placed in a niche on the epistle side — an arrangement adopted around 1733), there are objects and symbols of their office and rank: the abbatial cross and their princely crown. Among the paintings, the focus of interest is the so-called St George Triptych and — more of a curiosity — a Baroque painting which simultaneously represents Mlada's mission to Rome and the handing over of the foundation act of the diocese to Boleslav II.

To the right of the chapel entrance is the original of the semicircular high relief showing St George slaying the dragon: it can also be seen at a distance from the entry of the south wing. It was removed from the tympanum of the southern side door of the basilica (where a copy now stands). Originally, the clay relief was richly coloured and in some measure it resembles the technique of woodcarving. Its date is 1510-20. The interesting theory has been advanced that it may have been a kind of homage paid to Prince Louis Jagiello, who had been crowned in Prague in the spring of 1509; and that it predicted his destiny of resisting the Turkish threat.

In the south wing of the cloister the tombstones of thirteen abbesses of St George's, dating from various centuries, are built into the walls. At the foot of the tower, a glass partition affords a beautiful and imposing view of the adjoining St George's Basilica.

THE HISTORY AND NATURE OF THE ART COLLECTIONS

It is worth saying a few words about the institution of the Prague National Gallery to give those who are interested a rather more detailed account of the somewhat complex origins, development and nature of the collections that form such an important part of the nation's heritage.

The Private Society of the Patriotic Friends of the Arts, which was founded on 5 February 1796 'once more to encourage art and good taste...', was the origin of the present-day National Gallery. This Society, with its noble intentions so clearly declared in its act of foundation, aimed to halt the decline of the fine arts (which had reached their peak in the second half of the 18th century) and to check the systematic export of art works belonging to old collections. The foundation of an Academy of Fine Arts would achieve the first of these objectives, while the second would be assured by the creation of a permanent gallery in Prague. The idea for the Society came from the cultured and scholarly Count František Šternberk-Manderscheid. During the Society's initial period, the paintings were not the property of the gallery but of the different members of the Society, who provided them on loan. An annual auction was held where members could purchase the paintings acquired during the year by the Society out of its funds. This system was abolished in 1835.

Certain key dates mark the subsequent development of what was eventually to become the National Gallery. Thus the Modern Gallery of the Czech Kingdom, as envisaged by the Society of Patriotic Friends, was completed in 1901 and created by an edict of Emperor Franz Joseph. Credit for the organisation and efficient running of the gallery goes to Vincenc Kramář (director from 1919-39), an internationally recognised expert and collector of Cubist paintings. In 1933, the state took charge of the collections, establishing what became known as the State Collection of Ancient Art. During the Second World War, it functioned under the title of the Czecho-Moravian Territorial Gallery of Prague. In 1945 the collections of ancient and modern art were handed over to the National Gallery, heir to a two centuries-old tradition, during which time chance had frequently played a role in determining where the collections were housed. Early in its history, in 1811, the Society had acquired the Sternberg (Šternberk) Palace, at Hradčany, and had held its first exhibition there. In 1885 the Society's works of art found another suitable home in the Rudolfinum, which had just been built to hold concerts; this was a donation from the Czech Savings Bank for local cultural activities.

After the First World War, this building was handed over to the Parliament of the new independent nation, which had no seat of its own. Thus art lovers were once more faced with the problem, as they had been a century or so before, of looking for a new gallery. In 1945, at the end of the Second World War, the National Gallery collections were housed in the Sternberg Palace, and selected examples of ancient Czech and European art were exhibited together. After the transfer to St George's Convent of the Czech painting and sculpture collections of the Gothic and Baroque periods, the rooms of the Sternberg Palace were reserved exclusively for foreign art. So the two central collections of the National Gallery, each with a clearly defined, specialised character, finally found suitable homes.

Since then, both collections have grown so rapidly that new exhibition galleries have had to be acquired. In spite of this, only a tiny proportion of the art works in store is exhibited and accessible to the public. And even those works that form the core of the permanent exhibitions are likely to be subjected to essential changes in the near future. Although these are mainly owned by the National Gallery (through purchases, donations, legacies, etc.), many are works of art confiscated or stolen after the Communists seized power in 1948. They include the property of religious orders or church institutions, inheritances of aristocratic families, objects originally belonging to private collections, and so forth. Because the priority has been to establish the legal position and, where necessary, to make restitution in such cases, this has led to new relationships between the gallery and the various owners, taking the form of short- and long-term loans. Fortunately, all concerned are well aware of the historical and artistic importance of the nation's cultural heritage, and this provides a solid foundation for finding satisfactory solutions to the problem in the future.

As already mentioned, the Gothic works of art are exhibited in the basement, and those ranging from Late Gothic to the Renaissance on the ground floor of the convent. There are close to two hundred paintings and sculptures on display and, as far as circumstances permit, these follow a logical timescale and sequence of development. They represent a golden age of artistic achievement during the reigns of two monarchs of the Luxembourg dynasty, the emperors Charles IV (king of Bohemia from 1346 to 1378) and his son Wenceslas IV (king of Bohemia from 1378 to 1419), at a time when Czech art played an important and, to some extent, leading role in the countries north of the Alps.

Charles IV, one of the great statesmen of the Middle Ages and by far the most influential monarch of his time, was directly or indirectly associated with all contemporary developments in learning and culture, particularly in the field of fine arts. According to its reputed date, the oldest fragment of panel painting (known as the 'fragment of the Roudnice polyptich') coincides, almost symbolically, with the accession of Charles IV; and the date of the emperor's death with the appearance of the Master of the Třeboň Altarpiece, who raised the level of Czech painting to new heights. A number of factors — the quality of the mural paintings and illuminations that have survived, the maturity of the local milieu, the abundance of mid-14th-century painting on glass and, finally, comparison with what was going on in neighbouring regions — point to the hypothesis that the earliest development of painting on wood could have occurred much earlier, perhaps dating from about 1310 to 1320, namely during the time of John (the Blind) of Luxembourg, king of Bohemia from 1310 to 1346. Yet, in spite of the astonishing wealth of preserved fragments, these represent only an infinitesimally small proportion of the original production. Thus, before 1420, there were 104 public sanctuaries in Prague, and 89 altars in St Vitus's Cathedral alone; in 1348 a brotherhood of painters had been founded, which subsequently became the Guild of St Luke, the first professional body of its kind in Europe. Consequently, any attempt to trace the development of medieval Czech art can only be theoretical since it is based merely on objects that have been preserved by chance: miraculously they managed to survive the unimaginable destruction wrought by the Hussite uprisings and other disasters brought on by war, natural causes or fatal actions stemming from ignorance and illiteracy.

The imperial policy of Charles IV was based essentially on principles of Bohemian centralism as well as personal and dynastic sovereignty. The emperor was fortunate in surrounding himself with the ablest representatives of the church hierarchy, and his activities as a builder and patron attracted, from near and far, the greatest masters in their fields: Matthew of Arras, Peter Parler, Nicolas Wurmser and others. The interchange of ideas from Italy and western Europe with those of local tradition rapidly produced a syncretism of different

THE MASTER OF THE KRUMLOV
MADONNA (active from the 1380s until
the early 15th century)

St Peter, *c.* 1395, marl with traces of poly-
chròmy, height.91.5 cm (36 in). The right
hand and part of the keys are missing, the

influences and stylistic tendencies. Out of this
emerged a local plastic style that was given the
opportunity to develop and mature as a result of
innumerable commissions obtained from the court
of Charles IV and from other representatives of the
upper echelons of society, both secular and religious. The development of the schools of Czech
painting and sculpture (which in many respects
strongly influenced each other) was determined and
assured by a succession of creative geniuses: the
Master of the Vyšši Brod Cycle, the Master of the
Michle Madonna, Master Theodoric, the Master of
the Třeboň Altarpiece, the Master of the Týn
Tympanum, the Master of the Krumlov Madonna,
the Master of the Rajhrad Altarpiece, and others.

All in all, the work of these masters showed an
astonishing inner cohesion, for the creative impulse
of each individual was conditioned by a common
cultural and spiritual heritage. The formally late, but
refined, expression of the Flamboyant Gothic style,
dating from around 1400, was replaced by an art
that already reflected the anxiety and the spiritual
and social unease of pre-Hussite Bohemia; and this
boded ill for the future of local plastic arts as a significant force in the overall context of European culture. During the ensuing fifty years or so, artistic
output was sparse and uninspired. Not until the
1460s and the political changes associated with the
accession of George of Poděbrady (king of Bohemia
from 1458 to 1471) and the first of the two Jagiello
monarchs, Vladislav II (king of Bohemia from 1471
to 1516) was there any evidence of a revival in
architecture, painting and sculpture. Only then did
local culture once more react and adapt to outside
influences, stimulated by the example of its
European neighbours.

Bohemia initially became aware of the realism of
Flemish art, as evinced in varying measure by successive generations, through indirect contacts with
German centres of painting in the Rhineland,
Nuremberg and other places. Later still, this time
learning from native example, Czech art derived
inspiration from the Danubian school of land-

182

nose is broken and there is slight damage to the drapery.

On the basis of stylistic studies, this sculpture has been attributed to an anonymous artist who owes his name to a statue of the Virgin and Child (made around 1400) from the town of Český Krumlov (southern Bohemia) and now to be found in the Kunsthistorisches Museum, Vienna. Whereas the curve of the body and the form of the drapery conform to the more or less obligatory criteria of modelling for this genre of sculpture, the head of the old man is rendered in a wholly unusual manner, representing a masterly synthesis of aesthetic idealism and intensely realistic observation. The sculpture was loaned to the National Gallery by the parish church of St Peter of Slivice.

scapists. From 1470 onward, until well into the early 16th century, a number of important new artists appeared, whose works were the equal of anything currently being done in Europe: the Master of the St George Altarpiece, the Master of the Puchner Altarpiece, the Master of the Žebrák *Lamentation of Christ*, the Master of the Litoměřice Altarpiece, Master IP, etc.

In the last part of the exhibition, certain general tendencies are evident: for example, the persistence of ancient tradition in painting and sculpture and the gradual conception and expression of Late Gothic. The breakthrough achieved by an objective approach to naturalism and realism, the changes in the artistic perception of space, of the human face and of the pictorial setting, and the differences in iconographic representation, etc. — all this is interesting and revealing in the light of the ensuing transformation from Late Gothic to the new viewpoint of Renaissance aesthetics.

If, for convenience, the collections of St George's Convent are defined broadly as Gothic and Baroque, the last works of the first section date from around 1530 (Master IW and Master IP). The oldest Baroque paintings and sculptures on display were done around 1630 (Karel Škréta and Arnošt Jan Heidelberger). This gap of a hundred years is bridged by a small but select group representing socalled 'Rudolfian' Mannerism: an art style created at Emperor Rudolf II's court in Prague. Actually, it is a specific and unique form of artistic expression, and the fact that it is included in the exhibition should not convey the impression that it represents any kind of continuity, spanning the two styles. In the last few decades keen interest and detailed study have thrown much light on the phenomenon of Mannerism. This body of painting and sculpture, created by foreign artists working in Prague, is now deservedly recognised as occupying a very prominent position in the history of art.

Rudolf II officially transferred the capital of his empire to Prague in 1583, eight years after being crowned king of Bohemia in St Vitus's Cathedral.

He then lived in the castle permanently until his death in 1612 and directed all the complex royal activities associated with the Habsburg dynasty from Prague. But although his imperial policies often aroused controversy, there can be no denying that, as a monarch, his interest in and passion for art, and his appreciation and understanding of all forms of artistic creativity were unrivalled. In his capacities as collector, promoter and patron, he surrounded himself with brilliant artists from virtually every corner of Europe, a dazzling list of names ranging, alphabetically, from Arcimbolo to Vries. His collections at Prague Castle were, and still are, of incalculable historical and cultural importance: his network of agent-buyers covered the whole of Europe, and his local colony of artists made priceless contributions in every field of the fine arts — examples of which can be found today in all the great world collections. Some twenty or so key figures of 'Rudolfian' art are represented in the aforementioned small selection in the convent: there are paintings by Bartholomeus Spranger, Hans von Aachen, Josef Heintz, Roelant Savery and others; and sculptures by Adriaen de Vries and Hans Mont. These works were chosen so as to provide a fair sample of this refined court culture, its motivation and content, its method and style, and, not least, to show off the astonishing virtuosity of its creators.

The first floor of the cloister is devoted to the Baroque. The period covered by the exhibits ranges from the earliest works of Škréta (in the 1630s) to the Rococo works of Norbert Grund (late 1760s) and even to the late classical style of the Platzer studio (around 1800). Paradoxically, these dates, insofar as they reflect social and political life in Europe generally, and in the Czech-speaking lands specifically, coincide with shattering events affecting ordinary people everywhere, from the horrors of the Thirty Years' War to the dramas of the French Revolution. The dates also span the reigns of some ten monarchs of the Habsburg dynasty, from Ferdinand II to Leopold II. In the religious sphere, this period saw the cruellest forms of repression and

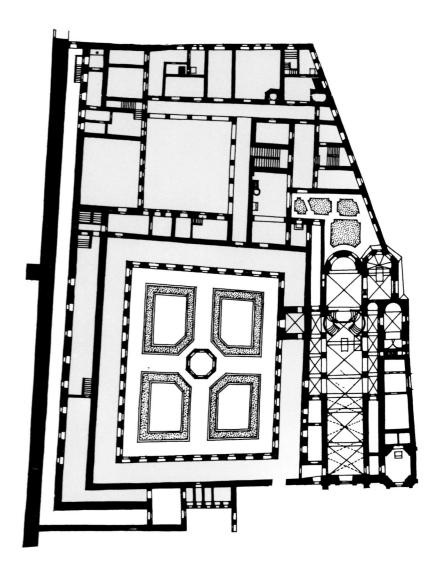

the resurgence of Catholicism after the battle of the White Mountain (1620), which was lost by the Protestants (it is estimated that more than a quarter of the professional and educated classes went into forced exile). This was roughly the period that began with the return of the Jesuit order to Prague (from which it had been driven out in 1618), to become the principal agent of the systematic Catholicising policy of Ferdinand II, and with the founding of its college, the Clementium, around 1656, and ended in 1781 with Joseph II's Edict of Tolerance and the secularisation of monasteries.

Broadly speaking, during this period of some one hundred and fifty years, the irreplaceable loss that Bohemia suffered as a result of the departure of its intellectuals proved to be Europe's gain, with the arrival of many important figures, such as the writer and philosopher Comenius (Jan Ámos Komenský) and the designer and engraver Václav Hollar. But, in compensation, this same period saw a regular flow of artists and craftsmen in the reverse direction, from many European countries towards Bohemia, where they helped to establish the Baroque style throughout the Czech-speaking lands and, particularly, in the capital city of Prague.

This continuous exchange of personalities and ideas, of such lasting significance on a spiritual and cultural level, was one of the principal features of the Baroque era. Among those forced to leave was Škréta, who returned from exile in Italy in 1638, the same year that the architect Carlo Lurago arrived in Prague. Jan Kupecký, born in 1667, was to spend his entire life in exile, travelling all over Europe; Petr Brandl, on the other hand, born in 1668, never left his native land. One year separates the erection of the first statue on Charles Bridge (that of St John of Nepomuk, in 1683) and the birth of Matthias B. Braun (1684), the genius from the Tyrol and master of the Baroque whose sculpture was to adorn the bridge, one of the most important and famous cultural monuments in Europe, and many of the city churches. In that same year (1689) two great artists were born: Kilián Ignác Dienzenhofer, the most gift-

ed of all local architects, who created the so-called Dienzenhofer Baroque and whose masterpieces include that most beautiful of all the Late Baroque churches, St Nicholas's Church in the Old Town; and Václav Vavřinec Reiner, frescoist and painter, a dazzling exponent of Baroque art at its zenith. And as if to re-emphasise the close links and reciprocal influences of the three principal areas of the plastic arts, the previous year (1688) had seen the birth of Ferdinand M. Brokoff, another major figure of Czech sculpture and the very antithesis of Braun.

Czech Baroque art, after the Gothic of Charles IV and Wenceslas IV, made a significant contribution to European plastic arts. It was a highly complex phenomenon, inherently founded upon the synthesis and interplay of the three principal creative areas: architecture, painting and sculpture. The St George's Convent collection cannot possibly give a complete picture of the scope, diversity and individuality, nor of the harmony and homogeneity of this artistic heritage. Yet, in spite of such inevitable shortcomings, it remains an indispensable experience, intellectually and emotionally stimulating, with a significance beyond time and place.

Opposite page: plan of St George's Basilica and cloister, signed by Niccolo Pacassi (1789). The coloured area corresponds to the present-day site of the National Gallery.

Right: the south isle of the cloister seen from the main entrance; in the background is a semicircular high-relief from the early 16th century representing St George slaying the dragon.

Below: the north corridor, with 15th-century works in the foreground.

CZECH MASTER FROM BEFORE 1350

Fragment of a polyptich with the figures of St Andrew, St John the Evangelist and St Peter; before 1350, distemper on maple wood, mounted on cloth, height 40 cm (15.75 in), width 91 cm (36 in).

This fragment, dating from 1345-9, is

this town or, more probably, for the castle, which served as a summer residence for the bishops of Prague. The style of the painting is notable for its expressive drawing and numerous Italian features. It shows every sign of being a transitional work in which ancient, traditional forms were subjected to strong Italian influence, possibly transmitted by the importation of manu-

regarded as the oldest Czech painting on wood. It was long thought to be the lower part of the predella of an altarpiece, but today it is considered to be a fragment of a larger polyptich which represented the twelve apostles in several superimposed ranks. It comes from St Joseph's Chapel of Roudnice, but was doubtless originally intended either for the Augustine abbey of

scripts and by the artistic atmosphere diffused by the entourage of Bishop Jan of Dražice (d. 1343).

186

THE MASTER OF THE
VYŠŠI BROD CYCLE
(active 1340-60)

*Christ on the Mount of
Olives*; before 1350, distemper on maple wood,
mounted on cloth, height

99.5 cm (39.25 in), width
91.5 cm (36 in). Scholars
now tend to agree that this
was part of a large square

altarpiece consisting of nine panels in three rows. The lower row of paintings would have represented the childhood of Christ; the centre row, his sufferings, and the upper row his apotheosis. On the basis of this reconstruction, the *Mount of Olives* would have appeared on the left-hand panel of the centre row. The nine panels which have been preserved thus make up a complete whole. They come from the Church of the Assumption of the Blessed Virgin in the Cistercian convent of Vyšší Brod (Hohenfurth). On the *Nativity* panel, the kneeling figure of the donor, Peter of Rožmberk (d. 1347), has been identified. His death probably indicates the latest date for the creation of the cycle. It has not yet been determined whether they originally came from Vyšší Brod or from Prague, but judging by the high quality it was undoubtedly created in one of the best court workshops. The Master of the Vyšší Brod Cycle was a dominant figure in the first generation of panel painters: as the founder of the Czech tradition of the genre, he had a profound influence not only on Czech painting but also, to a certain extent, on sculpture, elevating local production to European level.

MASTER THEODORIC
(active 1350-70)

St Elizabeth; *c.* 1365, distemper on beech wood, height 114.5 cm (45 in), width 86.5 cm (34 in).

Master Theodoric is the first Czech painter to be known by name, about whom we have personal information, and whose work has survived. Magister Theodoricus or Theodoricus pictor was court painter to Emperor Charles IV, first master of the confraternity of Prague painters and owner of a house in the Hradčany quarter. *St Elizabeth* was part of a series of paintings that Theodoric and his workshop did to decorate the Holy Cross Chapel in the dungeon of Karlštejn Castle: it comprised *The Crucifixion*, *The Man of Sorrows* and 127 panels with the figures of Christ's army. A letter from the emperor, dated 28 April 1367, announcing that the artist was to be paid for the finished work, makes it possible to affirm with certainty that the decoration of this chapel was completed by this date at the latest. The panels formed part of the overall ornamentation which included inlaid semi-precious stones in the walls, mural paintings, inlaid crystal in the vault, etc. The chapel was the repository of relics of the Passion of Christ and the Crown Jewels; and relics of various saints were also placed in the picture frames. Theodoric was the principal representative of the second generation of Bohemian painters on wood. Above: the room devoted to Master Theodoric.

THE MASTER OF THE TŘEBOŇ ALTARPIECE
(active 1370-90)

The Resurrection of Christ; *c.* 1380, distemper on spruce wood, mounted on cloth on both sides, height 132 cm (52 in), width 92 cm (36.25 in).

The panel is painted on both sides. On the reverse are figures of three apostles, St James the Just (the Less), St Bartholomew and St Philip; on the front is the *Resurrection of Christ*. This is one of the three surviving panels from a large altarpiece, since dismantled. The two others represent *Christ on the Mount of Olives* and *The Entombment*, with, on the back of each panel, the figures of three saints. There is no doubt that other panels are missing, so that views differ as to the likely initial appearance of the altarpiece. Originally it was in St Giles's Church at the Augustine abbey of Třeboň (southern Bohemia); after the altarpiece was dismantled, the panels were given, in the first half of the 18th century, to local churches of the region. The Master of the Třeboň Altarpiece was a brilliant artist and, thanks to his work, the third generation of Czech painting reached unequalled heights.

CZECH MASTER FROM BEFORE 1396

Madonna and Child known as *St Vitus's Cathedral Madonna*; before 1396, distemper on lime wood, mounted on cloth on both sides, height 51 cm (20 in), width 39.5 cm (15.5 in).

This is undoubtedly the best-known local Marian painting which, according to the second iconographical variant, shows the Mother and Child, the latter resting on Mary's right arm, directly facing the observer. In the corner quadrifoliate medallions of the carved frame, there are half-figures of four angels, with white ribbons bearing the abbreviations of the beginning of a Marian song. On the upper part of the frame, the half-figures of St John the Baptist and St John are placed in the six-lobed medallions. On the left of the frame are St Wenceslas and St Sigismund; on the right, St Vitus and St Adalbert. At the bottom of the frame, on the right, is the local St Procopius, particularly venerated by the donor, Archbishop Jan of Jenštejn, because of the extreme austerity of his monastic life. The archbishop is himself represented kneeling in the left-hand medallion. The blessing of the foundations of the three-aisled nave took place in 1392 and the archbishop gave up his functions in 1396; the work was painted between these dates and was undoubtedly a personal donation by Jenštejn to the cathedral.

THE MASTER OF THE RAJHRAD ALTARPIECE
(active 1415-60)

The *Rajhrad* or *Nové Sady Crucifixion*; before 1420, distemper on spruce wood mounted on cloth, height 101 cm (39.75 in), width 142 cm (56 in).

This panel, painted on one side, is from a large, dismantled altarpiece, only six panels of which survive. The second

panel, its width exceeding its height, shows the *Way of the Cross*, and the four others are smaller, but painted vertically. The two wide panels would have formed the centre of the altarpiece. The *Crucifixion* comes from the Church of St Philip and St James in Olomouc: it was brought there in 1784 from its original site, St Maurice's Church, in the same town. The iconographical subject of the altarpiece was Christ's Passion and the legend

of the Holy Cross. The Master of the Rajhrad Altarpiece headed a large workshop, doubtless situated in Brno, since the surviving works are mainly of Moravian origin. His style is in the tradition of the Master of the Třeboň Altarpiece and Flamboyant Gothic, but also shows close familiarity with contemporary pictorial production (from France, the Netherlands, northern Germany, etc.). In fact, he represents the culmination of

Czech panel painting and was the last important painter before the start of the Hussite troubles.

CZECH MASTER OF AROUND 1450

The Assumption in a Flower Garden, the so-called *Děstná Assumption*; *c.* 1450, distemper on spruce wood, mounted on cloth, height 144 cm (56.75 in), width 111 cm (43.75 in).

The Virgin Mary, hair in a halo, stands in a flower garden and holds the infant Jesus on her left arm; beneath her feet sin and evil are symbolically represented in a half-moon, while at the top of the picture the Madonna is crowned Queen of Heaven by two angels. The highly complex iconography of this painting is to be interpreted principally as a devout manifestation of the Marian cult: the inscriptions with fragments of Marian litanies testify to this. The painting comes from St John the Baptist's

Chapel in Děstná (southern Bohemia). There are references in the picture to the Flamboyant Gothic style but also significant Late Gothic elements, as in the descriptive realism of the natural features and the folds of the draperies.

MASTER OF THE ST GEORGE ALTAR-PIECE (active 1470-85)

Triptych with the Death of the Virgin Mary, the so-called *St George Triptych*; *c.* 1470, distemper on lime wood, mounted on cloth on the central panel and on the inside of the two wings; panel, height 192.5 cm (75.75 in), width 114 cm(45 in); each wing, height 192 cm (75.75 in), width 56.5 cm (22.25 in).

The central panel of the open triptych rep-

resents the death of the Virgin Mary: above, in a square, is Christ with the soul of the Virgin Mary and a choir of seven angels. At the top of the left wing is the Visitation and, below, the Adoration of the Magi. When the triptych is closed, the reverse side of the left wing shows, above, St Wenceslas and, below, St Philip and St Simon with the donatrix, the kneeling abbess. On the reverse side of the right wing, above, is St George, one foot placed on the dead dragon and, below, St Andrew with the donor, the kneeling canon. The placing of a key scene of the St George legend as well as the image of the saint himself on the outer side of a triptych wing is rather unusual, but is explicable here by the fact that the triptych was originally intended for St George's Basilica.

that such an altarpiece might have been destined for a chapel. *The Martyrdom of St Catherine* was bought in 1969 by a private Austrian collector; this work, as well as others by the same hand, show that the Master of the Litoměřice Altarpiece was one of the most important Czech painters during the first quarter of the 16th century.

CZECH MASTER FROM THE FIRST THIRD OF THE 13TH CENTURY

High-relief in three parts from St George's Basilica; 1210-28, gilded marl; centrepiece, height 88 cm (34.75 in), width 57 cm (22.5 in); wings height 66 cm (26 in), width 27 cm (10.5 in); traces of polychromy on central section; the left and right bases of the wings are broken and there is other slight damage. The central high-relief shows

THE MASTER OF THE LITO-MEŘICE ALTARPIECE (active 1490-1520)

The Martyrdom of St Catherine; after 1510 distemper on lime wood, height 77.5 cm (30.5 in), width 44.5 cm (17.5 in).

The wood panel is painted on both sides. On the reverse is *St Catherine in Alexandria Debating with the Pagan Philosophers*. This is a movable wing, difficult to identify with precision, from a dismantled altarpiece which has not been entirely preserved. Four other

paintings belonging to it are known, on panels painted on both sides that were sawn off: *St Catherine before the Emperor Maximilian; The Burial of St Catherine; The Vanity of St Catherine;* and *St Catherine Visiting a Hermit*. They are all in foreign collections.

The fragmentary character of the remains of this altarpiece makes it impossible to theorise as to its original appearance. What is certain is that a complete wing painted on both sides has been lost. The smaller format of the paintings suggests the Madonna in majesty, crowned by angels bearing monstrances. Kneeling at her feet are: left, the founder and first abbess of St George's Convent, Mary Mlada, and, right, the abbess Bertha known as the "second founder". On the right wing is the Přemysl king, Otakar I, on his knees, and on the left wing a nun, probably Agnes, half-sister of the king. The importance given to her suggests that she may have been the donatrix of the high-relief.

Experts do not agree as to where this sculpture was originally placed (either on the door of the Chapel of the Virgin Mary or on the main or south door of the basilica). The work is one of the most important examples of Czech Romanesque art.

CZECH MASTER FROM THE FIRST QUARTER OF THE 14TH CENTURY

Madonna and Child, the so-called *Strakonice Madonna, c.* 1300, fir wood, height 183 cm (72 in); sculpture carved on the back with traces of polychromy; the right hand of the Madonna is missing; the head and left hand of the infant Jesus (in lime wood) have been added.

The statue comes from the Way of the Cross of the Hospitallers' Convent of St John of Jerusalem, Strakonice. According to an inventory of

1742, it was then placed in the chapter room, namely St George's Chapel. It was acquired for the National Gallery in 1927. This Madonna ranks as one of the most important Central European works of art, exemplifying a phase of development towards an abstract post-classical style. The statue occupies an exceptional place in Czech Gothic sculpture by reason of its close link with monumental French sculpture and with the same trend of cathedral sculpture in the Rhineland.

MARTIN AND GEORGE OF KOLOSZVÁR (active in last quarter of 14th century)

Equestrian statue of St George slaying the dragon; 1373, special bronze (with addition of lead); overall height 196 cm (77 in); knight, 135 cm (53 in); the saint's lance is missing.

This equestrian statue of St George is considered to be one of the most important pieces of 14th-century sculpture. Its modeller is unknown: either Peter Parler or one of the members of the Prague workshop. The statue was cast from this model by the brothers Martin and George of Kolozsvár;

after 1562 Wolf Hofprucker and Tomáš Jaroš recast the horse and the dragon. It has been established that the statue was in Prague Castle from the 16th century, but the version now in the castle's Third Courtyard is a copy, the original having been loaned to the National Gallery. The statue was inspired by antique and Italian models, but the dynamism of the movements, the masterly combination of expressive features, the keenness and concentration of the rider's gaze (not to mention the naturalistic details of anatomy, equipment, etc.) — all these elements serve to endow it with a timeless quality unique in the context of similar European works of this genre.

THE MASTER OF THE LAMENTATION OF THE CHRIST OF ŽEBRÁK (active in first third of 16th century)

The Lamentation of Žebrák; *c.* 1510, lime wood, height 126 cm (49.5 in), width 121 cm (47.75 in); traces of original polychromy and later white painting, series of cracks and slight damage.

This remarkable work owes its name to its anonymous creator, an important sculptor in wood who ran a workshop at České Budějovice, in the south of the country. This sculpture is his only work that does not come from that region. The Prague Museum acquired it from a private owner in Žebrák early in the present century and loaned it to the National Gallery. Research has uncovered more works by this artist and deduced that in his early days he was taught by the Masters of the Kefermarkt Altarpiece (Austria), and that he developed this style in a very personal manner, notable particularly for a depth and tension of subjective feeling, a spiritual dimension and an authenticity of form and expressive means.

ADRIAEN DE VRIES (The
Hague, 1545 - Prague, 1626)

*Hercules in the Garden of the
Hesperides*; *c.* 1625, bronze
with original patina, height
162.5 cm (64 in).

The mythological hero holds
the golden apples of the
Hesperides (daughters of Atlas)
in his right hand, which rests
against his side, while the left
hand grips a club resting on his
shoulder. There is no way of
telling whether the subject is
standing or walking. The somewhat subdued dynamism of the
figure, the fluidity and rough-
ness of the modelling, and the
vague facial expression are
characteristic elements of the
artist's late style. The rich play
of light on the curves and
crevices of the statue, which
still retains traces of original
patina (due to always having
been kept indoors) produces a
remarkable effect. Like some
other mythological statues, it
was intended originally for the
garden of the Wallenstein
Palace, but in 1648 it was carried off to Sweden by General
Königsmark as a trophy of war.

BARTHOLOMEUS
SPRANGER (Antwerp, 1546 -
Prague, 1611)

*Painting to the Memory of the
Prague Goldsmith Mikuláš
Müller*; *c.* 1592, oil on canvas,
243 cm x 160 cm (96 x 63 in),
unsigned.

The goldsmith Mikuláš Müller,
who died in 1586, had been
summoned from Brussels to
Prague by Archduke Ferdinand
of Tyrol before 1566. His
daughter Christina was the wife
of Spranger, who did the painting in memory of his father-in-
law for St Matthew's Chapel of
St John's Church in Malá
Strana. The painting, which
originally hung beneath the portrait of *God the Father and Two
Putti* by Adriaen de Vries, later
adorned the tomb of Spranger
himself, before becoming private property when the church
was closed. At the feet of Christ
triumphant over Evil is the family of the deceased, this being a

transalpine convention. On the left is the deceased and his son Jacob; on the right is his wife in a hat and, behind her, their daughter Christina, with a little girl in the foreground. According to Karel Van Mander, the celebrated biographer of artists, Spranger regarded this as one of his best works from the viewpoint of coloration.

JOSEF HEINTZ THE ELDER (Basel, 1564 - Prague, 1609)

The Adoration of the Shepherds; *c.* 1598, oil on copperplate, 29.7 cm x 21.8 cm (11.75 x 8.5 in), unsigned, illegible inscription on back.

A remarkable example of Heintz's mastery of colour, this painting, although small, nevertheless makes a considerable impression. Heintz was inspired by the central part of Hans Holbein the Younger's *Altarpiece of Chancellor Hans Oberried* (the wings of which are today in Freiburg Cathedral). The shepherd standing at the far right, with his broad-brimmed hat (*detail above*), is almost identical in the two works, and experts surmise that this is not simply a return to the cultivated past on the part of Rudolfian Mannerism but a direct tribute by Heintz to Holbein the Younger, whom he considered an important source of artistic inspiration. The painting, which was originally in the collections of Rudolf II, came into the possession, at some undetermined time, of the gallery of the Premonstrant Convent in Strahov.

KAREL ŠKRÉTA (Prague, 1610 - Prague, 1674)

St Charles Borromeo Visiting Victims of the Plague in Milan; 1647, oil on canvas, 210 cm x 147.5 cm (82.5 in x 58 in), unsigned; the dedication on the altar, in the centre of the painting, reads: "E/EGO MAX ANTONIUS CASSINIS F.C. 1647".

The painting shows the future St Charles Borromeo, then cardinal, carrying out his pastoral duties during the plague epidemic of 1576. It emerges from the dedication that this painting was commissioned by M.A. Cassinis of Bugella, a member of the presidency of the Italian Congregation. The picture was designed for the high altar of

the painting: he is the bearded man pointing to the inscription, behind St Charles Borromeo, seen blessing the sick. The person standing behind the saint and looking outward is Škréta himself: this is the only self-portrait of the artist to have survived. Škréta painted this work nine years after returning from exile to Prague and three

the Church of St Charles Borromeo in the Italian hospital situated in the quarter of Malá Strana. The donor is represented in

years after his enrolment in the famous confraternity of painters of the Old Town, when he was already a recognised artist.

JAN KUPECKÝ (Prague, 1667 - Nuremberg, 1740)

Self-Portrait: the Artist Working on a Painting of His Wife; 1711, oil on canvas 93.5 cm x 74.5 cm (36.75 in x 29.25 in), signed on the back: "Joh. Kupezky pinx. 1711".

This is one of many self-portraits by Kupecký and resembles the more famous *Self-Portrait of the Artist Working on a Painting of a Man* (perhaps of A.B, de Löwenstadt, a citizen of Wroclaw) in the Österreichische Galerie of Vienna. The Vienna portrait is dated 1709, and that of Prague two years later. This was the year Kupecký, the son of emigrés, who in 1707 had settled in Vienna, and where he was to live until 1723, returned for the second time to his native land for a short stay in Karlovy Vary (Karlsbad), where he painted a commissioned portrait of Tsar Peter the Great. This self-portrait was in the collection of Prince Wenceslas Paar.

VÁCLAV VAVŘINEC REINER (Prague, 1689 - Prague, 1743)

Orpheus and the Animals; before 1720, oil on canvas, 199 cm x 167 cm (79 in x 65.75 in), unsigned.

The subject, known best from Ovid's *Metamorphoses*, relates to the mythological fable of Orpheus, founder of poetry, who, having lost his wife Eurydice, expresses his deep grief by playing his lyre and so enchants the different animals that they gather round to listen in a spirit of harmony and conciliation. It is an allegory that aims to underline the magical power of music and poetry, superior to the very forces of nature. This theme is found nowhere else in Reiner's body of work (though there is a similar painting, *Landscape with Birds and a Pointing Dog*, also in the National Gallery). It harks back to an older painting of Orpheus by Michael Leopold Willmann, dated 1670-5. Reiner's two pictures come from the collection of the Counts Nostitz (Nostic) and faithfully reflect the thinking and attitudes of the cultured aristocracy.

PETER BRANDL (Prague, 1668 - Kutná Hora, 1735)

Simeon with Jesus; shortly after 1725, oil on canvas, 78 cm x 60 cm (30.75 in x 23.5 in), unsigned.

This is among Brandl's most beautiful paintings and one of the greatest examples of Czech Baroque art. The painter has chosen the moment when the elderly Simeon recognises the child Jesus as the Messiah and thanks God in these words: "Now thou dost dismiss thy servant, O Master, according to thy word, in peace; Because mine eyes have seen thy salvation, which thou hast prepared before the face of all the peoples: A light of revelation unto the gentiles, and glory for thy people Israel." (*St Luke's Gospel*, ii, 29-32).

The picture is unique in its technique: it is possible to distinguish clearly in this deeply felt painting the areas in which the artist has used the other end of his brush and those where he has modelled the thick layers of paint with his fingers. The date given (just after 1725) is based on the fact that this was the period when Brandl's art reached its culmination. The first known owner of the painting was Count Fr. Šternberk (Sternberg), who had it in his collection.

NORBERT GRUND (Prague, 1717 - Prague, 1767)

The Sculpture Studio; before 1767, oil on beech wood, 25 cm x 34.7 cm (9.75 in x 13.75 in), unsigned.

This painting is the pendant to *The Painting Studio*, which dates from the same year.

The two paintings form part of a very large group of works which the doctor J. Hoser donated, in 1843, to the gallery of painting installed at the Sternberg Palace by the Patriotic Friends of the Arts. This painting in the intimist genre shows the studio of the sculptor František Platzer (1717-87), who worked in Prague and was one of Grund's generation. The sculpture is one of the two groups of *Fighting Giants* (the left-hand one) commissioned for the railings of the Court of Honour of Prague Castle. The original sandstone sculptures were delivered to the castle before 1769, but as they could not be preserved, in 1919 they were replaced by new copies. Small terracotta models are to be found in the National Gallery collections.

MATTHIAS RAUCHMILLER (Radolfzell, 1645 - Vienna, 1686)

St John of Nepomuk; 1681, terracotta with additions of plaster, height 41 cm (16 in); the sculpture is fully worked on the back; subsequent inscription on plinth: "Matthias Rauchmiller fec. Viennae Ao 1681".

Although this work is by a foreign artist, it appears here because it represents an eminent and highly popular local saint, and because of its unusual historical link with Prague. Rauchmiller submitted his small terracotta model in 1681 and it was from this that Jan Brokoff carved a larger model, from which, in turn, Wolff H. Heroldt, in 1683, cast the definitive bronze statue, in Nuremberg. That same year the statue was erected on the Charles Bridge; the first and oldest of its famous double line of statues (the eighth on the right as one comes from the Old Town). The model of the statue's plinth was by the distinguished architect Jean-Baptiste Mathey, and again it was Brokoff who cut it in stone. Of all the statues on the Charles Bridge, it is unrivalled for sheer majesty. It was commissioned by G.M. Wünschwitz as an ex-voto.

FERDINAND MAXIMILIÁN
BROKOFF (Červený Hrádek,
1688 - Prague, 1731)

St John of God; *c.* 1724, lime
wood, height 185 cm (73 in);
sculpture hollow on reverse,
with original polychromy; the
rayed halo is missing.

St John of God, founder of the
order of Hospitallers of St
John of God (canonised in
1690) is shown dressed in a
black robe and wearing a

crown of thorns, symbol of
deep repentance. In 1620 the
order obtained an abbey and a
hospital from Ferdinand II,
with the adjoining Church of
St Simon and St Jude. It is
known that in 1724 Brokoff
helped to decorate the church
organ. The effigy of this stern
saint can still be seen on a side
altar, painted by J.R. Byss, an
artist originally from Soleure
(Switzerland), who lived in
Prague intermittently between
1689 and 1737.

MATYÁŠ BERNARD BRAUN
(Oetz [Tyroll], 1684 - Prague,
1738)

St Judas Thaddeus; 1712, lime
wood, height 192 cm (75.75 in);
sculpture hollow on reverse;
later layer of white paint
applied to original surface,
whitened with chalk and polished.

This work is one of the jewels
of Czech Baroque sculpture,
Braun being the finest representative of the "school of
Bernini". It is interesting to
note that it is a fairly early
work. Braun settled in Prague
in 1710 and became instantly
famous for his two statues on
the Charles Bridge, of St
Ludmila (1711) and of St Ivo
(1712). The wooden carving of

St Jude Thaddeus was part of
the decoration prepared by
Braun for the altar of the
Church of the Virgin Mary
(built in the Middle Ages),
which was demolished in 1791
when outbuildings were erected
for the Clam-Gallas Palace.
This altar had been made in
1712 by the architect František
Maximilián Kaňka with the
assistance of Braun and Brandl.
The sculpture of the apostle,
furnished with a club and book
(current attributes of local
Baroque iconography), was
later found at the Clementium,
the oldest seat of the Jesuits in
Prague, and was added to the
National Gallery collections in
1939.

FRANTIŠEK IGNÁC WEISS
(Plzeň, 1695 - Prague, 1756)

Crucifix; *c.* 1740, lime wood, height 198 cm (78 in); solid sculpture with original polychromy.

Between 1734 and 1738 Weiss worked for the Dominican St Giles's (Jilja) Church in the Old Town quarter of Prague (notably on the high altar the side altars, the pulpit and the decoration of the organ). On the basis of stylistic studies, he is also attributed with the Crucifix, which hung in the adjoining cloister and which was undoubtedly made when he concluded work on this church.

Originally from western Bohemia, Weiss was a sculptor in wood and stone, having been the pupil and later the collaborator and successor of his father-in-law M.V. Jäckel, himself a leading Czech Baroque sculptor. Weiss did a good deal of decorative work for the interiors of various Prague churches, and the beautiful Crucifix, with its slightly larger than life-size Christ, falls into this category.

THE COLLECTION OF ANCIENT EUROPEAN ART AT THE STERNBERG PALACE

Leaving the castle's Court of Honour through the gate of the Rococo railings dating from the reign of Empress Maria Theresa, the visitor comes across the life-size version of the two *Fighting Giants* which appeared in miniature in Grund's painting (the sculptures are copies dating from 1912; the originals, accompanied by decorated vases of putti, were done in 1768 by Ignác Platzner the Elder). In front is the vast expanse of Hradčany Square where, back in the depths of time, a path ran through a dark forest, leading to what is today the Pohořelec and the Strahov quarter. Here is the last of Prague Castle's galleries of art. The most immediately striking of the buildings around the square, on the north side, is the façade of the Archbishop's Palace: this house, of Renaissance origin, was transformed between 1669 and 1694 into an Early Baroque palace by Jean-Baptiste Mathey (the main doorway and the central construction on the roof date from this period). The Rococo appearance of the façade is due to its reconstruction by Jan Josef Wirch at the time of Archbishop Antonín Příchovský (1764-5).

A passage in the west extension of the Archbishop's Palace leads to the hall of the Sternberg Palace where the National Gallery collections are exhibited: these comprise ancient European art and selections of modern European art and French 19th- and 20th-century art. This town mansion with gardens, situated below the level of Hradčany Square, has four wings enclosing an inner courtyard and a large cylindrical projection on the west wing, marking the original entrance to the small adjacent garden. It was Václav Vojtěch of Šternberk (Sternberg) who decided to build the palace, a masterpiece of Late Baroque architecture. The original plans by the Viennese architect Domenico Martinelli were realised around 1698-1708 by Giovanni Battista Alliprandi and Giovanni Santini Aichel. There is still no agreement as to which parts should be attributed to which architects, the relationship between the different projects, nor even on the exact history and date of the building.

The subsequent fortunes of the gallery are worth recording. On 1 July 1811 the Society of Patriotic Friends of the Arts bought the palace, adapted it as necessary and exhibited paintings in twelve rooms. The gallery remained intact until 1871; after 1872 the building was briefly used for charitable and military purposes, and later, as a result of the problems experienced by other Prague museums, the Sternberg Palace housed collections from the National Museum. After the Second World War — and by now it was part of the National Gallery — a selection of the huge store of European art was displayed on two floors of the palace and in the two ground-floor wings facing the garden and the Stag Moat.

As in all institutions of this type, growth of the various collections was conditioned by changes in the National Gallery's organisation and ownership of art works, and by alterations of distribution and layout. Here, too, the basis of the collections consists of both works owned by the National Gallery and loans from the Church or private persons, so it is to be expected that this collection of European art will be subject to the same changing circumstances as those of the St George's Convent.

Today the first-floor rooms house the works of the Italian Primitives, as Vasari described them in the 16th century without any pejorative connotation.

Coat-of-arms of the Šternberk family, dating from the 17th century, in the Burgrave's House.

They are works ranging from the *trecento* (14th century) to the first third of the *cinquecento* (1533). Naturally the Prague collection is far from complete and can merely reflect the evolution or representative styles of the many different Italian schools. The paintings come mainly from the collection of Archduke Francis Ferdinand d'Este. Among the truly representative works is a small triptych with a *Madonna in Majesty* by Bernardo Daddi, *The Lamentation of Christ* by Lorenzo Monaco, a large polyptich with saints by Nardo di Cione and another reredos by Antonio Vivarini and Giovanni d'Alemagna, works by Cosimo Rosselli, a rare Pasqualino Veneto, a Bartolomeo Montagna, etc.

Another group is made up of Dutch and Flemish paintings, of which the most important are *The Adoration of the Magi* by Geertgen tot Sint Jans, the large and beautiful composition of *St Luke Painting the Virgin Mary* by Jan Goessart, known as Mabuse, a *Landscape with Forge* by Herri met de Bles, paintings by Jan Mostaert, Cornelys Massys and Karel van Mander and a small group of paintings by the large Brueghel family. On of the jewels of this National Gallery collection is Pieter Brueghel the Elder's *Haymaking*. A third group comprises a large, but excellently chosen, collection of 15th- and 16th-century Russian icons.

The works on the second floor are displayed in rooms of various size which communicate freely within the four wings of the palace. Especially notable are the stucco ceilings of G.D. Frisoni and the murals of *The Death of Dido* and *The Sorrow of Artemis*, attributed to Halwachs or Bys, in rooms decorated with the motif of the Šternberk star.

The next collection (German painting from the Middle Ages and the Renaissance) is of paramount quality, with altarpieces by Hans Holbein the Elder and Bernhard Strigel, a series of paintings by Lucas Cranach, Albrecht Altdorfer and Hans Baldung Grien and, in the centre, the large and celebrated *Festival of the Rosary* by Albrecht Dürer. This is followed by the collection of 16th- to 18th-century Italian paintings, including works by Palma the Elder, Sebastiano del Piombo, Agnolo di Cosimo, known as Bronzino, Boccaccino, Tintoretto, Domenico Fetti, Alessandro Magnasco, known as Lissandrino, Sebastiano Ricci, Giovanni Battista Tiepolo, Francesco Guardi and, in particular, Giovanni Caneletto, represented by the magnificent *View of London with the Thames*, from the Lobkowicz collection.

The collection of Spanish art is not large, but paucity of numbers is redeemed by high artistic quality, as in two canvasses by Jusepe de Ribera, a marvellous *Bust of Christ* by El Greco and the *Portrait of Don Miguel de Lardizabal* by Francisco Goya. The numbers, the comparative cohesion and the quality of the collection of Dutch paintings testifies to the Czech preference for 17th-century Dutch art, chiefly attributable to commercial motives. Beginning with Rembrandt's *Old Scholar* and Frans Hals's *Portrait of Jasper Schade van Westrum*, the collection includes remarkable works in every genre: portraits (Ter Bosch), landscapes (Jan van Goyen, Salomon van Uyl, van de Velde, Willem Kalff, Abraham van Beyeren), figurative paintings (Jacob Ochtervelt, Arent Gelder, Gerbrandt van den Eeckhout, Gerard Dou, Gabriël Metsu, Jan Steen, Adriaen van Ostade), etc. Flemish painting is also worthily represented, with several magnificent works by Peter Paul Rubens, including the two compositions of the *Martyrdom of St Thomas and St Augustine*, commissioned in 1637 for St Thomas's Church in Prague. There are also works by Jacob Jordaens, Antony van Dyck, Frans Snyders, David Teniers and others.

At the very end of the section devoted to the collections of ancient European art, there are a number of paintings and sculptures (arranged in no particular order) showing the development of fine art in Europe to the present day: these include works by Gustav Klimt, Egon Schiele, Oskar Kokoschka, Max Lievermann, Lovis Corinth, Max Slevogt, Max Pechstein, Karl Hofer, Giorgio de Chirico, Carlo Carrà, Joan Miró, Manzu and Henry Moore.

The final group is French art. Although the oldest schools of painting are represented only in a fragmentary manner (Vouet, Mignard and Boucher), the 19th- and 20th-century collections are a delightful surprise, even for the connoisseur. Entrance to this part of the exhibition, on the ground floor, is by way of the courtyard, in the centre of which is a monumental sculpture by Antoine-Louis Barye. Arranged in chronological order, and with only a few gaps and, inevitably, some fluctuations of quality, the collection traces the evolution of French painting from Eugène Delacroix onward. Artists representing the schools and movements of the mid-19th century include Camille Corot, Honoré Daumier, Théodore Rousseau, Charles-François Daubigny and Gustave Courbet. There is then a natural progression to the artists of the Impressionist school — Claude Monet, Auguste Renoir, Alfred Sisley and Camille Pissarro — and on to the next generation: George Seurat, Paul Gauguin, Paul Cézanne and Vincent van Gogh. There are also portraits by Edgar Degas and Edouard Manet, and a marvellous painting by Henri de Toulouse-Lautrec. In addition to works by Pierre Bonnard, Henri Matisse, Maurice Utrillo, Le Douanier Rousseau and Marc Chagall, there is a large group of pictures by Pablo Picasso (particularly from the 1906-13 period), Georges Braque and André Derain. This section of the exhibition is also particularly rich in sculpture: works by François Rude, Antoine-Louis Barye, Jean-Baptiste Carpeaux, Antoine Bourdelle, Aristide Maillol, Charles Despiau, Henri Laurens and, above all, an important selection of sculptures by Auguste Rodin, whose first exhibition abroad, in 1902, was held in Prague.

Few galleries in the world, if any, can offer the visitor who is on the point of leaving such an enticing farewell present: a ravishing glimpse of more than five centuries of European art is followed by a view of the realm of monumental art: the city of which the National Gallery forms an organic part. Having enjoyed the riches of the Sternberg Palace collection, the visitor has only to cross Hradčany Square diagonally to reach the ramp of the castle, with its magnificent view of the river and the historic, beautiful and tragic city of Prague.

ALBRECHT DÜRER (Nuremberg, 1471 - Nuremberg, 1528)

The Festival of the Rose-Garlands; 1506, distemper on poplar wood, 161.5 cm x 192 cm (63.5 in x 75.75 in), signed and dated on the right of the painting, on the parchment held by Dürer, leaning against a tree; it reads: "Exegit quinquemestri spatio Albertus Dürer Germanus MDVI. AD."

The painting was bought in 1606 by Emperor Rudolf II for his collections in Prague. After various vicissitudes, it reached the Premonstrant Abbey in the Strahov quarter of Prague and was eventually bought from the canons in 1934 by the Czechoslovak state. The genesis of the painting is of interest, being related in detail in Dürer's correspondence with one of his Nuremberg friends, the humanist Willibald Pirckheimer. Dürer painted the work during his second trip to Venice for the local St Bartholomew's Church; it was commissioned by the Fondaco dei Tedeschi, a society of German merchants who administered this German church.
The painting shows a scene in which the Virgin Mary, with the infant Jesus and St Dominic, bless the onlookers and distribute small symbolic coronets of roses. This *Sancta Conversatione* comprises a series of portraits: on the right is Emperor Maximilian I, on the left, Pope Julius II and, behind him, Cardinal Domenico Grimani (all kneeling). Each of the persons in the picture can be identified. This celebrated painting by Dürer is one of the three most important works by foreign artists to be found in Czechoslovakia (the others being Brueghel and Titian).

213

PIETER BRUEGHEL THE ELDER
(Breda, 1525 to 1530 - Brussels, 1569)

Haymaking; 1565, oil on oak wood, 117 cm x 161 cm (46 in x 63.5 in), unsigned.

The painting belongs to the collection of the Lobkowicz family of Roudnice on the Elbe and its changing fortunes can be traced back to the exact date when they begin, on 21 November 1565. It is part of the cycle of *The Months* or *The Seasons*, five of which still survive: in addition to *Haymaking* in Prague, there are three in the Vienna Kunsthistorisches Museum (*Hunters in the Snow*, *The Dark Day* and *The Return of the Flocks*) and one in the Metropolitan Museum, New York (*Harvest*). Brueghel actually painted six, for his friend, a wealthy Antwerp banker, Niclaes Jongelinck. This cycle, which was sadly dispersed later, was a kind of variation on the subject of work in the fields in different months of the year. Such cycles were very fashionable at this time, particularly in France and Flanders, appearing in the form of calendars and Books of Hours. Judging by similar cycles (cf the miniaturist Simon Bening and his circle), the Prague painting would appear to show the month of July. Of the five surviving pictures, only the one in Prague bears neither date nor signature; it is considered by some to have been the first work of the cycle. The picture, which brilliantly suggests the harmony of nature, work and human destiny, epitomises Brueghel's thoughts and feelings about life and is one of the world's great artistic masterpieces.

REMBRANDT, HARMENSZ VAN RIJN (Leiden, 1606 - Amsterdam, 1669)

A Scholar in His Study (The Rabbi); 1634, oil on canvas, 141 cm x 135 cm (55.5. in x 53.5 in), signed lower left: "Rembrandt f. 1634".

This painting from the collection of the Counts Nostitz is regarded by experts as the only authentic work by Rembrandt in Czechoslovakia. It was done soon after he arrived and settled in Amsterdam (1631-2), the same year, in fact, that he married Saskia van Uylenburgh. The identity of the old man represented in the picture has not been satisfactorily resolved, although the same model is to be found in several of Rembrandt's works. The extraordinary maturity of the young artist at this period is evident from the searching gaze and expressive features of the scholar, abruptly interupted in his studies, and in Rembrandt's masterly handling of his different materials.

Rembrandt, triste hôpital tout rempli de murmures,
Et d'un grand crucifix décoré seulement,
Où la prière en pleurs s'exhale des ordures,
Et d'un rayon d'hiver traversé brusquement.

Charles Baudelaire: Les Phares (Excerpt)

HENRI ROUSSEAU, known as LE DOUANIER ROUSSEAU (Laval, 1844 - Paris, 1910)

Self-Portrait; 1890, oil on canvas, 146 cm x 113 cm (57.5 in x 44.5 in), signed lower left: "Henri Rousseau, 1890".

The artist entitled this painting *Moi-même, Portrait Paysage*. Painted in 1890, as the date attests, it was exhibited in the spring of the same year at the Salon des Indépendants, in the Pavilion de la Ville de Paris, on the Champs Elysées. Rousseau represents himself dressed in a sober black suit, wearing a beret and carrying a palette and brush. In the years that followed, he made some interesting modifications to the picture. He reduced the size of the human subject and made two minor changes that were not discovered until the painting was restored, in 1961: thus in 1901 he added to the lapel of his jacket the Ministry of Education badge he received on becoming professor of drawing at the rue d'Alésia. On the heart-shaped palette there are two names: Clémence and Joséphine. The former is that of his first wife, *née* Clémence Boitard, who died in 1888. Originally, the other name was Marie; but after marrying, in 1899, Joséphine Noury (who died in 1903), he substituted her name for that of Marie. The painting was exhibited in Prague in 1923 and bought locally for the Sergei Yastrebtzov collection.

JACOPO ROBUSTI, a.k.a.TINTORETTO
(Venice, 1518 - Vencie, 1594)

The Flagellation of Christ; between 1555 and 1560, oil on canvas, 165 cm x 128.5 cm (65 in x 50.5 in), unsigned.

This painting, listed in the inventory of the castle collection, dated 3 April 1685, had been bought in 1648 at the famous sale by auction of the Duke of Buckingham's collection in Antwerp. In 1635 it figured in the inventories of the Buckingham collection as an original work by Tintoretto, but in a bigger, squarer format. Subsequently, the work was somewhat roughly handled: it was literally cut in order to reduce it to the present format and some of the glazing was obliterated. Moreover, it was variously attributed in lists and invenories of the 18th and 19th centuries, and often moved around. Its final home was Opočno Castle where, in 1962, Jaromir Neumann recognised and identified it. *The Flagellation of Christ* was a theme frequently treated by Tintoretto. The Prague painting is distinguished by its dramatic contrast of light and shade — the contrast being equally marked in the case of the human figures viewed from the front and back, and in the details of their anatomy — and by the broad, confident brush-strokes.

BENEDIKT WURZELBAUER
(Nuremberg, 1548 - Nuremberg, 1620)

Venus with a Cupid; 1599, bronze, height 123 cm (48.5 in)

The group of sculptures representing Venus holding the hands of a Cupid who stands on a dolphin constitutes the upper part of the famous fountain, the lower part of which (together with a copy of this upper part) is in the garden of the Wallenstein Palace in Malá Strana. Originally the fountain was commissioned in 1599 by Christoph Popel of Lobkowitz, chief steward of the Czech kingdom, for the garden of his Hradčany house.

Wurzelbauer, the Nuremberg Mannerist influenced by Giambologna, cast the fountain and delivered it to Prague a year later. Albrecht of Wallenstein bought it for his palace before 1630. Eventually, in 1648, *Venus with a Cupid* was removed as booty by the Swedes and was subsequently found in the collection of Queen Christina. After varying fortunes, it fittingly found its way back to Prague (thanks to a purchase in Berlin in 1889) and still remains the only original work of art, out of all the war booty taken by the Swedes, to have returned to Prague.

CZECH MASTER OF THE THIRD QUARTER OF THE 14TH CENTURY

The Madonna of Aracoeli; *c.* 1370, distemper on new panel of laminated wood fibre, height 101 cm (39.75 in), width 64.5 cm (25.5 in).

This is a very important panel painting, frequently written about, but sometimes considered to be a 19th-century copy. Complete restoration in the 1980s, together with a detailed technological analysis, proved it to be a significant transitional work from around 1370 by one of the many followers of Master Theodoric. It bears a close technical resemblance to the latter's work, but in certain features anticipates that of the Master of Třeboň. The inspiration of the painting is the 5th-century Byzantine Virgin Agiosoritissa and its Romanesque version in the basilica of Sta Maria in Aracoeli, Rome. In 1368, on his visit to Rome for his second coronation, Emperor Charles IV had a copy made of it, since vanished, but which served as the model for this *Madonna* and, some twenty years later, for another painting of the subject from the workshop of the Master of the Třeboň Altarpiece. This *Madonna* was a royal gift to St Vitus's Cathedral. The drops of blood are a characteristic feature of Czech religious art.

THE GARDENS

Like other great cities, Prague owes much of its beauty to its gardens. But, in contrast to many other towns, the lie of the land, with its slopes, ridges and hollows, and the consequent absence of large, level expanses of ground, makes it necessary to construct terraces and lay out ornamental areas on a fairly small scale. Architects, therefore, have been forced to plan accordingly and to restrict themselves to sites that are easily shaped and modified.[1] This holds true, in general, for all the gardens of Prague, which harmonise perfectly with their surroundings.

The terrain on the north side is separated from the castle hill by the valley of the Rusnice stream, traditionally, though wrongly, called the Stag Moat (wrongly because it does not comprise part of the man-made fortifications and because its depth qualifies it more for the name 'ravine'; yet correctly in the sense that, from the late 16th century until 1741, red and fallow deer were raised here). Moreover, until the 16th century, the ground situated beyond the northern limit of the castle had nothing in common with it, and the vineyards there did not belong to the king. But in 1534 Ferdinand II bought the land and had it laid out as a garden of unprecedented size: the Royal Garden. For natural reasons, work began with the construction of the Powder Bridge, on five rectangular pillars supporting the wooden structure of the covered bridge. This *entresol* permitted the king to enter and leave the garden without being seen, which, according to texts that have underlined the point, suited the rather introverted Rudolf II very well. On the north side, outside the castle, the bridge terminated in a tower-shaped gate with a high roof, the appearance of which we know from an engraving[2] and a drawing by Stevens[3]. Furnished with a semicircular arch, the gate was framed by rustic work and the whole structure topped with a rounded cornice. These two architectonic features, typical of Mannerist architecture, were doubtless created only in the second half of the 16th century. On the castle side there must also have been a drawbridge at that time.

The site of the garden was almost rectangular or, more precisely, trapezoid, fairly long and very narrow; Giovanni Spatio, the builder of the bridge, was also instructed to enclose the garden with a wall. Existing sources provide us with more information about the names of the gardeners and the plants grown than about the garden's appearance. They name the Italian Francesco, Ludovico Brandis of Trieste, Hugo Venius of Flanders and the brothers Reinhardt of Germany. Tropical fruits, roses and select grape varieties were all grown.

In 1538 work commenced on a building described by the documents as a 'summer pleasure house', designed to be the dominant feature of the garden. This summer pavilion was built by King Ferdinand I for his wife, Queen Anna Jagiello. Known as the Royal Belvedere (Královský letohrádek), it is situated at the eastern end of the site, on ground that slopes down to the east: there are thus two levels on this side, but only one on the garden side.

The idea of a pavilion exclusively intended for summer relaxation was popular in Italy at the time of its construction, although not by any means in the countries of northern Europe. It is worth noting that the building which most resembles the Belvedere in general design is a 'pleasure pavilion' constructed in 1583-93 in the gardens of Stuttgart Castle, of which only a fragment remains today. Consequently, the Prague pavilion, intact apart from a few modifications, is of unique interest.

The story behind this fairly modest building is long and complicated. In the first instance, from about 1536 to 1538, while the basement and ground floor were under construction, the architect was Giovanni Spatio. He was then replaced by Paolo della Stella, who arrived in Prague with thirteen stonemasons: he was to supervise the project until his death, in 1552. It was apparently at this time that work was completed on the gallery of arcades surrounding the pavilion, the doors and windows (a magnificent achievement by the stonecutters to designs by Sebastiano Serlio), and, finally, the reliefs on the pedestals of the columns and above the spandrels of the arcades, constituting a group of sculptures unique in both subject and form. Boniface Wohlmut, the last architect in charge of the work (from 1556 to 1563), built the first storey and an interesting keeled roof.

The conclusion to be drawn from the various relevant surviving documents suggests that the first builder of the pavilion, Giovanni Spatio, did not actually draw up the plans, and that the most likely designer, though this cannot be established for certain, was Paolo della Stella. There is uncertainty, too, as to the origin of the artistic prototype for this remarkable structure: a fairly long rectangle of 51.5 m by 21 m (170 ft by 70 ft) which originally comprised three ground-floor rooms (two of which were almost square and the third twice as long as it was wide) and two above (a square room and the main room three times as long as it was wide). This layout is to be found nowhere else in the entire field of European Renaissance architecture. The horizontal plan of the pavilion is strongly reminiscent of a Greek *peripteros* (a building surrounded by isolated wall columns)[4]; but comparison of plans of Greek temples with that of the pavilion shows essential differences. The impression of lightness, the airy, immaterial character of the Prague arcades are further enhanced by the form of the balustrade, made of graceful banisters. The first-floor terrace balustrade appears at first sight to be solid, but it is actually a masterpiece of the stonecutter's art, resembling work in a much softer material.

If doubt remains as to where the overall design of the pavilion originated, the same is unfortunately true of the decorative sculptures. The inspirational source of the group by Paolo della Stella can almost certainly be found in contemporary Italy, as attested both by the mythological, historical and allegorical motifs and subjects, and by the narrative realism of the figures (including the representation of the builder himself and his wife), convincingly solid and contoured, usually portrayed in lifelike poses. Nevertheless, no close parallel has yet been established. It is clear that the sculptors must have drawn on many sources of reference. Of the 74 sculpted scenes, apart from a single religious subject depicting the meeting of Jacob and Esau, from the Old Testament, there is a series on the Labours of Hercules, Ovid's *Metamorphoses*, Livy's *History of Rome* and the Trojan War, scenes of Olympus and of the history of Alexander the Great; there are also bacchic and satirical episodes, hunting and battle scenes (legendary and historical) and, specifically, the victory of Emperor Charles V over the infidels at the port of La Goulette, in Tunisia.

There is also a singular absence of satisfactory information as to why the pavilion was built in the first place. It is probable that the kitchens and other offices were situated in a separate annex on one floor, implying that none of the rooms inside the pavilion needed to be used for any practical function. We know indirectly that the largest room served, among other things, as a ballroom: this information is contained in a letter from Archduke Ferdinand of Tyrol to the architect Wohlmut, reminding him not to tile the floor in marble because it would be too slippery for dancing[5]. Nor do we know anything about the interior decoration, either because it was unfinished (Ferdinand of Tyrol wanted an astronomical subject for the ceiling of the main hall) or because nothing is left of it.

After the reign of Rudolf II, who used the pavilion for his collections and astronomical observations (Tycho Brahe himself worked there), fate did not smile upon the building, and in the late 18th century it was turned over to the army service corps. Not until 1839 was it decided once more to use the summer pavilion for cultural purposes, as a picture gallery run by the Society of Patriotic Friends of the Arts. Soon afterwards, the staircase was rebuilt and the great hall was repainted with historical scenes, designed by Kristián Ruben.

Renaissance and Mannerist architectural and artistic activities in the Royal Garden were not restricted, however, to the Belvedere. During the 16th century two other important additions to the garden were the Singing Fountain and the Royal Ball Court.

In 1538 Ferdinand I had commissioned, in Innsbruck, designs for six fountains destined for the Royal Garden. There is no evidence that this plan was ever realised, but it does suggest that the place of honour given to the fountain, in the centre of the parterre in front of the Belvedere, had apparently been projected by its builder. In the event, it was the model submitted by the court painter Francesco Terzio, dating from 1562, that was accepted: in the same year, the woodcarver Hanuš Peisser prepared a wooden mould and the fountain (in bronze) was cast between 1564 and 1568 by Tomáš Jaroš, a bell-founder and gunsmith from Brno, and by his assistants Vavřinec Křička and Wolf Hofprucker. The most delicate parts of the fountain — the column, the upper basin and the little piper on top — were chiselled by the sculptor Antonio Brocco. The name Singing Fountain is doubtless explained by the melodious sound of the water splashing into the metal basin. In 1603 the traveller Pierre Bergeron compared the sound to the lilt of the pipe[6]. The rich ornamentation of the fountain is not confined to musical subjects: alongside classical motifs such as palmettes, masks, bucranes, festoons, etc., there is, on the shaft, Pan with a deer and shepherds.

Another 'marvel' of the Royal Garden which visitors never failed to mention in reports of their visit, was the Large House of the Ball Court, so named to distinguish it from a smaller games-court situated in the courtyard just beside the gate of the Powder Bridge. The two courts were of the same width, but the larger one was three times as long. Bergeron noted that it was a ball-court 'à la française, of extraordinary length'[7]. Evidently Boniface Wohlmut built both courts[8]. The smaller one was a simple, unpretentious building with seven round windows, apparently placed (given its function) as high as possible, near the roof. We do not know what it looked like originally, before it was transformed according to designs by Dietzler[9]. An inner gallery, against the south and west walls, was intended for spectators, among them, according to observers, Emperor Rudolf I in person, who watched the matches hidden behind a screen.

The construction of the Large Ball Court (1567-69) was much more difficult: it was raised on the slope just in front of the Stag Moat (its basement was intended as a stable for eighty horses) and the north façade, on the garden side, was an enormous colonnade broken by great arcades. This building is evidence of Wohlmut's partiality to massive and powerful forms, which has sometimes been described, not altogether correctly, as Palladianism. Ionic half-columns bear an entablature with a cylindrical frieze (of the type found in many villas and palaces built by Palladio). The composition of the north façade is very interesting: niches divide the two outermost axes of the two sides into two 'levels', thus seeming, by an optical illusion, to accentuate the size of the central arcades. But the most characteristic element of the façade is undoubtedly the deliberate, and typically local, sgraffito ornamentation — something not found in Palladio's work. The sgraffiti are, in fact, both decorative and pictorial. In the spandrels of the arcades is a cycle of the liberal arts (astrology, geometry, music, arithmetic, rhetoric, dialectic and grammar), personified by allegorical female figures based on graphic models by Frans Floris, published around 1560 by Hieronymus Cock. Then come the four elements (earth, air, water and fire), the seven virtues (the four cardinal virtues of courage, justice, prudence and temperance, and the three theological virtues of charity, hope and faith)[10]. The author of the sgraffiti certainly did not copy his models slavishly, but was inspired by them to create fairly condensed scenes that nevertheless give an impression of depth thanks to the smaller accompanying figures. The pictorial sgraffiti were modelled by Cornelis Bose, who was one of the leading exponents of *beschlagwerk*, i.e. hammered ornaments, together with compositions of grotesque fantasy. Such combinations were familiar themes of the northern variant of Mannerism.

After the fire of 1950, the interior, covered with barrel vaulting, was divided into three exhibition rooms. Across the large central room are balconies for spectators[11].

From the Middle Ages, menageries, usually situated in the castle moats, were important features of royal households. Although originally intended to be of practical use in guarding the castle, they soon assumed purely symbolic roles. For many European courts, the lion was a heraldic animal, not to mention its traditional connotations of strength and courage (as in the biblical story of Daniel in the lion's den). In the 16th and 17th centuries there were menageries at the Tower of London, in Versailles, Potsdam, Dresden, Kassel, the Hague, Turin and elsewhere. In the Austrian territories, there is a mention in 1552 of menageries at Ebersdorf, near Vienna, and others at Neugebäude, at the Belvedere and at Schönbrunn.

For the Prague menagerie, in contrast to others created later (like the menagerie at Versailles with its radial layout), a less elaborate design was chosen: simply a rectangular building comprising in all seven enclosures of the same size — 3.2 metres by 4.5 metres (10.5 ft by 15 ft) — all facing east, not by chance but taking into consideration the Bohemian climate. Even so, a number of the more delicate animals, by all accounts, were lost. The original construction was of wood; not until 1581-3 did the court architect, Ulrico Aostalli, replace this with a stone building.

Approaching the castle from the north, one can still see in the present-day Lion Court vestiges of the foundations of the old menagerie: these show that the courtyard stands on the site of the animal enclosure which was on the south side, while on the north side there was a small yard leading to a corridor which enabled the staff to clean the cages, bring in the food and make heating arrangements. In one corner of this little courtyard, on the garden side, a spiral staircase led from the lion enclosure up to the visitors' gallery. The west wing (the present entrance to the building) was added later as living quarters for the keepers of the wild animals.

This building, of little architectural interest, was originally adorned with a small sgraffito inscription and with decorative bosses to the small doorways. Yet although the story of how it was built is ordinary enough, that is by no means true of its animal occupants. There are colourful reports brought back by travellers of the time. In 1594, Fynes Moryson noted, after a trip to Prague, that the emperor kept 'twelve camels; an Indian ass, yellow, quite hairy, with hair like a lion. Then an Indian calf and two cheetahs which apparently were tame, as far as such a wild animal can be. They are yellow with black stripes, they have a head that is rather like that of a cat, the tail of an ass and the body of a greyhound. When the hunters go hunting, at their command, the cheetahs jump behind them and remain seated like dogs on the back of a horse. They run very fast, which doubtless makes them capable of bringing down a deer'[12].

The account of the journey of Jacques Esprinchard (in 1597) provides another source: 'Near the Ball Court, there is an enclosure where wild and domestic animals are kept; given that almost all of them had died the previous year, we only saw one big lion, a leopard and two large civets'[13]. In 1603 Pierre Bergeron wrote: 'Then there was a menagerie with lions, leopards and civets, as well as a crow as white as snow'[14]. In 1611, just prior to the death of Rudolf II, the inventory of live animals in the Lions' Court was 'one lion, two tigers, one bear and two wildcats'[15]. During the 17th century there were tigers, bears and lynxes, but by the end of the century all that remained were two bears and three elderly wolves; occasionally, some foxes were kept for hunting. Information on the animals ceased in 1720 and in 1740 the building was adapted for use as stables[16].

From these accounts, it is clear that the Lions' Court was not simply an enclosure for an animal of local emblematic significance, but a true menagerie, a kind of forerunner of the modern zoological gardens. Rudolf II, contrary to his portrayal in literature, until quite recently, as an adventitious collector of rarities and curiosities, emerges as a man of broad-ranging interests. As shown by his systematic acquisition of art treasures, in a similar manner to alchemists in their laboratories and observatories, he was intent on discovering the mysteries of the world, of seeking the links between the macrocosm and the microcosm[17].

The original overall plans of the Royal Garden have not survived, and nothing is known of them except for one project by Boniface Wohlmut. According to contemporary descriptions, however, the garden was divided into three sections: the western part, near the Powder Bridge, was a pleasure garden; the central part was more utilitarian, on the lines of an orchard; and the eastern part, the smallest, was a miniature pleasure garden in front of Queen Anna's summer pavilion (the Royal Belvedere).

The two ends of the garden were linked by a covered walk, planted in 1640 at the latest, and perhaps earlier, by L. Hartung. It appears on a series of 17th-century engravings, which show how access to the walk was provided, at given points, by three slightly larger circular areas in the form of pergolas. This broad corridor of interlaced hazel branches and osiers, covered with a variety of climbing plants[18] — still existed in the 18th century, as can be seen from surviving plans.

It would be reasonable to suppose that the garden also contained other sculptures similar to the Singing Fountain (the archives state that in 1598 Hans Vredeman de Vries, the eminent architect and artist, was paid retainers covering projects for seven fountains in all[19]); but there is no concrete evidence for this, and the same goes for other features: artificial grottoes, aviaries, mazes and the like, such as were found, in the early 17th century, for example, at Hellbrunn, near Salzburg, or the Wallenstein (Valdštejn) Palace in Prague. There was one other certified Renaissance building, namely the Fig House, a rectangular, unheated glasshouse with a detachable roof, located not far from the Belvedere.

On the same level, between the Royal Garden and the Stag Moat, there stood a shooting gallery which was converted into stables in 1723, on the occasion of Charles VI's coronation.

Whereas information about the Royal Garden is sparse, much more is known of the garden extending west of the path leading to the Powder Bridge. In 1572 (the date is preserved) a rectangular stable building was put up. Then, in the reign of Rudolf II, a pheasantry was built, still accessible through small doorways decorated with bosses, and a rectangular fishpond made for keeping rare tropical fish. This pond has survived until today.

The dominant feature of the western portion of this garden is certainly the Royal Riding School. At the beginning of the 17th century horses were groomed in the open air, as we know from *Equine Medicine* by Master Albrecht[20]. The Winter Riding School, designed by Jean-Baptiste Mathey was not built until 1694-5. Its dimensions are impressive, almost 90 m (300 ft) in length, and the main and lateral façades are characterised by splendid pilastered arcades. In the right-hand corner, a narrow, single-storey passage with twelve arcades, at right angles to the main building, formed a covered balcony for visitors to the Summer Riding School (a piece of terraced ground leading towards the Stag Moat).

The most important Baroque construction was undoubtedly Dientzenhofer's glasshouse. Kilián Ignác Dientzenhofer, appointed Master Mason of the Court in 1737, built the glasshouse when he began his activities on behalf of the Court Building Office. There were long discussions about improvements to the Royal Garden, in which three generations of gardeners had been involved: Mates Zinner, his son František Josef and, finally, his grandson František, who submitted a Baroque garden design[21].

The glasshouse project had been drawn up in 1731 by the court overseer, František Hoffe, but Dientzenhofer was responsible for the principal motif of the south front, with its central arched window placed higher that the side windows. This was, in fact, a classic variation of European architecture, described as the 'Serliana' or, later, the 'Palladian window'. In the whole of Czech architecture, only Dientzenhofer[22] seems to have used it. The importance of such a motif was evident: in a building that was essentially utilitarian, the glasshouse was in this way given special architectural emphasis. Contemporaries of Dientzenhofer clearly approved of his architecture, as was evident some time later when, in 1757, during the siege of Prague by the Prussians, the glasshouse was shattered by an artillery shell. The two wings with their three large square windows were never rebuilt but the architect Haffenecker transformed the central part of the glasshouse into a garden pavilion[23]. Nor did the changes of 1776 conclude the story of this small but charming building: in the 20th century it was transformed yet again (still retaining its historic central portion) into a presidential villa.

The original appearance of the glasshouse is known to us from a drawing of 1724 by J. Dietzler[24]. Its striking outline was derived from a very complex arrangement of roofs: the central part, with a single storey, had its own roof, which stood higher than the mansard roofs with skylights that covered the two wings of the building. This dynamic effect was accentuated by two ovals along the axis of the entry. The first oval is formed by the entrance hall, with a mythological fresco on the slightly raised semicircular vault; the second is created by two flights of stairs, each semi-oval and separated by a small central corridor.

Much less is known about another Baroque building in the Royal Garden — the theatre, built in 1681 by order of Leopold I, situated in front of the Riding School. The simplicity of the exterior does not appear to have changed over the centuries. On the other hand, according to plans dating from the mid-18th century, the interior was sumptuously furnished, with a curved balcony that extended on either side towards the stage, at the eastern end. This stage was fairly deep, approximately seven times the length of the side corridors. An idea of the quality of the décor in Prague at that time is suggested by paintings that show the stage sets for *Constanza e Fortezza* (Constancy and Fortitude), an opera by Johann Josef Fux, performed for the coronation of Charles VI in 1723 at Prague Castle, on the ramparts of the Virgin Mary (Mariánské hradby), which enclose the Royal Garden to the north. This décor was the work of Giuseppe Galli Bibbiena, one of the most famous theatrical designers of the 18th century[25]. The theatre itself certainly suffered the same fate as the other buildings in the garden: it was burned down and never rebuilt.

It would appear that the Baroque changes to the garden were concentrated more on the northern access route to the castle than on the ends. Evidence of this comes from the changing appearance of the large geometrical parterre close to the Lion Court and the theatre, which extended almost to the line formed by the east side of the Royal Ball Court. At this point the parterre had box edgings of shrubs that formed long, elegant volutes, while a composition of clipped limes and obelisk-shaped conifers added a vertical touch. A circular pool with a water jet formed an appropriate central feature of the parterre.

The sculptural decoration of the garden seems to have been fairly modest. The only two sculptures that survive are a Baroque fountain by J.J. Bendl, dating from 1670 and representing Hercules, and a magnificent allegory of *Night* by M.B. Braun, from the 1730s. The Braun studio evidently supplied other ornamental features, such as huge vases and sculptures of lions.

The garden retained its formal decorative character until the end of the 18th century. After the reconstruction of the castle by the court architect, Niccolo Pacassi, there were changes that affected the land north of the castle. Until the pillars of the Powder Bridge were knocked down in 1769-70 in order to create a broad entry road, the north garden had constituted a kind of enclave which, whilst being wholly independent, complemented the inimitably dramatic form of the castle. For this age of sober classicism, with its rational image, the unique qualities of the Stag Moat in the context of the landscape at large were considered somewhat odd and unremarkable. The utilitarianism of the era of Joseph II was soon made manifest: the Royal Belvedere, the Ball Court and the Riding School were all commandeered by the army service corps.

It was only with the arrival of European romanticism that the final change occurred which was to transform the north garden into a natural park, with winding paths and marvellous long vistas.

The unique significance of the Renaissance castle and all the buildings described in this chapter prompted the authorities, when an independent Czechoslovakia was created, to return at least a part of the Royal Garden to something like its original state. In 1938 and 1955, under the direction of the architects Pavel Janák and Otakár Fierlinger respectively, the little garden in front of Queen Anna's summer house was restored.

The gardens to the south of the castle have had as long a history as those of the northern side. The Paradise Garden, situated at the western end, was created in 1562, at the time of Archduke Ferdinand of Tyrol, and altered under Rudolf II, when a small pavilion with an aviary and pools were added: the archives mention a basin 1.8 metres (6 ft) deep. And in the reign of his brother Matthias, a charming bugler's pavilion was built alongside the wall enclosing the garden, opposite the new castle staircase. In the Baroque era the garden was divided into two parterres: the west parterre was square and box-edged with shrubs, surrounding a small central pool; the east parterre was rectangular, surrounded by six lawns and decorated with a flat edging in the shape of an ellipse.

The other part of the south gardens, extending eastward to form the Ramparts Garden, was created only in the 19th century on the site, as its name suggests, of the ancient Late Gothic fortifications. Originally this was simply an alley of trees that linked the Hradčany and Klárov quarters.

The two gardens acquired their present appearance when Prague Castle was adapted as the residence of the Czechoslovak president.

1. Z. Wirth: *Pražské zahrody* (The Gardens of Prague), Poláček, Prague, 1943, p. 4.
2. J. Krčálová: *Poznámky k rudolfinské architektuře* (Notes on Architecture in the Time of Rudolf II), Academia Umění, 1975, p.507, ill. 6.
3. E. Fučiková, B. Bukovinská, I. Muchka: *Die Kunst am Hofe Rudolfs II* (Art at the Court of Rudolf II), Dansien, Hanau, 1988, p. 34.
4. A. Mihulka: *Královský letohrádek zvaný Belvedere an Hradě Pražském* (The Royal Summer Pavilion called the Belvedere at Prague Castle), Kruh pro pěstování dějin umění, Prague, 1939, p.12.
5. J. Svoboda: *Královský letohrádek* (The Royal Summer Pavilion), Památky a příroda, Panorama, Prague, 1987, p. 7.
6. E. Fučiková: *Tři francouzští kavalíři v rudolfinské Praze* (Three French Knights in the Prague of Rudolf II), Mladá Fronta, Prague, 1989, pp. 82-3.
7. ibid.
8. J. Morávek, Z. Wirth: *Pražsky hrad v renesanci a baroku 1490-1790* (Prague Castle from the Renaissance to the Baroque, 1490-1790), Prague, 1947, p.10.
9. V. Fabian: *Dietzlerova kresba: Pohled z věže chrámu s. Vita na hradě Pražském k severu* (A drawing by Dietzler: View towards the north, from a tower of St Vitus's Cathedral to Prague Castle), Památky archeologické, 1921, p. 151.
10. M. Lejsková-Matyášová: *Florisův cyklus sedmexa svobodných umění a jeho odezva v české renesanci* (The Floris cycle on the seven liberal arts and its repercussion on the Czech Renaissance), Academia Umění, Prague, 1960, p. 396.
11. P. Janák: *Obnova sgrafit na mičovně* (Restoration of the sgraffiti of the Royal Ball Court), Academia Umění, Prague, 1963, p. 220.
12. F. Moryson, J. Taylor: *Cesta do Čech* (Voyage in Bohemia), Mladá Fronta, Prague, 1977, p. 33.
13. cf note 6, p. 33.
14. cf note 6, p. 82.
15. F. Kašička, M. Vilímková: *Lvi dvůrPražského hradu* (The Lion Court at Prague Castle), Panorama, Prague, 1970, pp. 34-41.
16. ibid., p. 40.
17. cf note 3, p. 22.
18. V. Procházka: *Zahrady pražského hradu* (The Gardens of Prague Castle), Obelisk, Prague, 1976, no pagination.
19. Cf *Jahrbuch der kunsthistorischen Sammlungen des allerhöchsten Kaiserhauses in Wien* (Yearbook of the Art Collections of the Mighty Emperor in Vienna), 1891, register no. 8317.
20. cf note 2, ibid.
21. M. Vilímková: *Stavitelé chrámi a palaci* (The Builders of the Churches and Palaces), Prague, 1986, p. 165.
22. Cf 'One of the variants of the plan of the Ursuline convent at Kutná Hora', in the book by H.G. Franz: *Bauten und Baumeister der Barockzeit in Böhmen* (Buildings and Architects of the Baroque Era in Bohemia), Seeman Verlag, Leipzig, 1962, ill. 261.
23. cf note 21, p. 230, note 16.
24. cf note 9, ibid.
25. P. Preiss: *Italští umělci v Praze* (Italian Artists in Prague), Panorama, Prague 1986, p. 419.

THE FORTIFICATIONS

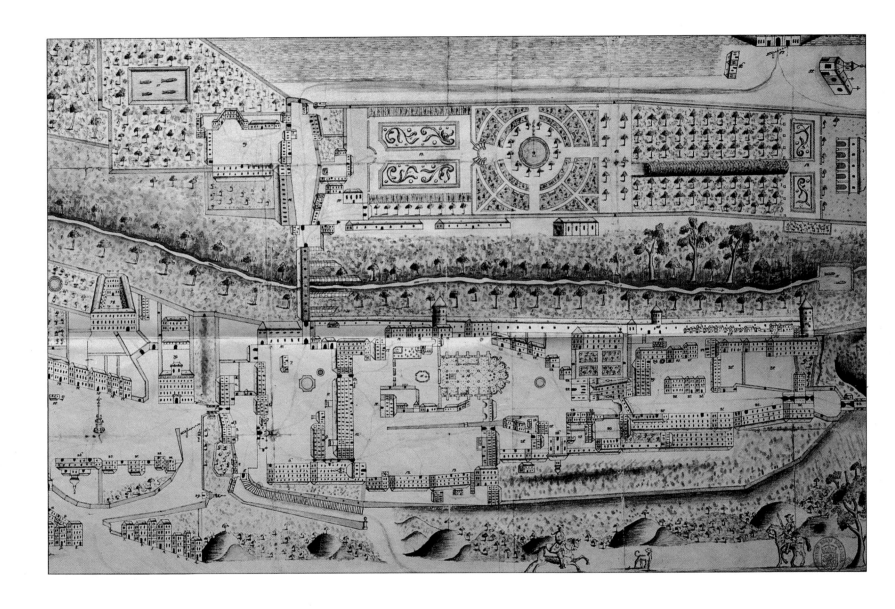

Plan of the site of Prague Castle and of a part of Hradčany, in the library of the Prague National Museum. Made during the second half of the 18th century, shortly before the reconstruction ordered by Maria Theresa, the plan includes, for the first time, all the buildings, with a semblance of perspective created by the inclination of the different façades of the buildings, except for St Vitus's Cathedral. Thus, the representation of the covered bridge, resting on its stone piers and linking the castle to the northern gardens, is very explicit.

Opposite page: *the Powder Tower*. In the northern section, the fortifications run very close to St Vitus's Cathedral, which is separated from them only by a few buildings in Vicar's Street (Vikárka) and a very narrow courtyard. Around 1500 the enclosing walls were reinforced with large round towers that accommodated cannon, the new form of firearms.

The castle's northern fortifications are located on the edge of the escarpment known as the Stag Moat, one of the site's important natural defences. After the invention of artillery, in the 15th century, the castle had to be protected against possible attack from the northern plain. Three round towers were therefore built, to designs by Benedikt Ried, with foundations deeply embedded in the Stag Moat: the Daliborka, the new White Tower and, mightiest of all, the Powder Tower.

"I climbed the silent, dark, echoless streets to the top of the high hill crowned by the immense castle of the kings of Bohemia. The sombre outline of the building was silhouetted against the sky; no light shone from its windows; its solitude was somewhat reminiscent of the site and grandeur of the Vatican or of the temple of Jerusalem as seen from the valley of Jehoshaphat..."

Chateaubriand: Mémoires d'outre-tombe, 24 May 1833

THE SUMMER PAVILION
OF QUEEN ANNA

After 1354 Emperor Ferdinand I converted the extensive area to the north of the castle into a garden that became known as the Royal Garden. It was enclosed, to the east, by this pavilion (known as the Royal Belvedere) which the emperor commissioned for his wife, Queen Anna. A small garden, one of the loveliest to be found north of the Alps, was laid out in front of the building. The parterres were reconstructed, quite freely, in the 20th century.

The Singing Fountain, detail. This fountain consists of two superimposed basins on a shaft with sculptures of Pan bearing a deer and shepherds. Carved by Antonio Brocco, court sculptor, they testify to the excellence of Renaissance sculpture in Prague.

237

Opposite page: *the arcades of the Summer Pavilion*. The type of construction used for the pavilion is a variant of the antique *peripteros*, a Greek temple consisting of a rectangular hall surrounded by a line of columns detached from the wall. The semi-circular arcades are enclosed at the base by an elegant balustrade, and the capitals, stylobates of the columns and areas above the spandrels are adorned with remarkable sculptures, made in the middle of the 16th century by Paolo della Stella and his assistants.

Below: *the Singing Fountain* in the centre of the little garden in front of the Belvedere was, based on the designs of the court painter, Francesco Terzio, and cast in bronze in 1564-8 by Tomáš Jaroš, bell-founder and armourer of Brno. It owes its evocative name to the melodious sound of the water splashing into the bowls.

Above: *two reliefs on Queen Anna's Summer Pavilion*. The upper one represents the forge of Vulcan with Venus, and the lower, Zeus metamorphosed into an eagle carrying Ganymede up to Olympus. Thirty-two rectangular reliefs constitute the main decoration of the pavilion. They treat various subjects from Greek mythology, Roman history and contemporary themes, such as hunting. The overall interest of the group derives not only from the subjects but also from the exceptional artistic quality displayed by the stonemasons of the workshop of the Italian sculptor Paolo della Stella.

239

THE LARGE HOUSE OF THE BALL COURT

Two ball courts catering for a sport much enjoyed during the Renaissance formed part of the amenities of the Royal Garden. The smaller of the two, situated near the covered bridge, in the service courtyard, is of no great artistic merit. The larger court, on the other hand, built in 1567-9 by Boniface Wohlmut, has a remarkable sgraffito façade and makes a distinctive artistic contribution to the central part of the garden.

Right: *Night*. The statues of the Royal Garden dating from the Baroque era are fairly sober in decorative style. Most of the sculptures come from the workshop of Matyáš Bernard Braun, who was responsible not only for the statues of lions and the large vases of the parterres but also for the admirable allegorical *Night* which stands in front of the Royal Ball Court.

THE ROYAL
RIDING SCHOOL

Because of the specific configuration of the castle site, a number of the buildings traditionally associated with the concept of an imperial residence lie outside the site proper, to the north of the Stag Moat.
In the 16th century this area boasted large stables, with an open-air riding school. The present building, the Winter Riding School, dates from 1694-5 and was constructed to the plans of Jean-Baptiste Mathey.
A narrow wing was later added at right angles to the rectangular building. Having semicircular arcades on the ground floor and first storey, it formed covered balconies for visitors to the Summer Riding School. Today the area is laid out as a garden, with parterres, which provides unusual views of the cathedral, the Spanish Room wing and the Powder Tower.

THE ROYAL GARDEN

"Prague is one of the noblest cities and my thoughts often turn to Rome, the city it most resembles. Nor can I refrain from mentioning the charm of the festivities in the gardens of the palace, the spring flowers and the aristocratic beauty of the Prague women, their sensuous bearing and their clothes, so charming and so elegant that they put me in mind of Dante's Paradiso."

Auguste Rodin in 1902

Originally the garden was laid out with parterres and box edging, bounded to the north by the enclosure wall and to the south by a glasshouse built to the plans of Kilián Ignác Dientzenhofer. This building, small but architecturally interesting, was renovated several times, most recently after the Second World War, when the castle was being refurbished as a residence for the presidents of the Republic.

PLEČNIK'S GARDEN WORKS

Left to right: *the Bugle Pavilion*, dating from the first half of the 17th century; renovations were carried out by Plečnik's assistants.

View from Plečnik's new staircase, which leads from the Third Courtyard of the castle to the Ramparts Garden. Plečnik used the pure classical form of Ionic columns.

Under the staircase of the Paradise Garden, Plečnik placed *a small wall fountain*, a fine example of the ironworker's craft.

The central point of the Paradise Garden is *a large granite basin* weighing forty tons.

In the Bastion Garden, Plečnik utilised the classical motif of *the double flight of semicircular steps*, concave and convex, a form that is found in European architecture, in the Vatican.

At the entrance to the Paradise Garden (reached via the ramp from Hradčany), Plečnik used the suggestive motif of *a narrow Greek vase*, placed in a rectangular niche. In the Ramparts Garden the *obelisk-pyramid* (right) serves as a very expressive vertical landmark in this part of the castle.

OTHER SECULAR BUILDINGS OF THE CASTLE

THE ROSENBERG (ROŽMBERK) PALACE

The building of this palace was doubly influenced by the fire of 1541 which destroyed much of the Malá Strana quarter (including the residence of the Rožmberk family) and of Hradčany where, from then on, plans were made to replace the former small buildings with larger ones. All the evidence shows that the undamaged rubble of older houses was used in the building of the Rosenberg Palace[1].

Initially, from 1545 to 1560, a palace was built under the direction of Hans Vlach[2], the four wings of which formed a closed courtyard with galleries of arcades. But there were no arcades on the ground floor and first floor except along the shorter lateral wings of the courtyard; and on the access side to the palace (George Street) there was a massive arcaded entrance (still existing today), the smooth façade of which may have been covered with ornamental sgraffiti. On each of the two floors of this south wing there was a large room, the one on the ground floor having direct access to the court through a doorway. On either side of these large rooms there were two smaller rooms of identical size. The strict symmetry of this layout, linked to the axis of the main entry, was very evident and was undoubtedly a novelty in the mid-16th-century architecture of Prague.

In contrast, the remains of the façades of the street and garden sides show a picturesque asymmetry that was more or less in accordance with contemporary architectural style: they had been constructed almost directly on the foundations of the Roman surrounding wall and the bases of this wall had been used to break up the south front with polygonal turrets. Apart from their bossed doorways, the principal decorative element of these façades were the gables, partly functional (since they provided a saddleback cover to the roofs of the shorter east and west wings) and partly *trompe l'œil*, devoid of any practical purpose. The picturesque

outlines of these large and small voluted gables (the garden front had ten in all) are more in keeping with local architectural tradition, as was the structure of the façades they surmounted. In any event, the main cylindrical cornice (placed on top of the western part and built later) is rightly regarded as the most characteristic feature of the palace.

The next stage was to enlarge the site of the palace westward (towards All Saints Chapel). In 1573-4 Ulrico Aostalli built a long rectangular garden in this area, lying on the same level as the first floor of the palace, because of the sloping ground. This garden was also surrounded by a gallery of arcades, with thirteen arches on the north and south sides and six arches on the west side. Above the arcades was an enclosed corridor with oblong windows surmounted by a straight moulding. In 1600, following an exchange, the Rosenberg Palace became the property of Emperor Rudolf II, and its subsequent fortunes were a royal concern. Nevertheless, this Renaissance palace, the biggest in Prague, retained its original appearance until the 1720s and it was only at this period that fundamental changes were made. The architect Tomáš Haffenecker heightened the palace by adding a second storey, partitioned the wings of the single block and connected the two parts with corridors giving on to the courtyard.

The present appearance of the palace is the result of changes ordered by Empress Maria Theresa when she decided to convert the building into the Institute of Noblewomen. Niccolo Pacassi was commissioned to enlarge the palace, adding the part contiguous to All Saints Chapel. This is where the present main entrance to the palace is situated, beneath a rounded portico, and where a large hall and staircase were also built. So the turrets were destroyed and the façades joined, while the Renaissance arcades inside were bricked up. The new building was impressively large, with some thirty-five windows opening on to George Street and almost fifty along the south front, which was still broken up by seven terraced bastions. Within the panoramic context of the castle as a whole, it created a counterbalance to the south wing of the Royal Palace, the façades of which, incidentally, were by the same architect.

Inside the old west wing of the Rosenberg Palace (between the courtyard and the garden) Pacassi built a chapel and its adjoining four-curved monumental staircase. The original garden was slightly shortened and a small garden-court was built on the west side. The two gardens had lawns with curved borders and an oval pool in the middle. The Institute accommodated thirty or so girls of noble families. Each had her own apartment comprising an antechamber, a bedroom (with no door leading to the corridor) and a small room for a maid. All the apartments were absolutely identical. The palace, as modified by Pacassi, has remained virtually unchanged to this day.

Until 1970 the Rosenberg Palace housed the Historical Institute of the Academy of Sciences. The palace was cleared during the programme of 'normalisation' that followed the invasion of Czechoslovakia by troops of the Warsaw Pact, more than seven hundred research students being dismissed and the building confiscated by the Ministry of the Interior, which still occupies it today.

Tu es dans le jardin d'une auberge aux environs de Prague
Tu te sens tout heureux d'une rose sur la table
Et tu observes au lieu d'écrire ton conte en prose
La cétoine qui dort au coeur de la rose

Epouvanté tu te vois dessiné dans les agates de Saint-Vit
Tu étais triste à mourir le jour où tu t'y vis
Tu ressembles au Lazare affolé par le jour
Les aiguilles du quartier juif vont à rebours
En montant au Hradchin et le soir en écoutant
Dans les tavernes chanter les chansons tchèques.

Poem by Apollinaire

Right and opposite page: *terracotta fragments*. Reconstruction during the Early Baroque era destroyed virtually all the original ornamentation of the Pernštejn Palace. Only a few fragments have been discovered to convey any idea of the wealth and quality of the terracotta decorations that framed the doors and windows, as in Italian palaces of the 15th century.

THE LOBKOWICZ (FORMERLY PERNŠTEJN) PALACE

In addition to the Rožmberks, there was a second noble family, the Pernštejns, whose representative could even lay claim to the royal crown. Only a narrow alley or passage separated the homes of the two families. The Pernštejn Palace dates from 1554-60, at which time it had four wings and a single storey with two prismatic towers of the original ancient south-side fortifications giving it an unmistakable outline. On the south wing there was a semicircular arcade decorated (like many other architectural features of the palace) with terracotta ornamentation unique of its kind. The Pernštejns had already used terracotta for other buildings, notably at Pardubice, in eastern Bohemia, but in that case it was apparently a matter of standardising construction methods because the Pernštejn brickworks turned out, among other things, shaped bricks for vaults and cornices, casings for doors and windows, etc. It would appear that terracotta was used in Prague for quite another reason, notably the artistic possibilities arising of this material, probably introduced to Prague by artists from Italy. There are numerous examples of the masterly employment of the terracotta technique in many parts of Europe, often far removed from one another (Wismar, Schallaburg, etc.). The basreliefs of the Pernštejn Palace in Prague are of exceptional artistic quality, even if they exhibit ornamental features that could be considered purely local and sometimes rather rustic: for example, the figurines of antique-type dolphins mingled with leaves and acorns.

The sumptuous façade that faces the street must have been created towards the end of the 16th century, judging by the large roof gables (known from a drawing dated 1622[3]). The entrance wing already had two floors with gemel windows, and even triplet in the centre of the façade, and straight mouldings. The main doorway or, more precisely, the triangular gable above it, its line broken by a segment of the cornice,

252

Putti. The gardens to the south of the castle contain more sculpture than the Royal Garden itself. The majority were executed in the 18th century, like these putti supporting a cartouche with the blazon of the Czech lion surmounted by a crown.

constituted a highly advanced stylistic feature.

The palace did not receive its present-day appearance until it passed into the hands of new Czech owners, the eminent Lobkowicz (Lobkovic) family. Carlo Lurago refurbished the palace in 1651-68 for Wenceslas Eusebius Lobkowicz; and it was after this owner's forename that the chapel on the first floor was dedicated to St Wenceslas, whose legend served as the subject of the paintings on the walls and ceiling. The paintings are by Fabián Hárovnik, while Domenico Galli[4] did the sculpted stucco work that frames them. These two artists also collaborated in other parts of the palace, notably in the hall, in the adjacent dining room and in the large reception room of the south wing. The interiors of the hall and dining room are almost wholly preserved, including the two hall chimney-pieces, whereas the reception room was later partitioned and only fragments of its original decoration scheme remain. As was often the case in the Baroque period, the theme of the paintings was associated with the purpose of the room: for example, the dining room contains a painting of the feast of the gods on Olympus, and so forth. When the palace was renovated between 1973 and 1987 in order to hold exhibitions of the National Museum, a number of Carlo Lurago's architectural features were rescued, such as the staircase with its stone door casing and the two principal doorways. Even so, the original layout was badly disrupted as, for example, by building a new staircase near the large reception room[5].

THE BURGRAVE'S HOUSE

The house of the grand burgrave was built in 1555, close to the beautiful Renaissance palaces belonging to the Rožmberk and Pernštejn families. The burgrave of the time was a member of the Lobkowicz family, John, who commissioned not only this mansion but also the splendid palace bearing his family name (today the Schwarzenberg Palace) on Hradčany Square. The Burgrave's House doubtless contained the offices associated with that functionary's official duties. (The burgrave was an important nobleman who managed royal business during the absence of the king.) For this building the Italian architect Giovanni Ventura utilised, for the first time in Bohemia, pierced gables, in which the vertical elements (the small pilasters) were omitted, so that they were segmented only by thin horizontal cornices. This solution reinforced the overall monumental effect[6]. Originally it had been a medieval building flanked by a Romanesque tower, which Ventura modernised, notably by adorning the façade with simple sgraffito work. It was then refurbished, during the 1590s, by the court architect Ulrico Aostalli. It was certainly in this period that the walls and ceilings of one of the first-floor rooms were decorated with paintings, which were discovered and restored in 1962-3 when the building was transformed into the Czechoslovak Children's Home by the architect Josef Hlavatý[7]. Until then, the original beamed ceiling had been covered by a false wooden ceiling, decorated with a fresco, *The Judgement of Solomon*, a theme highly suitable for a room devoted to matters of state. The allegorical figures of the five senses appear on another grotesquely ornamented wall frieze. Most interesting, however, are the genre landscapes on the side of the beams.

The building underwent further reconstruction in the Baroque period. Still visible on the door are the finely carved coats-of-arms of the four burgraves then in office.

GOLDEN LANE

Behind the Burgrave's House is one of the most fascinating parts of the castle complex, Golden Lane (Zlatá) which, according to the archives, was originally known as Goldsmiths' Lane (Zlatnická). The small houses that line the lane to this day are typical of the period when the castle area still resembled a little town, separate and enclosed. Tucked into the twenty or so Romanesque arches of Soběslav I's enclosure wall were tiny houses, usually of one storey, with a single door and window on either side, or sometimes with an upper storey, in a few cases projecting and supported by consoles. This was a typical feature of contemporary Bohemian bourgeois architecture: where conditions permitted, such an overhang was designed to increase the habitable space of the house. The houses, which also received some light through a window looking out on the Stag Moat, were extremely narrow, and the two storeys were linked by a little crooked staircase. It is interesting to see, in Golden Lane, built into the fortifications, surviving examples of the 'humble dwellings' that could also be found, until the reign of Rudolf II, in other areas of the castle: for example, in the outer moat, at the western entrance to the castle, or built very high up in the southern part of the castle, beneath Maximilian's kitchens (their existence is known from drawings by Rudolf II's court painters, for whom they were a picturesque subject). At the time of Rudolf II, the lane was mainly inhabited by the castle guards charged with entry gate and prison duties. Originally, the lane led to St George's Convent, but this section of it was destroyed at the request of one of the abbesses because of 'the stink and the smoke, as well as the din coming out of the taverns, disturbing the nuns'[8].

THE FORTIFICATIONS

Nothing is known for certain about the appearance, the layout or the exact extent of the most ancient fortifications of the castle. Archaeological discoveries here and there indicate that they consisted of a raised mound of earth strengthened by tree trunks on the inside and by rough stones on the outside. A shallow ditch encircled this mound. Nor is there much more information concerning the fortifications of the Romanesque period, which were begun in 1135, during the reign of Soběslav I. Traces of them can be seen in several places: for instance, in the passage between the Second and Third Courtyards, where an idea of their thickness can be obtained from an opening made in the enclosure wall: meticulously fashioned of marl rubble, the wall at this point measured an astonishing height of some 14 metres (45 ft). It is easy to reconstruct the outlines of this enclosure and of the three towers that gave access to the castle site. On the west side, the White Tower wall has been preserved in the wall up to the third storey; its interior is also intact and is accessible from the 'central' (perpendicular) wing. To the west of the Royal Palace was an entry gate on the town side; it has been partially preserved in the underground passages below the Vladislav Hall. To the east, entry was via the Black Gate, preserved in its entirety. The enclosure wall was additionally reinforced on the east and west sides by other prism-shaped towers and, on the south, by small turrets which were either polygonal (near the Royal Palace), semi-cylindrical (near what was to become the Institute of Noblewomen) or prismatic (near the future Lobkowicz Palace). The towers and turrets of the south side have also been partially conserved: for example, on the terraced bastions adjoining the castle façade, near the Ramparts Garden, and also farther west, near the Paradise Garden[9].

The next stage in the extension of the fortifications, dating from the Late Gothic, owed more to the development of firearms than to evolution of the

Wood engraving: the oldest view of Prague, from the *Liber Chronicarum* by Hartmann Schedel (1493). The principal features of the castle can be clearly seen: from left to right, the White Tower, St Vitus's Cathedral and the Black Tower.

arts. The castle had to be protected against artillery fire, mainly by the construction of powerful bastions to accommodate such weapons. These improvements were carried out by one of the most important architects in the castle's history, Benedikt Ried. Not only did he certainly build the three solid bastions for cannons in the new, outer zone of the castle's southern fortifications, but he was also responsible for the barbican situated to the east and the three round towers near the Stag Moat: the Daliborka, the New White Tower and, most important of all, the Powder Tower (wrongly called 'Mihulka'). There were loopholes on all four floors of the tower, so that 18 cannons of various calibre could be fired, aimed at the base of the tower, the Stag Moat and, finally, the terrain directly opposite, to the north. There were separate entrances to each storey. Originally, the Powder Tower was not roofed as it is today but encircled by a terrace with a parapet, making it easier to defend. In the course of recent reconstruction of the tower, the system of closing the loopholes was restored. This quite exceptional technique is perpetuated in another form, in Ried's Švihov Castle, in western Bohemia.

The last step in the rebuilding of the castle forti-fications, which left them looking more or less as they do today, came during the reign of Rudolf II, almost at the end of the 16th century. The south entry disappeared and a new main entrance was constructed to the north, from the two sides of the Powder Bridge which straddled the Stag Moat. In modern parlance it would be fair to say Rudolf II proceeded like a big property developer, merging into a single entity (with fixed outer boundaries) the patchwork medieval 'town' created by a large number of minor builders, independently of one another. He is sometimes described, not altogether incorrectly, as 'the greatest architect of the castle's secular buildings'.

The first feature to be completed was the east gate of the Black Tower: its outer portals have a semicircular archivolt with alternately long and short voussoirs. Another work with more or less the same appearance is the small portal of the Stromovka in Prague, bearing the monogram of Rudolf II and the date 1593. The interior portal of the Black Tower is bordered with typically Mannerist diamond-point bossage (rustication).

Around 1600 the North Gate was built, in front of which, in the time of Pacassi, a columned Mannerist portal was added. The upper part of the portal had been bricked up in the passage vault in the Baroque period. This part of the portal was discovered during the restoration of the flooring of the Spanish Room: in sharp contrast to the rough bossage, its beam was adorned with very delicate ovolo moulding, giving it an antique appearance.

The best-known example of Mannerism in the castle, however, is the Matthias Gate, bearing an inscription relating to the activities at the castle (1614) of Rudolf II's brother, Matthias II. Considering that this gate formed the main entrance to Prague Castle and that it once gave access, on the right, to the staircase leading to the staterooms of Rudolf's palace, it is probable that it was constructed earlier, around 1600, and merely completed, under Matthias, by the addition of a stucco plaque that differed, in both materials and artistic style, from the other parts in sandstone[10]. It was with the creation of these three large gateways that the development of the Prague Castle fortifications, extending over several centuries, came to an end.

'Prague will not let us go. Neither of us. This little mother has claws. We must submit, or else ... We ought to set fire to the two ends, at Vyšehrad and at Hradčany; perhaps then we could free ourselves of her. Think of this from now until Carnival.'

Franz Kafka: Letter of 20.12.1902 to Oskar Pollak

1. A. Kubiček: *Rožmberský palác na Pražském hradě* (The Rosenberg Palace in Prague Castle), Academia Umění, Prague, 1953, p. 308.
2. J. Krčálová: *Palác pánů z Rožemberka* (The Palace of the Lords of Rožmberk), Academia Umění, Prague, 1970, p. 469.
3. *ibid.*, p. 477, ill. 7.
4. A. Lewiová: *Doklady ke stavbě Lobkovického palác* (Documents on the building of the Lobkowicz Palace at Prague Castle), Památky archeologické, 1925, pp. 250-6.
5. V. Procházka, P. Chotěbor: *Lobkovický palác* (The Lobkowicz Palace), in: *Průvodce historickou expozicí Narodního Muzea* (Guide to the Historical Exhibition of the National Museum), Narodní Museum, Prague, 1987, pp. 7-11.
6. E. Šamánková: *Architektura české renesanse* (The Architecture of the Czech Renaissance), Nakladatelsví Krásné literatury hudby a umení, Prague, 1961, p.39.
7. J. Krčalová: *Obnovené renesanční malby purkrabství Pražského hradu* (The Restored Renaissance Paintings of the Burgrave's House at Prague Castle), Orbis, Prague, Památkova páče, 1964, p. 275.
8. P. Chotěbor, J. Svoboda: *Pražský hrad* (Prague Castle), Olympia, Prague, 1990, p. 86.
9. *ibid.*, p. 12.
10. *Ausstellungskatalog Prag um 1600, Kunst und Kultur am Hofe Rudolfs II* (Catalogue of the Prague Exhibition c. 1600, Art and Culture at the Court of Rudolf II), Villa Hügel, Essen, 1988, pp. 86-7.

Opposite page: *the Royal Garden*. The avenue of trees in the central part of the garden did not form part of the original scheme. The pleasure garden to the west and the Summer Pavilion at the eastern end were originally linked by a long arbour covered with climbing plants, as shown on a plan dating from the second half of the 18th century (see p. 232). It was not until the middle of the 19th century that the arbour was replaced by an avenue of trees leading to a niche with a statue of Hercules by Jan Jiří Bendl (1670).

THE LOBKOWICZ PALACE

This palace was created by the reconstruction of the Renaissance-style Pernštejn Palace. In the second half of the 17th century, the architect Carlo Lurago collaborated with the most famous Prague ornamentalist of the period, Diminik Galli, and the painter, Fabián Harovník, to do the interior decoration. On the first floor were the reception rooms, decorated, as was the Baroque custom, according to the function of the particular room. The ceiling of the dining room, for example, was adorned with a fresco showing a feast of the gods of Olympus. The oriental room, in the Black Tower of the fortifications, is of interest as the only example of decoration in the romantic style.

Right: *the music room*, with an exhibition of instruments: a square piano, Bohemian, from the first half of the 19th century; a basset horn by František Doleisch, Prague, 1796; a double-action harp from the early 19th century; a guitar by Jean Baptiste Dvořak, Prague, second half of the 19th century; a guitar by Gennaro, Naples, 1819.

THE BURGRAVE'S HOUSE

Left: *the beamed ceiling*. The residence of the burgrave was built in the 16th century, at which time the walls and ceiling of one of the first-floor rooms were decorated with wonderful paintings. The painter used the sides of the supporting beams very cleverly for interesting countryside scenes. The frieze below the ceiling, contains allegorical pictures of the five senses, a very popular subject at the time.

At the eastern end of the castle the Italian architect Giovanni Ventura built the palace of the grand burgrave of the Czech kingdom, the official who took the place of the sovereign during his absence (below). Above the main gate are the coats-of-arms of certain distinguished families whose representatives carried out this function.

Below: *George Street (Jiřská ulice,)* the oldest in the castle area. From the 9th century it was used for crossing the fortified site from east to west. To the east, the castle site is reached by way of the Black Tower, after climbing the picturesque Old Castle Steps (Stare zámecké schody).

GOLDEN LANE

This lane is certainly the castle's biggest tourist attraction, rich in legends concerning the alchemists who lived there in the reign of Rudolf II. The street was created by building tiny houses intended for the castle guards, in the gaps formed by the arcades of the Romanesque enclosing wall of Soběslav I. The picturesque charm of this lane derives particularly from the crooked overhangs and roofs. At one time the writer Franz Kafka had his study on the ground floor of the house numbered 22.

Page 264: *view of the north-eastern end of the castle fortifications, from Queen Anna's Summer Pavilion.* The large polygonal tower, known as the Black Tower, formed part of the Romanesque enclosing wall and served as the main entrance to the castle for visitors arriving from the east. In the Late Gothic period massive round towers were built to strengthen the fortifications. One of them, the Daliborka Tower, took its name from a legendary figure of Czech history, the nobleman Dalibor of Kozojedy, whose opposition to royal power caused him to be locked up in the tower and then executed. To pass the time, he learned to play the violin, attracting passers-by who, it is said, gathered outside his prison to listen.

APPENDICES

BIOGRAPHIES

EMIL M. BÜHRER (design). After an apprenticeship in graphic arts, he worked as an editor, photographer and art director for the journal *Camera*. In his capacity of book designer and art director, he created a number of internationally successful works, among them 'Leonardo', 'The Kingdom of the Horse', 'Journey Through Ancient China', 'The Sistine Chapel', 'The Silk Road', 'The Himalayas', 'Great Women of the Bible', 'Chess — 2000 Years of the Game's History'. Emil M. Buhrer died on January 2 1994 in Luzern.

IVO HLOBIL, born in 1942 at Přerov, has been teaching since 1990 at František Palacký University, Olomouc, where he had previously taught from 1974 to 1981. He is a specialist in the medieval art of Bohemia and Moravia, particularly in Moravian Late Gothic and Early Renaissance, and is also interested in the theoretical problems of conserving ancient monuments. After university studies at Prague, this art historian worked from 1970 to 1973 in the State Office in charge of the conservation of historic monuments in Ostrava. His research studies have appeared in translation in a number of publications. After 1981 he worked at the Art History Institute of the Czechoslovak Academy of Sciences, Prague.

MIROSLAV HUCEK (photography). Born in 1934 at Malacky, he has been a freelance press photographer since 1975. After studying at the Academy of the Cinema, in Prague, he worked as a television cameraman from 1958 to 1962; and then, until 1975 as a photographic reporter for the weekly *Mladý Svět* (World of Youth). He has contributed to various publications, brought out some ten albums of his own photographs and taken part in many exhibitions. He is included in the *International Encyclopedia of Photography from 1839 to the Present Day* (Michel Auer, Zurich, 1985), and some of his works can be found in the Bibliothèque Nationale of Paris. His wife Arita works closely with him and their daughter Barbara is following in their footsteps.

BARBARA HUCKOVÁ (photography). Since completing her studies at the Academy of Fine Arts, Prague, in 1988, Barbara has spent some time training in France with a FRAC grant. She has already exhibited in Prague, Paris, Milan and Stockholm and has contributed to several publications. She worked with her father in illustrating this book.

Other photographic sources:
JIŘÍ CESÁK pp 12-13; FOTO ČSTK pp 42-3, 44

LADISLAV KESNER, born in Prague, has been director, since 1991, of the Prague National Gallery's collection of ancient art at St George's Convent. After studying art history and aesthetics at Charles University, Prague, he worked from 1954 in the National Gallery as curator specialising in ancient art, serving as acting director from 1965 to 1969 when, for political reasons, he was removed from his post. In 1974 he was employed at St George's Convent, where the National Gallery had installed its ancient Bohemian art collection. He was appointed its director after a brief period as director of the National Gallery (from 1990 until early 1991).

IVAN P. MUCHKA, born in 1946 in Prague, has worked since 1986 at the Art History Institute of the Czechoslovak Academy of Sciences. This art historian specialises in the conservation of historical monuments and has been engaged in this work since graduating from Charles University, Prague, in 1969. Thanks to grants, he worked in Italy (1968), France (1973) and the United States (1990), which allowed him to attend many seminars and conferences. In 1985, in his Institute for the Preservation of Historical Monuments, he was put in charge of the department of state castles and historic houses. The following year he entered the Art History Institute. Author of numerous publications on the castles of Bohemia and Moravia, he has also helped to prepare exhibition catalogues, notably on art at the court of Rudolf II (Paris, 1990). He also contributed to the exhibition on Prague in the 1400s.

PRINCE CHARLES OF SCHWARZENBERG, former head of the chancellery of the presidency of the Czechoslovak Republic, was born in Prague in 1937. In 1948, the year of the Communist *coup d'état*, his family settled in Austria, in the village of Strobl on the Wolfgangsee. He studied forestry in Vienna, Munich and Graz, before taking over the administration of the family property. From 1984 to 1991 he was president of the Helsinki International Federation for Human Rights and in 1989, jointly with Lech Walesa, received the Council of Europe prize. Shortly after his election to the presidency of the Republic, on 1 January 1990, Václav Havel appointed Prince Charles director of his group of counsellors; then, after his re-election, to be head of his chancellery, a post he held until 1 July 1992. He is now director of the Bohemian Foundation, which aims to promote abroad the image of the Czech nation, its citizens and industries.

TOMÁŠ VLČEK, born in 1941, has been director of the Art History Institute of the Czechoslovak Academy of Sciences since 1990. This art historian, specialising particularly in the 19th and 20th centuries, is also director of the Central European University (installed at Prague), a college specialising in the history and philosophy of art and architecture. Since 1991 he has been chief editor of the journal *Estetika* (Aesthetics). He travelled widely abroad in the 1980s and belongs to various national and international organisations (including the AICA — Association Internationale des Critiques d'Art).

BIBLIOGRAPHY

Bondzio, Bodo, Feyfar, Petr and Ladwigová, Karla: *Prag*; Bucher Verlag, Munich and Berlin, 1990.

Burian, Jiří and Svoboda, Jiří: *Le château de Prague*; Olympia, Prague, 1974.

Coster, Léon de and Coster, Xavier de: *15 promenades dans Prague*; Casterman Coll. Déecouvrir l'architecture des villes, 1992.

Chotěbor, Petr and Svoboda, Jiří: *Pražský Hrad* (Prague Castle); Olympia, Prague, 1990.

Doležal, Jiří and Ivan: *Praha*; Olympia Prague, 1983.

Doležal, Jiří and Ivan: *Zlatá Praha* (Prague the Golden); Olympia, Prague, 1971.

Fernandez, Dominique: *Le Banquet des Andes, L'Europe de Rome à Prague*; Plon, Paris, 1984.

Galmiche, Xavier and Král, Petr: *Prague, Secrets et métamorphoses*; Autrement, Série Monde, H.S.N. 46, Paris, 1990.

Hlavsa, Václav: *Praha, očima staletí* (Prague, Seen through the Centuries); Panorama, Prague, 1984.

Hoensch, Jörg K.: *Geschichte Böhmens* (History of Bohemia); C.H. Beck Verlag, Munich, 1987.

Král, Petr: *Le surréalisme en Tchéchoslovaquie*; Gallimard, Paris, 1983.

Kutal, Albert: *L'art gothique en Tchéchoslovaquie*; Cercle d'Art, Paris, 1971.

Macek, Josef and Mandrou, Robert: *Histoire de la Bohême, des origines à 1918*; Fayard, Paris, 1984.

Mosler, Axel M., Kliment, Alexandr, Novák, Petr and Cmíral, Pavel: *Tschechoslowakei*; Bucher Verlag, Munich and Berlin, 1991.

Mráz, Bohumír: *Prague, coeur de l'Europe*; Librairie Gründ, Paris, 1986.

Mucha, Jiří: *Mucha* (Alfons), monograph; Flammarion, Paris, 1976.

Neubert, Karel: *Pražský Hrad* (Prague Castle); Panorama, Prague, 1990.

Porter, Tim: *Prague Art and History*; Flow East Ltd, Prague, 1991.

Staňková, Jaroslava, Stursa, Jiří and Voděra, Svatopluk: *Pražská architektura* (Prague Architecrture); Ing. arch. Jaroslav Stanek, Prague, 1990.

Stejskal, Karel: *L'art en Europe au XIVe siècle;* Librairie Gründ, Paris, 1980.

Vancura, Jiří: *Hradčany, Pražský hrad* (Prague Castle); SNLT, Prague, 1976.

COLLECTED WORKS

Exhibition catalogues:

1957 *L'art ancien à Prague et en Tchéchoslovaquie*, Paris, 1957, Musée des Arts décoratifs.

1966 *L'arte de Barocco in Boemia*, Milan, 1966, Palazzo Reale.

1968 *Petr Brandl*, Prague, 1968, Národní Galerie.

Josef Šima, Paris 1968, Musée d'Art moderne.

1969 *Baroque in Bohemia*, London, 1969, Victoria and Albert Museum.

1974 *Karel Škréta*, Prague, 1974, Národní Galerie.

1975 *Dix siècles d'art tchèque et slovaque*, Paris, 1975, Grand Palais.

1977 *Kunst des Barock in Böhmen*, Essen, 1977, Villa Hügel.

1978 *Rudolfinska kresba* (Rudolfian Drawing), Prague, 1978, Národní Galerie.

1981 *Le Baroque en Bohème*, Paris, 1981, Grand Palais.

1985 *Kunst der Gotik aus Böhmen*, Cologne, 1985, Schnutgen Museum.

1988 *Prag um 1600, Kunst und Kultur am Hofe Rudolfs II*, Essen, 1988, Villa Hügel, and Vienna, Kunsthistorisches Museum.

Staré české uměni (Ancient Czech Art), Prague, 1988, Národní Galerie.

1990 *Prag um 1400: Der Schöne Stil, Böhmische Malerei und Plastik in der Gotik*, Vienna, 1990, Historisches Museum der Stadt Wien.

INDEX

Numbers in *italic* indicate captions

A

Abondio, Alessandro: 21, *23, 34*
Abondio, Antonio: 21, *34*
Adalbert (St, a.k.a. Vojtěch): 17, 19, 20, 114, 117, 119, 120, 122, 141-144
Agnes (abbess): 165,*168, 197*
Aichel, Giovanni Santini: 49, 210
Albert II of Habsburg: *33*
Alexander the Great: 226
Alliprandi, Giovanni Battista: 210
Altdorfer, Alfrecht: 211
Anna Jagiello (queen): 50, 142, 225, 229, 231, *237, 263*
Anne of Bavaria: 121, *138*
Anne of Silesia: 138
Aostalli, Ulrico: *57,* 142, 143, 228, 249, 253
Apollinaire, Guillaume: 45, *250*
Arcimbolo, Giuseppe: 21, 183
Arnošt of Harrach (cardinal-arch-bishop): 143
Arnošt of Pardubice (archbishop): 113, 120
Arras, Matthew of: *see Matthew of Arras*
Auerbach, Johann Karl: *90*
Augustus III: 221

B

Babbiena, Giuseppe Galli: 230
Balbín, Bohuslav: 22, 143
Barye, Antoine-Louis: 212,
Bassano, Jacopo: 211, 221
Baudelaire, Charles: *217*
Bechteler, Caspar: 143, *150, 151*
Becker, Tobiáš Jan: *177*
Bedřich J. Schwarzenberg (cardinal-archbishop): 144, 147
Benda, Břetislav: 148
Bendl, Jiří: 230, *256*
Benedict XIII (pope): 144
Beneš, Edouard: 24, *30,* 165
Beneš Krabice of Weitmile (arch-bishop): 113, 118, 119, 120
Bening, Simon: *214*
Bergeron, Pierre: 227, 228
Bernini: *208*
Bertha (abbess): 165, 177, 197
Beyeren, Abraham von: 211
Blanche de Valois: 121, *138*
Bles, Herri Met de: 211
Boccaccino: 211

Boitard, Clemence: *218*
Boleslav I the Cruel: 18, *27,* 118
Boleslav II: 18, 165, 177, 179
Boleslav the Brave: 19, 46
Bonnard, Pierre: 212
Borch, Ter: 211
Borivoj I: 46, 165, 168
Borivoj II: *19,* 120
Bose, Cornélius: 227
Boucher, François: 212
Bourdelle, Antoine: 212
Brahe, Tycho: 21, *37,* 226
Brandl, Petr: 144, 178, 184, *205, 208,* 221
Braque, Georges: 212
Braudis of Trieste, Louis: 225
Braun, Georg: *51*
Braun, Matyáš Bernard: *94, 135,* 144, 178, 179, 184, 208, 230, *241*
Breuner, Jan J. (archbishop): 144
Brožík, Václav: 92
Broca, Giovanni Antonio: 81
Brocco, Antonio: 227, *237*
Brod, Max: 45
Brokoff, Ferdinand Maximillian: 179, 184, *208*
Brokoff, Jan: *206,* 278
Bronzino, il (Agnolo di Cosimo): 211
Bruegel, Pieter, the Elder: 211, *212,* 214
Brunner, Vratislav H.: 148
Bruno, Giordano: 21
Brus of Mohelnice, Antonín: *57,* 142
Břetislav I: 19, 46, 120
Buckingham, Duke of: *223*
Byss, J. R.: *208,* 211

C

Canaletto, Giovanni: 211
Čapek, Karel: *109*
Caratti, Francesco: *57,* 168
Carpeaux, Jean-Baptiste: 212
Carrà, Carlo: 212
Cassinis of Bugella, M. A.: *202*
Catherine of Lipoltice (abbess): 168
Cézanne, Paul: 212
Chagall, Marc: 212
Charlemagne: 115
Charles IV: *7, 10,* 19, 20, *22,* 30, 31, 47, 8, *62, 74, 78,* 113, 114, 115, 116, 117, 118, 119, 120, 121, 123, *124, 126, 135, 138,* 141, 142, 144, 148, *154, 156, 158, 160, 162,* 165, 174,

181, 184, *189, 224*
Charles V: 226
Charles VI: 221, 229, 230
Charles VII: *92*
Charles X: 23
Chateaubriand, René de: *235*
Chirico, Giorgio de: 211
Chody, Jindřich Hýrzl of: *37*
Christina (queen of Sweden): 22, 220, *223*
Cibulka, Josef: 147
Cione, Nardo di: 211
Claesz, Pieter: 211
Clement VI (pope): 113, 114, 116, 119
Cock, Hieronymus: 227
Colin, Alexandre: 142, *151*
Comenius, Jan Ámos: 184
Corinth, Lovis: 211
Corot, Camille: 212
Corradini, Antonio: *135,* 144
Courbet, Gustave: 212
Cranach, Lucas: 211
Cubr, František: 178, 220
Cunegonde (abbess): 165

D

Daddi, Bernardo: 211
Dalibor of Kozojedy: *263*
Dante Alighieri: *244*
Daubigny, Charles-François: 212
Daumier, Honoré: 212
Dětmar: 18, 19
De Vriendt, Frans Floris: 221
Dee, John: 21
Degas, Edgar: 212
Delacroix, Eugène: 212
Derain, André: 212
Despiau, Charles: 212
Dienzenhofer, Kilián Ignác: 184, 229, 230, *245*
Dietzler, Johan Joseph: 227, 230
Dittman, Kristian: 174
Dlouhoveský, Jan: *159*
Doleiš, František: *259*
Dou, Gérard: 211
Dražice, Jan de: *186*
Drahomíra (princess): 168
Dubček, Alexander: 44
Ducharda, Vojtěch: 148
Dürer, Albrecht: 211, *212,* 221
Dvořák, Jean Baptiste: *259*
Dvořák, Karel: *126*